THE VICTORIA HISTORY OF THE COUNTIES
OF ENGLAND

A HISTORY OF CORNWALL
VOLUME II

INSCRIBED TO THE MEMORY OF HER LATE MAJESTY

QUEEN VICTORIA

WHO GRACIOUSLY GAVE THE TITLE TO AND

ACCEPTED THE DEDICATION OF THIS HISTORY

THE VICTORIA HISTORY OF THE COUNTIES OF ENGLAND

JOHN BECKETT   DIRECTOR AND GENERAL EDITOR

ALAN THACKER   EXECUTIVE EDITOR

ELIZABETH WILLIAMSON   ARCHITECTURAL EDITOR

THE UNIVERSITY OF LONDON

INSTITUTE OF HISTORICAL RESEARCH

ECCLESIASTICAL HERALDRY OF CORNWALL

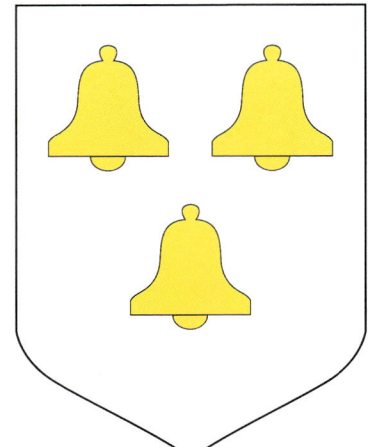

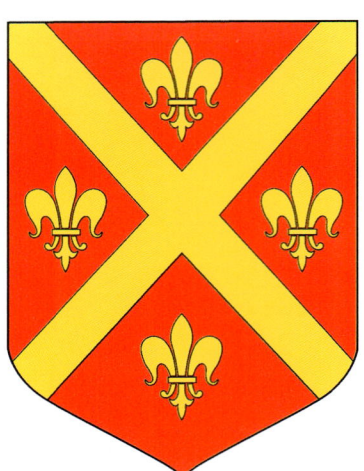

Bodmin Priory (top)
Launceston Priory (middle)
Thomas Vivian, prior of Bodmin (bottom)

St Germans Priory (top)
Tywardreath Priory (middle)
Thomas Colyns, prior of Tywardreath (bottom)

A HISTORY OF THE COUNTY OF CORNWALL

VOLUME II

RELIGIOUS HISTORY TO 1560

BY NICHOLAS ORME
with a contribution from Oliver Padel

PUBLISHED FOR THE
INSTITUTE OF HISTORICAL RESEARCH
BY BOYDELL & BREWER · 2010

© University of London and Nicholas Orme 2010

All rights reserved. Except as permitted under current legislation
no part of this work may be photocopied, stored in a retrieval system,
published, performed in public, adapted, broadcast,
transmitted, recorded or reproduced in any form or by any means,
without the prior permission of the copyright owner

First published 2010

A Victoria County History publication
in association with The Boydell Press
an imprint of Boydell & Brewer Ltd
PO Box 9 Woodbridge Suffolk IP12 3DF UK
and of Boydell & Brewer Inc.
668 Mt Hope Avenue Rochester NY 14620 USA
website: www.boydellandbrewer.com
and with the
University of London Institute of Historical Research

ISBN 978–1–904356–12–7
ISSN 1477–0709

A catalogue record for this book is available
from the British Library

Typeset by Tina Ranft, Woodbridge
Printed in Great Britain by
CPI Antony Rowe, Chippenham and Eastbourne

CONTENTS OF VOLUME TWO

	Page
Dedication	ii
Contents	vii
List of Illustrations, Maps and Plans	ix
Preface	xi
Editorial Note	xiii
List of Abbreviations	xv

RELIGIOUS HISTORY TO 1560
   1. FROM THE ROMANS TO THE NORMAN CONQUEST   1
   2. THE TWELFTH AND THIRTEENTH CENTURIES   22
   3. THE LATER MIDDLE AGES: THE CLERGY   46
   4. THE LATER MIDDLE AGES: THE PEOPLE   65
   5. THE REFORMATION   91
   6. CHRISTIANITY IN MEDIEVAL CORNWALL: CELTIC ASPECTS *by* OLIVER PADEL   110

RELIGIOUS HOUSES BEFORE 1066   126

RELIGIOUS HOUSES AFTER 1066   136

   ST ANTHONY-IN-ROSELAND
      Augustinian Priory of St Anthony   136

   BODMIN
      Minster, later Augustinian Priory   139
      Franciscan Friary   155
      Hospital of St Anthony   159
      Hospital of St George   160
      Hospital of St Laurence   160

   ST BURYAN
      Collegiate Church   163

   ST COLUMB MAJOR
      Arundell Chantry   171

   CRANTOCK
      Collegiate Church   173

   ST ENDELLION
      Prebendal Church   180

   ST GERMANS
      Minster, later Augustinian Priory   184

   HELSTON
      Hospital of St John Baptist   192
      Hospital of St Mary Magdalene   194

   ST KEVERNE
      Leper House of 'Nan(s)clegy'   195

   ST KEW
      Alleged Augustinian House   195

   LAMMANA
      Benedictine Priory   196

LANLIVERY	
Lamford Hospital	200
LAUNCESTON	
Minster, later Augustinian Priory	201
Hospital of St Leonard	221
Launceston Almshouse	224
LISKEARD	
Hospital of St Mary Magdalene	224
ST MICHAEL PENKEVIL	
Collegiate Church	226
ST MICHAEL'S MOUNT	
Benedictine Priory, later Chapel	228
MINSTER	
Benedictine Priory	240
PENRYN	
Glasney Collegiate Church	244
Penryn Almshouse	262
PROBUS	
Collegiate, later Prebendal, Church	262
SCILLY	
Benedictine Priory	266
ST TEATH	
Prebendal Church	270
TEMPLE	
Knights Templars' Property	272
TREBEIGH	
Knights Hospitallers' Preceptory	273
TREGONY	
Augustinian Priory	278
TRURO	
Dominican Friary	281
TYWARDREATH	
Benedictine Priory	284
ST VEEP	
Cluniac Priory of St Carroc	297
VERYAN	
'Sheepstall' Leper House	299
UNCERTAIN HOSPITALS AND LEPER COMMUNITIES	300
ANCHORITES AND HERMITS	304
Glossary	307
Bibliography	311
Index	323

LIST OF ILLUSTRATIONS, MAPS AND PLANS

Frontispiece: Ecclesiastical Heraldry of Cornwall

Figure		Page
1	Inscribed stones (W. Borlase, *Antiquities, Historical and Monumental, of the County of Cornwall*, 2nd edn (1769), plate 35, p. 391).	2
2	The South West of England, 400–900 (N. Orme; Cath D'Alton: University of London).	3
3	Inscribed stone at South Hill (photograph: English Heritage).	6
4	St Samson, from a former bench end at St Sampson, Golant (photograph: the vicar and churchwardens of St Sampson, Golant).	8
5	Land-holding churches of Cornwall, up to 1086 (N. Orme; Cath D'Alton: University of London).	13
6	St Neot and the pop e (photograph: S. Goddard).	17
7	The Gospel of Mark from the 'Bodmin Gospels' (The British Library, Add. 9381, f. 50).	19
8	Lands of the bishop of Exeter, rural deaneries, and peculiars (N. Orme; Cath D'Alton: University of London).	23
9	The tomb of Walter Bronescombe (d. 1280), Exeter Cathedral (photograph: N. Orme).	24
10	Parishes in Cornwall, 1291. (N. Orme; Helen Jones)	28
11	Religious houses in Cornwall, 1100–1560. (N. Orme; Helen Jones)	31
12	Reliquary from Bodmin parish church (photograph: N. Orme, copyright of the vicar and churchwardens of Bodmin parish church).	35
13	Parish church plans, 12th and 13th centuries (E. H. Sedding; Cath D'Alton: University of London).	40
14	Tintagel church (photograph: N. Orme).	45
15	A leper (The British Library, Lansd. 451, f. 127).	47
16	St Germans Priory, south-west view ('The South West View of St. Germans Priory' (1734)) (The Royal Institution of Cornwall).	50
17	The Cornish at Oxford University (N. Orme; Cath D'Alton: University of London).	58
18	Exeter College (Oxford) (Bodleian, Bodl. 13, f. 12v).	59
19	St Ive church, east end of the chancel (photograph: English Heritage).	62
20	Former brass of John Waryn, Menheniot church (Bodleian, printed book, Gough Cornwall 22 (R. Carew, *The Survey of Cornwall* (1602), opp. f. 155r)).	64
21	Church of St Mary Magdalene, Launceston (photograph: English Heritage).	66
22	Parish church plans, 15th and 16th centuries (E. H. Sedding; Alan Fagan: University of London).	67
23	Altarnun church, screen and seating (photograph: English Heritage).	68
24	Breage church, wall painting of St Christopher (photograph: N. Orme).	69
25	The sisters of St Neot parish, from a window in the church (photograph: English Heritage).	72
26	Domestic chapel, Cotehele, Calstock (photograph: English Heritage).	74
27	Parishes and chapels in central Cornwall (N. Orme; Cath D'Alton: University of London).	75
28	Chapel plans (N. Orme; Alan Fagan: University of London).	76
29	Well house, St Cleer (photograph: English Heritage).	78
30	Cult chapel, St Clether (photograph: N. Orme).	79
31	Church house, Poundstock (photograph: English Heritage).	81
32	Cult centres in Cornwall, 1100–1550 (N. Orme; Cath D'Alton: University of London).	85
33	St Kew church, Passion window (photograph: English Heritage).	89
34	Bodmin church, exterior (photograph: English Heritage).	94
35	The Church of St Probus. Its fine tower was added in the 1520s (photograph: English Heritage).	95
36	St Michael's chapel, Roche (photograph: English Heritage).	97
37	The 'Prayer Book Rising' of 1549 (N. Orme; Cath D'Alton: University of London).	102
38	The tomb of John Veysey (d. 1554), Sutton Coldfield church (photograph: English Heritage)	103
39	St Endellion church (photograph: English Heritage).	104
40	St Buryan and the parishes of West Penwith, *c.*1574 (The National Archives, MPF 1/332).	108
41	Parish churches with names containing **lann* and *egros* (O. J. Padel; Cath D'Alton: University of London).	117

42 St Anthony-in-Roseland, parish church (photograph: English Heritage). 137
43 The property of Bodmin Priory (N. Orme; Cath D'Alton: University of London). 141
44 Bodmin Priory, plan (N. Orme; Alan Fagan: University of London). 143
45 The splendid tomb of Thomas Vivian (d. 1533), prior of Bodmin and bishop of Megara (photograph: N. Orme). 151
46 The former Franciscan friary (Bodmin), 1716 (Drawing by Edmund Prideaux, Padstow, Prideaux Place, copyright of Mr P. Prideaux-Brune). 155
47 Crantock Collegiate Church, plan (E. H. Sedding; Alan Fagan: University of London). 177
48 Crantock Collegiate Church, exterior (photograph: English Heritage). 178
49 The property of St Germans Priory (N. Orme; Cath D'Alton: University of London). 185
50 St Germans Priory, plan (L. Olson and A. Preston-Jones; Alan Fagan: University of London). 187
51 Launceston Priory, reconstruction (Richard Parker, 2009). 205
52 Launceston Priory, plan (N. Orme; Alan Fagan: University of London). 205
53 The property of Launceston Priory (N. Orme; Cath D'Alton: University of London). 209
54 Indulgence of St Michael Penkevil, 1335 (private collection). 227
55 St Michael's Mount Priory, plan (P. A. S. Pool; Alan Fagan: University of London). 230
56 St Michael's Mount, present-day church interior (photograph: N. Orme). 231
57 St Michael's Mount, exterior in 1786 (F. Grose, *Supplement to the Antiquities of England and Wales* (London, 1787), opposite p. 38). 236
58 The property of Glasney Collegiate Church (N. Orme; Cath D'Alton: University of London). 247
59 Glasney Collegiate Church, plan (N. Orme; Alan Fagan: University of London). 249
60 Glasney Collegiate Church, from a lost drawing (Penryn Town Council). 251
61 Scilly Priory, plan (N. Orme; Alan Fagan: University of London). 267
62 Tresco, Isles of Scilly, priory ruins (W. Borlase, *Observations on the Ancient and Present State of the Islands of Scilly* (1756), 43–4 and plate IV). 267
63 The property of Tywardreath Priory (N. Orme; Cath D'Alton: University of London). 287

PREFACE

THE VICTORIA History of the Counties of England, usually known as the Victoria County History (VCH), is a national project originating in 1899 to publish a detailed history of every English county, encompassing general topics and individual towns and parishes. The first volume of the History of Cornwall was published in 1906, and two more sections of a volume appeared subsequently. This present volume is the result of a revival of the History of Cornwall in 2002 as a collaboration between the central organisation of the Victoria County History, the University of Exeter, and a supporting group in Cornwall: the Victoria County History of Cornwall Trust. The research for the volume has been funded by the Trust and the University, while the Heritage Lottery Fund has supported an associated project, 'England's Past for Everyone'.

Many people have contributed to the making of this volume. The revival of the VCH in Cornwall is due to the tireless and enthusiastic work of the VCH Cornwall Trust, especially that of its distinguished member, the late Sir Richard Trant. The Cornish volunteers of the 'Religious History Project' gave generously of their time and effort to collecting information on parish history and parish remains, information now preserved as a resource for historians. Dr Jonathan Barry, Head of the School of Humanities and Social Sciences, University of Exeter, has provided unfailing encouragement and essential practical support. Mr Eric Berry carried out a survey of eight churches representing former religious houses for the London office of the VCH, of which use has been made in the volume. Further individual help, often on a considerable scale, has been given by Mr John Allan, Mr Stewart Ainsworth and the staff of Channel Four 'Time Team', Miss C. Annesley, Dr Virginia Bainbridge, Mr Stuart Blaylock, Monsieur A.-Y. Bourgès, Ms Angela Broome, Professor James Carley, Mr R. I. Cole, Mrs Christine Edwards, Mr Colin Edwards, Professor Michael Gervers, Professor Malcolm Godden, Mr Steve Hartgroves, Dr Eddie Jones, Professor M. C. E. Jones, Dr Maureen Jurkowski, Dr H. Kleineke, Mr A. Langdon, Dr Evelyn Lord, Dr Joanna Mattingly, Dr Richard Mortimer, Dr E. A. New, Dr Helen Nicholson, Mr P. Northeast, Mr M. O'Connor, Dr Gregory O'Malley, Mr K. Paul, Dr Simon Phillips, Mrs Ann Preston-Jones, Dr M. Robson, Mr Peter Rose, Mrs Eve Ross, Mr Ifor Rowlands, Professor David Smith, Miss E. A. Stuart, Sir John Trelawny, Mr Raleigh Trevelyan, Dr James Whetter, Mr R. Harcourt Williams, Miss Pamela Willis, and Mr Arthur Wills. A special tribute should be paid to the published work and generous advice of Dr O. J. Padel, who has also contributed a chapter on Celtic aspects of Christianity in Medieval Cornwall.

The VCH and the author would also like to record their gratitude for the research facilities made available by the Bodleian Library (Oxford), Bodmin Town Museum, the British Library (London), Canterbury Cathedral Archives, the College of Arms (London), Cornwall County Council Historic Environment Service (Truro), Cornwall County Record Office (Truro), Cornwall Studies Library (Redruth), Devon County Record Office (Exeter and Barnstaple), The Devon and Exeter Institution (Exeter), the Duchy of Cornwall, Exeter Cathedral Archives, Exeter Cathedral Library, Exeter University Library, King's College (Cambridge), Hatfield House, Launceston Borough Archives, the Morrab Library (Penzance), the National Archives (Kew) and its Family Records Centre (London), the National Monuments Record, the Order of St John of Jerusalem (Clerkenwell), Mr P. Prideaux-Brune, the Royal Institution of Cornwall Courtney Library (Truro), the Sackler Library (Oxford), Somerset Record Office (Taunton), and the West Country Studies Library (Exeter).

Finally I appreciate the help of Matthew Bristow and Stephen Lubell on organising the cartography and illustrations, Cath D'Alton in drawing the maps, Alan and Lizzy Fagan the plans, and Barry Phillips of the University of Exeter for the scanning of images.

Nicholas Orme,
April 2010

*Publication of this volume
was greatly assisted by
a grant from*

the Isobel Thornley Bequest Fund

EDITORIAL NOTE

THREE FEATURES of the arrangement of this volume should be explained. First it accords with a long-standing tradition in publications about Cornwall by ignoring the prefix 'St' when arranging place-names in alphabetical order. This is because many churches and parishes are named after people regarded as saints, and practice has varied historically in applying or not applying the prefix 'St', resulting (for example) in both Constantine and St Constantine, Endellion and St Endellion. Secondly the treatment of the religious houses of medieval Cornwall is divided into two sections. One of these deals with evidence about such houses before 1066, and the other after that date. This reflects the fact that the houses in the first period mostly involve similar kinds of evidence, are mostly not recorded after 1066, and mostly only enable a little to be written about themselves, so that they constitute a group of foundations appropriate for separate treatment. Equally most of the houses that existed after 1066 were founded after that date and have generated more and different evidence, so that they too form a uniform body. Six houses – Bodmin (Minster, later Priory), St Buryan, Crantock, St Germans, Launceston (Minster, later Priory), and Probus – existed in both periods and receive treatment in each section.

Thirdly, the arrangement of the gazetteer of medieval sites requires a word of explanation. The many relatively small religious foundations in the county pose problems which render complete consistency almost impossible. Because so few were affiliated to the major orders we have not listed them under the divisions normal in VCH volumes of this kind. Instead, we have in general arranged them alphabetically and according to the ancient parish in which the site occurs. We have departed just occasionally from this principle, mostly when the site occurs in, and is identified with, a significant medieval town which did not have parochial status in the Middle Ages. For example, Glasney is placed under Penryn, not the medieval parish (Budock); the hospitals in Helston are placed under Helston, not Wendron parish; and the Dominican friary in Truro is placed under Truro, not Kea or Kenwyn. The hospital of St Mary Magdalene, normally associated with Liskeard, is placed under that parish even though it is sited just over the boundary in the neighbouring parish of Menheniot. The lists of uncertain hospitals and leper communities and of anchorites which follow the main gazetteer have been organised according to the same principles.

LIST OF ABBREVIATIONS

For further details of published works, see the bibliography, pp. 311–321.

Add.	Additional
adm.	admitted
BL	British Library, London
Bodleian	Bodleian Library, Oxford
BRUO, I–III	A. B. Emden, *A Biographical Register of the University of Oxford to AD 1500*, 3 vols (Oxford, 1957–9)
BRUO, IV	A. B. Emden, *A Biographical Register of the University of Oxford AD 1501 to 1540* (Oxford, 1974)
Cal. Inq. Misc.	*Calendar of Inquisitions Miscellaneous*
Cal. Inq. p. m.	*Calendar of Inquisitions Post Mortem*
Cal. Close	*Calendar of Close Rolls*
Cal. Papal Pets.	*Calendar of Papal Petitions*
Cal. Papal Regs.	*Calendar of Papal Registers*
Cal. Pat.	*Calendar of Patent Rolls*
Cant. & York Soc.	Canterbury and York Society
Cat. Anct. D.	*Catalogue of Ancient Deeds*
CCC	Cornwall County Council, Historic Environment Service
Ch.	Charter
Close R.	*Close Rolls*
coll.	collated
comp.	compounded for paying first-fruits to the crown
conf.	confirmed in office
CRO	Cornwall Record Office, Truro
Cur. Reg.	*Curia Regis Rolls*
d	dorse of membrane
D&C	Dean and Chapter documents in Exeter Cathedral Archives
DCNQ	*Devon and Cornwall Notes and Queries*
DCRS	Devon and Cornwall Record Society
DRO	Devon Record Office, Exeter
ECA	Exeter Cathedral Archives
edn	edition
el.	elected
Feudal Aids	*Feudal Aids*
f.	folio
fl.	floruit
Hist.	*Historical*
HMC	*Historical Manuscripts Commission* reports
inst.	instituted
Jnl	*Journal*
JRIC	*Journal of the Royal Institution of Cornwall*
L. & P. Hen VIII	*Letters and Papers, Foreign and Domestic, Henry VIII*
m.	membrane
new ser	new series
ODNB	*Oxford Dictionary of National Biography*
Pipe R	*Pipe Roll*
pres.	presented
prob.	probably
PRS	Pipe Roll Society
r	recto of folio
Rec. Com.	Record Commission

Reg.	Registers of bishops; *see* Bibliography: Register
repr.	reprinted
res.	resigned
RIC	Royal Institution of Cornwall, Truro, Courtney Library
Rot. Litt. Pat.	*Rotuli Litterarum Patentium*
RS	Rolls Series
Soc.	*Society*
SMR	Cornwall County Council, Sites and Monuments Register
TDA	*Transactions of the Devonshire Association*
TNA	The National Archives (formerly Public Record Office)
v	verso of folio
vac.	vacated
Valor Eccl.	*Valor Ecclesiasticus*
VCH	*The Victoria History of the Counties of England (Victoria County History)*

RELIGIOUS HISTORY TO 1560

1. FROM THE ROMANS TO THE NORMAN CONQUEST

CHRISTIANITY in Cornwall can be traced back with certainty to about the year AD 500. For the next three or four hundred years, it took root in a region that was ruled by local British kings, based in Devon or Cornwall. Not until the 9th century did Cornwall fall under the rule of English kings, first of Wessex and later of all England, and only in that century, as far as we know, did the Cornish clergy begin to accept the authority of the archbishop of Canterbury and to become a constituency of the English Church. Meanwhile, in the period preceding English rule, at least two monasteries were built in Cornwall and numerous other religious sites probably appeared: burial grounds, churches, standing crosses, and wells. Many of the names of these sites, later believed to contain the names of saints, are likely to go back to the same era. This means that to understand how the Church in Cornwall began, and how it acquired some of its distinctive features, we must know something of the history and nature of the region in which the Church first grew up. What was Cornwall like before it became an English county and its Church a part of the English Church?[1]

When the Romans conquered Britain in the 1st century AD, the South-West of the country was inhabited by people known to the Romans as the 'Dumnonii'. These people were 'Brittonic', in other words they shared the language and culture of most of Britain: the language that eventually became Welsh, Cornish, and Breton. Their centre of power was probably in Devon, which takes its name from them and contains Exeter, the administrative capital of the South West under the Romans. Roman writings called Exeter *Isca Dumnoniorum* ('the place on the Exe, belonging to the Dumnonii').[2] The territory of the Dumnonii seems to have included what is now Cornwall, since the geographer Ptolemy (fl. AD 125–150) refers to a place called the *promontorium Damnonium* ('promontory of the Dumnonii') that appears to have been Lizard Point.[3] However, a list of Roman place-names in southern Britain, preserved in late-medieval texts of the 'Ravenna Cosmography' (*c.*700), mentions one called *Purocoronavis* which apparently lay to the west of the River Tamar, the modern eastern boundary of Cornwall. This name has been conjectured to be a misreading of *Durocornovium* ('fort of the Cornish'), and if this is correct, it would suggest that there was a concept of the Cornish in Roman times, meaning the inhabitants of the 'horn' or peninsula.[4] It is not possible to say whether this was a geographical term or a reference to people with their own social or political organisation, wholly or partly distinct from that of the Dumnonians.

The same uncertainty applies to the period after unified Roman rule ended in Britain in the early 5th century. Urban life seems to have weakened in Exeter, and the subsequent centres of power in the region are not clear. We would expect the Dumnonii to have acquired one or more local rulers, and such a person is mentioned by the 6th-century British writer Gildas in his famous work, *On the Ruin and Conquest of Britain*: the 'tyrant' Constantine, 'whelp of the filthy lioness of

---

1 General surveys of the history and archaeology of the South West in the period from about 400 to 1000, include A. Fox, *South-West England*, 2nd edn (1973); M. Todd, *The South West to AD 1000* (1987); A. Preston-Jones and P. Rose, 'Medieval Cornwall', *Cornish Archaeology* 25 (1986), 155–85; B. Yorke, *Wessex in the Early Middle Ages* (1995); D. W. Probert, 'Church and Landscape: a study in social transition in south-western Britain A.D. *c.*400 to *c.*1200' (University of Birmingham, unpublished PhD thesis, 2002); and S. Turner, *Making a Christian Landscape: the countryside in early medieval Cornwall, Devon and Wessex* (2006). On S. M. Pearce, *South Western Britain in the Early Middle Ages* (2005), see the present writer's review in *TDA* 138 (2006), 416–19.

2 A. L. F. Rivet and C. Smith, *The Place-Names of Roman Britain* (1979), 342–3, 378.

3 Ibid., 344, 429. C. Thomas suggests that the Isles of Scilly were also part of the territory of the Dumnonii (*Explorations of a Drowned Landscape: Archaeology and History of the Isles of Scilly* (1985), 60).

4 Rivet and Smith, *Place-Names of Roman Britain*, 205, 350.

FIG 1. *Early inscribed stones from Cornwall. They carry the names of important people, usually in Latin, sometimes with Christian phraseology or symbols.*

Damnonia', a ruler of some kind, perhaps a king.[1] This is the earliest known reference to a territory called Damnonia or Dumnonia, formed from the name of the people who occupied it, but no other written evidence survives about the political organisation of this territory in the 5th or 6th centuries, apart from a very late tradition that another of its kings gave land to Glastonbury Abbey, allegedly in 601.[2] Instead the records take the form of inscribed stones, usually of a pillar type, mainly located in Cornwall but spreading into north and south-west Devon (Fig. 1). The stones are memorials of a kind that are also found in south Wales and share features with those in continental Europe.[3] Some may have marked graves and others roads or boundaries. They may extend in date from the 5th to the 11th centuries, but are typically of the 6th and 7th. All bear people's names, a few of which on the oldest stones are Irish names, occasionally written in Irish 'ogham' letters. Similar Irish names and letters are also found in Wales and need not imply a direct link between Ireland and Cornwall. Most of the names on the stones, however, are Brittonic, relating to people from Cornwall or Wales such as Conetoc, Rialobran, and Tegernomal, and the latest stones of all contain English personal names. The inscriptions are usually written in 'Insular' Latin script, sometimes with Christian phrases or emblems. Their language (except in the ogham inscriptions) is normally Latin too, and the names of the persons commemorated are often latinised. It is likely that the stones were erected for persons of high status: the aristocracy of Cornwall (mainly men), who seem to have been Christians when most of the stones were set up and who were supportive enough of Latin civilisation to display it on their memorials.

In the early 7th century the South West began to come under pressure from the English in the persons of the kings of Wessex (more correctly of the West Saxons), who ruled southern England from Somerset and Dorset to Berkshire and Hampshire (Fig. 2).[4] They sought to extend their control over Devon and Cornwall, but the task was a difficult one that took

---

1 Gildas, *The Ruin of Britain and Other Works*, ed. M. Winterbottom (1978), 29–30, 99–100 (chaps. 28–9).

2 William of Malmesbury, *Gesta Regum Anglorum*, ed. R. A. B. Mynors, R. M. Thomson, and M. Winterbottom (1998–9), I, 812–13; II, 405.

3 Seventy-nine such stones have been identified. The most recent inventory is by E. Okasha, *Corpus of Early Christian Inscribed Stones of South-West Britain* (1993) and idem, 'A Supplement to Corpus of Early Christian Inscribed Stones of South-West Britain', *Cornish Archaeology* 37–8 (1998–9), 137–52. For discussion and dating, see C. Thomas, *And Shall these Mute Stones Speak: Post-Roman Inscriptions in Western Britain* (1994); J. Knight, 'Seasoned with Salt: insular-Gallic contacts in the early memorial stones and cross slabs', in K. Dark (ed), *External Contacts and the Economy of Late Roman and Post-Roman Britain* (1996), pp. 109–20; and P. Sims-Williams, *The Celtic Inscriptions of Britain: phonology and chronology, c.400–1200* (2003).

4 On Wessex, see Yorke, *Wessex in the Early Middle Ages*, passim.

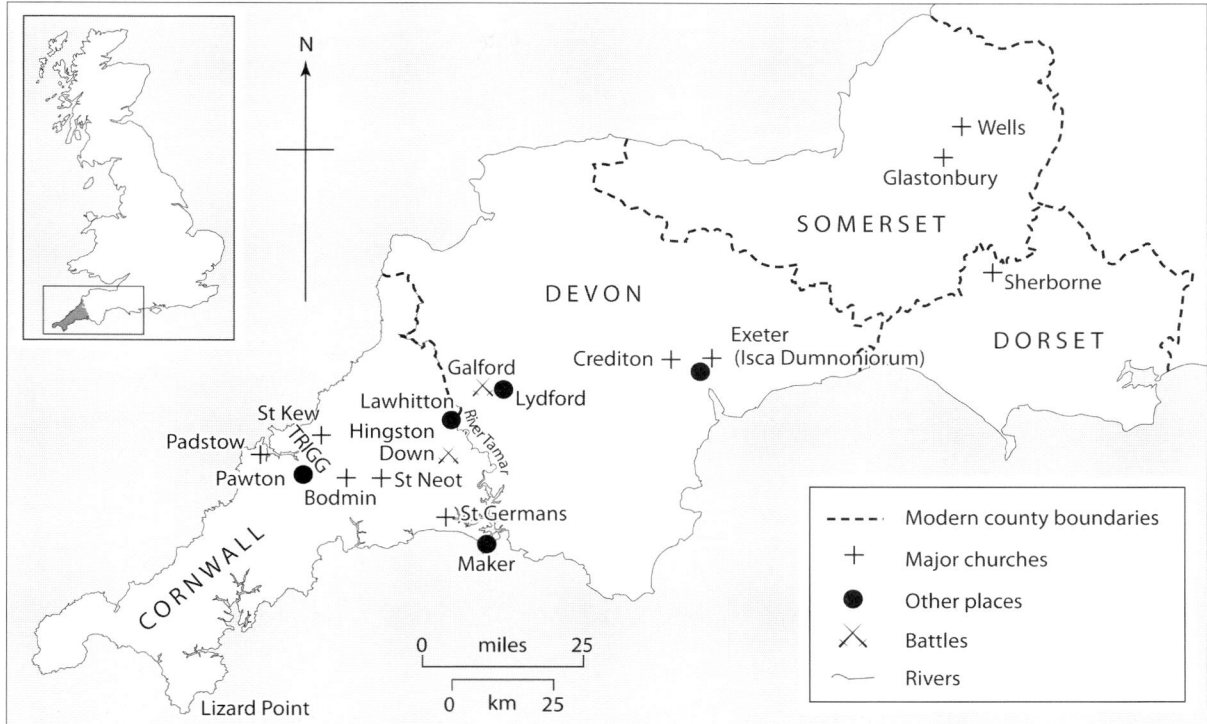

FIG 2. *The South West of England, 400–900.*

three hundred years to achieve and was not completed until the late 9th or 10th centuries.[1] The chief account of it is to be found in the Anglo-Saxon Chronicle, whose earliest text dates from round about 900 but is likely to have drawn on previous written sources. This 'A-Text' of the Chronicle records a series of struggles between the West Saxon kings and those whom it calls *Walas* ('Welsh', meaning foreigners) or *Bretwalas* ('British foreigners'), meaning the British people of the South West. In 614 and 658 the West Saxon kings are said to have gained victories over the *Walas* at *Beandune* and *Peonna*, probably in Dorset and Somerset respectively, which opened the way for English penetration into Devon during the second half of the 7th century.[2] In 682, according to the Chronicle, the West Saxon king Centwine 'drove the *Bretwalas* as far as the sea',[3] and within a few years of this, in about 690, it was possible for an English boy called Winfrith (later St Boniface) to enter a monastery in Exeter, ruled by an abbot with an English name.[4] In 693 Centwine's successor-but-one, King Ine, issued a code of laws for his subjects who included a number of 'Welsh', some paying tax to the king and others riding on his errands.[5]

Nonetheless there was still an important British ruler in the South West in the years around 700, when the English cleric St Aldhelm (d. 709) wrote a lengthy and carefully argued letter asking him and his clergy to adopt the current practices of the western Roman Church with regard to the calculation of the date of Easter and the shape of the clerical tonsure. The letter was addressed to 'the most glorious King *Geruntius*, the lord who guides the sceptre of the western kingdom, and to all the *sacerdotes* [bishops or priests] of *Domnonia*'.[6] *Geruntius* (Gerent in Old Cornish) is recorded as a king in two other sources, and Aldhelm's letter to him is worth scrutinising for its political as well as its religious significance. Its opening salutation is a curious one, since Gerent's kingdom is identified in an abstract geographical way whereas his clergy are placed in the precise and historic location of Dumnonia. By Aldhelm's time there was a concept of Dumnonia in the narrower sense of Devon as opposed

---

1 This view of the process as a lengthy one is shared by Probert, 'Church and Landscape', 241–90.

2 J. M. Bately (ed.), *The Anglo-Saxon Chronicle: a Collaborative Edition*, III (1986), 27, 30; *The Anglo-Saxon Chronicle*, trans. D. Whitelock (1965), 16, 21. Dates quoted from the Chronicle are as adjusted by the editors.

3 Bately (ed.), *Anglo-Saxon Chronicle*, 32; trans. Whitelock, 23.

4 W. Levison (ed.), *Vitae Sancti Bonifacii*, Monumenta Germaniae Historica, Scriptores Rerum Germanicarum 57 (1905),

6; trans. C. H. Talbot, *The Anglo-Saxon Missionaries in Germany* (1954), 28.

5 F. L. Attenborough (ed.), *The Laws of the Earliest English Kings* (1922), 43, 45, 47, 51, 55, 61.

6 Aldhelm, *Opera Omnia*, ed. R. Ehwald, Monumenta Germaniae Historica, Auctores Antiquissimi 15 (1919), 480–6; Aldhelm, *The Prose Works*, trans. M. Lapidge and M. Herren (1979), 155–60. The letter is discussed in detail by Probert, 'Church and Landscape' 267–78, who suggests the mid 690s as a possible date.

to Cornwall,[1] but he would hardly have restricted his message to the clergy of Devon; his hope would have been to bring the whole of the South West into harmony on the matters at issue. It is possible that the phrase 'the western kingdom' is a version of *Westwalas*, 'the west Welsh', the name by which the West Saxons called the south-western Britons and their land, but Aldhelm's tact is more likely to have led him to address Gerent by his official title. That might have been 'king of the west' or 'of the western people', but no evidence exists of such a title, and the most probable explanation for the phrase is that Aldhelm was obliged to avoid saluting Gerent as king of Dumnonia. Such an action would have offended the West Saxon kings who aspired to rule the territory and probably did rule it in east Devon and west Somerset. At the same time there is nothing in the address or the letter to suggest that Aldhelm regarded Gerent as someone whose pretensions could be ignored. Rather, the letter's deference and care to persuade not to threaten suggest a ruler and clergy of substance who had to be won over through respect and diplomacy.

Gerent has usually been regarded as a victim of the power of King Ine, a view originating in a statement by the Chronicle that Ine fought with Gerent 'king of the Welsh' in 710.[2] In fact the Chronicle does not identify the victor of this conflict, and an assumption that it was Ine appears only in later English chroniclers.[3] At one time there seemed to be confirmation of Ine's superiority over Gerent in a medieval record of Glastonbury Abbey that the West Saxon king granted land to the abbey at a place by the River *Tamer*, called *Linis* or *Linig*.[4] The historian H. P. R. Finberg used this belief to argue that Ine's power reached into Cornwall itself, since he was able to dispose of territory there,[5] but subsequent research has shown that the Glastonbury grant refers to Somerset, *Tamer* being an error for the River Tone.[6] This weakens the case for Ine possessing political control so far to the west. On the contrary, the Welsh source known as *Annales Cambriae* states that in 722 the British peoples of Britain were victorious in three battles, including one at '*Hehil* in [the land of] the Cornish people', an engagement that took place in Ine's reign since he ruled until 726.[7] True, the West Saxon kings were claiming authority well inside Devon soon after this date. Ine's successor, King Æthelheard, felt able to grant land to Glastonbury near the River Torridge in north Devon in 729, and to the bishop of Sherborne at Crediton near Exeter ten years later.[8] But neither grant proves that Gerent personally, or any of Cornwall, had come under Ine's control.

We can therefore view two other pieces of information about Cornwall at this time with less need to regard them as signs of West Saxon dominance. The first is a poem, written by Aldhelm at some point before his death in 709, describing a journey in the South West 'to dire Devon [*Domnonia*] through comfortless Cornwall [*Cornubia*]'.[9] This is the earliest recorded use of *Domnonia* to mean Devon alone and one of the first clear references to Cornwall as a region. During the journey a storm arose and he sheltered for the night in a church, attending worship led by local clergy. The poem, as a record of intercourse between Britons and West Saxons, is matched by a 14th-century list of royal benefactions to Sherborne Abbey (Dorset), which includes the statement that 'King *Gerontius*' granted an estate at Maker in south-east Cornwall.[10] Sherborne was in English hands by Gerent's time, but its church (or a church nearby) was named *Lanprobi* in 671 and may have commemorated the same saint as Probus church in Cornwall.[11] Gerent's grant may reflect links between Sherborne and Dumnonia, and such links might explain why Sherborne was chosen in about 705 to be the seat of an English bishop in charge of the lands further west. These lands were coming under West Saxon control but they were still partly populated by Britons. It may have been desirable to administer them from a church honoured by them, and no accident that Aldhelm, who had made contact with Devon and Cornwall, became the first bishop of Sherborne.

Three points emerge from this. First, now that Ine's power is less likely to have stretched into what is now Cornwall, west of the River Tamar, Aldhelm's mention of Cornwall need not mean that it had just become a separate political entity as a result of a West Saxon

---

1 Below. note 9.

2 Bately (ed.), *Anglo-Saxon Chronicle*, 33; trans. Whitelock, 26.

3 Henry of Huntingdon, *Historia Anglicana: The History of the English People*, ed. D. Greenway (1996), 222–4; *The Chronicle of John of Worcester*, ed. R. R. Darlington and P. McGurk, II (1995), 168–9.

4 L. Abrams, *Anglo-Saxon Glastonbury: Church and Endowment* (1996), 231–4.

5 H. P. R. Finberg, *The Early Charters of Devon and Cornwall* (hereafter *ECDC*) University of Leicester, Department of English Local History, occasional papers 2 (2nd edn, 1963), 17.

6 L. Abrams and J. P. Carley (eds.), *The Archaeology and History of Glastonbury Abbey* (1991), 123–4, 251–2; Abrams, *Anglo-Saxon Glastonbury*, 231–4.

7 *Nennius: British History and the Welsh Annals*, ed. J. Morris (1980), 47, 87.

8 P. H. Sawyer, *Anglo-Saxon Charters: An Annotated List and Bibliography* (1968) (hereafter S), 1676, 255; Finberg, *ECDC*, 7–8.

9 'Usque diram Domnoniam per carentem [strictly, meaning 'deficient'] Cornubiam' (*Aldhelmi Opera Omnia*, ed. Ehwald, 524–8; Aldhelm, *The Poetic Works*, trans. M. Lapidge and J. L. Rosier (1985), 177–9); discussed by Probert, 'Church and Landscape', 265–7.

10 M. A. O'Donovan (ed.), *Charters of Sherborne*, British Academy, Anglo-Saxon Charters 3 (1988), 81.

11 Ibid., 81, 85; K. Barker, 'The Early History of Sherborne', in S. M. Pearce (ed.), *The Early Church in Western Britain and Ireland*, British Archaeological Reports, British Series, 102 (1982), 77.

conquest of Devon. Rather his words imply that Cornwall and Devon were already different concepts, at least geographically. Secondly Aldhelm's journey, his presence at worship in a Dumnonian church (very likely a British one), his letter to Gerent, and Gerent's grant to Sherborne seem to represent free and equal intercourse between Dumnonian and English leaders. In the sphere of religion, at least, they look as much like friends as enemies. Finally, although Gerent's grant is the only known document issued by a Dumnonian king or indeed by anyone in the Brittonic South West apart from a profession of obedience made by a 9th-century bishop,[1] it need not have been a rare initiative or one borrowed from English usage. Three charters composed in Cornwall in the 10th century when it was under English rule contain features in common with those of Wales and Brittany, implying that there was a distinct tradition of charter-making among the Dumnonian people.[2] We should allow for a history of law and record-keeping in the region, as well as for the wars described in the Anglo-Saxon Chronicle.

These wars continued from time to time in the 8th century. The Chronicle states that the West Saxon king Cuthred 'fought against the *Walas*' in 753 and that his successor-but-one, King Cynewulf (757–86), 'frequently fought great battles against the *Bretwalas*'.[3] A charter allegedly granted by Cynewulf to the church of Wells (Som.) in about 774 states that he gave it partly to expiate his sins 'and also, what it is sorrowful to say, for a certain vexation of our enemies, the race of the Cornish people'. A Cornish raid into Somerset seems unlikely at this date, but the charter may be based on an earlier document, perhaps one in favour of Sherborne which had property in Devon.[4] Later, in 786, when Cynewulf was attacked and killed in his kingdom by a band of his enemies, his retinue included an unnamed British (*Bryttisc*) hostage who was badly wounded, apparently while defending the king to whom he had been entrusted.[5] The evidence suggests that the Britons still offered a challenge to the West Saxon kings during the second half of the 8th century, but the reference to them as Cornish is worth noting. It may reflect a situation in which most of Devon and its people had been integrated into the West Saxon kingdom, so that the Cornish beyond the Tamar had come to be seen as the principal enemies of the English in the South West.

In 802 a new and energetic king took the West Saxon throne: Ecgberht, the ancestor of all its later rulers and of most of those of England up to 1066. For whatever reasons, hostilities broke out between him and the Britons of the South West, and in 815, according to the Chronicle, he 'raided *Westwalas* from east to west'.[6] The term, by this time, must have meant the people or land of Cornwall, possibly with parts of west Devon. Ten years later, in 825, the *Walas* fought with the men of Devon at *Gafulford*: probably Galford two miles west of Lydford (west Devon).[7] The name *Gafulford*, meaning 'the tax ford', hints at a frontier here, a little east of the Tamar, with Lydford as an English border stronghold. Finally we are told that a 'great ship army' of Danes came to *Westwalas* in 835 and was put to flight by Ecgberht, along with the *Walas* who had joined them, at *Hengestdun*: very likely Hingston Down near Callington.[8] A letter of the late 10th century claims that Ecgberht 'gave a tenth of the land [to God] and disposed of it as seemed fit to him'. The same source states that he granted three estates in Cornwall 'to Sherborne', meaning its bishop and church.[9] If correct, this suggests that he acquired considerable power in the region. He did not necessarily annex Cornwall completely, however. It was common practice for a conqueror to allow a local ruler to remain as his deputy and servant. A British king may have ruled west of the Tamar until at least 876 when the *Annales Cambriae* record Dungarth, 'king of *Cerniu*' (i.e. Cornwall), as having drowned.[10] Dungarth bears a close resemblance to Doniert, the name of an important person inscribed on King Doniert's Stone at Redgate in the parish of St Cleer, and the annals and stone may refer to the very same man.[11]

The notice of Dungarth's death may also imply that he was the last king of Cornwall, since the *Annales* rarely mention Cornish affairs. Soon afterwards it is apparent that the West Saxon king, the famous King Alfred, who ruled from 871 to 899, was active in the region in a peaceful sense, not just as a conqueror. Alfred is said by his Welsh biographer Asser to have hunted in Cornwall and to have visited the shrine of St Gueriir, probably at St Neot.[12] Alfred's will mentions lands that he held in Cornwall, both in 'Triggshire' (the

---

1 Below, p. 9.
2 S 450, 810, 1207 ; W. Davies, 'The Latin Charter Tradition in Western Britain, Brittany and Ireland in the Early Mediaeval Period', in D. Whitelock et al. (ed.), *Ireland in Early Medieval Europe: Studies in Memory of Kathleen Hughes* (1982), 258–80.
3 Bately (ed.), *Anglo-Saxon Chronicle*, 36; trans. Whitelock, 30.
4 S 262, printed and discussed in S. E. Kelly (ed.), *Charters of Bath and Wells*, Anglo-Saxon Charters, 13 (2009), 193, 197.
5 Bately (ed.), *Anglo-Saxon Chronicle*, 37; trans. Whitelock, 31.
6 Bately (ed.), *Anglo-Saxon Chronicle*, 41; trans. Whitelock, 39.
7 Bately (ed.), *Anglo-Saxon Chronicle*, 41; trans. Whitelock, 40 and n. 2.
8 Bately (ed.), *Anglo-Saxon Chronicle*, 42–3; trans. Whitelock, 41.
9 D. Whitelock, M. Brett, and C. N. L. Brooke (ed.), *Councils & Synods I: A.D. 871–1204* (1981), I, 170.
10 D. N. Dumville (ed.), *Annales Cambriae, A.D.682–954* (2002), 12–13. A late manuscript of the work explains *Cerniu* as 'Cornwall'.
11 Okasha, *Corpus of Early Christian Inscribed Stones*, 213–17.
12 *Asser's Life of King Alfred*, ed. W. H. Stevenson (1959), 55; trans. S. Keynes and M. Lapidge, *Alfred the Great: Asser's Life of King Alfred and other Contemporary Sources* (1983), 89.

FIG 3. *An early inscribed stone, undated, from South Hill churchyard. It carries the name (in Latin) of Cumregnus son of Maucus.*

north-east) and elsewhere.¹ By about 900, therefore, parts of Cornwall were the estates of an English king, and some other parts those of the English bishop of Sherborne if the grants ascribed to Ecgberht had taken effect. There can no longer have been a British ruler in Cornwall possessing much in the way of kingship, and the most powerful men of the area were probably noblemen like Maenchi the 'count' (*comes*) who is recorded granting land to the church of Lansallos in the 920s or 30s.² Alfred's successor-but-one, King Æthelstan (924–39), ruled not only the West Saxon kingdom but most of England and was also active in Cornwall. He appointed or confirmed in office a bishop of Cornwall named Conan, who witnessed charters in England during the early 930s, and Conan, whose name indicates that he was of British race, was evidently integrated into the English Church and kingdom.³ Æthelstan also appears to have granted or confirmed the possessions of the church of St Germans in 936, and (with less certainty) those of St Buryan in the far west of the land.⁴ The authority that he held in Cornwall could be interpreted as having grown peacefully from that of Alfred, but the 12th-century historian William of Malmesbury believed that Æthelstan waged war on the Cornish and attacked them energetically (*impigne adorsus*). He drove them from Exeter, which they had hitherto shared with the English, and fixed the boundary of their territory at the Tamar.⁵

William's assertions are not confirmed by contemporary evidence, although Æthelstan's reign is admittedly poor in its written records. There is indeed a reference in the Anglo-Saxon Chronicle to Æthelstan having authority over Hywel, king of the 'West Welsh', but in that case the term relates to a ruler of south-west Wales, not south-west England.⁶ William's story about a significant presence of 'Cornish' people in Exeter in Æthelstan's time looks anachronistic in terms of the 10th century, although some immigrants may have lived there. Still, whether or not Æthelstan was the last conqueror of Cornwall or its ruler through a gradual peaceable growth of English power, it seems clear that the region was firmly under the control of the West Saxon kings by his reign. A number of royal charters survive after the middle of the 10th century granting or confirming lands and privileges west of the Tamar. In religious terms Cornwall was now a diocese subject to the archbishop of Canterbury, and politically on the way to becoming a county of the kingdom of England. By the second half of the 10th century some important men in Cornwall were adopting an English forename as well as their Brittonic one, at least when doing business with the English: Ælfeah Gerent, Wulfnoth Rumuncant, and Bishop Wulfsige Comoere.⁷ By the time of Domesday Book virtually all the leading nobility and clergy are recorded with Norman or English forenames, making it impossible to be sure any longer which of them was Cornish by race or culture.⁸

---

1 F. E. Harmer (ed.), *Select English Historical Documents of the Ninth and Tenth Centuries* (1914), no. 11; Keynes and Lapidge, *Alfred the Great*, 175.

2 S 1207, printed and discussed in O. J. Padel, 'The Charter of Lanlawren (Cornwall)', in K. O'Brien O'Keeffe and A. Orchard (ed.), *Latin Learning and English Lore* (2005), II, 74–85.

3 L. Olson, *Early Monasteries in Cornwall* (1989), 63.

4 Ibid., 63, 78–81.

5 William of Malmesbury, *Gesta Regum Anglorum*, ed. Mynors et al., I, 216–17.

6 *The Anglo-Saxon Chronicle*, trans. Whitelock, 68.

7 O. J. Padel, 'Two New Pre-Conquest Charters for Cornwall', *Cornish Studies* 6 (1978), 20–7 at 25 n. 2; idem, 'The Charter of Lanlawren (Cornwall)', 85 n. 25.

8 C. and F. Thorn (ed.), *Domesday Book*, vol. X: *Cornwall* (1979), 'Index of Persons'.

CHRISTIANITY BEFORE AD 900

It is possible that there were individual Christians in the South West, visitors or natives, from the 1st century onwards, but they have left no traces. The earliest known Christians in Cornwall may have been two bishops, Instantius and Tiberianus, who were deposed at the Council of Bordeaux in 384 on charges of heresy and exiled to an island beyond Britain called *Sylinancim*, which could be Scilly.[1] The Emperor Constantine granted toleration to Christians throughout the Roman Empire in 313, and in the following year three British bishops from London, York, and possibly Lincoln attended a Church council at Arles in modern France.[2] During the rest of the 4th century Christianity increased its status in the Empire and became the official religion, enabling it to establish bishops, clergy, churches and congregations.

Roman Christianity of an organised kind has left most traces in towns. In Exeter, the administrative centre of the South West, burials on the site of the former Roman basilica (the local centre of administration) point to the likely existence of a Christian church and Christian burial practices on the site in the 5th century.[3] It is less certain that such organisation had reached the rural majority of the region by the time that imperial rule in Britain evaporated in that century.[4] Evidence for Christianity in Cornwall begins to build up only after about 500. One indication of its presence is to be found on the inscribed stones, many of which appear to belong to the 6th and 7th centuries.[5] Some of these stones display the Christian 'chi-rho' symbol (the first two letters of Christ in Greek) and most have their texts in Latin, affirming a link with the Christian Latin culture of continental Europe. Another sign consists of Gildas's attack on Constantine, the 6th-century ruler of Dumnonia. He alleged that this man had killed two royal youths and their guardians in a church near an altar, to which they had presumably gone to refuge. The mention of the church, followed by an exhortation from Gildas that the tyrant should repent and seek forgiveness, indicates that the ruler and his family were Christians, at least in name.[6] If Constantine had been a practising pagan, Gildas would hardly have failed to say so. The South West adjoined late- and post-Roman Christian areas in southern Britain during the 4th, 5th, and much of the 6th centuries, and it had trading relations with western Gaul and the Mediterranean, shown by the presence of pottery from those regions at sites such as Bantham (Devon) and Tintagel.[7] It is therefore likely that much of the impetus of early Christianity in Devon and Cornwall came from southern Britain and, more widely, from links with continental Europe.

Those who later wrote about the origins of Christianity in Cornwall, from about the 8th century onwards, had different views about its arrival there. They did not retain memories of contacts with the east, but emphasised those with the north and west: Wales and Ireland.[8] The earliest manifestation of this is the so-called 'First Life of St Samson of Dol', the oldest written Life of a saint that contains information about Cornwall. Samson probably died in the decade or two after 562 and the Life therefore professes to deal with affairs in the middle of the 6th century, at about the time of Gildas. It claims to be the work of a cleric of Brittany who had visited Cornwall and gained information from an elderly man who lived there in a monastery founded by Samson.[9] This man's uncle, Henoc, had been Samson's cousin and companion, had been told stories about him by Samson's mother, and had written an account of him.[10] If true, these life-spans would suggest that the work was written in the first half of the 7th century, but the latest editor of the Life observes that it quotes from the English scholar Bede (active c.700–735), and proposes a date of about 750.[11] This shows that the version of the Life that we possess is not an account close to the events of the saint's life but a work, or at least a revision of a work, made much later. One of the episodes relating to Cornwall, concerning a serpent, is of a legendary kind.

---

1 Sulpicius Severus, *Libri qui Supersunt*, ed. K. Halm, Corpus Scriptorum Ecclesiasticorum Latinorum, I (1866), 104; discussed by Rivet and Smith, *Place-Names of Roman Britain*, 457–9.

2 R. Sharpe, 'Martyrs and Local Saints in Late Antique Britain', in A. Thacker and R. Sharpe (ed.), *Local Saints and Local Churches in the Early Medieval West* (Oxford, 2002), 75–154 at 77.

3 P. T. Bidwell et al., *The Legionary Bath-House and Basilica and Forum at Exeter* (1979), 2, 111–13; C. Henderson and P. T. Bidwell, 'The Saxon Minster at Exeter', in S. M. Pearce (ed.), *The Early Church in Western Britain and Ireland* (1982), 145–75.

4 On Christianity in Roman and post-Roman Britain, see C. Thomas, *Christianity in Britain to AD500* (1981); Sharpe, 'Martyrs and Local Saints'; J. Blair, *The Church in Anglo-Saxon Society* (2005), 10–34; and D. Petts, *Christianity in Roman Britain* (2003). The latter points to possible late-Roman Christian sites in the countryside of the South West at Holcombe (Devon) and Brean Down and Lamyatt Beacon (Som.) (ibid., 20, 69, 71, 74, 95).

5 Above, pp. 1–2.

6 Gildas, *Ruin of Britain*, ed. Winterbottom, 29–30, 99–100 (chaps. 28–9).

7 The evidence is summarised by Probert, 'Church and Landscape', 244–5 and fig. 4.1.

8 For further discussion see below, pp. 110–25.

9 The best edition is now P. Flobert (ed.), *La Vie ancienne de Saint Samson de Dol* (1997), with a French translation. The English translation by T. Taylor, *The Life of St. Samson of Dol* (1925) must be used with great caution.

10 *La Vie ancienne*, 138–43.

11 Ibid., 102–11, 186, 242.

Samson is described as having been the child of noble parents in south-west Wales (Fig. 4). He was brought up by St Illtud in the monastery of Llantwit Major (Glamorgan), becoming a monk and eventually a bishop. Later he came by ship to Cornwall with his father Amon and a company of followers. The author of the Life knew little about why this journey began or ended. All he recorded were three episodes from it, which he arranged in what he represents as their chronological order. First, after landing (probably in the estuary of the River Camel), Samson went to a monastery called *Docco*, identifiable with St Kew. Its monks refused to receive him on the excuse that his standards were too high for them, so Samson and his party travelled onwards through the *pagus Tricurius*, meaning Trigg, north Cornwall east of the Camel. Here local people were holding games at a pillar or image. Samson regarded what they were doing as pagan, but he won them over through a miracle and the nobleman who led them, named Vedian (*Vedianus*), asked him to confirm their baptisms. The count then told Samson about a huge serpent which lurked in a cave and troubled its neighbourhood. Samson destroyed the serpent, and went to live in the cave where a spring of water appeared in response to his prayer. He founded a monastery in the vicinity, leaving Amon to run it and ordaining his cousin Henoc as deacon. Then he crossed the English Channel to Brittany where he was based for the rest of his life.[1] More than one site has been suggested for Samson's monastery, but the location remains an open question.[2]

This information is interesting, but it is too limited and probably too late to be regarded as a literal and connected account of what happened. Its presentation of the events of Samson's visit to Cornwall may be an artistic one with an ascending sequence: rejection, struggle, triumph, and foundation. Its portrayal of 6th-century Cornish society as nominally Christian but still engaged in some pagan practices may not be far from the truth, but may equally be a romantic notion that enabled Samson's achievements to seem more dramatic. This notion appears in a more pronounced form in some later legends of Cornish saints, in which they are represented struggling with pagans, notably with a wicked ruler named Teudar. At least two saints, Columb and Gwinear, were alleged to have been martyred in the region on account of their faith,[3] but there is no evidence of martyrdoms in Cornwall, and even Samson's Life does not imply such happenings. Its most reliable evidence relates to the time in which it took its present form, the 8th century. By that time there had evidently been religious contact between south Wales and Cornwall. Samson is depicted as coming from Wales, and the

FIG 4. *St Samson, imagined as a bishop, from a pre-Reformation bench end at St Samson's church, Golant.*

monastery of *Docco* at St Kew certainly bore the name of a saint of that country, whose original monastery was at Llandough (Glamorgan).[4] The Cornish *Docco* must have been a daughter house of Llandough or a foundation inspired by it.

Samson's Life, then, emphasises the contribution of South Wales to the growth of Christianity in Cornwall. This is credible, since it accords with the common presence of the inscribed stones in both areas and the association by Gildas of the ruler of Dumnonia with those of Wales. Some subsequent Lives of saints venerated in Cornwall and Brittany also represent them as having travelled there from Wales, including the Lives of Paul of Léon (884), Cadoc and Petroc (11th century), and Nectan (12th century). Later still Irish origins were claimed for saints such as Piran (12th or 13th centuries), Gwinear (c.1300), and Breage (before 1542).[5] These Lives may have imitated that of Samson, however, and they are principally based on the beliefs and folklore of the times in which they were written

---

1 Ibid., 210–23.　　2 Below, p. 135.　　4 N. Orme, *The Saints of Cornwall* (2000), 108.
3 *La Vie ancienne*, 91–2, 136–7.　　5 On these Lives, see the entries for the saints in ibid.

rather than on trustworthy earlier evidence. Their picture of the evangelisation of Cornwall coming largely from other 'Celtic' countries has become deeply embedded in popular belief, but it exaggerates one direction of influence at the expense of the others. There are not many churches or chapels in the county dedicated to Welsh saints, and hardly any commemorating Irish ones.[1] The religious ties between Cornwall and southern Britain, which we have postulated in the 5th and 6th centuries, revived or continued around 700 through Aldhelm's relations with Dumnonia and Gerent's gift of land to Sherborne. Links with Brittany across the English Channel are suggested by the visit of Samson's Breton biographer (or at the very least by his interest in and knowledge of Cornwall) and, as we shall see in due course, by the dedication of several Cornish churches and chapels to Breton saints. The chronology of some of these latter dedications, however, may belong to the 10th and 11th centuries rather than to earlier times.

Assuming that Samson's Life, as we have it, comes from the 8th century, we can add its information about religion in Cornwall to that which emerges from Aldhelm's letter to Gerent of about 700 and the tradition of Gerent's grant. All three sources suggest that Christianity was by this time well established. Aldhelm addressed a Christian king whom he envisaged as an influential figure in the local Church. The Sherborne charter suggests that such a king might engage in the endowment of religious houses like his counterparts elsewhere in Britain. Samson's Life refers to two Cornish monasteries, and since it seems to be mainly concerned with central Cornwall, this leaves room for other such houses elsewhere. The clergy of such monasteries might have lived communally and celibately or alternatively have enjoyed a degree of personal privacy and property; there may have even been a mixture of life-styles on the same site.[2] Some of the clergy may have sought retirement from the world, while others have ministered within it. Aldhelm's letter indicates that the Cornish clergy shared the customs of the Welsh and Irish in cutting their hair and calculating the date of Easter in ways that were obsolete in the rest of the Catholic Church. To that extent the Cornish differed from the English, but the letter and Aldhelm's journey through Cornwall suggest that they were not unfriendly to their eastern neighbours. Indeed he felt able to express the hope that they would not behave like the clergy of Dyfed (south-west Wales), who refused even to worship with Englishmen.[3] His letter may even have had some effect. It was believed by Bede to have persuaded at least those Britons who lived in the West Saxon kingdom to adopt the modern Roman way of reckoning Easter.[4]

The glimpses of Cornwall given by these records are followed by another period of obscurity, which ends only after Ecgberht's conquests in the early 9th century. As has been mentioned, he is credited by a letter of the late 10th century with having granted three estates in Cornwall to the church of Sherborne. These are listed as *Polltun* (Pawton in St Breock), *Caellwic*, and *Landwithan* (Lawhitton near Launceston).[5] A separate tradition at Sherborne in the 14th century attributed Ecgberht with giving its church 12 hides of land at *Kelk* and 18 hides at *Ros* and *Macor* (Maker).[6] The king's intention was presumably to increase Sherborne's possessions in Cornwall, building on Gerent's grant to give the bishop of Sherborne bases from which to supervise and influence the local Church. For a long time to come, however, Cornwall was sufficiently remote and distinctive to need Church leaders who were Britons. Between 833 and 870, Kenstec, a bishop whose seat lay 'in the monastery of *Dinuurrin*', made a profession of obedience to the archbishop of Canterbury.[7] Kenstec's name was Brittonic and his seat, *Dinuurrin*, has been plausibly identified as Bodmin, a suitably important and central site for a bishop.[8] It is not clear if there was only one such person in Cornwall at this time since St Germans shows signs of having been another early bishop's seat,[9] whether similar bishops remained in being during the late 9th century, or how they related to the bishops of Sherborne.

The next recorded bishop in Cornwall after Kenstec appears to have been Bishop Asser, the biographer of King Alfred. Asser tells us in his biography that the king gave him the church at Exeter 'with all its *parochia* [i.e. territory] in the Saxon lands [*Saxonia*] and Cornwall'.[10] This was probably in about the 880s and is more likely to have involved a territory in the sense of a diocesan responsibility in Devon and Cornwall than a gift of landed property alone, because the church at Exeter is not known to have possessed such property outside south and east Devon before the Norman Conquest.[11] At the time of Alfred's gift, Asser was already a bishop and, as a native of Wales, a speaker of a language close

---

1 For discussion of this point, see ibid., 28–9, 53.
2 For possible late traces of a mixed community, see below, p. 12 note 8.
3 *Aldhelmi Opera Omnia*, ed. Ehwald, 480–6; Aldhelm, *Prose Works*, ed. Lapidge and Herren, 155–60.
4 *Bede's Ecclesiastical History of the English People*, ed. B. Colgrave and R. A. B. Mynors (1991), 514–15.
5 Whitelock, Brett, and Brooke (ed.), *Councils & Synods I*, I, 170. *Caellwic* is also read as *Caellincg*; see below, p. 123. The location is uncertain.

6 O'Donovan (ed.), *Charters of Sherborne*, 81; Finberg, *ECDC*, 17 no. 74. *Kelk* may be identical with *Caellwic* and *Ros* was presumably near Maker: possibly Rame.
7 Olson, *Early Monasteries in Cornwall*, 51–6.
8 Ibid., 53, a suggestion of O. J. Padel.   9 Ibid., 63–4.
10 *Asser's Life of King Alfred*, ed. Stevenson, 68; Keynes and Lapidge, *Alfred the Great*, 50–1, 97, 264–5.
11 N. Orme, *Exeter Cathedral: the First Thousand Years 400–1500* (2009), 5, 8–10, 76. For a different view of this difficult passage see below, pp. 121–2.

to Cornish. It looks as if the king put him in charge of the Church in Devon and Cornwall, possibly as an assistant to the bishop of Sherborne. When a new bishop of Sherborne was required in the 890s, Alfred gave the post to Asser, making him leader of the Church of the whole South West. This had the merit of placing the Cornish under a trusted royal servant, while catering for their special needs with a bishop whose speech and religious traditions resembled their own. After Asser's death in 909, the South West was regarded as too large for one bishop to serve, and the diocese of Sherborne was subdivided. Somerset was given a bishop based at Wells, and Devon one located at Crediton near Exeter.

The history of the Church in Cornwall after this subdivision is partly revealed by two West Saxon sources of the 10th century. One is a Latin document produced between 952 and 988 in the interests of the bishop and church of Crediton, known as the 'Plegmund letter' or the 'Crediton claim'. It gives an incorrect account of the Sherborne subdivision, which it ascribes to the intervention of Pope Formosus who was dead by that date, and adopts a hostile stance towards the Cornish.[1] The second is a letter in English, sent by Archbishop Dunstan of Canterbury to King Æthelred the Unready between 981 and 988.[2] This letter parallels the 'Crediton claim' in some respects and evidently knew of it, but provides more information about Cornwall, is favourable to the Cornish Church, and contains two later additions that are even more favourable in that respect. The 'Crediton claim' asserts that Crediton's first bishop, Eadwulf, was granted the three estates in Cornwall that had hitherto belonged to Sherborne. This was done 'so that every year he might visit the Cornish people and repress their errors, for formerly, in as far as they could, they resisted the truth and did not obey the apostolic decrees'. It goes on to allege that the estates were held by both Eadwulf (in office c.909–934) and his successor Æthelgar (934–952/3). Dunstan concurs about the three estates. He differs in saying that they were originally given to Sherborne by Ecgberht (which, as we shall see, was a point in favour of Cornwall) and he explains their grant to Eadwulf in a more temperate way: 'because its people had previously been disobedient, without awe of the West Saxons'. Whereas the 'Crediton claim' accused the Cornish of being unsatisfactory in their religious beliefs or practices, Dunstan reduced the charge to one of disobedience which he did not define as religious.

There is no reason to doubt the grant of the three estates to Crediton since both sources assert it and both were evidently linked with attempts by Crediton to retain the lands. It looks therefore as if at first, after 909, the bishops of that church were expected to exercise some authority in Cornwall by virtue of holding the three estates. But this authority did not continue in a full sense for very long because of the presence of Conan as bishop in Cornwall from at least 931 until at least the mid 940s.[3] An explanation of his presence is given by the additions to the text of Dunstan's letter, made at some point after 981, which say that King Æthelstan 'gave Conan the bishopric as far as the Tamar flows', in other words all the land west of the river.[4] This ascribes to Æthelstan the creation or revival of an independent bishop and diocese of Cornwall. It receives support from two documents attributed to Æthelstan in later sources. One is a charter seen in the 1530s or 40s by John Leland, probably at St Germans, from which he made a note that Æthelstan 'raised a certain Conan as bishop in the church of St Germans' on 7 December 936.[5] The second is a fragment of the same or another charter of 936, preserved in the medieval cartulary of Plympton Priory (Devon), in which the king said that 'I restore and freely bestow as a perpetual diocese all the territory of the bishopric, that is to say of St German, bishop of the region of Cornwall'.[6] The three references combine to make a powerful case for the creation or revival of an independent diocese in 936, perhaps converting Conan from a subordinate role to an authoritative one. The absence of this event from the 'Crediton claim' is not surprising; we might expect it to have been mentioned in Dunstan's letter, but he may not have thought it relevant since he was concerned with the three estates not the existence of the diocese. We can reconcile all the sources by concluding that an independent diocese came into existence in 936 but that Crediton held on to the three estates for another twenty years. During this period the bishop of Cornwall would have had to support himself from St Germans and its lands along with any others that Æthelstan may have granted to him.

The next known bishop of Cornwall after Conan is Daniel, who became bishop not later than 955. He was consecrated, according to Dunstan's letter, at the order of King Eadred of the West Saxons (946–55) and received from Eadred the three estates, to be held 'to St Germans to the bishopric'. Dunstan's mention of Ecgberht's grant is relevant here: what one king had given to one church, another king could transfer to another. Daniel, like Conan, was probably from one of the Brittonic lands, whose clergy adopted Old Testament names more often than their English counterparts, and this was undoubtedly true of Daniel's

---

1 BL, Add. 7138, printed in Whitelock, Brett, and Brooke (ed.), *Councils & Synods I*, I, 167–9.
2 Ibid., I, 169–73.
3 E. B. Fryde et al. (ed.), *Handbook of British Chronology* (1986), 214.
4 Whitelock, Brett, and Brooke (ed.), *Councils & Synods I*, I, 171–2.
5 J. Leland, *Collectanea*, ed. T. Hearne (1774), I, 75.
6 Padel, 'Two New Pre-Conquest Charters', 26–7.

successor whose Brittonic name was Comoere but was also known by the Anglo-Saxon name Wulfsige.[1] Dunstan's letter concludes by saying that when he consecrated Wulfsige as bishop (an event datable to between 959 and 963), he and all the bishops agreed that the new bishop should keep the three estates as long as he preached the faith correctly and was loyal to the king.[2] Their acquisition must have improved the resources of the Cornish bishops as much as their loss impoverished and embittered the bishops and clergy of Crediton, hence the hostility of the 'Crediton claim' to the Cornish. The claim must have been triggered by either the transfer of the estates to Daniel or their confirmation to Wulfsige Comoere, and Dunstan's letter implies that the claim was renewed when Wulfsige died, probably in the 980s, hence perhaps an appeal to Dunstan from Cornwall to set the record straight.[3] The additions to the letter may even point to a later dispute, but Crediton did not succeed in its challenges and the bishops of Cornwall kept at least two of the estates, Lawhitton and Pawton, for the rest of the life of the diocese.

THE CHURCH IN CORNWALL 900–1066

The West Saxon kings, later kings of England, who established their rule over Cornwall duly acted as patrons and protectors of the Church there. As well as the bishopric established or re-established by Æthelstan, two charters exist purporting to be grants by him and by a later king, Edgar (959–75), to the churches of St Buryan and St Kew.[4] This does not mean that the Church in Cornwall led a calm and untroubled existence under royal protection. Royal authority itself was disrupted from time to time, notably by the Viking invasions of the reign of Æthelred the Unready (978–1016). In 981 the Anglo-Saxon Chronicle recorded that '*Sancte Petroces stow* [either Padstow or Bodmin] was laid waste', presumably by a Viking attack, and at some point St Petroc's relics and clergy moved from Padstow to Bodmin, perhaps as a result of that event.[5] Even in peaceful times, churches could not always retain their property. The ancient monastery of St Kew forfeited lands to powerful laity during the 10th or 11th centuries.[6] Maker, which was given to Sherborne by Gerent and Ecgberht, was back in the hands of the king by 1066.[7] After the Norman Conquest, William the Conqueror ordered the restoration to Bodmin church of a piece of land that Earl Harold of Wessex (later King Harold II) was said to have seized from that church.[8]

There was also an exploitation of Cornish resources in favour of churches east of the Tamar. One aspect of this was the granting of land, in the manner of Ecgberht to Sherborne. Tavistock Abbey (Devon) acquired estates in eastern Cornwall towards the end of the 10th century, and further lands and churches were transferred to other religious houses after the Norman Conquest. Relics were removed, notably the bones of Neot and Rumon, which were taken to St Neot's (Hunts.) and Tavistock respectively.[9] The removal of holy remains from Cornwall may be judged as a species of plunder, but it may also be interpreted as a sign of respect by the English for Cornish spirituality. Such respect is most evident with regard to Petroc of Bodmin, who was chosen as the patron saint of more than a dozen churches in Devon, Somerset, and Hampshire, some of them probably founded during the 10th and 11th centuries, perhaps using bits of his relics.[10] The fact that one of the churches was in Winchester, the chief city of the English kings in those centuries, suggests that they deliberately added Petroc to the other saints whom they honoured and trusted to help them.

The bishops of Cornwall by the mid 10th century had their principal seat in the church of St Germans. This was in effect their cathedral and adjoined a large estate which supported them, their household, and the cathedral clergy. They also came to hold other important properties: Lawhitton, Pawton, and two large estates which belonged to the bishops of Exeter by the time of the Domesday survey in 1086. The latter were the manors of Treliever, consisting of the lands around Penryn, and Tregaire, encompassing much of the Roseland peninsula.[11] Five or six bishops of Cornwall are recorded from Conan in the 930s to Buruhwold in about the 1020s, and there may have been

---

1 W. M. M. Picken, 'Bishop Wulfsige Comoere: an unrecognised tenth-century gloss in the Bodmin Gospels', *Cornish Studies* 14 (1986), 34–8.
2 Whitelock, Brett, and Brooke (ed.), *Councils & Synods I*, I, 172.
3 Ibid., I, 165–7.
4 S 450, 810; Finberg, *ECDC*, 17 nos 77–8; 18 no. 84.
5 *The Anglo-Saxon Chronicle*, V, ed. K. O'Brien O'Keeffe (2001), 84; trans. Whitelock, 80.
6 Thorn (ed.), *Domesday Book: Cornwall*, 1/4, 5/7/6, 5/24/14.
7 Ibid., 5/2/14.

8 Ibid., 4/21.
9 Orme, *Saints of Cornwall*, 202, 226. Relics of a third saint, Moren of Lamorran, may have been conveyed to other churches in England (ibid., 195, 226–7).
10 Ibid., 218.
11 Thorn (ed.), *Domesday Book: Cornwall*, 2/1–15. In 1086 the bishop also owned some further lesser properties including Methleigh in Breage, which he held outright, and Burniere in Egloshayle, Gulval, Lanherne, Tinten in St Tudy, and St Winnow, held of him by tenants.

more.¹ After the 990s they had English names alone, reflecting the fact that, even if they were Cornish, there was coming to be a stronger English influence on the county. In the 10th century the diocese accorded with the Church organisation of southern England. Most of the counties of this region had their own bishop, and his seat often lay at a rural estate like St Germans, but during the 11th century opinion in England came to favour larger dioceses with richer, more powerful bishops and cathedrals based in towns. The diocese of Cornwall did not meet these criteria and, as the county became more closely integrated with England, it lost some of the special character that had caused it to be treated separately.

The new order of things was foreshadowed in 1027 when Lyfing became the bishop. He was an Englishman who had been abbot of Tavistock and was already bishop of Crediton, which he continued to hold in plurality with Cornwall.² In 1038–9 he added a third diocese, Worcester, to his portfolio, making it unlikely that he spent much time west of the Tamar. When Lyfing died in 1046 he was succeeded both in Cornwall and at Crediton by Leofric, who may have been Cornish or Welsh since he is once described as a Briton (*Brytonicus*).³ Leofric was a reformer who sought to build stronger Church institutions. In 1050 he got the agreement of the pope and the king to rationalise the linkage of the two dioceses by a formal act of union and the establishment of a new cathedral in the city of Exeter. This helped set a pattern for similar diocesan readjustments elsewhere in England. After 1050 Cornwall formed part of the diocese of Exeter, although it had some separate status as an archdeaconry by the 1120s, and it remained a part until the diocese of Truro was created in 1877.

Little is recorded about the organisation of the diocese of Cornwall during the 10th and 11th centuries. The diocese was a small one, and until Lyfing's reign its supervision need not have been a difficult task for the bishop and his household, since at least the first three bishops were probably speakers of Cornish. The bishop would have been based at St Germans and possibly Bodmin, administering the Church from those places, travelling through the diocese, or sending his servants on missions on his behalf. After 1027, when the bishop had responsibilities in at least one other diocese, he would have had to depute most of his Cornish affairs to others, but we do not know whom he employed to do them. No charters or records of acts of the bishops of Cornwall survive before 1050, other than some mentions of Wulfsige Comoere freeing slaves (or serfs) at the church of St Petroc (Bodmin or Padstow) in the second half of the 10th century.⁴ The bishops must have ordained clergy and provided some means for their education, probably at Bodmin and St Germans in particular. A pupil (*discipulus*) named Boia is mentioned at St Petroc's church (Bodmin or Padstow) in the 10th century,⁵ and some dialogues for teaching students Latin, now known as *De Raris Fabulis*, occur in a manuscript that has associations with St Germans. This may be a text that was used in a school at that church.⁶

In the 10th century we can begin to glimpse other churches in Cornwall for the first time since the Life of Samson. By this time they consisted of religious houses and lesser churches. The religious houses were now churches of the kind that would later be called minsters rather than monasteries.⁷ They were staffed by clergy described in contemporary sources as canons, priests, or clerks, although one or two individuals among them may have lived personally as monks.⁸ Churches of this kind likely to have existed between 900 and 1066 include Bodmin, St Buryan, Crantock, Kea, St Keverne, St Kew, Launceston, St Neot, Perranzabuloe, and Probus.⁹ Launceston in this period meant St Stephen-by-Launceston, the original site of Launceston before the growth of the modern town south of the River Kensey. All these churches held landed property, as did some others – Constantine, Goran, and Lansallos – where the existence of a body of clergy is less certain (Fig. 5).¹⁰ The minsters also acted as parish churches, providing worship and pastoral services to the people of their neighbourhoods. In England most minster clergy in the 11th century followed a more individual and less communal way of life than that of a monastery. They lived in separate houses rather than a common dormitory, and received a personal share of the lands or revenues of the church instead of sharing such revenues collectively. This was the case at St Buryan, Crantock,

---

1   The known bishops are Conan, Daniel, Wulfsige Comoere, Ealdred, possibly Ælfsige, and Buruhwold (Fryde et al. (ed.), *Handbook of British Chronology*, 214–15). A tradition of eleven bishops (who probably included Lyfing and Leofric, bishops also of Crediton) was preserved at St Germans (below, p. 188).

2   Biography in *ODNB*.

3   Biography in ibid., and in F. Barlow et al., *Leofric of Exeter* (1972).

4   M. Förster, 'Die Freilassungsurkunden des Bodmin-Evangeliars', in N. Bøgholm, A. Brusendorff, and C. Bodelsen (ed.), *A Grammatical Miscellany Offered to Otto Jespersen* (1930), 77–99, at 84, 86, 95–6, 98. For the dating of the documents in this source, see N. R. Ker, *Catalogue of Manuscripts Containing Anglo-Saxon* (1957), 159.

5   Förster, 'Die Freilassungsurkunden', 94.

6   S. Gwara, *Education in Wales and Cornwall in the Ninth and Tenth Centuries: understanding* De Raris Fabulis (Cambridge, Hughes Hall and Dept. of Anglo-Saxon, Norse, and Celtic, Kathleen Hughes Memorial Lectures, 4 (2004)).

7   On minsters from c.850–1100, see Blair, *Church in Anglo-Saxon Society*, 291–367.

8   An Abbot Germanus, possibly local, possibly a visitor, witnessed the freeing of a slave at Bodmin or Padstow in the early 10th century, and a *monachus* (monk) named Leucum later in the century (Förster, 'Die Freilassungsurkunden', 88, 96). There are examples in England of clergy following the monastic rule alongside colleagues who did not.

9   Below, pp. 126–35.   10   Below, pp. 128, 130, 132.

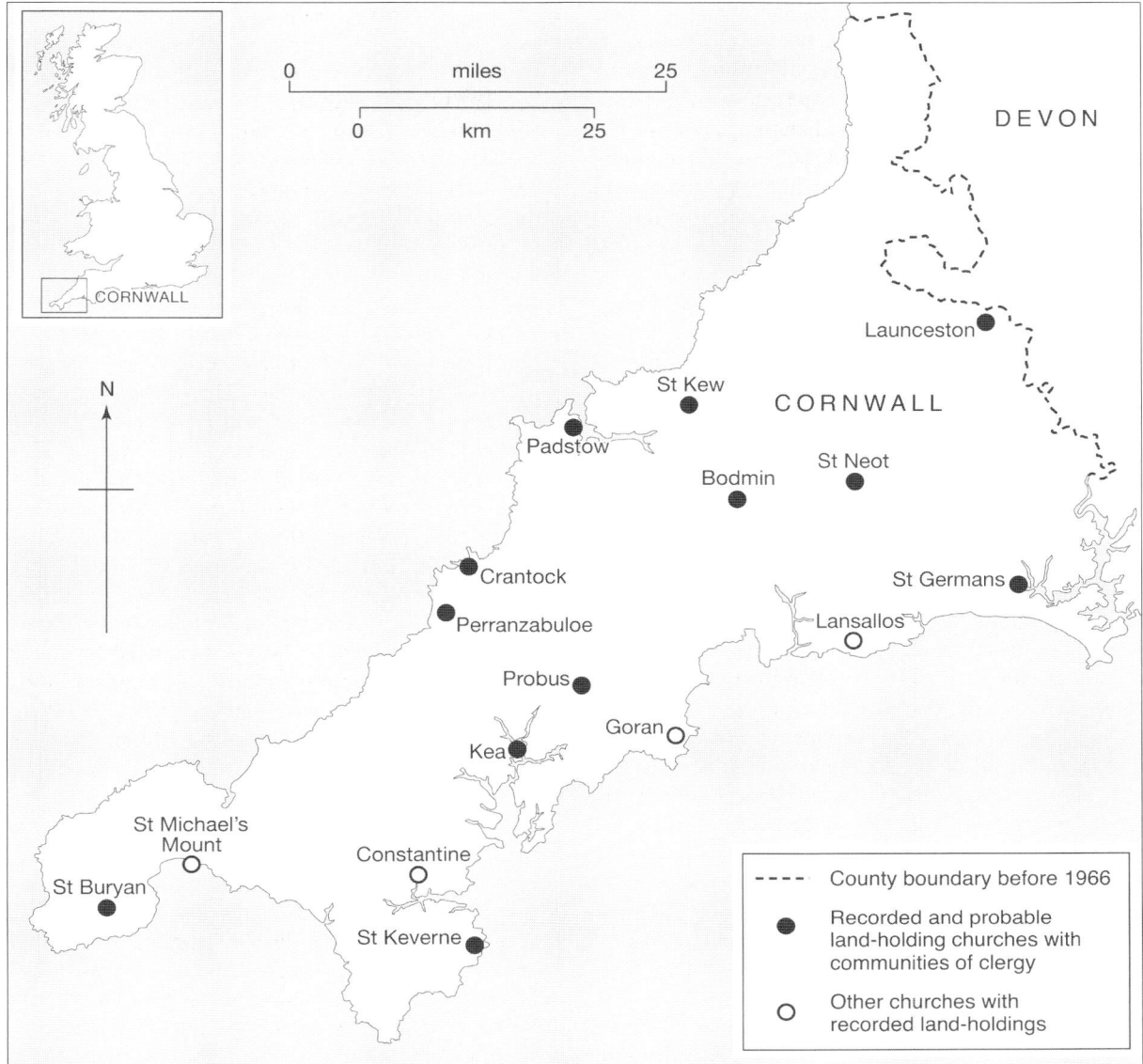

FIG 5. *Land-holding churches of Cornwall, up to 1086.*

and Probus by the 13th century, and such customs are likely to have been followed in the religious houses of Cornwall before the Norman Conquest.

The wealthiest of the Cornish minsters was Bodmin, which owned a large endowment of over 30 hides of land by 1066, part held directly by its clergy and part by tenants who paid them rents or services. A hide was roughly 120 acres of cultivated land. The other foundations had smaller estates ranging from four hides at Launceston to one or less at St Buryan, Probus, and St Keverne.[1] In no case do we know the number of clergy at these churches, but Hartland (Devon) in 1086 supported twelve canons from two hides of land plus the tithes of a large parish,[2] which would allow Bodmin and Launceston to have maintained at least as many. In the 13th century Crantock had ten canons, Probus six, and St Buryan four, and such figures may go back to earlier times. In Anglo-Saxon minsters one of the canons often presided over the others, and in Cornwall we hear of deans in charge of Bodmin, Launceston, and Perranzabuloe soon after the Norman Conquest, and at St Buryan, Crantock, and Probus later on. There may have been similar leaders before the Conquest.[3] The Domesday survey of 1086 states that

---

1 Thorn (ed.), *Domesday Book: Cornwall*, 2/6, 4/1–24; below, pp. 128, 131, 135.
2 H. Ellis (ed.), *Domesday Book: Additamenta* (Rec. Com. 1816), 421 (f. 456–b).
3 Below, pp. 134, 154, 220; for the titles of Anglo-Saxon presiding officers, see Blair, *Church in Anglo-Saxon Society*, 343 note 246.

nearly all the religious houses of Cornwall held their land free of taxation, a privilege particular to this county in the South West since it was not usual in Devon.¹ Either it originated in the period of Dumnonian rule or it was a deliberate concession by a king such as Æthelstan. Four churches – St Buryan, St Keverne, Padstow, and Probus – also had greater rights of sanctuary than other churches in later times, probably including lands beyond the church. These rights too may have been ancient privileges.²

The religious houses were outnumbered by lesser church-sites, meaning places that came to possess a church or chapel without large landed endowments or bodies of clergy. They came to be known in the Cornish language (as were the religious houses) by the words *lann* ('cemetery' or 'church-site') or *eglos* ('church'), giving rise to place-names such as Lanreath and Launceston, Egloshayle and Egloskerry. A third word, *merther* ('saint's grave'), is found in west Cornwall, often denoting chapels with a lower status than churches, such as Merthereuny in Wendron and Mertherderwa (now Menedarva) in Camborne.³ A revealing source about these early lesser sites is to be found in a list of names of 48 saints, compiled in Brittany or Cornwall in about 900, without any accompanying explanation of the origin, nature, or purpose of the list.⁴ Many of the names are those of saints of Cornish churches, and parts of the list follow a topographical order showing that the compiler was thinking not only of the saints but of the location of their church-sites. Thus the church saints of Roseland and nearby (Just, Entenin, Gerent, Fili, and Rumon) appear in sequence, and later on we encounter the saints of St Austell and its modern neighbours Creed, Goran, Mevagissey, and St Mewan. In these two regions most of the later parish church-sites were evidently in being by about 900, and there is no reason to suppose that this situation was untypical. The list itself seems to refer to Gwithian, St Levan, Mawgan-in-Meneage, and Phillack in other parts of Cornwall, and charter evidence from the 10th and 11th centuries adds some further names.⁵

Most of the minster churches lay close to the sea or to estuaries. Two likely reasons for their sites would have been the presence of lords' estates nearby, and the proximity of good communications by water. Bodmin and Launceston differed in being inland, but their sites probably also reflected travel and traffic since they were on or near the main road from Cornwall to southern England. A few church-sites, like the latter two, lay close to settlements or caused settlements to grow up beside them. The most typical Cornish church-site, however, tended to lie in rural isolation: on a road but adjoined by no more than a farm or a couple of cottages, a hamlet known in later times as a 'church town'. Isolated sites of this kind may have been chosen for more than one reason. Some were ancient graveyards, originally unenclosed, like those that have been found close to later churches such as St Endellion and Tintagel.⁶ Other sites show signs of having been 'rounds': the small farming settlements common in Cornwall during the Iron Age and Roman periods, enclosed by a bank and ditch.⁷ One such round, at Merthereuny in Wendron parish, has been excavated, showing that a chapel was built there in or after the 10th century.⁸ The nature of settlement in Cornwall was also a major factor, since it usually took the form of farms and hamlets rather than nucleated villages. Church-sites had to minister to a scattered population, and most were therefore placed in a fairly central part of the area that they served.

By about 800 it became usual to provide graveyards with enclosures, hence the use of rounds which were the right size and already had boundaries.⁹ Most graveyards also came to acquire church buildings and sometimes standing crosses and memorial stones. Churches spread all over Cornwall until, by about the Norman Conquest, there was one every three miles or so with the exception of the moorland areas of the interior. This Christianised the landscape, a process increased by the proliferation of crosses, stones, and holy wells.¹⁰ Crosses existed by the mid 10th century when they begin to occur in descriptions of territorial boundaries attached to charters conveying land. A

---

1 Thorn (ed.), *Domesday Book: Cornwall*, 2/6, 4/1–24.

2 J. Leland, *Itinerary*, ed. L. Toulmin Smith (1907–10), I, 179, 195, 319, 321; J. C. Cox, *The Sanctuaries and Sanctuary Seekers of Mediaeval England* (1911), 215–26, 262, 299–300; Olson, *Early Monasteries in Cornwall*, 72, 79, 107.

3 O. J. Padel, 'Cornish Language Notes: 5. Cornish Names of Parish Churches', *Cornish Studies* 4–5 (1976–7), 15–27; idem, *Cornish Place-Name Elements*, English Place-Name Society 56–7 (1985), 91, 142–5, 164. The asterisk indicates a word attested only in place-names.

4 L. Olson and O. J. Padel, 'A Tenth-Century List of Cornish Parochial Saints', *Cambridge Medieval Celtic Studies* 12 (1986), 33–37.

5 The charter evidence is listed in S 770, 832, and Finberg, *ECDC*, 17–20, to be supplemented by O. J. Padel, 'Two New Pre-Conquest Charters for Cornwall', 20–7; idem, 'The Charter of Lanlawren (Cornwall)', 74–85; and Della Hooke, *Pre-Conquest Charter-Bounds of Devon and Cornwall* (1994), 18, 41–5, 50–1.

6 P. Trudgian, 'Excavation of a Burial Ground at St Endellion, Cornwall', *Cornish Archaeology* 26 (1987), 145–52; J. Nowakowski and C. Thomas, *Grave News from Tintagel*, Truro Archaeological Unit (1992); Thomas, *Mute Stones*, 197–209.

7 A. Preston-Jones, 'Decoding Cornish Churchyards', in N. Edwards and A. Lane (ed.), *The Early Church in Wales and the West* (1992), 114–15, republished in *Cornish Archaeology* 33 (1994), 82–4.

8 'Decoding Cornish Churchyards', 114–15 (*Cornish Archaeology* 33 (1994), 82–4).

9 On graveyards and churchyards, see D. Petts, 'Cemeteries and Boundaries in Western Britain', in S. Lucy and A. Reynolds (ed.), *Burial in Early Medieval England and Wales* (2002), 24–46, and Preston-Jones, 'Decoding Cornish Churchyards', 104–24 (*Cornish Archaeology* 33 (1994), 71–95).

10 On the Christianisation of the landscape, see Turner, *Making a Christian Landscape*, passim.

crucifix at Tywarnhayle, originally in Perranzabuloe parish, is recorded in this context in 960 and a cross at St Keverne seven years later.[1] The erection of crosses went on throughout the Middle Ages in various forms, ranging from simple standing stones with crosses carved on them to fully sculptured examples with wheel-shaped heads and decorated shafts. Some are found in churchyards (possibly having been removed there) or built into churches. Here their function may have been to mark or embellish a graveyard, either before or after the erection of a church there. Many others occur in the secular landscape along roads or in fields, where they are likely to have been placed as waymarks or (as in the charter boundaries) to define a territory such as the landed property of a church or the edges of its parish.[2]

Holy wells may be defined as natural springs or man-made wells which were associated with saints or believed to possess supernatural qualities. The earliest recorded Cornish spring with sacred associations is the one in the First Life of St Samson, which is said to have flowed in a cave in response to his prayer.[3] Another, north of Padstow, occurs in the 11th-century Life of St Petroc, who was credited with striking it out of the rock,[4] and a third, St Cadoc's, also in Padstow parish, arose in the same way according to the Life of that saint written by the Welsh writer Llifris in about 1100. Llifris states that drinking from the latter well was effective against intestinal disorders, including worms, and that the Cornish of both sexes resorted to it.[5] Many more wells are recorded in later centuries. Some were linked with local saints and may have played a part in the veneration of such people; others, while having such links, were used to promote healing or for purposes of divination.[6] It is very likely that such practices were already in use in Cornwall by the Norman Conquest.

SAINTS, CLERGY, PARISHES, LANDS, TITHES AND PATRONS

As churches developed they acquired resources, spiritual and temporal, in the form of saints and relics, clergy, moveable property, and endowments. Of these the saints had a special importance. They offered protection in this world and intercession in the next, and were often regarded as the living owners of the property belonging to their churches.[7] They also gave their names to churches and to the place-names and parish names associated with churches. Of the 209 Cornish parish churches and major parochial chapels,[8] only 77 took their names from topographical features like Egloshayle ('church on an estuary') and Tintagel ('fort by a neck of land'), while 132 were known by the names of the saints to whom they were, or were thought to be, dedicated.[9] A majority of the church saints of Cornwall had names like Budoc, Gwithian, and Sithney that seem to go back to true personal names of Brittonic origin, although a few saints' names were probably conjectures based on place-names such as Kenwyn of Kenwyn and Ludewan of Ludgvan.[10] Brittonic personal names became attached to churches in Cornwall by the 8th century, as we have seen in the case of *Docco*, and by the 10th century there were many churches so named. By the latter century their name-givers were regarded as saints and in due course the word 'St' was often prefixed to church names, giving us names such as St Austell, St Buryan, and St Winnow, although the word was often omitted, especially in colloquial usage, as at Budock, Gwithian, and Sithney. The naming of churches after saints (most of them local saints) is paralleled on this scale in Brittany and Wales, but differed sharply from the practice in most of medieval England. There most churches outside the larger towns were not known by their saints' names, and the saints to whom they were dedicated were national or international saints rather than local ones.

Medieval Cornwall contained at least 185 places (parish churches, major chapels, and minor chapels) named after people who were believed to have been

---

1   S 684, 755, 832; Hooke, *Pre-Conquest Charter-Bounds*, 29, 38, 49.

2   The oldest large-scale work on Cornish crosses is A. G. Langdon, *Old Cornish Crosses* (1896). For recent inventories of crosses, discussion of their functions, and bibliography, see A. [i.e. Andrew] Langdon's works, listed in the bibliography of this volume, and for further discussion, Turner, *Making a Christian Landscape*, 161–3, and idem, 'The Christian Landscape: Churches, Chapels and Crosses', in S. Turner (ed.), *Medieval Devon and Cornwall: shaping an ancient countryside* (2006), 33–41.

3   Above, p. 8; Flobert (ed.), *Vie de Saint Samson*, 220.

4   P. Grosjean, 'Vie et Miracles de S. Petroc', *Analecta Bollandiana* 74 (1956), 490.

5   A. W. Wade-Evans (ed.), *Vitae Sanctorum Britanniae et Genealogiae* (1944), 92–5.

6   For further discussion, see below, pp. 78–9.

7   Thorn (ed.), *Domesday Book: Cornwall*, 4/6–22, 26, 29; 5/8/10.

8   For discussion of these terms, see below, pp. 26–7.

9   On what follows, see O. J. Padel, 'Cornish Language Notes', 15–27; idem, *Cornish Place-Name Elements*, passim; Orme, *Saints of Cornwall*, especially 17–27; and O. J. Padel, 'Local Saints and Place-Names in Cornwall' in Thacker and Sharpe (ed.), *Local Saints and Local Churches*, 303–60.

10 Other such 'saints' are Morveth (of Morvah), Tallan (of Talland), and perhaps Allen and Manacca.

saints from Cornwall, Wales, Brittany, and (with less justification) Ireland.[1] Just over half of these places (78) commemorated saints who were venerated only in Cornwall, usually at a single site, so that many of the church saints were unique to the places named after them. The rest of the places concerned (62) were named after people who were venerated as saints in Brittany or Wales as well as in Cornwall. Welsh saints, including Cybi and David, were honoured at a handful of churches and chapels, chiefly on the north coast of Cornwall and in the area north-west of Looe. Breton saints, such as Samson and Winwaloe, were patrons of a larger number of sites spreading widely across the county. By 1066 there were also churches honouring international saints. The earliest known are St Michael's Mount and Launceston ('church-site of St Stephen'), and a number of other Cornish churches came to be dedicated to these saints or to Martin, Mary, or similar well-known figures. This range of saint dedications points to various historical processes having taken place, but it is difficult to date them. We cannot say that the saints unique to Cornwall and to one site in the county are necessarily the earliest ones, since the first recorded saint dedication, *Docco*, is that of a Welsh saint. Equally the cult of St Neot, honoured in a single Cornish church, may have been a relatively late one that displaced an earlier saint.[2]

A simple way to summarise the complexity is to say that it reflects a variety of processes and influences. There were unique Cornish saints because there was indigenous religious activity within Cornwall; not all Christianity in the county can have been due to missionaries from outside. At the same time there were external influences from Brittany, England, Wales, and continental Europe which help to explain the presence in Cornwall of saints who were venerated in those places. The role of Brittany deserves a special mention. Saints whose cults probably originated in that country were adopted as the patron saints of at least fourteen parish churches and fifteen chapels and possibly of some others.[3] There is a marked concentration of these places on the south coast of Cornwall, especially in the Lizard and around the Fal estuary, but they also occur on the north coast and inland, reaching as far as Poundstock and Tremaine in the north-west. This partly reflects the regular links between Brittany and Cornwall through fishing or trade – links assisted by the closeness (indeed the virtual identity) of the language spoken in both countries in early times. The links are also apparent in surviving manuscripts, a topic to be mentioned presently. There were particularly close connections between Brittany and southern England in the 10th century when Viking attacks drove Breton nobility to take refuge with the English kings Edward the Elder and Æthelstan, and caused relics to be dispersed from Breton churches to England.[4] This may have enabled some Cornish churches to acquire such relics and therefore Breton names, but such acquisitions could have happened at other times thanks to the contacts between the two peninsulas.[5]

The identities of the Brittonic saints venerated in Cornwall are generally unknown. We have seen that even the First Life of Samson survives in a version from as much as 170 years after his death, and the next Lives to survive, those of Paul of Léon and Winwaloe, were composed in Brittany in the late 800s, some three hundred years after these saints were supposed to have lived. We possess no saint's Life written in Cornwall until the first Life of Petroc, which probably dates from the 11th century, and most of the Lives and legends of Cornish saints are later still. They are not based on older historical records, which it is clear that their authors did not possess, but on local folklore and contemporary views of what a saint should be like. The Lives imagined their heroes and heroines bringing Christianity to Cornwall in an 'age of the saints', which they did not define in date but seem to have envisaged as following Roman times in about the 5th and 6th centuries. They described the saints as coming to Cornwall from elsewhere, usually Ireland or Wales, founding a church and a holy well, and sometimes meeting a violent death for religious or other reasons. In fact there is little supporting evidence for the saints being Welsh, little or none that they were Irish, and none for their martyrdom by pagan rulers. The saints, as preserved in their legends, are not the creators of Christianity in Cornwall as is often supposed, but the creations of that Christianity long after it was well established in the region. It is more likely that many of them were important local people, clergy or laity, who founded churches or were buried in graveyards that came to be named after them. Graveyard names may then have been transferred to the churches built inside them. Most of the saints could have lived at any period before the 10th or 11th centuries, not excluding pre-Christian times.

Several Cornish churches claimed to possess the bodies of their saint: both large foundations like Bodmin (Petroc) and Perranzabuloe (Piran), and small ones such as Cardinham (Meubred), St Ives (Ia), and Sithney (Sithney).[6] The claim has some credibility where the church concerned was the saint's main site, as in the first two cases, or the unique site, as at Cardinham. It is less convincing in cases like St Ives and

---

1 The number of 132, mentioned above, rises to 185 by including lesser chapels which had little or no status in the parish system: for such chapels, see below, pp. 26–7, 74–7.
2 Orme, *Saints of Cornwall*, 200. 3 Ibid., 54.
4 C. Brett, 'A Breton Pilgrim to England in the Reign of King Æthelstan', in G. Jondorf and D. N. Dumville (ed.), *France and the British Isles in the Middle Ages* (1991), 43–70 at 44–8.
5 For further discussion see below, p. 112.
6 Orme, *Saints of Cornwall*, 69, 72, 86, 111, 113, 119, 129, 137, 144, 147, 173, 190, 196, 216, 221, 226, 236, 255.

FIG 6. *St Neot and the pope, an early Cornish saint on pilgrimage to Rome, as imagined in the early Tudor windows of St Neot church.*

Sithney, whose saints had important churches in Brittany where their cults may equally well have begun.[1] Most of the veneration and understanding of saints in medieval Cornwall was localised to their parishes. The saint was believed to have helped to shape the neighbouring landscape with hills, wells, or paths – a belief that explained such features. Sometimes a saint's legend represented him or her as having been more important than other local saints, reflecting a parish's jealousy about its status. Even when a church, like St Agnes or St Michael's Mount, did not have a local saint, people might still imagine the saint to have visited their parish and left a mark on the landscape there: a stone pillar or a rocky chair.[2] Most of the saint-cults that originated in Cornwall were also parochial in failing to spread outside their home parishes. Of those that did, Piran achieved only three church-sites in Cornwall, Euny five, and Petroc six. Neot (Fig. 6), Petroc, Piran, and Rumon alone became widely known in England through relics, church dedications, and inclusion in church calendars, lists of saints, or collections of saints' Lives. Petroc and Piran also established sites in Brittany and Wales.

Next to a saint, a church needed one or more clergy to serve it. By the 10th century there were several grades of clergy. The Bodmin Gospels, a manuscript of the late 9th or early 10th century, contains records of the freeing of serfs or slaves at St Petroc's church at Padstow or Bodmin between about 950 and 1100 in the presence of clerks, readers, deacons, and priests (the latter also called, in English, mass-priests).[3] Priests were expected to say daily prayers and they alone could celebrate the

---

1 Ibid., 144–5, 236–7
2 Ibid., 60, 194; below, p. 237.

3 BL, Add. 9381; Förster, 'Die Freilassungsurkunden', 83–99; Ker, *Catalogue of Manuscripts Containing Anglo-Saxon*, 159.

sacraments. These included baptism (which was coming to be administered on the day of birth), confession, marriage, and the eucharist or communion (known as the mass), together with funerals and burials which counted as pastoral services not sacraments. Clerks, readers, and deacons could say daily prayers but act only as assistants in the sacraments.[1] All such clergy might be married until the 12th century, although equally they might observe celibacy. A minster could function with a single priest, allowing its other clergy to be men of the lesser grades. An ordinary church needed to provide the whole range of services and sacraments through one person, who had therefore to be a priest, with a single clerk to assist him. It is not known, however, whether all Cornish churches were served by a priest before the Norman Conquest. Minster clergy worshipped on a daily basis, or should have done so. This involved saying eight services at intervals in the chancel of the church, beginning with matins at midnight and ending with compline in the afternoon or evening. In the lesser churches worship was more likely to be confined to Sundays and festivals.

A further requirement for a church was equipment for the clergy to use, such as vestments, holy vessels, crosses, and bells. Bodmin possessed St Petroc's bell, a portable one, by the 11th century, and there is a later reference to the church possessing his staff of office.[2] In 1281 Perranzabuloe church owned a silver bowl, two pastoral staffs (one jewelled, one of bone), and a little copper bell, all attributed to St Piran, while Veryan church had a 'small bell of St Symphorian', its patron saint.[3] No such objects exist today from pre-Conquest Cornwall, but a few books survive that may have been used there or by Cornish scholars elsewhere in the 9th, 10th, and 11th centuries, although certainty is not always possible. All are in Latin. A 9th-century copy of Boethius's work *On the Consolation of Philosophy*, made in France, contains a single gloss (an interlined note), *ud rocashaas* ('it hated'), which is in either Old Cornish or Breton.[4] The Vatican manuscript containing the list of saints includes *On Manners*, ascribed to Seneca, and *On Illustrious Men* by Jerome, and may have been used in Brittany by a Cornishman or brought from there to Cornwall.[5] The miscellany known as the *Codex Oxoniensis Posterior* comprises four independent sections written in the first half or middle of the 10th century. The opening section consists of a single leaf with material for masses in honour of St German at *Lannaled*, an old name for St Germans in Cornwall.[6] The second section is an *Exposition of the Mass*, with three glosses in Old Cornish or Breton, and the third an epistle by St Augustine of Hippo and one by Caesarius of Arles. The fourth is the school-text *De Raris Fabulis*, which contains some glosses that are either Old Cornish or Welsh. Given the linkage of the first leaf with St Germans, it is possible that the other sections had belonged to its church, and this was undoubtedly the case with a further manuscript, the so-called *Lanalet Pontifical*, a 10th-century book of the rites and sacraments carried out by bishops and hence an essential tool for those of Cornwall.[7] Finally there are the Bodmin Gospels (Fig. 7), which may have been used at Padstow before belonging to Bodmin when that became the centre of the cult of St Petroc,[8] and the 11th-century Life of Petroc, probably originating from Bodmin but extant only in later texts.[9] Taken together, these works indicate that religious and scholarly texts circulated in Cornwall and were studied there, especially (as one would expect) in the larger religious houses.[10]

Saints, clergy, and equipment were all to be found inside churches, but churches also acquired possessions beyond their walls and precincts. Chief here was the area over which the church had spiritual control: its parish. It is difficult to date the origins and boundaries of parishes, but they are likely to have developed into a common system in Cornwall during the 10th and 11th centuries as they appear to have done in England as a whole.[11] It is not until the 13th century, however, that we possess a complete list of the parish churches of Cornwall and can begin to analyse the nature of their parishes, a task to be addressed in the following chapter.[12] Parishes represent the turning of the Church from a missionary organisation into a ruling one, as society became more thoroughly Christian. The clergy of each parish church had spiritual authority over everyone who lived within their parish, and gained the right to take resources from the parish for their livelihood. Some church-sites that appear to be early ones never achieved parochial status or lost it after achieving it. Such places included Burlawn Eglos in St Breock (dedicated to St Weras), St Carroc in St Veep, St Derwa in Camborne, St Elvan in Sithney, and St Illick in St Endellion. These all bore the names of Brittonic people, generally names unique to each site, and,

---

1 On this subject, see F. Tinti (ed.), *Pastoral Care in Late Anglo-Saxon England* (2005).

2 Förster, 'Die Freilassungsurkunden', 88; Grosjean, 'Vie et Miracles de S. Petroc', 173.

3 ECA, D&C 2672A, ff. 7v, 10r.

4 P. Sims-Williams, 'A New Brittonic Gloss on Boethius: *ud rocashaas*', *Cambrian Medieval Celtic Studies* 50 (2005), 77–86.

5 Olson and Padel, 'Tenth-century List', 33–71.

6 Bodleian, Bodley 572 (S.C. 2026), discussed by Gwara, *Education in Wales and Cornwall*, 13–15.

7 Rouen, Bibliothèque municipale, A.27 (368); Olson, *Early Monasteries in Cornwall*, 62–3.

8 BL, Add. 9381; above, p. 11.

9 Grosjean, 'Vies et Miracles de S. Petroc', 470–96.

10 For another possible Cornish manuscript, see D. Dumville, 'Writers, Scribes and Readers in Brittany, AD 800–1100', in H. Fulton (ed.), *Medieval Celtic Literature and Society* (2005), 55–6.

11 Blair, *Church in Anglo-Saxon Society*, 368–504. Turner, *Making a Christian Landscape*, 155, cautions against supposing that the church-sites of the 10th-century list already had parishes as conjectured by Olson and Padel, 'Tenth-century List', 68–9.

12 Below, p. 26–9.

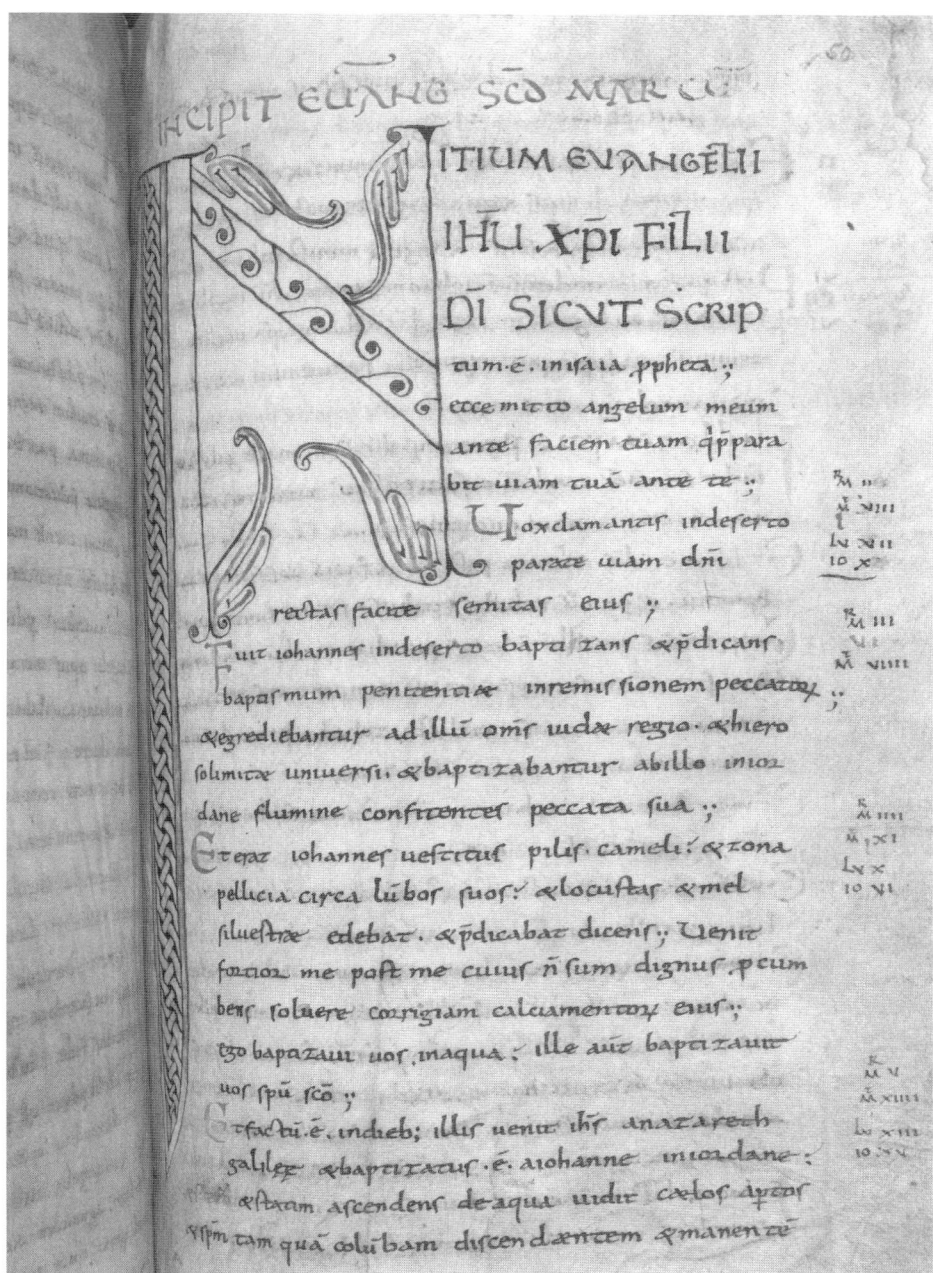

FIG 7. The opening of the Gospel of Mark from the Bodmin Gospels.

although not recorded until after the Norman Conquest, they look likely to have existed in earlier times. They were used for occasional worship but, by about the 12th century, they were classified as chapels not as churches, and local people were allowed to support them only in addition to their primary duty towards the church and clergyman in whose parish the chapel lay.

Two kinds of resources came to a church from its parish (and sometimes from outside): lands and tithes. Lands were significant only in the case of the religious houses already mentioned and of churches like Constantine, Goran, and Lansallos which may once have been religious houses or close in status to them. After the Norman Conquest, it became rare for an ordinary parish church to hold more than a modest endowment of land known as the 'glebe' or 'sanctuary' consisting of fields, often scattered within the parish, which the clergyman could farm or let for farming. In the 18th century, half of the recorded glebes of Cornish churches measured less than 30 acres and only 8 exceeded 100, with South Hill, the largest, at 177.[1]

---

1 The main information about glebes comes from 'terriers' compiled between 1601 and 1746 (CRO, ARD/TER series). Some are published in R. Potts (ed.), *A Calendar of Cornish Glebe Terriers 1673–1735*, DCRS new ser 19 (1974); sizes are discussed on p. xiii.

More important than glebes were tithes, which developed in early 10th-century England as a compulsory payment of a tenth of plant and animal products, including crops from the land, new-born animals, fish (important in Cornwall), and dairy foods such as milk, butter, and cheese.[1] Parish churches normally received tithes from the whole of their parishes, but in the 12th century important landholders sometimes assigned the tithes on their estates to churches elsewhere. Minster Priory, for example, received the tithes of certain lands in Altarnun parish, a parish that it did not otherwise own.[2] Religious houses established after the Conquest were exempt from paying tithes on their land and that of their home farms, and these exemptions sometimes survived the Reformation, leading to the existence of tithe-free areas down to modern times.[3] The value of tithes was substantial, and since they belonged wholly to the clergy or clergyman of each church, they enabled a parish to maintain its own clergyman even if it covered a relatively small area. In return the clergyman became responsible for maintaining his house and the chancel of the church, where services were said. He was expected to provide hospitality to travellers and alms to the poor, but the maintenance of the nave – the public part of the church building – became a charge on the parishioners in addition to the payment of tithes.

The possessions of churches, from saints to tithes, gave them and their clergy power, but this power was qualified by a measure of control by other people. The medieval Church existed in a hierarchical society whose ruling classes exerted a considerable influence over its affairs. Lords like Maenchi who endowed a church customarily regarded it and its endowments as still part of their property and continued to supervise its affairs including the appointment and governance of its clergy.[4] It is possible that the Anglo-Saxon kings who granted charters to St Buryan and St Kew considered themselves the lords of those churches, and very likely that the bishops of Sherborne and their successors at St Germans took a similar view of the churches on their property in places such as Bodmin and Padstow. Earl Harold of Wessex who held a good deal of property in Cornwall on the eve of the Norman Conquest may be expected to have behaved in the same way to the churches that lay on his lands.[5] Most parish churches in Cornwall by 1066, however, would have come under the power of the lords of the manors in which they were situated, enabling these lords to control the religious life of their neighbourhoods as well as the law and economy. Later, in the 12th century, the Church authorities succeeded in restricting the powers of lords over churches, and the arrangements that resulted will be outlined in the next chapter.[6]

Lords and their ladies are the only lay people in Cornwall of whose spirituality we can gain even the faintest glimpse before the Norman Conquest. Some were anxious for the well-being of their souls, seeking to gain merit by a charitable act such as freeing a serf or slave. 'Byrhtflæd [a woman] freed Huna and his sister Dolo on the altar of St Petroc for the redemption of her soul.' This is one of several such records in the Bodmin Gospels.[7] King Doniert's stone at Redgate requests prayers for Doniert's soul,[8] and a standing cross at Tintagel, of about the 11th century, tell us that 'Ælnat made this cross for his soul'.[9] Sometimes these people were concerned for the souls of their loved ones. Ermen freed slaves for his mother's soul, and Æthelflæd for her soul and that of her lord Æthelweard.[10] They wished for salvation in heaven and remembrance on earth by those who survived them, hence their commissioning of the stones that would carry their names to the future.

THE NORMAN CONQUEST AND THE DOMESDAY SURVEY

The Norman Conquest of 1066 led to further changes in Cornwall in respect of power and property, and therefore of the Church. The new king, William the Conqueror, took over the royal estates of the last Anglo-Saxon kings: Edward the Confessor and Harold, his short-lived successor. William needed a lieutenant in Cornwall and found one briefly in Brian, a member of the family of the dukes of Brittany, to whom he gave lands in the South West of England. Brian was active there in 1069 but his stay in England was apparently brief, and in 1076 William put Cornwall into the charge of his own half-brother, Robert count of Mortain, along with a good deal of land in the county. Robert's wealth and royal connection made him the most powerful figure in Church affairs in Cornwall for the next fourteen years until he died abroad in 1090. His

---

1 On tithes, see Blair, *Church in Anglo-Saxon Society*, 435–43, 447–51.
2 Below, p. 241.
3 For tithe-free areas in Cornwall, see the index, sub 'tithe-free areas'.
4 On what follows, see S. Wood, *The Proprietary Church in the Medieval West* (2006).
5 For Harold's property, see Thorn (ed.), *Domesday Book: Cornwall*, 1/1–13; 4/2, /21; 5/1/5; 5/2/17; 5/4/17.
6 Below, p. 25.
7 Förster, 'Die Freilassungsurkunden', 83, etc.
8 Okasha, *Corpus of Early Christian Inscribed Stones*, 213–17.
9 Ibid., 291–5.
10 Förster, 'Die Freilassungsurkunden', 88, 96.

power was enhanced by the lack of a strong bishop of Exeter. Bishop Leofric had died in 1072, and his successor Osbern was a Norman who had served Edward the Confessor and was also a distant relation of King William. Osbern's reign at Exeter, which lasted until 1103, is an obscure one that seems to reflect a quiet man who was in poor health from about 1093. He appears to have had little influence on Cornish affairs, leaving Robert with virtual freedom to do as he pleased.[1]

In 1086 William's officers carried out the valuation of all the landed property and livestock of his realm now known as Domesday Book. Its section on Cornwall provides us with the earliest detailed account of the major landed estates in the county and those who held them.[2] The survey was chiefly concerned with lay property, but it throws valuable light upon churches in two respects. First it mentions about thirty place-names derived from church-sites, nearly all of which probably possessed a church building in 1086. They include major places like Bodmin and Launceston, and minor ones such as St Gennys, Lanreath, and Pelynt.[3] Secondly it tells us something about eleven of the larger churches which owned landed property. These were Bodmin, St Buryan, Constantine, Crantock, St Germans, St Keverne, Launceston, St Michael's Mount, St Neot, Perranzabuloe, and Probus. Seven of these, excepting Constantine and the Mount, are said to have been staffed by canons (or in the case of St Neot 'priests' or 'clerks'), indicating that they were churches akin to minsters, served by bodies of clergy. Domesday describes their land and reckons its annual income, but it does not deal with their other revenues. All these churches received tithes and offerings from the parishes in which they lay, and the three largest and richest – Bodmin, St Germans, and Launceston – owned lesser churches in other parishes and therefore the tithes belonging to them. We need to make allowance for such tithes when reckoning the income of the minsters in William's reign.

The wealthiest of the minster churches was Bodmin. Its landed property included six manors in Cornwall and two in Devon, while a further estate at Pendavey in Egloshayle belonged to Bodmin later and may have done so in 1086. These manors comprised just over 16 hides in extent and were valued at £10 15s. per annum. A further 13 manors were held by tenants of Bodmin, and the Domesday survey identified some land that had been taken away from Bodmin's ownership. Bodmin also owned the tithes of its parish and probably those of the parishes of Cubert and Padstow whose churches belonged to it in later times. Next in wealth came St Germans, which had an estate of 12 hides worth £5 per annum situated at St Germans and Landrake, together with the churches and tithes of both places. Third in respect of land stood Launceston, with an estimated holding of 4 hides, as well as a further 2½ hides that, as we shall see, may have been new acquisitions. These properties together were valued at £5 per annum. In addition the count of Mortain had recently granted Launceston the tithes of Liskeard and of some other manors, and it may have owned some of the churches in the neighbourhood that are recorded in its possession later on, such as Laneast, North Tamerton, and Werrington.[4] The tithes of these properties may have made Launceston richer than St Germans.

The remaining land-holding churches had smaller possessions. At the time of the Norman Conquest Crantock and Perranzabuloe had held three hides of land each, St Michael's Mount and St Neot two each, St Buryan and Probus one each, and Constantine and St Keverne smaller amounts. To judge from what we know about St Buryan, Crantock, and Probus in later times, these hides of land generally lay near the church building, although the Mount possessed Truthwall on the adjoining mainland and Perranzabuloe owned an estate near Tintagel. In addition the churches concerned received the tithes of their parishes, parishes usually larger in size than the average. By the time of Domesday, however, some of the land-holding churches had suffered losses of lands to the count of Mortain, a matter to be dealt with presently. The Mount had lost one of its two hides, St Neot nearly all of its former two, and Perranzabuloe two manors. The values of the lands of each church had fallen too, thanks to the count's intervention, generally from £2 at the time of the Conquest to a quarter or even an eighth of that figure in 1086. The count probably assisted, although he did not begin, a process by which some of the minster churches declined into being ordinary parish churches served by a single clergyman. One such church was the ancient foundation at St Kew. It had once owned substantial resources, owning at least part of St Kew itself and outlying estates at St Gennys, Poundstock, and Treroosel in St Teath, but by 1086 its principal landed endowment was in the hands of the king. It still had minster clergy in 1158, but probably lost them soon afterwards, and became a possession of Plympton priory.[5] Other churches that lost their lands and

---

1 On Osbern, see F. Barlow (ed.), *English Episcopal Acta*, XI: *Exeter 1046–1184* (1996), pp. xxxii–xxxiii, and *ODNB*.
2 Thorn (ed.), *Domesday Book: Cornwall*.
3 The list includes Bodmin, Constantine, Crantock, St Enoder, St Gennys, St Germans, Gulval, Helland, St Juliot, Kea, St Keverne, St Kew, Landulph, Langunnet (not a parish church in historic times, but later a chapel site), Lanreath, Lansallos, Launcells, Launceston, Lawhitton, Marhamchurch, Mawgan-in-Meneage, St Mawgan-in-Pydar (Lanherne), St Michael's Mount, Padstow, Pelynt, Perranzabuloe, Philleigh, Probus, and St Winnow. Other possible former church-sites or chapel-sites are Lancarffe, Landinner, and Landreyne.
4 Below, pp. 209–10.
5 Below, p. 131.

bodies of clergy in the decades after the Conquest were St Keverne, St Neot, and Perranzabuloe.

Robert of Mortain's role in reshaping the churches of Cornwall was clearly substantial.[1] The Domesday survey usually depicts it as damaging. He had taken land or value from all of the land-holding churches except for Launceston and Probus. He had removed livestock from one of the properties of Perranzabuloe,[2] and wrongfully subtracted four manors in the Launceston area from Tavistock Abbey.[3] The major churches of Cornwall would have presented an easy target to a powerful Norman lord intent on enriching himself and rewarding his followers.[4] Yet it would be incorrect to regard Robert as a pioneer plunderer or a plunderer alone. People before him had robbed the churches of Cornwall, and while he seized some properties he reassigned others to a favourite church. Robert made Launceston his centre of power in Cornwall, and built a castle there. A Norman lord was accustomed to have links with a religious house whose members would pray for him and his family and (if nearby) provide for the spiritual needs of himself and his household. Some such lords established small monasteries of French monks in England for this purpose, and Robert too had friendly relations with monks. In about 1070 he granted St Michael's Mount to Mont St Michel (Normandy), and either he or his son William founded Montacute Priory (Somerset).[5] No monastery was founded in Cornwall during Robert's lifetime, however, since Mont St Michel does not seem to have established one at the Mount until the mid 12th century, and Robert turned to the minster at Launceston for the provision of religious services at his castle there. It may be that Cornwall was seen as still too strange or unsettled to support a community of monks from France.

In 1076 the count granted a charter to Launceston, which named its dean as another Robert, probably a Norman installed by the count to ensure that the minster satisfied his needs. The charter was granted in the name of the king, Count Robert, his wife Matilda, and their children, doubtless people for whom the clergy would pray. It listed a number of lands that the minster was to hold, estimated at 8½ hides, some of which are likely to have been its traditional holdings. Three of the lands, Bonyalva in St Germans and Bodigga and Bucklawren in St Martin-by-Looe, appear in Domesday Book where they were estimated at 2½ hides and were said to have been taken away from the manor of Pendrim in the same parish, suggesting that they represented gifts from the count to the minster. He also gave the tithes of six of his manors, notably Liskeard, for the personal use of the dean, whom he evidently wished to increase in status and wealth.[6] As a result Launceston became the chief church in Cornwall to benefit from the Norman Conquest. It entered into a relationship with the lords of Launceston Castle which outlived Robert of Mortain's family and continued through much of the 12th century. This link enabled it to acquire more property, to overtake Bodmin and St Germans in this respect, and to become the best endowed and wealthiest religious house in the county. For this reason at least Count Robert deserves to be remembered as a positive figure in Cornish Church history, as well as a negative one.

2. THE TWELFTH AND THIRTEENTH CENTURIES

BISHOPS, ARCHDEACONS, AND PARISHES

The dominance of the counts of Mortain in Cornwall ended in 1106. Count William, who had succeeded his father Robert in 1090, joined enemies of Henry I and lost his English lands and titles. No lord held comparable power in the county until Reginald, one of Henry's illegitimate sons, was created earl of Cornwall in 1140. Instead conditions favoured the bishops of Exeter. The quiet Bishop Osbern died in 1103 and after a four-year interval he was replaced by William Warelwast, a Norman close to Henry and a more active man.[7] William succeeded, although not immediately, in recovering control of the major churches of Cornwall. In 1123 he secured a charter from Henry restoring to his church of Exeter (and therefore to himself as well) the

---

1 On Robert, see B. Golding, 'Robert of Mortain', *Anglo-Norman Studies* 13 (1990), 19–44.
2 Thorn (ed.), *Domesday Book: Cornwall*, 4/26.
3 Ibid., 3/7.   4 Ibid., 4/22, /26.

5 P. L. Hull (ed.), *The Cartulary of St. Michael's Mount*, DCRS new ser. 5 (1962), pp. xiii, xviii–xix, 1–2; below, pp. 228–9.
6 Below, p. 202.
7 Biography in *ODNB*.

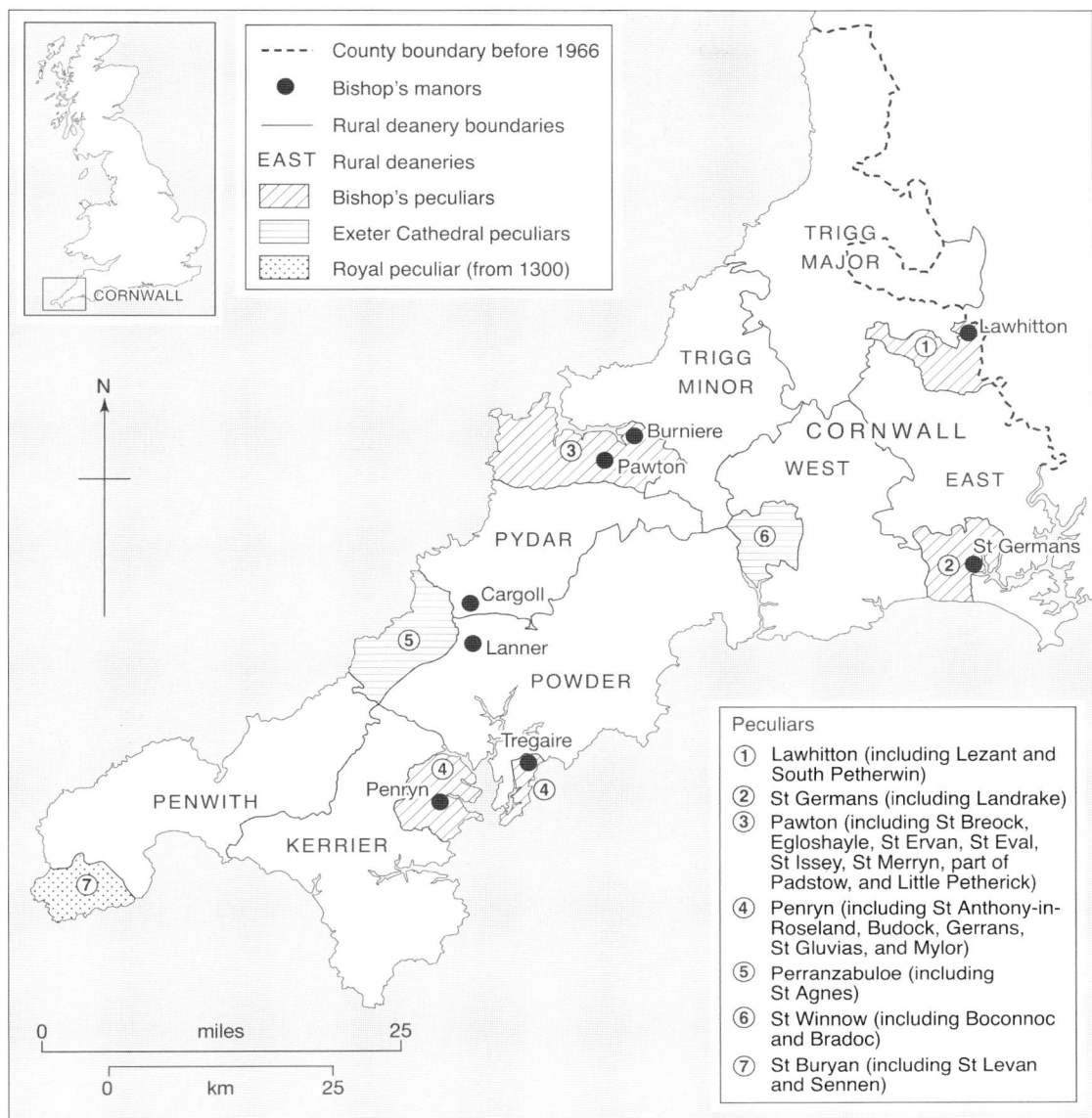

FIG 8. *Lands of the bishop of Exeter, rural deaneries, and peculiars.*

churches of Bodmin, Launceston, Perranzabuloe, and St Kew.[1] This enabled him to reorganise the first two and to use the others to endow his cathedral and his new foundation of Plympton Priory (Devon). From this time onwards the bishops of Exeter played a major part again in the affairs of the Cornish Church.[2] They were confronted by a new series of earls and dukes of Cornwall after Reginald's promotion, and by the crown when the earldom or duchy was vacant, but until the Reformation they were longer sidelined to the extent that had been possible in the late 11th century. Indeed a chronicler of King Stephen's reign (1135–54) assures us that when Earl Reginald plundered Church property during the civil wars of that period, he was excommunicated by the bishop of Exeter (Robert Warelwast) and suffered a series of personal disasters.[3]

The bishops were the wealthiest clergy in Cornwall during the 12th and 13th centuries. They held six major estates in the county: Burniere in Egloshayle, St Germans, Lawhitton, Pawton in St Breock, Penryn, and Tregaire in Roseland (Fig. 8), all with houses at which they could stay. A seventh estate, the manor of Cargoll in Newlyn East, was purchased by Bishop Walter Bronescombe in 1270 for £200, including Lanner, a residence in the adjoining parish of St Allen.[4] The bishops also had extensive lands in Devon where they

---

1 *Regesta Regum Anglo-Normannorum*, ed. H. W. C. Davis et al. (1913–59), II, 185; cf. 72.
2 For the bishops up to 1300, see J. Le Neve, *Fasti Ecclesiae Anglicanae 1066–1300, 10: Exeter*, ed. D. E. Greenway (2005), 1–7, and for their biographies, F. Barlow (ed.), *English Episcopal Acta*, XI, pp. xxxii–liv, and *ODNB*.
3 K. R. Potter (ed.), *Gesta Stephani* (1955), 68.
4 J. H. Rowe (ed.), *Cornwall Feet of Fines*, DCRS (1914), I, 118–19.

FIG 9. *The tomb of Walter Bronescombe (d. 1280), bishop of Exeter, in Exeter Cathedral. A frequent visitor to Cornwall, he is also the first bishop of Exeter to have left a register of his activities.*

spent most of their time unless they were elsewhere in England. Sometimes they lived at their palace at Exeter but more often at their Devon manors of Bishop's Clyst, Bishop's Tawton, Chudleigh, Crediton, and Paignton, or further away at houses that they owned in Hampshire and London. The Cornish saw them more rarely. How often it is hard to say, because records of their travels are sparse before the middle of the 13th century, but Robert Warelwast is mentioned going to Cornwall in 1150, Henry Marshal three times between 1196 and 1202, William Brewer in 1236, and Richard Blund in 1249.[1] The first bishop whose register of activities survives, enabling us to trace his journeys in detail, is Bronescombe (1258–80) (Fig. 9). He came to Cornwall a month after his enthronement in Exeter Cathedral, and returned in all but five of the 21 years of his reign, usually staying on his estates but sometimes travelling more widely.[2] For most of the time, however, each bishop of Exeter ruled the county from a distance by sending letters and using officers to act on his behalf. He held a consistory court which dealt with crimes by the clergy, or by the laity against the Church and its rules, and administered certain wills. The court met in Exeter and was supervised, after about 1200, by a deputy of the bishop known as his official.[3] Some Cornish people would have had to make journeys to this court, or to deal with the bishop and his senior clergy in Devon on other matters.

The bishop had local deputies throughout the diocese in the form of four archdeacons, each looking after a large district. There was an archdeacon in Exeter diocese by 1083, and it is probable that the historic system of four, including an archdeacon of Cornwall, was established by William Warelwast in the late 1120s.[4]

---

1 F. Barlow (ed.), *English Episcopal Acta*, XII: *Exeter 1186–1257* (1996), 292–300.
2 *Reg. Bronescombe*, ed. Hingeston-Randolph, 294–302.
3 For early names of officials, see Barlow (ed.), *English Episcopal Acta*, XII, 312.
4 Ibid., 306–9.

William d'Eu, the earliest known occupant of the office, was in post by about 1128.¹ The Cornish archdeaconry encompassed the whole of the area west of the River Tamar, including the arm of Devon which until 1966 stretched across Werrington to North Petherwin. It also extended east of the Tamar to take in St Giles-on-the-Heath in Devon, which belonged to the church of North Petherwin.² From the very beginning the archdeacons were normally based at Exeter. They had a stall in the cathedral choir and a house in the cathedral close that lay, by the end of the 13th century, at the far left-hand end of St Martin's Lane beside the city wall.³ When Bronescombe founded Glasney College at Penryn in 1267, it became the practice for the bishop to appoint the archdeacon to a canonry of Glasney with a residence there, and this arrangement became permanent, giving him a base in Cornwall if he chose to use it.⁴ The archdeacon was required to visit and inspect the parishes in the archdeaconry once a year, a process that allowed him to collect a fee from each place. If he was conscientious he examined the condition of churches and clergy houses, and ensured that deficiencies were remedied.⁵ He put orders from the bishop into effect and inducted some clergy into possession of parish churches.⁶ He also held a court that dealt with minor offences against Church law and administered wills.⁷ For much of this work he employed a deputy, known as the vice- or sub-archdeacon in the late 12th century and the 'official of Cornwall' by the early 13th.⁸ This person was normally one of the Cornish parish clergy, resident in the county itself.

The archdeaconry was divided into rural deaneries, each containing a couple of dozen parishes (Fig. 8).⁹ Rural deaneries came into existence in England during the 12th century, and Cornwall had them by about 1200 when a list survives naming seven, with the likelihood that the eighth existed too.¹⁰ By 1291 there were certainly eight. Six of the deaneries roughly coincided with the hundreds of Cornwall, the local divisions of secular government, and had similar names: East and West (the two halves of the district of Wivelshire), Kerrier, Penwith, Powder, and Pydar. In north-east Cornwall the deaneries and hundreds differed more widely. The deanery of Trigg Minor contained not only the hundred of Trigg but seven parishes in that of Lesnewth, while the deanery of Trigg Major (referred to in 1200 as *Wike*, i.e. Week St Mary) encompassed the rest of Lesnewth, the hundred of Stratton, and six parishes in the hundred of East. A factor here must have been the priory church of Launceston, since the parish churches belonging to it were included within Trigg Major. The post of rural dean was held for a year at a time, and by 1492 the bishop of Exeter formally admitted the deans to office each year.¹¹ In the later Middle Ages the Exeter custom was for the post to circulate in turn among the rectors and vicars of each deanery, but later on, in about 1700, a system of election was used.¹² The dean was the person locally responsible to the Church authorities and carried out orders from the bishop or archdeacon as required.

Alongside the authority of the bishop and his officers lay another kind of authority: the private control of churches by kings, bishops, monasteries, and lords of the manor. Before the Norman Conquest this control probably included the appointment of clergy and the entrusting to them of the church's property while they held office, but during the 12th century the Church authorities curbed these powers and those who held them were redefined as 'patrons'.¹³ A patron had the right to be consulted about the election of the head of a church if it was a religious house and to 'present' or nominate the clergyman in the case of a parish church. This right became known as an 'advowson' and was regarded as a piece of property which could be inherited or given away.¹⁴ In turn the bishop claimed the right to confirm elections and to 'institute' or 'admit' parish clergy to office, conferring the property of the church upon them and receiving an oath of obedience. After 1258 confirmations and institutions were usually recorded in the bishop's register. Parish

---

1 Ibid., 310. For the list of archdeacons to 1300, see Le Neve, *Fasti*, X: *Exeter*, 32–5.

2 This did not include certain parishes that were 'peculiars' outside the archdeacon's jurisdiction: see below, p. 27.

3 E. Lega-Weekes, *Some Studies in the Topography of the Cathedral Close Exeter* (1915), 129–35.

4 *Reg. Bronescombe*, ed. Hingeston-Randolph, 142; ed. Robinson, II, 68; see below, p. 253.

5 ECA, D&C 2851; *Reg. Grandisson*, II, 606–7.

6 On archdeacons and their duties, see A. Hamilton Thompson, 'Diocesan Organization in the Middle Ages: archdeacons and rural deans', *Proceedings of the British Academy* 29 (1943), 153–94; idem, *The English Clergy and their Organization in the Later Middle Ages* (1947), 57–63; and B. R. Kemp, *Twelfth-Century English Archidiaconal and Vice-Archidiaconal Acta*, Cant. & York. Soc. 92 (2001), especially pp. xlii–lv, 27–30.

7 Roughly speaking the archdeacon dealt with wills of people whose property lay only within the archdeaconry while the bishop's consistory court handled those whose property lay both within and outside it, as well as the wills of rectors, vicars, and important lay people (N. Orme (ed.), *Cornish Wills 1342–1540*, DCRS new ser. 50 (2007), passim).

8 Barlow (ed.), *English Episcopal Acta*, XII, 311.

9 On rural deaneries, see Hamilton Thompson, 'Diocesan Organization', 153–94, and idem, *English Clergy*, 63–9.

10 N. Orme and O. J. Padel, 'Cornwall and the Third Crusade', *JRIC* (2005), 71–7.

11 The bishop received a fee of 2s. from each dean every year (London, Lambeth Palace Library, Reg. Morton, I, f. 134v; Reg. Warham, II, f. 275r).

12 *Reg. Stafford*, pp. 244, 310; R. W. Dunning, 'Rural Deans in England in the Fifteenth Century', *Bull. of the Inst. of Hist. Research*, 40 (1967), 207–13; M. G. Smith, 'Bishop Trelawney and the Office of Rural Dean', *TDA*, 111 (1979), 14–15, 28.

13 S. Wood, *The Proprietary Church in the Medieval West* (2006), 883–921, 930–1.

14 On patronage of monasteries, see S. Wood, *English Monasteries and their Patrons in the Thirteenth Century* (1955), and of parish churches, F. Pollock and F. W. Maitland, *The History of English Law before the Time of Edward I*, 2nd edn (1952), II, 136–9.

clergy were subsequently put into possession of their churches by a further ceremony known as 'induction' and carried out locally by the archdeacon, his deputy, or the rural dean. Only the bishop could discipline or oust clergy after they had been confirmed or instituted, but patrons of religious houses continued to hold rights such as receiving hospitality during visits and burial after death, while those of parish churches retained a good deal of status and influence in them.

The basic local units of the Church in Cornwall were the parish church and parish, but it says a good deal about the Church's lack of organisation that we possess few documents listing all the Cornish churches and their parishes before the Reformation. Such lists as we have come from records aimed at estimating the incomes of the clergy for imposing taxes on them. The best lists relate to the papal taxation of England in 1291 and to a series of royal taxes: the 'ninth' of 1340–1, the poll-tax of 1381, and various 'subsidies' and 'tenths' imposed on the Church under Henry VIII in the 1520s and 30s.[1] The registers of the bishops of Exeter are also a useful source since they recorded the institution of rectors and vicars to parishes, but since not every parish had a rector or a vicar, even the registers fall short of including them all. In the end enumerating the medieval Cornish parish churches and parishes involves combining each of these sources to produce a composite total. The task is not possible before the end of the 13th century, when it can be achieved by using the papal taxation of 1291, the bishops' registers, and other material. By that date there were about 209 officially recognised parishes or parish-like areas in the archdeaconry of Cornwall, that is to say the ancient county of Cornwall together with North Petherwin, Werrington, and St Giles-on-the-Heath. About 167 of these units were fully parishes. They had a parish church with rights of worship, baptism, marriage, funeral, and burial. The clergyman of the parish church had jurisdiction over everyone in the parish for ordinary religious purposes, and every adult in the parish was expected to attend the parish church and to pay it tithes and other dues. Some parish clergymen were rectors, others vicars, and yet others chaplains or curates – distinctions to be explained later.[2]

Another 42 units fell into two categories. Most of them (37) were places like Advent, Germoe, Lostwithiel, or Warbstow, which may be termed 'sub-parishes'.[3] They had some of the characteristics of parishes, notably their own places of worship and probably definite boundaries within which people had responsibilities for that place of worship. Often they had their own chaplain to hold services. Legally, however, they were part of a larger parish: Lanteglos-by-Camelford, Breage, Lanlivery, and Treneglos in the examples just mentioned. Their place of worship was technically a chapel, not a church, and their chaplain was the employee of the clergyman of the mother church and answerable to him. Their parishioners paid tithes and dues to that clergyman, not to the priest of the chapel, and they were expected to attend the mother church on certain days of the year and sometimes for baptisms, funerals, and burials. A few of these chapels gained full parochial status during the later Middle Ages (1300–1500), while one full parish, Budock, lost some of its status to St Gluvias, originally its daughter church.

That leaves various oddities to consider. Three were islands. The Isles of Scilly formed a parish, chiefly served by monks of Tavistock Abbey, which is uniformly absent from official records, doubtless reflecting the islands' remoteness and lack of a normal clergyman. St Michael's Mount was not part of any other parish and was, in effect, a parish of itself, although it was run first by monks and later by an archpriest.[4] A third island, Lammana (nowadays Looe Island), constituted another distinct area, including a strip of territory on the adjoining mainland. This too was first administered by monks and later, after 1289, by a priest of its own.[5] A fourth parish, St Anthony-in-Roseland was a little area served by the Augustinian canons of the priory situated there; it would have operated as a parish but is rarely mentioned in records. A fifth small district, Temple, belonged first to the Knights Templars and later to the Order of St John of Jerusalem. Its church was described as a chapel in 1291, but formed an independent unit. In the 14th century the bishop regarded it as a normal part of the diocese, but it never seems to have had a straightforward rector or vicar, and after the Reformation it was regarded as a 'peculiar' exempt from part or all the normal diocesan administration.[6] There were also a few chapels which were locally regarded as having territories and 'parishioners'. These included St Luke in St Neot, St Constantine in

---

1 On 1291, see below, p. 00; on 1340–1, *Nonarum Inquisitiones* (Rec. Com. 1807); on 1381, TNA, E 179/25/5; and on the Henry VIII taxes, below, pp. 91–3.

2 Below, pp. 37–8.

3 The parishes with this lesser status in 1291 included most or all of the following: Advent, St Agnes, St Blazey, Bradoc, Callington, St Columb Minor, Cornelly, Cury, St Dennis, St Erney, Germoe, St Giles-in-the-Heath, St Gluvias, Golant, Gunwaloe, Gwithian, Helston, St Ives, Kenwyn, Laneast, Lanhydrock, St Levan, Lostwithiel, Luxulyan, Mabe, St Martin-in-Meneage, St Mary Magdalene (Launceston), Merther, St Michael Caerhays, Morvah, Perranarworthal, Sennen, St Thomas-by-Launceston, Towednack, Tremaine, Trewen, Warbstow, and Werrington. There were other sub-parishes whose status was less official and more local, such as St Nectan in St Winnow (*Reg. Grandisson*, II, 606), and possibly St Enodoc and Porthilly in St Minver.

4 Below, pp. 228–39.

5 Below, pp. 196–9.

6 *Reg. Grandisson*, II, 640; below, p. 273.

St Merryn, and St Nighton and Respryn in St Winnow.¹ They rarely or never figure in lists of churches or parishes as the sub-parishes did, and they are discounted from the statistics already mentioned.

A further complication was caused by the existence of peculiars, short for 'peculiar jurisdictions'. These were a feature of the English Church from at least the 12th century until the 19th, and existed all over the kingdom (Fig. 8). They reflected the wish of the king, bishops, cathedrals, and great monasteries to administer the churches belonging to them and the parishes surrounding these churches without interference from the normal diocesan officers. Sometimes a parish was taken out of its rural deanery and archdeaconry; occasionally it was removed even from its diocese and the power of its local bishop. At first the only authorities in Cornwall powerful enough to withdraw parishes in this way were the bishop and the cathedral. The bishops organised the 21 parishes and sub-parishes linked with their estates into four small rural deaneries: St Germans, Lawhitton, Penryn, and Pawton.² Within these deaneries Church affairs, including the Church courts and the administration of wills, were handled by special officers appointed by the bishop. The cathedral had two peculiars: the parishes of Perranzabuloe (including St Agnes) and St Winnow (including Boconnoc and Bradoc).³ These also had distinct administrators and courts, supervised by the cathedral. Religious houses were often peculiars too, in respect of their immediate sites, and the fact is recorded in the case of the collegiate churches of Crantock and Glasney, and the hospital of St John (Helston).⁴ All the peculiars in Cornwall up to 1300 remained within the diocese and were ultimately under the bishop's authority, but in that year the large parish of St Buryan was claimed by the king as a royal chapel outside the bishop's control. We shall examine this development in the following chapter.⁵

A conjectural map of parishes in Cornwall in 1291 appears as Fig. 10.⁶ This shows the boundaries of the areas that were fully parishes in continuous lines and those of the major sub-parishes within them in dotted lines. These boundaries can only be conjectural because sources for reconstructing them hardly exist in the Middle Ages. The earliest general body of information about them comes from documents called terriers in the early 17th century, which sometimes describe parish boundaries in words.⁷ A map of those in west Penwith survives from as far back as the 1570s, but the lines that it shows are merely schematic (Fig. 40).⁸ More helpful is the detailed map of Cornwall published by Joel Gascoyne in 1699, which professes to include the boundaries throughout the county, although their routes are not always accurately or fully depicted.⁹ The most reliable information comes only from the Tithe Assessments and Tithe Maps compiled in the years around 1840 as a result of the Tithe Act of 1836.¹⁰ There are some correspondences between the boundaries recorded in about 1840 with those of the earlier sources and with ancient landmarks such as roads and streams, which suggest that their routes may go back to the Middle Ages, but we cannot usually prove the fact for certain and the possibility of changes should be allowed for.

Given that caveat, the boundaries suggest that the parishes of Cornwall grew up organically over a period of time. They may have begun to appear as early as monasteries and churches were founded, and went on being formed up to about 1200 by which time the system was virtually complete. The majority of parishes covered between about 4 and 12 square miles (1036–3108 hectares), but a few were larger or smaller. The biggest parishes fell into two groups. Some of them belonged to churches that were staffed by groups of clergy before the Norman Conquest, such as St Buryan, St Germans, St Keverne, St Kew, and St Stephen-by-Launceston. In these cases parish size was linked with the superior status of the church, which either established a spacious territory in early times (St Kew might be such an example), or was strong enough to annex other areas (a process that can be traced at St Stephen-by-Launceston).¹¹ The other large parishes covered moorland areas, such as Altarnun, St Cleer, and Wendron; here largeness was not a mark of status but reflected a shortage of people to support a parish

---

1 P. L. Hull (ed.), *The Cartulary of Launceston Priory*, DCRS new ser. 30 (1987), 143–4; *Reg. Brantyngham*, II, 698–9; ECA, D&C 2672A f. 8r; *Reg. Grandisson*, II, 605.

2 St Germans included the parishes of St Germans and Landrake (with St Erney); Lawhitton those of Lawhitton, Lezant, and South Petherwin (with Trewen); Penryn those of St Anthony-in-Roseland, Budock, Gerrans, St Gluvias, and Mylor (with Mabe); and Pawton those of St Breock, Egloshayle, St Ervan, St Eval, and Little Petherick (*Reg. Bronescombe*, ed. Hingeston-Randolph, 466–7), as well as St Issey, St Merryn and the rural part of Padstow.

3 Ibid., 465; here St Issey is listed as a cathedral peculiar, although other records attribute it to the bishop's jurisdiction (e.g. RIC, Henderson 66, pp. 149–50, 161).

4 Below, pp. 175, 192, 248.

5 Below, p. 48.

6 A revision of the version first published in R. J. P. Kain and W. L. D. Ravenhill (ed.), *Historical Atlas of South-West England* (1999), 212, 214.

7 CRO, ARD/TER series.

8 TNA, MPF 1/332, illustrated and discussed in N. Orme, 'The Church and Clergy of St Buryan, c.1200–c.1574', *JRIC* (2006), 34–8.

9 J. Gascoyne, *A Map of the County of Cornwall, 1699*, ed. W. L. D. Ravenhill and O. J. Padel, DCRS new ser. 34 (1991).

10 On the tithe surveys and maps, see R. J. P. Kain and H. C. Prince, *The Tithe Surveys of England and Wales* (1985); R. J. P. Kain and R. R. Oliver, *The Tithe Maps of England and Wales: a cartographic analysis and county-by-county catalogue* (1995), 85–97; and R. J. P. Kain and H. C. Prince, *Tithe Surveys for Historians* (2000). The Cornish material is preserved in CRO, TA/ (tithe apportionments) and TM/ (tithe maps), and in TNA, IR 29/6/1–212 (tithe apportionments) and IR 30/6/1–212 (tithe maps).

11 On Launceston, see also below, pp. 132, 210.

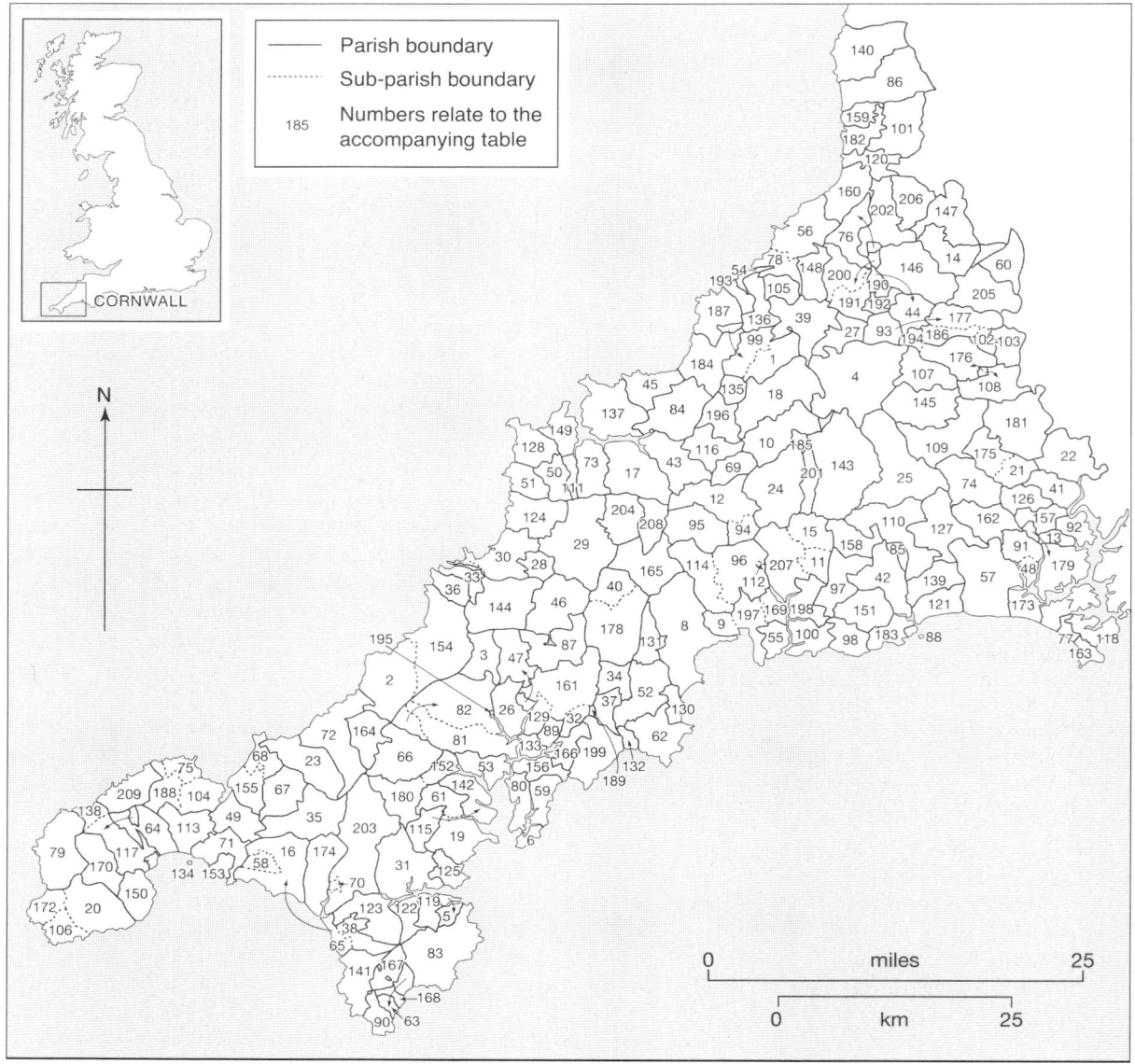

FIG 10. *Parishes in Cornwall, 1291.*

church and clergyman. Smaller than average parishes and sub-parishes include some based on towns like St Mary Magdalene (Launceston), Lostwithiel, St Thomas-by-Launceston, Tregony, and Truro, and others that lay in the countryside, such as St Keyne, Lammana, St Michael Caerhays, Perranuthnoe, and Temple. Small units of both kinds are likely to have taken shape after about the 10th century, since they reflect the growth of the tithe system which made it easier for such areas to maintain a clergyman. The urban parishes in particular followed the foundation or growth of towns in the 12th century, while Lammana and Temple arose from gifts of land to religious bodies in the same period.

The varied nature of the parishes – diversified by their size, location, economy, and society – shaped the character of the Church in Cornwall, as it did in England generally. Wealthy parishes produced large incomes (known as stipends) for their clergy, and plentiful resources to build and maintain the parish church. In poor parishes the opposite was the case. Clergy stipends ranged widely from parish to parish until the early 20th century, and the variety of church buildings caused by parish wealth can be seen at the present day. This variety meant that the Church authorities had an assortment of parishes and clergy to deal with, and that there was never uniformity in how the Church operated at a local level.

PARISHES IN THE ARCHDEACONRY OF CORNWALL, 1291
Parishes were in Cornwall unless otherwise stated

1 Advent	55 Fowey	107 Lewannick	160 Poundstock
2 St Agnes	56 St Gennys	108 Lezant	161 Probus
3 St Allen	57 St Germans	109 Linkinhorne	162 Quethiock
4 Altarnun	58 Germoe	110 Liskeard	163 Rame
5 St Anthony-in-Meneage	59 Gerrans	111 Little Petherick	164 Redruth
6 St Anthony-in-Roseland	60 St Giles-in-the-Heath (Devon)	112 Lostwithiel	165 Roche
7 Antony		113 Ludgvan	166 Ruan Lanihorne
8 St Austell	61 St Gluvias	114 Luxulyan	167 Ruan Major
9 St Blazey	62 Goran	115 Mabe	168 Ruan Minor
10 Blisland	63 Grade	116 St Mabyn	169 St Sampson (Golant)
11 Boconnoc	64 Gulval	117 Madron	170 Sancreed
12 Bodmin	65 Gunwalloe	118 Maker (partly in Devon)	171 Scilly
13 Botus Fleming	66 Gwennap	119 Manaccan	172 Sennen
14 Boyton (partly in Devon)	67 Gwinear	120 Marhamchurch	173 Sheviock
15 Bradoc	68 Gwithian	121 St Martin-by-Looe	174 Sithney
16 Breage	69 Helland	122 St Martin-in-Meneage	175 South Hill
17 St Breock	70 Helston	123 Mawgan-in-Meneage	176 South Petherwin
18 St Breward	71 St Hilary	124 St Mawgan-in-Pydar	177 St Stephen-by-Launceston
19 Budock	72 Illogan	125 Mawnan	
20 St Buryan	73 St Issey	126 St Mellion	178 St Stephen-in-Brannel
21 Callington	74 St Ive	127 Menheniot	179 St Stephen-by-Saltash
22 Calstock	75 St Ives	128 St Merryn	180 Stithians
23 Camborne	76 Jacobstow	129 Merther	181 Stoke Climsland
24 Cardinham	77 St John	130 Mevagissey	182 Stratton
25 St Cleer,	78 St Juliot	131 St Mewan	183 Talland
26 St Clement	79 St Just-in-Penwith	132 St Michael Caerhays	184 St Teath
27 St Clether	80 St Just-in-Roseland	133 St Michael Penkevil	185 Temple
28 Colan	81 Kea	134 St Michael's Mount	186 St Thomas-by-Launceston
29 St Columb Major	82 Kenwyn	135 Michaelstow	
30 St Columb Minor	83 St Keverne	136 Minster	187 Tintagel
31 Constantine	84 St Kew	137 St Minver	188 Towednack
32 Cornelly	85 St Keyne	138 Morvah	189 Tregony
33 Crantock	86 Kilkhampton	139 Morval	190 Tremaine
34 Creed	87 Ladock	140 Morwenstow	191 Treneglos
35 Crowan	88 Lammana	141 Mullion	192 Tresmeer
36 Cubert	89 Lamorran	142 Mylor	193 Trevalga
37 Cuby	90 Landewednack	143 St Neot	194 Trewen
38 Cury	91 Landrake	144 Newlyn East	195 Truro
39 Davidstow	92 Landulph	145 North Hill	196 St Tudy
40 St Dennis	93 Laneast	146 North Petherwin (Devon)	197 Tywardreath
41 St Dominick	94 Lanhydrock		198 St Veep
42 Duloe,	95 Lanivet	147 North Tamerton	199 Veryan
43 Egloshayle	96 Lanlivery	148 Otterham	200 Warbstow
44 Egloskerry	97 Lanreath	149 Padstow	201 Warleggan
45 St Endellion	98 Lansallos	150 Paul	202 Week St Mary
46 St Enoder	99 Lanteglos-by-Camelford	151 Pelynt	203 Wendron
47 St Erme	100 Lanteglos-by-Fowey	152 Perranarworthal	204 St Wenn
48 St Erney	101 Launcells	153 Perranuthnoe	205 Werrington (Devon)
49 St Erth	102 Launceston: St Mary Magdalene	154 Perranzabuloe	206 Whitstone
50 St Ervan		155 Phillack	207 St Winnow
51 St Eval	103 Lawhitton	156 Philleigh	208 Withiel
52 St Ewe	104 Lelant	157 Pillaton	209 Zennor
53 Feock	105 Lesnewth	158 St Pinnock	
54 Forrabury	106 St Levan	159 Poughill	

Key to FIG 10.

THE REVIVAL OF RELIGIOUS HOUSES

There were only a few dozen monasteries in England in the 11th century, and Cornwall, as we have seen, had none but minsters. The Normans were stronger supporters of monasticism and began to found more monasteries in England after the Conquest. At first the monks of these foundations were Benedictines, but during the 12th century the monastic revival branched out into new forms, such as houses of Cistercian monks and Augustinian canons. The counts of Mortain were sympathetic to monasteries to the extent of granting St Michael's Mount to the abbey of Mont St Michel and of founding Montacute Priory (Somerset). One or other of the counts must have given Montacute the Cornish minsters of Crantock and St Neot as endowments, since Montacute possessed both churches in the 12th century,[1] but nobody set up a monastery in Cornwall itself before 1100.

The earliest house of monks to appear in the county was the priory of St Nicholas on Tresco (Isles of Scilly) in about 1114.[2] This seems to have followed a grant by King Henry I of all the churches of Scilly to Tavistock Abbey (Devon), a Benedictine house. The abbey then founded the priory as a dependent house or 'cell', with a handful of monks from Tavistock to organise worship and pastoral services on the islands. Three more Benedictine priories made their appearance in the first half of the 12th century: Tywardreath and Minster at unknown dates, and St Michael's Mount perhaps between 1135 and 1144.[3] These too were cells, the first two belonging to the abbey of St Serge and St Bacche at Angers (Anjou) and the third to Mont St Michel. All were modestly staffed: Tywardreath by seven monks, Minster by two or three, while St Michael's Mount, although apparently intended for thirteen, is more likely to have supported six or less. Four other cells were opened during the second half of the 12th century or the early 13th, at dates that are also obscure. The priory of St Anthony-in Roseland, for two Augustinian canons, was a dependency of Plympton Priory (Devon); the priory of St Carroc, for two Cluniac monks, belonged to Montacute; the priory of Lammana, on Looe Island, for two Benedictine monks, was a daughter house of Glastonbury Abbey (Somerset); and the priory of Tregony, for two or more Augustinian canons, owed allegiance to the abbey of Sainte-Marie-du-Val (Normandy). A further cell of Tywardreath existed for a period during the 13th century at St Mary Vale in the parish of Cardinham.[4]

The most substantial monastic foundations in Cornwall came about through the conversion of minsters to Augustinian priories, a process that was fashionable in England during the 12th century. In 1123–4 Bishop William Warelwast introduced Augustinian canons to the minster at Bodmin, and in 1127 he did the same at Launceston. Somewhat later, perhaps in the early 1180s, Bishop Bartholomew of Exeter followed suit at St Germans. These changes, sometimes involving a transitional period in which the minster canons existed alongside the Augustinian ones, created three wealthier priories of canons following a modified version of the monastic life. Each lay under the patronage of the bishop of Exeter. They had larger numbers of clergy than the small cells: about eighteen canons at Bodmin by the early 14th century, perhaps as many at Launceston, and probably a dozen at St Germans. All three houses had a zone of power and influence in Cornwall. Bodmin's extended from Bodmin westwards and northwards towards the north coast. Launceston's occupied the east of the county between Bodmin Moor and the Tamar valley, while St Germans dominated the south-eastern corner. Bodmin and Launceston also profited from their location in towns and on the chief road that led through Cornwall and Devon to Exeter. Among the lesser houses Tywardreath held sway in the area around Fowey, while St Michael's Mount presided over Mount's Bay and attracted pilgrims from all over Cornwall. The other cells had only a local importance.

To this extent the 12th century was a monastic century in Cornwall as it was elsewhere in England (Fig. 11). Many people in that era saw monasticism as the best way to lead a religious life, and the leaders of society in the county did much to promote it. This was true of Bishops William Warelwast and Bartholomew, and of some of the heads of the chief landowning families. Reginald earl of Cornwall was a major benefactor of Launceston, and the next richest family, that of Richard fitz Turold, later known as the Cardinan family, was responsible for founding Tywardreath. Minster was the creation of the Botreaux family and Tregony that of the Pomeroys – both substantial landholders in the south-west of England. Two further houses received benefactions from more modest knightly families: St Carroc from Warin of Haccombe and Lammana from Hasculf de Soligny and predecessors of his. Nevertheless the monasteries were never strong in Cornwall in terms of their numbers of clergy. At the peak of their recruitment, in the 13th and early 14th centuries, they are unlikely to have included more than about 22 Benedictine and Cluniac monks and 50–60 Augustinian canons. The other major orders of monks and canons in England – Cistercians, Carthusians, and Premonstratensians – did not establish houses west of the Tamar, although an occasional Cornishman entered their houses

---

1 Below, p. 173.
2 Below, p. 266.
3 Below, pp. 229, 240, 284–5.
4 Below, pp. 136–7, 297, 196–7, 279, 285.

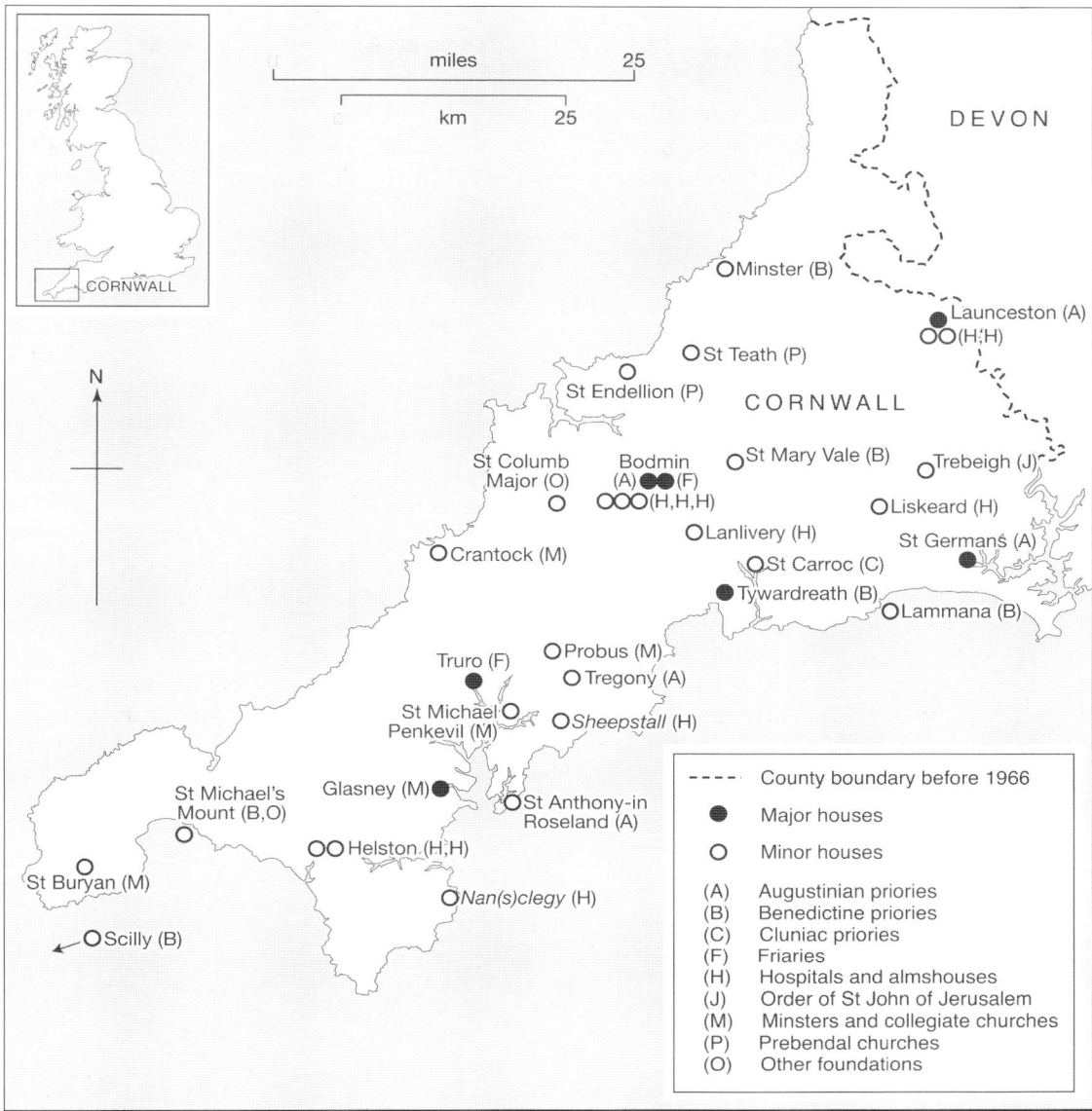

FIG 11. *Religious houses in Cornwall, 1100–1560.*

elsewhere.[1] The Knights Templars acquired some small properties, chiefly Temple on Bodmin Moor, but not enough to maintain any resident knights. The Order of St John of Jerusalem (also known as the Hospitallers) was represented by a single 'preceptory' at Trebeigh staffed by two or three brothers, a foundation due to one of the Pomeroys and to Reginald de Marisco in the late 12th century. There was never a nunnery in Cornwall, but a few Cornish women went to be nuns in other counties. We hear of Alice Reskymer as a sister of Buckland Priory (Somerset) in 1411, and Margaret, an anchoress living near Bodmin, was allowed to join Henry V's new Bridgettine abbey at Syon (Middx.) five years later.[2] Three other ladies came to be prioresses of nunneries in Devon: Joan Arundell of Lanherne at Canonsleigh in 1450, Honora Vyvyan at Cornworthy in 1461, and Isabel Trevarak at Polsoe in about 1500.[3]

The array of religious orders was completed by the arrival of the friars in the middle of the 13th century. They formed four major bodies in medieval England, two of which established houses in Cornwall: the Franciscans at Bodmin between 1240 and 1260, and the Dominicans at Truro in or shortly before 1259. Traditions at Bodmin varied in giving the credit for the foundation to the earl of Cornwall, John Fitzralph lord of Caerhays, and a merchant named John of London.[4]

1 e.g. Peter of Cornwall (Cistercian) in 1293–5 (*BRUO*, I, 490), Hugh Boscawen (Carthusian) in 1446 (below, p. 83), and William Tregooz (Carthusian) in *c*.1500 (E. M. Thompson, *The Carthusian Order in England* (1930), 324).

2 DRO, Chanter VIII, f. 218r, 323v; *Reg. Stafford*, 210, 406.

3 *Reg. Lacy*, ed. Hingeston-Randolph, I, 344–52; G. Oliver, *Monasticon Dioecesis Exoniensis* (1846), 236; TNA, C 1/349/61.

4 Below, p. 155.

Truro's foundation was claimed in later times by the royal family (probably as heirs of the earls of Cornwall) and by the Reskymer family of Constantine and Mawgan-in-Meneage.[1] A third order of friars, the Carmelites, established themselves just outside the county at Plymouth between 1289 and 1296, but developed links within it, especially across its eastern half.[2] The two Cornish friaries reinforced the presence of the religious orders by at least a dozen and possibly two dozen members each, but their importance, as we shall see, was greater and more distinctive than such numbers suggest.[3] Nonetheless it cannot be denied that Cornwall made a poor showing in the size and variety of its religious houses, compared with many other parts of England. The modest nature of the monastic foundations reflected the shortage of powerful wealthy people capable of providing the necessary endowments. Friars, on the other hand, who lived from voluntary donations and generally gravitated to towns, were hampered by the lack of large urban centres in Cornwall.

The Cornish monasteries did not account for the whole of the monastic presence in the county, however. Some Cornish churches and lands were granted to abbeys and priories elsewhere in England which administered them without establishing cells. During the second half of the 12th century William earl of Gloucester gave several churches in Cornwall to the priory of St James (Bristol), a cell of Tewkesbury Abbey (Gloucs.),[4] and the earls of Cornwall bestowed properties on the Cistercian abbeys of Beaulieu (Hants.), Hailes (Gloucs.), and Rewley (Oxford) during the 13th century. Earl Edmund of Cornwall also gave the church of St Buryan to Rochester Cathedral (Kent) in the 1270s.[5] Not all these gifts took effect. Several of Earl William's were abortive and Rochester returned St Buryan after a few years, perhaps because of its remoteness. Nonetheless a range of properties in Cornwall belonged to religious houses outside the county by 1291, allowing the houses to nominate rectors or vicars to churches and to receive tithes and land rents.[6] From Devon Hartland Abbey owned the manor and church of Launcells and some property in Bodmin, Newenham Abbey the church of Pelynt, Plympton Priory those of St Anthony-in-Roseland, St Kew, and Maker with some land in Menheniot, and Tavistock Abbey the church of North Petherwin with the manor of Werrington. From Somerset the Augustinian hospital of St John the Baptist (Bridgwater) held the churches of Davidstow and Lanteglos-by-Fowey, Cleeve Abbey the manors of Poughill and of Treglasta in Davidstow, and Montacute Priory its property at St Carroc with the churches of St Neot and St Veep. Further afield Beaulieu possessed the church of St Keverne with neighbouring lands, Hailes the church of Breage, Merton Priory (Surrey) those of Cuby and Tregony, Mottisfont Priory (Hants.) that of Mullion, Rewley those of Stithians and Wendron, and Tewkesbury those of Crowan and St Wenn (the latter with some land). Three nunneries were also represented. Wherwell Abbey (Hants.) held a small manor in Sennen,[7] while Wilton Abbey (Wilts.) had lands in Bodmin and Pelynt with the chapel of St Nennina in the latter parish. The furthest linkage of all joined the church of Tintagel to the nuns of Fontevrault Abbey in France.

There were some other religious houses that were neither monasteries nor friaries. Three of the pre-Conquest minsters survived the disturbances of the 11th century and the monastic reorganisations of the 12th. These were St Buryan, Crantock, and Probus, with four, ten, and six canons respectively, the presiding canon being styled the dean. The minsters had a profile similar to that of the monastic cells, in that their endowments and influence were chiefly confined to the parishes where they lay, and their impact was further weakened by the easy-going ways in which they were run. St Buryan lay under the patronage of the earls of Cornwall and later of the crown, while Probus and eventually Crantock belonged to the bishop of Exeter. These patrons appointed their servants as deans and canons with the intention of rewarding them, because minster clergy were usually able to receive their stipends without keeping residence as long as they arranged for others to do their duties. Many of these clergy were already absent from their churches by the 13th century, and in 1268 the bishop of Exeter suppressed the deanery of Probus and gave its endowments to the treasurer of Exeter Cathedral. Thereafter Probus was virtually only a parish church in practice, although it continued to support five canons who rarely or never resided. St Buryan shrank into a group of lowly-paid chaplains and clerks who deputised for an absent dean and canons, and only Crantock held on to some semblance of communal life.

More important than the ancient minsters was a

---

1 Below, p. 281.
2 Below, pp. 53–4.
3 Ibid.
4 *VCH Gloucestershire*, II, 74.
5 On Rochester, see below, p. 164.
6 For the Cornish possessions of these houses, except for Wherwell, see the papal taxation of 1291 in *Reg. Bronescombe*, ed. Hingeston-Randolph, 467–72, 476–7, 479. It should also be noted that the church of Lelant belonged to the collegiate church of Crediton (Devon) after 1272.

7 This property, which is not listed in the Cornish section of the papal taxation, was given by Isabel de Lucy in the 1220s and was worth £3 13s. 1¾d. per annum (BL, Egerton 2104 (A), ff. 79v–81r).

new foundation in the same tradition made by Bronescombe in 1265. This was Glasney College (Penryn), one of the earliest colleges or collegiate churches in England.[1] Colleges, like minsters, were staffed by canons and lesser clergy (vicars choral and chantry priests) who resembled parish clergy rather than members of the religious orders. They differed from minsters in possessing codes of statutes which laid down more precisely how they should work and prevented their communities dissolving through non-residence. During the next two hundred years this kind of foundation became popular among kings, noblemen, and bishops since it was less expensive to found than a monastery and could recruit its staff from among the parish clergy. Glasney was given a large church building and substantial endowments in the form of tithes of parish churches. It was closely modelled on Exeter Cathedral and the appointment of its canons belonged, like those of the cathedral, to the bishop. Bronescombe seems to have envisaged it as a sub-cathedral for Cornwall like the sub-cathedrals of the diocese of York at Beverley, Ripon, and Southwell. He probably saw its role as two-fold. One was to provide a model of worship for the parish clergy, since bishops regarded cathedrals as more suitable for this purpose than monasteries. The other was to be an administrative centre for Church affairs. A canonry of Glasney and house were allocated to the archdeacon of Cornwall, and it was common for other members of the church to hold posts in the bishop's service or to do duties for him. Glasney's history was not without problems, but it realised its founder's intentions in a reasonably faithful way until it was suppressed at the Reformation.[2]

A few more institutions call for attention. Two parish churches, St Endellion and St Teath, had multiple clergy, four prebendaries in the first case and two prebendaries and a vicar in the second, who shared their revenues.[3] One clergyman resided at each place to staff the parish, but the other posts were largely sinecures. They were usually held by absentees, and no communities of clergy developed at these churches. Six leper hospitals (Bodmin, Helston, Launceston, Liskeard, Maudlin in Lanlivery, and *Sheepstall* in Veryan) came into existence during the late 12th and 13th centuries, while Helston had a second hospital (St John's) for infirm people who were not lepers.[4] The hospitals catered chiefly for laymen and women and were served by chaplains from outside, but St John's had two or three resident clergy. A further leper community at *Nan(s)clegy* in St Keverne is mentioned in 1268 and may still have existed in 1481.[5] The number of Cornish hospitals is sometimes reckoned higher than this because, after Bishop Bitton of Exeter died in 1307, his executors (or someone on their behalf) travelled through Devon and Cornwall giving small sums of money to lepers in particular places, 22 of them in Cornwall.[6] Six of these were the places with leper hospitals, but the others are not recorded as having had such hospitals and the money may have been distributed to lepers who were living in private houses rather than institutions.

The numbers of the religious houses in Cornwall and of their inmates peaked in the middle of the 13th century, after which they began to decline. Some mother houses found their Cornish cells too costly to maintain. In 1267 the French abbey of Le Val exchanged its priory of Tregony with Merton Priory in return for lands in France, and Merton did not maintain Tregony for much longer, closing it between 1282 and 1286.[7] Soon afterwards, in 1289, Glastonbury Abbey withdrew its monks from Lammana and sold its property there to a local landowner.[8] St Mary Vale turned from a priory into a chapel during the late 13th or 14th centuries,[9] and by about 1300 the monks of Tavistock Abbey were trying to exchange their property in the Isles of Scilly with King Edward I in return for endowments elsewhere, although they were not successful in this respect.[10] During the 14th century the monasteries were to suffer further blows from plague and war, causing numbers of monks and canons to fall and two more houses to close soon after 1400.[11]

LIFE WITHIN THE RELIGIOUS HOUSES

The religious houses of Cornwall were scattered across the country in an irregular way, reflecting the various forces that had created them. Five were in towns – Bodmin (with two), Launceston, Tregony, and Truro – while Tywardreath near Fowey was close to another. Most of the rest lay in the countryside, sometimes off main roads like Crantock, St Germans, and Minster. There were slightly more houses in the eastern half of the county, which was closer to England and mainly English-speaking, but the western, Cornish-speaking half had St Buryan, Crantock, St Michael's Mount, Glasney, and the Truro friary, while the friary at Bodmin included men who were fluent in Cornish, at

---

1 There is no sign that Bishop Brewer, Bronescombe's predecessor-but-one, took an interest in collegiate churches. He acquired the patronage of Crantock, but did nothing to reform it.
2 Below, pp. 244–62.
3 Below, pp. 180–4, 270–1.
4 Below, see the houses named.
5 Below, p. 195.

6 N. Orme and M. Webster, *The English Hospital, 1070–1570* (1995), 170–7, and below, pp. 00–00.
7 Below, pp. 279–80.
8 Below, p. 199.
9 Below, p. 285.
10 Below, p. 268.
11 Below, pp. 50–1.

least in the 14th century. Nearly all the houses occupied ancient religious sites. This was the case with the minsters and the Augustinian ex-minsters as well as with St Anthony, St Carroc, Lammana, Minster, and Scilly, all of which stood where there had been a previous church or chapel, sometimes with a claim to a buried saint. Only St Mary Vale, Tregony, and Tywardreath seem to have been founded in virgin locations, the first two near Norman castles and the latter at the centre of its endowment of churches and lands. Remoteness was sometimes a feature too. Three houses were built on islands (Lammana, the Mount, and Scilly) and two in secluded valleys (St Mary Vale and Minster). Such foundations point to a wish by some founders and clergy to establish religion away from the everyday world – a wish that is paralleled in other parts of the British Isles.

The evidence about the religious houses of Cornwall in the 12th and 13th centuries is largely confined to charters which record their foundation and list their endowments. Little is known about their internal life until the bishops' registers begin in 1258. Some light is thrown on Launceston minster and priory in the 12th century by the writings of Peter of Cornwall, to be mentioned presently. His family, which came from Launceston, had a close relationship with the minster of St Stephen. Its first known member, Ailsi (died before 1123), acted as clerk of the works when the church's tower was built, and claimed to have had met the church's saint in a vision. Two of Ailsi's sons, Bernard and Nicholas, became clergy and made gifts to the church, including a banner depicting the saint, a carpet, and an ivory casket of relics. When their brother Jordan died in about 1180 the prior of Launceston, Osbert, was at his deathbed – all facts that witness to a monastery rooted in local society.[1] Launceston may have had a better relationship with its neighbourhood than was the case at Bodmin. The chief settlement at Launceston, the new town of Dunheved, was a self-governing borough whose dealings with the priory were more equal and consequently more equable. In contrast Bodmin was ruled by its local priory, a situation that led to disputes about government in the town and the rights of local people to exploit the neighbouring woods and waters. Internally, however, Bodmin shone as a centre of Latin writing in the 12th century. Four works were written about its patron saint, St Petroc, which form the principal Cornish examples of the contemporary vogue for writing Lives of indigenous English and Welsh saints. They include the so-called 'Gotha Life', an enlarged version of the earlier 11th-century Life of the saint;[2] a short Life of him in rhymed 'goliardic' verse; a list of miracles done through his intercession; and an account of the theft and recovery of his relics in 1171, the last of which was composed by one of the canons, Robert of Tauton.[3] When the relics (stolen by another canon and taken to France) were returned, they were conveyed back to Cornwall with much ceremony by the bishop of Exeter and the prior of Bodmin, pausing at Exeter and Launceston. Here too one gains a sense of the importance of the saint to the church (Fig. 12).

Once we reach the second half of the 13th century, incidents of monastic life begin to be recorded in the bishops' registers. These are chiefly of a constitutional and disciplinary nature, such as the elections of priors and the maintenance of good order. At Launceston Bronescombe did battle in 1259 with the prior, Robert Fissacre, over maladministration. Two years later Fissacre resigned. The election of his successor caused deep divisions and was improperly conducted in the bishop's view, which caused him to quash the election and appoint one of the two rival candidates. The next election in 1285 was also annulled by the bishop, although he approved the canon chosen as prior, William Teignterer.[4] Bodmin experienced problems of bad behaviour. Bronescombe apparently excommunicated Prior Richard in about 1274 for associating with people who had themselves been excommunicated. When the prior agreed to submit to the bishop, he was ordered to hold services in his church in a simple and muted way until the excommunications were lifted. In 1277 Richard was, or had been, in dispute with the archdeacon of Cornwall over tithes and other things, and in 1284, after he had incurred a further excommunication, the crown was asked to arrest him. Two years later one of his canons, William of Plympton, was imprisoned by the bishop for rebellion and disobedience.[5] Incidents like these were common in English monasteries during the later Middle Ages, and are sometimes seen as evidence of the decline of monastic life. They were certainly one aspect of that life, but not the whole of it.

The three large monasteries in Cornwall were independent houses and recruited most of their canons locally, so that they were primarily Cornish institutions. At the same time they belonged to a religious order, that of the Augustinian canons, and forged links through the order with the world beyond the Tamar. The first prior of Bodmin, Guy, came from Merton Priory (Surrey) and the first prior of Launceston, Teoric, from the priory of Holy Trinity Aldgate (London), both Augustinian houses.[6] In turn the

---

1 P. L. Hull and R. Sharpe, 'Peter of Cornwall and Launceston', *Cornish Studies* 13 (1985), 16–27.
2 Above, p. 16.
3 P. Grosjean, 'Vie et Miracles de. S. Petroc', *Analecta Bollandiana* 74 (1956), 131–88, 470–96, at 145–65, 166–71, 171–4, 174–88; G. H. Doble, 'The Relics of St Petroc', *Antiquity* 13 (1939), 403–15.
4 Below, pp. 213–14.
5 Below, pp. 146–7.
6 Below, pp. 140, 203.

FIG 12. *The ivory reliquary preserved at Bodmin parish church, perhaps the one given by Walter of Coutances in 1177 to store the bones of St Petroc.*

Cornish priories sent canons elsewhere. Bodmin did best in this respect. Its probable second prior, Algar, was made bishop of Coutances in Normandy in 1133, and four of its canons were dispatched at the request of an Anglo-Irish landlord to open an Augustinian priory in Ireland in 1193. Three of the four became priors of houses there and one of them, Hugh le Rous, also bishop of Ossory.[1] Launceston's most famous son in this period, Peter of Cornwall (1139/40–1221), came from the town rather than the priory, but his family was closely connected with the Augustinians and he joined Launceston's mother house of Holy Trinity Aldgate as a canon, rising to be the prior. He was the author of several theological works and of a large collection of evidence about visions, *Liber Revelationum*, in which he included the details of his own family history.[2] The smaller houses all had external connections because they were cells of houses elsewhere and their monks or canons came from outside, even from France in the case of St Michael's Mount, Minster, Tywardreath, and (until 1267) Tregony. These connections brought clergy to Cornwall from other places, and although monks were not primarily evangelists, they must have come into contact with many local people, chiefly through administering property but also by running churches. St Michael's Mount drew people to its shrine, while St Anthony, Minster, Scilly, and probably Tregony were parish churches as well as monasteries.

Monks and canons belonged to self-contained monasteries and lived their lives within them, travelling at most from a mother house to a dependent cell. The orders of friars, on the other hand, were international organisations as was the Order of St John of Jerusalem. Members of these orders were mobile. Cornish recruits were sent elsewhere to be educated or to spend their adult lives, and outsiders were drafted to work in Cornwall. There were other differences in being friars. Unlike monks and canons they had few endowments and depended chiefly on charity, hence the location of their houses in towns where donations were easier to come by. They had a more pastoral vocation than monks and canons, observing daily worship in their houses but spending time in the outside world preaching and hearing confessions. This work required greater learning than was needed by monks and canons, and the friars embraced university life soon after they established themselves in England. Some friars from Cornwall must have attended university during the 13th century, and two of them, both Franciscans, are known to have done so. The first, another Peter of Cornwall, studied logic and wrote a surviving work on the subject.[3] The second, Richard Rufus of Cornwall, appears to have entered the order at Paris in 1229 after which he taught at both Paris and Oxford, graduating as a doctor of divinity and writing (or being credited with) several works on theology.[4] In the following chapter we shall encounter more evidence of the learning of friars in Cornwall and its impact on Cornish people.

---

1 Below, p. 140.
2 R. Sharpe, *A Handlist of the Latin Writers of Great Britain and Ireland before 1540* (1997), 425–6; biography in *ODNB*.
3 Sharpe, *Handlist*, 426.
4 Ibid., 503–5; P. G. J. M. Raedts, *Richard Rufus of Cornwall and the Tradition of Oxford Theology* (1987); R. Wood, 'Richard Rufus of Cornwall and Aristotle's Physics', *Franciscan Studies* 52 (1996), 247–81; biography in *ODNB*.

THE PARISH CLERGY

The majority of Cornish clergy in the 12th and 13th centuries worked in the parishes. Two hundred or more of them served the 209 parish churches and the important chapels of the county, almost double the number of those in the monasteries and friaries. A similar number by about 1300 are likely to have served as assistant curates, chantry priests saying masses for the dead, and chaplains in private households. During the 13th century two of the bishops of Exeter held synods of their clergy, at which statutes were passed regulating clerical life. William Brewer's statutes date from an unknown year between 1225 and 1237 (these do not survive in a complete form), and Peter Quinil's, a lengthy and detailed code, from 1287. Both sets of statutes gave instructions about Church services, the sacraments, the functions and behaviour of the clergy, and the duties of the laity to the Church. This shows us how the authorities wished the Church to work and, more obliquely, how it worked in practice.[1]

The education and recruitment of the parish clergy before 1300 are obscure topics as far as Cornwall is concerned. There was no organised system for training them. A would-be priest had to acquire the necessary learning for Church work by attending a school or through private tuition from a clergyman. Both these means were probably available in Cornwall before 1300 but they have left no records. Education involved mastering Latin in the sense of reading, pronouncing, and understanding it correctly so that one could perform the church services, as well as learning how to sing services to plainsong chants and tunes. The cost of education was usually a private matter for the learner's family or for some other person willing to sponsor his studies. All that the Church did in a public way was to encourage the clergy to employ young scholars as parish clerks while they learnt to be priests. Quinil's statutes ordered that the post of clerk should always be given to a scholar in parishes within ten miles of the cathedral and the 'castles', probably meaning towns with castles like Launceston where there were likely to be schools.[2] Our sole record of what was taught in a school in Cornwall during the 12th and 13th centuries is the so-called 'Cornish Vocabulary', recorded in a single manuscript written in about 1100. It is a list of Latin words with their equivalents in the Cornish language, arranged by subjects: God, heaven, earth, mankind, birds, animals, plants, houses, and furniture. The work was modelled on a similar Latin and English vocabulary compiled by Ælfric of Eynsham in the 990s, and shows that Latin was being learnt in the Cornish-speaking areas of the county.[3] The study of the Bible or of theology by clergy was not required. Quinil demanded only knowledge of the Ten Commandments, the Seven Deadly Sins, the Seven Sacraments, and the articles of the Christian faith enshrined in the creeds.[4] He also produced a short abridgement of his statutes in Latin and ordered every parish church to acquire a copy, in effect a basic guide to all that the clergy should know.[5]

Some Cornish clergy took their studies further. These were a minority, chiefly sons of knightly or wealthy burgess families, who had the resources to travel to centres of learning outside the county. The emergence of universities at Paris, Oxford, and Cambridge in the late 12th and early 13th centuries offered the opportunity to study the liberal arts, chiefly made up of logic, philosophy, and science. This was a lengthy procedure which, in England, required seven years to gain the degree of master of arts (MA), with a further two years of 'regency' during which an MA graduate was expected to act as a university teacher. Besides the liberal arts, four other studies developed with their own degrees: medicine, civil (i.e. Roman) law, canon (i.e. Church) law, and theology. A notable Cornish pioneer of university education was John of Cornwall, who appears to have studied at Paris as early as the 1150s, where his teachers included Peter Lombard, the great Biblical commentator. John duly achieved the rank of MA and, after moving from Paris, seems to have become an early teacher of theology or law at Oxford, where he is named as a 'master' in the late 1170s. Three of his works on theology survive, along with a Latin poetical version of Geoffrey of Monmouth's 'Prophecies of Merlin' that he dedicated to the bishop of Exeter in the 1150s. John mentions Cornwall several times in the poem and in a commentary attached to it, as well as referring specifically to Fowey (now Bodmin) Moor, the River Tamar, Tintagel, and other places with an evident pride in his native region and a wish to emphasise its place in British history. He may have spoken Cornish, since he gives the Cornish name for Fowey Moor as *Goen Bren,* and in 1173 he was recommended to Henry II in 1173 as a suitable person to be made bishop of St David's because he knew Welsh, although he was not selected.[6]

John had close connections with Walter of Coutances, who was also a native of Cornwall, probably

---

1 F. M. Powicke and C. R. Cheney (ed.), *Councils & Synods II: A.D. 1205–1313* (1964), I, 227–37; II, 982–1077.

2 Ibid., II, 1026–7.

3 BL, Cotton Vesp. A.xiv, ff. 7r–10r; E. van T. Graves (ed.), 'The Old Cornish Vocabulary', Columbia University, New York, PhD thesis, 1962.

4 Powicke and Cheney (ed.), *Councils & Synods II*, II, 1017.

5 Ibid., 1059–77.

6 Biography in *ODNB*; M. J. Curley, 'A New Edition of John of Cornwall's *Prophetia Merlini*', *Speculum* 57 (1982), 217–49.

from a wealthy Anglo-Norman family. Walter studied at Paris, became deputy to the chancellor of Henry II, and rose to be archdeacon of Oxford, bishop of Lincoln, and finally archbishop of Rouen.[1] John seems to have been employed in Walter's household at Lincoln and to have received from him a canonry of Rouen before concluding his career as archdeacon of Worcester. Other men from Cornwall rose to middle-ranking posts in the English Church during the 13th century, but it is difficult to gauge how numerous they were. David of Cornwall, doctor of canon law of Oxford, became chancellor of Limerick Cathedral in Ireland, and two Oxford scholars named Richard of Cornwall gained promotion as cathedral canons of Lincoln and York respectively.[2] Master John of St Goran was appointed a canon of Exeter and put in charge of Bishop Brewer's consistory court, while Master Philip of St Austell was made archdeacon of Winchester.[3] A more literary figure, Michael of Cornwall, appears to have studied university subjects in England, including rhetoric under the eminent Latin poet Henry of Avranches. During the 1250s Henry and Michael wrote Latin verses for public contests in which they pretended to attack one another, once with the bishop of Ely as judge and once before the bishop of Winchester.[4] Michael eventually settled in London, but he remained proud of his Cornish origins and claimed to have the favour of King Arthur. The studies of all these scholars led them away from Cornwall, and they did not return home permanently afterwards.

Education prepared one for life as a clergyman, but entry to that life was gained through ordination which in Cornwall meant going to Exeter for the purpose, or even further, except on the rare occasions when the bishop crossed the Tamar. There were stages of ordination, beginning with the 'first tonsure', which could be conferred at the age of seven, and the order of acolyte at fourteen. These two orders were 'minor orders', which gave you clerical status but left you freedom to take up work as a layman and marry. Higher than these were the grades of subdeacon (for which you had to be at least seventeen), deacon (at least nineteen), and priest (at least twenty-four). By about the 12th century taking these 'major orders' required a permanent commitment to clerical life, including a vow of celibacy. Ordination as a priest enabled you to perform all the ecclesiastical functions required in parishes, but gaining an ecclesiastical post was a further process. The best posts were those of rector or vicar of a parish, posts known as 'benefices' and their occupants as 'beneficed clergy'.

The nomination of each rector and vicar belonged to the patron who held the advowson of the benefice. In 1291 a majority (97) of the 167 rectories or vicarages in Cornwall belonged to patrons who were clergy.[5] The bishop owned 11, the cathedral 13, and religious houses (inside and outside the county) 73. Lay people held the rest. Nine were in the gift of the earl of Cornwall; these subsequently came into the hands of the king and, at times, to the king's eldest son as duke of Cornwall. Sixty-one belonged to other lay patrons, generally local lords of the manor. An advowson could be bequeathed or sold, and Mullion's changed hands for £30 in 1309.[6] It followed that to become a rector or vicar one needed a patron's favour, something that was likely to go to men with higher rank, distinction in learning, or powerful friends to press their case. Bronescombe's register (1258–80), the first record of institutions in Exeter diocese, shows some benefices in Cornwall being given to members of Cornish or Devonian families of gentry such as Arundell, Bodrigan, Fitz-Henry, Lercevesque, and Pyne. Others went to Geoffrey de Bisimano (of an Italian family), Henry of Bollegh, and John of Esse, who were bishops' officials, or to men in the service of the earl of Cornwall like Arnold of Holland and Stephen Haym. Many clergy lacked such backing, at least to begin with, and had to take more lowly work as assistants to rectors and vicars or as chantry priests. They worked for comparatively low wages or salaries without security of tenure and, in the case of some of the chantry priests, for fixed periods of time.

The parish clergy, then, were not a uniform group. As well as the distinction just outlined between the beneficed clergy (rectors and vicars) and the unbeneficed (wage-earning chaplains and chantry priests), the beneficed clergy differed among themselves in terms of their income and where it came from. The wide range in the size and therefore the wealth of parishes led to a corresponding span of clergy incomes from glebe, tithes, and other revenues. As we shall see, the papal taxation of 1291 estimated the rector of St Columb Major as receiving £17 a year and the poorest, the vicar of Colan, only 6s. 8d. These were considerable underestimates, and the vicar's earnings may have come closer to £3, but his neighbour at St Columb could well have been ten times as rich. Another important distinction between the beneficed clergy related to rectors and vicars. The rector of a benefice received all the income of the benefice for his 'stipend' or earnings. By the 12th century, however, it became popular for patrons of benefices to give their advowsons to religious houses.[7] One motive for this

---

1 Biography in *ODNB*.   2 *BRUO*, I, 489, 490–1.
3 Barlow (ed.), *English Episcopal Acta*, XII, 312, 320; J. Le Neve, *Fasti Ecclesiae Anglicanae 1300–1541*, IV: *Monastic Cathedrals*, ed. B. Jones (1963), 50.
4 Sharpe, *Handlist*, 162–3, 376–7; biographies in *ODNB*.
5 See also M. Page, 'The Ownership of Advowsons in Thirteenth-Century Cornwall', *DCNQ* 37/10 (1996), 336–41. His method of counting differs slightly from that used here.
6 W. H. Hale and H. T. Ellacombe (ed.), *Accounts of the Executors of Richard Bishop of London 1303, and... Thomas Bishop of Exeter, 1310*, Camden Soc. new ser. 10 (1874), 44.
7 Page, 'The Ownership of Advowsons', 336–41.

was to endow the houses concerned. When a religious house acquired an advowson, it could, with the bishop's agreement, appoint itself as rector on a permanent basis and receive the rector's income. This process was known as 'appropriation' and such benefices as 'appropriated benefices' or 'vicarages'. Since a parish church still had to be served by a clergyman, the religious house appointed a 'vicar' (a term meaning deputy) to act in its place.

Rectors and vicars were identical in being presented to the benefice by the patron, instituted by the bishop, appointed for an indefinite period, and charged with similar spiritual duties. They differed in that the rector received the whole of the benefice income while the vicar shared it with the appropriating institution. By the 13th century the vicar's share was usually 'taxed' (i.e. assessed and fixed) by the bishop to ensure fair treatment, and several such 'taxations' of Cornish vicarages survive in the registers of Bronescombe and Quinil (1258–88).[1] The taxation usually gave the appropriating institution the tithes of grain from the parish, known as the 'great tithes', because these tithes were the most valuable, the easiest to collect, and the least perishable, so that they could be stored, transported, or sold. The vicar was generally given the rector's house, the glebe, and what was called the 'altarage'. This comprised the offerings given in church at weddings, churchings of mothers, deaths, and other occasions, together with the lesser tithes of the parish including hay, other crops, animals, dairy products, and fish. Where the altarage was considered to be more valuable than the vicar deserved, certain tithes might be omitted such as fish in the major fishing parishes or crops like peas and beans. Occasionally he was required to make a payment of money to the appropriators, and it was common to expect him to repair the chancel of the church and the house he lived in.[2] Quinil laid down that every vicar should receive a stipend of at least £3 6s. 8d. per annum.[3] In practice this amount was often exceeded, but it is worth remembering that rectors' and vicars' stipends came only partly in cash and mainly in kind. Tithes had to be collected, their value fluctuated with good and bad seasons, and a clergyman might not be able to extract all the income to which he was entitled. Moreover rectors and vicars were expected to give some hospitality to visitors and alms to the poor.[4]

Some appropriators took more of the benefice income. The priories of Bodmin, St Carroc, and Tywardreath saved money by lodging the vicars of their nearby churches in their monasteries, feeding them there, and paying them small salaries in cash. The priories then took the whole of the parish tithes.[5] Several of the churches belonging to Launceston Priory were not even served by vicars. This was the case at Boyton, Egloskerry, St Giles-in-the-Heath, Laneast, North Tamerton, Tremaine, Tresmeer, Werrington, and the three churches of Launceston itself. Here the priory appointed chaplains who were not presented to the bishop for institution and did not have tenure for life, although it is possible that such clergy held office for long periods. The same happened in the parishes of St Germans and Minster, where there were also priory churches.[6] Brewer ordered that chaplains serving in parishes should receive at least £2 per annum, which Quinil increased to £2 10s., less than the £3 6s. 8d. allowed to vicars.[7] It is likely that this £2 rate also held good for chantry priests and domestic chaplains, but it was only just enough on which to live.

CHURCH BUILDINGS AND POPULAR RELIGION

We know the names of the parish churches of Cornwall in the 12th and 13th centuries, but few documentary sources exist about them. Most of the surviving written evidence relates to the religious houses and suggests that they experienced a good deal of building work during this period. St Stephen-by-Launceston, the original minster of Launceston, is recorded acquiring a tower in the early 12th century.[8] Later, after it became a priory church in the 1120s, it was rebuilt on a new site, as was Bodmin Priory. The other religious houses – St Germans, St Michael's Mount, Tywardreath, and their lesser sisters – also gained new buildings or refurbished ones, as did Glasney in the 13th century. Little is known from documents about the construction of the ordinary parish churches. In 1259–60 Bronescombe dedicated twenty-five such churches in Cornwall, but it is not certain whether this was because they had been rebuilt.[9] In 1237 an English Church council deemed that many ancient churches had never been dedicated, and ordered that this lack should be made good, so Bronescombe may have been attending to churches that could not show that they had received the rite in earlier times.[10]

---

1 *Reg. Bronescombe*, ed. Hingeston-Randolph, 32, 64, 196, 203, 205, 222, 231, 239, 244, 246–7, 249–51, 253–4, 256, 263, 285, 372; ed. Robinson, III, 125 s.v. 'taxation'.
2 See also *Reg. Grandisson*, II, 605–11.
3 Powicke and Cheney (ed.), *Councils & Synods II*, II, 1025.
4 Ibid., I, 232.
5 Below, pp. 145, 289, 298.
6 Below, pp. 188, 242.
7 Powicke and Cheney (ed.), *Councils & Synods II*, I, 236; II, 1025.
8 Hull and Sharpe, 'Peter of Cornwall', 16–21.
9 *Reg. Bronescombe*, ed. Hingeston-Randolph, 65–7; ed. Robinson, III, 121, s.v. 'dedication'.
10 N. Orme, *English Church Dedications, with a Survey of Cornwall and Devon* (1996), 5.

That leaves surviving remains as the principal source, and these are less obvious than in some other parts of England because of the almost universal rebuilding of parish churches in the 15th and early 16th centuries, coupled with the loss of the monasteries at the Reformation. Many Cornish parish churches, however, still contain portions of fabric in the Norman style of architecture dating from the 12th century, and in the Early English style from the 13th century, indicating that the construction or reconstruction of churches took place on a wide scale over both periods of time.[1] About 100 churches have fabric of the 13th century, much of it with features such as stiff leaf capitals and lancet windows, the latter disposed singly or grouped as at St Anthony-in-Roseland. Building stone appears to have often found from neighbouring sources: Tintagel, for example, was constructed from local slate-stone. The bringing of stone from granite quarries only became widespread at the end of the Middle Ages, but good-quality stone was occasionally procured from a distance for buildings of higher status or for decorative purposes. Caen stone from Normandy was used for the priory church of St Anthony-in-Roseland and also for Mylor parish church (which belonged to the bishops of Exeter). The west doorway of St Germans appears to be built of Hurdwick stone from Tavistock.

The largest and most ornate church buildings in 12th- and 13th-century Cornwall were those of the religious houses, most of which (apart from Bodmin, Launceston, and Tywardreath) were also parish churches. One of their principal features was often a tower of a large and significant kind like that of Launceston, although it is not known whether the latter was free-standing or part of the building. A lateral tower survives from the minster church of Bodmin on the north side of the later parish church on the site, and this may have stood on its own or at the end of a transept which was subsumed into a later aisle. Cruciform plans incorporating a central tower were often a feature of minster churches in England, and in Cornwall this was the case at Crantock and Glasney, the former perhaps from the 12th century and the latter from the second half of the 13th or later (Fig. 47). Crantock had some additional distinctions. Its choir was raised above the level of the nave (as in a cathedral or large monastery) and there were aisles alongside the choir, enabling the clergy to go in processions outside the choir. St Buryan, another minster, of which little survives from before the 15th century, appears to have had similar choir aisles. Both Crantock and St Buryan were surpassed by Glasney, begun in the mid 13th century. This was the largest and wealthiest of the minster or collegiate churches, similar in size to the biggest monastic churches at Bodmin and Launceston,

and having an elaborate plan of choir, nave, aisles, and transepts, as well as a central tower (Fig. 58). Influence from Devon is apparent at Glasney, both in its plan which resembled that of Crediton church (a church associated with Glasney's founder Bishop Bronescombe) and in its structure, which included the use of Beer stone from east Devon.

Turning to the monastic churches, St Germans, the best preserved today, was an imposing building with two western towers flanking a grand entrance into the nave (Figs. 49–50). The nave had north and south aisles down which clergy could go in procession, and east of it lay the choir (or chancel), apparently lacking such aisles. There may have been transepts, but this is not clear.[2] Bodmin Priory (at least by the 15th century) seems to have had a main entrance on the west, leading to a nave and chancel each with aisles on both sides, which gave access to a shrine of the patron saint, St Petroc, at the east end of the church (Fig. 44).[3] Launceston Priory, another house known chiefly from its layout at the end of the Middle Ages, appears to have been built in the 12th century as a long aisleless nave and chancel. Eventually the nave included a north aisle and the chancel north and south aisles, parts or all of which may have been added to the original building (Figs. 51–2).[4] The only friary church of which anything is known is that of the Franciscans at Bodmin, which was probably the larger of the two Cornish friaries. This was a long narrow aisleless building with a high roof, probably topped by a little tower and spire supported on walls between the nave and chancel (Fig. 46).[5] The remaining religious houses were smaller and had little to distinguish them from ordinary parish churches. St Anthony included a nave, chancel, and transepts (Fig. 42), but St Michael's Mount had only the first two of these elements, and Minster and Scilly were probably similar to the Mount (Figs. 55, 61).[6] St Carroc's church was so small that it was generally referred to as a chapel. All the religious houses had further ancillary buildings to accommodate their staff and domestic activities. In the case of the monasteries these buildings were compact and enclosed, with at least Launceston's lying around a cloister. Minsters like Glasney and Crantock, on the other hand, had a more open precinct comprising individual houses, like a cathedral close in miniature.

The basic plan of the parish churches in Cornwall during the 12th and 13th centuries consisted of a simple nave and a chancel, a plan best seen today at St John and Tremaine (Fig. 13). Naves and chancels were usually separated from one another by a wall pierced by an archway, the chancel arch, giving a view from the nave to the altar in the chancel. Such arches were often smaller than those of later times, and the fixing of a wooden rood screen across them probably became

---

1 E. H. Sedding, *Norman Architecture in Cornwall* (1909), passim.
2 Below, p. 187.
3 Below, pp. 143–4.
4 Below, pp. 204–6.
5 Below, pp. 155–6.
6 Below, pp. 138, 230, 241, 267.

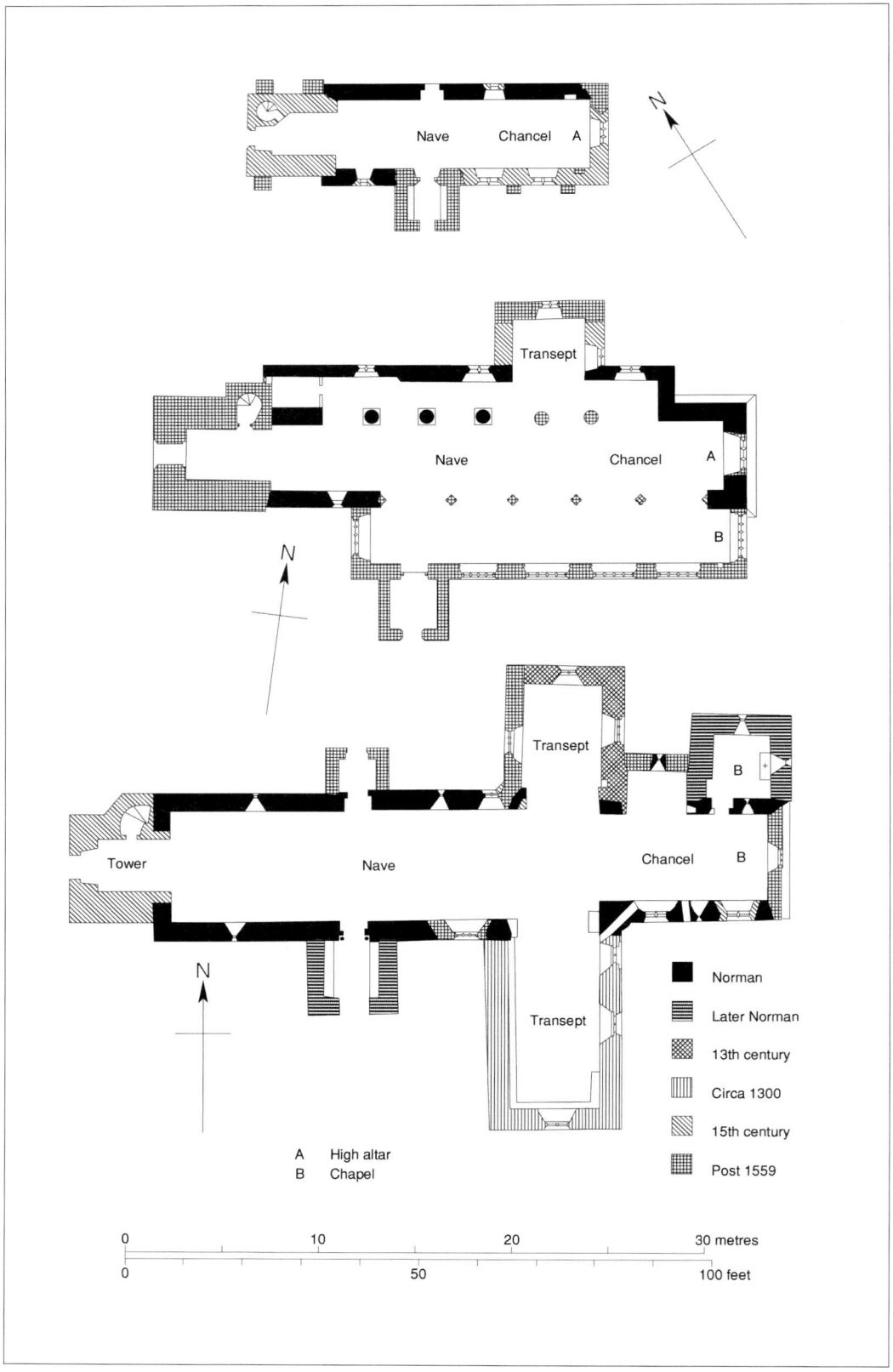

FIG 13. *Parish church plans, 12th and 13th centuries. Tremaine (top); St Breward (middle); Tintagel (bottom).*

common only towards the end of the 13th century or even later.[1] Parishioners gained access to the nave through a doorway, usually placed on the south side of the nave and often decorated with carving around it (Kilkhampton, Morwenstow) or on a tympanum above it (St Michael Caerhays, Treneglos). Some churches, like Egloskerry and Tintagel, had an additional north entrance, generally less elaborate. All parish churches possessed a font for baptisms, and this was an important sign of status since fonts were normally forbidden in lesser religious buildings such as chapels. Ancient fonts were frequently kept in use, perhaps for this reason, and Cornwall still possesses over 100 that stem from the Norman period, many of them in churches such as Altarnun and Fowey where all other evidence of early work has gone. High-quality stone was often used for Norman fonts, including Catacleuse from near Padstow and Purbeck, imported from Dorset. This enabled such fonts to be embellished with carving, and there are similarities between particular fonts, such as the Catacleuse examples with palmette decoration at Fowey, Lanlivery, and elsewhere. Interior walls might be decorated, and Tintagel formerly had painted geometrical designs consisting of Romanesque arches and zig-zag ornament.

There were three ways of elaborating the basic church plan. One was to add aisles to the nave, divided from it by arcades of pillars. These survive or can be traced on the north side of the naves of St Breward, Morwenstow, North Petherwin, and elsewhere, and they were narrower than the aisles of the later Middle Ages. Their function in church worship is unclear unless it was to enable processions to take place, but they certainly gave a church status since they were more expensive to build and called to mind the processional nave aisles of the larger religious houses The second kind of elaboration was to attach one or more extensions to the east end of the nave in the manner of a transept, as can be seen at St Enoder and Tintagel. It is sometimes supposed that such extensions were common in Cornish churches of the Norman period and represent cruciform plans, but those that survive or are recorded may equally well be later additions. Tintagel's north and south transepts were probably added in the mid and late 13th century respectively, while the north transept at Lanlivery has the thinner walls used in Cornwall later in that century, as well as a triple lancet window.[2] The early transepts tended to be long and narrow lateral wings, sometimes on one side of the church, sometimes on both, and in the latter case (as at Tintagel) not always equal in length. Transepts too gave status to a church by making it bigger, and are likely to have originated as chapels and burial areas for important families, such as lords of the manor. Creed's transept has a Norman piscina pointing to the presence of an altar, while Lanlivery's has revealed traces of an altar and a granite coffin.[3] The third method of embellishment was to build a tower where bells could be hung and rung. Towers from the Norman period survive on the north side of Bodmin parish church and St Enodoc chapel, and at the west end of St Gennys and St John. Lawhitton has a south tower of the 13th century, while Crantock and Glasney, as we have seen, were topped with central towers.

The statutes of Brewer and Quinil, especially the latter, give us some insight into the interiors and workings of Cornish churches by laying down what each should possess in terms of equipment. Quinil ordered that chancels and naves should have glass windows, and forbade church buildings to be used for holding courts or markets.[4] Brewer had already prohibited 'scotales' in churches, meaning ale feasts held to raise money.[5] Each church was expected to have a set of ornaments and books for services, Quinil specifying as many as 52 items.[6] The high altar was to be dressed with a frontal cloth and to have a canopy above it, from which hung a locked capsule or 'pyx' containing a consecrated wafer. Images of the patron saint and the Virgin Mary were to stand beside the high altar. Two surplices were to be provided for the priest as well as a rochet (a sleeveless surplice, perhaps for the parish clerk), a silver chalice for mass, a silver cup for sick communions, corporal cloths for use on the altar at mass, cruets for wine and water, a thurible for burning incense, and vessels to contain incense and holy water. A large veil was to hang in front of the altar during Lent, and a big standing candlestick was to hold a candle to burn at Eastertide. Small bells were required for ringing during mass or while taking communion to the sick, a cross and banners for processions, a woman's veil for marriages, a pall to cover bodies at funerals, and a font with a cover and lock. The font was to be kept full of water, which was changed once a week in case it was needed for a baptism, the lock ensuring that the water was protected. Twelve books were specified, some of which may have been contained within a single volume. They included Quinil's summary of his statutes, an ordinal (guide to services), a breviary (containing the daily services), a legend (including Bible and other readings for ordinary days and festivals), a missal (for mass), and a manual (for pastoral services like baptisms, marriages, and funerals). Finally an antiphonal, a gradual, a hymnal, a psalter, a troper, and a venitary contained the texts sung at services, often with musical notation.

---

1 C. D. Cragoe, 'Belief and Patronage in the English Parish before 1300: some evidence from roods', *Architectural History* 48 (2005), 21–48, and see below, p. 68.

2 W. Rodwell, 'Lanlivery church: its archaeology and architectural history', *Cornish Archaeology*, 32 (1993), 91, 98.

3 Ibid., 100–2.

4 Powicke and Cheney (ed.), *Councils & Synods II*, II, 1006, 1008–9.

5 Ibid., I, 231–2.

6 Ibid., II, 1005–8.

This tells us what the authorities wanted churches to have, not what they had. The earliest evidence of real conditions in Cornwall comes from a visitation of 1281 in which two clergy of Exeter Cathedral reported on the state of eight of its churches and one of its chapels. They recorded the condition of the chancels, the state of the ornaments and books, and the nature and value of the church endowments.[1] They did not take notice of naves or nave furnishings, however, since these were the responsibility of the parishioners and came under the archdeacon's supervision. Six of the chancels were in good order: well roofed and provided with windows. Veryan's is mentioned as being whitewashed. Altarnun and St Erth had defective roofs, St Breward's windows were unsatisfactory and made the chancel dark, while one window at St Erth needed repair; its chancel was also censured for not being whitewashed. All the churches in 1281 had most of the ornaments and books which Quinil was to require six years later, but there was usually some deficiency. A few of the items were missing or were old and in a decrepit condition. Pyxes and fonts were not always furnished with locks. Even when sound the articles were often simple in form. Chalices indeed accorded with the bishop's statutes in being of silver, sometimes gilded, but cruets and candlesticks were commonly of tin.

A similar visitation took place in 1331, encompassing fourteen churches and three chapels.[2] This painted much the same picture, although there were deteriorations in some places. Only two churches, St Breward and Gwinear, were judged to be more or less satisfactory. Altarnun, Gwennap, and St Issey each had structural defects in the roofs, walls, or windows of their chancels, and Veryan was now criticised for the darkness of that part of the church. Most of the others were lacking in some of their ornaments and books. The three chapels were particularly short in these respects, perhaps because the priest brought what he needed from the mother church. Such visitations warn us against assuming that there was ever a golden age of well-maintained churches and devout clergy and parishioners. Indeed at St Erth in 1331 we are told that thieves had entered the church through the chancel windows and stolen the chalice, books, wax, and other things. Nevertheless the evidence shows that clergy and parishioners were not too far adrift from what they were supposed to provide, and that the authorities tried, at least occasionally, to keep them up to the mark.

Beyond this we are obliged to conjecture the layout and furnishings of Cornish churches from what is known in England as a whole. The chancel contained the high (i.e. chief) altar. In the larger religious houses with several priests there may have been lesser altars in other parts of the building, but these are likely to have been rare in most parish churches before the 13th century. The font was probably situated in the nave near the principal doorway, as was the case in later centuries. Lay people were allowed to enter and use the nave, but the chancel was reserved for the priest (or clergy), the parish clerk, and (one may reasonably conjecture) the patron of the church with his or her family. There was seating in the chancel for the clergy and probably for the important laity, and some churches had seats in the nave by Quinil's time. His statutes refer to disputes that had arisen about such seats, and he laid down that no one could claim a personal right to one except members of the *nobilitas* (nobility and gentry).[3] Floors in religious houses might be paved or tiled, but some parish churches may have had no more than bare earth strewn with rushes. Open spaces on the church floors were sometimes used for the burials of important people. Priors of monasteries were usually entombed inside their churches, and a countess and some knights shared this privilege in Launceston Priory.[4]

In the religious communities – monasteries, friaries, and collegiate churches – a cycle of daily services was performed in the chancel by the adult clergy. This began with matins at about midnight, and continued at intervals until compline in the early evening. At least one daily mass was celebrated at mid-morning by the clergy at the high altar, and those of the clergy who were priests might celebrate additional masses at lesser altars. The priests who served the ordinary parish churches were also expected to say the daily services, but it was left to them to decide whether they did so in church or in their houses, at least on ordinary days. On Sundays and major festivals, however, they were required to say matins in church in the morning followed by a mass for parishioners, with evensong in the mid afternoon. Mass was a dialogue for two people. In a monastery one monk or canon could help another, while in parish churches the priest had the parish clerk to assist him. The parish clerk, or holy-water clerk as he was usually called in the 13th century, was an adolescent or young adult who, as we have seen, might be a scholar training to be a priest. The clerk rang the church bells, prepared the altar, served the priest at mass, said the responses in the service, and read the epistle. He accompanied the priest to rites such as baptisms, weddings, and funerals, and dispensed holy water, for which he gained small fees.

The bishops' statutes tell us a little about what the

---

1 ECA, D&C 2672A, ff. 7v–8r, 9r–11r. The churches were Altarnun, St Breward, St Erth, Gwennap, St Issey, Perranzabuloe, Veryan, and St Winnow, and the chapel St Nectan in St Winnow parish.

2 ECA, D&C 2851, printed in *Reg. Grandisson*, II, 605–11. The churches were Altarnun, Boconnoc, Bradoc, St Breward, Constantine, St Erth, Gwennap, Gwinear, St Issey, Mullion, Perranzabuloe, Sancreed, Veryan, and St Winnow, and the chapels St Agnes (in Perranzabuloe), and St Nectan and Respryn (in St Winnow).

3 Powicke and Cheney (ed.), *Councils & Synods II*, II, 1007.

4 Below, pp. 206–7.

Church required of ordinary people.¹ All children had to be baptised in a ceremony which, by the 13th century, was normally done on the day of their birth. Immediate baptism was so common that the statutes do not even stipulate it. They merely order that the older Christian practice of baptising only at Easter and Pentecost should be followed when a baby was born in the week immediately before these festivals. Both festivals involved baptisms being done on the previous Saturday, and recently born babies were used for that purpose. People named Pascow ('Easter') and Pentecost may have owed their names to their birth at such times. Children could be confirmed at any age after baptism, a rite that had to be done by a bishop, something not easily achieved in Cornwall. Both Brewer and Quinil ordered the parish clergy to compel parents to have their children confirmed, but both accepted that remoteness from a bishop was an excuse and in practice many people may have reached adulthood without being confirmed. Children were expected to learn three basic prayers in Latin: the Paternoster (Lord's Prayer), Credo (Apostles' Creed), and Ave Maria (Hail Mary). Brewer told the clergy to teach these prayers and call children into church for the purpose, but it was probably more usual for the task to be done by parents or godparents.² After the 12th century there was a greater distinction in the Church between the status of children and adults.³ Children were regarded as minors until they reached puberty: innocent of sins and free of most Church obligations. At puberty they were believed to gain adult knowledge and capabilities, including the power to sin, making it appropriate for them to go to confession, receive holy communion, and pay church dues. The Church encouraged everyone to confess before Christmas, Easter, and Pentecost, but in practice the major time for confession was the beginning of Lent. Confession had to be done in church 'openly' by the priest sitting with the penitent so as to be seen but not overheard, lest he be suspected of dalliance with women. Communion was received only at Easter and before life-threatening events such as childbirth, a long pilgrimage, departure for war, or terminal sickness.

The practice of religion by lay people is poorly recorded in Cornwall before 1300. This reflects the lack of bishops' registers until 1258 and for twenty years after 1288. Even within the period when they survive, they do not deal with religious affairs beneath the level of knights or beneficed clergy. There are no extant parish or personal records, with the exception of Peter of Cornwall's memories of his family in Launceston. Most is known about the religion of knightly families, thanks to their gifts of property to religious houses recorded in charters. The benefactions of the families of Botreaux, Cardinan, and Pomeroy indicate that wealthy people in Cornwall followed fashion in favouring monks and canons during the 12th and 13th centuries. Such gifts also reveal the devotion of their givers to some of the well-known saints of Christendom: St Andrew at Tywardreath, St James at Tregony, and St Stephen at Launceston. Equally the foundation of the priory of Minster by the Botreaux and the gifts of property by some local knights to the priory of St Carroc suggest a continuing or reviving interest in Brittonic saints, Mertherian and Carroc respectively.

There is no reason, however, why lay religion should not have been as rich and diverse in the 12th and 13th centuries as we know it to have been in the later Middle Ages when better records survive. The network of parish churches already existed, and chapels were becoming common, some of them at ancient religious sites and others (such as West Looe) serving new settlements (Fig. 27).⁴ Guilds or fraternities, devoted to fellowship and worship, existed in the rural parishes around Exeter by about 1100, and may have done so in Cornwall.⁵ The earliest clear record of one relates to a guild of St Nicholas at Truro in about 1278, and another may have existed at Nancekuke in Illogan by the same period.⁶ Pilgrimages were already taking place. The claim of St Michael's Mount that those who went there would be excused a third of their penance probably originated in the 13th century, and we are told of three miracles experienced by pilgrims at the Mount in 1262.⁷ In 1238 Brewer granted an indulgence to those who visited St Buryan church on the anniversary of its dedication, and some other churches are likely to have had similar privileges.⁸ Finally there is a rare and valuable glimpse of popular religion at the time of the Third Crusade of 1188. In the previous year the Saracens had recaptured Jerusalem from the Christians, causing consternation throughout western Europe. It appears that numerous people in Cornwall, as elsewhere, vowed to join the campaign to recover the city in that year and were marked with a cross by a priest as a sign of their promise, a process known as 'taking the cross'. In about 1200 the Church authorities in England made enquiries about those who had not fulfilled their vows, and a list of 44 names was forwarded from Cornwall. Their owners came from seven of the eight rural deaneries, and seem to have been mostly people of middling importance, chiefly from towns.⁹ This sequel suggests that although the Crusade had an impact on Cornwall, not all those who rallied to the cause sustained their initial fervour towards it.

---

1 On what follows, see Powicke and Cheney (ed.), *Councils & Synods II*, I, 228, 233–5; II, 987–99.
2 Ibid., I, 228.
3 N. Orme, *Medieval Children* (2001), 200–36.
4 Below, pp. 74–7.
5 D. Lepine and N. Orme, *Death and Memory in Medieval Exeter*, DCRS new ser. 46 (2003), 259–61.
6 *Cat. Ancient Deeds*, IV, 449; see below, pp. 301–2.
7 Below, p. 232.
8 Below, p. 164.
9 Canterbury Cathedral Archives, DCc B/A/7; Orme and Padel, 'Cornwall and the Third Crusade', 71–7.

THE CHURCH IN CORNWALL IN 1291

The papal taxation of 1291, the 'Taxation of Pope Nicholas IV', as it is known, is an exceptionally valuable source for the history of the Church in medieval England. It represents the most comprehensive attempt to value the Church's income before 1500, and was used by both the popes and the kings of England as the basis for taxing the English clergy until the 1530s. The valuation aimed to identify and tap significant wealth, so it concentrated on the possessions of the religious houses and of the parish rectories and vicarages. It excluded the friars because of their poverty, the Templars and Hospitallers who were already supporting crusades, the hospitals, and the poorer wage-earning clergy – parish chaplains and chantry priests.[1]

The taxation is therefore not a complete guide to Church institutions and clergy, and it is further impaired by the undervaluation of its figures. This undervaluation is well known nationally, and can be demonstrated in Cornwall by comparing the net incomes of the eight Cornish vicarages recorded in the cathedral visitation of 1281 with those of the papal taxation ten years later. The cathedral visitors were able to enquire in detail into the affairs of each parish, whereas the values of 1291 were estimated by panels of clergy who took a lenient view of one another's incomes:

TABLE 1. *Estimated Incomes of Cornish Vicarages, 1281–91*[2]

	1281	1291
Altarnun	£5 0s. 0d.	£2 0s. 0d.
St Breward	£10 0s. 0d.	£1 0s. 0d.
St Erth	£6 3s. 4d.	£1 6s. 8d.
Gwennap	£10 0s. 0d.	£1 6s. 8d.
St Issey	£6 0s. 0d.	£2 10s. 0d.
Perranzabuloe[3]	c.£5 0s. 0d.	£1 6s. 8d.
Veryan	£5 0s. 0d.	£2 0s. 0d.
St Winnow	£4 0s. 0d.	£1 10s. 0d.

In these cases the 1291 figures fall to as little as 10% of those of 1281 and rise to no more than 40%. The papal taxation data are consequently more helpful in showing relative values than absolute ones.

The Taxation within each diocese was divided into two sections: 'ecclesiastical goods' and 'temporalities'. The first estimated the income of the rectors and vicars of the parishes, and stated (with respect to the vicars) how much of the parish income was appropriated to a cathedral or monastery. The second section calculated the income of the lands held by the bishop and the religious houses. The whole income of the clergy of Cornwall was reckoned at about £1,543, of which the ecclesiastical goods formed the larger element at about £1,166 (75%) and the temporalities £377 (25%). The biggest incomes in the county were those of the bishop of Exeter, Exeter Cathedral, and the larger religious houses. Their incomes came from tithes and from land, but there are often difficulties in estimating the totals. Some of the religious houses seem not to have been assessed on the home estates that supported their everyday life, so the figures that follow must be regarded as approximate even by the standards of 1291. The bishop drew the largest amount from Cornwall, his seven estates and their churches producing about £242 per annum. The next richest after the bishop were the big priories of Launceston with about £88, Tywardreath with about £73, Bodmin (perhaps under-represented) with about £60, and the college of Glasney with between about £50 and £60. St Germans was credited with about £30, and St Michael's Mount with about £28. Exeter Cathedral was attributed with £17, and the small cells of St Anthony, St Carroc, and Minster with £9, £7, and £6 respectively.[4] The priory of Scilly was omitted altogether.

The Taxation listed 167 parishes or, more accurately benefices, since it was concerned to value the income of the rector or vicar. Sub-parishes were regarded as part of the benefices of their mother parishes and did not appear separately. The benefices were listed under the eight rural deaneries, with separate sections for those in the peculiars of the bishop and of the dean and chapter. At the summit, in terms of wealth, were St Keverne (valued at £27 per annum), St Buryan (over £25), Probus (over £23), Crantock (over £20), and St Columb Major (over £17). Most benefices were rated at somewhere between £3 and £10, and were worth at least twice as much in practice. The poorest were Forrabury, Lamorran, and Warleggan, each of which was valued at only £1. Not all the parish income necessarily belonged to the clergyman of the parish, of course, because so many parishes were appropriated to a religious house. Most of the revenues of St Keverne went to Beaulieu Abbey, while St Buryan, Probus, and Crantock were minsters staffed by several canons who shared the profits between them. That left the wealthiest clergyman in Cornwall as the dean of St Buryan with

---

1 For the Cornish sections of the Taxation, see *Reg. Bronescombe*, ed. Hingeston-Randolph, 466–73, 479–80, and for analysis of the whole Taxation, R. Graham, *English Ecclesiastical Studies* (1929), 271–301, and the forthcoming edition of the 'Taxatio Project'.

2 Based on D&C 2672A, ff. 7v–8, 9–11, and *Reg. Bronescombe*, ed. Hingeston-Randolph, 466–73.

3 In 1281 the vicar's income was £9 6s. 8d., but from this he had to maintain two chaplains.

4 For the figures relating to the religious houses, see the individual histories in Part 2 of the volume.

FIG 14. *Tintagel church, a characteristic example of a 13th-century Cornish church without aisles but with elongated transepts.*

£20, followed by the rector of St Columb Major with £17. The poorest rectors were the clergy of the three poorest benefices mentioned above, since although they received the whole of the benefice income, it came from a small or impoverished area. Some vicars may have been even worse off. Seven of them were assessed at less than £1 per annum,[1] and four others at Egloshayle, Fowey, Poughill, and St Veep were not required to pay anything 'on account of poverty'.

About 76 of the 167 benefices resembled St Keverne in being appropriated to the bishop, the cathedral, or various religious houses.[2] As a result about £516 per annum, or 44% of the benefice income in Cornwall, was taken out of these parishes for the benefit of the appropriators. The amount and percentage increased still further after 1291, since another 19 benefices were appropriated between then and the early 16th century.[3] There were also several cases where a benefice was not appropriated but had to pay an annual pension to some other ecclesiastical body or person. Thus the abbot of Hartland received 7s. from the rectory of Forrabury, the priors of Merton and Tywardreath took 5s. each from the rectory of Lesnewth, while the Order of St John of Jerusalem drew £6 13s. 4d. from the rectory of Madron. There were three destinations to which the income from the Church in Cornwall might go. First it might stay in the county, at least to begin with. This was the case with the income of the Cornish rectors and vicars and that of the independent religious houses in Cornwall such as Bodmin, St Germans, and Launceston. Wealth of this kind amounted to about £861 per annum, according to the assessment of 1291, or about 55% of the total. In fact some of this money left Cornwall in the end. The clergyman of a Cornish benefice (especially one of the richer kind) might be a servant of the king or the bishop, or be a scholar at a university. In consequence he lived outside the county, and used much of his income to support himself there, paying only a chaplain to deputise for him in Cornwall.

A second stream of income left Cornwall for places

---

1 St Anthony-in-Meneage, St Clement, Colan, Feock, Padstow, St Wenn, and Tywardreath.

2 Budock, St Gluvias, Manaccan, and Sithney were not reported as appropriated, although they had become vicarages of Glasney College by this time. Morval and Scilly should probably be added to the list of appropriations. Duloe had both a rector and a vicar.

3 Below, p. 48.

elsewhere in England. This stream included the revenues taken by the bishop, the cathedral, and the dozen or so English monasteries that held land or appropriations inside the county. Six non-Cornish monasteries drew substantial incomes from lands west of the Tamar in 1291: Hartland and Newenham (about £13 each), Plympton (about £12), and Beaulieu, Cleeve, and Tavistock (about £11 each). Income of this kind amounted to about £565, or about £37% of the total, although not all of it left the county. Some would have stayed there, maintaining the small priory cells or paying local agents to manage lands and revenues. A third category of income travelled abroad. Some of it belonged to the Templars and the Order of St John, and was used to support their crusading work in the Mediterranean. This income was not taxed in 1291, and cannot therefore be measured. Further sums went to the French abbeys that had been given property in Cornwall after the Norman Conquest. By 1291 they consisted of Fontevrault, the owner of Tintagel parish church (Fig. 14); Mont St Michel, the mother house of St Michael's Mount; and St Serge at Angers, which held this role with regard to Minster and Tywardreath. Together the French houses drew a gross income from Cornwall that amounted to about £125, or 8% of the total. In practice less of their income would have passed overseas, since some of it remained behind to support the four Cornish cells of these abbeys.

In the end it is impossible to provide a financial statement of what Church wealth left Cornwall and what stayed there. Nevertheless a good deal was undoubtedly subtracted from the county each year from the late 11th century onwards. In 1291 it could well have been about a third. Every English county suffered losses of this kind, but in most of them the losses were offset by gains of income coming from elsewhere. Cornwall was unfortunate because it had no resident bishop and no large monastery with significant lands beyond the county boundary. Bodmin and Launceston each had some property in Devon, but of so modest a nature that it did little to counteract the outflow of wealth across the Tamar. In this respect the Cornish gained less than others from the dues they paid to the Church.

3. THE LATER MIDDLE AGES: THE CLERGY

During the 14th and 15th centuries (the later Middle Ages) a new series of events and developments affected the Church in Cornwall. Some of these originated in continental Europe. One was the ambition of the 14th-century popes to gain control of ecclesiastical patronage. This involved the growth of 'papal provisions', the claim of the popes to appoint clergy to benefices normally in the gift of bishops, cathedrals, and monasteries. A number of benefices in Cornwall were filled through such provisions in the 14th century, notably the provostship of Glasney.[1] Another external factor was the Hundred Years War, the intermittent conflicts between the English and the French that lasted from 1294 to 1453. During the wars marauders of one side or another attacked the priories of St Anthony, Scilly, and Tywardreath.[2] More peacefully, but still in a damaging way, the English crown took control of the four 'alien priories' in Cornwall that belonged to French abbeys – a process that threatened the life of these priories and, in two cases, led to their extinction.

The Black Death, a major epidemic of the plague, also arrived from the Continent. It was not the only cause of mortality during the later Middle Ages, since many other diseases and conditions caused fatalities, notably the great famine of 1316–17, but it had dramatic effects in the short term.[3] Contemporaries believed that the plague came to England during the summer of 1348, but most of the deaths that it caused in Cornwall and Devon appear to belong to the early months of 1349. Some of its greatest ravages took place in Bodmin where the priory lost its prior and all but two of the community of about 15–18 canons by 17 March, and where 1,500 townspeople were later believed to have died.[4] Most of what we know about the effects of the plague on the Church comes from the register of John Grandisson, the bishop at that time. His register records the institutions of most (but not all) rectors and vicars of parish churches, but it does not throw much light on monks, canons, friars, chaplains, or chantry priests.[5] During the five years from 1343 to 1347 the average number of clergy recorded as being instituted to rectories and vicarages in Cornwall was 9 per annum. The total in 1348 was 14, and in 1349 it rose to 85. Within 1349 the recorded figures were: 1 (January), 2 (February), 6 (March), 11 (April), 14 (May),

---

1 Below, p. 261.
2 Below, pp. 138, 268, 289.
3 M. Prestwich, *Plantagenet England* (2005), 538–46.
4 W. Worcester, *Itineraries*, ed. J. H. Harvey (1969), 94–5; *Reg. Grandisson*, II, 1076–7.
5 *Reg. Grandisson*, III, 1338–1425.

FIG 15. *A leper asks for alms ('Some good, my gentle master, for God sake'). There were at least seven leper houses in medieval Cornwall, and lepers lived independently in other places. Leprosy declined in the later middle ages, but this was offset by the arrival of plague in England in 1348–9.*

14 (June), 15 (July), 5 (August), 7 (September), 4 (October), 5 (November), and 1 (December). There were 17 institutions in 1350, 5 in 1351, and 11 in 1352. Not all these institutions followed deaths. Some were due to the previous clergyman moving benefices, but there must have been more deaths than usual. We can probably backdate the deaths from the institutions by two or three months, because it might take that long for the patron of a benefice to find a new candidate, especially if there was a shortage of clergy. Making that allowance suggests that most of the deaths of rectors and vicars took place in the early months of the year, as was the case at Bodmin Priory. How many clergy died in Cornwall, or what percentage of the whole, cannot be known.

There were certainly demographic and economic changes in Cornwall during the second half of the 14th century, partly (but not wholly) caused by the plague. It is likely that population levels fell: in England as a whole there may have been only three million people by 1400, as opposed to five or six million a century earlier.[1] Records show that in and after 1350 some settlements on the lands of the duchy of Cornwall were depopulated, tenements left vacant, and rents reduced in value.[2] The yields of tithes must have fallen too, while wages and prices rose as labour grew scarcer. All this bore on the clergy, whose incomes were depleted while their outgoings increased. Religious houses found it harder to find recruits and to maintain those they got. The three largest Cornish monasteries were left with fewer canons. Appropriators of rectories sometimes found it necessary to increase the revenues they allowed their vicars, because the old amounts were no longer enough. Fewer clergy were willing to do lowly paid jobs as chaplains, chantry priests, and vicars choral, and although such clergy continued to exist, they were less numerous by 1400 than they had been a century before. The effects on the laity are still little known. There is no evidence that the plague brought about a religious revival of a significant kind, or a religious decline due to despair or scepticism. In general the framework of people's religious lives appears to have continued much as before, and the changes that took place to this framework during the 14th and 15th centuries were gradual ones caused by various social and cultural processes, of which the plague was but one.

Other influences on Cornwall during the later Middle Ages were national in origin, and these tended to dilute and weaken those that came from abroad. England as a whole grew more insular in its religion and culture. The popes' attempts to increase their patronage were defeated by about 1400, weakening their power. The alien priories were closed or turned into independent English houses, and Church architecture evolved into a more distinct national style that we now call Perpendicular. The use of the French language fell into decline both for spoken and written purposes. In 1336 some of the more important people in St Buryan were able to promise obedience to the bishop in French, and a former rector of Warleggan is mentioned speaking the language in 1356.[3] By the end of the century French was rarely spoken except by courtiers, lawyers, and those who were directly involved with France in war or commerce. It was still used for writing some documents until the early 15th century, and some wealthy literate people went on reading French romances until the time of Caxton in the 1470s. Nevertheless by about 1400 English was becoming the predominant language for writing popular literary works and less formal documents such as letters and financial accounts. Cornwall shared in this process; indeed, as we shall see, two Cornishmen played key roles in advancing the use of English during the 14th century.[4]

---

1 A. Hinde, *England's Population* (2003), especially 38–52, 68–73.
2 J. Hatcher, *Rural Economy and Society in the Duchy of Cornwall, 1300–1500* (1970), 102–21; for illustrations, see TNA, E 368/126, m 54, and SC 6/817/1.
3 *Reg. Grandisson*, II, 820, 1180.
4 Below, pp. 89–90.

The major political and religious events in England during the late 14th and the 15th centuries were less important for Cornwall. The Peasants' Revolt of May and June 1381, centred on London, inspired a group of Cornish people to make an attack on the property of Bodmin Priory, but the Revolt had no wider effects in the county.[1] In the following year the radical religious views of the Oxford scholar John Wycliffe led to the formation of a Wycliffite or Lollard movement in religion, which survived in covert groups of followers until the Reformation. Cornwall had already produced a religious dissenter in the 1350s, Ralph Tremur whose story is told below,[2] and another, Laurence Stephen, fellow of Exeter College (Oxford), was one of Wycliffe's early Oxford disciples. During the spring of 1382 he toured Hampshire, preaching Wycliffe's views, and in the summer he did the same in Cornwall. The Church authorities took action against both men. Tremur apparently fled the county, while Stephen was arrested and persuaded to recant his beliefs. He later became rector of Lifton in Devon.[3] Neither cleric appears to have made significant converts, and Lollardy did not establish itself in Cornwall as it did in other parts of England. By the 1540s the Cornish were to be notorious for their religious conservatism.

The Wars of the Roses disrupted English life at intervals between the 1450s and the 1490s, but they too largely passed the county by. There were small-scale disorders in 1473, when St Michael's Mount was briefly occupied by the Lancastrian earl of Oxford, in 1483 when a few local gentry tried to defy Richard III, and more seriously in 1497 when some Cornish people rebelled against Henry VII, once over taxation and once in support of the pretender Perkin Warbeck.[4] None of these events, however, was significant for the religious history of Cornwall.

THE DIOCESE AND THE BISHOPS

The diocese of Exeter in Cornwall experienced little change in its structure between 1291 and the Reformation. Two parishes, Tregony and Cuby, had been joined together as one benefice under a single incumbent in 1286, but they remained separate parishes and Tregony kept its parish church until the 16th century.[5] Three sub-parishes that had been served by chaplains gained recognition as parishes and benefices in their own right: Bradoc as a rectory and Lostwithiel and Luxulyan as vicarages.[6] Within the structure there were some shifts of patronage. About ten benefices that belonged to lay patrons in 1291 were subsequently given by these patrons to religious houses,[7] so that by the end of the Middle Ages about 94 (59%) of the 160 parishes served by a rector or vicar in Cornwall were in the hands of the bishop, cathedral, and religious houses, and further parishes like St Germans and St Juliot were served by chaplains appointed by monasteries. A single benefice, Minster, went in the opposite direction, its advowson passing to the Botreaux family following the extinction of the priory of Minster soon after 1400.[8] The great wave of appropriations, by which rectories and their tithes were given to monasteries and replaced by vicarages, was almost over by 1291, but about 19 more vicarages were created in this way between then and 1500.[9] As a result well over half of the parishes in Cornwall came to have their tithes appropriated.

During the 14th century the English crown intervened in the sphere of patronage. In 1300–1 King Edward I became patron of St Buryan on the death of Edmund, earl of Cornwall. He and his officers immediately claimed that the church was a royal chapel exempt from normal Church authority, despite the bishops' long-standing rights over the church, its clergy, and its parish. The bishop, Thomas Bitton, and his successors, Walter Stapledon and Grandisson, fought the claim, both inside the diocese and in the royal courts, but they failed to defeat it. By the middle of the 14th century St Buryan with its dependent chapelries of St Levan and Sennen constituted a peculiar jurisdiction outside the diocese. Deans of the church were appointed by the crown without going to the bishop for institution, and the deans took charge of the supervision of moral matters and wills in the parish, matters that normally belonged to the bishop and the archdeacon.[10] The crown also tried to dispute the bishop's patronage of the priories of Bodmin, St

---

1 Below, p. 146.
2 Below, p. 60.
3 *Reg. Brantyngham*, I, 158, 480–1; biography in *BRUO*, III, 1772, and *ODNB*.
4 Below, pp. 237–8.
5 Below, p. 280.
6 A fourth church, Boconnoc, is described as a chapel of St Winnow in 1269, but rectors of Boconnoc are mentioned from 1268 onwards (*Reg. Bronescombe*, ed. Hingeston-Randolph, 115, 256; ed. Robinson, II, 19, 28, 81).
7 i.e. Gwinear, St Just-in-Penwith, Menheniot, Mevagissey, Morwenstow, Mullion, Poundstock, Quethiock, St Stephen-by-Saltash, and Stithians.
8 Below, pp. 243–4.
9 i.e. St Allen, Antony, St Clether, Gwinear, St Just-in-Penwith, Lanteglos-by-Fowey, Madron, Manaccan, Menheniot, Mevagissey, Morwenstow, Mullion, Paul, Poundstock, Quethiock, Sancreed, Sithney, St Stephen-by-Saltash, and Stithians. In addition Lostwithiel and Luxulyan, which were separated from the appropriated vicarage of Lanlivery after 1291, were thereby appropriated parishes from their beginning.
10 Below, pp. 164–7.

Germans, and Launceston, on the grounds that these were royal foundations. Here there were some short-term royal victories, but the bishops managed to hold their ground and the crown at last abandoned its attempts.[1] It had more success in taking over the patronage and income of the alien priories – a process that we shall examine presently – and in imposing pensioners on five of the largest religious houses (Bodmin, St Germans, Launceston, St Michael's Mount, and Tywardreath), especially the latter two. The pensioners were former royal servants, whom the monasteries concerned had to supply with board and lodging for life.[2]

Fourteen bishops ruled the diocese of Exeter between 1300 and 1500. Five of them are notable for the length of their reigns – Stapledon (1308–26), Grandisson (1327–69), Thomas Brantingham (1370–94), Edmund Stafford (1395–1419), and Edmund Lacy (1420–55) – and these five are the easiest to study because their activities were recorded in registers that have been edited and published.[3] The bishops of this period travelled frequently until they grew too old to do so. Their travels took them to London, Exeter, their manors in Devon and Cornwall, and occasionally more widely around the two counties. Predictably they came to Cornwall less often than Devon. The usual pattern was for a new bishop to make a tour through the county early after his appointment, during which he would visit his major properties and go to St Michael's Mount. Grandisson alone went as far as St Just-in-Penwith, and then only once. The bishops varied in the total extent of their visits. Stapledon did the best, coming 14 times in 19 years, while Grandisson managed only 6 times in 42 years, Brantingham 8 times in 25 years, Stafford 4 times in 25 years, and Lacy 8 times in 35 years.[4] This relative infrequency reflected the long, expensive, and fatiguing task of travelling with a household and of organising food and accommodation. Even in Cornwall the bishops did not always get further west than Glasney, and as age wore them out they ceased to be able to cope with the journey at all. Grandisson crossed the Tamar just once in the final 26 years of his reign, merely to Lawhitton, and Lacy made a single visit during his own last 15 years. This does not mean that the bishops neglected Cornwall. They kept in touch with it by letters and officials, and there were large areas of Devon and elsewhere in England where bishops went with equal rarity.

The complex duties of late-medieval bishops, involving national affairs in London and local ones in the diocese, meant that many of their tasks had to be done by deputies. One of these was the vicar general who carried out the bishop's administrative tasks in his absence; another was the official principal who ran the bishop's consistory court. Both these men were based in Exeter and were often canons of the cathedral. A third official was the suffragan bishop who helped with the bishop's spiritual tasks. He travelled round the diocese on an occasional basis to confirm children, ordain clergy (especially clerks who needed only tonsuring), and consecrate churches, chapels, and churchyards. There was no permanent post of suffragan bishop in the Middle Ages; the bishops of Exeter appointed one as they felt necessary. The earliest recorded suffragans in Exeter diocese were clergy from Ireland: Thomas, bishop of Leighlin, in 1275 and Robert Le Petit, bishop of Clonfert, in 1324.[5] Later bishops employed a series of such men, some from Ireland and others specially appointed by the pope with titles taken from extinct dioceses in or around the Mediterranean Sea like Selymbria and Tenos.[6] Both kinds of suffragan were often monks or friars, and it was common to pay them by appointing them as rectors or vicars of parish churches.

The bishop's chief lieutenant in Cornwall, along with the officials just mentioned, continued to be the archdeacon, of whom there were about 27 between 1300 and the Reformation.[7] Most of them had studied at university, generally law. There was no special policy of employing Cornishmen in the post. Only four archdeacons in this period fell into that category: William of Bodrugan (by 1297–1308), Richard Penels (1418–19), Walter Trengoff (1436–45), and Henry Trevilian (1446–9), and their terms of office were not long. As we have seen, the archdeacon had a house at Glasney College, but how much time he spent in Cornwall is uncertain. If he was not there himself he continued to appoint an 'official' to deputise for him, and the bishop often addressed his letters on Cornish matters to 'the archdeacon or his official'. Most of the officials were probably Cornish rectors or vicars, and during the 15th century some of them also held canonries of Glasney, making it likely that some of the business of the archdeaconry and its court was transacted there.[8] Other duties in Cornwall continued to be done by the rural deans and the officials of the peculiars, and the clergy and laity remained liable to visit the bishop on important spiritual matters wherever he was staying, or to attend his consistory court at Exeter.

---

1 Below, pp. 142–3, 186, 211.
2 Below, pp. 145, 189, 212, 231–2, 289.
3 *Regg. Stapeldon, Grandisson, Brantyngham, Stafford,* and *Lacy*, vol. I, ed. Hingeston-Randolph, and *Reg. Lacy*, ed. Dunstan, vols I–V; biographies in *BRUO*, passim, and *ODNB*.
4 For bishops' itineraries, see *Reg. Stapeldon*, 547–60; *Reg. Grandisson*, III, 1524–32; *Reg. Brantyngham*, II, 890–6; *Reg. Stafford*, 476–9; and *Reg. Lacy*, ed. Hingeston-Randolph and Dunstan, passim.
5 *Reg. Bronescombe*, ed. Hingeston-Randolph, 202; ed. Robinson, II, 74; *Reg. Stapeldon*, 384.
6 For a provisional list, see E. B. Fryde et al. (ed.), *Handbook of British Chronology* (3rd edn 1986), 284–7.
7 Listed by J. Le Neve, *Fasti Ecclesiae Anglicanae, 1300–1540*, IX: *Exeter Diocese*, ed. J. M. Horn (1964), 15–17.
8 *Reg. Lacy*, ed. Dunstan, I, 285, 291; II, 367, 374; III, 213.

THE MONASTERIES

FIG 16. *St Germans Priory church, originally built in about the late 12th century, with twin western towers. To this a south transept and south aisle were added in the 14th and 15th centuries. The choir was removed in the 16th century.*

In 1300 the religious houses of Cornwall fell into four groups (Fig. 11). The monasteries, a little depleted in number after the closure of two or three houses in the 13th century, now totalled nine. There were three independent foundations (Bodmin, St Germans (Fig. 16), and Launceston), and six smaller dependent ones (St Anthony, St Carroc, St Michael's Mount, Minster, Scilly, and Tywardreath). With the monasteries we may group the preceptory of the Order of St John of Jerusalem at Trebeigh in St Ive. During the 1310s or 20s this house acquired the property of the Knights Templars at Temple, following their suppression in 1312.[1] The friars continued to possess their houses at Bodmin and Truro, and three collegiate churches still remained: two old minsters at St Buryan and Crantock, and the new foundation of Glasney. Finally there was the handful of small hospitals with some other less formal communities of lepers.

This situation changed somewhat between 1300 and 1500. The monasteries suffered losses, and the collegiate churches and hospitals experienced gains and losses. In the first place the Hundred Years War caused short-term harm to three of the religious houses on the coast through attacks by the French and, in the case of Scilly, by the king of England's forces as well.[2] Secondly major alterations were made to the alien priories of St Carroc, St Michael's Mount, Minster, and Tywardreath. From 1294 to 1303, at a time of war with France, the crown took control of all such priories in England. This control was repeated between 1324 and 1327, 1337 and 1361, 1369 and 1399, and from 1402 onwards.[3] The priories were not closed during these periods but their activities were restricted. Many of their revenues and moveable assets were confiscated to enrich the crown and prevent any surplus income reaching France. Eventually there were impediments to the French mother houses appointing priors and monks to the dependent houses, and in 1378 foreign monks (except for heads of houses) were ordered to leave the kingdom.

The alien priories struggled to survive in these constraints, not altogether unsuccessfully. French priors continued to rule St Michael's Mount until about 1380, Minster until about 1382, and Tywardreath until 1433.[4] After the middle of the 14th century, however, the priors of these houses were sometimes appointed not by the mother house but by the crown or the bishop, usually from among the other French monks resident in the priory. The expulsion of foreign monks in 1378 made the task of maintaining a monastic community almost impossible. By the 1380s it is doubtful whether any monks other than the prior remained at the three houses mentioned, and the duties of prayer may have been done by hired chaplains from Cornwall. In 1383 a prior was appointed to the Mount

---

1 Below, pp. 272, 275.
2 Below, pp. 138, 268, 286.
3 D. J. A. Matthew, *The Norman Monasteries and their English Possessions* (1962), 72–142.
4 Below, pp. 233, 243, 290–1.

who was not even a monk but an Augustinian canon from St Germans, Richard Harepath, although Harepath was succeeded by Richard Auncell, a monk from Tavistock Abbey. In 1386 the bishop appointed an English monk named John Stratton as prior of Minster, and in 1399 and 1406 the king, Henry IV, brought in monks from St Pierre-sur-Dives (Normandy) to be priors of Tywardreath, not men from the mother house of St Serge (Angers). St Pierre, although a French monastery, was one with close links to the king. Minster was the first house to lose its monastic character absolutely. In 1408 the king appointed a secular priest as rector of the church, which thus became an ordinary parish church. The Mount fell next, between 1417 and 1420, when Henry V granted it and its possessions to his new abbey of Syon (Middx.). Thereafter the church was served by a group of three chaplains.

The other two alien priories were luckier. St Carroc survived because its English mother house, Montacute Priory, itself a French dependency, gained 'denizen' status in 1407 and ranked thereafter as an English monastery.[1] Tywardreath too lived on, perhaps because its last French prior, John Roger, seems to have made himself useful to Henry V in France. In 1416 he gained recognition of the priory as a 'conventual' house (i.e. a community), although it is not clear if he had any monastic colleagues. This recognition made Tywardreath an independent denizen house. When Roger resigned in 1433, the crown appointed a prior of English birth, John Brentyngham, but the French link was maintained to the extent that Brentyngham had been a monk of the abbey of St Vigor at Cerisy-la-Forêt (Normandy). He began to recruit English monks and gradually re-built a community, including the industrious Walter Barnecote, who succeeded him as prior. Under Barnecote the priory energetically pursued its claims to lapsed or lost property, and even tried to recover the priory of Minster, which it alleged had been its daughter house. This claim was not successful, but by 1492 Tywardreath had regained its original complement of seven monks after staging a remarkable recovery that made it the one success among the four Cornish alien priories.[2]

There were two further losses of religious houses in the 15th century – one military establishment and one priory. The preceptory of Trebeigh, belonging to the Order of St John, was still fully functioning in the 1370s and 1380s, but by the early 15th century the preceptors who ran the houses of the order were allowed to hold more than one simultaneously, and by about the 1430s Trebeigh was permanently linked with the preceptory of Ansty (Wilts.). After this the order's Cornish affairs were managed from Ansty, and the staff at Trebeigh was reduced to a chaplain and perhaps a few servants.[3] The closure of the priory of Scilly had been foreshadowed as early as 1300 when its mother house, Tavistock Abbey, tried to exchange it with the crown for other property. Tavistock actually withdrew its monks from the islands for some twenty years after 1345, pleading the dangers of war, and was reluctant to send them back when the war ended. The monks returned in the 1360s under pressure from Bishop Grandisson, and some kind of priory appears to have been maintained until the middle of the 15th century. Although the wars with France ended in 1453, the Isles of Scilly continued to suffer from attacks by pirates and in 1461 the pope was persuaded to place the islands under his protection. His intervention probably had little or no effect, and the abbey seems to have disbanded the community at about this time or a little later. By 1492 its affairs were managed by a single monk in the islands.[4]

More information survives about the Cornish monasteries after 1300 than before but, as in much of England, it covers only parts of monastic life. Even the numbers of canons and monks are not fully recorded. Bodmin is the only large house for whom we have a list of canons before the Black Death. The list, from 1312, which totals 18, implies that Launceston may have had slightly more and St Germans perhaps about 12. After the Black Death all three places had fewer clergy, as was commonly so throughout England. Losses of staffing caused by the plague were hard to make up, for two reasons. First the general population was smaller and there were more opportunities than before for those with religious vocations to gain rectories and vicarages. Secondly the less favourable balance between income and expenditure made it more costly to run a monastery with the old numbers of clergy. By 1381 Launceston housed about 13 canons, Bodmin 11, and St Germans 8, totals that were generally sustained in the 15th century although they fell at times until the house made up the vacancies, sometimes at the insistence of the Church authorities. In 1500 there were probably about 30 canons in the three large houses, seven monks at Tywardreath, two monks or canons each at St Anthony and St Carroc, and one in the Scillies – a total of just over 40.

The records of monastic life are uneven. Bishops' registers provide numerous details of the elections of priors, visitations, and disciplinary problems, but for the rest of what went on in a monastery we have to gather bits of evidence from many different sources. The registers, by tending to expose divisions and breaches of procedure, show us the least attractive aspects of the houses. Bodmin and St Germans seem to have elected priors without too much trouble, but Launceston had some unhappy experiences. After a contested election between two candidates in 1261, the bishop quashed the proceedings and appointed one of

---

1 Below, p. 298.
2 Below, pp. 290–1.
3 Below, p. 276.
4 Below, pp. 269–70.

the two. His successors overruled the elections of 1285 and 1346, although in each case they confirmed in office the man whom the canons had chosen. In 1430 there was a bitter contest between William Shyre and John Yerle, the bishop (Lacy) apparently favouring Yerle for whom the older canons voted, while Shyre had the support of the younger canons who formed the majority. Shyre was declared elected, but the bishop refused to confirm the election. The canons defied the bishop, appealed to the archbishop of Canterbury and the crown, and spread rumours that Yerle had connived at the poisoning of the previous prior. Lacy was forced to give way, but he took revenge several years later by forcing Shyre to make a public retraction of slanders against him and to promise him obedience.[1] There was to be yet another disputed election in 1534.[2]

The management and discipline of the three larger houses was also a cause of concern from time to time. Grandisson fought a series of battles to improve what he considered to be the unsatisfactory state of Launceston under Prior Adam of Knolle (1327–46). Adam was charged by the bishop with spending time outside the monastery with secular persons, some of them women. He had too many servants and was impoverishing the monastery. He had stopped giving alms to the poor. The canons were drinking too much in their refectory as well as in private. They were keeping dogs and hawks, presumably for hunting. In 1344 Grandisson removed Adam from practical control of the monastery and appointed two canons to govern it. The canons began to carry out reforms, but the prior resisted. He assigned other people to do the administration, abstracted money, and continued to spend time with a married woman friend. The angry bishop denounced the prior as 'a son of damnation', a man 'who has for many years led a life detestable to God and man, scorning and undermining our commands, punishments, and sentences with damnable audacity'. Adam managed to hold out for a couple more years, but in the end the bishop was too strong for him and on 19 June 1346 he was forced to agree to resign.[3] In the following year Grandisson turned his attention to Bodmin. Its affairs were little better. The canons were wearing secular clothes such as buttoned and hooded tunics, thigh boots, and pointed shoes. They were playing dice, backgammon, and chess, and talking to women. Some of them were living in private rooms, dogs were being kept, and the monastery was badly in debt.[4]

These kinds of problems surface in one bishop's register after another, all over England. They arose because the larger monasteries were independent bodies with complex affairs. A prior was expected to live in some style, to entertain visiting bishops, judges, and gentlemen, and to show favours both to the powerful and to those who depended on the monastery as tenants and neighbours. The prior of Bodmin had country residences: one at St Margaret's outside Bodmin and another at Rialton near Newquay. The rest of the canons needed servants to enable them to concentrate on the religious life, and all these commitments ate into a monastery's resources. Nor was monastic recruitment the kind of process familiar in modern institutions where several candidates are interviewed for a post. In the later Middle Ages it is likely that a small group of novices were brought in at rare intervals to make up numbers that had fallen, and a monastery might be limited to the recruits available at the time. Requests on behalf of tenants' sons or the relatives of existing canons would have mattered as well. The result was to produce a body of adequate rather than committed men with strong secular leanings and a not unnatural tendency to become bored and discontented, given the small size of the community and its repetitive activities.

It is easy to overestimate the negative evidence about monasticism through knowing so little of its more positive sides. The major activity of Cornish monasteries between 1300 and 1500 was the daily round of services and masses, read, intoned, and sung to plainsong.[5] Yet this is hardly ever mentioned in records except to allege that it was not being properly done. Elsewhere in England monasteries began to supplement the basic plainsong with polyphonic music during the 15th century, such music being produced by non-monastic men and boys especially in the form of masses and antiphons in honour of the Virgin in the Lady chapel. Virtually nothing is known about such music in Cornwall, but since Tywardreath appointed a clerk of its Lady chapel in 1522, who appears to have taught a few boys, it is possible that polyphony of this kind made its way into the four largest monasteries in Cornwall.[6] More certainly monastic prayers had an appeal to people outside. In 1274 visitors to Bodmin on days of county court business are said to have entered the priory church to listen to the services. That church had the shrine of St Petroc behind the high altar, and an image and light of the Virgin Mary in the Lady Chapel to which offerings were made.[7] St Germans acquired a relic of its patron saint in the 14th century, and the pope and the bishop granted indulgences to those who came to the church to honour the saint.[8] Even St Carroc appears to have benefited from donations to the saint

---

1 Below, pp. 215–16.
2 Below, pp. 217–18.
3 Below, p. 214.
4 Below, p. 148.
5 Fragments of liturgical texts containing plainsong, possibly used in Cornish religious houses or other churches, survive as binding materials in CRO, RS/60, ff. 211r–v, 222r–v; TF/677; and TF/678/2.
6 N. Orme, 'Music and Teaching at Tywardreath Priory, 1522–1536', *DCNQ* 36/8 (1990), 277–80, and below, p. 292.
7 Below, p. 144.
8 Below, p. 188.

allegedly buried in its chapel.¹ By 1300 the days when wealthy founders gave estates to monasteries were over, but the Cornish houses continued to receive smaller gifts in return for prayers. Bodmin benefited from the charity of Robert Olyver, a wealthy man of Bodmin, who paid for the making and glazing of a new window in the church, enabled the remaking of the great cross, and gave the priory a sum of £100 – gifts that the priory requited by setting up a chantry to pray for his soul.² Tywardreath, despite its small size and comparative remoteness, established a confraternity or group of supporters that included men and women from all over Cornwall. They included families of the gentry such as the Bevills of Killigarth, the Grenvilles of Stowe, the Treffrys of Fowey, and the Tregians of St Ewe. The members of this confraternity assisted the monastery with gifts, and it held obits for them (masses for the dead) on the anniversaries of their deaths.³

Another difficult topic to investigate is the role of monasteries as places of study and learning. Only a few surviving manuscripts can be traced to the Cornish houses, and these are mostly books employed for worship.⁴ The best evidence comes from about 1300 when the Franciscan friars of Oxford set out to compile a union catalogue of standard theological works, indicating the places in England where they existed. The friars evidently asked their colleagues in Cornwall to investigate the priory book collections at Bodmin and Launceston, and this produced a report of 41 titles held by Launceston and 52 by Bodmin, including works by Augustine, Jerome, John Chrysostom, and Bede.⁵ Later, in 1426, John Waryn, rector of Menheniot and a former Oxford student, felt Launceston a sufficiently scholarly place to bequeath it Robert Holcote's commentary on the Biblical 'Book of Wisdom'.⁶ A few men from Cornish monasteries were licensed to study at university. Permissions were granted for Prior Kenegy of Bodmin to go to Oxford in 1405, Prior Shyre of Launceston to Oxford or Cambridge in 1438, Prior Vivian of Bodmin to Cambridge in 1455, and Prior Barnecote of Tywardreath to Oxford in 1455.⁷ The bishop gave the permission, usually for three years. Heads of houses were not typical monastic clergy, however, and the only junior member of a Cornish house recorded at university is Thomas Fort, allegedly a canon of Bodmin and a master of arts in 1492 when he was made bishop of Achonry in Ireland.⁸

Most Cornish canons and monks probably had more practical or popular interests in literature. William Shyre, later prior of Launceston, was bequeathed a copy of Jacopo da Varazzo's Latin dictionary of saints, *The Golden Legend*, by the rector of Lawhitton in 1428 – a well-known handbook rather than a scholarly treatise.⁹ One of the canons of Bodmin in the late 15th century, John Bowyer, compiled an anthology of religious and moral poems in English which will be mentioned in the following chapter.¹⁰ At about the time that Bowyer lived, the antiquary William Worcester passed through Bodmin on his way to St Michael's Mount in 1478. He met and talked to two canons, William John (later prior) and John Stevyns, who were interested in 'physic' (what we would call natural science, especially medicine). John showed Worcester 'several ancient books' on the subject.¹¹

FRIARIES

The friaries resemble the monasteries in being better recorded after 1300, but still imperfectly so. No details of their staffing survive until the Reformation, but it is possible that the friaries of Bodmin and Truro each housed about two dozen friars before the Black Death, after which the number of friars in England declined like those of monks and canons. Friars' buildings were more modest than those of monasteries (Fig. 46), and friars did not possess significant endowments. Only the Dominicans interpreted their rule liberally enough to acquire a few small pieces of land in Truro, and the two Cornish houses would have lived largely from voluntary donations. Gifts of timber, wine, and food were made to them by the Black Prince (duke of Cornwall) and the Arundell family of Lanherne, and small bequests of cash are commonly found in Cornish people's wills.¹² A third group of friars, the Carmelites of Plymouth, continued to operate inside the county during the later Middle Ages. They too attracted legacies in wills and gained Cornish recruits, notably Godfrey of Cornwall (fl. 1347) and John Stanbury of Morwenstow (d. 1474).¹³

---

1 Below, pp. 298–9.
2 Below, p. 144.
3 Below, p. 292.
4 For records, see N. R. Ker, *Medieval Libraries of Great Britain* (2nd edn 1964), and idem, *Supplement to the Second Edition*, ed. A. G. Watson (1987).
5 Below, pp. 149, 213.
6 N. Orme (ed.), *Cornish Wills 1342–1540*, DCRS new ser. 50 (2007), 61–2.
7 Below, pp. 149, 213, 291.
8 Below, pp. 149–50.
9 Below, p. 213.
10 Below, p. 150.
11 Ibid.
12 Orme (ed.), *Cornish Wills*, entries indexed on 269, 285.
13 On Cornwall and Stanbury, see below, p. 60. Other Cornish Carmelite recruits included John Lanrake (*BRUO*, II, 1103), and William Clerk, John Landewarnek, and William Trethevyn (*Reg. Lacy*, ed. Dunstan, V, 45, 160). For further evidence of Carmelite influence, see *Reg. Stafford*, 380.

Critics of the friars accused them of associating with the rich rather than ministering to the poor. The Cornish houses certainly had links with wealthy people. Worcester transcribed the names of twenty-six 'nobility and gentry in the calendar of the friars of Bodmin', who would have been prayed for on the anniversaries of their deaths.[1] At Truro he noted the names of seven members of the county gentry who were buried or commemorated in the friary church.[2] The illegitimate brother of Sir John Arundell of Lanherne (d. 1433), named William Clerk, entered the Carmelite Order and was rewarded (against the spirit of the order) with the family's rectory of St Columb Major.[3] Our information is distorted, however, because the sources available to us favour the wealthy. The relationship of the friars with lesser folk has left little trace, but they were able to recruit members from all over Cornwall including the Cornish speaking area, suggesting that they had goodwill among the general population from whom such members came. In Bodmin they may have been seen as more sympathetic to the townspeople than were the canons of the priory. Two friars are even mentioned working as parish chaplains in 1474: the Dominican Philip Arundell at Penzance and a certain Friar Adam at Poundstock.[4]

Friaries were not self-contained houses like monasteries. Cornish friars would have been drafted to houses elsewhere in England from time to time, and perhaps even abroad, while friars from outside were brought into Cornwall. We hear of men with Germanic surnames at Bodmin in the 15th century.[5] Some of this movement was connected with education. Friars embraced learning more enthusiastically than monks, since they saw it as an essential preparation for their work of preaching and hearing confessions. All their orders developed systems of learning. Novices were taught grammar in their own friaries, if necessary, and sent to regional centres to learn theology of a basic and practical kind to enable their work. Education was viewed as a life-long process, and the study of basic theology continued throughout adulthood. A minority of friars with appropriate qualifications went on to tackle the liberal arts and theology at a university level, graduating in some cases as bachelors and doctors of theology. There are indications that both Cornish friaries promoted learning.[6] Early in the 14th century Henry, dean of Crantock, gave a copy of Peter Comestor's *Historia Scholastica* to the friars of Bodmin, and Truro's 14th-century copy of Witelo's treatise on perspective is still in existence. We hear of a lecturer at Bodmin in 1328 and one at Truro in 1397, and a few distinguished scholars were based in the Cornish houses during the 14th and 15th centuries. John Somer, famous for his astronomical work on the calendar, was briefly the warden or presiding officer of Bodmin in the early 1380s, while Truro was home to Benedict Lugans and Thomas Truro in the same period, both graduates in theology.

The learning of the Cornish friars was utilised for pastoral purposes by the bishops of Exeter. In 1309 Stapledon authorised two friars of Truro to hear confessions inside the friary – presumably of outsiders. In 1328 Grandisson commissioned a Truro Dominican to hear them in the Isles of Scilly, while the warden of Bodmin and one of his colleagues were licensed to do the same in the county at large, with the power to handle confessional issues normally reserved to the bishop. Similar appointments of Bodmin or Truro friars were made by Grandisson, Brantingham, and Lacy until at least 1435. One of the attractions of friars to the bishops was the ability of some of them to speak the Cornish language. In 1331 Grandisson empowered the Bodmin friar Alfred of Drefe to hear confessions of parishioners and grant absolutions throughout Cornwall, praising his purity of conscience, circumspection, and expertness 'in the idiom of those parts'. Since Drefe is the modern Drift in Sancreed parish, Alfred was evidently a native speaker of Cornish from the far west of Cornwall.[7] Later, in 1355, Grandisson appointed another Bodmin friar, John, as a confessor 'to those in Cornwall who know either language', and Roger Tyrel from the Truro friary to hold the same office 'for the merely Cornish [speakers] who do not know English'.[8] Appointments of this kind are not found in later times, either because they were not recorded or because they became unnecessary as monolingual Cornish speakers grew less common. Nevertheless the evidence points to the likelihood that Cornish was known and spoken in both friaries during the 14th century, and that some of the friars must have been among the most learned members of the Cornish-speaking community.

COLLEGIATE CHURCHES

Unlike the friaries, which were units of highly developed international organisations, the collegiate churches were disparate and independent bodies. Two of them, St Buryan and Crantock, were the last survivors of the early minsters, Probus having become little more than a parish church with some non-resident prebendaries. Both consisted of a group of secular canons, each of whom held a distinct prebend

---

1 Worcester, *Itineraries*, 84–7, 92–3.
2 Ibid., 98–9.
3 *Reg. Lacy*, ed. Hingeston-Randolph, I, 32–3.
4 TNA, C 85/81/25.
5 Below, p. 158.
6 On what follows, see below, pp. 157–8, 282–3.
7 *Reg. Grandisson*, II, 632, 1146.
8 Ibid., 1146.

or share of the church's wealth. The practice of non-residence by these canons, which we noted in the 13th century, continued into the later Middle Ages, their posts continuing to be regarded as rewards for servants of the bishop or the king. The dean and canons of St Buryan spent most of their lives elsewhere, and only a modest community life survived at the church in the form of three lowly-paid chaplains, a chantry priest, and three clerks, who worshipped together and ministered to the people of the parish.[1] Crantock nearly went the same way. Some of its canons were also absentees by about 1300, and the church was largely run by a handful of vicars choral who deputised for them. In this case, however, two of the bishops tried to improve the situation. Stapledon reformed the office of dean of the church in 1309, financing it with two of the canonries and making it a resident post. Grandisson strove to make the rest of the canons reside, but he was defeated in this respect and the changes in clerical manpower and wealth after the Black Death forced him to reconstitute the clergy on a smaller scale. In 1352 he laid down that they should consist of a dean, four vicars choral, two clerks, and two or three boys. The rest of the canons were given the option of paying a tax instead of residing, and most of them chose it. After this Crantock pursued an unobtrusive existence, maintaining common worship but probably little more. Its remoteness and poverty stopped it from playing much part in the life of the county.[2]

Glasney, the earliest collegiate church in Cornwall, stood apart from the older minsters. It had statutes to regulate the conduct of its affairs, although it retained something of the older customary law of the minsters through the ruling of its founder, Bronescombe, that the usages of Exeter Cathedral should be followed in matters not covered by the statutes. The college was distinguished in three respects. Its church was one of the biggest in Cornwall, it had a larger clerical staff than most other religious houses in the county, and its endowments exceeded those of any foundation apart from the four largest priories. There were thirteen canons headed by a provost, thirteen vicars choral, and smaller numbers of chantry priests, clerks, and boys. The canons did not all keep residence permanently. Many also held parish benefices or did duties for the bishop, and they shared the privilege of the cathedral canons that they could be absent for half of each quarter of the year while still receiving their stipends. Nevertheless the resident members of the college must have usually have numbered at least twenty men and boys, allowing the daily services of plainsong to be supplemented by a polyphonic mass and antiphons in the Lady chapel. In 1438 one of the canons, James Michell, owned a booklet of 'songs of music', and by 1548 the college employed a clerk of the Lady Chapel who may well have taught and directed the polyphony.[3] The college was also a centre of learned men. Some of the canons were graduates who owned or studied books, and by the Reformation one of the vicars choral was teaching a grammar school for the public, the origin of which is not yet known.[4]

After 1300 Cornwall acquired three more churches with collegiate features, but these were smaller foundations. During the early 14th century, when tithes were relatively productive and chaplains were cheap to hire, it became fashionable to convert parish churches into small chantry colleges. This reflected the popularity of prayers for the dead. The patron of a parish church could approach the bishop to allow the church income that had hitherto sustained the rector to maintain four or five chantry priests. This not only increased the number of prayers that could be said, but enabled the patron to set up a chantry without sacrificing his or her own land or money to do so. Four foundations of this kind were planned or made in Exeter diocese between 1320 and 1337, the earliest at St Michael Penkevil in Cornwall and the others at Bere Ferrers, Haccombe, and Whitchurch in Devon.[5] St Michael's owed its creation to Sir John Treiagu, the patron of the church, who received the bishop's permission in 1320 to convert the revenues to support a rector (now styled archpriest) and four other priests. The church was not a wealthy one and the four priests are unlikely to have survived the Black Death of 1349, which made such institutions unviable due to rising wages and prices. Not long after this event the church reverted to being a normal rectory.[6] For the rest of the 14th century economic conditions were unfavourable to the establishment of small cheap collegiate churches, but Grandisson's reorganisation of Crantock in 1352 came close to being a foundation of this kind although its worship did not centre on prayers for the dead.[7]

Two other institutions of a similar nature appeared in the 15th century. One was St Michael's Mount. After it passed into the hands of Syon Abbey in the late 1410s, it was staffed by three priests, the senior of whom held the title of archpriest. Their duties were to say the daily services and to pray for the dead, but they were paid employees of the abbey and did not form an independent self-governing body.[8] The other new foundation was established by Sir John Arundell of Lanherne in the church of St Columb Major in 1428. This was an unusually large and well-endowed chantry for five priests, saying prayers and masses for the souls

---

1 Below, pp. 163–8.
3 Below, p. 258.
4 Below, p. 259.
5 For the Devon foundations, see *Reg. Stapeldon*, 402–5, and

2 Below, pp. 176–7.

Reg. Grandisson, II, 731–4, 852–5.
6 Below, pp. 226–8.
7 Below, pp. 176–7.
8 Below, p. 234.

of the Arundell family in a new chapel built to the south of the church's chancel. The church did not become collegiate like St Michael Penkevil. It remained a parish church in the hands of its rector, and the priests of the chantry merely functioned inside it. However, the senior priest held the title of 'warden', the priests lived together in a single house, and local people called the building 'the college'. The Arundell chantry survived, as did St Michael's Mount, until chantries in England were abolished in 1548.[1]

HOSPITALS, HERMITS, AND ANCHORITES

The Cornish hospitals were the smallest and poorest of the religious foundations.[2] There were still seven of them in 1300: six for lepers at Bodmin, St Mary Magdalene (Helston), Lanlivery, Launceston, Liskeard, and *Sheepstall* (a lost place in Veryan), and one for non-lepers at St John Baptist (Helston). All probably offered long-term care, rather than short-term medical help like their modern successors. They usually had small endowments of land or income which they supplemented from donations. Hospitals were characteristically sited outside towns (because of their links with disease) but on major roads, often by bridges where traffic slowed and passers-by could be waylaid for alms. They were religious foundations in that they all had chapels and came under the jurisdiction of the Church, but all except one were run by their senior male inmate, known as the prior. The exception was St John's, which had a cleric as prior assisted by one or more clergy brethren. During the 14th and 15th centuries hospitals in England underwent changes. Leprosy grew rarer among the population, and foundations for lepers either closed or turned into places for other kinds of infirm or elderly people. At least two of the Cornish leper hospitals, St Mary Magdalene (Helston) and *Sheepstall*, appear to have shut down during the 15th century, and Lanlivery may have been a third unless it became an almshouse for the poor. Bodmin, Launceston, and Liskeard continued to provide care for 'lazars' until at least the mid 16th century, but it is not clear whether the word, by that time, meant only lepers or included other kinds of sick people.

During the 15th century a new fashion developed in England for founding almshouses, a name that is a coinage of that period. Almshouses shared some of the characteristics of earlier hospitals. They provided accommodation rather than medical help, and they expected their inmates to say daily prayers in a specially provided chapel or a nearby church. They differed in usually ministering to people suffering conditions other than leprosy, especially old age, and they often possessed few resources, providing no meals and having no resident clergy. Three such almshouses were founded in Cornwall between after 1400, although the details of their foundations are elusive. One is mentioned at Launceston in 1446, and two at Bodmin (St Anthony and St George) in 1492. Launceston's appears to have been created by the borough corporation of Dunheved, while at Bodmin (where the corporation had less power) the initiative was due to two local guilds which each maintained a chapel and almshouse. All were modest schemes that probably centred on providing accommodation for a few elderly or disabled people; Launceston is mentioned as having six inmates. A fourth foundation at Penryn was being planned in 1501 when a local gentleman gave money towards it, but seems not to have come into being. That leaves St John Helston, which followed a different path that is paralleled elsewhere in England. Here the resident clergy gradually used their power to absorb all the income of the foundation. By the Reformation the house had turned into a benefice for a single clergyman without any charitable functions.

A few people followed a religious vocation by withdrawing from everyday life without joining a community.[3] Some (always men) became hermits, living a simple life alone in a dwelling. This might involve seeking solitude or, on the contrary, a role in the community looking after a chapel, a road, a bridge, or a lighthouse. The earliest document mentioning such a man in Cornwall dates from the late 12th century, very likely relating to Lostwithiel, and hermits are recorded later in four other places. A favourite spot was a secluded location close to a centre of population or public resort, like the parks of Liskeard and Restormel or the island of St Michael's Mount. Some hermits may have begged for alms, but the more fortunate were paid small stipends by noblemen or, in the case of the Mount, by Syon Abbey. Little is known of what they did, but the hermit of the Mount carried out some small administrative tasks on behalf of his church.[4] More austere than the hermit was the anchorite, who left the world for a cell in which to follow a life of prayer and contemplation. Such men or women often acquired high reputations for holiness and were visited by people seeking spiritual counsel. One, Cecily or Lucy Moys, received permission from the bishop of Exeter to live in a house in the churchyard of Marhamchurch in 1403. Another, that Margaret who

---

1 Below, pp. 171–3.
2 On hospitals in medieval England, see N. Orme and M. Webster, *The English Hospital, 1070–1570* (1995). The articles on Cornwall in that book have been updated in the present volume.

3 Anchorites and hermits in Cornwall are listed below, pp. 304–5 for context, see R. M. Clay, *The Hermits and Anchorites of England* (1914) and A. K. Warren, *Anchorites and their Patrons in Medieval England* (1985).
4 Below, p. 235.

became a nun of Syon, was based at Bodmin in the same period, and both were well-enough known for a canon of Exeter to bequeath them each £2 in 1406.[1] There may have been a few widows known as 'vowesses' who lived a life of chastity and prayer while living in the world. Such women, along with the anchoresses, were the nearest that Cornwall came to having nuns within its borders.

THE PARISH CLERGY

EDUCATION

On 21 December 1308 Walter Stapledon, who had just arrived in his diocese for the first time as bishop, made his way to Crediton where a huge crowd of clergy was awaiting him. They had come to be ordained from all over Cornwall and Devon, and there were 1,005 of them, leading to the largest ordination ever recorded in the diocese. The Cornish were well represented. As many as 106 received tonsures and 326 were made acolytes; these were probably schoolboys, boys who helped in church services, and parish clerks. A further 116 were young adults: 74 ordained as subdeacons, 22 as deacons, and 6 as priests, together with 14 who were already parish clergy and needed one or other of these orders to qualify.[2] These high numbers arose partly from the fact that there had been no ordination for some time, due to the age of the previous bishop and the vacancy that followed. But the crowd also mirrored the society of the day. The population of England had reached a peak that was not equalled until the 17th century. At a time when the countryside was over-crowded with people and work in towns was limited, a career as a priest had its attractions despite the often modest wages.

How such candidates for ordination were educated is little clearer after 1300 than before. Knowledge of reading, song, and some Latin grammar continued to be required for admission to the major orders of subdeacon and above, and bishops are occasionally found rejecting candidates until they were fully qualified.[3] Yet there was still little systematic help for those who sought such knowledge. As before, a youth had to learn grammar at his family's expense in a town school or through private tuition.[4] A few religious houses – Crantock, Glasney, and possibly the larger Cornish monasteries – provided board, lodging, and some education for a few boys who acted as servers or choristers, but the boys concerned were likely to be the kinsfolk of the clergy in the houses or the sons of their friends and tenants. The ancient practice of appointing teenage students as parish clerks continued during the 14th century but weakened in the 15th, as these posts came to be held by older men for longer periods.[5] In consequence education was most easily gained by the wealthy and the well-connected, and as in previous centuries they were also the best placed to find a patron to give them a rectory or vicarage. The fall in the population made more such benefices available after 1350, but many clergy still had to take work as parish chaplains, domestic chaplains, or chantry priests, at least when they were younger. Work of this kind remained poorly paid and was still often short-term or liable to be ended by employers whenever they wished.

Most of the parish clergy after 1300 were probably educated inside the county, but an important minority went further afield to study, continuing the practice that we saw developing in the 12th century. Such study was now centred largely on Oxford while Paris fell out of favour, another example of English insularity (Fig. 17).[6] Some of those who went to Oxford were teenagers studying grammar because the city was well-known for its grammar schools, one of which was run by a Cornishman in the mid 14th century. Others, who had wealthy families or friends, went at the age of about eighteen after going to school elsewhere, and followed university courses during their late teens and early twenties. Hugh Boscawen bequeathed £2 13s. 4d. per annum in 1447 to support two poor youths at Oxford, each for seven years.[7] Yet others delayed their studies until well into adulthood after they had gained a rectory or vicarage, rather than doing so beforehand as we would consider appropriate. Church benefices gave them an income to pay for their higher education, and they would seek the bishop's permission to be absent from their parishes to go to university – permission that was generally granted.[8] The students who went from Cornwall to Oxford came from both the English-speaking east of the county and the Cornish-speaking west. Five men from Camborne alone are known to have gone there during the 15th century, and a number of others are recorded with surnames taken from places in the western parishes.[9]

---

1 DRO, Chanter VIII, ff. 64r, 218r, 313r; *Reg. Stafford*, 25, 251, 394.
2 *Reg. Stapeldon*, 448–50, 452–5. Even this figure does not exhaust the Cornish at the ordination, since there were other people from peculiar jurisdictions unattributed to Cornwall or to Devon.
3 *Reg. Stapeldon*, 523; *Reg. Brantyngham*, II, 787, 789.
4 On medieval schools in Cornwall, see below, pp. 87–8.
5 N. Orme, *Medieval Children* (2001), 231.
6 On this subject, see N. Orme, 'The Cornish at Oxford University, 1180–1540', *JRIC* (2010).

7 Orme (ed.), *Cornish Wills*, 75.
8 For Bishop Grandisson's irritation at, but tolerance of, repeated requests, see A. B. Emden, *An Oxford Hall in Medieval Times* (1968), 107–8.
9 John Gentill, Stephen Lanivry, Richard Leyty (or Layty), and Reginald and Thomas Mertherderwa, all recorded in a prayer list from Camborne (CRO, PD/322/1, f. 53r-v; N. Orme, 'Prayer and Education in Fifteenth-Century Camborne', *JRIC* (2006), 95–104).

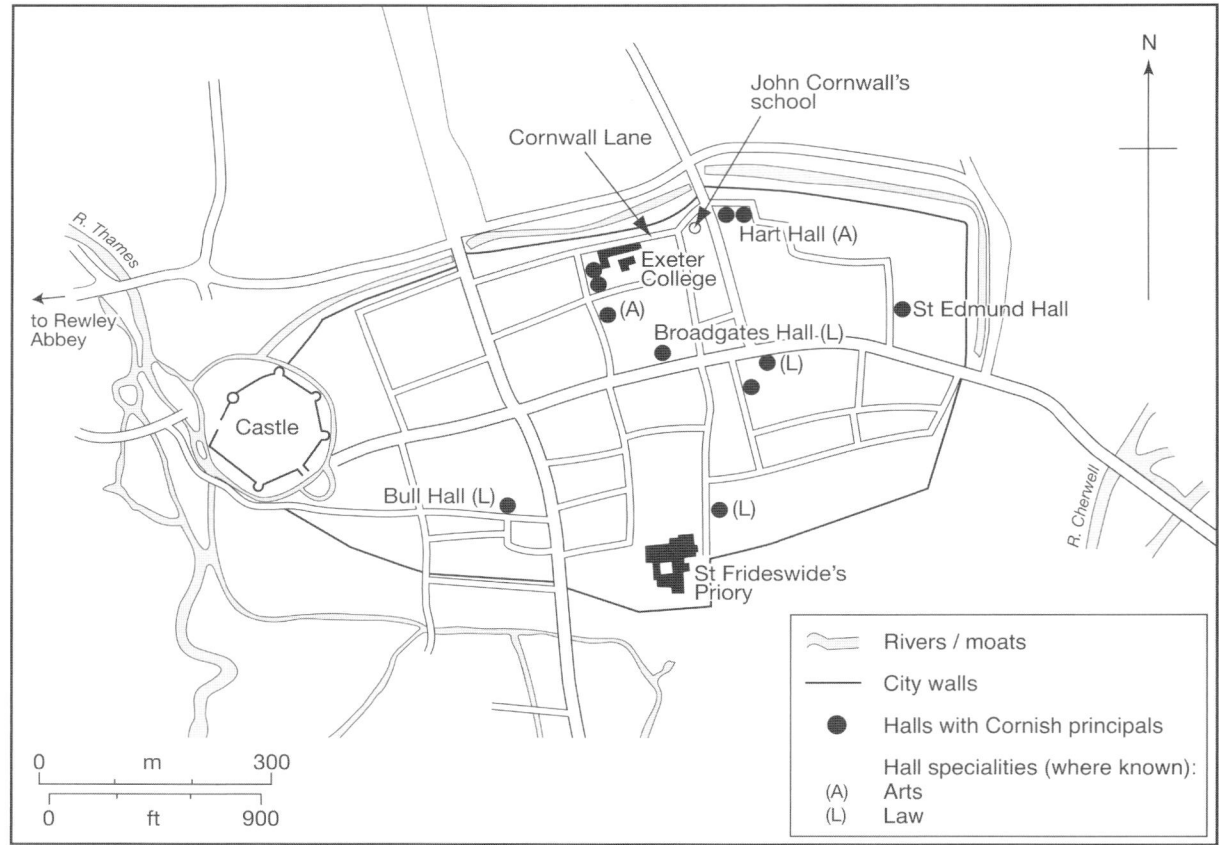

FIG 17. *The Cornish at Oxford University, showing John Cornwall's grammar school, Exeter College, and some of the halls associated with Cornish students.*

Students at Oxford up to about 1500 usually shared a room in a university hall, which was simply a rented house managed by a principal appointed by the university authorities. The principal, a graduate in his twenties or thereabouts, had charge of a dozen, two dozen, or three dozen students who paid for their board and lodging. He might also act as their guardian, keeping their money and arranging for their tuition. Halls tended to gather students according to the degrees for which they were reading (arts, law, or theology) and from particular regions of the country, although these affiliations might change as principals came and went. One hall, St Edmund, may have attracted Cornishmen in the early 14th century when it was ruled by two men from the county in succession.[1] Another, Hart Hall on the site of the present-day Hertford College, was purchased by Bishop Stapledon at about the same time and given to Exeter College which he had founded. It was later rented out by the college and became a popular lodging place for students from the west of England.[2] Cornishmen studying law in the first half of the 15th century may have congregated at Broadgates Hall in High Street or Bull Hall in Pembroke Street, both of which had Cornish principals for parts of the period.[3] Unfortunately records linking students with particular halls are virtually non-existent in the later Middle Ages, inhibiting the search for those who lived in them. A rare exception is an account book kept by a Cornish principal, John Arundell senior, at an unnamed hall in 1424, probably near Exeter College of which he was a fellow. In the book Arundell listed the money he received for several students to whom he acted as guardian and the payments he made on their behalf. One of his students, Penpons, was Cornish, but the names of the others are not distinctive to the county, perhaps implying that he had taken over a hall of students from other regions.[4]

After the 1260s the halls were gradually

---

1 Emden, *Oxford Hall*, 105–10.

2 N. Saul, 'The Pre-History of an Oxford College: Hart Hall and its Neighbours in the Middle Ages', *Oxoniensia* 54 (1991), 327–43.

3 For Cornish principals, see *BRUO*, I, 49–50, 355, 490; II, 1114, 1176, 1266–7, 1361–2; III, 1892, 1894–5, 1905, 1927, 1996.

4 Barnstaple, North Devon Record Office, B 1/3960, f. 39r; H. E. Salter, 'An Oxford Hall in 1424', in H. W. C. Davis (ed.), *Essays on History Presented to R. L. Poole* (1927), 421–35; A. B. Cobban, 'John Arundel, The Tutorial System, and the Cost of Undergraduate Living in the Medieval English Universities', *Bull. John Rylands Univ. Lib.* 77 (1995), 143–59. For Penpons, see *BRUO*, III, 1458.

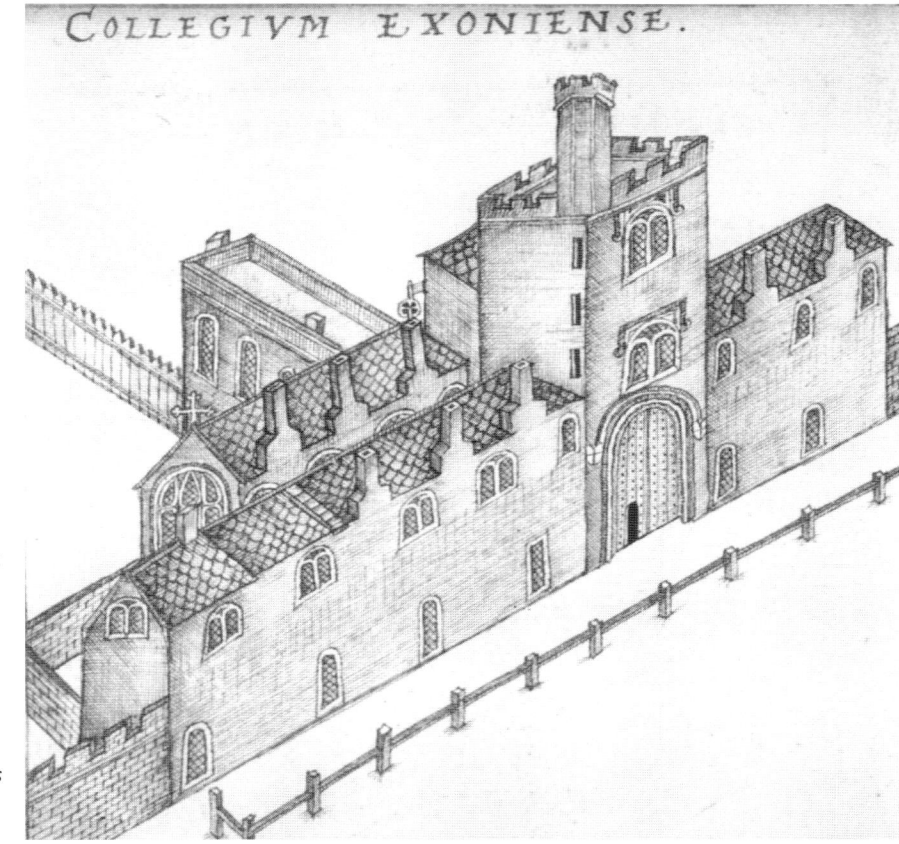

FIG 18. *Exeter College (Oxford) in the 16th century, the college founded by Bishop Stapledon for students from Devon and Cornwall. The picture shows the original frontage of the college onto what was sometimes known as Cornwall Lane.*

supplemented by colleges offering free board and lodging, but the colleges were small in size and numbers until the 1380s and catered chiefly for postgraduates. They too favoured entrants from particular counties or dioceses. The college for men from the South West of England was 'Stapledon Hall', later known as Exeter College, founded by Bishop Stapledon in 1314 (Fig. 18).[1] It provided places for eight men from Devon and four from Cornwall to study the arts course from the beginning of their studies or from a little way into them.[2] They were then housed and fed for up to ten years until they graduated as masters of arts and for two or three further years during which they undertook 'regency' or teaching. This made the college a community of young men in their twenties, apart from a thirteenth older scholar who acted as chaplain and was required to study theology or canon law. Stapledon also planned a school foundation in the city of Exeter, which was put into effect in 1332 after his death. This enabled thirteen boys to board in the local hospital of St John and to study grammar at the city high school, which was effectively the cathedral school of the diocese of Exeter. Up to two of the boys could be chosen from Cornwall.[3] In planning a school and a college, Stapledon anticipated what William Wykeham was to do fifty years later at Winchester College and New College (Oxford), but Stapledon's schemes, unlike Wykeham's, were not formally linked. No provision was made for the Exeter boys to proceed to Oxford, in the way that the scholars of Winchester were maintained and trained until they could become undergraduates of New College. Nor, given the small size of his foundations, would free places have come up very often. Still his benefactions were better than nothing, and enough is known about the college to show that it provided a valuable resource for some Cornish scholars, a few of whom went on to hold high posts in the English Church.

It is likely that at least a couple of dozen Cornishmen were to be found in Oxford at any time between 1300 and 1550, totalling a few hundred across

---

1 On the history of the college, with lists of fellows, see C. W. Boase, *Registrum Collegii Exoniensis*, Oxford Hist. Soc. 27 (1894).

2 From 1355 the college contained two fellows from Salisbury diocese, notionally in addition to the twelve but possibly sometimes occupying two of their places (ibid., pp. xxix–xxxi).

3 N. Orme, *Education in the West of England, 1066–1548* (1976), 48–9.

the period.¹ Most of them chose to study arts or law. Arts gave a broad liberal education, whereas canon and civil law provided the legal and administrative skills helpful to underpin a career in the Church. Theology had fewer students, and only a handful followed medicine. Ordinary students were expected to gain an MA degree before embarking on theology, and the subject was most popular with monks and friars who were allowed to study it after preparatory work in their own religious houses. Notable Cornish scholars in the 14th century, all of whom gained doctoral degrees, were Stephen of Cornwall in medicine, Stephen Pempel and Ralph Tregrisiow in civil law, and Friar Godfrey of Cornwall, John Landreyne, Richard Redruth, and William Polmorva in theology. Doctorates in the 15th century were achieved by John Arundell senior in medicine, John Gentill and Reginald Mertherderwa in civil law, and Friar David Cornu, Walter Lyhert. Richard Reddew, Friar John Stanbury, Walter Trengoff, Michael Tregury, and Michael Trewynnard in theology. Two other scholars, John Nans and Thomas Tomyowe, took a new path by studying in Italy and graduated as doctors of canon and civil law at Bologna in 1481 and 1483. Since Exeter College provided for only one postgraduate, the Cornish who tackled degrees other than the MA had to maintain themselves or to gain places in colleges where such studies were supported. Stephen of Cornwall secured such a place at Balliol, Landreyne, Lyhert, and Redruth at Oriel, and William Trevelles and John Trevisa at the Queen's College. Major roles in academic life were played by Polmorva, Redruth, and Trengoff, who served as chancellors of the university (the highest office), while Landreyne and Tregrisiow were involved with the condemnation of John Wycliffe's writings between 1380 and 1382.² Altogether the Cornish in Oxford were prominent enough for the street that went past Exeter College to be sometimes known as 'Cornwall Lane',³ and there are traces of relationships among them. John Arundell's account book mentions small loans of money passing between himself, Walter Lyhert, and Michael Tregury, while Reginald Mertherderwa made bequests in his will to two or three of his fellow-countrymen in and around the city.⁴

One further graduate stands out as an oddity. This was Ralph Tremur, who succeeded his uncle as rector of the small moorland parish of Warleggan in 1331. He was already described as 'Master' and the bishop (Grandisson) allowed him to leave his benefice for three years to do further study at Oxford on condition that he was ordained, an example of the procedure by which ordination and study might follow the acquisition of a benefice. In 1334 Tremur resigned from Warleggan and, still only a deacon not a priest, became in Grandisson's words a fugitive and wanderer in the diocese and elsewhere in England. A year later the bishop was horrified to hear that Tremur had developed heretical opinions that he was secretly teaching to others, notably that the communion bread and wine, when consecrated, did not become in substance the body and blood of Christ. Grandisson ordered him to be excommunicated and had the order published throughout the diocese, but Tremur appears to have fled to London, prompting Grandisson to warn its bishop about his activities. In his warning Grandisson conceded that Tremur was a distinguished man: a master of arts, learned in grammar and in four languages. His opinions, however, were detestable. He taught that only manual work was truly good and that priests achieved nothing by opening their mouths and digesting communion wafers. He had called St Peter 'a bad, hollow rustic' and St John the Evangelist a liar. Finally he had stolen a pyx from a church containing a consecrated wafer, thrown the wafer in a fire, and absconded with the pyx. Reformer or eccentric? It is hard to be sure, since we have only Grandisson's charges on record, but the communion, priests, and saints were to become the targets of Wycliffe and the Lollards some twenty-five years later. Tremur may have anticipated some of the views that they were to express more rationally and effectively.⁵

Some university men came back to Cornwall after their studies. About one fifth of the rectors and vicars instituted to parishes in the county under Bishop Lacy (1420–55) were graduates, either natives or incomers. The provosts of Glasney College after 1427 were generally Cornishmen who had graduated or at least studied at university.⁶ Other such men found employment in Devon rather than Cornwall, sometimes as clergy serving the bishops of Exeter. There was usually at least one Cornish canon of Exeter Cathedral and three or four held posts there at the same time for a period around 1400.⁷ Three deans of the cathedral came from Cornwall: Ralph Tregrisiow from Creed (1384–1415), John Cobbethorn from Launceston (1419–58), and John Arundell junior from the Lanherne branch of that family (c.1482–96).⁸ A further group of Cornish graduates did not return to any part of the

---

1 Biographies of most known scholars of Oxford University up to 1540 are listed in *BRUO*, I–IV.

2 Orme, 'The Cornish at Oxford', and *BRUO* passim; biographies of the two John Arundells, Lyhert, Stanbury, Tregury, and Trevisa also appear in *ODNB*.

3 A. Wood, *Survey of the Antiquities of the City of Oxford*, ed. A. Clark, vol. I, Oxford Hist. Soc. 15 (1889), 111, 113.

4 Orme (ed.), *Cornish Wills*, 76–9; H. E. Salter (ed.), *Registrum Cancellarii Oxoniensis 1434–1469*, vol. I, Oxford Hist. Soc. 93 (1932), 151–4 (David Carnu, Pascow Noel, and possibly Ralph Carnehille).

5 On Tremur, see *Reg. Grandisson*, II, 621–2, 627, 660, 1147–9, 1179–81; III, 1305.

6 Below, pp. 261–2.

7 D. Lepine, *A Brotherhood of Canons Serving God: English Secular Cathedrals in the Later Middle Ages* (1995), 47.

8 For the list of dignitaries and canons of Exeter Cathedral, 1300–1540, see Le Neve, *Fasti, 1300–1540*, IX: *Exeter Diocese*, ed. Horn. For Cobbethorn, see R. and O. B. Peter, *The Histories of Launceston and Dunheved* (1885), 13, 116. 149.

South West, but followed careers elsewhere in England. William Polmorva scored an early success by becoming a royal clerk and the confessor to Philippa, queen of Edward III, until his death in 1362. Tregrisiow's uncle, Stephen Pempel, rose to be dean of Wells (1361–79), and John Gentill gained a senior post in the royal court of admiralty (1428–35). Most notable is a group of graduates that formed at the court of Henry VI and his queen, Margaret of Anjou. It included John Arundell senior (d. 1477), probably from the Lanherne family, who became Henry's chaplain and physician, and later bishop of Chichester; Walter Lyhert (d. 1472) from Lanteglos-by-Fowey, Margaret's confessor and subsequently bishop of Norwich; John Stanbury (d. 1474) from Morwenstow, Henry's confessor, bishop of Bangor and afterwards of Hereford; and Michael Tregury (d. 1471) from St Wenn, also close to Margaret, sometime rector of the university of Caen and later archbishop of Dublin. Such achievements were rarer in the second half of the century, but posts of distinction were gained by Thomas Fort (d. c.1503), canon of Bodmin, bishop of Achonry in Ireland, and later prior of Huntingdon, while John Arundell junior (d. 1504) became a chaplain to Edward IV and chancellor of Prince Arthur, son of Henry VII. After serving as bishop of Lichfield, he was translated to Exeter, the only medieval Cornishman to hold the senior post in the diocese with the possible exception of Leofric.

These men's achievements were unusual. Most medieval Cornish clergy were non-graduates who spent their adult lives in the county as rectors and vicars, or as chaplains and chantry priests. Many must have been speakers of Cornish, especially in west Cornwall, as we happen to know was the case with Henry Marsely, rector of St Just-in-Penwith in 1335, Ralph Tremur a year later, and John Polmarke, chaplain of St Cadoc in Padstow in 1339.¹ Some of the graduate clergy who came from the west of the county and returned to parishes there would also have been fluent in the language. Conversely we hear of a few clergy in the Cornish-speaking areas who claimed to encounter difficulties from not knowing Cornish: at Glasney (1318), St Erme (1437), St Ewe (1450), Goran (1477), and St Mewan (1512).² The references in these latter cases, however, relate to clergy wishing to acquire new benefices or receive pensions. This involved them justifying their requests, and the issue of the Cornish language may have been more useful for that purpose than it was a problem in practice.³

DAILY LIFE

The everyday life of the parish clergy, like that of monks and friars, centred on saying the eight daily services. There was no requirement to say them in church except on Sundays and festivals, and many parish clergy may have done so in their houses. The common medieval word for the breviary that contained the daily services, the 'portas', came from the French words 'carry outside'. It could be used at home, in which case a priest may have said his daily services in blocks in the early morning and afternoon, freeing the rest of the day for other activities, but little is known of this matter. Baptisms, visits to the sick, and funerals might be required at any time, since baptism took place on the day of birth and a funeral on the day of death or soon afterwards. The year was punctuated by the sequence of feasts and fasts and by the collection of tithes and offerings. The parish was not a unit of civil government until Tudor times, but a medieval rector or vicar had to maintain his chancel and house (Fig. 19), supervise the affairs of his church, take his turn as rural dean, or be assigned by the bishop to investigate, for example, a dispute over church patronage or a crime that had been committed against Church law.

Parish life did not always follow a calm routine. There could be tensions between the clergy and their parishioners over refusals to pay tithes, attend church, or keep the Church's moral code. In 1342 the archdeacon of Cornwall, Adam Carleton, petitioned the bishop to allow him to exchange the post for a parish in Huntingdonshire, asserting that his health was inadequate to deal with 'a people... so extraordinary, rebellious, and difficult to teach and correct.' A more powerful man than himself, he thought, was needed to handle them.[4] Occasionally clergy were victims of crimes. A clerk of Poundstock was wounded in his church in 1357 and the provost of Glasney in his precinct in 1375.[5] The dean of Crantock was dragged from his church in 1382, and a priest of Penryn was violently attacked in the town in the following year.[6] The rector of Whitstone died mysteriously by murder or suicide in 1359, a priest of St Hilary was stabbed and beheaded in 1380, and the vicar of Linkinhorne was killed in 1411 after falling out with local people.[7] On such occasions the bishop excommunicated the perpetrators, and ordered the fact to be given wide publicity. The death at Whitstone caused a local sensation that led to the veneration of the dead man as a saint.[8] Such evidence is worth remembering lest we be tempted to regard all medieval Cornish people as good Catholics.

---

1 *Reg. Grandisson*, II, 820, 910, 1180.
2 *Reg. Stapeldon*, 219; *Reg. Lacy*, ed. Hingeston-Randolph, I, 225; *Reg. Lacy*, ed. Dunstan, III, 173–4; Chanter XII(ii), Reg Bothe, ff. 41v–42r; *CPL*, IX, 354.
3 Compare the monks of Minster, who complained of the language problem in 1355 and 1374 although they lived in a non-Cornish speaking area (*Cal. Pat.* 1354–8, 247, 252; *Cal. Pat.* 1374–7, 7).
4 *Reg. Grandisson*, II, 957–8.
5 Ibid., 1193–5; *Reg. Brantyngham*, I, 148, 354–5.
6 *Reg. Brantyngham*, I, 466, 490.
7 *Reg. Grandisson*, III, 1231–4; *Reg. Brantyngham*, I, 156, 434, 438; *Reg. Stafford*, 242.
8 Below, pp. 84–5.

FIG 19. *The east end of the chancel, St Ive church, probably embellished by Bartholomew de Castro, rector of the church (1314-c.1349). Unusually for Cornwall, it imitates the highly decorative style currently in use at Exeter Cathedral, apparently involving the same craftsmen.*

Each parish contained a house for the rector or vicar, which he was expected to keep in repair. If he let it become dilapidated, he or his heirs might be pursued for costs. The earliest house of which a record survives is St Neot's in 1314, which was described as having a hall and chamber linked by a door, with other buildings.[1] Veryan's in 1331 included a hall, chamber, *garderoba* (which might mean a store room or privy), cellar, and kitchen.[2] The incumbent would have had one or more male servants, depending on his wealth, and sometimes a chaplain to assist him. If he was not resident, the chaplain might occupy the house in his absence. We know little of the lives of rectors and vicars, since we lack their personal records except for a few of their wills, and the latter only after 1400.[3] Wills are problematical documents too, because they were often made near to death and followed conventional forms. Those of the Cornish clergy mention modest possessions: gowns, bedding, a few pieces of silver (cups, bowls, and spoons), and livestock such as sheep and cattle – reflecting the fact that many rectors and vicars were involved in agriculture, usually through servants or tenants rather than personally. A few clergy refer to their books, generally Latin ones: prayer-books, grammars, books on canon law, and an occasional work of theology. One priest's book is still extant: a breviary owned by Thomas Greke of the parish of Lanteglos-by-Fowey, in which he noted the names of his family members.[4] There is little evidence that the clergy wrote books themselves, although it is possible that they helped produce some of the Latin Lives of Cornish saints or the plays in Cornish that feature Bible stories and saintly legends.[5] Some of the saint cults introduced into parish churches were probably due to them. John Waryn of Menheniot was a devotee of St Anne, and left money in 1426 to build a chapel and found a guild in her honour in his parish church.[6]

The lowest clergy of all were the chaplains and chantry priests. Shortage of clergy after the Black Death caused their wages to rise, but this left them only

---

1   *Reg. Stapeldon*, 342.
2   ECA, D&C 2851; *Reg. Grandisson*, II, 606.
3   Orme (ed.), *Medieval Wills*, passim.
4   Aberystwyth, National Library of Wales, NLW 22253A, described in N. Orme, 'A Fifteenth-century Prayer-Book from Cornwall: MS NLW 22253A', *JRIC*, new ser. II, 3/2 (1999), 69–73; idem, 'The Lanteglos Prayer-Book: a further note', *JRIC*, new ser. II, 3/3–4 (2000), 67. Thomas Greke, priest, sued John Richard of Polruan in 1475×1485 over detention of deeds (TNA, C 1/ 53/311).
5   Below, pp. 88–91.
6   Orme (ed.), *Cornish Wills*, 60; below, p. 73.

slightly better off. The rises were paralleled by increases in prices, and governments tried to stop wages from rising. In 1351 the famous Statute of Labourers fixed the earnings of lay workers, and this was followed by similar measures aimed at the lesser clergy. In 1362 stipends for chantry priests were set at £3 6s. 8d. and those for parish chaplains at £4, figures that were raised to £4 13s. 4d. and £5 6s. 8d. respectively in 1414.[1] As there was limited scope for employment as a priest in Cornwall, some of the lesser Cornish clergy sought careers in Devon or elsewhere in England. If they were lucky they might find a permanent post in a perpetual chantry or a guild where, although they earned no more, they were less liable to sudden dismissal. A fortunate few were able to join the staff of Exeter Cathedral as vicars choral or perpetual chantry priests: posts that were better paid, had security of tenure, and sometimes led to promotion as parish rectors or vicars. Several clergy with Cornish surnames held such posts, but it is likely that their success was due to patronage from canons of the cathedral who came from Cornwall.[2] Favour was important even for gaining this work.

Little is recorded about such lowly clergy in Cornwall until after the Black Death and the minimum total of two hundred that we have postulated before that event can be only a conjecture. The earliest list of them comes from the poll-tax of 1381, when there were 157, a figure that stayed much the same until the Reformation, so that they formed about half of the parish clergy.[3] Chaplains worked as assistants to rectors and vicars, or took their places if they were absent, and a few may have served in the households of the gentry. They were perceived to be in short supply after 1349 when the population was smaller and more opportunities existed, inside and outside the Church, to earn better wages. By the 15th century, a clergyman who could not find a chaplain willing to serve his parish might ask the bishop to order one to do so, such as a priest who prayed for the dead. The bishop would take the view that serving a parish could be done in tandem with such prayers. In 1438, for example, the rector of Trevalga, who wished to live elsewhere, got the bishop to issue a 'compulsion' to John Gregory, a chaplain of Tintagel. Gregory was told to serve Trevalga parish in return for an adequate salary, and to present himself before the bishop within twelve days if he had any objection to doing so.[4]

Chantry priests were of two kinds. Some were hired by the year to say masses for the dead, causing their masses to be known as 'annuals' and themselves as 'annuellars'. They would establish themselves in the church of the dead person's parish and say their masses at an altar there. Others served perpetual chantries endowed by a wealthy person or supported by a religious guild, and received a salary for as long as they held the post. In that respect they were better off than their temporary colleagues, and some of them were formally instituted to their posts by the bishop like rectors and vicars. In 1548, when chantries were abolished in England, there were about 27 perpetual chantries in Cornwall, employing about 31 priests. Most were founded by individual donors but in a few cases (Davidstow, St Stephen-by-Saltash, and Truro) they were maintained by guilds or town councils.[5] It is unlikely that there had ever been many more perpetual chantries, so that when people today talk of chantry chapels in parish churches, they are really referring to side chapels with altars where a priest (such as the incumbent of the church) might occasionally celebrate mass, rather than chapels with priests of their own. Some perpetual chantry priests were expected to help run the church or the nearby parish; a few served chapels-of-ease as at Boscastle and Penzance. By the 1540s a handful taught schools as well, but there is no evidence as yet that any did so in Cornwall before 1500.[6]

The poll-tax records of 1381 also contain the names of 81 clerks. A few of these were junior clergy in monasteries or collegiate churches, but most were probably parish clerks. There is a problem here in that Cornwall had 209 parishes, each of which would have needed at least one parish clerk and possibly more. In 1427 John Walle, rector of Sheviock, left bequests in his will to the clerk of the 'town', meaning the settlement by the church, and to the clerks 'on the land', signifying the rural areas, but the will may relate to Tiverton (Devon), an unusually large parish, not typical of Cornwall.[7] Many such clerks may have done the duty as a part-time supplement to a lay career, however, and have paid the poll-tax as laymen. The 81 clerks of 1381 are likely to have been young men intending to follow careers as priests, and some of them can be identified in the lists of clergy being ordained in the following years. Very few of the cohort of 1381 seem to have become rectors or vicars of parish churches, although John Sore, a clerk in Trigg Minor deanery in 1381, was appointed dean of Crantock in 1410.[8] Before this he had been a chantry priest at St Austell, while Thomas Cook, also a clerk of Trigg Minor in 1381, became chaplain of the chapel of St Illick in St Endellion parish in 1382.[9] These lesser posts were probably more typical of clerks who rose to be priests. Richer clergy, of the kind who became rectors and vicars spent their youth

---

1 *Statutes of the Realm*, I, 373–4; II, 188; W. Lyndwood, *Provinciale seu Constitutiones Angliae* (1679), 240–1.
2 N. Orme, *The Minor Clergy of Exeter Cathedral* (1979), e.g. names on p. 162.
3 TNA, E 179/25/5.
4 *Reg. Lacy*, ed. Dunstan, II, 114; cf. II, 400; III, 16, 47–8, 49, 92.
5 L. S. Snell, *Documents towards a History of the Reformation in Cornwall*: vol. I, *The Chantry Certificates for Cornwall* (c.1953).
6 Below, p. 94.
7 Orme (ed.), *Cornish Wills*, 62.
8 *Reg. Stafford*, 159.
9 *Reg. Brantyngham*, I, 82.

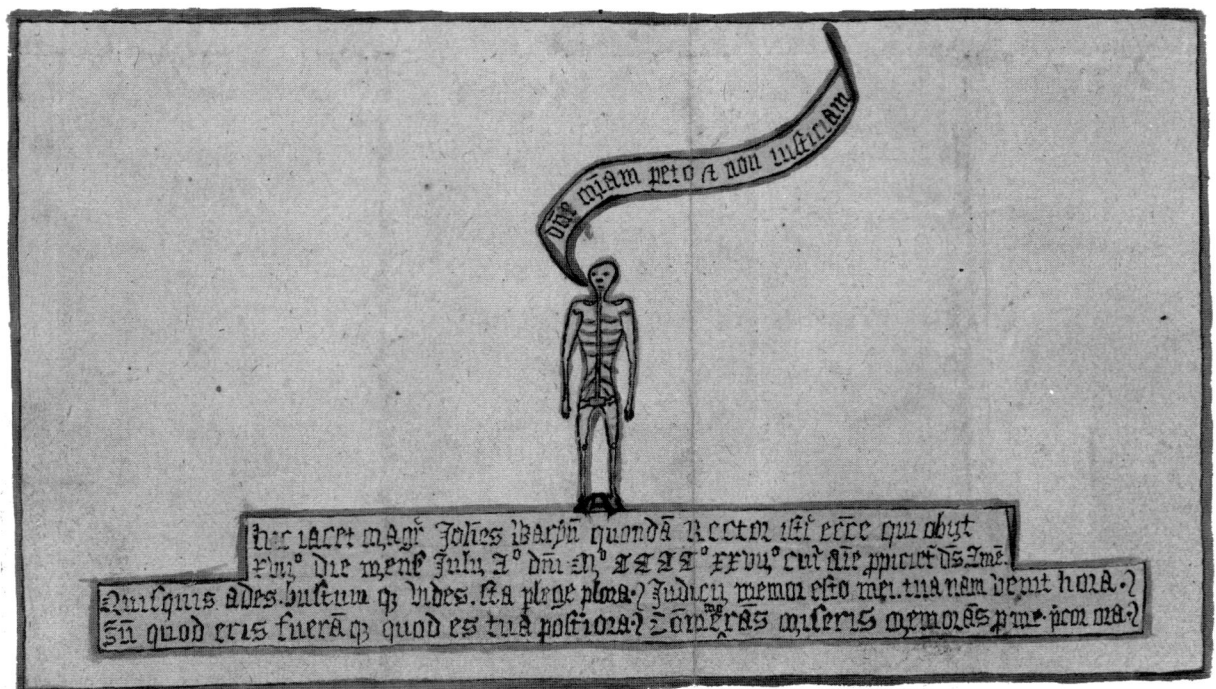

FIG 20. *A drawing of the brass (now lost) of John Waryn, rector of Menheniot (died 1426), displaying the newly fashionable image known as a cadaver.*

solely at school, and did not need to work their way up the clerical ladder as parish clerks.

Contemporaries tended to envisage the clergy as youthful men (like Chaucer's Clerk of Oxford) or mature ones (such as his Parson). In reality, in Cornwall as elsewhere, there were those who developed infirmities and disabilities (especially blindness or lameness), or grew into an old age that made it hard for them to work.[1] The solution usually adopted in the early 14th century was for an elderly or infirm rector or vicar to ask the bishop to appoint someone as his coadjutor or assistant, or for the bishop to appoint such a person on his own initiative. The coadjutor might be a neighbouring clergyman, or a chaplain who moved into the incumbent's house and helped run his affairs. In the early 15th century it became more common for the incumbent to resign his benefice in return for receiving a proportion of the income as a pension. Such an arrangement had to be sanctioned by the bishop, who approved the amount (usually a third of the income) and made the new incumbent promise to pay it. This system worked well for rich clergy but not for those who were poor. A rector or vicar with a small stipend faced difficulty in negotiating a pension, because the stipend could not support both him and his successor. Occasionally we find rectors or vicars becoming perpetual chantry priests, a move that may have been prompted by a need to find work that did not require much effort. Hired curates or temporary priests who became too old or ill to work had no resources to fall back on. If they became destitute the bishop had to take responsibility for them. In 1309–12 Bishop Stapledon addressed this problem by founding a hospital at Clyst Gabriel, east of Exeter, for infirm priests who had no livelihood. A few of the priests admitted to the hospital had Cornish names and probably came from the underclass of poor hired clergy.[2] What happened to the majority of such clergy when they grew sick or old is not recorded.

When death came, status ruled as it did in life. The grandees of the Cornish Church – the priors of the monasteries – were given elaborate funerals and monuments inside their churches. John Leland, visiting Cornwall in 1542, noticed the tomb of Thomas Vivian, prior of Bodmin and titular bishop of Megara, and those of Roger of Horton and Stephen Trediddan, priors of Launceston.[3] Cornwall lacked bishops or dignitaries to commission such objects in the parish churches: most of the successful Cornish clergy got posts at Exeter or elsewhere and were buried far away. The prosperous beneficed clergy, rectors and vicars, made their wills and told their executors to hold their

---

1 On this subject, see N. Orme, 'Sufferings of the Clergy': illness and old age in Exeter diocese, 1300–1540, in M. Pelling and R. M. Smith (ed.), *Life, Death, and the Elderly: historical perspectives* (1991), 62–73.

2 N. Orme, 'The Clergy of Clyst Gabriel, 1312–1508', *TDA* 126 (1994), 107–121, especially 114–21.

3 J. Leland, *Itinerary*, ed. L. Toulmin Smith (1907–10), I, 175, 180.

funerals, sometimes defining the masses to be said for their souls and the alms to be paid to the poor. They claimed the privilege of burial in their chancels, usually beneath a ledger-stone flush with the floor and incised with their name, their date of their death, and a prayer for God to have mercy on their soul. The resting places of the poor unbeneficed clergy are hardly ever recorded, and it is an open question whether they were buried in church or, like the majority of the population, under an unmarked mound in the churchyard.

The ledger-stones of the wealthier clergy were sometimes decorated with an inlaid brass memorial, showing a priest in vestments: not a life-like portrait but a conventional image supplied by a workshop. We still possess a few of these portrait brasses, including those of Thomas Aumarle (*c*.1401) at Cardinham, John Balsam (1410) at Blisland, and John Trembras (1515) at St Michael Penkevil. Aumarle's and Trembras's gravestones display their social status by showing their coats of arms, and Aumarle's reinforces the point by showing him girt with a sword.[1] John Waryn of Menheniot (1426), on the other hand, sought to teach passers-by rather than to proclaim his own importance. His brass, no longer extant, followed a fashion popular with some clergy in 15th-century England by depicting himself as a skeleton (Fig. 20). The Latin inscription warned those able to read it, 'I am what you will be, and I was what you are!'[2]

4. THE LATER MIDDLE AGES: THE PEOPLE

PARISH CHURCHES

For most people in medieval Cornwall, the Church meant their parish church. There they attended services, at least occasionally. There they were christened, confessed, married, and buried. The building featured largely in local life. It had to be maintained, and there was often a desire to improve it if resources allowed. This desire led to the widespread rebuilding or restoration of churches in Cornwall during the later Middle Ages. Some of this took place in the 14th century, as can be seen in details such as the south transept of St Germans and the east end of the chancel of St Ive (Figs. 16, 19). Here, and at the vanished college of Glasney, Beer stone from Devon was used for decorative features and fittings, probably shaped by masons of Exeter Cathedral with which all three of these churches had connections.

The majority of rebuilding projects, however, took place in the 15th and early 16th centuries, which constitute one of the greatest periods of such activity in Cornish history. Rebuilding obliterated most of the fabric of churches that had existed previously, making it hard for us to recapture what they had been like. More positively it filled the county with a distinct and often uniform kind of church, which we today regard as typically medieval but which only dates from the very end of the Middle Ages. The rebuilt or restored Cornish churches of this period were typically constructed of granite or 'moorstone' as it was known, quarried or gathered from loose blocks on the county's moorlands.[3] For long such stone was difficult to acquire, and as late as about 1470 Bodmin church was built of freestone although it lay close to a moor, but by the 16th century granite became widely available and tended to replace an earlier variety of stones of more local origin. It is a hard and often coarse material, capable of being dressed for building walls but difficult to carve satisfactorily, so that the mouldings of windows, doors, and piers had generally to be simple. Only in the early 16th century, in wealthier churches like St Mary Magdalene (Launceston) and Truro, was there funding to procure high-grade granite and skilled craftsmanship so that buildings could be ornately carved, in Launceston's case with shields, decorative leaves and flowers, and inscriptions (Fig. 21). Cornish slate was generally used for roofing. For small-scale decorative work, such as church fittings or tombs, stone of finer texture was often employed such as elvan and Catacleuse, both found in Cornwall itself. These were used for objects like the holy-water stoups and probable saint's shrines at St Endellion and St Issey, both apparently the work of a single master craftsman.[4]

---

1 For medieval Cornish brasses, see E. H. W. Dunkin, *The Monumental Brasses of Cornwall* (1882), especially 9–11; M. Stephenson, *A List of Monumental Brasses in the British Isles*, 2nd edn (1964), 70–7, 731; and, most thoroughly, W. Lack, H. M. Stuckfield, and P. Whittemore, *The Monumental Brasses of Cornwall* (1997).

2 Bodleian, Gough Cornwall 22 (printed book: R. Carew, *The Survey of Cornwall* (1602)), drawing opp. f. 135r; Lack et al., *Monumental Brasses of Cornwall*, 85.

3 On building stone, see A. Clifton-Taylor, 'Building Materials', in N. Pevsner, *Cornwall*, The Buildings of England, rev. edn (1970), 29–34; a new edition of this work by P. Beecham is about to appear.

4 On St Endellion, see below, p. 182.

FIG 21. *The church of St Mary Magdalene, Launceston. Its porch is magnificent, carved from granite.*

The rebuilding of churches generally made them bigger and more striking visually (Figs. 21–2, 34–5). Externally towers were added or enlarged, usually of three stages with battlements and often buttresses. Spires were less common, but Glasney had one while others have come down to modern times at places like Gerrans, St Hilary, Lostwithiel, and St Minver. Porches were provided or extended, for reasons to be explained presently. Internally aisles were built alongside many naves: sometimes a single aisle, sometimes one on each side. In the most ambitious schemes, as at Bodmin and St Columb Major, the aisles extended alongside the chancel as well. The new aisles were wider than those of the 12th and 13th centuries, and formed oblongs lying east to west, unlike the transepts of earlier periods which they often incorporated. Chancel aisles formed chapels devoted to saints, especially the Virgin Mary. Lady chapels in her honour became popular in religious houses during the 13th century. Launceston Priory had one by 1312 and Bodmin Priory by 1343, and this provision was probably imitated in the larger parish churches during the 14th and 15th centuries.[1] Nave aisles provided further space for images and altars at their east ends, and seats for the congregation further west. By leaving an alley alongside the seats, the aisles could also be used as processional ways.

The energy and resources for church building and decoration came from various sources. Rectors, as we have seen, were responsible for chancels, and religious houses which had appropriated parish tithes might

---

1 ECA, D&C 1145; Oliver, *Monasticon*, 413 (Launceston); *Reg. Grandisson*, II, 982 (Bodmin, reference to an altar of St Mary, implying a Lady chapel).

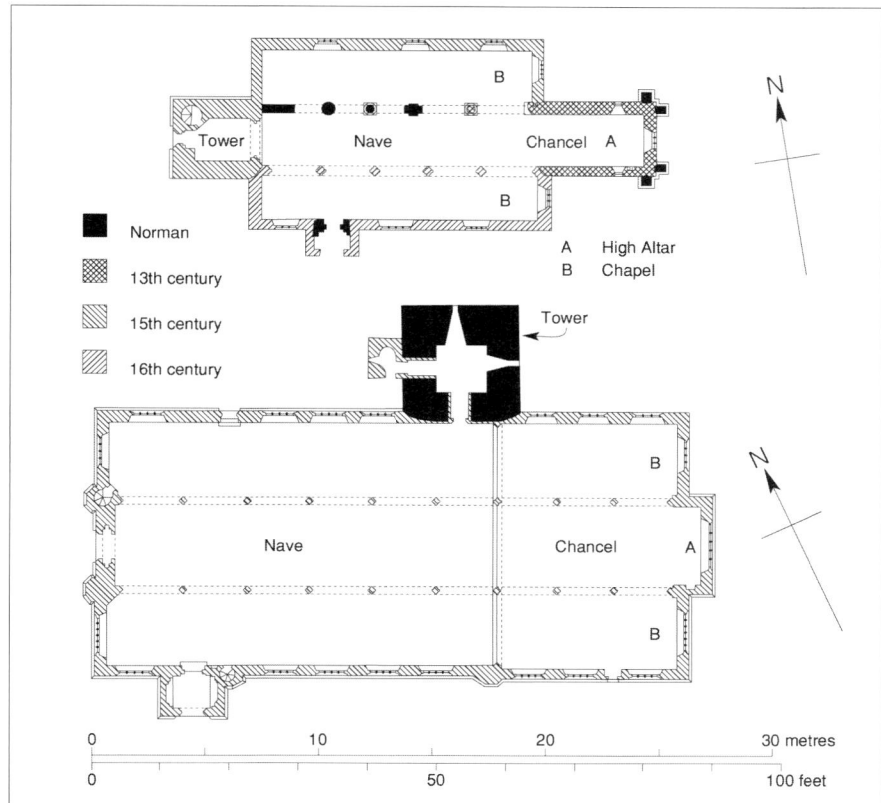

FIG 22. *Parish church plans, 15th and 16th centuries, Morwenstow (top) and St Petroc Bodmin.*

assist with church building. Exeter Cathedral paid just over £30 to rebuild the chancel of St Merryn in 1422, the cost including masonry, rafters, tiling, and four glazed windows.[1] Gentry might contribute to the general improvement of a church or build a transept, aisle, or chapel in which they would worship and be buried. Some wealthy Cornishmen with interests in tin-mining gave profits from their mines, or even the mines themselves, to churches, chapels, or religious houses. Udy Philpot of Roche bestowed a mine on Bodmin church before 1448, and William Martyn of Lostwithiel gave portions of three to Lostwithiel church, Luxulyan church, and Tywardreath Priory in 1493.[2] Peter Bevill of St Allen used mines to finance a chantry in his parish in 1512,[3] and Tristram Colen presented the friars of Truro with half of a tin-working in 1517.[4] In 1528 Thomas Tretherff bequeathed the whole of his tin-workings in Cornwall to his wife while she lived, and then to the wardens of the shrine of St Enoder in the church of that name.[5] The early 16th-century stained-glass windows of St Neot included a picture of a miner, perhaps acknowledging that the glass was partly funded from the industry of such men or from their wages.[6]

Not all churches were so lucky. Parishioners might struggle to do their duty of maintaining the nave, or try to avoid the responsibility. In 1377 the bishop was obliged to order the people of Crantock to contribute to the repair of the central tower, and when the tower fell, damaging the nave, another bishop granted an indulgence to help the parishioners, remarking that they were too poor to afford the repairs.[7] At other times the people of a parish might join in heroic efforts to raise money for ambitious building projects. This happened at St Neot, where the windows commemorate not only the gentry who contributed individually but the young men, 'sisters', and wives of the parish who did so as groups.[8] Shared efforts of this kind are most fully recorded at Bodmin, where the parish church was rebuilt between 1469 and 1472 to create the structure that exists today (Fig. 34). The work cost £268, not counting gifts of materials and labour. Some £24 of this came from a levy, agreed by the community, under which certain people paid 1d. or ½d. per week, but most of it consisted of voluntary donations from the craft and religious guilds of the town, the congregations of the outlying chapels, and individual men and women,

1 ECA, D&C 1403.
2 TNA, C 1/17/232; N. Orme (ed.), *Cornish Wills 1342–1540*, DCRS new ser. 50 (2007), 103–4.
3 Orme (ed.), *Cornish Wills*, 140.
4 Ibid., 164.
5 Ibid., 177.
6 J. Mattingly et al., 'A Tin Miner and a Bal Maiden: further research on the St Neot windows', *JRIC* (2001), 96–100.
7 *Reg. Brantyngham*, I, 379–80; II, 891; *Reg. Stafford*, 74.
8 Below, p. 72.

FIG 23. *A pre-Reformation church interior, Altarnun. The rood screen (lacking its images) runs across the church. The extensive seating includes bench-ends elaborately carved with instruments of the Passion and musicians; one commemorates the carver, Robert Daye.*

including servants. The contributions ranged from 1*d*. to 13*s*. 4*d*. and a list was made of the donors. It contains the names of about 447 people of Bodmin, of whom about 70 were women and the remainder men. The smaller number of women may reflect the fact that most husbands gave on behalf of their wives, but sometimes both partners are listed separately.[1]

Much care and money was spent on furnishing churches. During the 13th century it became fashionable to have a larger opening between the nave and the chancel, framed by a higher and wider chancel arch, and by the end of the century such openings were coming to be filled by a wooden screen surmounted by a 'rood' or crucifix and nowadays known as a 'rood screen'.[2] The origin of rood screens in Cornwall is hard to date. Bishop Quinil's statutes of 1287 do not list them along with the furnishings required in churches; nor do the visitations of the Cornish churches belonging to Exeter Cathedral in 1331.[3] This suggests that if they existed at this time they were not mandatory, but they probably became common during the 14th century. Rood screens were panelled up to a height of about four feet (1.2 metres) and had open windows above, with a door or doors in the middle. Above the windows was a loft or gallery on which stood the rood. The screen formed a conspicuous boundary between the clergy in the chancel and the people in the nave, but it gave the latter a relatively good view of the service – probably better than in the old churches with narrow chancel openings. This visibility is particularly striking at Altarnun (Fig. 23). The congregation had to take charge of the screen because it stood in the nave, and since it was the principal object that they looked at, it often received a good deal of care and attention. Its woodwork might be elaborately carved and painted, and saints be commemorated in paintings on the panels or in sculpted images on or near the screen. In 1531, for example, the parishioners of Stratton contracted with two 'carvers', John Dow of Lawhitton and John Parys of North Lew (Devon), to provide a rood screen right across the church, in the manner of the screen at St Kew. Standing upon it were to be figures of Christ, Mary, and John the Evangelist, modelled on those of Liskeard, with windows over Christ, as at Week St Mary. An altar was to be placed at either end of the screen, on the nave side, with statues of St Armel and the Virgin

---

1 CRO, B/BOD/244, printed in J. J. Wilkinson, 'The Receipts and Expenses in the Building of Bodmin Church', *The Camden Miscellany: Vol. VII*, Camden Soc. new ser. 14 (1875), 1–49.

2 C. D. Cragoe, 'Belief and Patronage in the English Parish before 1300: some evidence from roods', *Architectural History* 48 (2005), 21–48.

3 F. M. Powicke and C. R. Cheney, (ed.) *Councils & Synods II: A.D. 1205–1313* (1964), II, 1005–8; ECA, D&C 2851, printed in *Reg. Grandisson*, II, 605–11.

FIG 24. *One of the fine series of late medieval wall paintings in Breage church, showing St Christopher carrying Christ. Another painting features the 'Sunday Christ' wounded with implements used by Sabbath breakers.*

Mary respectively, and two further screens called 'intercloses' were to divide the chancel from the chapels that flanked it, in the style of St Columb Major. The parishioners undertook to pay £2 6s. 8d. per linear foot for the work, and the carvers bound themselves to forfeit £200 if they did not complete it in a satisfactory way.[1]

The nave of the church continued to be the part of the laity. We have seen that some people had (or claimed to have) seats there as early as 1287, and by the 15th century the ambitions of parishioners to have a well-furnished church extended to installing seating for everyone or improving the seating that existed already (Fig. 23). In 1491 the parishioners of Bodmin commissioned Matthy More, 'carpenter', to fit chairs and seats in four 'renges' or lines like those of Plympton St Mary (Devon). The nave was to have two renges and the nave aisles one each, which would have produced four blocks of seating with alleys between them. A pulpit was to be built replicating that of Moretonhampstead (Devon), and the whole work was to take four years and to cost £92, the church providing the timber.[2] Seating usually took the form of benches with backs, while the ends alongside the alleys were often embellished with carvings. Such carvings might feature the instruments associated with the Crucifixion (the lance, nails, and crown of thorns), humorous scenes from everyday life, or, by the 16th century, initials and coats-of-arms commemorating those who sat in the seats or paid for their installation.[3] Some churches like Blisland, Landewednack, and Lanlivery acquired new fonts but many kept their Norman ones – perhaps to proclaim their ancient baptismal rights.

Walls, windows, and floors might also be decorated. It would be hazardous to say that such decoration was universal or always very elaborate, but it took well-developed forms in some places. A tympanum or partition across the upper half of the chancel arch, above the screen and behind the rood, might carry a picture of the Last Judgment. No such picture survives in Cornwall, but a few wall paintings are still visible. One favourite subject was St Christopher carrying the infant Christ, as may be seen at Breage (Fig. 24), St

---

1 R. W. Goulding, *Records of the Charity known as Blanchminster's Charity* (1898), 91–4.
2 J. Maclean, *The Parochial and Family History of the Deanery of Trigg Minor* (1873–9), I, 154.
3 J. Mattingly, 'The Dating of Bench-ends in Cornish Churches', *JRIC* new ser. II, 1/1 (1991), 58–72.

Keverne, and Poughill.¹ Another depicted the 'Sunday Christ', a motif popular in England from about the mid 14th century and often known as 'St Sunday'. Four such paintings are extant in Cornwall. They show Christ's body, wounded by the tools and playthings of people who spent Sunday at work or in sport, and seek to warn people to keep the Lord's Day piously.² Floors might have tiles, particularly churches that were also religious houses and therefore wealthier. The chancel of Launcells preserves many 15th-century tiles, manufactured at Barnstaple (Devon). Decorative glazing reached its acme at St Neot in the early 16th century, where a complete series of windows was installed showing Christ, saints, the donors of the work, and scenes from the Life of the church's patron saint (Fig. 6).³ This may have been exceptional, but a substantial amount of late-medieval stained glass survives at St Kew and St Winnow, and many fragments in other churches, so that such glass may have been widespread by the Reformation in the 1530s, albeit not in every church or window.

Parish churches were built not only to be impressive and beautiful but to be practical. Their plans reflected the uses to which they were put. A church was not a single space but a series of rooms of greater or lesser holiness. The outermost was the porch, which was used for the ceremonies that brought people out of secular life into the arms of Holy Church. The baptism service began here with the exorcism of the baby, making it capable of going into the church to be christened. Marriages took place in the porch, because marriage (although regarded as a sacrament) was basically a contract between lay people. It was encouraged to happen at church but outside the door, and only after the couple had made their vows did the priest lead them inside for a blessing. Mothers were met in the porch by the priest after childbirth and taken into church in the ceremony known as 'churching', which stemmed from the Jewish practice of purifying such women, although the Catholic Church regarded the rite more as one of thanksgiving. Passing from the porch one entered the nave, often sanctifying oneself with drops of water from a holy-water stoup by the nave door. The nave was holier than the porch. It contained the font near the door and the rood screen at the east end. Other images – statues or wall paintings – were likely to be present in the nave and to serve as objects of devotion.

Holier still was the chancel and, in many churches, the chapels that lay on either side of it or in the transepts or elsewhere. The rood screen closed off the chancel, and only special people, or people on special occasions, went through its door. The first group included the priest and his clerk, the male choir maintained in a few large churches, and the patron of the church (if such a person lived locally) with his or her family. The second group consisted of couples receiving their wedding blessing and adults confessing their sins during Lent. Chapels too were often private places, reserved for wealthy people or for guild members. Thomas Killigrew, one of the leading inhabitants of Penryn, had his own chapel in St Gluvias church in 1501, and we may imagine him kneeling there with his wife, his two sons, and his daughters, like figures on a monumental brass.⁴ Chancels and chapels were also holier because the Church's prayers were offered in them and mass was celebrated. In the view of the Catholic Church, when the priest consecrated the wafer of bread and chalice of wine during mass they became, in substance, the real body and blood of Christ. This called for the consecration to happen in a special area, removed from ordinary people and fit for Christ to manifest himself.

WORSHIP

Public worship was meant to happen in church on every Sunday and major festival day. The priest and clerk would read matins in the early hours of daylight, celebrate mass in the middle of the morning, and read evensong in the afternoon. Beyond this priests, like monks, were required to say all the eight services each day, and in a few large parish churches with several priests, like Bodmin, St Columb Major, and Liskeard, they may have gathered in church to do so, although not necessarily at the regular times observed in monasteries. Most parish clergy, as has been suggested, may have said weekday prayers in their homes, so that there would not necessarily have been formal services in most parish churches on ordinary weekdays.

The principal Sunday service was the Latin mass, and we can visualise its shape in the 14th and 15th centuries from prayer books and from the ways in which churches were built and furnished. By this period most parish clergy in southern England were using prayer books of the 'Use of Sarum', which contained the forms of the services followed at Salisbury Cathedral.⁵ This applied to the material of the service; the way in which it was done would have been simpler in a parish church than a cathedral, reflecting the single priest and clerk

---

1 J. D. Enys et al., 'Mural Painting in Cornish Churches', *JRIC* 15 (1901–2), 136–60; J. E. Coomber, 'Medieval Painting in Cornwall', University of Exeter, unpublished MA thesis (1980).

2 A. Reiss, *The Sunday Christ: Sabbatarianism in English medieval wall painting*, British Archaeological Reports, British Series 292 (2000).

3 J. Mattingly, 'Stories in the Glass: reconstructing the St Neot pre-Reformation glazing scheme', *JRIC* new ser. II, 3/3–4 (2000), 9–55; J. Mattingly et al., 'A Tin Miner and a Bal Maiden', 96–100;

and J. Mattingly, 'Pre-Reformation Saints' Cults in Cornwall, with particular reference to the St Neot windows', in J. Cartwright (ed.), *Celtic Hagiography and Saints' Cults* (2003), 249–70.

4 Orme (ed.), *Cornish Wills*, 111.

5 For the earliest Latin text, see J. Wickham Legg (ed.), *The Sarum Missal* (1916), 205–29, and for a text based on later printed editions, F. H. Dickinson (ed.), *Missale ad Usum Insignis et Praeclarae Ecclesiae Sarum* (1861–83). The Sarum texts were probably widely used in Cornwall by 1428 (below, p. 172).

who performed it. The priest said or sang most of the mass while the clerk pronounced the responses, and no spoken words were required from anyone else. Indeed the rood screen made the point that the congregation were spectators, not performers, of the worship. The first part of the mass consisted of prayers and Bible readings (an epistle and a gospel). After the gospel there was an opportunity to preach a sermon, but it is unlikely that most Cornish parish clergy did so: only 14 out of 124 were recorded as preachers in 1561.[1] More usually the priest would come to the screen, or to a separate pulpit, to ask the parishioners to pray for particular causes, or to announce bishops' letters, indulgences, or excommunications. A common practice by the 15th century was to keep a parish 'bead-roll' on which people paid to have their names inscribed. This was read by the priest on Sundays, often from a free-standing pulpit which may have been used for this purpose more often than for preaching. Several Cornish parishes are recorded possessing bead-rolls, and a prayer list survives from Camborne that may have been copied from one.[2] It is in Latin, apart from the surnames, making it close in character to the rest of the service.

The second part of the mass, held at the altar in the chancel, centred on consecrating a wafer of bread and a small chalice of wine. This part of the service was so holy that the priest muttered the words inaudibly, and the congregation was alerted to the progress of the service by his actions. When the wafer had been consecrated, he held it above his head, and likewise the chalice. At this, the holiest moment of the mass, men were expected to remove their headgear (as they did in the presence of a social superior), and it is likely that people tried to get a glimpse of the wafer and chalice – Christ's real body and blood, as the Church taught – so that they could receive his power and blessing. Windows, nowadays known as hagioscopes or squints, still visible in churches such as St Cleer and Germoe, were sometimes cut through the walls of side-chapels or transepts to extend the view to those parts. The priest alone consumed the wafer and wine, and if there were more than one priest present only the priest who celebrated mass ate and drank them. Substitutes took the place of communion for the congregation. One of these was the pax – a small disk of ivory or metal with a Christian symbol upon it. This was kissed by the priest at the altar after he had consecrated the wafer and chalice, and taken by the clerk to be kissed by the congregation. After mass had finished there was another ceremony. The priest came to the screen door and read in Latin the opening words of the Gospel of John: 'In the beginning was the Word'. The clerk sprinkled the congregation with holy water, and the priest blessed a loaf of bread and distributed it to the people. The loaf was provided by households in turn, and was merely blessed, not consecrated like the wafer. Parishioners received communion in church only at Easter, and then only if they were adults over the age of puberty. They came to the screen, probably in order of rank, knelt, and had a consecrated wafer put into their mouths with a sip of ordinary wine (the consecrated wine being considered too precious to give them in case it was spilt).

Parish worship, then, took a different form from that of most modern churches. It was not educational. Little attempt was made in it to teach parishioners about the Bible or Christian behaviour beyond the basic matters mentioned above. Rather worship was medicinal. It offered spiritual benefit, especially at mass when Christ became present, healing your sins and afflictions. The laity had a degree of freedom in what they did during mass, since they were not involved in saying the service and were physically removed from it. A gentleman or his wife might own a psalter, a breviary, or a missal, take it to church, and follow the priest exactly. John Urban of Southfleet (Kent), who came from Cornwall, bequeathed 'my missal' in 1420, and Katherine Arundell of Lanherne 'my psalter book' in 1479.[3] More commonly such people owned simpler kinds of prayer books known as primers and books of hours, which they read devoutly although the words were not those of the service. Parishioners who could not read or did not own books were recommended to say the three basic prayers in Latin, as in previous centuries, and rosaries (often mentioned in wills) were used to say them repetitively. Some of those who went to church were young, others were inattentive, and complaints were voiced about the disturbances caused by such people. If a church lacked much seating, it was easy for the congregation to stand, form groups, or walk about, as it chose. As benches and pews became common during the 15th and early 16th centuries, however, they restricted people's movements and encouraged them to act in similar ways. This development anticipated the Reformation when more deliberate attempts were made to make congregations behave in a uniform way by standing, sitting, or kneeling all together.

Every parish church contained holy objects. Christ himself was present in the form of a consecrated wafer placed in the pyx that hung above the high altar as a focus for devotion. That altar had relics of saints inside its structure. The rood screen carried the great image of Christ on the cross, and there were statues of the patron saint on the north side of the high altar and the Virgin Mary on the south side.[4] We have seen that a majority

---

1 Below, p. 107.
2 e.g. Creed and Duloe in 1411 (DRO, Chanter VIII, f. 323r; *Reg. Stafford*, 405), St Gluvias in 1501 (PROB 11/12, f 164v), Menheniot in 1509 (PROB 11/16, f. 184v), and an unspecified church in 1528 (BL, Harley 597, ff. 28r–29r). On the Camborne bead-roll material (CRO, PD/322/1, f. 53r–v), see N. Orme, 'Prayer and Education in Fifteenth-Century Camborne', *JRIC* (2006), 95–104.
3 Orme (ed.), *Cornish Wills*, 55, 93.
4 N. Orme, *English Church Dedications* (1996), 6–7.

FIG 25. *The 'sisters' of St Neot parish, one of the early Tudor guilds or companies of parishioners that helped raise money for the church's magnificent stained-glass windows.*

of the Cornish churches venerated a Brittonic saint, some of whom were thought to be buried locally and had tombs or shrines in their honour.[1] During the later Middle Ages, however, they had to compete with the universal saints of the Catholic Church and the popular saints of England. The images of these saints – especially Christopher, George, James, Katherine, Mary Magdalene, and Thomas Becket – made their way into parish churches as statuary beside altars, paintings on walls, and figures in window glass. A substantial minority of Cornish churches came to have patron saints from outside Cornwall – Andrew, Martin, Mary, Michael, Peter – and in others the Brittonic saint came to share the patronage with a more famous figure. Illogan was joined by Edmund at Illogan, Manac by Dunstan at Lanreath, while Cuby and Dilic each acquired Leonard as their colleague at Duloe and Landulph respectively.

Many of these images had organisations dedicated to supporting them. These were of three kinds: stores, companies, and guilds. Stores were simply funds in the form of money, sheep, cattle, or bees. The parish church itself had a store, often named after the patron saint, such as the 'store of St Ervan' or 'of St Mawgan', and there were stores belonging to the individual images. William Trenowyth, a peasant farmer of St Cleer in 1400, bequeathed two sheep to the store of St Mary in his parish church, and one each to the stores of the Holy Cross and St James.[2] A store had one or more wardens to look after the offerings made to its image and to pay for a light in front of it, but the supporters of the store did not necessarily form a society. A company possessed a stronger social framework, and there were three kinds of these although not every church may have had them all: the young men, the maidens, and the wives (Fig. 25). They reflected the fact that people were expected to attend church and contribute to its maintenance once they reached puberty. The young men and maidens were the unmarried in the parish, aged from the early teens up to about the mid twenties, when most people wed. The wives were the married women or widows. Each company raised money during the year through social events such as ales, through money collections (notably on Hock Monday and Tuesday, in the second week after Easter), or through keeping sheep or bees. This money was given to the maintenance of the church, and sometimes perhaps to an image or light supported by the members.

Guilds (also known as fraternities) were social

---

1 Above, pp. 16–17.

2 Orme (ed.), *Cornish Wills*, 42–3.

groups as well.¹ We have already noticed their first recorded appearance in Cornwall in 1278,² and they were very common indeed between the 14th and the early 16th centuries. Mentions survive of four guilds in the churches of Liskeard, Poughill, and South Petherwin, five at Stratton, eight at St Mary Magdalene (Launceston), and ten at Antony and Camborne, the latter suggesting that the smaller numbers may be selections rather than totals. Bodmin, one of the most populous parishes in Cornwall, may have had as many as 29.³ There must have been hundreds of parish guilds across the whole county, but little is known about their membership. Many may have been dominated by adult men in view of the formation of companies to cater for other social groups. Some guilds, especially in towns, were restricted to particular kinds of people. Launceston, for example, supported a guild of minstrels in 1440,⁴ while Bodmin, about thirty years later, had guilds of cordwainers (i.e. shoemakers), millers, and skinners jointly with glovers.⁵ Guilds like these were both craft guilds, regulating their members' work, and religious guilds, maintaining an image in a church or chapel and paying for prayers for dead members. People in a neighbourhood might also form a guild. In Bodmin there were guilds based in Bore Street, Fore Street, and Pole Street, while the rural chapel of Gwarnick in St Allen had a guild of supporters, doubtless those who lived nearby.⁶ A few guilds acquired enough resources to pay a priest to say masses regularly for their souls, as was the case at Davidstow, or to maintain an almshouse like the guilds of St Anthony and St George in Bodmin.⁷ Most guilds were humbler bodies, however, with small stores and modest social activities such as fund raising and an occasional feast or visit to church for a mass.

A Cornish church between 1300 and 1500 was a miniature of the Church as a whole. Visually it proclaimed its allegiance to Christ, both on the cross and presiding at Judgment Day, as well as to his mother and the saints. It was a church not only of the living but the dead, or at least the more important dead who were buried beneath its floors and named in its bead-roll. It was a mirror of society, with the clergy in the holiest part, the patron or other gentry in privileged places, and the congregation almost certainly arranged in social order, especially once seating was installed. It was a developing, not a static church, which underwent rebuilding and embraced new religious cults. During the later Middle Ages several Cornish parishes introduced chapels, images, or services in honour of the Name of Jesus, St Anne the mother of the Virgin, St Roche the patron of plague victims, St Syth the patroness of servants, keys, and lost objects, and the murdered King Henry VI.⁸ It was a church with several focuses, not one. Although the chancel was important, there was also the rood screen with its images; the aisles and chapels for additional masses; the nave for announcements, processions, and baptisms; the porch for services of introduction; and the tower for ringing bells to send messages from the church to the world. These subdivisions reflected the fact that the Catholic Church itself was complex and offered a good deal of choice. True, it demanded obedience to certain doctrines, duties, and modes of behaviour. But it also provided a range of options: various places in which to worship, an array of saints to venerate, and a huge assortment of good practices to follow and causes to support. We shall now proceed to explore some of these alternatives and how the people of Cornwall chose between them.

A warning should be signalled at this point. Describing how institutions work implies that they worked properly. This was not always the case with the Church in the Middle Ages. One has only to read the writings of Langland, Chaucer, and the Lollards in the 14th and 15th centuries to hear many allegations that the clergy were ignorant or negligent and the laity slack in their church attendance and religious duties. These allegations are themselves over-simplified, but they caution us against believing that the Middle Ages was simply an age of faith. We know of thefts of church property (like that at St Erth) and attacks on clergy.⁹ The Church courts of Exeter diocese have left no records from before the period of the Reformation, but the 'significations of excommunication' survive which the bishop sent to the king about the most obstinate offenders. These were people who had refused to submit to the authority of the courts, had been excommunicated, yet still remained defiant, and the king was asked to tell the sheriff to arrest and hold them until they complied. The charges against such people in Cornwall included fornication, slander, perjury and breach of contract, the misadministration of wills, failure to pay tithes or other dues, assaulting a rector, shedding blood in a church, and (in one case) pretending to be a priest.¹⁰ As for church attendance,

---

1 J. Mattingly, 'The Medieval Parish Guilds of Cornwall', *JRIC* new ser. 10/3 (1989), 290–329, and idem, 'Going A-Riding: Cornwall's late-medieval guilds revisited', *JRIC* (2005), 78–103.
2 Above, p. 43.
3 Mattingly, 'Medieval Parish Guilds', 311–12.
4 *Reg. Lacy*, ed. Dunstan, II, 197.
5 Wilkinson, 'Receipts and Expenses', 5–6.
6 Ibid.; Orme (ed.), *Cornish Wills*, 139.
7 L. S. Snell, *Documents towards a History of the Reformation in Cornwall*: vol. I, *The Chantry Certificates for Cornwall* (c.1953), 21–2; below, pp. 159–60.
8 N. Orme, *The Saints of Cornwall* (2000), 63–4, 141–2, 150–1, 225, 241–2; a further store of St Anne is mentioned at St Ive as early as 1387 (Orme (ed.), *Cornish Wills*, 41).
9 Above, pp. 42, 61.
10 TNA, C 85/71–84, covering the period 1264–1558. All the documents name the offenders but most do not identify their crimes. For the pretended priest, see C 85/77/16, and for the pollution of North Tamerton church, C 85/81/6.

Bishop Veysey of Exeter observed in 1523 that at Crediton, one of the major churches of the diocese, most local people scarcely attended mass four times a year.[1] One might observe that they probably went even then only because it was compulsory to make religious offerings at four major festivals. No census of church attendance exists in the periods with which this volume deals, and the surviving records tell us more about people who were devout and active than about those who were not.

CHAPELS

Parish churches and religious houses were not the only places of worship in the Middle Ages. By the late Anglo-Saxon period they were supplemented, in England generally and in Cornwall particularly, by chapels in the sense of free-standing buildings, often located a long way from the parish churches.[2] Some chapels were ancient religious places which failed to gain full parochial status or, perhaps, lost it in early times. These were often dedicated to a unique saint, like many parish churches,[3] and functioned as what was later known as chapels of ease. They served local communities who lived at a distance from the parish church, and some of them, like Advent and Germoe, were virtually parish churches with full-time chaplains, although they were legally under the control of a neighbouring parish church and its rector or vicar.

After the Norman Conquest evidence survives about other chapels. Some of these were built in or alongside the castles or houses of the nobility and gentry. Launceston Castle had one by about 1127,[4] and others are mentioned later in the castles of Restormel and Tintagel. Eventually they became common in Cornish manor houses like Cotehele, where the chapel can still be visited (Fig. 26). Numerous chapels of ease were founded during the 12th and 13th centuries to serve the towns and other new settlements that grew up in Cornwall. Boscastle, Camelford, Grampound, East and West Looe, Launceston, Mitchell, Penzance, and Wadebridge all had buildings of this kind. A further kind of chapel was the cult chapel, whose primary purpose was to maintain a cult of God or a saint. It did not restrict its ministry to a family or a neighbourhood, like the other two groups, but sought to draw in people from as widely as possible. Early examples of such chapels were St Michael's Mount and St Mary Vale in Cardinham, first documented in the 11th and 12th centuries respectively, although they were also monastic in character for parts of their history. Others

FIG 26. *The 15th-century domestic chapel of Cotehele House near Calstock. Inside the chapel retains a stained-glass east window and a rood screen.*

1 N. Orme, 'The Church in Crediton from Saint Boniface to the Reformation', in T. A. Reuter (ed.), *The Greatest Englishman: Essays on St Boniface and the Church at Crediton* (1980), 122.

2 On medieval chapels, see N. Orme, 'Church and Chapel', *Transactions of the Royal Hist. Soc.* 6th ser. 6 (1996), 75–102, and idem, 'The Other Parish Churches: Chapels in Late Medieval England', in C. Burgess (ed.), *Parish Churches in Late Medieval England* (2006), 78–94.

3 Above, p. 18; Orme, *Saints of Cornwall*, passim.

4 P. L. Hull (ed.), *The Cartulary of Launceston Priory*, DCRS new ser. 30 (1987), 17–18.

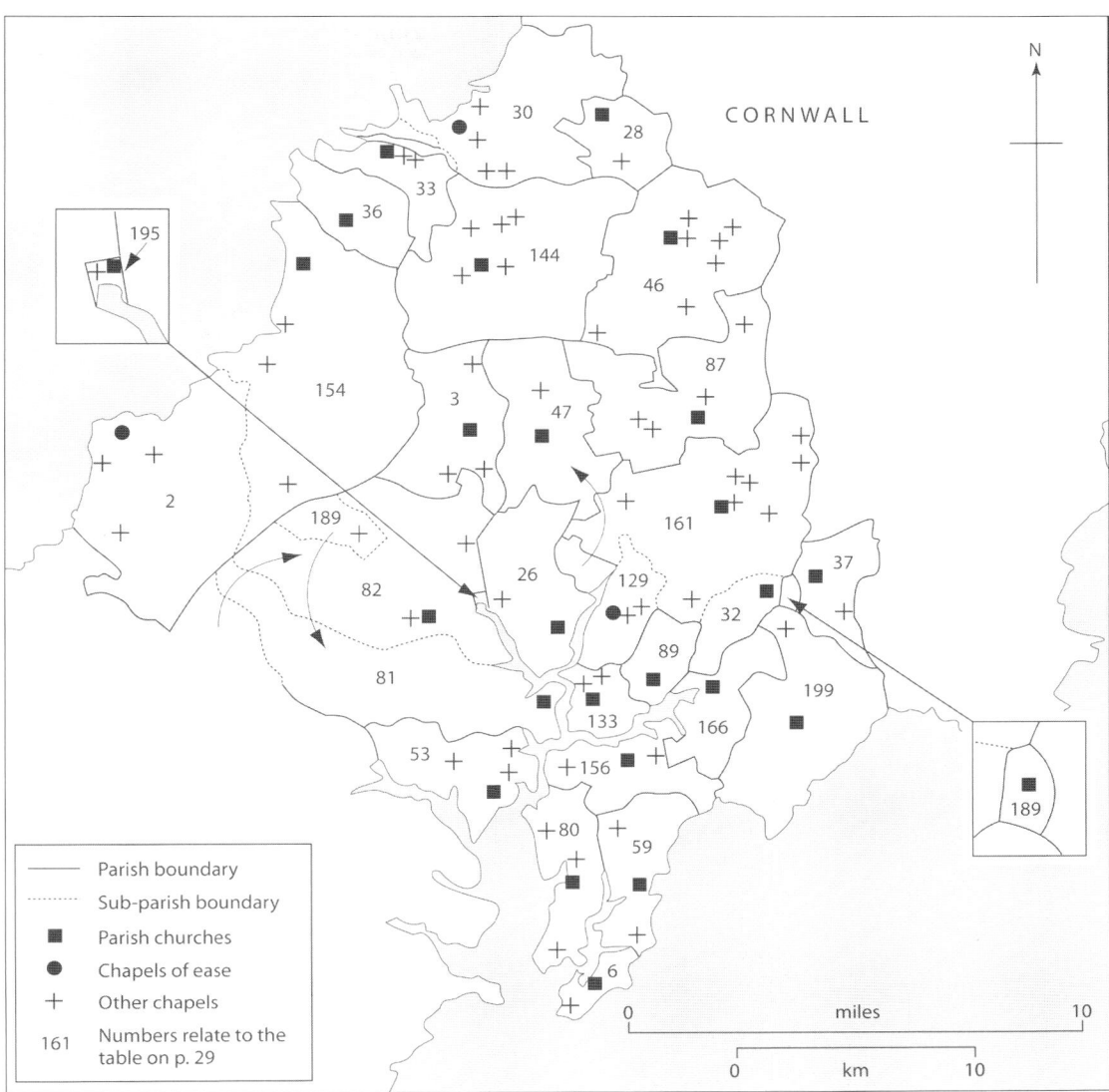

FIG 27. *Parishes and chapels in central Cornwall.*

were the chapels of St Mary in the Park at Liskeard, St Mary Magdalene at Cosawes in St Gluvias, St Saviour at Padstow and at Polruan in Lanteglos-by-Fowey, and most famously the chapel of the Trinity at St Day in Gwennap, first mentioned in 1269, which became an important centre of pilgrimage. Nearly all the post-Conquest chapels were dedicated to English or international saints, with one or two exceptions like the chapel of St Nectan in Newlyn East.

Until the 14th century references in documents to chapels in Cornwall occur only by chance. After 1308 this changes, thanks to the bishops of Exeter insisting on licensing new chapels and on recording the licences in their registers. Hundreds of such licences are recorded being granted to places or people in Cornwall and Devon but it is difficult to estimate from them how many chapels there were in either county.[1] Some grants were for an unspecified number of chapels, some chapels received more than one grant, and some grants may have escaped record, especially after 1455 when they cease to appear in the registers. Nevertheless the total was undoubtedly a large one (Fig. 27). Charles Henderson, who made a careful count of chapels in the 95 parishes of west Cornwall found evidence of 188, a number double that of the parish churches. Since the whole county contained about 170 such churches, this would suggest a Cornish total of at least 350 chapels, and one calculation has suggested as many as 650–700.[2] Devon was equally well endowed, if not more so. A survey of its 409 parishes has discovered

---

1 For the documents, see *Reg. Stapeldon*, 299–302; *Reg. Grandisson*, III, 1716–18; *Reg. Brantyngham*, II, 947–55; *Reg. Stafford*, 270–83; and *Reg. Lacy*, ed. Dunstan, passim.

2 J. H. Adams, 'The Mediaeval Chapels of Cornwall,' *JRIC* new ser. 3 (1957–60), 48–65.

about 1,300 chapels, over three times as many as the churches, and this does not include all the evidence supplied by place-names or archaeological remains which might well add to the total.[1]

Chapels, then, became ubiquitous features of the Cornish scene, urban and rural, inland and maritime, highland and lowland. The larger towns had several: Bodmin at least eight and Launceston about the same number. Padstow could boast about nine.[2] Smaller places, like those already mentioned, acquired one or two. Nor were chapels built only in populous places. Many were sited in isolated spots to which access was difficult, such as small islands. A voyager along the south coasts of Cornwall would have passed chapels on Looe Island, St Michael's Mount, St Clement's Island by Mousehole, and at least five on the Isles of Scilly. There were promontory chapels at St Ives, Padstow, and Polruan, possibly acting as marks for ships at sea. Inland hills had chapels, such as Carn Brea, Roche rock (Fig. 36), Michaelstow Beacon, and Rough Tor, and there were chapels hidden from view in woodland like the Cornish parks of Liskeard and Restormel, or in secluded valleys such as St Mary Vale in Cardinham and St Illick in St Endellion. The effect of such buildings, supplemented by crosses and wells, was to make the landscape yet more Christian than before.

Chapels in manor houses often formed part of the house. Cotehele chapel was entered from the ground floor but had a small high window inside communicating with the upper storey of the house, so that privileged people could watch the service from there. Cult chapels were usually oblong freestanding buildings no higher than a one-storey house (Figs. 28–9). Chapels of ease tended to be larger and some grew almost to the size of parish churches, with aisles, transepts, or towers (Fig. 28). Most chapels were probably divided internally by a screen as in a parish church, separating the outer 'antechapel' for the laity from the inner part with the altar where services took place. Few had resident clergy, and we should not envisage daily worship inside their walls. Instead formal services probably centred on an occasional mass performed by a visiting priest when he was able or was paid to do so, which might not happen very often. Bishop Lacy licensed services in the chapels of St John Baptist at Polapit Tamar in Werrington in 1447 and St Laurence in Lezant in 1450 solely on the feast-days of these saints.[3] Admittedly such conditions were not common in chapel licences but, even if bishops did not impose them, it may not have been easy to pay or procure a priest for frequent masses. Many small chapels were in remote places, and the fall in the

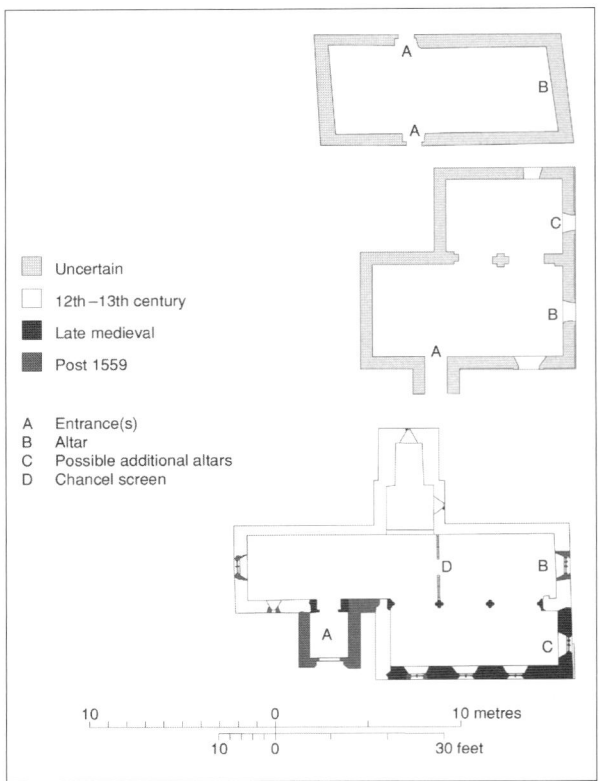

FIG 28. *Chapel plans, St Ia, Camborne (top); St Elide, Isles of Scilly (centre); St Enodoc, St Minver (bottom).*

number of clergy after the Black Death left a shortage of men for such work. Most worship in a small chapel may not have been formal or clergy-led. The building, perhaps, remained open (or was unlocked by arrangement) so that local people or passers-by could enter, light a candle, say a Paternoster, Ave Maria, and Credo, and ask for the saint's intercession. A chapel of this kind might be operated, for most of the year, by the laity for the laity. In this respect, as well as in their often rural locations and their tendency to draw people away from the parish churches, medieval chapels foreshadowed their Nonconformist successors, although their worship was Catholic in nature.

Chapels were only allowed to exist in subordination to the churches of the parishes where they lay. It was for this reason that bishops claimed the right to licence them and to set out the conditions under which they could function. In the case of domestic chapels, there seems to have been a liberal practice in granting licences. But that does not mean that such applications were not carefully scrutinised and, at least sometimes, discussed with other interested parties. A licence for a

---

1 J. James, 'The Medieval Chapels of Devon' (University of Exeter, unpublished MPhil thesis, 1997).

2 On Bodmin, see Wilkinson, 'Receipts and Expenses', 5–7; on Launceston, below, pp. 00–00; and on Padstow, C. G. Henderson, 'The Ecclesiastical History of the 109 Parishes of West Cornwall', *JRIC* new ser. 3 (1957–60), 376–9. The chapels of St Saviour and Trinity at Padstow were probably identical.

3 *Reg. Lacy*, ed. Dunstan, II, 389; III, 75.

domestic chapel at Binnerton in Crowan, dated 1415, stated that its terms were not to apply to the chapel of St Augustine nearby, an issue that could only have been raised by the vicar of the parish or the archdeacon.[1] Licences for domestic chapels in Cornwall usually mention the name of the grantee and sometimes, in a man's case, that of his wife. Occasionally their children are also named, but it is more usual for the licence to specify the children as a group and sometimes the servants as well. Some licences identify the place or places to which they apply, while others are general and allow the recipients to have a chapel or oratory in any of their houses. Some state that services may not be held on Sundays and festivals, implying that gentry, their families, and servants were expected to go to the parish church on such days, but most have no such proviso. One grant prohibits a chapel from having a bell, because it is not a parish church but 'only an oratory'.[2] There are also differences in whether the grant is made for a period of time, such as a year, or during the bishop's pleasure.

Chapels of ease were also subject to episcopal regulation of greater or lesser stringency. Ancient foundations that were virtually parish churches, like Gwithian or Mabe, existed by tradition rather than licence and had most of the features of parish churches. There was a full-time priest, a distinct territory, complete freedom of worship, and sometimes the right to baptise, marry, confess, and bury. The chapels of ease founded from about the 13th century onwards came into existence with the bishops' permission and were carefully limited in their powers. Their congregations had to pay tithes and offerings to the parish church and go there for baptisms, burials, and other rites. Sometimes services could not be held in the chapel on Sundays or festivals, since attendance was required at the parish church. Donations of money to the chapel belonged to the parish rector or vicar, and the chapel congregation was expected to pay for its upkeep and services on top of their financial obligations to the parish church. In England as a whole these restrictions often led to friction between the chapel community on the one hand and the parish church, its rector, and patron on the other. Attempts might be made by a chapel congregation to break its links with the parish church and establish its own independence. Such attempts were usually opposed by the bishop, who did his best to defend the parish churches. In 1434 Bishop Lacy instituted proceedings against certain men of Polruan for inciting a chaplain to bless the chapel of St Saviour, ask for prayers in its pulpit, distribute holy bread on Sundays, and make wills for sick people – privileges reserved to the vicar of Lanteglos-by-Fowey.[3]

The foundation and running of chapels varied according to type. Nobility and gentry provided and maintained them in their houses. Groups of local people built and cared for chapels of ease, and individual devotees or groups were responsible for cult chapels. One such group occurs in relation to the ancient chapel at Chapel Amble in St Kew, where Bishop Stafford licensed Nicholas and Emmot Helygan, a local gentleman and his wife, their two children, and eleven other named people, husbands and wives, to worship in 1405.[4] Later in the same century, between 1496 and 1501, Bishop Redman permitted a group of people to administer the chapel of St Anta at Chapel Ainger, on the sea coast of Lelant.[5] A third parish, Camborne, contained a number of outlying chapels: St Anne at Baripper, St Derwa at Menadarva, St Ia at Troon, St James at Treslothan, St Mary in the parish churchyard, and 'Gwynwala' – the latter apparently a chapel of St Winwaloe, perhaps at Kehelland. Each of these was operated by a guild that contributed money to the parish church, money that appears in the accounts of the churchwardens.[6] The Camborne accounts do not mention any guild officers, but these appear in another instance, the chapel of St Weras at Burlawn Eglos in St Breock. Here two 'store wardens' are mentioned, who would have been in charge of handling income and expenditure, and two 'ale wardens', who evidently looked after fundraising.[7]

It cost money to maintain a chapel, and this had to come from local gentry, the chapel congregation, or travellers and pilgrims. Many chapels secured indulgences from the bishop for those who contributed to their upkeep, but indulgences were so common that their impact may have been limited. The guild of the chapel of St Mary at Camborne transferred sums of between 10s. 10d. and 14s. 6d. per annum to the churchwardens between 1538 and 1543, St Derwa's chapel about 14s. a year, and the others amounts of between 3s. 9d. and 8s. 6d.[8] These sums must have excluded money spent on repairs and on costs of worship: indeed when the bishop approved the arrangements for St Anta's chapel in 1496–1501, he allowed its guild to keep all the offerings for this purpose as long as it rendered 6s. 8d. to the parish church.[9] The income of the Camborne chapels was possibly higher for this reason, at 10s., £1, or a little more each, but their financial activities were clearly small in scale.

---

1 *Reg. Stafford*, 271.
2 At Tremoddrett in Roche, 1242 (CRO, ME/595, /596 pp. 24–5).
3 *Reg. Lacy*, ed. Dunstan, I, 285–8.
4 *Reg. Stafford*, 276.
5 Orme, *Saints of Cornwall*, 65.
6 CRO, PD/322/1, ff. 1r–14r.
7 CRO, P/19/5/1, ff. 4r, 6r.
8 CRO, PD/322/1, ff. 1r–14r.
9 Orme, *Saints of Cornwall*, 65.

WELLS AND OTHER LANDSCAPE FEATURES

The Christianisation of the landscape which had made such progress before the Norman Conquest remained and even increased in the later middle ages. As well as churches and chapels it encompassed holy wells, crosses, and natural features given supernatural associations without alterations by human hands. Many wells in Cornwall today are reputed to be holy, but the antiquity of their reputation is often not traceable before the 19th century.[1] Those recorded in earlier times included wells lying near a parish church (Bodmin), by an outlying chapel (Gwinear), by a road (St Keyne), or in a remote place such as a cave (Holywell in Cubert). Some were defined with stonework, often in the form of a small well-house covering the spring, with a low doorway through which to reach the water. Other structures were larger and higher, including seats where people could sit to wash themselves, as at St Constantine in St Merryn parish.[2] The biggest surviving buildings, almost of chapel size, are those of St Cleer (Fig. 29) and Dupath in Callington. A further development was the provision of a chapel beside the well or incorporating it. This was the case at St Clether (Fig. 30), St Columb Major, Gwinear, St Issey, Madron, Merther, Padstow, and Chapel Euny in Sancreed parish.[3] Some Cornish saints were believed to have lived at the well or to have been martyred there

FIG 29. *The elaborate late medieval well-house at St Cleer. The vaulted granite building enabled bathing to be done in the water.*

---

1 M. and L. Quiller-Couch, *Ancient and Holy Wells of Cornwall* (1894); A. Lane-Davies, *Holy Wells of Cornwall* (1970); and J. Meyrick, *A Pilgrims Guide to the Holy Wells of Cornwall* (1982) – the latter valuable for including many sites but weaker on history.

2 Orme, *Saints of Cornwall*, 95.

3 Ibid., 89, 90, 92, 120, 137, 148, 169–71, 203, 216.

FIG 30. *The late-medieval chapel at St Clether, half a mile from the parish church. A typical small chapel building, it has an adjoining holy well from which water runs through the chapel itself.*

before their bodies were buried on the site of the parish church.[1] There were also at least one or two well chapels in Cornwall dedicated to international cult figures: Jesus in St Minver and apparently Our Lady at Lady Nant Well in Colan.[2]

Little is recorded about how Cornish holy wells were used in the Middle Ages, or by whom. They may have supplied water for church fonts, but this is not stated. They may have attracted offerings of money like the well of St Paternus in North Petherwin, where receipts are mentioned in the churchwardens' accounts of 1496–7.[3] Observers writing after the Reformation tell us that wells were visited by individuals or by groups of parishioners on certain days of the Church year: Lady Nant Well on Palm Sunday, Madron on Corpus Christi Day, and Chapel Euny (Sancreed) on New Year's Eve.[4] One motive for such visits was the hope of receiving healing. The reputation of St Cadoc's well for curing intestinal worms, already noted in about 1100, was still alive in 1478.[5] Altarnun well was remembered in about 1600 as having been used to give therapeutic treatment to the insane.[6] In the 18th century St Levan's well in St Levan was thought to be wholesome for the eyes and for toothache.[7] The chapel near Madron well drew visitors long after the Reformation, apparently for more than one kind of affliction. A sensational cure there in about 1638–40 involved a cripple who was able to resume normal life.[8] The other use of Cornish holy wells, at least in late Tudor, Stuart, and Hanoverian times, was for divination. The people of Colan threw their palm crosses into Lady Nant well on Palm Sunday and drew conclusions from whether these floated or sank,[9] while those who went to Gulval learnt whether those they loved were ill or well by pronouncing their names and watching how the water bubbled up.[10]

A variety of other minor holy sites existed in late-medieval Cornwall. The inscribed stones and standing crosses of earlier times continued to dot the landscape in the later middle ages, and additions to the crosses continued to be made. As before they were placed to mark roads and cross-roads, sometimes those leading to parish churches or holy wells, or to indicate the boundaries of glebes or parishes.[11] Some would have had religious functions. People passing crosses in other parts of England were sometimes prompted to say a prayer, such as the Paternoster.[12] In Cornwall Reginald Mertherderwa, rector of Creed, left money in his will in 1448 for nine stone crosses 'such as they have in those

1 Ibid., 90, 92, 137, 148, 169–70, 187, 228.
2 Ibid., 150–1, 180.
3 CRO, P/167/5/1, ff. 8v, 11v.
4 Orme, *Saints of Cornwall*, 120, 170, 180.
5 Ibid., 80–2; above, p. 15.
6 Orme, *Saints of Cornwall*, 206.
7 Ibid., 228.

8 Ibid., 170–1.
9 R. Carew, *Survey of Cornwall* (1602; repr. 2004), f. 144r–v; J. Norden, *Speculi Britanniae Pars: Cornwall* (1728), 66.
10 Orme, *Saints of Cornwall*, 135, 171, 180.
11 Above, pp. 14–15.
12 *The Merry Devill of Edmonton* (London, Arthur Johnson, 1608), sig. B1 verso.

parts of Cornwall' to be erected in his native parish of Camborne from Reskajeage in the north west to the parish church. They were to stand 'in the places where the bodies of the dead being carried to burial are laid down, for prayers to be offered there and for the alleviation of the bearers'. Mertherderwa originated from Menadarva near Reskajeage and evidently wished the crosses to mark the route from that district towards the parish church.[1] There was a saint's chair at St Mawes and another at St Michael's Mount, where the archangel was believed to have sat in a lofty part of the rock.[2] A possibly similar structure still exists at Germoe in the form of a small stone arcade in the churchyard containing three seats; its purpose is unknown. A holy tree is mentioned in the Life of St Gwinear, written in about 1300, as having grown on the site of the saint's martyrdom, probably at Roseworthy in Gwinear.[3] Other trees linked with saints are recorded by the Cornish writer Nicholas Roscarrock as having existed at St Breward and St Illick in the second half of the 16th century. The latter was cut down in that period.[4] We hear of paths associated with saints in the parishes of St Endellion and St Levan, ditches in Padstow, cliffs at St Agnes, a hill at Breage, and a rock at Camborne.[5] In this way the aetiology of parishes – the explanation of how their features originated – came to be closely linked with the cults of local saints.

THE RELIGION OF THE COMMUNITY

The Church involved people as communities and as individuals. All adults in a parish had the duty of attending church, keeping the Church's laws, and supporting the clergyman with tithes and offerings. They had to maintain the nave of the church, the furnishings of the whole building, and the books, ornaments, and materials required for services. Bishop Quinil's statutes of 1287 laid down that each parish church should have a store or fund for its maintenance, administered by wardens [*custodes*] who were to render an account of their stewardship once a year before the clergy and five or six of the parishioners. The account was to be recorded in writing and submitted to the archdeacon during his visitation.[6] During the 13th, 14th, and 15th centuries most English parishes acquired churchwardens to carry out this duty. There were normally two wardens, chosen to serve for a year, sometimes according to a rota which ensured that all major householders took their turn. Women, if widows, might therefore hold the office.

Although the statutes talk of written churchwardens' accounts, records of this kind do not survive in England until the late 14th century.[7] The oldest in Cornwall are some accounts of St Mary Magdalene (Launceston), kept as part of the borough records after 1461, and an account book relating to the rebuilding of Bodmin parish church in 1469–72.[8] Accounts are extant from eight other Cornish parishes before 1559, chiefly from the early 16th century and often with gaps in the sequence.[9] They are illuminating about how money was raised and what it was spent on. Parish income came chiefly from voluntary contributions: freewill offerings, fees for seats and for burials inside the church, sales of candles, and 'church ales' – the selling of ale to be drunk at home or in sociable gatherings of parishioners. Some parishes, by the later Middle Ages, held such gatherings in a specially built 'church house' close to the church, the best remaining example of which is at Poundstock (Fig. 31). Expenditure included the wages of the parish clerk and sometimes those of a sexton, the maintenance of the nave and church furnishings, and the materials used in services. By the early 16th century some larger and wealthier parish churches in England were imitating religious houses by financing the purchase of an organ, the payment of a director of music, and the expenses of a small choir of men and boys to sing a regular polyphonic mass or antiphon in honour of Jesus or of Our Lady, copying what was done in cathedrals, colleges, and larger monasteries.[10] In Cornwall the borough authorities of Bodmin paid several pounds in 1529–30 to bring 'organs' from London by sea to Fowey, by river boat to Lostwithiel, and thence by land. A further sum was spent on an organ case, and a donor gave two books of 'pricksong' or polyphony.[11]

The communal life of a parish was framed by the

---

1 H. E. Salter (ed.), *Registrum Cancellarii Oxoniensis 1434–1469*, vol. I, Oxford Hist. Soc. 93 (1932), 152; Orme (ed.), *Cornish Wills*, 77. It is not known if the crosses were ever erected.
2 Orme, *Saints of Cornwall*, 182, 194.
3 Ibid., 137.
4 N. Roscarrock, *Lives of the Saints: Cornwall and Devon*, ed. N. Orme, DCRS new ser. 35 (1992), 61, 79.
5 Orme, *Saints of Cornwall*, 60, 72, 107, 189, 215, 228.
6 Powicke and Cheney (ed.), *Councils & Synods II*, II, 1008.
7 On the subject in general, see J. C. Cox, *Churchwardens' Accounts* (1913), and for the earliest accounts in England, ibid., 15–52.
8 CRO, B/LAUS/148–172, extracted in R. and O. B. Peter, *The Histories of Launceston and Dunheved* (1885), 140–88; Wilkinson, 'Receipts and Expenses', pp. iii–vii, 1–49. Later Bodmin accounts are preserved in CRO, B/BOD/314/4–6, and the borough accounts (B/BOD/314/3) also include some parish church items.
9 BL, Add. MSS 32,243–4 (Stratton); CRO, P/7/5/1 (Antony); P/19/5/1 (St Breock), P/102/5/1 (Kilkhampton), P/144/5/2 (Menheniot), P/167/5/1 (North Petherwin), P/192/5/1 (Poughill), and P/322/1–3 (Camborne).
10 In the west of England such choirs are recorded at Ashburton, Cirencester, and Lyme Regis (N. Orme, *Education in the West of England, 1066–1548* (1976), 111, 130, 150).
11 CRO, B/BOD/314/3/22d; J. Wallis, *The Bodmin Register* (1827–38), 41.

FIG 31. The late medieval church house at Poundstock. Such houses were built by the parish community for church and social use.

calendar as well as by the upkeep of the church.[1] Religious observances changed as the seasons passed, and everyone was expected to follow these changes. The Church year, then as now, included a cycle of events based on the life of Christ and, to a greater extent than today, feast days of saints. Advent, the four weeks before Christmas, was a time of penitence and preparation; indeed the Church authorities tried to encourage people to treat it as a Lent in terms of fasting and going to confession. Christmas Day itself, although a great religious festival, had little to distinguish it apart from the celebration of a midnight mass to mark the birth of the Christ child, and its festivities chiefly took place at home, especially among the wealthy. Lent, beginning in February or March, had a wider impact. During its first few days all adults were required to attend confession in their parish church,[2] and there were set times for the people of Lelant to come for this purpose in 1429, a practice that may have been observed elsewhere.[3] During Lent, which lasted six weeks, all adults had to abstain from meat and dairy products. Palm Sunday, the Sunday before Easter, was the first of seven spring and summer days on which parish processions were held, in this case around the outside of the church. The following 'Holy Week', the last week of Lent, included penitential observances culminating on Good Friday when bells were not rung, mass was not celebrated, and people took part in 'creeping to the cross' – dragging themselves on their bellies across the church floor from the porch to the rood screen.

Easter Day was a communal festival, and adults received their annual holy communion on that day or the day before.[4] Fasting stopped and diets changed again. There were more parish processions on St Mark's Day (25 April), the Monday, Tuesday, and Wednesday of Rogation Week (the sixth week after Easter), Ascension Day (the Thursday of the same week), and Corpus Christi (the second Thursday after Pentecost). Rogation week was regarded as a holiday season, which may have stretched as far as Pentecost or Whit Sunday, ten days after Ascension Day, along with the Monday and Tuesday following Pentecost. Pentecost was the third great festival of the Church, commemorating the coming of the Holy Spirit to Christ's apostles and the foundation of the Church, and people were urged to go to confession beforehand, as before Easter and Christmas, but with what success is unknown. Pentecost completed the 'Christ cycle', but the whole year was punctuated by saints' days. Some of these were observed as popular festivals, notably the feast-day of the church's patron saint. Even local Cornish saints had feast-days, and Richard Carew recorded how, as late as around 1600, people entertained their friends from other parishes on such days.[5] Other days kept as holidays in England were probably observed in Cornwall too, such as those of St John Baptist, 24 June; St Thomas Becket, 7 July; and the days in late autumn, St Clement and St Katherine, 23 and 25 November, when children (particularly boys) dressed as priests or women and went round the parish singing, dancing,

---

1 On the calendar, see A. R. Wright, *British Calendar Customs: England*, ed. T. E. Lones, Folk-Lore Soc. 97, 102, 106 (1936–40); R. Hutton, *The Rise and Fall of Merry England: The Ritual Year 1400–1700* (1994); and idem, *The Stations of the Sun: A History of the Ritual Year in Britain* (1996).

2 N. Orme, 'Confession in a Fifteenth-Century Devon Parish', *TDA* 134 (2002), 57–68.

3 *Reg. Lacy*, ed. Dunstan, IV, 260, 265.

4 Parishioners at Lanteglos-by-Fowey are mentioned receiving communion on the evening before Easter in 1504×1515 (TNA, C 1/363/39).

5 Orme, *Saints of Cornwall*, 67, 69, 72, et passim; R. Carew, *The Survey of Cornwall*, ed. J. Chynoweth, N. Orme, and A. Walsham, DCRS new ser 47 (2004), f. 69r.

and asking for food or money. The choosing of a boy bishop to lead the church services on St Nicholas's Day (6 December) and Holy Innocents' Day (28 December) must have also been common, and these days were also accompanied by jollifications and begging, especially by boys.

The parish processions call for special consideration, particularly those of Rogation Week. During this week clergy and people travelled through the parish to its borders and sometimes met other processions by arrangement. With the procession went the church relics, banners, a cross, and a dragon. The parishioners of Perranzabuloe carried round the relics of St Piran by 1331 and did so up to the Reformation.[1] Processions with the relics of St Buryan are mentioned in 1478, although in this case no calendar date is mentioned and the journeys apparently extended beyond the parish.[2] The parishioners of St Hilary visited St Michael's Mount on one of the Rogation days from the 1460s onwards. Once they were accompanied by the people of Perranuthnoe, and the clergy of the Mount routinely provided refreshments for those who carried the relics and banners.[3] The fullest evidence may come from a chapel licence granted to the vicar of Davidstow in 1441. This permitted the vicar to hold worship on the Rogation days in three chapels in the parish (St Augustine, St Helen, and St Michael), suggesting that a procession was made to a different chapel each day, culminating in the celebration of mass inside them.[4]

Further accounts of processions come from Nicholas Roscarrock, writing after the Reformation but recalling the practices in use before that time. One of his anecdotes concerns the chapel of St Nectan in Newlyn East, a chapel sited on the parish boundary and used as a rendezvous by four local parishes in Rogation week. This chapel, Roscarrock tells us,

> had a yard belonginge unto it in which ther were foure stones on a little mount or hill at the Northwest corner, wher the crosses and reliques of St Piran, St Crantocke, St Cuthbert, [and] St Newlan were wont to be placed in the Rogation weeke, at which time they used to meete ther and had a sermond made to the people.[5]

In other words, the parishioners of four parishes – Crantock, Cubert, Newlyn East, and Perranzabuloe – used to journey there at Rogationtide with their crosses and relics. Some other chapels stood on or near parish boundaries, and although this may sometimes reflect the desire to serve an outlying community or to draw worshippers from other parishes, Rogation processions may have been a motive for their creation. From one point of view we might interpret such journeys as expressions of parochial independence, promoting solidarity and the maintenance of the borders. When more than one church was involved they may have signified the opposite: the hallowing of links between communities through prayer and fellowship.

THE RELIGION OF THE INDIVIDUAL

The chief events of everybody's life were blessed and validated by the Church. Birth continued to be followed by immediate baptism in one's parish church, at which one received godparents and a forename. Forenames, after about 1100, were generally similar to those throughout England, but local saints' names are sometimes found in Cornwall, such as Gerent, Petroc, and Rumon for boys and Dilecta, Minefred, and Sidwell for girls.[6] Each baptised person was expected to be confirmed by the bishop, a ceremony that could be done at any time after birth, and the employment of suffragan bishops may have made confirmation easier to obtain in the later Middle Ages than before or for a long time afterwards. At puberty adolescents were likely to make their first Lenten confessions and receive their first Easter communion, after which they were regarded as having the same responsibilities as adults. Men and women were recommended to marry at the church door, but it was not compulsory to do so and the Church recognised marriages made elsewhere, provided they could be authenticated by witnesses. When people were gravely ill or dying, the parish priest heard their confessions, anointed them with holy oil, and gave them communion. Death was followed by a funeral at the parish church, usually on the following day, and the dead were buried in their parish churchyard. Money would be spent on the funeral and often on the saying of mass for the departed person a week, a month, a year, or several years later. In 1387 the wife of a peasant farmer, John Keych of St Ive, whose goods were valued at under £13, claimed to have bestowed over £5 in this way.[7] The rich, as their wills show, envisaged much greater expenses.[8]

For many people these rites and duties were sufficient. Others, with greater piety, embraced their religion with more zeal. They might ask a priest to bless a new house or new well, and might decorate the house with religious art in the form of statuettes, paintings, or (after the late 15th century) printed engravings or texts. If wealthy they might have rosaries for saying prayers,

1 Orme, *Saints of Cornwall*, 221–2.
2 Below, p. 168.
3 Below, p. 236.
4 *Reg. Lacy*, ed. Dunstan, II, 336.

5 Roscarrock, *Lives of the Saints*, 94.
6 Orme, *Saints of Cornwall*, 106, 127, 187, 217, 227, 235.
7 Orme (ed.), *Cornish Wills*, 41.
8 Ibid., 32, 37, 188, 198.

rings or seals depicting Christ or the saints,[1] or religious books. Most such books were prayer-books, notably the short Latin versions of the daily services known as the 'hours of the Virgin Mary' contained in the 'primer' or 'book of hours'. These were read aloud by their owners, either as a private devotion or while attending mass in a church or chapel. One such book survives that appears to have belonged to a lay owner in Cornwall: a book of hours containing notes referring to the dedication festival of Fowey parish church and listing the births of seven children between 1512 and 1523.[2] Devotional books in French or English might also be used, including Lives of saints, works of instruction, and (especially in the later Middle Ages) mystical writings describing spiritual insights and experiences. Sir Ranulph Blanchminster (d. 1348), a wealthy knight of Binhamy in Week St Mary parish, owned at least four such books in Latin or French, all of which he bequeathed to women – a sign that this rank of society included readers of both sexes.[3]

In or outside the house there were many other religious practices with which individuals might choose to involve themselves, or not. These encompassed prayers, pilgrimages, the support of religious houses, donations to roads and bridges, and charity to the poor. In one exceptional case, Hugh Boscawen, a gentleman and widower, abandoned his young son and heir in 1446 to embrace the lonely silent life of a Carthusian monk at Witham Priory (Somerset).[4] Another activity, crusading, engaged few or no Cornish directly but still had its well-wishers. The Order of St John at Trebeigh raised over £18 per annum in Cornwall in 1338 for its activities in the Mediterranean, and went on soliciting gifts for the purpose until 1536.[5] By the later Middle Ages many good causes were backed by indulgences (Fig. 54).[6] Those who supported them with prayers, work, or money were offered remissions of penance, measured in days or years. Indulgences did not forgive one's sins, which could only be done by a priest after confession, but they replaced the penances due for sins. Bishops could issue indulgences of up to forty days worth of penance (a 'lent'), while the pope could grant multiple lents and whole years of penance, or cancel somebody's penance absolutely with what was known as a plenary indulgence. The latter was originally given only to those undertaking arduous tasks such as crusades or pilgrimages to Rome or Jerusalem, but by the 14th century it could be obtained from the papal administration for a modest fee on condition that it were used only once, generally on the deathbed. Roger and Joan Trewethenek, for example, were granted plenary indulgences in 1414, and Richard and Joan Trevanion in 1423.[7] A small collection of such documents survives that belonged to the Arundell family of Lanherne in the early 16th century. It includes four or five plenary grants made to the family by the pope or by officers empowered to act in his place, as well as a petition to the pope for a plenary indulgence from a group of gentry families including Sir John Arundell of Lanherne and his wife, John and Alice Arundell of Tolverne, John and Joan Reskymer, and William and Margaret Seyntmaur.[8]

People in Cornwall would have had the opportunity to gain a wide variety of other indulgences. Some could be obtained for saying prayers or visiting churches, like Bishop Stafford's indulgence for anyone who prayed for Lady Matilda Chyverston in St Issey church (1399) or Lacy's for pilgrims to St George's chapel near Truro (1435).[9] Others required monetary donations but an amount was never specified, and it was left to people's consciences and confessors to decide if they had given enough. When Exeter Cathedral was rebuilt in the 14th century, letters were sent to churches throughout the diocese each year, offering an indulgence to contributors.[10] Certain institutions like the hospital of St Mary Rounceval (London) made use of agents known as 'questors' or 'pardoners' to raise money throughout England. Two pardoners, William Marke and John Yong, are recorded living at Liskeard in 1507, of whom Marke gathered money in Cornwall and Devon for the Jesus Guild of St Paul's Cathedral (London) and doubtless for other organisations.[11] Most religious houses in Cornwall probably gained support in this way (Bodmin Priory acquired an indulgence of twenty days as early as 1177) but the majority of the recorded grants in the county date from after 1300 and were awarded to those who visited or helped parish churches, chapels, images, guilds, hospitals, bridges, or named individuals. Lacy (1419–55), for example, gave grants to institutions and projects such as Padstow parish church, the chapel of St Winnols in St Germans parish, the image of St Mary Magdalene in Creed church, the guild of minstrels in Launceston, the leper hospital of Helston, a road near

---

1 e.g. Truro, Royal Cornwall Museum, 1990.59 (ring depicting St Margaret, found at Linkinhorne 1990).
2 Bodleian, Dugdale 47, described in N. Orme, 'A Fifteenth-century Prayer-Book from Cornwall: MS NLW 22253A', *JRIC* new ser. II, 3/2 (1999), 69.
3 Below, p. 89.
4 Orme (ed.), *Cornish Wills*, 75–6, 216–17.
5 Below, pp. 275, 277.
6 On this subject in general, see R. N. Swanson, *Indulgences in Late Medieval England* (2007), and N. Orme, 'Indulgences in Medieval Cornwall', *JRIC* new ser. II, 1/2 (1992), 149–69.
7 *Cal. Papal Regs.* VI, 408; VII, 313.
8 Orme, 'Indulgences in Medieval Cornwall', 163.
9 *Reg. Stafford*, 316; *Reg. Lacy*, ed. Dunstan, I, 306.
10 A. M. Erskine (ed.), *The Accounts of the Fabric of Exeter Cathedral, 1279–1353*, 2 parts, DCRS new ser. 24, 26 (1981–3), I, 162, 172; II, 218, 228, 237, 247, 253.
11 CRO, B/LIS 171; Bodleian, Tanner 221, ff. 37v, 43v, 49r; references kindly supplied by Dr J. Mattingly and Dr E. A. New respectively.

Liskeard, Lostwithiel bridge, Marazion causeway, and the new quay at Newquay.[1] None has yet been found for a holy well. Indulgences for individual people fell into two categories. Some were granted for prayers for deceased members of the gentry and higher clergy like Clarice de Bolleit in St Buryan church, Matilda Chyverston of St Issey, and John Roger, prior of Tywardreath.[2] Others were issued for donations to needy people, such as a man whose house and goods had been burnt by fire and a wounded soldier burdened with a wife and children.[3]

Hardly anything can now be said about the spirituality of individual Cornish men and women in the later Middle Ages, except that it must have varied along with their opinions and resources. Wills hint at these, although only about 120 survive from before the Reformation with significant information about Cornwall, mostly of men of substantial wealth.[4] William Trenowyth of St Cleer, whose bequests to the stores in his parish church in 1400 have been mentioned, was probably typical of peasant farmers in chiefly supporting his parish church and its images, although he was aware of the friars of Bodmin, Plymouth, and Truro to whom he left small donations.[5] James Lannargh, a minor gentleman of Sithney parish, making his will in 1458, had wider horizons. He made bequests not only to his own church but to churches and chapels in the surrounding countryside: the relics of the Holy Cross at St Buryan and Grade, the image of St Mary at Constantine, the church of Germoe, and the chapels of Bonallack and St Degaman. He also left token sums of money, as many Cornish people did, to the three major shrines in the county: the Holy Trinity at St Day, St Michael at the Mount, and St Piran at Perranzabuloe.[6] Finally the will of Thomas Killigrew of Penryn, 1501, demonstrates the more extensive contacts and interests of the richer gentry. Not only did he remember all three great shrines and his parish church, but Glasney College, four other parish churches, three chapels, two friaries, and three hospitals. His bequests carried his name to be prayed for and remembered over most of the county.[7]

PILGRIMAGE

Pilgrimage offered another wide range of choices. The majority of journeys to holy places were local ones, because such journeys best suited everyday life. Each religious house, parish church, chapel, and some wells had one or more festivals during the year relating to the patron saint, the dedication of the building by a bishop, or the images or altars inside. Such days were likely to attract visitors from the neighbourhood to hear mass, receive the benefit of a small indulgence, and take part in social festivities. Beyond this certain religious sites had a greater reputation for sanctity, embodied in holy relics, images, or wells (Fig. 32). Several of the religious houses owned relics of saints, including Bodmin, St Carroc, St Germans, Launceston, St Michael's Mount, and Minster.[8] The Mount's relics, about which we know most, comprised some milk of the Virgin, a portion of her girdle, stones from the Holy Sepulchre, and bones of SS Agapitus, 'Apolina', Felix, and Mansuetus.[9] Parish churches and chapels also boasted relics of saints. Some were the remains of the local Brittonic saint,[10] notably those of St Piran at Perranzabuloe. Its church claimed to have a shrine containing the saint's bones and a reliquary enclosing his head; in 1433 Sir John Arundell of Lanherne bequeathed 40s. to improve the reliquary.[11] Others acquired important relics of Christ, Mary, or some other well-known saint which gave them fame, such as the fragments of the Holy Cross already mentioned.

No one in Cornwall was canonised as a saint between the Norman Conquest and the Reformation, but one cult sprang up around a human body after the death of Richard Bovyle, rector of Whitstone, in the early spring of 1359. Local opinion seems to have been divided as to whether he was murdered or committed suicide, but his body was treated with little respect and received an inferior burial either in the churchyard or in unconsecrated ground. Shortly afterwards pilgrims began to frequent the burial-place and miracles were claimed. The rector was reburied in the parish church, and pilgrims continued to visit his grave for the next two and a half years. By August 1361 Bishop Grandisson had heard of the cult, with evident disapproval. He forbade the veneration of Bovyle until the Church should permit it, and ordered an enquiry into the miracles. A jury of six local clergy and six laymen duly forwarded to the bishop a list of ten people allegedly cured at the rector's grave. One had been deranged, three blind, and six crippled. They had come from north Cornwall, north Devon, and in one case Plympton in south-west Devon. Five were women, three men, and one a child. None was of gentry rank or a cleric, and they give the impression of being, at best, burgesses, yeomen

---

1 Orme, 'Indulgences in Medieval Cornwall', 162–9.
2 Ibid., 163.
3 Ibid., 162–3.
4 Orme (ed.), *Cornish Wills*, passim.
5 Ibid., 42–3.
6 Ibid., 82–3.
7 Ibid., 110–12.
8 Orme, *Saints of Cornwall*, 86, 124, 128, 190, 215–16.
9 Below, p. 238.
10 Orme, *Saints of Cornwall*, 69, 72, 111, 113, 114, 119, 129, 137, 144, 147, 155, 173, 190, 196, 202, 207, 221, 236, 255.
11 *Reg. Lacy*, ed. Dunstan, IV, 20–2.

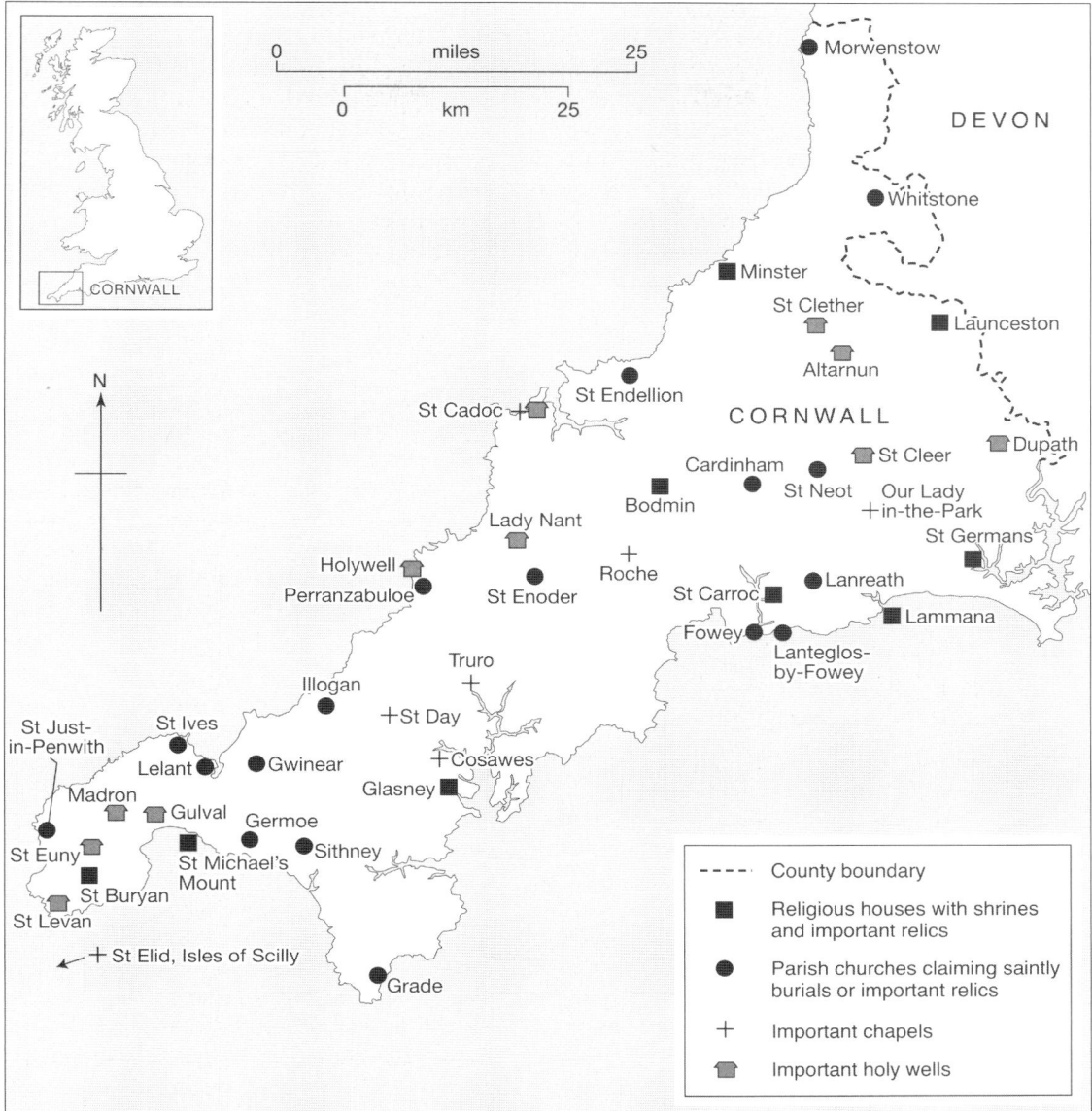

FIG 32. *Cult centres in Cornwall, 1100–1550.*

farmers, craftsmen, or inferior folk. One man is described as being a smith. The evidence of the miracles was reported to the bishop and copied into his register, but nothing more is heard of the cult. The bishop may have been unconvinced and may have maintained his embargo. Grandisson was hostile to enthusiasm of this kind, and had already acted to suppress or discourage popular cults in Exeter and north Devon.[1]

All churches supplemented their relics with holy images: statues or paintings. These were especially popular in the later Middle Ages because they were easier to acquire than relics, and some were regarded as equally holy. The Virgin Mary was universally popular and many not only had her statue by the high altar but a Lady chapel solely in her honour. Visitors are recorded making offerings to her image in the Bodmin Priory, and probably did so in the Lady chapel at the Mount.[2] She was also worshipped in free-standing chapels, two in particular. One was the chapel of Our Lady in the Park near Liskeard, a foundation already in existence in the early 14th century. John Leland, the Tudor topographer, described it in 1542 as having been a place 'of great pilgrimage', and its fame spread far enough for a wealthy tradesman from as Bury St Edmunds (Suffolk) to leave money in 1509 for a priest to travel there on his behalf.[3] Further west Mary had

---

1 N. Orme, 'Bishop Grandisson and Popular Religion', *TDA* 124 (1992), 107–18. The surname comes from the north of England.

2 Below, pp. 144, 235.

3 J. Leland, *Itinerary*, ed. L. Toulmin Smith (1907–10), I, 208; Orme (ed.), *Cornish Wills*, 266 and entries indexed on 272.

an important shrine at the chapel of St Mary of the Portal outside Truro, first mentioned in 1420, which possessed her image as well as a priest to say services and a bead-roll of benefactors.[1] Other places of saint veneration, probably also centred on images, included the altar of St John Baptist in Bodmin parish church, to which the pope gave a large indulgence of three years and three 'lents' of forty days in 1476,[2] and the chapel of St Mary Magdalene at Cosawes, a place that seems to have had more than a local reputation.[3]

The two principal places of pilgrimage in medieval Cornwall also featured images. These were the chapel of the Holy Trinity at St Day in Gwennap, and the priory (later the chapel) of St Michael's Mount. The chapel of St Day is first mentioned in 1269 and contained an image of the Trinity, whose form has not been recorded. It received bequests in many Cornish wills and the 16th-century geographer John Norden wrote in about 1604 that 'men and women came in times past from far in pilgrimage' to go there.[4] Some of this pilgrim traffic must have come from St Day's location on the main route to the Mount, so that both places could be visited on a single journey. The Mount was an important pilgrimage destination by at least 1262, when three miracles are recorded there, attributed to the intercession of the Archangel Michael.[5] All involved women: one from Gulval close by, a second from Glastonbury (Somerset), and a third from Hereford or its vicinity, indicating that the Mount's reputation had spread widely. By the late 14th century, when the cartulary of the Mount's possessions was compiled, it included a charter attributed to Bishop Leofric of Exeter, stating that he had been commanded by Pope Gregory VII to grant visitors and contributors to the church remission of one third of all their penance.[6] The document was an invention, but its promise (the same remission that was available at Compostella in Spain) probably helped encourage pilgrimage.

In about 1400 the Mount adopted the legend, hitherto that of its mother house, Mont St Michel in France, that its church had been founded at Michael's direction and that the archangel had manifested himself there – one of only three places on earth where this had happened.[7] When William Worcester visited the church in 1478, he was told of the three manifestations (including the one at the Mount) and he transcribed the text of the Leofric charter, apparently from a copy displayed in the church.[8] The Mount had a strong appeal to the Cornish in the 15th and early 16th centuries, and most surviving wills from the county made a small donation to it. Anecdotal evidence of pilgrims coming from outside Cornwall includes several bishops of Exeter, John Peeche – a leading London merchant (1359), John Jerrard of Netherbury (Dorset) (mid or late 15th century), and Thomas Clerk of Ware (Herts.) (1476). William Worcester made the journey from Norwich, gentlemen servants from Syon Abbey (Middx.) in 1517, and friars from Nottingham in 1521.[9] Other people made the journey by proxy. A Bedfordshire knight, Sir Gerard Braybrook, and the Cornish archbishop of Dublin, Michael Tregury, both stipulated in their wills that people should go on their behalf.[10] The Mount is one of the few places in Cornwall for which there are records of the amount of money and goods donated to the shrine. In 1454 these totalled over £36, apparently falling to between £17 and £22 per annum in the 1460s before rising again to nearly £44 in 1517 and £38 in 1519. Most of the donations were made in coin but some took the form of barley or fish.[11] Altogether the Mount was the major shrine of Cornwall and the chief one in the county to feature on the national 'shopping list' of shrines, albeit with a modest place in the latter respect. For English people it may have had the attraction that Land's End has today, as apparently the furthest western point to which one could travel.

There was a further dimension of pilgrimage: the making of journeys by Cornish people to shrines in the outside world. This can only be illustrated from scattered references that fail to do justice to the numbers of journeys and the variety of people who would have made them. Agnes, a widow of Cornwall, visited the shrine of Thomas Becket at Canterbury barefoot and wearing linen clothes in the late 12th century. Her prayers to the saint caused her stepson to restore the dower property that he had taken from her.[12] There must have been many more such pilgrimages to Canterbury in later times. Some Cornish people in the early Tudor period travelled to Windsor to venerate the tomb of King Henry VI. One of the priests of St Michael's Mount was healed of a fever there in 1484–5, and a sympathiser with the Reformation expressed his disapproval of the crowds of pilgrims from Devon and Cornwall who came to the tomb in the 1530s with offerings of candles and wax images.[13]

Further afield there were those who set out for the three great international shrines of St James at Compostella, the apostles Peter and Paul at Rome, and Christ himself at Jerusalem. Compostella was the nearest of these, a not-too-arduous passage by sea, and licenses were granted to Cornish mariners during the

---

1 Orme, *Saints of Cornwall*, 180.
2 *Cal. Papal Regs.* XIII(2), 494.
3 Orme, *Saints of Cornwall*, 176.
4 Ibid., 246.
5 Below, p. 232.
6 P. L. Hull (ed.), *The Cartulary of St Michael's Mount*, DCRS new ser. 5 (1962), xiv–xvi, 2–3.
7 N. Orme, 'St Michael and his Mount', *JRIC* 10/1 (1986–7),

35–6, and below, p. 257.
8 W. Worcester, *Itineraries*, ed. J. H. Harvey (1969), 100–1.
9 Below, pp. 236–7.
10 *Reg. Chichele, Canterbury*, II, 411; Orme (ed.), *Cornish Wills*, 90.
11 Below, p. 236.
12 J. C. Robertson (ed.), *Materials for the History of Thomas Becket* (RS, 1875–85), II, 248.
13 Orme, *Saints of Cornwall*, 142.

14th and 15th centuries to transport pilgrims there.[1] In 1434, for example, seven ships from Falmouth, Fowey, Landulph, St Michael's Mount, Penzance, and Saltash were allowed to take passengers on the journey in groups of 25–60.[2] The variety of places shows that, contrary to modern belief, there was no 'pilgrim's way' through Cornwall to a particular port; in any case pilgrims used ordinary roads, on which they were a small part of the traffic. A few names survive of Cornish people who went to Compostella or planned to do so. Among the gentry, for example, Thomas Tregoz intended to go in 1318, Sir Ote Bodrugan in 1324, and John Mohun of Lanteglos-by-Fowey in 1507.[3] A 15th-century register of documents associated with Launceston Priory includes a list of the saints buried at Compostella and of the indulgences available there.[4] Further afield the vicar of St Erth got leave of absence to visit Rome in 1334, the vicar of St Cleer likewise in 1437, and documents survive from the priories of Launceston and Tywardreath allowing members of these houses to do the same.[5] John Hoggs, a poor scholar of Camelford, is recorded visiting the city in 1505.[6]

The most exacting pilgrimage was to Jerusalem because of its distance, danger, and expense. In the 16th century it was believed that a knight of the Whalesborough family had visited the Holy Land a long time before, and had brought back the pieces of the Holy Cross that were venerated at St Buryan and Grade.[7] In 1331 Ote Bodrugan tried to cap his Compostella pilgrimage with one to Jerusalem, but he died on the way and was buried at Montpellier in France.[8] Another Cornish gentleman, John Dabernon of Calstock, took the safer precaution of leaving money in his will for a man to make the journey for him.[9] The sum was a large one, £26 13s. 4d., reflecting the financial and personal cost involved by the journey. References like these show that Jerusalem had a place in the minds of some Cornish people, and it is not unlikely that a few of them managed to get there.

EDUCATION, LITERACY, AND LITERATURE

Christians are a 'people of the book', and medieval Christianity (for all its visual imagery) made extensive use of education, literacy, and literature. Clergy and parish clerks had to be able to read and sing Latin, and preferably to understand what it meant. Schools came into existence to teach boys who might become clergy or might remain as laity. Wealthy lay people like the gentry, the merchant class, and eventually the prosperous yeomen farmers of the countryside valued school education. It gave them the skills to keep accounts, send letters, and read books: prayer books, practical treatises, and recreational literature. By modern standards, medieval schooling was limited in two ways. It was largely confined to boys and it was not generally free. Schools taught Latin which boys needed to know for careers as clergy or literate laymen. Teachers charged fees and lived from the proceeds, so that the pupils in their classes were those whose parents or patrons could pay for the privilege. Girls from wealthier families also learnt to read, but this generally happened at home and to a more limited extent. Their knowledge of Latin was usually confined to recognising and pronouncing the words of Latin prayer books rather than fully understanding them, and they were more fluent in reading French or English.[10]

The system of education in England is better recorded in the later Middle Ages than in earlier times. Most boys who went to school probably started at around the age of seven. They began by learning to read the Latin alphabet, pronounce Latin words, and sing them to plainsong. This might be done in an elementary school, or in the junior branch of a grammar school. The 15th-century Cornish play *Bewnans Meriasek*, written in or for the parish of Camborne, depicts a class of children learning the alphabet, a scene suggesting that elementary education was familiar even in the Cornish-speaking areas of the county.[11] Boys able to do so progressed from reading and song to grammar, the study of how to read, understand, write, and speak Latin; a study that took a few years to complete and usually took place in a grammar school. Schools of this kind existed in most English towns by the later Middle Ages, but we know little about them in Cornwall. Launceston appears to

---

1 Listed in C. M. Storrs, *Jacobean Pilgrims from England to St. James of Compostella* (1994, repr. 1998), 173–82.

2 TNA, C 76/116, mm. 9–14, printed in T. Rymer, *Foedera* (1704–35), X, 567–82.

3 *Cal. Pat.* 1317–21, 119, 556, 565; 1321–4, 391, 399; Orme (ed.), *Cornish Wills*, 128.

4 Bodleian, Tanner 196, pp. 227–9.

5 *Reg. Grandisson*, II, 741; *Reg. Lacy*, ed. Dunstan, II, 44; Bodleian, Tanner 196, f. 125r (model letter of permission for a canon, mid 15th century); CRO, ART/5/10 (permission for a monk in 1518).

6 W. C. Trevelyan, 'Names of Pilgrims from England to Rome', *Collectanea Topographica et Genealogica* 5 (1838), 69.

7 BL, Harley 2252, ff. 50v–51v; H. Jenner and T. Taylor, 'The Legend of the Church of the Holy Cross in Cornwall', *JRIC* 20 (1915–21), 295–309.

8 *Cal. Pat.* 1330–4, 69; P. L. Hull, 'Thomas Chiverton's Book of Obits', *DCNQ* 33/6 (1976), 190.

9 Orme (ed.), *Cornish Wills*, 32.

10 N. Orme, *Medieval Schools* (2006), passim.

11 N. Orme, 'Education in the Cornish Play *Beunans Meriasek*', *Cambridge Medieval Celtic Studies* 25 (1993), 1–13.

have had one by the mid 14th century, Bodmin by about 1470, and Penryn and Saltash by the 1540s.¹ From the 1380s onwards wealthy people in England endowed grammar schools to provide free schooling, but Cornwall lagged behind in this respect until Thomasine Percival, the Cornish widow of a lord mayor of London, founded one at Week St Mary in 1506–8.² Cornish pupils of grammar are likely to have studied the standard texts and topics common in the rest of England and, in many cases, in western Europe. One former pupil, John Waryn, rector of Menheniot in 1426, possessed the Latin grammar *Memoriale Juniorum* by Thomas Hanney, the Latin dictionary of Papias, and Isidore of Seville's *Etymologies*.³ Another, Reginald Mertherderwa, rector of Creed in 1448, owned copies of Alexander of Ville-Dieu's *Doctrinale* and Evrard of Béthune's *Grecismus*, two popular school grammars both in Latin verse.⁴ All these books were widely used in classrooms.⁵

Reading by lay people in England is recorded as early as Anglo-Saxon times, and we have seen how, by the end of the 13th century, it was becoming fashionable for the wealthy to own prayer-books such as psalters and books of hours. Words had been carved on stones for people to read ever since the Roman times, and tomb inscriptions were common in churches by the later Middle Ages. Sometimes longer pieces of writing were displayed. Worcester read the indulgence of St Michael's Mount on his visit in 1478, apparently in some public format, and took notes from a rhymed history of Glasney College from a board exhibited there.⁶ Inscriptions and writings in churches, like prayers, were mostly in Latin which was felt to convey the dignity and orthodoxy proper for such places. Latin was used as late as the early Tudor period for the captions in the windows of St Neot: *Hic Dominus fecit Evam de Adam* ('Here the Lord made Eve from Adam').⁷ Only very gradually did some inscriptions use languages that would reach out to non-Latin readers. A few tombs were inscribed in French during the 13th and 14th centuries, like that of Clarice of Bolleit at St Buryan.⁸ English made its first recorded appearance in a Cornish church on the monumental brass of Nicholas Aysshton, a royal judge who was buried in Callington church in 1465, and its use became common on tombs in the early 16th century.⁹ At St Kew the early-Tudor window depicting the Passion of Christ abandoned Latin for its subtitles and used phrases in English dialect (Fig. 33). 'Here owr Lord rydeth ynto Jherusalem.' 'Here a [i.e. he] prayyth to the Fader.' 'Here [he] ys ybrot byfore Pilat.'

Latin writings by medieval Cornishmen survive on a range of topics. We have already encountered scholars who wrote on grammar, prophecy, visions, logic, and academic theology, as well as producing poetry.¹⁰ Such writing generally took place outside the county, however. Far fewer literary works can be shown to have originated locally, chiefly Lives of saints.¹¹ The 11th- and 12th-century Lives of St Petroc, probably written at Bodmin, were followed by a Life of St Piran composed in Cornwall or at Exeter Cathedral during the 12th or 13th centuries.¹² Altarnun church possessed a lost Life of its saint, Nonn or Nonnita, by 1281,¹³ and a Life of Gwinear was written in about 1300 by a Breton cleric named Anselm. He was so well informed about the parish of Gwinear that he must have visited it or have used an earlier work on the subject from Cornwall.¹⁴ In 1330 Grandisson complained about the lack of knowledge of the county's saints and ordered that such written Lives as survived should be copied for posterity.¹⁵ Whether or not because of this command, we hear of some more works of this kind later on. A Life of Paternus was written or copied at North Petherwin in 1510–11,¹⁶ and when John Leland toured Cornwall in 1542, collecting antiquities, he found and made notes from Lives of Breage and Ia, notes that imply the existence of further Lives of Gwinear and of Elwen, the saint of a chapel in Sithney parish.¹⁷

The wide use of French in England for speaking, reading, and writing from the mid 12th century onwards also affected Cornwall, as we have seen from tomb inscriptions. This was particularly so in the writing of documents, such as letters, deeds, and financial accounts, and the records of the Arundells of Lanherne contain such documents until as late as 1409.¹⁸ Many larger works of literature or instruction came to England from France or were written in England in French, and Cornwall figures in romantic

---

1 Orme, *Education in the West of England*, 100–1, 111–14, 148–50, 167–8. On Bodmin, see also Wilkinson, 'Receipts and Expenses', 47, and CRO, B/BOD314/3/42d – a reference to a schoolmaster in 1524–5.
2 Orme, *Education in the West of England*, 173–82.
3 Orme (ed.), *Cornish Wills*, 61.
4 Ibid., 78.
5 Orme, *Medieval Schools*, 86–127.
6 Worcester, *Itineraries*, ed. Harvey, 100–1, 104–5. For a text displayed in St Columb Major church, see below, p. 172. The four lines of Latin verse preserved on a later board in St Neot church may also date from the later Middle Ages.
7 BL, Egerton 2657, f. 87r–v.
8 Other tombs with inscriptions in French survive at Bodmin, St Breock, and Little Petherick.
9 Dunkin, *Monumental Brasses of Cornwall*, 16–18.
10 Above, pp. 35–7.
11 In addition Geoffrey of Monmouth shows a knowledge of Cornwall in his *History of the Kings of Britain*, and had probably visited it (O. J. Padel, 'Geoffrey of Monmouth and Cornwall', *Cambridge Medieval Celtic Studies*, 8 (1984), 1–28.
12 Orme, *Saints of Cornwall*, 214–15, 220–1.
13 Ibid., 205.
14 Ibid., 136–7.
15 *Reg. Grandisson*, I, 585.
16 Orme, *Saints of Cornwall*, 211.
17 Ibid., 72, 112, 137, 144–5.
18 CRO, O. J. Padel and L. McCann, 'Catalogue of Arundell Deeds', passim.

FIG 33. *Jesus washing Peter's feet, from the early Tudor Passion window in St Kew church. St John is on the left, holding a book. Each scene from the Passion has a sub-title in English.*

stories, notably the 12th-century *Tristan* by Beroul and the 13th-century *Roman de Silence* by Heldris de Cornuälle, the former of which shows some acquaintance with the county.[1] The chief piece of evidence about the reading of works in French by the Cornish relates to the six books named in Sir Ranulph Blanchminster's will of 1348, which are typical of the kinds of writings owned and read by wealthy men and women of that period. Two were secular works – *Brut* (a chronicle history of Britain) and a volume of romances. Four were religious texts: a psalter, a book of Sunday gospels, the *Apocalypse* (a version of the Biblical 'Book of Revelation'), and Peter of Peckham's theological handbook *Lumiere as Lais* ('a light for lay people'). All six books were probably in French, although the psalter and gospels could have been in Latin.[2] Meanwhile the reading and writing of English had never entirely stopped in England, and after about the time of the Black Death in 1348–9 it began to overtake French in terms of numbers of works produced, the copies made of them, and the people who read them.

Two Cornishmen played leading parts in this process. One, John Bryan (more often known today

---

1 Beroul, *The Romance of Tristran*, ed. A. Ewert, vol ii (1970), 32–3, discussed by O. J. Padel, 'The Cornish Background of the Tristan Stories', *Cambridge Medieval Celtic Studies*, 1 (1981), 53–81;
Heldris, *Le Roman de Silence*, ed. L. Thorpe (1972), 15–17. Heldris wrote in France, and the significance of his surname is not clear.
2 Orme (ed.), *Cornish Wills*, 27–8.

as John Cornwall) was a foremost teacher of Latin in Oxford until his death in 1349. He was credited with abandoning a custom by which boys were taught Latin in French and with speeding up the pace at which they learnt by teaching them in English.[1] This judgment is probably an exaggeration, since some medieval schoolmasters are likely to have taught Latin in English long before Cornwall, but Cornwall certainly composed a grammatical treatise in Latin containing material in English, one of the first of its kind to survive since the Norman Conquest. True, the material consisted only of a few illustrative sentences, but it anticipated the production of Latin grammars for schools written wholly in English, which was in train by about 1400. The other outstanding Cornish contributor to the development of English was John Trevisa, born in about 1340, probably in the parish of St Enoder. Trevisa studied arts and theology at Oxford, was ordained as a priest, and ended his life in 1402 as vicar of Berkeley (Gloucs.).[2] Thomas, Lord Berkeley, the local magnate, was interested in reading the standard Latin handbooks of the day, and commissioned Trevisa and other writers to turn them into English for his convenience. Trevisa undertook the translation of the chief history of the world that was read in England, the *Polychronicon* by Ranulf Higden, and one of the major medieval encyclopaedias, *On the Properties of Things* by Bartholomew the Englishman.

Trevisa took the English language seriously, and wrote a treatise advocating its use for translations, even of religious works. He was also proud of being Cornish. It was he who attributed to his fellow countryman, John Cornwall, the enhanced use of English in schools,[3] and he intervened three times in the *Polychronicon* to correct or add information about his native county. His translations circulated widely, first in manuscript copies and later in printed editions. During the 15th century readers and writers in Cornwall must have been using English on a wide scale, particularly in the eastern English-speaking part of the county. The best evidence for this comes from a damaged manuscript miscellany compiled by a canon of Bodmin named John Bowyer in about the 1470s or 1480s. It includes a 'Good Contemplation', which is part of a prayer or meditation directed to Jesus, and two works in verse: 'The Infancy of the Saviour', telling the story of the childhood of Christ, and 'How the Wise Man Taught his Son', giving prudent and practical advice for a young man.[4] Both of the latter two works occur in manuscripts from elsewhere in England, suggesting that the canons of Bodmin shared in the common literary culture of the day.

Meanwhile the Cornish language went on being spoken west of a line running from Padstow through Wadebridge and Bodmin to Fowey.[5] Stories and legends in the language probably circulated orally, but the extent to which it was used for writing is not clear.[6] There are no private letters or financial records in Cornish, although it is not impossible that such things were written. What exists is chiefly religious in nature and comes from about the 15th century. It includes *Pascon agan Arluth* (a poem on the Passion of Christ),[7] five religious plays, and the so-called 'Charter Endorsement' – speeches about a marriage, perhaps from another such play.[8] Further religious literature survives from the following century in the form of some homilies, and there was once a Life of St Columb (no longer extant) that was reported to Nicholas Roscarrock round about 1600.[9] Three of the extant plays form a trilogy based on the Bible: *The Creation of the World*, *The Passion of Christ*, and *The Resurrection of Christ*.[10] The other two recount the Lives of saints: *Bewnans* [i.e. *The Life of*] *Meriasek* on the patron saint of Camborne,[11] and the recently discovered *Bewnans Ke* on the patron saint of Kea.[12] Calling these works religious plays is insufficient, however, since they include legendary material, such as King Arthur in *Bewnans Ke*, and vignettes of everyday life like the school scene in *Bewnans Meriasek*. The trilogy contains

---

1 Ranulf Higden, *Polychronicon*, ed. C. Babington (RS, 1865–86), II, 158–61. For discussion of this issue, see N. Orme, *Medieval Schools* (2006), 105–6, and for Cornwall's biography, *BRUO*, I, 490; *ODNB*; and Orme (ed.), *Cornish Wills*, 30–1, 218. Cornwall's innovation is said to have been adopted by another Oxford schoolmaster, Richard Pencrich (*BRUO*, III, 1456), who has sometimes been identified as Cornish, but Dr O. J. Padel informs me that, on linguistic grounds, his surname cannot have originated in Cornwall. It is more likely to have come from Penkridge (Staffs.).

2 For Trevisa's biography, see *BRUO*, III, 1903–4; D. C. Fowler, *John Trevisa* (1993); idem, *The Life and Times of John Trevisa, Medieval Scholar* (1995); and *ODNB*.

3 Above, note 1.

4 BL, Harley 2399, ff. 47r–64v; below, p. 00.

5 For documentary evidence on the speaking of Cornish, see M. Spriggs, 'Where Cornish Was Spoken and When: a provisional synthesis', *Cornish Studies*, 11 (2003), 228–69. I am grateful to Dr Padel for advice on the linguistic boundary; published maps of the Cornish-speaking area in the Middle Ages should be used with caution.

6 For a good survey of medieval Cornish, see O. J. Padel, 'Oral and Literary Culture in Medieval Cornwall', in H. Fulton (ed.), *Medieval Celtic Literature and Society* (2005), 95–116.

7 W. Stokes (ed.), *The Passion* (1861).

8 L. Toorians (ed.), *The Middle Cornish Charter Endorsement: the making of a marriage in medieval Cornwall*, Innsbrucker Beiträge zur Sprachwissenschaft, 67 (1991); O. J. Padel, 'Notes on the New Edition of the Middle Cornish "Charter Endorsement"', *Cambrian Medieval Celtic Studies* 30 (1995), 123–7; E. S. Newton, 'The Middle Cornish Interlude: Genre and Tradition', *Comparative Drama*, 30/2 (1996), 266–81.

9 Below, p. 105; Roscarrock, *Lives of the Saints*, 67-8.

10 Bodleian, Bodley 791; E. Norris (ed.), *The Ancient Cornish Drama* (1859). For a modern study, see J. A. Bakere, *The Cornish Ordinalia: a critical study* (1980).

11 Aberystwyth, Nat. Lib. of Wales, Peniarth 105; W. Stokes (ed.), Beunans Meriasek: *The Life of St Meriasek* (1872); M. Combellack, *The Camborne Play* (1988).

12 Aberystwyth, Nat. Lib. of Wales, 23,849D; *Bewnans Ke*, ed. C. G. Thomas and N. J. A. Williams (2007).

numerous references to places in Cornwall, especially in and around Penryn. This has led to the suggestion that it was composed by one or more of the clergy of Glasney College. The college owned the church of Kea and three of its provosts between 1476 and 1507 were, at one time, rectors of Camborne, so a link is possible between the college and all five plays, although firm evidence on the point is elusive. There were other clergy in western Cornwall capable of writing such works, and possibly even lay people. All the plays provide valuable evidence about popular religion and culture in the Cornish-speaking areas before the Reformation.

People in Cornwall, then, used three or four oral and written languages at the same time during the later Middle Ages. What language they used might change with their situation or purpose. Many men and women spoke Cornish, English, or both, and some of these could write in English, a few in both. There were also a small number who knew a third language, Latin or French, or even four like Ralph Tremur.[1] Far from being peripheral and primitive, Cornwall had a rich linguistic and literary culture that mingled its own traditions with those of the wider world.

5. THE REFORMATION

THE EARLY 16TH CENTURY

Three bishops presided over the Church in Cornwall during the first half of the 16th century. They were John Arundell, born in the county itself (1502–4), Hugh Oldham from Lancashire (1505–19), and John Veysey, a Warwickshire man (1519–51).[2] Oldham came to Cornwall at least twice, in 1506 and 1509, and Veysey apparently went there in 1541, but journeys of this kind were now unusual.[3] Oldham lived chiefly at his Devon manors, as previous bishops had done, and Veysey was often based outside the South West altogether. He was president of the Council of Wales and the Marches for a long period and frequently stayed at his birthplace, Sutton Coldfield, where he built a house, endowed a school, and made other charitable bequests. Both Oldham and Veysey employed a vicar general to do much of their administrative work and suffragan bishops to carry out confirmations and ordinations. There were four major suffragans during this period: Thomas Cornish, warden of Ottery St Mary collegiate church (Devon), from 1487 to 1505, Thomas Chard, prior of Kerswell (Devon), from 1508 to 1534, Thomas Vivian, prior of Bodmin, from 1517 to 1533 (Fig. 45), and William Fawell from 1532 to 1544.[4] Of these only Vivian was based in Cornwall, where he carried out over twenty ordinations between 1527 and 1532, generally at Bodmin Priory but once, in 1532, at St Cadoc's chapel in the parish of Padstow.[5]

The archdeacon of Cornwall remained the bishop's other important deputy during this period. His duties were summarised in a valuation of his income made in 1535, which reckoned that he received £1 per annum from fees for inducting clergy to benefices, £3 14s. 8d. from fees for proving wills, and £44 5s. 7½d. from the fees known as procurations. The latter were paid at the visitations of parishes made each year by the archdeacon or his official,[6] and by 1538 the archdeacon had a registrar based at Launceston, where some of the archdeaconry business may have been done.[7] In 1537 Veysey gave the post of archdeacon to Thomas Winter, the illegitimate son of Cardinal Wolsey, who did not come to Exeter diocese but leased his rights to William Body, a gentleman usher of the king's household. Body's lease was to run for 35 years during which he would pay an annual sum of £30, leaving him free to act as archdeacon and to make what profit he could. The lease led to disputes between Winter and Body, but Body maintained his claim and, when Winter resigned the archdeaconry in 1543, he secured a fresh lease for a further 34 years from the new archdeacon, John Pollard, this time for a mere £10 per annum.[8]

We are fortunate in having several sources that cast light on the Church in Cornwall in the 1520s and 30s as an institution, an economy, and a society. The earliest is the 'military survey of 1522', which lists the Cornish

---

1 *Reg. Grandisson*, II, 1180; above, p. 60.
2 Biographies in *ODNB*.
3 DRO, Chanter XIII, ff. 87v, 98r (Oldham); Chanter XV, f. 110v–111r, printed in Oliver, *Monasticon*, 53 (Veysey, a reference to a visitation of Glasney, possibly personal).
4 E. B. Fryde et al. (ed.), *Handbook of British Chronology* (3rd edn, 1986), 286–7. Cornish was titled bishop of Tenos, Chard of Selymbria, Vivian of Megara, and Fawell of Hippo.
5 DRO, Chanter XIV, ordination lists.
6 *Valor Eccl.* (Rec. Com. 1810–34), II, 296.
7 For the will of the registrar, Thomas Harris, see N. Orme (ed.), *Cornish Wills 1342–1540*, DCRS, new ser. 50 (2007), 191–3; cf. the will of Thomas Busan of Launceston, also proved there in 1514 (ibid., 155–6).
8 On Winter, Body, and Pollard, see A. L. Rowse, *Tudor Cornwall* (1941), 149–51, and for the lease of 1543, DRO, Chanter 1073.

parish clergy, their incomes, and the wealth of their moveable goods.¹ Unfortunately this survives for only five of the nine hundreds of Cornwall and undervalues the incomes of rectors and vicars, although it is more accurate about those of chaplains and chantry priests. Next, in 1534, the clergy were made to acknowledge Henry VIII as head of the Church of England and to renounce the pope's authority, a process that has left us the names of all the parish clergy and many of those in the religious houses.² In the following year an audit of the income of the Church was undertaken throughout England, now known as the *Valor Ecclesiasticus* ('ecclesiastical valuation'). This was concerned to estimate the annual earnings of all religious houses and beneficed clergy (chiefly rectors and vicars). It was a more rigorous enquiry into income than the papal taxation of 1291, but it may still have fallen short of reality by as much as a quarter, and hardly concerned itself at all with chaplains, chantry priests, or the finances of parish churches.³ It is complemented in this respect by a list of all the parish clergy of Cornwall making small monetary contributions, which dates from about the year 1536 and may relate to the payment of a fine offered to the king by the Church in 1532.⁴ A further source is provided by the Chantry Certificates of 1546–8, which are concerned with chantries and their clergy in particular, including the latter's functions and their incomes.⁵

These records enable us to compile a list of all the religious institutions in Cornwall at the beginning of the Reformation, roughly in about 1530. There were six monasteries: the three Augustinian priories of Bodmin, St Germans, and Launceston, the Benedictine priory of Tywardreath, and the two small cells of St Anthony-in-Roseland and St Carroc, while a single Benedictine monk represented Tavistock Abbey on the Isles of Scilly. There were two friaries (Bodmin and Truro), three collegiate churches (St Buryan, Crantock, and Glasney), three churches with prebends but without significant collegiate life (St Endellion, Probus, and St Teath), and one former hospital, St John (Helston), now a sinecure post for a single clergyman. Three other hospitals or almshouses functioned in Bodmin, two in Launceston, and one outside Liskeard, but these were all small institutions without full-time clergy and were largely ignored by the valuations and surveys of the period. Finally there were the parishes or parish-like areas, still 209 in number, served by a rector, vicar, or curate. As in previous centuries additional clergy served in some of the parishes: curates assisting rectors and vicars, chantry priests, and perhaps a few chaplains in the households of the gentry. Some of the chantry priests were still hired on a temporary basis while others had a longer-term or permanent employment in the 27 endowed chantries and religious guilds in the county. Most of these chantries and guilds maintained a single priest but the Arundell chantry at St Columb Major had five, and the church of St Michael's Mount, which shared some of the features of a chantry, had three. All the parish clergy below the level of rectors and vicars operated largely outside the bishop's supervision, at the beck and call of those who employed them.

We can pass beyond listing these institutions to estimating the number of clergy that they supported. There were at least 61 members of the religious orders in the 1530s, all resident in Cornwall – a figure that may need to be supplemented by a few novices and some additional friars, since the figures for the latter relate to the dissolution of their houses in 1538 after possible losses of members. The largest group within the religious orders were the Augustinian canons (totalling 31), of whom Launceston had 12, Bodmin 10, St Germans 7, and St Anthony-in-Roseland 2. There were 10 monks: 7 at Tywardreath, 2 at St Carroc, and the one on the Scillies. The Franciscans of Bodmin numbered at least 9 friars and the Dominicans of Truro at least 11. The collegiate and prebendal churches had a nominal strength of 58, divided between Glasney with 23 clergy, Crantock with 13, St Buryan with 8, Probus with 6, St Endellion with 4, St Teath with 3, and St John Helston with one. However some of the prebendaries of these churches did not live in Cornwall and others were also parish rectors or vicars, making it likely that the resident clergy of the collegiate and prebendal churches numbered only 18 at Glasney, 6 at Crantock, 4 at St Buryan, and one each at the others – a total of 31. Moving to the parishes, there were 160 beneficed clergy (rectors and vicars), of whom 15 held more than one benefice, reducing the total to about 145. Some of the 145 (at least a dozen) did not reside in Cornwall, so that the resident number may have fallen to about 130. Below them were 196 other clergy, all resident. About 28 of these were curates in charge of parishes that had no rector or vicar, 49 were curates assisting rectors or vicars or deputising for those who were absent, and 119 were chantry priests, guild priests, and chaplains in private houses. This adds up to a maximum of about 350 parish clergy with a benefice or a post in Cornwall, of whom about 310–320 may have lived in the county for most of the time. We might add to them 200 or more parish clerks and probably at least 300 servants of the clergy, ranging from noblemen and gentlemen who acted as honorary stewards of the largest monasteries

---

1 T. L. Stoate (ed.), *The Cornwall Military Survey 1522* (1987), 1–127. The surviving records omit the hundreds of Lesnewth, Powder, Pydar, and Stratton.

2 Acknowledgments survive for the monasteries of Bodmin, St Germans, and Launceston, the friary of Bodmin, and the colleges of Crantock and Glasney (TNA, E 25), and renunciations for the parish clergy (TNA, E 36/64, pp. 35–46).

3 *Valor Eccl.*, II, 392–408; material relevant to Cornwall appears elsewhere in the work. 4 ECA, D&C 3688.

5 TNA, E 301/15, /9, printed by L. S. Snell, *Documents towards a History of the Reformation in Cornwall:* vol. I, *The Chantry Certificates for Cornwall* (Exeter, c.1953).

down to the ordinary domestics (almost invariably male) of the religious houses and the beneficed clergy. The Church's personnel could be enlarged further with about 600 churchwardens and sextons.

The *Valor Ecclesiasticus* provides total figures for the gross and net incomes of the chief dignitaries, monasteries, and parish clergy of Cornwall during the 1530s, with the caveat that its figures were still underestimated, at least in the case of the monasteries. The largest income was still that of the bishop of Exeter with £436 per annum from his lands and churches in the county. This was made up of £105 from Pawton, £64 from St Germans, £63 each from Cargoll and Penryn, £62 from Lawhitton, £40 from Tregaire, and £35 from Burniere. Of the monasteries, Launeston had £354, Bodmin £270, and St Germans £245. Exeter Cathedral's income was reckoned at £239, all from the tithes of its churches. That of Glasney was assessed at £210, and Tywardreath's at £151; in fact the latter's was over £200. The rest of the religious houses were less well endowed. Crantock was deemed to have £94 per annum, St Buryan £74 (most of which went to the dean), St Anthony about £28, and St Carroc £11. No figures were recorded for the friaries or the monastic property on the Scillies. Sixteen or so religious houses outside Cornwall still drew revenues from the county, although the sums were mostly fairly small. They included the abbeys of Beaulieu, Cleeve, Hailes, Hartland, Rewley, Syon, Tavistock, Tewkesbury, and Wilton, the priories of Bridgwater, Merton, Montacute, and Plympton, Exeter College (Oxford), St George's Chapel (Windsor), and the preceptor of the house of the Order of St John of Jerusalem at Ansty in Wiltshire.

The parish clergy, as in times past, ranged widely in their incomes or wages and the terms of their duties. The 160 beneficed clergy were divided between 74 rectors and 86 vicars. Their incomes are best set out as a table:

TABLE 2. *Stipends of Rectors and Vicars in Cornwall, 1535*

Stipends	No. of rectors	No. of vicars
Under £5	2	3
£5–£9	12	26
£10–£14	13	26
£15–£19	14	19
£20–£24	9	7
£25–£29	6	3
£30 and above	18	2
Total	74	86

Five of the beneficed clergy received no more than hired chaplains: these were the rectors of Forrabury and Ruan Minor and the vicars of St Anthony-in-Meneage and Manaccan, each with just under £5, while the vicar of Lostwithiel was reported as having only £2 13s. 4d. – perhaps an underestimate. The two rectors were in tiny parishes with few tithes, while two of the vicars served in churches appropriated to Tywardreath Priory which took as much of the income as it could. A further 12 rectors and 26 vicars with between £5 and £9 were little better off, because a reasonable salary began at about £10 by the standards of the 1530s. As in 1291, vicarages tended to be closer in value than rectories, partly because they were subject to some regulation by bishops, so that most vicars got between £5 and £19 and very few more than £20, whereas 31 rectors enjoyed more than the latter figure. The two wealthiest vicars were those of Breage with £33 and Madron with £50. There were nearly twenty rectories worth over £30, the richest of all being St Columb Major with £53 and the deanery of St Buryan, effectively the rectory of that parish, with £58. Not all of this was profit, however. Both Breage and St Buryan had dependent chapels of ease within their parishes, and the rector or vicar had to pay the stipends of the priests who served them.

The majority of the clergy, the non-beneficed chaplains and chantry priests, still fared poorly in their salaries and sometimes in their conditions of service. The most fortunate were the curates in charge of parishes that were part of a larger benefice. They were largely left alone to run their churches and could develop links with local people. Their conditions of tenure are unclear, but as there was no reason to remove them, they may have served for long periods. Curates who assisted a rector or vicar, or who deputised for an absent one, were in a more precarious state. They might be dismissed when their employer ceased to require their services, or if he died or left the parish, since his successor was under no obligation to employ them. The curate of Marhamchurch claimed in about 1540 that he was offered his post for four years at a salary of £6, with notice of three months before termination, but was later dismissed without warning.[1] A salary of £6 was relatively high. The military survey of 1522 shows that the maximum rate for a curate was about £6 13s. 4d. but that this could fall to as little as £3, or to £2 if food and clothes were provided as well. Launceston Priory paid four of its parochial curates between £5 and £6, depending on the importance of the parish.[2] Priests employed by guilds or serving endowed chantries generally earned between £4 and £6. Some could stay as long as they wished; others might find themselves discharged if they fell out with their employers, and those chantry priests who were hired for a year or so had constantly to seek for re-employment. The best paid of the non-beneficed clergy was the chantry-priest of Week St Mary, who also

---

1 TNA, C 1/1055/34, /35.

2 TNA, SC 6/HenVIII/454.

FIG 34. *Bodmin church, rebuilt in the early 1470s as a large aisled church, the biggest parish church in Cornwall. The costs were met by heroic fund-raising by the people of the town.*

taught the grammar school there. He was required to be a university graduate and received over £12. A few other chantry priests were teaching schools by the 1540s in Bodmin, Launceston, Saltash, and Truro. They received no greater salaries for doing so but may have been able to increase their earnings by charging some fees from their pupils.[1]

The activities of parish churches in the early 16th century seem to have broadly followed the pattern established during the later Middle Ages. Rebuilding continued in many places and money was spent on renewing screens and seating. Rivals to Bodmin's great church (Fig. 34) emerged at St Mary Magdalene (Launceston), magnificently rebuilt in carved granite, and Probus with its spectacular tower (Fig. 35). In 1534 the vicar of Altarnun commissioned a 'carver' to fit a new roof and two new windows in his chancel (Fig. 23).[2] Work on Kilkhampton church was still in progress in the early years of Elizabeth I; the south porch bears the date 1567. Churchwardens went on producing their accounts, although it is not certain if all churches were well organised in this respect. Stores, guilds, and companies continued to exist in large numbers, raising money for their churches and indicating that people continued to honour the images to which the stores belonged. Chapels were still well supported. Bishop Vivian dedicated one at Stowe in Kilkhampton to St Christina in 1519, and another, in honour of St Katherine, was being planned at Treviddo in Menheniot as late as 1532.[3] Pilgrimage continued to St Michael's Mount, where the receipts at the shrine were still at a high level in the 1510s.[4] The Arundell family of Lanherne, a family that would remain staunchly Catholic after the Reformation, was carefully keeping the indulgences already mentioned, and by the 1510s Sir John Arundell and Peter Bevill of St Allen had links with the reformed branch of the Franciscan friars known as 'Observants', based at Greenwich (Kent) and Richmond (Surrey).[5]

Some historians have used sources like the above to argue that traditional religion was flourishing in England on the eve of the Reformation. Certainly much continued in the accustomed ways, especially in the parishes. Patrons presented clergy, clergy led services and dispensed the sacraments, while parishioners paid tithes and offerings and served as churchwardens and other officers. The varied religious culture outlined in the previous chapter continued up to the 1530s, but it must be recalled that church buildings, wardens' accounts, and even wills are by nature records of achievement. They testify to the sympathy of many

---

1 N. Orme, *Education in the West of England, 1066–1548* (1976), 113–14, 149, 169, 172–3, 180–1.
2 TNA, STAC 2/17/209; ECA, D&C 606.
3 Orme, *The Saints of Cornwall* (2000), 87; CRO, AR/24/21; Orme (ed.), *Cornish Wills*, 188. Stowe was not necessarily a new chapel; one is recorded there in 1386 (*Reg. Brantyngham*, II, 621).
4 Below, p. 236.
5 Above, p. 83; Orme (ed.), *Cornish Wills*, 140, 153.

FIG 35. The Church of St Probus. Its fine tower was added in the 1520s.

people with the religion of the day – a sympathy that was to be affronted by the events of the Reformation. Equally they tell us little of those who held aloof from religious activities, either because of their worldliness or their dissent, and it would be wise to allow for the existence of such people. There is no trace of Lollard unorthodoxy in early 16th-century Cornwall, but there would have been plenty of non-conformity in terms of disobedience to the Church's moral laws, failure to attend church or pay tithes, and sometimes attacks on churches and clergy. Even scepticism and disbelief may have existed without being recorded, because it was not expressed or identified as heresy.

Changes were also in progress that would help to bring about the forthcoming Reformation. One was a deeper respect for the king, shown by the display in churches of royal motifs like the Tudor rose or portcullis. Another was the growth of seating in naves, turning the congregation into a more uniform and orderly gathering, potentially a school for instruction. In schools themselves classical or 'humanist' Latin was replacing late-medieval Latin between 1480 and 1520, a process that must have extended to Cornwall. The new technology of printing was increasing the supply of books, some printed in England after 1476 and others imported from the Continent, and by the 1520s the leaders of Church and state were becoming aware of the need to control the trade in books. All these developments – royal power, uniformity, literacy, and printing – were to help change the Catholic Church of the later Middle Ages into a new and somewhat different Church of England.

THE EARLY REFORMATION, 1529–38

The English Reformation is conventionally said to begin in 1529 with the summoning of the Parliament which, for the next seven years, enacted a series of statutes that remodelled the English Church. At first the statutes were largely confined to the clergy. In 1529 their rights and powers were restricted with regard to mortuaries (the gifts they claimed from dead parishioners), charges for the probate of wills, pluralities (the holding of more than one benefice at once), and involvement in business activities.[1] In 1530 they agreed to pay a huge fine to the king over five years, as a penalty for having infringed his laws, and in 1532 they promised not make new religious laws without his authority.[2] In 1534 Parliament passed the Act of Supremacy, making Henry the earthly head of the Church of England instead of the

---

1 *Statutes of the Realm*, III, 285–8, 288–9, 292–6.   2 Ibid., 334–8, 460–1.

pope,¹ and the clergy were required to assent to this through the acknowledgements and renunciations already mentioned.

Once the king had secured the headship of the Church, he and his chief minister, Thomas Cromwell, made it effective in two respects. The first and more immediate was financial. In 1534 the parliamentary Act of First Fruits and Tenths gave the king power to impose taxation on the Church at a heavier rate than had been previously levied by either the king or the pope. All religious houses and beneficed clergy were in future to pay the crown one tenth of their income each year. Anyone who in future obtained a new benefice, be it as a bishop, canon, rector, or vicar, was to forfeit the whole of the first year's income to the king, ten tenths as it were for that year, and all candidates for benefices had to provide guarantors to ensure that the sum would be paid.² The only existing valuation of Church incomes was still the papal one of 1291, which had remained in use as the basis of taxing the clergy. To update this, the new assessment of the *Valor Ecclesiasticus* was made in 1535, which was more searching and rigorous than its predecessor. Even so the task of valuing the income of the clergy was so vast that the *Valor* fell short of perfection. As has been mentioned, it underestimated the incomes of the Cornish religious houses, making it likely that there was also a shortfall with regard to the incomes of the beneficed clergy. Moreover the commissioners concentrated on the rich or relatively rich – the religious houses and the beneficed clergy – and overlooked most of the chantry priests and all the chaplains.

The other new application of royal policy towards the church was spiritual and aimed at reform. This was broader in its effects than the financial one and affected the religion of lay people more directly. One change followed naturally from the removal of the power of the pope, although it was not enacted in law: the disuse of indulgences. True, these had been issued by bishops as well as by popes, and Veysey (a conservative in some respects) granted one in favour of Cowley Bridge near Exeter as late as Christmas Day 1536.³ Nevertheless indulgences were so intimately associated with papal claims of power that people instinctively abandoned them during the mid 1530s, and an act of Parliament in 1536 made it illegal to teach or maintain any aspect of the pope's authority.⁴ In the autumn of 1536 Cromwell issued royal injunctions to the clergy requiring them to preach regularly against the powers of the pope and in favour of those of the king. They were warned not to promote the undue worship of saints, images, or pilgrimages, but to encourage the laity to please God through their work and by giving charity to the poor. They were reminded of a recent law that the keeping of holy days was to be drastically reduced.⁵ Feasts commemorating the days when churches had been dedicated were to be held only on 1 October. Feasts in honour of the patron saint of the church were not to be kept as holidays unless the saint was a major figure whose day was generally observed – a threat to Cornwall where so many saints were uniquely local. Finally the clergy were told to teach the laity to say their basic prayers in English not Latin – a major change of habit. The basic prayers were specified as the Lord's Prayer, Apostles' Creed, and Ten Commandments, the latter replacing the long-used Hail Mary, and printed prayer-books began to include them in English.⁶ In May 1538 Veysey issued injunctions of his own for his diocese, reinforcing those of the king. In them he made the concession that the basic prayers might be taught and learnt 'in the Cornish [language] where the English tongue is not used'.⁷

In October 1538 Cromwell sent out a second and more radical set of injunctions. These had a wider impact on lay people, contradicting the view, sometimes stated, that Henry VIII's Reformation was limited to the clergy. Positively the movement in favour of the English language continued. Bible translation now received approval, and each church was ordered to provide itself with a Bible in English, a new translation being published for this purpose in 1539. Parishioners coming for confession in Lent were to be tested on their ability to say the Lord's Prayer and Creed in English, and warned that they might be denied communion at Easter if they did not learn them. The clergy were told to record every baptism, marriage, and burial in a register maintained for the purpose. This measure was claimed as helping to authenticate legitimate births for legal purposes, but it probably also aimed at ensuring that everyone was baptised, married, and buried according to law. The 1520s and 30s had seen the emergence of Anabaptists in Germany who practised adult baptism, and registration made certain that parents in England would have their children baptised as infants.⁸ Equally important in the injunctions of 1538 were their prohibitions. No images or relics were to be venerated by worship, lighting of candles, or by pilgrimage. Any that had been venerated were to be removed.⁹ In a pendant to this a royal proclamation of November 1538 forbade the cult of Thomas Becket altogether, because he had championed the Church against an earlier King Henry. His images were to be

---

1 Ibid., 492.
2 Ibid., 493–9.
3 DRO, ED/M/1036; N. Orme, 'Indulgences in the Diocese of Exeter 1100–1536', *TDA* 120 (1988), 26.
4 *Statutes of the Realm*, III, 663–6.
5 D. Wilkins (ed.), *Concilia Magnae Britanniae et Hiberniae* (1737), III, 823–4.
6 W. H. Frere and W. M. Kennedy (ed.), *Visitation Articles and Injunctions of the Period of the Reformation*, Alcuin Club 14–16 (1908–10), II, 1–11.
7 Ibid., II, 61–4.
8 Ibid., II, 34–7.
9 Ibid., II, 38–42.

FIG 36. *The ruins of the late-medieval chapel of St Michael, Roche, a casualty of the Reformation, which forbade the veneration of images and pilgrimages to holy places.*

removed, his festivals abolished, and his name expunged from service books.[1]

The attack on images had an immense and permanent impact on popular religion in England. It was not confined to words. During the year 1538 some images were publicly destroyed by the authorities in London and elsewhere, including the Welsh image of Darfell Gadern and the Rood or crucifix of Boxley (Kent), the latter of which had wires to move its eyes.[2] We do not know what happened to the two chief pilgrim shrines in Cornwall, St Michael's Mount and St Day, but their activities must have been greatly curtailed. Comments by John Leland, who visited the county in 1542, imply that public pilgrimage had ceased by that time. Writing about St Elide's chapel on the Isles of Scilly, he used the past tense, 'in times past at her sepulchre was great superstition', and similarly with regard to the chapel of Our Lady in the Park near Liskeard, 'where was wont to be great pilgrimage'.[3] The attacks on images, pilgrimages, and indulgences had serious effects on chapels, whose functions and resources were often bound up with such things. There was no formal abolition of chapels, but most of them ceased to be used and were demolished or converted to other purposes (Fig. 36). Leland mentioned St Katherine's chapel in Launceston as already 'prophaned' (i.e. turned to secular use).[4] Even chapels of ease eventually disappeared in some small towns, and the only ones to survive in the long term were those that were virtually parish churches like Advent, Germoe, and Helston, together with a few others such as Marazion in St Hilary, St Enodoc and Porthilly in St Minver, St Nectan in St Winnow, and Penzance in Madron.

The religious changes of the 1530s caused some discontent in Cornwall, especially the prohibition of local saints' days in 1536. In September 1536 John Tregonwell, a Cornish-born lawyer who was acting as a royal commissioner in his native county, told Cromwell of rumours afoot that he, Tregonwell, was about to remove crosses, chalices, and images from churches, but said that he had personally found the county loyal and quiet.[5] By April 1537, however, Sir William Godolphin of Breage was informing Cromwell that a fisherman named Carpyssacke of St Keverne had tried to commission a banner showing a wounded Christ

---

1 P. L. Hughes and J. F. Larkin (ed.) *Tudor Royal Proclamations* (1964–9), I, 275–6.

2 On image-destruction in general, see M. Aston, *England's Iconoclasts* (1988), and E. Duffy, *The Stripping of the Altars* (1992),

402–10.

3 Leland, *Itinerary*, ed. Toulmin Smith, I, 190, 208.

4 Ibid., 175.

5 *L. & P. Hen VIII*, XI, 166.

with an inscription petitioning that the old holy days might be kept. St Keverne's day (5 March) fell into the forbidden category. The banner was intended for display on Pardon Monday (probably Rogation Monday), but Carpyssacke was arrested and consideration was given to trying him for treason.[1] On the following 29 May a ship named the *Maudlyn* left Truro for Treguier in Brittany, carrying what Alexander Carvanell, a deputy searcher (or customs officer), called a company of 'riotous' pilgrims feigning to go on a 'pope-holy pilgrimage'. They included two clergy, a merchant of Truro, and over fifty others. Carvanell and two assistants tried to enter the vessel at Truro, ostensibly to inspect the cargo, but were thrown into the sea. They managed to get on board when the ship stopped at St Mawes, but the mariners would not allow the inspection to proceed and carried Carvanell to Brittany from whence he had to return in another boat.[2] Although pilgrimage had not yet been forbidden, it was being discouraged, and the participants were probably as aware as Carvanell that they were defying official policy by going on such a journey.

THE DISSOLUTION AND AFTER, 1536–47

Soon after Parliament recognised Henry VIII as head of the Church of England, Cromwell and other royal servants began to make plans for the crown to take control of Church property. In April 1536 an act of Parliament authorised the dissolution of small monasteries. It began by asserting that houses of less than thirteen clergy were unsatisfactory in their religious life, unlike larger communities which kept it well. It ordered the closure of such houses, however, not on the basis of their numbers of clergy but on whether they had an income of £200 or less. The monks and canons of the houses to be closed were given the option of leaving the monastic life or of being transferred to another house.[3]

Only one Cornish monastery was dissolved under the act of 1536. This was Tywardreath whose income was reckoned at £151 in the *Valor*, although it was worth more in practice. The prior, Nicholas Guest, who had been imported from St Germans only recently, chose to withdraw from monastic life and was granted a pension of £16. Two years later he became vicar of St Winnow; the fate of his fellow monks is largely unknown.[4] The compulsory dissolutions of 1536 were followed by a 'voluntary' process in which the friaries and the remaining monasteries were persuaded to surrender themselves and their property into the king's hands. The two Cornish friaries capitulated in September 1538, and the three largest monasteries followed suit early in 1539. There was no active resistance. The king's commissioner, John Tregonwell, received the surrender of Launceston on 24 February, Bodmin on 27 February, and St Germans on 2 March. The closure dates of the small cells at St Anthony and St Carroc, and the withdrawal of Tavistock's last monk from the Isles of Scilly, are not known because records only survive in respect of their mother houses. The cells cannot have survived beyond 1539, and it is possible that one or both were closed in the previous year. Last of all fell the Order of St John in 1540, bringing to an end whatever activities still went on at Trebeigh.

Monks and canons who surrendered in 1539 were granted pensions, since there was no option to go to another house. In contrast friars got nothing, since they were regarded as having chosen to live in poverty. The priors of the three largest Cornish monasteries were handsomely treated. Robert Swymmer of St Germans and Thomas Wandsworth of Bodmin received pensions of £66 13s. 4d. per annum, while John Shere of Launceston obtained £100, allowing them a comfortable retirement. Swymmer, who was already rector of Minster, continued to hold that parish along with his pension, and Wandsworth acquired two new parish benefices, including Lanlivery. His later career was anything but comfortable, however, since he was charged with involvement in Catholic activities during the reign of Edward VI, condemned to death for high treason, reprieved, imprisoned, and deprived of his parishes.[5] Ordinary canons were allocated anything from £10 down to £2 and they were allowed to work as parish clergy, as were the friars. Their subsequent careers appear to have varied. Some acquired rectories or vicarages and one, Stephen Gourge, became master of Launceston grammar school. Others are not recorded holding parish benefices and must have joined the crowd of ill-paid parish chaplains and chantry priests.

The dissolution of the monasteries had major effects upon Cornwall. Two towns, Bodmin and Fowey, escaped from the control of the priories that had hitherto run their affairs, and became self-governing institutions. Religious property passed into lay control. The crown itself kept the lands of Launceston Priory and the Isles of Scilly, some of which still belong to the duchy of Cornwall. Other lands were sold or leased by the crown to courtiers or to wealthy bidders from outside the court. Thomas Sternhold, groom of the robes in the royal household, gained a lease of Bodmin Priory, and Gawen Carew, courtier and soldier, was granted the premises of Launceston. Some Cornish gentry families also did well out of the Dissolution, especially from Bodmin's possessions. Its prior, Thomas Wandsworth, foresaw the crown's intention of dissolving all the

---

1 *L. & P. Hen VIII*, XII(1), 450–1, 522; XII(2), 220.
2 *L. & P. Hen VIII*, XII(2), 124, 476.
3 *Statutes of the Realm*, III, 575–8.
4 Below, p. 295.
5 Below, p. 153.

monasteries as early as 1537, and leased as many of the priory's lands as possible to his family and friends. Bodiniel went to Sir John Chamond, Fursnewth to John Tubbe, Kingswood Hill to Thomas Lytelton, and Withiel to Laurence Kendall. Wandsworth arranged marriages between the children of his brother John and those of Humphrey Prideaux, and three of the best Bodmin properties – the manors of Padstow, Rialton, and Reterth – were leased to the partners concerned to sweeten the arrangements. The establishment of the Prideaux family at Padstow dates from this time.[1]

Churches and tithes changed hands as well as lands. In the early 1530s the patrons of the 160 rectories and vicarages in Cornwall were still predominantly churchmen. The bishop, the cathedral, and various monasteries appointed clergy to about 94 benefices (59%), and the crown and laity to about 66 (41%). The patronage of the bishop and the cathedral was largely left alone during the Reformation, and when it was over they (along with a few other religious bodies) still controlled about 39 benefices. The patronage of the monasteries and other religious houses, on the other hand, was either taken over by the crown or sold to lay purchasers. About 66 advowsons changed hands in this way, so that by the 1560s the crown or other lay people appointed clergy to about 121 benefices (75%), while the share of the churchmen fell to 25%. The percentage change would rise a little higher in favour of the laity if we added the parishes served by chaplains like Boyton and North Tamerton, some of which also passed from religious to lay control at this time. Tithe-paying was affected too. Since the 12th century tithes had belonged to the clergy alone, and lay lords had not been allowed to receive them. Now the crown sold off the tithes that had once belonged to the monasteries, and a new situation arose by which the great tithes of grain in many of the former vicarages had to be paid to the lay people who purchased the right to receive them, 'impropriators' as they were subsequently known. Tithe-free areas were transferred in the same way, and remained in being despite the disappearance of the religious houses to which they had been attached.

During 1539–40, when the crown was rich with the property of the monasteries, it considered using some of their buildings and endowments to create new dioceses and cathedrals. One of these was proposed for Cornwall, financed from the priories of Bodmin, St Germans, and Launceston; it is not clear which of the sites was intended for use. Plans were drawn up for a bishop and a cathedral foundation of a dean, six prebendaries, various minor clergy, lay clerks, choristers, servants, a schoolmaster, and four almsmen, at an annual cost of £669 19s. 9d. A candidate to be bishop was even identified: William Tresham, DD, canon of Chichester, Lincoln, and Oxford.[2] In the end the crown diminished its plans for reasons of cost and criticism, and a mere six new foundations were eventually made, omitting the scheme for Cornwall. It was a sign that religious changes were slowing down. In 1539 the crown caused Parliament to pass the 'Act of Six Articles', which defended the traditional doctrines about the mass, the celibacy of the clergy, and confession, and threatened draconian penalties against anyone who dissented. The veneration of images remained forbidden, but most of the images in parish churches survived and so did many of the stores and guilds devoted to maintaining them.[3]

The final years of Henry's reign, from 1540 until 1547, did not produce dramatic alterations to the Church in Cornwall, but the Reformation continued to edge forward in small steps. In 1541 a royal proclamation abolished the custom of choosing a boy-bishop to lead the church services on St Nicholas Day and Holy Innocents Day (6 and 28 December), and tried (less successfully) to suppress the folk-customs associated with these and some other saints' days.[4] During the early 1540s there was a resumption of the closure of religious houses, now affecting collegiate churches and hospitals, although this did not involve Cornwall. Finally in 1545 a Chantry Act was passed by Parliament allowed the king to take control of colleges, chantries, and their property during his lifetime, although Henry made a verbal promise to Parliament that he would use the power to safeguard the clergy, education, and the poor.[5] During the spring of 1546 royal commissioners investigated the chantries in each county by extracting returns or 'certificates' from every parish. Parishioners were required to identify the founders, purposes, endowments, revenues, and clergy of any chantry within their boundaries. In Cornwall the commissioners reported on the six remaining collegiate and prebendal churches (St Buryan, Crantock, St Endellion, Glasney, Probus, and St Teath), the chapel of Lammana, the former hospital of Helston, and 18 chantries in parish churches.[6] Their enquiries were not wholly successful, since there were at least another 8 chantries that they did not discover, but before this lack was remedied Henry died on 28 January 1547 and the Chantry Act lapsed in consequence. The colleges and chantries gained a brief respite.

---

1 Below, pp. 152–3.
2 H. Cole (ed.), *King Henry VIII's Scheme of Bishopricks* (1838), 68–9, 74; *L&P Hen. VIII*, XIV(2), 152; Addenda, I(2), 498. On Tresham, see *BRUO*, IV, 576–7.
3 *Statutes of the Realm*, III, 739–43.
4 Hughes and Larkin, *Tudor Royal Proclamations*, I, 302.
5 *Statutes of the Realm*, III, 988–93; E. Hall, *Chronicle Containing the History of England [from] Henry IV to Henry VIII* (1809), 864–5.
6 The Cornish certificates are preserved in TNA, E 301/15, printed in Snell, *Chantry Certificates* (entries marked 'Chantry Certificate 15'). On the procedure followed in 1545–6, see N. Orme, 'The Dissolution of the Chantries in Devon, 1546–8', *TDA* 111 (1979), 78–80.

THE REFORMATION UNDER EDWARD VI

Henry was succeeded in name by his nine year-old son Edward VI and in practice by a government led by the young king's uncle, Edward Seymour, duke of Somerset. This government soon made plain its intention of continuing the Reformation to establish a fully Protestant Church. In the autumn of 1547 teams of royal visitors toured England, addressing enquiries to the clergy and publicising a fresh set of injunctions, those of Edward VI. The injunctions began to make changes to worship in church. The epistle and gospel at mass were to be read in English, and English lessons from the Bible were introduced at morning and evening prayer. The clergy were told to preach the *Homilies* published by Cranmer in 1547: sermons expounding the official doctrines of salvation, obedience, almsgiving, and so on. Most religious processions were forbidden. Clergy were no longer allowed to lead the bodies of the dead to the church from their homes, but only to receive the dead at the churchyard. The Latin prayers said at public processions, such as Rogationtide, were replaced by prayers in English, the litany, now to be said in church while kneeling. The warnings against shrines and images were reinforced, and the removal of venerated images was required even from window glass. No lights were allowed in churches, except for two on the high altar beside the hanging pyx containing the sacrament – the only object of worship still allowed. Instead, the regime strove to turn people's devotion to Bible reading, Sunday observance, and works of charity. Each church was told to acquire a chest to receive donations for the needy, and the resources of the church guilds and stores were to be put into the chest for that purpose.[1]

More radical reforms came with the enactment of the second Chantry Act by Parliament in December 1547. Unlike the previous act, which had been non-committal about the future of the chantries, this began with a robust Protestant attack on prayers for the dead. It sanctioned the dissolution of a wide range of institutions and endowments and the seizure of their property by the crown. They included the remaining collegiate churches, the chantries, religious (but not craft) guilds, obits (masses on the anniversaries of people's deaths), and lights in churches. Collegiate churches and chantries were to cease their activities on Easter Day, 1 April 1548, and a promise was made that chantry property would be applied 'to good and godly uses' such as founding grammar schools, augmenting the universities, and providing better relief for the poor.[2] During the spring of 1548 commissioners in Cornwall made fresh enquiries in each parish about chantries, religious guilds, obits, and lights and these form the second or 'Edwardian' series of chantry certificates. The process was more efficient than it had been in 1546. St Michael's Mount was now included with the collegiate and prebendal churches, the number of chantries identified rose to 26, and 19 additional endowments were discovered for the support of masses, obits, and lights.[3]

The second Chantry Act had another substantial impact upon Cornwall. Glasney College, the largest remaining religious house in the county, was closed, as was the ancient minster of Crantock. St Buryan, St Endellion, Probus, and St Teath lost their prebendaries, and all the chantries were dissolved (Fig. 40). Several chapels were shorn of their endowments, notably the chapels of ease at Boscastle and Camelford, the cult chapel of Our Lady in the Park near Liskeard, and the chapels and priest of Lammana that had replaced the priory there. The Mount was spared to the extent of keeping the church and two priests to serve it, chiefly to minister to a royal garrison stationed on the island. St Buryan too kept some of its distinction. The chantry commissioners intended to abolish the dean as well as the prebendaries, but this turned out to be impractical and the church continued as a royal peculiar down to the 19th century, staffed by the dean (a wealthy absentee) and three poorly-paid parish chaplains. All the clergy of the colleges and the priests of the chantries and guilds were granted pensions. The three heads of houses, St Buryan, Crantock, and Glasney, received £25 17s. 3d., £12 6s. 6d., and £18 7s. 1d. respectively, representing half of their previous stipends.[4] The rest of the clergy were treated on a graduated scale. Those who had been paid £5 or less got the same amount, and those above were awarded sums of between £5 and £6 13s. 4d. Some became parish chaplains and others rectors and vicars, like the ex-monks and canons.

Despite the promises of the Chantry Act, no significant amount of chantry property was applied in Cornwall for new educational or charitable purposes. The king's officers merely safeguarded some of the schools that existed in connection with Glasney and with a few of the chantries.[5] Six places with schools were reported to the chantry commissioners of 1548. At Glasney a clerk had taught children the ABC and one of the vicars choral had kept a grammar school. At Launceston an elderly man and a chantry priest

---

1 Frere and Kennedy (ed.), *Visitation Articles and Injunctions*, II, 103–30.

2 *Statutes of the Realm*, IV(1), 24–33.

3 TNA, E 301/9, printed in Snell, *Chantry Certificates* (entries marked 'Chantry Certificate 9'). On the procedure followed in 1547–8, see Orme, 'Dissolution of the Chantries in Devon', 81–5.

4 Probus had no head, the headship having been devolved to the bishop (below, p. 263).

5 On what follows, see Orme, *Education in the West of England*, 113–14, 148–50, 167–9, 172–182.

arranged their teaching similarly. Chantry priests at Bodmin, Saltash, and Week St Mary taught grammar, and one at Truro ran a school of an unspecified nature. The crown ignored the teaching of the ABC, which was regarded as so widely available that it needed no support, but most of the Cornish grammar schools were preserved although they lost their endowments and received an annual payment from the crown for the schoolmaster's salary, frozen at the level of 1548. On the death or resignation of the current chantry priest, the post became open to any teacher: cleric or layman. The crown did a modest service to education in Cornwall by drafting the last archpriest of the Mount, John Arscott, MA, to be schoolmaster of Penryn. A greater disservice was done at Week St Mary, where Thomasine Percival had founded the first endowed Cornish grammar school in 1506–8. The chantry priest in charge of the school was a good teacher and the school apparently attracted the sons of the local gentry, but the king's officers considered that it was hampered by its remote location and the authorities at Launceston appear to have suggested that it should be moved to their town. The salary due to Week was therefore added to that of Launceston school, and Thomasine's foundation came to an end.

The first three years of Edward VI's reign saw a succession of further reforms to the Church, aiming to make it Protestant in its doctrines and observances. In 1547 Parliament abolished Henry's Act of Six Articles and the medieval heresy laws, opening the way for Protestant doctrines to become lawful.[1] Rumours spread that the government was planning to seize church silver and jewels, and when William Body, who was effectively the archdeacon, visited the deanery of Penwith in December 1547, a riot broke out because of fear that he was coming with that intention.[2] In January 1548 the king's council forbade the popular Church customs of lighting candles at Candlemas, receiving ashes on Ash Wednesday, carrying palms on Palm Sunday, and creeping to the cross on Good Friday. In February all images were ordered to be removed from churches, and pyxes above high altars later followed them.[3] On 1 April, Easter Day, a new *Order of Communion* was introduced, bringing some English prayers into the Latin mass alongside the English epistle and gospel, and requiring communion to be given to the laity 'in both kinds': the bread and the consecrated wine. In the spring of 1549 the issue of church silver arose again. Royal commissioners told parishes to declare what they had, and lists were made of the objects, a procedure only too likely to confirm the fear that the government wanted to seize them.[4]

The culmination of these changes was a new prayer book, Cranmer's *Book of Common Prayer*, which was prescribed for use in all churches as from Pentecost (9 June) 1549. All worship was now to be held in English. The nine daily services hitherto said by the clergy were reduced to two, morning and evening prayer, and the clergy remained obliged to say them both each day. The mass became the service of holy communion, and pastoral services continued in the form of baptism, confirmation, marriage, churching of women, and funerals. The mass and the pastoral services retained a traditional shape and continued to involve substances that were regarded as holy – water, chrism, bread, and wine – but their ceremonies were simplified and their material was made more instructive. Baptism and marriage both began with explanations of what they involved, and funerals became occasions to teach the living as well as to send off the dead.[5] The introduction of the new Prayer-Book on Pentecost, the day of the foundation of the Church by the Holy Spirit, was admirable in principle but maladroit in practice. Pentecost fell in the holiday period, when people had time to spare from work and when the roads allowed easy passage. This was an ancient season of unrest. The Peasants' Revolt of 1381 had taken place in May and June, as had the first Cornish rising of 1497. The new book followed a long series of unpopular changes affecting parish life, including the abolition of saints' days, guilds, and images. Body's presence in Penwith had caused a riot as early as 1547. When he visited Kerrier deanery early in 1548 and tried to enforce the removal of images, matters grew worse. Men from St Keverne and the neighbouring parishes attacked his lodgings in Helston and murdered him on 5 April. Their leaders announced demands in the market-place that no more religious changes should be made until the king was twenty-four. Gentry loyal to the government restored order and at least three ringleaders were executed, but the events showed how easily religious changes could now provoke violent reactions.[6]

The Prayer-Book had the same effect on a larger scale.[7] In Devon the people of Sampford Courtenay rose in protest on Monday 10 June, the day after Pentecost, having heard the new service once. In Cornwall unrest began at Bodmin on Thursday 6 June before the introduction of the Prayer-Book, perhaps when copies of the volume arrived. The Cornish protesters gained two leaders from the gentry,

---

1 *Statutes of the Realm*, IV(1), 18–22.
2 Rowse, *Tudor Cornwall*, 253–4.
3 Duffy, *Stripping of the Altars*, 547–8.
4 TNA, E 117, printed in L. S. Snell, *Documents towards a History of the Reformation in Cornwall*: vol. II, *The Edwardian Inventories of Church Goods for Cornwall* (c.1955), 1–25.
5 *Statutes of the Realm*, IV(1), 37–9. The best edition of the 1549 prayer book is F. E. Brightman (ed.), *The English Rite*, 2nd edn (1970).
6 Rowse, *Tudor Cornwall*, 253–4, 257–9; J. P. D. Cooper, *Propaganda and the Tudor State* (2003), 58–61.
7 On the rising, see F. Rose-Troup, *The Western Rebellion of 1549* (1913); Rowse, *Tudor Cornwall*, 253–90; I. Arthurson, 'Fear and Loathing in West Cornwall: seven new letters on the 1548 rising', *JRIC* new ser. II, 3/3–4 (2000), 68–96; and Cooper, *Propaganda*, 61–8 (which may overestimate the issue of the Cornish language).

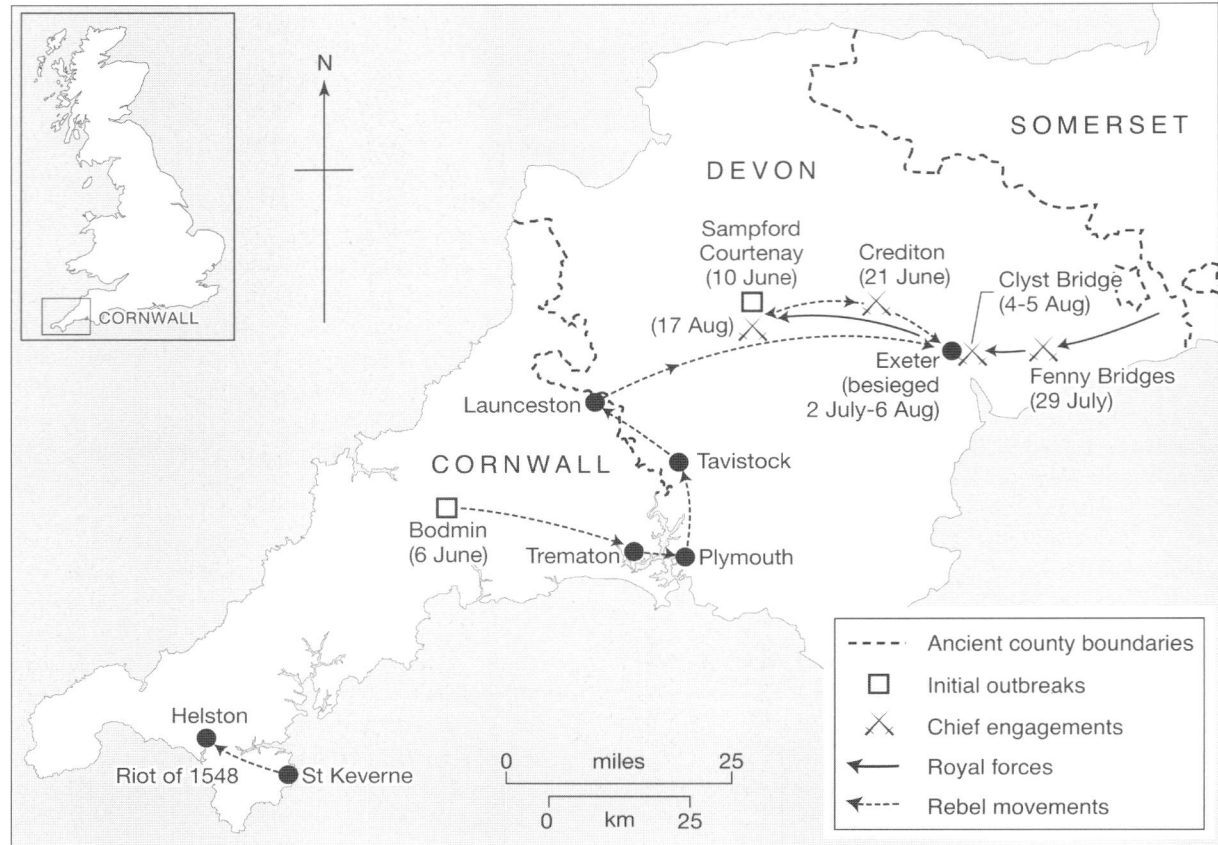

FIG 37. The 'Prayer Book Rising' of 1549.

Humphrey Arundell and John Winslade, and some of the clergy of Cornwall were later accused of involvement.[1] The number of their followers is still unknown, as are the totals of those killed in the fighting or in subsequent executions, and it should not be assumed that every active man in the county approved of the rising or, if he did approve, took part in it. The Cornish joined up with their fellow dissenters in Devon, besieged Exeter (2 July to 6 August), and fought three battles with the forces of the crown, ending with the victory of the latter at Sampford Courtenay on 29 August. This quashed the rising as an organised movement (Fig. 37). While it was in progress the leaders produced petitions which they sent to the crown, without receiving a satisfactory response. The chief set of these was produced during the siege of Exeter in July.[2] There were fifteen petitions in all, each introduced by the words 'we will have', and all religious in nature except for one, but there was a reference to 'particular griefs' that the leaders wished to explain to the king, and these may have included non-religious matters.

Most of the petitions involved undoing the reforms that had been made under Edward VI. Doctrinally they called for the Act of Six Articles to be re-established, and the death penalty reintroduced for heresy. In worship the Latin mass should be restored, along with the Latin matins, evensong, and processions. The protesters refused to accept the new service 'because it is but like a Christmas game', probably meaning a play in English, such as might be staged at Christmastide, and pointed out that some of them understood no English in any case. Other traditions to be restored including the hanging of the pyx above the high altar, the distribution of holy bread and water after services, and the giving of communion only in the form of bread and only at Easter. Ashes were to be given to the people again on Ash Wednesday and palms on Palm Sunday. Baptism was to take place on weekdays (in other words as soon as babies were born), images to be venerated again, and the dead to be prayed for. Two further demands hinted at undoing the break with Rome and the dissolution of the monasteries. Cardinal Pole, the leading Catholic exile, should be recalled and made a member of the king's council. Half of the monastic lands and chantry properties in anyone's possession should be surrendered to finance two religious houses in each county – their nature being unspecified. Whether these demands reflected the views of all the Cornish protesters is impossible to say; their strongly liturgical bias may owe something to the influence of clergy.

---

1 For some names of clergy allegedly involved, see Rose-Troup, *Western Rebellion*, 497–501.   2 Ibid., 220–2.

FIG 38. *John Veysey (d. 1554), as represented on his tomb in Sutton Coldfield church. Bishop for much of the Reformation, he complied with the demands of successive rulers until he was removed in 1551 by Edward VI's government, but was restored to office by Queen Mary in 1553.*

The suppression of the rising allowed the crown not only to maintain its reforms but to extend them further. The marriage of the clergy had already been permitted in 1548.[1] In 1550 a process began of removing all altars in churches and of replacing them by a single wooden table in the chancel for the purpose of communion. In 1552 the Prayer-Book was reissued in a more radical form. The medieval ceremonies, substances, and vestments retained in the 1549 book were mostly omitted, and services became almost wholly centred on the reading of Bible lessons and prayers. At communion, the priest was told to wear only a surplice and to stand on the north side of the new table. This was to be placed in the middle of the chancel on an east-west axis rather than the north-south axis of the old high altar. The communion bread was to be given in the form of a piece of white loaf bread rather than the traditional wafer, and the service was conceived as a memorial of Christ's Last Supper and sacrifice on the cross, not (as before) as a re-creation in some sense of that sacrifice and of his body and blood. Having made services simpler, the crown considered that churches no longer needed the vestments or ornaments that they had used hitherto. In the same year, 1552, commissioners were appointed to make inventories of all such things and to take charge of them. Churches were to be left with only a surplice for the clergyman, table cloths for the communion table, a cup for the communion, and a bell.[2] One aspect of these changes attracted a little support. At least seven Cornish rectors and vicars appear to have married during Edward's reign, including the incumbents of Antony, Calstock, St Kew, St Michael Penkevil, North Hill, Pelynt, and Tywardreath.[3] Their boldness was to bring them into trouble.

Throughout the religious changes from the break with the pope to the Prayer-Book rebellion, Bishop Veysey continued to rule the diocese (Fig. 38). Courtly and careful, he followed a policy of limiting damage by co-operating with the crown. He did not manage to prevent any of the major religious changes, however, and in 1550 he was made to surrender two of his Cornish properties, the manor of Pawton and the rectory of St Breock, to Sir Andrew Dudley, a gentleman of the royal household. He lost other property in Devon at the same time, and the wealth and power of the bishops declined in consequence.[4] In 1534 an act of Parliament provided for the appointment of suffragan bishops, who had hitherto been validated by the pope. The bishop of Exeter was empowered to have a suffragan named after St Germans,

---

1 *Statutes of the Realm*, IV(1), 67, 146–7.

2 Duffy, *Stripping of the Altars*, 476–7; Snell, *Edwardian Inventories*, xxiii, 35–6.

3 DRO, Chanter XVI, ff. 21r–31v. For further discussion, see Rowse, *Tudor Cornwall*, 307–10.

4 *Cal. Pat.* 1549–51, 7, 333. A rental of Pawton survives from 1548 (TNA, DL 43/1/13, printed in T. L. Stoate (ed.), *Cornwall Manorial Rentals and Surveys* (1988), 97–114). The bishop kept his other Cornish estates at Burniere, Cargoll, Lawhitton, Penryn, and Tregaire.

presumably with the thought that Cornwall might need separate oversight, but no such bishop was ever appointed.¹ Veysey used his existing suffragan, William Fawell, bishop of Hippo, until 1544, and after that had none. Only a trickle of candidates was now coming forward for ordination and little provision was made for confirmations, so that few Cornish can have been confirmed in the mid 16th century. Eventually, in 1551, the government decided that it needed a more active Protestant bishop, and Veysey (now in his eighties) was told to resign. He was allowed a substantial pension, and retired to Sutton Coldfield. In his place the crown appointed Miles Coverdale, the translator of the Bible and a distinguished Reformer. During his reign of two years Coverdale did what he could to forward the Reformation, persuading the conservative archdeacon of Cornwall, John Pollard, to recant his beliefs in the cathedral. He also made an ill-starred visit to Cornwall, where he fell seriously sick after drinking something at Bodmin that was contaminated or, it was rumoured, poisoned.²

THE REIGN OF MARY I

With the death of Edward VI in July 1553, and the succession of his elder sister Mary I, there was a return to Catholicism, although it lasted for little more than five years. In the autumn of 1553 Parliament repealed the statutes of Edward that dealt with religion.³ The English prayer-book lapsed in favour of the old Latin ones and it became lawful again to venerate saints and to pray for the dead. In 1554 the heresy laws were revived, the statutes of Henry VIII against the pope were repealed, and the English Church acknowledged the pope as its head.⁴ A clause of one of the statutes of repeal calmed the fears of those who had acquired religious property by recognising their rights to what they held. This concession made it difficult to revive the monasteries or chantries and none reappeared in Cornwall. The sole institutions to be re-established in the county during Mary's reign were the prebendal church of St Endellion (Fig. 39) and the preceptory of the Order of St John at Trebeigh, or rather its property. The crown had seized the prebends of St Endellion in 1548, leaving only the rector, but their endowments were not sold or granted during Edward's reign, no doubt because the lands and tithes concerned were mingled with those of the rector in a complicated manner. This allowed Mary's bishop of Exeter to institute new prebendaries in 1555 and 1559, and by the 1560s the church once more supported a rector and three (normally non-resident) colleagues.⁵ The crown restored Trebeigh to the Order of St John in 1558, but the order held it for only a year before the next monarch, Elizabeth I, withdrew it again.⁶

Meanwhile in September 1553 Coverdale was

FIG 39. *The prebendal church of St Endellion, rebuilt in the 15th century. Three of the four prebends were abolished in 1548, but restored in the 1550s.*

1 *Statutes of the Realm*, III, 509–10.
2 DRO, Exeter City Archives, Book 51, f. 350r.
3 *Statutes of the Realm*, IV(1), 202.
4 Ibid., 246–54.
5 Below, p. 183.
6 Below, p. 277.

removed as bishop of Exeter and Veysey returned. Despite being now in his eighties, he travelled to Exeter for a short stay before returning to Sutton Coldfield where he died in October 1554. His second period of office, although brief, saw the eviction of seven Cornish rectors and vicars from their benefices between June and October 1554, probably for the offence of having married, and the number may have been a little higher since the records are not complete.[1] Clergy willing to renounce their wives were allowed to occupy new parishes and Nicholas Nicolls, the former vicar of St Kew, moved to Marhamchurch under this provision, while William Lamb, expelled from Pelynt, started afresh at St Keyne. When Veysey died it was not easy for the crown to replace him, given that so many senior clergy had cooperated with the regimes of Henry and Edward. The choice eventually fell on James Turberville, who was consecrated as bishop in September 1555. He was a learned man (a doctor of divinity) from a gentry family in Dorset, who had been a cathedral canon in recent times and not prominent in Church life.[2] His younger contemporary, the Exeter historian John Hooker who was a Protestant, characterised him as 'very gentle and courteous', 'most zealous in the Romish religion', but not personally 'cruel or bloody', although Hooker blamed him for his part in the persecution of Agnes Prest, to which we shall come.[3] Little is known of Turberville's time in office. He was in power for only four years, and his register records hardly more than the names of the clergy whom he ordained and instituted to benefices.

It was less easy to re-establish Catholic worship. Much of the equipment of the old religion had disappeared from the parish churches, such as church silver, service books, and images, all of which had to be procured again. The crown helped a little, since most of the church plate seized in 1553 was still being stored, and this was returned to the parishes.[4] Cornish churchwardens' accounts from Mary's reign list payments relating to the restoration of church interiors and worship, but there may have been much variation in the speed at which this was done. At Camborne payments were made in 1554 for altar linen, holy oil, a holy cross, a holy candle, and a holy-water bucket, while the pyx to hold the sacrament above the altar is mentioned in the following year.[5] At Menheniot, on the other hand, although money was spent on the altar in 1554, it was not until 1557 that the pyx and the 'crucifix', presumably the rood, were set up again, or until 1558 that processional books were acquired, while a box for holy bread and rails for altar curtains were not paid for until 1559.[6] Nevertheless some wills of the mid 1550s confirm the evidence of the accounts that many Catholic practices and objects were reinstated. Ralph Thomvy of Perranzabuloe left money for a priest to sing five masses of the five wounds of Christ for his soul.[7] Richard Hore of St Ervan asked to be buried before the picture of St Erasmus in the parish church and gave 13s. 4d. to have his name put on the bead-roll.[8] James Speryer of Mabe bequeathed a ewe to a guild in the parish named after the Holy Ghost.[9]

One Cornish cleric tried to provide preaching material for the Catholic revival. In 1555 Edmund Bonner, bishop of London, and others published a set of twelve homilies in English for reading in church, intended to replace those of Cranmer which had been in use up to 1553. Towards the end of the 1550s, John Tregear, vicar of St Allen, translated Bonner's homilies into Cornish, although his version now exists in a single manuscript and we do not know how far or even whether it was used in churches.[10] A wider form of revival was that of popular processions. Nicholas Roscarrock, born in St Endellion parish in the late 1540s, remembered in later life that the relics of St Piran of Perranzabuloe 'were wont to be carried up and down in the country upon occasion, and I have seen them so carried in the time of Queen Mary'.[11] Presumably the relics had been preserved since 1538 when their veneration was forbidden. Roscarrock also recorded the revival of the Rogationtide processions by the parishioners of Crantock, Cubert, Newlyn East, and Perranzabuloe to the chapel of St Nighton at their common central point. Henry Crane, rector of Withiel, was said to have preached the last sermon to such a gathering, perhaps in 1558.[12] Some pilgrimage to St Michael's Mount and St Day may have been resumed, although it is not known what objects of veneration survived or were restored at these places. In 1556, for example, Walter Sawell of Gerrans made small bequests of 4d. each to the Holy Trinity of St Day, the Mount, St Piran of Perranzabuloe, and St Mary Magdalene – the latter probably meaning the chapel of the saint at Cosawes near Penryn.[13]

Not everyone was active in supporting the restoration of Catholicism. There was a notable reluctance by young men to be ordained as clergy. In 1557 and 1558, for which complete figures survive, only three and five men respectively were ordained as priests

---

1 DRO, Chanter XVI, ff. 14r–31v; Rowse, *Tudor Cornwall*, 307–10. Not all institutions of clergy in this period state what had happened to the previous incumbent, and the records after October 1554 are less informative.
2 Biography in *BRUO*, IV, 579, and *ODNB*.
3 J. Hooker, *A Catalog of the Bishops of Excester* (1584), sig. Iiiv.
4 Snell, *Edwardian Inventories*, 37–51.
5 CRO, PD/322/1, ff. 35v–40r.
6 CRO, P/144/5/2, ff. 6r–10v.
7 RIC, Henderson 66, p. 159.
8 Ibid., p. 149.
9 Ibid., p. 150.
10 BL, Add. 46397. On Tregear and his homilies, see D. H. Frost, '*Sacrament an Alter*: a Tudor Cornish Patristic Catena', *Cornish Studies* 11 (2003), 291–307.
11 N. Roscarrock, *Lives of the Saints: Cornwall and Devon*, ed. N. Orme, DCRS new ser. 35 (1992), 107.
12 Ibid., 94, 159–60.
13 Henderson 66, p. 149.

in the whole of Devon and Cornwall.[1] We hear of a few lay dissenters. When John Come left the Christmas Eve service at Linkinhorne in 1553, he expressed his pleasure at hearing mass again and receiving holy bread and water. But Sampson Jackman allegedly replied to him, 'I would all priests were hanged', after which (according to Come) Jackman and a visitor from Stoke Climsland, John Cowlyn, slandered the queen and said that if a woman were to reign, it ought to be her sister the Princess Elizabeth.[2] In the parish of Boyton, Agnes Prest of Northcott voiced anti-Catholic views to such an extent that she got into trouble with the Church authorities. This woman, a wife in her fifties, had learnt Protestant ideas from sermons during the reign of Edward VI. During the 1550s she voiced her disbelief in transubstantiation and the veneration of images, falling out with her husband and children and eventually leaving them. In due course she was accused by her neighbours of heresy and sent to Exeter to be examined by the bishop and his chancellor. She was kept at first in the bishop's prison, but was transferred to the gaoler's private house on the grounds that she was naive rather than heretical. Only when she persisted in maintaining her beliefs and declaring them to other people was she eventually found guilty of heresy and handed over to the lay power for execution. She was burnt in Southernhay, outside the city walls of Exeter, in August 1558 – the only person from Cornwall ever to have suffered this punishment, as far as we know, and the only one in the diocese during Mary's reign.[3]

THE ELIZABETHAN CHURCH SETTLEMENT

Mary died and Elizabeth succeeded her on 17 November 1558. A new Parliament assembled in January 1559 and, in a session lasting until May, enacted statutes restoring the Protestant Church of England.[4] The Church was again made subject to the English crown, with the more tactful use of the phrase 'supreme governor' to describe the monarch instead of 'supreme head'. The *Book of Common Prayer* was re-established in a version based on the second, more radical, Prayer Book of 1552, with a few conservative alterations. With one exception, the bishops currently in office refused to cooperate with the new regime, and voted against the new legislation in Parliament. The government hoped to win them over, and although they were suspended from power in the summer of 1559 and imprisoned in the Tower of London, it was not until March 1560 that a new bishop of Exeter was nominated in the person of William Alley. He was consecrated on 14 July. Bishop Turberville remained in the Tower until 1563, when he was transferred to the custody of the bishop of London. The crown allowed him to live in London under supervision early in 1565, but he was brought back to the Tower six months later and probably died there in about 1570.[5]

Meanwhile in September 1559 a fresh royal visitation of the Church took place throughout England. The usual teams of commissioners addressed articles of enquiry to the local clergy, delivered injunctions to them, and required them to swear an oath of allegiance to the queen as supreme governor.[6] Bishop Jewel of Salisbury, who took part in the visitation of Exeter diocese and was a Devon man himself, said when it was over that he and his companions found people everywhere 'well disposed towards religion', in other words to its reformed variety, 'even in those quarters where we expected most difficulty'. He complained, on the other hand, of the wilderness of superstition that had sprung up in Mary's reign. 'We found in all places votive relics of saints, nails with which the infatuated people dreamed that Christ had been pierced, and I know not what small fragments of the sacred cross.'[7] This points to the concealment of relics during the 1540s and their veneration again after 1553, suggesting that even in 1559 people's attitudes were not always as progressive as Jewel assumed. Many older people still clung mentally to the religion of their childhood. A few, like the Arundells of Lanherne and some members of the Roscarrock family of St Endellion, remained true to Catholicism throughout Elizabeth's reign, despite disapproval and eventually persecution.[8]

The injunctions of 1559 embodied a return to the policies of Henry VIII and Edward VI in most respects. The placing of English Bibles in churches, the keeping of parish registers and poor boxes, and the abolition of shrines and images were all prescribed once more. Clergy were again permitted to marry, although (in a reflection of Elizabeth's dislike of this practice) they were allowed to do so only after gaining the approval of the bishop, two local justices of the peace, and the future wife's parents. As we shall see, this did not deter some of the Cornish clergy from taking the step.[9] The new edition of the *Book of Common Prayer* issued in the

---

1 DRO, Chanter XVIII, ordination lists.
2 TNA, SP 11/2, f. 2r.
3 On Agnes Prest, see J. Foxe, *Acts and Monuments*, ed. J. Pratt (1877), VIII, 737–8, and DRO, Exeter City Archives, Book 51, f. 352r. The other two known heretics burnt at Exeter were Drew Steyner in 1431 and Thomas Benet in 1532.
4 *Statutes of the Realm*, IV(1), 350–8, 359–64, 397–400.
5 G. E. Phillips, *The Extinction of the Ancient Hierarchy* (1905), 198, 204–8, 232, 245–9, 343, 357.
6 Frere and Kennedy (ed.), *Visitation Articles and Injunctions*, III, 1–29.
7 J. Jewel, *Works*, ed. J. Ayre, Parker Soc. (1847–50), IV, 1216–18.
8 *ODNB* s.n. 'Arundell Family'; Roscarrock, *Lives of the Saints*, 1–14.
9 Frere and Kennedy (ed.), *Visitation Articles and Injunctions*, III, 18–20.

spring of 1559 restored church worship to a Protestant form largely based on the Prayer Book of 1552.[1] Normal Sunday worship in parish churches now came to consist of morning prayer, the litany, and the antecommunion (the first half of the communion service) in the morning, with evening prayer in the mid afternoon. Communion services became confined to about four occasions each year: at Christmas, Easter, Pentecost, and Michaelmas (29 September) or All Saints tide (1 November). Services in most churches were led by the clergyman and parish clerk from reading desks and a pulpit at the east end of the nave. Rood screens remained without images, but the chancel was only used in that part of the communion in which the bread and wine were consecrated at the table and distributed from there to the laity.

At the same tide the Elizabethan Church Settlement marked a retreat from some of the more radical changes of the later years of Edward VI. The communion table (when not in use) was ordered to be placed where the high altar had formerly been. The communion bread returned to the traditional form of wafers, and it and the wine were again considered to be consecrated objects, not merely symbols of the Last Supper, causing a London clergyman to get into trouble in 1573 when he ran out of communion wine and dispensed more without praying over it.[2] Music in parish churches was declared to be lawful, to the extent that choirs of men and boys could be organised and a hymn sung at the end of a service provided that it was in English. In practice, however, music in Elizabethan churches tended to centre on the singing of the psalms by the congregation in metrical versions rather than according to the chant of the later Middle Ages. People were once again directed to bow at the name of Jesus, and although processions in general remained forbidden, an exception was made for Rogationtide, reflecting its great popularity. It became lawful again for clergy and people to make their customary tours around their parishes on one of the Rogation days, saying Psalm 103 and other prayers, and such processions continued to be accompanied by eating and drinking, as they had been until the 1540s.[3]

In 1561 Bishop Alley sent a report about his beneficed clergy (rectors and vicars) to the archbishop of Canterbury, Matthew Parker.[4] He set out to list them by name, but in Cornwall his report identified only 124, falling short of the total by a couple of dozen. In one case, that of Hamond Hanfort, vicar of St Austell, the bishop was unable to make any contact at all. The list states, in most cases, whether the clergy were or were not graduates, ordained as priests, learned, preachers, married, and resident in their benefices giving hospitality to the poor. Every one of the beneficed clergy named was a priest, with the exception of the rector of Lawhitton, William Aylworth, who was a boy of 12 at school in Oxford – the kind of exception that was strictly against canon law but had sometimes occurred in the Middle Ages. About 92 of the clergy were described as non-graduates, compared with about 30 who possessed degrees. In reality graduate clergy were less common in Cornwall than this suggests, because some of them did not reside in their parishes and were represented there by non-graduate curates. In terms of learning, the incumbents were categorised as moderately learned, sufficiently learned, and learned.[5] Here 35 were moderate, 66 sufficient, 10 learned, and one 'studious', while only the vicar of Davidstow was altogether 'unlearned'.

Whether less or more learned, their main parochial work still centred on leading Sunday worship and on providing baptisms, marriages, churchings, and funerals when needed. Hardly any of them preached. Only 14 were stated as doing so, and of the 14 over half did so only in their own parishes. A mere handful, six or less, had licences to preach more generally. No less than 85 were returned as non-preachers, suggesting one reason why Elizabeth's regime, like that of Edward VI, issued authorised *Homilies* for the clergy to read instead. Ninety-three parishes were recorded as having a resident clergyman, who provided hospitality, meaning alms for the poor and possibly lodging for travellers. Forty-one parishes had an absent incumbent. The absent were either pluralists, who held more than one parish, or men with other reasons for living away from their benefices. Both practices continued to need permission, and (as in the past) this was most easily obtained by the well-connected. Of the 41 absent clergy in the survey, 23 lived in the county on one of their parishes, 14 resided outside the county, and 4 were of unknown whereabouts. Four were at university, one in London, two with the earl of Pembroke, one with Sir Richard Edgcumbe, and one (the rector of Ruan Major) with a local gentleman because the income of his parish was allegedly too small for his upkeep. Where the incumbent was not resident, he was still expected to pay a curate to do his duties, but the document does not list such men. Many of the clergy were probably still conservative in outlook – 1561 was only twelve years after the Prayer-Book rebellion – but, as in Edward's reign, a few of them were up-to-date in choosing to get married. Although only two years had passed since the

---

1 For modern editions, see W. K. Clay (ed.), *Liturgies and Occasional Forms of Prayer set forth in the reign of Queen Elizabeth*, Parker Soc. (1847), 23–245, 272–98, and E. Benham (ed.), *The Prayer-Book of Queen Elizabeth 1559* (1890).

2 *ODNB*, s.n. Robert Johnson (d. 1574).

3 Frere and Kennedy (ed.), *Visitation Articles and Injunctions*, III, 15; J. C. Cox, *Churchwardens' Accounts* (1913), 264–5.

4 Cambridge, Corpus Christi College, 97, ff. 156r–183r. There is a photostat and transcript in DRO, Z 19/10/1a–b.

5 Some university graduates were described as 'sufficiently learned' and some as 'learned'.

marriage of clergy was allowed, and despite the new restrictions, 16 clergy had found themselves wives while at least 105 of their colleagues remained unmarried.

The list of 1561 does not tell us everything we would like to know, particularly about the non-beneficed clergy who served the parishes of the non-residents. But, in the case of the beneficed clergy, it paints a not unsatisfactory picture. Almost all had some learning, and some were graduates. Most were resident, giving hospitality, and would have been capable of performing services and reading the *Homilies*. Christopher Walker, the vicar of Davidstow was indeed an exception. He had a female partner (it was not known whether wife or concubine), he was deemed unlearned, and he did not live on his benefice, where 'all things are ruinous'. But he was the only cleric to prompt such an adverse report.

CHANGES AND CONTINUITIES

How far did the Church change in Cornwall during the Reformation, and how far did it continue as before? This question can be answered in three respects: landscape, worship, and people. By Elizabeth's reign the Cornish landscape was not quite the same as before. In four of the towns – Bodmin, Launceston, Penryn, and Truro – large churches that had dominated the skyline had been pulled down or converted to other uses. In the countryside Tywardreath Priory disappeared, St Anthony-in-Roseland and St Germans lost their chancels, and hundreds of chapels closed. Many former religious structures were adapted to new uses. Bodmin Friary became a civic building, and several chapels were turned into sheds or dwellings. The gentry who bought monastic sites often converted the residential parts of the buildings into houses for themselves, a transformation visible at Bodmin, St Carroc, St Germans, and Trebeigh, as well as at Rialton, the country residence of the priors of Bodmin. As a result the Cornish landscape became less religious in appearance, although not completely so. Holy wells and wayside crosses remained, thanks to their smaller size or popular support, and the lesser concern of the authorities to remove them. Parish churches, too, continued along with their clergy houses and glebes (Fig. 40). In one respect the churches grew in strength, both institutionally and visually. The religious houses and chapels that had competed with them disappeared, and there were now no other places at which to worship or to be buried. As landscape elements, however, they stopped growing altogether. Rebuilding petered out during the middle of the 16th century. The outsides of church buildings were frozen in time. For the next three hundred years the characteristic church in the Cornish (and indeed in the English) landscape was a 15th- or early 16th-century building, usually with a tower and aisles. What the builders of that period had achieved became what people understood churches to be, an understanding that is still with us.

Churchscapes, the internal appearances of churches, did not freeze in this way. Their walls and pillars remained the same, and so did two important parts of their furnishings. Chancels continued to be divided from naves by the screens that had been introduced in about 1300. Naves remained full of the seating that had appeared or had been upgraded during the 15th and early 16th centuries. Yet much else changed between the 1530s and the 1560s. Holy objects were removed: altars, lights, and nearly every image, whether sculpted or painted. Such images as survived did so chiefly in stained-glass windows or as carvings in lofty places. The people of St Neot were notable in defending the grand

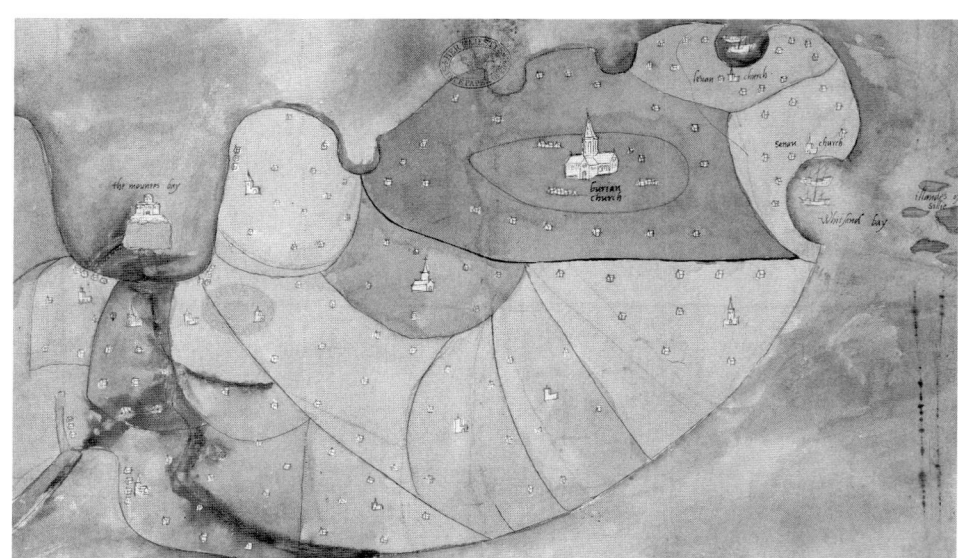

FIG 40.
St Buryan church, shown unrealistically large and magnificent, on a map of c. 1574. The map is one of the oldest known attempts to depict parish boundaries in England, albeit in a simplified way.

set of windows that they had recently installed,[1] and other windows with images of saints remained in churches such as Cardinham, Feock, St Kew, and St Winnow. Nevertheless such images were no longer focuses of devotion, and churches lacked anything to venerate apart from whatever respect people might pay to the communion table or font. Visual aids still had a place in church, but they now consisted of texts: the Lord's Prayer, the Creed, the Ten Commandments, inscriptions on tombs, or boards describing charitable benefactions. Texts in churches, as we have seen, long antedated the Reformation, so their proliferation afterwards represented a development of tradition rather than something quite new. From at least Elizabeth's reign onwards the royal coat of arms began to be displayed as well, signifying the fact that the monarch was the ruler of both Church and state. Even this was not entirely new, given the popularity of royal emblems by the early 16th century.

The parish church also changed inside by expressing unity rather than variety. Before the Reformation it had consisted of two or more rooms containing several areas of devotion and activity: the chancel, the side chapels and altars, images, the font, and the porch. Now there was a single focus on most Sundays: the nave, especially the area in front of the chancel screen. Nearly every service was centred here except for baptisms, which were still done at the font, and the consecration and reception of communion in the chancel. Other parts of the church ceased to have religious functions. The porch was reduced to a shelter, and the side chapels were filled with seating or tombs. A church was now a unitary space in which people gathered for almost identical services each Sunday. Most of the material was repeated on every occasion. Only the psalms, the lessons, and the homily ran through a sequence, although later, as preaching developed, the sermon became something individual to the service. Every church did the same, so that those who ignored the requirement to attend their own church had nothing to gain by attending another, unless a sermon was preached. Whereas the medieval mass had been something to watch and adore, rather than to understand, the services of the Church of England became occasions of instruction. The churchscape came to resemble a schoolroom. The clergyman read the service from a special seat like that of a master in a school, to people seated on benches as if they were pupils, amid texts that could be learnt. It was a service that sought to instruct them in the nature of God, the history of his relationship with the world, and the duties that he required of his people.

The clergyman's duties did not change in many respects. He continued to lead the service and his clerk to lead the responses. The congregation was allocated some prayers to say, but its role remained comparatively small. You still addressed him as 'Sir' John or whatever his forename was in Elizabeth's reign, and he was still the chief spiritual person in the parish. Economically he retained his tithes and glebe, although he was more heavily taxed than before the 1530s. His status even improved in certain respects. During the mid and late 16th century the Tudor monarchs turned the parish into a unit of civil government with responsibility for poor relief, roads and bridges, and military matters. The clergyman became the leader of what became the 'vestry' or parish administration for these purposes. In this way he gained powers over his parishioners that his predecessors had not held before the Reformation. He was also free of competition from monks, friars, guild priests, and chantry priests. There were now fewer clergy than before. From the mid 1530s to the late 1550s the numbers of men being ordained as priests in Exeter diocese fell considerably, as can be seen in Table 3:

TABLE 3. *Numbers of Priests Ordained in Exeter Diocese, 1520–1569.*

(Years for which complete figures are available)[2]

1520	58	1530	41	1557	3
1521	62	1531	30	1558	5
1522	54	1532	55	1561	19
1523	43	1533	47	1562	14
1524	34	1534	55	1563	16
1525	61	1537	14	1564	18
1526	38	1540	4	1566	27
1527	33	1541	6	1567	22
1528	49	1542	7	1568	44
1529	47	1552	1	1569	32

This reflected the uncertainty about a career in the Church that set in during the 1530s, and the loss of openings caused by the dissolution of the monasteries, colleges, and chantries. For a time, too, in the 1540s and 50s, there were many former members of these bodies available to act as assistant clergy or to fill vacancies as rectors or vicars. In the early years of Elizabeth's reign the number of new priests increased again, although it remained lower than it had normally been in the 1520s. The clergy became less of an 'estate' of the realm, a widely assorted group like the gentry and the labourers, as they had been before the Reformation. In future they would come closer to being a profession with a uniform way of life and public roles.

Lay people had a parallel experience of change and continuity. Much stayed the same for them. They still

---

1 J. Mattingly, 'Stories in the Glass: reconstructing the St Neot pre-Reformation glazing scheme', *JRIC* new ser. II, 3/3–4 (2000), 9–55.

2 The figures are taken from the ordination lists in DRO, Chanter XIV, XVI, XVIII, and XIX.

entered the Church, like it or not, by baptism, now usually done on the Sunday after the birth rather than on the birthday itself. They continued to be subject to the Church's laws, laws supported as before by the power of the crown. They were still expected to learn the basic prayers, to be confirmed (although that remained hard to achieve), to attend church on Sundays, to keep the Church's times and seasons including the Lenten fast, and to be buried in the parish church or churchyard. They had to pay tithes as before (some of which now went to lay impropriators), as well as monetary offerings four times a year and dues at weddings and funerals. Inside church social distinctions continued to matter. The gentry had their own space; indeed the disappearance of chapels and images gave them more scope to erect private seating and tombs. Lesser parish worthies also displayed their importance in where they sat. Senior parishioners continued to act as churchwardens and, these officers, like the clergyman, acquired new parochial responsibilities. There were still Church courts to police tithe-paying and moral behaviour, especially slander and sexuality. Outside church it was possible for some old religious customs to continue. Richard Carew, writing his *Survey of Cornwall* (1602), pointed out that the Cornish still held church ales to raise money, organised by young men of the parish. People still commemorated the days of the patron saints of their churches: no longer in church, but by entertaining friends from other parishes.[1] Carew might have mentioned that other folk-customs survived in association with these days, like those of the tinners of Perranzabuloe on 5 March (St Piran's day) and Helston's 'furry day' on 8 May (a feast of St Michael, the town's patron saint).[2] But, as a Protestant writer he wished to play down the appeal of the religious past, just as he avoided discussing the popularity of the old holy wells. These too went on attracting people for purposes of healing or of divining the future.[3]

Historians have long argued over whether the Reformation should be seen as a process of destruction or one of development and renewal. In truth it was both. Much that had been lovingly created during the Middle Ages was destroyed. Equally much of what happened during the Reformation grew out of that creation. The Church in Cornwall, in Elizabeth's reign, embodied not only new ideas and new laws of the 16th century but the institutions, buildings, revenues, education, and social relationships that had taken shape in the previous thousand years.

6. CHRISTIANITY IN MEDIEVAL CORNWALL: CELTIC ASPECTS

BY OLIVER PADEL

Christianity in Cornwall has functioned within the mainstream of Western Christendom from the Roman or post-Roman period until the present. The idea that there was a distinctive 'Celtic Church' in the earlier Middle Ages, although it was widespread during the 20th century, is not accepted today by historians.[4] It is misleading both because it exaggerates the significance of certain differences in practice which existed temporarily in the 7th and early 8th centuries, and because it creates an impression of unity between the different Celtic-speaking regions. Nevertheless, certain aspects of Christianity in Cornwall distinguished it from the rest of England throughout the Middle Ages; mostly they were features shared with other Celtic-speaking regions, and were inherited or developed from the pre-English period.

Consideration of their extent and significance is necessary for a full understanding of medieval Christianity in the county. These features are seen principally in the cult of saints, the physical geography and landscape of Christianity, and, to a limited extent, in aspects of church organisation and practice, mainly in the earlier Middle Ages. Distinctive aspects of the cult of saints and the ecclesiastical landscape are apparent in Cornwall from the earliest times to the Reformation, and to some extent even today. In so far as these characteristics were shared with other Celtic-speaking regions, especially Brittany and Wales (but to some extent also with Ireland, the Isle of Man, and parts of Scotland), they are part of the cultural inheritance in Cornwall, and can reasonably be called 'Celtic'.

---

1 R. Carew, *The Survey of Cornwall* (1602; repr. 2004), ff. 68r–71r.
2 A. R. Wright, *British Calendar Customs: England*, ed. T. E. Lones, Folk-Lore Soc. 97, 102, 106 (1936–40), II, 162, 247–51.
3 Carew, *Survey of Cornwall*, ff. 123r, 126v–127r, 129v–130r, 144r–v. On the survival of religious traditions in Cornwall after the Reformation, see N. Orme, 'Popular Religion and the Reformation in Cornwall', in J. D. Tracy and M. Ragnow, *Religion and the Early Modern State* (2004), 365–74.
4 W. Davies, 'The Celtic Church' (review article), *Journal of Religious History*, 8 (1974–5), 406–11; K. Hughes, 'The Celtic Church: is this a valid concept?' *Cambridge Medieval Celtic Studies*, 1 (1981), 1–20; W. Davies, 'The myth of the Celtic Church', in N. Edwards and A. Lane (eds.), *The Early Church in Wales and the West* (1992), 12–21.

THE CULT OF SAINTS

The distinctive character of the cult of saints in medieval Cornwall can be shown through comparison with Devon, a typical English county, and particularly in the dedications of parish churches.[1] Cornwall has 142 different dedicatory saints, of whom 103 bear distinctive Brittonic names such as Carantoc, Kea and Mawgan, and many are unique to Cornwall, such as St Bryvyth at Lanlivery, St Ildiern at Lansallos, and St Coan at Merther. In the rather larger county of Devon, with over 450 parishes, compared with about 196 in Cornwall, only 60 different dedications are known, of which the great majority (43) are to universal saints. Mary, Michael, Andrew, Peter, and All Saints alone account for 185 dedications of parish churches in Devon, compared with 19 in Cornwall. Only about seven dedications are distinctively Devonian, and a few churches have either imported Cornish or a few other Insular saints, including English ones, as patrons. The difference is further emphasised by the fact that the medieval dedications (if any) of 143 Devonshire churches are unknown, but of only 11 Cornish ones.

This difference between the two counties did not arise during the central or later Middle Ages, for it is evident at all periods for which records are available, back to the 8th century. By 1100, cults of more than 35 local or common-Brittonic saints are attested in Cornwall, nearly all as dedications of later parish churches, whereas only three universal saints (Stephen, Michael and German) are known as dedications. In Devon by the same date cults of seventeen universal saints are known, but of only six local ones, two of them acquired from Cornwall.[2] In 1330 the energetically authoritarian Bishop John de Grandisson, three years into his episcopacy at Exeter, remarked upon the obscure nature of many dedications in his diocese, particularly in Cornwall, and instructed that Lives of otherwise unknown saints were to be written and kept in duplicate or triplicate.[3] On the eve of the Reformation Cornish distinctiveness is again in evidence, for twenty or more parish churches, plus two non-parochial chapels, still honoured the bodies of their patron saints; by contrast Devon, though so much larger, had six such sites.[4] Even today the difference is immediately apparent from the many obscure saints who have entered into the local toponymy, and so appear on the modern map.[5] Since Cornish-language personal names had largely gone out of use by 1100, cults of saints with such names must have arisen before that date, except perhaps in a few cases where they may have been imported later from a neighbouring Brittonic area.[6] Such borrowing was itself a manifestation of the cultural community between the regions.

By contrast, in the characteristic later-medieval manifestations of saints' cults such as gilds, town chapels, church-stores and manorial chapels, the usual western European and Insular saints appear in Cornwall as in any other county, and the characteristic local saints appear only occasionally.[7] Evidently such international cults had been added more recently to the longer-established native diversity. By the late Middle Ages the two cultures happily co-existed, jostling for devotional space, as seen in the 16th-century windows at St Neot, where local and international saints appear side-by-side within individual windows. Evidence in the 15th and 16th centuries suggests that the local saints were honoured especially by the poorer classes, while the wealthier tended to favour better-known saints, although there is not a rigid separation.[8]

Such a profusion of distinctive local cults has caused discomfort to conformists since at least Bishop Grandisson's time; it raises the question of what precisely counts as a saint. The process of formal canonisation which arose in the 12th century created a clarity and rigidity which has to be discarded in considering these early local cults; indeed, uncertainty remained even after that date, owing to the ambiguity of Latin *sanctus*, both 'holy' and 'saint'.[9] At earlier periods saints emerged locally, sometimes regionally or even internationally, through more informal processes, their names becoming attached to the sites of churches and chapels without necessarily any intervention by the ecclesiastical authorities.[10] Once established at a single

---

1 Data from N. Orme, *English Church Dedications, with a Survey of Cornwall and Devon* (1996); and see above, 'From the Romans to the Norman Conquest'.

2 O. J. Padel, 'Local saints and place-names in Cornwall', in A. Thacker and R. Sharpe (eds.), *Local Saints and Local Churches in the Early Medieval West* (2002), 303–60 (at 330); the evidence examined by C. Cubitt, 'Universal and local saints in Anglo-Saxon England', *ibid.*, 423–53, shows that Devon was typical of England.

3 Padel, 'Local saints', 338–9.

4 Padel, 'Local saints', 341–4 and 354–60; to the four in Devon listed there (344) can be added St Brandwellan at Branscombe and St Sativola in a chapel at Exeter (J. H. Harvey (ed.), *William Worcestre: Itineraries* (1969), 124); also the 12th-century 'saint' Walter of Cowick: *Worcestre*, 124, and D. H. Farmer (ed.) *The Oxford Dictionary of Saints* (1978), 398.

5 For example, Sts Veep, Eval, Germoe, and Phillack, among many others.

6 For example, St Day (below).

7 J. Mattingly, 'The medieval parish guilds of Cornwall', *Journal of the Royal Institution of Cornwall*, n.s., 10 (1986–90), 290–329.

8 J. Mattingly, 'Stories in the glass: reconstructing the St Neot pre-Reformation glazing scheme', *Journal of the Royal Institution of Cornwall*, [3rd series], 3 (1998–2000), 9–55; Padel, 'Local saints', 347–50; N. Orme, *The Saints of Cornwall* (2000), 34–5.

9 Compare *sanctus* Walter of Cowick, at Exeter; so termed by William Worcester, but never formally canonised (above, note 5).

10 Below, 'Physical geography'.

site their cults might spread, but even then it would be misleading to think of these people as 'saints' in the later, formal, sense.

In the Brittonic world the very limited evidence suggests that these people were sometimes priests living at an early period, some probably in the 6th or 7th centuries, although contemporary evidence is lacking. A good example of a later cult is that of St Neot, who apparently died in eastern Cornwall in c. 865 × 93, and whose cult had become sufficiently prominent for his body to be removed to Eynesbury (Hunts.) by about 1000; despite the loss of his corporal remains in Cornwall, the cult remained sufficiently active locally for his name to remain attached to the site, for his life to be portrayed in a window in the church in around 1530, and for a poem explaining his importance, and drawing on his written dossier, to appear on a wall-panel in the later 17th century.[1]

These local cults and the possession of a saint's body were not restricted to major, minster-like, churches, as they generally were in Anglo-Saxon England.[2] In Cornwall, several parish churches which had saints' bodies lacked other attributes of minsters. Indeed, some were technically chapelries of other churches (themselves minster-like): Germoe (with the body of St *Germocus*) was a chapelry of Breage parish, though a Norman or earlier font suggests that it also had baptismal rights; St Ives (with the body of St *Ia*) was a chapelry of Lelant parish, which had the body of another saint, Euny; and Merther was a chapelry of Probus, but its place-name indicates that it had the body of its own saint, Coan.[3] At an even lower level, some of the numerous minor rural chapels provide evidence of distinctive local cults, but do not conform to the usual range of later-medieval chapels found elsewhere, and are often known by the saint's name alone. They include the chapels of St Illick in St Endellion parish, of St Ildrayth in St Dominick parish (probably the Irish saint Indract, honoured also at Glastonbury), and of St Day, a major destination of pilgrimage in Cornwall, dedicated to a Breton saint whose cult is otherwise unknown in Britain.[4] A chapel in the parish of Newlyn East dedicated to St Nectan (of Hartland) is not attested until the 17th century, although its existence is indicated by bequests made to that saint in 1470 and 1503;[5] and it was used as the destination of special Rogationtide processions, reminiscent of the Breton *pardons*, whereby the people of the four adjoining parishes would meet with their relics.[6] Although the processes are not understood whereby some sites remained as chapels while others became ordinary parish churches or minsters, the dedications of these sub-parochial chapels are likely to be just as ancient as those of sites which gained parochial status.[7]

The profusion of local cults, expressed primarily through dedications, is a characteristic shared with all other Celtic areas: Wales, Brittany, Ireland, Scotland and the Isle of Man. The most mysterious aspect of such dedications is the way in which some of them recur, particularly in the other Brittonic-speaking areas (Wales and Brittany), but also in Somerset, which was probably fully anglicised by the end of the 7th century, though it may have continued to receive cultural influences across the Severn estuary from Wales. St Degeman or *Decumanus*, honoured at a chapel in Wendron parish mentioned in 1397 (and attested there a century earlier as a place-name), provides a typical example. This saint was also honoured in Wales, at a chapel in Breconshire (Llanddegyman) and at one, perhaps two, parish churches in Pembrokeshire; and he is also the patron saint of Watchet parish church in Somerset.[8] The parish church of St Mewan provides a Breton example: in Cornwall it is overshadowed by the larger parish of St Austell adjoining it, whereas in Brittany St Méen's is a major church, while St Austol has no dedication but was known there as St Méen's close companion, who died a week after him and was buried with him.[9]

These two dedications (St Austell and St Mewan), and others to saints honoured primarily in Brittany, were already established at local sites in Cornwall in the early 10th century,[10] before Viking attacks brought

---

1 S. Keynes and M. Lapidge, *Alfred the Great: Asser's Life of King Alfred and other Contemporary Sources* (1983), 89 and 254–5; Mattingly, 'Stories in the glass', 46–9; G. H. Doble, *Saint Neot, Abbot and Confessor*, Cornish Saints, no. 21 (1929), 59–60 (poem).

2 J. Blair, 'A saint for every minster? Local cults in Anglo-Saxon England', in Thacker and Sharpe (eds.), *Local Saints and Local Churches*, 455–94.

3 Padel, 'Local saints', 336 (St Coan), 342 (St Germoe), and 358–9 (Sts Euny and Ia).

4 Orme, *Saints of Cornwall*, 106–7 (St Illick), 145–7 (St Ildrayth), and 103–4 (St Day).

5 N. Orme, *Cornish Wills 1342–1540*, Devon and Cornwall Record Society, n.s., 50 (2007), 88 and 115. Brief archaeological investigation of the site before it was destroyed by road-works indicated a building of the 14th or 15th century: anon., 'St Nighton's chapel, Newlyn East', *Cornish Archaeology*, 7 (1968), 83.

6 N. Roscarrock, 'Cornwall and Devon' in N. Orme (ed.), *Lives of the Saints,* Devon and Cornwall Record Society, n.s., 35 (1992), 94 and 159–60; L. Olson, 'Cornish rural religious processions', *Australian Celtic Journal*, 1 (1988), 22–9. These ceremonies seem to have been rather different from the single-parish perambulations of parish bounds known elsewhere in England, and more widely (e.g. Orme (ed.), *Roscarrock*, p. 42 and references, n. 197).

7 For a different view see Orme, *Saints of Cornwall*, e.g. 119 and 258.

8 Grid reference ST0642; so attested in c. 1190 (Orme, *Saints of Cornwall*, 104).

9 G. H. Doble, *Saint Mewan and Saint Austol*, Cornish Saints, no. 8, 2nd edn (1929); Orme, *Saints of Cornwall*, 67 and 191–2; K. Jankulak, 'Adjacent saints' dedications and early Celtic history', in S. Boardman et al. (eds.), *Saints' Cults in the Celtic World* (2009), 91–118 (at 113–16).

10 B. Lynette Olson and O. J. Padel, 'A tenth-century list of Cornish parochial saints', *Cambridge Medieval Celtic Studies*, 12 (1986), 33–71 (at 39–40, 68–9).

Bretons, and relics of Breton saints, to other parts of England, particularly through the patronage of King Athelstan (924–39).[1] It is unknown to what extent, if at all, Cornwall participated in the reception of Breton saints at that period; but in any case saints shared with Wales, such as St Degeman and about twenty others, cannot be so explained; nor can those unique to Cornwall. The profusion of local saints in Cornwall arose from its indigenous culture, as in Wales and Brittany, not from overseas influence.

Recurrent dedications are generally assumed to be to saints shared by the different regions, rather than to separate saints who happen to have had the same name; but proof is elusive. Circumstantial evidence can suggest that particular saints are shared ones. The fact that the parishes of St Austell and St Mewan are adjacent in Cornwall, while St Austol was recognised as a companion of St Méen in Brittany, is typical. Another such pointer, itself a further mystery, is the occasional combination of a saint's name with the same words in widely dispersed place-names. Thus the four places in Britain named from St Ke all show a distinctive place-name form, comprising Brittonic *lann* 'church-site' plus *to* 'thy', used as a prefix in hypocoristic (pet) names of saints. The name of *Landegea*, St Ke's church-site in Cornwall, is identical in derivation to Landkey (Devon), where the church is now dedicated to St Paul, *Lantokai* (Somerset; now Leigh-in-Street), and Llandygai (Caernarvonshire). In Somerset and Devon these place-names can hardly have been created after about A.D. 700 at the latest; and in none of these regions is there any other place named from St Ke, with a variant name. In Brittany, on the other hand, the place-name St Quay occurs several times, without any suggestion of a composite name like Landegea. No reason for the repetition of this place-name form, nor for its absence in Brittany, has been suggested.

No theory satisfactorily accounts for the range of repeated dedications. In all, Cornwall has dedications to about 20 saints honoured primarily in Wales, and to about 34 saints honoured primarily in Brittany, as well as ones to about 15 more saints known in both countries. The traditional explanation for such repetitions is offered in saints' Lives, mostly written from the late 9th to the 12th centuries. The writers assumed that the dedications provide a record of the travels of the saints themselves, showing the churches which they founded as they journeyed. This explanation, which remained popular until the mid-20th century, is now generally discounted.[2] There were other ways in which dedications could travel, and the hagiographers probably had no reliable information about their subjects, but were themselves trying to explain the dedications. It is now considered that local cults could be spread by individuals or groups at a variety of dates. Thus the Cornish cult of St Petroc was perhaps taken to Brittany by Bretons returning from Cornwall after the diaspora in the earlier 10th century,[3] while a dedication to St Winwaloe, primarily a Breton saint, at the coastal parish of East Portlemouth (Devon) may have arisen from maritime links with Brittany at any time before its first attestation in 1450.[4] The subject is complicated by uncertainty over which names can actually be equated, since hypocoristic forms of saints' names were sometimes far removed from the original.[5] Some authorities therefore combine saints having a range of different name-forms as a single cult.[6]

In Ireland the same phenomenon is partly attributed to scattered ecclesiastical estates owned by a single church or community, or to travelling kin-groups which imposed their stamp upon newly-settled lands by implanting their favoured saint.[7] The former of these explanations has also been convincingly invoked to explain repeated dedications within Wales,[8] and to a lesser extent in Brittany.[9] It may have some limited application in Cornwall, where St Piran's monastery at Perranzabuloe had, by 1086, been deprived of a distant estate in the north of the county, of uncertain identification but perhaps traceable from a later chapel near Tintagel dedicated to St Piran.[10] However, there is

---

1 For example, P. W. Conner, *Anglo-Saxon Exeter: a Tenth-Century Cultural History* (1993), 23–9; G. H. Doble, *Saint Melor, Patron of Mylor and Linkinhorne, and of Amesbury (Wilts.)*, Cornish Saints, no. 13 (1927), 24–5.

2 E. G. Bowen, *The Settlements of the Celtic Saints in Wales* (1954), and *Saints, Seaways and Settlements in the Celtic Lands* (1969).

3 K. Jankulak, *The Medieval Cult of St Petroc* (2000), 101–14.

4 N. Orme, *English Church Dedications*, 157; but St Winwaloe is probably older as patron saint of Landewednack, Gunwalloe, and presumably Towednack churches in west Cornwall.

5 Thus *Towennoc* is a hypocoristic form for St Winwaloe, but is St Winnow (*Winnocus*) the same saint? Compare Orme, *Saints of Cornwall*, 256–9, and P. Russell, 'Patterns of hypocorism in early Irish hagiography', in J. Carey et al. (eds.), *Studies in Irish Hagiography: Saints and Scholars* (2001), 237–49.

6 Notably P. Ó Riain, 'Towards a methodology in early Irish hagiography', *Peritia*, 1 (1982), 146–59, and 'The saints of Cardiganshire', in J. L. Davis and D. P. Kirby (eds.), *Cardiganshire County History*, I, *From the Earliest Times to the Coming of the Normans* (1994), 378–96.

7 For example, T. M. Charles-Edwards, 'Érlam: the patron-saint of an Irish church', in *Local Saints and Local Churches*, edited by Thacker and Sharpe, 267–90; and P. Ó Riain, 'Irish saints' cults and ecclesiastical families', *ibid.*, 291–302.

8 J. R. Davies, 'The saints of south Wales and the Welsh Church', in Thacker and Sharpe (eds.), *Local Saints and Local Churches*, 361–95.

9 B. Tanguy, 'Les cultes de saint Gildas, sainte Trifine et saint Trémeur et les abbayes de Saint-Gildas-de-Rhuys et de Saint-Gildas-des-Bois', *Mémoires de la Société d'histoire et d'archéologie de Bretagne*, 83 (2006), 5–27.

10 St Piran's unidentified manor of *Tregrebri* (*Domesday Book: Cornwall*, edited by Thorn, 5.8.10) is tentatively equated with modern Genver (grid reference SX085887), because of a nearby chapel of St Piran attested in 1457: J. Maclean, *The Parochial and Family History of the Deanery of Trigg Minor*, 3 vols (1873–9), III, 224 and n. 5 (chapel); Orme, *Saints of Cornwall*, 220–2.

little evidence to suggest that many early Cornish churches held scattered estates of this kind, and most repeated dedications within the county cannot be so explained, such as those to St Winwaloe,[1] nor those to St Euny at Lelant and Redruth churches, and at the chapels of Merthereuny in Wendron parish and Chapel Euny in Sancreed parish.[2] Moreover, in the cases of transmarine repetitions this explanation would require us to envisage pre-Conquest ecclesiastical estates embracing lands in more than one Brittonic region, and such estates are unknown and seem improbable. Nor is anything known about movements of kin-groups in the Brittonic world, of the kind that are well attested in the Gaelic world; there may have been such movements between Wales, Cornwall and Brittany at a very early period, but evidence is lacking.

A few Lives of Cornish saints were written in Cornwall, although there is little to show whether Bishop Grandisson's instruction of 1330 concerning this matter had a significant effect. Three Lives of St Petroc were written, presumably at Bodmin since they show local knowledge; the earliest has been dated to the 11th century on stylistic grounds, but may be slightly later.[3] John Leland reported brief details of two other saints' Lives, which he probably found in their respective parish churches.[4] Doble deduced that a lost Breton-Latin Life of St Ke, summarised by Albert Le Grand in 1636, was derived from one written at Glasney College (Penryn), because Glasney possessed the advowson and great tithes of that parish, and the lost Life incorporated local detail about the parish;[5] his conclusion has been strengthened by the discovery of *Bewnans Ke*, a Cornish-language play of the saint. The writing of vernacular Lives of local saints in dramatic form was a significant late development. Two such plays survive, of St Meriasek, patron saint of Camborne (dated 1504), and St Ke, patron saint of Kea parish (perhaps a little earlier).[6] As vernacular plays of local saints they are unique in England, but are paralleled in Brittany and more widely on the Continent.[7] The two texts are verbally and thematically related, and since both parishes had close links with Glasney College at Penryn, the textual relationship of the two plays is readily explained through that institution.[8] *Rad'* Ton, the copyist or author of *Bewnans Meriasek*, was probably Richard Ton, a parish priest who in 1536 was serving at Crowan, the adjacent parish to Camborne, as curate to Ralph Trelobys, vicar of Crowan and a long-serving canon of Glasney.[9] *Bewnans Meriasek* is based on a Breton-Latin Life of the saint, and on other sources including a Life of St Silvester, the first pope;[10] its composition may have arisen from the appointment of John Nans, a provost of Glasney, as rector of Camborne in 1501.[11] Similarly the author of *Bewnans Ke* made close textual use, not only of a lost Latin Life of the saint, but also of Geoffrey of Monmouth's *Historia Regum Britanniae*, again probably available at Glasney, for a long, unimaginative digression about King Arthur (the only medieval dramatic treatment of that figure in any language). These two dramas depend closely upon Latin learning, and they presumably arose from cultural links with Brittany in the later 15th century; they vividly illustrate how distinctive some aspects of Cornwall's religious culture remained right down to the Reformation.

In fact all the substantial texts extant in Middle Cornish have links, direct or indirect, with either Glasney College or Penryn town, suggesting that Glasney may have been the only centre of Cornish-language literary production in the Middle Ages;[12] not that the texts were necessarily written by its clergy, but by men who had connections with it and could benefit from its resources. The college may also have served to alleviate the difficulties which arose for the bishops of Exeter from the linguistic and cultural distinctiveness of the westernmost quarter of their diocese.[13] It lay at

---

1 King Athelstan's gift of relics of St Winwaloe to Exeter minster (Conner, *Anglo-Saxon Exeter*, 184, 196, and 204) may subsequently have aided the popularity of his cult within the later diocese; but the dedications in west Cornwall are unlikely to have arisen thus.

2 Orme, *Saints of Cornwall*, 118–220.

3 P. Grosjean, 'Vies et miracles de S. Petroc', *Analecta Bollandiana*, 74 (1956), 131–88 and 470–96 (at 474–8); Jankulak, *Cult of St Petroc*, 4 and n. 27.

4 N. Orme, 'Saint Breage; a medieval virgin saint of Cornwall', *Analecta Bollandiana*, 110 (1992), 341–52.

5 G. H. Doble, *Four Saints of the Fal*, Cornish Saints, no. 20 (1929), 16–18.

6 W. Stokes (ed.), *Beunans Meriasek, the Life of Saint Meriasek, Bishop and Confessor: a Cornish Drama* (1872; = BM); G. Thomas and N. Williams (eds.), *Bewnans Ke: the Life of St Kea* (2007; = BK).

7 É. Ernault (ed.), *L'ancien mystère de saint-Gwénolé* (1932–4); Y. Le Berre et al. (eds.), *Buez santez Nonn, mystère breton: vie de sainte Nonne* (1999); there are also Breton plays of universal saints (St Barbara, St Patrick), and further post-medieval plays of local saints.

8 O. J. Padel, 'Oral and literary culture in medieval Cornwall', in H. Fulton (ed.), *Medieval Celtic Literature and Society* (2005), 95–116 (at 105 and 110); close verbal parallels appear, for example, at lines BK 169, etc. (BM 3295); BK 928–9 (BM 3201); BK 1041 (BM 3983); BK 1176 (BM 2327–8); BK 1275 (BM 3215); BK 1397–9 (BM 3369–70); and BK 2120 (BM 2457).

9 D. H. Frost, 'Glasney's parish clergy and the Tregear manuscript', *Cornish Studies*, 2nd series, 15 (2007), 27–89 (at 65–8): *Rad'* would normally be understood as 'Ralph', but Frost has shown (with parallels) that it could also signify 'Richard' at this period.

10 G. H. Doble, *Saint Meriadoc, Bishop and Confessor*, Cornish Saints, no. 34 (1935); B. Murdoch, *Cornish Literature* (1993), 99–126.

11 T. C. Peter, *The History of Glasney Collegiate Church, Cornwall* (1903), 79.

12 Padel, 'Oral and literary culture in medieval Cornwall', 97–9; and now Frost, 'Glasney's parish clergy and the Tregear manuscript'.

13 Compare the difficulties raised in Bishop Grandisson's time over the obscurity of the saints and the treatment of St Piran's relics (below); and occasional hints of linguistic difficulties experienced by clergy in the western half of Cornwall at this period: e.g. F. C. Hingeston-Randolph, *Register of Bishop Grandisson*, I, 97–8 (general western Cornwall, 1329); II, 820–1 (St Buryan, 1336); II, 910 (St Merryn, 1339); II, 957–8 (Glasney, 1342).

the mid-point of the Cornish-speaking half of the county, on land which the bishops had held since before the Norman Conquest, and at a flourishing south-coastal port which provided easy communication with Exeter itself, as well as giving wider international links (especially with Brittany), of which the fruits can be seen in the texts. As a college of secular clergy, Glasney served as a focus for the Cornish-speaking priests who were needed in the western half of the county, and Penryn's close links with Brittany and the wider Continent would have generated a lively intellectual atmosphere. The college was well placed to facilitate the two-way transmission of news and ideas between the Cornish-speaking sector and the diocesan see.

Likewise the cult of corporal relics in Cornwall remained distinctive within England down to the Reformation. As already noted, a striking number of parish churches (one in ten) and a few non-parochial chapels claimed to have their saint's body in the late 15th or early 16th century. The importance of bodily relics is witnessed in Cornwall from the time of the earliest records, in the 9th century (St *Gueriir*, at St Neot) and in the 10th (St Neot himself; St German; St Petroc; Sts Docco and Kew at St Kew; St Rumon at Ruan Lanihorne).[1] Relics in private hands (though of unspecified type) are mentioned in one of the 10th-century Bodmin manumissions.[2] These relics, however, were not honoured in the way that Anglo-Saxon, and subsequently Norman, observers might have expected, and there is little evidence that they were used for curative purposes at any date.[3] The cultural difference gave rise to the impression among outsiders that the bodies were not actually valued locally, although that was demonstrably untrue in some cases. This difference in perception is known to have been the reason for the removal of St Winifred's relics from Holywell (Flints.) to Shrewsbury in the 12th century, and it may similarly explain the removal of St Neot's and St Rumon's bodies in the 10th century, to Eynesbury (Hunts.) and Tavistock (Devon) respectively, and possibly the theft of St Petroc's relics in the 12th to Brittany, though that was attributed to a disaffected monk of his own community.[4] A similar lack of emphasis in Brittany and Wales upon the healing powers of corporal relics has been noted.[5] In many cases the relics were perhaps not translated to an above-ground shrine until comparatively late, if at all.[6] Nor did they tend to become the objects of pilgrimage from outside the parish, as often elsewhere: the chief sites of pilgrimage in Cornwall were St Michael's Mount and St Day, neither of them among the sites claiming the corporal remains of a saint. Only St Piran's relics, at Perranzabuloe, are known to have been an object of pilgrimage by the 14th century; and even there their main function seems to have lain in their use in *pardon*-like inter-parochial processions which were themselves (predictably) a cause of admonition during Bishop Grandisson's episcopacy, in 1331.[7]

Yet the frequency with which relics are mentioned, from the 9th century to the 16th, shows that they were important locally; in the Brittonic world (perhaps in the Celtic world in general) the importance of the saint's body seems to have lain rather in the way in which its presence sanctified the site and gave it historical authority.[8] In 1086 obscure saints such as Ke, Goran and Probus appeared among the principal landholders of the county in the Geld Inquest, alongside King William, the bishop of Exeter, and the Norman barons. This powerful link between the saint and his *locus* created a resistance to moving the relics. The body of St Petroc seems to have remained at Padstow probably for some while after the chief site of his monastery had moved inland to Bodmin, for safety from maritime attack.[9]

Thus the cult of saints in medieval Cornwall was characterized by two conflicting attitudes, pulling in different directions. On the one hand, as widely in western Christendom, a saint was expected to be local, to such an extent that a local saint might develop out of an international figure (St German is a probable example), or from a saint shared with another Brittonic area (such as St Carantoc or St Docco), or occasionally out of a secular place-name.[10] On the other hand there was also sometimes a desire, often encouraged from above, to equate a local saint with a better-established one elsewhere: the local St Piran was equated with the Irish St Ciarán of Saighir (Seirkieran, Co. Offaly), to provide St Piran with a written Life; St Meriasek was replaced (though never entirely so) by St Martin at

---

1 Padel, 'Local saints', 345; O. J. Padel, *Slavery in Saxon Cornwall: the Bodmin Manumissions* (2009), 21, for St Petroc's relics in the 10th century.

2 Padel, *Slavery in Saxon Cornwall*, 18.

3 Padel, 'Local saints', 345–7; three persons were recorded as having been healed in about 1477 at Minster by St Mertherian, presumably at her shrine: Harvey (ed.) *William Worcestre: Itineraries*, 30.

4 Padel, 'Local saints', 345–7 and 351; Jankulak, *Cult of St Petroc*, especially 18–31; above, 'From the Romans'.

5 J. Smith, 'Oral and written: saints, miracles, and relics in Brittany, *c.* 850–1250', *Speculum*, 65 (1990), 309–43; Padel, 'Local saints', 346–7.

6 At Altarnun ('altar of St Nonn') an above-ground shrine of St Nonn was sufficiently noteworthy to give the place its unique name, at some date before *c.* 1100: Padel, 'Local saints', 315–16.

7 Hingeston-Randolph, *Register of Bishop Grandisson*, 3 vols (1894–9), II, 608; the phrase *diversa et remota loca* of the reprimand suggests journeys further afield than merely within the parish. Compare Padel, 'Local saints', 342; and above, 'Later Middle Ages; People'.

8 Smith, 'Oral and written', 342; Padel, 'Local saints', 350–2.

9 Padel, *Slavery in Saxon Cornwall*, 6–7.

10 Padel, 'Local saints', 351; Orme, *Saints of Cornwall*, 83–5, 108–9 and 242.

Camborne; and the local St *Felec*, who gave Phillack parish its name, was latinised as St *Felicitas*, though it is unclear which of the saints of that name in the Roman calendar was intended.[1]

In most cases nothing is known about the saints, for lack of contemporary information: all that we have, in Cornwall as in Wales and Brittany, are the dedications and the place-names, *nuda tantum nomina*, 'just bare names', in William of Malmesbury's phrase.[2] It is therefore unhelpful to think in terms of where the saints 'came from', which is irrecoverable; what may be ascertainable is the location of their chief cult centres, from which the cults could spread. In the later Middle Ages there was a fashion for claiming an Irish origin for saints, in Cornwall as elsewhere in England; but in fact few cults seem to have been introduced from there.[3] However, a tradition in north Cornwall that twenty-four saints were all offspring of the saintly King Broccan, who gave his name to Breconshire (Brycheiniog) in central Wales, does seem to reflect some historical truth, since the area covered by their identifiable dedications is roughly the same as that which received Irish settlement in the 5th to 6th centuries, as evidenced by ogham and other inscriptions; and this Irish settlement may itself have come from Breconshire, which had received Irish settlement from further west in Wales at about that period.[4] The inscriptions, however, prove only a general cultural influence in the area, not that any of the patron saints of chapels or churches were themselves immigrant settlers; and not many saints' cults are actually shared with Breconshire. In the case of the many Cornish cults shared with other areas, such as Brittany, other parts of Wales, and Somerset, the direction of travel of each cult will be ascertained, if at all, only by detailed local work.

THE PHYSICAL GEOGRAPHY OF CHRISTIANITY

Cornwall also differs from the rest of England in the physical geography of Christianity, the manner in which the religion has accommodated itself to the landscape. The profusion of local saints' cults is associated with a profusion of small-scale religious sites, contrasting with the nucleation of local devotion into fewer, larger-scale, sites in much of England.[5] The differences can be examined by starting with the types of names borne by the parishes today. About three-quarters of Cornwall's ancient parishes (147 out of 196) have an ecclesiastical name, consisting of either a saint's name alone, or an ecclesiastical place-name element such as *Lann-* 'church-site' (Fig. 41) or *Eglos-* 'church' plus another word. By contrast, in Devon only 29 out of 454 parishes have names of this kind.[6] The ecclesiastical system in Cornwall was less closely linked to the secular settlement-pattern, and thus to the medieval manorial system, than in the rest of England. Thus only 28 per cent of the names of Cornish parishes appear in Domesday Book, whereas in Devonshire over 90 per cent appear as the names of (secular) manors.

A more visual manifestation of the difference is the frequency of isolated churches, sited not in population-centres but having often only a single farm nearby. The most intriguing of these sites are coastal churches lying at one end of their parish, and inconveniently located for the population of the area which they served; the extreme example is Kea, where the church was at the south-eastern coastal tip of a parish over seven miles in length.[7] There is no evidence that villages or ports have ever surrounded many of these churches; they seem to owe their coastal location to some other cause. They were already considered isolated in the central Middle Ages, when the writers of saints' Lives portrayed them as the landing-places of wandering saints, who arrived by boat from overseas and established communities which were deliberately isolated; but there are also similar churches at inland sites, where the explanation as landing-places cannot apply. The distinctive pattern is related to the fact that, typically for upland Britain, settlements in Cornwall are less nucleated than in most of England and remain scattered and rural; towns are considered to be predominantly introductions made in the central Middle Ages, after the parochial system had been established.

The key word designating the early sites of churches is *lann*, which is recognised as crucial for understanding early Christianity in the Brittonic world, although its precise meaning is uncertain.[8] It was in use by the 7th century at the latest, as shown by its occurrence in place-names in Devon, Somerset and Dorset, where Brittonic names can hardly have been created any later than that date. There are also indications that it was being used in place-names in

---

1 Olson and Padel, 'Tenth-century list', 48–9; Orme, *Saints of Cornwall*, 121–2.

2 *Gesta Pontificum* (Rolls Series), 202.

3 R. Bartlett, 'Cults of Irish, Scottish and Welsh saints in twelfth-century England', in B. Smith (ed.), *Britain and Ireland 900–1300* (1999), 67–87; Orme, *Saints of Cornwall*, 28.

4 Orme (ed.), *Nicholas Roscarrock*, 45–51; C. Thomas, *And Shall these Mute Stones Speak? Post-Roman Inscriptions in Western Britain* (1994), 113–29 and 238–53.

5 J. Blair, *The Church in Anglo-Saxon Society* (2005), 19–21 and 302–4.

6 O. J. Padel, 'Cornish names of parish churches', *Cornish Studies*, 4–5 (1976–7), 15–27; Padel, 'Local saints', 304–10.

7 Other examples, less extreme, include the parish churches of Mylor, Mullion, St Gennys, Talland and St Germans.

8 Padel, 'Cornish names of parish churches'; O. J. Padel, *Cornish Place-Name Elements* (1985), 142–5, and references.

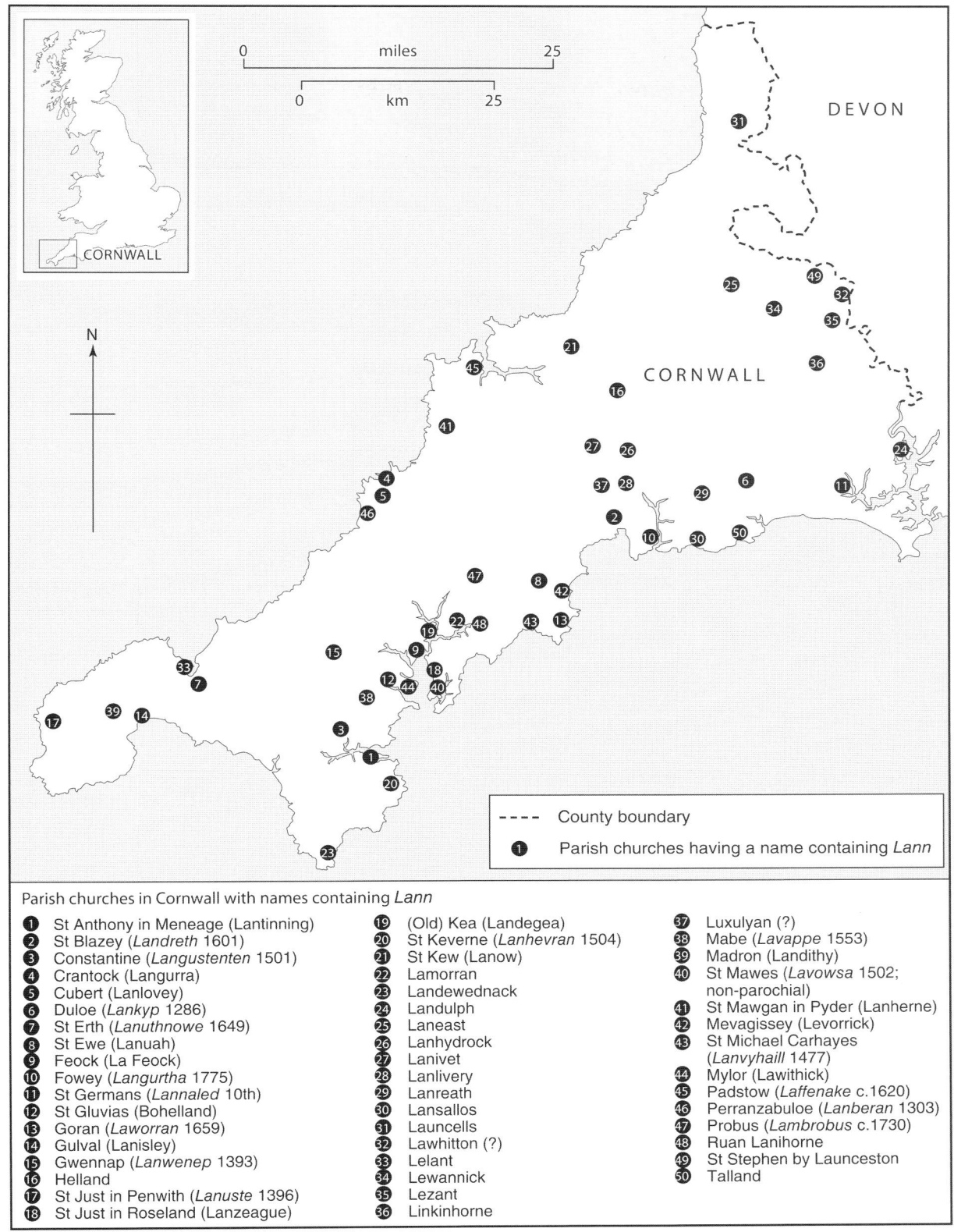

FIG 41. *Parishes churches in Cornwall with names containing Lann.*

Wales by then, and its shared usage in Wales, Cornwall and Brittany presumably goes back to a very early period. In Cornwall place-names containing the word are well attested in the earliest extant records. Implied in the 8th-century Life of St Samson,[1] it appears in the mid-10th century in the names *Lannaled* (St Germans), *Lannmoren* (Lamorran), and *Landochou* (St Kew), and in Domesday Book in the names of at least 14 further manors.[2] Of the three 10th-century names, two refer to minster-like churches, but the third (Lamorran) to a small church with no minster-like attributes. The word seems likely to have gone out of general use, as a formative element, by about the 10th century in Cornwall, perhaps as late as the 11th; a similar period of use has been suggested, independently, in both Brittany and Wales (although the word itself has remained current in Welsh, meaning 'church', to the present day).[3] It is nowhere attested as a word in surviving Cornish-language texts, from the 12th to the 18th centuries.

The suggested Dark-Age meaning of *lann used to be given as 'enclosed cemetery', but in the present state of knowledge it is perhaps better rendered as 'church-site within a curved enclosure', though it remains uncertain what precisely that implied. Both its period of use and its meaning have been usefully questioned from an archaeological perspective, primarily because it is known archaeologically that unenclosed burial-sites continued in use into the 5th and 6th centuries, when *lann is likely to have been current.[4] Probably the difficulty lies in an over-emphasis upon burials and cemeteries in Dark-Age archaeology, for the understandable reason that those features constitute the most visible form of material evidence in a very obscure period. Burials comprised only one aspect of the new religion, not necessarily the most distinctive. *Lann may be envisaged rather as a habitative place-name element, designating the dwelling-site of a small community of clerics, perhaps with variable functions, either ministering to a lay population or leading monastic lives, or both; living possibly with associated family or other lay people; and dwelling within, or by, a curved enclosure, within which their burials may also have taken place.[5] This meaning would be compatible with such archaeological evidence as is available concerning early church-sites in the Brittonic world. Burials in enclosed and unenclosed sites may have overlapped chronologically, perhaps according to local or family preference, or for different sectors of the population; to begin with it may have been only members of the communities dwelling at such sites who were buried within the enclosures. No Cornish word signifying an unenclosed burial-site has been identified.

Overall *lann is known to occur in the names of about 50 parish churches in Cornwall, and additionally in those of an uncertain number of non-parochial sites, very approximately perhaps another 50; an unknown further number must have been lost altogether.[6] Not all need have been in use at the same time; some might have been quite short-lived as ecclesiastical sites, at some date between about the 6th and 10th centuries. This level of density invites comparison with Ireland, where the evidence suggests an early profusion of ecclesiastical sites, of which some became secular farms (if they survived as settlements at all), while others remained as chapel-sites or expanded to become the sites of future parish churches.[7] Thus most of the surviving non-parochial *lann-names in Cornwall probably refer to early sites which failed to develop into parish churches, rather than ones which developed after the parochial system had begun to take shape. The visible structure at the farm of Helland in Mabe parish (*Hen-lann 'old, disused *lann') gives the best idea of what might be envisaged at such sites. The site had probably gone out of use by the 10th century at the latest, and there is no documentary record of its ecclesiastical use at any period. Burials took place within the raised curvilinear enclosure, which is significantly smaller than any existing parochial churchyard.[8]

A good number of the isolated churches, inland as well as waterside ones, have names in *lann, suggesting that some early Christian communities were indeed situated deliberately in out-of-the-way locations, as claimed in later legends;[9] presumably by about the 9th or 10th century these sites were serving wider areas as centres for worship, including burial. Such sites may have coexisted with less isolated ones, perhaps also designated by names in *lann. Later, in about the 10th to 12th centuries, there was probably infilling, with the

---

1 *monasterium quod Docco uocatur* 'the *lann called *Docco* (10th-century *Landochou*): P. Flobert (ed.), *La Vie ancienne de saint Samson de Dol* (1997), 212.

2 H. Jenner, 'The Lannaled mass of St Germanus in Bodl. MS. 572', *Journal of the Royal Institution of Cornwall*, 23 (1929–32), 477–92 (at 482–3); Sawyer, nos 770 (*Lannmoren* 969) and 810 (*Landochou* 961×3).

3 R. Largillière, *Les Saints et l'organisation chrétienne primitive dans l'Armorique bretonne* (1923), 27–33 and 43–4; Davies, 'Saints of south Wales', 374–6 and 393–4.

4 D. Petts, 'Cemeteries and boundaries in western Britain', in S. Lucy and A. Reynolds (eds.), *Burial in Early Medieval England and Wales* (2002), 24–46 (at 40–2); S. Turner, 'Making a Christian landscape: early medieval Cornwall', in M. Carver (ed.), *The Cross Goes North: Processes of Conversion in Northern Europe, A.D. 300–1300* (2003), 171–94 (at 171–4); S. Turner, *Making a Christian Landscape* (2006), 5–7; compare Blair, *Church in Anglo-Saxon Society*, 21.

5 Compare the evidence of the 6th-century Letter to Lovocat and Catihern (below).

6 Padel, 'Cornish names of parish churches'; Padel, *Cornish Place-Name Elements*, 145; between 20 and 90 surviving non-parochial names might be a fairly confident estimate.

7 R. Sharpe, 'Churches and communities in early medieval Ireland: towards a pastoral model', in J. Blair and R. Sharpe (eds.), *Pastoral Care before the Parish* (1992), 81–109 (at 86, 88–91, and 95).

8 A. Preston-Jones, 'Decoding Cornish churchyards', in N. Edwards and A. Lane (eds.), *Early Church in Wales and the West* (1992), 104–24 (at 116–17).

9 Preston-Jones, 'Decoding Cornish churchyards', 115–20.

addition of further churches (perhaps primarily manorial ones) in areas which had not been catered for in the earlier process. Ann Preston-Jones has suggested that such later churchyards can be identified archaeologically by rectilinear rather than curvilinear boundaries; these sites tend to have names beginning with *Eglos-*, indicating that this word was in use later than **Lann-* as a formative element in place-names.[1] Overall, the implication of this scheme would be that many parish churches in Cornwall had rather different origins from those in most of England. They were neither former minsters nor manorial churches, but originated perhaps as small early-Christian communities endowed with small plots of land for their chapels, dwellings, burials, and presumably subsistence.

Some of these sites developed further still, continuing as recognised landholding communities of clergy. By 1086 Cornwall was distinctive within England in showing a dozen such communities where the priests held land in the name of their patron saint.[2] As a group, these institutions are distinctive by their small size, the geld-free nature of their land, their place-names in *Lann-*, and the phrasing of their entries in Domesday Book which lays emphasis on the patron saint, both in the place-name and sometimes as landholder. 'The canons of St *Achebrann* hold *Lannachebran*' is typical.[3] The size of their estates ranged from half a hide to three hides; most probably had never owned more extensive lands, although St Piran's and St Kew had done so. Several of these communities survived into the later Middle Ages, sometimes refounded as priories in the 12th century; but four of them (Goran, Kea, Constantine and St Kew) ceased to exist shortly before or after 1086, continuing simply as parish churches, although one of these (St Kew) was revived in the 12th century as a cell of Plympton Priory.[4]

Many of the rural chapel-sites, having their distinctive dedications and being of a type which does not conform to the late-medieval types of chapel usual elsewhere in England, also probably belong to this early period, whether or not they have names in **Lann-*.[5] The chapels already mentioned of St Illick (where a burial-ground existed, presumably from before the consolidation of the parochial system in the 11th or 12th century), St Nectan (also with a burial-ground, in Newlyn East parish), and of St Decuman and St Sowanna, both in Wendron parish, are typical of the many sites which made the Cornish ecclesiastical landscape so rich in the early Middle Ages.

By 1086 these landholding communities could resemble Anglo-Saxon minster-churches. However, their distinctive characteristics, and the features which they share with other Cornish churches and chapel-sites which never had the status of minsters, suggest that they had rather different origins from Anglo-Saxon minsters, but had grown to resemble them, probably during the 250 years of Anglo-Saxon rule and assimilation which had preceded Domesday Book. Perhaps those churches which already by *c.* 900 had come to resemble minsters prospered in the 10th and 11th centuries, while those which were too small declined and became ordinary parish churches; patronage during the period may have encouraged the process.[6] St Petroc's monastery in particular (assuming that it existed before the 10th century) was exceptional: it prospered and expanded in the 10th and 11th centuries, gaining a new site at Bodmin and holding 26 manors by 1066, though by 1086 the count of Mortain had reduced these to 18.

This profusion of small-scale sites extended below the level of churches and chapels, to minor built features such as holy wells and crosses. Up to 192 holy wells have been identified in Cornwall, though some are of doubtful status.[7] Such features tend not to be mentioned in historical records, so most are poorly documented; but holy wells in Cornwall are referred to in some saints' Lives, including ones written outside the county, from as early as the 8th century (St Samson).[8] Both the Cornish-language saint's plays mention healing springs created by their saints. That of St Meriasek, in Camborne parish, was valued for treating insanity, while that of St Ke, at Killiow in Kea parish, cured a leper; another one attributed to St Ke, at Old Kea itself, continued to be used for treating toothache after the Reformation.[9]

---

1 Preston-Jones, 'Decoding Cornish churchyards', 112–13.

2 Nine are listed in *Domesday Book: Cornwall*, edited by Thorn, 4.1–2 and 4.23–9; three more defunct ones (Kea, Goran, and St Kew) are mentioned elsewhere in Domesday Book (DB 1.4, 5.7.6, and 5.24.14) or in the Geld Inquest (Exeter Domesday, fol. 72r). See also Olson, *Early Monasteries in Cornwall* (1989), 86–97, and W. M. M. Picken, 'The manor of Tremaruustel and the honour of St Keus', *Journal of the Royal Institution of Cornwall*, n.s., 7 (1973–7), 20–30.

3 *Domesday Book: Cornwall*, edited by Thorn, 4.3; three of the sites do not have names in Lann-: St Michael's Mount, St Buryan (*Eglosberrie*) with *Eglos-*, and St Neot (*Neotestov*) with the distinctive south-western use of English *-stow*: M. Gelling, 'Some meanings of *stōw*', in S. M. Pearce (ed.), *The Early Church in Western Britain and Ireland* (1982), 187–96.

4 See the individual chapters, below; and Blair, *Church in Anglo-Saxon Society*, chapter 6, 'Minsters in a changing world', especially 304–6.

5 See above, 'Later Middle Ages: People'.

6 Compare Blair, *Church in Anglo-Saxon Society*, 305–6.

7 J. Meyrick, *A Pilgrim's Guide to the Holy Wells of Cornwall* (1982); also still useful are M. and L. Quiller-Couch, *Ancient and Holy Wells of Cornwall* (1894), and A. Lane-Davies, *Holy Wells of Cornwall* (1970).

8 Flobert (ed.) *Vie ancienne de saint Samson*, 220; well of St Cadoc (Padstow parish), *Vita Sancti Cadoci* (*c.* 1100), in A.W. Wade-Evans (ed.), *Vitae Sanctorum Britanniae et Genealogiae* (1944), 92–4, and H. Harvey (ed.) *William Worcestre: Itineraries*, 72; wells of St Petroc, First Life of St Petroc (*c.* 1100), in Grosjean, 'Vies et miracles de S. Petroc', 490 and 494.

9 W. Stokes (ed.), *Beunans Meriasek* (1872), lines 664–71; Thomas and Williams (eds.), *Bewnans Ke*, lines 781–822; A. Le Grand, *Les Vies des saints de la Bretagne-armorique*, new edition (1837), 678; C. Thomas, *Christian Antiquities of Camborne* (1967), 123–5.

Enthusiasm for holy wells was still flourishing in the 15th and early 16th centuries, and they benefited from the surge in building activity at that period. The best surviving examples are those at Dupath and St Cleer in eastern Cornwall, both situated in areas which by then had long been English-speaking; many others have (or formerly had) minor structures dating from this period. The large well-chapels of St Clether and Madron are less datable. By this late period such features can be considered a distinctive regional manifestation of the western European cult of saints. Holy wells are known in other counties of England; it is their number which is exceptional in Cornwall, and paralleled in Wales and Brittany.[1] As with other, better-documented, types of site, the cultural roots of this class of features lay in the pre-English past.

The practice of erecting stone crosses was shared with Devon, where crosses comparable with Cornish ones mark routeways across Dartmoor.[2] They are difficult to date, because of their stylistic simplicity; many are probably late-medieval.[3] From as early as the 5th or 6th century there are chi-rho stones, and crosses are also found on some of the inscribed stones of that period.[4] However, the practice of erecting free-standing crosses seems to have been an innovation resulting from increased Anglo-Saxon cultural influence in the later 9th century, especially in King Alfred's reign. The two at St Cleer and the nearby one at St Neot date from c. 900 and resemble ones known further east, such as that at Copplestone, near Crediton (Devon).[5] Two crosses, therefore, which are mentioned in the boundaries of 10th-century west-Cornish charters were perhaps recent constructions, rather than older monuments used as boundary-markers.[6]

The crosses had various purposes. Besides waymarking functions, they might be commemorative, like the stone in St Cleer parish standing on a moorland trackway and bearing the name Doniert, probably referring to Dungarth, the last king of Cornwall (d. 875/6).[7] The exceptional number of crosses in St Buryan parish perhaps marked the extended sanctuary-ground of that church.[8] In eastern Cornwall the crosses, if dating from the 14th and 15th centuries, were erected in an English-speaking environment. Their presence in that area, like the saints' relics and holy wells, represents a regional distinctiveness in religious culture, which continued after the language had died out. At that late period stone crosses, other than grave-markers, do not seem to be common in other Celtic-speaking regions, except in Brittany, where many are more elaborate though some are very similar to Cornish ones.[9] The south-western crosses constitute a distinct group, a product of the interaction of English and Celtic tastes. Their use in western Devon may be due to a spread of this distinctive culture beyond the limits of Cornwall itself, perhaps in the 12th to 15th centuries.

Finally, three church-sites in west Cornwall had structures claiming to be the 'chairs' of their saints. That at Germoe resembles an elaborate holy well, but in about 1540 Leland distinguished St Germoe's chair from his well at the site; the designation may have been connected with a local claim (first attested around 1700) that the saint was a king.[10] The other two 'chairs', at St Michael's Mount and St Mawes, seem to have been natural rocks rather than man-made structures.[11] There are parallels in Brittany and Ireland for this designation of features: two 'Chairs of St Maudet' in Brittany (as well as an 'Oven'), and a *cathedra* of St Ciarán of Saighir, in his cemetery there.[12] Such names are reminiscent of the naming of rocks and other local landmarks as the seat, bed, oven or other furniture of the legendary Arthur.[13]

---

1 J. Rattue, *The Living Stream: Holy Wells in Historical Context* (1995); F. Jones, *The Holy Wells of Wales* (1954); P. Audin, *Guide des fontaines guérisseuses du Finistère*, and *Guide des fontaines guérisseuses du Morbihan* (both 1983), lists 236 curative wells in those two departments of Brittany.

2 W. Crossing, *Guide to Dartmoor*, 2nd edn (1912), 16, and index, 'Crosses, stone'.

3 A. Preston-Jones and A. Langdon, 'St Buryan crosses', *Cornish Archaeology*, 36 (1997), 107–28 (at 115–21); above, 'Later Middle Ages: People'.

4 A. Langdon, *Stone Crosses in West Penwith* (1997), 25 (chi-rho, St Just in Penwith); A. Langdon, *Stone Crosses in West Cornwall (including the Lizard)* (1999), 54 (chi-rho, Phillack); E. Okasha, *Corpus of Early Christian Inscribed Stones of South-West Britain* (Leicester, 1993), 233 (St Endellion), 265 (Southill).

5 A. Langdon, *Stone Crosses in East Cornwall* (2005), 35–6 (St Cleer) and 50 (St Neot); R. Cramp et al., *Corpus of Anglo-Saxon Stone Sculpture*, VII, *South-West England* (2006), 82–3 (Copplestone), 86–7 (Exeter).

6 Sawyer, nos 684, 755, and 832; D. Hooke, *Pre-Conquest Charter-Bounds of Devon and Cornwall* (1994), 28–9, 37–9, and 49; A. Langdon, *Stone Crosses in Mid Cornwall*, 2nd edn (2002), 61.

7 Nine crosses in Camborne parish were ordered in a bequest of 1448 (Orme, *Cornish Wills*, 77); and one at Penhalvean (Stithians parish) was described in 1423 as 'erected for the soul of the lord of *Talgullow*' (Cornwall Record Office, Truro, ME/193).

8 Preston-Jones and Langdon, 'St Buryan crosses', 114–15; see below.

9 Examples in Y.-P. Castel, *Atlas des croix et calvaires du Finistère* (1980).

10 L. T. Smith (ed.), *The Itinerary of John Leland in or about the Years 1535–1543*, 5 vols (1906–10), I, 188; Thomas Tonkin (c. 1700), in [Joseph Polsue], *A Complete Parochial History of the County of Cornwall*, 4 vols (1867–72), III, 65.

11 Smith (ed.), *Itinerary of John Leland*, I, 200 (St Mawes); P. A. S. Pool, 'The ancient and present state of St Michael's Mount, 1762', *Cornish Studies*, 3 (1975), 29–47 (at 30).

12 G. H. Doble, *Saint Mawes, Abbot and Confessor*, Cornish Saints, no. 1, 2nd edn (1938), 10–12; Latin Life of St Ciarán of Saighir, §35, in C. Plummer (ed.), *Vitae Sanctorum Hiberniae*, 2 vols (1910), I, 232.

13 O. J. Padel, 'The nature of Arthur', *Cambrian Medieval Celtic Studies*, 27 (1994), 1–31 (at 5–6, 25–6, and 29).

CHURCH ORGANISATION AND PRACTICE

In so far as significant differences in church organisation and practice are detectable at all, they appear mainly in the earliest, pre-English, period, although in some cases they left a legacy. Some such differences are related to the distinctive ecclesiastical landscape. In the earliest period one piece of documentary evidence about Brittonic religious life is an admonitory letter of the 6th century, addressed to two Breton priests, Lovocat and Catihern, by the bishops of Tours, Rennes, and Angers. They reprehended the priests for celebrating mass in the houses of ordinary people, for allowing women to assist them in the celebration, and for permitting women other than close blood relations to dwell with themselves under the same roof.[1]

By definition this letter is concerned with unorthodox practices, and it is unknown how widespread in the Brittonic world these practices were; nevertheless its contents merit careful attention. The idea of priests taking mass to the people, rather than expecting them to come to a church, would fit well in the context of the isolated locations of many Cornish churches; it may not have been that practice itself which was reprehensible, but that of actually entering the houses of lay-people. The implication that a few priests might live together in a community with permitted relations, including kindred women (though not unrelated ones), is useful for considering the meaning of *lann. Such communities could have had a dual function, pastoral and monastic; if so, then the difference from early Anglo-Saxon practice may lie in the relative emphasis placed upon the two functions. The physical location of churches in Cornwall and other Celtic lands suggests an emphasis on the monastic role, while in early Anglo-Saxon society the pastoral one was stronger.

There is little evidence relating to church governance in the pre-English period. A passage in the Welsh law-books suggests that before the 9th century there were seven bishoprics in the kingdom of Dyfed, corresponding to its seven *cantrefi*.[2] A Welsh *cantref* corresponded roughly to an administrative hundred in England, of which Cornwall originally had seven; so if Dyfed was typical of Wales, and if Cornwall were similarly governed, we could envisage, by extrapolation, that there might have been up to seven bishops in Cornwall before the Anglo-Saxon conquest in the 9th century. The letter of Aldhelm (*c.* 700) addressed to King Gerent and all the *sacerdotes* dwelling throughout *Domnonia* bears upon this point.[3] The word *sacerdotes* is ambiguous, meaning either 'bishops' or 'priests'. If it meant 'bishops' here, the plural would suggest that at that date there was more than one bishop in Cornwall; but that is not a necessary interpretation.[4]

As late as the 9th century there may have been more than one bishop in Cornwall, for one is known, probably at Bodmin, and there was possibly another at St Germans. In the mid 9th century Bishop Kenstec, in his profession of obedience to Archbishop Ceolnoth of Canterbury (833–70), called himself bishop 'in the Cornish race in the monastery called *Dinuurrin* in the language of the Britons';[5] the name *Dinuurrin* is not known from any other source, but Bodmin is the best identification.[6] At St Germans there may already have been a bishopric before King Athelstan's creation of a see there in about 930.[7] The incorporation of Cornwall into the Anglo-Saxon see of Sherborne began in King Ecgbert's reign (802–39), so Kenstec's period of office must have overlapped with that process, which probably became complete when his episcopacy ended. Cornwall thus lay within Sherborne diocese from the mid-9th century until about 909. During that period, at some date before 890, King Alfred placed the minster-church at Exeter, 'together with the whole jurisdiction (or territory, *parochia*) belonging to it in *Saxonia* and *Cornubia*', in charge of the Welsh bishop Asser, along with two other minsters in Somerset and further gifts.[8]

---

1 A. Jülicher, 'Ein gallisches Bischofsschreiben des 6. Jahrhunderts als Zeuge für die Verfassung der Montanistenkirche', *Zeitschrift für Kirchengeschichte*, 16 (1896), 664–71 (at 665–6); P. de Labriolle, *Les Sources de l'histoire du montanisme* (1913), 226–30; compare A. Chédeville and H. Guillotel, *La Bretagne des saints et des rois* (1984), 121–2, and P.-R. Giot et al., *The British Settlement of Brittany* (2003), 136–8.

2 T. Charles-Edwards, 'The seven bishop-houses of Dyfed', *Bulletin of the Board of Celtic Studies*, 24 (1970–2), 247–62 (at 252 and 262 for the date).

3 *Geruntio regi simulque cunctis Dei sacerdotibus per Domnoniam conuersantibus*, in R. Ehwald (ed.), *Aldhelmi Opera*, Monumenta Germaniae Historica, Auctores Antiquissimi, 15 (1919), 480–6 (at 480–1); *Aldhelm: the Prose Works*, translated by M. Lapidge and M. Herren (1979), 155; above, 'From the Romans to the Norman Conquest'.

4 In the same letter Aldhelm also used *sacerdotes* of those who attended a church council.

5 The manuscript form *Kenstec* (14th-century) may be a scribal error for *Keustec*, which is perhaps more likely as a 9th-century Cornish name; *Kenstec* is used here because it seems to be the form intended in the manuscript, and has become the conventional form used in modern accounts.

6 Olson, *Early Monasteries in Cornwall*, 52–6; Jankulak, *Cult of St Petroc*, 57–9; not St Germans, since the 10th-century name for that place was *Lannaled*.

7 Olson, *Early Monasteries in Cornwall*, 64–6; Jankulak, *Cult of St Petroc*, 62 and 64–5; above, 'From the Romans to the Norman Conquest'; below, 'Religious Houses before 1066'.

8 *cum omni parochia quae ad se pertinebat in Saxonia et Cornubia*, in W. H. Stevenson (ed.), *Asser's Life of King Alfred* (1904), 68 (§81); Keynes and Lapidge, *Alfred the Great*, 97.

The meaning of *parochia* here is uncertain. It evidently refers to some sphere of jurisdiction which belonged to the minster at Exeter, seemingly before Asser was placed in charge of it. One of its meanings was 'area of episcopal jurisdiction', but it also had broader meanings of 'territory', including 'lands belonging to a major church'.[1] Since Exeter lay within the diocese of Sherborne and did not become a bishopric until 1050, any episcopal responsibility which Asser exercised within Sherborne diocese would have been in a personal capacity, rather than a role attached to the minster at Exeter; there are anyway reasons to think that he was probably a bishop in Wales before coming to England.[2] Therefore the lands in Devon and Cornwall for which Asser was responsible (whether as bishop or not) were presumably estates which the minster at Exeter owned in both counties. Little is known about the lands of that minster before the 11th century, and it could well have owned estates west of the River Tamar by King Alfred's time, as Sherborne did in the 8th and 9th centuries, and Tavistock did in the late 10th. If so, such lands would be among the twelve Cornish estates which belonged to the bishop of Exeter in 1066, although they cannot now be identified among those properties, which had come to the bishopric from various sources.[3] When Asser himself became bishop of Sherborne in the 890s, his role included episcopal care for the whole of Cornwall. At that period the Cornish language and his native Welsh were only separating dialects, so he was well suited to the position, irrespective of the precise nature of his former role at Exeter.

With the subdivision of the impractically large diocese of Sherborne, after Asser's death in 909, a new see was created at Crediton for the whole of Devon and Cornwall. This arrangement was still unwieldy, and a generation later, in about 930, King Athelstan created a specifically Cornish bishopric at St Germans. The older name of that church (*Lannaled*) indicates an earlier church at the site, and it is possible that Athelstan was simply reviving a former see.[4] If so, it must have coexisted with the one at *Dinuurrin*, and with any other Cornish see still in existence in the 9th century. In 994 King Æthelred confirmed the position of the see of St Germans, declaring that Bishop Ealdred was to govern his province of Cornwall freely like other bishops in the kingdom. The phraseology of this charter, which was made 'for love of our lord Jesus Christ and the holy confessor German and also the blessed excellent Petroc',[5] seems to allow St Petroc (and, by implication, his church) a special role within the diocese alongside St Germans. However, the charter goes on to specify, with unusual wording, 'and the site and rule of St Petroc shall be always in his [Bishop Ealdred's] power and that of his successors'.[6] Commentators have been unsure how to understand this curious clause. It cannot mean that Bodmin priory and its lands were given to St Germans, both because it does not say so (with no mention of the lands of the church, nor of any gift at all), and because there is no hint in other sources that St Germans ever had any rights of ownership over St Petroc's monastery at Padstow and Bodmin. The purpose of the clause was presumably to resolve any dispute between St Germans and St Petroc's, arising perhaps from continuing claims made by St Petroc's to some degree of diocesan independence.[7] Such claims would be particularly understandable if Bodmin had had bishops of its own until about a century earlier, as would be the case if Kenstec's 9th-century see of *Dinuurrin* was located there. St Petroc's minster had recently acquired the inland site at Bodmin (probably after the Viking attack on Padstow in 981), and the acquisition of that prestigious central site would have been a cause of pride.

There may have been an additional reason for the unusual clause. The charter was granted to Bishop Ealdred, who had succeeded Bishop Wulfsige Comoere at St Germans at some time during the 980s. Wulfsige himself had come to St Germans from St Petroc's, having risen through the ranks there; King Edgar appointed him to the bishopric soon after coming to the throne in 959.[8] After becoming bishop Wulfsige continued to visit St Petroc's, presumably still at Padstow, and to be engaged with its affairs: he appears as bishop in eleven of the fifty entries which constitute the Bodmin Manumissions.[9] In some of these entries he himself freed slaves, which could even imply that he was in charge of St Petroc's estates, since he is unlikely to have chosen Padstow for freeing slaves belonging to the St Germans estates. It may even have been Bishop Wulfsige who obtained the prestigious site which

---

1 C. Etchingham, 'The implications of *paruchia*', *Ériu*, 44 (1993), 139–62 (at 162, 'connotations of a temporal asset or resource'); C. Etchingham, *Church Organisation in Ireland A.D. 650 to 1000* (1999), 14–44, 105–30, and 172–7; R. E. Latham et al. (eds.), *Dictionary of Medieval Latin from British Sources* (1975–), s.v. *paroecia*, especially senses (1) 'district or territory under ecclesiastical control' (distinct from (3) 'diocese, bishopric') and (7) 'district, territory' (in the 10th-century Chronicle of Æthelweard). For a different view, see above, p. 9.

2 J. E. Lloyd, *A History of Wales, from the Earliest Times to the Norman Conquest*, 3rd edn, 2 vols (1939), I, 226 and n. 159; Keynes and Lapidge, *Alfred the Great*, 52.

3 Thorn (ed.), *Domesday Book: Cornwall*, 2.1–2.12.

4 Olson, *Early Monasteries in Cornwall*, 63–6; below, 'Religious Houses before 1066'.

5 *pro amore domini nostri Ihesu Christi atque sancti confessoris Germani necnon et beati eximii Petroci*, J. M. Kemble, *Codex Diplomaticus Aevi Saxonici*, 6 vols (1839–48), III, 276 (no. 686; Sawyer, no. 880).

6 *locus atque regimen sancti Petroci semper in potestate eius sit successorumque eius*, ibid.

7 Olson, *Early Monasteries in Cornwall*, 74–8.

8 Padel, *Slavery in Saxon Cornwall*, 10–11 (and note 40), 22, and 32.

9 M. Förster, 'Die Freilassungsurkunden des Bodmin-Evangeliars', in N. Bøgholm et al.(eds.), *A Grammatical Miscellany offered to Otto Jespersen* (1930), 77–99 (nos 3, 6–7, 16, 17, 39, 40, 42, 44, 46, 47, and 50).

enabled St Petroc's to move inland to Bodmin after the Viking attack in 981, although it is not certain that he was still in office then. If Wulfsige remained in charge of St Petroc's after becoming bishop at St Germans, or even if he merely allowed St Petroc's a special place within his diocese, problems would have arisen for his successor at St Germans. The new bishop, Ealdred, had no known connection with St Petroc's, and his accession would therefore have lowered the status of Bodmin within the diocese, a development which St Petroc's community may have found hard to accept. The clause in Æthelred's charter may have been designed to formalise and clarify officially what had previously been an informal arrangement residing in the person of Bishop Wulfsige, namely that in diocesan matters St Petroc's was now unequivocally subordinate to St Germans.

Thus Cornwall had a separate see at St Germans from about 930 until 1027, when it was united with Devon under a single bishop, Lyfing, although they still constituted two dioceses. (Lyfing also became bishop of Worcester in 1038–9.) This arrangement continued under Lyfing's successor, Leofric, in 1046, but when Leofric moved his see from Crediton to Exeter four years later, in 1050, he formally united the sees, and they were to remain so until 1877. Even on that occasion a gesture was made towards Bodmin: King Edward the Confessor's charter effecting the merger stated that the diocese of Cornwall had formerly been created 'in memory of the blessed Germanus and veneration of Petroc'.[1] Perhaps it was only merging the see of Cornwall with that of Devon that finally ended the rivalry between the two Cornish ecclesiastical centres.

As far as church practice is concerned, Aldhelm's letter to Gerent shows that the church in Cornwall, like those in Ireland and Wales, had been slow to adopt the newer Roman method of calculating the date of Easter and the new form of monastic tonsure.[2] By the early 8th century the Irish church had accepted the change, in both Ireland and Britain, and if it was Aldhelm's letter that prompted the Cornish to do the same, it may have been the Cornish whom Bede had in mind when he stated that 'some of the British in Britain' had conformed by about 703, and that Aldhelm's efforts were successful among those British 'who were subject to the West Saxons', although at this date such a description need not necessarily have included Gerent's realm.[3] Bishop Kenstec's profession of obedience to Archbishop Ceolnoth shows that Cornwall had conformed at least by the mid-9th century.

Therefore it is curious that a Cornish failure to conform in certain (unspecified) religious matters was cited in the 10th century as the reason for three Cornish estates to have been transferred from Sherborne to the bishopric of Crediton at its creation in about 909: 'they gave [to Bishop Eadulf of Crediton] additionally three estates in Cornwall, called Pawton, *Cællincg* and Lawhitton, so that he might every year visit the Cornish to eradicate their errors'. The statement appears twice, first in a narrative of the mid-10th century describing the subdivision of the sees of Wessex in *c*. 909,[4] and thirty years later in a letter (981 × 8) from Archbishop Dunstan to King Æthelred recounting the same event.[5] It is uncertain what the difficulty may have been. In the 9th century the Welsh church was still using an archaic liturgy (older than that promulgated by Pope Gregory the Great in *c*. 592), together with the Old Latin version of the Bible instead of the Vulgate, and 'in liturgical matters at least … may have been conservative in the extreme'.[6] Perhaps it was matters of this kind which provided the excuse for claiming, in the mid-10th century, that in 909 the church in Cornwall had still needed to amend certain errors. The use of the Lanalet pontifical, an Anglo-Saxon episcopal service book, at St Germans in the later 10th century shows that it was then following normal practice.[7]

Such conservatism, in liturgical matters as over Easter and the tonsure, was not a 'Celtic' phenomenon, but merely due to a tendency of peripheral areas to change more slowly than ones nearer to Rome. However, in at least one respect ecclesiastical usage in Cornwall was innovative in the first half of the 10th century. One of the earliest examples in England of Carolingian script, newly introduced from the Continent, was written in Cornwall, presumably at Padstow, in the 940s.[8] It is very likely that Cornwall's

---

1 *olim in beati Germani memoria atque Petroci ueneratione*, Kemble, *Codex Diplomaticus*, IV, 118–21 (no. 791); Sawyer no. 1021.

2 Above, 'From the Romans'.

3 *Nonnulla [pars] de Brettonibus in Britania*, Bede, *Historia Ecclesiastica*, V, 15; *multosque eorum qui Occidentalibus Saxonibus subditi erant Brettones ad catholicam dominici paschae celebrationem huius lectione perduxit*, V, 18.

4 *Insuper addiderunt illi tres uillas in Cornubia quorum nomina Polltun, Cællincg, Landuuithan, ut inde singulis annis uisitaret gentem Cornubiensem ad exprimendos eorum errores*: the 'Plegmund Narrative' (so named from Archbishop Plegmund who oversaw the subdivision): J. Armitage Robinson, *The Saxon Bishops of Wells* (1918), 7–28 (at 22); the estate of *Cællincg* has eluded identification.

5 A. S. Napier and W. H. Stevenson (eds.), *The Crawford Collection of Early Charters and Documents* (Oxford, 1895), 18–19 and 102–10 (no. VII; Sawyer, no. 1296).

6 M. Lapidge, 'Latin learning in Dark Age Wales: some prolegomena', in D. Ellis Evans et al. (eds.), *Proceedings of the Seventh International Congress of Celtic Studies* (1986), 91–107 (at 93); compare Davies, 'Myth of the Celtic Church', 18–19; and for the possible use of a conservative biblical text in Wales even in the 11th century, J. Stevenson, 'Introduction' to a reprint of F. E. Warren, *The Liturgy and Ritual of the Celtic Church* [1881] (1987), lxxvi–lxxvii.

7 G. H. Doble (ed.), *Pontificale Lanaletense (Blbliothèque de la Ville de Rouen, A.27 cat. 368)*, Henry Bradshaw Society, 74 (1937).

8 D. N. Dumville, *English Caroline Script and Monastic History* (1993), 142; Dumville, *Liturgy and the Ecclesiastical History of Late Anglo-Saxon England* (1992), 116–117, n. 150.

precocity in this respect was due to its close contacts with Brittany, where Caroline script had been adopted in the 9th century.

One particularity of practice retained by Cornwall long after the Norman Conquest related to church sanctuary. Every church in England could provide temporary sanctuary to a fugitive criminal, who could then abjure the kingdom and gain legal protection while travelling to a port for departure. The English system can be seen operating in the county as soon as there are records capable of showing it, in 1201.[1] But a few major churches in England, such as Durham cathedral and Westminster abbey, possessed additional chartered rights of sanctuary, extending over land surrounding the church, and allowing convicted criminals to continue living indefinitely within their precincts. Cornwall was unusual because four lesser collegiate churches, all in the west of the county, claimed such a special privilege of extended sanctuary in the later Middle Ages. The churches of St Buryan, St Keverne, Padstow and Probus thus stand out as distinctive within England.[2] All four had been among the geld-free Cornish churches mentioned in Domesday Book.

The privileged sanctuaries of St Buryan and Padstow are the best documented of the four. That at St Buryan appears in a charter of confirmation issued to the church in 1238 by William Brewer, bishop of Exeter, in which the privilege, already ancient, was ascribed to King Athelstan.[3] However, it was not mentioned in the actual charter ascribed to King Athelstan which was recited at the same time.[4] Perhaps such a privilege was, in the 10th century, part of customary law for such churches in Cornwall, so did not need to be mentioned; but by the 13th century it was unusual and needed to be articulated. The privilege was still known at St Buryan in the 16th century.[5] At Padstow, although ordinary (temporary) sanctuary was frequently used because it was a port, the only known evidence for the use of the privileged form is of a fugitive who in 1284 was said to have lived 'in the church' for two months, and a similar case in 1521.[6] The privilege there, as at St Buryan, was ascribed to King Athelstan, and it presumably goes back to a time before the move of the chief site of the minster from Padstow to Bodmin, probably soon after 981, for otherwise we might expect it to have been granted to the new site at Bodmin instead.[7] As at St Buryan, it therefore dates from the mid-10th century, or earlier.

The privileged sanctuary at Probus is known only from a claim registered in the Assize Roll of 1302, which suggests an ancient right of which the usage had declined, and may soon have disappeared altogether.[8] At St Keverne there is uncertainty as to how ancient the privilege was. In the 13th and 14th centuries St Keverne provided protection like that of an ordinary church, and the claim to more extensive rights appears only in the 16th century, when Leland said that the sanctuary included 10 or 12 dwelling-houses.[9] Here the privilege could have arisen from the fact that the church and its cell belonged, from the mid-13th century, to the Cistercian parent-house of Beaulieu (Hants.), one of the great national sanctuaries;[10] such a transfer could have been eased by the custom of extended sanctuary found elsewhere in west Cornwall. However, no parallel has been cited for such a transfer of privileged sanctuary from a mother-institution to one of its dependencies; and in 1525 the rector of the adjacent parish of Grade asserted that St Keverne's privilege was ancient, and did not come from Beaulieu.[11]

These rights at St Buryan and Padstow, at least, are likely to date from the 10th century or earlier. The claim that they were granted by King Athelstan is shared with several of the great northern sanctuaries;[12] at the Cornish sites it need not be correct, and could have arisen from the esteem in which both the privilege and that king were held in Cornwall; but ancient rights might well have been confirmed by English kings in the

---

1   In Illogan parish (west Cornwall): D. M. Stenton, (ed.), *Pleas before the King or his Justices, 1198–1202*, vol. II, *Rolls or Fragments of Rolls from the Years 1198, 1201 and 1202*, Selden Society, 68 (1952), 48–9 (no. 244); examples from 1284 and 1302 in J. C. Cox, *The Sanctuaries and Sanctuary Seekers of Mediæval England* (1911), 298–302.

2   Cox, *Sanctuaries*, 214–26 (St Buryan, Padstow); C. Henderson, 'The cult of S. Pieran or Perran and S. Keverne in Cornwall', in G. H. Doble, *Saint Perran, Saint Keverne, and Saint Kerrian*, Cornish Saints, no. 29 (1931), 36–68 (at 63–5); C. Henderson, 'The ecclesiastical antiquities of the four western hundreds of Cornwall', *Journal of the Royal Institution of Cornwall*, n.s., 2 (1953–6) and 3 (1957–60) (pagination consecutive throughout), at 415–16 (Probus); see also Olson, *Early Monasteries in Cornwall*, 72–3 and 107; below, 'Religious Houses before 1066'; 'Religious Houses after 1066'.

3   *ad confirmationem, protectionem, et ad defensionem sanctuarii sui et libertatis ab annis antiquis concesse sibi a felicis et clare recordationis Ethelstano rege Anglorum … ne privilegium et scriptum sanctuarii ac libertatis predicte, ab antiquo confectum, deperire posset propter vetustatem*, in F. Barlow (ed.), *English Episcopal Acta*, XII, *Exeter 1186–1257* (1996), 260 (no. 287).

4   W. de G. Birch, *Cartularium Saxonicum*, 3 vols and index (1885–99), II, 527–8 (no. 785; Sawyer, no. 450); compare Olson, *Early Monasteries in Cornwall*, 78–81. In fact the charter was probably issued in 943, four years after Athelstan's death, and ascribed to him owing to the high esteem which he enjoyed in Cornwall.

5   Leland, *Itineraries*, I, 189 (compare 319); C. B. Crofts, *A Short History of St Buryan* (1955), 36–7.

6   Cox, *Sanctuaries*, 223–6 and 299–300; C. Henderson, 'Padstow church and parish', in G. H. Doble, *Saint Petrock, Abbot and Confessor*, Cornish Saints, no. 11, 3rd edn (1938), 51–9 (at 53–4); Henderson, 'Ecclesiastical antiquities', 375–6.

7   Leland, *Itineraries*, I, 179, 'the toune there takith King Adelstane for the chief gever of privileges onto it'.

8   Henderson, 'Ecclesiastical antiquities', 415–16.

9   Henderson, 'Ecclesiastical antiquities', 265–6; Henderson, 'Cult of S. Pieran and S. Keverne', in Doble, *St Perran*, 63–5; Leland, *Itineraries*, I, 321.

10 Cox, *Sanctuaries*, 183–9.

11 Henderson, 'Cult of S. Pieran and S. Keverne', 64; Henderson, 'Ecclesiastical antiquities', 265–7.

12 Cox, *Sanctuaries*, 126, 151–2, and 163.

10th century. The distinctive situation seen in western Cornwall invites comparison with the practice of church sanctuary in Wales, and also in Brittany, where some medieval sanctuaries extended over wide territories.[1] In extant Welsh law-texts the focus is different from that in Cornwall, laying emphasis on the conditions under which sanctuary might be claimed, and the penalties imposed for harming someone within its protection; but the Cornish evidence is broadly suggestive of the Welsh system.[2] The Cornish custom is likely to have been inherited from pre-English times, though not necessarily so at individual sites; the attested examples may represent survivors of a more widespread practice, perhaps a standard feature of Cornish monastic churches such as those which survived to appear in Domesday Book. At most sites, lacking written confirmation, the privilege presumably lapsed, perhaps because it was liable to be superseded by the more widely accessible, though more limited, English legal sanctuary available at any church.

CONCLUSION

There were various ways in which Christianity in Cornwall differed from the rest of England in the Middle Ages. These features were ancient, and were shared with other Brittonic lands and to some extent with Gaelic-speaking lands as well.[3] The profusion of small-scale sites, with its associated quantity and diversity of obscure saints' cults, many unique to a single place, is apparent from the earliest times; but the phenomenon of dedications which recur between the different regions is still not understood. Even in the 16th century the corporal relics of these local saints and the two Cornish-language saints' plays were notable manifestations of this particular aspect of religion. To some extent the cult of saints had similarities with what is found in some areas of the Continent, especially the Mediterranean;[4] so it might be argued that it was not the Celtic-speaking regions that were exceptional in this respect, but England, or perhaps Germanic culture in general; further work on saints' cults across Europe generally might show how far the shared Brittonic features seen in Cornwall were particular to the Celtic-speaking regions.[5] The many early sites included those designated by the term *lann, which were often quite isolated originally, suggesting that their purpose in the 6th to 9th centuries may have included an emphasis on monasticism, though not to the exclusion of pastoral work. Some of these sites later became parish churches, but their origins caused the parish system in Cornwall to be less closely associated with the secular settlement-pattern than elsewhere in England. A few of these sites had, by the 10th and 11th centuries, developed to become land-owning, minster-like institutions, and by 1086 these Cornish churches were distinctive in Domesday Book, perhaps through a combination of their different origins and of having not yet developed as had happened elsewhere in England; and a few of these churches had one attribute, the privilege of offering extended sanctuary to criminals, which survived until the 16th century. Even today the saints and their churches provide a constant reminder of Cornwall's distinctive past, because the physical geography of early Christianity caused the names of many of the obscure saints to become fixed in the later patterns of parishes and settlements, and so to appear on the modern map.

---

1 H. Pryce, *Native Law and the Church in Medieval Wales* (1993), 164 and note 8.

2 H. Pryce, 'Ecclesiastical sanctuary in thirteenth-century Welsh law', *Journal of Legal History*, 5 (1984), 1–13; Pryce, *Native Law and the Church*, 163–203.

3 Compare Davies, 'Myth of the Celtic Church', 18–20, 'Some similarities' (between Celtic-speaking areas).

4 Compare I. Wood, 'Constructing cults in early medieval France: local saints and churches in Burgundy and the Auvergne 400–1000', in Thacker and Sharpe (eds.), *Local Saints and Local Churches*, 155–87.

5 G. Jones (ed.), *Saints of Europe: Studies towards a Survey of Cults and Culture* (2005), provides accounts of cults in various parts of Europe; it is hoped that the work of the Trans-National Database and Atlas of Saints' Cults at the University of Leicester will, as it progresses, assist further study of such matters.

RELIGIOUS HOUSES BEFORE 1066

THERE were more than a dozen churches in Cornwall staffed by groups of clergy before the Norman Conquest. Two communities of clergy are implied in the first life of St Samson of Dol, written in about 750, and several minsters served by canons, priests, or clerks, are recorded in the 10th and 11th centuries. Evidence about these houses comes directly from written sources: saints' lives, charters, and Domesday Book. There is also indirect evidence pointing to the existence of other houses for which there is no documentation. The known houses tended to have certain types of saint cults, privileges of taxation and sometimes of sanctuary, and more extensive parishes. It follows that when we find these features attached to other churches, they may indicate that such places housed religious communities, at some time or another, before 1066. The evidence, both direct and indirect, is summarised below, and there may be other churches worth considering as having once been houses of clergy. The term 'pre-Conquest' refers to the Norman Conquest of 1066.

ST ANTHONY-IN-ROSELAND

There was a religious site at St Anthony-in-Roseland by about 900, dedicated to a saint *Entenin* who was also commemorated at St Anthony-in-Meneage.[1] Robert Warelwast, bishop of Exeter, gave the Roseland church to Plympton Priory between 1138 and 1155, together with other local property, and the priory eventually established a small house of Augustinian canons at the site of the church.[2] It is possible that Bishop Warelwast's gifts had been the property of a pre-Conquest religious house based at the Roseland church, but there is no evidence to this effect.[3] The parish of St Anthony-in-Roseland in later times was a tiny one, untypical of those of most ancient Cornish religious houses.

BODMIN

Bodmin is first mentioned as a place in *c.*975,[4] and possessed a major church, staffed by a body of clergy, by at least the 11th century. Three pieces of evidence suggest that the religious community was much older. One is the place-name itself, meaning 'dwelling by church-land'.[5] Another is the first known Cornish bishop Kenstec's professing of obedience to Ceolnoth, archbishop of Canterbury (833–870), which described this episcopal seat as the monastery of the *Dinuurrin* [or *Dinnurrin*]'.[6] It has been plausibly suggested that *Dinuurrin* might be a copying-error for *Dinuurron* which would then mean 'the fortification of *Uuron*', the latter name recalling an incident in the 11th-century Cornish Life of St Petroc.[7] The Life describes how Petroc went to Bodmin, where he found a hermit named *Uuron*, who agreed to vacate the place in Petroc's favour, after which Petroc founded a monastery there.[8] Although the Life is not a trustworthy account of events in earlier centuries, it may preserve a tradition linking *Uuron* with Bodmin, in which case *Dinuurrin* might be identifiable with Bodmin or a place close by it.

By 1066 Bodmin had become the centre of the cult of St Petroc, possessing a church dedicated to the saint, which housed his relics and was served by a body of clergy. The cult appears to have moved to Bodmin from Padstow, but there is no clear evidence about when this event took place. One view would place it in the first half of the 9th century after King Ecgberht of Wessex granted land at Pawton in St Breock to the bishop of Sherborne – a grant that might have isolated the community at Padstow and robbed it of endowments.[9] Another would link the move to Bodmin with a statement in the Anglo-Saxon Chronicle, under the year 981, that '*Sancte Petroces stow* was laid waste', presumably by a Viking attack.[10] The name *Sancte Petroces stow* ('St Petroc's holy place') might refer to Padstow or, if the transference had already taken place, to Bodmin, but if it concerns the former it would provide a motive for a migration to Bodmin by the Padstow clergy with the body of their saint. A list of the resting places of saints in England, dating from the first third of the 11th century, states that Petroc's relics lay

---

1 L. Olson and O. J. Padel, 'A Tenth-Century List of Cornish Parochial Saints', *Cambridge Medieval Celtic Studies* 12 (1986), 45.
2 Below, p. 136.
3 The question is discussed by L. Olson, *Early Monasteries in Cornwall* (1989), 103–4.
4 O. J. Padel, *A Popular Dictionary of Cornish Place-Names* (1988), 55.
5 Ibid.
6 W. de Gray Birch, *Cartularium Saxonicum*, 3 vols (1885–99), II, no. 527; Olson, *Early Monasteries*, 51–6.
7 Olson, *Early Monasteries*, 53. For further discussion of the early history of the church of Bodmin, see ibid., 51–6, 66–78.
8 P. Grosjean, 'Vie et miracles de S. Petroc', *Analecta Bollandiana* 74 (1956), 131–88, 470–96, at 495, transl. G. H. Doble, *Saint Petrock*, Cornish Saints Series, 11, 3rd ed. (1938), 8–22, at 20.
9 C. G. Henderson in Doble, *Saint Petrock*, 35.
10 *The Anglo-Saxon Chronicle*, vol. V, ed. K. O'Brien O'Keeffe (2001), 84.

near *Hæglæmutha* ('Hayle mouth'), meaning Padstow; this might seem to push the migration even later, but it is possible that the entry in the list was copied from an earlier source.[1] By about the middle of the 11th century the earliest surviving Life of Petroc linked him with Bodmin as well as with Padstow.[2]

In 994 King Æthelred the Unready granted privileges to the bishop of Cornwall 'for love of... St German, confessor, and the blessed excellent Petroc'. He ordered 'that the place and rule of St Petroc' should be forever in the power of the bishop and his successors.[3] This grant apparently gave the bishop, whose primary church had hitherto been St Germans, authority over the church of Petroc, either at Padstow, Bodmin, or both – perhaps to ensure that he was not challenged by any tradition of episcopal or independent status attaching to Petroc's church. When the diocese of Exeter was formed in 1050 by uniting the previous dioceses of Cornwall and Crediton, the foundation charter referred to the diocese of Cornwall as having been founded in veneration of both German and Petroc.[4]

The principal surviving record of St Petroc's church before the Norman Conquest is the 'Bodmin Gospels', a text used for reading the gospels in church, written in Brittany during the late 9th or early 10th century.[5] The manuscript was into the possession of St Petroc's by the middle of the latter century. The volume contains, besides the text of the gospels, some fifty manumissions (grants of free status to men and women), generally at the altar of St Petroc.[6] The manumissions range in date from the time of King Edmund (941–6) to the mid 11th century or later, indicating that the manuscript belonged to Petroc's major church by Edmund's reign. They were often witnessed by clergy, referred to individually as priests, deacons, clerks, once as a *lector* or reader, and twice collectively as 'the clerks of St Petroc'.[7] There is also one mention of *Petrocys stow* as a place.[8] Unfortunately the 10th- and early 11th-century manumissions are not clear about whether Petroc and *Petrocys stow* refer to Padstow or Bodmin. Only in the middle of the 11th century do two of them mention 'the church door at Bodmin', confirming other evidence that Petroc's principal church and body of clergy was then based at that place.[9] Altogether the proofs of a community of clergy at Bodmin from the 9th century to the early 11th fall short of the standard one would like, although the existence of such a community is likely.

Firmer evidence comes at about the time of the Norman Conquest. The 'Exon' text of the Domesday Survey of 1086 refers to the church of Bodmin as being staffed by canons and as having been so in 1066; this indicates that, like most other Cornish religious houses, Bodmin church in the 11th century was a minster served by secular canons.[10] The two manumissions that mention 'the church door at Bodmin' are complemented by a third of mid 11th-century date, witnessed by Boia the dean, who was evidently the presiding officer of the community, together with two priests, four deacons, and one clerk who may have been his colleagues.[11] It was a well-endowed community, since the Domesday survey lists far more land belonging to it than was held by any other religious house in Cornwall. The survey credited St Petroc, now meaning Bodmin, with having held twenty-two manors in 1066, and some smaller pieces of property. Nine of the manors had been managed by the church directly: Bodmin, Ellenglaze in Cubert, Padstow, Rialton in St Columb Minor, St Tudy, Treknow in Tintagel, and Withiel in Cornwall, together with Hollacombe and Newton St Petrock in Devon. The other thirteen had been held by tenants, these being Bossiney in Tintagel, Callestick and Tywarnhayle in Perranzabuloe, Cargoll in Newlyn East, Coswarth in Colan, St Enoder, Fursnewth and Trengale in St Cleer, Halwyn in Crantock, Nancekuke in Illogan, Polroad in St Tudy, Treloy in St Columb Minor, and Trevilley in St Teath. St Petroc's lands had totalled about 34 hides with an annual income of £46 plus rents in kind, to which we need to add ecclesiastical income, such as tithes, which was not included in the Domesday survey. Several of the manors, including Bodmin and Padstow, were described as having never paid tax, a distinctive characteristic of land belonging to pre-Conquest religious houses in Cornwall.[12]

The distribution of the Bodmin lands may provide clues about the earlier history of the churches of both Bodmin and Padstow. Over half of the lands and income, in terms of size and wealth, lay to the south of

---

1 D. W. Rollason, 'Lists of Saints' Resting-Places in Anglo-Saxon England', *Anglo-Saxon England* 7 (1978), 61–93, at 64, 68, 92.
2 Grosjean, 'Vie et miracles', 487–96; Doble, *Saint Petrock*, 8–22.
3 P. H. Sawyer, *Anglo-Saxon Charters* (1968), no. 880; J. R. Kemble (ed.), *Codex Diplomaticus Aevi Saxonici* (1839–48), III, 275–8.
4 Sawyer, *Anglo-Saxon Charters*, no. 1021; Kemble (ed.), *Codex*, IV, 118–21.
5 BL, Add. 9381; H. Jenner, 'The Bodmin Gospels', *JRIC* 21 (1922–5), 113–45; idem, 'The Manumissions in the Bodmin Gospels', ibid., 235–60.
6 M. Förster, 'Die Freilassungsurkunden des Bodmin-Evangeliars', in N. Bøgholm et al. (ed.), *A Grammatical Miscellany offered to Otto Jespersen* (1930), 77–99.
7 Ibid., nos XIV, XXII.
8 Ibid., nos XLIX.
9 Ibid., nos XXX, XXXIII.
10 Exon Domesday, in H. Ellis (ed.), *Domesday Book, IV: Additamenta* (Rec. Com. 1816), p. 183 (f. 200).
11 Förster, 'Die Freilassungsurkunden', no. XXXI.
12 C. and F. Thorn (ed.), *Domesday Book*, vol. IX: *Devon* (1985), I, 51/15–16; vol. X: *Cornwall* (1979), 4/3–5, 4/18–20; Ellis (ed.), *Domesday Book, IV: Additamenta*, pp. 183–7 (ff. 202–5), p. 471 (ff. 507b–8). For two corrections to the identifications in *Domesday Book*, vol. X: *Cornwall*, see W. M. M. Picken, 'Tremail and Turgoil in Doemsday Book', *DCNQ*, 38.8 (1990), 269–73.

Padstow, between Withiel and Illogan, suggesting that the church that they endowed was originally Padstow, although they did not adjoin it closely. Significantly the 'hundred' or local district of this part of Cornwall came to be known as 'Pyder', a name that seems likely to mean the hundred of Petroc.[1] A smaller scatter of lands lay north and east of the Camel estuary in the hundred of Trigg, including Bodmin itself, Bodiniel nearby, and Lanhydrock, and this scatter might have been ancient possessions of the church of Bodmin. Both groups of lands encountered encroachments during the 11th century. The Domesday survey records that Earl Harold (later King Harold II) had wrongfully taken away one (unidentified) hide of land from St Petroc before 1066,[2] and further losses occurred after the Norman Conquest. By 1086 Coswarth had been appropriated by William the Conqueror, and his chief lieutenant in Cornwall, Robert count of Mortain, had taken over most of the lands formerly held by the tenants, although he was still regarded as holding these from the church. They included the large wealthy manor of Tywarnhayle.[3] Nevertheless the church and clergy of Bodmin survived the Norman Conquest with substantial assets, and the community of canons continued until the 1120s, when it adopted the Rule of St Augustine and became a priory of regular canons.[4]

BREAGE

Breage church had a unique female saint, and a late-medieval tradition in the parish regarded her as a leader among other local saints.[5] The parish was a relatively large one, and by the 13th century the chapels of Cury and Gunwalloe were dependencies of the church and parish – giving Breage some resemblance to an English minster with subordinate chapels. There is no documentary evidence, however, of a pre-Conquest religious house.

ST BURYAN

There was a church at St Buryan by about 900, and a charter dated 943 and attributed to King Æthelstan (925–39), but in view of the date more probably granted by his successor Edmund (939–46) gave the church (or perhaps more truly recognised its possession of) one hide of land in St Buryan, located in seven named places.[6] Churches given grants of land in pre-Conquest Cornwall were generally staffed by groups of clergy, and this may have been the case at St Buryan by the mid 10th century. A body of clergy is not mentioned by name, however, until the Domesday survey which states that, in 1066, the canons of St Buryan held one hide of land there, free of tax.[7] Tax-free status is another indicator of an ancient religious house in Cornwall, and further pointers in the same direction include St Buryan's large parish (originally including St Levan and Sennen) and its possession, by the 13th century, of a sanctuary – a privilege shared by Padstow and Probus where there were also religious houses.[8] In 1086 the Domesday survey refers to the canons as still holding one hide of land, but valued it at only 10s., as against 40s. when Robert count of Mortain 'received the land'. Evidently Robert had appropriated some of the church's wealth, and he may have made himself patron of the church. Later this patronage, with the right to appoint the dean of the church, appears to have passed to the crown, but a body of four canons (including the dean) continued to exist down to the Reformation, possessing the landed endowments of the church and the tithes of the parish.[9]

CONSTANTINE

The Domesday survey states that in 1066 'St Constantine' held half a hide of land, exempt from tax. This land presumably lay around the church of Constantine, as was usual with other such church estates.[10] The land had been worth 40s. but by the date of the survey, in 1086, was valued at only 10s. because Robert count of Mortain had 'received the land' and had evidently taken resources from it.[11] No mention is made of a body of clergy in the Domesday survey or the contemporary geld-accounts, but holdings of land free of tax were characteristic of other pre-Conquest religious communities in Cornwall, and it is possible that one existed here up to the time of Count Robert in the late 1070s or early 1080s.

CRANTOCK

The Domesday survey states that in 1066 the canons of St Carantoc had held just under three hides of land there, which had never paid tax. The value had been 40s., but was only worth 5s. by the time of the survey in 1086, because Robert count of Mortain had taken possession of the land, here as at other churches.[12] Crantock is an undoubted pre-Conquest religious

---

1 Usually nowadays spelt Pydar, and so in this volume.
2 Thorn (ed.), *Domesday Book: Cornwall*, 4/21; Ellis (ed.), *Domesday Book, IV: Additamenta*, p. 186 (f. 204b).
3 Thorn (ed.), *Domesday Book: Cornwall*, ed. Thorn, 4/7–15, 4/22; Ellis (ed.), *Domesday Book, IV: Additamenta*, pp. 186–7 (f. 205), p. 471 (ff. 507b–8).
4 Below, pp. 139–40.
5 N. Orme, *The Saints of Cornwall* (2000), 71–2.
6 Sawyer, *Anglo-Saxon Charters*, no. 450; printed in *Reg. Grandisson*, I, 84–6. For discussions of the document, see Sawyer; Olson, *Early Monasteries*, 78–81; and, for the topography, Della Hooke, *Pre-Conquest Charter-Bounds of Devon and Cornwall* (1994), 22–7.
7 Thorn (ed.), *Domesday Book: Cornwall*, 4/27; Ellis (ed.), *Domesday Book, IV: Additamenta*, p. 65 (f. 72), p. 188 (f. 207).
8 Below, pp. 134–5.
9 Below, p. 163.
10 Olson, *Early Monasteries*, 90.
11 Thorn (ed.), *Domesday Book: Cornwall*, 4/29; Ellis (ed.), *Domesday Book, IV: Additamenta*, p. 66 (f. 72), p. 188 (f. 207).
12 Thorn (ed.), *Domesday Book: Cornwall*, 4/25; Ellis (ed.), *Domesday Book, IV: Additamenta*, p. 187 (f. 206).

house, although its antiquity is unknown. Other signs of the church's importance include the large size of the parish in later times, including St Columb Minor, and the commemoration of the church saint in churches at Carhampton (Somerset) and Llangranog (Cardiganshire), to which his cult may have spread from Crantock.[1] It is probable that Count Robert made himself patron of the church, since the monks of Montacute Priory (Somerset), who later owned it and its property, believed that it had been granted to them by Robert's son William.[2] Such a grant would have to be dated between 1090 when Robert died and 1106 when William lost his estates and was imprisoned by Henry I. Despite the statement of Domesday that Robert had taken the land, the church appears to have kept all or most of it in the long term. It owned a substantial local estate in later times that appears to have been an ancient endowment, and a body of ten canons still served the church in the 13th century. Their subsequent history and that of the church is related below.[3]

ST ENDELLION

By the middle of the 13th century the church of St Endellion possessed an unusually large glebe of about 86 acres, which were divided (along with the tithes of the parish) among four clergy. The Domesday survey, however, does not list St Endellion as a land-owning church staffed by a group of clergy, and the four may have emerged only in the 12th or early 13th century. If the glebe is older, it may have been the endowment of a monastery or minster that came to an end well before 1066, or it may have been that of a church that never had a community of clergy.[4] The origin of the four clergy of St Endellion is examined in more detail below.[5]

ST GERMANS

The earliest evidence for a church and religious community at St Germans comes from two 10th-century manuscripts known respectively as the *Codex Oxoniensis Posterior* and the 'Lanalet Pontifical'. The *Codex*, a miscellany of texts, opens with a single folio containing an incomplete liturgical text entitled *Missa propria Germani episcopi* ('the proper mass of Bishop German').[6] The folio contains prayers, one of which talks of the 'place [called] *Lannaled*', famous and notable everywhere, where the relics of German the bishop are preserved'.[7] Another refers to Bishop German as having been 'sent to us by St Gregory, apostle of the Roman city' and describes German as 'the lamp and pillar of Cornwall'. The 'Lanalet Pontifical' is a manual of the kinds of texts used by bishops. The bishop for whom it was produced is not known, but it contains a formula of excommunication, added to the volume probably in the 11th century, which mentions 'the bishop... of the *monasterium* of *Lanalet*', implying that it was later associated with that place.[8]

The linkage of *Lannaled/Lanalet* with St German and with a bishop indicates that both texts were associated with St Germans in Cornwall which, by at least the end of the 10th century, was the seat of a bishop. *Lannaled*, the better form, appears to mean 'church-site at *Aled*', an older or alternative name for St Germans.[9] The earlier text, that of the mass, appears to assume that the saint German to whom it refers was German of Auxerre (d. 448), commemorated on 31 July.[10] It represents him as having been sent to Cornwall by Pope Gregory the Great (590–604), an impossibility, but one perhaps inspired by a wish to claim for St Germans an antiquity equal to that of Canterbury, to which Gregory sent St Augustine in 597. The church of St Germans may have originated before the 9th century, but there is no independent evidence to that effect. The mass further shows that the church claimed to possess relics of the saint, and refers (at least in hope) to the coming of pilgrims to the place. It does not mention a body of clergy, but St Germans possessed one in later times and is likely to have to have done so in the 10th century. By that time the church is more likely to have been a minster served by canons than a monastery of monks.

In 936 King Æthelstan founded or confirmed a bishopric based at St Germans. This is attested by three different sources. A letter of Dunstan, archbishop of Canterbury, to King Æthelred the Unready dating from 981–8 contains an interpolation, probably from a few years later, claiming that 'King Æthelstan gave to *Cunun* the bishopric as far as the Tamar flowed'. The letter itself states that the bishop's seat was at St Germans by the time that Daniel became bishop of Cornwall in about 955.[11] In 1533 the antiquary John Leland reported finding a charter at St Germans in which Æthelstan 'established a certain Bishop Conan [or a certain Conan as bishop] in the church of St Germans on 5 December in the year of the Lord 936'.[12] Notes made in the 17th century from a lost register of Plympton Priory

---

1 L. Olson, 'Crantock, Cornwall, as an Early Monastic Site'. in S. M. Pearce (ed.), *The Early Church in Western Britain and Ireland* (1982), 177–85; Orme, *The Saints of Cornwall*, 83–5.
2 Below, p. 173.
3 Ibid.
4 Compare Lansallos, below p. 132.
5 Below, p. 180.
6 Bodleian, Bodley 572, described in F. Madan and H. H. E. Craster (ed.), *A Summary Catalogue of Western Manuscripts in the Bodleian Library at Oxford* (1922–53), II(i), 170–4.
7 Bodley 572, f. 1, printed in G. H. Doble (ed.), *Pontificale Lanaletense*, Henry Bradshaw Soc. 74 (1937), pp. xxi–xxii.
8 Rouen, Bibliothèque municipale, A. 27 (368), ff. 183r–184r.
9 O. J. Padel, *Cornish Place-Name Elements*, English Place-Name Society 56/57 (1985), 4; idem, *Popular Dictionary of Cornish Place-Names*, 87.
10 The liturgical material is partly borrowed from the mass of SS Abdon and Sennen, commemorated on the previous day, 30 July.
11 A. S. Napier and W. H. Stevenson (ed.), *The Crawford Collection of Early Charters and Documents now in the Bodleian Library* (1895), 18–9, 104–5.
12 J. Leland, *Collectanea*, ed. T. Hearne (1774), I, 75.

(Devon) include part of the same or a different charter allegedly granted by Æthelstan in the year 936, in which the king is said to 'restore and willingly bestow… all the territory of the bishopric, that is to say of the Blessed German, bishop of the region of Cornwall', with freedom from all royal impositions except for military obligations.[1] The word 'restore', if authentic, points to St Germans having been the seat of a Cornish bishop, or of the bishop of Cornwall, before that date. However a bishop is recorded elsewhere in Cornwall in the 9th century, possibly at Bodmin, and this must be allowed for when reconstructing the previous history of St Germans.[2]

Conan is the first recorded of a series of bishops who ruled the whole of Cornwall from the 930s to the year 1050, under the authority of the kings of England and the archbishops of Canterbury. By 955 at the latest, as stated above, their seat was at St Germans, and by the 990s they also had authority over the church of St Petroc, at Padstow or Bodmin.[3] A bishop of this period would have had a staff of clergy at his principal church. The word *monasterium* in the 11th-century formula of excommunication points in the same direction, and should probably be understood as a minster. In later times it was believed that King Cnut (1016–35) had also granted or confirmed property to the church.[4] The earliest distinct reference to clergy at St Germans occurs in the Domesday Survey of 1086, which states that in 1066 the canons of that church had held twelve hides of land at St Germans, exempt from tax, alongside twelve that were held by the bishop. The canons' portion was worth 100s.[5] Exemption from tax was a feature of the lands of most pre-Conquest Cornish religious houses, and is mentioned, as we have seen, in the charter attributed to Æthelstan. St Germans also resembled most of these houses in possessing, in later times, a large parish.

The existence of two manuscripts linked with the church makes it possible to glimpse something of its religious and cultural life. The 'Lanalet Pontifical' is less helpful here than the *Codex*, because it only contains the kinds of liturgical material commonly used by bishops. The *Codex* is more varied. Apart from the 'Mass of St German' it is made up of three parts, all in Latin. The third part, written in France in the 9th century, contains three works on penance and a sermon. The first part, apparently compiled in Cornwall in the 10th century, includes an 'Exposition of the Mass', probably by Theodulf, bishop of Orleans, and the Biblical 'Book of Tobias' (or Tobit). The second part, also of the 10th century and apparently produced or used in Wales and Cornwall, consists of a 'Letter of Augustine to Proba', a homily by Caesarius of Arles, and *De Raris Fabulis* – the name now given to a series of dialogues probably used in school for developing pupils' vocabulary, syntax, and conversational powers in Latin.[6] Only the 'Mass' is specifically linked with St Germans, but the presence of glosses in Old Cornish or Welsh to 'Tobias' and *De Raris Fabulis* may imply that these texts were used in Cornwall. If the whole *Codex* was used there, it would show that Cornwall, and perhaps St Germans specifically, was in touch with learning from a wide range of northern Europe, encompassing Latin texts from England and the Continent, Welsh glosses, Scandinavian runes, and script both 'insular' and continental in style. *De Raris Fabulis*, in particular, implies the provision of education in Latin to a standard of that of schools elsewhere in Britain.

St Germans continued to be the seat of a bishop until 1050 when Leofric, bishop of the two dioceses of Crediton and Cornwall, gained permission to unite them and to move his seat to Exeter. A body of canons continued to exist at St Germans until the second half of the 12th century, when the church was reorganised as a priory of Augustinian canons.[7]

GORAN

There may have been a church at Goran by the 10th century, when its saint, *Guron*, appears in the important list of saints, including Cornish saints, compiled in Brittany or Cornwall at that time.[8] The church is not mentioned in the Domesday survey of 1086, but the geld accounts which date from the same period list 'St Goran' as holding half of a hide of land in Powder hundred.[9] A saint's name employed in this way indicates a church that held land in its own right, often one staffed by a community of clergy. It is therefore possible that Goran church had such a community at some point before the middle of the 11th century; however in later times it was only a parish church with a single clergyman.

KEA

The church of Kea possessed a large parish in historic times, including Kenwyn, Tregavethan, and possibly formerly Truro. The geld accounts, dating from about the time of the Domesday survey in 1086, state that 'St Che' held half a hide of land in Powder hundred: this is likely to refer to the church of Kea.[10] Domesday itself attributes a small tenement at *Tremaru(u)stel* (probably Treroosel in St Teath parish) to the 'honour of St Che'; this on the other hand must refer to the church of St

---

1 Bodleian, James 23, p. 170; O. J. Padel, "Two New Pre-Conquest Charters for Cornwall', *Cornish Studies* 6 (1978), 26–7.
2 Above, p. 126.
3 Above, p. 127.
4 Below, p. 186.
5 Thorn (ed.), *Domesday Book: Cornwall*, 2/6; Ellis (ed.), *Domesday Book, IV: Additamenta*, p. 182 (f. 199b), p. 470 (f. 507).
6 Discussed and edited by S. Gwara, *Education in Wales and Cornwall in the Ninth and Tenth Centuries: Understanding* De raris fabulis (Cambridge, Kathleen Hughes Memorial Lectures, 4, 2004).
7 Below, p. 184.
8 Olson and Padel, 'A Tenth-Century List', 60–1.
9 Ellis (ed.), *Domesday Book, IV: Additamenta*, p. 66 (f. 72).
10 Ibid.

Kew, to which Treroosel is known to have belonged.[1] Kea's possession of land and the size of its parish suggest the presence of a pre-Conquest religious house, one that disappeared in about the middle of the 11th century. In later times the church was an ordinary parish church.

ST KEVERNE

St Keverne church must have existed by the 10th century when its saint, *Achobran*, occurs in the early list of saints compiled in Brittany or Cornwall.[2] The parish, in later times, was a large one, and the church, by the 11th century, was staffed by a body of canons, mentioned in the Domesday survey of 1086 as having held eleven acres of land there in 1066.[3] The geld accounts of the same period, however, credit 'St *Achabran*' with holding one hide of land.[4] Neither record mentions the land as being exempt from tax, although this exemption was common among ancient religious communities in Cornwall. Domesday valued the property at 40*s*. 'when the count received it' and afterwards 5*s*., Robert count of Mortain having, as usual, appropriated some of the wealth of the church. His intervention may have caused or hastened a loss of endowments by the church, helping to bring about the disappearance of the canons, who are not mentioned after this date. St Keverne subsequently became an ordinary parish church, and was granted by Richard, earl of Cornwall, to Beaulieu Abbey (Hants.) by 1235.[5] In the later Middle Ages it was sometimes claimed as having special privileges of sanctuary – a claim, if true, that replicated those of three other important pre-Conquest churches in Cornwall: St Buryan, Padstow, and Probus.[6]

ST KEW

St Kew is the oldest recorded religious house in Cornwall, being mentioned in the earliest Life of St Samson, written in Brittany probably in about 750. According to the Life, Samson (who lived two centuries earlier, in the middle of the 6th century) was travelling towards a monastery called *Docco* in Cornwall when its 'brothers' sent one of their number, named *Viniauus*, to ask the saint tactfully not to visit the place.[7] *Docco* was the name of a saint associated with an early monastery at Llandough near Cardiff (Glamorgan), suggesting that the Cornish *Docco* was founded from or inspired by its Welsh counterpart. In later times *Docco* was known as *Landochou*, *Lanohoo*, or *Lannou*, meaning 'church-site of *Docco*', and by the 10th century the church had also become associated with St Kewa, whose name eventually eclipsed that of *Docco*. The next reference to the church, after the Life of Samson, occurs in a charter of King Edgar, datable to between 961 and 963. By it the king granted (or more probably confirmed) two hides of land at St Kew to the monastery of SS *Docco* and Kew.[8] The clergy of such a 'monastery' might have been monks or clergy living a less strict life; either are possible in the 8th century, and the latter more likely by the 10th. In later times the parish of St Kew, like that of other ancient religious houses in Cornwall, was a relatively large one.

By 1066 the manor of St Kew was held by Earl Harold, later Harold II, from whom it passed to William the Conqueror.[9] The church is not listed among other landowning churches in the Domesday survey of 1086, but it is mentioned twice in relation to pieces of land in Cornwall. The first of these states that a small tenement at *Tremaru(u)stel* (probably Treroosel in St Teath parish) belonged to the 'honour [i.e. lordship] of St *Che*'.[10] This must be a reference to St Kew (rather than to Kea), since Treroosel was claimed by Plympton Priory, owners of St Kew church, in the 12th century.[11] The second reference says that the manors of Poundstock and St Gennys had been taken from St Kew and were now held by a tenant of Robert, count of Mortain, suggesting that the church of St Kew may also have held these manors as outlying possessions.[12] The church was granted to the church of Exeter (in effect to the bishop) by Henry I in 1123, and the bishop, William Warelwast, gave it to Plympton Priory.[13] There were apparently still clergy at St Kew in 1158 when Henry II confirmed Plympton's possession of the church and ordered that the prebends of the 'clerks' should pass to the priory on their deaths.[14] Their presence probably came to an end in the 1160s or 70s.[15]

---

1 Thorn (ed.), *Domesday Book: Cornwall*, 5/24/14; Ellis (ed.), *Domesday Book, IV: Additamenta*, p. 225 (f. 245b). For discussion, see W. M. M. Picken, 'The Manor of Tremaruustel and the Honour of St Keus', *JRIC* n.s. 7 (1973–7), 220–30, and Olson, *Early Monasteries*, 91.

2 Olson and Padel, 'A Tenth-Century List', 47–8.

3 Thorn (ed.), *Domesday Book: Cornwall*, ed. Thorn, 4/23; Ellis (ed.), *Domesday Book, IV: Additamenta*, p. 187 (f. 205b).

4 Ellis (ed.), *Domesday Book, IV: Additamenta*, p. 66 (f. 72).

5 C. Henderson, 'The Ecclesiastical History of the 109 Parishes of West Cornwall', *JRIC* n.s. 3 (1957–60), 263.

6 Ibid., 265–7.

7 P. Flobert (ed.), *La Vie ancienne de Saint Samson de Dol* (1997), 212–15.

8 Sawyer, *Anglo-Saxon Charters*, no. 810, printed by W. M. M. Picken, 'The "Landochou" Charter', in W. G. Hoskins, *The Westward Expansion of Wessex*, University of Leicester, Department of English Local History, Occasional Papers, 13 (1960), 36–44, discussed by Olson, *Early Monasteries*, 81–4, and topographically by Hooke, *Pre-Conquest Charter Bounds*, 33–7.

9 Ellis (ed.), *Domesday Book, IV: Additamenta*, 92–3 (f. 101).

10 Thorn (ed.), *Domesday Book: Cornwall*, 5/24/14; Ellis (ed.), *Domesday Book, IV: Additamenta*, p. 225 (f. 245b).

11 W. M. M. Picken, 'The Manor of Tremaruustel and the Honour of St Keus', *JRIC* new ser. 7 (1973–7), 220–30; Olson, *Early Monasteries*, 91.

12 Thorn (ed.), *Domesday Book: Cornwall*, ed. Thorn, 1/4, 5/7/6; Ellis (ed.), *Domesday Book, IV: Additamenta*, pp. 92–3 (f. 101).

13 *Regesta Regum Anglo-Normannorum*, ed. H. W. C. Davis et al. (1913–59), II, 72, 185; F, Barlow (ed.), *English Episcopal Acta*, XI: *Exeter 1046–1184*, 24.

14 G. Oliver, *Monasticon Dioecesis Exoniensis* (1846), 135.

15 For a possible later priory, see below, p. 195.

LAMMANA

Lammana was a name, first recorded in 1144, of the island off the south coast of Cornwall near Looe, known today as St George's or Looe Island. The name was also applied to the part of the mainland opposite the island. By 1144 both island and mainland belonged to Glastonbury Abbey, and by 1199–1220 there was a chapel on the island, dedicated to St Michael, which was staffed for a period in the 13th century by two monks of Glastonbury.[1] The name 'Lammana' appears to mean 'church-site of a monk',[2] and the island has been suggested as the possible site of a pre-Conquest religious community.[3] No documentary evidence survives to this effect, however. The chapel was not a parish church in the normal sense, and the territory attached to it on the island and mainland was much smaller than those of most ancient religious communities.

LANSALLOS

A charter of the reign of King Æthelstan (924–39), preserved in a 15th-century transcript, contains a grant by a nobleman (*comes*) named *Maenchi* of land at *Lanlouern* (Lanlawren in the parish of Lanteglos-by-Fowey) to 'God and St *Heldenus*', the latter saint being identical with Ildiern or Hyldren, later recorded as the patron saint of the neighbouring parish of Lansallos.[4] A grant to a saint meant one to the church of the saint, and the record shows that Lansallos church held some land, possibly indicating the presence of a religious community. No documentary reference survives to such a house at Lansallos, however, and Domesday Book states that by 1066 the manor of Lansallos was in lay hands as, by 1182, was Lanlawren.[5] The parish in later times was not significantly large in size.

LAUNCESTON

Launceston (meaning 'church-site of Stephen') takes its name from the church of St Stephen-by-Launceston. The name passed first, by the time of the Norman Conquest, to a settlement beside the church (nowadays St Stephen's) and later, after the Conquest, to the present town south of the River Kensey. According to the 'Exon' text of Domesday Book, the church existed by 1066 when its property was held by Earl Harold, later King Harold II. Harold's tenure probably interrupted an earlier possession by a body of canons, who are definitely mentioned in Domesday (1086) as owning the property. They are stated as holding four hides of land at or near Launceston, which had never paid tax, a freedom enjoyed by several of the ancient Cornish religious communities and unlikely to have been of recent origin. The value of the canons' property was said to have been £8 'when the count received it' and £4 in 1086. Here as elsewhere it is implied that Robert count of Mortain had appropriated some of the wealth of the church. In particular he was said to have removed the canons' market at St Stephen's, worth £1, to his new castle south of the river. The canons, however, were now holding two and a half hides from the count at Bonyalva in St Germans and at Bodigga and Bucklawren in St Martin-by-Looe – evidently as his gift to their church.[6]

The Domesday account gives no clue to the antiquity of St Stephen's church and community before the middle of the 11th century. It is also too brief to give us an adequate picture of either the church's endowments or the role of Robert count of Mortain. As we shall see from the history of the church after the Norman Conquest, Robert granted a charter to the canons in 1076 giving them 26 pieces of property amounting to five or even eight hides of land. In this respect he acted as their protector, not their predator, and the charter may represent less of a gift than a confirmation of property that the canons had once held; indeed it may even signify the return of property taken by Harold.[7] The properties listed in the charter lay not only in St Stephen-by-Launceston itself but in the nearby parishes of Boyton, Egloskerry, Laneast, South Petherwin, and Tresmeer, with outliers in St Germans and in St Martin-by-Looe. Neither the charter nor the Domesday survey was concerned to enumerate St Stephen's spiritual property, such as churches and tithes, but the church held a number of these in the surrounding area by the 12th century and may have done so earlier. By 1076, and probably earlier, it was the best-endowed religious house in Cornwall apart from Bodmin, and exercised a wide jurisdiction as a mother house over the churches north and west of Launceston. This made it more similar to an important English minster church than were most Cornish religious houses before the Conquest, a fact that probably reflects the fact that St Stephen's lay close to the county boundary with Devon and was an administrative centre of the kings of England, with its own mint, during the 11th century.

MANACCAN

The church of Manaccan is first mentioned in 1259 as that of *Ministre*, and subsequently as *Menstre* or similar

---

1 Below, p. 196.
2 Padel, *Popular Dictionary*, 86.
3 Olson, *Early Monasteries*, 98–103.
4 Sawyer, *Anglo-Saxon Charters*, no. 1207; E. H. Bates (ed.), *Two Cartularies of the Benedictine Abbeys of Muchelney and Athelney*, Somerset Record Soc. 14 (1899), 156; O. J. Padel, 'Two New Pre-Conquest Charters for Cornwall', 20; idem, 'The Charter of Lanlawren (Cornwall)', in K. O'Brien O'Keeffe and A. Orchard (ed.), *Latin Learning and English Lore* (2005), II, 74–85.
5 Thorn (ed.), *Domesday Book: Cornwall*, 5/3/7; Padel, 'Pre-Conquest Charters', 22.
6 Thorn (ed.), *Domesday Book: Cornwall*, 1/7, 4/2; Ellis (ed.), *Domesday Book, IV: Additamenta*, pp. 93 (f. 101b), 188 (f. 206v); W. M. M. Picken, 'The Domesday Book and East Cornwall', *Old Cornwall* 2.11 (1936), 24–7.
7 Below, pp. 201–2.

forms.¹ *Ministre* and *Menstre* appear to be forms of the English word 'minster',² usually meaning a church served by a community of clergy, and raise the question (as at Minster) whether such a church existed at Manaccan in earlier times. 'Manaccan' may be a personal name, like that of many other Cornish churches or, with less likelihood, 'place of monks'.³ The church lies in the district of Meneage, meaning 'monkish land', but it is not known whether this district name arose from one or more local monasteries or from its possession by a monastery elsewhere, such as St Keverne or St Michael's Mount.⁴ In short there is no documentary evidence for a pre-Conquest religious house in Manaccan, and the small size of the parish does not suggest the existence of one.

MAWGAN-IN-MENEAGE

There is no documentary reference to a pre-Conquest community of clergy at this church. A hypothesis about such a community might be based on the relatively large size of the parish (formerly including St Martin-in-Meneage) and its central position and relatively important rank in the scattering of churches dedicated to the patron saint, Maugan, in Brittany, Cornwall, and Wales.⁵

ST MICHAEL'S MOUNT

The case for a pre-Conquest church and religious community at St Michael's Mount rests on a charter in the 12th-century cartulary of the Benedictine abbey of Mont St Michel (Manche), by which King Edward the Confessor granted the abbey 'St Michael, which is by the sea' (in other words St Michael's Mount), together with the land of *Vennesire* and the port of *Ruminella*.⁶ The grant would have to be dated between 1027 and 1035, when Edward was an exile in Normandy where he was regarded as the legitimate king of England. If the grant is genuine, it points to a church holding property on the nearby mainland, a church that would have been likely to support a community of clergy.⁷

MINSTER

Minster is not mentioned in Domesday Book as a church holding land or served by a body of clergy. It was granted to the monks of the abbey of St Serge, Angers, in about the middle third of the 12th century, and the abbey established a small priory of monks at the church.⁸ The name 'Minster', first recorded at that time, may simply have arisen to describe this priory rather than implying an earlier religious community. There are, however, hints that this region had a long-standing religious importance, given that Minster church had the same patron saint, Mertherian, as its neighbour Tintagel, the latter of which was situated beside an early cemetery and close to a promontory (later the castle) which seems to have been a site of high status.

ST NEOT

The church of St Neot may have existed by the 890s, when the Welsh bishop Asser appears to allude in his Life of King Alfred to the saint of that name as being buried in Cornwall.⁹ There is an impressive carved shaft of a standing cross in the churchyard, dating from about 900. Most of the saint's bones were removed to the church of St Neot's (Huntingdonshire) in about the late 10th century, but the Cornish church kept some importance as the centre of a large parish, holding an endowment of land, and staffed, in the 11th century, by a body of clergy. The Domesday survey recorded that in 1066 the clergy of St Neot held two hides of land there, formerly worth 20s., which had never paid tax – a privilege common to some other ancient religious houses in Cornwall. Two references to the clergy call them 'priests' and one 'clerks'. By the time that the survey was made, twenty years later, Robert count of Mortain had taken this land away from the church except for a single acre, worth 5s.¹⁰ He evidently also acquired the patronage of the church, and by 1106 he or his son William had given it to the priory of Montacute (Somerset).¹¹ The community of clergy probably ceased to exist as a result of these changes. The tithes of the parish were appropriated to Montacute Priory, and St Neot became an ordinary parish church served by a vicar appointed by the priory.

NORTH AND SOUTH PETHERWIN

North Petherwin church was the centre of an unusually large parish north of Launceston, which included Werrington and St Giles-on-the-Heath in the 12th century. Another large parish dedicated to the same saint, Paternus, was centred on the church of South Petherwin, which originally included Trewen and what later became the parishes of St Mary Magdalene (Launceston) and St Thomas-by-Launceston. The two Petherwin parishes were, however, separated by that of St Stephen-by-Launceston. The size of these parishes is suggestive of

---

1 *Reg. Bronescombe*, ed. Hingeston-Randolph, 152–3; ed. Robinson, I, 26–7; II, 15, 87; III, 55.

2 Padel, *Cornish Place-Name Elements*, 167; idem, *Popular Dictionary*, 114.

3 Padel, *Cornish Place-Name Elements*, 156; idem, *Popular Dictionary*, 114, 118–19.

4 Olson, *Early Monasteries*, 108–9.

5 Orme, *The Saints of Cornwall*, 182–3.

6 Printed in P. L. Hull (ed.), *The Cartulary of St. Michael's Mount*, DCRS new ser. 5 (1962) 61, and M. Fauroux (ed.), *Recueil des actes des ducs de Normandie de 911 à 1066* (1961), 217–18.

7 Discussed below, p. 228.

8 Below, p. 240.

9 *Asser's Life of King Alfred*, ed. W. H. Stevenson (1959), 55.

10 Thorn (ed.), *Domesday Book: Cornwall*, 4/28; Ellis (ed.), *Domesday Book, IV: Additamenta*, p. 66 (f. 72b) (which estimates the land at one hide and one virgate), pp. 198–9 f. 207.

11 Below, p. 297.

PADSTOW

The evidence for a pre-Conquest religious house at Padstow is indirect but significant. According to the oldest Life of St Petroc, written in about the middle of the 11th century, probably in Cornwall, Petroc established a 'monastery' at Padstow at an unstated but early date, followed by a second foundation at Bodmin.[1] The Life has no value in establishing when any monastery at Padstow was founded, but shows that there was a tradition of such a monastery when it was written. The cult of St Petroc was an important one, which inspired the dedication of churches in Cornwall, Brittany, Wales, and southern England, and seems more likely to have originated at Padstow than Bodmin, where it was eventually centred. A list of the resting places of saints in England, dating from the first third of the 11th century, states that Petroc's relics lay near *Hæglæmutha* ('Hayle mouth'), meaning Padstow.[2] Other factors point to Padstow as a place of religious importance, probably embodied by a religious house rather than a mere parish church. Much of the property held by Petroc's other major church at Bodmin in the late 11th century lay south of Padstow. In 1086 Bodmin church held one hide of land at Padstow itself, which was stated to have never paid tax – a common feature of ancient religious houses in Cornwall.[3] Padstow enjoyed a special privilege of sanctuary in the Middle Ages, something shared by St Buryan and Probus which also housed religious communities.[4] Finally, although the parish of the church was not large in historic times, the southern boundaries of the next parishes to the south of it – St Eval, St Ervan, Little Petherick, St Issey, and St Breock – follow a continuous line that suggest an extensive territory, which might once have belonged to Padstow church.

By about the middle of the 11th century the centre of Petroc's cult was the church of the canons of Bodmin, which eventually claimed to possess his body. Padstow was often known, by about 1200, as *Aldstow*, 'the old holy place', implying a belief that it had been superseded in this respect, presumably by Bodmin. It looks as if the cult of Petroc was transferred from Padstow to Bodmin, and that any community of clergy devoted to maintaining the cult moved likewise. As has already been stated in connection with Bodmin, there is no clear evidence as to when this might have happened.[5] One suggestion has placed the event in the first half of the 9th century and another in the late 10th, when the Anglo-Saxon Chronicle states that '*Sancte Petroces stow* was laid waste' in 981, presumably by a Viking attack.[6] The latter entry might refer to Padstow or to Bodmin, but if it relates to Padstow it would provide a motive for the Padstow clergy to have moved to Bodmin with the body of their saint. We are left with a strong sense of there having been a religious house at Padstow, perhaps housing a monastic community that eventually turned into a minster of canons or clerks. Neither its origins nor its terminus can be dated, however, beyond the possibility that it still existed in the 10th century and the certainty that it had ceased to do so by the middle of the 11th.

PERRANZABULOE

The church of Perranzabuloe was an important one in medieval Cornwall. It possessed one of the largest parishes in the county, and its saint, Piran, was commemorated at two other churches – Perranarworthal and Perranuthnoe, as well as attracting bequests in Cornish wills from outside the parish. The church is not mentioned in documents until the Domesday survey of 1086, but a charter of 960 which granted a large estate similar in size to the later historic parish of Perranzabuloe, and which mentions a rock called *Carn Peran*, implies the existence of the church by this date.[7] Domesday states that in 1066 its canons had held three hides of land at Perranzabuloe, worth 40s. The land had been free of tax, like that of other ancient Cornish religious houses. Since then the canons had lost two pieces of land, only one of which is named: a hide of land at *Tregrebri*, probably *Tregenver* a former place at Trethevy in Tintagel parish. The two lost properties had formerly paid four weeks' revenues to the canons and 20s. to the dean.[8] This shows that Perranzabuloe, like the minsters at Bodmin and Launceston, had acquired a presiding cleric called the dean, and he may have received a larger stipend than the rest of the canons, as his counterparts did at the other two churches.[9]

By the time of the Domesday survey Perranzabuloe was still staffed by canons but it had suffered like other Cornish churches from Robert count of Mortain. The count had given the property at *Tregrebri* to one of his men, who now held it from him, and he had taken away the stock from another hide, which his tenant Odo now held from the canons. It is likely that Robert also

---

1 Grosjean, 'Vie et miracles de S. Petroc', 487–96, at 491, 495; translated by Doble, *Saint Petrock*, 8–22, at 14, 20.
2 D. W. Rollason, 'Lists of Saints' Resting-Places in Anglo-Saxon England', *Anglo-Saxon England* 7 (1978), 61–93, at 64, 68, 92.
3 Thorn (ed.), *Domesday Book: Cornwall*, 4/4; Ellis (ed.), *Domesday Book, IV: Additamenta*, p. 183 (f. 202) (*Languihenoc*).
4 Doble, *St Petrock*, 36.

5 Above, p. 126.
6 *The Anglo-Saxon Chronicle*, vol. V, ed. O'Keeffe, 84.
7 Hooke, *Pre-Conquest Charter-Bounds*, 28–33.
8 Thorn (ed.), *Domesday Book: Cornwall*, 4/26, 5/8/10; Ellis (ed.), *Domesday Book, IV: Additamenta*, p. 188 (f. 206b–7), p. 220 (f. 240b).
9 Above, p. 127; below, pp. 139, 202.

appropriated the patronage of the church and that this passed, after the downfall of Robert's son William in 1106, to Henry I, who granted it to the bishop and cathedral of Exeter in 1123.[1] At some unknown point after 1086 the community of canons disappeared, and the church became an ordinary parish church, the cathedral receiving its major tithes and appointing the vicar who served it.

PROBUS

Probus church existed by the 10th century, when its saint occurs in the early list of saints compiled in Brittany or Cornwall, next to Ladoc the saint of the adjoining parish.[2] The church may be older than this, given that a saint of the same name appears to have given his name to a church at Sherborne by the 7th century.[3] In later times the parish was large and the church possessed special privileges of sanctuary. According to the Domesday survey of 1086 it was staffed by canons who held one hide and one virgate of land there, worth 40s. This land had never paid tax – a privilege typical of similar ancient Cornish religious houses.[4] The church was unusual in apparently not having experienced, by 1086, control or expropriation by Robert count of Mortain, and by 1123 at the latest it was granted to the bishop and cathedral of Exeter. A community of canons appears to have survived throughout the late 11th and 12th centuries, and emerges in the thirteenth as a body of six, including a dean.[5]

SAMSON'S MONASTERY

The author of the earliest Life of St Samson, who wrote in Brittany in about 750, credited Samson, who lived historically in the middle of the 6th century, with the foundation of a monastery in Cornwall. Traditions collected by the author alleged that the monastery was sited near a cave from which Samson had expelled and killed a dangerous serpent, and that its first leader was Samson's father Amon, whom Samson chose for this purpose before he himself departed from Cornwall to Brittany. The monastery still existed when the author wrote his Life, and he claims that he had visited it.[6]

Several attempts have been made to identify the site of this monastery. One school of thought has wished to place it at Golant or South Hill, whose churches were both dedicated to Samson by the 12th and 14th centuries respectively.[7] This case is weakened by the fact that the dedications to Samson in Cornwall, of which there were four, were all or almost all chapels and appear to be relatively late foundations.[8] A religious house in Cornwall like Samson's monastery could be expected to have become a parish church in later times and to have acquired a large parish. Fowey, which has also been suggested, equally lacks traces of having owned such a parish.[9] In fact more than one of the churches which supported communities of clergy in the 10th and 11th centuries might be candidates for the site of Samson's monastery, since the church need not have been dedicated to him.

ST WINNOW

The case for a pre-Conquest religious house at St Winnow rests on the location of the parish church in a maritime position with a large surrounding parish, features characteristic of some other such houses in Cornwall.

---

1 *Regesta Regum Anglo-Normannorum*, ed. Davis et al., II, 185; cf. 72.

2 Olson and Padel, 'A Tenth-Century List', 51–2.

3 K. Barker, 'The Early History of Sherborne', in S. M. Pearce (ed.), *The Early Church in Britain and Ireland*, British Archaeological Reports, British Series, 102 (Oxford, 1982), 77–116; Orme, *The Saints of Cornwall*, 223–4.

4 Thorn (ed.), *Domesday Book: Cornwall*, 4/24; Ellis (ed.), *Domesday Book, IV: Additamenta*, p. 66 (f. 72), p. 187 (f. 206).

5 Below, p. 262.

6 Flobert (ed.), *Vie de Saint Samson*, 140–3, 220–3.

7 G. H. Doble, *Saint Samson in Cornwall*, Cornish Saints Series, 36 (1935), reprinted in idem, *The Saints of Cornwall*, ed. D. Attwater and R. L. Ravenscroft (1960–97), V, 80-103; Olson, *Early Monasteries*, 12–14.

8 Orme, *The Saints of Cornwall*, 229–30.

9 C. Thomas, *And Shall These Mute Stones Speak? Post-Roman inscriptions in western Britain* (1994), 232.

RELIGIOUS HOUSES AFTER 1066

THE sections that follow describe the histories of the religious houses of Cornwall after the Norman Conquest. They are listed in alphabetical order of location, ignoring the prefix 'St'. Where there was more than one religious house in a place, as in Bodmin and Launceston, the houses are ranked in order of importance. Each house is treated within a single article, irrespective of whether it changed its nature from minster to monastery or monastery to chantry.

The religious houses of Cornwall after 1100 belonged to several different types. Pre-Conquest minsters survived for a time at Bodmin, Launceston, and St Germans, and were reorganised during the twelfth century as priories of Augustinian canons. Three other pre-Conquest minsters survived for longer at St Buryan, Crantock, and Probus, and there were two prebendal churches – St Endellion and St Teath. All these institutions were staffed by 'secular clergy' similar to parish clergy, as were the collegiate churches of Glasney and St Michael Penkevil, and two large chantries at St Columb Major and St Michael's Mount. The 'regular' or monastic orders of clergy were represented by five priories of Benedictine monks at Lammana, St Michael's Mount, Minster, Scilly, and Tywardreath, one priory of Cluniac monks at St Carroc, and four of Augustinian canons (the three former minsters mentioned above, and a small priory at Tregony). A further doubtful Augustinian house at St Kew is also discussed in this volume. The Order of St John of Jerusalem (the Hospitallers) owned a preceptory at Trebeigh, and the Knights Templars acquired property at Temple, although there is no evidence that they founded a religious establishment there. Two houses of friars, Franciscans at Bodmin and Dominicans at Truro, made their appearance during the thirteenth century. There were leper hospitals at Bodmin, Helston, Lanlivery, Launceston, Liskeard, and *Sheepstall* in Veryan, and a hospital for others than lepers at Helston. Other hospitals – almshouses in nature – were founded at Bodmin (two: St Anthony and St George) and Launceston, and planned at Penryn. A number of leper communities existed that are not certainly known to have been hospital institutions. These are discussed in the section entitled 'Uncertain Hospitals', and the book concludes with the records relating to anchorites and hermits.

ST ANTHONY-IN-ROSELAND

AUGUSTINIAN PRIORY OF ST ANTHONY

The origins of the priory of St Anthony-in-Roseland are linked with the ecclesiastical history of the Roseland peninsula. Most of the peninsula lay within the manor of Tregaire, which belonged to the bishops of Exeter and contained the churches and parishes of St Anthony-in-Roseland, Gerrans, St Just-in-Roseland, and Philleigh. Bishop William Warelwast refounded the Anglo-Saxon minster of Plympton (Devon) as a house of Augustinian canons in 1121, and William's nephew and successor as bishop, Robert Warelwast (1138–1155), gave Plympton two of the Roseland churches, St Anthony and St Just, 'with lands, tithes, liberties, and all their appurtenances'. His grant was subsequently confirmed by Henry II (1154–89).[1] Plympton appears to have gained possession of St Anthony without difficulty, but its claim to St Just was challenged by the family of le Soor, lords of Tolverne in Philleigh parish. In about 1188 John the Chanter, bishop of Exeter, approved an agreement between Plympton and John le Soor which settled that John was to hold the advowson of St Just in return for a payment to Plympton of 13s. 4d. per annum.[2] An attempt by the prior of Plympton to appoint a cleric to the benefice in 1201 was foiled by John, who produced Bishop John's charter in his favour.[3] In 1202 the next bishop of Exeter, Henry Marshal, granted Plympton part of the income

---

1 W. Dugdale, *Monasticon Anglicanum* (1817–30), VI.1, 53–4. On the history of Plympton, see A. D. Fizzard, *Plympton Priory* (2008).

2 F. Barlow (ed.), *English Episcopal Acta*, XII: *Exeter 1186–1257* (1996), 153–4.

3 D. M. Stenton (ed.), *Pleas before the King or his Justices 1198–1202*, vol. II, Selden Soc. 68 (1952), 148–9.

FIG 42. *The parish church of St Anthony-in-Roseland preserves the cruciform shape of the medieval priory church and contains some of its ornately carved stonework inside.*

of Gerrans, another of the Roseland parishes. The bishop was to receive the tithes of his demesne in the parish, and the two parties were each to take half of the remaining tithes and offerings, the bishop having the responsibility of finding a chaplain to serve the church.[1]

The priory of St Anthony was founded by Plympton after it acquired its Roseland properties, probably as a base from which to administer them. Its staff may also have supervised Plympton's other possessions in Cornwall: the rectory of St Kew and some small landed properties in the hundreds of East and Powder.[2] The date of the foundation lies between 1138 (the earliest possible year of Bishop Robert's grant) and 1231 (when the priory was certainly in existence).[3] It may be possible to place the date before about 1200, when the gazetteer of religious houses in England attributed to Gervase of Canterbury lists one called St Anthony in Cornwall, stated as being staffed by Benedictine monks from Angers in France. At first sight this would indicate the church of St Anthony-in-Meneage, which belonged to Tywardreath Priory, a cell of Angers, but nothing is known of a religious house in the Meneage parish, making it plausible that the author meant St Anthony-in-Roseland but gave it the wrong religious affiliation.[4] In 1291, when the revenues of the English Church were assessed for papal taxation, Plympton possessed four sources of income from its Roseland properties. The spiritual revenues of the parish of St Anthony were assessed at £3, the temporal revenues of the parish at £3 11s. 2d., the 'portion of the prior of St Anthony in Gerrans' (i.e. the half share of its tithes) at £2 6s. 8d., and the pension from St Just-in-Roseland at 13s. 4d. This totalled a little over £9, and like most of the assessments of 1291 was much less than the real value. Since the priory of St Anthony did not have a legal existence independent of Plympton, the mother house would have appropriated the income over and above the expenses of running the priory.

The priory was sited in a sheltered spot at the head of a short inlet off the estuary of Percuil River, with access by boat to the River Fal and to the English Channel (SW 8549 3204). It consisted of a church with domestic buildings on its northern side, the latter now subsumed into the mansion of Place. The site had been that of a church or chapel since at least the 10th century, dedicated to a Brittonic or Brittonicised saint named Entenin, whose name was also linked with the church of St Anthony-in-Meneage and with a holy well at Ventontinny in Probus parish.[5] By the 12th century this saint was identified with the martyr Antoninus of Alexandria, and was believed in Cornwall to have been a king. The name of the church, however, was often spelt in Latin as *Antonius*, and there may have been a further identification with the well-known hermit saint Anthony of Egypt.[6] Nothing is known of the cult of the saint at the church. In view of the church's antiquity and

1 Barlow (ed.), *English Episcopal Acta*, XII, 190–1.
2 *Reg. Bronescombe*, ed. Hingeston-Randolph, 471, 478.
3 *Cur. Reg. R.* 1230–2, 308.
4 Gervase of Canterbury, *Historical Works*, ed. W. Stubbs, vol. II (RS 1880), 424).

5 L. Olson, 'Saint Entenyn', *Cornish Studies* 3 (1975), 25–8; above, p. 126.
6 N. Orme, *The Saints of Cornwall* (2000), 65–6, 115–16.

its later status as a priory, the question has been raised as to whether it was a monastery before the Norman Conquest. The answer is not known for certain, but it seems unlikely that a religious community existed up to the time of the foundation of St Anthony by Plympton, an act that appears to have been a new initiative.[1] The priory site may have been chosen for the sake of its spiritual past, or for practical reasons. Plympton held both St Anthony church and its adjoining manor, which was not the case at Gerrans or St Just.

The priory seems to have been normally staffed by two canons sent from the mother house, one of whom was prior. They had no independent status or seal, and their revenues belonged wholly to Plympton apart from what was used to maintain the priory. It is possible that the canons acted as the clergy of the parish, a permissible task for members of the Augustinian Order, or that they employed a chaplain to do so, although no such person is recorded.[2] The oldest features of the surviving church are a highly decorated Romanesque south doorway; this along with the presence of pieces of Caen stone suggest that the building was rebuilt or adapted to a good standard during the 12th century for the use of the priory. During the 13th there was a further rebuilding or restoration of the church using local slatestone for the walls. This resulted in a cruciform plan comprising an aisleless chancel and nave, two transepts, and a tower over the crossing, supported inside by carved freestone shafts and arches of high quality (Fig. 42).[3] The church was dedicated by Bishop Bronescombe of Exeter on 3 October 1259.[4] Constitutionally the building served as both a priory church and a parish church, so that the canons would have said daily services in the chancel while the parishioners (when present) used the nave. As well as the high altar in the chancel there were eventually altars in both transepts, the piscinas of which survive. Two bodies are known to have been buried on either side of the high altar, and two coffin-shaped ledger stones are recorded in the pavement of the church.[5] These were probably burials of canons; there was an exterior graveyard for parishioners. The parish was a small one, occupying only the eastern finger of the Roseland peninsula up to Porth Creek and covering 753 acres. In the 19th century the southern part of it, extending from a little way east of the church to St Anthony Head, constituted a tithe-free area of 284 acres, which no doubt represented the barton or home-farm of the priory.[6]

Little has survived about the history of the priory. Its maritime siting made it vulnerable to attack from the sea in wartime, and in 1338, when Bishop Grandisson of Exeter allowed Plympton to appropriate the tithes of the parish church of Newton St Cyres (Devon), he accepted as a reason the burden of repairing the cell of St Anthony which had been burnt 'by hostile incursions'.[7] An unnamed prior is mentioned in 1348–9, however, buying wine from a wrecked ship.[8] In 1381 the priory was staffed by Nicholas Walforde, described as *custos*,[9] and in 1492 by John Austyn, entitled prior, each with a canon colleague.[10] John Leland, who made his first visit to Cornwall in about 1533, recorded that 'upon the south side of this creek [Percuil River] is a cell belonging to the house of Plympton, called St Anthony's, having but two canons'.[11] Two years later in 1535 the *Valor Ecclesiasticus* or royal valuation of Plympton estimated the spiritual revenues of St Anthony at £5 a year (evidently the rent paid by a farmer or lessee) and the half share of the tithes of Gerrans at £13 6s. 8d. (which are stated as being farmed to John Reswycke). St Just-in-Roseland church still paid the pension of 13s. 4d.[12] A more detailed account of the revenues comes from the accounts of the king's receiver in 1540, after the dissolution of the monasteries. This valued the spiritual revenues of St Anthony at £5, those of Gerrans at £12, the farm or lease of the priory and its lands at £6 13s. 4d., the rents of free tenants at 19s. 10d., and the rents of customary tenants at £3 11s., total £28 4s. 2d. A chaplain was paid £5 per annum to serve St Anthony parish; it is not clear how far back this practice stretched.[13]

Plympton Priory surrendered to the crown on 1 March 1539, and the priory of St Anthony must have come to an end by this date.[14] On 20 January 1540 its property was leased by the crown to Henry Thomas, alias Kyllavoes, of London, king's servant, for twenty-one years at a rent of £27. The lease included the cell (i.e. priory) of St Anthony, lands called *Sande Parke*, *Wenyat Down*, *Lang Parke*, *Hall Parke*, and *The Lodge*, two water-mills, and the rectories of St Anthony and Gerrans – in other words the whole tithes of the former and the half-tithes of the latter.[15] Subsequently, on 10 August 1546, the cell and its demesne lands were sold,

---

1 L. Olson, *Early Monasteries in Cornwall* (1989), 103–4. Ancient religious houses in Cornwall tended to have much larger parishes than St Anthony's.

2 On the parochial work of canons, see J. C. Dickinson, *The Origins of the Austin Canons and their Introduction into England* (1950), 214–41.

3 For site information, see CCC, HER 22807.

4 *Reg. Bronescombe*, ed. Hingeston-Randolph, 65; ed. Robinson, I, 44. He dedicated many churches in that year, so there no certainty that the rededication reflected a recent rebuilding.

5 J. Polsue, *A Complete Parochial History of the County of Cornwall* (1867–72), I, 37–8.

6 CRO, TA/6, p. 16.

7 *Reg. Grandisson*, II, 872.

8 M. A. Kowaleski (ed.), *The Haveners' Accounts of the Earldom and Duchy of Cornwall, 1287–1356*, DCRS new ser. 44 (2001), 194.

9 TNA, E 179/24/5. A *custos* could be a temporary head, or an alternative title for a prior.

10 *Reg. Morton, Canterbury*, II, 82.

11 J. Leland, *Itinerary*, ed. L. Toulmin Smith (1907–10), I, 322.

12 *Valor Eccl.* (Rec. Com. 1810–34), II, 377–8.

13 TNA, SC 6/HenVIII/597.

14 *8th Deputy Keeper's Report* (1847), Appendix II, 37.

15 TNA, E 315/212 f. 60r–v; /235 f. 52v; *L&P Hen. VIII*, XV, p. 562; DRO, DD 22905.

subject to Thomas's lease, to Thomas Godwyn of London, who was licensed on 1 September to convey them to Nicholas and Elizabeth Fortescue.[1] The priory buildings were converted into the manor house of Place, and the post of clergyman of the parish became a 'donative' to which the lord of the manor made appointments without involving the bishop. The choir of the church was demolished after the Reformation. In 1850 the nave and south aisle were largely rebuilt and the chancel completely so, leaving the north transept, crossing, and the Romanesque south doorway as the chief surviving medieval features. Vestiges of the other priory buildings may be preserved within Place.

PRIORS OF ST ANTHONY-IN-ROSELAND

Peter of St Antoninus	before 1273[2]
Nicholas Walforde	occurs 1381[3]
James Davy	occurs 1443[4]
John Austyn	occurs 7–17 July 1492[5]

BODMIN

MINSTER, LATER AUGUSTINIAN PRIORY

FROM MINSTER TO MONASTERY

Bodmin was the wealthiest of the Cornish minsters that survived the Norman Conquest.[6] In the Cornish section of Domesday Book (1086) its clergy are identified as canons and in that of Devon as priests, indicating that they retained their late Anglo-Saxon form as a community of secular clergy rather than monks. Their landed property, according to the Domesday survey, included eighteen manors in Cornwall and two in Devon, excluding properties that had been taken away from the church's ownership in recent times.[7] Most of these properties, as already noted, lay in the hundred of Pydar, east of the River Camel.[8]

Eight of the manors were administered directly by the church and its clergy, these being Bodmin, Ellenglaze in Cubert, Padstow, Rialton in St Columb Minor, Treknow in Tintagel, and Withiel, all in Cornwall, and Hollacombe and Newton St Petrock in Devon. These properties totalled a little over 16 hides and were worth £10 15s. per annum in 1086. A further ten manors were held by lay tenants, accounting for another 18 hides.[9] Altogether this was the largest landed endowment of any Cornish minster at that date, and much greater than that of Launceston, the next in size.

The Bodmin canons must also have owned several parish churches by 1086, although these are not mentioned in the Domesday survey. They probably included, as they did in later times, Bodmin itself, Cubert, Hollacombe, Newton St Petrock, Padstow, and Withiel. The canons would have appointed the clergy of these churches and, in some cases, would have appropriated some of the parish tithes, thereby increasing their influence and revenues. A further estate may need to be credited to Bodmin in 1086: Pendavey in Egloshayle which belonged to it subsequently. According to Domesday this was said to be held by Boia the priest, who may have been the dean or presiding officer of the body of clergy, holding the property by virtue of his office.[10]

The church is next mentioned in an account of a money-raising tour of England made by the canons of Laon (France) in 1113, carrying a shrine of the Virgin Mary and relics of saints. Arriving at Bodmin, they were received with honour by a 'clerk' named Algar who had once lived at Laon – a fact that probably explains their journey to Cornwall. Their shrine appears to have been placed in the church of Bodmin where it caused three miracles of healing, but when an argument arose between a Frenchman and a Cornishman as to whether

---

1 *L&P Hen. VIII*, XXI(1), p. 761; XXI(2), p. 99.
2 *Reg. Bronescombe*, ed. Hingeston-Randolph, 162; ed. Robinson, II, 62: a conjecture based solely on the surname.
3 Described as *custos* (TNA, E 179/24/5).
4 C. G. Henderson, 'The Ecclesiastical History of the 109 Parishes of West Cornwall', *JRIC* new ser. 2 (1953–6), 23, quoting 'a charter at Kellian'. It is odd, however, that Davy should be described as a 'clerk', and a James Davy was the canon colleague of John Austin in 1492, in the next reference.
5 *Reg. Morton, Canterbury*, II, 80, 82. There is an unspecified reference to a prior named David Bercle in about 1507 (Polsue, *A Complete Parochial History*, I, 37–8); a contemporary prior of Plympton had that name.
6 The principal previous histories of Bodmin Priory are G. Oliver, *Monasticon Dioecesis Exoniensis* (1846), 15–21; J. Maclean, *The Parochial and Family History of the Deanery of Trigg Minor* (1873–9), I, 120–42; C. G. Henderson, 'Concerning Bodmin Priory', *Journal of the Royal Polytechnic Society of Cornwall* new ser. 8.3 (1936), 27–39; and, for the period up to 1200, K. Jankulak, *The Medieval Cult of St Petroc* (2000).
7 C. and F. Thorn (ed.), *Domesday Book, IX: Devon* (1983), I, 51/15–16; C. and F. Thorn (ed.), *Domesday Book, X: Cornwall*, (1979), 1/6, 4/3–5, 4/18–20; H. Ellis (ed.), *Domesday Book, IV: Additamenta* (Rec. Com. 1816), p. 183 f. 200.
8 Above, pp. 127–8.
9 Ibid.
10 For a dean of Bodmin named Boia, of mid eleventh-century date, see M. Förster, 'Die Freilassungsurkunden des Bodmin-Evangeliars', in N. Bøgholm, A. Brusendorff, and C. Bodelsen (ed.), *A Grammatical Miscellany offered to Otto Jespersen* (1930), 92 (no. 31), dated by N. R. Ker, *Catalogue of Manuscripts Containing Anglo-Saxon* (1957), 159.

King Arthur was still alive, a riot broke out in the church that had to be quelled by Algar's intervention.[1] His status appears to have been an important one, and a writer of the mid 12th century refers to him both as 'Master Algar' and as *procurator* (person in charge) of the church – probably its dean.[2] A few years later the church was reformed by William Warelwast, bishop of Exeter from 1107 to 1137. William, who originated from Normandy, was an active bishop who combined the reorganisation of his diocese with service to the king, Henry I.[3] After he had begun to rebuild the cathedral at Exeter in 1114, he turned his attention to some other major churches in Devon and Cornwall, refounding Bodmin, Launceston, and Plympton as priories of Augustinian canons during the 1120s. This was a time when the Augustinian Order was spreading through England, buoyed by a reputation for providing a better-regulated and holier way of life for the clergy of minster churches than that of secular canons.[4] Plympton was refounded as a house of the Order in 1121, and the remodelling of Bodmin can be approximately dated to 1123–4.[5] In 1123 William secured a grant from Henry I restoring to him five former minsters in the diocese, including those of St Petroc (Bodmin) and St Stephen (Launceston).[6] This confirmed his legal status as patron of these churches, and left him free to reform them.

An approach was made to Merton Priory (Surrey), which had recently been established as an Augustinian house, to find a suitable person to start the new community. The prior of Merton responded by sending Guy, one of his senior canons, and a short life of Guy written by Rainald, canon of Merton, between 1132 and 1151, attributes to Algar the request that Guy should be sent to Bodmin. Guy was an Italian and a former schoolmaster, who became a canon of Merton and was ordained as a priest. In about 1120 he was seconded to be prior of the former minster of Taunton (Somerset), so that he might establish the Augustinian order there, returning to Merton soon afterwards at his own request. According to Rainald Guy was despatched to Bodmin as prior in the winter of 1123–4, but his tenure was cut short by a riding accident while he was travelling to meet the bishop on business, and he died at Exeter on 15 May 1124. Although Guy's priorship was brief, Rainald avers that Algar and several others of the Bodmin canons joined the Augustinian Order under his leadership. Algar was with Guy at his deathbed, and after a funeral in Exeter Cathedral the first prior was buried in an honourable place 'of his monastery', meaning Bodmin.[7] A reference to 'Prior Algar' in Cornwall in 1131 suggests that Algar later came to be prior himself, but he must have resigned by 1133 when he was appointed bishop of Coutances in Normandy.[8] In the 16th century he was regarded as having played an equal role with Bishop William in founding the priory.[9]

Algar was not the only Bodmin cleric to build a career elsewhere. In 1193 Geoffrey fitz Robert, a Wiltshire knight with property in Ireland, arranged for four of its canons to open the Augustinian priory of St Mary founded by him at Kells in County Kilkenny.[10] A later tradition at Kells told how Geoffrey 'crossed the sea to Bodmin in Cornwall and took back with him to Ireland from the house of Bodmin four canons: Reginald de Aclond, Hugh le Rous, Alured, and Algar, and then the said Reginald was created prior, whom Hugh le Rous succeeded – who was afterwards the first English bishop of Ossory' (c.1202–c.1218). Subsequently, in about 1206, Thomas fitz Anthony, another Anglo-Irish landlord, founded the Augustinian priory of Inistioge in the same region and obtained the services of Alured and Algar to reform and instruct its canons. Alured became the prior there, while Algar was believed to have been sent to the papal court in Italy to seek privileges for Inistioge and Kells. He was said to have stayed in Italy and to have been appointed by the pope as bishop of a diocese in Lombardy, but this appointment has yet to be verified.[11] Another Bodmin canon was to become an Irish bishop and English priory head in the 15th century.[12]

The priory's chief spiritual possession was the body of Petroc, its patron saint.[13] A Latin Life of Petroc had been written in the 11th century, probably at or for the church of Bodmin,[14] and during the second half of the following century four further works about the saint were composed there, forming one of the chief surviving bodies of Latin literature from Cornwall

---

1 Hermann, 'De Miraculis S. Mariae Laudunensis', in J. P. Migne, *Patrologia Latina* 156 (1880), col. 983.

2 M. L. Colker, 'The Life of Guy of Merton by Rainald of Merton', *Mediaeval Studies* 31 (1969), 250–61 at 253–4, 259–61.

3 On William, see F. Barlow (ed.), *English Episcopal Acta*, XI: *Exeter 1046–1184* (1996), pp. xxxiii–iv, and *ODNB*.

4 J. C. Dickinson, *The Origins of the Austin Canons and their Introduction into England* (1950); D. M. Robinson, *The Geography of Augustinian Settlement*, 2 parts, British Archaeol. Reports, British Series 80 (1980).

5 Barlow (ed.), *English Episcopal Acta*, XI, 13.

6 *Regesta Regum Anglo-Normannorum*, ed. H. W. C. Davis et al. (1913–59), II, 72, 185; P. L. Hull (ed.), *The Cartulary of Launceston Priory*, DCRS new ser. 30 (1987), 1–2. The properties were said to have been originally given by William the Conqueror to Bishop William while he was the king's chaplain. There are two versions of the charter, both undated but one datable to 1123, the latter being generally regarded as the more authentic.

7 Colker, 'Guy of Merton', 250–61.

8 *The Pipe Roll of 31 Henry I*, ed. J. Hunter (Rec. Com. 1833, repr. 1929), 160.

9 J. Leland, *Collectanea*, ed. T. Hearne (1774), I, 176.

10 On Geoffrey, see D. Crouch, *William Marshal* (1990), 197.

11 BL, Lansdowne 418, ff. 28v–29 (a 17th-century transcript of part of a medieval cartulary of the priory). No bishop named Algar is recorded in northern Italy around 1200 in P. B. Gams, *Series Episcoporum Ecclesiae Catholicae* (Regensburg, 1873).

12 Thomas Fort (below, p. 149).

13 On the cult of Petroc, see N. Orme, *The Saints of Cornwall* (2000), 214–19, and Jankulak, *Cult of St Petroc*.

14 P. Grosjean, 'Vie et Miracles de. S. Petroc', *Analecta Bollandiana* 74 (1956), 131–88, 470–96, at 487–96.

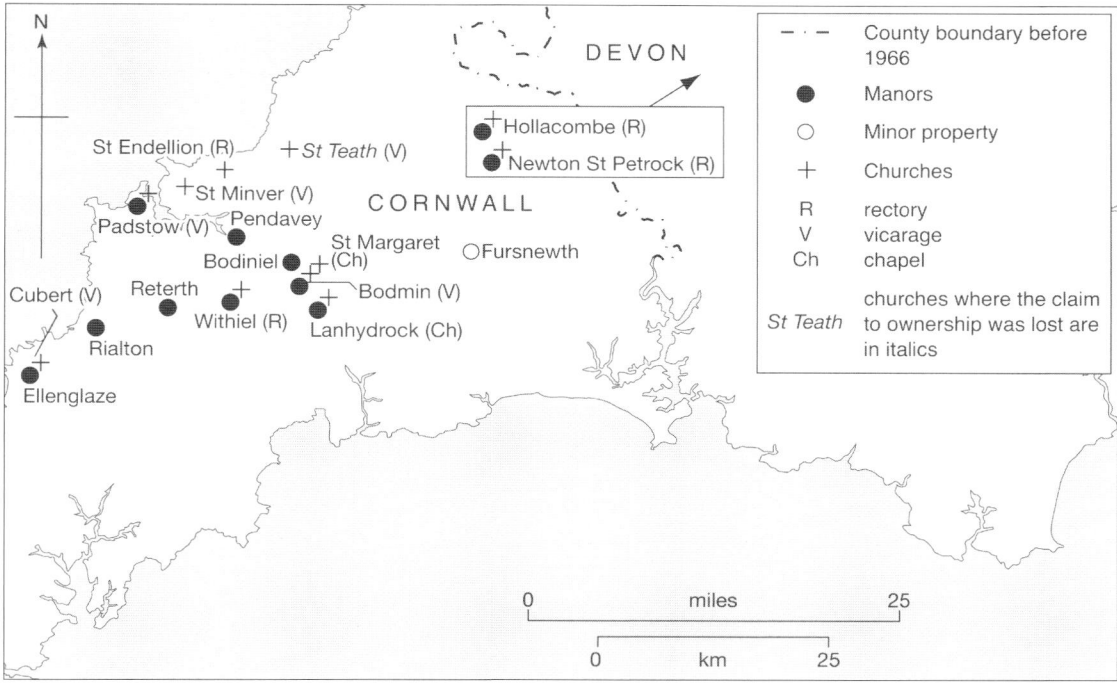

FIG 43. *The property of Bodmin Priory.*

during that period. The first work was an enlarged Life of Petroc, the so-called 'Gotha Life', which gives more information about the places in Cornwall associated with the saint, especially at Bodmin and Padstow.[1] The second was a short Life of the saint in rhymed 'goliardic' verse, and the third a list of miracles done through his intercession.[2] Finally a canon named Robert of Tauton wrote an account of the theft and recovery of Petroc's relics, which happened in 1171.[3] The theft was the work of a discontented canon named Martin, who secretly removed the saint's bones from the shrine and took them to the abbey of Saint-Méen in Brittany. News of this was sent from the abbey of Mont Saint Michel to the bishop of Exeter, Bartholomew, who ordered the shrine to be opened, revealing the fact of the robbery. The bishop sought assistance from the king, Henry II, and Roger the prior of Bodmin travelled to Brittany with royal letters to demand the return of the bones. These were recovered from the unwilling monastery and brought back to Winchester, where the king helped himself to three small bones and a rib, the latter of which he encased in silver and sent to Saint-Méen as a peace offering. Henry presented the relics with an embroidered pall, and one of his clerks, Walter of Coutances (who had been born in Cornwall and became archbishop of Rouen), donated a casket to hold them.[4] The casket may be identical with that which is now preserved in Bodmin parish church (Fig. 12). The bishop and the prior carried the relics home with much ceremony, pausing at Exeter and Launceston, and on arriving at Bodmin on 14 September the head and certain bones were placed in the casket while the rest of the bones were enclosed in a gilt box or shrine. The bishop granted an indulgence of twenty days to all who attended the church on that date in future.

The Tudor antiquary John Leland, who visited Bodmin in 1542, noted a local tradition that William Warelwast appropriated for himself 'part of th'ancient lands of Bodmin monastery'.[5] This is unlikely. A comparison between the evidence of Domesday Book with the next surviving account of the priory's property, the papal taxation of 1291, shows that the only piece of land to have disappeared was the estate at Treknow in Tintagel, which the canons are known to have exchanged with Richard earl of Cornwall (1227–72) for a rent and some woodland in Bodmin.[6] The priory appears to have retained all the other properties mentioned in the Domesday survey, both the manors held directly and those in the hands of feudal tenants (Fig. 43).[7] The five churches of Cubert,

---

1 Ibid., 145–65. 2 Ibid., 166–71, 171–4.
3 Ibid., 174–88, transl. G. H. Doble, 'The Relics of St Petroc', *Antiquity* 13 (1939), 403–15. The episode is briefly noticed in the contemporary chronicles of Benedict of Peterborough (W. Stubbs (ed.), *Gesta Regis Henrici Secundi* (RS 1867), I, 178–80) and Roger of Howden (*Chronica Magistri Rogeri de Houedene*, ed. W. Stubbs (RS 1868–71), II, 136).
4 For Walter, see *ODNB*.
5 J. Leland, *Itinerary*, ed. L. Toulmin Smith (1907–10), I, 180.
6 *Reg. Bronescombe*, ed. Hingeston-Randolph, 470–1, 479; *Cal. Pat. 1374–7*, 26.
7 Cargoll was still regarded as tenanted (by the bishop) in 1311 (*Cal. Pat. 1307–13*, 377–8) and Nancecuke (*Lanceys*) by Alan Bloyou in 1306 (*Feudal Aids*, I, 327).

Hollacombe, Newton St Petrock, Padstow, and Withiel, which have been conjectured as belonging to Bodmin in 1086, certainly belonged to it in 1291, as did the parish church of Bodmin and its dependent chapel of Lanhydrock. The priory also acquired interests in three other churches. One was St Minver, of which it owned at least a half share by 1256 and the whole church by 1272.[1] Another was St Endellion, which was divided among four clergy called portionists or prebendaries, of whom Bodmin Priory appointed the resident rector by 1272 and one of the three non-resident prebendaries by 1314.[2] A third church in the same part of Cornwall, St Teath, which was shared between two prebendaries and a vicar, had its vicar presented to office by the priory in 1259, but here the canons did not succeed in retaining their rights and the bishops of Exeter later assumed the patronage of the vicarage.[3] At one time the priory had further claims to the churches of St Allen and Newlyn East, which it renounced in the bishop's favour in 1269.[4]

Few records survive of the administration and income of the priory's property. No cartulary is known or any royal charter confirming its principal possessions, and a single brief rental of the mid 15th century covers only some of the manors.[5] This leaves us dependent on exterior sources, notably the taxation of 1291 which was not only undervalued by half or more but fails to give a complete account of Bodmin's resources. It rated the priory's income from temporal property (land and rents) at £26 4s. and from spiritual property (chiefly tithes of corn) at £23 16s. 8d., a total of just over £50. The annual values of seven manors were given, in descending order: Ellenglaze in Cubert (£8 11s.), Bodmin (£7 5s.), Withiel (£4 2s.), Pendavey in Egloshayle (£3 18s.), Reterth in St Columb Major (£1), Lanhydrock (£1), and Fursnewth in St Cleer (8s.). Bodmin manor, however, appears to have been undervalued if we refer to the later and more accurate valuation of Henry VIII's government in 1535, while the manors of Hollacombe, Newton St Petrock, and Rialton in St Columb Minor – the latter the most valuable of all – were not included in the taxation. The priory's spiritual revenues came from the four of its churches that were appropriated benefices in which the priory acted as rector, receiving the great tithes of grain and leaving the small tithes to the vicar who served the parish. Here the most valuable great tithes were those of St Minver (£7) followed by Bodmin (£6 13s. 4d.), Padstow (£5 6s. 8d.), and Cubert (£4 16s. 8d.). The taxation of 1291 omitted the spiritual revenues from Lanhydrock as well as from some other minor sources that Bodmin possessed by this time. These included tithes from the priory's lay property at Rialton, tithes from its former property at Treknow, and pensions from the churches of Egloshayle, Hollacombe, Newton St Petrock, and Withiel.[6] The latter three churches were not otherwise appropriated, and continued to have rectors appointed by the priory until the Reformation. If the missing revenues had been counted, Bodmin's total receipts would doubtless have reached at least £60, and the undervaluation of the tax suggests that the priory's real income came to well beyond £100.[7] This made Bodmin the second richest religious house in Cornwall, Launceston having overtaken it in that respect during the 12th and 13th centuries.

CHURCH AND COMMUNITY

The bishop of Exeter held the patronage of the priory by virtue of Henry I's grant of 1123 and William Warelwast's foundation. He had the right to be told when a prior resigned or died, to permit a new election to be made, and to administer the priory during the vacancy. Each new prior swore him an oath of obedience, and the bishop could visit the priory or intervene in its affairs at will. The crown appears to have challenged this state of affairs in the reign of John (1199–1216), who gave his protection to the priory as belonging to his donation and founded on his demesne.[8] In 1215 the bishop, Simon of Apulia, pressed his claim and John told the sheriff of Cornwall to let Simon have the priory until he had shown the king his charters.[9] The issue arose again in March 1349, after the Black Death devastated the community, when the bishop wished to appoint a prior without the usual process of election. An inquisition at Lostwithiel on behalf of the Black Prince as duke of Cornwall reported that the priory had originally been founded by a king (whose name the inquirers did not know), but that the bishop of Exeter had possessed the patronage and the custody of the priory during vacancies, time out of mind, and the priory held none of its lands from the duke.[10] In spite of this verdict Edward III took Bodmin Priory into his own hands during the 1360s (as he also did in the case of St Germans),[11] on the grounds that he had 'long been defrauded of his right of patronage' and that the present prior had been appointed without royal

---

1 J. H. Rowe (ed.), *Cornwall Feet of Fines*, DCRS (1914–50), I, 80–1, 208; *Reg. Bronescombe*, ed. Hingeston-Randolph, 175; ed. Robinson, II, 60.

2 *Reg. Bronescombe*, ed. Hingeston-Randolph, 171; ed. Robinson, II, 60; *Reg. Stapeldon*, 251.

3 *Reg. Bronescombe*, ed. Hingeston-Randolph, 178; ed. Robinson, I, 30–1, 50–1; II, 126.

4 *Reg. Bronescombe*, ed. Hingeston-Randolph, 43–4; ed. Robinson, III, 56–7. On a composition between the priory and Bishop Henry Marshal concerning the church of Egloshayle, see *Reg. Bronescombe*, ed. Hingeston-Randolph, 291.

5 DRO, CR 655.

6 ECA, D&C 2125; *Reg. Bronescombe*, ed. Hingeston-Randolph, 402 and n. 5 (an account of Bodmin's church property, dated 1299).

7 *Reg. Bronescombe*, ed. Hingeston-Randolph, 470–1, 479.

8 Undated grant confirmed in 1424 (*Cal. Pat. 1422–9*, 262–3).

9 *Rot. Litt. Claus.* I, 193.

10 *Reg. Grandisson*, II, 1077.

11 Below, p. 186.

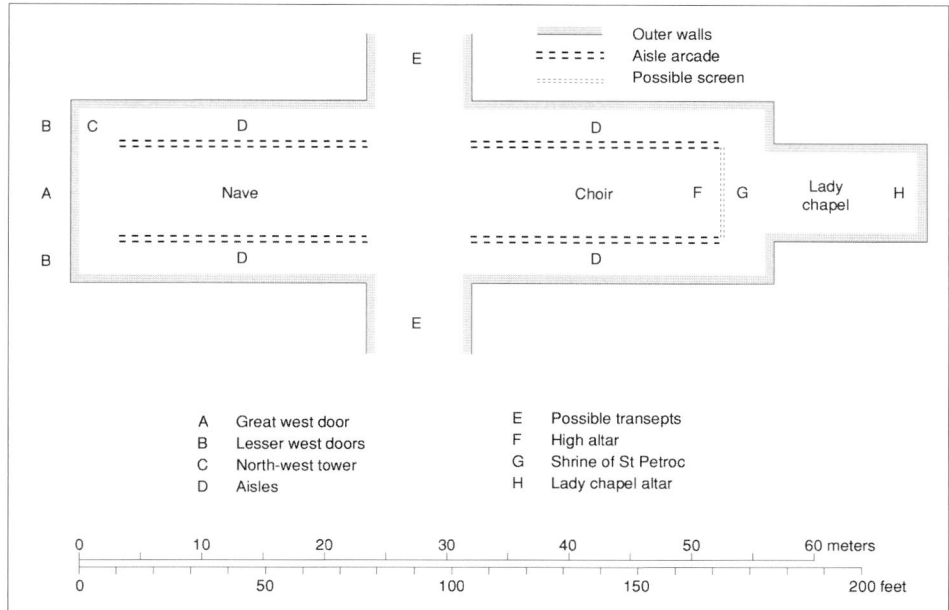

FIG 44.
Bodmin Priory,
schematic plan.

licence. On 5 May 1366 the king restored the priory to the care of the prior, but only on condition of a payment of £20, an agreement to receive a royal pensioner, and the reservation to the crown of the patronage and the possession of the priory's temporalities during vacancies, together with any rights that might belong to the duchy of Cornwall.[1] After 1366, however, the crown did not normally assert these claims, and the bishop's rights held good until the priory was dissolved in 1539.

The minster church occupied the site of the present-day parish church to the east of the town, but the parish church was rebuilt in the 15th century and the only remaining trace of the minster is the Norman tower now attached to the north side of the parish church. After the reorganisation of 1123 the Augustinian canons may have used the minster building for a time, but before long they moved to a new location on the opposite side of the road to the parish church (SX 0740 6690).[2] Surviving fragments of masonry suggest that the new priory church was built in the Norman transitional style, probably in the second half of the 12h century.[3] There was some subsequent rebuilding in the 13th and 15th centuries: in 1453 the church was described as in a falling condition, due to its age, and the 15th-century rebuilding may be related to this.[4] A little about the layout of the church after the rebuilding can be conjectured from excavations carried out at the west end in 1985 and from a few documentary references, notably the observations of the antiquary William Worcester who visited the church in 1478 (Fig. 44).[5] Worcester measured the length of the main building as approximately 192 feet (58 metres) and its width as 51 feet (15.4 metres).[6] The church had a large west door, opening to the nave, flanked by smaller doors leading to north and south nave aisles which probably continued alongside the choir.[7] The nave aisles had stone vaulted roofs and were separated from the nave by arcades supported on cylindrical piers. A tower and belfry were constructed at the north-west corner of the nave in the 15th century, which Worcester estimated as 21 feet (6.3 metres) in length.[8] At the east end of the nave there were probably transepts and, between them, a screen topped with a great cross or rood. In 1451 there is a reference to an altar beneath the cross, 'on the north side of the church', which hints at the presence of two

1 Cal Fine 1356–68, 330; Cal. Pat. 1364–7, 241.

2 For site information, see CCC, HER 4355, 4356–4355.19, 4357.

3 On the building, see E. H. Sedding, Norman Architecture in Cornwall (1909), 34–6; H. L. Douch, 'New Discovery on Site of Bodmin Priory, Cornish Guardian 9 Dec 1965; B. B. Clarke, 'Bodmin Medieval Priory Church', Old Cornwall 9 (1979–85), 177–82; P. O'Hara, 'Bodmin Priory', Cornish Archaeology 24 (1985), 212; and unpublished reports of Cornwall County Council, Historic Environment Service.

4 Cal. Pat. 1452–61, 111, 139. Some rebuilding may also have been related to defects in the priory buildings, mentioned in 1339 (Reg. Grandisson, II, 898).

5 The principal documentary sources are Reg. Lacy, ed. Dunstan, III, 278–80, 320–4; Worcester, Itineraries, ed. Harvey, 86–7, 90–1; and Leland, Itinerary, I, 180.

6 Worcester, Itineraries, ed. Harvey, 86–7 (in paces and steps), 90–1 (in yards).

7 The presence of St Petroc's shrine and a public Lady chapel at the east end of the church points to choir aisles along which lay people could reach them.

8 Ibid., 90–1. A pictorial map of Cornwall, drawn in 1539, appears to show the priory with a battlemented tower at the west end (BL, Cotton Aug. I.i.35, 36, 38, 39).

altars against the choir screen, on either side of a door from the nave to the choir, as was the case at Exeter Cathedral.[1]

The choir was enclosed with screens, possessing doors that could be shut. Its western end would have contained stalls for the canons, and its eastern the presbytery and sanctuary. The high altar stood in the sanctuary, probably with a statue of St Petroc at one end and one of the Virgin Mary at the other.[2] East of the choir, apparently in a retrochoir behind the high altar, lay the shrine of St Petroc, described by Worcester as 'beautiful'. The shrine faced the chapel of St Mary, or Lady Chapel, which he measured as being about 42 feet long (12.6 metres); this presumably abutted from the main church and may have been a later addition.[3] The Lady Chapel contained an altar and image of the Virgin Mary; it had a clerk to care for it, and was visited by members of the public, some of whom made offerings of money.[4] Other altars in the church would have been required, since the canons were usually priests and might wish to say daily masses, and these may have been sited in corners such as transepts or the east ends of the choir aisles, if such places existed. A chapel of St Mary Magdalene is mentioned in 1435.[5] The minster church must have served as the parish church of Bodmin, and it continued to do so when the canons moved to the new site. It is first mentioned as a parish church in its own right in 1252.[6] The priory church, therefore, did not play a parochial role but members of the public could enter it to listen to services or to visit the shrine, images, and altars. In 1274 a penance imposed on the prior required that services on 'county days' (days of county business in Bodmin) should be said in low voices with the choir doors shut, suggesting that visitors would normally have been present on these occasions.[7] In about 1447 the west door of the church was ordered to be locked, except at service times.[8]

The priory had religious links with some leading local people. In 1451 it established a chantry for Robert Olyver, a wealthy man of Bodmin who had paid for the making and glazing of a new window in the church, enabled the remaking of the great cross, and given the priory a sum of £100.[9] The chantry was based at the north altar beneath the cross, and involved the celebration of mass at dawn each day by a canon, serving for a week at a time for a fee of 12d. Similar masses in other great churches were sometimes attended by pious lay people.[10] In 1474 the king licensed the executors of another Bodmin man, John Naylor, to found a chantry in the priory or parish church, but in the end they opted for the latter.[11] Gifts to the priory are mentioned in the wills of two wealthy Cornish expatriates: a sum of 20s. from John Urban of Southfleet (Kent) in 1420, and six silver-gilt bowls and a cover from Dame Thomasine Percival of London in 1512.[12] The church would have been used for burial purposes, housing the tombs of priors (especially in the choir) and perhaps of canons, but Leland recorded only one notable monument, that of Prior Vivian (d. 1533), described below.[13] A few privileged laity may have been granted graves inside the church; one, John Carminow, asked to be buried in the priory in 1492 if he should die in Cornwall.[14] There was an outdoor cemetery too, which appears to have lain to the north and west of the church.

A high perimeter wall surrounded the priory buildings, pierced by a gatehouse on the western side towards the town. Immediately south of the church was a cloister with a door on the north side opening into the church and another giving access to the priory court or outer yard. Documents mention a dormitory, refectory, chapter-house, the subprior's chamber, and the prior's chamber with its own chapel. An almonry, also referred to, would have been situated on the outer edge of the precinct; here visitors were entertained and food dispensed to the poor. Service facilities included a kitchen, a great malthouse, a brewhouse, stables, a circular dovecote, and a mill (near the gatehouse). A fishpond survives to the south of the priory site, and a number of tiles from floors have been recovered.[15] In 1840 a corridor of land free of tithe stretched eastwards from the priory site, past a farm called Prior's Barn to the boundary of the parish with Cardinham.[16] This probably represents the home estate that supplied the priory. On the eastern part of this estate was a place called St Margaret (nowadays Margate), containing a chapel and residential accommodation that served as a rural retreat from the priory. In 1310 the elderly prior German was allowed to retire there, with a brother canon

---

1 *Reg. Lacy*, ed. Dunstan, III, 278–80, 324–5; N. Orme, *Exeter Cathedral: the first thousand years* (2009), 44.

2 On the priory's seal Mary appears on the left and Petroc on the right (see below, p. 153).

3 Worcester, *Itineraries*, 86–7.

4 *Reg. Grandisson*, II, 982; *Reg. Morton, Canterbury*, II, 79. In 1535 offerings to the Virgin Mary were estimated at 10s. 6d. per annum (*Valor Eccl.* (Rec. Com. 1810–34), II, 400).

5 *Reg. Lacy*, ed. Hingeston-Randolph, I, 198.

6 P. L. Hull (ed.), *The Cartulary of St Michael's Mount*, DCRS new ser. 5 (1962), 54–5.

7 *Reg. Bronescombe*, ed. Hingeston-Randolph, 31; ed. Robinson, II, 66–7.

8 *Reg. Lacy*, ed. Dunstan, III, 320, 323–4.

9 Ibid., 278–80.

10 Orme, *Exeter Cathedral*, 62.

11 *Cal. Pat. 1467–77*, 468–9; TNA, E 301/15, ff. 47v–48r; E 301/9, m. 5, printed in L. S. Snell, *Documents towards a History of the Reformation in Cornwall: vol. I, The Chantry Certificates for Cornwall* (1953), 10–12.

12 N. Orme (ed.), *Cornish Wills 1342–1540*, DCRS new ser. 50 (2007), 55, 144.

13 Leland, *Itinerary*, ed. Toulmin Smith, I, 180.

14 Orme (ed.), *Cornish Wills*, 103. He may have been buried in the Franciscan friary, however (below, p. 156).

15 For the tiles, see W. Iago's drawings in Royal Cornwall Museum, Truro.

16 CRO, TA/ and TM/13.

to keep him company. He was granted the offerings made in the chapel together with an allowance from the priory for his food, clothes, and other necessaries, but was required to maintain the buildings.[1] The site was used again in 1347 to accommodate an unsatisfactory prior, John of Kilkhampton.[2] The priors of Bodmin had one or more country houses further afield: possibly at Pendavey in Egloshayle, where they were licensed to have mass said in their chapel in 1421,[3] and certainly at Rialton. The latter, which came to include a hall, prior's chamber, chapel, and tower was used and rebuilt by successive priors down to Thomas Vivian in the early 16th century.[4]

From time to time the head of the house was expected to do administrative tasks for the Church or the crown. The year 1275 found Prior Richard supervising the collection of the lay tax known as the fifteenth, and in 1340 John of Kilkhampton was responsible for gathering the ninth from the clergy.[5] In 1301 the king appointed a prior as controller of mines in Cornwall, and in 1378 entrusted William Carnellow with the profits of gold and silver mines.[6] The priors participated in the affairs of the Augustinian Order, acting as 'diffinitors' or organisers of chapter meetings, or as visitors of other houses of the order in the southwest of England.[7] They lived in a quasi-aristocratic style, with a separate lodging and household of servants. Since Bishop Grandisson cut down the servants of an unsatisfactory prior to three, the prior's retinue may have been much larger at times. Priors were probably expected to give hospitality to visiting notables, and when Bishop Lacy wished to impose economies on the priory in the 1440s he sent the prior to study at Cambridge, probably to avoid the expenses incurred by entertaining people in Bodmin.[8] As late as the 1530s the prior complained of the burdens of accommodating travellers.[9] The priors' resemblance to nobility was also expressed in the tours they made of the house's estates in company with their household, a life-style that might involve them in too much extravagance (at least in the bishop's view).[10]

Responsibility for the oversight of the community lay with the prior, together with officers whom he was meant to choose from among the canons in consultation with them. We hear at various times of the almoner (in charge of charity), cellarer (responsible for provisions), precentor (who supervised the chant in the choir), sacristan (who cared for the church and its furnishings), steward (financial officer), and subprior (the prior's general deputy).[11] The earliest indication of the size of the community occurs in 1310 when there were a prior and fourteen canons who were priests; this must have excluded junior members, since eighteen canons were named in 1312.[12] The priory was dealt a devastating blow by the Black Death in the early months of 1349, which killed the prior and all the canons save two, necessitating the appointment of a new prior from Launceston.[13] The community was re-established, and by 1381 there were eleven canons (excluding ones not yet ordained as priests), but the earlier number was never regained.[14] In 1435 there were a prior and eight canons, in 1492 a prior and at least six, in 1534 a prior and nine, and at the suppression of the house in 1539, a prior and eight.[15] Augustinian canons were allowed to do pastoral work, and two from Bodmin gained papal permission to serve parish churches.[16]

A variety of other people lived in the precincts outside the cloister. Some may have been novices who were not yet fully professed as canons; others included the prior's servants, those of the monastery in general, and perhaps a few boys in the almonry acting as servers in church. In 1269 the vicar of Bodmin appears to have lived on the premises, because his stipend was defined as including a daily allowance of food like that of a canon together with a modest payment of money.[17] During the 14th century the English kings sent their superannuated servants to monasteries to be given corrodies: accommodation and board at the cost of the clergy concerned. All the five largest priories in Cornwall endured this burden. The first known holder of a corrody at Bodmin was despatched by Edward II (1307–27), but when his place became vacant in 1358 and a successor was proposed, the prior resisted for several years until he was cited before the king's justices.[18] A series of other royal nominations are recorded down to 1451, including two clerks, a falconer, and a launderer, until Edward IV exempted the priory from the duty in 1465, recognising that it belonged to the patronage of

---

1 *Reg. Stapeldon*, 49–50.
2 *Reg. Grandisson*, II, 1012.
3 *Reg. Lacy*, ed. Dunstan, I, 74.
4 C. Henderson, 'Rialton', *Old Cornwall* 2/12 (1936), 1–10; N. J. G. Pounds (ed.), *The Parliamentary Survey of the Duchy of Cornwall*, part 1, DCRS new ser. 25 (1982), 113–14.
5 *Cal. Close 1271–9*, 250; *Cal. Close 1339–41*, 437; cf. *Reg. Brantyngham*, I, 195, 201, 205, 207.
6 *Cal. Pat. 1292–1301*, 577; *Cal. Pat. 1377–81*, 259.
7 H. E. Salter (ed.), *Chapters of the Augustinian Canons*, Cant. & York Soc. 29 (1922), 52, 59, 103, 112, 132.
8 Below, p. 149.
9 Below, p. 152.
10 *Reg. Grandisson*, II, 982, 1012.
11 Ibid., II, 981–3; Worcester, *Itineraries*, 90–1.

12 ECA, D&C 2152, printed in G. Oliver, *Additional Supplement to the Monasticon* (1854), 2; *Reg. Stapeldon*, 50.
13 *Reg. Grandisson*, II, 1077.
14 TNA, E 179/24/5. In 1391 some Bodmin witnesses said that there were twelve canons and had formerly been twenty-six, but their evidence was hostile and may not be reliable about the past (*Cal. Inq. Misc.* V, 175).
15 *Reg. Lacy*, ed. Hingeston-Randolph, I, 200; *Reg. Morton, Canterbury*, II, 79; *7th Deputy Keeper's Report* (1846), App. II, 280; *8th Deputy Keeper's Report* (1847), App. II, 10.
16 Richard Trenakys and John Thomas (*Cal. Papal Reg.* XIII(2), 659, 712; XV, 22–3).
17 *Reg. Bronescombe*, ed. Hingeston-Randolph, 32; ed. Robinson, II, 34.
18 *Cal. Close 1354–60*, 528; *1364–8*, 327.

the bishop of Exeter.[1] In 1463 the prior agreed to accommodate the elderly vicar of Cubert, who wished to resign.[2]

The priory's property gave it influence over a segment of Cornwall stretching from Bodmin to Cubert in one direction and St Endellion in another, as well as part of north-west Devon (Hollacombe and Newton St Petrock).[3] Its status was further increased by its location on the main road from Exeter and Launceston into Cornwall, and by the presence of the nearby town – probably the most populous settlement in the county by the end of the later Middle Ages.[4] The town's commercial importance went back to the late Saxon period, and Richard earl of Cornwall granted privileges to its burgesses between 1227 and 1257, including the right to have a merchant guild and freedom from tolls throughout Cornwall.[5] These benefits were granted in the first instance to the priory as lord of Bodmin, however, and it was the prior and canons, not the burgesses, who exercised justice and supervised trade in the town.[6] The burgesses had only limited rights, although they sent representatives to Parliament by 1295 and elected a mayor from about 1340.[7] This situation led to tensions between the canons and the community, as it commonly did in towns that lay under the control of religious bodies. In 1345 the king commissioned judges to hear the prior's complaints against the mayor and others who hindered his policing powers (the view of frankpledge) and his judicial right to hold a court dealing with trespass, debt, covenant, and detinue.[8] In 1351 the Black Prince, duke of Cornwall, ordered the sheriff to intervene in disputes between the prior and the men of Bodmin so as to favour the prior as much as he could.[9] The town did not gain corporate status and rights of self-government until 1563, well after the dissolution of the priory.[10]

The woods and water outside the town were another cause of friction. In 1199–1200 the priory paid 20 marks to King John to gain or recover the wood of Ruthern (*Rodan*) and a fishery upon the River Alan (nowadays known as the River Camel), to which Richard earl of Cornwall added the woods of Callywith and Kingswood.[11] The priory's rights in these places (it also owned Dunmere wood) were resented by local people, who wished to draw on these resources themselves. In 1345 royal justices were ordered to investigate complaints against twelve men who had fished in the prior's fishery on the Alan, carried off fish from his nets, made assaults on his servants, and even besieged the priory.[12] In 1379 a similar investigation was ordered, again respecting men who had broken the prior's closes and his weir in the Alan and taken away his fish and timber.[13] Two years later news of the Peasants' Revolt, which was taking place in London, led to further disturbances. According to a local inquisition, held on 5 July 1381, Richard Eir of Trelissick, William Godman, chaplain, and Peter Aude of Lelant, knowing of the revolt, gathered a large band of men and usurped the royal power in Cornwall. On Saturday 15 June, the day that the revolt collapsed in London, they came to the priory's water at Dunmere, broke down a weir, and destroyed a building belonging to the priory.[14] During the 15th century disputes about woodland arose with the Flamank family of Boscarne Vean near Bodmin. In 1432 Richard Flamank asserted that the prior, two canons, and others had assaulted him and abstracted his timber.[15] In 1456 the prior complained that James Flamank and others had fished in his fishery for a year, broken the weir of his mill, and entered the priory on three occasions. The complaint alleged that a crowd of a hundred people had invaded the priory on Whit Monday (during the holiday season, as in 1381), assaulting the prior and canons, imprisoning two of them for five hours, carrying away goods worth £200, and doing damage estimated at £1,000.[16]

INTERNAL HISTORY, 1250–1508

The priory's internal history emerges only in the second half of the 13th century, with the survival of the bishops' registers and other ecclesiastical records. These records centre on the elections of priors and on visitations by bishops, restricting our view to legal and disciplinary matters. Problems in the priory are first manifest in the reign of Prior Richard (fl. 1256–86), who was apparently excommunicated by Bishop Bronescombe and had to visit the pope's penitentiary at Lyons in 1274 to be absolved and given a penance. He was forbidden to associate with certain other people who had received

---

1 *Cal. Close* 1364–8, 481; 1374–7, 232; 1381–5, 18; 1389–92, 281, 492; 1429–35, 157; 1435–41, 250–1; 1447–54, 278; TNA, C 1/16/134; *Cal. Pat.* 1461–7, 441.

2 DRO, Chanter XII(i), f. 21r.

3 The priory's privileges included rights over waifs and strays in the hundred of Pydar (*Placita de Quo Warranto* (Rec. Com. 1818), 110).

4 On the town, see P. Sheppard, *The Historic Towns of Cornwall* (1980), 57–9.

5 *Cal. Chart.* 1257–1300, 323; 1300–26, 218; 1327–41, 340.

6 *Placita de Quo Warranto*, 110; A. J. Horwood (ed.), *Year Books of the Reign of King Edward the First [Year 30–31]* (RS, 1863), 500–3.

7 On the history of the borough, see J. Wallis, *The Bodmin Register* (1827–38), 150–62, 298–313, and Maclean, *Trigg Minor*, I, 204–18.

8 *Cal. Pat.* 1345–3, 577.

9 *Black Prince's Register*, II, 19.

10 *Cal. Pat.* 1560–3, 511–13; Wallis, *Bodmin Register*, 154–62.

11 *Pipe R* 1200 (PRS n.s.12), 224; *Rot. Chart.* I(i), 63; *Cal. Chart.* 1257–1300, 303, 323; *Cal. Pat.* 1374–7, 26. Leland attributed the grant of Dunmere to King John (*Collectanea*, ed. Hearne, I, 75–6).

12 *Cal. Pat.* 1343–5, 577.

13 *Cal. Pat.* 1377–81, 421.

14 *Cal. Inq. Misc.* IV, 102. Bodmin thus became one of several religious houses that suffered attacks in 1381, including Bury St Edmunds, Dunstable, and St Albans.

15 *Cal. Pat.* 1429–36, 198.

16 *Cal. Pat.* 1452–61, 308–9.

the same sentence, and it was on this occasion that he was required to hold services in his church in a simple and muted way until the excommunications were lifted.[1] In 1277 he was, or had been, in dispute with the archdeacon of Cornwall over tithes and other things, and in 1284, after he had incurred a further excommunication, the crown was asked to arrest him.[2] Two years later one of his canons, William of Plympton, was imprisoned by the bishop for rebellion and disobedience.[3]

The next bishop whose register survives, Walter Stapledon, was involved with the priory on several occasions. In 1309, having visited Bodmin and found German the prior encumbered with age and illness, he gave him a coadjutor and, in the following year, received his resignation and arranged for his care in retirement.[4] In 1312 the bishop excommunicated eighteen of the canons who had defied him, and in the following year the new prior, John of Kilkhampton, was excommunicated and reported to the crown for arrest.[5] These actions may relate to a confession made to Stapledon by Kilkhampton in 1314 that one of the canons, Odo Denisel, had beaten a secular clerk in the priory two years previously, polluting the place with blood, in spite of which the canons had continued to hold services and bury the dead. Kilkhampton asked Stapledon to reconcile the church, and the bishop fined the priory £20.[6] Meanwhile the prior himself got into trouble with Edward II for making an unauthorised visit overseas. The king retaliated by seizing the priory's temporalities, but restored them in 1313.[7] The priory at this time was in debt to the bishop in respect of a sum of £266 13s. 4d., most of which was subsequently repaid.[8] When Bishop Grandisson took over the diocese in 1327, he perceived a good deal wanting in the running of the house. After a visitation in the following year he complained that its goods had been dispersed and dissipated by the carelessness of its bailiffs and officials. Judging Kilkhampton to be an inadequate leader, he appointed one of the canons and a neighbouring rector to assist the prior with his administration, and declared in 1329 that this arrangement was such a success that the prior should leave all business to his assistants.[9] In 1330 the violent Denisel was again causing trouble. He had discarded his habit, left his order, and was said to be living at Huish near Hatherleigh (Devon), where he was holding services in public. The bishop told the local archdeacon to excommunicate him.[10]

Grandisson's initiative did not lead to a permanent improvement in the priory's affairs. In 1339 the prior and canons informed him that their chapter-house and dormitory had grown ruinous through age and high winds, and that they could not afford to repair them unless they raised money by selling a corrody. This the bishop allowed on condition that all the money was used for repairs.[11] In 1343 he intervened for a second time. Confronting the prior and canons in their chapter house, he ordered an inquiry into the government and discipline of the house which, he had heard, was falling in standards due to the rule of the prior and certain canons and servants, threatening irremediable opprobrium and ruin. He was vexed that this should have occurred after he had provided the prior with two assistants through whose prudence the priory was removed from debts and burdens. Further ills had arisen because he had allowed the prior to resume his involvement with government. On 30 November, having heard the results of the inquiry, he removed the prior from all administration and appointed a coadjutor. He also drew up a list of ordinances which the prior and canons were to observe on pain of excommunication and, in the prior's case, of removal from the priory.[12]

The ordinances indicate what the bishop felt to be lacking. The daily services must be said at the proper times, and the proper fasts, vigils, silences, and prayers observed. The prior was to eat in the refectory and come to chapter meetings, at least once a week in each respect, and attend the choir at least three times a day on Sundays and major festivals. He was not to stay on the priory's manors without good cause, with a large household, or in an extravagant way. Kilkhampton had apparently spent little time at Bodmin. The prior was not to alienate property or concede corrodies without the bishop's approval. Offerings at the altar of the Virgin Mary and reliefs (money paid by feudal tenants on inheriting their estates) were to be applied to the common benefit, not that of the prior. The cellarer, Nicholas of Estone, whom the prior had appointed without consultation, was to be replaced. The subprior, William Hole, who had long been negligent in attending the choir, dormitory, and refectory (presumably through adopting a private life-style), was to take these duties seriously under threat of removal, although he could still eat outside the refectory if he did not receive more food than the other canons. Thirteen named servants were to be dismissed because they were useless and burdensome, but they might stay if they were deployed effectively. Alms to the poor were to be given as accustomed, and the

---

1 *Reg. Bronescombe*, ed. Hingeston-Randolph, 31; ed. Robinson, II, 66–7.
2 *Reg. Bronescombe*, ed. Hingeston-Randolph, 31–2, 315; ed. Robinson, II, 111.
3 *Register of Bishop Godfrey Giffard*, ed. J. W. Willis Bund, III, Worcs. Hist. Soc. (1900), 293.
4 *Reg. Stapeldon*, 48–50.
5 Ibid., 50; TNA, C 85/75/62.
6 *Reg. Stapeldon*, 51.
7 *Cal. Close* 1313–18, 21.
8 *Reg. Stapeldon*, 50–1.
9 *Reg. Grandisson*, I, 185–6, 417, 484–5.
10 Ibid., I, 581.
11 Ibid., II, 898.
12 Ibid., II, 979–81.

almoner was to account for the almsgiving twice a year. In future the prior, with the canons' consent, was to appoint two canons as stewards and administrators of the prior's goods with responsibility for making repairs. He himself was to receive no money beyond what he needed for his household, the sum for which was not to exceed £6 13s. 4d. per annum.[1]

Bodmin's response to these orders was disappointing. In the winter of 1346–7 the bishop appointed local clergy to investigate yet more rumours of improvident government, and ordered the prior to appear before him at his manor of Chudleigh (Devon).[2] The prior sent representatives, after which the bishop issued a further set of ordinances on 20 April 1347 which reveal that many of his previous commands had been ignored. Services were to be properly held, and alms given. The almoner, who had not rendered accounts for six years, was to do so immediately, and so were the sacrist and other officers. The canons were not to wear secular clothes such as buttoned or hooded tunics, thigh boots, or pointed shoes. They were not to play dice, backgammon, or chess, or to consort or converse with women. No allowances of wine were to be made to them until the house's debts had been paid. None of them, even the subprior, was to occupy a separate chamber. No dogs were to be kept, except the guard dogs of the bakery and stable. The number of servants was to be reduced and six named men were to leave within a week. Servants and outsiders were not to enter the cloister or, during meal times, the refectory. Finally Grandisson took stringent action against the prior, forcing him to retire in all but name. Castigating his 'simplicity', the bishop removed him from all administration and confined him to St Margaret with one canon and three servants. There he was to receive a carefully defined allowance of food and money.[3] In his place Roger Honiton, one of the canons, and John Oldstowe, rector of St Mabyn, were appointed as administrators and governors of all the temporal goods of the priory.[4]

The bishop's efforts to reform the community were overtaken by a more remorseless power in the early months of 1349, when the Black Death killed the prior and all the canons except for Roger Honiton and William Tregawythan. The two survivors asked Grandisson to give them a new leader, and in March he appointed Oger Bante, a canon of Launceston, with the consent of the prior of that house.[5] This should have begun a fresh era but, although the community was gradually re-established, the bishop suspended Bante from office by 1362, only to be obliged to restore him conditionally because the affairs of the priory deteriorated during his absence.[6] After this Bodmin enters an era of obscurity as far as episcopal records are concerned. The register of the next bishop, Brantingham, has nothing to say about the priory, and although his successor Stafford visited it in 1405 no evidence survives from his visitation.[7] During the reigns of these two bishops the priory's internal affairs are mentioned only in secular sources. In 1379 the king ordered the arrest of Prior William Carnellow on unspecified charges of misprisions against the king's peace,[8] and in 1391 the king's escheator heard complaints against the priory by the inhabitants of Bodmin. They accused the canons of withdrawing their accustomed alms to the poor on Saturdays, of acquiring a messuage at Padstow without the king's licence, and of unlawfully setting up a weir for salmon on the Alan.[9]

The priory's affairs next come before us in detail during the reign of Bishop Lacy in the 1430s and 1440s. In 1435 the elderly prior Alan Kenegy resigned and went into retirement, obliging the bishop to appoint a canon to look after him because laymen had appropriated his pension.[10] The next prior, William Vivian, was so far from a success that, in about 1447, the bishop intervened to straighten matters again. He identified two basic problems. The priory was heavily in debt and the canons were slack in their life. They attended the choir at will, wandered outside the cloister by day and night, and allowed laymen and women to visit their chambers. Accordingly he issued injunctions for the priory, modelled on ones that he had produced for Launceston in 1445, although the records do not make clear when or even whether they were imposed in the form that survives. The injunctions have resemblances to Grandisson's a century earlier, and may have drawn on them.[11] Services were to be recited by day and night; fastings, vigils, and silences should be observed. The subprior was to be diligent in attending church and observing the rules of the order. No one should leave the cloister without permission, except the steward, cellarer, and others on duty. No women should enter the cloister and chambers, or join the canons in eating, drinking, and idle conversation. The three doors of the cloister area should normally be locked to enforce this policy. All meals must be eaten in the refectory, with reading as prescribed in the Augustinian Rule, and canons were not to have private chambers. Respectable friends of the canons might be entertained in public in the refectory; otherwise only the subprior was allowed a chamber where he might entertain. The priory seal was to be kept under three locks and used solely with the

---

1 Ibid., II, 981–3.
2 Ibid., II, 1009–11.
3 Ibid., II, 1011–13.
4 Ibid., II, 1013–14.
5 Ibid., II, 1076–8.
6 Ibid., III, 1238.
7 DRO, Chanter VIII, f. 48r.
8 F. Devon (ed.), *Issues of the Exchequer* (1837), 213; *Cal. Pat.* 1377–81, 517, 569.
9 *Cal, Inq. Misc.* V, 175.
10 *Reg. Lacy*, ed. Hingeston-Randolph, I, 197–8; *Reg. Lacy*, ed. Dunstan, II, 201–2.
11 *Reg. Lacy*, ed. Dunstan, III, 320–4.

agreement of the majority of the canons. No pensions or corrodies were to be granted without the bishop's permission. Dogs were to be excluded from the church and cloister.

Lacy's injunctions continued with forceful measures to deal with the administration of the priory and to discharge its debts. Canon Thomas Courteys (later prior) was to be appointed steward, receiver, and cellarer for a two-year period. He was to expend quarterly what was needed to feed the community at the rate of 2s. per canon per week.[1] All superfluous servants were to be removed. The prior himself was told to withdraw to Cambridge University for three years to reduce his expenses. There he was to live in an honest, religious, and scholarly way on an allowance of £10 for the first year and £20 for each of the others. He was allowed servants, but in view of his small resources they must have been few in number. The success of these measures is not recorded, but they did not prevent occasional lapses of discipline in subsequent years. One canon, William Mullyng, was imprisoned for incontinence and waste of the priory's goods. He escaped from Bodmin and stayed out for some time before returning in 1451, with Lacy's permission, to undergo penance.[2] Another, John Thomas, absconded in or before 1479 when the prior requested the king to have him arrested.[3] On 21 May 1492 the priory was visited by the commissary or deputy of the archbishop of Canterbury, who interviewed the prior, William John, and six canons. John's evidence was not recorded, but the subprior complained of the depletion of the community since there should have been ten canons by ancient custom. He censured John Richard (possibly the sacrist) for refusing to carry a lantern, to observe the ceremonies of the rule, or to obey the orders of the prior and subprior. One canon objected to minor irregularities in the distribution of alms, and implied that there was no longer an almoner to supervise the process. Two others drew attention to the absence of a clerk of the Lady chapel and to the lack of a candle to burn before the Virgin Mary's image there. The commissary ordered the subprior and four other monks holding offices to render accounts to the prior, and commanded the latter to remedy all the deficiencies by 1 August.[4]

Bodmin's economic and disciplinary problems did not rule out the canons' involvement with spirituality and learning. They continued to venerate the priory's patron saint down to the Reformation. By the time that Worcester visited Bodmin in 1478 three festivals were held in Petroc's honour: the original one of 4 June, his 'exaltation' on 14 September, and his translation on 8 October.[5] Worcester was shown an antiphonal lying in the choir, the calendar of which contained the feast days of Cornish saints associated with parishes belonging to the priory: Cadoc (Padstow), Enodoc and Menfre (St Minver), Goran (Bodmin), and Hydroc (Lanhydrock).[6] Two other liturgical volumes formerly owned by the priory or its members are extant: the famous Bodmin Gospels and a 15th-century manual containing services such as the baptism and the funeral.[7] The canons had a book collection by the early 14th century, some of whose holdings are listed in the catalogue of theological books in England drawn up at that time by the Franciscan friars of Oxford, presumably on information from the Bodmin friary. Fifty-two titles of works held by the priory are mentioned, including 20 by St Augustine, the inspiration for the Augustinian Order, 22 by other patristic and early Christian writers, and ten by writers of the 11th and 12th centuries.[8]

By the early 14th century the Augustinian Order encouraged its houses to engage in study. In 1325 it ordered them to send scholars to the 'schools' (meaning universities), and in 1334 to appoint teachers (*lectores*) in each monastery to instruct the canons, and to assign them times and places to do so.[9] In 1339 the papal bull *Ad Decorem Ecclesiae* required all Augustinian monasteries to provide a teacher (internal or external) to teach their canons grammar, logic, and philosophy. Communities of more than twenty canons were to despatch one of their members to university.[10] Bodmin fell below the threshold of numbers in the latter respect, but two or three of the canons appear to have gone to Oxford or Cambridge during the 15th century, or to have planned to do so. One was Prior Alan Kenegy, who received the bishop's licence to spend three years at Oxford from May 1405.[11] The second may have been William Vivian, the prior in 1447 who was envisaged as studying in Cambridge as an economy measure.[12] The third was Thomas Fort, canon of the monastery of St Mary and St Petroc (Bodmin) in 1492 when the pope appointed him as bishop of Achonry in Ireland, the documentation stating that he was a master of arts and a priest.[13] If this is correct, Fort was unusual among the Bodmin canons both in the extent of his learning and in his public career. He acted as a suffragan bishop in the dioceses of

---

1 Perhaps an error for 2s. 8d., the comparable sum prescribed at Launceston.
2 *Reg. Lacy*, ed. Dunstan, III, 129–30.
3 TNA, C 81/1789/1.
4 *Reg. Morton, Canterbury*, II, 79.
5 Worcester, *Itineraries*, ed. Harvey, 86–9.
6 Ibid.
7 N. R. Ker, *Medieval Libraries of Great Britain* (1964), 10. The manual is Bodleian, Douce 22.
8 R. H. and M. A. Rouse (ed.), *Registrum Anglie de Libris Doctorum et Auctorum Veterum*, Corpus of British Medieval Library Catalogues, 2 (London, 1991), 281.
9 Salter (ed.), *Chapters of the Augustinian Canons*, 13, 17.
10 C. Cocquelines (ed.), *Bullarum Privilegiorum ac Diplomatum Romanorum Pontificum Collectio* (1739–62), III(2), 270–1.
11 *Reg. Stafford*, 26.
12 *Reg. Lacy*, ed. Dunstan, III, 324.
13 *Cal. Pap. Reg.* XVI, 27–8, 42.

Lichfield and Lincoln, under Bishop William Smith, and was head of the Augustinian priory of Huntingdon from 1496 to 1503.[1]

The 15th-century canons had other interests too. One of them, John Bowyer, copied some literary texts in English into a manuscript now damaged and incomplete.[2] They include a 'Good Contemplation' which is part of a prayer or meditation directed to Jesus, and two works in verse that occur in other English sources. The first of these, 'The Infancy of the Saviour', tells the story of the childhood of Christ, while the second, 'How the Wise Man Taught his Son', contains prudent and practical advice for a young man. A fourth item, a short verse letter by a man to his brother, appears to partake of a cryptic or humorous nature. Worcester talked to two canons during his visit, William John (later prior) and John Stevyns, who were interested in 'physic' (natural science, especially medicine). John showed him 'several ancient books' on the subject.[3] The community was aware of its history. Worcester was told that the church had originally been for monks, then for canons, and had been founded three times: by King Æthelstan, William de Warelwast, and Bishop Grandisson.[4] Leland heard two versions of Bodmin history in 1542. One came close to being accurate: a monastery until Æthelstan's time, then clerks, then the foundation of Warelwast.[5] The other was fanciful: 'There hath been monks, then nuns, then secular priests, then monks again, and last canons regular.'[6]

THE FINAL YEARS, 1508–39

After the death of William John in 1508 the canons chose the subprior, Thomas Vivian, to succeed him. Vivian was a strong figure who played a larger role than most of his predecessors.[7] In 1509, soon after his accession, he was allowed to hold the vicarage of Egloshayle, an unprecedented privilege for a prior, which suggests that he was already in favour with the bishop and the cathedral, to whose subdean the patronage belonged. Later, in 1523–4, Vivian acquired other benefices: the Bodmin prebend in St Endellion and the rectory of Withiel. Meanwhile he was made bishop of Megara by the pope in 1517, a titular appointment that allowed him to act as a suffragan bishop in Exeter diocese under Bishops Oldham and Veysey.

Vivian was not popular in the town. In 1524–5, and again in about the early 1530s, the inhabitants petitioned Henry VIII against the restrictions and encroachments that the prior and canons laid on them.[8] The townsmen called themselves 'the king's burgesses and no one else's', and argued that they had (or should have) rights of self-government, considering that they held assemblies, appointed constables, and elected and paid MPs. They claimed that Vivian had stopped their access to local lime-pits and to Dunmere wood, where they had customarily pastured animals and lopped branches. Public ways through the wood had been closed, and poor women who gathered fuel had been robbed of the cords with which they tied their faggots. Religion in the town was impaired, because the prior had withdrawn the priests who had said twice-weekly masses in the chapels of St Leonard and St Thomas. His brother (also named Thomas), the vicar of the parish, lived in London, where he engaged in vexatious litigation with the burgesses, and the prior had appointed a priest of evil life to serve the church in the meantime. The prior's servants insulted the townsmen, promising that their master would make them wear halters and hang them like their predecessors at Blackheath – a reference to the Bodmin men who rebelled against Henry VII in 1497. Finally the prior was a worldly man: active in leasing churches and temporal property, enclosing land, and manufacturing and selling tin. Charges of this kind could have been levelled at many religious leaders of the day, but Vivian certainly lived in some grandeur. He assumed a personal coat of arms, recognised by the College of Arms in London,[9] and added to the prior's residence at Rialton, where an inscription records his work.[10] The historian William Hals further credited him with building the south aisle of Egloshayle church and the rectory of Withiel, in the latter case on the basis of his arms in the window glass, while William Borlase observed the arms on the inner and outer walls of the

---

1 Also spelt 'Ford'; biography in *BRUO*, II, 711. No corroborative evidence of his link with Bodmin has yet been found, but records of canons are poor between 1465 and 1492. A later canon of Launceston was called John Forte (below, p. 217).

2 BL, Harley 2399, ff. 47r–64v; C. Brown and R. H. Robbins, *The Index of Middle English Verse* (1943), nos. 250 (printed in C. Horstmann, *Sammlung Altenglisches Legenden* (1878), 101–10), 1985 (printed in R. Fischer (ed.), *How the Wyse Man Taught hys Sone* (1889), 42–9), and 4232 (printed in T. Wright and J. O. Halliwell (ed.), *Reliquiae Antiquae*, (1841–3), II, 173–4); R. H. Robbins and J. L. Cutler, *The Index of Middle English Verse: Supplement* (1965), 711.5. Bowyer states that he was a canon of Bodmin and born there (Harley 2399, ff. 47r, 61r), but he has not yet been found in other documents. He may have been, like Fort, a canon in the period when records are poor. Another hand has added a reference to 'King Edward', suggestive of 1461–83 (f. 56r).

3 Worcester, *Itineraries*, ed. Harvey, 88–91.

4 Ibid., 86–7.

5 Leland, *Collectanea*, ed. Hearne, I, 75–6.

6 Leland, *Itinerary*, ed. Toulmin Smith, I, 180.

7 Biography in *BRUO*, III, 1951; his academic links, however, are not proven.

8 Wallis, *Bodmin Register*, 298–313; Maclean, *Trigg Minor*, I, 134. The surviving documents are in CRO, B/BOD/245 and B/BOD/314/7/10–12.

9 London, College of Arms, L 10, f. 71r; M 3, f. 79v; Bodleian, Ashmole 763, f. 68 right hand. The arms were: or, on a chevron azure between three lions' heads erased purpure, as many annulets of the field, on a chief gules as many martlets argent. MS Ashmole gives the field colour as argent. They copied or inspired those of the Vivian family of Trenowth.

10 Henderson, 'Rialton', 6–9.

FIG 45. The splendid tomb of Thomas Vivian (d. 1533), prior of Bodmin and bishop of Megara.

chancel of Bodmin parish church.[1] After his death on 1 June 1533 his body was buried in the choir of the priory church beneath a magnificent altar tomb, surmounted by an effigy (Fig. 45). The tomb, which bears the coat of arms, was transferred to the parish church after the closure of the priory in 1539.[2]

Vivian's demise was followed by the election of John Symon, who was confirmed as prior by the bishop of Exeter, John Veysey, on 6 July 1533.[3] In less than a year Symon was coaxed to resign with a pension of £40 to make way for another candidate, Thomas Wandsworth, born as Thomas Mundy in about 1480. He is likely to have come from Wandsworth (Surrey) and to have taken the name as a surname on joining the Augustinian priory of Merton in that county, where he occurs as the most junior canon in 1501.[4] Wandsworth had long-standing Cornish links, the origins of which are mysterious. In 1518 he was a canon of Launceston Priory when he was censured by the visitors of the Augustinian Order for disobedience and sowing discord among the canons, and threatened with imprisonment unless he returned to his senses.[5] By 1530 he was back at Merton, but apparently remained in touch with Cornwall. The Cornish lawyer Nicholas Prideaux later claimed that Prior Vivian wished Wandsworth to be his successor, but that this wish had been forestalled by the intervention of Sir John Arundell of Lanherne and others to secure the election of Symon.[6] By the spring of 1534 Bishop Veysey of Exeter was working to make Wandsworth prior of Bodmin, with the knowledge and very likely the encouragement of the king's secretary, Thomas Cromwell.[7] Cromwell may well have identified the Merton canon as a suitable person from the London area to reform monastic life in Cornwall and to do the bidding of the crown there. Wandsworth was confirmed as prior on 19 May 1534,[8] and on 5 August he, Symon, and eight other canons acknowledged Henry VIII as head of the Church of England.[9]

In the following year a new royal valuation, the *Valor Ecclesiasticus*, was made of all religious and parish churches. Bodmin's annual revenues were estimated at £289 11s. 11d. gross and £270 0s. 11d. net. About three quarters of the priory's income (£217 9s. 11d.) were now identified as coming from temporal sources: rents, farms, and sales of woods. The most lucrative were the

---

1 BL, Add. 29762, ff. 11v, 243r; Egerton 2657, f. 71r. The arms also survive in the south-east window of Withiel church.
2 W. Iago, 'The Tomb of the Suffragan Bishop Vivian', *JRIC* 5 (1874–8), 342–8; P. D. Cockerham, *Continuity and Change: Memorialisation and the Cornish Funeral Monument Industry, 1497–1660* (2006), 25–31.
3 DRO, Chanter XIV, ff. 67r–v, 72v.
4 A. Heales, *The Records of Merton Priory in the County of Surrey* (1898), 311, 331. He was ordained in 1503 (London, Lambeth Palace Library, Reg. Warham, ff. 9v, 10v). Merton canons often used surnames based on place-names, so there is no need to suppose like A. L. Rowse (*Tudor Cornwall* (1941), 175) that Wandsworth was illegitimate.
5 Salter (ed.), *Chapters of the Augustinian Canons*, 136.
6 Rowse, *Tudor Cornwall*, 174–5.
7 *L&P Hen. VIII*, VI, 78, there dated 18 Feb 1533 but perhaps more correctly 1534.
8 Chanter XIV, f. 72v.
9 TNA, E 25/14, printed in *7th Deputy Keeper's Report* (1846), App. II, 280.

manors of Bodmin and Lanhydrock (£74 15s. 7d.), followed by those of Rialton Libera (£27), Pendavey (£24), Rialton Infra (£22), Ellenglaze (£14 10s.), Withiel (£11 12s. 5d.), Reterth (£10 13s. 4d.), Padstow (£10 7s. 5d.), Newton St Petrock (£7 9s. 6d.), Bodiniel in Bodmin (£7 0s. 8d.), and Hollacombe (£5 0s. 1d.). The principal spiritual revenues, chiefly tithes, came from the parishes of Padstow (£20 9s. 6d.), Cubert (£17 10s.), St Minver (£14 13s. 6d.), Bodmin (£13 16s. 10d.), and Lanhydrock (£5 12s. 2d.). The priory retained Sir John Chamond, knight, as its chief steward at an annual sum of £5, and other fees were paid to a steward of courts, an auditor, and various bailiffs. Alms for the poor were distributed at the rate of one shilling a week.[1] The *Valor*'s figures were somewhat undervalued, since the king's officers who began to administer the priory revenues after its dissolution, produced new ones that raised the total income to £341 6s. 8½d.[2] As before Bodmin ranked second to Launceston in wealth among the religious houses of Cornwall, Launceston being valued at about £100 higher.

Five letters from Wandsworth to Cromwell are extant, together with a sixth to their mutual friend, the London mercer William Lock, which provide some insights into the priory during its final years.[3] The prior was careful to cultivate Cromwell's favour, sending him conger eels, assisting him in finding hawks and hounds, and granting an annuity of £3 6s. 8d. to one of Cromwell's servants. Eventually, in 1538, Bodmin joined numerous other houses in bestowing an annuity on Cromwell himself, in this case £6.[4] Wandsworth did not use the letters to pass on local news or information, but to report the troubles he faced in the priory and to ask for Cromwell's help in solving them. He complained that the monastery was burdened with debt and the expenses of hospitality, through accommodating ambassadors and strangers. He sought Cromwell's support to acquire the church of Lanteglos-by-Camelford – a benefaction which, he claimed, had been promised to the priory by Henry VII. The prior confided that he was not impressed by his canons, whose vocations were weak especially after 1536 when stricter rules on monasteries were imposed by the Church authorities. Hitherto, Wandsworth alleged, the canons had lived 'unthriftily and against the good order of religion'. Most of them now intended to secure 'capacities' or licences to leave the monastic life, and one had already done so. The prior had restrained that canon from leaving, and feared that if he let him go no canon would stay in the house.[5]

Outside the priory local conflicts continued. Roger Arundell of Helland was a cause of trouble. According to Wandsworth he had taken one of the canons from the priory by force, and had issued a commission for the destruction of one of its weirs.[6] Friction continued with the mayor and burgesses, particularly over the right to fish in the Alan. The prior complained that men from Bodmin invaded his woods and waters, cutting his nets and forbidding his men from fishing. One night nine or ten people seized fish from his servants by force, saying insolently that as Wandsworth trusted so much in his link with Cromwell, let Cromwell mend the matter if he could![7] By the winter of 1537 the prior had issued a bill of complaint against the townspeople, and the latter had drawn up a statement of their own claims.[8] Royal commissioners were appointed to hear the case, and Wandsworth asked Cromwell to intercede with them in his favour – which Cromwell apparently did.[9] Nevertheless the life of the priory in its last years need not have been wholly without spirituality. In 1537 the canons granted an annuity of £4 to the distinguished Dominican friar of Truro, John de Coloribus, 'for his good and salubrious service in preaching the word of God' to them in the past and the future.[10]

The practice of granting pensions and leases to lay people was common in monasteries during the late 1530s, as their clergy came under pressure and tried to gain friends or reward supporters. After the dissolution of the monasteries the crown became suspicious that such grants had robbed it of monastic property, and a commission was appointed in February 1546 to investigate those made at Bodmin.[11] Depositions were taken from witnesses, who portrayed Wandsworth's role in the matter as worldly and self-seeking. It was alleged that at Midsummer 1537 he summoned the canons to the chapter house and told them that he had heard 'that the king's majesty would take his pleasure upon their house, and therefore he thought it good to give unto such as [had] been good to the house some leases or other preferments, to th'intent they should be the better to them hereafter'.[12] In the following autumn he and the canons made numerous leases of their property.[13] They soothed the feelings of the town by granting the

---

1 *Valor Eccl.*, II, 400–1.
2 W. Dugdale, *Monasticon Anglicanum* (1817–30), II, 465–6; Oliver, *Monasticon*, 21.
3 *L&P Hen. VIII*, VII, 87; IX, 306; X, 409; XI, 55; XII(1), 82–3, 518.
4 TNA, E 315/96, f. 118v.
5 Permissions to hold benefices were granted to two canons, John Bawdyn and Benedict Carter alias Smyth, in 1535, provided they had the prior's permission. Bawdyn's was later cancelled, but he was not in the priory in 1539; Carter, however, stayed until the end (D. S. Chambers, *Faculty Office Registers 1534–1549* (1966), 26–7).
6 *L&P Hen. VIII*, IX, 306.
7 Ibid., XI, 55.
8 Ibid., XII(1), 82–3, 518; CRO, B/BOD/248.
9 *L&P Hen. VIII*, XII(1), 82–3, 518; B/BOD/245 no. 2 (fragmentary letter from Cromwell).
10 TNA, E 315/102, f. 158r. On Coloribus, see below, p. 283.
11 Maclean, *Trigg Minor*, I, 136.
12 Ibid., I, 135.
13 The leases survive in later confirmations by the Court of Augmentations (TNA, E 315/93–104).

mayor and burgesses the judicial rights of court leet and view of frankpledge for ninety-nine years, allowing them to build a market-house and to hold a fair or market nearby at the Berry. In return the town gave up its claims on Dunmere wood.[1] Leases of priory lands were made to important individuals. Laurence Kendall received the manor and advowson of Withiel, Thomas Lytelton the church of Lanhydrock and Kingswood Hill, and John Tubbe the manor of Fursnewth, while Sir John Chamond gained the manor of Bodiniel not only by lease but by outright grant. Wandsworth was said to have expedited these grants by offering the canons money, and his own family figured largely in the transactions. His brother John Mundy's son William had married Elizabeth, daughter of Humphrey Prideaux, and John's daughter Joan was intended to marry Humphrey's son William. On 18 October 1537 the priory leased the manors of Rialton and Reterth to John, William, and Elizabeth Mundy, and two days later the manor of Padstow to Humphrey, William, and Joan Prideaux, for ninety-nine years in each case. Kendall too had married a Mundy niece. In the end the commission of 1546 allowed the leases to stand and merely converted Chamond's grant to a lease.[2]

On 27 February 1539 the prior and eight canons surrendered their house to the king's commissioner, the Cornishman John Tregonwell.[3] Wandsworth received a pension of £66 13s. 4d., the same as his colleague at St Germans but less than the prior of Launceston. The subprior, Richard Olyver, got £8, two canons £6 each, three £5 6s. 8d. each, and two young canons, probably novices, £2 each. Two other inmates, said to be blind and aged, were also pensioned. One was an ancient canon, Richard Luer, described as 100 years old, who had featured in the archbishop's visitation of 1492.[4] He was awarded £10 per annum and six dozen loads of wood, while Thomas Rawlyns, who held a corrody, was granted £2.[5] It is likely that the canons were all licensed to leave the religious life and to hold parochial benefices, as happened at Launceston and St Germans, but the record of this does not survive. Five of them appear to have gained such benefices during the following years, notably the ex-prior.[6] In 1540 he acquired the vicarage of Lanlivery on the presentation of Laurence Kendall's brother Nicholas, and two years later he added the rectory of St Leonard Foster Lane (London). His religious sympathies, however, were sufficiently conservative to cause him to be tried and convicted of treason in 1547. The charges involved aiding a former monk of the Carthusian priory in London to flee the country, and of assisting another to smuggle abroad the arm of the Carthusian martyr John Houghton, executed in 1535 for refusing to recognise Henry VIII as head of the Church. Wandsworth was condemned to be hanged, drawn, and quartered, but the sentence was not carried out and he merely suffered a period of imprisonment in the Tower of London and lost his benefices.[7] In February 1549 he fell sick and made his will. It centres on a recital of the sums of money he had given or loaned to other people, including Sir John Chamond, Humphrey and Nicholas Prideaux, and John Tubbe, and contains the protestation that his gifts to the Prideaux were the price of the Mundy marriages. A more attractive side is revealed by his concern for the future of two of his old servants. He asked to have ten masses and dirges said for his soul, but he appears to have survived for a few more years since his will was not proved until February 1555.[8]

During 1539–40 the crown considered establishing a diocese for Cornwall, endowed with the resources of Bodmin Priory and those of St Germans and Launceston.[9] This plan was not pursued, and in 1541 the site of the priory was leased to Thomas Sternhold, groom of the robes in the royal household and coincidentally the first Tudor translator of the Psalms into English verse.[10] On 2 July 1544 he was granted the priory site and demesne lands for the price of £100.[11] After his death in 1549 the property was divided between his two daughters until they and their husbands disposed of it 1567 to John Rashleigh, merchant of Fowey, whose family held the site for the next two hundred years.[12] Four of the priory's bells were sold to the parishioners of Lanivet for £36 13s. 4d.[13] Parts of the prior's lodging were still standing in the early 18th century, but no substantial remains of the church or other buildings are visible on the site today.[14] The priory seal, by the 14th century, displayed the Virgin Mary on the left and St Petroc on the right, each standing beneath an ornamental canopy. Beneath them was a shield containing the priory's coat of arms, and around them the legend SIGILLU[M] CO[MMUN]E

---

1 CRO, B/BOD/314/7/2–5; Wallis, *Bodmin Register*, 296–7; Maclean, *Trigg Minor*, I, 135

2 Maclean, *Trigg Minor*, I, 137; DRO, Chanter 854(a), ff. 128v–129v.

3 TNA, E 322/23, printed in *8th Deputy Keeper' Report* (1847), App. II, 10.

4 *Reg. Morton, Canterbury*, II, 79.

5 *L&P Hen. VIII*, XIV(1), 147.

6 Rowse, *Tudor Cornwall*, 207, 209.

7 C. Wriothesley, *A Chronicle of England*, ed. W. D. Hamilton, vol. I, Camden Soc. n.s. 11 (1875), 184–5.

8 PROB 11/37, ff. 142v–143r, dated 17 Feb 1549, proved 6 Feb 1555; J. Maclean, 'The Last Will and Testament of Thomas Wandsworth, Last Prior of Bodmin', *JRIC* 5 (1874–8), 349–57; Rowse, *Tudor Cornwall*, 208–9.

9 Above, p. 99.

10 TNA, E 315/213, f. 65r; *L&P Hen. VIII*, XVI, 728; biography in *ODNB*.

11 *L&P Hen. VIII*, XIX(1), 617.

12 *Cal. Pat.* 1566–9, 111; Maclean, *Trigg Minor*, I, 140.

13 E. H. W. Dunkin, *The Church Bells of Cornwall* (1878), 50.

14 BL, Egerton 2657, f. 70v.

PRIORATUS B[EAT]E [or SANCTE] MARIE ET SANCTI PETROCI DE BODMYN. Prior Vivian had a personal seal as bishop of Megara, showing him kneeling before the Virgin and Child.[1] The priory's arms ('azure, three salmon naiant argent palewise') appeared on buildings by the early 16th century.[2] They may have been suggested by the legend that St Petroc was sustained by a single fish for the seven years that he spent on a desert island.[3]

DEANS OF BODMIN

Boia	occurs mid 11th century[4]
Algar	probably dean, occurs 1113–1123[5]

PRIORS OF BODMIN[6]

Guy	app. winter 1123–1124; died 15 May 1124[7]
Algar	occurs 1130; vacated by 1132[8]
William	occurs 1140 × 1149[9]
Robert	occurs before 1149[10]
Reginald	died 1149[11]
William	occurs 1155 × 1158; 1171[12]
Roger	occurs c.Jan 1177; 19 June 1177[13]
Hugh	occurs 1200 × 1220[14]
John	occurs c.1220 × 1230[15]
Baldwin	occurs after 1227, 1236[16]
Richard	occurs 13 Oct 1256, 25 Aug 1286[17]
Edmund	occurs 22 Feb 1296, summer 1297[18]
German	occurs 27 Oct 1302; res. 10 May 1310[19]
John of Kilkhampton	coll. 20 May 1310; died 27 Feb 1349[20]
Oger Bante	coll. 22 March 1349, occurs autumn 1364[21]
William Carnellow	occurs 22 July 1372; died c.10 Nov 1403[22]
Alan Kenegy	el. 14 Dec 1403, conf. 22 Dec 1403; res. 10 Sept 1435[23]
William Vivian	el. 30 Sept 1435, conf. 8 Oct 1435, occurs 12 July 1456[24]
Thomas Courteys	occurs Michaelmas 1457, 4 March 1477 × 3 March 1478, probably still in Sept 1478[25]
William John, alias John William	el. between Sept 1478 and 30 Sept 1480; died by 13 Apr 1508[26]
Thomas Vivian	el. by 13 Apr 1508, conf. 13 Apr 1508; died 1 June 1533[27]
John Symon	el. c.June 1533, conf. 6 July 1533; res. by 19 May 1534[28]
Thomas Wandsworth alias Mundy	conf. 19 May 1534; till surrender 27 Feb 1539[29]

---

1 Oliver, *Monasticon*, 17, plate between 408 and 409; *Catalogue of Seals in the British Museum*, vol. I (1887), 450 no. 2677.

2 Bodleian, Ashmole 763, f. 65 right hand (impaling Vivian's arms); *Old Cornwall* 2.12 (1931–6), 7.

3 *Analecta Bollandiana* 74 (1956), 156, 493.

4 Förster, 'Die Freilassungsurkunden des Bodmin-Evangeliars', 92 (no. XXXI).

5 Hermann, 'De Miraculis S. Mariae Laudunensis', col. 983; Colker, 'Guy of Merton', 253–4, 259–61.

6 The assistance of D. Knowles, C. N. L. Brooke, and V. C. M. London (ed.), *The Heads of Religious Houses: England and Wales*, vol. I, 2nd edn (2001), and D. M. Smith and V. C. M. London (ed.), *The Heads of Religious Houses: England and Wales*, vol. II (2001), is gratefully acknowledged.

7 Colker, 'Guy of Merton', 253–4, 259–61.

8 *The Pipe Roll of 31 Henry I*, ed. Hunter, 160. He was bishop of Coutances 1132–61.

9 Hull (ed.), *Cartulary of Launceston Priory*, 141.

10 Ibid., 34.

11 F. Liebermann (ed.), *Ungedruckte Anglo-Normannische Geschichtsquellen* (1879), 29.

12 Barlow (ed.), *English Episcopal Acta*, XI, 53–4, 59–60, 127–8.

13 Stubbs (ed.), *Gesta Regis Henrici Secundi*, I, 179; Doble, 'The Relics of St Petroc', 403–15.

14 CRO, AR 1/793–5; a Winchester Cathedral calendar noted the death of a prior of Bodmin named Hugh on a 30 Dec (BL, Add. 29436, f. 44r).

15 AR 1/800–1; Hull (ed.), *Cartulary of Launceston Priory*, 194.

16 *Cal. Pat.* 1374–7, 26; AR 1/802.

17 Rowe (ed.), *Cornwall Feet of Fines*, I, 80–1; *Reg. Bronescombe*, ed. Hingeston-Randolph, 315; *Register of Bishop Godfrey Giffard*, ed. Willis Bund, III, 293.

18 *Cal. Close* 1288–96, 474; TNA, CP 40/119, m.41d.

19 Rowe (ed.), *Cornwall Feet of Fines*, I, 208; *Reg. Stapeldon*, 49–50.

20 *Reg. Stapeldon*, 49–50; *Reg. Grandisson*, II, 1077.

21 *Reg. Grandisson*, II, 1078; III, 1238; TNA, KB 27/416, rex roll m.10.

22 TNA, E 40/10365; *Reg. Stafford*, 25–6.

23 *Reg. Stafford*, 25–6; *Reg. Lacy*, ed. Hingeston-Randolph, I, 197.

24 *Reg. Lacy*, ed. Hingeston-Randolph, I, 200–4; *Cal. Pat.* 1452–61, 308.

25 TNA, CP 40/787; Chanter XII(i), ff. 21r, 51v; DRO Chanter XII(ii) (Reg. Bothe), f. 77r; E. Smirke, *The Case of Vice against Thomas* (1843), 66. In Sept 1478 Worcester (*Itineraries*, ed. Harvey, 38–9) refers to the next prior, William John, as merely a canon.

26 Ibid.; Smirke, *The Case of Vice against Thomas*, 70; DRO, Chanter XIII, f. 22r-v.

27 Chanter XIII, f. 22r-v; DRO Chanter XIV, f. 67r-v; tomb in Bodmin church.

28 Chanter XIV, ff. 67r-v, 72v.

29 Ibid., f. 72v; *8th Deputy Keeper' Report*, (1846), App. II, 10.

FRANCISCAN FRIARY

FIG 46. *The former Franciscan priory at Bodmin (centre), from a drawing of 1716 when it had been turned into a civic building.*

The Franciscan Friars, also known as the Friars Minor or Grey Friars, founded their house at Bodmin in the middle of the 13th century. Traditions about the date of its foundation and the people responsible were collected by the antiquary William Worcester, who visited the friary in 1478. His notes include the contradictory statements that it was founded on 19 June 1239 by Edmund earl of Cornwall, that the 'first founder' was John FitzRalph, lord of Caerhays (who is known to have died in 1242), and that the foundation was carried out in 1239 by Richard earl of Cornwall.[1] John Leland, who came to Bodmin in 1542, shortly after the dissolution of the friary, recorded that 'one John of London, a merchant, was the beginner of this house. Edmund earl of Cornwall augmented it.'[2] The date 1239 is not impossible but would be early, since the Franciscan friary at Exeter, a house in a much larger town, is documented only from 1240.[3] Local men such as John FitzRalph or John of London may well have helped to initiate the project, but if the earl of Cornwall was involved at that point, he must have been Richard, king of the Romans and brother of Henry III, who held the title from 1227 to 1272. His son Edmund, earl from 1272 to 1300, can only have assisted the house later on. The first contemporary reference to its existence occurs on 18 September 1260, when Bishop Bronescombe of Exeter ordered some sinners in Bodmin to do penance by walking barefoot from the Augustinian priory to the church of the Franciscans.[4]

SITE AND CHURCH BUILDING

The friary was situated in the centre of Bodmin near the junction of Fore Street, Honey Street, and St Nicholas Street (SX 0710 6690). Leland described it as being south of the market place, so that it lay at the heart of one of the chief towns of Cornwall and alongside one of the main roads leading through the county.[5] That the Franciscans settled at such a prime site suggests that they reached Cornwall before the Dominicans, the only other order of friars to found a house west of the Tamar, who chose the smaller community of Truro by 1259.[6] The main entrance to the friary was via a gatehouse in Fore Street,[7] and the church stood some way south of the gatehouse and street, apparently with a cemetery on its north side. It is mentioned as 'the church of St Francis' in 1284, which may indicate its dedication unless the reference is merely to the order of friars.[8] Many English Franciscan churches were enlarged or rebuilt in the late 13th and early 14th centuries in order to provide more space for preaching and for burials.[9] Bodmin appears to have followed this trend, albeit a little later, since Worcester recorded that

---

1 W. Worcester, *Itineraries*, ed. J. H. Harvey (1969), 84–5, 86–7, 90–1.
2 J. Leland, *Itinerary*, ed. L. Toulmin Smith (1907–10), I, 180, 184.
3 D. Knowles and R. N. Hadcock, *Medieval Religious Houses: England and Wales* (1971), 222–3.
4 *Reg. Bronescombe*, ed. Hingeston-Randolph, 30; ed. Robinson, I, 90–1.
5 P. Sheppard, *The Historic Towns of Cornwall* (1980), 57–9.
6 On the Dominican friary at Truro, see below, p. 281.
7 *L&P Hen. VIII*, XXI(1), 76.
8 TNA, JUST 1/111, m. 27d; 1/112, m. 8d. The suggestion that the dedication was to St Nicholas (G. Oliver, *Monasticon Dioecesis Exoniensis* (1846), 17), presumably comes from the friary's site in St Nicholas Street: actually named after a local chapel.
9 On Franciscan churches, see A. R. Martin, *Franciscan Architecture in England* (1937).

the church was dedicated by Bishop Grandisson of Exeter in 1352, an action that would have been appropriate after a large-scale reconstruction.[1] At the Reformation the structure was said to include a choir, nave, vestry, and steeple (i.e. tower or turret).[2]

Much of the church remained in use from the Reformation until the early 19th century as an assize hall and corn market. A map of 1822–3 depicts the building as a narrow structure, about six times longer than wide, on an east-west alignment.[3] A hundred years previously William Hals described it as having a single roof, 60 feet high and 150 feet long, 'with two stone windows admirable for height, breadth, and workmanship'.[4] A drawing, apparently of the north elevation, made by Edmund Prideaux in 1716, shows (from left to right) four bays of uniform size, a wider bay, and three further bays of the first size, with buttresses dividing the bays and reaching to the roof edge (Fig. 48).[5] The roof is depicted as continuous, except for a line of division at the commencement of the three right-hand bays. Two storeys of arched windows appear in the left-hand bays. This evidence may indicate a choir of four bays and a nave of four, divided by a transverse passage, since Franciscan choirs and naves elsewhere in England were often of similar length. In other such churches the passage might lie between a rood screen on the side towards the nave and a further screen towards the choir, with a slim steeple being often placed on the roof above the passage.[6] The windows may have undergone alteration by 1716, due to the division of the church into two storeys, since friars' churches generally had a single long window in each bay; those mentioned by Hals are likely to have been the great east and west windows.

There is no clear evidence about the interior layout of the church. Pillar stones from the friary site have survived into modern times, but it is not known if these formed an aisle or aisles inside the building. There were, however, chapels within the church. In 1442–3, a craftsman named William Ford was paid £14 13s. 4d. for work on the tomb of Thomas Peverel, esquire, which he had done from a design on parchment using French stone 'in a goodly chapel' within the friary church.[7] In 1480 Thomas Whalesborough, esquire, of Marhamchurch chose to be buried 'in my chapel, that is to say in the north part of the church of the Friars Minor of Bodmin, as is specified in a certain indenture made between me and ... the convent of the same place'.[8] It is possible that these chapels were contrived within the main walls of the nave by means of screens, but equally one or both of them may have been exterior additions to the nave joined to it by doors and windows. By the Reformation the church contained four altars besides the high altar. One of these was known as the altar of John Carminow in 1529, when Thomas Carminow asked to be buried before it in his will.[9] A tomb set into a wall along with vaults and graves beneath the church floor were discovered in the early 19th century.[10]

The domestic buildings of the friary may have stood south of the church. These, by the Reformation, included a great chamber, other chambers, a frater (i.e. refectory), kitchen, brewhouse, and buttery.[11] Further south lay a meadow belonging to the friars, and they held a small amount of other property and income. In 1539 this was stated as comprising a house, 2½ acres of land, a close, and four rent charges, producing a total income of about £10 10s. including the gatehouse which was let for £1 10s.[12]

THE FRIARS AND THE COMMUNITY

Apart from the small sums derived from their property, the Franciscans of Bodmin followed their order in living mainly from voluntary donations of food or money, some of which have left traces in documents. In 1297 Edward I, while visiting Plympton (Devon), sent them 40s.; in 1307–10 they were given £7 2s. 0d. to pray for Bishop Bitton of Exeter; in 1354 the Black Prince told his receiver in Cornwall to assign them 20s. in alms; and in 1466–7 the steward of the Arundell family of Lanherne recorded a gift of fish (four hake and thirty-five whiting) 'to the friars', probably of Bodmin.[13] Bequests of money to them often occur in the wills of Cornish people from the mid

---

1 Worcester, *Itineraries*, 90–1. The dedication is not recorded in Grandisson's register, but the bishop visited Cornwall in July of that year (*Reg. Grandisson*, III, 1531).

2 *L&P Hen. VIII*, XIII(2), 153; H. Michell Whitley, 'Inventories of the Cornish Friaries at the Time of their Dissolution', *JRIC* 8 (1883–5), 24–6.

3 RIC, MMP/22,1.

4 BL, Add. 29762, f. 12v. A comparison with other friaries suggests that this measurement is likely to refer to the whole church.

5 Padstow, Prideaux Place, in private ownership.

6 The steeple is depicted as a four-sided tower at the west end of the church on a map of the south coast of Cornwall, drawn in about 1540, but this could be a conventional sign for a church (BL, Cotton Aug. I.i.35, 36, 38, 39).

7 J. Maclean, *The Parochial and Family History of the Deanery of Trigg Minor* (1873–9), I, 188.

8 N. Orme (ed.), *Cornish Wills 1342–1540*, DCRS new ser. 50 (2007), 94.

9 TNA, PROB 11/23, f. 53v; Orme (ed.), *Cornish Wills*, 179.

10 Maclean, *Trigg Minor*, I, 191.

11 *L&P Hen. VIII*, XIII(2), 153; Whitley, 'Inventories of the Cornish Friaries', 24–6.

12 TNA, SC 6/HenVIII/7300. In 1350–1 an inquisition was held to determine whether Thomas le Goldsmyth of Bodmin might grant them messuages and land in the town (TNA, C 143/299/10). Parts of the friary's site can be identified from tithe-free properties in the vicinity known as 'Frieries' in 1840 (CRO, TA/ and TM/13).

13 BL, Add. 7965, f. 7(2)r; W. H. Hale and H. T. Ellacombe (ed.), *Accounts of the Executors of Richard Bishop of London 1303, and... Thomas Bishop of Exeter 1310*, Camden Soc. new ser. 10 (1874), 23, 28, 30; *Black Prince's Reg.*, II, 65; H. L. Douch, 'Household Accounts at Lanherne', *JRIC* new ser. 2 (1953–6), 27.

14th to the early 16th centuries, usually coupled with legacies to the Dominicans of Truro.[1] A legal dispute of 1465–7 throws further light on the kinds of gifts that friars might receive and how they were dealt with. During the early 1460s Friar Stephen Rauff, DD, a senior member of the Franciscan Order and possibly based at Bristol, was given goods and money worth £5 13s. 4d. by various persons in return for prayers. Following the friars' strict rules about handling money, he gave these assets to John Lokyer, a locksmith of Bristol, for safe keeping, and secured the permission of the Franciscans' head or 'general' to dispose of them for the benefit of the Bodmin friary. Rauff having died before this was done, Lokyer refused to deliver up the property to Bodmin's representative, Friar James William, and the head or 'provincial' of the English branch of the order was driven to seek redress from the chancellor of England.[2]

Friars established links with important in their localities, able to give them substantial support. When Worcester visited the house in 1478, he transcribed the names of twenty-six 'nobility and gentry [listed] in the calendar of the friars of Bodmin'. As well as the founding figures already mentioned they included Bishop Bronescombe, described as a 'special benefactor', John, earl of Cornwall (i.e. John of Eltham, 1328–36), and knights and ladies from the families of Arundell, Beaupré, Bleuet, Carminow, Cergeaux, Cleverton, Daune, FitzWalter, Hywys, Kent, Peverel, Rodney, Trelothryk, Trewynt, and Wythiel.[3] Some of these, including Sir Hugh Peverell, Sir Thomas Peverell, and Margery Sergeaux, were entombed in the friary.[4] In turn the friars prayed for their benefactors, and celebrated obit masses on the anniversaries of their deaths. A man named John Serle of Liskeard granted the Franciscans 2s. per annum from his lands during the 1460s to keep an annual obit, but the friars complained that his stepson withheld the payment after Serle's death.[5] The community's relationships with these wealthy families are likely to have reflected the fact that its members worked not only in Bodmin but in much of Cornwall through preaching, pastoral visiting, and hearing confessions. Their connections with lesser folk have left fewer traces, but it is likely that they were close to the people of Bodmin. Unlike the Augustinian priory they claimed no jurisdiction in the borough and may have been an alternative focus of religious loyalty. A pointer to this is the fact that the borough officers began their financial year on St Francis's Day (4 October), perhaps reflecting a civic ceremony involving the friary.[6] The borough paid Friar Fayne for mending books in 1500–1, and three sums to Friar John Kentysbery for mending and binding four volumes in 1504–5, the latter all being liturgical texts, probably from the parish church.[7] In 1503–4 Friar John Smith was given 3s. 4d. by the borough 'as a reward'.[8]

RECRUITMENT, TRAINING, AND WORK

We know little about the life and work of the friars of Bodmin. Even their number is unknown until 1538 when, at the very end of its existence, the community comprised a warden and eight brethren.[9] It is probable, however, that the Franciscans suffered badly in the Black Death of 1348–9, since Worcester saw a note in a friary register that 1,500 people died in the town of Bodmin at that time.[10] Some of the Bodmin Franciscans were men from Cornwall. Ordinations of friars in Exeter diocese, some specified as from Bodmin and others unspecified, include men with topographical surnames such as Kerneck, Kildreyneke, Landege, Roseweke, and Weneppa, as well as men called simply 'of Cornwall'.[11] Friars differed from monks, on the other hand, in being organised internationally, each house being supervised from above and its members moving from house to house as required. The English province of the Franciscans was divided into seven districts known as 'custodies', Bodmin being one of ten houses in the custody of Bristol.[12] Friars were often recruited in their teens, and are likely to have been schooled in Latin grammar in the friaries that they first entered. By the end of the 13th century the Franciscans also provided instruction in basic theology in their houses, and suitable students were sent away to local centres to study logic, philosophy, and academic theology. A friar named Alfred is mentioned in 1328 as a former lecturer (*lector*) at Bodmin, probably in basic theology.[13] In 1337 the Exeter friary was one of the major Franciscan study centres for academic theology, and some Bodmin friars probably travelled there for that purpose.[14] Students who made the most progress would be sent to continue

---

1 Notably £9 3s. 4d. from John Dabernon of Calstock in 1368, £2 13s. 4d. from Sir Thomas Carminow of Mawgan-in-Meneage to four named friars (Richard Pole, Richard Boscarn, John Trefolyn, and Ralph Parleben) in 1369, and £2 from John Treffry of Fowey in 1500 (Orme (ed.), *Cornish Wills*, 32, 36 109). Other will bequests are indexed in ibid., 269.
2 C 1/31/444.
3 Worcester, *Itineraries*, 84–7, 92–3.
4 Leland, *Itinerary*, ed. Toulmin Smith, I, 180. In 1375 William Cranewell, sheriff of Cornwall and steward of the Black Prince, requested burial in the friary if he died in Cornwall (London, Lambeth Palace Library, Reg. Sudbury, f. 83v; Orme (ed.), *Cornish Wills*, 37).
5 TNA, C1/48/521.
6 CRO, B/BOD/314/3/1–57.
7 B/BOD/314/3/16d, /314/3/21d.
8 B/BOD/314/3/20d.
9 Below, p. 158.
10 Worcester, *Itineraries*, 94–5.
11 *Reg. Stapeldon*, 464–533 passim.
12 Knowles and Hadcock, *Medieval Religious Houses*, 222–3.
13 *Reg. Grandisson*, I, 420–1.
14 A. G. Little, 'Educational Organisation of the Mendicant Friars in England (Dominicans and Franciscans)', *Transactions of the Royal Historical Society* new ser. 8 (1894), 68–9.

their studies at a university, such as Oxford,[1] and conversely friars from elsewhere might be drafted to Bodmin to study or work. The names of four Franciscans from Bodmin who were ordained in Exeter diocese between 1421 and 1455 – Christian de Bonna, Raymond de Bordigla, Herman Taminek, and Arnald de Wesalia – suggest that they were men from overseas.[2]

The friary is likely to have had a library. Early in the 14th century Henry, dean of Crantock, gave a copy of Peter Comestor's *Historia Scholastica* to 'the community of the Friars Minor of Bodmin'. His gift was channelled through two friars, Richard of St Columb and Geoffrey Werdour, who were allowed the use of the volume during their lives.[3] At about the same time the Bodmin friars were probably responsible for making a list of theological works in the library of Bodmin Priory, which they passed to their colleagues in Oxford who were compiling a union catalogue of such works in England.[4] John Somer (fl. 1380–1409), an important friar scholar of the late 14th century, was apparently based at Bodmin for a time. He was the author of a calendar with astronomical tables, compiled at Oxford in 1380, which circulated in many copies. One of these, apparently originating from before 1384, refers to him as warden of the priory of Bodmin, but his stay there cannot have been long since his home convent was Bridgwater and much of his life was passed at Oxford.[5] Two other Bodmin friars are named in manuscripts that they may have owned in some private capacity: Richard Pole (alive in the 1370s) in a Latin astronomical tract, and Gregory Bassett (who flourished in the 1520s) in a printed copy of the theological commentary on the *Sentences* of Peter Lombard by the Franciscan scholar Richard Middleton.[6] Another Franciscan active in Cornwall in 1535–8 was Alexander Barclay, doctor of divinity and a former English poet, but it is not known if he was based at the Bodmin convent.[7]

The ethos of study among the English orders of friars made many of them skilful in preaching and hearing confessions, and Franciscans and Dominicans in Cornwall were utilised by some of the bishops of Exeter to provide pastoral services to the people of the county. In 1328 Bishop Grandisson appointed the warden or head of the Bodmin friary, Adam of Trekelad, and Alfred, the former lecturer, as public confessors with power to deal with some matters normally reserved for the bishop's own attention.[8] In 1331 he authorised Alfred of Drefe, who may have been identical with Alfred the lecturer, to hear confessions of parishioners and grant absolutions throughout Cornwall, praising Alfred's purity of conscience, circumspection, and expertness 'in the idiom of those parts'. Since Drefe is the modern Drift in Sancreed parish, Alfred was evidently a native speaker of Cornish from the far west of Cornwall.[9] Later, in 1355, Grandisson appointed another Bodmin friar, John, as a penitentiary (a confessor to the clergy and to lay people with serious sins) 'to those in Cornwall who know either language', meaning Cornish or English.[10] At least seven licences were issued to wardens or friars of Bodmin to work as confessors by Grandisson's successor, Thomas Brantingham, between 1371 and 1390, and although these do not mention the linguistic issue, some of the friars concerned may well have been expert in Cornish, helping to bring the learning and law of the Church to people who spoke that language.[11]

THE DISSOLUTION

The friary was dissolved on 20 September 1538, in the same year as all the remaining orders and establishments of friars in England. On that day the warden, Walter Rodde, and eight of his brethren surrendered their house to the king's visitor, who made an inventory of all the moveable possessions. The buildings, as their later history confirms, were still substantial. Leland, who visited Bodmin four years later, used the term 'a good place' to describe them,[12] and a survey of friaries carried out by the crown in about 1538 listed the house as one that possessed a significant amount of lead roofing.[13] According to the inventory the goods of the choir included 'a fair table of alabaster' at the high altar, stalls for the friars in good condition, and books for services. The nave contained four altars, the vestry several vestments and altar cloths, and the steeple two bells. Tables, benches, and cupboards were mentioned in the domestic buildings, but the equipment in the kitchen and brewhouse was described as 'all poor stuff'. As at Truro there was a chest containing documents belonging to local gentry, placed in the house for safety.[14] The friary's debts were reckoned at £16, and 286 ounces of silver and plate were taken for the king's use.[15]

Friars did not receive pensions at the dissolution, like monks, since they were considered to have embraced a life of poverty. However on 5 December

---

1 Possible Cornish Franciscans at Oxford include Richard Trevers and John Trevilian (*BRUO*, III, 1902; IV, 578).
2 *Reg. Lacy*, ed. Dunstan, V, 19.
3 BL, Royal 7.A.X; G. F. Warner and J. P. Gilson, *British Museum: Catalogue of Western Manuscripts in the Old Royal and King's Collections*, 4 vols (London, 1921), I, 167.
4 Above, p. 149.
5 *ODNB*; BL, Add. 10,628, f. 10r; L. Mooney, *The 'Kalendarium' of John Somer* (1998), 57–9.
6 N. R. Ker, *Medieval Libraries of Great Britain* (1964), 11, 230. On Bassett, see *BRUO*, IV, 30.
7 Below, pp. 190, 219.
8 *Reg. Grandisson*, I, 420–1; cf. I, 558, 566.
9 Ibid., II, 632.
10 Ibid., II, 1146.
11 *Reg. Brantyngham*, I, 238, 322, 374, 388, 401; II, 692.
12 Leland, *Itinerary*, I, 180.
13 *L&P Hen. VIII*, XIII(2), 190.
14 For a dispute about documents held by the friars, see C 1/469/8.
15 Ibid., 153; Whitley, 'Inventories of the Cornish Friaries', 24–6.

1538 all the Bodmin friars were granted dispensations to change their dress and to hold benefices as if they were parish clergy.[1] The site of the friary, its buildings, gatehouse, and gardens, and its possessions in Bodmin were purchased from the crown by William Abbott, serjeant of the king's cellar, on 30 January 1546.[2] In 1566 the property, then in the hands of William Vyvyan and John Hewet, was sold to the mayor and burgesses of Bodmin, who converted the church for civic purposes to which, in due course, the holding of the assizes was added. Most of the former church was replaced by a new Shire Hall in the early 19th century, but the western part of it, including a great west window, remained in use as a corn market until it was demolished in 1891.[3] Funerary remains from the church have been found beneath the Shire Hall and in the former friary cemetery on Mount Folly, the area north of the hall. The only visible structure is part of the gatehouse inside No. 4, Fore Street.[4] Some pieces of stonework, including a sculptured human head and a column with a capital, are preserved in Bodmin Town Museum.[5]

WARDENS OF BODMIN FRIARY

Adam of Trekelad	occurs 27 Oct 1328–16 Feb 1330[6]
Richard Boscarn	occurs 15 Feb 1374[7]
John Stephens	occurs 20 Nov 1376–22 Aug 1378[8]
John Somer	occurs before 1384[9]
Roger Rosemelian	occurs 19 Feb 1390[10]
Ralph	occurs 1473–4, before 4 Aug 1480[11]
Walter Rodde	occurs 1515 × 1518–20 Sept 1538[12]

HOSPITAL OF ST ANTHONY

The hospital or almshouse of St Anthony in Bodmin is first mentioned in the will of John Carminow of Bodmin in 1492, who bequeathed 3s. 4d. 'to the poor of the hospital of St Anthony' along with similar sums to the other two Bodmin hospitals of St George and St Laurence.[13] There are five further references to the hospital, all in wills. In 1501 Thomas Killigrew of Arwenack near Penryn left 6s. 8d. 'to the poor of St Anthony of Bodmin' to be equally divided;[14] in the following year Thomas Poyle of Tregony gave 20d. 'to the almshouse [*domo elemosinale*] of St Anthony of Bodmin;[15] in 1531 Christopher Tredeneck bequeathed 20d. 'to the people of St Anthony';[16] and in 1542 Joyce Flamank bestowed 1d. on every poor man and woman in St Anthony's and St George's chapels.[17] The last known bequest, also of 20d., 'to the poor people of the house of St Anthony in Bodmin', occurs in the will of John Adam, rector of Bradoc, in 1553.[18]

The six references, with their slightly different terminology, indicate that the hospital was associated with a chapel of St Anthony. It catered for the poor, both men and women, and was supported by well-wishers not only from Bodmin but more widely in Cornwall. It was probably an almshouse in form, consisting of a number of small dwellings, and the legacies imply that it was unendowed or poorly endowed, making its inmates reliant on public charity for at least part of their support. The chapel existed until the early 19th century in Chapel Lane off Bore Street,[19] and a chancery petition of 1529 × 1532 mentions a tenement adjoining it 'on the east side'.[20] The almshouse was presumably in the same vicinity. It is possible that the chapel and almshouse were maintained by a guild, like the guild almshouses found in several other English towns in the 15th century, but the building accounts of Bodmin parish church, which survive from 1469 to 1472 and are very informative about the chapels and guilds of Bodmin, do not refer to a guild of St Anthony, so if one existed it is likely to have been established after 1472.[21] The almshouse was perhaps the foundation noted by the antiquary John Leland on his visit to Cornwall in 1542, when he

---

1 D. S. Chambers, *Faculty Office Registers 1534–1549* (1966), 167.
2 *L&P Hen. VIII*, XXI(1), 76.
3 For site information, see CCC, HER 4354, and Maclean, *Trigg Minor*, I, 191–2; for the layout in 1822–3, RIC, MMP/22,1; and for a photograph of the west window in 1891, Bodmin Town Museum (unclassified photo).
4 An early photograph of the gateway is preserved in Bodmin Town Museum, P90.
5 The Bodmin market bell, held in the Town Museum, is traditionally linked with the friary but without conclusive evidence (Maclean, *Trigg Minor*, I, 192–3, with an engraving; E. H. W. Dunkin, *The Church Bells of Cornwall* (1878), 62).
6 *Reg. Grandisson*, I, 420–1, 558. 'Crekelad' would be a more likely surname, but the initial T is clear in the MS register (DRO, Chanter IV, f. 78r); alternatively a Cornish 'tre' name.
7 *Reg. Brantyngham*, I, 322.
8 Ibid., I, 374, 388.
9 BL, Add. MS 10,628, f. 10r; Mooney, *Kalendarium*, 57–9.
10 *Reg. Brantyngham*, II, 692, 811.

11 C 1/48/521; Orme (ed.), *Cornish Wills*, 94.
12 Also Redde, Rodda (C 1/384/40; C 1/469/8; *L&P Hen. VIII*, XIII(2), 153)
13 N. Orme (ed.), *Cornish Wills 1342–1540*, DCRS new ser. 50 (2007), 102.
14 Ibid., 111; J. Whetter, 'The Thomas Killigrews', *Old Cornwall* 10/7 (1988), 338–49.
15 Orme (ed.), *Cornish Wills*, 114.
16 Ibid., 186.
17 CRO, AD/103/2.
18 RIC, HC 66.
19 D. and S. Lysons, *Magna Britannia*: vol. III, *Cornwall* (1814), 351; J. Maclean, *The Parochial and Family History of the Deanery of Trigg Minor* (1873–9), I, 199. The site is marked in P. Sheppard, *The Historic Towns of Cornwall* (1980), 58.
20 TNA, C 1/608/28.
21 J. J. Wilkinson, 'The Receipts and Expenses in the Building of Bodmin Church', *The Camden Miscellany: Vol. VII*, Camden Soc. new ser. 14 (1875), pp. i–viii, 1–49.

observed that 'there is another chapel in Bodmin beside that in the west end of the town, and an almshouse, but not endowed with lands'.[1] It is not mentioned in the survey of chantries and hospitals carried out for Henry VIII in 1546, possibly because it had no endowments, but it seems to have continued. 'A hospital joining with St Anthony's chapel' is mentioned by a visitor to Bodmin, probably Edward Lhuyd, in about 1700,[2] and a little later William Borlase referred to 'a chapel now a poor house, I think dedicated to St Anthony', as lying 'in the middle of the town'.[3] The foundation appears to have become extinct only during the 18th century.[4] There are no visible remains.

HOSPITAL OF ST GEORGE

There was a chapel of St George in Bodmin by 1405,[5] and guilds of St George and St Mary based in the chapel gave money towards the reconstruction of Bodmin parish church in 1469–70.[6] In about 1700 the chapel building is said to have stood on the north side of the town.[7] Evidence for a hospital or almshouse near or associated with the chapel comes from wills, as is the case with the neighbouring hospital of St Anthony. In 1492 John Carminow bequeathed 3s. 4d. 'to the poor of the chapel of St George at Bodmin;[8] in 1501 Thomas Killigrew of Arwenack near Penryn left 6s. 8d. 'to the poor of St George of Bodmin' to be equally divided';[9] in 1531 Christopher Tredeneck gave 12d. 'to the people of St George of Bodmin';[10] and in 1542 Joyce Flamank bestowed 1d. on every poor man and woman of St George's chapel.[11] The foundation, like that of St Anthony's, was probably a hospital of almshouse type, consisting of some small dwellings close to the chapel, supporting poor men and women, and probably providing them mainly or solely with accommodation – hence the need for public donations. Why there were two almshouses in Bodmin and what distinguished them are not clear. The history of the foundation is not known after 1531.

HOSPITAL OF ST LAWRENCE

The hospital of St Laurence near Bodmin is first mentioned in 1288, when Margery of Caerhays granted the manor of Caerhays (Cornwall) and other rights and properties, including her lordship over the hospital, to Roger of Inkpen and Emmeline his wife.[12] Margery was the daughter of Sir Ralph and the granddaughter of John of Caerhays, and probably inherited the lordship from her ancestors – one of whom had evidently patronised the foundation of the hospital. Its date of origin could lie anywhere in the previous hundred years or so. The hospital was a community of lepers, a fact recorded in 1302 when the prior of Bodmin and Laurence of Treueygon, the bailiff of the lepers of Bodmin, were accused before the king's justices at Launceston of levying new tolls on buyers and sellers of goods at Bodmin Fair.[13] The accusation arose because such tolls could be levied only on purchasers who were merchants; there may have been an arrangement whereby the tolls were used to benefit the lepers, as happened with market tolls in some other towns. Shortly after this, between 1307 and 1310, the executors of Thomas Bitton, bishop of Exeter, granted 17s. 'to the lepers of Bodmin' whom they distinguished from the lepers of Dunmere, a mile and a half north of Bodmin, and who received a larger sum of 22s. 6d.[14]

It was common to place leper hospitals on parish boundaries and by major roads, where their inmates could gain alms from passers by. Bridges were popular locations because they slowed and defined the traffic. St Laurence occupied a typical site of this kind beside the road from Bodmin to St Columb Major, originally a chief route leading into west Cornwall, at a point where the road crossed a stream by a bridge about a mile outside the town. The stream was the boundary of the parishes of Bodmin and Lanivet, and the hospital was situated on the east side of the bridge to the north of

---

1 J. Leland, *Itinerary*, ed. L. Toulmin Smith (1907–10), I, 180.
2 Bodleian, Rawl. D 997, f. 13r.
3 BL, Egerton 2657 (W. Borlase, 'Parochial Memorials'), f. 71r.
4 Maclean, *Trigg Minor*, I, 199.
5 *Reg. Stafford*, 25.
6 J. J. Wilkinson, 'The Receipts and Expenses in the Building of Bodmin Church', *The Camden Miscellany: Vol. VII*, Camden Soc. new ser. 14 (1875), 5, 8, 29.
7 Bodleian, Rawl. D 997, f. 13r.
8 N. Orme (ed.), *Cornish Wills 1342–1540*, DCRS new ser. 50 (2007), 102.
9 Ibid., 111; J. Whetter, 'The Thomas Killigrews', *Old Cornwall* 10/7 (1988), 338–49.
10 Orme (ed.), *Cornish Wills*, 186.
11 CRO, AD/103/2.
12 R. W. Dunning (ed.), *The Hylle Cartulary*, Somerset Record Soc. 68 (1968), 79.
13 TNA, JUST 1/118, m. 58. On the history of the house, see also M. I. Somerscales, 'Lazar Houses in Cornwall', *JRIC* new ser. 5.1 (1965), 76–82.
14 W. H. Hale and H. T. Ellacombe (ed.), *Accounts of the Executors of Richard Bishop of London 1303, and of the Executors of Thomas Bishop of Exeter 1310*, Camden Soc. new ser. 10 (1874), 28.

the road (SX 0500 6600).[1] Margery's grant of 1288 (or rather the surviving later copy of it) calls the place 'Pempoya', a late 15th-century seal of the hospital 'Penpo[ns]', and a royal charter of 1582 'Ponteboy', Penpons meaning 'the head of the bridge' and Ponteboy 'the wooden bridge'.[2] The right of patronage over the hospital seems to have descended with the manor of Caerhays, and in 1546 the inmates of St Laurence acknowledged the Trevanion family of that place to be their first founder, paying a token rent of 1d. in recognition.[3]

In 1368 John Dabernon, a gentleman of Calstock, bequeathed 40s. 'to the lepers of St Laurence near Bodmin' to pray for him.[4] This is the earliest clear reference to the hospital as having a religious dedication and hence a chapel. Six years later, in 1374, Bishop Brantingham of Exeter granted permission to the *nuncius* or proctor of the hospital of St Laurence outside Bodmin to collect alms for one year, and granted the house an indulgence of twenty days, presumably to encourage such alms.[5] Two further indulgences are known to have been given by bishops of Exeter, both of forty days, one by Edmund Stafford in 1395 to the 'leper house of St Laurence' and the other by Edmund Lacy in 1436 'to sustain the brothers and sick of the house or hospital of St Laurence near Bodmin'.[6] Whether the reference to brothers refers to healthy brothers in charge of the hospital, or to the inmates being wholly male at this time, is not certain. The indulgences suggest that the house placed much reliance on voluntary alms for its support, and in 1419 a London pewterer who originated from Truro, John Megre, bequeathed 12d. 'to be shared among the lepers of the chapel of St Laurence'.[7] There were also some modest endowments. The antiquary John Leland, who visited Bodmin in 1542, noted that Sir Hugh and Sir Thomas Peverel were buried in Bodmin Priory and reported that 'one of the Peverels gave a little annuity unto this house', i.e. the hospital.[8] The Peverels were a family of gentry with property in Cornwall and Devon, including the manor of Hamatethy in St Breward parish, and the obituaries of James (d. 1314), Elizabeth (d. 1342), and Sir Hugh (d. 1372) were commemorated in Bodmin's Franciscan friary, so it is possible that the annuity was given in the 14th century.[9]

St Laurence possessed its own seal, a late 15th-century version of which is now preserved in the Royal Institution of Cornwall. It depicts St Laurence holding a gridiron above a small figure in prayer, and is inscribed S[IGILLUM] SANCTI LAURENCII BODMONS DE PENPO[NS].[10] By that date the house was ruled by a prior who was probably the senior lay inmate, as in other small leper communities. In 1476 Prior John Cole sued William Luke, chaplain, in the stannary court at Lostwithiel,[11] and in 1478–9 the hospital was involved in a dispute with the vicar of Bodmin, William Brewe, over certain 'oblations and obventions' claimed by the vicar. These were presumably either offerings due from the lepers to Brewe as their parish priest, or offerings made in the hospital chapel that the vicar regarded as his perquisite. The rector of the nearby church of Lanivet, John Gody, an elderly man aged eighty or more (so he said) intervened on the side of the lepers, and Brewe then successfully prosecuted Gody in the archbishop of Canterbury's court of audience.[12] His success suggests that the vicar held recognised rights over the hospital similar to those of the parish church of St Stephen-by-Launceston over the lepers of that town.[13] At some date between 1476 and 1485 Cole was succeeded as prior by John Hopkyn, who tried to recover deeds and muniments relating to the hospital's rights, which he alleged that Cole had entrusted to Thomas Hogge of Bodmin. Hogge denied the charge and Hopkyn then accused John Raulyn, a local baker, of keeping them.[14]

Like the other two Bodmin hospitals, St Laurence benefited from bequests in wills. In 1492 John Carminow bestowed 3s. 4d. on 'the poor of the hospital of St Laurence';[15] in 1501 Thomas Killigrew of Arwenack near Penryn left them 6s. 8d. to be equally divided;[16] in 1531 Christopher Tredeneck gave 'the

---

1 Two sources indicate a site to the west of the bridge: J. Leland, *Itinerary*, ed. L. Toulmin Smith (1907–10), I, 181, and J. Gascoyne, *A Map of the County of Cornwall*, ed. W. L. D. Ravenhill and O. J. Padel, DCRS new ser. 34 (1991), sheet 6A. But the hospital is stated as lying in Bodmin parish in 1582 (below, note 2), and its property appears in the Bodmin parish Tithe Award of 1841 (CRO, CL/52).

2 J. Maclean, *The Parochial and Family History of the Deanery of Trigg Minor* (1873–9), I, 195; A. Way, 'Charter of Queen Elizabeth to the Hospital of St Laurence de Ponteboy, Bodmin, AD 1582', JRIC 3 (1868–70), 1–33.

3 CRO, CF/3582.

4 N. Orme (ed), *Cornish Wills 1342–1540*, DCRS new ser. 50 (2007), 34.

5 *Reg. Brantyngham*, I, 335. No evidence has been found for the assertion that Bishop Brantyngham consecrated the hospital chapel on 27 August 1382 (Maclean, *History of Bodmin*, p. 94; Somerscales, 'Lazar Houses', 78). He cannot have done so, because he was not in Cornwall that year (*Reg. Brantyngham*, II, 893).

6 DRO, Chanter VIII, ff. 5v–6r (*Reg. Stafford*, 25); *Reg. Lacy*, ed. Dunstan, I, 326.

7 Orme (ed.), *Cornish Wills*, 52.

8 Leland, *Itinerary*, ed. Toulmin Smith, I, 184.

9 W. Worcester, *Itineraries*, ed. J. H. Harvey (1969), 86–7, 92–3. For the family property see *Feudal Aids*, I, 199, 205, 214, and Maclean, *Trigg Minor*, I, 345–6, 382–3.

10 Maclean, *Trigg Minor*, I, 197; W. Jago, 'The Ecclesiastical Seals of Cornwall', JRIC 8 (1883–5), 64–5.

11 TNA, SC 2/157/11, m. 2.

12 TNA, C 1/5/86.

13 Below, pp. 222–3.

14 C 1/52/128, C 1/58/340. These documents date from either 1476–8 or 1483–5.

15 Orme (ed.), *Cornish Wills*, 102.

16 Ibid., 111; J. Whetter, 'The Thomas Killigrews', *Old Cornwall* 10.7, 338–49.

people of St Laurence' 3s. 4d.;[1] and in 1542 Joyce Flamank bequeathed 20d. 'to the poor sick people at St Laurence'.[2] In 1537 Nicholas Harry of Bodmin granted the hospital an annual rent of 10s. from a tenement in Pole Street.[3] For all that, Leland called the place only 'a poor hospital or lazar house' – the term 'lazar' possibly indicating lepers specifically, possibly a wider range of sick people.[4] Bodmin Priory was dissolved in 1539, but the hospital survived as an independent foundation. When the Chantry Commissioners of Henry VIII made their survey of chantries and hospitals in the spring of 1546, they were told that the hospital's founder was unknown and that the foundation was intended to maintain nineteen lazar people, two healthy men, two healthy women, and a chaplain ministering in the hospital chapel. We are not told whether the healthy were ministers to the lazars or were almsfolk themselves. The commissioners learnt that hospital possessed lands but that the annual income was only £4 14s. 1d., which was entirely employed for the benefit of the poor lazar 'men', a word that could have meant 'people' including women. The value of the plate in the chapel was 30s.[5] During the next thirty-five years the hospital continued to rely on alms for much of its support. The churchwardens of St Breock paid 12d. in 1564 to help a sick woman to enter St Laurence, and 16d. in 1574 for a poor man of St Columb Major to be brought to the hospital – which was evidently not restricted to people from Bodmin.[6] The wardens of Blanchminster's charity at Stratton gave 12d. to a poor man gathering alms for St Laurence in 1571 and 8d. likewise in 1578.[7]

In 1582 the community was put on a firmer legal footing by Elizabeth I, probably in response to a local request. The queen, noting that it had existed without legal incorporation for a long time under the name of a prior, brethren, and sisters, and currently included thirty-six leprous people, incorporated the house under the name of the 'Hospital or Almshouse of Elizabeth, Queen of England, of St Laurence de Ponteboy in the parish of Bodmin'. The hospital was to maintain a master or governor and thirty-nine poor men and women who were leprous people, Lewis Shessel being appointed the first master. In future the brethren and sisters were empowered to choose masters themselves and to admit new inmates to fill up vacancies. They were to meet daily for prayer, using the appointed prayers of the Church (i.e. matins and evensong), and were obliged to find a minister to say services within their chapel and to administer the sacraments. The hospital was confirmed in the possession of its house, one acre of land, two mills, an annual fair lasting three days at St Laurence tide (10 August) held in the Fair Field near the hospital, and various other nearby tenements let out to local tenants.[8] There is no sign that the crown increased the endowments of the hospital, and the only known additional resource was due to Richard Carter, a merchant of St Columb Major, who gave a sum of £10, also in 1582 that was used to build a house in Bodmin for renting out.[9] The hospital went on raising money from voluntary donations, the churchwardens of St Neot paying 2s. 8d. to a collection on its behalf in 1606.[10] In 1602 the county historian Richard Carew mentioned St Laurence as one of three Cornish lazar houses and asserted that it was 'well endowed and governed'.[11] Shortly afterwards James I granted the hospital a weekly market every Wednesday and an additional fair on St Luke's Day.[12]

Recruitment to the hospital changed during the 17th century to include non-lepers, and fell away altogether in the 18th. By 1805 there were only a handful of inmates, and in 1810 the property of the hospital was transferred to the Cornwall County Infirmary. The chapel was used until about 1800, but was in ruins by 1814.[13] In its later days it is said to have consisted of two aisles, divided by arches: perhaps representing a building that had once segregated men and women, or lepers and non-lepers.[14] In this period, and probably earlier, the hospital site and the nearby lands belonging to it were free of great tithes, i.e. tithes of grain, but not of small tithes.[15] There are no visible remains of significance.[16]

PRIORS OF THE HOSPITAL OF ST LAURENCE TO 1580

John Cole	occurs 1476[17]
John Hopkyn	occurs 1476 × 1485[18]
Henry Parkyn	occurs 8 Oct 1537[19]
William Curtys	died 1580[20]

---

1 Orme (ed.), *Cornish Wills*, 186.
2 CRO, AD/103/2.
3 BL, Add. 2657 (W. Borlase, 'Parochial Memorials), f. 71r (or 64r).
4 Leland, *Itinerary*, ed. Toulmin Smith, I, 184.
5 TNA, E 301/15, ff. 47v–48r, printed in L. S. Snell, *Documents towards a History of the Reformation in Cornwall: vol. I, The Chantry Certificates for Cornwall* (c.1953), 11.
6 CRO, P/19/5/1, ff. 14r, 32v.
7 R. W. Goulding, *Records of the Charity known as Blanchminster's Charity* (1898), 68-9; cf. R. and O. B. Peter, *The Histories of Launceston and Dunheved* (1885), 206. In 1577 John Dollson of St Ewe bequeathed the hospital 6s. 8d (RIC, HC 66, p. 156).
8 Way, 'Charter of Queen Elizabeth', 21–33.
9 Maclean, *Trigg Minor*, I, 196–7.
10 CRO, P/162/5/1, f. 9v.
11 R. Carew, *The Survey of Cornwall* (1602, repr. 2004), f. 68r.
12 Maclean, *Trigg Minor*, I, 195.
13 On the later history of the hospital, see ibid., 195–7, and C. T. Andrews, *The Dark Awakening: a history of St Laurence's Hospital, Bodmin* (1978).
14 C.S. Gilbert, *Historical and Topographical Survey of the County of Cornwall* (1817–20), II, 633; Maclean, *Trigg Minor*, I, 197.
15 CRO, CL/52; J. Polsue, *A Complete Parochial History of the County of Cornwall* (1867–72), I, 101, which lists the hospital properties.
16 For site information, see CCC, HER 4350.
17 SC 2/157/11, m. 2.
18 C 1/52/128, C 1/58/340.
19 BL, Add. 29762, f. 71 (or 64).
20 CRO, P/13/1/1.

ST BURYAN

COLLEGIATE CHURCH

The minster or collegiate church of St Buryan (SW 4092 2572), first documented in the 10th century,[1] survived the Norman Conquest and is mentioned as *Eglosberrie* ('church of Buryan') in the Domesday survey of 1086. It was held at that time by a body of canons who possessed land estimated at one hide that was described as formerly 'free', that is to say of tax. The land was currently valued at 10s. per annum, but had been worth 40s. 'when the count received the land'.[2] This person, Robert count of Mortain (d. 1090), half-brother of the Conqueror, was a powerful figure in late 11th-century Cornwall, who took property away from some of its religious houses.[3] There is a dearth of evidence about St Buryan for over a hundred years after 1086, and its history during the 12th century can only be conjectured from its character when it reappears in records in the 1210s. On this basis Robert of Mortain did not injure the church to the extent of dissolving the community of canons, who survived as a group of four, the chief of whom was styled the dean. Robert may have made himself patron of the church, however, with the right to appoint the dean, and this patronage may have been seized by Henry I in 1106 when he confiscated the possessions of Robert's son William. It may have passed to Henry's son Reginald, earl of Cornwall in 1140, and back to the crown after Reginald's death in 1175, since it belonged to King John in 1214.[4] It was held by John's younger son Richard, earl of Cornwall, in 1259, probably having come to him with the earldom in 1227, and it remained in the hands of the earls and dukes of Cornwall until the Reformation, except at times that the earldom or duchy was vacant, when it passed to the crown.

The revenues of the church consisted of its land and the tithes of the parish, of which the latter were the more valuable since the parish was a large one that included St Levan and Sennen, now separate units. These revenues were shared between the dean and the canons in a manner that favoured the dean. He seems to have held the main piece of land, around the church, and received most of the tithes of the whole parish. In 1480 his perquisites were said to include religious offerings, fines, escheats, wreck, flotsam, and jetsam.[5] The papal taxation of 1291 (which greatly underestimated church revenues) valued the church of St Buryan, meaning the dean's share, at £20 per annum: over three times that of the other canons together.[6] In return he was responsible for the cure of souls in the parish and the provision of chaplains to serve St Levan and Sennen, where there were chapels of ease. He and the canons were also expected to say daily services in the church in person or by deputy. Each of the other three canons held a prebend consisting of a small share of the church's lands and some tithes. These prebends were of unequal value, estimated in 1291 at £2 10s. 0d., £2 6s. 8d., and 15s. 0d.[7] The most valuable of the three was known by the 14th century as Rospannel (a place in St Buryan) and the next as *Trethyn* (now Treen in St Levan), presumably named because they included property there. The remaining prebend, with the lowest value, was called the 'Small', 'Minor', or 'Third'. In 1548 Rospannel and *Trethyn* each possessed a messuage and six acres of land, and the Small Prebend a single acre.[8] King John granted a pension of £5 from the church to the Breton abbey of St Mathieu-de-Fineterre (Finistère) but, although this grant was confirmed by Henry III in 1233, its subsequent history is lacking.[9]

By the early 13th century the deanery was regarded as a lucrative benefice for men in favour with the king and later with the earls and dukes of Cornwall. The earliest known occupant is Walter de Gray, John's chancellor and supporter, who also held the archdeaconry of Totnes and the deanery of Probus until his election as bishop of Worcester in 1214.[10] John then gave all three of these benefices to another of his associates, Walter provost of St Omer in France, whose interests, like Walter de Gray's, lay well away from Cornwall and can rarely if ever have taken either man to St Buryan.[11] The next deans, William of St Aubin (1220) and Arnold of Holland (1259), followed in this tradition. William represented Henry III at the papal court from 1218 to 1232, and Arnold acted as prothonotary of Richard earl of Cornwall, helping Richard in his attempt to establish

---

1 Above, p. 128.
2 C. and F. Thorn (ed.), *Domesday Book*, vol. X: *Cornwall* (1979), 4/27.
3 B. Golding, 'Robert of Mortain', *Anglo-Norman Studies* 13 (1990), 19–44, especially 140–1.
4 *Rot. Litt. Pat.*, 111.
5 C. G. Henderson, 'The Ecclesiastical History of the 109 Parishes of West Cornwall', *JRIC* new ser. 2 (1953–6), 55.
6 *Reg. Bronescombe*, ed. Hingeston-Randolph, 470.
7 *Reg. Bronescombe*, ed. Hingeston-Randolph, 470.
8 Bodleian, Rawl. D 363, ff. 263v–4r; *Cal. Pat.* 1549–51, 104.
9 *Rot. Chart.* 196; *Cal. Chart.* 1226–57, 123. It is not mentioned in the papal taxation of 1291.
10 *Rot. Litt. Pat.*, 111.
11 On Walter, see F. Michel (ed.), *Histoire des Ducs de Normandie et des rois d'Angleterre* (Paris, Société de l'Histoire de France, 1840), 116; G. G. Dept, *Les Influences anglaise et française dans le comté de Flandre* (Gent and Paris, 1928), 128; and E. Warlop, *The Flemish Nobility before 1300*, vol. II (Kortrijk, 1976), 1109.

himself as 'king of the Romans' in Germany.¹ At this time, and throughout the 13th century, the church was subject to the authority of the bishops of Exeter in the normal way. Bishop Brewer visited it on 26 August 1238 and dedicated the building in the names of God, Andrew, Thomas Becket, Nicholas, Buryan, and all the saints. He granted an indulgence of thirty days to those who visited the church on the anniversary of the dedication, confirmed the church's liberties including its right of sanctuary, and ratified the charter ascribed to King Æthelstan in its favour.² The sanctuary, paralleled in Cornwall at St Keverne, Padstow, and Probus, covered a larger area than that of an ordinary church and probably extended over the church land nearby. It was under the control of the dean's bailiffs, and claimed immunity from all lay officers except for the king's justices.³

The earliest surviving register of a bishop of Exeter, that of Walter Bronescombe, includes three appointments of deans of St Buryan between 1259 and 1275, each candidate being presented by the earl of Cornwall to the bishop who instituted him to the benefice.⁴ Four appointments of prebendaries are also recorded between 1264 and 1273, two being 'collated' (chosen and instituted) by the bishop and two instituted by him on the presentation of the dean.⁵ In later times the deans always claimed the right of nominating the prebendaries, and it is not clear why the bishop intervened to do so; at least one of the collations, in 1271, was made while the deanery was occupied. One wonders if the bishop had ambitions to gain patronage over the prebends of St Buryan like that which he held over those of similar churches in Cornwall: Crantock, Glasney, and Probus. Between 1274 and 1277 Edmund earl of Cornwall granted the advowson of St Buryan to the bishop and cathedral of Rochester, including the right to appoint to the prebends and chapels in the parish.⁶ This arrangement did not last long, perhaps because of the distance involved, and in 1287 the bishop of Rochester acknowledged the return of the church to the earl's possession in exchange for grants of churches and land in Oxfordshire and Suffolk.⁷

When Edmund died without an heir in 1300, the patronage over St Buryan reverted to the crown in the person of Edward I, and this was soon followed by a claim on the part of the crown that the church was a royal free chapel over which the bishops of Exeter had no right of jurisdiction. According to Bishop Stapledon of Exeter, in a petition to the king in 1324–5, the author of this change was Ralph of Manton, a royal clerk of Edward I, who suggested to the king that the church was and ought to be a free chapel of the king, to which the king might appoint him as dean without reference to the bishop.⁸ Manton's appointment took place in 1301, but the fact that he was granted the deanery by the king without reference to the bishop, in a document that names the church as a royal free chapel, shows that the crown had already decided to change the status of the church.⁹ Later, in 1352, Bishop Grandisson of Exeter told Edward III, that the idea came from Manton's predecessor, William of Hambleton, who resigned in 1301. According to Grandisson, William wished to hold the deanery of St Buryan together with that of York and, being unable to occupy both benefices under canon law, proposed to the king that St Buryan was a royal free chapel and therefore a benefice without cure of souls.¹⁰ In fact the impetus for the change of status probably came from as much from the crown itself as from Hambleton or Manton. During his reign Edward I consistently defended the immunities of royal chapels against the Church authorities, and advanced new claims in this respect on behalf of at least three churches not hitherto regarded as such chapels, including St Buryan.¹¹ History would have suggested reasons why St Buryan could claim royal status. Its alleged founder was King Æthelstan, and Domesday Book had stated that the church was 'free before 1066', a phrase that may well have been interpreted to mean freedom from episcopal jurisdiction.¹² The royal chancery held records of the appointments of deans by John and Henry III, and if the bishops had been encroaching on the dean's right to appoint prebendaries, that fact may have been a further motive for excluding their authority.

The bishops of Exeter could not tolerate the withdrawal of a major church and parish from their control, and they strove to maintain their traditional rights. In 1302 Edward I prohibited Bishop Thomas Bitton and his officials from doing anything prejudicial to the free chapel, which the king asserted had 'newly reverted to the crown as to its founder'.¹³ Two years

---

1 On William, see *Cal. Pat.* 1216–25, pp. 84, 237, 261, 328, 408, and *Cal. Pat.* 1225–32, 508, and on Arnold, N. Denholm-Young, *Richard of Cornwall* (1947), 92. However, William witnessed at least one deed in Cornwall: P. L. Hull (ed.), *The Cartulary of St Michael's Mount*, DCRS new ser. 5 (1962), 47.

2 F. Barlow (ed.), *English Episcopal Acta*, vol. XII: *Exeter 1186–1257* (1996), 259–61; *Reg. Grandisson*, I, 84–6.

3 *Parliament Rolls*, II, 601; J. C. Cox, *The Sanctuaries and Sanctuary Seekers of Mediaeval England* (1911), 215–20.

4 *Reg. Bronescombe*, ed. Hingeston-Randolph, 167; ed. Robinson, I, 32–3; II, 19, 91.

5 *Reg. Bronescombe*, ed. Hingeston-Randolph, 167; ed. Robinson, II, 11, 50, 56, 61.

6 *Reg. Grandisson*, I, 86–7.　　　　　　　　　　7 Ibid., 86.

8 TNA, SC 8/8/361; *Rot. Parl.*, I, 421.

9 *Cal. Pat.* 1292–1301, 617–18.

10 *Reg. Grandisson*, II, 73–4.

11 J. H. Denton, *English Royal Free Chapels 1100–1300* (1970), 103–16; idem, *Robert Winchelsey and the Crown 1294–1313* (1980), 289–90.

12 *Reg. Grandisson*, II, 73–4.

13 *Cal. Close* 1296–1302, 587.

later the issue was the subject of litigation in the court of king's bench.¹ In 1314 Bitton's successor, Walter Stapledon, sought to enforce his authority by making a visitation of St Buryan. He arrived at the church in person on 13 February, made an inventory of the church's moveable possessions, and examined one of its chaplains on a charge of sexual incontinence. He also commissioned two Cornish clergy to hear ecclesiastical cases involving the parish.² The king, now Edward II, replied by ordering the keepers of the great seal and one of the justices of the king's bench to defend his rights, and in due course Stapledon, like Bitton, was summoned before the court of king's bench to answer for wrongs that he had committed against the free chapel.³ In June 1318 the king prohibited the bishop from exercising jurisdiction over St Buryan, pending a judicial decision,⁴ but in the following August Stapledon boldly collated a cleric named Richard of Beaupré to the prebend of *Trethyn*, although the document with which he did so agreed to respect any rights that the king might have in the matter.⁵ In 1324–5 the bishop made the petition to the king, already mentioned, asking for the restoration of his power to institute deans against the recent practice of making appointments by mere royal grants, but the petition was merely remitted to the king's justices for consideration and the dean and canons of St Buryan petitioned the crown in their turn against the claims of Beaupré.⁶ Despite all Stapledon's efforts and his closeness to Edward II as treasurer of England in the early 1320s, the issue was still unsettled when the bishop was murdered in 1326.

In 1327 John Grandisson became bishop of Exeter and took up the challenge with spirit. A document in his register, dated 15 July 1328 and headed 'Mandate to cite people of St Buryan', ordered the rector of Ladock to summon four men and one woman before him or his representative on charges that seem to have been related to Church discipline and to have aimed to demonstrate the bishop's authority over the parish.⁷ By November the bishop and the dean, now John de Maunte, were involved in litigation in the court of the archbishop of Canterbury.⁸ In the same month Grandisson made a progress into western Cornwall and on 4 November at St Michael's Mount, supported by the prior of the Mount and other clergy, he excommunicated John Kaer, parish chaplain of St Buryan, Richard of Penros who acted as the dean's official or ecclesiastical judge, Richard Vyvyan, allegedly the author of many evils and scandals in the parish, and all who impeded the bishop's jurisdiction. One of the clergy accompanying the bishop was Richard of Beaupré, whose attempts to establish his rights in the church had brought about armed clashes.⁹ The bishop's excommunication covered both those responsible for resisting his authority and any who communicated with them. Grandisson did not proceed to the parish but his pronouncement caused sufficient alarm for eighteen parishioners to come to the bishop, make their submission, and receive absolution. The bishop's register, which lists their names, states that they recognised him as their spiritual father and promised never again to resist his authority.¹⁰

This victory did not resolve the war. On 24 March 1329 the king complained about the bishop's exercise of jurisdiction over the church, pending the settlement of their respective claims in the king's court, and ordered him to desist.¹¹ In August the bishop, who was collecting a tax on the clergy for the benefit of the king, reported to Edward III that he could not collect it in St Buryan because the people there would not recognise his authority.¹² In December he said that none of his officers dared go to the parish for fear of death or mutilation.¹³ In 1333 Grandisson had the pleasure of excommunicating John de Maunte for failing to contribute to the tax, and when in August 1336 he was ordered to certify what goods de Maunte held in the diocese, he complained that de Maunte did not reside on his benefice and feared no ecclesiastical censures.¹⁴ Meanwhile, in July 1336, Grandisson undertook a visitation of the archdeaconry of Cornwall and decided to use the occasion to go to St Buryan in person. Mindful of the threats or violence with which his agents had been greeted there, he went with three knights, two archdeacons, the chancellor of the cathedral, and many other clergy and servants. They arrived in the parish on 12 July and encountered a crowd of parishioners. The bishop began by telling the assembled people that they had rebelled against God, the Church, and himself, and asked them if they wished to return to the Church. He addressed the 'major parishioners' himself, presumably in English or French, and Henry Marsely, rector of St Just-in-Penwith, translated his words into Cornish for the benefit of 'the others', in other words the common people. The parishioners, having discussed the matter, replied that nothing should be done to prejudice the

---

1 Denton, *Robert Winchelsey*, 289–90; *Cal. Chancery Warrants 1244–1326*, 205; *Reg. Grandisson*, II, 73–4.
2 *Reg. Stapeldon*, 327–8, 498.
3 *Cal. Chancery Warrants, 1244–1326*, 402–3, 489.
4 *Cal Close 1313–18*, 624.
5 *Reg. Stapeldon*, 248.
6 TNA, C 81/105/4748B; SC 8/8/361, 8/33/1629, 8/91/4528, 8/92/4565, 8/110/5964, 8/169/8447, 8/205/10205, 8/257/12814; *Rot. Parl.* I, 421; II, 19.
7 *Reg. Grandisson*, I, 359.
8 Ibid., I, 188.
9 SC 8/33/1629 (the dean's account, claiming that Beaupré had tried to enter the church by force with armed men).
10 *Reg. Grandisson*, I, 422–3. On Beaupré, see also ibid., I, 39–41, 44.
11 Ibid., I, 41.
12 Ibid., I, 43.
13 Ibid.
14 Ibid., II, 706. In January 1336 Grandisson asked the king to arrest de Maunte for defying excommunication (TNA, C 85/76/16).

king's rights, but they undertook to obey the bishop and his officers in future. The major parishioners made their promises in English and French, and the rest did so in Cornish. All knelt, holding up their hands in supplication, and after the singing of the hymn *Veni Creator Spiritus* the bishop absolved them. He then preached on the First Epistle of Peter (ii.25): 'you were straying like sheep, but now you have turned towards the shepherd and guardian of your souls'. The sermon was also rendered into Cornish. After this the bishop tonsured many clerks from the parish, confirmed 'innumerable' children, and received oaths of obedience from the priests who served the church, of whom there were five.[1]

The visitation was more than symbolic, since on 14 July Grandisson appointed Marsely as steward of the goods of John de Maunte, thereby threatening to cut off the dean's income.[2] This had the effect of bringing the dean to heel, and on 15 August he appeared at the bishop's manor of Bishop's Clyst (Devon). He swore to obey the bishop in all questions concerning the jurisdiction of the Church, apologised for his offence in not paying the tax, and was absolved from excommunication. The bishop then told Marsely to allow de Maunte to resume his rights and revenues, except those that related to the question of jurisdiction.[3] Unfortunately the bishop was unable to exert his authority beyond these rare and dramatic gestures.[4] The crown maintained its claims. It went on appointing deans without reference to the bishop, and the deans continued to ignore the bishop's authority. Grandisson's sole lever was the supply of those ecclesiastical services that only a bishop could provide. In February 1352 both the king and the Black Prince, duke of Cornwall, wrote to the bishop asking why he was refusing to ordain the clergy of St Buryan, confirm its children, and send chrism for baptisms and anointing the sick. This caused Grandisson to write a long letter, reviewing the history of the dispute: the letter in which he traced its origin to William of Hambleton. He went on to complain that the dispute had never been legally settled, and that although the dean, prebendaries, and parishioners had formerly acknowledged their duties to him, those of the present day had withdrawn their obedience.[5] Grandisson undoubtedly did all he could in terms of research, correspondence, and visitations to solve the St Buryan problem in his favour. His register contains copies of the charter attributed to Æthelstan, Brewer's dedication document, and two charters relating to the grant of St Buryan to Rochester Cathedral whence Grandisson had obtained them.[6] After 1352, however, the issue disappears from his register and from those of his successors, a sign that they were obliged to accept the changes that had occurred, although as late as 1427 the dean felt it wise to obtain a confirmation of his church's rights and liberties from Pope Martin V, including Æthelstan's charter.[7] In the end St Buryan acquired definitive status as a royal free chapel. Its dean was directly appointed by the king or the duke of Cornwall, and its parish was reconstituted as a peculiar jurisdiction in which the dean and his official exercised the powers that normally belonged to the bishop, including the enforcement of Church law and the probate of wills.

St Buryan's removal from the diocese deprives us of a major source for its later history: the bishops' registers. All that survives of the church's own medieval archives is a fragment of a dean's register, chiefly listing appointments of prebendaries between 1473 and 1485.[8] Even the appointments of deans do not always appear among the records of the crown, and the names of prebendaries survive largely by accident.[9] Most of our information about the church between Grandisson's time and the Reformation arises from the grant of the deanery by Henry VI to his new foundation of King's College (Cambridge) on 11 November 1445.[10] The grant, which refers to the deanery as an 'alien' benefice as if it had been one of the former French 'alien priories', was deferred until the death or resignation of the current dean, Peter Stukeley.[11] He died in 1451, and the college was in possession of the deanery by 1454.[12] The change of masters made little difference in St Buryan. King's College was an absentee like previous deans, and continued to appoint prebendaries and chaplains to serve the parish, as they had done. There was a benefit for historians, however, since King's commissioned surveys of the deanery's revenues that remain in the

---

1 *Reg. Grandisson*, II, 820–1.

2 Ibid., II, 821.

3 Ibid., II, 824–5.

4 He had excommunicated de Maunte again by 1341, when he again asked the king to have him arrested for refusing to pay clerical taxation (C 85/76/35).

5 *Reg. Grandisson*, II, 73–4.

6 Ibid., I, 84–7, 267.

7 Cambridge, King's College, SBU/8.

8 Cambridge Univ. Lib., Ee.5.34; Anonymous, 'Part Register of St. Buryan College, *temp.* Dean Robt. Knollys, 1473–1485', *JRIC* 15 (1901–2), 86–96. A so-called 'chronicle' of St Buryan, preserved in BL, Harley 6600, ff. 2v–15r, and transcribed in BL, Harley MS 7048, pp. 343–5, and Lansdown 766, ff. 12v–15r, is a late-medieval compilation of documents from the bishops' registers and elsewhere relating to the dispute between the king and the bishop, without independent value.

9 Known names of prebendaries are listed in N. Orme, 'The Church and Clergy of St Buryan, *c*.1200–*c*.1574', *JRIC* (2006), 39–41. In addition Henry Merston exchanged the prebend of Rospannel with Robert Bolton on 28 June 1422 (York, Borthwick Institute, Reg. 18, f. 283r).

10 *Cal. Pat.* 1441–6, 390; King's College, SBU/1–2; *Parliament Rolls*, XI, 449.

11 The crown may have regarded the deanery as alien because the crown had briefly taken over its possessions in 1337 when the dean, John de Maunte, was a Frenchman (below, p. 167).

12 *BRUC*, 555–6; King's College, Ledger Books, KCAR/3/3/1, f.

college archives. The fullest of these, which dates from about September 1454, estimated the gross income at £70 4s. 0d. This consisted of the 'great tithes' of corn, worth £36 18s. 3d., the 'small tithes' of other produce especially fish (£16 4s. 8d.), rents from the land belonging to the deanery (£8 13s. 11d.), and miscellaneous revenues such as mortuaries and offerings (£8 7s. 2d.). Charges on the deanery totalled £23 5s. 4d., chiefly made up by the salaries of four chaplains and by the fees paid to the steward of the dean's court and the official of his ecclesiastical jurisdiction, leaving a net income of £46 18s. 8d.[1]

By 1458 King's was leasing the revenues of St Buryan for an annual rent of £38,[2] but it did not enjoy this rent for very long. Henry VI was deposed in March 1461, and much of the property that he had given to King's and its sister foundation, Eton College, was restored to its former possessors. The next king, Edward IV, reappropriated the patronage of the deanery of St Buryan, and appointed a new dean, Robert Knolles, on 14 November 1462.[3] Knolles incurred charges of neglecting his obligations as dean. In July 1473 Edward IV commissioned five canon lawyers, some of whom were Cornish clergy, to visit St Buryan, enquire into defects and waste of its property caused by the negligence of the deans, and make reforms. It was alleged that the ministers and officers were men of dissolute life, and that the resources of the foundation were being misapplied. The commission was revoked in December of the same year for reasons that remain mysterious,[4] but between 1474 and 1480 three parishioners of St Buryan, including two members of the Boscawen family, petitioned the chancellor of England for redress against Knolles, claiming that he had allowed the chancels of St Buryan and its dependent churches to become ruinous and had failed to provide books and ornaments.[5] Knolles, as we shall see, countered with his own claims about the irresponsibility of the parishioners.

The deans of the 14th and early 15th centuries resembled their predecessors in gaining the office through the favour of the king or the duke of Cornwall, often being their administrators or clergy. Matthew and John de Maunte were both Frenchmen, the former being chaplain of Queen Margaret of France, the second wife of Edward I. John, who was presumably Matthew's relative, encountered problems from his nationality during the Hundred Years War. He suffered sequestration of his revenues in the mid 1320s, and in August 1337 he was briefly replaced as dean on the grounds of being an alien before he was restored in November in consideration of his long tenure and residence in England.[6] Grandisson stated on one occasion that John did not reside in Exeter diocese, and on another that he sometimes did so in Cornwall and sometimes elsewhere.[7] The deans after John were Englishmen with numerous benefices and widely scattered interests in the Church. Nicholas Slake, a close associate of Richard II, was dean of St Stephen's Chapel (Westminster), and his successor William Lochard was a canon of Hereford Cathedral and of other churches. In September 1438 Lochard's successor Adam Moleyns, clerk of the king's council, complained that Lochard had dilapidated and wasted the deanery, and the sheriff of Cornwall was ordered to inquire into the matter.[8] Yet Lochard at least regarded the saint of the church as his patroness, and left £10 in his will to his poor parishioners of St Buryan, St Levan, and Sennen.[9] By 1484 the crown had adopted the practice of granting the next presentation to the deanery as a favour to courtiers or as a means of raising money, which opened the post to men with more varied connections.[10] There was a strong link between St Buryan and Exeter Cathedral from the mid 15th to the early 16th centuries. Dean Stukeley of St Buryan (1439–45) was archdeacon of Exeter, Dean Ryse (1509–22) was cathedral treasurer, and Dean Knolles (1462–85) conferred prebends on several members of the cathedral chapter.[11] Prebendaries, like deans, usually held more than one benefice and had concerns outside Cornwall. Neither category of clergy had much incentive to visit so remote a church, whose revenues they could lease in return for money. When the antiquary John Leland visited Cornwall in about 1533, he wrote that the dean and prebendaries 'almost be nether [i.e. none of them] there'.[12]

Little survives about the history of the collegiate church of St Buryan as opposed to that of its senior clergy. The church building, in about the 12th century, appears to have been a substantial Norman structure, chiefly represented today by two round arches and a pillar built into the north wall of the chancel.[13] This points to the presence of a north chancel aisle or chapel besides the chancel and nave. The whole building was reconstructed on an ample scale, probably in the early

---

1 King's College, SBU/4–9, SMM/9.
2 King's College, SMM/7.
3 *Cal. Pat.* 1461–7, 73.
4 *Cal. Pat.* 1467–77, 427; 'Part Register of St. Buryan College', 94–6.
5 TNA, C 1/66/269: a fragmentary and faded document.
6 *Cal. Memoranda Rolls* 1326–7, 78–9; *Cal. Pat.* 1334–8, 492; *Cal. Close* 1337–9, 211; and TNA, E 106/9/30 (a royal valuation of the deanery in 1337).
7 *Reg. Grandisson*, I, 53, 59.
8 *Cal. Pat.* 1436–41, 268.
9 N. Orme (ed.), *Cornish Wills 1342–1540*, DCRS new ser. 50 (2007), 203.
10 Grants of this kind were made in 1484, 1485, 1529, and 1536 (BL, Harley 433, f. 101r; *Cal. Pat.* 1485–94, 112; *Parliament Rolls*, XV, 253; *L&P Hen. VIII*, III(1), 2436; XI, 489).
11 Knolles's Exeter appointments included John Combe, John Dunmow, Nicholas Gosse, Owen Lloyd, William Sylke, and William Wagett ('Part Register of St. Buryan College', 86–91; *BRUO*, I, 473, 606; II, 795, 1153–4; III, 1701–2, 1954).
12 J. Leland, *Itinerary*, ed. L. Toulmin Smith (1907–10), I, 319.
13 The arches suggest either early chancel aisles or a north chancel chapel.

16th century. No circumstances of this event are recorded, but it must have involved cooperation between the dean and the parishioners, possibly under Dean Ryse (occurs 1509–22 and probably in office for longer) who lived in Exeter. The new structure, chiefly built of ashlar cut from local granite moor-stone (a prestige material at the time), included a west tower, porch, nave, chancel, and two aisles extending from the west end of the nave almost to the east end of the chancel.[1] One aisle may have been the chapel of St Nicholas, mentioned in the 1470s as lying within the free chapel of St Buryan.[2] The magnificent rood screen, now in a restored state, probably dates from the period of the rebuilding. Daily services in the church were meant to be said by the dean and prebendaries, and four oak stalls may represent their seats. In practice these duties, and the care of the parish, were carried out by deputies. Grandisson, as we have seen, took oaths of obedience from five chaplains in 1336,[3] and by about 1454, the dean was responsible for appointing four parish clergy: a chaplain of St Buryan (paid £7 6s. 8d.), chaplains of St Levan and Sennen (£5 each), and the so-called 'king's priest' (£4).[4] The latter was a chantry priest who said a daily mass for the soul of Æthelstan and probably those of all the kings of England, a duty that was stated in 1546 to have been instituted by Æthelstan himself.[5] The chantry is first mentioned in about 1327, however, and is more likely to have been a recent creation as part of the campaign to make the church a royal chapel.[6] In 1546–8 the prebendaries were described as bound to pay three clerks to serve in the choir of St Buryan church; these men may have also acted as the parish clerks of the church and its two chapels of ease.[7] One medieval gravestone survives in the church, that of Clarice wife of Geoffrey of Boleit, and advertises an indulgence to those who prayed for her.[8] Leland described the church as still possessing a sanctuary and implies that it was an isolated building, adjoined by 'not above eight dwelling houses'.[9] The churchyard was used to bury not only the inhabitants of St Buryan but those of Sennen, until the pope permitted the latter to have a cemetery of their own in 1430.[10]

The church, being also a parish church, appears to have shared the spiritual and social characteristics of other such churches in Cornwall. Its parishioners were required to make monetary offerings four times a year: at Easter, St Buryan's Day (1 May), All Saints Day, and Christmas. The inhabitants of the two outlying communities had to do the same in their chapels, the day of the chapel's own saint replacing that of Buryan at Sennen and probably at St Levan. Further small offerings are recorded being made to the Holy Cross, the relics, and the image of Buryan, all in the parish church.[11] The Holy Cross, according to a legend recorded in the 16th century, was a splinter of wood from Christ's cross, another part of which was claimed by the parish church of Grade.[12] In 1458 James Lannargh of Sithney parish made small bequests to the Holy Cross at both St Buryan and Grade, implying that these relics attracted devotion beyond the immediate neighbourhood.[13] There are also mentions of four fraternities, devoted to SS Christopher, Eloy, James, and John; these may have been based in the parish church or at chapels elsewhere in the parish.[14] In 1478 Dean Knolles complained to the pope that the church contained many precious relics of saints, which he tried to keep in an honourable way and displayed for popular devotion on solemn days and festivals. Certain clerks and laymen, on the other hand, desiring gain, took them away without leave and carried them round the diocese to unsuitable places, begging alms – a practice which the pope forbade at the dean's request.[15] This custom recalls that of taking the relics of St Piran around the parish of Perranzabuloe, and the practice of making parochial processions with relics at Rogationtide elsewhere in Cornwall.[16]

The economy and personnel of the church emerge clearly once more at the Reformation. In 1533 the dean, Thomas Baugh, leased the deanery to a relative of his, David Baugh, for eighty years at an annual rent of £53 6s. 8d.[17] Thomas continued to appoint prebendaries until as late as April 1548,[18] and on 5 June 1547 he arranged for the lease of 1533 to be confirmed by himself and his chapter under the chapter seal of the

---

1 J. D. Sedding, 'Notes on S. Buryan Church', *Transactions of the Exeter Diocesan Architectural Soc.* 6 (1861), 259–69. A 1539 map of the south coast of Cornwall shows the tower topped by a spire (BL, Cotton Aug. I.i.35, 36, 38, 39), as does the map described on p. 170.
2 C 1/66/269.
3 *Reg. Grandisson*, II, 820–1.
4 King's College, SMM/9.
5 TNA, E 301/15, ff. 54v–55r; printed in L. S. Snell, *Documents towards a History of the Reformation in Cornwall: vol. I, The Chantry Certificates for Cornwall* (c.1953), 13–14.
6 SC 8/33/1629.
7 E 301/15, ff. 54v–55r; E 301/9, m. 2d; Snell, *Chantry Certificates*, 13, 15.
8 First drawn by William Jones in 1700 (BL, Stowe 1023, f. 3r); cf. BL, Add. MS 29762, f. 20r, reproduced in D. Gilbert, *The Parochial History of Cornwall* (1838), I, 142.
9 Leland, *Itinerary*, ed. Toulmin Smith, I, 319.
10 *Cal. Papal Regs*, VIII, 173.
11 King's College, SBU/4, /6.
12 BL, Harley 2252, ff. 50v–51v; H. Jenner and T. Taylor, 'The Legend of the Church of the Holy Cross in Cornwall', *JRIC* 20 (1915–21), 295–309.
13 Orme (ed.), *Cornish Wills*, 82.
14 King's College, SBU/4, /6. There appears to have been a chapel of St Eloy in the parish (N. Orme, *The Saints of Cornwall* (2000), 105).
15 *Cal. Papal Regs*, XIII(2), 590–1.
16 Orme, *Saints of Cornwall*, 221–2, cf. 99, 217. The account does not identify the relics.
17 Duchy of Cornwall, E/6/1; TNA, C 3/26/20.
18 TNA, E 334/3, f. 14r, 120r; E 334/4, f. 6v.

collegiate church – a rare reference to a corporate meeting of the clergy and to the use of a common seal.[1] Comparable, but slightly different, estimates of the dean's revenues were reported to the *Valor Ecclesiasticus* (the royal valuation of church property) in 1535 and to chantry commissioners of Henry VIII and Edward VI in 1546 and 1548. The *Valor* distinguished what it called the annual revenue of the deanery from that of the rectory. The former included the secular income from rents of tenants and perquisites of courts, and totalled £9 15s. 11d. The latter consisted of the spiritual revenues, chiefly the greater and lesser tithes, which produced £48 12s. 0d., giving the dean a gross income of over £58.[2] He paid 13s. 4d. to James Gentill, dean of Crantock and Glasney, who exercised the dean's ecclesiastical jurisdiction, 20s. to Robert Vyvian, the steward of his lands, 13s. 4d. to his bailiff, and probably the wages of the four priests but they are not mentioned. The prebend of Rospannel was valued at £7 7s. 8d. per annum in 1535, Trethyn at £7, and the Small Prebend at £2.[3] In 1548 the chantry commissioners estimated the revenues of the collegiate church at similar levels.[4] The dean's temporalities were now reckoned as £9 14s. 1½d.[5] and his spiritual revenues as £54 1s. 0d., of which nearly £34 came from the great tithes. The prebendary of Rospannel received £7 6s. 8d., and his colleagues of Trethyn and the Small Prebend £6 19s. 4d. and £2 4s. 0d. respectively. Their incomes came from a mixture of rents, great tithes, small tithes, and offerings. The three parish chaplains were now paid £6 each, the chantry priest £5, and the three clerks £2 apiece.

In 1538 the crown considered granting St Buryan to Thomas Cranmer, archbishop of Canterbury, in exchange for Maidstone College (Kent), but nothing came of this plan.[6] The church retained its status until the spring of 1548 when it was dissolved, like most other collegiate churches, under the second Chantry Act of December 1547. Its property reverted to the crown, and pensions were awarded to the dean, the prebendaries, and the king's priest. The dean, Thomas Baugh, was allocated £25 17s. 4d., half of his stipend. He subsequently lived in London and died in the autumn of 1557; his will shows him to have been a man of conservative religious sympathies.[7] The three prebendaries received £7 6s. 0d., £6 12s. 0d., and £2, roughly similar sums to their stipends as valued in 1548.

The king's priest was pensioned with £4 10s. It then became necessary to consider what provision should be made for the parish. The chantry commissioners of 1546 had been told that about 1,050 people received communion in the church of St Buryan, and 400 each in each of the two chapels of St Levan and Sennen. Their successors in 1548 noted a total figure of 1,500. Since one became a communicant at puberty, these estimates (if correct) would imply a population in the jurisdiction of St Buryan, including children, of between about 2,200 and 2,700 at this time. The commissioners recommended that the parishioners' needs should be met by endowing three vicarages for the three churches, with stipends of £20 at St Buryan and £10 each at the other two. In the meantime it ordered the existing chaplains to remain in office with wages of £8 at the mother church and £6 10s. 0d. at each of the two chapels. The crown took control of all the property of the collegiate church, and on 21 July 1549 sold a number of named pieces of land, including those belonging to the prebends, to Sir Thomas Pomeroy.[8]

It proved more difficult to dispose of the tithes and the dean's endowments. Apart from the lease of the deanery to David Baugh, the crown itself in 1536 had granted the right to present a dean at the next vacancy to a group of three men,[9] who later sold it for £80 to Richard Gayer of Market Jew (now Marazion). The chantry commissioners of 1548 described Gayer as 'an ancient gentleman', and filed a request that his purchase should be respected.[10] In 1538 the advowson of the deanery itself had been granted to Charles Brandon, duke of Suffolk, in 1538, and this grant apparently remained in the Brandon family until 1566, when a division of property between the duke's heirs, led to one of them, William Stanley, Lord Mounteagle, securing a confirmation in his favour.[11] In 1556 William Gayer, Richard's son and heir, was engaged in pursuing the Gayer claim – he tried to register it with the bishop of Exeter[12] – and he seems to have succeeded in the end, since the incumbent of the deanery by about 1574 was a certain John Guyer whose surname is a likely variant of Gayer.[13] After the accession of Elizabeth I in 1558, however, a practice developed by which informers exposed what they alleged to be pieces of religious property that had been concealed from appropriation by the crown, and allegations of this kind were made

---

1 Duchy of Cornwall, E/6/1.

2 *Valor Eccl.* (Rec. Com. 1810–34), II, 395. This account talks of the rectory of St Levan as being appropriated to the dean, although St Levan seems usually to have been regarded as a chapelry of St Buryan.

3 For the acreages, see *Cal. Pat.* 1549–51, 104.

4 E 301/9, m. 2d; Snell, *Chantry Certificates*, 13–15; with more detailed evidence in Bodleian, MS Rawlinson D 363, ff. 263v–4v.

5 Divided into two sums: £1 9s. 6d. and £8 4s. 7½d.

6 *L&P Hen. VIII*, XII(1), 471.

7 Alias Williams. For his career see J. and J. A. Venn, *Alumni Cantabrigienses, Part I: to 1751* (1922), I, 110, and J. Le Neve, *Fasti Ecclesiae Anglicanae 1300–1541*, vol. V: *St Paul's London* (1963), 19; and for his will, PROB 11/39, ff. 212v–213r.

8 *Cal. Pat.* 1549–51, 104.

9 *L&P Hen. VIII*, XI, 489.

10 E 301/9, m. 2d; Snell, *Chantry Certificates*, 14. For Gayer (also Geyre and Gyer), see T. L. Stoate (ed.), *Cornwall Subsidies in the Reign of Henry VIII* (Almondsbury, 1985), p. 17; CRO, AR/3/554; and C 3/73/20.

11 *L&P Hen. VIII*, XII(2), 494; XIV(1), 261; *Cal. Pat.* 1560–3, 558.

12 DRO, Chanter XIX, f. 6v.

13 Below, p. 170 note 2. A John Gayre was instituted as rector of St Mawgan-in-Pydar in 1563.

against St Buryan. In 1573 the English crown leased the deanery, the two chapelries, and the tithes of the three former prebends to one Richard Senhouse for twenty-one years at an annual rent of £60 7s. 8½d., on the grounds that the properties had been concealed and that Senhouse was offering to recover them for the crown at his own cost, presumably through legal processes.[1]

The lease to Senhouse prompted a petition from the inhabitants of St Buryan to the court of the exchequer, probably in 1574, in which they asserted that the status of their parish and benefice had already been examined in the court and recognised by it. Despite that recognition, 'certain covetous persons' were attempting to unseat their incumbent by arguing that the benefice was a deanery or collegiate church. The inhabitants evidently feared that Guyer might not contest these claims, no doubt because he possessed only a life interest in the benefice. They therefore asked the exchequer officials to call the objectors into court to show cause why the previous judgment in favour of the parish should be set aside, and expressed their willingness to be represented at such a hearing and to abide by the result.[2] Their petition was accompanied by a map of the peninsula of west Penwith, depicting the church, sanctuary, and parish of St Buryan (Fig. 40). The map shows the boundaries of all the parishes of the area, drawn in a simple way, so as to emphasise the place of St Buryan as part of the normal parochial system, and is an unusual – perhaps even pioneering – piece of English cartography in its depiction of parish boundaries.[3]

The threat of 1573 to the church and its parish appears to have made no headway, and both survived this period with their ancient rights and possessions, although further litigation continued during the reign of Elizabeth I over the patronage of the deanery and to the right to lease its revenues.[4] In the end the deanery also avoided extinction, the titles 'dean' and 'deanery' (carefully avoided by the petitioners of the 1570s) came back into use, and the patronage eventually reverted to the duchy of Cornwall. The deans recovered most of the ancient revenues of their office (enlarged by the tithes of the prebends), their jurisdictional rights over the parish, and their duty merely to pay assistant priests to look after the parish church and the two chapels.[5] The clergy appointed to the deanery went on being absentees, usually with crown connections, except between the Restoration and 1707 when the deanery was held by the bishops of Exeter to enlarge their income.[6] It was abolished on the death of the last incumbent, the Hon. Fitzroy Stanhope, in 1864.[7] The church building remains.[8]

DEANS OF ST BURYAN TO 1559

Walter de Gray	res. c.20 Jan 1214[9]
Walter of St Omer	granted 7 Feb 1214[10]
William of St Aubin	coll. by 14 Dec 1220[11]
Arnold of Holland	inst. 11 July 1259[12]
Stephen Haym	inst. 26 May 1266[13]
John of Kirkeby	granted custody 21 Oct 1275 until 1 Apr 1276; occurs c.1277, perhaps till 1286[14]
William of Hambleton	inst. by 1300; res. by 8 Nov 1301[15]
Ralph of Manton	granted 8 Nov 1301, occurs 5 Sept 1302[16]
Matthew de Maunte	granted 10 March 1303; res. by 2 May 1318[17]
John de Maunte	granted 2 May 1318; depr. c.Aug 1337[18]
Thomas of Crosse	granted 17 Aug 1337[19]
John de Maunte	restored 8 Nov 1337; occurs 6 Feb 1343[20]
John of Hale	occurs 12 Jan 1349[21]
Richard of Wolveston	conf. 13 Oct 1349; occurs 2 July 1352[22]

---

1 *Calendar of Patent Rolls 1572–5*, p. 52.
2 TNA, SP 12/99, no. 58.
3 TNA, MPF 1/332, illustrated and discussed in Orme, 'Church and Clergy of St Buryan', 34–8.
4 e.g. TNA, C 2/Eliz/F8/25, C 3/26/20, and C 3/73/20.
5 On 19 June 1583 William Forthe compounded for paying first-fruits of the deanery of St Buryan and of all the prebends (TNA, E 334/10).
6 For the names of deans after the Reformation, see Oliver, *Monasticon*, 7, and Henderson, 'Ecclesiastical History', 59–60.
7 J. Polsue, *A Complete Parochial History of the County of Cornwall* (1867–72), I, 164.
8 For site information, see CCC, HER 28683.
9 *Rot. Litt. Pat.*, 111; he had also been archdeacon of Totnes and dean of Probus. The date 20 Jan was that of his election as bishop of Worcester; biography in *ODNB*.
10 Ibid., succeeding to his predecessor's three benefices.
11 He had been collated by the papal legate Pandulf; the date is the king's order to the sheriff to admit him (*Rot. Litt. Claus.*, I, 444). He was still alive in 1232 (*Cal. Pat. 1225–32*, 508).
12 *Reg. Bronescombe*, ed. Hingeston-Randolph, 167; ed. Robinson, I, 32–3. *Magister*.
13 *Reg. Bronescombe*, ed. Hingeston-Randolph, 167; ed. Robinson, II, 19.
14 *Reg. Bronescombe*, ed. Hingeston-Randolph, 167; ed. Robinson, II, 91; *Rot. Parl.*, I, 14. He was elected bishop of Ely on 26 July 1286; biography in *ODNB* s.n. 'John Kirkby'.
15 *Rot. Parl.*, I, 421; *Cal. Pat.* 1292–1301, 617–18; biography in *ODNB* s.n. 'William Hamilton'.
16 *Cal. Pat.* 1292–1301, 617–18; *Cal. Close* 1294–1302, 599.
17 *Cal. Pat.* 1301–7, 122; *Cal. Pat.* 1317–21, 140. Also known as Matthew Boileau.
18 *Cal. Pat.* 1317–21, 140. The deprivation is indicated by the presentation of Thomas of Crosse, which follows.
19 *Cal. Pat.* 1334–8, 492. The presentation was not effective for long, if at all, since John de Maunte was restored soon afterwards.
20 *Cal. Close* 1337–9, 211; *Cal. Pat.* 1343–5, 66, 74.
21 *Cal. Pat.* 1348–50, 226.
22 Ibid., 404 (a royal confirmation of a previous collation by Edward, prince of Wales); *Black Prince's Reg.* II, 34–5.

John Sancey, BCL	granted 12 Sept 1352; exch. c.21 June 1353[1]	Adam Moleyns, DCL	granted 25 Sept 1438; occurs 12 Dec 1438[7]
David Maynard	by exch. c.21 June 1353; order to induct 14 July 1353; died by Oct 1361[2]	Peter Stukeley, BCan&CL	occurs 19 June 1439, 11 Nov 1445; perhaps till death, shortly before May 1451[8]
Alan Stokes	granted 22 Oct 1361; re-granted 16 Apr 1381; died late in 1393[3]	The deanery was annexed to King's College, Cambridge between about 1451 and 1462.	
John Boor	granted 1 Jan 1394[4]	Robert Knolles, BCanL	granted 20 Nov 1462; occurs 12 Nov 1485[9]
Nicholas Slake	granted 1394, after 1 Jan; estate ratified 1 June 1400[5]	John Ryse, BCL	occurs c.June 1509, 1522; perhaps till death on 7 May 1531[10]
William Lochard	occurs 15 Feb 1410; estate ratified 24 Feb 1410; died by 25 Sept 1438[6]	Thomas Baugh alias Williams, DD	occurs 1 Aug 1533; pensioned spring 1548[11]

ST COLUMB MAJOR

ARUNDELL CHANTRY

The church of St Columb Major was the wealthiest benefice in medieval Cornwall that belonged to the patronage of a lay family, the Arundells of Lanherne. In 1291 the rector's income was inadequately estimated as £17 13s. 4d., and more accurately in 1535 as £53 6s. 8d.[12] The parish church (SW 9125 6365) was the favourite burial place of the Lanherne Arundells and was rebuilt on a lavish scale in the 15th century, partly with their help.[13] In 1428 Sir John Arundell (d. 1435) endowed a chantry of five priests in the parish church, the largest chantry founded in the county, located in a new chapel (still extant) on the south side of the chancel. Its foundation was linked with Sir John's arrangements for the endowment of his youngest son, Sir Thomas Arundell, the ancestor of the Tolverne branch of the family. On 24 March 1428 Sir John issued a private charter, later registered on the close roll of the royal chancery, by which he granted five Arundell manors in Cornwall (Bodbrane in Duloe, Pengwedna in Breage, Prospidnick in Sithney, Reperry in Lanivet, and Tolverne in Philleigh) to Sir Thomas and three other grantees (Sir John Herle, Thomas Henry, clerk, and John Tresithney).[14] Tolverne was intended to be Sir Thomas's inheritance, and the other manors were to support the costs of the chantry. The charter bound the grantees, within two years of Sir John's death, to maintain five chaplains and a clerk to serve them, one of the chaplains being named warden of the other four. Sir John stated his intention of building an aisle or chapel in the church of St Columb, called 'Arundell's chapel', where he would be buried and the chaplains would say their services. The priests were to be chosen by the grantees and eventually by the heirs of Sir Thomas Arundell. If his line failed, or if there was any neglect to appoint the chaplains, the estate was to revert to Sir John's elder son, Remfrey. Provision was made for the warden to receive a salary of £6 13s. 4d. per annum, the other chaplains £5 6s. 8d., and the clerk £2 13s. 4d. The grantees were to provide them with vestments, chalices, cruets, and books, and to pay £1 6s. 8d. per annum for bread, wine, and wax.

Legally the chantry remained a separate entity within

---

1 *Black Prince's Reg.* II, 38, 49; biography in *BRUO*, III, 1637.

2 *Black Prince's Reg.* II, 49, 51, 184

3 Ibid., 184; *Cal. Pat.* 1377–81, 615 (an apparently new grant, by the king); *Cal. Pat.* 1391–6, 349.

4 *Cal. Pat.* 1391–6, 349.

5 Ibid., 529; *Cal. Pat.* 1399–1401, 279

6 Lambeth Palace Library, Reg. Arundel, II, f. 97r (when ordained acolyte, as dean); *Cal. Pat.* 1408–13, 117; *Cal. Pat.* 1436–41, 203

7 *Cal. Pat.* 1436–41, 203, 268; possibly resigned on becoming a canon of Lincoln cathedral in March 1439; biography in *BRUO*, II, 1289–91, and *ODNB*.

8 *Cal. Papal Regs.* IX, 67; *Cal. Pat.* 1441–5, 390; J. Le Neve, *Fasti Ecclesiae Anglicanae 1300–1541*: VIII, *Bath and Wells*, ed. B. Jones (1964), 11, 78; biography in *BRUC*, 555–6.

9 *Cal. Pat.* 1461–7, 73; 'Part Register of St. Buryan College', 91; biography in *BRUO*, II, 1059–60.

10 *L&P Hen. VIII*, I(1), 244; T. L. Stoate (ed.), *The Cornish Military Survey 1522* (1987), 20; J. Le Neve, *Fasti Ecclesiae Anglicanae 1300–1541*, vol. IX: *Exeter Diocese*, ed. J. M. Horn (1964), 12.

11 Duchy of Cornwall, E/6/1; C 3/26/20; Bodleian, Rawl. D 363, f. 265v; biography in *BRUO*, IV, 32.

12 *Reg. Bronescombe*, ed. Hingeston-Randolph, 470; *Valor Eccl.* (Rec. Com. 1810–34), II, 400.

13 R. Carew, *The Survey of Cornwall* (1602, repr. 2004), f. 144r. On the history of the church and parish, see C. G. Henderson, *St. Columb Major Church & Parish, Cornwall* (1929, 1930); on the chantry, ibid., 38–45; and for site information on the church, CCC, HER 21607.

14 H. S. A. Fox and O. J. Padel (ed.), *The Cornish Lands of the Arundells of Lanherne*, DCRS new ser. 41 (2000), pp. xxii–xxiv; *Cal Close* 1429–35, 35–7; TNA, C 179/32 no 19.

the church. It did not involve the conversion of the church into a college, nor was it officially known as a college although, as we shall see, the word was used by local people apparently to describe the house in which the clergy lived. Sir John's foundation grant described in detail the daily work of the priests. They were to say the canonical hours, including matins and vespers, according to the use of Sarum, and to celebrate at least three masses at the altar in the chapel. One was to be a mass of the Virgin Mary, one of the Trinity or of requiem, and one the ordinary mass of the day. Twice a week the priests were to say the funeral services of *Placebo* and *Dirige*, and every day they were to repeat the psalm *De Profundis*, the Paternoster (Lord's Prayer), and other prayers around the founder's tomb. On the day of Sir John's death they were to keep his 'obit' or anniversary, singing *Placebo* and *Dirige* on the previous evening and celebrating a mass of requiem on the day itself. Every Sunday and festival day they were required to join the other clerical staff of St Columb Major in singing the daily services in the choir of the parish church. The prayers of the chantry were to be offered for the souls of Sir John Arundell, his wife Annora, his children, kinsfolk, and ancestors, as well as Ralph Soor and other people whose names were to be written on a little tablet or schedule set above the altar in the Arundell chapel. The chapel had been built by 18 April 1433, when Sir John made his will and requested burial 'in the middle of the new chapel annexed to the chancel of the church of St Columb Major'. He gave £20 to the 'new work' of the church bell-tower and the bells, and £6 13s. 4d. to Richard Clegher or another chaplain to celebrate a trental of masses of St Gregory for his soul.[1] A reference of 1484 shows that the chapel was dedicated to the Virgin Mary.[2] Sir John was duly buried there in 1435 beneath a memorial (not extant) that described him as 'formerly steward of the lord king, and patron of this church, who caused this chapel to be made'.[3]

The foundation document did not transfer the endowments to the chantry priests themselves but retained them in the hands of members of the Arundell family. Later in the 15th century John Arundell, Remfrey's son and the head of the elder line of the family, claimed that the manors should revert to him because the Tolverne branch was failing to maintain the chantry.[4] This reversion duly took place, but the four manors devoted to supporting the chantry were kept apart from the family's ordinary estate and had their own roll of rentals.[5] The history of the chantry remains obscure until the Reformation. It is not mentioned in the *Valor Ecclesiasticus*, the royal assessment of Church property in 1535, but a list of clergy in Exeter diocese in 1536–7 names Richard Vyvyan as the warden and identifies four other priests who were probably his colleagues.[6] In 1546 the first survey of chantries, by commissioners of Henry VIII, recorded that the institution still consisted of five priests, who each received £5 12s. out of the four manors of the endowment. The value of the ornaments and goods of the chantry was estimated at £1 15s. 4d.[7] By 1548, when the second survey of chantries was carried out by commissioners of Edward VI, there were four priests (one post being vacant) and a clerk. Their salaries were stated to be what they were in the foundation charter: £6 13s. 4d. for the warden, £5 6s. 8d. for the other priests, and £2 13s. 4d. for the clerk, the chantry ornaments being valued at £3. The warden reported that the income of the four manors had become insufficient to cover the costs of the chantry, and that the late Sir John Arundell (d. 1545) had been accustomed to make up the shortfall himself.[8] No schooling, preaching, or poor relief were provided.

The chantry qualified for dissolution under the second Chantry Act of 1547, and pensions were awarded to the staff: £6 to the warden, £5 to each chaplain, and £2 13s. 4d. to the clerk.[9] It came to an end, as did all chantries, in the spring of 1548, but the Arundells argued that since they had retained the endowments, the crown was entitled to confiscate only the income that had been applied to support the chantry. This led to lengthy legal challenges to the family's right of possession, which were not settled until the court of the Exchequer made a judgment in the Arundells' favour in 1628, in return for the payment to the crown of a sum of £30 10s. 11d. per annum. During this process, in 1604, two elderly witnesses described their memories of the chantry in the 1530s and 40s. Richard Hawke, aged 74, remembered there being five priests, and said that he had been at school under one of them. This was probably as a single pupil or at a private school, since the chantry had no official function of teaching. John Merryfield, aged 80, also recalled five priests and their clerk, and stated that he had sometimes deputised for the latter. His elder brother used to bring the priests' wages from Lanherne, and the priests would come to the Merryfields' house to receive them.[10] Both witnesses talked of the 'college of St Columb', which seems to refer to the house where the priests lived together, provided by the Arundells. This is said to have stood near the west end of the church, and to have been burnt

---

1 N. Orme (ed.), *Cornish Wills 1342–1540*, DCRS new ser. 50 (2007), 66–7.
2 Will of Richard Tomyowe of St Columb Major (ibid., 95).
3 Bodleian, Wood C 11, f. 46r–v. He died on 11 January 1435: writ of *diem clausit extremum* issued 21 January (*Cal. Fine* 1430–7, 215, 242).
4 Henderson, *St. Columb Major*, 40–1.
5 Fox and Padel (ed.), *Cornish Lands*, 143–5.

6 ECA, D&C 3688, f. 33r.
7 TNA, E 301/15, ff. 52v–53r, printed in L. S. Snell, *Documents towards a History of the Reformation in Cornwall: vol. I, The Chantry Certificates for Cornwall* (c.1953), 18.
8 E 301/9, m. 5; Snell, *Chantry Certificates*, 17–18.
9 E 301/10; Snell, *Chantry Certificates*, 16.
10 TNA, E 134/2 James I, Hilary, no. 7; Henderson, *St. Columb Major*, 41.

down in 1701.¹ The Arundell chapel survives in the parish church in a modified form.

Two other endowments for priests existed in St Columb Major church by 1548. One was for a 'stipendiary' celebrating at the altar of the Trinity in the chapel on the north side of the chancel, who received a stipend of £4 12s. from an endowment worth £6 4s. gross, from which £2 0s. 8d. was given to the poor and others.² The term 'stipendiary' often indicates a priest endowed or maintained by a guild, and the chapel and store of the Holy Trinity are mentioned in the will of Richard Tomyowe, merchant of St Columb Major, in 1484. He bequeathed money to the store and requested burial in the chapel, but he is unlikely to have been the sole author of the endowment.³ The other priest served a chantry in the Jesus chapel, located in the south transept. This was said to have been founded by Sir Emmanuel 'Esamus' and his wife Avice for a priest to sing mass in the chapel three times a week. The incumbent received the whole net income of its property which was £7 15s. 4d.⁴ Emmanuel Assanus, alias Suffianus, a knight of foreign origin, appears briefly in the history of St Columb Major in 1480, having married Joan, the widow of Richard Penpons, esquire, and settled at Tregoose in the parish.⁵ The crown dissolved both of these other endowments in 1548, and their priests were awarded pensions.⁶

WARDENS OF THE ARUNDELL CHANTRY

John Alyn	occurs 4 Nov 1486⁷
Richard Vyvyan	occurs 1536 × 1537⁸
Richard Payne	buried 9 March 1543⁹
John Lucow	occurs spring 1546; buried 3 Apr 1546¹⁰
Richard Nanskevell	occurs spring 1548¹¹

CRANTOCK

COLLEGIATE CHURCH

Crantock takes its name from Carantoc, the saint of the early monastery or minster at Crantock, a church also known in early times as *Langorroc* ('church-site of Carantoc') (SW 7904 6056).¹² The minster survived the Norman Conquest and is first documented in the Domesday survey of 1086, which states that its property was held by canons, indicating a group of clergy under some kind of rule. They possessed three hides of land minus two acres, and their land was traditionally exempt from taxation. The value of the land was 5s., but had been 40s. 'when the count took possession of the land';¹³ to this should be added the tithes of the parish, which did not fall within the concern of the Domesday survey.

The count referred to in the survey was Robert count of Mortain (d. 1090), who appropriated parts of the property of several churches in Cornwall, including Crantock.¹⁴ His son and successor William count of Mortain was later believed to have granted the church, along with three or four others in Cornwall, to the Cluniac priory of Montacute that he founded in Somerset. This would have been between 1090, when William succeeded his father, and 1106, when he forfeited his property in England and was imprisoned by Henry I. The evidence for the grant is contained in charters copied into the early 14th-century cartulary of Montacute, some of which appear to be reconstructions, but since William left no heir in England, there is no better candidate than himself.¹⁵ Montacute held Crantock until July 1236, when it surrendered its rights over this and a second Cornish church, Altarnun, to William Brewer, bishop of Exeter.¹⁶ The surrender was made in exchange for the bishop's permission to appropriate the tithes of five other churches in Exeter diocese belonging to Montacute.¹⁷

---

1 Ibid., 38, 43; P. Sheppard, *The Historic Towns of Cornwall* (1980), 41. For site information, see CCC, HER 21587.
2 E 301/9, m. 4d; Snell, *Chantry Certificates*, 16–17.
3 Orme (ed.), *Cornish Wills*, 95.
4 E 301/9, m. 4d; Snell, *Chantry Certificates*, 17.
5 *Cal. Pat.* 1476–85, 198; TNA, C 1/51/199, C 1/55/103.
6 Snell, *Chantry Certificates*, 16.
7 CRO, AR/3/32.
8 ECA, D&C 3688, f. 33r.
9 A. J. Jewers (ed.), *The Registers of the Parish of St. Columb Major, Cornwall, 1539 to 1780*, Harleian Society Publications, Register Section 6 (1881), 180. Payne headed a list of chaplains at the church in 1534 (TNA, 36/64) but is not mentioned among them in 1535–6 (D&C 3688, f. 33r).
10 Or Lycow (E 301/15, ff. 52v–53r; Snell, *Chantry Certificates*, 18; Jewers (ed.), *Registers of St. Columb Major*, 182).
11 E 301/9, m. 5; L. S. Snell, *The Chantry Certificates for Cornwall* (c. 1953), 16, 18.
12 On the earlier history of the minster, see above, pp. 128–9.
13 C. and F. Thorn (ed.), *Domesday Book*, vol. X: *Cornwall* (1979), 4/25.
14 B. Golding, 'Robert of Mortain', *Anglo-Norman Studies* 13 (1990), 19–44, especially 140–1.
15 Bodleian, Trinity College Oxford D 85, ff. 1r, 2r, 3r, 6r, 8r, 23r; T. S. Holmes (ed.), *Two Cartularies of the Augustinian Priory of Bruton and the Cluniac Priory of Montacute*, Somerset Record Soc. 8 (1894), 119–22, 124–6.
16 *Reg. Bronescombe*, ed. Hingeston-Randolph, 5.
17 F. Barlow (ed.), *English Episcopal Acta*, vol. XII: *Exeter 1186–1257* (1996), 251–2.

After this the patronage of Crantock church remained with the bishops of Exeter until the Reformation.

We know nothing about the internal history of Crantock church for over a hundred years after the Domesday survey. When it reappears in documents in the 13th century, its possessions seem to have been intact and it was still staffed by canons. Montacute Priory was a distant and rather weak house, and its involvement with Crantock may have centred on appointing the canons rather than appropriating their resources. A dean of the church is recorded in 1214 during Montacute's rule, as we shall see, and there is nothing to suggest that Bishop Brewer refounded the church as a college of canons after a period of closure.[1] Although he played an important part in the constitutional development of Exeter Cathedral,[2] he seems to have lacked interest in reforming the other ancient minsters of the diocese (such as St Buryan, Crediton, and Probus), and no statutes for their government survive from his reign. His motive for acquiring Crantock may have been to gain the right to appoint the canons, thereby increasing his stock of patronage in Cornwall. There were ten canons by 1291, compared with six at Probus and four at St Buryan, perhaps reflecting the larger endowment of land in Crantock's case. At the papal taxation of 1291 the income of the church was valued at £21 3s. 4d., a sum that was understated by as much as a half.[3]

The fullest account of the church's endowments and income, which dates from 1548, states that its lands lay at Langurrow (a version of the ancient name of the church, probably in its immediate vicinity), at Vosporth south-east of the church, and at St Columb Minor. Each canon had a prebend or endowment, causing the canons to be often known as prebendaries, and every prebend included a small part of the church's land, usually of 15 acres or less. In one case two men took half shares of a single part. The canons each received a further share of the great (or grain) tithes of the parish, which included the modern parishes of Crantock and St Columb Minor, the church of the latter being a chapel dependent on Crantock church.[4] As was usual in minster churches the division of revenues was not equal, and the incomes of the prebends, as estimated in 1291, varied from £3 to £1 10s. 0d., with an additional tiny prebend of 6s. 8d. Most of the canons' prebends had no names and were identified by reference to the clerics who currently held them or who had last held them, not, as in some other churches, by the names of the places from which the prebends drew their revenues. This may have been because the places concerned were small or intricately divided. An exception to this rule was the prebend called, by 1359, St Columb Minor, whose occupant was responsible for maintaining the chapel there and presumably held the church land nearby.[5]

The canons formed a community, at least in the 13th century, and we hear of two dignitaries: a dean in 1214 and a precentor in 1258.[6] Most of our knowledge relates to the canons, 31 of whom are mentioned in the earliest two registers of the bishops of Exeter which survive from 1258 to 1288. Some of the those concerned are not recorded holding other benefices and may have resided at Crantock, but others were men of some importance, including John of Esse, a bishop's official, Geoffrey of Bisimano, archdeacon of Cornwall, and Michael of Northamtone, a clerk of Richard earl of Cornwall. These people can have spent little time at the church, and their appointments were primarily rewards from the bishop. The earliest mention of the dean arises from a dispute before the king's justices in the spring of 1214 as to whether five acres of land at Treago in the parish belonged 'to the deanery of Hugh of Wells of *Langero* [i.e. Crantock] or to the lay fee of Terri fitz Simon'. A later document relating to the case differs in calling Hugh 'archdeacon of Bath' and Terri 'dean of *Langero*', suggesting that the two men were either claimants to the office or successive occupants of it.[7] The post appears again in 1250 when Henry III prohibited the dean of Wells Cathedral from implementing a papal provision (or appointment) of a dean of Crantock, the king affirming that the prebends of Crantock lay in the gift of the crown when the bishopric of Exeter was vacant.[8] A third reference to the dean occurs in 1282 when the bishop ordered him to relax the sequestration of the revenues of one of the canons.[9] The dean of Crantock in this period was a less powerful figure than his counterparts at St Buryan and Probus, who had disproportionately large shares of the church income and appointed their fellow canons. The papal taxation records of 1291 do not mention a dean's portion at Crantock, and the church revenues there were shared more evenly among the canons. Moreover the bishop 'collated' or appointed the canons, and there is no record of the appointment of a dean before 1309. It may be that the office, up to that time, was based on seniority, election, or rotation.

The first known attempt to reform or develop the church was made by Bishop Quinil of Exeter through

---

1 As suggested by C. G. Henderson, 'The Ecclesiastical History of the 109 Parishes of West Cornwall', *JRIC* new ser. 2 (1953–6), 106–21 at 107.

2 A. M. Erskine, 'Bishop Briwere and the Reorganization of the Chapter of Exeter Cathedral', *TDA* 108 (1976), 159–71.

3 *Reg. Bronescombe*, ed. Hingeston-Randolph, 471.

4 Bodleian, Rawl. D 363, ff. 250r–1v. Fields called Vosporth are mentioned in the 19th-century tithe apportionment, south of Trevella (CRO, TA/40 nos. 186–93).

5 *Cal. Papal Pets*, I, 311, 339; *Cal. Pat.* 1247–58, 611.

6 *Cur. Reg.* 1213–15, 55; *Cal. Pat.* 1247–58, 611.

7 *Cur. Reg.* 1213–15, 55, 65.

8 *Close Rolls* 1247–51, 351–2. It is difficult to understand this intervention, since the bishopric of Exeter had not been vacant since 1245.

9 *Reg. Bronescombe*, ed. Hingeston-Randolph, 371.

the creation of an office of vicar of the parish. Crantock was a parish church, as well as a college of clergy, but the previous arrangements for providing pastoral care are unclear: they may have been the responsibility of the dean, or of vicars hired by the canons. In 1284 Quinil appointed Master Robert of Marsh (*Marisco*) as vicar of Crantock and of the chapel of St Columb Minor, and made arrangements for his duties and stipend. The vicar was evidently required to provide pastoral services at Crantock, and he was ordered to supply a chaplain for St Columb Minor at his own expense. His accommodation and stipend were provided by making them a charge on two of the prebends: those held by Nicholas of Brimmore and John of St Keran. The vicar and his successors were to occupy John's house and to receive the profits of the two prebends, in return for paying £4 per annum to each of the two canons concerned, who thereby acquired 'bursal' or monetary prebends.[1] This scheme did not work satisfactorily, probably because the vicar's two prebends produced less income than expected. In 1291 the two bursal canons are recorded as receiving only £2 each, and on 20 October 1309 Bishop Stapledon made a fresh arrangement, observing that the burden on the two prebends (i.e. the cost of the vicar and chaplain) was too great and left insufficient resources to enable their holders to reside at the church. He declared that the two canons had resigned their prebends into his hands and that, after consulting with the other clergy of Crantock and the canons of Exeter Cathedral, he had decided to establish a new officer to rule the church and care for the parish. This person was given the title of dean. He was to be collated by the bishop, and to be a literate man who was at least a deacon, in which case he was to become a priest at the next ordination. He was to swear to reside at Crantock for at least three quarters of the year, continuously or intermittently. All new canons were to take an oath of obedience to him, and he was to exercise the cure of souls in the parish – a cure not defined in Stapledon's ordinance but one that came to involve employing two chaplains to do parish duties at Crantock and St Columb Minor. The dean was to receive the income of the two prebends, as before, together with the offerings in the chapel of St Ambrusca in Crantock churchyard, from which he was to pay one bursal prebend of £4 in place of the previous two.[2]

Stapledon's reforms at Crantock were not only related to the pastoral care of the parish but to the state of the church itself. Visiting it on 15 March 1309, he found some of the canons absent, leading to a decline of worship and hospitality. Such a situation was common in minster churches of this type, where canonries and prebends were often given as rewards and their holders received their stipends irrespective of whether they resided. To counteract it Stapledon's reform of 1309 required all the canons to keep residence on the same terms as the canons of Exeter Cathedral: for at least thirty days and nights in each of the four terms of the year, a proportion of one third of the time. During that time they were to serve the church, in other words by attending the daily services, on pain of losing the income of their prebends. Only the holder of the £4 prebend was excused from residence. In 1315 the bishop made a further order about Crantock, stating that it was not to be subject either to the official in charge of the bishop's peculiar jurisdiction in Cornwall or to the archdeacon of Cornwall. This recognised it, in effect, as an independent religious house, subject to the bishop himself. The archdeacon, on the other hand, was to have power over the inhabitants of the parish, and the parish chaplains of Crantock and St Columb Minor were to appear before him when ecclesiastical business so required.[3] The order of 1315 also contains the earliest reference to vicars of Crantock alongside the dean and canons, meaning vicars choral who deputised for the canons, especially in saying the daily services. When they originated is unknown.

Stapledon's first dean, Henry of Trefeuwa, was evidently Cornish and is likely to have resided.[4] The next known dean (apart from a very brief incumbent) was William Skyn(n)ard, who first comes to notice in 1322 when he was described as 'called "of Lelant [*Lananta*]", priest', evidently coming from a family in that locality.[5] He may have been dean at this date, although not so described, since the record relates to his being excommunicated by Stapledon and reported to the crown for arrest for refusing to accept the judgment of the Church in a legal case brought by Peter of Honeton, one of the Crantock canons. Skynard was more than a local Cornish priest since, as we shall see, he acquired influential connections and two records of the 1330s refer to him as 'Master', as if he were a university graduate.[6] These connections availed him little, however, when the masterful Bishop Grandisson began to take an interest in Crantock in 1328, having been bishop for less than two months and learnt (so he said) that the college's affairs were badly ordered. On 17 July he wrote to the dean (unnamed, but probably Skynard) that some of the canons were failing to reside

---

1 Ibid. Bursal prebends had been introduced at Crediton church in 1272 (*Reg. Bronescombe*, ed. Hingeston-Randolph, 60–2; ed. Robinson, II, 58–9).

2 ECA, D&C 1384; G. Oliver, *Monasticon Dioecesis Exoniensis* (1846), 56–8.

3 *Reg. Stapeldon*, 328–9.

4 He is probably the 'Sir H., dean of Crantock' who owned a manuscript of Peter Comestor that later passed to the Franciscan friars of Bodmin (above, p. 158).

5 For a later Skynard of Lelant, see *Year Books of Richard II: 11 Richard II, 1387–8*, ed. I. D. Thornley (1937), 95, and for other clergy of the same name, TNA, C 85/75/62; *Reg. Stapeldon*, 264; and *Cal. Pat.* 1348–50, 61.

6 *Cal. Pat.* 1330–4, 107; *Reg. Grandisson*, II, 737.

and had leased their prebends and houses to laymen without the bishop's permission. Lay people were living in the houses around the church, taverns were operating inside them, and secular traffic and animals were brought in and out of the precincts.

The bishop instructed the dean to inquire into these matters and into the goods of canons who had left or died, goods that should have been applied to the repair of the church but had been dissipated. Culpable people were to be cited before the bishop or his official.[1] On 20 September the bishop wrote afresh to the dean, naming fourteen people of the parish, chiefly laity, who had been excommunicated for contumacy: probably in refusing to appear at or to obey the judgment of the Church courts. The dean was told to pronounce their excommunication in public and to cite them to appear before the bishop.[2] By 27 October it was manifest to Grandisson that Skynard was far from innocent himself. He was being sued for damages by two of the canons, and Grandisson ordered the sequestration of his goods.[3] Skynard buttressed his position on 21 March 1329 by securing a royal grant that he might hold his benefice for life, and he later became a collector of papal taxation in the west of England.[4] In this role he was accused of extortions as a tax-collector, arresting even the executors of the dead and dragging them away to come to terms, while failing to contribute his own share of the tax.[5] On 12 January 1331 Grandisson asked the king to arrest Skynard, 'pretending himself to be dean', whom he had excommunicated for refusing to pay tax himself and presumably had suspended from office.[6]

Skynard was still acting as dean in the following July, when the bishop charged him with misappropriating goods at Crantock,[7] but he was forced out soon afterwards and went to be rector of the parish of St Mary Magdalene (Canterbury).[8] Grandisson may have achieved this result by enrolling the help of the French papal nuncio, Ithier de Concorès, to whom he granted the next presentation to the deanery on 20 October.[9] Ithier nominated his fellow countryman Bernard de Mayrinhac from the diocese of Cahors, and the bishop collated him on 28 April 1332.[10] Mayrinhac's tenure was neither long nor, it seems, satisfactory. When it ended, probably in the first half of 1336, Grandisson was able to appoint a nominee of his own. His choice was William of Lunday, whom he praised as being pure of life and devoted to the Church. Collating him on 8 October, the bishop bemoaned the damage that had been caused to the office of dean by the carelessness and neglect of its last occupant (Mayrinhac) and his predecessor (Skynard). Grandisson's first charge to Lunday was to improve the capabilities of the vicars choral, who must not be admitted unless they were literate, expert in singing, and ordained as priests.[11] Next, on 28 November, he wrote to Lunday reviving the issue of non-residence by the canons, some of whom were still absent from Crantock despite Stapledon's ordinance. Lunday was to proclaim in the church that all the canons should return there within thirty days and keep their residence personally; names of defaulters were to be sent to the bishop.[12] It is not clear how effective such measures were in the short term, but in the long term, here as elsewhere, the battle to enforce residence was gradually lost. By 1348 Grandisson was writing to the dean that the canons were once more leasing their houses to lay people (a sign of non-residence), and ordering the removal of the occupants. No one was to lease a prebend in future without the bishop's permission.[13]

In 1348–9 the Black Death came to England. The resulting depopulation led to a greater choice of benefices for clergy and to rises in wages and prices. All over the Church it became more difficult to fill lowly paid posts for chaplains and vicars choral, and Grandisson responded by making new arrangements for the vicars of Crantock in an ordinance issued on 1 February 1352. Hitherto, he noted, there had been seven vicars, who had received the small tithes of the prebends: in other words all tithes of animals and of crops other than the great tithes of grain. This arrangement shows that the vicars were not simply hired by the canons individually, but formed an established group with recognised perquisites.[14] Nowadays, the bishop observed, this level of support was inadequate, and insufficient people were being recruited to maintain daily services. With the consent of the dean and five of the canons, he reduced the number of vicars to four and gave their appointment to the dean. Next he turned to the issue of residence by the canons. He admitted for the first time that this was difficult for those who worked in his service, and gave them the option of not residing in return for paying a tax, the amount of which was set for each prebend individually, ranging from 4s. per annum to 30s. If those absent failed to pay, the income of their prebends was to be sequestrated. The money raised by the tax was

---

1 *Reg. Grandisson*, I, 359–60.
2 Ibid., I, 400.
3 Ibid., I, 420–1, 426, 464–5.
4 *Cal. Pat.* 1327–30, 378; *Cal. Pat.* 1330–4, 107.
5 *The Register of Ralph of Shrewsbury, Bishop of Bath and Wells*, ed. T. S. Holmes, vol. I, Somerset Record Soc. 9 (1896), 267; *Reg. Grandisson*, I, 596.
6 *Reg. Grandisson*, I, 596.
7 Ibid., II, 622–3.
8 Ibid., II, 736–7.
9 Ibid., II, 636.
10 Ibid., III, 1287–8. Cahors, Concorès, and Mayrinhac are all in the département of Lot.
11 Ibid., II, 828.
12 Ibid., II, 833–4.
13 Ibid., II, 1039–40.
14 The number seven, as compared with ten canons, probably reflects the fact that the dean was assisted by a chaplain rather than a vicar, one prebend was bursal, and another was very small in value.

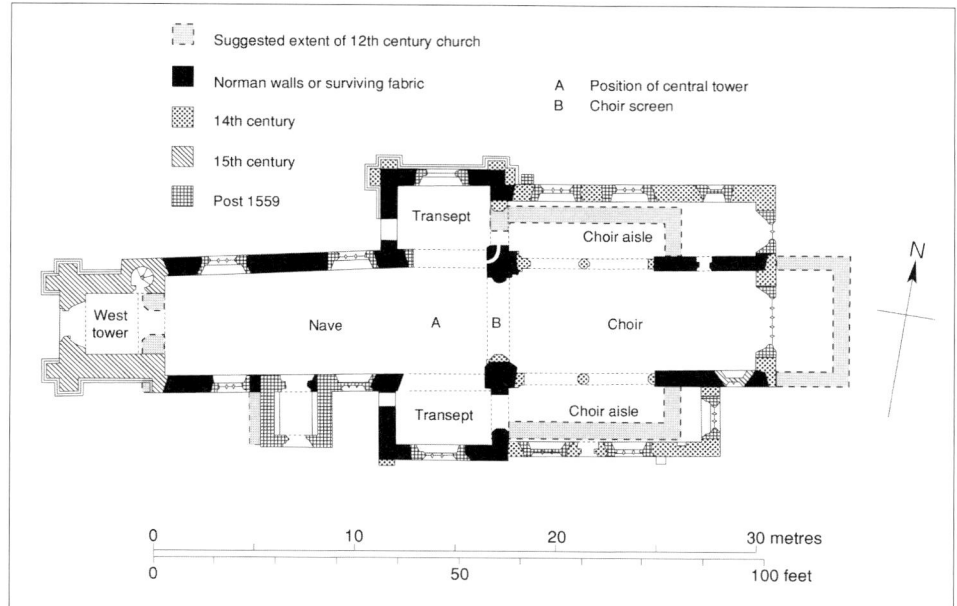

FIG 47. Crantock Collegiate Church, plan.

designated to maintain two clerks and two or three boys to help the vicars say the daily services. The clerks were to receive 16s. per annum, the boys 8s., and they were all to live with the vicars, implying residence in a common house with common meals. This reform effectively changed the character of Crantock from a minster church staffed by canons to a small late-medieval college with a dean, four vicars, clerks, and boys.[1] Otherwise the campaign to enforce residence was abandoned. In 1381 only the dean, two canons, three priests, and two clerks paid poll-tax,[2] and when the commissary of the archbishop of Canterbury formally visited Crantock on 14 May 1384, he noted that the dean was poor and that 'there is not any canon resident there'.[3]

Grandisson's reforms lasted, at least in outline, until the Reformation, and the attention of his successors turned to the state of the building rather than that of its clergy. Crantock church, in the 12th and 13th centuries, appears to have possessed a choir with (probably narrow) aisles, transepts, a central tower, a nave without aisles, and a west tower (Fig. 47). The fabric of the transepts survives largely in its original form, as does the lower masonry of the Norman crossing piers. The choir originally stretched 2.7 metres (9 feet) further east than at present.[4] A large burial ground surrounded the church, and 17th-century folklore spoke of seven neighbouring churches going in procession to the ground with their relics,[5] but no special rights of sanctuary are recorded as existed at St Buryan and Probus. In 1375 Bishop Brantingham visited the church and found it in need of repair. Work was subsequently done on the choir aisles at the expense of the canons, and the surviving wider choir aisles may date from this time. A dispute arose with the parishioners about the responsibility of maintaining the central tower, causing the bishop to rule in May 1377 that the parishioners should contribute to its repair and complete the work by November.[6] The tower remained a concern, however, and in 1393 Brantingham bequeathed £20 to restore it as well as giving the church a vestment and two service-books.[7] By 1412 the tower had fallen, causing damage to the nave, and Bishop Stafford granted an indulgence to all who donated to the repair of the nave, noting that the local community was too poor to support the work.[8] In 1417 he ordered the dean to repair the choir and to raise the required money; the canons were to contribute and the bishop was to be told of any defaulters.[9] This process may have involved the shortening of the choir, which is known to have been abridged by nine feet (2.7 metres). The central tower was never rebuilt, and the west tower was developed

1 *Reg. Grandisson*, II, 1112–14.
2 TNA, E 179/24/5.
3 Lambeth Palace Library, Reg. Courtenay, f. 116r. In 1437 and 1455 only vicars choral were available to induct new deans (*Reg. Lacy*, ed. Hingeston-Randolph, I, 223, 395–6).
4 E. H. Sedding, *Norman Architecture in Cornwall* (1909), 68–72.
5 N. Roscarrock, *Lives of the Saints: Cornwall and Devon*, ed. N. Orme, DCRS new ser. 35 (1992), 66. The churchyard contains a stone coffin from the church or churchyard, which may relate to one of the clergy of the church.
6 *Reg. Brantyngham*, I, 379–80; II, 891.
7 Ibid., II, 745; N. Orme (ed.), *Cornish Wills 1342–1540*, DCRS new ser. 50 (2007), 199. Canon Roger Bolter bequeathed £1 6s. 8d. in 1435 to repair the church's ornaments (Orme (ed.), *Cornish Wills*, 202).
8 *Reg. Stafford*, 74.
9 Ibid.

FIG 48. *The collegiate church of Crantock. Originally the church had a central tower and a longer choir with narrow choir aisles. The tower fell in the early 15th century, a western tower was developed instead, the choir was shortened, and its aisles widened.*

instead, leaving the church in its modern form with a porch, nave, transepts, choir, and choir aisles. The north aisle extends to be level with the east wall of the chancel, but the south aisle is slightly shorter. The wagon roofs over the nave and chancel may date from the 15th century (Figs. 47–8).[1]

Daily services would have been said in the choir by the clergy, and those who were priests are likely to have celebrated some daily masses. The church, by the 15th century, probably contained two altars for this purpose in the choir aisles and possible others in the transepts, but nothing is recorded about them or their dedications. Nor is anything known of the cult of the saint, Carantoc, who was also venerated in Somerset and south Wales.[2] The deans of the later Middle Ages mostly resembled the rectors and vicars of Cornwall in their careers and probably in their birth and attainments, and several had Cornish surnames. It is not clear why a number of men invaded the church in 1382 and violently took away the dean and other ministers while divine service was in progress, but the outrage caused the bishop to order the offenders to be excommunicated in every parish church in Cornwall.[3]

In 1492 a visitation of the church was held by the archbishop of Canterbury. This resulted in the dean, John Edmund, being told to keep continual residence according to the statutes, implying that he had not complied with the rules in this matter. The canons were listed, but it is not stated how many of them resided. There were still four vicars but only one clerk and no boys – deficiencies that were ordered to be corrected.[4] Polyphonic music became popular in collegiate churches and monasteries during the 15th century, requiring the services of boys as well as adults, but Crantock's small staff and the absence of mentions of boys in and after 1492 make it uncertain whether the college supported such music.

John Leland, who first visited Cornwall in about 1533, passed by Crantock but noted it simply as 'a little house of canons secular'.[5] In 1534 the dean, James Gentill, and one canon, Richard Heynson, acknowledged Henry VIII as head of the English Church.[6] They were presumably the only senior clergy then resident, but neither can always have been so, since Gentill was also provost of Glasney College, Penryn, while Heynson held a post at Exeter Cathedral.[7] In the following year, the

1 The west tower is shown with four pinnacles at the topmost corners on a 1539 map of Cornwall, which otherwise depicts church towers conventionally (BL, Cotton Aug. I.i. 35, 36, 38, 39).
2 On the saint, see N. Orme, *The Saints of Cornwall* (2000), 83–5.
3 *Reg. Brantyngham*, I, 466.

4 *Reg. Morton, Canterbury*, II, 79–80.
5 J. Leland, *Itinerary*, ed. L. Toulmin Smith (1907–10), I, 317.
6 TNA, E 25/69/2, printed in *7th Deputy Keeper's Report* (1846), App. II, 299.
7 On Gentill, see below, p. 259, and on Heynson, N. Orme, *The Minor Clergy of Exeter Cathedral* (1979), 2, 12, 46.

royal survey of Church property known as the *Valor Ecclesiasticus* described the church as founded by William Warelwast, bishop of Exeter. It assessed Gentill's income at £21 9s., Heynson's at £12, and those of the other canons at between £6 and £1 6s. 8d. The four vicars received £5 each.[1] Crantock duly shared the fate of other collegiate churches in being surveyed by the chantry commissioners in 1546 and 1548, and being suppressed in the spring of the latter year. The commissioners of 1546 estimated the total income of the college at £94 5s. 1d., and their successors in 1548 at £94 11s. 9d.[2] During the latter year detailed information was collected about the college's revenues and stipends. The dean, Christopher Saunders, was estimated to receive rents worth £2 13s. 4d., two prebends worth £12, and some great tithes worth £27 6s. 8d., totalling £42, so that the office could no longer be termed a poor one. The stipends of the eight canons fell between £12 and about £1, each made up of a small amount of rent from their portion of land and a larger sum from the great tithes. Thirty-five years previously the dean had undertaken to collect the small tithes for the vicars choral and to pay them salaries. This enabled him to make a slight additional profit, since the small tithes produced £27 6s. 8d. while the salaries cost only £25.

By 1548 the posts of the vicars choral had been combined with those of the parish chaplains, so that one vicar doubled as curate of Crantock and a second likewise of St Columb Minor, while a third celebrated mass in the college and the fourth was clerk of the college (in effect parish clerk). Their salaries were £8, £7, £6, and £4 respectively. No report of the Reformation period refers to any other clerks or to boys, and no schooling, preaching, or almsgiving was reported. The chantry commissioners of 1548 awarded a pension of £12 6s. 11d. to the dean, and the canons received sums similar to or scaled down from their former stipends. The commissioners praised Saunders as learned and fit to be vicar or curate of the parish, and proposed that vicarages should be endowed at Crantock and St Columb Minor with stipends of £23 11s. 8d. and £10. In the meantime an order was given that the existing curates should continue to receive £8 to work at Crantock and £7 at St Columb Minor. The third vicar was given a pension of £5, and the fourth, the clerk, who is not mentioned, probably remained in office. The proposed endowments were never made, and the parish was left only with the two poorly paid curates.

On 1 August 1550 the crown sold the college lands as part of a large collection of religious property to two gentlemen of Yorkshire: Silvester Leigh of Pontefract and Leonard Bate of Wakefield.[3] It retained the tithes for longer, but on 24 March 1612 James I granted them to Francis Morice and Francis Phelips, gentlemen. The income of the tithes was then valued at £60, and the grantees were required to pay the two curates the rates laid down in 1548.[4] Nothing of the college survives on the site except for the church.[5] Grandisson's ordinance of 1352 is stated to have been sealed with the seal of the dean and chapter of Crantock, but the only recorded seal impression appears to belong to a private seal of the dean, of 14th-century date. It is said to have shown a mitred bishop, presumably representing St Carantoc, holding a cross in his left hand while he delivered a blessing with his right.[6]

DEANS OF CRANTOCK

Terri fitz Simon	occurs spring 1214[7]
Hugh of Wells	occurs spring 1214[8]
Henry of Trefeuwa	coll. 20 Oct 1309; vac. by 9 May 1311[9]
John of Pultone	coll. 22 Sept 1311; exch. 1 Nov 1311[10]
Henry of Trefeuwa	inst. by exchange 1 Nov 1311[11]
William Skynard	occurs 27 Oct 1328, 27 July 1331[12]
Bernard de Mayrinhac	coll. 28 Apr 1332; occurs 12 Sept 1334[13]
William of Lunday	adm. in commendam 2 Aug 1336; coll. 7 Oct 1336[14]
Siger of London	coll. 2 Oct 1337; exchanged 4 Nov 1337[15]
John of Nortone	inst. by exchange 4 Nov 1337; died by 19 March 1347[16]

---

1 *Valor. Eccl.* (Rec. Com. 1810–34), II, 399. It is difficult to see why Warelwast (bishop 1107–37, while Crantock belonged to Montacute Priory) was regarded as founder. Was this a mistake for William Brewer?

2 TNA, E 301/15, ff. 52v–53r; E 301/9, m. 2, printed in L. S. Snell, *Documents towards a History of the Reformation in Cornwall*: vol. I, *The Chantry Certificates for Cornwall* (c.1953), 19–21. Further detailed evidence of great value, dating from 1548, occurs in Bodleian, Rawl. D 363, ff. 250r–1v. There are minor discrepancies between the statistics in the chantry certificate of 1548 and those in the Rawlinson manuscript.

3 *Cal. Pat.* 1549–51, 260, 262.

4 Oliver, *Monasticon*, 54.

5 For site information, see CCC, HER 25368, 25368.2.

6 *Catalogue of Seals in the Dept. of Manuscripts, British Museum*, vol. I (1887), 729, no. 3956: presumably the same as the seal described by Oliver, *Monasticon*, 54. The inscription was not fully legible, but seems to have included the Latin word *privatum* ('private') rather than *prepositi* ('provost'), as thought by Oliver, the latter word not being a title of the dean of Crantock.

7 *Cur. Reg.* 1213–15, 55, 65.

8 Ibid., 55, 65. For his career, see J. Le Neve, *Fasti Ecclesiae Anglicanae 1066–1300*: VII, *Bath and Wells*, ed. D. E. Greenway (2001), 29.

9 *Reg. Stapeldon*, 249, 252.

10 Ibid., 249.

11 Ibid.

12 *Reg. Grandisson*, I, 420–1; II, 622–3.

13 Ibid., III, 1287–8; II, 764.

14 Ibid., II, 822; III, 1313–14.

15 Ibid., III, 1318–19.

16 Ibid., III, 1319, 1357.

Thomas atte Brigge	coll. 19 March 1347[1]	John Kelly	coll. 16 Jan 1430; exch. 13 Aug 1437[10]
William Jaune, alias of Trebursy	coll. 30 June 1348, occurs 4 June 1349[2]	John Carbura	inst. by exchange 13 Aug 1437; res. by 6 Aug 1455[11]
William of Trevenwythe	occurs 1 Feb 1352[3]	John Michell, BCL.	coll. 6 Aug 1455; occurs 18 Apr 1477[12]
William	occurs 16 Jan 1372, 16 June 1382[4]	John Edmund	occurs 4 July 1492; res. by 14 March 1514[13]
Thomas Hendeman, DD	occurs 10 Dec 1390; exch. 25 Feb 1410[5]	Richard Carlyon	coll. 14 March 1514[14]
William Cullyng	papal reservation 20 July 1406[6]	James Gentill, BCanL.	occurs 23 Aug 1534; died by 23 Apr 1546[15]
John Soor	inst. by exchange 25 Feb 1410; res. by 27 July 1414[7]	Christopher Saunders	comp. 20 May 1546; coll. 6 Sept 1546; till surrender, spring 1548[16]
John Waryn, BCL	coll. 27 July 1414; res. by 11 May 1418[8]		
William Talkarn, MA	coll. 11 May 1418; died by 16 Jan 1430[9]		

ST ENDELLION

PREBENDAL CHURCH

St Endellion church (SW 9971 7866) stands near an ancient, probably early Brittonic, cemetery, so that the church-site may have origins stretching back long before documentary records.[17] In later times the church possessed a substantial endowment of land but it is not listed in the Domesday survey of 1086 among the land-holding churches of Cornwall, staffed by groups of clergy. It is first mentioned indirectly in the 12th-century life of St Nectan of Hartland (Devon), where the church saint Endelient, in the form *Endilient*, occurs in a list of saints next to those of the neighbouring churches, St Minver and St Teath, suggesting that all three churches existed at that date.[18] The earliest direct evidence comes from 1260, when the register of Bishop Walter Bronescombe (the oldest surviving register of a bishop of Exeter) records the admission of John Blohiou, clerk, to a 'portion' of the church.[19] This indicates that the revenues of the church already supported more than one parish clergyman, the clergy being known as 'portionists' or 'prebendaries'.

By 1291 there were four clergy, as there have generally been ever since.[20] The number before that date is uncertain, since in 1272 William of Tragev was admitted to a half (*medietas*) of the church, formerly that of John of Winchester.[21] Either these two men held half the church and the other half was divided into two prebends, making three, or they each held two prebends out of an earlier division into four.

---

1 Ibid., III, 1357. Also called 'of Blokkele' (probably Blockley, Gloucs.)

2 Ibid., III, 1366; private archive, Treago, 2.

3 *Reg. Grandisson*, II, 1113.

4 *Reg. Brantyngham*, I, 143, 466. These may be further references to William Trevenwythe, or to a different man or men.

5 Ibid., II, 712; *Reg. Stafford*, 159; biography in *BRUO*, II, 907–8.

6 *Cal. Papal Regs*, VI, 114–15. Cullyng was provost of Glasney; the reservation seems not to have been effective.

7 *Reg. Stafford*, 159.

8 Ibid.; biography in *BRUO*, III, 1996.

9 *Reg. Stafford*, 159; *Reg. Lacy*, ed. Hingeston-Randolph, I, 123; biography in *BRUO*, III, 1847.

10 *Reg. Lacy*, ed. Hingeston-Randolph, I, 123, 223. There is a monumental brass to his mother, Joan, in Tintagel church.

11 Ibid., 223, 395–6.

12 Ibid., 395–6; *Cal. Papal Regs*, XIII(2). 556; biography in *BRUO*, III, 1332.

13 *Reg. Morton, Canterbury*, II, 79; DRO, Chanter XIII, f. 54v. For a possible identification, see *BRUO*, I, 625–6.

14 DRO, Chanter XIII, f. 54v. He was the brother of John Carlyon, prior of Launceston, and held three of that priory's benefices (see below, p. 217, 219).

15 *7th Deputy Keeper's Report*, App. II, p. 299; DRO, Chanter XIV, ff. 119r, 120r–v; biography in *BRUO*, IV, 679.

16 TNA, E 334/3, f. 87v; Chanter XIV, f. 120r–v; E 301/9, m. 2; Snell, *Chantry Certificates*, 19–21.

I am grateful for the advice and research of Professor A. D. E. Lewis in writing the article on St Endellion.

17 P. Trudgian, 'Excavation of a Burial Ground at St Endellion, Cornwall', *Cornish Archaeology* 26 (1987), 145–52. For site information, see CCC, HER 26293, 26293.01.

18 P. Grosjean, 'Vie de S. Rumon, Vie… de S. Nectan', *Analecta Bollandiana* 71 (1953), 397–8 (a text preserved in a 14th-century manuscript).

19 *Reg. Bronescombe*, ed. Hingeston-Randolph, 170–1; ed. Robinson, I, 92–3.

20 *Reg. Bronescombe*, ed. Hingeston-Randolph , 471.

21 *Reg. Bronescombe*, ed. Hingeston-Randolph, 171; ed. Robinson, II, 60.

Whichever is correct, the half share seems to have been divided or re-divided into two in 1275, making four prebends altogether.[1] During the 13th and 14th centuries the prebends had no permanent names. Each was identified simply as 'the prebend held by so-and-so', this being the name of the cleric who had last held it or was currently doing so – a practice also followed at Crantock and Probus. Later one prebend came to be called the rector's prebend and the other three took the names of the patrons who appointed their clergy. At first the name was that of the current patron (the earliest such reference is to a Bodrugan prebend in 1414),[2] but eventually permanent titles arose: Bodmin (renamed King's after the Reformation), Marny, and Trehaverock. All four prebendaries shared the revenues of the church, but not equally. In the papal taxation of 1291, two prebends (the rector's and Bodmin) were reported to be worth £4 2s. per annum and two (Marny and Trehaverock) £3.[3]

Each prebendary had a share of the church's land (i.e. glebe) and of the tithes of the parish. In 1601 the rector was said to hold 20 acres of land, and two years later the lands of Marny were estimated at 18 acres, Trehaverock at 15 or 18, and King's at 15.[4] The fullest and most accurate account of the lands and tithes is to be found in the tithe survey of 1841, when the entitlements of the clergy still survived largely unchanged from the Middle Ages. At that time the acreage of the rector's share of glebe was measured as 27, Marny 22, Trehaverock 21, and King's 16. Most of the clergy's income came from tithes, however. In 1841 the rector received the whole tithes of 405 acres of the parish and shared those of 1,236 acres equally with the prebendary of King's. The prebendaries of Marny and Trehaverock had an equal share of 1,334 acres. The tithes of a further 162 acres at Higher and Lower Scarrabine were distributed equally between the four clergy, while those of the neighbouring estate of Roscarrock (498 acres) were allocated in the proportion of one third to the rector and two-ninths to each of his colleagues.[5] Sharing arrangements of similar complexity are recorded at Probus.[6] There was also an inequality in the duties of the clergy. As early as 1275 the Bodmin prebend was termed as being 'without cure of souls',[7] and this was also true of Marny and Trehaverock. The care of the parish devolved solely on the holder of the rector's prebend, who was officially known as rector by 1331.[8]

How did the four-fold division of St Endellion begin, and what was its significance? It is worthy of note that all three parishes adjoining St Endellion show evidence of having been divided into portions. To the west a moiety or half-share of the church of St Minver was recognised as belonging to Bodmin priory in 1255, implying that the church had formerly been shared by two patrons and perhaps by two clergy, although it was subsequently a single benefice.[9] To the east St Teath was divided into two prebends and a vicarage by 1266, and remained so until the Reformation.[10] To the south St Kew, having been a minster church until about the middle of the 12th century, would also have shared its revenues among several clergy.[11] Bodmin priory was another common factor in three of these parishes. Its canons were patrons of St Minver church by 1272, of the rector's and Bodmin portions of St Endellion by the same date, and of the vicarage of St Teath in 1259, although they lost their rights to the latter by 1279.[12] These portionary parallels and Bodmin links may be significant, but in themselves they do not explain the origins of St Endellion's prebendal status. One possibility is that the church was originally a land-holding monastery or minster staffed by a group of clergy. This would account for the church's later endowment of land, which was approximately equal in size to one hide, the endowment of the minsters of St Buryan and Probus. Such a monastery or minster is unlikely so close to St Kew, however, and its disappearance as a religious community would have to be dated well before the Domesday survey of 1086 which does not mention it among the existing or recently existing churches of this kind. Elsewhere in England some small communities of clergy were founded after the Norman Conquest in the late 11th and 12th centuries, generally near a castle or town, but this too looks improbable in the case of St Endellion which fell into neither category.

Nor is there much evidence, by the 13th century, that the clergy formed a community. The medieval registers of the bishops of Exeter commonly call St Endellion a 'portionary' or 'prebendal' church, not a 'collegiate' one.[13] In 1444 Bishop Lacy took the view that the three prebendaries other than the rector were obliged to keep residence, maintain houses in the parish, and contribute to the upkeep of the chancel and the church books.[14] His intervention came about, however, because the three clergy concerned were refusing to do these

---

1 *Reg. Bronescombe*, ed. Hingeston-Randolph, 171; ed. Robinson, II, 74, 77.
2 *Cal. Inq. PM*, XX, 61.
3 *Reg. Bronescombe*, ed. Hingeston-Randolph, 471.
4 CRO, ARD/TER/189–191.
5 CRO, TA/55; J. Maclean, *The Parochial and Family History of the Deanery of Trigg Minor* (1873–9), I, 479, 488–9.
6 Below, p. 264.
7 *Reg. Bronescombe*, ed. Hingeston-Randolph, 171; ed. Robinson, II, 74.
8 *Reg. Grandisson*, I, 598, 627.
9 J. H. Rowe (ed.), *Cornwall Feet of Fines*, DCRS (1914–50), I, 80.
10 Below, pp. 270–1.
11 Above, p. 131.
12 *Reg. Bronescombe*, ed. Hingeston-Randolph, 171, 175, 178; ed. Robinson, I, 30–1; II, 60.
13 For exceptions in 1341 and 1417, see *Reg. Grandisson*, II, 971, and N. Orme (ed.), *Cornish Wills 1342–1540*, DCRS new ser. 50 (2007), 200.
14 *Reg. Lacy*, ed. Dunstan, II, 314–16.

duties, and there is little likelihood that the kinds of prebendary appointed (other than the rectors) resided, or actual evidence that they did so. The four clergy may have discussed their revenues or church responsibilities with one another, but they had no corporate legal status or seal. They were presented to their prebends by four different patrons, not a single one, and there is no evidence (save for the rectors) that they appointed vicars or curates to do their duties in their absence. All this marks them as different from the prebendaries of the ancient Cornish minsters of St Buryan, Crantock, and Probus. An occasional prebendary may have resided in the parish. In 1381 Henry Bodulgate, prebendary of Trehaverock, is listed at St Endellion in a return of clergy paying poll-tax, and he is not known to have held another benefice so may have lived there.[1] The Trehaverock house is mentioned again in 1603 and 1680,[2] and by the 19th century the Marny prebend was stated as owning a house, that of Trehaverock lying opposite the east end of the church while Marny's stood between the west end of the church and the main road (it has since been demolished).[3] Most prebendaries apart from the rector, however, had other benefices or concerns and it is probable that the majority were usually non-resident.

The lack of a strong corporate history among the clergy of St Endellion suggests an alternative explanation of their origin through a division of the church between different claimants to the patronage, made at some point during the 12th or early 13th centuries.[4] This would account for there being four patrons and a weak community of clergy. The patronage of parish churches, both in England generally and Cornwall in particular, was often disputed by rival claimants. Normally it was not possible to divide the patronage of a church between two or more such claimants, since most churches could support only one clergyman, and claims had to be settled by law or by one party buying out the claims of another. St Endellion church may have acquired land in pre-Conquest times without necessarily having supported a religious community. Constantine, Goran, and Lansallos are other parishes where this appears to have happened.[5] The existence of this land along with substantial tithes may have permitted disputes about the patronage of the church to be solved by dividing the endowment and creating separate benefices belonging to different patrons. Disputes about the church are certainly recorded. We hear of one in 1302, when Richard of Roscarrock, a landholder in the parish, attempted to claim the patronage of the church from Bodmin priory,[6] and litigation is mentioned taking place in 1314–16 between the rector and the holder of the prebend later known as Bodmin.[7]

Little is recorded of the history of St Endellion church from the 13th century to the Reformation. One glimpse comes from the will of William Doune, archdeacon of Leicester and prebendary of the church, made in about 1361. He bequeathed £10 to repair the chancel; if that could not be done, half the money should be used to repair the nave and half to feed the poor. A further £2 was given for buying or repairing vestments.[8] Lacy's intervention of 1444 provides us with another brief insight, but there is no account of what resulted from it and although the church was rebuilt in the 15th century, it is not possible to say if the two events are connected. The rebuilt church, which survives today, consists of a chancel, nave, and two wide nave aisles (Fig. 39). According to Nicholas Roscarrock (c.1550–c.1633), the Catholic scholar who was born at Roscarrock in the parish, the church contained St Endelient's 'tomb' in the form of a 'table' or altar-tomb of black polished stone; its original location is not stated. He went on to say that the tomb was defaced in the reign of Henry VIII (presumably in 1538) and was later used as monument for a lay person buried in the south aisle of the church. This tomb is probably identical with the present-day altar in the same aisle, a 15th-century structure of catacleuse stone with recessed niches along the sides.[9] Roscarrock collected local folklore about the church saint and about another saint of the parish, Dilic or Illick, who had an important chapel at St Illick near Port Gaverne (SX 016 801).[10] It is not known how far the cults of these two saints were confined to the parish, or whether they attracted devotees from elsewhere.

Most of the records about the church relate to its patrons and prebendaries.[11] The patronage of the rector's prebend belonged to Bodmin priory until the Reformation, when it passed to the Crown from which it was transferred to the lord chancellor by 1917. The patronage of the Bodmin prebend was also held by the priory until its dissolution, after which it was appropriated by the Crown and granted to Sir John St

---

1 TNA, E 179/24/5.
2 ARD/TER/191; R. Potts (ed.), *A Calendar of Cornish Glebe Terriers 1673–1735*, DCRS new ser. 19 (1974), 33.
3 Maclean, *Trigg Minor*, I, 500, 504. However in 1603 King's and Marny were said to possess no houses (ARD/TER/191).
4 After 1200 there is an increasing likelihood that any division of the church would have been recorded in Rowe (ed.), *Cornwall Feet of Fines*.
5 Above, pp. 128, 130, 132.
6 Maclean, *Trigg Minor*, I, 489.
7 *Reg. Stapeldon*, 251.

8 A. H. Thompson, 'The Will of Master William Doune', *Archaeological Jnl* 72 (1915), 268–9; Orme (ed.), *Cornish Wills*, 198. The prebendary Richard Bruton made a bequest of 40s. to the church fabric in 1417 (Orme (ed.), *Cornish Wills*, 200).
9 N. Roscarrock, *Lives of the Saints: Cornwall and Devon*, ed. N. Orme, DCRS new ser. 35 (1992), 71–3.
10 Ibid., 71–3, 78–9; N. Orme, *The Saints of Cornwall* (2000), 106–7, 113–14.
11 Patrons and prebendaries are listed in E. Stark, *Saint Endellion* (1983), 43–65, and (more fully) in forthcoming work by Professor A. Lewis.

Leger in 1543.¹ It subsequently descended through the families of Boteler and Basset. A number of lay families held the patronage of the Marny prebend in turn, including those of Bodrugan, Cergeaux, Marny, Howard of Bindon, and Robartes. The same was true of the Trehaverock prebend, which passed through the families of Modred, Trehaverock, Cavell, Richardson, and Gray. The occupants of the rector's prebend before the Reformation resembled the incumbents of modestly endowed churches elsewhere in Cornwall, while the non-resident prebendaries were a more varied assortment of clergy, usually connected in some way with their patrons. They included a few canons of Exeter cathedral and a prior of Bodmin (Thomas Vivian) who held the Bodmin prebend himself up to 1524, but as these men are unlikely to have resided, their status had little impact on the church or parish.

In 1535 the annual income of the rector's prebend was estimated as £10 and that of the other three prebends as £5 each.² The list of clergy renouncing the pope's supremacy over the Church in the previous year included only the rector and a curate from the parish, and a taxation list of about 1535–6 is confined to them and to a recently deceased chaplain, so that there is no evidence of the prebendaries residing in this period.³ During the spring of 1546 the church foundation was investigated by the chantry commissioners of Henry VIII, and this process was repeated by similar commissioners under Edward VI in the spring of 1548.⁴ Neither enquiry concerned itself with the rector or his income, but each valued the revenues of the King's (formerly Bodmin) prebend at £6 per annum, the Trehaverock prebend at the same, and the Marny prebend at £7. These sums were paid by three lay 'farmers' who collected the tithes and presumably also the glebe rents on behalf of each prebendary. Both investigations reported that the duty of the prebendaries was to 'help in the ministry of divine service within the parish church', but it was observed in 1548 that 'they [were] not resident there at any time'. Under the terms of the Chantry Act, the chantry commissioners were to dissolve all collegiate churches and chantries and transfer their endowments to the Crown, but the application of the Act to prebendal and portionary churches was not clear. The commissioners spared three foundations of this kind in Devon – Chulmleigh, Tiverton, and the chapel of Exeter castle – apparently regarding them as sinecure benefices without chantry duties or collegiate life. In Cornwall a stricter policy was followed. At St Endellion and St Teath the Crown exempted only the rectory and the vicarage respectively, and confiscated the three prebends of St Endellion as well as the two of St Teath. The St Endellion prebendaries were each awarded pensions of £5 per annum, which were paid until at least 1554–5.⁵ These pensions witness to the fact that the government of Edward VI intended to dissolve the prebendal church and did so, contrary to some modern statements that the prebends escaped dissolution.⁶

Much of the property seized by the Crown in consequence of the second Chantry Act was sold in the following years, but this seems not to have happened in the case of the three St Endellion prebends. A problem would have arisen because the endowments were leased to three different farmers and were difficult to detach from those of the rector, especially in the case of the King's prebend. In consequence the endowments had not been alienated when Roman Catholicism was re-established under Mary I in 1553 and a more sympathetic view was taken of traditional Church institutions. No official decision to revive the St Endellion prebends is recorded, but on 21 April 1555 William Cavell was instituted to the Trehaverock prebend on the presentation of Nicholas Cavell.⁷ Later, on 17 February 1559, Bishop Turberville of Exeter instituted Ralph Hartopp to the Marny prebend,⁸ and in 1564 Giles Boteler gained possession of the Bodmin prebend, probably on the presentation of the Boteler family of Parkham (Devon).⁹ By the 1560s, therefore, all four prebends had been re-established, a process likely to have been driven by their patrons as much as by more tolerant attitudes on the part of the Crown and Church authorities.

The prebends continued with little change until the late 19th century, escaping the major Church reforms of that period. In 1880 the Bodmin prebend began to be used to support a clergyman to serve the village of Port Isaac in the parish, and its endowments were applied for that purpose in 1913. In 1928 the lord chancellor transferred the patronage of the rectory to the bishop of Truro, Walter Howard Frere, and his example was eventually followed by the patrons of the other three prebends. Frere, an historian sympathetic to medieval institutions, at once encouraged the four clergy to form a chapter or collective body. The first recorded chapter meeting was held in 1929, the bishop issued statutes for the chapter in the same year, and it was granted a coat of arms on 27 November 1950.¹⁰ The chapter's existence

---

1 *L&P Hen. VIII*, XVIII(1), 449.
2 *Valor. Eccl.* (Rec. Comm. 1810–34), II, 401.
3 TNA, E 36/64, pp. 43–4; ECA, D&C 3688, f. 35r; Stark, *Saint Endellion*, 49.
4 TNA, E 301/15, ff. 55v–56r; E 301/9, m. 4d, printed in L. S. Snell, *Documents towards a History of the Reformation in Cornwall: vol. I, The Chantry Certificates for Cornwall* (c.1953), 22–3.
5 BL, Add. 8102, f. 35r–v.
6 e.g. C. G. Henderson, *The Cornish Church Guide* (1927), 60; Stark, *Saint Endellion*, 37.
7 Maclean, *Trigg Minor*, II, 160.
8 DRO, Chanter XVIII, ff. 45r, 78r.
9 TNA, E 334/8, f. 29r.
10 Per chevron wavy azure and vert, in chief a crown vallary between two bulls heads caboshed, and in base a cow couchant guardant or.

gives the impression that the church is an ancient collegiate foundation that survived the Reformation. In fact the modern chapter is a recent creation with the status of a society not a corporation with legal functions.[1] For practical purposes the church is a parish church, to which three prebendaries are attached on historic grounds without legal responsibilities or emoluments.

ST GERMANS

MINSTER, LATER AUGUSTINIAN PRIORY

REFORMATION AND PROPERTY

The union of the dioceses of Cornwall and Crediton in 1050 reduced the status of the church of St Germans.[2] It remained a church of the bishop of the diocese, but ceased to be a cathedral containing his seat and housing his administrative staff, both now established at Exeter.[3] By 1304 there was a belief in Cornwall that the first bishop of Exeter, Leofric (d. 1072), changed not only the status of St Germans church but also its clergy, replacing the 'secular' canons who had hitherto served it with 'regular' canons of the Augustinian Order.[4] This belief is not credible, however, since the order was not active in England until about 1100. The Domesday survey of 1086, which provides the first evidence about St Germans after 1050, describes its clergy simply as 'canons', but there is no reason to think that they differed in their way of life from the secular canons who had staffed the church hitherto. Domesday Book records that they shared the adjoining manor of St Germans with the bishop of Exeter, the bishop and canons each holding half of the manor's 24 hides of land, of which the canons' portion was exempt from taxation.[5] No further information survives about the church or its clergy for a hundred years, but the canons apparently continued in their traditional form until the reign of Bishop Bartholomew of Exeter (1161–84). It was he who reorganised the church as an Augustinian priory following a monastic rule.[6]

Bartholomew issued a charter refounding the church, but only a single clause of it survives in a note made by the Tudor antiquary John Leland who visited St Germans in about 1533 and in 1542. As the charter was subsequently confirmed by Baldwin, archbishop of Canterbury (1184–90), it seems to date from about the early 1180s, towards the end of Bartholomew's reign. Leland's note of the charter records the bishop as saying 'I have converted the church of St Germans in Cornwall, whose life was being conducted in an insufficiently ecclesiastical and almost secular manner, to the life of regular canons, for the sake of religion and piety.'[7] This implies that he reformed an existing community, not one that had died out. Bartholomew was a well-educated Frenchman likely to have wished to raise the staff of the church to the higher standards of the Augustinian Order, which was well established in England by this time. His reform must have involved introducing a prior from elsewhere, and perhaps other canons, but nothing is known of this process or whether he sought help from the two houses of the order already established in Cornwall: Bodmin and Launceston.

Most of the endowments of the new priory are likely to have been ones that had long pertained to the bishop or to the previous body of canons (Fig. 49). Their scope and value are not substantially described until the papal valuation of English Church property in 1291, and even then not fully. By that time they consisted partly of land and partly of tithes. At St Germans itself the bishop's share of the land was estimated as worth £17 17s. 5d., while the priory's was reckoned at only £1 12s. 8d, but the latter sum must exclude substantial revenues that supported the priory itself.[8] The priory's largest incomes from land elsewhere came from Landrake (£5) and Tinnel in Landulph (£1 10s. 2d.), both of which had belonged to the bishop or to St Germans since at least the 11th century.[9] Landrake was held with the privileges of 'infangthief', the assizes of bread and ale, and the right to waifs and

---

1 A. Lewis, 'The College of Prebends and the Living of Littleham', *Newsletter and Annual Report, Friends of St Endellion* (2005), 20–6.

2 On St Germans before 1050, see above, p. 129.

3 The principal previous histories of the monastery are by G. Oliver, *Monasticon Dioecesis Exoniensis* (1846), 1–6, and C. G. Henderson, *Records of the Church and Priory of St. Germans in Cornwall* (1929). Studies of the building are listed below, p. 186 note 14.

4 Below, p. 190.

5 C. and F. Thorn (ed.), *Domesday Book*, vol. X: *Cornwall* (1979), 2/6.

6 On Bartholomew, see A. Morey, *Bartholomew of Exeter, Bishop and Canonist: a study in the twelfth century* (1937); F. Barlow (ed.), *English Episcopal Acta*, XI: *Exeter 1046–1184* (1996), pp. xxxix–xli; and *ODNB*.

7 J. Leland, *Collectanea*, ed. T. Hearne (1774), I, 75.

8 *Reg. Bronescombe*, ed. Hingeston-Randolph, 479. In 1535 the priory's share of land revenue at St Germans was valued at £13 12s. 10d. (below, p. 190).

9 P. H. Sawyer, *Anglo-Saxon Charters* (1968), no. 951.

strays.[1] Other small sums were received from holdings at Carracawn in St Germans, *Gonethode*, and Lambest in Menheniot. In the 19th century the land immediately around the former priory at Port Eliot and Lethiock, together with holdings at Bake and Long Colling, was stated to be free of tithe.[2] This probably represents the area of the 'home farm' that supplied the priory.

The priory's ecclesiastical property in 1291 consisted of the churches of St Germans, Gulval, Landrake, Morval, and South Petherwin, at each of which the canons held the advowson, conferring the right to appoint the parish clergy and to a share of the tithes of the parish, usually the 'great' tithes of corn. Here too the annual income from St Germans (£2) was greatly undervalued (in 1535 it was £70). Of the other churches South Petherwin produced £6, Landrake £4 13s. 4d., and Gulval £3 6s. 8d. Morval's income is not stated, but to judge from its value in 1535 it was similar to Gulval's.[3] Smaller amounts of tithe came from the priory's land in Landulph, and there were pensions from South Petherwin church and from its dependent chapel at Launceston Castle. The churches of Gulval, Landrake, and South Petherwin were former possessions of the bishops of Exeter, and their connection with the priory may go back to Bartholomew's time or before. Morval belonged to the canons by 1244,[4] and they had a claim to the church of Sithney until they renounced it in 1230.[5] Altogether the priory's income amounted to £27 9s. 6d. according to the valuation of 1291, and since this was defective by a half or more the real total may have reached £50 or £60 – more than that of most religious houses in Cornwall but less than the sums enjoyed by Bodmin and Launceston.[6]

The priory's history was shaped by its location and endowments.[7] With the exception of Gulval in west Cornwall, its possessions were concentrated in the south-eastern corner of the county between Landulph and Morval, confining the monastery's dominance to that district. This was a smaller sphere of influence than those of the priories of Bodmin and Launceston, and St Germans lacked their advantages of lying on the major northern road across Cornwall close to substantial towns. The priory site adjoined an inlet of the River Tiddy, now infilled, which gave it access to Plymouth Sound and the English Channel, but in terms of land communications it stood some way from the principal southern road through the county, which passed to the north of it from Saltash to Liskeard. Its relative isolation is perhaps reflected by the rarity with which it received bequests in surviving Cornish wills.[8] The parish belonging to the

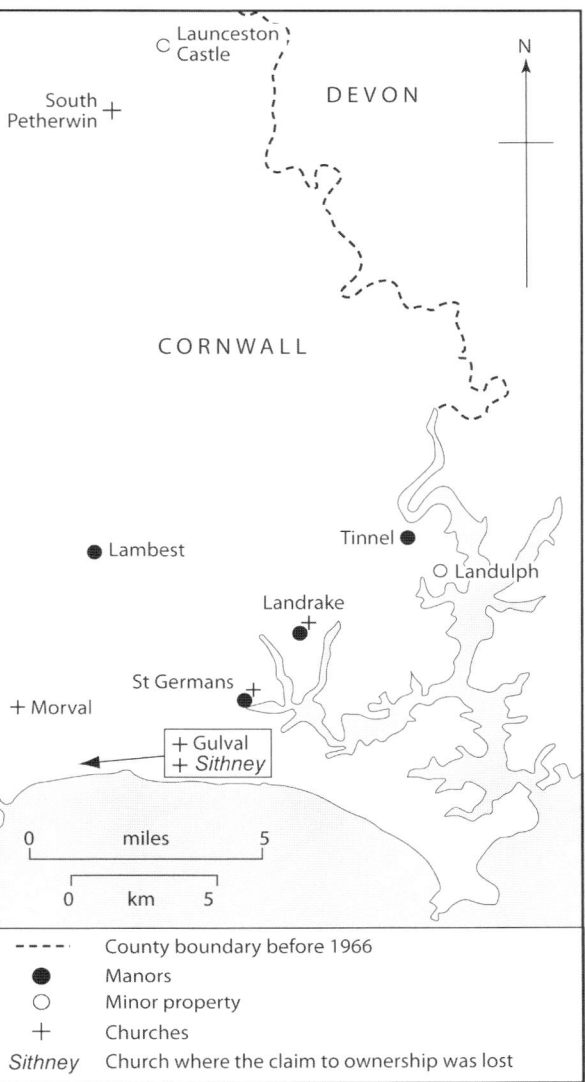

FIG 49. *The property of St Germans Priory.*

church was a large one by Cornish standards, and was described by the county historian Richard Carew in 1603 as fertile and housing several gentry and wealthy farmers,[9] but it lacked a significant town. The church's ancient Sunday market was reported, as early as the Domesday survey, to have been ruined by the opening of a rival one at Trematon.[10] By 1284 the priory held a two-day fair on the vigil and feast day of St German (probably at the end of May), as well as a market, and in 1343 the bishop was authorised to hold a three-day fair between

---

1 *Placita de Quo Warranto* (Rec. Com. 1818), 108.
2 CRO, TA/68, pp. 7, 17–18, 32, 40.
3 Below, p. 190.
4 J. H. Rowe (ed.), *Cornwall Feet of Fines*, DCRS (1914–50), I, 43; cf. 54 (Gulval).
5 *Cur. Reg.* XIV, 23–4; Rowe (ed.), *Cornwall Feet of Fines*, I, 23.
6 *Reg. Bronescombe*, ed. Hingeston-Randolph, 466–7, 470, 472–3, 479.
7 On the location, see P. Sheppard, *The Historic Towns of Cornwall* (1980), 53–4.
8 Modest bequests occur in the wills of John Dabernon of Calstock, 1368, William Wynard of Exeter, 1442, Alexander Carew of Anthony, 1492, and John Treffry of Fowey, 1500 (N. Orme (ed.), *Cornish Wills 1342–1540*, DCRS new ser. 50 (2007), 33, 103, 108–9, 203–4).
9 R. Carew, *The Survey of Cornwall* (1602, repr. 2004), ff. 108v–109r.
10 *Domesday Book: Cornwall*, ed. Thorn, 2/6.

31 July and 2 August.¹ However neither the bishop's share of the land in the parish (the manor of Cuddenbeak) nor the priory's (the manor of St Germans) was highly developed as a borough in either a governmental or commercial sense. The priory never reaped the advantages of ruling its own urban community, but equally it avoided the tensions that such rule often produced. When Leland made his second visit shortly after the priory's dissolution, he remarked that 'St Germans is but a poor fisher town. The glory of it stood by the priory.'²

Another defining factor in the priory's history was its close connection with the bishops of Exeter. They kept their estate at St Germans until the Reformation, including a palace at Cuddenbeak which they visited from time to time, a quarter of a mile south-east of the church.³ The bishop acted as patron of the monastery, as he did at Bodmin and Launceston, enjoying the right to be told of the death of each prior and to give permission for a new one to be elected. During the consequent vacancy he appointed sequestrators to administer the priory's spiritual and temporal goods and affairs, and the newly elected prior went to the bishop to have his election confirmed and to swear an oath of obedience.⁴ As a result of this patronage the parishes of St Germans and Landrake did not form part of the neighbouring rural deanery of East Wivelshire, but constituted a peculiar jurisdiction belonging to the bishop, called the deanery of St Germans.⁵ Claims to authority over the priory were also advanced by the crown. In 1279 Edward I informed the sheriff of Cornwall that it was held in chief of the king because the kings of England had founded the canons there, and in 1304 an inquisition by the escheator of Cornwall reported that King Cnut (1016–35) was one of its founders.⁶ Eventually the crown asserted its right to the patronage of the priory. This was apparently influenced by a plea in a royal court between Bishop Grandisson of Exeter (1327–69) and other parties concerning certain tenements in Landrake, during which the prior of St Germans stated that the patronage belonged to the king's ancestors as a result of Cnut's foundation.⁷

The patronage issue appears to have come to a head in the 1350s. When John Prechour was elected prior in 1355 and went to Grandisson for confirmation at Chudleigh (Devon), the bishop delayed his assent for eight days to allow time for objections to be made – an action that may have reflected the royal claim.⁸ In 1358 Grandisson wrote to the Black Prince, as duke of Cornwall and possessor of certain royal rights in the county, complaining of interference by the duke's officers with his rights as patron.⁹ The Prince wrote to them to ask why, but the challenge to the bishop's patronage, far from being withdrawn, was pushed further. On Prechour's death in 1367 Edward III issued a licence for the canons to elect a successor, and ordered the escheator to take control of the priory's temporal possessions. The canons were obliged to ask the king's consent to the election of the new prior, William Treskelly, after which the king informed the bishop of his consent and told the escheator to restore the sequestrated properties.¹⁰ Eventually Grandisson's successor, Thomas Brantingham, took steps to recover his rights. On 24 April 1385 he wrote to the prior and canons asking them to provide him with the charters and muniments relating to the foundation and patronage of the monastery, which he used to convince the crown of the truth of his claims.¹¹ On the following 22 June Richard II, with the assent of his council, admitted the error and restored the patronage to the bishop.¹² It stayed in episcopal hands until the dissolution of the priory, but the practice continued by which the bishop delayed confirming the elections of priors for a few days during which anyone who opposed the election might appear before him.¹³

BUILDINGS AND COMMUNITY

The priory church (located at SX 3597 5780) survives more fully than any of its monastic siblings in Cornwall, since most of its nave remains as the present-day parish church (Fig. 50).¹⁴ The building accommodated both the canons and the parishioners throughout the medieval centuries, as opposed to the Augustinian priories at

---

1 W. M. M. Picken, 'St German of Cornwall's Day', *DCNQ* 27 (1956–8), 103–7.

2 J. Leland, *Itinerary*, ed. L. Toulmin Smith (1907–10), I, 210.

3 e.g. F. Barlow (ed.), *English Episcopal Acta*, XII: *Exeter 1186–1257* (1996). 294, 297; *Reg. Bronescombe*, ed. Hingeston-Randolph, 295–301; *Reg. Lacy*, ed. Dunstan, V, 177.

4 *Reg. Bronescombe*, ed. Hingeston-Randolph, 247–8; ed. Robinson, II, 129; *Reg. Grandisson*, II, 950, 1162–3; *Reg. Stafford*, 314.

5 *Reg. Bronescombe*, ed. Hingeston-Randolph, 247–8, 466; ed. Robinson, II, 129.

6 *Cal. Inq. Misc.* I, 344; *Cal. Pat.* 1385–5, 316; Oliver, *Monasticon*, 4. The Cnut charter, on which this evidence was based, is listed in Sawyer, *Anglo-Saxon Charters*, no. 951.

7 *Cal. Pat.* 1385–9, 8; see also Henderson, *St. Germans*, 16.

8 *Reg. Grandisson*, II, 1166–73. The documentation of this prior's election in the bishop's register is unusually extensive.

9 *Black Prince's Reg.* II, 143.

10 *Cal. Pat.* 1364–7, 376, 385, 388.

11 *Reg. Brantyngham*, I, 164.   12 *Cal. Pat.* 1385–9, 8.

13 e.g. *Reg. Lacy*, ed. Hingeston-Randolph, I, 69–78, 162–70.

14 For site information, see CCC, HER 6395.05, 07. The most recent discussion of the building is by L. Olson and A. Preston-Jones, 'An Ancient Cathedral of Cornwall? Excavated remains east of St Germans Church', *Cornish Archaeology* 37–8 (1998–9), 153–69. Other discussions include Browne Willis, *Notitia Parliamentaria* (1715–50), II, 150–2; J. Whitaker, *The Ancient Cathedral of Cornwall Historically Surveyed* (1804), I, 69–153; J. Furneaux, 'A paper on St. German's Priory Church, Cornwall', *Transactions of the Exeter Diocesan Architectural Soc.* 3 (1849), 82–9; F. C. Hingeston-Randolph, *The Architectural History of St Germans Church, Cornwall* (1902); R. Gem, 'St Germans Priory Church', *Archaeol. Jnl* 130 (1973), 289–91; and C. A. Ralegh Radford, 'The Church of Saint Germans', *JRIC* new ser. 7 (1973–7), 190–6. Early depictions of the church include S. and N. Buck, *Perspective Views of the Most Noted Abbeys and Castles of England* (1726–39); 'The South West View of St. Germans Priory' (1734); and J. Britton and E. W. Brayley, *A Topographical and Historical Description of the County of Cornwall* (1801), I, 374–5 (a view from the north-west).

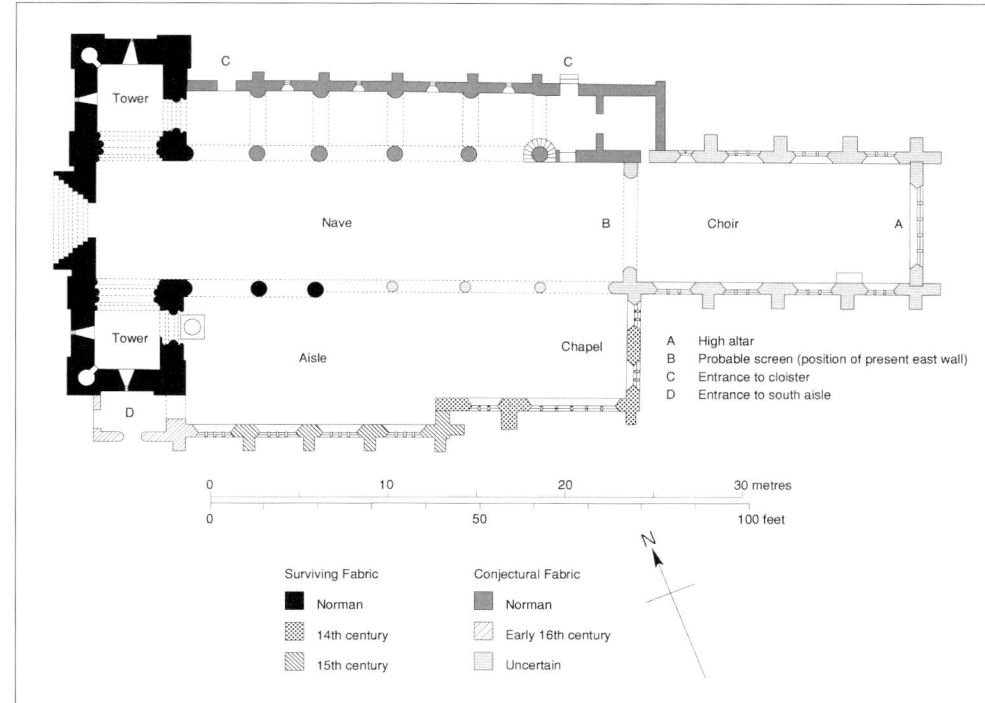

FIG 50.
St Germans
Priory, plan.

Bodmin, Launceston, and Plympton (Devon) where the monastic and parish churches were separate structures. The extant Norman work at the west end of the nave suggests that there was a major rebuilding of the church in or after the time of Bishop Bartholomew. Augustinian priories at this time were usually given either a narrow aisleless nave or a wider aisled one, Launceston receiving the former and St Germans the latter.[1]

The church was mostly built from local slate-stone with dressings of elvan and Beer stone. Its western façade contains a central gabled porch containing one richly decorated west doorway, probably built of Hurdwick stone from Tavistock (Devon). This façade was flanked by towers at the corners and the doorway led to a nave about 100 feet (30.2 metres) long and 24 feet (7.2 metres) wide (internal measurements). Two nave arcades with two-centred Transitional arches, resting on massive round piers, opened onto narrow aisles along the north and south sides; the north aisle was removed in 1802. The aisles and arcades added a further 14 feet (4.2 metres) of internal width, the aisles being probably covered with a low pentice roof and the arcade eventually surmounted by a clerestory. Beyond the nave stood the choir or chancel, with an estimated internal length of 49 feet (15 metres).[2] This has long been destroyed but was as wide as the nave (excluding the nave aisles).[3] The canons would have occupied the choir and the parishioners the nave, with screening between the two parts. Bishop Bronescombe of Exeter dedicated the whole church on 28 August 1261.[4] In about the 1330s a grand and lofty south chapel about 20 feet (6 metres) long internally was built at the south-east end of the nave in the Decorated style, projecting beyond the south nave aisle. This had two east and two south windows and two niches, one a sedile and one perhaps for a tomb. Later the rest of that aisle was extended to a line slightly further south than the end of the chapel, including a new porch and entrance next to the south-west tower. The windows of this aisle can be dated to the reign of Bishop Lacy of Exeter (1420–55), whose coat of arms appears on a dripstone stop.[5] The two western towers were probably both originally rectangular, but the upper part of the north tower was rebuilt in the 13th century as an octagon, producing an asymmetrical appearance (Fig. 16).

Little is known of the church's interior layout and furnishings. The choir was floored with encaustic tiles dating from the late 13th or early 14th centuries,

---

1 Other Augustinian churches with aisled naves included Christchurch (Hants.), Llanthony (Mon.), Waltham (Essex), and Colchester (Essex) – the latter further resembling St Germans in having western towers from which the nave aisles opened.
2 Willis, *Notitia Parliamentaria*, II, 151; *Cornish Archaeology*, 37–8 (1998–9), 167.
3 Olson and Preston-Jones have suggested the presence of a north choir aisle (*Cornish Archaeology* 37–8 (1998–9), 167), but if there was a south choir aisle it is odd that it was not retained within the fourteenth-century south transept.
4 *Reg. Bronescombe*, ed. Hingeston-Randolph, 68; ed. Robinson, 126–7.
5 Henderson, *St. Germans*, 37, which also mentions the arms of the Arches, Dinham, and Hamley families.

decorated with fleur-de-lys and herringbone patterns.¹ There must have been stalls for the canons, and parts of a misericord survive depicting a hunter and hounds which may have belonged to one such stall. In about 1533 Leland observed what he called a tomb in the wall on the right-hand side of the high altar 'with an image of a bishop, and over the tomb eleven bishops painted with their names and verses, in token of so many bishops buried there or that there had been so many bishops of Cornwall that had their seat there'.² This shows the canons' pride in their episcopal traditions. The nave, which served as the parish church, may have contained a single altar in front of the choir screen as at Launceston, or two placed side by side as at Crediton (Devon), another ancient church shared by parishioners and canons.³ The east ends of the nave aisles probably housed altars, that on the south side being replaced by the new 14th-century south chapel, the altar piscina of which is still extant. This new chapel could well have been identical with the chapel of St Mary (i.e. Lady chapel), mentioned in 1535.⁴ In the early 18th century the antiquary Browne Willis noticed armorial glass in the nave windows, including the arms of the diocese and those of Bishops Stafford (1395–1419) and Courtenay (1478–87).⁵ The late 12th-century font survives in the nave, and it is likely that some important lay people were buried beneath the nave floor. John Trelawny and Richard Moyle requested burial in the church in 1504 and 1525 respectively, and both referred in their wills to St Thomas, probably indicating that his image stood in the church.⁶ The care of souls in the parish belonged to the prior and canons, but although Augustinian clergy had more freedom than monks to do pastoral work and may have done this at St Germans, the priory employed a parish chaplain partly or wholly for that purpose.⁷

St Germans acknowledged St German of Auxerre in France as its patron saint by at least the 10th century.⁸ The feast-days of this saint were 31 July and 1 October, and the priory appears to have celebrated an additional feast at the end of May, when it held its annual fair.⁹ In 1342 the reeve and burgesses of Saltash, whose ancestors had been excommunicated for injuring the prior, undertook to offer a candle weighing one pound every year at the priory on 31 July.¹⁰ In 1358 Sir Nicholas Tamworth, a professional soldier in the war with France, persuaded the abbot and monks of Auxerre to give him a small bone from the saint's arm and a part of the shroud on which the body lay, together with a letter authenticating the grant. Tamworth (died 1377) was a distinguished warrior and royal servant, who rose to be captain of Calais and one of the king's admirals. He held property in several English counties, including the manor of St Winnow (Cornwall) where he was a tenant of the bishop of Exeter in the latter's capacity as lord of the church of St Germans – a fact that explains his interest in the relics.¹¹ After enclosing them in a silver-gilt capsule, he presented them to the priory and, having submitted his letter of authenticity to Bishop Grandisson in 1361, secured from him an indulgence of forty days to all who visited the priory by way of pilgrimage on 31 July and 1 October.¹² Subsequently Nicholas or the priory applied to the pope for a larger indulgence, mentioning the bone and its ornamentation in gold and silver, and claiming that 'in the monastery, after its oblation, many miracles have been done by the prayers and merits of the aforesaid saint'. Accordingly in 1364 Pope Urban V granted remission of penance of one year and forty days to those who frequented the church on German's festivals during the next ten years, all of which points to a revival of the cult of the saint at the priory.¹³

The monastic buildings lay to the north of the church. They included a refectory, still extant as the hall of the present-day house of Port Eliot and formerly containing armorial glass of the early 16th century which featured the arms of the diocese and of Bishop Oldham (d. 1519).¹⁴ The house also contains an

---

1 CCC, HER 6395.07; E. S. Eames, *Catalogue of Medieval Lead-Glazed Earthenware Tiles in the… British Museum* (1980), ii, nos 2,117–19; *Cornish Archaeology*, 37–8 (1998–9), 165–6.

2 Leland, *Itinerary*, ed. Toulmin Smith, I, 324. Right-hand is likely to mean north, as viewed from the altar. There are now known to have been eight bishops of Cornwall; the eleven may have included others, such as Bartholomew, and the 'tomb' may have been the shrine of German.

3 Below, p. 206; N. Orme, 'The Church in Crediton from Saint Boniface to the Reformation', in T. A. Reuter (ed.), *The Greatest Englishman: Essays on St Boniface and the Church at Crediton* (1980), 112–13.

4 *L&P Hen. VIII*, VIII, 126. Hingeston-Randolph (*St Germans Church*, 32, 34) preferred to place the Lady chapel at the east end of the north aisle, envisaging the south chapel as a shrine of the relic of St German, discussed next. However the south chapel seems earlier than the date of the relic; its grandeur would befit the cult of Mary; and Lady chapels existed on the south sides of the Augustinian monasteries of Waltham (Essex) and Dorchester (Oxon.). The relic could have been housed within the Lady chapel, like the shrine of St Birinus at Dorchester.

5 Willis, *Notitia Parliamentaria*, II, 151.

6 Orme, (ed.), *Cornish Wills*, 117, 176.

7 The chaplain is mentioned in 1329 (*Reg. Grandisson*, I, 509), 1416–19 (DRO, Chanter VIII, ff. 217r, 238r, 245v), 1381 (TNA, 179/24/5), and 1450 (*Reg. Lacy*, ed. Dunstan, III, 60). See also Henderson, *Church and Priory of St. Germans*, 12–13.

8 Above, p. 129.

9 The May feast may have been influenced by a different saint, German of Paris, whose day was the 28th (N. Orme, *The Saints of Cornwall* (2000), 128). Picken ('*DCNQ* 27 (1956–8)', 103–7) preferred to see it as the feast of a local saint whose cult was subsequently superseded by that of German of Auxerre.

10 DRO, Chanter V, f. 86v; Oliver, *Monasticon*, 5; *Reg. Lacy*, ed. Dunstan, I, 232–4.

11 For his career, see *Cal. Pat.* 1354–1374 passim, and for his Cornish connections *Reg. Brantyngham*, I, 208, and *Cal. Pat.* 1354–8, 215, and 1364–7, 408. His death is noted in *Cal. Fine* 1369–77, 407.

12 *Reg. Grandisson*, III, 1226.

13 *Lettres communes des papes du XIVe siècle: Urbain V, letters communes*, 3 (1974–6), 542.

14 Willis, *Notitia Parliamentaria*, II, 150.

undercroft with 13th-century lancet windows. No records indicate the size of the monastic community before the Black Death, but the founder is likely to have envisaged at least a dozen clergy. After the Black Death there were, besides the prior, ten canons in 1355, eight (counting only canons who were priests) in 1381, nine in 1424, seven in 1434 and 1492, four in 1509, six in 1534, and seven in 1539.[1] These figures may exclude one or two junior canons or novices.[2] From the 14th century onwards, when the names of most of the canons survive, the priors all appear to have been chosen from within the house, some having been subpriors and others ordinary members of the community. The priory would have employed a body of servants, with an additional small household to serve the prior, but nothing is known of their numbers. During the 14th century St Germans, like the other major Cornish religious houses, was required by the king to board and feed one of his retired household servants. A pensioner of this kind is mentioned in 1365, and his place continued to be filled by the crown until 1409.[3] In 1535 a man named Robert Goldson held a similar 'corrody' or pension granted to him by the bishop of Exeter.[4] By the latter date the priory was accustomed to provide bread and fish for four poor people during Lent, and to give further alms to the poor on Maundy Thursday.[5]

LATER HISTORY, 1300–1539

The internal history of the priory is largely confined to the elections of priors and to visitations by bishops and representatives of the Augustinian Order. Bishop Stapledon, who made the earliest recorded visitation in 1315, ordered the prior, Henry, to give up the office of chamberlain which he held unlawfully. He was to consult his brethren about appointing a substitute, and to ensure that the person appointed rendered accounts, including payments for novices and sick canons staying in the infirmary.[6] Stapledon's successor Grandisson has left no record of a visitation, and the affairs of the priory next emerge in the reign of William Treskelly, prior from 1367 to 1385. Two canons at this time got into trouble. One, John Averay, left his habit and withdrew from the priory without licence, but was restored to it by the pope at his request in 1368.[7] Another, John Mychel, was indicted by a jury at Callington in 1370 on a charge of breaking into the prior's chamber and forcing open a chest containing £26, which he carried off to Landrake. He was apparently put into the sheriff's custody.[8] By 1377 Treskelly was feeble with age and blindness, and the bishop ordered him to choose a coadjutor.[9] The prior's choice was Averay, whom Bishop Brantingham (not surprisingly) regarded as unsuitable and removed in 1379, complaining as he did so of the trouble caused by Averay and similar contradictors and rebels.[10] In 1384 he ordered the prior of Launceston and others to report on the state of the community, where he had identified faults and decreed remedies which, to his vexation, the prior and canons had ignored.[11] In 1385 Treskelly resigned and was succeeded by Richard Harepath, who had replaced Averay as coadjutor before leaving St Germans to be prior of St Michael's Mount.[12] Brantyngham approved the candidate but not the election procedure which he quashed, collating Harepath by his own authority.[13]

Harepath's successor was the egregious Averay, whose rule of the community appears to have been unsatisfactory. When the next bishop, Stafford, visited the priory in 1400, he found four canons guilty of scandalous and immoral conduct – presumably sexual. He ordered three of them to be confined to the church and cloister, and to do public penance on Fridays by sitting on the floor of the refectory at meal times with only bread and water; the fourth received a lesser punishment.[14] John Piper was elected on Averay's death in 1404; he too stood accused of adultery but was able to clear his name.[15] In 1410 the bishop told him to purge himself again of certain unspecified charges before a jury of clergy in Liskeard, and it seems that he did so successfully since he remained as prior.[16] During his priorate the prior of Launceston visited St Germans in 1413 on behalf of the Augustinian Order, and laid down that all its officials should render accounts of their offices to their fellow clergy, at least annually. Two more canons should be professed within the following year to bring up the number of clergy to its ancient level, and the prior should provide bread, drink, and other victuals that were both sufficient and decent. Piper was apparently slow to comply, since the prior of Launceston repeated his injunctions in 1419. This time he demanded that two canons should be professed within seven months and two more within a year. Further

---

1 *Reg. Grandisson*, II, 1169; TNA, E 179/24/5); *Reg. Lacy*, ed. Hingeston-Randolph, I, 72, 163; *Reg. Morton, Canterbury*, II, 81; DRO, Chanter XIII, ff. 31v–33v (a fifth canon had absconded from the house); see below, p. 190.

2 e.g. two canons were ordained subdeacons in Sept 1381 (*Reg. Brantyngham*, II, 832), in addition to those listed as priests in the poll-tax levied earlier in the year (E 179/24/5). Leland in about 1533 noted a prior and eight canons, either as a real or as an ideal number (*Collectanea*, ed. Hearne, I, 75).

3 *Cal. Close 1364–8*, 167; *1392–6*, 482; *1399–1402*, 130; *1402–5*, 502; *1405–9*, 57, 466; *1409–13*, 64.

4 *Valor Eccl.* (Rec. Com. 1810–34), II, 405.

5 Ibid.

6 *Reg. Stapeldon*, 331.

7 *Lettres communes, Urbain V*, 7 (1981), 317.

8 TNA, C 258/17, no. 1.

9 *Reg. Brantyngham*, I, 382–3.

10 Ibid., I, 410, 414, 447.

11 Ibid., I, 508–9. There was also a visitation by Archbishop Courtenay of Canterbury in 1384, but this has left no records (Lambeth Palace Library, Reg. Courtenay, f. 115r).

12 Below, p. 233.

13 *Reg. Brantyngham*, I, 93.

14 DRO, Chanter VIII, f. 48r–v; *Reg. Stafford*, 314.

15 DRO, Chanter IX, ff. 78v–79r; *Reg. Stafford*, 314.

16 Chanter IX, ff. 232v–233r; *Reg. Stafford*, 314.

directions were given about the burning of candles in the choir during vespers, mattins, and high mass.[1]

Little is known of the positive achievements of the house, but the lack of recorded interventions by Grandisson and by the bishops after 1400 may indicate that much of its history passed satisfactorily. The canons knew something of their church's history and, like all medieval communities, were inclined to expound and embroider it. This had been so in the 10th century, when their predecessors believed that Pope Gregory had sent St German to evangelise Cornwall.[2] In 1284 the priory asserted that its fair had been granted by King Æthelstan,[3] and, as we have seen, its members were aware that Cnut had given their church a charter and that it had been the seat of bishops. In 1304 the king's escheator in Cornwall was told the story that Bishop Leofric removed the original canons from St Germans and installed Augustinian ones, a story that is likely to have come from the canons since Leland recorded it, probably on his visit in about 1533.[4] This version of history would have enabled the priory to claim seniority as an Augustinian house over Bodmin and Launceston; indeed, it would have made it the oldest in England. The priors of St Germans played minor roles in Church affairs as collectors of clergy taxation, and at least two of them acted as visitors to the houses of the Augustinian Order in the south-west of England.[5] In 1436 the prior was appointed by the pope to help the people of Callington acquire a graveyard for their church.[6]

The next recorded visitation of the priory was carried out on behalf of the archbishop of Canterbury in 1492, but it produced no comments or injunctions. The visitors merely noted a complaint by the prior that one of the canons, John Jamys, lately professed, had left the priory and his religious observance without permission, and that his whereabouts was unknown. The other canons said that all was well.[7] In 1498–9 Prior John Serle obtained a grant from Pope Alexander VI allowing him the privilege of having a mitre, staff, and the other insignia of a bishop.[8] The last prior, Robert Swymmer, supplemented his income by holding the vicarage of Talland from 1520 until 1538 and the rectory of Minster from 1537 onwards. He and six canons acknowledged Henry VIII as supreme head of the church in 1534.[9] In the following year the royal valuation of Church property, *Valor Ecclesiasticus*, estimated the gross income of the priory at £243 8s. 0d., a sum divided almost equally between temporal and spiritual resources. In the first category £84 18s. 6d. came from rents and farms of lands in Landrake, £21 from Tinnel in Landulph, and £13 12s. 10d. from St Germans. The most valuable tithes were those of St Germans (£70), followed by Landrake (£16), South Petherwin (£15 13s. 4d.), Gulval (£10 6s. 8d.), and Morval (£10). Smaller sums still came from tithes in Landulph and from the pensions of Launceston and South Petherwin. An annuity of £2 was paid to Henry Courtenay, marquess of Exeter, who was chief steward of the priory, and the canons employed a sub-steward, auditor, and receiver general. After payments to cover their fees, almsgiving to the poor during Lent, an obit in Callington church, and the cost of a pensioner assigned by the bishop of Exeter, the net income was £228 4s. 8d.[10] The valuation was somewhat underestimated; in 1539 the king's officials charged with administering the revenues of the now dissolved priory found the total annual revenue to be £279 8s. 2¼d.[11]

Unlike Bodmin, Launceston, and Tywardreath whose internal affairs were troubled during the 1530s, St Germans figures little in the records of the period. The subprior, Nicholas Guest, was promoted to be prior of Tywardreath in March 1536, but his stay there was brief since that house was closed later that year, after which he left the monastic life and became vicar of St Winnow.[12] On 12 October 1538 William Dinham wrote a letter to the king's minister, Thomas Cromwell, stating that he had recently had supper with Prior Swymmer in the company of the ex-friar, theologian, and former poet, Alexander Barclay, who was visiting the priory and had preached a sermon in honour of the Virgin Mary.[13] Barclay, who was currently employed at Launceston Priory, was notorious at that time for his conservative views on religion, and Dinham gave a circumstantial account of his criticisms of the destruction of images that marked the year 1538 and of innuendoes against the king, but no disloyalty was attributed to Swymmer.[14] The prior and seven canons surrendered the priory to the king's commissioner, the Cornishman John Tregonwell, on 2 March 1539.[15] The prior received a pension of £66 13s. 4d., one canon

---

1 H. E. Salter (ed.), *Chapters of the Augustinian Canons*, Cant. & York Soc. 29 (1922), 171–4.

2 Above, p. 129.

3 TNA, JUST 1/111, m 36d; Picken, *DCNQ* 27 (1956–8), 104.

4 Oliver, *Monasticon*, 4; *Cal. Pat.* 1381–5, 316; Leland, *Collectanea*, ed. Hearne, I, 75.

5 *Reg. Lacy*, ed. Dunstan, I, 86, 229, 262, 300, 324, etc.; Salter (ed.), *Chapters of the Augustinian Canons*, 52, 174–5.

6 *Cal. Papal Regs* IV, 166; VIII, 581; *Reg. Lacy*, ed. Dunstan, II, 90–7.

7 *Reg. Morton, Canterbury*, II, 81.

8 *Cal. Papal Regs* XVII(1), 643.

9 TNA, E 25/57/2, printed in *7th Deputy Keeper's Report* (1846) App. II, 300.

10 *Valor Eccl.*, II, 405. A more detailed valor of 1539 is printed in Oliver, *Monasticon*, 409.

11 W. Dugdale, *Monasticon Anglicanum* (1817–30), II, 470.

12 Below, p. 295. Guest (or Gyst) was vicar of St Winnow until his death in 1545. He gave evidence about a property dispute at St Germans in 1544, and signed his deposition 'Guest' (TNA, E 315/118, f. 232r).

13 On Barclay, see *ODNB*, and for his link with Launceston at this time, below, p. 00.

14 *L&P Hen. VIII*, XIII(2), 232.

15 TNA, E 322/209, printed in *8th Deputy Keeper's Report* (1847) App. II, 26. One of these canons, Martin Powtrayn, was not pensioned; perhaps he was listed incorrectly or was a chaplain.

£6 13s. 4d., four £5 6s. 8d., and the single novice, Robert Capell, £2.[1] All but one were given permission to change their habits and to hold benefices.[2] Swymmer continued to hold the rectory of Minster until his death (by January 1559), along with the rectory of North Hill which he acquired in 1554.[3] A sum of £12 6s. 8d. per annum was assigned to pay for the chaplain who ministered in the church and a colleague who served 'the court', presumably Cuddenbeak manor.[4]

In 1541 the crown leased the priory site, buildings, and 19 acres of land in St Germans and Landrake to John Champernown, a squire of the king's household, for 21 years at a rent of £6 15s. 11d.[5] A year later, after his death, his widow Katherine and two gentlemen purchased the reversion of the property for a sum of £434.[6] In 1564 it passed to the Eliot family. In 1547 the crown gave the rectory of St Germans, comprising the tithes and revenues of the parish, to the dean and chapter of Windsor (Berks.), who appointed a series of curates, modestly paid, to serve the parish until the 19th century.[7] Following the dissolution of the priory the nave continued to serve as the parish church, but the choir fell into disuse. Part of it collapsed in 1592.[8] The opening between the nave and the choir was built up, and a Perpendicular window, perhaps the former east window of the choir, was inserted into it. A few specimens survive of seals of the priory, both those of the whole community and the private seals of Priors Henry and Hawkyn. The latter, dated 1431–2, displays the priory's coat of arms, consisting of three bells, arranged 2 and 1. The arms appear on an early 16th-century bench-end in Landulph church (where the priory had property), and in a window of Antony church where the tincture of the bells is or.[9]

PRIORS OF ST GERMANS

William	occurs 1194 × 1195[10]
Auger	occurs 25 June 1201, 8 July 1202[11]
Alfred	occurs summer 1224, 1225[12]
Godfrey	occurs 16 June 1230, 25 June 1245[13]
Walter	occurs c.1262[14]
Adam	occurs c.1265[15]
Richard	died by 11 Aug 1279[16]
Geoffrey	conf. 16 March 1280[17]
Henry	occurs 16 July 1293, 31 Aug 1315[18]
Richard Michael	occurs 1332 × 1333, vac. by 14 Sept 1341[19]
Richard of Polgover	el. c. Sept 1341, died c. 7 Aug 1355[20]
John Prechour	el. 14 Aug 1355, conf. 27 Aug 1355, died by 22 Jan 1367[21]
William Treskelly	el. by 16 March 1367, royal assent 16 March 1367, res. c. 20 Aug 1385[22]
Richard Harepath	el. Aug–Oct 1385, conf. 12 Oct 1385, coll. 4 Nov 1385[23]
John Averay	occurs 29 Sept 1401, died 8 Sept 1404[24]
John Piper	el. 23 Sept 1404, conf. c.8 Oct 1404, died 1 Feb 1424[25]
John Hawkyn	el. 12 Feb 1424, conf. 19 Feb 1424, died 26 Apr 1434[26]
John Kylkeham	el. 22 May 1434, conf. 29 May 1434, occurs 16 June 1437, prob. occurs 4 Feb 1453[27]
William Hancock	occurs 12 July 1462, 1483 × 1485[28]
John Serle	occurs 13 July 1492; died 28 Feb 1509[29]
Robert Swymmer	el. 13 March 1509, conf. 27 March 1509; till surrender, 2 March 1539[30]

---

1 *L&P Hen. VIII*, XIV(1), 169. For their subsequent careers, see A. L. Rowse, *Tudor Cornwall* (1941), 203.

2 D. S. Chambers, *Faculty Office Registers 1534–1549* (1966), 183.

3 For North Hill, see Chanter XVI, f. 27v and TNA, E 334/4, f. 201r. The next rector of Minster was instituted in January 1559 (Chanter XVIII, f. 44v).

4 TNA, SC 6/HenVIII/454.

5 TNA, E 315/212, f. 191r; *L&P Hen. VIII*, XVI, 722. The lands are listed, with their acreages, as *Pounde Mead*, *Kethyk Parke*, *Barne Park*, *Cowe Parke*, *Penmans Doune*, *Three Cornerd Parke*, *North-* and *South-furze Parke*, and *Deare Parke*.

6 *L&P Hen. VIII*, XVII, 101.

7 *Cal. Pat.* 1547–8, 148–51.

8 Carew, *The Survey of Cornwall*, f. 109v.

9 W. Iago, 'The Ecclesiastical Seals of Cornwall', *JRIC* 8 (1883–5), 50–1; *Catalogue of Seals in the Dept. of MSS, British Museum*, vol. I (1887), 728 no 3955; R. and O. B. Peter, *The Histories of Launceston and Dunheved* (1885), 17; Henderson, *Church and Priory of St. Germans*, 23.

10 S. Hobbs (ed.), *The Cartulary of Forde Abbey*, Somerset Record Soc. 85 (1998), 96.

11 Rowe (ed.), *Cornwall Feet of Fines*, I, 13; *Reg. Bronescombe*, ed. Hingeston-Randolph, 249; Barlow (ed.), *English Episcopal Acta*, XII, 190–1.

12 *Cur. Reg.* XI, 334–5; P. L. Hull (ed.), *The Cartulary of Launceston Priory*, DCRS n.s. 30 (1987), 194.

13 Rowe (ed.), *Cornwall Feet of Fines*, I, 23, 54. Rowe proposed a prior named Henry in 1244 (ibid., I, 43); if correct, there were two named Godfrey.

14 Hull (ed.), *Cartulary of Launceston Priory*, 153.

15 CRO, ME/595, /596 p. 153.

16 *Reg. Bronescombe*, ed. Hingeston-Randolph, 247–8; ed. Robinson, II, 129.

17 *Reg. Bronescombe*, ed. Hingeston-Randolph, 248; ed. Robinson, II, 134.

18 Hull (ed.), *Cartulary of Launceston Priory*, 20; *Reg. Stapeldon*, 331; *Reg. Grandisson*, II, 950.

19 TNA, C 270/11/17; *Reg. Grandisson*, II, 950; *Black Prince's Reg.*, II, 114.

20 *Reg. Grandisson*, II, 950, 954, 1162–3.

21 Ibid., II, 1166–73; *Cal. Pat.* 1364–7, 376; TNA, C 84/29/8.

22 *Cal. Pat.* 1364–7, 385, 388; *Reg. Brantyngham*, II, 585; cf. I, 165.

23 *Reg. Brantyngham*, I, 93, 165; II, 586–7.

24 ECA, D&C3773, f. 44v; Chanter IX, f. 78v.

25 Chanter IX, f. 78v; *Reg. Lacy*, ed. Hingeston-Randolph, I, 69–70.

26 *Reg. Lacy*, ed. Hingeston-Randolph, I, 69–78, 162.

27 Ibid., I, 162–70; *Reg. Lacy*, ed. Dunstan, II, 47; III, 164.

28 DRO, Chanter XII(i), f. 51v, 53r; TNA, C 1/65/4. For references to his surname, see also C 1/20/77 and DRO, CR 163, m. 1-1d.

29 *Reg. Morton, Canterbury*, II, 81; Chanter XIII., ff. 31v-33r.

30 Chanter XIII, ff. 31v-33r; *8th Deputy Keeper's Report* (1847) App. II, 26.

HELSTON

HOSPITAL OF ST JOHN BAPTIST

The hospital of St John Baptist (Helston) was an example of an institution common in England but unique in Cornwall before the 15th century: the small hospital caring for, or accommodating, the short-term sick or long-term infirm who were not lepers. The earliest evidence of its existence comes from a deed of about 1240 by which Henry, son of Henry fitz William, lord of Kellygreen in St Tudy, confirmed a grant of property made by his father Henry to the chapel of St John Baptist at *Menedklodou* and to the brothers who served God there, doing works of charity and ministering to the poor.[1] The grant gave the chapel and its brethren one acre of land at *Menedklodou*, the right to take materials (perhaps for fuel or building) from Henry's wood at Penventon, and permission to pasture three pigs there.[2] It looks as though the hospital was founded by the elder Henry in about 1220, unless he endowed an institution that already existed. *Menedklodou*, the modern Menaclidgey (perhaps 'the hill of ditches'), lies half a mile west of Helston in the parish of Sithney, by the side of Gipsy Lane: the old road from Helston to Breage and Marazion (SW 639 276).

By about 1260 the community, now called a hospital, had moved from Menaclidgey to a site next to Helston Bridge. This emerges from a confirmation of the hospital's property made at about that date by a third Henry, son of the second one, in favour of the hospital 'by the bridge of Helston' and the brethren serving God there.[3] The new site stood on the west side of the River Cober, just inside Sithney parish and on the south side of the old road to Marazion at the junction with Ratcliffe's Lane (SW6542 2754).[4] The old site at Menaclidgey continued to belong to the hospital and, since it seems to have retained a chapel, the suggestion was plausibly made by Charles Henderson that the place was occupied by the leper hospital of St Mary Magdalene (Helston) when the brothers of St John had left.[5] During the second half of the 13th century St John's received a number of small grants of property by way of endowment. Most of these were in Sithney parish, but there were outliers in Constantine, Crantock, St Enoder, Newlyn East, and Truro, so that the hospital acquired links with some of the parishes of mid-Cornwall as well as with its own vicinity.[6] The deeds that conveyed these properties do not always make clear the donors, since the signatories were sometimes people releasing claims rather than benefactors, but the Reskymer family of Mawgan-in-Meneage seems to have played an important role alongside the family of Kellygreen. Sir Richard Reskymer witnessed the earliest surviving hospital charter of about 1240; he appears to have been involved with the grant of the property at Constantine, and later tradition regarded his family as co-founders or benefactors of the hospital.[7] Another founder or benefactor, according to an inquest of 1396, was Master John Bollegh,[8] and John Boleghe or Boleigh was reported as the sole founder to the Chantry Commissioners in 1546 and 1548.[9] No person of that name is known, but Henry of Bollegh was a leading Cornish cleric of the late 13th century, being provost of Glasney college and, from 1284, archdeacon of Cornwall.[10] By 1331 his successor as archdeacon claimed to be 'patron, rector, protector, and disposer' of the house and its brethren,[11] and the hospital was subsequently a peculiar jurisdiction outside the normal administration of the diocese and under that of the archdeacon. This situation may well have come about through the intervention of Henry of Bollegh while he held the office.

During the late 13th and early 14th centuries the hospital was locally governed by a cleric who was sometimes entitled the prior, sometimes the warden. He was assisted by brothers who numbered two in 1324 when their names are given.[12] By 1331 at least one of them was a priest; an agreement of that year, following a dispute between the hospital and Roger Reskymer, knight, provided that Sir Roger and his heirs should

---

1 On the history of the hospital, see also C. G. Henderson, 'Records of St John's Hospital near Helston', *JRIC* 22.3 (1928), 382–407. Most of the records there printed, and some others, are now held in TNA, E 40, catalogued in *Cat. Anct D*; CRO, Rashleigh of Menabilly Deeds, R/3143–58; and Antony House. Of the latter Henderson transcribed a few more in RIC, Henderson 19, pp. 407–12 than now survive as Antony, HD/11/92–99.

2 Henderson, 'Records', 394–5; R/3144.

3 Henderson, 'Records', 395–6; R/3145.

4 It is not clear from the Sithney tithe apportionment of 1845 whether the hospital and its grounds were ever tithe free (TA/209, pp. 15–17, 39, 58, 75–6).

5 Henderson, 'Records', 394.

6 Ibid., 388, 396–9; R/3146–7; HD/11/92–98.

7 Henderson, 'Records', 387–8, 403.

8 Ibid., 403.

9 TNA, E 301/15, ff. 49v–50r; E 301/9, m. 5d; printed in L. S. Snell, *Documents towards a History of the Reformation in Cornwall*: vol. I, *The Chantry Certificates for Cornwall* (*c*.1953), 26–7.

10 For his career, see *Reg. Bronescombe*, ed. Hingeston-Randolph, 32, 315; ed. Robinson, III, 78.

11 Henderson, 'Records', 401.   12 Ibid. 400.

have the right in future to appoint one of the brothers, the person thus appointed saying mass daily for Sir Richard son of Gilbert Reskymer, Sir Roger, his wife and their ancestors. The hospital undertook to pay a fine of 6*d*. for every mass omitted.[1] Worship must have been a principal function of the house and the commemoration of benefactors may reflect the burial of some of them in its chapel: a 13th-century coffin slab from the hospital site is now preserved in Sithney church.[2] The surviving records of St John's, however, throw no light on the charitable work of the house, although the brethren seem to have sold at least one corrody or pension. In 1324 a cleric called Henry of Penhal sued the hospital for depriving him of his chamber and allowance of bread, wine, ale, pottage, meat, fish, and other victuals as the brothers of the hospital had them, together with wood for his hearth, a robe, footwear and linen.[3] In 1354 the prior still had brother colleagues, but by this time the hospital must have begun to suffer, like all ecclesiastical institutions after the Black Death of 1349, from the effects of rising prices and a falling population.[4]

In 1396 the crown ordered an inquest to be held into land that St John's had allegedly acquired without licence, and the escheator of Cornwall was subsequently instructed to confiscate and sell the property at issue.[5] The hospital still had a public profile in 1420 when John Urban of Southfleet (Kent), who originated from Helston, bequeathed it 40*s*. to buy a pair of vestments,[6] but during the 15th century its functions of care to the sick or poor probably faded away – a process observable in some other small English hospitals.[7] In 1486 the prior was John Carewe, a graduate of canon law and a pluralist cleric, who held the post with the rectories of Lanreath and Phillack and a canonry of Glasney college.[8] It is unlikely that he was often or ever resident. Not content with his other income, Carewe appears to have tried to suppress the priest in the hospital responsible for saying mass for the Reskymers. In 1487 he forged two deeds by which John Reskymer, the head of the family, allegedly released his rights over the hospital property and over all masses and prayers to be said for his soul and his parents' souls. The fraud was discovered, and the deeds were cancelled and returned to the Reskymers.[9] Presumably at least one priest remained at the hospital to celebrate the necessary masses.

Carewe continued as prior until at least 1502 and probably until his death in the summer of 1504.[10] He was succeeded by John Nans, a distinguished man who had graduated as a doctor of canon and civil law at Bologna and resembled Carewe as the holder of several benefices. Vicar-general of the bishops of Exeter and Wells, subdean of Wells cathedral, and rector of Camborne, Nans too can have spent little if any time at Helston during the period of his priorship.[11] He even failed to remember the hospital in his will, although he left bequests to six other local churches.[12] When Nans died in 1508 his successor was appointed by the archdeacon of Cornwall – a practice that probably went back earlier but is only recorded at this date.[13] The archdeacon, Thomas Harrys, chose John Harrys, a young man of about twenty who may have been his nephew and was still undergoing his education: he graduated as a bachelor of civil and canon law at Oxford in 1512–13.[14] This confirms that the office of prior was now a sinecure, but because Harrys was not resident or a priest, there must have been a chaplain at St John to say the necessary masses and we are told of one called Richard William in 1522.[15] After graduating, Harrys was ordained priest and embarked on yet another career as a pluralist, becoming vicar of Gulval in 1513 and later canon of Glasney college. He too must have been often non-resident at Helston, but that it did not prevent him from succeeding where Carewe had failed and gaining the income of the hospital for his sole benefit. In 1522 he was receiving £7 for his stipend and the chaplain £4 13*s*. 4*d*.[16] By 1546 Harrys was the only member of staff and had appropriated the whole net income.[17]

In 1535 St John Helston was the only hospital in Cornwall to be assessed for the new royal taxation of the Church: first fruits and tenths. The gross income was estimated at £14 7*s*. 2½*d*. and the net income at £12 16*s*. 4*d*., a total of 19*s*. 2*d*. being paid as fees to the steward, auditor, and bailiff who presumably managed the hospital's property in the prior's absence.[18] When John Leland visited Helston in 1542, he found the hospital of St John 'yet standing at the west south west end of the town, of the foundation of one Kylligrin',[19] but the fabric may not have been in a good state since the prior's dwelling house was said in 1548 to be 'in decay and ruin'.[20] In 1546 and 1548 the chantry commissioners described the institution as a chantry, and assessed the

---

1 Ibid. 401; E 40/11590.
2 P. Sheppard, *The Historic Towns of Cornwall* (1980), 11.
3 Henderson, 'Records', 400–1.
4 Ibid. 402–3.   5 Ibid. 403; R/3154–5.
6 N. Orme (ed.), *Cornish Wills 1342–1540*, DCRS new ser. 50 (2007), 55.
7 N. Orme and M. Webster, *The English Hospital, 1070–1570* (1995), 129–30, 221–2, 266–7.
8 Biography in *BRUO*, I, 354.
9 Henderson, 'Records', 403–4; E 40/10023.
10 Henderson, 'Records', 404; biography in *BRUO*, I, 354.
11 Biography in *BRUO*, II, 1336–7.
12 Orme (ed.), *Cornish Wills*, 129–30.
13 Henderson, 'Records', 404–5.
14 Biography in *BRUO*, IV, 270, which may conflate the benefices of more than one man.
15 T. L. Stoate (ed.), *The Cornwall Military Survey 1522* (1987), 32.
16 Ibid.
17 E 301/15, ff. 49v–50r; Snell, *Chantry Certificates*, 26.
18 *Valor Eccl.* (Rec. Com. 1810–34), II, 393.
19 J. Leland, *Itinerary*, ed. L. Toulmin Smith (1907–10), I, 194.
20 E 301/9, m. 5d; Snell, *Chantry Certificates*, 27.

net income as £15 19s. 1½d. and £16 11s. 10d. respectively, all of which went to Harrys.[1] A contemporary rental of the endowments survives, which lists the tenements, tenants, and rents in Crantock, St Enoder, Kea, Sithney, Truro, and Helston itself.[2] The chapel contained ornaments worth £3 and had bells weighing one and half hundredweight. There seems to have been no work of charity, since the commissioners of 1548 noted 'poor people having relief out of the premises, none'. The institution was dissolved under the Chantry Act of 1547, with effect from 1 April 1548, and Harrys was awarded a pension of £6 13s. 4d.[3] The site and lands were sold to Sir Thomas Pomeroy and his brother Hugh on 21 July in the same year.[4] St John Helston was the only hospital in Cornwall or Devon to suffer dissolution during the Reformation, apart from the much larger foundation of St John Exeter in 1539, but the term 'former hospital' would be a more just description in this case. No remains of the buildings are visible.[5]

WARDENS OR PRIORS OF THE HOSPITAL OF ST JOHN

John Coynt	occurs 3 Nov 1269[6]
Michael	occurs 29 Sept 1302, 18 May 1304[7]
Laurence	occurs 1328[8]
Urban	occurs 1324[9]
William of Rosmeber	occurs 1 Aug 1332, 7 Apr 1344[10]
Thomas	occurs 3 Jan 1352, 24 May 1354[11]
John Carewe, BCanL	occurs 10 Apr 1487, 22 Aug 1502 × 21 Aug 1503[12]
John Nans, DCan&CL	died by Sept 1508[13]
John Harrys, BCL	coll. 22 Sept 1508, till dissolution 1548[14]

HOSPITAL OF ST MARY MAGDALENE

There were lepers at Helston by 1307–10, when the executors of Bishop Bitton of Exeter gave them a sum of 15s. 6d,[15] and by the early 15th century their community had acquired the status of a hospital with a chapel. In 1398 John Kembell, vicar of Sithney, was licensed to celebrate mass in the chapel of St Mary Magdalene, Helston,[16] and Bishop Stafford of Exeter granted an indulgence of forty days in 1411 to those contributing to the support of the 'hospital of St Mary Magdalene near Helston'.[17] A similar indulgence of forty days was issued by Bishop Lacy in 1435, but this mentions the place only as a chapel.[18] The will bequest by John Megre, a London pewterer in 1419, of 6d. 'to each lazar of the church of St Margaret near Helston' is best interpreted as a further but confused reference to St Mary Magdalene.[19] These mentions of the hospital and its chapel as near Helston and in Sithney parish suggest that its site lay outside the town towards the west. Charles Henderson conjectured that it was at Menaclidgey (SW639 276), about half a mile west of Helston by the side of the old road to Marazion. This was the original site of the hospital of St John before it moved to a new location by Helston Bridge in the mid 13th century. In 1786 Menaclidgey included fields called 'Chapel field' and 'Parc-chapel', which hint at the existence of a chapel on the site after the removal of the other hospital, and in the 1540s the property of St John included tenements called 'Aidenford juxta Maulyn' and 'Mawlen', both mentioned in association with Menaclidgey.[20] If Henderson's conjecture is correct, the leper community came into being between about 1250 and 1307–10, and existed until at least 1419 in close association with St John. The fact that its property was in the hands of St John by the 1540s suggests that it had ceased to exist by that date. No visible remains survive.[21]

---

1 E 301/15, ff. 49v–50r; E 301/9, m. 5d; Snell, *Chantry Certificates*, 26–7.
2 Bodleian, Rawl. D 363, ff. 258v–61v; Henderson, 'Records', 406–7.
3 E 301/10; Snell, *Chantry Certificates*, 26–7.
4 *Cal. Pat.* 1549–51, 104.
5 For site information, see CCC, HER 30096.
6 Henderson, 'Records', 396.
7 R/3151; E 40/10427.
8 TNA, CP 40/272, m. 13d.
9 Henderson, 'Records', 400.
10 Ibid., 401–2; E 40/11590, 12011.
11 Henderson, 'Records', 402–3 (RIC, Henderson 19, p. 410); HD/11/96.
12 Henderson. 'Records', 403–4; E 40/10023.
13 Henderson, 'Records', 404.
14 HD/11/99; E 301/9, m. 5d; Snell, *Chantry Certificates*, 27.
15 W. H. Hale and H. T. Ellacombe (ed.), *Accounts of the Executors… of Thomas Bishop of Exeter 1310*, Camden Soc. new ser. 10 (1874), 29; M. I. Somerscales, 'Lazar Houses in Cornwall', *JRIC* new ser. 5.1 (1965), 89–90.
16 *Reg. Stafford,* 225.
17 Ibid., 127; DRO, Chanter VIII, f. 135r–v.
18 *Reg. Lacy,* ed. Dunstan, I, 300.
19 N. Orme (ed.), *Cornish Wills 1342–1540*, DCRS new ser. 50 (2007), 52.
20 C. G. Henderson, 22.3 (1928), 384–5, 393–4, 406.
21 For site information, see CCC, HER 28952.2.

ST KEVERNE

LEPER HOUSE OF 'NAN(S)CLEGY'

On Thursday 22 March 1268 (new style) Thomas Conwenian granted to Ralph, prior of St Michael's Mount, his rights in the moor and water lands near the leper house (*leprosarium*) of 'Nanclegy'. The boundaries of the property in question also mention the highway in front of the leper house and the ford of 'Nansclegy', a name that means 'valley with a sick house'.[1] In 1842, the tithe apportionment of St Keverne parish refers to a field called Lazarus field near Trenoweth farm (SW 7975 2205), and if this was on or near the site, the valley was that of the stream which enters the sea at Porthoustock; if not, the valley may have been that of the stream running down to Porthallow.[2] The fact that the leper community had given its name to a valley suggests that it had been established for some time by 1268, and it seems to have been still or recently in being in 1481 when the reeve of St Michael's Mount's manor of Traboe in St Keverne recorded a payment of 2*d*. 'from the farm [i.e. rent] of the leper house (*domus leprosorum*) there' – presumably the same house.[3] The house at 'Nan(s)clegy' thus appears to have had a more than temporary existence, but it was unusual in the remoteness of its situation (most developed leper communities were sited on main roads), and the registers of the bishops of Exeter make no mention of it.

ST KEW

ALLEGED AUSTINIAN HOUSE

In 1123 Henry I granted the church of St Kew to Exeter cathedral, whose head was the bishop of Exeter,[4] and the bishop, William Warelwast, gave it to the priory of Plympton (Devon), which he had refounded as a house of Augustinian canons in 1121.[5] Later, in 1158, Henry II confirmed the grant to Plympton, and ordered that the prebends of the clerks still serving the church should revert to the priory on their deaths.[6] An account of the subsequent history of the church of St Kew was given, very much later, by Bishop Bronescombe of Exeter when he took action against Plympton priory in 1261 for allegedly holding three churches in his diocese without proper title, including St Kew. Bronescombe contended that William Warelast's grant was invalid, because it did not receive the consent of the cathedral clergy until long afterwards. He went on to claim that St Kew was staffed by secular canons while William was bishop (1107–37), and that these were later replaced by regular canons: presumably Augustinians from Plympton. He stated that no canons of any kind were now serving God there, and concluded by asserting that the church had devolved into his own hands.[7] Despite this assertion St Kew remained in or returned to the hands of Plympton priory by 1283 when the next bishop of Exeter, Peter Quinil, instituted a vicar to serve the church, who was presented by the prior and canons and was assigned a share of the parish revenues by Quinil.[8]

The claim that St Kew church had been staffed by canons from Plympton surfaced again in 1302, when a complaint was made to the king's justices of eyre in Cornwall about the priory's administration of the church.[9] A local jury asked to report on the matter said that King Edgar (d. 975) had given the canons of Plympton two carucates of land, 100*s*. of rent in St Kew, and the church of the place on condition of maintaining two canons there to celebrate divine service, provide alms for the poor, and offer hospitality to pilgrims and other guests. These duties, the jury claimed, had been performed until fifteen years previously, when the priory had discontinued them. The prior of Plympton replied that his house held the

---

1 P. L. Hull (ed.), *The Cartulary of St Michael's Mount*, DCRS new ser. 5 (1962), 29–30; C. G. Henderson, 'The Ecclesiastical History of the 109 Parishes of West Cornwall', *JRIC* new ser. 3 (1957-60), 274–5; M. I. Somerscales, 'Lazar Houses in Cornwall', *JRIC* new ser. 5.1 (1965), 88–9.

2 CRO, TA/99, p. 30 (no. 351).

3 CRO, AU/1d.

4 *Regesta Regum Anglo-Normannorum*, ed. H. W. C. Davis et. al. (1913–59), II, 185; G. Oliver, *Monasticon Dioecesis Exoniensis* (1846), 134. See also above, p. 131.

5 *Reg. Bronescombe*, ed. Hingeston-Randolph, 224; ed. Robinson, I, 130–1.

6 Oliver, *Monasticon*, 135.

7 *Reg. Bronescombe*, ed. Hingeston-Randolph, 224–5; ed. Robinson, I, 128–33.

8 *Reg. Bronescombe*, ed. Hingeston-Randolph, 354, 372.

9 The justices were appointed to hold the eyre as from Michaelmas 1302 (*Cal. Pat.* 1307–7, 57).

church by a grant of Bishop Warelwast, confirmed by one of Henry II, and that these grants did not specify the duties alleged by the jury. The evidence available to us today supports his case, but the judges accepted the jury's evidence and ruled that the obligations should be restored.[1] Plympton responded by petitioning the king that the conditions on which it held St Kew had been misrepresented, and asked to be allowed to keep the property according to the terms of its charters.[2] The result was a compromise in 1307 by which Edward I upheld the justices' decision but gave the priory permission to provide the necessary prayers, alms, and hospitality by means of a vicar and chaplain: parish clergy instead of canons.[3]

If the history of St Kew was correct as narrated by Bronescombe, the church was served by regular canons of Plympton from about the middle of the 12th century to the middle of the 13th. Canons living away from their mother house generally did so in pairs, so those at St Kew would have been likely to form a small cell or priory under Plympton's authority. Bronescombe's assertions, however, were made long after the events they profess to describe, and the evidence of the jury of 1302 is less trustworthy still. Its claim that there were regular canons of Plympton at St Kew until 1287 runs counter to Bronescombe's statement that none existed in 1261 and to Quinil's institution of a vicar to serve the church in 1283. It is possible that Plympton sent canons to St Kew between the judgment of 1302 and the king's licence of 1307, but the existence of any long-term Augustinian cell attached to the church remains to be confirmed.[4]

LAMMANA

BENEDICTINE PRIORY

Lammana is the ancient name of the island known today as St George's or Looe Island (SX 25 51), and of the adjoining part of the mainland west of Looe which is now in the parish of Talland.[5] The name first appears in the form *Lamene* as one of the landed possessions confirmed as belonging to Glastonbury Abbey by Pope Lucius II in 1144.[6] A similar confirmation by Pope Alexander III in 1168 spells it as *Lamane*.[7] The island and mainland each acquired a religious building, generally described as chapels in medieval records. One lay towards the western end of the island on its summit (SX 2569 5137), and the other opposite to it on a hillside of the mainland (SX 2510 5228). The earliest document clearly to differentiate the two is a legal judgment based on the findings of a jury of local people in 1290, who believed that the island chapel was the earlier and that its counterpart on the mainland came into existence later, a belief that seems likely to be true.[8] The island chapel may have ancient origins. It was sited at one end of an oval enclosure formed by a bank and ditch, in the latter of which a handful of Roman coins was found in 2008.[9] The name Lammana appears to mean 'church-site of a monk' (*lann managh*),[10] and the island has been proposed as a possible location of a pre-Conquest monastery.[11] No evidence of such a foundation has yet emerged, but there may have been a lesser ecclesiastical site such as a graveyard or chapel.

The confirmation of Pope Lucius extended to the churches and chapels belonging to the properties that it names, which may indicate that Lammana had such a building by 1144. More certainty comes from a charter issued by a local landholder, Hasculf de Soligny,

---

1 TNA, JUST 1/118, m. 58; J. Maclean, *The Parochial and Family History of the Deanery of Trigg Minor* (1873–9), II, 269–70. On the affair, see Maclean, *Trigg Minor*, II, 84–7, and W. M. M. Picken, 'The "Landochou" Charter', in W. G. Hoskins, *The Westward Expansion of Wessex*, University of Leicester, Department of Local History, Occasional Papers 13 (1960), 36–44.

2 Maclean, *Trigg Minor*, II, 270.

3 *Cal. Pat.* 1307–7, 512.

4 Allegations similar to those of 1302 were repeated in 1391 (*Cal. Inq. Misc.* V, 175). Further information on the history of the church may be found in Maclean, *Trigg Minor*, and W. M. M. Picken, 'The Manor of Tremaruusel and the Honour of St Keus', *JRIC* new ser. 7.3 (1975–6), 220–30. For site-information, see CCC, HER. 17950(cf. 17934, 17948).

5 The sites mentioned in this article were investigated by Channel Four 'Time Team' (2008) and recorded in Wessex Archaeology, 2009, St Michael's Chapel and Lammana Chapel, Looe, Cornwall', unpublished report for Videotext Communications Ltd.; copy deposited with CCC, HER. I am grateful to 'Time Team' for involving me in the investigation and especially to Stewart Ainsworth for his advice on topography. The other principal works on Lammana are W. M. M. Picken, 'Light on Lammana', *DCNQ* 35.8 (1985), 281–6; L. Olson, *Early Monasteries in Cornwall* (Woodbridge, 1989), 98–103; O. J. Padel, 'Glastonbury's Cornish Connections', in L. Abrams and J. P. Carley (eds.), *The Archaeology and History of Glastonbury Abbey* (1991), pp. 253–6; and L. Olson, 'Lammana, West Looe; C. K. Croft Andrew's excavations of the chapel and Monks House, 1935–6', *Cornish Archaeology*, 33 (1994), 96–129.

6 Adam of Domerham, *Historia de Rebus Gestis Glastoniensibus*, ed. T. Hearne (1727), II, 323.

7 A. Watkin (ed.), *The Great Chartulary of Glastonbury*, Somerset Record Soc. 59, 63–4 (1947–56), I, 129.

8 Picken, 'Light on Lammana', 283, 284–5.

9 Wessex Archaeology, 2009 report.

10 O. J. Padel, *A Popular Dictionary of Cornish Place-Names* (1988), 86.

11 Olson, *Early Monasteries in Cornwall*, 98–103.

between about 1199 and 1220, confirming a grant to Glastonbury Abbey by his predecessors (who are not identified or dated) of 'the whole island of St Michael of *Lammana* with all its appurtenances and lands and tithes', as well as the tithes of his demesne of Portlooe on the mainland. The witnesses to the charter were led by 'Helias, then prior of the same place [i.e. Lammana], and his fellow monk John'.[1] Hasculf held property at Kilmersdon (Somerset) in 1212 and Ralph de Soligny, presumably a relation, did so at Fawton in St Neot (Cornwall) in 1228–9, which helps explain the gift of property in the second county to a monastery in the first.[2] By the time of Hasculf's charter, in about 1200, the island definitely had a church or chapel dedicated to St Michael, and the witnesses to his grant reveal that a small priory staffed by two monks, doubtless from Glastonbury Abbey, existed in the vicinity: either on the island or the adjoining mainland. This evidence is supported by a report of the bishop of Ely and two other clergy that the patronage of the priory of Lammana belonged to the monks of Glastonbury – a report made soon after 1202, when it was commissioned by Pope Innocent III.[3] An undated charter of about the mid 13th century states that a Glastonbury tenant named Robert de Colerne held property in return for providing a horse to carry monks from the abbey to Lammana.[4]

The chapel on the island is shown on a map of the south coast of Cornwall in 1539 as a small rectangular edifice one-storey high, without a tower.[5] A partial excavation of the site in 2008 uncovered sections of the north and west walls, and revealed a burial within the chapel, probably of a cleric or a layman of high status.[6] Two large carved stones preserved on the site may have been part of a chancel arch, subdividing the building inside. The chapel on the mainland stood on a small platform just below the top of a hillside, opposite the island chapel and immediately beneath a lane shown on the tithe map of 1839.[7] The lane (still partly visible) appears to be of ancient origin. It leads from Hasculf's property at Portlooe straight to the chapel, after which it turns east to descend by a gentle gradient to level ground beside the shore and thence to Looe. A short branch from the lane once led to a landing place opposite the island, and part of one wall of a stone building conjecturally known as the Monks House stands a little above the landing place beside the modern coastal path (SX 252 522). This building and the mainland chapel were excavated by C. K. Croft Andrew in 1936 and partially re-excavated in 2008.[8] The chapel site appears to relate to Portlooe, to the island chapel (which it faces, at about the same height), to the surrounding coast of the mainland (including Looe, a mile away), and to the landing place and the sea. The shape of the chapel was also a rectangle, internally measuring about 8.22 metres (27 feet) in length and 4.72 metres (15.5 feet) in width, perhaps having been extended at some time towards the east. It eventually included a chancel, nave, and a substantial south porch, while steps in the north wall opposite the porch suggest another doorway which may have been accessed from the lane above. Two or three burials have been traced inside the building. Its patron saint is not recorded, but may have been St Michael like the island. The jury of 1290 talked of Glastonbury's monks having celebrated divine service in the island chapel,[9] but it is not certain whether this was the only place of their ministry. There would have been advantages in living on the mainland close to the island, the lords of Portlooe, and the community of Looe, whereas residence on the island might have been more difficult. A large field south of the chapel and west of the Monks House has well-defined boundaries, and may indicate the curtilage of the priory if the latter was on the mainland, in which case the Monks House may represent part of its buildings.

The priory enjoyed certain holdings and rights. These were said in 1289 to include a messuage and a carucate of land 'in Lammana',[10] apparently on the mainland beside the island. Another endowment was granted by Robert (III) of Cardinan (fl. 1200–1227), lord of the honour of Cardinham, to Glastonbury Abbey, St Michael of Lammana, and the brothers serving God there, in the form of one ferling of land called *Fentenfilgi* at *Trewodlowan* (probably Trelawne in Pelynt), with the right to take timber from Robert's wood at *Trewodlowan* to maintain and mend their houses at *Fentenfilgi*, and firewood from the same place for their fire.[11] The most valuable piece of property, however, would have been the tithes of the demesne of Portlooe, as granted or confirmed in Hasculf's charter. By the middle of the 13th century there was an obligation on the monks of Glastonbury to pay 10s. a year to the earl of Cornwall in respect of their

---

1 Somerset Record Office, DD/WO/23/1, printed with commentary by Padel, 'Glastonbury's Cornish Connections', 254–5. A later copy of the deed, preserved in Cambridge, Trinity College, R.5.33, f. 105v, was printed in Adam of Domerham, *Historia*, ed. Hearne, II, 599–600, and in G. Oliver, *Monasticon Dioecesis Exoniensis*, (1846), 70.

2 *Book of Fees*, I, 83, 394, 437.

3 Adam of Domerham, *Historia*, 420, 423; Watkin (ed.), *Great Chartulary*, I, 78.

4 Watkin (ed.), *Great Chartulary*, II, 328.

5 BL, Cotton Aug. I.i.35, 36, 38, 39.

6 Wessex Archaeology, 2009 report.

7 CRO, TA/ and TM/218.

8 Olson, 'Lammana, West Looe', 96–129; Wessex Archaeology, 2009 report.

9 Picken, 'Light on Lammana', 283, 284–5.

10 P. L. Hull (ed.), *The Cartulary of Launceston Priory*, DCRS new ser. 30 (1987), 168.

11 Adam of Domerham, *Historia*, 600–1. For Robert's dates, see I. J. Sanders, *English Baronies* (1960), 110, and below, p. 284. The Cardinan family held property at Trelawne in 1241 (J. H. Rowe (ed.), *Cornwall Feet of Fines*, DCRS (1914–50), I, 37).

possessions at Lammana; this sum was eventually waived by Richard, earl of Cornwall and brother of Henry III, who died in 1272.[1] At the time of Hasculf's grant, the parish church of most of the surrounding area was Talland which belonged to a lay patron, but in about the early 13th century the patron transferred the church to the canons of Launceston Priory.[2] The canons duly became rectors of the parish and appropriated the great tithes, deputing the care of the church to a vicar. Disputes then arose between the canons and the monks of Lammana, since Portlooe and its demesne constituted a virtually autonomous parish of its own, the monks receiving its tithes and apparently ministering to its inhabitants in return.[3]

The first record of these disputes occurs in 1238 when Pope Gregory IX commissioned the abbot of Muchelney (Somerset) and the archdeacon of Wells to judge a claim by Glastonbury against Launceston for the restitution of tithes on the land between the way from *Porthpighan* (West Looe) to *Ternent* (Trenant) on one side and the water of Looe on the other, which formed part of the demesne of Sir Odo of Portlooe. An additional issue concerned the baptism of children, perhaps indicating that the infants of the demesne tenants were christened at the mainland chapel of Lammana rather than at Talland church. The quarrel was settled in 1239 in favour of Launceston, in return for a payment of 5s. per annum to Glastonbury by way of indemnity.[4] A second dispute resulted in an agreement in 1279 by which Launceston recognised Glastonbury's possession of tithes from the sea at Looe along the highway from *Porthpighan* to the court of the lord of Portlooe and thence to the sea, except for the tithes of the men of the settlement at *Porthpighan*. Glastonbury in turn recognised Launceston's right to tithes north of these boundaries, on condition that the former payment of 5s. was increased to 6s. 8d.[5] The tithe survey of Talland parish in 1839 reveals that the district still known as Lemain, west of Looe, paid no tithe to the vicar, and this approximates to the territory allocated to Glastonbury in 1279.[6]

Why did the priory come into being, and what were its functions? The lords of Portlooe may have wished to have monks at hand to organise worship and pray for them, as other Cornish lords possessed at Minster and Tregony. The mention of baptism in 1238, together with later references to the clergy of Lammana ministering to the dwellers in the demesne of Portlooe, make it possible that some pastoral work was done from the priory and its chapels, although Benedictine monks like those of Glastonbury were not normally active in this respect. Since, as we shall see, Lammana's revenues were small and the abbey had no other churches or lands in Cornwall, the monks can have spent little time on administrative tasks. One of their chief functions is likely to have been to maintain a religious presence on the island, possibly to minister to pilgrims to its chapel. Glastonbury may have been attracted to Lammana because it was already a holy site or through the hope of developing a cult of St Michael on the island in imitation of the saint's more famous island shrine at St Michael's Mount.[7] The jury of 1290 thought that the mainland chapel was built 'because in days of old many of those people who, through devotion, would have wanted to visit the [island] chapel on St Michael's Day, often lost their lives in the stormy sea'.[8] There were in fact three festivals in the saint's honour during the year: 8 May, 29 September, and 16 October, but further evidence for pilgrimages to Lammana is elusive. William Worcester, who visited Cornwall in 1478, noted the names of several places where St Michael was honoured, but Lammana was not among them.[9] John Leland, on his first journey through the county in about 1533, referred to the island as 'St Nicholas Isle', stating that it was six or seven acres in extent and supported sheep, rabbits, and seabirds. He too made no mention of the chapel there or its mainland counterpart, although he alluded to the chapels in the villages of East and West Looe.[10] If pilgrimage took place, it may have been largely restricted to people from the immediate neighbourhood.

Richard earl of Cornwall's undated remission of the 10s. due to him from Lamanna allowed the monks of Glastonbury to put the church (*ecclesia* – a rare usage), the island, and the other properties to farm, or to alienate or dispose of them without impediment from the earl or his heirs.[11] Putting to farm meant leasing the revenues in return for an annual rent, rather than collecting them directly via the abbey's monks or servants. Later tradition at Glastonbury stated that Abbot Michael of Amesbury (1235–53) 'put Lammana in Cornwall to farm and assigned it to the sacristy [or to the office of sacrist] (*sacristarie*)',[12] but this did not immediately bring about the end of the priory. There was still a monastic presence on the island in 1277, when the abbot of Glastonbury sued persons who had broken into the 'cell' at Lamanna and had assaulted his monk, William of Bolevill, its *custos* – a term found

---

1 Watkin (ed.), *Great Chartulary*, III, 580; Adam of Domerham, *Historia*, 603–4.
2 Below, p. 210.
3 In 1727 the vicar and churchwardens referred to the area as the 'ancient parish' of *Lemane* (R. Potts (ed.), *A Calendar of Cornish Glebe Terriers 1673–1735*, DCRS new ser. 19 (1974), 156).
4 Adam of Domerham, *Historia*, 602–3.
5 Hull (ed.), *Cartulary of Launceston*, 167.
6 CRO, TA/ and TM/218.
7 Olson, *Early Monasteries in Cornwall*, 101.
8 Picken, 'Light on Lammana', 283, 284–5; Potts, *Cornish Glebe Terriers*, 156.
9 W. Worcester, *Itineraries*, ed. J. H. Harvey (1969), 14–15.
10 J. Leland, *Itinerary*, ed. L. Toulmin Smith (1907–10), I, 324.
11 Adam of Domerham, *Historia*, 603–4.
12 Ibid., 518.

elsewhere in monastic usage for a person of lesser or more temporary status than a prior.[1] During the 1280s, however, the abbey decided to withdraw from Lammana, on grounds that may have included distance from the Glastonbury, lack of other interests in Cornwall, and insufficiency of revenues. The patronage of the island chapel, together with its lands and possessions, was sold to Ralph Bloyou on behalf of Walter of Treverbyn, the lord of the manor of Portlooe, and the sale took effect on Midsummer Day, 24 June, 1289.[2]

On taking over the property Walter 'presented' a secular chaplain named Andrew to the bishop of Exeter for institution as rector of Lammana, presumably of both the island and mainland chapels and their rights and territories. The term 'rector' probably signified an attempt to maintain or create a parish separate from Talland, and the prior of Launceston immediately opposed Walter's presentation on the grounds that the chapels of Lammana lay within Talland's jurisdiction. Rights of patronage were a matter for the king's justices, not for the bishop, so Walter secured a royal writ of *quare impedit* and had the case heard before the justices of the court of common pleas at Westminster in November 1289, adding a claim for damages of £40 against the prior of Launceston. The court ordered the sheriff of Cornwall to find a jury of twelve local men to testify to the truth of the matter, and they returned a verdict at Westminster in October 1290 in favour of Walter. They stated that the abbot of Glastonbury, time out of mind, had held the island and mainland chapels, had maintained monks celebrating divine service on the island, and had possessed all the tithes, dues, and offerings within the boundaries mentioned above. The court endorsed this view, granted Walter damages of £10, and authorised the issue of a writ to the bishop of Exeter to institute Walter's nominee to the benefice of Lammana.[3] There is no bishop's register for this period, but Andrew appears to have been instituted since he is mentioned as 'portionary' of the chapel of Lammana in 1297.[4]

From 1290 until the Reformation the two chapels and their rights and revenues formed a separate benefice in the patronage of Walter and his heirs; by 1388 the patron was the earl of Devon. Institutions of clergy occur irregularly in the bishops' registers during the 14th and 15th centuries, and these are always said to be to the 'chapel' or 'chantry', not the rectory, of Lammana, implying (like the word 'portionary') that the bishops of Exeter did not recognise the benefice as having full parochial status.[5] Nevertheless its rights continued to overlap with those of Talland, to the extent that the inhabitants of the demesne of Portlooe paid tithes to the chaplain of Lammana and received some ministrations in return.[6] In 1291 the income of the chapel was valued at 30s., probably an underestimate but one that indicates the small size of the monks' endowment.[7] The income was still modest when the chantry commissions of Henry VIII (1546) and Edward VI (1548) reported it to be worth £4 12s., defined in 1548 as consisting of tithes worth £4 from the mainland and 12s. from the island.[8] Henry's commission found that the benefice existed to support a priest celebrating divine service in the chapel on the island, but said that there were no ornaments or goods belonging to the chapel because 'the service in the chapel hath of late [been] discontinued'. Edward's commission received more positive reports that may have been inspired by local attempts to keep the benefice in being. These stated that the incumbent, David Hynkley, ministered in the mainland chapel to 70 adult people from three nearby townships on five or six occasions in the year, including Easter Sunday when he gave them communion. Nonetheless the crown dissolved the benefice and seized the endowments in the spring of 1548, as it did in the case of most such chapels and chantries, and awarded Hynkley a pension equal to his former stipend.[9] On 17 August 1548 'the island of *Lamane*' and the chapel and lands belonging to it were sold with other chantry property to Thomas Bell, knight, of Gloucester and Richard Duke, esquire, of London.[10] The footings of parts of the walls of the mainland chapel are preserved and may be visited, as may an 8-metre stretch of a wall of the Monks House.[11] The site of the chapel on the island is identifiable, but nothing is visible there above the ground.[12]

PRIORS OF LAMMANA

Helias	occurs c.1199 × 1220[13]
William of Bolevill	occurs 1277[14]

---

1   TNA, KB 27/30, m. 18d.
2   Hull (ed.), *Cartulary of Launceston*, 168.
3   Ibid., 168–9; TNA, CP 40/80, m. 151d, discussed by Picken, 'Light on Lammana', 283–5.
4   *Cal. Chanc. Rolls, Various 1277–1326*, 29.
5   *Reg. Grandisson*, III, 1276, 1338, 1370, 1424; *Reg. Brantyngham*, I, 74, 105; *Reg. Lacy*, ed. Hingeston-Randolph, I, 157.
6   This is shown by the evidence of 1548, below. Picken's suggestion ('Light on Lammana', 283) that the lords of Portlooe appropriated the tithes of Lammana after 1290 is unlikely. Lay possession of tithes was common only after the 1530s.
7   *Reg. Bronescombe*, ed. Hingeston-Randolph, 468.
8   TNA, E 301/15, ff. 50v–51r; E 301/9, m. 4; printed in L. S. Snell, *Documents towards a History of the Reformation in Cornwall*: vol. I, *The Chantry Certificates for Cornwall* (c.1953), 47–8); Bodleian, Rawl. D 363, ff. 239v–40r.
9   E 301/10; Snell, *Chantry Certificates*, 48.
10 *Cal. Pat. 1548–9*, 40.
11 For site information, see CCC, HER 126547.
12 For site information, see CCC, HER 6535.
13 Above, p. 197 note 1.
14 Described as custos (KB27/30, m. 18d).

LANLIVERY

LAMFORD LEPER HOSPITAL

The leper hospital of Lamford, as the place was originally called, stood by the road from Bodmin to Lostwithiel, about three miles south of the former and two miles north of the latter, where the road crosses a small bridge at a place now known as Maudlin (SX 0830 6240). The place is close to the parish boundary between Lanhydrock and Lanlivery, and lands called Maudlin appear in the 19th-century tithe apportionments of both parishes. That of Lanhydrock (1840) mentions a tenement called Maudlin covering 44 acres and including 'Magdalen Chapel, orchard, cottage, and garden' – a reference that has led to an assumption that the chapel and hospital lay in Lanhydrock.[1] The first surviving record of the hospital, however, is a list of customs dated 15 August 1258, drawn up by its patron, Sir Thomas de Tracy, a major landlord in Lanlivery, and by the vicar of Lanlivery, indicating that the hospital stood in that parish.[2] The earliest maps of Cornwall to show parish boundaries (Joel Gascoyne's of 1699 and Thomas Martin's of 1748) also place Maudlin in Lanlivery, while the tithe apportionment of Lanlivery (1841) includes Maudlin as a place where the poor of the parish held six acres and four cottages.[3] This property lay by the road, close to the parish boundary, and may represent the site of the medieval hospital. All the evidence suggests that the main site of the hospital was in Lanlivery, but the Lanhydrock chapel was only a few yards north across the parish boundary and may have been the hospital chapel, slightly detached from the residential buildings, unless it was a chapel of separate origin.

The document of 1258 prepared by Tracy and the vicar of Lanlivery laid down six customs to be observed in the hospital. The inmates, who are described as leper brothers and sisters, were not to admit anyone to their fraternity (i.e. the hospital) without the consent of the patron. All gifts made by new entrants were to be applied to the common use of the hospital, with the exception of 2s. for a dinner – the customary feast provided by incomers to religious communities. Once a brother or sister entered the house, their property (except for food or clothing) was to be used for the common benefit, and no inmate could sell or dispose of anything except for a charitable purpose. If anyone made a gift to the brothers and sisters, an equal share was to be given to the general purposes of the house. Once a year the prior of the hospital was to render the patron an account of all the common hospital goods and expenses. Any brothers or sisters who resisted the customs or suffered conviction for wrongdoing were to lose their personal goods and communal rights until they had made satisfaction to the patron. It is not clear whether the document was a code of practice for a new community or for an older one that needed to be organised. In either case those who supervised the hospital would have wished to regulate the behaviour of the inmates with regard to property. Hospital inmates in England were prone to divide any gifts and income among themselves, without regard to the needs of their institution (such as building repairs), and to give away their property individually or to bequeath it when they died. All hospitals depended for part of their income on entry payments, bequests from outsiders, and the goods of deceased inmates, so it was natural for the supervisors of Lamford to lay down rules to be followed. Similar ones are forthcoming from Launceston in 1584.[4]

The document of 1258 shows that Lamford hospital already possessed an institutional structure. It had a lay patron who claimed the right of appointing the inmates, and Tracy probably filled this role by virtue of his marriage to Isold of Cardinan, heiress of Bodardle, the principal manor of Lanlivery parish. The hospital was dedicated to St Mary Magdalene and so must have possessed a chapel. It was locally run by a prior (probably the senior leper) who had to render an annual account, and the community had its own seal, a damaged specimen of which is still attached to the document.[5] The community is next recorded in the accounts of the executors of Bishop Bitton of Exeter in 1307–10, who gave 14s. to the lepers of 'Lanford', the name occurring in the list between Bodmin and Fowey.[6] It continued to exist for at least a further century, since John Dabernon of Calstock left 40s. to

---

1 CRO, TA/109, p. 3; M. I. Somerscales, 'Lazar Houses in Cornwall', *JRIC* new ser. 5.1 (1965), 83.

2 CRO, AR/50/1 (formerly ARB 123/644), printed in N. Orme and O. J. Padel, 'The Medieval Lepers of *Lamford*, Cornwall', *Historical Research* 69 (1995), 102–7.

3 CRO, TA/111, p. 57.

4 Below, p. 223.

5 The legend on the seal probably read 'S. DOMUS [or HOSPITALIS or LEPROSORUM] DE LAMFORD', but only the last word is still legible.

6 W. H. Hale and H. T. Ellacombe (ed.), *Accounts of the Executors... of Thomas Bishop of Exeter 1310*, Camden Soc. new ser. 10 (1874), 28; C. G. Henderson, 'The Ecclesiastical History of the 109 Parishes of West Cornwall', *JRIC* new ser. 3 (1957–60), 285.

the lepers of Lamford to pray for him in 1368,[1] and John Megre, a London pewterer from Truro whose daughter had married into the Cornish family of Lercedekne, bequeathed the sum of 9*d*. in 1419, 'to be shared among the lazars at "Lamport" near Lostwithiel' in return for prayers for his soul.[2] Lamford thus emerges as a comparatively long-lived and well developed institution: perhaps in effect the leper house of the nearby borough of Lostwithiel.[3] No later reference has been discovered to the leper community, but the fact that the 1841 tithe apportionment states that the land at Maudlin was held by (or for) the poor of the parish may indicate that the hospital or its property survived to become an almshouse for people other than lepers, or an endowment for poor relief. There are no visible remains.[4]

LAUNCESTON

MINSTER, LATER AUGUSTINIAN PRIORY

The church of St Stephen-by-Launceston was one of the ancient Cornish minsters staffed by secular canons that survived the Norman Conquest.[5] It lay at the site of the present-day parish church of that name (SW 3250 8568), in the place now known as St Stephens but, at the time of the Conquest, as Launceston (meaning 'church-site of Stephen'), which originally denoted this church and a settlement beside it. Only later was the name transferred to what is now known as Launceston: a new town that grew up after the 1070s, south of the church and beyond the River Kensey. The earlier settlement at St Stephens was a centre of commercial activity by late Saxon times, including a Sunday market whose profits belonged to the canons.[6] In 1076 there were eight burgesses over whom they had lordship.[7] It is possible that the bishop of Cornwall (later of Exeter) was the patron of the minster before the Conquest, since he held the nearby manor of Lawhitton, including what became the site of Launceston Castle.[8] The patronage was certainly gained or regained by Bishop William Warelwast of Exeter during the reign of Henry I.

A decade after the Conquest, in about 1075–6, William the Conqueror assigned the chief power in Cornwall to his half-brother Robert count of Mortain, who made Launceston a centre of his authority.[9] Robert exchanged land with the bishop for the hill of *Dounhed* or *Dunheved* (an English name meaning 'hill-end'),[10] nearly a mile south of St Stephens, and built a castle there: the ancestor of the present Launceston Castle.[11] He took away the market from St Stephens and established it by the castle – a change that encouraged the growth of a new town there, eclipsing the settlement at St Stephens.[12] The new town was commonly known as Launceston like the old one, but for administrative purposes it came to be called the borough of Dunheved. In other respects Count Robert extended his protection over the minster, associating it with himself and his castle rather than founding a monastery for the purpose as was done by some other Norman lords. In 1076 he granted a charter to the canons giving them property in the name of the king, himself, his wife Matilda, and their children.[13] Those named were evidently meant to gain merit from the gift, and doubtless to be prayed for at the minster. Robert's charter enumerates the lands of the church and some of its ecclesiastical revenues, providing us with a more detailed account of its property than exists for most Cornish minsters in the 11th century. The document is not straightforward, however, since although it is cast as a grant, some if not most of the properties it describes were evidently in the

---

1 N. Orme (ed.), *Cornish Wills 1342–1540*, DCRS, new ser. 50 (2007), 34.

2 Ibid., 52.

3 On Lostwithiel, see M. W. Beresford and H. P. R. Finberg, *English Medieval Boroughs* (1973), 79, and C. G. Henderson, *Essays in Cornish History* (1935), 44–8.

4 For site information, see CCC, HER 21386.

5 The principal previous works on the history of Launceston minster and priory include G. Oliver, *Monasticon Dioecesis Exoniensis* (1846), 21–28; R. and O. B. Peter, *The Histories of Launceston and Dunheved* (1885); O. B. Peter's articles on the priory buildings (below, p. 205 note 1); idem, 'Launceston Priory, Cornwall: Notes from MSS. in the Bodleian Library', *JRIC* 18 (1910–11), 197–218; P. L. Hull and R. Sharpe, 'Peter of Cornwall and Launceston', *Cornish Studies* 13 (1986), 5–54; and P. L. Hull (ed.), *The Cartulary of Launceston Priory*, DCRS new ser. 30 (1987).

6 C. and F. Thorn (ed.), *Domesday Book*, vol. X: *Cornwall* (1979), 4/2; P. Sheppard, *The Historic Towns of Cornwall* (1980), 79 and fig. 28.

7 Hull (ed.), *Cartulary of Launceston Priory*, 3.

8 H. P. R. Finberg, 'The Castle of Cornwall', *DCNQ* 23 (1947–9), 123.

9 On Robert, see B. Golding, 'Robert of Mortain', *Anglo-Norman Studies* 13 (1990), 19–44.

10 On the names Launceston and Dunheved, see O. J. Padel, *A Popular Dictionary of Cornish Place-Names* (1988), 107–8.

11 Finberg, 'The Castle of Cornwall', 123.

12 Thorn (ed.), *Domesday Book: Cornwall*, 4/2. On the history of 'new' Launceston, see Peter, *Histories of Launceston and Dunheved*, and Sheppard, *Historic Towns of Cornwall*, 75–80.

13 Hull (ed.), *Cartulary of Launceston*, 2–4. Hull's commentary on the charter (ibid., pp. xii–xiii) contains some misunderstandings of its terms and meaning.

minster's possession already. It also needs to be studied in tandem with the account of St Stephen's church in Domesday Book (1086).[1]

The charter identifies 26 pieces of land ranging in size from one and a half hides to one acre. Most of them lay in the parishes of St Stephen and Boyton (north of the Kensey), South Petherwin (south of it), and Egloskerry, Laneast, and Tresmeer (to the west of Launceston). There were also three distant holdings at Bonyalva in St Germans and at Bodigga and Bucklawren in St Martin-by-Looe. Domesday Book is less specific about the properties but more precise about their legal status and value. It records that the canons held Launceston (St Stephen's, probably including other nearby lands) independent of any overlord other than the king. Their property there had never paid tax – a privilege of ancient minster land in Cornwall, implying that the property had long belonged to St Stephen's. Bodigga, Bonyalva, and Bucklawren were held by the canons as tenants of the count of Mortain, and these three places were stated to have been taken away from the manor of Pendrim, making it likely that they represented gifts from the count to St Stephen's. The Launceston property was formerly worth £8 but now £4, the lost market being valued at £1. The other three lands were formerly worth £2, now £1. There are discrepancies between the charter and Domesday Book as to the total amount of the minster's lands. The charter summarises it as eight and a half hides and 5 acres, of which half was cultivated and half lay waste. The measurements of the individual properties, however, add up to five and a half hides, 7 virgates, and 24 acres, and a further overall figure is given of eight hides and three (or more) acres. Domesday, on the other hand, estimated the Launceston property at four hides and the other three lands at two and a half: a total of six and a half. Neither source mentions any parish churches as belonging to the minster, but to anticipate the discussions that follow, it is possible that Launceston already owned some of the churches and chapels that belonged to it in the 12th century, such as Laneast, North Tamerton, and Werrington.[2] These would have added to the income recorded in Domesday.

The charter throws some light on the organisation of the minster. It states that the count had appointed a priest named Robert as dean of the church. This man is likely to have been a Norman, installed to make the church compatible with the new order of things. Neither the charter nor Domesday explains how many other canons there were, but some notion may be had by comparing St Stephen's with neighbouring minsters whose staffing is known. St Buryan (with one hide) later possessed a dean and three canons, Probus (with one hide) a dean and five, and Crantock (with three and a half) a dean and nine, while Hartland in Devon (with two hides) had twelve canons in 1086.[3] Launceston, with its larger resources, could well have had as many as Hartland, if not more.[4] It is not known if Robert was the first dean, or how the canons were appointed. The charter states that the clergy (probably including the dean) shared four hides and certain acres of the endowment in common, and that a further four hides and three acres were divided between them individually. This meant that each canon's 'prebend' or means of support consisted partly of a share of communal resources and partly of some land exclusive to him.

These sharing arrangements look as if they were long-standing in 1076, and support the view that many of the six or eight hides of the charter and of Domesday had belonged to the minster for some time. Given the likelihood that St Stephen's owned other parish churches, its possessions raised it above most other Cornish minsters of that time, whose property was largely confined to their own parishes. Rather it seems to belong with Bodmin as a church with more substantial assets and influence, although at the time of Domesday it was the less well-endowed of the two. However the count was not without impact on the minster. He established or raised the office of dean to a high level by granting it the tithes of six of his manors: Fawton in St Neot, Helstone in Lanteglos-by-Camelford, Liskeard, Rillaton in Linkinhorne, Treglasta in Davidstow, and Tywarnhayle in Perranzabuloe. These tithes were subject to deductions for the support of the priests of the parishes concerned. A further perquisite of the dean, an annual sum of £2 13s. 4d. from the chapel of Launceston Castle, may also go back to the time of Robert of Mortain.[5] At St Buryan and Probus the dean received a far larger share of resources than any other canon, and the count's endowment of the office at Launceston probably led to a similar situation.[6]

The revenues of the church, apart from the dean's share, are likely to be have been allocated to the canons on an unequal basis, as was the case at St Buryan, Crantock, and Probus. The common revenues may or may not have been shared out equally, but the lands assigned to each canon would almost certainly have varied in size and income. The shares would then have become permanent, each new canon receiving whatever

---

1 Thorn (ed.), *Domesday Book: Cornwall*, 1/7, 4/2.

2 Boyton was another of these churches, but its manor in 1086 was held by a tenant of the count of Mortain, and the count was alleged to have taken it from Tavistock Abbey (ibid., 3/7, 5/5/4), so it may have come to Launceston later on.

3 Above, pp. 163 and 174, below, p. 262, and for Hartland, H. Ellis (ed.), *Domesday Book: Additamenta* (Rec. Com., 1816), 421 (f. 456r–v).

4 Hull (*Cartulary of Launceston*, p. xiii) envisaged a dean and five canons, interpreting the tithes of six manors given by Count Robert as an endowment for six clergy. This view is not supported by the charter or by the evidence from the other minsters.

5 Hull (ed.), *Cartulary of Launceston*, 18.

6 This may have been true at Perranzabuloe (above, p. 134).

his predecessor had enjoyed. Neither the charter nor the Domesday Survey was concerned to define the duties of the Launceston clergy, but, as was the case in all minsters, the basic task of the dean and canons was to say the daily services in church. Minster clergy also had pastoral duties to baptise, confess, marry, and bury their parishioners – duties for which the dean was primarily responsible in other such churches. Apart from joining together in worship, the clergy of the minster did not live in communal premises but each in a separate house, probably with a servant or two.[1] Some canons in 11th-century churches regarded their prebends as outright possessions, and bequeathed them to members of their families, even to their children, since the marriage of minster clergy was tolerated until the 12th century. It is noteworthy that, as late as 1136, King Stephen promised to safeguard Launceston Priory (by then a monastery) against claims by relatives to the prebends formerly held by the minster canons.[2]

Count Robert appears to have made one or two other concessions to the minster: a grant of 20s. per annum paid by the reeve of the castle as compensation for the market, and a grant of borough status to St Stephens.[3] After his death in 1090 his title and property were inherited by his son William, but William lost the favour of Henry I in 1104 and his status as count two years later. This may have affected the minster's properties – it lost touch at some point with its rights in Helstone and Tywarnhayle – and duly brought about a change of patron. The bishop of Exeter, now William Warelwast, was able to reassert his influence in Cornwall and to secure a charter from King Henry in 1123, granting him five ancient minsters in the county, including Launceston.[4] William was a reformer who would have seen the religious life of the minsters as weakened by the worldly concerns of their clergy. He sought to improve matters by introducing the newly fashionable Rule of St Augustine, under which minsters became monasteries and their clergy 'regular canons' living a communal and celibate life without personal incomes. William established the Augustinian Rule in three of the leading minsters of his diocese: Plympton (Devon) in 1121, Bodmin in 1123–4, and Launceston in 1127.[5] In the latter year he issued a charter stating that he had decided to institute the rule at Launceston with the advice of the king, the archbishop of Canterbury, the other bishops, and the best people of the region. The new canons, living under the rule, were to hold all the previous rights of the church free of customary duties or exactions.[6] These arrangements were confirmed by Henry I.[7]

There would have been a gradual rather than an immediate change to the new arrangements. Henry's charter provided that the existing secular canons might become regular canons if they wished, in which case they might continue to hold their prebends while they lived. The new regular canons were to receive only such goods of the church as were already in the hands of the bishop, together with the prebends of the existing canons as they died.[8] At some point in or after 1127 the secular dean, Ralph Pullo, formally resigned and was granted his existing prebend and certain other lands of the church for the rest of his life.[9] This made it possible for the bishop to appoint an Augustinian canon to organise the conversion of the church and community their rule. The records of one of the earliest priories of Augustinian canons, Holy Trinity Aldgate (London), state that its first prior, Norman, sent one canon to each of five new houses of the Order, including Launceston and Plympton.[10] According to an early 17th-century note in the medieval cartulary of Launceston Priory, the first prior was *Teoricus* (Teoric, modern French Thierry), 'a Norman by nation', and the statement accords with the appearance of a certain 'Teoderic, canon' as a witness to Dean Ralph's resignation of c.1128.[11] He may have been present as Bishop William's prior-in-waiting. Some of the secular canons may have survived for a period after Teoric's arrival, however, since the devolution of their prebends to the new priory was still an issue as late as the 1150s, when Henry II issued a charter confirming that this was to happen.[12]

The minster church underwent rebuilding during the late 11th or early 12th centuries. Some remains of its fabric survive in the present-day parish church of St Stephen-by-Launceston, which suggest that the rebuilding was in the Norman style using local slatestone. It encompassed a nave, choir, a south and probably a north transept, and possibly chapels on either side of the chancel.[13] There is also literary evidence for the building of a large tower, apparently constructed by the year 1106 but destroyed in about 1140.[14] The first Augustinian canons would have used

---

1 Hull and Sharpe, 'Peter of Cornwall', 18–19.
2 Hull (ed.), *Cartulary of Launceston*, 8–9.
3 Ibid., 10.
4 *Regesta Regum Anglo-Normannorum*, ed. H. W. C. Davis et al. (1913–59), II, 72, 185; Hull (ed.), *Cartulary of Launceston*, 1–2. The charter exists in two versions, both undated but one datable to 1123, the latter date according with Bishop William's church reforms of the 1120s.
5 Above, pp. 22–3.
6 Hull (ed.), *Cartulary of Launceston*, 4–5.
7 Ibid., 4.
8 Ibid.
9 Ibid., 13.
10 G. A. J. Hodgett (ed.), *The Cartulary of Holy Trinity, Aldgate*, London Record Soc. 7 (1971), 278.
11 Hull (ed.), *Cartulary of Launceston*, pp. viii, 13.
12 Ibid., 9.
13 E. H. Sedding, *Norman Architecture in Cornwall* (1909), 363–7. For site information, see CCC, HER 2615–2615.12.
14 Hull and Sharpe, 'Peter of Cornwall', 16–21. A date before 1106 is suggested by the reference to a count of Mortain (ibid., 20–1).

this church, but by 1135 there seems to have been a project to transfer the priory to a different site, since King Stephen in a charter of that year granted permission for the canons to move to a more suitable place.[1] The migration may have reflected a wish to be closer to the flourishing town of Dunheved, rather than to stay in the relative isolation of the old site. A second motive may have been the need to provide new communal buildings – cloister, dormitory, and refectory – which the minster had not possessed. A third resulted from the civil war in England that broke out between Stephen and Matilda in 1139. Matilda conferred the earldom of Cornwall on her illegitimate half-brother, Reginald de Dunstanville, in 1140, and Reginald gained possession of Launceston Castle, hitherto in the hands of the crown. Stephen made a rapid expedition to Cornwall, recovering the castles that Reginald had taken, and Reginald, who is recorded as having destroyed the tower of the minster church, may have done so at this time to prevent his enemies from using it as a stronghold.[2] Accordingly a new site was chosen on the south side of the Kensey, and the new church and buildings were sufficiently complete for the canons to move to them by 1155, very likely on 7 February of that year.[3] The old church remained as the parish church of the area north of the river and in some respects (as we shall see) of Dunheved as well. It was dedicated in 1259 along with several other Cornish churches, perhaps simply through uncertainty as to whether this had been done before.[4] Parts of the church were subsequently added or rebuilt in the 15th or early 16th centuries, namely the north and south transepts, chancel chapels, south nave aisle, south porch, and west tower.

Further light is cast on the minster and the early years of the priory by the *Liber Revelationum* ('book of revelations'), compiled by Peter of Cornwall in 1200 and shortly afterwards. Peter was the son of Jordan of Trecarrel (d. *c.*1171–80) and the grandson of Ailsi (d. before 1123), both burgesses of Launceston. He spent his adult life as an Augustinian canon at Launceston's mother-house of Holy Trinity Aldgate, where he rose to be prior. His book is an anthology of dreams and visions, some of which came from traditions within his family and enabled him to tell stories about its members. Ailsi was involved with the building of the minster tower that Earl Reginald later destroyed. He acted as custodian of the building fund and paid the workmen on a weekly basis. Wagon-loads of stone were brought from a quarry, and scaffolding was erected while the tower was built. He identified a place two miles from the church, possibly at Cannapark, where limestone could be dug for making mortar. Ailsi owned property south of the river, which was traditionally part of the parish of South Petherwin, but the encroachment of the new town on this area led him to pay the tithes of the property to the minster. Eventually he received a vision in which St Stephen told him to pay them to St Paternus, the patron saint of South Petherwin, and this vision was later used as evidence when the regular canons of Launceston tried to regain the tithes. Two of Ailsi's sons, Bernard and Nicholas, became clergy, scribes in the king's chapel, and thereby prosperous men. They made gifts to the church of St Stephen (meaning perhaps, by this time, the priory), including a banner depicting the saint, a carpet, and an ivory writing case. When their brother Jordan died the prior of Launceston, Osbert, was at his deathbed, and Jordan was subsequently buried at the church of St Stephen, which in this case appears to denote the former minster church, since that church remained in use for the funerals and burials of the people of both old and new Launceston.[5]

BUILDINGS AND ENDOWMENTS

After 1155 the priory occupied a valley site, a little way south of and above the River Kensey (SX 3280 8500), with the church and churchyard of St Thomas-by-Launceston on its north side, dividing it from the river.[6] South of the priory rose a hillside, covered with woodland when the Tudor antiquary, John Leland, visited Launceston in about 1533 and in 1542.[7] The site was probably chosen to utilise the stream later known as Harper's Lake, which ran west of the new town and into the river at that point. Leland noted that the stream was channelled through the 'offices' of the monastery, presumably to supply water and remove sewage.[8] Similar locations close to towns but outside them were adopted by Augustinian houses at some other places, such as Bristol and Gloucester.

Archaeological evidence of the priory's plan emerged between 1886 and 1893 during the installation of railway lines and a gas works. Footings of the walls of much of the church and of the cloister area were found, and those of the eastern end of the church are still exposed to view. The evidence was collected and interpreted by the local historian, O. B. Peter, who produced an overall plan, and the surviving remains were

---

1 Hull (ed.), *Cartulary of Launceston Priory*, 8.
2 K. R. Potter (ed.), *Gesta Stephani* (1955), 67–8; Hull (ed.), *Cartulary of Launceston*, 10–11.
3 Hull (ed.), *Cartulary of Launceston*, p. xvi.
4 *Reg. Bronescombe*, ed. Hingeston-Randolph, 66; ed. Robinson, I, 49.

5 Hull and Sharpe, 'Peter of Cornwall', 16–27; biographies of Bernard the Scribe and Peter of Cornwall in *ODNB*.
6 For site information, see CCC, HER 2613–2613.01.
7 J. Leland, *Itinerary*, ed. L. Toulmin Smith (1907–10), I, 302 (earlier visit), 175 (later one).
8 Ibid., I, 175, 302.

FIG 51. *Launceston Priory, reconstruction.*

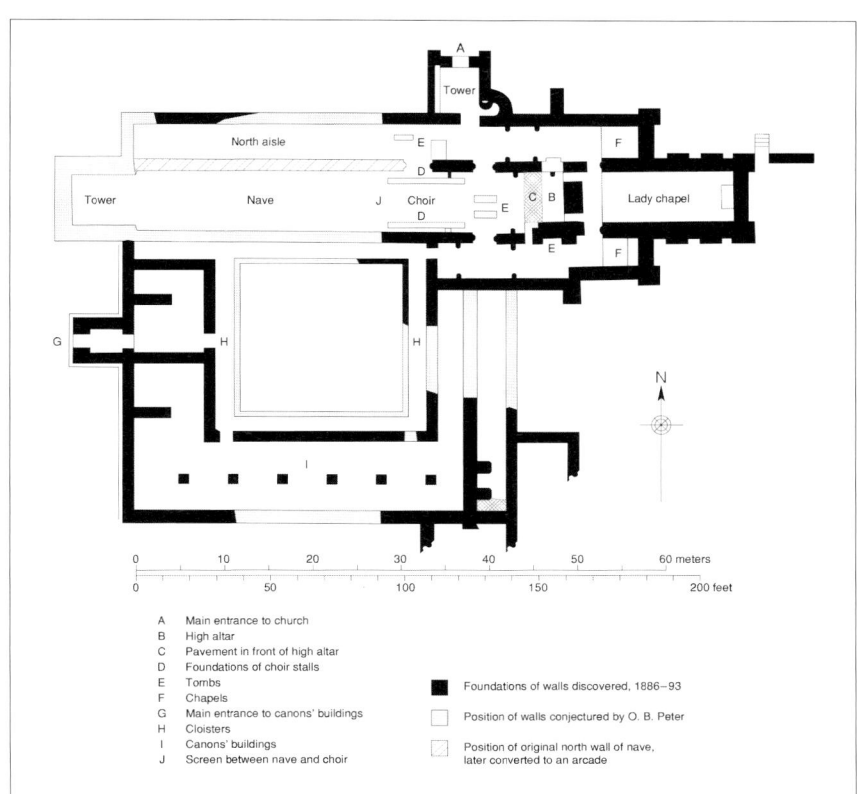

FIG 52. *Launceston Priory, plan.*

reappraised in 2002 (Fig. 52).[1] Most of the available information about the layout of the priory relates to the 15th or early 16th centuries rather than to the building of the 1150s, but comparison with other early Augustinian houses suggests that the original church may have included a narrow nave without aisles, a

---

[1] On what follows, see O. B. Peter, 'Launceston Priory: the substance of a lecture' (Launceston, 1889); idem, 'Excavations on the Site of Launceston Priory', *JRIC* 11 (1891–3), 1–6; idem, 'Note of Further Excavations on the Site of Launceston Priory', *JRIC*, 11 (1891–3), 249–50; Anon., 'Launceston Priory: some interesting particulars', *Western Weekly News* 22 July 1893, reproduced as 'Notes on Archaeology and Kindred Subjects: Launceston Priory', *The Reliquary and Illustrated Archaeologist* 1 (1894), 113–16; O. B. Peter, 'Notes on Encaustic Tiles', *Archaeologia Cambrensis* 5th series 13 (1896), 307–14; J. Gossip, *St Thomas' Priory, Launceston, Cornwall*, Cornwall Archaeological Unit, 2002R004 (2002) and J. Allan, *Notes towards an Architectural History of Launceston Priory*, Exeter Archaeology, Report No. 09.58 (2009).

choir, and possibly transepts.[1] This church was subsequently enlarged in the 13th or early 14th centuries, including the addition of a north aisle alongside the nave and choir. A south choir aisle, still visible, may have been added at the same time. The enlargement was probably the reason for Bishop Stapledon's dedication of the whole church and two altars in the north aisle in 1318.[2] Fragments of stonework point to further rebuilding during the 15th century, perhaps extending into the early 16th. The stonework of this period was carved to a high standard from moorstone and from quarried granite, pointing to significant expenditure by the priory on its own embellishment.

In its final state the church consisted, from west to east, of a bell-tower, nave with north aisle, choir with north and south aisles, and a retrochoir and Lady Chapel, the latter flanked by two smaller chapels at the east ends of the choir aisles. The Lady Chapel is documented in 1312.[3] North of the choir, beyond the north aisle, was a porch containing a staircase, apparently leading to a small tower. This porch was probably the main public entrance and identical with what Bishop Lacy referred to in 1445 as 'the great north door of the church, leading into the cemetery'.[4] In 1478 the priory was visited by the antiquary William Worcester, who measured the length of the church as 100 of his own steps and its width as 24 steps. In modern terms this amounts to about 175 feet (52.8 metres) and 42 feet (12.6 metres), which roughly corresponds to the length of the north aisle alongside the nave and choir, and to the width of the north aisle and nave.[5] Peter measured the church externally as 260 feet (78.5 metres), including the western bell-tower and Lady chapel. Internally the nave was about 90 feet (27 metres) long and 24 feet (7.2 metres) wide; the choir about 75 feet (22.8 metres) long; and the retrochoir and Lady Chapel about a further 55 feet (16.7 metres) long. The choir and Lady Chapel had similar widths to the nave.

The choir included seating for the canons at the west end and the high altar at the east end, the latter probably flanked by images of St Stephen and the Virgin Mary. Richard, earl of Cornwall, the brother of Henry III, gave a rent of 5s. 10d. from the revenues of Dunheved to maintain a perpetual light before an image of the Virgin in the church.[6] A screen divided the choir from the nave, with a single altar in front of it on a raised platform. Since the priory was not a parish church, the nave would have been used chiefly for celebrating masses, devotions by members of the public, and possibly preaching. As well as the two altars in the north aisle there would have been others in the south choir aisle and Lady Chapel. A daily mass was celebrated at the Lady Chapel altar in honour of the Virgin by 1312, when William Bauceyn, canon of Crantock and rector of Lansallos, founded a chantry at the same altar for a further mass to be said for his soul by a priest-canon of Launceston, immediately following the mass of the Virgin.[7] The later history of this chantry is not recorded. Another chantry was established by Prior John Honyland in 1428 to support a daily mass for the souls of the bishop (Edmund Lacy), the prior, the canons, and the benefactors of the priory. This mass was also to be celebrated by a canon, chosen for a week at a time and paid 12d. for his services by the chamberlain from the profits of the churches of Linkinhorne, North Tamerton, and Werrington. It took place at the altar of St Margaret and St John of Bridlington, the site of which is unknown.[8] Outside the priory but nearby were several free-standing chapels. These included the parochial chapel of St Thomas the Martyr (now the parish church of St Thomas-by-Launceston) and the devotional chapels of St James, near Newport Bridge, and St Katherine, on the west side of the priory.[9] The latter received an indulgence from Bishop Lacy in 1447 for those who visited or contributed to it.[10] In 1542 Leland described it as 'prophaned' or desecrated, often a sign of a flourishing saint cult suppressed when the veneration of saints was forbidden in 1538.[11]

Archaeological fragments show that the interior of the church was vaulted, plastered, and painted in vermilion, yellow, and black. Much of the floor was paved with tiles bearing geometrical patterns, letters of the alphabet, and coats of arms. The arms included those of England, Scotland, France, the earldom of Cornwall, and some local families.[12] Some floor space was used for burials, and four tombs can still be identified: two in the choir between the stalls and the sanctuary, and one in each of the two choir aisles. The two latter may be those of priors: Leland noted that Roger of Horton (died early 14th century) 'had a fair tomb in the south aisle' and that Stephen Trediddan (d. 1403) was 'richly tombed'. William Bauceyn was

---

1 For discussion of Augustinian plans, see D. Robinson, *Darley Abbey*, English Heritage, Historical Analysis and Research Team, Reports and Papers 45 (2001), 16–19, 52–62.

2 *Reg. Stapeldon*, 137.

3 ECA, D&C 1145; Oliver, *Monasticon*, 413.

4 *Reg. Lacy*, ed. Dunstan, III, 333.

5 W. Worcester, *Itineraries*, ed. J. H. Harvey (1969), pp. xvii, 82–3.

6 Hull (ed.), *Cartulary of Launceston*, 14, 99, 192.

7 ECA, D&C 1145; Oliver, *Monasticon*, 413.

8 *Reg. Lacy*, ed. Dunstan, IV, 278–80.

9 Hull (ed.), *Cartulary of Launceston*, 38; Peter, *Histories of Launceston and Dunheved*, 15; for the approximate location of St Katherine, see CRO, TA/ and TM/221.

10 *Reg. Lacy*, ed. Dunstan, II, 403.

11 Leland, *Itinerary*, ed. Toulmin Smith, I, 175.

12 Peter, 'Notes on Encaustic Tiles', 307–14. Some tiles and other pieces of carved stone are preserved in Lawrence House Museum, Launceston, and others in the British Museum (E. S. Eames, *Catalogue of Medieval Lead-Glazed Earthenware Tiles in the... British Museum* (1980), i, nos. 11,339–41).

offered the option of a grave in the Lady Chapel if he chose,[1] and Leland heard that the Countess Mabilia was buried in the chapter house.[2] She was the wife of Earl Reginald and the sister of Robert fitz William, lord of Cardinham and benefactor of Tywardreath Priory, who gave land to Launceston in about 1155–62 to fund prayers for her soul.[3] Reginald himself was buried in Reading Abbey. During the 13th century the Botreaux family of Boscastle adopted the church as their family mausoleum in preference to their priory at Minster. In a legal case of the 1340s it was alleged that William (IV) de Botreaux (d. 1242), who granted (or returned) three chapels to the priory, did so on condition that when he or any of his heirs was buried there, an armed man should ride in front of the corpse and the rider be given a 'corrody' or pension in the priory for the rest of his life. This procedure was said to have been followed at the funerals of William, his brother Reginald (d. 1272–3), Reginald's son William (V) (d. 1302), and the latter's son William (VI) (d. 1340).[4] There were outdoor burial places as well: the grass within the cloisters and a cemetery to the north of the church, known as 'Sextonhaye'. These areas were probably used for the interment of canons, priory servants, and perhaps other laity to whom the privilege was extended.

The cloister lay south of the church, with a door on its north side leading into the nave.[5] Around or near it were a refectory, dormitory, chapter-house, infirmary, and a prior's lodging, the three latter each with a chapel or altar.[6] These buildings were approached from outside by a courtyard on the west side of the cloister with an entrance porch into the monastic accommodation. Outside the cloister were ancillary buildings including a hall, which formed the centre of daily life for the layfolk of the community. Here the servants ate, charity was dispensed, and probably guests were received. In 1342 Bishop Grandisson referred to the practice of feeding the poor and elderly in the hall. He forbade such hospitality to be given to women and the able bodied, but told the canons to extend it to 'some poor boys suitable and apt to learn grammar'. These are likely to have come from a grammar school in the town, since similar boys are recorded receiving meals in religious houses elsewhere.[7] By the 15th century the hall included four tables allocated to grooms (*valetti*), clerks, workmen (*operarii*), and gentlemen and squires. Each table had an inscription above it in English verse, presumably on the wall.[8] The verses, most of which are recorded elsewhere, urged those beneath them to be economical, tolerant, restrained, and well mannered. At one end of the hall were two texts in Latin verse. One, a commonly found medieval couplet, urged 'When Christ comes to you in the form of a poor person, impart to him what he has given to you'.[9] This must have been aimed at those in charge of receiving the poor. The other, in rhymed 'goliardic' metre, was evidently addressed to the poor scholars. A modern translation might be: 'It is good, while you are young, Learning's house to fare to. They are foolish people who neither know nor care to'.[10]

The priory gained importance from its location in a town on the main road from Exeter to Bodmin and to other places in Cornwall. Its jurisdiction over the town, however, was more restricted than that of Bodmin Priory over Bodmin or Tywardreath Priory over Fowey. Geographically the priory had temporal authority only on the northern and western fringes of the new town, including St Stephen's and its neighbourhood north of the River Kensey together with the priory site and its lands south of the river and west of Harper's Lake.[11] Between about 1154 and 1165 Earl Reginald granted and confirmed that the canons should hold their lands 'with sake and soke, and toll and team, and infangthief', signifying the right to hold courts for judging tenants, to take tolls and hear property disputes, and to try and execute thieves. The canons and their men were to be free of attending shire and hundred courts, doing castle guard, and other secular duties. Reginald also confirmed that the canons' borough of Launceston, meaning St Stephens, was to have the privileges of a free borough.[12] This freedom applied to property and trading rights, not self-government, since the inhabitants of St Stephens were ruled by the priory. The new town of Dunheved, on the other hand, belonged to the lords of the castle: the counts of Mortain and the earls of Cornwall. It was itself a borough with a provost and burgesses by the middle of the 12th century, and during the 13th century it

---

1 ECA, D&C 1145; Oliver, *Monasticon*, 413. His may be the tomb formerly visible in the north east wall of the Lady chapel.

2 Leland, *Itinerary*, ed. Toulmin Smith, I, 175, 302.

3 Hull (ed.), *Cartulary of Launceston*, 94–5. She was presumably identical with Beatrice, wife of Reginald, earl of Cornwall (G. E. Cokayne, *The Complete Peerage*, ed. V. Gibbs and H. A. Doubleday (1910–59), III, 429).

4 Hull (ed.), *Cartulary of Launceston*, 104 (misdated). For the Botreaux family, see J. Maclean, *The Parochial and Family History of the Deanery of Trigg Minor*, 3 vols. (1873–9), 632–9.

5 *Reg. Lacy*, ed. Dunstan, III, 333.

6 These are mostly mentioned in documents in the published bishops' registers; the infirmary chapel occurs in Bodleian, Tanner 196, f. 11v (p. 22).

7 *Reg. Grandisson*, II, 955. Alternatively the bishop wished the priory to introduce 'almonry boys', commonly maintained and taught in monasteries: see p. 212.

8 Bodleian, Bodley 315, f. 268r, printed by F. Rose-Troup, 'Verses in the Hall at Launceston', *DCNQ* 19 (1936–7), 154–6, and (with full discussion) by R. H. Robbins, 'Wall Verses at Launceston Priory', *Archiv für Neueren Sprachen und Literaturen* 200 (1964), 338–43.

9 H. Walther, *Proverbia Sententiaeque Latinitatis Medii Aevi* (1963–9), no. 20998.

10 Rose-Troup and Robbins both printed the two Latin couplets as one stanza, although they are addressed to different people in different metres.

11 Hull (ed.), *Cartulary of Launceston*, 21.

12 Ibid., 9–10; cf. *Placita de Quo Warranto* (Rec. Com. 1818), 110; *Cal. Pat.* 1340–3, 536–7.

received further privileges from Richard, earl of Cornwall (1227–72) and 'king of the Romans'. Richard gave Dunheved self-government with the right to choose officers (who came to include a mayor and two provosts), to erect a guildhall, and to hold a borough court. All the inhabitants were to be free of serfdom, spared from taxation except for that of the king, and exempt from tolls throughout the earl's lands.[1] By 1295 the town was returning two members to Parliament.

Richard's charter reinforced the superiority of Dunheved over St Stephens. The latter, as we have seen, declined when the castle and market were established south of the river, and the priory was left with only a small borough to rule and draw revenues from. It managed to exploit the prosperity of Dunheved to the extent of encouraging the growth of a suburb on the north side of the river inside its own territory: the suburb known by 1284 as Newport.[2] Newport shared the privileges granted to the canons in respect of St Stephens, and in 1529 it too was granted representation in Parliament. The restrictions on the priory's temporal jurisdiction, however, did not apply to its spiritual authority which extended over the whole of Launceston, old and new. This authority was exercised through the church of St Stephen, whose parish covered the area north of the river, including St Stephens and Newport, but also came to include the new town which lay in territory that originally belonged to the parish of South Petherwin. St Stephen's encroachment upon this area reflected the greater status and power of the minster and the priory, helped by the favour of Count Robert and Earl Reginald. It was in progress, as we have seen, in the time of Ailsi. By the 13th century South Petherwin had lost most of its control over the living inhabitants of Dunheved, and in about 1291 its clergy were obliged to concede that the dead of Launceston (here meaning Dunheved) should be buried at St Stephen. In return it was agreed that the clergy of both parishes could visit the sick in Dunheved, and that offerings made at funerals should be shared by both parish churches.[3]

The parochial needs of the people of Dunheved were provided by two chapels in the new town, both dependent on St Stephen and therefore under the control of the priory. One of these, the chapel of the castle, may well have been founded by Count Robert. A half-share of it was given to the priory in about 1127, but after 1215 it seems to have been wholly in the priory's hands.[4] By 1291 this chapel was dedicated to St Mary Magdalene.[5] Historians have debated its relationship with Launceston's present-day church of St Mary Magdalene, which existed as a chapel by 1395 when it is described as lying in the High Street, as it does today.[6] The suggestion has been made that the chapel moved from the castle to the High Street and from being a private chapel to a public one,[7] but since the High Street chapel was described in 1521 as 'next to [*iuxta*] Launceston castle',[8] it is possible that there was only one chapel and one site, although the building certainly evolved from a castle chapel to a borough chapel. In the early 12th century the chapel was served by two clergy, but one may have been the rule in later times. The High Street chapel was substantially enlarged into its modern form in the early 16th century,[9] and in 1521 the priory granted it a burial ground and burial rights in return for a promise by the mayor and burgesses to maintain the chancel, books, and ornaments.[10] The other parochial chapel lay next to the priory and survives as the church of St Thomas-by-Launceston. Its foundation is not recorded, but its dedication to Thomas the Martyr (i.e. Thomas Becket) indicates a date between his canonisation in 1173 and 1291, when it appears in records.[11] Whereas St Mary Magdalene served the borough of Dunheved, St Thomas did so in the area to the west and north of the castle and borough and to the south of the river. In 1333 Bishop Grandisson consecrated a burial ground for its use, presumably to inter the inhabitants of this area.[12] Eventually, after the Reformation, both chapels became parish churches in their own right. We hear of other devotional chapels in the neighbourhood besides St James and St Katherine, including St Gabriel, St John of Bridlington, and St Leonard. The latter was the chapel of the leper hospital – an institution that also came under the priory's supervision.[13]

The priory was endowed with lands and churches, the relative value of the lands in the 13th century being about half that of the churches (Fig. 53). Both kinds of property lay chiefly in east Cornwall to the north, west, and south of Launceston, with notable outliers in north-west Devon and in the parishes of St

---

1 *Cal. Pat.* 1381–5, 263; 1399–1401, 334; 1413–16, 267; translated in Peter, *Histories of Launceston and Dunheved*, 72–4.
2 Hull (ed.), *Cartulary of Launceston*, 100–1.
3 Ibid., 19–20, giving the pastoral role on St Stephen's behalf to the chaplain of the castle, a person under St Stephen's jurisdiction.
4 Ibid., 16–19.
5 Ibid., 20.
6 Ibid., 20–1.
7 Ibid., pp. xxi–xxii.
8 CRO, B/LAUS/107.

9 For early mentions of the chaplain, see Hull (ed.), *Cartulary of Launceston*, 19–20, 22.
10 CRO, B/LAUS/105, /107; Peter, *Histories of Launceston and Dunheved*, 311.
11 Hull (ed.), *Cartulary of Launceston*, 21, 114–15; *Reg. Bronescombe*, ed. Hingeston-Randolph, 472. The dedication was changed to St Thomas the Apostle at the Reformation.
12 *Reg. Grandisson*, II, 718. For the parish boundary in 1841, see CRO, TA/ and TM/21.
13 On the leper hospital, see below, p. 221.

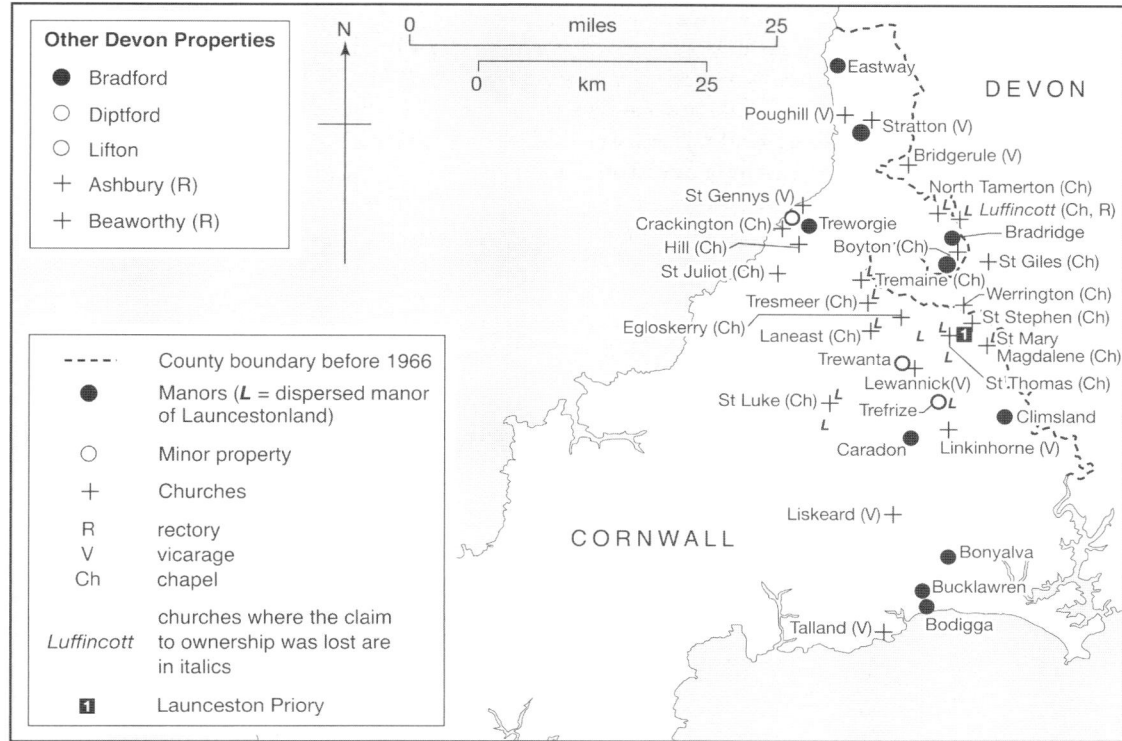

FIG 53. *The property of Launceston Priory.*

Germans and St Martin-by-Looe.[1] The priory inherited the lands of the minster, including all or most of the places mentioned in Earl Robert's charter. Those around Launceston constituted the manor of Launcestonland, which possessed the liberties already mentioned as being granted by Earl Reginald. The lands of this manor lay in St Stephen-by-Launceston, eight neighbouring parishes, and various outlying places (St Gennys, Linkinhorne, and St Neot in Cornwall, and Bridgerule, Diptford, Lifton, and Luffincott in Devon). In 1841 much of the parish of St Thomas-by-Launceston, west of the priory, was tithe free, probably indicating that it formed the home estate that supplied the canons.[2] Other properties going back to the days of the minster included Bonyalva, Boyton, Bradridge, and Bucklawren, and further estates were acquired after the transference of the priory in 1155. Earl Reginald played an important part in these new acquisitions. He gave what became the manor of Caradon Prior (formerly part of Rillaton), and further donations were made by his tenants William de Acy at Stratton, Osbert of Bikelegh at Trefrize in Linkinhorne, William de Botreaux at St Gennys, and Richard of Raddon at Trewanta in Lewannick.[3] Land at Climsland Prior in Stoke Climsland and at Stratton was confirmed by John, count of Mortain (later King John), between 1189 and 1199.[4] Reginald's successors as earls of Cornwall in the 13th century largely restricted themselves to ratifying the priory's existing property, but Earl Richard (1227–72) granted a two-day fair at the chapel of St James near the priory as well as the payment for a lamp, while his son Edmund (1272–1300) gave trading privileges to the priory's tenants.[5] While they were earls some more substantial lands were bestowed by lesser landowners: notably by Henry de Heriz at Bradford (Devon), Richard of Lewannick at Eastway in Morwenstow, and Robert of Tintagel at Treworgie in St Gennys.[6]

The earliest list of the priory's churches and chapels occurs in a papal confirmation of its possessions issued by Pope Alexander III (1159–81). This defines them as Boyton, Egloskerry, St Gennys, Laneast, the half of the castle chapel of Launceston, Lewannick, North Tamerton, St Stephen-by-Launceston, Stratton (including the chapel of Efford), and Tresmeer in Cornwall, with Beaworthy, Bridgerule, and Werrington in Devon.[7] The list omits Liskeard and Linkinhorne,

---

1 A substantial rental of all the priory's lay properties survives from 1474–5 (Launceston, Borough Archives, Rental of Launceston Priory, summarised in Peter, *Histories of Launceston and Dunheved*, 18–26). Two rentals of the manor of Launcestonland, dated 1463 (TNA, SC 11/968) and c.1535 (TNA, LR 2/207), have been published in T. L. Stoate (ed.), *Cornwall Manorial Rentals and Surveys* (1988), 56–64, 65–74).

2 CRO, TA/ and TM/221.
3 Hull (ed.), *Cartulary of Launceston*, 10–11, 17, 47–8, 141, 152–3, 157, 182, 195–6, 203.
4 Ibid., 195–6, 199–200.
5 Ibid., 12–14, 28–9, 100.
6 Ibid., 130, 144, 164.
7 Ibid., 6.

although the priory cartulary states that these were given by Earl Reginald in 1155, and St Juliot which was a dependency of St Gennys. It also fails to name St Giles-in-the-Heath and Tremaine, which later belonged to Launceston and may have done so by this time; perhaps they were subsumed under Werrington and Egloskerry respectively, to which they belonged.[1] No charters survive to show when or how the priory obtained any of these churches, apart from Liskeard and Linkinhorne. Some of those near Launceston such as Egloskerry, Laneast, and North Tamerton may have belonged to the pre-Conquest minster.[2] Although these nearby churches were parochial in most respects, they were usually referred to as chapels and were served by chaplains rather than rectors or vicars. The churches further afield may have been ancient possessions or gifts of the counts of Mortain or Earl Reginald. Much depends on whether Count Robert's grant of tithes at Liskeard, Linkinhorne, and elsewhere was a new donation or a confirmation of what the minster already held. Whichever the case, Launceston by the second half of the 12th century had come to resemble an English minster with a wide territory containing several subordinate churches, unlike the other ancient Cornish religious houses whose parishes were smaller.

Some other churches and chapels were acquired after Pope Alexander's confirmation. They included Ashbury (Devon), granted by a certain Robert and his father Alfred in about 1242–54; Crackington chapel in St Gennys parish, donated by William de Botreaux in about 1221–42; Hill chapel in the same parish, given by the same donor; Poughill, conceded to Launceston by Cleeve Abbey (Somerset) in about 1228; and Talland, allegedly bestowed by Gilbert of Talland and John Gervays in the early 13th century.[3] At one time the priory had rights over Luffincott (Devon). In the late 12th century the lay patron of this church promised that its priest should swear fealty to the prior and pay a pension of 2s. per annum, and that the bodies of the dead should be taken to Launceston for burial.[4] The priory also received tithes from three estates that it owned in parishes outside its patronage. One was Fawton in St Neot, mentioned in Count Robert's charter, where the priory enjoyed two-thirds of the tithes.[5] Another was Bucklawren in St Martin-by-Looe, served by its own chapel of St John Baptist from which the priory received most of the tithes.[6] The third was the chapel of St Luke at Drywork in Altarnun, together with nearby land held by Launceston on Bodmin Moor.[7] Some other small pensions came to the priory from churches both in and outside its patronage.[8]

Constitutionally and economically Launceston's churches fell into three categories. The tithes and revenues of the first group were wholly appropriated to the priory, and the parish was served by a chaplain without rights of tenure and probably paid modest wages in cash or kind.[9] This was the case at Boyton, Egloskerry, St Giles, Laneast, North Tamerton, Tremaine, Tresmeer, Werrington, and the three churches of Launceston. In other parishes the priory took some of the tithes (especially the great tithes of corn) but the work of the parish was done by a vicar, who was presented to the bishop for institution, received the lesser tithes and offerings, and held office until he died or resigned. This applied to Bridgerule, St Gennys, Lewannick, Linkinhorne, Liskeard, Poughill, Stratton, and Talland. A third kind of church was represented by Ashbury and Beaworthy in Devon, where the tithes were never appropriated and the priory merely presented the clergy, who were styled rectors. In 1398 Launceston tried to move three churches from the second category to the first by taking all the tithes and putting in chaplains, but this threatened the interests of the parishioners concerned and provoked strong opposition as we shall see.

The earliest surviving audit of the priory's revenues is provided by the papal valuation of the English Church in 1291. This valuation, which was underestimated by a half or more, reckoned the priory's income at £88 11s., of which just under one third (£26 8s. 4d.) came from temporal sources and the rest (£62 2s. 8d.) from ecclesiastical ones. The most lucrative of the priory's temporal possessions was the manor of Launcestonland, valued at £11 14s. 2d., followed by the manors or lands of Bucklawren (£3 9s. 8d.), *Tottesdoune* (£2 8s. 8d.), Climsland with Caradon (£2 0s. 6d.), Treworgie (£2), Eastway (£1 18s. 6d.), Bradridge (£1 11s. 6d.), *Trebruret* (£1 10s.), and *La Berne* near Exeter (5s. 4d.). The ecclesiastical revenues, chiefly tithes, ranged from St Stephen-by-Launceston (£10) to Liskeard and Talland (each £8), Bridgerule and Stratton (each £6 13s. 4d.), St Gennys (£5), Linkinhorne (£4 6s. 8d.), Lewannick (£4), Poughill (£2 13s. 4d.), North Tamerton (£2 6s. 8d.), Egloskerry and Laneast (each £2), Boyton, St Thomas-by-Launceston, and Werrington with St Giles (each £1 10s.), and St Juliot, the chapel of

---

1 St Giles is first distinctly mentioned in 1194–9, when it was being disputed between Launceston and Tavistock Abbey (ibid., 112), but it may be the 'chapel of Werrington' mentioned in Alexander's charter (ibid., 6). Tremaine was granted to Launceston by William de Botreaux in about 1221–42, but the grant also included Egloskerry, to which the priory had long held rights (ibid., 104).

2 Above, p. 202.

3 Hull (ed.), *Cartulary of Launceston*, 87, 104, 150, 157, 166–7, 217.

4 Ibid., 32–3.

5 Ibid., 3, 90, 172–3, 176–7.

6 Ibid., 39, 173–5.

7 Ibid., 36–8.

8 e.g. Linkinhorne (*Reg. Bronescombe*, ed. Hingeston-Randolph, 467); Lapford (Devon) (Hull (ed.), *Cartulary of Launceston*, 216); and various others (*Valor Eccl.* (Rec. Com. 1810–34), II, 402–3).

9 At the time of the dissolution of the monastery the chaplains were paid £5 each at St Giles and Tresmere, £5 6s. 8d. at St Thomas-by-Launceston, and £6 at St Stephen-by-Launceston (TNA, SC 6/HenVIII/454).

Launceston Castle, and Tresmeer (each £1 6s. 8d.). The prior had a further pension of £1 6s. 8d. from the church of Linkinhorne, and the chapel of Drywork in Altarnun produced 13s. 4d. Since Bodmin Priory was valued at just over £50 in 1291, Launceston had overtaken it to become the wealthiest religious house in Cornwall.[1]

THE COMMUNITY AND ITS LIFE

The bishop of Exeter held the role of founder and patron of the priory from the 12th century down to the dissolution of the monasteries, except when the bishopric was vacant and its rights lapsed to the crown. On the death or resignation of a prior the bishop took temporary charge of the house through a representative or 'commissary', and granted permission for the canons to elect a successor. If he was satisfied with the legitimacy of the result, he confirmed it and received an oath of obedience from the new prior. The charters and endowments given to Launceston by Count Robert and Earl Reginald, however, laid open the priory to claims of patronage from their heirs, the dukes of Cornwall. After Prior Honylond was elected to succeed Prior Combrygge in 1410, a local official of the duchy of Cornwall, the havener John Clynk, seized the temporalities of Launceston in January 1411 at the command – so he said – of the duke, Prince Henry (later Henry V), on the grounds that the prince was patron. The prior immediately went to the prince's council at Westminster to deny the claim, and was granted possession of the temporalities and their revenues while he gathered evidence to support his case. Later, in April, he reappeared before the council with the documents required, and the council conceded that the prince had no rights as founder or patron.[2] Similar claims were extended by the crown or the dukes to patronage over the priories of Bodmin and St Germans, with equal lack of success in the long term.[3]

The prior was required to rule the house in consultation with the canons, a practice that bishops sometimes judged to be lacking. Occasionally he carried out tasks within the Augustinian Order as a 'diffinitor' (organiser of general chapter meetings) and as a visitor of other monasteries.[4] He also served as a collector of taxes levied by the pope or the king upon the clergy in the diocese of Exeter.[5] The senior canons assisted the prior in carrying out particular duties. We hear at various times of a subprior, third prior, almoner (who organised the giving of food to the poor), cellarer, chamberlain, and steward (all concerned with finance and supplies), precentor (who directed the choir), and sacrist (custodian of the church goods). Charters and records were kept, and during the 15th century those that established the priory's title to its rights and possessions were copied into a cartulary, now in Lambeth Palace Library.[6] Another volume survives from this century, mainly containing documents relating to recent controversies, such as the election of Prior William Shyre in 1430. The compiler seems to have been interested in the form of documents as much as the contents, with the result that the collection is a formulary as well as a register. It also includes material relating to the Augustinian Order in general.[7]

The number of canons is first implied in 1381 when thirteen were priests, to whom one or two novices may need to be added.[8] The normal size of the community was said to be fifteen in 1402.[9] There were thirteen canons in 1410,[10] fourteen in 1431,[11] ten in 1492,[12] nine in 1507,[13] twelve in 1534,[14] and nine when the house was dissolved in 1539.[15] Most probably came from Launceston or the priory's sphere of influence in north Cornwall. Four 12th-century canons gave the priory pieces of property when they entered it: two at Bridgerule.[16] Prior Trediddan was a Launceston man, to judge from his surname, and Prior William Shyre was certainly one. Other canons had surnames based on nearby places such as Altarnun, [St] Gennys, Launcells, Otterham, and Treludick in Egloskerry. One or two names – St Eval and St Germans – point to origins further afield. Apart from the canons who rose to be priors of Launceston, two gained similar posts in other houses: Henry of Trewinnek at Canonsleigh (Devon) in 1260, and Oger Bante at Bodmin in 1349.[17] Most Augustinian canons were probably priests by the 14th century, and the customs of their order permitted them to undertake parish duties. Simon Anstewylle, a subprior, was appointed to hear confessions in northeast Cornwall between 1417 and 1419,[18] and Canon Robert Parys was vicar of Liskeard from 1457 to 1460 and subsequently of Milton Abbot (Devon). The priory's parish churches, however, were generally

---

1 *Reg. Bronescombe*, ed. Hingeston-Randolph, 459, 467–8, 472, 480.
2 Bodleian, Tanner 196, ff. 3v–4v (pp. 6–8).
3 Above, pp. 142–3, 186.
4 H. E. Salter (ed.), *Chapters of the Augustinian Canons*, Cant. & York Soc. 29 (1922), 59, 61, 63, 66–7, 169–72.
5 *Cal. Close* 1302–7, 119; *Cal. Close* 1307–13, 227; *Reg. Grandisson*, I, 432.
6 Hull (ed.), *Cartulary of Launceston*, pp. vii–x.
7 Bodleian, Tanner 196, described in *Catalogi Codicum Manuscriptorum Bibliothecae Bodleianae, 4: Codices... Thomae Tanneri*, ed. A. Hackman (1860, repr. 1966), cols 633–6.

8 TNA, E 179/24/5.
9 *Parliament Rolls*, VIII, 203–4.
10 *Reg. Stafford*, 237.
11 *Reg. Lacy*, ed. Hingeston-Randolph, I, 133.
12 *Reg. Morton, Canterbury*, II, 78–9.
13 DRO, Chanter XIII, ff. 13v–16v.
14 *7th Deputy Keeper' Report* (1846), App. II, 290.
15 *8th Deputy Keeper's Report* (1847), App. II, 26.
16 Hull (ed.), *Cartulary of Launceston*, 31, 158, 160–1.
17 *Reg. Bronescombe*, ed. Hingeston-Randolph, 41; ed. Robinson, I, 96–7; *Reg. Grandisson*, II, 1078.
18 DRO, Chanter VIII, ff. 231r, 238r, 245v.

served by vicars or chaplains, and a plan to send canons to serve three of them in 1398 was abortive.[1]

A body of servants lived in the outer parts of the priory buildings – too many, according to Bishop Grandisson, who insisted on a reduction of their numbers.[2] The four ranks of servants recognised in the 15th century have already been mentioned: grooms, clerks, workmen, and gentlemen or squires. In 1342 Grandisson accused some canons of having personal servants – a practice that he forbade.[3] A chaplain in the priory is mentioned in 1450,[4] and in 1506 it was agreed that the parish clerk of St Thomas-by-Launceston should sleep 'in a certain chamber of the tower of the [priory] church'.[5] Boys may have been housed and fed in return for serving the canons at masses or, towards the end of the priory's history, for singing in the Lady chapel. A man named Walter Froste of Launceston recalled that he was brought up in the house as a boy in about the 1520s.[6] The priory occasionally granted corrodies to benefactors or friends, who afterwards boarded there. One such grant was claimed by John of Skewys in the 1340s as having been established by the Botreaux family for the horsemen who rode at their funerals – a claim denied by the prior.[7] In 1328 Grandisson sent his cook, Henry of Shene, to receive, food, drink, and clothes equal to those of a squire, with an allowance for his groom.[8] Edward III and his successors were also prone to dispatching their former servants to Cornish religious houses for similar maintenance. When Edward sent Nicholas Dinham to Launceston in 1337, however, Grandisson objected that it prejudiced the priory and himself.[9] The king, undaunted, asked for a place for another candidate in 1348, although he promised that this would not set a precedent.[10] In 1381 Richard II (or his courtiers, since he was young) nominated a man called John Elys, but the prior refused to admit him and Elys was still awaiting admission in 1392 when the prior was prosecuted in the court of king's bench to show why this was the case.[11] At least one other pensioner was proposed by Henry VI in 1446,[12] but Launceston's resistance kept the number lower than was so at St Michael's Mount and Tywardreath, whose priories were less able to resist royal pressure.

The life of the priory centred on the daily round of services in the choir, together with a high mass at the high altar and other masses at the side altars, celebrated by those of the canons who were priests. Some obit masses would have taken place on the anniversaries of the deaths of important people. In 1434 Ralph Dolbear of Ashburton (Devon) bequeathed a rent of 4s. for ten years to maintain an obit for himself and his wife.[13] Launceston Priory is unique among medieval Cornish churches in possessing a late 14th-century calendar of its liturgical observances, attached to a book of hours that once belonged to the priory or to one of its members.[14] A major feast of 'the translation of relics' in the calendar on 7 February has been plausibly interpreted as the day on which the canons moved to the new priory church in 1155.[15] This church may well have been dedicated in the 12th century, but there is no record of such a ceremony until Bishop Stapledon carried out his dedication on 18 August 1318 – an event, as we have noted, that may have reflected a significant amount of rebuilding.[16] The priory subsequently observed 18 August as its feast of dedication until 1401, when Bishop Stafford changed the date to 22 October.[17] This change was presumably by request, perhaps because 18 August fell shortly after another major observance, the Assumption of the Virgin, and during harvest time. The days of Stephen's martyrdom on 26 December and the 'invention' or finding of his tomb on 3 August were naturally kept as feasts of the first rank.[18]

The priory acquired a second saint when Richard of Raddon gave it the church of St Gennys between about 1150 and 1165, a church that took its name from an unknown saint Guinas.[19] The cult of this person, apparently along with his head, duly passed to the priory where they were identified with the well-known saint Genesius of Arles, martyred in c.303. By the end of the 14th century the priory kept feast-days of Genesius on 2 May and 26 August, with a further feast of the 'translation of the head of St Genesius' on 19 July. When William Worcester visited the priory in 1478 he was told that Genesius was a martyr whose head was preserved in the church and that there had been three brothers called Genesius, each of whom had carried his (severed) head after martyrdom.[20] This story probably tried to explain how Launceston possessed such a head while the bones of Genesius of Arles lay elsewhere. The

---

1 However in 1506 the priory undertook to staff the church of St Thomas-by-Launceston with either a regular priest (i.e. a canon) or a secular one (Chanter XIII, ff. 182v–183r; Oliver, *Monasticon*, 26).
2 See below, p. 214.
3 *Reg. Grandisson*, II, 955–6.
4 *Reg. Lacy*, ed. Dunstan, III, 61.
5 Chanter XIII, ff. 182v–183r; Oliver, *Monasticon*, 27.
6 A. F. Robbins, 'The Closing Days of Launceston Priory', *Notes and Gleanings... Devon and Cornwall* 4 (1891), 3–7, 20–4, 42–5, 53–6, 71–5, 84–7, at 54.
7 Hull (ed.), *Cartulary of Launceston*, 104–5; cf. 87, 91, 128.
8 *Reg. Grandisson*, I, 187.
9 Hull (ed.), *Cartulary of Launceston*, 22.
10 *Cal. Close* 1346–8, 587.
11 *Cal. Close* 1377–81, 514; Hull (ed.), *Cartulary of Launceston*, 124.
12 *Cal. Close* 1441–7, 370.
13 *Reg. Lacy*, ed. Dunstan, IV, 18–20.
14 F. Wormald, 'The Calendar of the Augustinian Priory of Launceston in Cornwall', *Jnl of Theological Studies* 39 (1938), 1–21.
15 Ibid., 8; Hull and Sharpe, 'Peter of Launceston', 44.
16 *Reg. Stapeldon*, 137.
17 *Reg. Stafford*, 237.
18 Wormald, 'Calendar of Launceston', 5, 8.
19 Hull (ed.), *Cartulary of Launceston*, 124–5.
20 N. Orme, *The Saints of Cornwall* (2000), 124–5; Worcester, *Itineraries*, ed. Harvey, 84.

14th-century calendar includes the feast-days of several saints with Cornish connections. Some of these were well-known names, such as Nectan, Neot, Nonn, Petroc, Piran, and Rumon. Others were the patron saints of churches belonging to the priory, including Melor (Linkinhorne), Olave (Poughill), Sidwell (Laneast), Tallan (Talland), and Winwaloe (Tremaine).[1] At least one further saint was adopted by the priory in the early 15th century. This was John Thwing, prior of Bridlington (Yorks.), who died in 1379 and was canonised in 1401, one of the last Englishmen to be so honoured before the Reformation. Bridlington was an Augustinian priory, and its sister houses must have been proud of the order's new saint. We have seen that the priory church possessed an altar dedicated to Margaret and John of Bridlington by 1428, and in the same year there is a reference to a fraternity in John's honour at *Trecarfford*, now Chapple in the vicinity of Launceston (SX 3275 8414).[2] As the modern name suggests, the fraternity honoured the saint in a chapel – probably identical with that of St John built by the mayor and corporation of Launceston in 1414.[3]

Less has survived about the history of education and learning within the priory, but they were not absent. In 1325 the general chapter of the Augustinians laid down that scholars from the order should be sent to the 'schools', meaning the universities, adding in 1334 that heads of houses should provide teachers in their monasteries. The latter would have taught the novices and junior monks.[4] Pope Benedict XII reinforced these orders in 1339 with legislation requiring all Augustinian houses to appoint schoolmasters from inside or outside their communities to teach their brethren grammar, logic, and philosophy. Those who mastered such studies were to be sent to university to learn canon law or theology.[5] It is not known how conscientiously these orders were followed at Launceston, and we possess information about the learning of only one or two canons. Prior William Shyre had some interest in books. In 1428, before he was elected prior, he was bequeathed a copy of Jacopo da Varazzo's Latin dictionary of saints, *The Golden Legend*, by the rector of Lawhitton.[6] Ten years later he was licensed by the bishop to study at Oxford or Cambridge for three years, provided that the priory was properly ruled in his absence.[7] Stephen Gourge, the last subprior of Launceston, became master of the town grammar school after the dissolution of the priory and was described in 1548 as 'a man well learned, meet for the education of youth in the Latin tongue'.[8]

The house encouraged learning inasmuch as it had a book collection. In the early 14th century, when the Franciscan friars of Oxford were compiling a union catalogue of theological works in English libraries, they listed 41 titles belonging to Launceston Priory. The titles (some of which may have been contained within a single volume) included thirty by St Augustine whose writings had inspired the foundation of the Augustinian Order, six by St Jerome, three by St John Chrysostom, and one by Bede.[9] Two other theological works belonging to the priory are recorded. One, a 13th-century copy of *In Unum ex Quatuor*, a concord of the four gospels by Zacharias of Chrysopolis, survives in Cambridge University Library.[10] The other, Robert Holcote's commentary on the Biblical 'Book of Wisdom', was bequeathed to Launceston by a former Oxford student, John Waryn, rector of Menheniot, in 1426.[11]

THE 13TH AND 14TH CENTURIES

The internal affairs of the priory become clearer, as happens elsewhere, after the bishops of Exeter began to keep registers of their activities in 1258. Since Launceston lay within the bishop's patronage it often features in the registers, largely in matters of government and discipline. In 1259 Bishop Bronescombe did battle with the prior, Robert Fissacre, over the latter's administration. Bronescombe accused the prior of ruining the priory's goods, in particular by leasing the churches of St Gennys and Linkinhorne without the bishop's permission. When Fissacre attempted defiance he was excommunicated on 17 September, and suffered the indignity of having the sentence published in his own chapter house. On the 20th he appeared in penitence at the doors of the priory and was absolved in return for a promise to obey the bishop's commands. In November Bronescombe reassigned the leases, and two years later Fissacre resigned.[12] The election of his successor caused deep divisions and, in the bishop's opinion, was conducted in an irregular way – features that were to recur in the priory down to the 1530s. On this occasion, in 1261, two candidates claimed to have been elected. Bronescombe

---

1 The calendar also features an unknown saint *Helerus* (6 November), but it does not mention Keri, the patron saint of Egloskerry. For the saints concerned, see Orme, *Saints of Cornwall*, passim.

2 *Reg. Lacy*, ed. Dunstan, IV, 11.

3 Ibid., 152.

4 Salter (ed.), *Chapters of the Augustinian Canons*, 13, 17.

5 C. Cocquelines (ed.), *Bullarum Privilegiorum ac Diplomatum Romanorum Pontificium Amplissima Collectio*, (1739–62), III(2), 270–1.

6 *Reg. Lacy*, ed. Dunstan, IV, 10–11.

7 Ibid., II, 79.

8 TNA, E 301/9, m. 3, printed in L. S. Snell, *Documents towards a History of the Reformation in Cornwall*: vol. I, *The Chantry Certificates for Cornwall* (c.1953), 29; N. Orme, *Education in the West of England, 1066–1548* (1976), 149.

9 R. H. and M. A. Rouse (ed.), *Registrum Anglie de Libris Doctorum et Auctorum Veterum*, Corpus of British Medieval Library Catalogues 2 (London, 1991), 281–2.

10 Kk.2.2; N. R. Ker, *Medieval Libraries of Great Britain* (1964), 112.

11 N. Orme (ed.), *Cornish Wills 1342–1540*, DCRS new ser. 50 (2007), 61–2.

12 *Reg. Bronescombe*, ed. Hingeston-Randolph, 200–2; ed. Robinson, I, 40–5, 48–51, 126–7.

quashed the election, secured the withdrawal of one of the contenders, Brother Laurence, and appointed the other, Richard of Uppeton.[1] Further defects were identified in the next election of 1285. Once more the bishop, this time Quinil, annulled the proceedings but approved the canon who had been elected, William Teignterer.[2]

The priory figures less in the early 14th-century register of Bishop Stapledon. In 1308 Roger of Horton was elected prior and had to gain a dispensation to hold the office because he was illegitimate.[3] Later, in 1316, when Roger was blind and infirm, Stapledon appointed one of the canons as his coadjutor to help him manage affairs.[4] The next prior, Adam of Knolle, had the ill luck to coincide with Bishop Grandisson, who gave close attention to improving the discipline of his clergy. Grandisson visited the priory in 1328, and within two years was complaining of the damage caused by the maintenance of a 'superfluous and useless household', in other words the servants. He ordered those who were useless to be removed within eight days and replaced by useful ones.[5] By 1337 the bishop was concerned about Adam himself, having heard that he was living a dissolute life outside the priory with secular persons – possibly even with women. The priory was said to have deteriorated in its spiritual and temporal affairs, and two clergy were told to enquire into the situation and report back to the bishop.[6]

In 1342 Grandisson issued detailed injunctions, the result of a further visit to the priory. These criticised the prior obliquely for negligence and failure to consult with his canons. The alms traditionally given, but withdrawn by Adam, were to be restored, and it was on this occasion that the bishop ordered them to be extended to scholars. The sacrist was to provide the accustomed lights in the form of candles and lanterns, and damaged books and dirty vestments were to be cleaned and repaired. The canons were to abstain from immoderate drinking, both in the refectory and in private, and no dogs or birds for hunting were to be kept in the monastery. The bishop again called for the burdensome household to be reduced. Canons were not to have individual servants, except with the permission of the prior and cellarer, and servants were not to enter or leave the house after curfew. The prior was to gain the consent of the majority of the canons before appointing receivers and bailiffs to run the priory's estates or nominating clergy to its churches and chapels. The parish chaplain of St Stephen-by-Launceston was to be replaced, the bishop having found him unsuitable.[7]

During the next two years relations between the bishop and Prior Adam deteriorated further. In December 1344 Grandisson appointed two of the canons as coadjutors to the prior, in view of his imprudence and poor health. Adam was to remain in charge of spiritual affairs but the coadjutors were to handle temporal ones, especially the still unsettled issue of the servants.[8] It is possible that these canons refused to assist, for in January 1345 the bishop appointed three others of their colleagues with the same instructions, and directed them to seek help from clergy outside the monastery if necessary.[9] The new coadjutors began to reform the household and other matters, but the prior disrupted the process. By February Grandisson was referring to him as 'a son of damnation, we fear, who has for many years led a life detestable to God and man, scorning and undermining our commands, punishments, and sentences with damnable audacity'. Adam was in contact with a man who had been excommunicated for attacking a canon, and with three insolent servants whom the coadjutors had dismissed. He had taken away a quantity of arms from the monastery, appropriated money from St Stephen-by-Launceston church, and was sending food from his table to a married woman named Joan Cosyn with whom he was known to associate. He had stopped the subprior from administering the monastery's fabric fund, and had appointed two junior canons to do so, one of whom was said to be his nephew. Finally he had ceased to say the daily services, celebrate mass, or even hear it celebrated, and was devoting himself to meals and drunkenness.

The bishop took action. He ordered Adam and the excommunicated man, John Langa, to appear before him. The insolent servants were to be removed, and the prior was to return the arms he had taken. He was to give nothing more to Joan, and to refrain from being with her in any place that suspicion of sin might arise. Her husband was to restore the goods of the priory that he was holding.[10] The events of the next two years are not recorded, but eventually, by 19 June 1346, Adam was compelled to submit to the bishop and to promise to resign. On that day the bishop wrote to the subprior, ordering the canons to meet in the chapter house to receive the resignation and authorising them to elect a successor. A week later Adam formally gave up his office, reporting the fact to the bishop on the following day, and very shortly afterwards Thomas of Burdon was elected instead.[11] Once more the bishop took exception to the legality of the election and nullified it, but he appointed Thomas

---

1 *Reg. Bronescombe*, ed. Hingeston-Randolph, 202; ed. Robinson, I, 140–1, 146–7.
2 *Reg. Bronescombe*, ed. Hingeston-Randolph, 361.
3 *Cal. Papal Regs*, II, 63; *Reg. Stapeldon*, 180.
4 *Reg. Stapeldon*, 279.
5 *Reg. Grandisson*, I, 564–5.
6 Ibid., II, 837.
7 Ibid., II, 955–6.
8 Ibid., II, 989–90.
9 Ibid., II, 990.
10 Ibid., II, 990–2.
11 Ibid., II, 1003–4.

nevertheless.¹ He then issued a new set of injunctions which Thomas agreed to obey. The canons were to perform the day and night services in church, and to observe the Augustinian rule in the chapter-house, cloister, refectory, and dormitory. No one was to have private rooms, cupboards, or possessions, unless specially permitted by the prior. Personal usage of servants, horses, dogs, gardens, and dovecotes was forbidden. No canons were to leave the monastery without the leave of the prior or his deputies, and when this was necessary they were to go in threes. Food and drink were not to be sent outside the priory, but a suitable canon was to be almoner and to supervise the distribution of leftovers from his colleagues' dinners and suppers in the refectory.²

The Black Death reached Cornwall in 1348–9. Its effects on the priory are not known, but they were apparently less severe than at Bodmin. Thomas of Burdon remained in office and Canon Oger Bante was chosen by Grandisson to become the new prior of Bodmin.³ In about 1361 a former official of Grandisson, William Doune, archdeacon of Leicester, held the priory in sufficient respect to bequeath a silver cup and cover to the prior and half a mark to every canon.⁴ After this the priory's affairs largely disappear from the bishops' registers for about seventy years, leaving little record of the reign of Burdon and his short-lived successor Roger Leye. The prior who followed Leye, Stephen Trediddan, experienced unpopularity locally. In January 1400 John Holland, earl of Huntingdon, attempted a rising against Henry IV who had overthrown Holland's half-brother, Richard II, in the previous year. Holland was captured and executed, and in February royal commissioners visited Launceston and Lostwithiel to enquire into his goods and affairs. During this process some local people accused Trediddan of being one of Holland's adherents. He was charged with gathering men to support the earl, including his cousin, another Stephen Trediddan, and was reported to have said 'that he would give all the goods that he had – lands and moveables – in covenant that the earl of Huntingdon should be made king of England'.⁵ These charges cannot have been proved, since the prior remained in office till his death, and they are primarily evidence that he had enemies in the county.⁶

The antagonism to him may have reflected his role in a project by the priory to raise additional revenue from its parishes of Linkinhorne, Liskeard, and Talland.

Launceston received the great tithes of these places, but not the lesser tithes and revenues which supported the parochial vicars. In 1398, however, the priory gained permission from the pope to appropriate the vicarages too, allowing it to take the whole of the parish revenues after the departure of the current incumbents and to serve the parishes by canons from Launceston or by secular priests.⁷ This probably meant in practice chaplains hired for minimal wages. Later in the same year the crown approved the change in return for a fee of 100 marks (£66 13s. 4d.), on condition that money was allocated to support the poor – a normal obligation of parish clergy.⁸ The proposal aroused opposition, probably from the bishop of Exeter (Edmund Stafford)⁹ and certainly from the people of the parishes concerned, who faced the prospect of being served by visiting canons or poorly paid chaplains. Representations were made to the pope, and in 1401 the papal grant was revoked.¹⁰ When the priory tried to reverse the revocation, the people of the three parishes petitioned Parliament. They pointed out that they had been served from time immemorial by vicars who held services and provided hospitality. They claimed that the priory's proposals had been considered by the bishops at a convocation of clergy in London and found dishonest, since Launceston's income was £1,000: sufficient for fifteen canons. They accused the priory of trying to annul the papal revocation, at great cost and without the king's leave. Finally they asked for a prohibition against the priory's appeal to Rome and for the imposition of statutory penalties if it persisted. The parliamentary records note that the king ordained a sufficient remedy.¹¹ Its nature is unknown but the priory's plans were evidently frustrated, since all three parishes retained their vicars.

THE 15TH AND 16TH CENTURIES

The principal event of the early 15th century was another disputed election. In July 1427 Prior John Honylond, who had ruled since 1410, called in John Lovell, 'leech' of Launceston, who made incisions in his leg to bleed him. Lovell subsequently cared for Honylond's health until the prior died on 28 September 1430.¹² The bishop, Edmund Lacy, gave the canons permission to elect a successor, and on 19 October fourteen canons met to do so in the chapter-house under the presidency of the subprior.¹³ They delayed their proceedings for two days before attempting an election on the 21st. This proved impossible, so they

---

1 Ibid., II, 1004–6.
2 Ibid., II, 1007–8.
3 Ibid., II, 1077.
4 A. H. Thompson, 'The Will of Master William Doune', *Archaeological Jnl* 72 (1915), 274.
5 *Cal. Inq. Misc.* VII, 55–6, 58–9.
6 However, the abbots of Colchester, Beeleigh, and St Osyth (Essex) were also accused of treason against Henry IV in 1404.
7 *Cal. Papal Regs* V, 156.

8 *Cal. Pat.* 1396–9, 447.
9 CRO, B/LIS/77 is a notification of 1402 by Bishop Stafford, distancing himself from the prior's plans.
10 *Cal. Papal Regs* V, 357–8, 391.
11 *Parliament Rolls*, VIII, 203–4 (dated 1402).
12 For Lovell, see below, p. 216 note 1.
13 For the bishop's record of the election, see *Reg. Lacy*, ed. Hingeston-Randolph, I, 132–43, and for the priory's, Bodleian, Tanner 196, ff. 8r–54r (pp. 15–107).

adjourned the process until the 27th, only to meet and make a further adjournment until 16 November, when they finally agreed to choose a prior by the method of scrutiny, in modern terms by voting in writing. There were two candidates, Richard Yerle and William Shyre, both about halfway up the hierarchy. The four senior canons voted for Yerle, and the eight junior for Shyre, while the two candidates each voted for one of their supporters. After this Robert Parys, one of the three scrutineers of the voting and an adherent of Shyre, announced the result to the canons and declared that Shyre had won the election on all three grounds required by canon law: a majority of votes, the zeal of his supporters, and his merit as a candidate. The canons all gave their consent, and Shyre agreed to serve. Four proctors were then appointed (chiefly from Shyre's supporters) to ask the bishop to confirm the election, but Lacy refused, alleging defects in the proceedings.

The canons subsequently claimed that the bishop's refusal reflected his discontent with the outcome. They alleged that he had sent his commissary, James Carslegh, archdeacon of Exeter, to tell them that he wished them to choose Yerle. The canons had asked to be able to make a free election, but Carslegh had refused. When, towards the end of the year, it was clear that the bishop would not give his approval, the canons (nearly all of whom now endorsed Shyre) appealed to the archbishop of Canterbury, Henry Chichele. On 4 January 1431 they appointed Robert Parys to administer the priory's temporal property, defying the bishop to whom this power belonged during vacancies, and they (or others) levelled grave charges at Yerle. On 10 January Lovell and Yerle were accused before the king's justices at Bodmin of having murdered Prior Honylond: Lovell through his incisions and Yerle by poisoning the prior's food and drink.[1] On 14 January Yerle left Launceston, possibly fearing arrest and imprisonment. In June he surrendered to the authorities in London and was granted bail. Lovell gave himself up in the autumn and was found not guilty by a jury in January 1432. Yerle remained on bail for a further six years until it was decided, early in 1438, that the case against him should be dropped in view of Lovell's acquittal. He stayed away from the priory for much of this period, and on 20 February 1433 Shyre asked the king to arrest him for involving himself in secular affairs and living an apostate life outside the monastery.[2] Yerle had returned by 1439 when Lacy appointed him as a penitentiary to hear confessions in north Cornwall.[3] The appointment implies that he had the bishop's approval and throws doubt on the accusation of murder.

Meanwhile the canons pursued their fight with the bishop. On 18 February 1431 they signed a letter of protest about Lacy's proceedings. On 6 April they appointed John Degendon and Robert Toker to testify before the archbishop, and two days later they persuaded the mayor and council of Launceston to write a statement that Shyre was born in the town in 1394, of legitimate status and free condition. Two letters were sent to the leader of the government, Humphrey, duke of Gloucester, thanking him for support and complaining that Yerle was seeking to hinder the election. The canons also found the ear of another powerful figure, Cardinal Beaufort, bishop of Winchester, who wrote asking Lacy to recognise Shyre as prior. Yerle, claimed Beaufort, had agreed with the others to abide by the judgment of Parys, yet although Shyre had been elected, the bishop had committed the administration of the priory to Yerle. Lacy was obliged to give way. On 21 August he received Shyre and confirmed the election, recording that he did so despite its defects and because of his reverence for the duke of Gloucester and the archbishop of Canterbury.

The bishop was mortified by this defeat and did not forget it. In 1443 Shyre and Parys were obliged to appear before him, with the dean and chapter of Exeter Cathedral alongside him, in the chapter-house of the cathedral. Lacy complained that the two men had made false suggestions and libels about him to Beaufort, Chichele, and Gloucester at the time of the vacancy. They had untruthfully stated that the bishop had ordered Carslegh to manage the election and that Carslegh had said that they might only choose Yerle. They had wrongfully alleged that when Shyre and his attendants had come to Exeter seeking confirmation, in November 1430, the bishop had refused them fire and water and had appointed two commissaries to undo the election. They had impeded the bishop's right to send representatives to visit the priory, and had challenged his immemorial power to govern it in vacancies. Shyre and Parys knelt at the bishop's feet, and denied their intention of wrongdoing. If they had suggested or written anything against him, they begged for his mercy. They recognised his powers over the priory, and promised to record what they said in writing, sealed with the priory's seal. The bishop then forgave them. It would not have escaped anyone's notice that Chichele had recently died and that, with Henry VI having outgrown his minority, the power of Beaufort and Gloucester was weaker than it had been a dozen years earlier.[4]

Two years later, in 1445, Lacy imposed detailed injunctions on Launceston, as the result of his grave concern about the community.[5] He perceived it to be lacking in discipline and heavily burdened with debt. To restore discipline, the daily services were to be

---

1 On the allegations and the legal process, see TNA, KB 27/680, rex roll 1; KB 27/681, rex roll 6, 12, 19; KB 27/686, rex roll 4d; KB 9/225, nos 39–40. I am grateful to Dr H. Kleineke for this information.

2 TNA, C 81/1789/21.

3 *Reg. Lacy*, ed. Dunstan, II, 132.

4 Ibid., II, 300–2.

5 Ibid., III, 320–1, 329–40; the cathedral kept a copy (ECA, D&C 2331).

properly recited, roaming about was to cease, and fasts, vigils, prayers, and times of silence were to be kept. Excessive eating and drinking were forbidden, as was sexual incontinence. The canons were to go into the choir two by two, and none of them was to leave the priory without permission except for the steward, cellarer, and others with legitimate reasons to do so. Women were to be barred from the cloister area. The subprior was to ensure that the cloister doors were kept locked, and the church doors too except at times of services. The canons were to live communally, and all meals were to be taken in the refectory. An exception was made in favour of the subprior, who was allowed a private chamber and permitted to entertain men there, but other guests were to be fed in the infirmary and only to a modest extent. Dogs were to be excluded from both church and cloister. The economic state of the priory was so bad, the bishop claimed, that exceptionally prudent measures were needed to save it from debt. Stringent cuts in expenditure were ordered. The most dramatic of these was to send the prior away (as was proposed at Bodmin shortly afterwards). He was ordered to live at Bruton priory (Somerset) or Hartland abbey (Devon) for the next three years, with three servants only, on a total allowance of 40 marks (£26 13s. 4d.) per annum. This no doubt was meant to stop him from living expensively at home, where he was called upon to entertain guests. Next the bishop appointed John Denbawde as steward and receiver, and Robert Parys as cellarer, and told the steward to allow only 2s. 8d. per canon per week for feeding the community. Thirdly he ordered all the superfluous servants to be dismissed, referring to three by name. No one outside the priory was to receive allowances except for pensions and fees to those who gave counsel to the canons. The prior and canons agreed to observe these injunctions.

In 1492 the priory was visited by a representative of the archbishop of Canterbury. He found a community of ten canons, including the prior, although the subprior conceded that there ought to be thirteen. The prior, now William Hopkyn, claimed that his brethren behaved decently, and six other canons said that all was well. A canon named Walter Bent was reported to have absconded from the priory without permission, and his whereabouts was unknown. The only criticism was made by Canon William Symon, who accused the subprior, John Carlyon, of selling a gold chalice, giving away a law book, and pawning goods to local people, notably a bed and its trappings.[1] This complaint did not prevent Carlyon from remaining as subprior or from election as prior in September 1507. In the following December the priory was obliged to pay a heavy fine of 500 marks (£333 6s. 8d.) imposed by the crown in return for granting the prior a pardon.[2] In 1509 Bishop Oldham granted Carlyon and his successors the right to wear a grey almuce: a furred cape similar to those of the canons of Exeter cathedral.[3] Carlyon's rule was less successful in other respects. In 1509 the chapter of the Augustinian Order, meeting at Leicester, censured him for refusing to obey its command that canons should not be paid money to buy food. He was fined £5. At the same time the chapter ordered that the subprior of Launceston should be sent to Ixworth priory (Suffolk) and Canon John Forte to Leeds priory (Kent) because both had resisted the authority of the order's visitors, the priors of Plympton and Taunton.[4]

Augustinian visitors went to Launceston again in 1518. This time another canon, Thomas Wandsworth, was found to be in need of discipline. He was both disobedient and a sower of discord within the community, and was threatened with imprisonment at the next visitation unless he mended his ways.[5] What Wandsworth was doing at Launceston is unclear, since he had entered the order at Merton priory (Surrey). He later returned there but enjoyed a further career in Cornwall as the last prior of Bodmin from 1534 to 1539.[6] John Baker, who succeeded Carlyon in about 1521, was later said to have had a prosperous term of office, but by the early 1530s there were further tensions in the house. When Baker resigned in the spring of 1534, allegedly frustrated at the unruliness of some of the canons, the election of his successor caused renewed divisions. There were two candidates, William Gennys and John Shere, both younger canons. After an apparent deadlock between their supporters, the bishop's vicar general, John Gybbons, who was supervising the election, recommended the canons to adopt what was known as the 'way of compromise'. This meant committing the decision to an arbitrator, who was effectively Sir William Courtenay of Powderham (Devon), a powerful layman influential in the priory, although the role was ostensibly undertaken by John Stubbes, the curate of Powderham church. Stubbes selected Shere, the steward and cellarer, and Gybbons confirmed him as prior in the chapter house on 6 June. Baker was awarded a substantial pension of 100 marks (£66 13s. 4d.).[7]

Within six months of his confirmation Shere had fallen out with Gennys, the subprior (John Morlegh),

---

1 Reg. Morton, Canterbury, II, 78–9.
2 BL, Lansdown 160, f. 311r. The reason is not clear.
3 Chanter XIII, ff. 182v–183r. In 1512 Dame Thomasine Percival, a wealthy London widow who came from Week St Mary, bequeathed the priory three gilt goblets and a cover. She also left 20 marks towards the building of a new tower of St Stephen's in Launceston, evidently the parish church (Orme (ed.), Cornish Wills, 144).
4 Salter (ed.), Chapters of the Augustinian Canons, 128. For the name of John Forte, see Chanter XIII, ff. 13v–16v.
5 Salter (ed.), Chapters of the Augustinian Canons, 136.
6 Above, p. 151.
7 DRO, Chanter XIV, f. 73r. John Stubbes occurs as curate of Powderham in 1537 (ECA, D&C 3688 f. 3) and was later its rector.

and others of the brethren.[1] In November or December they petitioned the king, probably in the court of requests which dealt with pleas by poor litigants, to quash the election. The petitioners began by praising the work of Prior Baker during his thirteen years in office. He had brought the priory out of £1,000 of debt, roofed the church at a cost of £200, and spent £400 on copes and vestments. Then he had been deposed on Courtenay's initiative. Gybbons had promised them a free election and the canons had agreed on a suitable candidate, but the vicar general, finding he was not to receive a fee, refused to consent to the person concerned and forced upon them Shere, who three years earlier had been no more than the prior's chamberlain. Since his advancement he had incurred debts to the tune of 1,000 marks (£666 13s. 4d.), pledged the priory's plate, and sold its woods. The canons asked the king to give credence to William Kendall of Launceston, agent of the marquess of Exeter in Cornwall, and begged the king to allow them to re-elect a prior or to appoint one himself.[2] On 23 January 1535 the king wrote to Bishop Veysey of Exeter after being told that Shere had usurped the office of prior without lawful election and had imprisoned some of the brothers who resisted him. Veysey was ordered to examine Shere and the canons about the allegations, and to inform the king.[3]

Shere produced answers to the charges, which survive in two versions.[4] He accused Morlegh and Gennys of conspiring with Kendall, who was aggrieved with Shere for refusing to lease him the tithes of St Thomas-by-Launceston. The prior admitted that Baker's reign had been prosperous, although he estimated that the priory's debts were only £200 when Baker took office. Baker's departure, he claimed, had been forced on him by his inability to control Morlegh, Gennys, and other canons. Gennys had then exerted himself to gain the office and had promised money to various gentlemen, including Courtenay, to a total of more than 700 marks (£466 13s. 4d.). Gennys, Shere alleged, was a man of vices, openly reputed to commit adultery with Ellen Offe, a married woman of Launceston,[5] and to possess a child by another mistress. For these reasons, the prior asserted, Gennys lost Courtenay's favour, and in the end Gybbons (at Courtenay's suggestion) advised the canons to transfer the choice to Stubbes, who had chosen Shere because he was an officer of the priory. The more senior canons were either unlearned or defamed with vices. All the brethren had agreed to the election, and matters had gone well until Kendall fell out with Shere. As to the allegations of maladministration, Shere had pledged the priory's plate to the value of £80 to redeem certain debts and to buy bedding and household goods. He had sold the timber of Bradridge Wood with the consent of his brethren, but otherwise only coppice wood. To the charge that he had dealt cruelly with the canons, he said that Morlegh, Gennys, and a third brother, John Laurence, haunted ale-houses and suspicious places in the town, and ran up debts there, for which reason he posted a notice on the church doors asking local people to report the debts they owed. The three canons tore down the notice, and for that he imprisoned them according to the Augustinian Rule.

Kendall drew up a list of four witnesses and drafted six questions to ask them. These centred on whether Shere had sought their help to make him prior, and whether money was given to Courtenay for that purpose. Veysey examined the men concerned on 15 February 1535, and another local worthy, Sir John Chamond, interviewed a further witness on the following day. One of those questioned was the mayor, Thomas Hicks, the brother of one of the canons; another was Richard Carlyon, vicar of Stratton and brother of the previous prior-but-one.[6] Their evidence must have disappointed Kendall, since although three of them admitted offering or giving money to Shere, they did not link this with the election, about which they claimed to know nothing. Veysey duly reported in favour of Shere. Baker, he said, had confessed to retiring because he could not make the canons observe their religion. Shere had been confirmed and installed as prior with the consent of all his brethren. He was sufficiently learned and was commended by Sir Piers Edgcumbe, Sir John Chamond, and others. The three imprisoned canons had admitted tearing down the prior's notice, and the prior's statements about borrowing money and selling timber were correct.[7] Courtenay took the same view. Writing to the king's chief minister, Thomas Cromwell, on 20 April, he asked him to be good to Shere 'who is troubled with that wretch Kendall, and four or five unthrifty monks'.[8] On 8 May he sent another letter to the same effect, claiming that he had been offered large sums to make another canon prior (presumably Gennys), and calling the prior's opponents men 'of no name or fame'. One of them, Stephen Lamprey, whom the prior had dismissed from being priest of St Mary Magdalene, was a common lecher and maintainer of thieves.[9]

Shere was exonerated and Gennys left the priory, but

---

1 The documents relating to what follows are listed in *L&P Hen. VIII*, V and VIII, and transcribed in Robbins, 'Closing Days', 3–7, 20–4, 42–5.
2 *L&P Hen. VIII*, VIII, 88.
3 Ibid., 30.
4 TNA, REQ 2/6 no. 7; *L&P Hen. VIII*, V, 396.
5 Wife of John Offe, an inhabitant of Dunheved in 1544 (T. L. Stoate (ed.), *Cornwall Subsidies in the Reign of Henry VIII* (1985), 123).
6 Richard Carlyon held the priory churches of Ashbury (to 1510), Liskeard (1526–9), and Stratton (to 1541). He was also dean of Crantock (above p. 180).
7 *L&P Hen. VIII*, V, 396–7; VIII, 88, 202.
8 Ibid., VIII, 215.
9 Ibid., 259–60; TNA, E 134/27Eliz/Hil19.

he remained in the neighbourhood and made another attempt to bring down the prior two years later. According to Gennys he and Shere were riding together from Okehampton to Launceston on 19 January 1537 when Shere allegedly referred to the current rising in the north (the Pilgrimage of Grace), and said that if it continued the king might be in danger of his life or be forced to leave the realm. Gennys reported the words to Kendall and Lamprey, and confronted Shere with them in the prior's chapel.[1] Shere sent off a hasty letter to Cromwell: 'My old mortal enemy William Gennys has most devilishly invented a lie against me'. He said that Sir John Chamond and Richard Powlerde would testify to his innocence.[2] Once more, it seems, Shere's enemies were foiled, for he remained as prior until the house was dissolved two years later. Meanwhile the Reformation was casting its shadow. On 28 August 1534 Shere and eleven other canons acknowledged Henry VIII as head of the Church of England,[3] and in the following year the revenues of Launceston were assessed for the new royal valuation of the Church, the *Valor Ecclesiasticus*.

The new assessment rated the income of the priory at £392 11*s*. 2¼*d*. gross and £354 0*s*. 11¼*d*. net. About three fifths of the income, £229 2*s*. 6¼*d*., now came from the temporal properties, led by Launcestonland with £101 6*s*. 8*d*., followed by the revenues of the office of chamberlain (£26 0*s*. 5*d*.) and the manors of Bucklawren (£18 4*s*. 6*d*.), Caradon Prior (£13 8*s*. 0¾*d*.), Bradridge (£8 10*s*. 8½*d*.), Boyton (£8 2*s*.), Bonyalva (£7 10*s*. 11*d*.), Treworgie (£7 8*s*. 6*d*.), Stratton (£7 2*s*. 6*d*.), Climsland Prior (£7 1*s*. 4¼*d*.), and Bradford (£5 11*s*. 3½*d*.). All the other holdings produced less than £5. The rest of the income, £159 8*s*. 8*d*., came from spiritual sources. These included the farms of the tithes of Liskeard (£20), Linkinhorne (£18), Poughill and Stratton (jointly £16), St Giles-in-the Heath and Werrington (jointly £13 6*s*. 8*d*.), Egloskerry (£11), Lewannick (£10), Talland (£9), St Stephen-by-Launceston (£8 6*s*. 8*d*.), St Gennys (£8), North Tamerton (£7 13*s*. 4*d*.), Boyton (£6 13*s*. 4*d*.), St Thomas-by-Launceston (£6 6*s*. 8*d*.), St Juliot (£6), Laneast (£5), and Tresmeer (£2 15*s*. 8*d*.). A few other small tithe farms and pensions from churches were recorded, but the tithe income from Bridgerule escaped inclusion. The only expenses listed were those permitted under the rules of the valuation: fees paid to officers (notably to Sir John Chamond, the chief steward), pensions to other religious houses, the salary of the chaplain of Launceston Castle, the cost of providing three masses a week at Penheale chapel in Egloskerry parish, and £7 8*s*. 10*d*. per annum of alms to the poor. These latter consisted of donations to the prisoners in the castle, the hospital of St Leonard, and poor people on certain days during Lent.[4] The *Valor* was a more searching enquiry than the taxation of 1291, but it still fell short of the truth. When the priory came into the possession of the crown in 1539, the king's administrators estimated the annual income at £443 16*s*. 1¼*d*., an increase of some 13 per cent.[5]

Shere, like other monastic leaders, did his best to win the favour of Thomas Cromwell, the king's powerful minister. In 1536 he sent Cromwell a fee, and in the following year asked him for permission to interrogate Richard Carlyon, on the grounds that Carlyon had meddled in the affairs of the priory, defrauding it of money.[6] Later, in November 1538, shortly before the suppression, Launceston followed numerous other religious houses in granting an annuity of £5 to Cromwell and his son Gregory.[7] Other grants were made in the last few years of the priory, but Shere does not seem to have copied his fellow-prior Thomas Wandsworth at Bodmin in issuing extravagant leases of priory property. Two of the grants were to Franciscan friars. On 6 July 1535 Launceston gave an annuity of £4 to Alexander Barclay, and on 2 October 1536 one of £13 6*s*. 8*d*. to John Taylour.[8] Barclay, formerly a leading Tudor poet, was a doctor of divinity and at this time a man with a reputation for religious conservatism.[9] Taylour, alias Cardmaker, was a bachelor of divinity, currently warden of the Franciscan friary in Exeter and later a strong supporter of the Reformation, dying at the stake under Mary Tudor.[10] They may have been imported, as was John de Coloribus at Bodmin, to preach or to give the daily lecture on holy scripture imposed on monasteries in 1535. The canons were obliged to surrender the monastery to the king on 24 February 1539, when the king's commissioner, the Cornishman John Tregonwell arrived for this purpose.[11] They all complied by doing as they were asked, and Tregonwell reported to Cromwell on the following day that he found them 'very conformable' and all things in order. The house was not in debt, and it and its contents, plate, and bells were now in the king's hands.[12] On 1 April the former canons were given dispensations to change their clothes and to hold Church benefices.[13] On the 20th they were awarded pensions, Shere receiving £100, one canon £10, three £6 13*s*. 4*d*. each, and four £5 6*s*. 8*d*. each.[14]

In 1540 the majority of the priory's temporal property, ten manors, was taken to increase the

1 *L&P Hen. VIII*, XII(1), 133; Robbins, 'Closing Days', 73–4.

2 Ibid., XII(2), 482; Robbins, 'Closing Days', 74.

3 TNA, E 25/76/1, printed in *7th Deputy Keeper's Report* (1846), App. II, 290.

4 *Valor Eccl.*, II, 402–3. The chaplain of Laneast served Penheale three times a week (*Reg. Lacy*, ed. Dunstan, III, 241).

5 W. Dugdale, *Monasticon Anglicanum* (1817–30), VI(1), 212.

6 *L&P Hen.VIII*, XI, 308; XII(1), 482.

7 Ibid., XII(1), 72; TNA, E 315/96, f. 122v; E 315/93, ff. 106v–7.

8 TNA, SC 6/HenVIII/7300.

9 Biography in *ODNB*; for his conservatism, see above, p. 190.

10 *BRUO*, IV, 101.

11 TNA, E 322/122, printed in *8th Deputy Keeper's Report* (1847), App. II, 26.

12 *L&P Hen. VIII*, XIV(1), 140.

13 D. S. Chambers, *Faculty Office Registers 1534–1549* (1966), 182.

14 *L&P Hen. VIII*, XIV(1), 139; TNA, E 315/233, f. 260r–262r. For their subsequent careers, see A. L. Rowse, *Tudor Cornwall* (1941), 214.

endowments of the prince of Wales and duke of Cornwall, the future Edward VI.[1] In March of the same year the priory site was granted to the courtier and soldier Gawen Carew, together with the advowsons and tithes of some of the neighbouring churches.[2] The church and buildings were converted to other uses and eventually so wholly demolished that by 1880 the site consisted of an open field known as 'Priory Meadow'.[3] Much of the site was then destroyed by the building of the railway and gasworks, but the accompanying excavations revealed the lowest courses of the walls of the choir, choir aisles, and north tower, which are now preserved. A priory seal exists from the 13th century, displaying a church with a central tower.[4] Later the house possessed a coat of arms, recorded in a heraldic visitation of 1531 as (in modern terminology): argent gouté de sang, a cock gules; on a chief of the last three roses or.[5] The arms are preserved on a label end of a chancel window at Lewannick church, on a bench end in Poughill church, and (in colour) in the east window of the south aisle of St Thomas-by-Launceston.[6]

DEANS OF LAUNCESTON

Robert	occurs 1076[7]
Ralph Pullo	occurs by c.1127, res. c.1128[8]

PRIORS OF LAUNCESTON[9]

Teoric	allegedly first prior, c.1128[10]
Robert	died 24 June 1149[11]
Richard	occurs 1149[12]
Geoffrey	occurs c.1162, 1171[13]
Osbert	occurs c.1180 × 1183[14]
Adam	occurs 1184 × 1190[15]
Walter	occurs 3 or 4 Sept 1196[16]
Godfrey	occurs 29 Apr 1202, possibly still c.1220[17]
Richard	occurs c.1220 × 1233, c.1228 × 1233[18]
William	occurs 28 Oct 1232 × 27 Oct 1233, 2 June 1238[19]
Henry	occurs 1 May 1244[20]
Robert of Fissacre	occurs by 1256, res. 4 Sept 1261[21]
Laurence	election candidate; election quashed 17 Oct 1261; res. claims 24 Jan 1262[22]
Richard of Uppeton	election candidate; election quashed 17 Oct 1261; later el. or coll.; occurs 31 May 1271; died by 13 Jan 1273[23]
Henry	occurs 28 Feb 1277, 21 Feb 1285[24]
William Teingterer	election quashed and coll. 27 Aug 1285; vac. by 10 Apr 1289[25]
Richard of Brykevile	occurs 10 Apr 1289, died by 26 Dec 1307[26]
Roger of Horton	el. by 5 Apr 1308, conf. 5 Apr 1308, occurs 29 Oct 1320, possibly 13 Sept 1322[27]
Adam of Knolle	occurs 20 June 1327, res. 26 June 1346[28]
Thomas of Burdon	el. by 3 July 1346, election quashed and coll. 13 July 1346, occurs 19 May 1368[29]
Roger Leye	occurs 20 July 1370, 22 Nov 1373[30]

---

1 *L&P Hen. VIII*, XV, 213.
2 Ibid., 565; Leland, *Itinerary*, ed. Toulmin Smith, I, 175.
3 Photograph in Launceston Borough Archives.
4 Oliver, *Monasticon*, 23 and plate.
5 Bodleian, Ashmole 763, f. 68 right-hand; O. B. Peter, 'Launceston Priory: Notes from Manuscripts', 217–18. A late-medieval English ballad, 'Seynt Stevene was a clerk', tells how St Stephen was a clerk of King Herod and was martyred on 26 December when he testified to the birth of Christ on the previous day, a testimony supported by the roast capon on the king's table which crew 'Christ is born' (C. Brown and R. H. Robbins, *The Index of Middle English Verse* (1943), no. 3058). The cockerel may allude to this legend.
6 O. B. Peter, 'Launceston Priory: Notes from Manuscripts', 217–18. In St Thomas Church the gouté tincture is or and the roses are centred argent.
7 Hull (ed.), *Cartulary of Launceston*, 4.
8 Ibid., 4, 13.
9 The assistance of D. Knowles, C. N. L. Brooke, and V. C. M. London (ed.), *The Heads of Religious Houses: England and Wales*, vol. I, 2nd edn (2001), and D. M. Smith and V. C. M. London (ed.), *The Heads of Religious Houses: England and Wales*, vol. II (2001), is gratefully acknowledged.
10 Hull (ed.), *Cartulary of Launceston*, pp. viii (a late 16th- or 17th-century note), 13.
11 F. Liebermann (ed.), *Ungedruckte Anglo-Normannische Geschichtsquellen* (1879), 30.
12 Hull (ed.), *Cartulary of Launceston*, 34.
13 Ibid., 32; Barlow (ed.), *Early English Acta*, XI, 128; cf. Hull (ed.), *Cartulary of Launceston*, 6, 28, 169.

14 BL, Add. Charter 29000, printed in A. Morey, *Bartholomew of Exeter, Bishop and Canonist* (1937), 158; cf. Hull and Sharpe, 'Peter of Cornwall', 26–7.
15 Bodleian, Tanner 196, p. 491; N. Orme, 'The Origins of the Lepers of Launceston', *JRIC* (2003), 109–12.
16 *Calendar of Documents Preserved in France*, ed. J. H. Round (1899), 321.
17 J. H. Rowe (ed.), *Cornwall Feet of Fines*, 2 vols, DCRS (1914–50), I, 6; Hull (ed.), *Cartulary of Launceston*, 178.
18 Hull (ed.), *Cartulary of Launceston*, 119, 115.
19 Ibid., 85, 129; Rowe (ed.), *Cornwall Feet of Fines*, I, 28–9.
20 Rowe (ed.), *Cornwall Feet of Fines*, I, 43; Hull (ed.), *Cartulary of Launceston*, 206.
21 Hull (ed.), *Cartulary of Launceston*, 170; *Reg. Bronescombe*, ed. Hingeston-Randolph, 201–2; ed. Robinson, I, 126–7.
22 *Reg. Bronescombe*, ed. Hingeston-Randolph, 202; ed. Robinson, I, 140–1, 146–7.
23 *Reg. Bronescombe*, ed. Hingeston-Randolph, 202; ed. Robinson, I, 140–1; Hull (ed.), *Cartulary of Launceston*, 14–15, 13.
24 Hull (ed.), *Cartulary of Launceston*, 130–1,156, 208.
25 *Reg. Bronescombe*, ed. Hingeston-Randolph, 361; Hull (ed.), *Cartulary of Launceston*, 96.
26 Hull (ed.), *Cartulary of Launceston*, 96; TNA, C 84/16/3.
27 *Reg. Stapeldon*, 180; *Cal. Pat.* 1307–13, 43, 69; Hull (ed.), *Cartulary of Launceston*, 190–1, 137.
28 Hull (ed.), *Cartulary of Launceston*, 102–3; *Reg. Grandisson*, II, 1003–4.
29 *Reg. Grandisson*, II, 1004–6; Orme (ed.), *Cornish Wills*, 35.
30 Hull (ed.), *Cartulary of Launceston*, 172; *Reg. Brantyngham*, I, 303, 319.

Stephen Trediddan	occurs 1 June 1379, died 8 Dec 1403[1]	William Hopkyn	occurs 25 March 1491, died 10 Aug 1507[6]
Roger Combrygge	el. after 12 Dec 1403, died 18 June 1410[2]	John Carlyon	el. 3 Sept 1507, conf. 22–25 Sept 1507, probably res. or died c.1521[7]
John Honyland	el. 28 June 1410, conf. 5 July 1410 died 28 Sept 1430[3]	John Baker	occurs 1 Aug 1521, res. by 6 June 1534[8]
William Shyre	el. 16 Nov 1430, conf. 21 Aug 1431, occurs c.2 June 1463[4]	John Shere	conf. 6 June 1534, till surrender 24 Feb 1539[9]
Robert Waryn	occurs 3 May 1474, 28 Dec 1480[5]		

HOSPITAL OF ST LEONARD

A community of lepers probably existed at Launceston by about 1162, when a man named Wulfric 'of Spitel' (meaning hospital) witnessed a local charter. Land called 'Spitel' is also mentioned in a list of the possessions of Launceston Priory drawn up between 1159 and 1181.[10] Further light is cast on the community by a charter issued in their favour by the abbot and monks of the Cistercian abbey of Forde (Devon), between 1184 and 1190. The abbot, Robert, states in the charter that Reginald, earl of Cornwall (died 1175), left a sum of 44½ marks (£29 13s. 4d.) to 'Bartholomew of Exeter', who was probably the bishop of Exeter so named (died 1184). The money was intended by Bartholomew to buy a 'rent' for the lepers of Launceston, meaning a regular annual income in cash, and was entrusted to the abbot for this purpose. Robert experienced difficulties in finding a suitable source of income, but solved the problem after some lapse of time by transferring to the lepers three revenues that his monastery already owned, totalling 30s. a year. The abbey undertook to pay the sum in two equal instalments at Christmas Day and Midsummer Day, and promised to satisfy the lepers in some other way if the income was not paid.[11] It is not certain that the charter was effective in the long term, since it is not included in the official cartulary of Forde Abbey and there is no subsequent mention of the payment in documents relating to the lepers.[12] Its chief historical value is to suggest that they existed as a permanent body by the time of Earl Reginald's death, possibly having received his patronage.

The next historical evidence for the leper community comes from a charter issued in their favour by the canons of Launceston Priory in the mid 13th century.[13] This charter does not bear a date but must have been issued between 1245 and 1254, since it was witnessed by Richard Blund, bishop of Exeter (1245–57), and John Rof, archdeacon of Cornwall (resigned by 1254).[14] It states that the lepers had hitherto occupied a tenement in Launceston given to them by 'Earl Brian of Cornwall', a tenement that included a chapel dedicated to St Leonard (a saint who was patron of several other leper houses in England). The only Brian approaching this description was Brian son of Eudo count of Penthièvre, who was given lands in the South West of England by William the Conqueror and may have been briefly earl of Cornwall in 1069.[15] The latter date, however, is earlier than that of any known leper hospital in England and lacks credibility in view of Brian's brief connection with the South-West region and the lateness of the source. Perhaps Brian was a mistake for Reginald. The main purpose of the charter was to move the lepers from their Launceston site to a new one east of the town. It does not identify the earlier site in any more detail, but such communities often settled on parish boundaries and by a road (compare Bodmin, *Lamford*, and Liskeard) as was to be the case with the new location.

---

1 Hull (ed.), *Cartulary of Launceston*, 132; *Reg. Stafford*, 237.

2 *Reg. Stafford*, 237; Bodleian, Tanner 196, f. 3v (p. 6).

3 *Reg. Stafford*, 237; *Reg. Lacy*, ed. Hingeston-Randolph, I, 133.

4 *Reg. Lacy*, ed. Hingeston-Randolph, I, 138, 141; Bodleian, Tanner 196, ff. 237v–238r; DRO, Chanter XII(i), ff. 51v, 53r.

5 Rental of Launceston Priory, p. 13; Peter, *Histories of Launceston and Dunheved*, 18, 20; *Cal. Close 1476–85*, 219. He was ordained deacon as a canon of Launceston on 22 May 1456 (Chanter XII(i), f. 142v). For other references to him, see Hull (ed.), *Cartulary of Launceston*, 218; *Cal. Pat. 1476–85*, 179; and TNA, C 1/66/19.

6 *Cal. Pat. 1485–94*, 335; Chanter XIII, ff. 13v–16v. Peter (*Histories of Launceston and Dunheved*, 26) states that he occurs as prior in 1483.

7 Chanter XIII, ff. 13v–16v. A document of c.1534 implies that the next prior, John Baker, ruled for thirteen years, i.e. 1521–34 (*L&P Hen. VIII*, VIII, 88).

8 CRO, B/LAUS/105; DRO, Chanter XV, f. 38r; Chanter XIV, f. 73r.

9 Chanter XIV, f. 73r; *8th Deputy Keeper's Report* (1847), App. II, 26.

10 P. L. Hull (ed.), *The Cartulary of Launceston Priory*, DCRS new ser. 30 (1987), 6, 74.

11 Bodleian, Tanner 196, p. 491; N. Orme, 'The Origins of the Lepers of Launceston', *JRIC* (2003), 109–12.

12 S. Hobbs (ed.), *The Cartulary of Forde Abbey*, Somerset Record Soc. 85 (1998).

13 CRO, B/LAUS/641; printed in G. Oliver, *Monasticon Dioecesis Exoniensis* (1846), 25.

14 F. Barlow (ed.), *English Episcopal Acta*, XII: *Exeter 1186–1257* (1996), 303, 311.

15 D. C. Douglas, *William the Conqueror* (1964), 267.

By the charter of 1245×1254 the priory granted the lepers all the land at *Gillemartin* (later spelt *Gilmartin*) with its chapel, houses and fields. The land lay north of the River Kensey and west of the River Tamar, just off the main road from Devon into Cornwall after it passed over Polston Bridge (SX 3506 8475).[1] This was a typical location for a leper community or a hospital, enabling alms to be solicited from passing travellers. The boundaries of the site were described as going up the Kensey from the Tamar to the ditch of *Wittemore*, from the ditch to the spring at the head of the causeway, along the causeway to the wall of the chapel cemetery, thence northwards to the park, via *Meddelonde* and *Holemede* to the stream called *Colevorde Lake*, down the stream to the Tamar and back to the Kensey. The area comprised about 18 acres.[2] Besides the chapel and its cemetery there was a spring for the use of the community. The charter laid down that the lepers were to receive all the offerings made in the chapel and to be free of paying tithes on their land.[3] They were to continue to enjoy an annual payment of 12s. 9d. from the priory to support themselves and their resident chaplain, as well as a whole loaf of bread made of corn every day, the same as the canons received, 'for the soul of Earl Reginald'. On their part the lepers surrendered their existing tenement and chapel in Launceston, and this earlier chapel of St Leonard was to be destroyed, the canons promising never again to build one on or near the site. The priory also reserved certain rights over the hospital. The lepers might elect a prior of their own but had to present him to the prior of Launceston, and likewise each new candidate for admission. The chaplain of the lepers was to be subject to the priory, and the parish chaplain of Launceston (appointed by the priory) had the right to visit the lepers pastorally during Lent to counsel them, confess them, and receive their confessional offerings. He was also empowered to celebrate mass in the new chapel at Christmas, Easter, All Saints Day (1 November), and St Leonard's Day (6 November), the lepers each making an offering of ½d. on these occasions (¼d. at All Saints). The picture emerges of a largely self-governing body of lepers with economic resources from which they could afford to make offerings like healthy people.

Richard, earl of Cornwall, who consented to the charter and witnessed it, was an important patron of the town to which he gave a charter confirming the place as a borough and granting various rights to the burgesses, in return for obligations that included an annual payment of 100s. (£5) to the lepers of St Leonard. The charter, which survives in a royal confirmation of May 1383, is not dated but may have originated between 1227 and 1240, since Richard was made earl in the former year and granted to Liskeard in the latter the privileges he had given to Launceston.[4] In 1337 the burgesses of Launceston were paying 'the ancient alms of the realm' to the lepers of Gilmartin at the rate of 100s. a year at 2s. a week except for the two weeks before Michaelmas.[5] Shortly after Earl Richard's charter was confirmed in 1383, the reigning king of England, Richard II, asked his escheator in Cornwall to inquire into the liberties held by the burgesses of Launceston. The inquiry found that the burgesses had the right to levy customs on all merchandise crossing the Tamar in either direction, and had to pay from this income the lepers' 100s., now described as 'free alms of kings from time immemorial'. Such words as 'realm' and 'kings' suggest that Earl Richard may not have initiated the payment to the lepers but have reiterated an earlier royal grant, of which there are numerous examples elsewhere in England during the second half of the 12th century. The inquiry also stated that 'from time immemorial it has been the custom that no leper shall enter within the gates of the borough to do anything, and should he do so, the mayor's bailiff shall take away his upper garment and lead him outside the gate'.[6] This shows that Launceston, like other towns, forbade lepers to come inside its boundaries.

The hospital, then, had an endowment income of at least £5 12s. 9d., but it probably depended for its survival on alms as well. In 1307–10 the executors of Bishop Bitton of Exeter granted the large sum of 30s. 'to the lepers of Launceston',[7] and John Dabernon of Calstock bequeathed 50s. in 1368 'to the lepers of St Leonard at Launceston'.[8] John Megre, the London pewterer, who left 12d. in 1419 'to be shared among the lazars of the church of St Margaret near Launceston', probably also had St Leonard in mind.[9] Megre seems to have been ill-informed about Cornish hospital dedications, since he also refers to the lepers of St Margaret (correctly Mary Magdalene) near Helston. 'St Margaret' may be a scribal mistake influenced by the Helston reference that precedes it, or represent a confused memory of the prominent chapel in Launceston dedicated to St Mary Magdalene. One would expect the house to have solicited indulgences to encourage almsgiving and it is odd that

---

1 For a study of the site, with maps, see P. A. Harding and others, 'The Evaluation of a Medieval Leper Hospital at St Leonards, Cornwall', *Cornish Archaeology* 36 (1997), 138–50.

2 CRO, TA/213, p. 16 (but estimated at 13 acres in Parliamentary Papers, *Commissions of Inquiry into Charities in England and Wales, Thirty-second Report*, Part I (1837), 406). There is a map of the property in R. and O. B. Peter, *The Histories of Launceston and Dunheved* (1885), 194–5.

3 The area was still tithe-free in 1840 (CRO, TA/213, p. 16).

4 *Cal. Pat. 1381–5*, 263; A. Ballard and J. Tait, *British Borough Charters, 1216–1307* (1923), 5, 20, 104, 132.

5 P. L. Hull (ed.), *The Caption of Seisin of the Duchy of Cornwall (1337)*, DCRS new ser. 17 (1971), 4. The second payment of 2s. per week may simply be an elucidation of the sum of 100s. per annum.

6 *Cal. Inq. Misc. 1377–88*, IV, 146–7.

7 W. H. Hale and H. T. Ellacombe (ed.), *Accounts of the Executors… of Thomas Bishop of Exeter 1310*, Camden Soc. new ser. 10 (1874), 28.

8 N. Orme (ed.), *Cornish Wills 1342–1540*, DCRS new ser. 50 (2007), 34.

9 Ibid., 52.

none is recorded being granted by the late-medieval bishops of Exeter, but this may reflect shortcomings in their registers. Most of the information about the hospital in the 14th and 15th centuries comes from the borough records of Launceston, which mention the names of some inmates of the hospital entering the religious guild of St Mary Magdalene.[1] In 1467–8 three lepers were admitted, William Symons, William Chapelyn and William Stoke, with the observation that 'the prior of St Leonard and his brother lepers of the same place cannot be rejected'.[2] John Northecote came in likewise in 1478, John Gurde in 1493, and three unnamed lepers of Gilmartin in 1543, while in 1492 Eleanor Greston, laundress of St Leonard, was admitted as being a burgess.[3] All paid entrance fees of 6s. 8d. We can only speculate about how much and how closely the lepers associated with the healthy members of the guild. The hospital possessed its own seal, bearing the legend 'SIGILLUM HOSPITAL[IS] S[AN]C[T]I LEONARDI DE INT[ER] AQUAS', the phrase 'inter aquas' referring to its situation between the two rivers.[4]

In 1535 the royal valuation of Launceston Priory found 6s. 8d. being paid each year 'to the poor of the hospital of St Leonard, for the soul of the founder'.[5] This bears no obvious relation to the earlier sum of 12s. 9d. and its significance is obscure. In the spring of 1546 the Chantry Commissioners of Henry VIII, whose remit included hospitals, were told that a hospital existed in Launceston, 'founded by the late duke of Cornwall' for the relief of an unspecified number of poor men. The reference was probably to St Leonard. The inmates received their dwelling houses and a total income of £5 6s. 8d.[6] Two years later, in 1548, the Chantry Commissioners of Edward VI, whose brief excluded hospitals, were told of a sum of 20s. a year given by one Richard Carlyon and administered by the churchwardens of St Stephen Launceston for 'a priest to minister in a poor spitalhouse within the said parish, where be many sick and lazar people'.[7] This is likely to relate to the ministrations, regular or occasional, of a chaplain at St Leonard.

The hospital survived the Reformation, and continued with its land, its modest endowment, and some reliance on charity collections. The charter granted to Launceston by Philip and Mary I in 1556 specified the obligation on the burgesses to pay 100s. to the lepers of St Leonard 'of our alms', a point which echoed the royal alms mentioned by Earl Richard.[8] The churchwardens of St Breock made various small payments between 1568 and 1591 to the poor house or lazar house of St Leonard Launceston; on two occasions the 'gatherer' of the house is mentioned.[9] The wardens of Blanchminster's Charity at Stratton likewise paid 6d. to a poor man gathering for the 'lazar house' of Launceston in 1578 and 3d. to a gatherer called Hugh Williams in 1587.[10] In 1577 John Dollson of St Ewe bequeathed 6s. 8d. to the hospital.[11] The prior of the 'spital house' of St Leonard was charged in 1568 with not repairing the barn belonging to the hospital, and in 1584 the prior and brethren petitioned the mayor and community of Launceston in an interesting document which throws some light on the internal life of the community.[12] In it the prior and brethren wrote to ask for guidance on their customs, in humble tones that demonstrate their dependence on the borough authorities. They claimed that all the diseased persons who entered the house brought with them 'our house duty' (presumably an admission payment) and also goods, chattels, and household stuff. If they did not make an agreement to the contrary at their entrance, they could not subsequently dispose of any goods they brought in without the consent of the prior and other inmates, the goods remaining to the use of the house when they died. The document goes on to list eight inmates who had died in recent years, apparently in chronological sequence, and explains how their goods were disposed at their deaths. Their names were Thomas Edwards of North Tamerton, Prior Gryffynge (a man with a wife and child), Prior Robert Harrys, Prior Rawlinge, Prior John Rodde (a married man), Elizabeth Cornedon, Michael Ymbe, John Toker and Prior Gervais Gill. In most cases these people's goods passed to the house or were bequeathed elsewhere with permission, but Gill disposed of his without consent, which may have caused the appeal to the authorities. The mention of the 'prior and brethren' and the presence of only one woman in the list of eight inmates suggest that the community was dominated by men, a bias that is often observable in late-medieval and Tudor hospitals.

In 1602 the Cornish historian Richard Carew referred to the lazar house of 'St Thomas by Launceston' as one of three Cornish leper hospitals along with those of Bodmin and Liskeard, and mentioned that the inmates, like those of Liskeard, considered themselves to be defrauded of their rights.[13] 'St Thomas' must be a mistake for St Leonard but the mistake has led to the appearance of a phantom

---

1 In 1302–3 a fugitive took sanctuary in St Leonard's chapel (J. C. Cox, *Sanctuaries and Sanctuary Seekers of Mediaeval England* (1911), 301, quoting Assize Roll 1302–3).
2 Peter, *Histories of Launceston and Dunheved*, 43.
3 Ibid., 43–4.
4 Ibid., 47; W. Jago, 'The Ecclesiastical Seals of Cornwall', *JRIC* 8 (1883–5), 66.
5 *Valor Eccl.* (Rec. Com. 1810–34), II, 403.
6 TNA, E 301/15, ff. 46v–47r, printed in L. S. Snell, *Documents towards a History of the Reformation in Cornwall: vol. I, The Chantry Certificates for Cornwall* (c.1953), 30–1.
7 E 301/9, m. 3; Snell, *Chantry Certificates*, 31.
8 Peter, *Histories of Launceston and Dunheved*, 193–4.
9 CRO, P/19/5/1, ff. 20r–42v.
10 R. W. Goulding, *Records of the Charity known as Blanchminster's Charity* (1898), 69, 72.
11 RIC, HC 66, p. 156.
12 CRO, B/LAUS/106, printed in Peter, *The Histories of Launceston and Dunheved*, 44–6.
13 R. Carew, *The Survey of Cornwall* (1602, repr. 2004), f. 68r.

hospital of St Thomas in at least three modern works.[1] St Leonard seems to have decayed during the 17th century, and in 1685 its government was granted by James II to the mayor and burgesses of Launceston, with permission, if there were no lepers to be supported, to apply the land and revenues to support other poor people of the borough.[2] The hospital became extinct during the 18th century.[3] No visible remains survive.[4]

PRIORS OF LAUNCESTON HOSPITAL TO 1600

Gryffynge, 16th century, before 1584[5]
Robert Harrys, 16th century, before 1584[6]
Rawlinge, 16th century, before 1584[7]
John Rodde, 16th century, before 1584[8]
Gervais Gill, 16th century, before 1584[9]

LAUNCESTON: ALMSHOUSE

Almshouses developed in England after the middle of the 14th century, with the intention of providing accommodation for the long-term infirm. The earliest example in Cornwall appears at Launceston in 1446 when the borough council paid money for the upkeep of a building with that name. The founder and date of foundation are not recorded; we know only that in 1478 the mayor and burgesses of Launceston stated that they and their predecessors partly employed the profits of their possessions on 'the maintenance of the almshouse, wherein be six poor people'. The building continued to be mentioned in the borough accounts when repairs were carried out until as late as 1544, but in 1566 it was reported to be in decay 'for lack of reparation'.[10] The borough accounts imply that the almshouse was a small-scale enterprise, providing only accommodation and leaving the inmates dependent on organised or casual charity from local people.

LISKEARD

HOSPITAL OF ST MARY MAGDALENE

The earliest contemporary evidence for lepers at Liskeard occurs in 1307–10, when the executors of Bishop Bitton of Exeter made them a payment of 20s.[11] A document drawn up in the 14th or 15th centuries, however, attributes them with a history going back about 1200. In form this document is an undated Latin text purporting to have been issued by or for the 'brothers and sisters of the hospital of St Mary Magdalene of Liskeard', offering spiritual benefits to all who contributed to their needs or to their church. Those who did so would receive a share in all masses, hours, fasts, vigils, alms and good works performed by the brothers and sisters; in 10,005 masses said in nine other religious houses in Cornwall and Devon; and in a number of indulgences allegedly granted to the hospital by six popes and eighteen bishops, amounting to 14 years and 400 days of remission of penance.[12]

The document presents some problems of interpretation. It appears to have been drawn up between 1323 and 1326, since it mentions John bishop of Winchester, i.e. John Stratford, who became bishop in the former year, and Walter 'who is now bishop of Exeter', i.e. Walter Stapledon, who died in the latter. However four of the bishops mentioned in the document cannot be identified,[13] and the scribe's calligraphy is curious, appearing to combine features that could be as late as the 15th century with ones that seem to be imitating the conventions of the 12th and

---

1 Oliver, *Monasticon*, 22; R. M. Clay, *The Mediaeval Hospitals of England* (1909), 283; D. Knowles and R. N. Hadcock, *Medieval Religious Houses: England and Wales* (1971), 324, 369.

2 Peter, *Histories of Launceston and Dunheved*, 49–50.

3 M. I. Somerscales, 'Lazar Houses in Cornwall', *JRIC* new ser. 5.1 (1965), 73.

4 For site information, see CCC, HER 37129.

5 CRO, B/LAUS/106, printed in Peter, *Histories of Launceston and Dunheved*, 44-6.

6 Ibid.

7 Ibid.   8 Ibid.

9 Ibid.

10 R. and O. B. Peter, *The Histories of Launceston and Dunheved* (1885), 129, 131, 137, 151, 159, 167, 169, 187, 202.

11 W. H. Hale and H. T. Ellacombe (ed.), *Accounts of the Executors... of Thomas Bishop of Exeter 1310*, Camden Soc. new ser. 10 (1874), 28; M. I. Somerscales, 'Lazar Houses in Cornwall', *JRIC* new ser. 5.1, 75–6.

12 R. M. Haines, 'A Confraternity Document of St Mary Magdalene's Hospital, Liskeard', *Bulletin of the Institute of Historical Research* 45 (1972), 128–35, reprinted with an illustration and additions in idem, *Ecclesia Anglicana: Studies in the English Church of the Later Middle Ages* (1989), 192–200.

13 Haines noted five as unidentified but, since he wrote, E. B. Fryde et al. (ed.), *Handbook of British Chronology* (1986), 376, have listed two bishops of Waterford called Robert.

early 13th. This raises the question whether he was deliberately trying to forge a text in an earlier style. The most likely conclusion, shared by the editor of the document, is that he was copying a text of the 1320s at a later date. The nineteen identifiable popes and bishops in the document all lived before 1326, and the amounts of indulgence they are supposed to have given accord with the practices of their days. The four unidentifiable bishops could be innocent mistakes by the writer or mistakes in an exemplar that he was using. If the writer intended a pure fabrication, he would surely have invented more largely and included more famous popes and bishops than he did. True the list of indulgences is longer than that of any other religious house in the South West except for Exeter Cathedral, but most indulgences survive by chance. We know of only a small proportion of those that existed, and there is no reason why Liskeard Hospital should not have been given those that it claimed.[1]

Even if the text is a bona fide copy of one of the 1320s, we can only be certain that the hospital existed by that date (and probably by 1307–10), but there is nothing against the assertions of the text that its history went back for more than a further century. The earliest bishop mentioned as granting an indulgence is Henry Marshal, bishop of Exeter, who died in 1206, implying that the house was then in being. Many leper hospitals existed in England by that time and there is no improbability in Liskeard having acquired one. The other indulgences also carry conviction. They include one from each of the seven bishops of Exeter who followed Henry Marshal, six from other English bishops (allegedly from the neighbouring sees of Bath, Salisbury, and Winchester), four from bishops of Dublin and Waterford in Ireland, and six from popes. We would expect the diocesan bishops to have favoured the hospital with indulgences; the other English bishops are from nearby southern dioceses, and the Irish ones could be explained by visits to England by the bishops concerned. All the papal indulgences are of one year and 40 days and all the episcopal ones (save one) of 40 days or less, which accord with the values of indulgences then in force. The list implies that the hospital gained indulgences first from its local bishops and then, as it grew in resources and contacts, from the papacy and from bishops elsewhere, which is plausible. The document also alleges that the leper community was an organised hospital of brothers and sisters by 1326, that it had a dedicated chapel and one or more clergy who celebrated mass there at least occasionally, and that it had a relationship with the monasteries of the diocese, by which each shared in the masses celebrated by the others. There are parallels for all these features elsewhere and they are possible at Liskeard. If the document is true, it shows that a small south-western hospital could be better organised and enjoy more indulgences than other records suggest. Usually, we know little about the organisation of hospitals or their indulgences; the Liskeard document may be nearer to the truth in this respect.

The site of the hospital lay not in Liskeard itself but half a mile east of the town in the parish of Menheniot, at a place now known as Maudlin Farm (SW 26 64). In the 19th century the Charity Commissioners estimated the land formerly belonging to the hospital at eighteen acres, of which nine formed the core tenement of Maudlin in 1841. By that date the land was subject to tithe.[2] Further information about the foundation is forthcoming from 1368, when John Dabernon of Calstock left 40s. in his will to 'the lepers of St Mary Magdalene by Liskeard' to pray for him,[3] and 1379 when Bishop Brantingham licensed the rector of Menheniot to celebrate mass in the chapel of St Mary Magdalene.[4] Brantingham's licence was repeated by Bishop Stafford in 1400.[5] Since John Dabernon's reference to the hospital dedication implies that it had a chapel by his time, Brantingham's license cannot relate to a new building. Rather it suggests a change of use or personnel: the lepers' chapel was becoming a general place of worship or the local rector was being employed to celebrate mass instead of a hospital chaplain. Indulgences of forty days to those who contributed to the 'hospital' of St Mary Magdalene were granted by Bishop Stafford in 1395 and Bishop Lacy in 1436.[6] They tend to confirm the attribution of the undated document to 1323–6; if it was a later fabrication it would surely not have failed to include them. A bequest of 9d. 'to be shared between the lazars at Liskeard' was made by the London pewterer John Megre in 1419.[7]

The hospital survived the Reformation but continued to depend on public charity, sending proctors in search of alms throughout Cornwall. The churchwardens of St Breock made three small payments of about 6d. each to the 'poor house' or 'lazar house' of Liskeard between 1568 and 1577, the mayor of Launceston gave 6d. in 1574, and the wardens of Blanchminster's charity at Stratton in 1582–7 distributed money to a poor man of the house and to

---

1 On indulgences in the South West, see N. Orme, 'Indulgences in the Diocese of Exeter', *TDA* 120 (1988), 15–32, and 'Indulgences in Medieval Cornwall', *JRIC* new ser. II, 1.2 (1992), 149–70.
2 Parliamentary Papers, *Commissions of Inquiry into Charities in England and Wales, Thirty-second Report*, Part I (1837), 403; CRO, TA/144, p. 11.
3 N. Orme (ed.), *Cornish Wills 1342–1540*, DCRS new ser. 50 (2007), 34.
4 *Reg. Brantyngham*, I, 407.
5 *Reg. Stafford*, 242.
6 Ibid. (the number of days is implied in DRO, Chanter VIII, f. 6v); *Reg. Lacy*, ed. Dunstan, II, 7.
7 Orme (ed.), *Cornish Wills*, 52.

one John Marke who had a testimonial letter to gather on its behalf.[1] In 1577 John Dollson of St Ewe bequeathed 6s. 8d. to the poor people of 'the Maudlyn of Liskeard'.[2] The house included men and women in the late 16th century, some of whose burials are recorded in the parish registers of Liskeard although not in those of Menheniot. They include a poor woman of the Magdalen in 1553, Margaret of Magdalen in 1578, John Biskyr, lazar, in 1614, and William Webb of the Maudlin house in 1624.[3] In 1602 Richard Carew, the county historian, mentioned the hospital with Bodmin and Launceston as an example of a lazar house, but (as at Launceston) referred to complaints that the hospital or its inmates were defrauded of their rights.[4] By 1665 the house was empty. A report of that year made to Bishop Ward of Exeter states, under Menheniot, 'Hospitals there are none under that *notion*, only a lazar-house ... with a chapel for the lazar people, now in the custody and possession of one Mr Hodge, worth by common esteem ten pounds per annum. There is now no lazar in it; the house and chapel are kept in good repair ready to entertain any such person when presented.'[5] By about 1700 the historian William Hals referred to a hospital having 'formerly' existed in the parish, whose lands and revenues had been 'dismembered'.[6] No visible remains survive on the site.[7]

ST MICHAEL PENKEVIL

COLLEGIATE CHURCH

The parish church of St Michael Penkevil (SW 8578 4214) was converted into a small college of chantry priests in 1320 – an initiative that occurred elsewhere in early 14th-century England.[8] Similar foundations in the South West of England included three in Devon: Whitchurch, an abortive project, in 1322, Bere Ferrers in 1334, and Haccombe in 1337.[9] They were generally made by members of the gentry, who wished to establish chantries to pray for their souls in churches of which they were patrons. Being patrons enabled them, with their bishop's permission, to use church tithes to fund the institutions. Under these schemes the rector of the church remained in charge of the parish but acquired the duty of governing and maintaining three or four chantry priests, and received the title of 'archpriest' to reflect his responsibility. This was the time that the population of England was close to its medieval peak, when vocations to be clergy were correspondingly numerous. Many priests were available or obliged to work for low wages, which must have made it seem possible to support a group of them even from the modest revenues of St Michael Penkevil. At the papal taxation of England in 1291 the income of the church was reckoned to be worth only £2 a year, and although this sum was probably a large underestimate, the benefice was hardly a wealthy one.[10]

The patronage of the church belonged to the lords of the manor of Fentongollan in St Michael Penkevil, and had been held by the Treiagu family since at least the middle of the 13th century.[11] On 7 February 1320 Bishop Stapledon of Exeter issued an ordinance sanctioning the reorganisation of the church into a chantry of four chaplains, at the request of the patron, Sir John Treiagu, who had newly repaired the whole of the church at his own expense. Sir John was a close associate of the bishop, who made him his steward in Cornwall in 1308.[12] One of the chaplains was to be archpriest and to head the foundation; he was to be chosen by the patron, presented to the bishop for institution, and entrusted with the care of the parish. All the revenues of the parish were to be paid to him and he had responsibility for the goods of the church. He was to choose the other three chaplains and to maintain them from his income, paying each of them £1 6s. 8d. per annum for salary and clothes, an amount so small that it must have been assumed that they would live and eat free of charge in the archpriest's house. The archpriest and chaplains were to say the canonical hours (daily services) in the church, and to celebrate mass each day. They also had the duty of praying for various people, including John and Joan Treiagu, his parents, their children, and other members of their families, as well as Bishop Stapledon, his parents, his brother, and King Edward I. The prayers were to consist of the matins and vespers of the

---

1 CRO, P/19/5/1; R. and O. B. Peter, *The Histories of Launceston and Dunheved* (1885), 210; R. W. Goulding, *Records of Blanchminster's Charity* (1898), 71–2.

2 RIC, HC 66, p. 156.

3 CRO, P/126/1/1.

4 Carew, *The Survey of Cornwall* (1602, repr. 2004), f. 68r.

5 *Letters Relating to the Hospitals in the Diocese of Exeter, communicated at the instance of Bishop Seth Ward* (1665), 2.

6 BL, Add. 29762, f. 178r, printed in D. Gilbert, *The Parochial History of Cornwall* (1838), III, 170.

7 For site information, see CCC, HER 10365.

8 Although the terms 'college' and 'collegiate church' are used in this article, the ordinance setting up the foundation calls it an 'archpresbytery'.

9 D. Knowles and R. N. Hadcock, *Medieval Religious Houses: England and Wales* (1971), 413–19, with some inaccurate dates; *Reg. Stapeldon*, 402–5; *Reg. Grandisson*, II, 731–4, 852–5.

10 *Reg. Bronescombe*, ed. Hingeston-Randolph, 469.

11 Ibid., 175.

12 *Reg. Stapeldon*, 392.

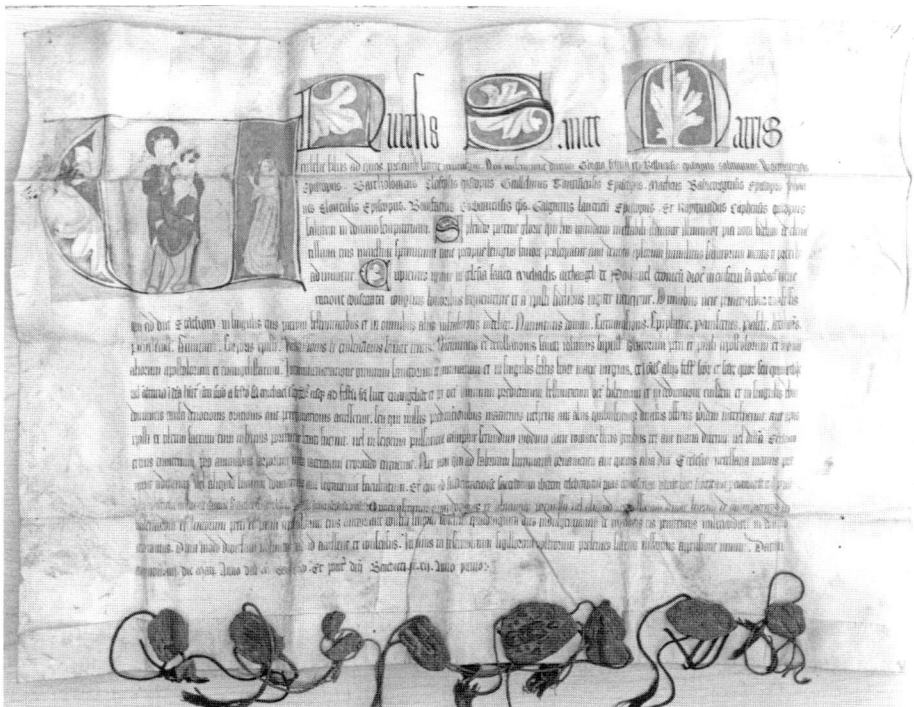

FIG 54. St Michael Penkevil. The indulgence issued in favour of the church by nine bishops at Avignon in 1335.

dead (*Placebo* and *Dirige*), the commendation of the dead, and three masses of intercession. Alternatively two masses of intercession might be said, and the third mass devoted to the Virgin Mary.[1]

The church of St Michael Penkevil was extensively restored by G. E. Street between 1862 and 1866, but it still bears marks of the refurbishment carried out by Sir John Treiagu at the time of his chantry foundation.[2] The chancel contained the high altar and would have included seats for the clergy to say the canonical hours. Two transepts were constructed or reconstructed next to the nave, each with a recess for a tomb at the outer end and an altar with a reredos against the east wall. Both transept altars were provided with piscinas and with seats for clergy nearby: three seats in the north transept and two in the south. There was a fourth altar on the first floor of the church tower, placed under a recessed arch against the east wall and also furnished with a piscina. The dedications of the altars are not known, apart from the high altar which was dedicated to Michael, but one may have been to the Virgin. No arrangements were made in the ordinance to provide clerks to say the responses at the daily masses, so either the chaplains helped one another or else there was a parish clerk who did the duty to all four. The church had the benefit of at least one indulgence (Fig. 54). This was issued at Avignon on 4 May 1335 by nine bishops, presumably ones whose sojourns there coincided with a visit to the papal court by an agent or well-wisher of the Treiagu family. The bishops included those of Aleria in Corsica, Bagnorea and Belluno-Feltre in Italy, Cloyne in Ireland, Krbava in Croatia, Tabriz in Iran, and Worms in Germany. Their document, which still exists, is beautifully illuminated with an initial letter depicting the Virgin and Child, and retains their seals attached to it. Each bishop granted 40 days of indulgence to anyone who attended the church on Sundays or major festivals, contributed to its expenses, prayed for the Treiagu family, or performed other specified good deeds.[3]

On 23 April 1320 Bishop Stapledon ordered the precentor of Exeter to give possession of the church to a suitable person, presented by the patron, but the person's name is not given. He was presumably William, who is named as the first archpriest in the indulgence of 1335. The next known incumbent is Benedict of Tresuswal, who was instituted in 1349.[4] On this occasion he was described as rector, the traditional title, but a reference to his appointment as a confessor in the rural deanery of Powder in 1355 calls him archpriest.[5] It is unlikely that the complement of chaplains was maintained for long after the Black Death of 1348–9. That event reduced the number of clergy,

1 Ibid., 339–41.
2 There are admirable descriptions of the church before the restoration and of Street's work, by the architect himself: G. E. Street, 'The Restoration of the Church of St. Michael Penkevel, Cornwall', *Jnl of the Royal Institute of British Architects*, 1st series 13 (1862–3), 32–53.
3 Private archive; N. Orme, 'Indulgences in Medieval Cornwall', *JRIC* new ser. II, 1.2 (1992), 155, 160 (illustration), 168.
4 *Reg. Grandisson*, III, 1392.
5 Ibid., II, 1147.

freed more attractive benefices for those who were left alive, and led to a rise in wages which would have made it difficult to pay appropriate stipends from the income of the church. The probability is that the chantry disappeared in the mid 14th century, except for the archpriest who resumed his former role as rector. In 1459 Maud Trenowth, dowager lady of the manor of Fentongollan, founded a new chantry of one priest in the church.[1] This lasted until the Reformation in 1548.[2] The early 18th-century historian William Hals refers to 'a convent house in the churchyard still extant for the chanter's residence'.[3] That was probably the house of the later chantry priest, as Hals believed, since it is likely that the earlier chaplains lived with the archpriest in the rectory. The church survives in its restored state.[4]

ARCHPRIESTS OF ST MICHAEL PENKEVIL

William	perhaps inst. 1320; occurs 4 May 1335[5]
Benedict of Tresuswal	inst. 18 June 1349; occurs 23 Feb 1355[6]

ST MICHAEL'S MOUNT

BENEDICTINE PRIORY, LATER CHAPEL

There is likely to have been a church at St Michael's Mount, and perhaps a religious community, before the Norman Conquest.[7] A charter in the 12th-century cartulary of the Benedictine abbey of Mont St Michel (Manche), which has a claim to be the earliest written evidence, consists of a grant to the abbey by King Edward the Confessor of 'St Michael, which is by the sea, with all its appurtenances', in other words St Michael's Mount, with the land of 'Vennesire' and the port of 'Ruminella'.[8] The authenticity of this charter has been much debated. The witnesses to it are wholly French, showing that it could not have been made while Edward was king of England (1042–66). Moreover later evidence does not firmly establish that Mont St Michel had possession of the Mount in the years immediately after 1066, causing some historians to doubt that the charter is genuine.[9] Against this it has been argued that the fabrication of a grant with such unusual witnesses is unlikely, and that Edward may have issued it between 1027 and 1035 while he was an exile in Normandy during the reign of Cnut. There he was regarded as the legitimate king of England, and might well have made such a grant without it becoming effective in subsequent years.[10]

THE MOUNT AFTER THE CONQUEST

The next written evidence chronologically appears to be a grant by Robert count of Mortain.[11] It is preserved in a much later text in the cartulary of the priory of St Michael's Mount, compiled towards the end of the 14th century, but it could be genuine and, if so, can be dated by its witnesses to between 1075 and 1084. In the charter the count gave the abbey of Mont St Michel the island of St Michael's Mount, half a hide of land, a weekly market on Thursday (which gave name to Market Jew near Marazion), and three acres of land at Traboe ('Traaraboth') in the Meneage district. The latter consisted of pieces of property that grew into a manor lying in the parishes of St Keverne and St Martin-in-Meneage.[12] Later, between 1087 and 1091, Robert made a further gift to the abbey of the manor of Ludgvan and a

---

1 Private archive, modifying C. G. Henderson, 'The Ecclesiastical History of the 109 Parishes of West Cornwall', *JRIC* new ser. 3 (1957–60), 386–8.

2 TNA, E 301/15, ff. 53v–54r; E 301/9, m. 6, printed in L. S. Snell, *Documents towards a History of the Reformation in Cornwall*: vol. I, *The Chantry Certificates for Cornwall* (c.1953), 35–6.

3 J. Polsue, *A Complete Parochial History of the County of Cornwall* (1867–72), III, 343.

4 For site information, see CCC, HER 22619.12, 14.

5 Orme, 'Indulgences in Medieval Cornwall', 155.

6 *Reg. Grandisson*, III, 1392: II, 1147.

7 The principal general publications on the religious history of the Mount include G. Oliver, *Monasticon Dioecesis Exoniensis* (1846), 28–33; T. C. Peter, 'Notes on St Michael's Mount', *JRIC* 14 (1899–1900), 221–46; T. Taylor, *St. Michael's Mount* (1932) (to be used with caution); C. Henderson, 'Ecclesiastical History of the 109 Parishes of Western Cornwall', *JRIC* new ser. 3 (1957–60), 217–23; J. R. Fletcher, *Short History of St. Michael's Mount Cornwall* (1951); P. L. Hull (ed), *The Cartulary of St. Michael's Mount*, DCRS new ser. 5 (1962); idem, 'The Foundation of St.-Michael's Mount in Cornwall: a Priory of the Abbey of Mont St.-Michel', in *Millénaire monastique du Mont Saint-Michel: mélanges commemoratifs: I. Histoire et vie monastique* (1967), 703–24; N. Orme, 'Saint Michael and his Mount', *JRIC* new ser. 10.1 (1986–7), 32–43; and P. Herring, *An Archaeological Evaluation of St Michael's Mount* (1993).

8 Printed in Hull (ed.), *Cartulary of St Michael's Mount*, 61, and M Fauroux (ed.), *Recueil des actes des ducs de Normandie de 911 à 1066* (1961), 217–18. 'Vennesire' is unidentified; 'Ruminella' has been suggested as a form of 'Treiwal' (Truthwall in St Hilary), which features in the following paragraphs (Hull (ed.), *Cartulary of St Michael's Mount*, p. xi).

9 For sceptical views, see Hull (ed.), *Cartulary of St Michael's Mount*, pp. x–xiii, and idem, 'Foundation of St.-Michael's Mount', 703–24.

10 S. Keynes, 'The Æthelings in Normandy', *Anglo-Norman Studies* 13 (1990), 190–6.

11 On Robert of Mortain, see B. Golding, 'Robert of Mortain', *Anglo-Norman Studies* 13 (1990), 119–144, especially 143.

12 Hull (ed.), *Cartulary of St Michael's Mount*, 1–2. For the suggested date, see I. N. Soulsby, 'The Fiefs in England of the Counts of Mortain, 1066–1106', University of Wales (Cardiff), MA thesis (1975), 41.

piece of land in Truthwall (in St Hilary), but this donation never took effect.[1] Robert's charter is followed in the cartulary by a copy of it containing a grant of religious privileges by Leofric, bishop of Exeter (1050–72) made 'at the order and exhortation' of Pope Gregory. The grant exempted the church of the Mount from episcopal authority, and offered pilgrims and contributors to the church a remission of one third of their penance.[2] This indulgence, as such grants were known, was a generous one, matching what pilgrims earned by journeying to the shrine of St James at Compostella, but it is clearly spurious.[3] Leofric's lifespan does not agree with the dates of the witnesses to Robert's charter, or with the reign of Pope Gregory VII, which began a year after Leofric's death. The grant is a later forgery and was not successful in gaining freedom for the Mount from the bishop of Exeter's jurisdiction, although it came to be regarded as valid in terms of the indulgence it offered to pilgrims.

We reach firm evidence about the Mount with the Domesday survey of 1086 and the geld accounts (taxation records) of about the same period. The fuller south-western text of the survey, known as the 'Exon Domesday', contains an entry headed 'Land of St Michael of Cornwall' (*Terra Sancti Michahelis de Cornugallia*), which in the more concise 'Exchequer' Domesday is simply called 'Land of St Michael' and in the geld accounts as 'St Michael'.[4] These entries refer to the Mount. They state that the land lay in Truthwall and was held in 1066 by Brismar, who is described in one entry as a priest. His tenure of the land suggests that the Norman abbey, whatever it may have been given by Edward the Confessor, did not have control of the Mount and its property in 1066. The land consisted of two hides and had never paid tax – a characteristic of property in Cornwall held by churches staffed by several clergy before the Norman Conquest, and a further pointer to the likelihood of such clergy at the Mount at some point before 1086.[5] One of the two Truthwall hides of land had been taken away from the church since 1066 by Robert of Mortain, who is noted in the Domesday survey as having expropriated Church property elsewhere in Cornwall. The value of St Michael's remaining hide in 1086 was 20s., and that of the count's hide was the same.

It is not clear how Robert of Mortain's charter and the Domesday survey relate to each other. Domesday fails to mention that the Mount belonged to Mont St Michel, whereas it records the fact that the abbey held Otterton (Devon) and might therefore be expected to have noticed the possessions of the abbey in Cornwall if Robert's charter had taken effect. Robert appears as a benefactor in the charter and as an expropriator in Domesday; he could well have been both. His grant to Mont St Michel is silent about the presence of a religious community on the Mount, but it is likely that a church building continued to stand on the site, possibly served by one or more non-monastic clergy. In the 16th century Leland heard that 'the count of Mortain… made a cell of monks in St Michael Mount',[6] but it is not until the mid 12th century, that written evidence survives about the presence of monks on the island. The evidence comes from an account of the Mount in the 13th-century cartulary of Mont St Michel's other south-western possession, Otterton priory. This states that Bernard, abbot of Mont St Michel, constructed the church of the Mount in 1135 and that the church was consecrated by Robert Warelwast, bishop of Exeter, in Bernard's presence, during the ninth year of King Stephen (December 1143–December 1144). The account goes on to state that the abbot with the advice of the bishop, 'Ranier' (perhaps Reginald, earl of Cornwall), and the barons of the region, constructed buildings suitable for the religious life, and installed thirteen monks in allusion to Christ and his apostles, one of whom was to act as prior. It was laid down that the prior should be appointed by the abbot of Mont St Michel from one of its monks, and could be removed from office if unsatisfactory. He was to pay an annual sum of 16 marks (£10 13s. 4d.) to the mother house. The Mount could recruit monks from Cornwall, but they were to be blessed (i.e. admitted) by the abbot of Mont St Michel, giving him control over entrants to the community. All this is suggestive of a new foundation, or at least of a substantial reorganisation of an earlier one, and points to the years between 1135 and 1144 as the significant date for the establishment of the priory of the Mount.[7] There were certainly monks on the site by 1193, when they were ejected by Henry de Pomeroy who fortified the island on behalf of Richard I's brother John. Henry himself was expelled in the following year.[8]

EARLY BUILDINGS AND PROPERTY

The priory church stood on the summit of the island, reached by a stepped path from the island's north side.[9]

---

1 Hull (ed.), *Cartulary of St Michael's Mount*, pp. xvii, 62.
2 Ibid., 2–3. For discussion, see ibid., pp. xiv–xvi; D. J. A. Matthew, *The Norman Monasteries and their English Possessions* (1962), 22–4; and Golding, 'Robert of Mortain', 126–8.
3 The 17th-century historian of Mont St Michel, Jean Huynes, who gives a chapter to its indulgences, mentions nothing similar there (E. Robillard de Beaurepaire (ed.), *Histoire générale de l'abbaye du Mont-St-Michel* (1872–3), II, 57–61).
4 *Domesday Book*, vol. I (1783), f. 120v; 'Exon Domesday' in H. Ellis (ed.), *Domesday Book: Additamenta* (1816), 65, 189, 471; C. and F. Thorn (ed.), *Domesday Book*, vol. X: *Cornwall* (1979), section 4/1.
5 L. Olson, *Early Monasteries in Cornwall* (1989), 89–90.
6 J. Leland, *Itinerary*, ed. L. Toulmain Smith (1907–10), I, 188.
7 Oliver, *Monasticon*, 414; translated in *Cal. Doc. France*, 264–5, where 'novo' is read as 'nono'.
8 Roger of Howden, *Chronicon*, ed. W. Stubbs (RS, 1868–71), III, 237–8.
9 Leland, *Itinerary*, I, 320.

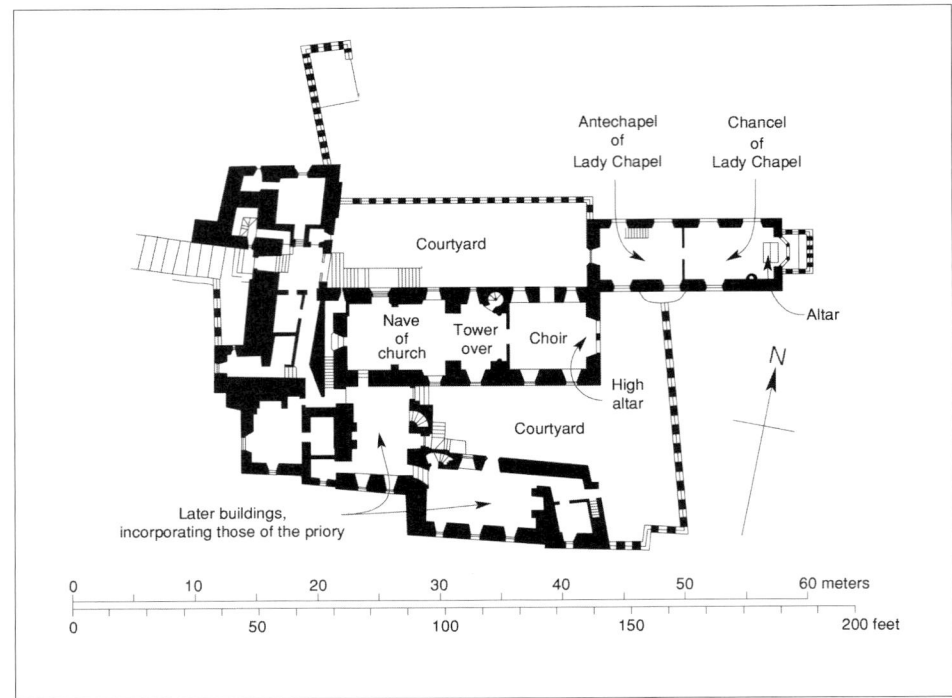

FIG 55. St Michael's Mount Priory, plan.

It is now represented by the chapel of the present-day house on the site (SW 5145 2984).[1] The original church was once thought to have collapsed in the great English earthquake of 1275, but the building in question was that of St Michael on the Tor outside Glastonbury.[2] The Mount's church appears to have undergone gradual renewal rather than major replacement, notably during the 15th century.[3] That being the case, the plan and dimensions of the surviving chapel – a choir and nave without aisles or transepts – may well reproduce those of the original church, especially in view of the constraints of the site (Figs. 55, 56). South and west of the church lay the monks' quarters, chiefly embodied today by the 'Chevy Chase' room which is now regarded as having been the refectory. There would have been a cemetery for the burial of monks, and in 1314 Bishop Stapledon of Exeter allowed the inhabitants of Market Jew to be buried at the Mount if they chose.[4] The church therefore had a parochial function of burial, and may well have acted as a parish church in other respects for people who lived on the island and on the lands held by the priory on the nearby mainland. All the island of the Mount belonged to the priory, which had (by 1352) an ancient right to take a bushel of corn or equivalent wares from every ship or boat that anchored there.[5] The rest of the priory's endowments, comprising lands, tolls, churches, and tithes, lay in west Cornwall except for the church of St Clement near Truro and a rent of 5s. from Trematon Castle in St Stephen-by-Saltash.[6]

On the mainland the priory's properties included part of Marazion in St Hilary parish and the manor of Traboe in the parishes of St Keverne and St-Martin-in-Meneage. It held three mills (St Michael's Mill in St Keverne, Trelowarren in Mawgan-in-Meneage, and Trevabyn in St Hilary), the Thursday market at Market Jew, and a further market at Marazion nearby (a name that means 'the little market').[7] The priory also received an annual rent of 10s. from the important fair held at Goldsithney, nearby in Perranuthnoe parish. By 1179 the monks held the advowsons of the churches of St Clement and St Hilary, conferring the right to appoint their clergy, and in 1205 Bishop Marshal of Exeter gave permission for Mont St Michel to appropriate the tithes of both parishes with the exception of revenues to support the vicars who

---

1 For site information, see CCC, HER 29222–29222.31.

2 Taylor, *St Michael's Mount*, 3, quoting H. R. Luard (ed.), *Annales Monastici* (RS, 1864–9), II, 386. The latter reference might permissibly be read as referring to the Mount, but other contemporary evidence states that the ruined church lay 'outside Glastonbury' (e.g. W. Stubbs (ed.), *Chronicles of the Reigns of Edward I. and Edward II.* (RS, 1882–3), I, 85). See also J. P. Carley, *Glastonbury Abbey* (1988), 35–6.

3 Below, p. 236.

4 *Reg. Stapeldon*, 333–4.

5 *Black Prince's Register*, II, 40–1, 45, 49.

6 On what follows, see Hull (ed.), *Cartulary of St Michael's Mount*, pp. xviii–xxv, and *Placita de Quo Warranto* (Rec. Com. 1818), 109.

7 Market Jew and Marazion were originally distinct but neighbouring places, which eventually became known by the latter name (O. J. Padel, *A Popular Dictionary of Cornish Place-Names* (1988), 115).

FIG 56. *The interior of the present-day church of St Michael's Mount, preserving much of the shape of the Benedictine priory and the later chantry chapel. In the 15th century there was a rood screen between the choir and the nave, an important image of St Michael, and at least one other altar.*

ministered in them.[1] In terms of tithes the monks received all those of the island, the tithes of corn and fish of St Hilary, the tithes of corn of St Clement, and shares of the tithes of certain estates within other parishes: Reskajeage in Camborne, Treworgan in St Erme, Tehidy in Illogan, Alverton in Madron, and the priory's own manor of Traboe. The earliest surviving evidence about the Mount's income comes from the papal valuation of English Church property in 1291. This reckoned it at £28 6s. 4d. per annum comprising temporal income from Market Jew (£4 14s. 2d.) and Traboe (£7 5s. 6d), tithe income from St Hilary (£3 13s. 4d.) and St Clement (£6), and offerings and payments at the church on the Mount (£6 13s. 4d.).[2]

EARLY HISTORY OF THE PRIORY

The abbots of Mont St Michel appointed a series of priors from the mid 12th century until 1362. All whose surnames survive appear to have been French. The earliest to be named is Richard de Wenilla in 1187.[3] By 1266 the prior was not only appointed by the abbot but instituted by the bishop of Exeter, who exacted an oath of obedience.[4] This disproves the spurious claim that the church of the Mount was not subject to the bishop's authority. Unlike the clergy of some other dependent religious houses in Cornwall, however, the prior and monks had a degree of autonomy, expressed in the possession of a seal which is mentioned as early as the time of Wenilla.[5] The size of the monastic community during the 13th and 14th centuries was probably smaller than the thirteen monks mentioned in 1143–4. A reference of 1262 alludes to the prior and three named *socii* ('fellows', probably monks), all apparently French,[6] and in later times there were only six stalls in the chancel of the church.[7] There was also a lay presence on the Mount in terms of servants, pensioners, visitors, and eventually soldiers. In addition, like most English religious houses, it was subject not only to its religious superiors but to an external patron, in this case the heirs of its founder, the count of Mortain. The heirs consisted of the Crown during the 12th century, the earls of Cornwall during the 13th, and the dukes of Cornwall from the 14th to the 16th.[8] Normally the Crown assumed the right of patronage when there was no duke, but the Black Prince's widow Joan held it as part of her dower from 1379 to 1385.[9] The Crown and the other patrons sometimes granted corrodies, usually to former royal servants, conferring the right to receive board and lodging in the priory at the monks' expense. Corrodies could also be purchased, or sold by one holder to another, and the names of more than a dozen men

---

1 F. Barlow (ed.), *English Episcopal Acta*, XII: *Exeter 1186–1257* (1996), 186–7.
2 *Reg. Bronescombe*, ed. Hingeston-Randolph, 469–70, 479.
3 Hull (ed.), *Cartulary of St Michael's Mount*, 29.
4 *Reg. Bronescombe*, ed. Hingeston-Randolph, 175; ed. Robinson, II, 20–1, 97.
5 Hull, 'Foundation of St. Michael's Mount', 721.
6 Avranches, Public Library, 159, f. 3r, printed in G. H. Doble, 'Miracles at St. Michael's Mount in Cornwall in 1262', *Truro Diocesan Gazette* (October, 1934), 130–1, and in Fletcher and Stéphan, *Short History*, 67–9.   7 Below, p. 235.
8 P. L. Hull (ed.), *The Caption of Seisin of the Duchy of Cornwall (1337)*, DCRS new ser. 17 (1971), 140.
9 *Cal. Close 1377–81*, 266; *Cal. Pat. 1381–5*, 314.

who held them at the Mount survive between 1316 and 1410.¹

The church on the Mount attracted pilgrims as early as the late 11th century, since the Life of St Cadoc by Llifris, written in Wales at that time, claims that Cadoc visited the place and talks of the archangel being venerated by all who come there.² The spurious document in the Mount's cartulary, with its generous remission of penance, was regarded as genuine in the later Middle Ages and probably helped to encourage visits to the archangel and his church.³ Evidence of individual pilgrims is recorded in a manuscript of Mont St Michel, now in the public library of Avranches (Manche). It refers to four miracles that took place at the Mount in 1262, of which three are described. In one case a woman named Matilda was brought by her parents from the nearby parish of Gulval, after losing consciousness and the power of speech for two days. In a second a certain Christina from Glastonbury came after losing her sight for six years, and in a third a girl called Alice, from the region of Hereford, arrived after suffering a similar loss for seven. All were cured through the archangel's intercession. The origins of the pilgrims suggest that the Mount's reputation was not confined to the neighbourhood but extended more widely, at least into the south-western quarter of England.⁴

DECLINE OF THE PRIORY

In 1328 the redoubtable John Grandisson, bishop of Exeter, visited the Mount, and the prior, Peter de Carville, assisted him in pronouncing excommunication on the rebellious clergy of St Buryan.⁵ Eight years later Peter himself was in trouble with the bishop on account of his alleged mismanagement of the priory. He was said to have dissipated its goods through improvidence, and Grandisson ordered the treasurer of Exeter cathedral, Richard Wydeslade, to investigate. The treasurer visited the Mount on 7 May 1336 and reported that the income of the priory was potentially worth about £100 per annum. The house was only £5 in debt, but the prior had leased lands at inadequate rents, alienated goods worth £12, and allowed one of his relatives to waste the priory's assets. Wydeslade's report talked of the prior and monks, but observed that the prior had recently spent a month alone in the monastery (i.e. without any colleagues), against the rule that religious persons should dwell at least in pairs. This suggests that the community had become a small one. Carville was ordered to appear before the bishop to answer the charges against him, but since he survived for another six years he was presumably dismissed with a warning.⁶ In 1340 the bishop of Exeter reported to the king that Carville resided in person with his fellow monks.⁷

By this time the Mount, like other French houses in England, was experiencing difficulties as enmity grew between the kings of England and France. In 1294 the Crown began a practice of taking control of such 'alien priories' during times of war with France. The king appropriated their rights, moveable property, and revenues, and left them only whatever resources were considered sufficient to maintain their religious life.⁸ Royal officials made a valuation of the priory's grain and animals in 1324, and a fuller inventory of furnishings, livestock, and income in 1337.⁹ The second of these included the church's books and ornaments, which were left in the keeping of the monks; the goods in the prior's chamber and elsewhere; and the livestock, represented by three heifers. The tithes of St Clement were valued at £15, those of St Hilary at £23 6s. 8d., the rents from Traboe at £22, and those in Penwith (presumably at Marazion) at £1 9s. 7½d. – a total (embracing the moveable property) of £82 3s. 11d. In 1379 the Crown estimated the priory's income at 100 marks (£66 13s. 4d).¹⁰ At first the abbots of Mont St Michel were able to appoint priors of the Mount despite the Crown's intervention, but the king took over the patronage of the priory's two parish churches and leased the revenues of the Mount to 'farmers'. These men, who sometimes included the prior himself, were responsible for conveying the surplus revenues to the Crown.¹¹ The king's interventions were compounded by the potential status of the Mount as a fortified site, and by 1338 royal appointments of keepers of the fort were being made, which suggests that the buildings were used as a defence and doubtless augmented for that purpose.¹² Further pressure on French monks in England came from the fear that they might be considered spies or agents of the French king.

---

1 Hull (ed.), *Cartulary of St. Michael's Mount*, pp. xxv–xxvii, 34–5; *Black Prince's Register* II, 208–9, 211; *Cal. Close* 1313–18, 437; *Cal. Close* 1318–23, 706; *Cal. Close* 1341–3, 142; *Cal. Close* 1346–9, 258; *Cal. Close* 1364–8, 281; *Cal. Close* 1368–71, 279; *Cal. Close* 1377–81, 343; *Cal. Pat.* 1385–9, 291; *Cal. Close* 1402–5, 116–17, 319; *Cal. Close* 1409–13, 119.

2 A. W. Wade-Evans (ed.), *Vitae Sanctorum Britanniae et Genealogiae* (1944), 93–4; N. Orme, *The Saints of Cornwall* (2000), 162.

3 Above, p. 229, and below, p. 236.

4 Avranches, 159, f. 3r; Doble, 'Miracles at St. Michael's Mount', 130–1; Fletcher and Stéphan, *Short History*, 67–9.

5 *Reg. Grandisson*, I, 422–3; above, p. 165.

6 *Reg. Grandisson*, II, 813.

7 Ibid., I, 59.

8 On this subject, see C. W. New, *History of the Alien Priories in England to the Confiscation of Henry V* (1916), 55–82; Matthew, *Norman Monasteries*, 72–142; *Cal. Close* 1327–30, 18–19. The chief periods of seizure were 1294–1303, 1324–7, 1337–61, 1369–99, and 1402 onwards.

9 TNA, E 106/6/11, mm. 2, 22; E 106/9/30; printed in Oliver, *Monasticon*, 29, and E. Smirke, 'An Inventory of the Property of the Alien Priory of St. Michael's Mount, in Cornwall, in the year 1337', *JRIC* 2 (1866–7), 1–6 at 4–5.

10 *Cal. Close* 1377–81, 266.

11 e.g. *Cal. Pat.* 1345–8, 15, 104, 211; *Cal. Close* 1381–5, 320.

12 *Cal. Pat.* 1338–40, 99.

In 1356 Prior John Hardy was indicted at Launceston assizes for sending his brother to Normandy with letters and money, and for keeping two of the king's enemies on the manor of Traboe, but he was acquitted by a jury.[1]

Peace between England and France in 1361 was followed by the restitution of the priory's rights and revenues, and the return of war in 1369 by their renewed confiscation.[2] The last French prior to be appointed by Mont St Michel was John le Volant in 1362,[3] and in 1374 he was reported by the bishop as residing at the Mount with two monks.[4] Three years later, Parliament ordered all French monks to leave England by February 1388, except for priors with life tenure, and the replacement of even the latter by Englishmen when they died or resigned. If English monks could not be found to fill the places of the French ones, chaplains could be appointed instead.[5] John le Volant ceased to be prior between 1380 and 1383, and in the summer of the latter year an Englishman laid claim to the office in the person of Richard Harepath, who was not even a Benedictine monk but an Augustinian canon of St Germans priory. Harepath's appointment was contentious. On 15 June 1383 Bishop Brantingham of Exeter instructed the archdeacon of Cornwall not to proceed with his induction as prior, having heard allegations from the Crown that Harepath had gained the office by means of false letters issued by the escheator of the county of Cornwall, and had taken control of the priory by force. The induction was to be delayed until the question of patronage had been settled in the king's court.[6]

Harepath was more respectable than these charges suggest. He appears to have established his position as prior, and resigned in December 1385 only to become prior of his own home monastery.[7] The king, Richard II, then presented another Englishman, Richard Auncell, a Benedictine monk of Tavistock abbey who had been prior of its cell in the Isles of Scilly.[8] During the mid 1390s the king was disposed to make peace with France, and in 1395 he granted a petition by Mont St Michel that it might appoint persons to govern the Mount, on condition that they recognised the Roman pope acknowledged in England (a reference to the Great Schism in the Church between two rival popes).[9] Richard's grant did not apparently affect Auncell, who remained as prior. In 1399 Henry IV restored to him and to several other heads of former alien priories control of the finances of their houses, and he held his office until his death in 1410.[10] The patron of the day, Henry prince of Wales and duke of Cornwall (later Henry V), then presented William Lambert, a monk from another alien priory, Tutbury (Staffs.).[11] This priory belonged to the patronage of the prince's father, Henry IV, and the prince had already promoted one of its monks to be prior of the Cornish monastery of Tywardreath.

THE MOUNT AS A CHAPEL

The events of the late 14th century turned the Mount in effect into a small independent English monastery. This process was not without positive results. The compilation of the priory's cartulary appears to have taken place at this time, no doubt to facilitate the administration and defence of its possessions, and, as we shall see, the church began to assert a relationship with its patron saint equal to that of Mont St Michel. The word 'monastery', however, may be inappropriate to describe the Mount after about 1380, since it is not clear if any monks remained beside the prior. We have seen that as early as 1336 the prior was accused of spending a month without a colleague, and by 1383 the church is stated as being served by a prior and chaplains.[12] The last three priors may have provided the sole monastic presence, and when in 1413 Henry V, now king, asked the bishop if the church was 'conventual', meaning a religious community, the bishop replied merely by citing past institutions of priors.[13] Eventually Henry either brought its residual monastic status to an end or intervened because this status had evaporated. In 1415 he founded a new religious community near London: the Bridgettine abbey of Syon (Middx.), a community of nuns assisted by a body of male clergy.[14] Between 1417 and 1420 he granted the Mount and its possessions, with many other lands, to a group of trustees as part of the abbey's endowment.[15] Lambert appears to have died or left by this date, since no mention was made of any life-interest of his, and the grant had taken effect by 20 November 1421 when the bishop of Exeter's vicar general noted that the priory was appropriated to Syon.[16] The trustees did not appoint attorneys to deliver the priory and its property

---

1 *Cal. Pat.* 1354–8, 460.
2 *Cal. Pat.* 1358–61, 558–9; *Cal. Pat.* 1367–70, 410.
3 *Reg. Grandisson*, III, 1461–2.
4 *Reg. Brantyngham*, II, 194.
5 *Parliament Rolls*, VI, 48; Matthew, *Norman Monasteries*, 108–12.
6 *Reg. Brantyngham*, I, 497.
7 Ibid., I, 93.
8 *Cal. Pat.* 1385–9, 62; *Reg. Brantyngham*, I, 94; see below, p. 269.
9 *Cal. Pat.* 1391–6, 625.
10 *Cal. Pat.* 1399–1401, 70; *Reg. Stafford*, 204, 320.

11 *Reg. Stafford*, 204, 320.
12 *Reg. Grandisson*, II, 813; *Cal. Close* 1381–5, 314.
13 *Reg. Stafford*, 321. Auncell was described in 1399 as a monk of Tavistock Abbey, as if that was his only monastic community (*Cal. Pat.* 1399–1401, 70).
14 On the history of Syon, see *VCH Middlesex*, vol. I (1969), 182–91.
15 Undated grant (datable to 1417–20 by the mention of Edmund Lacy, bishop of Hereford), ratified in 1424 (*Parliament Rolls*, X, 164; *Cal. Pat.* 1422–9, 205–7).
16 *Reg. Lacy*, ed. Dunstan, I, 54.

to Syon, however, until 3 March 1425.[1] In due course the abbey gained all the endowments of the priory, including the patronage of St Clement and St Hilary.

From about the 1420s onwards the staff of the church on the Mount consisted of three chaplains, who may represent continuity from similar chaplains under the last three priors. By 1427 William Morton appears to have been the senior chaplain, when he is mentioned forwarding sums of money to Syon.[2] Round about 29 September 1430 Syon entrusted him with various documents relating to the privileges of the Mount,[3] and with the ornaments and goods of the church, defined in an inventory.[4] By this date he held the title of 'archpriest', and was further granted the right to farm or administer the priory's property for twenty years in return for an annual payment of 100 marks (£66 13s. 4d.).[5] No statute survives setting up a new institution, and the church continued to be sometimes described as a priory, but it was now effectively a chantry chapel.[6] Its clergy no longer formed a legal body. They were simply the employees of Syon, and the only known document that sets out their duties is Syon's appointment of Ralph Crabbe as archpriest in 1460. This bound him to reside personally, say mass and the daily services with the other priests, and keep safe custody of the priory as Morton had done. He was to pray especially for Edward IV the current king, Henry V as the founder of Syon abbey, the benefactors, parishioners, and others buried there, and all the faithful departed.[7] This suggests that the clergy gathered in the choir to say daily services and each celebrated a daily mass at an altar. No doubt they also ministered to pilgrims.

Syon did not enjoy an undisturbed possession of the Mount after 1421. Its ownership was threatened when Henry V's successor Henry VI reached the age of majority and began to make his educational foundations at Eton and King's College (Cambridge). In 1440 he ordered the Mount to be taken into his own hands and commissioned a valuation of its revenues by the sheriff of Cornwall. The sheriff reported that the manor of the Mount was worth £5 per annum, the manor of Traboe £7 6s. 8d., the tithes of St Clement, St Hilary, and the other estates £14, and the offerings in the church £7, a total of about £33. This sum is smaller than the figures given in earlier and later times, but may discount the costs of maintaining the Mount and its staff.[8] On 15 March 1442 Henry VI gave the Mount and its properties to King's College – a decision that was probably influenced by the Mount's proximity to the deanery of St Buryan, a benefice in royal patronage which Henry conveyed to King's at the same time.[9] This confiscation must have been unwelcome to Syon and its supporters, and not long after Henry had been ousted from the throne in the spring of 1461, Edward IV restored the Mount to Syon on 29 November 1461.[10] King's was obliged to recognise the restoration in the following February.[11] When Henry briefly recovered the throne in 1471, the grant to Syon was confirmed and it remained in force until the dissolution of the monasteries.[12]

The disappearance of the monastic community modified but did not destroy the status of the Mount as a religious centre. Indeed the changes of the 15th century may have brought about revival in certain respects. By 1425 the people of Market Jew had begun to build a stone jetty in Mount's Bay to provide a haven for ships. Bishop Lacy of Exeter granted an indulgence to help the work in that year.[13] By 1427 William Morton had involved himself in the project and persuaded the Crown to grant tolls on local ships for seven years to fund it.[14] The tenure of the Mount by King's, although brief, led to the making of surveys and accounts that are helpful in reconstructing the nature of the church and community during the middle of the century. In 1454 the college's officers estimated the gross income of the Mount at about £110 7s. 7d., made up of rents from Traboe (£17 4s. 2d.), rents from the Mount's other properties (£14), tithes and other small receipts (£42 10s. 1d.), and offerings in the church (£36 13s. 4d.). These revenues were farmed to a local agent who remitted 100 marks (£66 13s. 4d.) per annum to the college, paid the staff of the Mount, bore the cost of repairs, and took the rest of the income as profit. Morton appears to have continued to hold the farm for much of the period up to 1460.[15]

The information supplied by the archives of King's College is complemented, after 1461, by a series of

---

1 TNA, E 329/150.

2 E 329/204; cf. *Cal. Pat.* 1422–9, 447–8. A William Morton from Durham diocese was ordained acolyte, subdeacon, and deacon in London in 1419–20 (London, Guildhall Library, 9531/4, ff. 88v, 89v, 91r).

3 They included documents issued by Henry, William, and Simon, bishops of Exeter, John, archbishop of Canterbury, and a Pope Clement (TNA, E 315/50/29).

4 TNA, E 106/12/33, E 326/4386, printed by H. Mitchell Whitley, 'An Inventory of the Ornaments and Jewels Delivered to the Archpriest of Saint Michael's Mount, Cornwall, 1st October 1430', *DCNQ* 8 (1915), 171–4.

5 TNA, E 326/4384.

6 *Reg. Lacy*, ed. Dunstan, I, 32, 53, 81, 100; II, 250; *Cal. Pat.* 1422–9, 20.

7 TNA, E 329/167.

8 Oliver, *Monasticon*, 414.

9 *Cal. Pat.* 1441–6, 111–12; *Parliament Rolls*, XI, 443. On St Buryan, see above, p. 166–7.

10 *Cal. Pat.* 1461–7, 56–7.

11 Cambridge, King's College Archives, Ledger Books, KCAR/3/3/1, f. 38r–v; *Cal. Close* 1461–8, 132; *Cal. Pat.* 1461–7, 177.

12 *Cal. Pat.* 1467–77, 238, printed in *Rot. Parl.*, V, 456–7.

13 *Reg. Lacy*, ed. Dunstan, I, 126–7.

14 TNA, SC 8/124/6187; *Cal. Pat.* 1422–9, 447–8.

15 King's College, SMM/4–9; KCAR/3/3/1, f. 9v.

receivers' accounts relating to Syon's resumption of the property.¹ The accounts, which run with gaps from 1461 to 1517, indicate that the annual revenue of the Mount and its properties (including arrears) ranged from £107 to £118 during the 1460s, fell to around £60–£70 in the late 1470s, and rose again to between £286 and £299 in the early 1480s. In 1517 it was £135. In the middle of the 15th century the archpriest was paid £10, the second priest £6 13s. 4d., and the third £6 6s. 8d., but between 1470 and 1479 the archpriest's stipend was reduced to £6 13s. 4d. and those of his colleagues to £5 6s. 8d. or £6. The other staff of the church included a clerk who would have served the priests in church, rung the bells, and looked after the altars and offerings, receiving £4 per annum, later £4 13s. 4d., along with a porter and an assistant porter paid £4 and £2 respectively.² In 1435 Syon granted an annuity of £4 to a hermit named Stephen Gildeford on condition that he behaved honestly and obeyed the abbey and its officers. He must have been a young man, since the grant was valid for sixty years unless he died in the meantime.³ From 1456 the annuity was paid to a hermit named Stephen Treher' alias Symond, who was either the same man or a successor. Treher is recorded helping to compile one of the receivers' accounts and handling the collection of tithes.⁴

The clergy after 1420 appear to have been generally recruited from Cornwall. The first two archpriests, Morton and Knyfton, were probably exceptions to this, brought in from outside by Syon and King's respectively, but Knyfton (appointed in 1460) was only briefly in office since Syon appointed another cleric, Robert Thomas, after it recovered the Mount in the following year. The assistant priests appear to have belonged to the rank-and-file unbeneficed clergy of the county, and apart from those who became archpriests, it was unusual for them to rise to hold parish benefices. Syon promoted two of the archpriests, Thomas and his successor Ralph Crabbe, to be vicars of its parish of St Hilary, and the next holder of the office, William Michell, to the corresponding post in its parish of St Clement.⁵ The last recorded archpriest, John Arscott, was either from Cornwall or Devon. He was born in 1497–8 and graduated as a master of arts, perhaps at Oxford.⁶ In 1537 he received licence to hold a benefice in plurality with the archpresbytery and was presented by Syon to St Clement, but resigned the latter after a short period, although he remained at the Mount.⁷ During his incumbency he recovered the £10 salary that had been given to the archpriests up to the 1470s, perhaps in recognition of his graduate status.

THE CHURCH BUILDING AFTER 1400

The church of the Mount can be more clearly visualised in the 15th and early 16th centuries than in earlier times. This is partly due to contemporary sources and partly to an account by the Cornish antiquary William Borlase in 1762, when more of the building and its contents were extant than are visible today.⁸ It was longitudinal in shape, internally about 62 feet (18.8 metres) long by 18 feet (5.4 metres) wide, divided into a choir 20 feet (6 metres) long and a nave 42 feet (12.8 metres) long. The nave was entered by a west door surmounted by a rose window. Between it and the chancel stood a rood screen and rood loft, the screen being carved and painted with the history of the Passion. By 1430 there was a secondary altar in the church dedicated to the crucified Jesus.⁹ This altar, together with the one in the Lady chapel, would have given each priest a place for saying mass. The chancel possessed two east windows surmounted by a rose window, and contained three stalls on either side. A staircase from a door in the south wall near the high altar descended to a chamber under the chancel. Above the east end of the nave was a tower containing five bells, each dedicated to one of the orders of angels in heaven and to a particular saint or angel.¹⁰ In 1508 John Bevill, of a family of gentry in St Allen parish, asked to be interred inside the church.¹¹

North-east of the church and extending beyond it was the Lady chapel, which stood on a lower level and had to be entered separately from the church. It was about 48 feet (14.5 metres) long by 14 feet (4.2 metres) wide, and contained an antechapel, screen, and chapel (Fig. 57). The antiquary William Worcester, who visited the Mount in 1478, called this chapel 'newly built', but it or a predecessor existed by 1430 when it contained an altar with appropriate frontals and a vestment for its priest.¹² Some of the monastic buildings remained

---

1 Hatfield House, 10/2, 14/20–24, 20/7, 35/5, 104/2–4, 104/6–9, 108/4. A stray from this series (an account for 1480–1) survives as CRO, AU/1.

2 AU 1; Fletcher and Stéphan, *Short History*, 63.

3 TNA, E 326/4385.

4 Hatfield House, 104/2, 14/21.

5 Thomas was instituted as vicar of St Hilary in 1462. Crabbe was ordained priest in 1454 to the title of Tywardreath Priory (*Reg. Lacy*, ed. Dunstan, IV, 178, 243, 251), and resigned as vicar of St Hilary in 1500 (DRO, Chanter XII(ii), (Reg. Redmayn) f. 17v). Michell died as vicar of St Clement in 1489 (ibid., (Reg. Fox) f. 140v).

6 For Arscott's age, see below, p. 239. He was ordained priest in 1531 to the title of Bodmin Priory (DRO, Chanter XIV, ordination lists.)

7 D. S. Chambers, *Faculty Office Registers, 1534–49* (1966), 114; DRO, Chanter XIV, ff. 91r, 96r).

8 P. A. S. Pool, 'The Ancient and Present State of St. Michael's Mount, 1762', *Cornish Studies* 3 (1976), 29–47 at 35–6, with plan; measurements are based on the plan rather than on those given by Borlase.

9 Whitley, 'An Inventory, 1430', 173.

10 The saints were Nicholas, Paul, and Margaret, and the angels Gabriel, Raphael, and probably Michael.

11 N. Orme (ed.), *Cornish Wills 1342–1540*, DCRS new ser. 50 (2007), 132.

12 W. Worcester, *Itineraries*, ed. J. H. Harvey (1969), 100–1; Whitley, 'An Inventory, 1430', 173.

FIG 57. *The church of St Michael's Mount from the south east, as it was in 1786. The former Lady Chapel is seen on the right, at a lower level than the church itself.*

south of the church, and these provided lodgings for the chaplains and clerk of the Syon and King's regimes.¹ King's sought to rebuild the church (a petition survives asking Henry VI for authority to collect donations),² and work on its fabric and on other buildings is recorded being done during its ownership. The lease granted to Morton in 1448 bound him not only to carry out general maintenance but to 'repair well a certain wall on the eastern side of the kitchen of the said priory, now in disrepair, and to make it embattled and crenellated with stones and mortar' within two years, and likewise to have the bell-tower 'well and sufficiently embattled with stones and mortar' during the same period.³ Fragmentary building accounts of this period mention work being done on the 'steeple' (i.e. church tower), four windows, a vault, and a further ten windows of which two were in the east end of the church and eight at the sides.⁴

PILGRIMAGE AND LEGEND

The church remained an important centre of popular devotion in Cornwall during the later Middle Ages (1300–1500), although the paucity of evidence before 1400 makes it impossible to put such devotion into perspective. By 1478 the spurious Leofric grant had been recast as a grant by 'Pope Gregory' himself, dated to the year 1070; this was exhibited at the Mount with the exhortation that it should be publicised in churches elsewhere.⁵ The offerings that had reached over £36 in 1454 fell to between £17 and £22 per annum in the 1460s, before rising to £43 19s. 1d. in 1517 and £38 in 1519. Most of the offerings were made in coin, including some broken and 'refuse' or odd money, but some came in the form of barley and fish. Visits for religious purposes were made from the neighbourhood, the rest of Cornwall, and beyond. From 1461 to 1483 there are references to a procession to the Mount by the vicar and parishioners of St Hilary with their relics and banners on the Monday of Rogation week, an activity referred to in 1466 as 'the pley' – possibly implying a drama, possibly meaning simply the procession.⁶

A widespread devotion to the Mount by Cornish people is suggested by the frequency of bequests to it in their wills up to 1569, often with gifts to the two other major county shrines of St Day and Perranzabuloe.⁷ This devotion doubtless brought many from Cornwall to the Mount on pilgrimages, but the surviving evidence for those who came is limited to visitors from beyond the Tamar, who apparently came to a significant extent. In 1359 the Black Prince, as duke of Cornwall, gave orders that John Pecche, an important London merchant and future lord mayor, might hunt in the ducal chases and warrens in Cornwall and Devon on his forthcoming pilgrimage to the Mount.⁸ In 1465–6 the Mount paid 14s. for a pipe of wine in readiness for the coming of the lord chancellor, George

---

1 Leland, *Itinerary*, ed. Toulmin Smith, I, 320.
2 BL, Harley Ch. 44 B 45.
3 SMM/8; BL, Harley Ch. 44 B 45, is a petition by King's College to Henry VI to grant letters patent for the collection of money to rebuild the church of the Mount.
4 SMM/1.

5 Worcester, *Itineraries*, ed. Harvey, 100–1.
6 Hatfield House, 14/21–3, 25/5; CRO, AU/1; Fletcher and Stéphan, *Short History*, 63. In 1464 people from Perranuthnoe also took part (Hatfield House, 14/22).
7 For will references, see Orme (ed.), *Cornish Wills*, indexed on 279.
8 *Black Prince's Register*, IV, 332.

Nevill.¹ Folklore of the late 16th century believed that John de Vere, earl of Oxford, and eighty of his followers who seized the Mount on behalf of the Lancastrian cause in 1473, did so by entering disguised as pilgrims.² The seizure certainly took place on 30 September, the day after Michael's principal festival, and may have reflected de Vere's expectation that the island would be crowded with people.³ Other 15th-century visitors included a man named John Jerrard of Netherbury (Dorset), who claimed to have been on his way to the Mount when he was arrested and imprisoned for debt in Exeter,⁴ and a certain Thomas Clerk, who made the journey from Ware (Herts.) in 1476. Clerk's notes or memories about his route were utilised two years later by William Worcester when he came from Norwich, partly, it seems, for reasons of pilgrimage and partly to collect historical and topographical data about south-west England.⁵ Gentlemen of the abbess of Syon made the journey in 1517, and two friars from Nottingham in 1521.⁶ Journeys were also made by proxy and at least four men asked for them to made in their wills, notably the Cornishman Michael Tregury, archbishop of Dublin, in 1471.⁷

The focus of the pilgrimages, as in earlier times, was the cult of the archangel. He was a popular saint in medieval Cornwall, where a number of churches, chapels, altars, and other objects were dedicated to him, which may have helped promote his cult at the Mount. Indeed two of these sites, the island chapel of Lamanna (Looe Island) and the inland rock chapel at Roche, look like attempts to imitate the Mount.⁸ In 1430 the church possessed an image of Michael and the dragon, and a painted cloth displaying his history.⁹ The saint had three annual festivals: his principal feast on 29 September (Michaelmas Day) and the feasts of his appearances at Monte Gargano in Italy (8 May) and at Mont St Michel (16 October). A short surviving text containing the lessons for the second feast was written for the church at the order of John Taylour, chancellor of Exeter cathedral, in 1489,¹⁰ and offerings at the Mount are recorded on that day – a day still commemorated in west Cornwall by the 'furry day' festivities at Helston whose church is also dedicated to Michael.¹¹ When Mont St Michel lost control of the Mount in the late 14th century, it became possible for the clergy of the latter to adopt some of the legends that had hitherto belonged primarily to the mother house. Ever since the 10th century Mont St Michel had claimed, in a text known as the *Revelatio Sancti Michaelis in Monte Tumba* ('the revelation of St Michael at Mount Tomb'), that the Archangel Michael had instructed and helped its founder, Aubert, to build the monastery at a place called *Mons Tumba*. This place was so called, states the account, because it stood up from the surrounding lands like a tomb, in a place that had once been surrounded by dense woods until the sea broke in and made it an island.¹²

Up to the late 14th century references in England to *Mons Tumba* relate to Mont St Michel, the Mount being called simply *Mons Sancti Michaelis*. In 1402, however, a royal writ provides an early example of the application of the term St Michael of *Mons Tumba* to the Mount, rather than to its mother house.¹³ At about the same time John Mirk, canon of Lilleshall abbey (Shropshire), described in his *Festial* (a book of model sermons for festival days) the occasions on which the Archangel had manifested himself, and stated that the second was 'to another byschop at a place that ys called now Mychaell yn the mownt in Corneweyle'.¹⁴ The details that follow are taken from the *Revelatio*, and show that the legend of the foundation of Mont St Michel was becoming transferred to the Mount. References to the Mount during the 15th century, especially in wills that made it donations, often called it St Michael *in Monte Tumba*, demonstrating the acceptance of the claim among English people. Worcester, during his visit in 1478, learnt that the archangel had made four 'apparitions' or appearances on earth, the second of which had been at the Mount.¹⁵ By the end of the 16th century visitors were shown St Michael's chair, 'a bad seat in a craggy place… somewhat dangerous for access', where the archangel was said to have sat.¹⁶ Later, by the early 18th century, 'Michael's Chair' or 'Kader Migell', was identified as 'a kind of seat, artificially made or cut in the stones of the garrets' on the top of the church tower.¹⁷

This was not the only cult at the Mount. The community possessed a small collection of relics which

---

1 Hatfield House, 14/21.
2 Richard Carew, *The Survey of Cornwall* (1602, repr. 2004), f. 155r.
3 Worcester, *Itineraries*, ed. Harvey, 102–3. Oxford held the Mount until 15 February 1474.
4 TNA, C 1/11/422, dated 1431×1443 or 1467×1473.
5 Worcester, *Itineraries*, ed. Harvey, 12–15.
6 Hatfield House, 20/7; *HMC Report of the MSS of Lord Middleton* (1911), 335.
7 Orme (ed.), *Cornish Wills*, 90. Similar requests were made by Sir Gerard Braybrook, a Bedfordshire knight, in 1429 (*Reg. Chichele, Canterbury*, II, 411); Robert Hoberd of Stradbroke (Suffolk) in 1450 (Orme (ed.), *Cornish Wills*, 266); and John Parsey of Bury St Edmunds in 1509 (ibid.), all further witnesses to the Mount's reputation outside Cornwall.
8 Orme, *Saints of Cornwall*, 192–3. On Lamanna, see above, pp. 197–8.
9 Whitley, 'An Inventory, 1430', 173.
10 BL, Cotton Jul. A.vii, ff. 124v–131r; it is followed by the material for 8 May in a different hand.
11 Hatfield House, 14/22–3.
12 On this subject and what follows, see Orme, 'St Michael and his Mount', 32–43.
13 *Cal. Close* 1402–5, 116; *Reg. Stafford*, 320.
14 J. Mirk, *Festial*, ed. T. Erbe, London, Early English Text Soc. extra series 96 (1905), 258.
15 Worcester, *Itineraries*, ed. Harvey, 98–9.
16 Carew, *Survey of Cornwall*, f. 154v; J. Norden, *Speculi Britanniae Pars: Cornwall* (1728), 38; N. Roscarrock, *Lives of the Saints: Cornwall and Devon*, ed. N. Orme, DCRS new ser. 35 (1992), 92.
17 BL, Add. 24762, f. 112r.

reposed in a coffer. This included some milk of the Virgin, a portion of her girdle, stones from the Holy Sepulchre, and bones of SS Agapitus, Appolina, Felix, and Mansuetus.[1] Under Syon's influence the cult of St Bridget of Sweden, one of the abbey's patron saints, reached the Mount along with that of her daughter St Katherine, to the extent that their images were displayed on a banner.[2] There seems also to have been an image of the Archangel Raphael, esteemed by Bishop Lacy for his healing powers.[3] Towards the end of the 15th century the Mount became a centre of veneration for Henry VI (d. 1471). This may have been helped by Oxford's seizure of the island in 1473, which was in favour of Henry's party. The miracles later attributed to Henry alleged that a priest of the Mount was healed of a fever in 1484–5 by visiting the king's tomb at Windsor,[4] and the Mount's church came to possess 'a sword and a pair of spurs of copper and gilt that was King Henry of Windsor's'.[5] Henry's cult, like Michael's, became popular with some Cornish people. A chapel dedicated to him was erected at King Harry Ferry in Philleigh parish by 1528, and during the 1530s pilgrims from Devon and Cornwall are said to have been a notable element among those who visited the Windsor tomb and made offerings there.[6]

The Mount became associated with legends too, doubtless because of its romantic appearance and situation. Its mention in the late 11th-century Life of St Cadoc, already noted, is followed by another in the 12th- or 13th-century Life of St Keyne, which states that Cadoc and Keyne met there, apparently while on pilgrimage.[7] The late 12th-century French romance of *Tristran* by Beroul features it as a place where Ogrin the hermit bought fine clothes for the heroine Yseut,[8] but the Mount where King Arthur killed a giant in Sir Thomas Malory's 15th-century Arthurian romances was Mont St Michel.[9] A miscellany of literary texts and prophecies, compiled between about 1320 and 1340, now in the British Library, contains ten lines of Latin verse which, it claims, 'were found written on a certain high rock at St Michael's Mount in Cornwall, in a certain very ancient schedule'. The lines were inspired by the prophecies of Merlin in Geoffrey of Monmouth's 12th-century *History of the Britons*, and appear to predict the victory of the contemporary king, Edward III, in his wars with the French.[10] They and their Mount context were a topic of interest as late as 1536, when Hugh Latimer sent a copy of them to Thomas Cromwell.[11] Worcester's notes on the Mount state that it was originally called 'le Horerok in the Wodd', i.e. 'the grey [or white] rock in the wood'. This, he had learnt, was because the place was originally clad in dense forest and lay six miles from the sea. 'There were both woods and meadows and ploughland between the said Mount and the Scilly Islands, and 140 parish churches were submerged between that Mount and Scilly'.[12] These statements seem to combine the evidence of the *Revelatio* relating to Mont St Michel, the legend of the lost land of Lyonesse, and the geological evidence of a petrified forest in Mount's Bay. The phrase 'Hoar Rock in the Wood' was still known in the late 16th century, when it is mentioned in Richard Carew's *Survey of Cornwall* (1603), along with an equivalent term in Cornish: *Cara clowse in cowse* (correctly *Carrek los y'n cos*).[13]

FINAL YEARS

The occupation of the Mount by the earl of Oxford in 1473–4 led to an alarm about its safety after the death of Edward IV in 1483, and soldiers were stationed on it for much of that year, which saw an abortive rebellion against Richard III in the South West.[14] The Mount was again caught up in politics in 1497, when Perkin Warbeck passed by it during his attempt to challenge Henry VII. His wife Katherine Gordon was left there for a time. For much of the 16th century the church and its properties were leased to the Militon family of Pengersick in Breage. John Militon arranged a lease with Syon in 1516, and this was renewed in 1534 at a rent of £26 13s. 4d. The second lease, for thirty years, made him captain and keeper of the Mount, and administrator of its revenues. Syon retained the appointment of the archpriest, to whom Militon was required to pay at least £8 3s. 4d. and up to £10 if Syon was unable to find a candidate for less money. He also undertook responsibility for the salaries of the second priest (£6 10s.), the third priest (£6 3s. 4d.), a sacrist to keep the altar offerings (£4 13s. 4d.), and a clerk and porter at the accustomed wages. Finally he was required to repair all the premises, excepting the pier of the

---

1 E 106/12/33, E 326/4386; Whitley, 'An Inventory, 1430', 173. For identifications of the saints, see Orme, *Saints of Cornwall*, 60, 66, 122, 173–4.

2 TNA, E 117/10/59, printed in L. S. Snell, *Documents towards a History of the Reformation in Cornwall: vol. II, The Edwardian Inventories of Church Goods for Cornwall* (c.1955), 26, 29.

3 Hatfield House, 14/21.

4 P. Grosjean (ed.), *Henrici VI Angliae Regis Miracula Postuma*, Société des Bollandistes, Subsidia Hagiographica 22 (Brussels, 1935) 115–16. The priest's name as given as Richard Whytby, but no such priest is recorded; one called Richard Hygo, however, occurs in 1477–8 (Hatfield House, 10/3, 14/23).

5 E 117/10/59; Snell, *Edwardian Inventories*, 27.

6 Orme, *Saints of Cornwall*, 142.

7 Ibid., 80, 162

8 Beroul, *The Romance of Tristran*, ed. A. Ewert (Oxford, 1939–70), I, line 2733.

9 T. Malory, *Works*, ed. E. Vinaver and P. J. C. Field, 3rd edn (1990), I, 200–5.

10 BL, Royal 12.C.XII, f. 15r; also found in Bodleian, Digby 196, f. 55v, and Tours, Bibliothèque municipale, MS 520, f. 14r.

11 *L & P Hen. VIII*, XI, 307.

12 Worcester, *Itineraries*, ed. Harvey, 98–101.

13 Carew, *Survey of Cornwall*, ff. 3r, 154v. I am grateful to Dr O. J. Padel for the correct version.

14 Hatfield House, 14/24.

Mount for which the abbey was to find materials.[1] When we have taken his profit into account, the lease suggests that the annual income of the Mount at this time was at least £70 and possibly more. A stray receiver's account for the financial year 1516–17, however, shows that there was no archpriest, and that the two remaining priests were paid only £5 6s. 8d. each and the clerk £2 13s. 4d.[2] In 1535 the royal valuation of Church property reported that Syon received £26 13s. 4d. from the farm of the Mount and £6 13s. 4d. from offerings there 'in common years'. The latter sum is much lower than the figures for earlier years, but it may have been simply an estimate and is not a safe guide to the extent of devotion to Michael and his shrine in the 1530s.[3]

In 1538 the second set of royal injunctions for the clergy issued by Henry VIII prohibited pilgrimages and the veneration of images, and must have had a considerable impact on the Mount, as was the case at other shrines. Pilgrimage still enjoyed some public support, however, and in late July and August of that year a rumour was current in Salisbury that Henry VIII had experienced a vision, in which he was commanded to visit the Mount and to offer a gold coin there. Several people repeated the rumours and one woman said, 'I trust we shall go a-pilgrimage again, for I hear say that his Grace will go a-pilgrimage to St Michael's Mount'.[4] The expectation was false; pilgrimage remained under official disapproval and in November 1539 the abbey of Syon was dissolved by the Crown.[5] This did not at first affect the status of the Mount, since the responsibility for paying the staff devolved upon John Militon.[6] It was not until the spring of 1548 that the church foundation was dissolved by the chantry commissioners of Edward VI, as a consequence of the second Chantry Act of December 1547. The commissioners reported that the Mount was a chapel staffed by an archpriest and two colleagues appointed 'to celebrate', i.e. to say mass and divine services. Arscott, described as 'a man well learned' (aged fifty), still received his stipend of £10, and his colleague John Wente (aged thirty) £6. The third post had been vacant for the last five or six years. The ornaments of the church were valued at £1 10s., while the bells were estimated as weighing two hundredweight and the plate as 32 ounces. The commissioners seem to have intended that all or part of the church should remain for the use of the garrison. A note was made that Arscott and Wente should continue at the Mount, and a chalice was spared for communion purposes.[7] In the end, although Arscott kept his stipend, he appears to have moved to another Crown appointment: that of master of the grammar school at Penryn.[8]

The Mount and its property were not sold by the Crown but leased as before to the Militon family. In 1560 Elizabeth I renewed their lease in favour of William, son of John, for forty years at the same rent. He was required to maintain a single priest and five soldiers, defend the Mount, and repair the pier as well as the other premises.[9] Eventually, in 1611, James I sold the place to Robert Cecil, earl of Salisbury after which it passed as a private house first to the family of Basset and later to that of St Aubyn. The church survives as the chapel of the house and the walls of the Lady chapel as the drawing room and boudoir. The monastic refectory is said to be preserved in the 'Chevy Chase' room. Some Cornish people continued to venerate the Mount for some time after 1548, especially during the reign of Mary I (1553–8) when such veneration could be expressed again. A register of wills relating to the parish of Perranzabuloe in the 1550s, now destroyed, shows that its yeomanry and husbandmen resumed the practice of leaving small sums of money to the Mount and to the chapel of St Day.[10] As late as 1569, when pilgrimage was once more forbidden and alms could lawfully be given only to the poor, Thomas Prowse of Mylor bequeathed 6d. 'to the poor men's boxes' at St Michael's Mount and St Day in an attempt to honour the shrines within the constraints of Protestantism.[11] No copy of the priory seal is known, but the matrix of the seal of Prior Auncell was discovered in the 19th century. It is described as portraying St Michael transfixing the dragon.[12] An unidentified coat of arms at the beginning of John Taylour's manuscript of 1489 may be that of the Mount: azure, on a cross patté argent, five torteaux.[13]

PRIORS OF ST MICHAEL'S MOUNT[14]

Richard de Wenilla	occurs 1187[15]
William d'Argenton	occurs c.1201 × 1212 or slightly earlier[16]
William de Valcan	occurs before 1215[17]
Ralph de Cancale	occurs c.1209 × 1214[1]
John	occurs before 1226[2]
R.	occurs 1249 or before[3]

---

1 Cal. Pat. 1558–60, 319. The sacrist was probably the same as the 'clerk' of earlier times; the additional clerk mentioned here is not found in other sources.
2 Hatfield House, 20/7.
3 Valor Eccl. (Rec. Com. 1810–34), I, 426.
4 L & P Hen. VIII, XIII(2), 23.
5 VCH Middlesex, I, 189.
6 TNA, E 301/9, m 7, printed in L. S. Snell, Documents towards a History of the Reformation in Cornwall: vol. I, The Chantry Certificates for Cornwall (c.1953), 34–5.
7 TNA, E 301/10; Snell, Chantry Certificates, 34–5.
8 TNA, E 301/12, printed in A. F. Leach, English Schools at the Reformation, 1546–8 (1896), part ii, 42.
9 Cal. Pat. 1558–60, 319.
10 RIC, Henderson 66.
11 Ibid.
12 Oliver, Monasticon, 29.
13 BL, Cotton Jul. A.vii, f. 124v.
14 The assistance of D. M. Smith and V. C. M. London (ed.), The Heads of Religious Houses: England and Wales, vol. II (2001) is gratefully acknowledged. French surnames based on place-names have been modernised where possible; principal original forms are listed in the notes.
15 Hull (ed.), Cartulary of St Michael's Mount, 29.
16 Ibid., 45 (Argentein).
17 Ibid., 46 (Walchin).

Aluin	occurs 16 Aug 1261[4]	Richard Auncell	pres. 1 Nov, inst. 7 Dec 1385; died by 31 July 1410[16]
Ralph Vyel	occurs 1 May 1262, c.1262 × 1266[5]	William Lambert	pres. by 31 July 1410, inst. 21 Oct 1410[17]
William de Pratellis	granted custody, 23 Sept 1266[6]		
Ralph de Carteret	inst. 21 Dec 1266; occurs 31 March 1267[7]	ARCHPRIESTS OF ST MICHAEL'S MOUNT	
Richard Perer	coll. 11 Apr 1276[8]	William Morton	occurs as a priest by 7 Aug 1427; archpriest by 29 Sept 1430; probably vac. c.29 Sept 1460[18]
John	occurs 18 June 1282[9]		
Geoffrey de Servon	adm. 9 July 1283; res. 3 Aug 1316[10]	Matthew Knyfton	granted office 6 Aug 1460[19]
Peter de Carville	inst. 12 Sept 1316; res. by 24 Sept 1342[11]	Robert Thomas	occurs 29 Sept 1461–29 Sept 1462[20]
Nicholas Isabel	inst. 24 Sept 1342; occurs 12 June 1348; depr. by 3 Oct 1349[12]	Ralph Crabbe	granted office 1 Sept, as from 29 Sept, 1462, vac. c.24 June 1482[21]
John Hardy	inst. 3 Oct 1349; died by 24 Apr 1362[13]	William Michell	granted office as from c.29 Sept 1482; occurs 25 March 1484; vac. by 1489[22]
John le Volant	inst. 24 Apr 1362; occurs 1380 × 1381[14]		
Richard Harepath	occurs 15 June 1383; depr. by 4 Nov 1385[15]	John Arscott	occurs 20 Nov 1537; till dissolution, spring 1548[23]

MINSTER

BENEDICTINE PRIORY

The priory of Minster probably owed its origin to William son of Nicholas, ancestor of the Boterel or Botreaux family, an important land-holding family in north-east Cornwall and elsewhere.[24] William is mentioned as being alive in 1130.[25] By an undated charter, perhaps from about that time, he granted the church of St Mertherian of *Laminst'* to the Benedictine abbey of St Serge and St Bacche at Angers in France.[26] The name *Laminst'*, apparently signifying 'the minster', invites the question whether there was an earlier religious community on the site, but there is no sign of such a community in Domesday Book or other records.

William's charter is the oldest surviving document relating to Minster church and does not mention any previous grant or previously existing church, implying that he gave the endowment on which the priory depended. St Serge already possessed property at Swavesey (Norfolk), Totnes (Devon), and (by 1149, at the latest) Tywardreath (Cornwall), at each of which it established a priory of monks. A similar small house was duly created at Minster, probably by the abbey at William's request, but the date cannot be established more precisely than in about the middle third of the 12th century. The priory was sometimes called by the

---

1 Ibid., 14 (Kankale).
2 Ibid., 15–16.
3 Ibid., 44.
4 G. Oliver, *Additional Supplement to the Monasticon Diocesis Exoniensis* (1854), 4.
5 Hull (ed.), *Cartulary of St Michael's Mount*, 24–5, 27.
6 *Reg. Bronescombe*, ed. Robinson, II, 20.
7 *Reg. Bronescombe*, ed. Hingeston-Randolph, 175; ed. Robinson, II, 21; Hull (ed.), *Cartulary of St Michael's Mount*, 29–30 (Cartaret).
8 *Reg. Bronescombe*, ed. Hingeston-Randolph, 175; ed. Robinson, II, 97.
9 Hull (ed.), *Cartulary of St Michael's Mount*, 4.
10 *Reg. Bronescombe*, ed. Hingeston-Randolph, 354; *Reg. Stapeldon*, 256 (Gernon, Jernon, Sernon).
11 *Reg. Stapeldon*, 256; *Reg. Grandisson*, I, 59, 422–3; II, 764; III, 1336; *Cal. Pat.* 1348–50, 107 (Cara Villa, Karavilla).
12 *Reg. Grandisson*, III, 1336; *Cal. Pat.* 1348–50, 107; *Cal. Fine* 1348–56, 97.

13 *Reg. Grandisson*, III, 1399, 1481–2.
14 Ibid., III, 1481–2.
15 *Reg. Brantyngham*, I, 93, 497; TNA, E 179/24/5, m. 4.
16 *Cal. Pat.* 1385–9, 62; *Reg. Brantyngham*, I, 94; *Reg. Stafford*, 204, 320.
17 *Reg. Stafford*, 204, 320.
18 TNA, E 329/204; E 106/12/33; E 326/4384, /4386; Whitley, 'An Inventory, 1430', 171–4; King's College, SMM/5.
19 King's College, KCAR/3/3/1, f. 33r.
20 Hatfield House, 104/2.
21 TNA, E 329/167; CRO, AU/1.
22 Hatfield House, 14/24; above, p. 235 note 5.
23 Chambers, *Faculty Office Registers*, 114; E 301/9, m. 7; Snell, *Chantry Certificates*, 34–5.
24 J. Maclean, *The Parochial and Family History of the Deanery of Trigg Minor* (1873–9), I, 631–41; *Feudal Aids* I, 201, 207–8.
25 *Pipe R* 1130 (HMSO), 160.
26 CRO, ART/6/5; G. Oliver, *Monasticon Dioecesis Exoniensis* (1846), 64.

alternative name of the site, *Talcarn* or *Talkarn*, meaning 'hill brow with a tor or rock-pile'.¹

Minster priory lay at the location of the present-day parish church of Minster, in an isolated spot on a minor road half a mile east of Boscastle (SX 1106 9508). Boscastle takes its name from a castle belonging to the Botreaux family, and in medieval times was a village with a little harbour, regarded as a borough for taxation purposes.² The priory can therefore be compared with other small houses of monks founded by the Anglo-Norman aristocracy near their castles and boroughs, of which Tregony is the chief example in Cornwall. Minster differed in being placed at some distance from the castle and settlement, apparently through a wish to exploit a pre-existing holy site associated with a saint named Mertherian, to whom the nearby parish church of Tintagel was also dedicated. Nothing is known about the saint except that the name was regarded as female and that its owner was believed by 1478 to lie in Minster church. Miracles at her shrine were recorded in the previous year.³ The church was and still is awkwardly placed on a steep hillside, further testifying to the desire to honour that particular site.

The church was both a priory and a parish church. Its building has been reshaped since medieval times, but it is likely that its medieval predecessor was of approximately similar length and consisted of a choir or chancel to accommodate the monks with a nave for the parishioners. The church's parish extended over the countryside to the south of the church as well as stretching westwards to the River Jordan, so as to include the castle and the upper part of the modern village of Boscastle, the rest of which lay in Forrabury parish.⁴ An ancillary chapel, dedicated to St James, was eventually established in the village, which provided a further source of revenue for the priory, valued at £5 7s. 5½d. per annum in 1374, presumably from offerings.⁵ It is not known if any members of the Botreaux family were buried in the church, but that is unlikely to have happened between 1242 and 1340, when the heads of the family were laid to rest in Launceston Priory.⁶ The domestic buildings of the priory lay on the north side of the church, apparently standing on three revetted terraces contrived on a downward sloping site. These buildings were partly residential and partly agricultural, since the priory employed servants to farm the surrounding glebe. In 1680, when the priory had long disappeared, the buildings consisted of two parallel ranges projecting northwards with a courtyard between them. The east range then contained three lower rooms, three chambers, and a study, while the west range included a parlour, kitchen, chamber, dryhouse, stable, barn, other outhouses, and probably a hall.⁷ The north wall of the church still reveals the outline of a door that may have led from the choir to the east range.

The original charter granted the monks of Angers the church and its appurtenances, the lands called *Kennegi* (Carnegie) and *Trelai* (Trela) in Minster parish, the manor of Polyphant in Lewannick, and half of the tithes of five estates belonging to the founder: *Woluedeston* (Woolstone in Poundstock), *Trefoward* (Trefoward in St Clether), *Tredawell* (Tredaule in Altarnun), *Treuaga* (Trevage in Altarnun), and *Holwode* (perhaps Holwood in Quethiock).⁸ Later the charter was confirmed by Henry Marshal, bishop of Exeter (1194–1206)⁹ and by William (III) de Botreaux (d. 1221), the grandson of the founder, who also issued a second charter confirming the grants of his ancestors William son of Nicholas and Aufred son of Ruald, the latter of whom had been a witness to the earlier charter. The second charter granted Angers the church of Minster, the lands of Carnegie and Trela, and a piece of land with specified boundaries that appears to be identical with the glebe of the church recorded from 1628 to 1839.¹⁰ This glebe consisted of about 50 acres of land extending eastwards from the church to the parish boundary, defined on the south by the road to Lesnewth and on the north by the River Valency. In addition the second charter confirmed the grant of Polyphant, the tithes of rents paid by tenants on 1 May, and the half tithes of the five estates already named. The monks of Minster were also allowed certain privileges if they wished to use William's mill, rights of pannage in his wood, pasture on his common, and fuel from his turbary.¹¹ A confirmation of the second charter was made by William (IV) de Botreaux, between 1221 and 1242.¹² The monks encountered opposition to their rights at Polyphant, and between 1198 and 1216 Pope Innocent III ordered three senior clergy from Exeter to enquire into a complaint by the prior of Talcarn that Thomas of Duneham and others had detained lands and other things belonging to him there. The clergy reported that the dispute had been amicably settled, Thomas having resigned all his rights in Polyphant to the prior in return for a payment of £20.¹³

---

1 O. J. Padel, *Cornish Place-Name Elements*, English Place-Name Society 56/57 (1985), 38–40, 214, 306.

2 M. W. Beresford and H. P. R. Finberg, *English Medieval Boroughs: a handlist* (1973), 76; P. Sheppard, *The Historic Towns of Cornwall* (1980), 71–2.

3 N. Orme, *The Saints of Cornwall* (2000), 189–90; W. Worcester, *Itineraries*, ed. J. H. Harvey (1969), 28–31.

4 CRO, TA/ and TM/153.

5 *Reg. Brantyngham*, I, 195.

6 P. L. Hull (ed.), *The Cartulary of Launceston Priory*, DCRS new ser. 30 (1987), 104; see above, p. 207.

7 R. Potts (ed.), *A Calendar of Cornish Glebe Terriers 1673–1735*, DCRS new ser. 19 (1974), 110.

8 The rector of Minster was recorded as still being entitled to receive tithes in St Clether parish in 1628 (CRO, ARD/TER/84).

9 CRO, ART/6/5.

10 CRO, ARD/TER/84; Potts (ed.), *Cornish Glebe Terriers*, 110; CRO, TA/153.

11 CRO, ART/6/5; Oliver, *Monasticon*, 64.

12 CRO, ART/6/5.

13 CRO, ART/6/5; Oliver, *Monasticon*, 64–5.

The priory was staffed by Benedictine monks sent from Angers or from its other dependent priories in England. Many (perhaps all) were of French birth. The priory was subject to the government of the bishop of Exeter and the priors were normally sent to him to be admitted or instituted to office; he also granted them leave of absence from time to time.[1] The earliest known prior, Geoffrey of Swavesey, from the Norfolk priory of that name, was admitted in 1263.[2] In the papal taxation of 1291 the spiritual revenues of Minster (tithes and offerings) were valued at £5 and the manor of Polyphant at £1, but values were much underestimated in this taxation.[3] It is likely that the priory's income supported the prior and one or two monks during the 13th century, and since Benedictines did not normally carry out parochial duties, a chaplain may have been employed to do so as was said to be the case by 1355. Any surplus income originally belonged to Angers, but the possession of property and income in England by French monasteries became an issue in the late 13th century, when periodic wars broke out between the kings of England and France.[4] In 1294 the crown began a practice, during times of war, of taking control of the 'alien priories' dependent on French mother houses.[5] This involved appropriating their moveable property and revenues, over and above what was needed to support the monks in England. When the second such seizure happened, in 1324, an inventory was made of the goods of Minster Priory, revealing that it possessed a store of grain worth £3 17s. 4d. and livestock worth about £5 5s. 0d. The latter included draught animals, twelve oxen, two cows, a small flock of sheep, and a horse for the prior to ride; these were all left to the priory while the king appropriated the grain. Three servants were kept at wages of 4d. a week, and three at 3d.[6] An inquisition in 1337, at the third seizure, found grain and hay worth £10, livestock worth £3, and rents worth £3 6s. 8d., the total value being £29 3s. 0½d. The latter enquiry also mentions the prior's chamber, his bed, a bed for his fellow monks, and a laver and basin.[7]

During the 14th century a series of priors received admission from the bishop of Exeter. All appear to have been French: Richard Portel (1314), William de Bouges (1323), Joel le Fertrer (1335), William de la Hune (1341), William Decimarius (1349), and Miletus Andreas (1375). Bouges and Andreas are both described as monks of Angers. Minster appears to have had a close connection with Tywardreath Priory, although it is no record of any formal link. A monk named William de la Minstre is mentioned at Tywardreath in 1329, and Le Fertrer is stated to have come from there.[8] In 1331 Bouges acted as coadjutor to the prior of Tywardreath and became prior of the house himself two years later.[9] The disruption of communications with Angers by the Hundred Years War, and the crown's seizure of assets and revenues, caused problems for Minster Priory as it did for other alien houses. When Bouges left towards the end of 1333, the office of prior appears to have been vacant for a year until the bishop of Exeter gave it in commendation to le Fertrer in December 1334, but Angers did not formally present him to the bishop for institution and he was eventually collated (directly appointed) by the bishop in October 1335.[10] In 1341 the bishop again collated a prior, William de la Hune, complaining that Angers had presented him with a monk unworthy in literary skills and other things.[11] The priors seem to have administered the priory revenues during the war, on condition of paying any surplus to the crown. In 1355, however, the king restored the priory's possessions to the prior free of payment, because the priory was so poor that its income was scarcely enough to maintain the prior, his fellow-monk, and an English chaplain whom the prior claimed that he kept to serve the parish church since neither he nor his colleague knew the English or Cornish languages.[12] The priory's possessions were reappropriated by the crown after 1369, when war broke out again, and were restored to the prior once more in 1374 by a similar grant to that of 1355, mentioning a prior and one monk, their inability to speak English or Cornish, and their employment of a chaplain.[13] In 1378, on the other hand, the revenues were said to be scarcely sufficient for the prior and one chaplain.[14]

From the middle of the 14th century attempts were made by the crown to appoint secular clergy to the church of Minster, either as a deliberate policy to supersede the monastery or through confusion about a priory that was also a parish church. The crown claimed the patronage of parish churches belonging to the alien priories under its control, and after Prior William de la Hune died in 1349 it presented John of Ledes to the church of Minster on 26 August, asserting that the church lay in the king's gift because the priory of Tywardreath (sic) was in his hands.[15] This presentation was forestalled by the institution of Prior William Decimarius by the bishop of Exeter on 8 July, and did

---

1 *Reg. Stapeldon*, 290; *Reg. Grandisson*, II, 633.
2 *Reg. Bronescombe*, ed. Hingeston-Randolph, 156; ed. Robinson, II, 3 (incorrectly as Swansea).
3 *Reg. Bronescombe*, ed. Hingeston-Randolph, 471, 479.
4 On this subject, see D. Matthew, *The Norman Monasteries and their English Possessions* (1962), 72–142.
5 The main periods of royal control were 1294–1307, 1324–7, 1337–61, 1369–99, and 1402 onwards (C. W. New, *History of the Alien Priories in England to the Confiscation of Henry V* (1916), 55–82).
6 TNA, E 106/6/11, mm. 5, 21; Maclean, *Trigg Minor*, I, 677–8.
7 E 106/9/30; Oliver, *Monasticon*, 65.
8 *Reg. Grandisson*, I, 455; III, 1304.
9 Ibid., II, 631, 695–6; III, 1296.
10 Ibid., III,. 1304, 1310.
11 Ibid., III, 1332.
12 *Cal. Pat.* 1354–8, 247, 252. It is unlikely that Cornish was spoken in Minster by this date.
13 *Cal. Pat.* 1374–7, 7.
14 *Cal. Pat.* 1377–81, 102.
15 *Cal. Pat.* 1348–50, 367.

not become effective. In 1375 Miletus Andreas took office, the last French monk to be prior, but like two of his predecessors he was collated by the bishop of Exeter 'through lapse', presumably because Angers did not present a suitable candidate in the required time.[1] In 1378 French monks were expelled from England, but priors and some others were allowed to remain and their number apparently included Andreas who was still prior in 1380–1. He seems to have died in office in about July 1382 when the bishop, Thomas Brantingham, in an undated document of about that time, ordered the rural dean of Trigg Minor to excommunicate evildoers who had invaded the priory after the announcement of the death of the minister of the place and had carried off ecclesiastical goods.[2] A long vacancy appears to have followed. In February 1384 the crown made a second attempt to appoint a member of the secular clergy, when Richard II presented John Macclesfield, a royal clerk, to the church of Talcarn, which he claimed to be a possession of Minster Priory.[3] This presentation was opposed by William de Botreaux, who argued that the advowson belonged to his grandfather Reginald and that his family had presented a succession of clergy: John Kellygore, William Decimarius, and Miletus Andreas. The case was heard before the justices of assize for Cornwall at Launceston on 4 April, when the jury judged in favour of William in spite of the fact that the last two named priors had really been collated by the bishop.[4] The king was given leave to appeal and in due course asked Brantingham for information about previous presentations to the church, which the bishop provided on 14 March 1385.[5] This revealed the falsity of William's claims and re-established the character of Minster as a priory church. In the end neither the king nor William gained their point and Brantingham collated an English monk named John Stratton on 26 January 1386, again through lapse.[6]

Stratton was destined to be the last prior. In the following June the bishop gave him permission to leave Minster and to stay in Westminster Abbey until the following February, on condition of maintaining divine service and the cure of souls and providing a proctor to rule the priory.[7] No more is known about his priorship until 16 June 1402 when the next bishop, Edmund Stafford, wrote to Henry Nansmuer, chaplain, perhaps the parish chaplain of Minster, informing him that he had sequestrated the revenues of the priory because Brother John Stratton, the prior, had allowed its buildings to fall into disrepair and 'on account of various other causes'. The care of the revenues was committed to Nansmuer, except for a portion to be allocated at his discretion for Stratton's support.[8] Nothing is said about any other monk and it looks as though Stratton was the sole survivor of his order, who may or may not have resided at Minster. On 8 June 1408 the crown presented a secular clerk named Reginald Welleslegh to the church, presumably vacant by Stratton's death, although when the bishop instituted Welleslegh eight days later the presentation was attributed to the prince of Wales (later Henry V).[9] Welleslegh came from Exeter diocese and was not a priest when appointed, but remedied this lack eighteen months later.[10] He was the illegitimate son of a married man and unmarried woman, and the papal dispensation allowing him to be ordained called him 'of baronial race'.[11] This time the presentation of somebody not a monk was effective and Minster was subsequently regarded as a parish church solely.

No document survives to explain the transformation of things, but it is likely that the priory succumbed both to a lack of suitable monks to serve it and to the wish of powerful interests to make it a lay benefice. The appropriation of the patronage by the crown or the duchy of Cornwall may replicate the assumption of 1349 and 1384: that the patronage belonged to the king by reason of the war with France. In the longer term the Botreaux asserted their claim. The advowson of the church was recognised as belonging to them by 1417, and they made the next known presentation in 1434.[12] Later in the century the prior of Tywardreath, Walter Barnecote, tried to recover the patronage of Minster church and the manor of Polyphant from the patron, Lady Margaret Hungerford (heiress of the Botreaux family), and from the rector, Richard Oliver. In a legal submission made between 1468 and 1478 Barnecote argued that his predecessor John Maslyn, prior of Tywardreath from 1399 to 1406, had been the rightful possessor of both church and manor until he was wrongfully deprived by Lady Elizabeth Botreaux, who presented Welleslegh to the church.[13] The prior received support from the bishop of Exeter, John Booth, and in 1468 they promoted an action to regain the patronage in the archbishop of Canterbury's court of Arches in London.[14] In 1476 the bishop confirmed the five early charters of the church, already discussed, which Barnecote brought to London for the purpose.[15]

---

1 *Reg. Brantyngham*, I, 36.
2 Ibid., I, 474.
3 *Cal. Pat.* 1381–5, 379.
4 Maclean, *Trigg Minor*, I, 597–8.
5 *Reg. Brantyngham*, I, 568–9.
6 Ibid., I, 94.
7 Ibid., II, 614. A monk named J. Stratton occurs at Westminster Abbey from 1378/9 to 1382/3, but he was not apparently there up to 1386 and is not certainly identifiable with the prior of Minster (E. H. Pearce, *The Monks of Westminster* (1916), 115).
8 DRO, Chanter VIII, f. 61r; *Reg. Stafford*, 257.
9 *Cal. Pat.* 1405–8, 444; *Reg. Stafford*, 188.
10 *Reg. Stafford*, 366, 466, 474.
11 *Cal. Papal Regs.* VI, 227. Was he a scion of the Botreaux family, in which the name Reginald was used?
12 *Cal. Close* 1413–19, 436, 439; *Reg. Lacy*, ed. Hingeston-Randolph, I, 173.
13 CRO, ART/6/4. Richard Oliver became rector of Minster in 1468, and Lady Margaret Hungerford died in 1478.
14 ART/6/3.
15 ART/6/5.

Despite the prior's possession of these muniments, his claim was a weak one given that the priory had been founded by the Botreaux family and was never formally linked with Tywardreath. The patronage claim did not succeed, and a separate action in a lay court between Barnecote and Oliver over the manor of Polyphant resulted in a judgment in Oliver's favour with an award to him of damages of £150.[1]

Minster thus remained a parish church under the patronage of the Hungerfords and their heirs the Hastings family, its rectors retaining the rights and revenues of the former priory in Minster, Polyphant, and elsewhere. Subsequent rectors were active in defending their claims to the tithes of Tredaule, Trevage, and Woolstone.[2] In 1535 the value of the rectory was estimated at £22 17s. 10½d.[3] The priory buildings became the rector's dwelling house and, as has been mentioned, still largely existed in 1680.[4] Part of the buildings, described as 'an old house' 40 feet long and 20 feet wide, was demolished in 1765,[5] and the whole of the site has since been cleared. The chancel of the priory church, built in about 1200, appears to survive as the chancel of the present parish church, albeit with the insertion of a Perpendicular east window. The nave of the church was rebuilt with a south aisle in the early 16th century, and the tower was reconstructed in 1870.[6]

PRIORS OF MINSTER[7]

Geoffrey of Swavesey	adm. 26 Aug 1263[8]
Nicholas	occurs Michaelmas 1279 × Michaelmas 1280[9]
Robert	occurs Easter 1276[10]
Ralph	occurs Nov 1296 × Nov 1297, and Easter 1300[11]
Philip	occurs 2 Apr 1311[12]
Richard Portel	inst. 26 Feb 1314[13]
William de Bouges	coll. 20 July 1323, occurs 18 Sept 1331, vac. by 17 Nov 1333[14]
Joel le Fertrer	commendation 10 Dec 1334, coll. 7 Oct 1335, occurs 31 Jan 1340[15]
William de la Hune	coll. 20 Sept 1341, died 26 Apr 1349[16]
William Decimarius	inst. 8 July 1349, died by 12 March 1375[17]
Miletus Andreas	coll. 12 March 1375, occurs 1380 × 1381, died by about July 1382[18]
John Stratton	coll. 26 Jan 1386, occurs 16 June 1402, vac. by 8 June 1408[19]

PENRYN

GLASNEY COLLEGIATE CHURCH

The collegiate church, or college, of Glasney at Penryn was founded by Walter Bronescombe (Fig. 9), bishop of Exeter in 1265, according to traditions recorded in the college's 15th-century cartulary and noted by the antiquary William Worcester during his visit to Glasney in 1478.[20] The cartulary states that Bronescombe was staying in Canterbury after undertaking business for Henry III in Germany, when he fell dangerously ill. During his sickness he saw three visions of St Thomas Becket, who promised that he would recover his health

---

1 ART/6/4.
2 [Year Books, Henry VI:] *De Termino Michaelis Anno XXX Henrici Sexti* (1556), ff. 13v–14v; *Cal. Pat.* 1452–61, 120; ECA, D&C 3498/28–9, /83.
3 *Valor Eccl.* (Rec. Com. 1810–34), II. 402.
4 Potts (ed.), *Cornish Glebe Terriers*, 110.
5 J. Maclean, *Trigg Minor*, I, 674.
6 For site information, see CCC, HER 617.4, and J. Allan, *Archaeological Recording at Minster Church Boscastle*, Exeter Archaeology, Report no. 05.19 (Exeter, 2005).
7 This list is indebted to D. M. Smith and V. C. M. London (ed.), *The Heads of Religious Houses: England and Wales, II. 1216–1377* (2001), 176–7.
8 *Reg. Bronescombe*, ed. Hingeston-Randolph, 156; ed. Robinson, II, 3.
9 TNA, E 159/53, m. 11d.
10 TNA, CP 40/14, m. 75.
11 E 106/14/2, m. 1d; E 106/4/14, m. 2.
12 *Reg. Stapeldon*, 235
13 Ibid., 235; *Reg. Brantyngham*, I, 568.
14 *Reg. Stapeldon*, 235; *Reg. Brantyngham*, I, 568; *Reg. Grandisson*, II, 633; III, 1296.
15 *Reg. Grandisson*, III, 1304, 1310; II, 924.
16 *Reg. Grandisson*, III, 1332; *Reg. Brantyngham*, I, 569; CRO, RS/60, p. 22.
17 *Reg. Grandisson*, III, 1394; *Reg. Brantyngham*, I, 36, 195, 569.
18 *Reg. Brantyngham*, I, 474, 569; TNA, E 179/24/5, m. 4.
19 *Reg. Brantyngham*, I, 94; *Reg. Stafford*, 257; *Cal. Pat.* 1405–8, 444.
20 CRO, RS/59/1, ff. 1r–2v, translated in J. Rashleigh and J. A. C. Vincent (ed.), *Abstract of the Glasney Cartulary* (1879), 6–8; W. Worcester, *Itineraries*, ed. J. H. Harvey (1969), 104–5. The principal previous works on the history of Glasney are G. Oliver, *Monasticon Dioecesis Exoniensis* (1846), 48–53; C. R. Sowell, 'The Collegiate Church of St. Thomas of Glasney', *JRIC* 1.3 (1864–5), 21–34 with 4 plates; Rashleigh and Vincent (ed.), *Abstract of the Glasney Cartulary*; T. C. Peter, *The History of Glasney Collegiate Church, Cornwall* (1903), which lists most of the known clergy of the college; J. Whetter, *The History of Glasney College* (1988); and D. Cole et al., *Glasney College, Penryn, Cornwall*, Cornwall County Council, Historic Environment Service, Report No. 2005R061 (2005).

and told him to found a collegiate church in Becket's honour in the wood of Glasney on the bishop's manor of Penryn. The saint gave the bishop directions about the site. He was to search near the river Antre for a spot called by local people 'Polsethow' ('the pool of the arrow'), where he would find a willow tree containing a swarm of bees. There he was to place the high altar of the church and fulfil an ancient Cornish prophecy that 'in Polsethow shall habitations, or marvellous things, be seen'. The bishop duly went to the place, found the tree and swarm, and caused the site to be drained and levelled. He had the tree dug up, and its trunk was preserved in the church as a memorial. He laid the foundation of the church on Lady Day (25 March) 1265, and consecrated the church and churchyard exactly two years later. On 26 March 1267, the day after the alleged date of the consecration, Bronescombe did indeed issue a foundation charter, which is the earliest documentary evidence for Glasney's existence.[1]

This legend has much in common with other origin stories of religious houses, involving the threefold appearance of a saint and the commandment to found a church on a new and unlikely site. It seeks to attribute the foundation to heavenly intervention rather than earthly motives. Whatever the truth about Bronescombe's visions, however, his creation of Glasney also took place for practical reasons and reflected conditions in the mid 13th century. Bronescombe was an active bishop, who ruled the diocese of Exeter from 1257 until his death in 1280 and was a pioneer in keeping a register of his activities.[2] He had a care for the Cornish part of his diocese, first visiting the county in 1259 and making his final thirteenth visit in 1278.[3] Penryn lay on one of his Cornish estates. While not antipathetic to monks or friars, he developed a particular interest in communities of secular clergy: those who lived in the world like parish priests. He issued statutes for one such institution, his cathedral of Exeter in 1268 and 1275,[4] increased the number and stipends of another, the ancient minster church of Crediton (Devon), between 1269 and 1272,[5] and began the construction of a new Lady chapel at the cathedral in a way that shows he envisaged at least part of the rebuilding of the whole church which took place after his death.[6] Glasney college dates from the same period as his activities at Crediton and Exeter, and accords with his concern for such communities and their clergy.

Colleges – primarily bodies of secular clergy, academic in nature only in the case of university colleges – superseded monasteries and friaries as the most popular kind of religious foundations in England during the 14th and 15th centuries. Earlier bishops of Exeter, like William de Warelwast and Bartholomew, had seen the future of the Church in terms of Augustinian priories, and had turned three ancient minsters of the diocese into such houses. Colleges represented a return to the minster model, in which the clergy lived closer to the world than monks. They were also cheaper than monasteries to found and to run. Bronescombe was one of the earliest founders of colleges in England, and the earliest in the South-West.[7] His predecessor-but-one, William Brewer, acquired the patronage of the minster at Crantock in 1236, but did nothing to develop either Crantock or the other remaining Cornish minsters: St Buryan and Probus.[8] At the same time the creation of Glasney did not set a trend in Exeter diocese. Only Ottery St Mary (Devon), founded by Bishop Grandisson of Exeter in 1338, followed a similar pattern and scale, a reflection of the fact that Cornwall and Devon lacked wealthy landowners with the resources to undertake such projects. The principal collegiate foundations of later medieval England were made in other parts of the country.[9]

EARLY HISTORY AND ENDOWMENT

The earliest document relating to Glasney is the bishop's grant of the churches of Budock, Feock, and St Gluvias to the college in 1267, which is described as the 'charter of foundation' in the 15th-century cartulary.[10] This listed some of the clergy and certain of their duties and stipends. Later Bronescombe also issued statutes, a common practice when founding colleges since they did not possess a standard religious rule like monks and friars. The statutes are not dated, but were evidently delivered between 1276 and 1280.[11] They give no reasons for the foundation and are limited in their scope. We

---

1 *Reg. Bronescombe*, ed. Hingeston-Randolph, 94–5; ed. Robinson, III, 50–2.

2 Biographies in *Reg. Bronescombe*, ed. Hingeston-Randolph, pp. ix–xxiii, and *ODNB*.

3 *Reg. Bronescombe*, ed. Hingeston-Randolph, 294–302.

4 Printed in *Reg. Bronescombe*, ed. Robinson, III, 62–72.

5 N. Orme, 'The Church in Crediton from Saint Boniface to the Reformation', in T. A. Reuter (ed.), *The Greatest Englishman: essays on St Boniface and the Church at Crediton* (1980), 103–4.

6 A. M. Erskine (ed.), *The Accounts of the Fabric of Exeter Cathedral, 1279–1353*, DCRS new ser. 24, 26 (1981–3), I, p. xxvi–xxvii; II, p. ix.

7 Other early founders included Giles of Bridport, bishop of Salisbury (De Vaux college, Salisbury, 1262) and Walter of Merton, Henry III's chancellor (Malden, Surrey, and Merton College, Oxford, 1264).

8 On Crantock, see above, p. 174.

9 There were also some small and mostly short-lived college foundations in Cornwall and Devon, such as St Michael Penkevil (above, p. 226).

10 RS/59/1, ff. 43r–44v, transl. in Rashleigh and Vincent (ed.), *Glasney Cartulary*, 19–20; *Reg. Bronescombe*, ed. Hingeston-Randolph, 94; ed. Robinson, III, 50–2.

11 RS/59/1, ff. 24v–27r, transl. in Rashleigh and Vincent (ed.), *Glasney Cartulary*, 15–18. They mention Henry Bollegh as being in charge of the college during the vacancy of the provostship, a role he took up in 1276; the bishop died in 1280.

can reconstruct Bronescombe's motives only from hints in the grant of 1267, in which he stated his wish to provide suitable persons to augment divine worship – the usual claim of medieval church founders. The same document also suggests a care for Penryn, the manor of which belonged to the bishops of Exeter. As early as 1259 Bronescombe had secured it a royal grant of a weekly market and an annual fair of three days, centring on the feast-day of St Thomas Becket.[1] In the 1267 document he referred to the poverty of the parish church of St Thomas of Penryn. There was no historic church of this name, so either Bronescombe founded a short-lived one before his plans expanded in favour of Glasney, or else he renamed St Gluvias, the previous parish church of the manor, in Thomas's honour. In practice Glasney never acquired parochial status and St Gluvias retained its name and status as the parish church of Penryn, supplemented by a chapel-of-ease in the town dedicated to St Mary. Nevertheless medieval witnesses testify to the fact that Glasney became the chief church of the area, to which local people and travellers resorted for at least part of their worship, so it is likely that the bishop intended to benefit the locality by his foundation.

Bronescombe's grant of 1267 envisaged the college as being staffed by thirteen canons, who were to serve the church in person or through deputies called vicars. The statutes also referred to chantry priests, clerks, and boys, without specifying their numbers. Neither document defined how these clergy were to be appointed: in practice the bishop chose the canons, and the canons the rest of the clergy except for the chantry priests. The grant allotted each canon a prebend (or allowance) of £4 per annum, and if he resided and attended matins or high mass he was to receive a further daily distribution from the college revenues. Vicars were to be paid 20s. per annum by their canons. The practice of paying the canons a small unconditional sum and a larger amount dependent on their attendance at services followed the system in use at Exeter cathedral, and would have been valued by Bronescombe because it encouraged canons to keep residence. Older minsters, like St Buryan and Probus, gave each canon the stipend of an estate irrespective of whether he resided, with the result that most canons failed to do so. The 20s. assigned to each vicar was also the ancient stipend of the vicars of Exeter cathedral, and had been adopted or confirmed by Bronescombe for the vicars of Crediton.[2]

The statutes were largely concerned with two matters: discipline in the church, and the administration of the college revenues. Canons and vicars were to perform the divine office (the eight daily services in the choir) every day and to attend a daily chapter meeting. This meeting (which at Exeter cathedral enabled the clergy to be briefed on the liturgical tasks for the following day) included the exercise of discipline by the canons over the lesser members of the church, if necessary. Punishment was to take the form of standing in the nave before the crucifix on the choir screen for 24 hours. Chantry priests, when added to the foundation, were to attend all services, and any canon, vicar, or priest wearing secular clothes in the choir was to have them confiscated. Obits (masses on the anniversaries of people's deaths), when established, were to be duly celebrated, and a canon and vicar, called stewards of the obits, were to organise them. Two clerks called proctors were to keep order in the church – presumably order among the laity, and no business was to be done there. Two statutes dealt with financial matters. The college revenues (which chiefly consisted of tithes from its parish churches) were to be 'farmed' or administered by the resident canons individually. Farming meant that the canons submitted tenders, offering to collect the tithes of a particular parish. The one who offered most was to be granted the farm, and had to pay the amount he offered in prompt and regular instalments to the college exchequer. If he could collect more tithes than his tender, he kept the profits, but no canon could hold more than one farm. The canons of Exeter cathedral farmed its churches and estates in similar ways.

The many resemblances between Bronescombe's arrangements for Glasney and those of the cathedral suggest that the former was deliberately modelled on the latter. Indeed he asserted the fact in his charter of 1267, stating that the college should observe 'the laudable, approved, and approvable customs of the church of Exeter'.[3] The cathedral exemplar points to other likely motives of Bronescombe in making his foundation. It provided not simply worship but worship approaching the standard of a cathedral, perhaps as a model for the parish churches of west Cornwall. Until the Reformation parish worship in England followed the practices of cathedrals, notably Salisbury and York. The presence of a body of secular canons able to operate freely in the world, unlike the more secluded Augustinian canons, gave the bishop posts to distribute in Cornwall and provide him with people to do administrative and pastoral duties there. A religious community in Penryn could also provide hospitality to the bishop's servants when travelling in the area, and to travellers embarking or disembarking by ship in Falmouth Haven. Glasney lay in the Cornish-speaking part of Cornwall, and it represented, along with the Dominican friary in Truro opened in about 1259, the first new religious house to be founded in that area since the mid 12th century. How far Bronescombe

---

1 *Cal. Chart.* 1257–1300, 16.
2 N. Orme, 'The Medieval Clergy of Exeter Cathedral: I. The Vicars and Annuellars', *TDA* 113 (1981), 79–102 at 81; *Reg. Bronescombe*, ed. Hingeston-Randolph, 61; ed. Robinson, II, 58.
3 *Reg. Bronescombe*, ed. Hingeston-Randolph, 94; ed. Robinson, III, 50–2; cf. *Reg. Grandisson*, II, 1044; III, 1213–15.

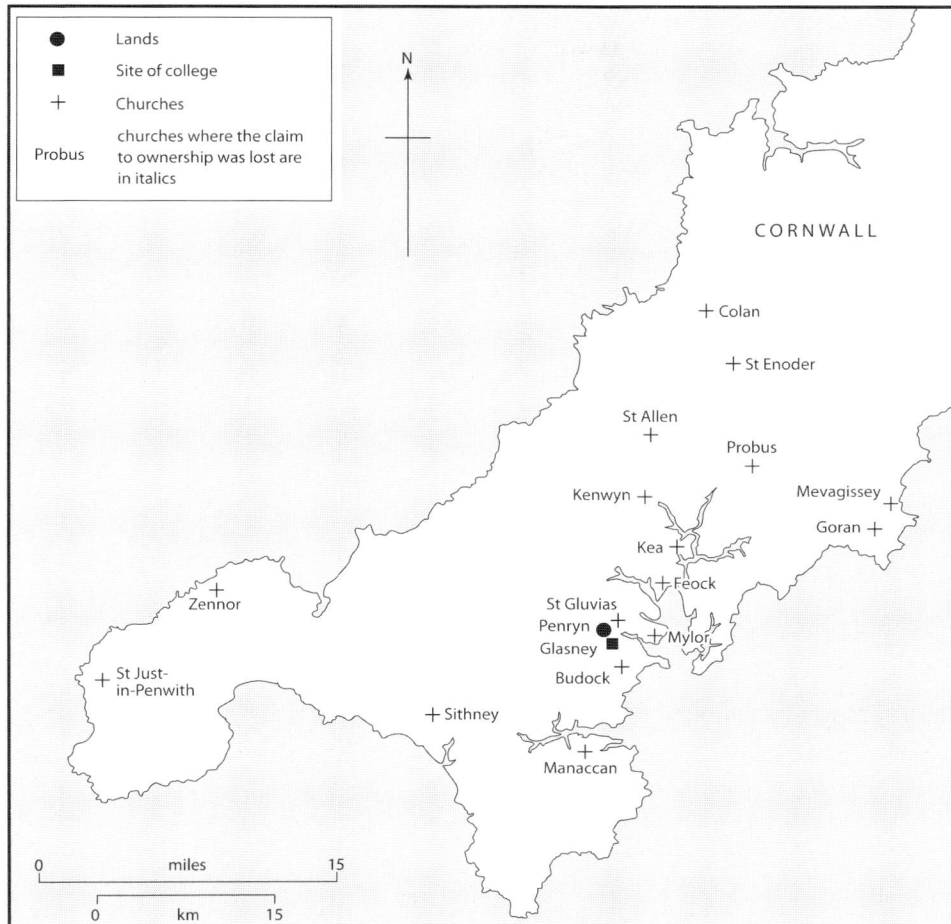

FIG 58. *The property of Glasney Collegiate Church.*

was conscious of a Cornish-speaking area, and how anxious to provide for its spiritual needs, remain open questions.

Bronescombe was not wealthy enough to endow the college with lands or tenements. Instead he acquired the advowsons of several parish churches and appropriated them to Glasney, so that the college took possession of the 'great tithes' of grain, while the lesser tithes were left to the vicars who served the parish (Fig. 58). The college did not gain the right to nominate these vicars, however, and they were normally collated by the bishops of Exeter.[1] One of the churches, Budock, already belonged to the bishopric of Exeter, although it was divided into two portions whose clergy had to be persuaded to resign their places in 1265.[2] This church included St Gluvias – effectively the parish church of Penryn but originally a chapel dependent on Budock. A third church, Feock, was granted to the bishop by Walter Peverel,[3] and appropriated to Glasney with Budock and St Gluvias in 1267 as the college's first endowments.[4] Five more churches were conveyed and appropriated in 1270: St Enoder (obtained from John of Trejagu), Goran (from Philip of Bodrugan), Kea (from Stephen Haym), Sithney (from Joce of Antrenon and Roger of Skyburiow), and Zennor (formerly a church of Tywardreath priory).[5] Finally Manaccan was appropriated in 1275, specifically to provide two chaplains, and Colan in 1276 to support the feast of St Gabriel.[6] Later, as we shall see, Bronescombe's successor, Peter Quinil, added Mylor and St Allen, and

---

1 There were a few occasions on which Glasney was allowed to nominate to these parishes, and its canons nominated the vicars of St Just-in-Penwith and Mevagissey, benefices given to the college by private benefactors.

2 *Reg. Bronescombe*, ed. Hingeston-Randolph, 167; ed. Robinson, II, 14–15.

3 RS/59/1, f. 51r, transl. in Rashleigh and Vincent (ed.), *Glasney Cartulary*, 22.

4 *Reg. Bronescombe*, ed. Hingeston-Randolph, 94–5; ed. Robinson, III, 50–2; RS/59/1, ff. 43r–44v, 51r, transl. in Rashleigh and Vincent (ed.), *Glasney Cartulary*, 19–20, 22–3.

5 RS/59/1, ff. 47r, 52v–55r, 95r, transl. in Rashleigh and Vincent (ed.), *Glasney Cartulary*, 20–1, 24–25, 47; *Reg. Bronescombe*, ed. Hingeston-Randolph, 95; ed. Robinson, II, 42. The date and circumstances of the acquisition of Zennor are unclear.

6 RS/59/1, ff. 48r–50v, transl. in Rashleigh and Vincent (ed.), *Glasney Cartulary*, 21–2; *Reg. Bronescombe*, ed. Hingeston-Randolph, 96–7, 244–5; ed. Robinson, II, 86–7, 100–1.

two further churches – St Just-in-Penwith and Mevagissey – were given in the 14th century. Some small pieces of land in and around Penryn were gradually donated by private donors to finance obits.¹ The earliest evidence about the value of these endowments comes from the papal taxation of 1291, an assessment underestimated by about a half. This gives the college's income from the most valuable parish, Kea, as £8 6s. 8d., followed by Goran (£6 13s. 8d.), St Enoder (£6 6s. 8d.), Colan and Zennor (each £4), and Feock (£3 6s. 8d.). The incomes of the college's other churches are presented as a whole, without deductions for the stipends of the parochial vicars. These include Mylor (£6 13s. 4d.), Sithney (£6 6s. 8d.), Budock (£6), St Allen (£5 6s. 8d.), Manaccan (£4), and St Gluvias (£2). Making the necessary deductions in those five cases would produce a total college income of between £50 and £60, which may well represent a real sum twice as high.²

Bronescombe's plans for Glasney were incomplete by his death in 1280. This particularly affected the headship of the college. In 1267 the bishop envisaged the appointment of a 'procurator' to supervise the community until he had taken a final decision about the headship.³ By 1272 he had settled on the title 'provost' for the office, a departure from 'dean' which was used at the ancient Cornish minsters, perhaps to indicate a more active, resident head. In that year Henry of Bollegh, dean of Probus and later archdeacon of Cornwall, occurs as provost, but Bollegh resigned in 1276, presumably at Bronescombe's wish, and was re-appointed to administer the college until the bishop made arrangements to fund the office of provost.⁴ This task was unfulfilled when Bronescombe died, and another important post that he visualised, that of sacrist, had not been fully established either. The next bishop, Quinil, dealt with the provostship. In 1283 he laid down that its holder should be a priest residing for two-thirds of the year, continuously or with interruptions. He was to have jurisdiction over all the canons and clerks, including the care of their souls, just as the dean of Exeter cathedral had in that community, and William of Bodrugan was appointed to the office with a stall in the choir, a seat in the chapter-house, and the house of Roger of St Constantine, one of the founding Glasney canons. This house was to be changed for a better one when opportunity offered. To finance the post the bishop conveyed to the provost the collegiate church of Probus, including all six of its prebends as they became vacant, saving only an endowment for a parochial vicar.⁵

Quinil's grant ignored the fact that a previous bishop, William Brewer, had given most of the revenues of Probus to the treasurer of Exeter cathedral. It was probably driven as much by Quinil's hostility towards the contemporary treasurer of Exeter, John Pycot, as by a desire to patronise Glasney.⁶ Pycot was engaged in a struggle with the bishop over his claim to be dean of Exeter cathedral, a struggle in which he was eventually worsted, losing both deanery and treasurership in 1285. Quinil subsequently recognised the inappropriateness of his grant to Glasney, and in 1288 he confirmed the annexation of Probus to the treasurership of Exeter.⁷ He compensated the provost, in the same year, with the church of Mylor, and the college as a whole with that of St Allen.⁸

SITE AND BUILDINGS

The college lay immediately to the south of Penryn in Budock parish, separated from the town by the River Antre but linked to it by a road and bridge (SW 7857 3410).⁹ East of the college, across the road, lay the palace of the bishops of Exeter, and also to the east, adjoining both college and palace, was the shore of King Road, part of Falmouth Haven. Glasney thus resembled the priories of Bodmin, Launceston, and Tywardreath in adjoining a significant town, although it differed from them in having no temporal jurisdiction in the town, which belonged to the bishop. For ecclesiastical purposes the town lay within the parish of St Gluvias, which was legally a chapelry of the parish church of Budock. Since Glasney owned both churches, its clergy were effectively in charge of the spiritual life of Penryn. For diocesan purposes the college lay within the bishop's peculiar jurisdiction of Penryn, and was subject to the bishop, represented by a local official in charge of the jurisdiction, not to the archdeacon of Cornwall. In 1331 Bishop Grandisson forbade the archdeacon to meddle with the college,¹⁰ and in 1513 the provost is recorded as supervising the probate of the will of one of the college chaplains.¹¹ The college gained advantages from the town, partly because it acquired a certain amount of urban property which it rented to tenants, and partly because Penryn was a port, supplying Glasney with goods and bringing travellers. The college was also the largest church of the Fal area, and the parishes it owned gave it wide influence in Cornwall west of Truro.

---

1 RS/59/1, ff. 5v, 7r, 8r–10r, 11v–12r, transl. in Rashleigh and Vincent (ed.), *Glasney Cartulary*, 11–12.
2 *Reg. Bronescombe*, ed. Hingeston-Randolph, 466, 468–9.
3 *Reg. Bronescombe*, ed. Hingeston-Randolph, 94–5; ed. Robinson, III, 50–2.
4 *Reg. Bronescombe*, ed. Hingeston-Randolph, 96–7; ed. Robinson, II, 57, 95.
5 ECA, D&C 1006; *Reg. Bronescombe*, ed. Hingeston-Randolph, 330–1.
6 Below, p. 264.
7 DRO, Chanter XII(ii), Reg. Bothe, f. 44(1); Oliver, *Monasticon*, 61–2.
8 *Reg. Brantyngham*, II, 652–4; Oliver, *Monasticon*, 50; *Cal. Pat. 1313–17*, 280.
9 For site information, see CCC, HER 18660–18660.5. The college lands were not free of tithe by 1843 (CRO, TA/22, pp. 5–6, 16–17).
10 *Reg. Grandisson*, I, 600–1.
11 N. Orme (ed.), *Cornish Wills 1342–1540*, DCRS new ser. 50 (2007), 154–5.

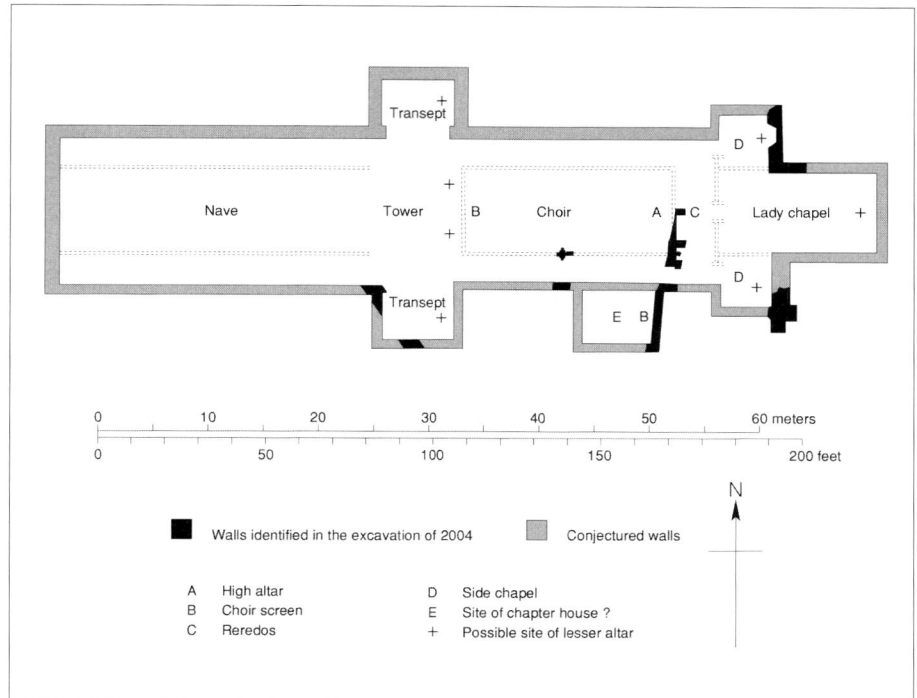

FIG 59. *Glasney Collegiate Church, conjectural plan.*

The church was probably begun in the 1260s, but received substantial additions and repairs later on, notably in about the 1330s. Excavations on the site in 2003 uncovered numerous fragments of stone.[1] These indicate that much of the fabric was built from local granite and greenstone, with shale for infilling walls, but that decorative work, such as piers, vaulting ribs and bosses, some window mouldings and internal furnishings, was in Beer stone from east Devon. The use of Beer stone suggests that work was being been done in the 1330s when that stone was also used at Exeter cathedral. This implies that Grandisson played an important role, perhaps seeking to complete a previously unfinished building at much the same time that he was founding his college at Ottery St Mary. There are also close stylistic parallels with work done at Exeter cathedral by the master mason, Thomas of Witney (fl. 1316–42), suggesting that Exeter masons were employed at Glasney or prepared materials to send there. Other imported objects included floor tiles decorated with griffins, birds, fish, and flowers, probably from south Devon. The quality of the surviving stonework shows that Glasney was a more sophisticated building than most Cornish parish churches, made as they were of purely local materials with simpler decorations. It was also bigger in scale than any except for the priories of Bodmin and Launceston, making it one of the three largest churches in Cornwall.

Our only medieval witness to the shape and size of the church is William Worcester, who visited Glasney on his return from a pilgrimage to St Michael's Mount in 1478. He mentions a nave, transepts, choir, and ambulatory, and attempted some measurements.[2] A detailed plan of the building was made by C. R. Sowell in the 1860s, when the footings of the north walls were still visible,[3] and this plan was refined by the excavations of 2003 (Fig. 59).[4] The church followed a symmetrical plan in its layout. Its nave was about 126 feet (38.4 metres) long and 46 feet (14 metres) wide, the width including north and south nave aisles. The east end of the nave formed a crossing extending into north and south transepts, measuring about 82 feet (25 metres) from north to south, and about 30 feet (9 metres) from east to west. East of the crossing lay a choir and sanctuary, both having a slightly raised floor and stretching for about 62 feet (19 metres) with a width like that of the nave including similar north and south aisles. East of the high altar in the sanctuary was a Lady chapel flanked by two smaller chapels a little way beyond the choir aisles. The Lady chapel was also about 62 feet (19 metres) long, with a width of about 24 feet (7.5 metres), but the western end of this section may have formed a retrochoir separate from the chapel itself. The foundations of the walls were substantial, in order to cope with the watery site. Most of the church was apparently vaulted with Beer stone inset with greenstone, with a roof above the vaults described in 1549 as covered

---

1 J. P. Allan, S. Blaylock, and L. Keen, in Cole et al., *Glasney College*, 32–47.

2 Worcester, *Itineraries*, ed. Harvey, 104–7. There are two conflicting sets of measurements. In modern terms the length of the nave and the choir are given as 87 feet (26.2 metres) and 105 feet (31.7 metres) each, and the width of the church at 87 feet (26.2 metres).

3 Sowell, 'The Collegiate Church of Glasney', 21–34.

4 Cole et al., *Glasney College*, 18–19, 30–32, 47, 107.

partly with lead and partly with slate.[1] Over the crossing was a central tower containing, by that date, five large bells and a small bell rung for the early morning mass, surmounted by a spire clad also in lead.[2] The church's plan resembled that of Crediton, a church with which Bronescombe had been involved and one that, in his day, would have been a more practical model for Glasney than the cathedral, which was out-of-date in its layout and waiting to be rebuilt.[3] Compared with other religious houses Glasney was close in area and volume to Bodmin and Launceston, the other two largest churches in Cornwall, and slightly bigger than Crediton

The choir, as usual in large churches, would have been separated by a choir screen from the nave and by lesser screens from the choir aisles. Here the daily services were said, and a daily mass celebrated at the high altar. Statues of the Virgin Mary and St Thomas Becket, the two patron saints of the church, would have flanked the altar. Above the choir screen stood a great crucifix with two lights burning before it, and there may well have been two altars in the nave against the choir screen as there were in the cathedral and at Crediton. The latter church had five further altars: in the Lady chapel, at the east ends of both choir aisles, and in the two transepts, and Glasney may have had a similar number.[4] An additional altar, used for a daily 'capitular mass', probably stood in the chapter-house,[5] a building that may have been sited south of the south choir aisle. Masses would have been said by the vicars and chantry priests at all these altars each day. The sequence would have begun with an early-morning or 'morrow' mass (indicated by the mention of a bell that rang to announce it), celebrated at dawn at one of the lesser altars. At Exeter cathedral this mass took place at the nave altar on the north side of the choir screen, and was attended by devout members of the laity.[6] The rest of the masses would have followed between dawn and about 10.00am. Two of them were celebrated by chantry priests at particular altars, which acquired the names Beaupré and Bodrugan from the founders of the masses concerned. These altars may have stood in the chapels that flanked the Lady chapel, but there are no documents to elucidate this matter.

A further important focus of worship was the Lady chapel, where the Virgin received veneration in the form of morning and evening prayers and a daily mass.

A guild of the Blessed Mary of Glasney is mentioned in the will of Richard Enys, one of the chaplains, in 1513, who bequeathed it 3s. 4d., along with a similar sum to repair 'the relics of Glasney'.[7] There was a light in honour of St Thomas, perhaps in front of his statue near the high altar, to which in 1438 Canon James Michell made a bequest, and Michell also mentioned an image of the Archangel Michael, in front of which he wished to be buried.[8] Bronescombe had already established the feast-day of another archangel, Gabriel, at Glasney in 1276, the feast being held on the second Monday in September.[9] Worcester refers to the 'foundation board' of the college: a display board presenting a short history of the church in Latin, examples of which are recorded in other large churches at this time. The Glasney history was in rhyming 'goliardic' Latin verse, of which Worcester quotes two couplets.[10] There must have been tombs in the church, chiefly of provosts and possibly of canons, as well as those of a few outsiders. Most of these may have been simple ledger stones, as they were in Exeter cathedral. Sybil Bodrugan (d. 1311), of the Bodrugan family of Goran, is mentioned in 1329 as being buried in the church.[11] Her son Sir Ote and Sir John Beaupré both founded chantries at Glasney and it is possible that Beaupré was buried there, but Ote died abroad.

Bequests in wills suggest that the church building was envisaged as needing repair or reconstruction for much of its history. The executors of Bishop Bitton of Exeter gave £13 6s. 8d. in 1307–10; William Doune, archdeacon of Leicester, bequeathed £2 to repair the church in 1361; and seven years later Bishop Grandisson added £13 6s. 8d. 'for the new work there'.[12] A canon, William Carslake, left £20 'to the new fabric' in 1379,[13] and in 1403 Bishop Stafford referred to the church as requiring amendment and still incomplete. He noted that the canons had each traditionally contributed 26s. per annum to restore and complete the church – especially the choir and its aisles, arcading, and vaulting – but that these sums were inadequate for the purpose. All were now anxious to forward the work, and the canons had agreed to give the whole of their stipends for one year except for the sacrist and one other who could give only part of their stipends because their resources were limited. The bishop approved the plan

---

1 TNA, E 315/67, f. 176v; Rashleigh and Vincent (ed.), *Glasney Cartulary*, 50.

2 TNA, E 315/67, f. 176v; Rashleigh and Vincent (ed.), *Glasney Cartulary*, 50. The tower and spire are shown on a map of Cornwall of c.1540 (BL, Cotton Aug. I.i.36–9; Facs. 1014(ii)).

3 B. Cherry and N. Pevsner, *Devon*, The Buildings of England, 2nd edn (1989), 296. However some of the surviving work at Crediton is later than the foundation of Glasney College.

4 Orme, 'The Church in Crediton', 112–13. The dedications of most of the Crediton altars are known, as are those of Exeter Cathedral, but it would be unsafe to assume that they were repeated on similar sites at Glasney.

5 *Reg. Grandisson*, I, 502.

6 N. Orme, *Exeter Cathedral: the first thousand years* (2009), 62.

7 Orme (ed.), *Cornish Wills*, 155.

8 Ibid., 70.

9 *Reg. Bronescombe*, ed. Hingeston-Randolph, 244–5; ed. Robinson, II, 100–1.

10 Worcester, *Itineraries*, ed. Harvey, 104–5.

11 *Reg. Grandisson*, I, 502.

12 W. H. Hale and H. T. Ellacombe (ed.), *Accounts of the Executors of Richard Bishop of London... and Thomas Bishop of Exeter*, Camden Soc. new ser. 10 (1874), 29; A. H. Thompson, 'The Will of Master William Doune', *Archaeological Jnl* 72 (1915), 271; *Reg. Grandisson*, III, 1514, 1551.

13 *Reg. Brantyngham*, I, 409–10.

FIG 60. *A view of Glasney's church and close from a 19th-century reconstruction based on a lost drawing associated with Sir Ferdinando Gorges (d. 1647). The canons' houses lay to the south of the church.*

and appointed a vicar and a chantry priest to administer the money.[1] A further 40s. was given to the fabric by Hugh Hyckeling, a former canon, in 1415,[2] but in 1445 Bishop Edmund Lacy came to Glasney and found the restoration project incomplete and the church in a ruinous condition. He reimposed the previous levy of 26s. per annum on each of the canons to fund the work.[3] Three bequests in the early 16th century point to work on the church still being needed or in progress. In 1501 Thomas Killigrew of Penryn bequeathed 100 marks (£66 13s. 4d.) 'to the building of the new fabric of the body [i.e. the nave] of the church',[4] and sums of £5 and 6s. 8d. were contributed to the fabric by John Nans, a former provost, in 1507 and by Richard Enys in 1513 respectively.[5] Even so Bishop Veysey, after a visitation of the college in 1541, found the church threatened with 'great and dangerous ruin in timbers, roofing, lead, and wood', requiring £40 worth of work, which he ordered the canons to pay by means of a levy on their allowances.[6] Some of these references reflect the need of any large building to be maintained, but their frequency implies that the condition of the church was more of a preoccupation than usual, perhaps because it was never wholly finished and lay on an unstable marshy site.

The church lay in a precinct, eventually walled and gated, resembling in these respects the cathedral at Exeter. Gates are mentioned in 1334 when, as we shall see, arrangements were made for a porter, and by this date the precinct was known as 'the close' like its counterpart at the cathedral.[7] Information about the topography of the precinct comes from scattered references in documents, from the particulars of the sale of the site in 1549,[8] and from three depictions of the college on maps or plans made between about 1540 and 1640 (Fig. 60).[9] Close to the church or within it were

---

1 *Reg. Stafford*, 112–13.
2 Orme (ed.), *Cornish Wills*, 200.
3 *Reg. Lacy*, ed. Dunstan, II, 330–1.
4 Orme (ed.), *Cornish Wills*, 111.   5 Ibid., 130, 155.
6 DRO, Chanter XV, f. 110v–111r; printed in Oliver, *Monasticon*, 53.
7 *Reg. Grandisson*, II, 757; RS/59/1, ff. 72r–76v, transl. in Rashleigh and Vincent (ed.), *Glasney Cartulary*, 34 (incorrectly dated); cf. *Reg. Brantyngham*, I, 148, and below, p. 255.

8 TNA, E 315/67, f. 176v; Rashleigh and Vincent (ed.), *Glasney Cartulary*, 50.
9 BL, Cotton Aug. I.i.35–9 (Facs. 1014(ii)), of *c*.1540; BL, Royal 18 D.III., ff. 15r–16v, of about the 1580s; and a map associated with Sir Ferdinando Gorges (d. 1647) now extant only in nineteenth-century copies, the best (Fig. 60) being in Penryn Museum, (D. Wingfield, *Penryn: Archaeology and Development – A Survey* (Institute of Cornish Studies and Cornwall Committee for Rescue Archaeology, 1979), 7, and Whetter, *History of Glasney*, p. vi).

the chapter-house and an exchequer (for keeping money and records), the former, as already noted, possibly standing south of the south choir aisle. A cloister is mentioned in 1549, but its nature is unknown.[1] Immediately south of the church lay an outdoor cemetery, shown in the latest of the three depictions with a cross on steps at its centre. Further south of the cemetery, separated from it by a lane, lay most of the clergy houses. Those of the canons were built on thirteen acres of land donated to them for this purpose by Bronescombe in 1270. Two years later, noting that the canons had built their dwellings and enclosed their grounds at their own expense, he ordered that those who succeeded them should each pay 8s. per annum to maintain an obit mass on the anniversaries of the deaths of each of these founding canons.[2] According to the 15th-century cartulary's account of the college foundation, one canon (Stephen Haym) erected his house on the other side of the road from the rest of his colleagues. Bronescombe decided that this location was unsuitable for a canon and, when Haym died, took it for his own use. He assigned Haym's successor a new site to the north of the church, beyond the river, and in 1300 Bishop Bitton ruled that this area, not originally part of the college grounds, should be joined to them and receive the freedom from secular dues and obligations enjoyed by the rest of the precinct.[3]

Each canon kept a separate household and probably employed two or three servants. In consequence each house would have included a hall, chambers, and a kitchen; some, by the late 14th century, contained private chapels.[4] Canons had to maintain their houses, and action was taken at least twice against those who allowed dilapidations to occur.[5] Bronescombe talked of the canons' houses having enclosures, meaning grounds with hedges or walls, but in about 1330 Grandisson complained about malefactors entering the bishop's park because the canons' gardens, which adjoined the park, were either not enclosed or possessed private gates leading into the park. He ordered the gardens to be enclosed and the gates stopped up.[6] The sale particulars of 1549 refer to eleven messuages inhabited by or belonging to the canons or other clergy. Some are described as having gardens, and two included three-quarters of an acre of enclosed land made up of woodland and heathland. In addition the particulars mention eight chambers called 'Vicars' Chambers'. These existed in some form by the 14th century, probably within a single building as was the case at Crediton.[7] The vicars' premises included a common hall for meals, and therefore presumably a kitchen, and a further chamber was assigned to the succentor and choristers. The succentor was the vicar choral in charge of the music of the choir who lived with and supervised the choristers, as did his counterpart at the cathedral.[8]

The location of the college near an inlet of Falmouth Harbour made it vulnerable to raids from the sea. Given the recorded attacks on the priories of St Anthony-in-Roseland and Tywardreath, it is not surprising that Glasney acquired much stronger defences than were needed to seclude it from public access. John Leland, who visited Penryn in about 1533 and in 1542, described the college as 'strongly walled and incastellated, having three strong towers and guns at the butt of the creek'.[9] The king's chantry commissioners took the same view in 1548, characterising 'the walls of the said college on the south side' as 'well fortified with towers, and ordnance [i.e. guns] in the same, for the defence of the said town and the river coming to the same, which ordnance pertain to the men of the said town'.[10] The early depictions of the college show its defences as consisting of three or four towers linked with battlemented walls on the east side of the close towards the river. On the other sides of the college the walls were of smaller dimensions.

CLERGY AND FUNCTIONS

The college never acquired a systematic code of statutes. Instead it was governed by Bronescombe's rudimentary code of 1276–80 supplemented by his grant of 1267, the various other charters conferring property, and the orders and injunctions of later bishops. These documents were collected together in the 15th-century cartulary, along with Bronescombe's statutes of 1268 and 1275 for Exeter cathedral. Here too the college imitated the cathedral, which observed a similar sequence of statutes and orders, not organised into a code until the 16th century. Glasney's personnel, as has been mentioned, consisted of a provost, twelve other canons, thirteen vicars, and undefined numbers of chantry priests, clerks, and boys. The number of canons remained the same throughout the college's

---

1 TNA, E 315/67, f. 176v; Rashleigh and Vincent (ed.), *Glasney Cartulary*, 50. It may have been a single covered walkway leading to, for example, the chapter house.
2 *Reg. Bronescombe*, ed. Hingeston-Randolph, 95–6; ed. Robinson, II, 57.
3 RS/59/1, ff. 2r–4v, transl. in Rashleigh and Vincent (ed.), *Glasney Cartulary*, pp. 8–10.
4 *Reg. Brantyngham*, I, 310, 322; II, 645; *Reg. Stafford*, 280.
5 *Reg. Brantyngham*, II, 597; *Reg. Morton, Canterbury*, II, 80.
6 *Reg. Grandisson*, I, 246.

7 *Reg. Brantyngham*, II, 700; *Reg. Stafford*, 112; *Cal. Pat.* 1548–9, 176.
8 *Reg. Lacy*, ed. Dunstan, II, 331; *Cal. Pat.* 1548–9, 176; cf. *Reg. Bronescombe*, ed. Hingeston-Randolph, 77–8; ed. Robinson, II, 95–6.
9 J. Leland, *Itinerary*, ed. L. Toulmin Smith (1907–10), I, 197, 322.
10 TNA, E 301/9, m. 1–1d, printed in L. S. Snell, *Documents towards a History of the Reformation in Cornwall*: vol. I, *The Chantry Certificates for Cornwall* (c.1953), 36.

history, although at the end, in 1548, two canonries were vacant.¹ Although the founder set out to encourage the canons to reside through the mechanism of distributions, he and later bishops never insisted that they should all do so continuously or even at all. Practice at Glasney followed the cathedral in paying canons their share of the church's revenues at the end of every quarter of the year, provided they had resided for 46 days within that quarter, in other words for half of it. Each day had to involve attendance at either the early or the high mass, and the eating of a main meal except on the day of their arrival.² Further payments, principally at obit masses, were made if the canon actually turned up to them. Those who did not reside to the extent of 46 days per quarter merely received their basic prebend of £4. In 1381 the provost and five canons paid poll-tax, probably all who were living there.³ In 1492 the provost and six canons were resident, in 1534 apparently the provost and four, and in 1548 the provost and seven.⁴

At first Glasney had only one designated officer, the provost. He presided in the choir and at chapter meetings, and exercised jurisdiction over all the clergy, but he could punish only those below the rank of canon since the discipline of the canons belonged to the bishop.⁵ There was no precentor to supervise the singing, as there was at Exeter, Crediton, and later Ottery, but Bronescombe envisaged a person to look after the altars, vestments, and ornaments. This duty was done at Exeter and Crediton by a treasurer, but Bronescombe preferred the title 'sacrist' and the same term was later adopted at Ottery. The first mention of the sacrist of Glasney occurs in 1275, and his office was outlined more fully in the following year.⁶ He was to be a canon and a priest, to organise the feast-day of St Gabriel, and presumably to have duties in supervising the ornaments and worship of the church. His stipend was to come from the tithes of Colan, but Bronescombe died before the arrangement was completed. After this the post seems to have lain vacant until, as we shall see, it was revived and filled first by a vicar-choral and later by a canon. By the mid 14th century the sacrist had become both a subdean, deputising for the provost, and a treasurer in charge of the articles needed for worship. The canons formed a chapter, including the provost and sacrist, which consulted and took decisions on matters affecting the church and its property. Two canons were elected each 2 November to serve as stewards of the exchequer, with the duty of receiving the revenues of the church and distributing payments to the clergy. This was another practice borrowed from Exeter.⁷

The farming of the parochial tithes by the canons continued throughout the history of Glasney. In 1316 a chapter meeting resolved that the farm of Goran, estimated as worth £40, should provide £13 6s. 8d. to maintain the fabric of the collegiate church. At the same time the farm of St Enoder was set at £27, Kea at £26 2s., Budock at £20 7s. 5d., Sithney at £17, Zennor at £12, St Gluvias at £10 7s. 4d., and Feock at £9 8s. 2d. These figures were to stand until the farms were surrendered through the departure of the canons concerned, after which they might be increased if canons were willing to pay more for them.⁸ Occasionally there were disputes about the farms. In 1321 Bishop Stapeldon intervened in the matter after receiving a complaint from Canon Richard of Beaupré that Adam of Carleton should have forfeited the farm of Goran for failing to pay the income on time. Beaupré possessed no farm and had offered a better rate for Goran, but the chapter had refused his offer. The bishop ordered it to give him justice.⁹ Grandisson, on visiting the college in 1328, found the canons disagreeing about whether farms should be allocated by seniority or juniority; he ruled in favour of the former.¹⁰

The bishops of Exeter used the canons to do business for them in Cornwall.¹¹ Bronescombe appointed the archdeacon of Cornwall to a canonry as early as 1274, and this practice was so often followed that in 1397 we find Bishop Stafford referring to the canonry and prebend 'annexed to the archdeaconry'.¹² By 1548 one of the houses in the close was known as the 'archdeacon's house', and evidently passed to each holder of the office.¹³ The appointment gave the archdeacon a base in west Cornwall, and it is possible that the 'official' who deputised for him in the county conducted some business at Glasney. In 1375 Simon Withiel, the official in charge of the bishop's peculiar jurisdiction, held a canonry, and the bishop allowed him to keep only half of the required period of residence in view of his duties elsewhere.¹⁴ Provosts and canons were often used pastorally as confessors. In 1331 and 1355 Grandisson licensed the provost to hear confessions throughout Cornwall, including cases reserved to the

---

1 For a list of canons, see Peter, *History of Glasney*, 106–171, and for an analysis of them, Whetter, *History of Glasney*, 52–65.
2 RS/59/1, f. 69v, translated in Rashleigh and Vincent (ed.), *Glasney Cartulary*, 31–2; cf. *Reg. Brantingham*, I, 359.
3 TNA, E 179/24/5.
4 *Reg. Morton, Canterbury*, II, 80–1; *7th Deputy Keeper's Report* (1846), App. II, 297; E 301/9, m. 1–1d; Snell, *Chantry Certificates*, 37.
5 *Reg. Brantyngham*, I, 150–2; cf. I, 153–4. On the office and its holders, see also Peter, *History of Glasney*, 81–92
6 *Reg. Bronescombe*, ed. Hingeston-Randolph, 96, 244–5; ed. Robinson, II, 87, 100–1.
7 *Reg. Stapeldon*, 167; cf. I, 536; II, 835; RS/59/1. f. 94v, transl. in Rashleigh and Vincent (ed.), *Glasney Cartulary*, 47.
8 RS/59/1, ff. 56v–58v, transl. in Rashleigh and Vincent (ed.), *Glasney Cartulary*, 26–8.
9 *Reg. Stapeldon*, 167.
10 *Reg. Grandisson*, I, 422; cf. I, 536.
11 e.g. *Reg. Grandisson*, II, 784, 812, 959.
12 DRO, Chanter IX, f. 35r.
13 *Cal. Pat.* 1548–9, 176.
14 *Reg. Brantyngham*, I, 359.

bishop, and similar commissions were given by Bishops Stafford, Lacy, and Neville to provosts, sacrists, or canons.[1] Canon William Noe was authorised to preach in the diocese in 1413, and five years later his colleague Richard Olyver received permission to do so in the college and the churches appropriated to it.[2] Canons also had concerns of their own. In addition to their farms they were often rectors or vicars of a parish benefice in tandem with their canonry. This did not involve a special dispensation, since it was lawful to hold a canonry with one parish church, but the canon concerned was meant to arrange for a curate to do his duties during his residence at Glasney.

Bronescombe talked of canons appointing vicars to do their work in the college if they were non-resident, but it is likely that all canons were expected to have vicars from the beginning and this was stated to be the case in 1288.[3] Once the bishop intervened to make an appointment when a canon failed to do so.[4] The vicars' numbers are not recorded until 1404 when there were eleven;[5] this had fallen to seven by 1492 and apparently remained at that level until shortly before the dissolution of the college.[6] Bronescombe speaks of them being either priests or in lesser holy orders,[7] but later on they all seem to have been required to be priests, as was so at the cathedral. When Grandisson allowed the admission of a man in 1338 who held the minor order of acolyte, this was clearly meant as a special favour.[8] One of the vicars was appointed as a *custos* in 1315, the title at Exeter of the senior and presiding vicar; the term implies that the Glasney vicars had some kind of organisation among themselves.[9] At Exeter the vicars originally lived and ate individually with the canons to whom they belonged, and this may have happened at Glasney to begin with. Later they acquired the common hall already mentioned, first recorded in 1387 when Bishop Brantingham ordered them to eat in it 'as used to be done'. He permitted them, however, to have meals with their own canons if the latter were resident, or with other canons who invited them.[10]

The staff of Exeter cathedral included two junior groups: fourteen boy choristers and twelve adolescent or young adult clerks called 'secondaries' or 'clerks of the second form'.[11] Bronescombe's statutes for Glasney mention boys and clerks, but do not expand on their numbers or functions, and he made no provision for payments to them on St Gabriel's Day. Very likely a clerk or two existed from the beginning to ring bells, dress altars, and assist at masses, but we do not hear of such persons until 1334, when the sacrist was told to appoint a clerk to carry out these duties.[12] A further two clerks were added in 1355, together with two more boy choristers.[13] By 1535 the latter constituted a group of six.[14] From the 1220s the cathedral began to acquire chantry priests, known at Exeter as 'annuellars', who were supported by private funds to pray for the dead. They celebrated mass each day at side altars in the church, and were expected to attend the daily services in the choir.[15] Glasney gained priests of a similar kind. In 1275 Bronescombe granted the church of Manaccan to the college to support two chaplains: one celebrating a daily mass in honour of the Virgin Mary and one doing so for the souls of himself, Henry of Bollegh, and Walter of Fermesham (one of the early canons). The two chaplains were to be appointed by the provost and the sacrist, or by one of them, and to live together in houses constructed by Bollegh and Fermesham near Glasney Bridge.[16] Later they were often referred to as the chaplains 'of the bridge' (*de Ponte*).[17] Two other chantries were subsequently endowed at Glasney, one for a vicar choral and one for two chantry priests, and there were generally about three clergy employed in this way down to the dissolution of the college in 1548.[18]

The resident clergy – canons, vicars, and others – were expected to carry out the daily round of services followed in all religious houses, beginning with matins at midnight and ending with vespers and compline in late afternoon. A high mass, meaning the principal mass of the day, was inserted into this round of services in the middle of the morning, and celebrated at the high altar. The daily services were said in the choir, which at Exeter cathedral was divided into three levels or 'forms', with canons and vicars in the highest row, secondaries and chantry priests in the middle, and choristers in the lowest. Glasney with its smaller establishment may have had only two rows. In practice, since canons needed to attend only matins and high mass, the weight of the

---

1 *Reg. Grandisson*, I, 597; II, 1146; *Reg. Stafford*, 112; *Reg. Lacy*, ed. Dunstan, III, 138, 165, 194, 205; DRO, Chanter XII(i), ff. 34v, 40v.
2 *Reg. Stafford*, 114.
3 *Cal. Pat.* 1313–17, 280; printed in Oliver, *Monasticon*, 50.
4 *Reg. Stafford*, 113.
5 TNA, E 179/25/183.
6 *Reg. Morton, Canterbury*, II, 80–1; E 301/15, ff. 49v–50r; E 301/9, m. 1–1d; Snell, *Chantry Certificates*, 37.
7 *Reg. Bronescombe*, ed. Hingeston-Randolph, 96; ed. Robinson, II, 57.
8 *Reg. Grandisson*, II, 888.
9 N. Orme, 'Vicars Choral and Annuellars', 87.
10 *Reg. Brantyngham*, II, 672.
11 On the Exeter choristers and secondaries, see N. Orme, 'The Medieval Clergy of Exeter Cathedral: II. The Secondaries and Choristers', *TDA* 115 (1983), 79–100.
12 *Reg. Grandisson*, II, 755.
13 Ibid., II, 1154.
14 *Valor Eccl.* (Rec. Com. 1810–34), II, 392.
15 On the Exeter chantry priests, see Orme, 'Vicars Choral and Annuellars', 91–102.
16 *Reg. Bronescombe*, ed. Hingeston-Randolph, 96–7; ed. Robinson, II, 86–7.
17 For a list of priests, see Peter, *History of Glasney*, 172–4.
18 A reference to a chantry priest of Bishop Thomas Brantingham in 1535 (*Valor. Eccl.*, II, 392) must be a mistake for Walter Bronescombe, i.e. 'of the bridge', since the stipends attributed to each chantry were similar (E 301/9, m. 1–1d; Snell, *Chantry Certificates*, 37).

services fell on the shoulders of the vicars. They had also to carry out the services in the Lady chapel, and some of them would have celebrated masses at the side altars in the college like the chantry priests. The vicars choral of Exeter raised money by offering to celebrate for the dead, and their counterparts at Glasney may have done so too. Obit masses also took place at the high altar. These were masses on the anniversaries of people's deaths, voluntarily endowed by members or friends of the college who gave money to be distributed in fees to the clergy who attended them. Thirty-two are listed in the 15th-century cartulary, chiefly in memory of bishops of Exeter and canons of Glasney, but four were held for knights and their wives and three for couples who appear to have been commoners, probably from Penryn.[1]

An intriguing document of 1372 points to the presence of other Cornish clergy in the college. In that year Brantingham complained that certain rectors were leaving their parishes in order to live at Glasney, 'onerating rather than honouring' the church by their presence. He ordered them to return to their parishes within six days.[2] The practice suggests the attractiveness of the college community to other clergy, and there is at least one example of a rector being licensed to reside there: John Hesyll of Jacobstow in 1398 and 1404.[3]

THE 14TH CENTURY

Glasney entered the 14th century still incompletely formed. Quinil had strengthened the office of provost with the appropriation of Mylor, but there was apparently no sacrist until 1315 when Stapledon (1308–26) intervened to make good the lack. He recalled that Bronescombe had intended that the sacrist should be a canon, but had died before establishing the office. No canon was willing to do the duty, so the bishop appointed one of the vicars of Glasney to do so, Robert of Tredowel, until other arrangements could be made.[4] The principal alterations to the college after Bronescombe's time, however, were not made until the reign of Grandisson (1327–69). These began in 1329, when Grandisson co-operated with a project by Sir Ote Bodrugan to improve the revenues of the college and to establish a chantry there. Bodrugan gave Glasney the advowson of his church of Mevagissey, and Grandisson assigned to the college the rent of the church glebe and various tithes amounting in value to £8 13s. 4d. Part of this money was to be used to pay an additional vicar-choral, nominated by Bodrugan and paid £3 6s. 8d. per annum. He was to join the others in the daily services and to say a daily mass at the altar called Bodrugan altar for the souls of the Bodrugan family. This mass seems to have designed as a 'morrow mass', said at dawn for the convenience of travellers. The college also promised to keep Sir Ote's obit every year on the anniversary of his death and to pay 8s. to the clergy who attended, as was done for the obits of canons.[5]

Grandisson next turned his attention to the office of sacrist. In 1329 he scolded the canons for having dismissed Robert of Tredowel, and ordered his restitution to the office and to its revenues.[6] In 1334 the bishop promoted Tredowel to be a canon and granted him the income of the parish of Colan, apart from £6 13s. 4d. to maintain the parochial vicar. In return the sacrist was to pay the clergy attending the feast of St Gabriel in September, to distribute £3 worth of bread to the poor on that day, as directed by Bronescombe, and to employ a clerk described by Grandisson as 'of the second form', like the secondaries of Exeter cathedral. This clerk was to attend the choir, ring the bells, and open and shut the gates of the close. The gate keys were to be kept by the provost or sacrist. The bishop concluded his ordinance for the sacrist with a detailed series of orders about the administration of the church and of services. This was at a time when Grandisson was drawing up the detailed manual for the conduct of services at the cathedral, known as *Ordinale Exon*. The sacrist was to furnish bread and wine for the eucharist, candles and torches for the high altar, and two lights to burn before the great crucifix. Other lights were prescribed to be lit on major festivals. He was to have custody of service books, vessels, vestments, and ornaments, and was to provide incense and charcoal, mats and straw for the church, and ropes for the bells. Together with the provost he was to see silence observed in the choir. In return for these expenses he was to receive £4 per annum from the stewards of the exchequer, all the wax offered in church, and certain payments when canons were installed.[7] At first Grandisson required the sacrist to keep residence continuously, but in 1336 he relaxed this condition and reduced the requirement to three quarters of the year, provided that the sacrist was present at major feasts.[8] In 1348 the bishop reminded the canons that they should all follow the cathedral statutes in being priests when admitted and in attending all the daily services, unless they had good reason to be absent.[9]

The summer of 1348 saw the beginning of the Black

---

1 RS/59/1, ff. 18v–25v, transl. in Rashleigh and Vincent (ed.), *Glasney Cartulary*, 14–15. To these should be added an obit intended to be endowed by Robert Hulle and his wife Joan née Bodrugan in 1407 (*Cal. Pat.* 1405–8, 338), and one requested by Thomas Killigrew of Arwenack near Penryn in 1501 (Orme (ed.), *Cornish Wills*, 111).
2 *Reg. Brantyngham*, I, 273–4.
3 *Reg. Stafford*, 112.
4 *Reg. Stapeldon*, 165–6.
5 *Cal. Pat.* 1327–30, 229; *Reg. Grandisson*, I, 364, 501–5; RS/59/1, ff. 83r–88r, transl. in Rashleigh and Vincent (ed.), *Glasney Cartulary*, 39–41.
6 *Reg. Grandisson*, I, 525–6.
7 Ibid., II, 754–7; RS/59/1, ff. 72r–76v, transl. in Rashleigh and Vincent (ed.), *Glasney Cartulary*, 33–5.
8 *Reg. Grandisson*, II, 821.
9 Ibid., II, 1044.

Death in England, which swept through the diocese of Exeter during the following nine months. Its impact on religious communities was both immediate, causing vacancies among their existing members, and long-term, changing economic conditions in ways that were adverse to churches. A smaller population meant that ecclesiastical revenues often declined, while wages rose. It was harder to recruit clergy to lower-paid posts, and more expensive to hire servants or carry out repairs. By 1355 Grandisson was observing that the vicars choral of Glasney no longer received sufficient support because of the plague and the mutability of the times. He praised Sir John Beaupré who had come forward to strengthen the vicars' resources by giving Glasney the advowson of St Just-in-Penwith, and he granted the knight's request for the appropriation of its revenues to the college. These revenues were to support two Beaupré chantry priests with salaries of £4 6s. 8d. each, two Beaupré secondary clerks receiving 8d. per week (£1 14s. 8d. per annum) apiece, and two Beaupré choristers each having 4d. per week (17s. 4d. per annum). A further annual sum of £4 6s. 8d. was to be paid to the thirteen vicars, raising their individual stipends by 6s. 8d. The two priests were to be appointed by the heirs of Beaupré. They were to say the daily services in the choir and each was to celebrate a daily mass for the souls of the Beaupré family: one a mass in honour of the Virgin Mary at sunrise and the other a mass of requiem after the service of prime in mid morning. The thirteen vicars were to take turns in saying a further daily mass for the Beauprés and certain former clergy of the church; this was to be a mass of the day and was normally to be said in the Beaupré aisle, meaning the part of the church whose altar had been designated for the use of the Beaupré chantry priests.[1]

Grandisson's successor, Thomas Brantingham, found fault with the state of the college. In January 1387 he recalled that he had visited the place and had tried to reform what he had found to be excesses and offences by the canons and other ministers. Despite his interventions, he had learnt that the offenders were still living dissolute lives and harbouring women of suspicious character in their houses. Two clergy were charged with enquiring into the situation.[2] In the following September the bishop issued injunctions to the clergy. All of them should perform the daily services, and the church should be used for prayer not for conversations or bad behaviour. The provost should correct the misdeeds of the lesser clergy in the chapter-house. No women, or men suspected of crimes, should be allowed in the clergy's houses, and female servants should be removed. The vicars should eat dinner and supper in their common hall, as was accustomed, and they should not dine in lay people's houses, especially where women might be. However they might accept invitations from their canons, other canons, or honest laity outside the close, provided they did not frequent taverns. The canons should keep their houses in repair, and the college stewards should sequestrate the revenues of those who refused to do so. Each new sacrist should produce within one month an inventory of all the books, vessels, and ornaments under his custody.[3] In a postscript, a week later than the injunctions, the bishop drew attention to the fact that 500 marks worth of arms, ornaments, and vestments from the church's treasury had been dispersed into various people's hands, almost alienating them from the church. An enquiry was ordered into this.[4]

The next bishop, Edmund Stafford, visited the college in September 1400 and issued injunctions on similar lines to those of Brantingham, but with more precise directives. Canons were to be present in their proper habits at the daily services and mass. Each canon in residence was to take turns in celebrating high mass at the high altar for a week at a time, and the vicars were to say their private masses at hours that did not interfere with the services in the choir. Vicars and lesser clergy guilty of neglect in services were to be punished by the provost 'in chapter' with the canons in the chapter-house, not privately. No canon was to give household chores to a vicar, thereby hindering his work for the church. The common seal of the college was to be kept securely. The sacrist, through his clerk, was to ensure that the bells were rung for services, the doors closed in good time, bread and wine provided for mass, and vessels cleansed. If negligent the clerk should be dismissed. The rest of the injunctions dealt with the repair of the church, already mentioned.[5] In 1405 the church was allegedly polluted, probably by bloodshed, and was temporarily closed. During the closure the bishop allowed the celebration of masses in the canons' houses and the common hall of the vicars.[6]

A series of disputes took place in Brantingham's reign about the right to be provost. Richard of Gomersale, Grandisson's last appointment to the office, died towards the end of 1367. The pope, Urban V, claimed the right to provide a successor, and appointed Robert Hoo, described by the papal chancery as a scholar of arts.[7] Hoo belonged to a family of knightly rank based in Hertfordshire and Sussex.[8] He evidently had some

---

1 *Cal. Pat.* 1350–4, 350; *Reg. Grandisson*, II, 1153–6; RS/59/1, ff. 76v–82r, transl. in Rashleigh and Vincent (ed.), *Glasney Cartulary*, 36–8.
2 *Reg. Brantyngham*, I, 174.
3 Ibid., II, 671–3. 4 Ibid., I, 176.
5 RS/59/1, ff. 88r–94v, transl. in Rashleigh and Vincent (ed.), *Glasney Cartulary*, 41–6; *Reg. Stafford*, 112–13.
6 *Reg. Stafford*, 112.
7 *Lettres Communes des Papes du XIVe Siècle: Urbain V, Lettres Communes*, VIII (1982), 85.
8 On the family, see W. D. Cooper, 'The Families of Braose of Chesworth and Hoo', *Sussex Archaeological Collections* 8 (1856), 97–131; G. E. Cokayne, *The Complete Peerage*, ed. H. A. Doubleday and V. Gibbs (1910–59), VI, 565–7.

influence at the papal court, since the pope had already reserved him a benefice in the diocese of Lincoln and a canonry of Lichfield, although he had not gained possession of either.[1] He was also unsuccessful in acquiring the provostship of Glasney up to 1369, at which point Grandisson died and the bishop's patronage lapsed to the king, Edward III, until a new bishop was appointed.[2] In due course Edward presented his own candidate, Reynold Calle, to be provost on 8 Oct 1370, and Calle took up residence but in February 1374 he asked permission to appoint a coadjutor because he had lost his sight like Tobit in the Old Testament book of that name.[3] Hoo, apparently having failed in other attempts to pursue his claims, went to Glasney in about the following November, and, according to the bishop, now Brantingham, laid violent hands on Calle, mortally wounding him within the close of the church.[4] Brantingham excommunicated Hoo, and by March 1375 Hoo was obliged to provide the king with sureties of £100 that he would not leave the country without permission or do anything prejudicial to the Crown.[5] The Crown seems to have been primarily interested in pursuing Hoo for challenging its powers in foreign lands – presumably at the papacy – and he was eventually sent to prison in London for this offence, until he was bailed in 1383.[6] He did not pursue his claim to the Glasney provostship.

After the death of Calle, Brantingham appointed Thomas Walkington, a respectable candidate who was already a doctor of canon and civil law. Unfortunately Walkington was not a canon of Glasney, a pre-requisite for becoming a provost, and had to resign, be given a canonry, and reappointed.[7] In 1375 the bishop permitted him to receive his stipend without residing, in view of his work for the bishop, the cathedral, and the papal court.[8] Three years later Walkington was promoted to be dean of Exeter cathedral but, since he had held the rank of papal chaplain, the right to fill his post lapsed again to the pope, now Urban VI. The pope appointed John Edneves, alias Souffere, another doctor of canon law, and also reserved for him a benefice in the gift of Plympton priory (Devon).[9] Meanwhile the bishop, in ignorance or defiance of the papal appointment, filled the provostship with his own candidates, first Adam Sparke in 1378 and then Walter Myn in 1380.[10] By January 1384 Edneves had succeeded in gaining control of the provostship, at least de facto, to the annoyance of the bishop, an annoyance compounded when Edneves also claimed the church of Plymouth (Devon) which he argued to be the Plympton benefice to which he was entitled.[11] Brantingham retaliated by ordering an investigation into charges that he had slandered the pope, the king, and the bishops of England,[12] and in June 1385 the bishop declared the provostship to be vacant and appointed his own candidate, John Rauf.[13] Edneves then began litigation with Rauf at the papal court, but died in about 1393 without recovering possession.[14]

The pope, by now Boniface IX, tried to maintain his authority by substituting a new candidate for Edneves in 1393: William Cullyng, rector of Upton Pyne (Devon).[15] Cullyng gained possession by 1395, and Rauf resigned or was demoted, receiving a Glasney canonry.[16] In 1396 the king, Richard II, granted the provostship to a Yorkshireman, Thomas Yokeflete,[17] but Cullyng was able to hold on to the office, obtaining a royal licence to accept it in 1397 and having his title ratified later that year. He held the post till 1423.[18] The complicated story of the provostship between 1367 and 1397 has many parallels in 14th-century England, a period of conflict between popes, kings, and bishops over ecclesiastical patronage.

THE 15TH AND 16TH CENTURIES

The next bishop to make a formal visitation of Glasney was Lacy, who issued injunctions in 1445. His perception of the ruinous condition of the building and his imposition of a tax to fund repairs have already been mentioned. As in Stafford's time the bishop was concerned about the administration of money. Some of the canons who had served as stewards had failed to present accounts, and were ordered to do so retrospectively. Some had taken to their houses sums of money belonging to the church; these were to be returned to the common chest in the college exchequer. In future all disbursements of money were to be made in the exchequer. The bishop discovered that the choristers had been ejected from the chamber in which

---

1 *Lettres Communes, Urbain V*, VIII, 101.

2 In 1372 the king was said to have recovered the presentation of the provostship in his court from Bishop Grandisson and Robert Hoo, so there may have been some litigation before Grandisson died (*Reg. Brantyngham*, I, 179–80) or afterwards (*Cal. Pat.* 1370–4, 98).

3 *Cal. Pat.* 1367–70, 463; *Reg. Brantyngham*, I, 323.

4 *Reg. Brantyngham*, I, 148, 354–5; cf. I, 150–2: an enquiry into Hoo's claims.

5 *Cal. Close* 1374–7, 211.

6 *Cal. Close* 1381–5, 287.

7 *Reg. Brantyngham*, I, 38.

8 Ibid., I, 363.

9 *Cal. Papal Regs* IV, 458–9; *Reg. Brantyngham*, I, 430. Dr O. J. Padel informs me that Edneves may be a surname based on Ethnevas in Constantine parish; if so, John had Cornish connections.

10 *Reg. Brantyngham*, I, 54, 60.

11 Ibid., I, 510–11.

12 Ibid., I, 160.

13 Ibid., I, 91–2.

14 He must therefore be distinguished from another John Edneves, non-graduate vicar of Newton St Cyres (Devon) by 1411; died 1430 (Chanter VIII, f. 138r–v; *Reg. Lacy*, ed. Hingeston-Randolph, 125).

15 *Cal. Papal Regs*, IV, 458–9.

16 *Reg. Stafford*, 112.

17 *Cal. Pat.* 1396–9, 15. Yokefleet is in Yorkshire; he did not gain possession.

18 *Cal. Pap. Regs*, IV, 458–9; *Cal. Pat.* 1396–9, 140, 154; *Reg. Lacy*, ed. Hingeston-Randolph, I, 60.

they had formerly lived with the succentor. They now roamed the town by night and day without supervision, and Lacy ordered them to be restored to their chamber.[1] In 1449 he commissioned three senior clergy to correct abuses at Glasney where, by report, disputes had broken out,[2] and in 1451 he ratified a papal privilege allowing the sacrist to hold his post in tandem with that of a parish church, on the grounds of the poverty of the sacrist's income. In future the sacrist was required to reside at Glasney for only half of each term like the other canons, leaving him free to spend the rest of the time in the parish.[3]

Lacy enhanced the college through the quality of the provosts whom he appointed. He himself was a doctor of divinity and a highly spiritual man. All three of the provosts he chose were Oxford graduates, Nicholas Harry or Henry (1423–7) being a master of arts, while William Trengoff (1427–36) and Richard Reddew (1436, still in 1451) were doctors of divinity, as was Michael Trewynnard (died 1471) who succeeded Reddew. With the possible exception of some of the friars of Bodmin and Truro, these would have been the most learned men in Cornwall in the middle of the 15th century. Furthermore two of the four sacrists appointed in Lacy's time were graduates, as were just over half of the canons and even one of the chantry priests. Some of the senior Glasney clergy must have been native Cornish speakers – Trewynnard, for example, came from St Ives – in which case, like the friars, they had the opportunity to bring their learning to other such speakers in sermons and confessions.[4] It is difficult to assess the importance of the college as a religious and cultural centre between 1400 and the Reformation, for the usual reason that the sources for its history are largely constitutional and economic. Nevertheless it must have ranked high, perhaps highest of all, among the religious houses in Cornwall in terms of its worship. The potential number of clergy in the choir (about twenty) exceeded that in the Cornish monasteries, and contacts with the cathedral, the regional centre of excellence, were strong.

During the 15th century polyphony (harmonised music) increased its importance in large English churches. The basic chant of the choral services was supplemented with special anthems or settings, especially for the services performed in the Lady chapel and for singing the evening antiphon in honour of the Virgin. It is likely that Glasney cultivated such music and did so more fully than most of the other Cornish religious houses. In 1438 Canon Michell bequeathed another Cornishman his quire of 'songs of music' which lay in Bishop Lacy's chapel – almost certainly works of polyphony, of which Lacy was a notable patron.[5] By 1548 the college employed Ralph Coche as clerk of the Lady chapel, with a salary of £6 12s. as well as food and drink.[6] Coche was probably responsible for organising harmonised music, using the voices of the boys and some of the adult clergy, and may have replaced the succentor in teaching the choristers, as happened at Exeter.[7] There must have been books in the close and Glasney may have had a library in the sense of a cupboard or chest of books. In 1430 Martin Lercedekne bequeathed it his concordances on condition that he was still a canon when he died.[8] Provosts Evelyng and Reddew in the 15th century and Corke in the 16th are known to have owned books or to have borrowed them from other people: a commentary on the *Sentences* of Peter Lombard, the Sunday sermons of Jacopo da Varazzo, the guide to parish work called *Pupilla Oculi*, and a work on the sacraments.[9]

Until at least 1506 Glasney lay within the area of Cornish speech. A Venetian ambassador who visited Falmouth in that year observed that the language of the district was unintelligible to people in the rest of England, and it is likely that many of the college clergy and their servants could speak it.[10] As has already been noted, the college has been suggested by scholars as the place of origin of the five surviving late-medieval plays in Cornish: the *Ordinalia*, a trilogy based on the Bible, and the two lives of St Kea and St Meriasek.[11] The *Ordinalia* certainly include several references to places in the vicinity of Penryn, while St Kea was the patron saint of one of the college's parishes and St Meriasek that of Camborne, of which three provosts of Glasney (John Pascow, Alexander Penhyll, and John Nans) were rectors of Camborne. This evidence is suggestive, but it is not conclusive. The Penryn references are primarily indications of a Penryn audience, not of a Glasney authorship, and caution is needed lest we overvalue the college's importance as a centre of literary culture when so little is known of that culture among the other clergy and laity of the vicinity. More certainly the college came to be an educational centre, although the origin of that is also unclear. By 1548 its bellringer John Pounde, who must have been identical with the clerk employed by the sacrist, received £2 from the college for teaching the children of the poor, so that he may have taught others for fees. There was a grammar school too by that year,

---

1 *Reg. Lacy*, ed. Dunstan, II, 329–33.
2 Ibid., III, 43, 45.
3 *Cal. Pap. Regs* X, 94; *Reg. Lacy*, ed. Dunstan, III, 130–1; further ratified by Bishop Neville in 1458 (Chanter XII(i), f. 41r–v). The sacrist's office remained relatively poorly endowed, and in 1508 Bishop Oldham relieved its holder of certain burdens and added a payment of 13s. 4d. (DRO, Chanter XIII, f. 157r–v).
4 Worcester, *Itineraries*, ed. Harvey, 104–5.
5 *Reg. Lacy*, ed. Dunstan, IV, 34. On Lacy's patronage of music, see N. Orme, 'The Early Musicians of Exeter Cathedral', *Music and Letters* 59 (1978), 399–403.
6 E 301/9, m. 1–1d; Snell, *Chantry Certificates*, 37.
7 Orme, 'Secondaries and Choristers', 86–8.
8 *Reg. Chichele, Canterbury*, II, 478.
9 *BRUO*, I, 487–8, 653; III, 1560.
10 *Cal. SP Venetian*, I, 314.
11 Above, pp. 90–1.

which had been taught by one of the vicars who had recently died, but it is not possible to say when either school was instituted.¹

William Worcester's visit to the college in the autumn of 1478 led him to note its foundation by Walter 'the Good' in 1265, the name of the site ('Glasneyth' or 'Polsethow'), the name of the current provost, John Pascow, and that of his predecessor-but-one, Michael Trewynnard, who had died in 1471.² In 1492 the college received a formal visitation from the official of the archbishop of Canterbury. The provost, John Oby, appeared, together with the sacrist, five resident canons, seven vicars, and four chantry priests. Oby admitted that they did not say matins in the middle of the night, as the statutes required – a fact confirmed by one of his colleagues. The sacrist drew attention to the decline of the statutory number of thirteen vicars to seven, and other people to the poor state of the houses of three of the non-resident canons. There were complaints about the lack of written statutes, and about the failure to give any alms to the poor. The visitor ordered the provost to restore the vicars to their proper strength, to provide new copies of the statutes, and to sequestrate the prebends of canons with disrepaired houses.³ He made no provisions concerning the other matters, however, and it is probable that the increase of the number of vicars remained a dead letter. Like the withdrawal of alms, the staffing of the college reflected its limited resources. Oby came to a sad end. He was appointed a justice of the peace in Cornwall in 1496,⁴ and a commissioner for collecting royal taxation in the following year. The taxation was so unpopular that it caused the Cornish rebellion of May–June 1497, which culminated in the battle of Blackheath. Later in the year, when discontent was still simmering in Cornwall, the pretender Perkin Warbeck landed in Whitesand Bay and led a second rebellion as far as Taunton. Oby had the misfortune to be captured by a party of Cornish under 'one James, a rover [i.e. a pirate]', which was making its way to join Warbeck. The rebels brought him into Taunton, probably on 21 September, 'and there in the market place slew him piteously, in such wise that he was dismembered and cut in many and sundry pieces'. The king's forces took the town on the following day, too late to save him.⁵

The early 16th-century provosts included John Nans, doctor of civil and canon law, who was a major figure in diocesan administration, but they lacked the intellectual distinction of Lacy's appointments. James Gentill (1526–46), the longest serving provost of this period, was a graduate in canon law who combined his office with the deanery of Crantock, the vicarage of Lelant, and the administration of the peculiar jurisdiction of St Buryan.⁶ Allegations were made against him by William Carvanyon, a lessee of the bishop's property in Penryn, accusing him of allowing the colleges to decay so that services were not properly held. He was also charged with misappropriating the chantries of Glasney and behaving, with his servants, like a temporal man, hawking, hunting, and thereby breaking hedges, damaging crops, and killing domestic animals.⁷ In 1534 Gentill, the sacrist, and three other canons acknowledged Henry VIII as head of the Church of England, presumably comprising the senior clergy then in residence.⁸ In the following year the king's commissioners assessed the revenues of the college. The gross income was estimated at £210 13s. 2d., of which £4 came from rents and leases of temporal property and the rest from the tithes and glebe rents of the college's fourteen parish churches. In descending order of value the churches were St Enoder (£27 13s. 4d.), Kea (including Kenwyn) (£24 3s. 4d.), Goran (£22), St Just-in-Penwith (£21 7s. 8d.), Mylor and Sithney (each £20), Budock (£17 8s.), St Allen (£10 12s.), St Gluvias (£10 10s.), Zennor (£8 12s. 2d.), Feock (£7 13s. 4d.), Manaccan (£7), Colan (£5 6s. 8d.), and Mevagissey (£3 6s. 8d.). The clergy's stipends were variable because they consisted partly of regular payments, partly of fees for attending obit masses, and (in the case of canons) a share of divided revenues. In 1535 this was estimated to give the provost £32 18s. 7d., the sacrist £10 4s. 7d., the other eleven canons £8 18s. 7d.,⁹ the seven vicars choral £6 2s. 2¼d., and the six choristers 18s. The three chantry priests of Walter Bronescombe,¹⁰ Odo Bodrugan, and John and Margaret Beaupré received £7 1s. 10d., £4 8s. 10d., and £4 8s. 6d. respectively. Fees of 20s. and 10s. were paid to an auditor and a steward, and £3 12s. 8d. was distributed to the poor on Maundy Thursday, St Gabriel's Day, and the founder's obit day.¹¹

DISSOLUTION

The college was surveyed by the chantry commissioners of Henry VIII in the spring of 1546 and by those of Edward VI in the same season two years later. The first survey was brief. It stated that Glasney lay in a populous town with traffic through its port, and described the college as staffed by a dean (*sic*), seven resident canons,

---

1 E 301/9, m. 1–1d; Snell, *Chantry Certificates*, 38–40; N. Orme, *Education in the West of England 1066–1548* (1976), 167–8.

2 Worcester, *Itineraries*, ed. Harvey, 102–7.

3 *Reg. Morton, Canterbury*, II, 80–1.

4 *Cal. Pat. 1494–1509*, 633.

5 C. L. Kingsford (ed.), *Chronicles of London* (1905), 218; I. Arthurson, *The Perkin Warbeck Conspiracy 1491–1499* (1994), 163, 187–8.

6 Above, pp. 169, 180. He witnessed a will at St Ives in 1503 (Orme (ed.), *Cornish Wills*, 116).

7 TNA, STAC 2/9, no. 63.

8 TNA, E 25/58/3, printed in *7th Deputy Keeper' Report* (1846), App. II, 297.

9 An odd entry, since canons' stipends depended on the extent to which they resided.

10 Wrongly described in the *Valor* as Thomas Brantingham (above, p. 254 note 18).

11 *Valor Eccl.*, II, 392.

five non-resident, seven vicars, and one chantry priest. The college was not a parish church but was the best frequented church in the town, because the parish church (i.e. St Gluvias) was small. Glasney's revenues were estimated at £227 13s. 7d. gross and £227 8s. 4d. net., and the ornaments, plate, goods, and chattels were worth £153 0s. 8d., excluding the bells.[1] The commissioners of 1548 observed that the traffic in the port sometimes amounted to a hundred ships, which led to people attending the college for worship. More accurately than in 1546 they enumerated the staff of Glasney as a provost, seven resident canons, three non-resident (two places being unfilled), five vicars (with two vacancies), three chantry priests, a chapel clerk, a bellringer, and four choristers. John Lybbe, the provost, had a salary of £36 14s. as well as holding other benefices,[2] while the resident canons received £11, the non-resident 26s., the vicars £7 10s., the Bronescombe chantry priest the same, and his two colleagues £5. The chapel clerk enjoyed £6 12s. together with food and drink, the bellringer £2, and the choristers £1. The gross value of the revenues was now estimated at £228 3s. 7d., and the net value £221 18s. 4d. The college plate weighed 986 ounces, the lead 40 fothers, and the bells 40 hundredweight; the ornaments were worth £26 and the vestments and altar cloths £4.[3]

In 1538 the Crown suppressed the cult of Thomas Becket, which may explain a statement ten years later that the church was 'now commonly called Our Lady of Glasney'.[4] The college was dissolved under the terms of the second Chantry Act which became effective on 1 April, 1548. The members of the college all received pensions, apart from the choristers. Lybbe was awarded half his salary (£18 7s. 1d.), the resident canons £6 13s. 4d., the non-resident £1 6s., the chapel clerk £6 13s. 4d., the vicars and the Bronescombe chantry priest £6, the other two chantry priests £4 12s., and the bellringer £2.[5] The commissioners of 1548 recommended Penryn as 'a meet place to establish a learned man to teach a grammar school or to preach God's word, for the people thereabouts be very ignorant'. The Crown respected this advice with regard to the grammar school, an order being given that it should continue and that the schoolmaster should receive the accustomed vicar-choral's stipend of £6 18s. In the first instance John Arscott, MA, who had just been pensioned as the archpriest of St Michael's Mount, was imported to run the school.[6] In 1552 the Crown made a grant to the archdeacon of Cornwall to recompense him for the canonry that he had previously held by virtue of his office.[7] Otherwise the college ceased to exist. On 1 June 1549 the Crown sold the residential buildings and their grounds, together with the churchyard, to John Southcote of London and Henry Chyverton of Bodmin, gentlemen,[8] and on the following 22 December Sir John Peryent and Thomas Reve, gentleman, purchased the church of Glasney including the tower, bells, walls, stone, timber, tiles, and lead.[9] The Crown took the tithes of the churches appropriated to Glasney and its landed property, but the bishops of Exeter continued to hold the patronage of most of the churches, having never relinquished it to the college. Only the advowsons of St Just-in-Penwith and Mevagissey, given by other benefactors, passed into the hands of the Crown.

Glasney did not disappear without some opposition. In April 1550 the royal commissioners responsible for the two sales reported that 'certain gentlemen' in Cornwall were trying to get the sales cancelled and to have the church, which had already been partly dismantled, converted into a parish church. The commissioners recommended that the purchasers should be safeguarded in their grants, and in the event nothing was done to disturb them.[10] Despite the dismantlement, parts of the fabric of the church and the surrounding fortifications remained visible well into the 17th century.[11] In about 1654 the voyager Peter Mundy referred to 'the ruins of the church and steeple [i.e. tower], yet to be seen; many strong towers remaining yet entire'.[12] The last tower was demolished in the early 18th century, and by the middle of the 19th little remained except for the footings of the north walls of the church.[13] At present most of the church site lies in an open field, the chief standing features being the window arch of the chapel at the east end of the north choir aisle, with some adjoining masonry, and the south wall of the cemetery of the church. Pieces of carved masonry from the site are preserved in Penryn Town Museum. The common seal of the college survives in a damaged specimen of 1330. It appears to have shown the martyrdom of Thomas Becket.[14]

---

1 E 301/15, ff. 49v–50r; Snell, *Chantry Certificates*, 38–9.

2 He was rector of Cheverell Magna (Wilts.) and vicar of Hatherleigh (Devon).

3 E 301/9, m. 1–1d; Snell, *Chantry Certificates*, 36–8. Some of these figures were slightly modified later (E 309/10; Snell, *Chantry Certificates*, 39–40). A list of tenants of the college's temporal property in 1548 is contained in Bodleian, Rawl. D 363, ff. 225r–227v.

4 TNA, E 315/67, f. 174v; Rashleigh and Vincent (ed.), *Glasney Cartulary*, 50.

5 E 301/10; Snell, *Chantry Certificates*, 39–40.

6 Orme, *Education in the West of England*, 168.

7 *Cal. Pat.* 1550–3, 320.

8 *Cal. Pat.* 1548–9, 176.

9 *Cal. Pat.* 1549–51, 13.

10 *HMC Salisbury I*, 74. The date there given, 1549, must be a year too early.

11 For the later history of the site, see J. Palmer, *Searching for Glasney: the evidence of the records*, Friends of Glasney Occasional Paper, 2 (1991).

12 Bodleian, Rawl. A 315, f. 218v; BL, Add. 33420, f. 106r.

13 J. Polsue, *A Complete Parochial History of the County of Cornwall* (1867–72), II, 79; Sowell, 'The Collegiate Church of Glasney', 21–34.

14 CRO, ME/335. A monumental brass in the church of St Just-in-Roseland may portray Alexander Geffrey (d. 1529), canon of Glasney and rector of St Just.

PROVOSTS OF GLASNEY[1]

Henry of Bollegh	occurs 22 Oct 1272, res. by 8 March 1276, when reappointed as administrator[2]
William of Bodrugan	coll. on or by 17 Apr 1283[3]
Walter of Fermesham	coll. c.24 Feb 1288[4]
William FitzRoges	occurs 8 Apr 1297, res. c.20 June 1311[5]
Richard of Braylegh	adm. *in commendam* 16 July 1312[6]
William Bloyou	adm. *in commendam* 9 Jan 1313[7]
Benedict Arundell	coll. 23 Oct 1313[8]
Richard Seneschal	occurs 18 Nov 1328, 12 May 1335[9]
William Heghes	adm. *in commendam* c.Nov 1347[10]
Richard of Todeworthe	coll. 3 Dec 1347, exch. 2 Jan 1348[11]
Richard of Gomersale	coll. after exch. 2 Jan 1348, died c.1 Nov 1367[12]
Robert of Hoo	papal reservation 1 Nov 1367, occurs as claimant 29 Feb 1375[13]
Reynold Calle	royal grant 8 Oct 1370, died by 21 Nov 1374[14]
Thomas Walkington, DCan&CL	coll. 2 Dec 1374, res. and re-coll. 10 Sept 1375, occurs 6 Apr 1377, res. by 25 May 1378[15]
John Edneves, DCanL	papal provision c.May 1378, claimant 17 Jan 1384, depr. by 7 June 1385, still claimant in 1389 or later, died by 25 Aug 1393[16]
Adam Sparke	coll. 25 May 1378, died by 31 March 1380[17]
Walter Myn	coll. 31 March 1380, occurs 1381[18]
John Rauf	coll. 7 June 1385, estate ratified 14 Nov 1390, royal grant 15 Nov 1392, apparently vacated by 8 June 1395[19]
William Cullyng	papal provision 25 Aug 1393, occurs 8 June 1395, royal licence to accept 6 Feb 1397, estate ratified 28 May 1397, died by 18 Feb 1423[20]
Thomas Yokeflete	royal grant 31 July 1396[21]
Nicholas Harry, MA	coll. 18 Feb 1423, died by 19 Sept 1427[22]
Walter Trengoff, DD	coll. 19 Sept 1427, res. by 23 Oct 1436[23]
Richard Reddew, DD	coll. 23 Oct 1436, occurs 20 Sept 1451[24]
Michael Trewynnard, DD	died 11 Apr 1471[25]
John Evelyng, BD	exch. 30 Nov 1476[26]
John Pascow	coll. after exch. 30 Nov 1476, res. by 4 Dec 1491[27]
John Oby	coll. 4 Dec 1491, died c.21 Sept 1497[28]
John Nans, DCan&CL	coll. 29 Nov 1497, exch. 5 June 1501[29]
Alexander Penhyll	coll. after exch. 5 June 1501, res. by 24 March 1507[30]
William Uryn	coll. 24 March 1507, died by 19 June 1519[31]

1 Biographical details of provosts appear in Peter, *History of Glasney*, 55–80.
2 *Reg. Bronescombe*, ed. Hingeston-Randolph, 96–7; ed. Robinson, II, 57, 95.
3 ECA, D&C 1006; *Reg. Bronescombe*, ed. Hingeston-Randolph, 330–1.
4 *Reg. Brantyngham*, II, 652–4.
5 *Cal. Pat.* 1292–1301, 285; *Reg. Stapeldon*, 165, 219.
6 *Reg. Stapeldon*, 219. *In commendam* signifies a commission to administer the office without full possession of its rights and revenues.
7 Ibid., 163, 219.
8 Ibid., 219.
9 *Reg. Grandisson*, I, 426; II, 784.
10 Ibid., II, 1037.
11 Ibid., III, 1364
12 Ibid.; Urbain V, *Lettres Communes*, VIII, 85. Gomersal is in Yorkshire.
13 Urbain V, *Lettres Communes*, VIII, 85; *Cal. Pat.* 1370–4, 98; *Reg. Brantyngham*, I, 148, 150–2.
14 *Cal. Pat.* 1367–70, 463; *Reg. Brantyngham*, I, 349–50.
15 *Reg. Brantyngham*, I, 35, 38, 150–2, 153–4, 356. He resigned in order to be elected as dean of Exeter Cathedral. Walkington is in Yorkshire; biography in *BRUO*, III, 1964–5.
16 *Cal. Papal Regs*, IV, 458–9; *Reg. Brantyngham*, I, 91–2, 160, 510–11; II, 597.
17 *Reg. Brantyngham*, I, 54, 60.
18 Ibid., I, 60; TNA, E 179/24/4.
19 *Reg. Brantyngham*, I, 91–2; *Cal. Pat.* 1388–92, 322; 1391–6, 45, 322; *Reg. Stafford*, 112; *Cal. Pap. Regs*, IV, 458–9.
20 *Cal. Papal Regs*, IV, 458–9; *Reg. Stafford*, 112; *Cal. Pat.* 1396–9, 140, 154; *Reg. Lacy*, ed. Hingeston-Randolph, I, 60.
21 *Cal. Pat.* 1396–9, 15; biography in *BRUO*, III, 2133–4. He did not gain possession.
22 *Reg. Lacy*, ed. Hingeston-Randolph, I, 60, 94–5; biography in *BRUO*, II, 910.
23 *Reg. Lacy*, ed. Hingeston-Randolph, I, 94–5, 214; biography in *BRUO*, III, 1896.
24 *Reg. Lacy*, ed. Dunstan, I, 214, 362; Peter, *History of Glasney*, 77, gives his latest occurrence as 29 Sept 1463; biography in *BRUO*, III, 1560.
25 Worcester, *Itineraries*, ed. Harvey, 104–5; biography in *BRUO*, III, 1905.
26 Chanter XII(ii) (Reg. Bothe), f. 38r–v; Peter, *History of Glasney*, 78, gives his first occurrence as 1471; biography in *BRUO*, I, 653.
27 Chanter XII(ii) (Reg. Bothe), f. 38r–v; (Reg. Fox), f. 116v.
28 Chanter XII(ii) (Reg. Fox), f. 116v; Kingsford (ed.), *Chronicles of London*, 218.
29 Chanter XII(ii) (Reg. Redman), ff. 3v, 22r; biography in *BRUO*, II, 1336–7.
30 Chanter XII(ii) (Reg. Redman), f. 22r; Chanter XIII, f. 11r.
31 Chanter XIII, ff. 11r, 81r.

John Corke, MA	coll. 19 June 1519, res. by 2 Nov 1526[1]	John Lybbe, BCanL	comp. 24 Sept 1546; coll. 30 Sept 1546; till dissolution, spring 1548[3]
James Gentill, BCanL	coll. 2 Nov 1526, died by 23 Apr 1546[2]		

PENRYN: ALMSHOUSE

Thomas Killigrew of Penryn, in his will dated 22 May 1501, left a sum of £5 'for the building of a house of the poor [*domus pauperum*] at Penryn for four poor people'.[4] Such a small sum suggests that Killigrew was subscribing towards a general project to build an unendowed almshouse to provide accommodation for needy people in the borough of Penryn. The houses would have resembled those in Bodmin and Launceston as a rather humble piece of charity, unlike the well-endowed foundations established in Devon and elsewhere in England. There is no evidence that the almshouse came into being, but if it consisted of dwellings without endowments it may have left little trace in records.

PROBUS

COLLEGIATE, LATER PREBENDAL, CHURCH

The church of Probus (SW 8990 4772) was another of the ancient Cornish minsters first fully recorded in the Domesday survey of 1086.[5] The Domesday account states that the church of 'Lanbrebois' was held by the canons of Probus, together with one hide and one virgate of land; the land had never paid tax and was worth 40s.[6] The mention of canons indicates a body of clergy living under a rule or observance, whose resources included a piece of land surrounding the church, later known as the manor of Lamprobus, and the tithes of the parish of Probus. The parish was large, including the chapelries of Cornelly and Merther, and the church had special privileges as a sanctuary.[7] The church saint was unique within Cornwall, but nothing is known of his cult in the parish.[8] At some point after the Norman Conquest the church was granted to the church of St Mary and St Peter, Exeter, meaning the cathedral, but in practice to its head: the bishop of Exeter. The earliest evidence for this is a charter of Henry I, datable to 1123, which states that the grant was made by his predecessors and confirms it.[9] King Stephen confirmed the grant in 1136, and John on 26 March 1200.[10] Nothing else is known about the church in the 12th century, but the evidence that survives about it in the 13th shows that the bishops, on gaining control of the church, did not extinguish the canons. The latter survived, six in number, including a dean who was not elected by his fellow clergy but collated (chosen and instituted) by the bishop of Exeter. The dean ruled the parish and had responsibility for its spiritual life; he appointed the canons, and shared with them the income of the church, taking the lion's share of it himself.

In the autumn of 1224 the patronage of the deanery was the subject of a lawsuit before the king's justices, which throws some light on appointments to the office in recent times.[11] A cleric named Thomas of Hertford claimed on behalf of the king, Henry III, that the right to appoint the dean of Probus belonged to the Crown and not to the bishop. The Crown's case was that King John had appointed Walter de Gray as dean and, after him, the provost of the church of St Omer in France, who had now ceased to hold office. The deanery was therefore vacant and eligible for a

---

1 Chanter XIII, f. 81r; DRO, Chanter XIV, f. 29r; biography in *BRUO*, I, 487–8.

2 Chanter XIV, ff. 29r, 119r, 120v; biography in *BRUO*, IV, 679.

3 TNA, E 334/3, f. 98v; Chanter XIV, f. 120v; E 301/9, m. 1–1d.; E 301/10; Snell, *Chantry Certificates*, 37, 39; biography in BRUO, IV, 367, to which add that he was vicar of Hatherleigh (Devon) from 1541 to c.1554.

4 N. Orme (ed.), *Cornish Wills 1342–1540*, DCRS new ser. 50 (2007), 111; J. Whetter, 'The Thomas Killigrews', *Old Cornwall* 10.7 (1988), 338–49.

5 Above, p. 135.

6 C. and F. Thorn (ed.), *Domesday Book*, vol. X: *Cornwall* (1979), 4/24.

7 C. G. Henderson, 'The Ecclesiastical History of the 109 Parishes of West Cornwall', *JRIC* new ser. 3 (1957–60), 411–24, especially 415–16.

8 On the saint, see N. Orme, *The Saints of Cornwall* (2000), 223–4.

9 *Regesta Regum Anglo-Normannorum*, ed. H. W. C. Davis et al. (1913–59), II, 72, 185; P. L. Hull (ed.), (ed.), *The Cartulary of Launceston Priory*, DCRS new ser. 30 (1987), 1–2. There are two versions of the charter, both undated but one datable to 1123, the latter being generally regarded as the more authentic.

10 ECA, D&C 2073, printed in *Regesta Regum Anglo-Normannorum*, III, 106–7, where doubt is expressed about authenticity; D&C 2080.

11 *Cur. Reg.* XI, 407.

Crown appointment. Indeed, although the judicial proceedings do not say so, the Crown had already presented Hertford to the post on 14 November 1223.[1] The bishop of Exeter replied that the patronage of the deanery belonged to him, and that the office was occupied. John, he declared, had given the church of Probus to Henry Marshal, bishop of Exeter (a reference to the charter of 1200), and although the king had subsequently appointed Walter de Gray and the provost, he had done so while the bishopric was vacant between 1206 and 1214, as he had a right to do. The bishop went on to state that after Simon of Apulia was elected as bishop in 1214, ending the vacancy, Simon appointed Simon the Clerk as dean who was still in office in 1224. The judges reserved their judgment and it is not recorded, but the fact that the patronage of the deanery remained in the bishop's hands in subsequent years shows that the Crown did not win its case.

Walter de Gray, the first recorded dean, was John's chancellor and leading supporter, for which he was made archdeacon of Totnes and dean of both Probus and St Buryan, but he is unlikely to have been much involved with either except in taking their revenues. He was promoted to be bishop of Worcester in January 1214, and Walter the provost of St Omer replaced him in all three offices, by royal presentation, on the following 7 February.[2] The provost's continental connections suggest that his relationship with Cornwall was no closer than his predecessor's. The next dean, Simon the Clerk (in office by 1223), was probably the nephew of Bishop Simon, who made him archdeacon of Cornwall in about 1216.[3] He too had wider concerns than Probus. In short the office of dean was already regarded not as a post with local duties but as a lucrative piece of patronage, and the next step was to take away its revenues from Probus altogether. In about the spring of 1241 Bishop Brewer of Exeter, the successor of Bishop Simon, granted the church of Probus to augment the stipend of the treasurer of Exeter cathedral and to pay for the cost of lighting the church on major festivals. This grant, once implemented, made the treasurer ex-officio dean of Probus. He retained the dean's right to appoint the five canons, or prebendaries as they were also known, and became responsible for appointing a vicar to care for the parish and maintain its church. The bishop reserved to himself the right to allocate the vicar's stipend.[4]

A document in the cartulary of St Michael's Mount states that in July 1248 Simon, dean of Probus, renounced his claim as dean to the tithes of Treworgan in St Erme in favour of the prior of the Mount in return for a pound of wax each Michaelmas.[5] This suggests that Simon the Clerk was still in office and that Brewer's grant had not yet taken effect, since the treasurer of Exeter in 1248 was William des Molines. It is possible that William, who died in 1251, succeeded Simon as dean, or that William's successor as treasurer, Walter FitzPeter, did so before his death in about 1267, but no-one is recorded as being appointed as dean or holding the office until Henry of Bollegh, early in 1268. He was given custody of the deanery by Bishop Bronescombe on 3 January, and full possession of it nineteen days later.[6] It is not known whether Bollegh was treasurer of Exeter, although this is likely, but his appointment as dean of Probus involved his consent to a change that Bronescombe wished to bring about in the relationship between the church and the treasurer. On 19 January, two days before he was given full possession, Bollegh surrendered the appointment of the prebendaries of Probus to the bishops of Exeter in perpetuity.[7] This surrender seems to have marked the end of the deanery. The treasurer continued to receive the dean's revenues from Probus, but he and his successors were not called deans and appear to have had no further responsibilities in the church and parish, since the bishop also took over the appointment of the vicar of Probus.[8] From 1268 the church was no longer a collegiate institution, jointly held and governed by a dean and canons. Instead it was an appropriated church, much of whose income went to the treasurer of Exeter, and a prebendal or portionary church in which certain other clergy had rights and revenues.

In 1283 the link between Probus and the treasurer was briefly broken. On 17 April of that year Bronescombe's successor, Peter Quinil, gave the church of Probus to endow the provost of Glasney college, together with each prebend (i.e. the rights and revenues of each canon) as it became vacant, and all the revenues except those belonging to the vicar of the parish. The vicar was to receive the altarage (i.e. offerings) of the parish church and of the parochial chapels of Cornelly and Merther, the house and land that belonged to Canon Nicholas of Peyntone when it became vacant, and pasture for sixty sheep and twelve other animals. In return he was to provide two chaplains for the

---

1 *Cal. Pat.* 1216–25, 415. 2 *Rot. Litt. Pat.*, 111.
3 F. Barlow (ed.), *English Episcopal Acta*, vol. XII: *Exeter 1186–1257* (1996), 311.
4 DRO, Chanter XII(ii), Reg. Bothe, f. 44(1); G. Oliver, *Monasticon Dioecesis Exoniensis* (1846), 61. This text is a registered copy, made in 1429, of four earlier charters relating to the treasurership of Exeter Cathedral.
5 P. L. Hull (ed.), *The Cartulary of St. Michael's Mount*, DCRS new ser. 5 (1962), 57.
6 *Reg. Bronescombe*, ed. Hingeston-Randolph, 177; ed. Robinson, II, 29.
7 *Reg. Bronescombe*, ed. Hingeston-Randolph, 255; ed. Robinson, III, 60–1.
8 e.g. *Reg. Grandisson*, III, 1390. In 1451, however, Bishop Lacy collated on the nomination of the treasurer (*Reg. Lacy*, ed. Hingeston-Randolph, I, 366).

parochial chapels and bear the costs of maintaining the church and the chapels, except for the obligations that belonged to the parishioners.¹ Quinil later claimed that he gave Probus to Glasney in ignorance of Brewer's grant, but his action may have arisen in part from his hostility towards the current treasurer of Exeter, John Pycot. Pycot had been elected dean of Exeter cathedral in 1280, but Quinil refused to recognise the election and took a number of measures against Pycot's property in the following years. In 1283 the animosity between the two parties and their supporters helped to bring about the murder of the cathedral precentor, Walter of Lechlade, causing Edward I to visit Exeter in 1285 to supervise the trial of those accused of the crime. Pycot, who was implicated in it, was forced to resign his Exeter benefices and enter a monastery.² This enabled Quinil to appoint a new treasurer and probably caused him to take a more favourable view of the treasurer's rights. He had already collated a prebendary to Probus on 17 March 1285, against the spirit of his grant to Glasney,³ and on 24 February 1288 he arbitrated between the claims of the treasurer and the provost of Glasney, confirming the treasurer's possession of Probus except with regard to the appointment of prebendaries.⁴

The papal taxation of 1291, which generally under-assessed by a half or more, valued the income of the church of Probus at £27 3s. 4d. The treasurer was estimated to receive £12 of this, the five prebendaries sums ranging from £3 6s. 8d. to £1, and the vicar £1 6s. 8d.⁵ Quinil's allocation of resources to the vicar in 1283 seems to have been inadequate, and in 1312 Bishop Stapeldon of Exeter decided that the canons were taking too high a proportion of the parish revenues. He increased the vicar's stipend by supplementing the altarage with the small tithes of the parish (the tithes of everything but grain) and with a pension of 6s. 8d. from the prebend of William of Harpedene. The vicar was confirmed in his possession of a house and land, now defined as that which belonged to the prebend of Martin of Suttone, in return for an annual payment of 10s. to that prebend. He was also required to provide books and ornaments for the church and the chapels, pay procurations (fees) to the archdeacon but not to the bishop, and presumably find the salaries of the two parish chaplains, although the latter duty is not specified.⁶ The mentions of canons' houses in 1283 and 1312 shows that they had once resided, and there is another reference to such a house in 1370.⁷ In the clerical poll-tax lists of 1381 one canon, Benedict Catisby, appears under Probus along with the vicar, but the likelihood is that most prebendaries rarely or never resided there after the 13th century.⁸ Their posts were small favours from the bishop, awarded to augment the resources of clerks or priests who served him or whom he was patronising. Royal appointments were occasionally made when the bishopric was vacant.⁹

The treasurer continued to enjoy the revenues of the manor of Lamprobus for the rest of the Middle Ages, and indeed long afterwards. By 1301 he was holding a three-day fair in Probus, centred on St John Baptist's day (24 June), and in 1321 Treasurer Thomas of Henton secured a royal grant of a weekly market at Probus on Mondays and a grant of two three-day fairs, one based on St George's day (23 April) and the other being the fair of St John Baptist.¹⁰ Each of the prebendaries held a prebend consisting a piece of the church's land, rented to one or more tenants,¹¹ together with a share of the great tithes (of grain) from the parish. The five prebends were known by the names of the canons who held them, not by the names of their property as at St Buryan, because they were not associated with a single piece of land. A document of the mid 15th century explains that the great tithes of Probus were allocated by dividing the parish into fourteen parcels of land, each consisting of one or more farmsteads.¹² The treasurer received all the tithes from eight of these parcels and shared those of five others with one or more of the prebendaries. The prebendaries shared the tithes of these five and of a sixth parcel, one prebendary having shares in six parcels, one in five, and three in three. There were further complications in that some participants had to give parts of their shares to their colleagues. In practice the treasurer and the prebendaries probably leased the collection of their tithes to local 'farmers' who paid a rent with the expectation of making a profit. The vicarage was certainly farmed in this way by the late 15th century, since a petition survives to the bishop of Exeter from

---

1 ECA, D&C 1006; *Reg. Bronescombe*, ed. Hingeston-Randolph, 330–1.

2 On the episode, see F. Rose-Troup, *Exeter Vignettes* (1942), 38–57.

3 *Reg. Bronescombe*, ed. Hingeston-Randolph, 355.

4 DRO, Chanter XII(ii), Reg. Bothe, f. 44(1); Oliver, *Monasticon*, 61.

5 *Reg. Bronescombe*, ed. Hingeston-Randolph, 469.

6 *Reg. Stapeldon*, 343–4. He had previously ordered the revenues of the church to be sequestrated, and accounts sent to him (ibid., 343).

7 *Reg. Brantyngham*, I, 223.

8 TNA, E 179/24/5.

9 e.g. *Cal. Pat.* 1307–13, 415; *Cal. Pat.* 1367–70, 368; *Cal. Pat.* 1377–81, 307.

10 Henderson, 'The Ecclesiastical History of the 109 Parishes of West Cornwall', 415; *Cal. Chart.* 1257–1300, 435.

11 The tenants and rents are recorded in 1548 (Bodleian, Rawl. D 363, ff. 248v–9v).

12 DRO, Chanter XII(ii), Reg. Bothe, f. 44(2) (also in BL, Harley 6600, ff. 2r–3v); Oliver, *Monasticon*, 62–3. The document is not dated, but the prebendaries whom it mentions were in office from 1448 until a few years before 1473. The locations of the prebendaries' tithes can also be reconstructed from the tithe survey of 1843, when they belonged to C. H. T. Hawkins (CRO, TA/194).

William Holcomb who became vicar of Probus in 1478, complaining that his farmer, Peter Bevill, had defrauded him of his rights.[1]

When so much revenue from the parish was permanently alienated to clergy elsewhere, the parishioners could only hope that the consciences of the absentees would move them to give something back. One or two did. In 1436 Roger Bolter, precentor of Exeter cathedral and also a Probus prebendary, told his executors to donate 20s. to the poor of the parish or to the ornaments of the church, and in 1509 Treasurer Thomas Austell left similar directions for £20 to be given to the church in return for prayers.[2] It is possible that the large scale of the late medieval parish church owes something to the clergy, although the Tudor historian Richard Carew believed that the famous early 16th-century tower, the largest in Cornwall, was the work of local people: 'the well disposed inhabitants'.[3] By the time that the tower was built even the post of vicar was sometimes held by senior clergy in the diocese, who must have deputed the work to a chaplain.[4] In 1535, the treasurer received £22 10s. 7d. from tithes and rent of the glebe, and the vicar £13 6s. 8d.[5] The prebendaries' incomes were not reported in 1535, but they were identified by the chantry commissioners in 1546, by which time there were still five prebends, valued at £5 6s. 8d., £4, £3, £3, and £1 6s. 8d.[6] The commissioners of 1548 gave slightly different values: £4 19s. 4d., £4, £3, £3, and £1 10s. Each of these was made up partly of rents of tenants and partly of great tithes, the latter being the larger element; in total the church's revenues produced well over £50 for its various clergy in the mid 16th century. None of the prebendaries was resident in 1548, and no schooling, preaching, or poor relief were provided.[7]

The Crown confiscated the prebends in 1548, and the prebendaries were awarded pensions equal to the stipends they had received. On 21 July 1549 one prebend was purchased as part of a large body of religious possessions by Sir Thomas Pomeroy, and in 1612 James I sold those that remained in Crown hands.[8] The rights and revenues of the bishop and the treasurer, on the other hand, did not undergo change at the Reformation and remained with them down to the 19th century. When the tithes of the parish were surveyed and valued in 1843, the medieval economy of the church was still largely intact, with the possession of some parish tithes by the treasurer, some by the vicar, and some by the impropriator who had acquired the prebends.[9] There are no visible remains of the medieval collegiate foundation, other than the parish church itself.[10]

DEANS OF PROBUS

Walter de Gray	pres. 1206 × 1214; res. c.20 Jan 1214[11]
Walter of St Omer	pres. 7 Feb 1214; possibly vac. c. Dec 1220[12]
Simon the Clerk	inst. by 9 Sept 1223; occurs autumn 1224; apparently still in office in July 1248[13]
Thomas of Hertford	pres. 14 Nov 1223, apparently ineffectively[14]
[William des Molines?]	occurs as treasurer of Exeter cathedral c.1241; died 10 Sept 1251[15]
[Walter FitzPeter?]	occurs as treasurer of Exeter cathedral 1257–1267[16]
Henry of Bollegh	granted custody 3 Jan 1268, coll. 22 Jan 1268, perhaps till he ceased to be treasurer c.25 Dec 1275[17]

From 1268 the revenues of the deanery, but not the title or other rights of the dean, belonged to the treasurers of Exeter cathedral, with the exception of the years between 1283 and 1288.[18]

---

1 ECA, D&C 1469 (undated). The collation of Holcomb as vicar is in DRO, Chanter XII(ii), Reg. Bothe, f. 45r.

2 N. Orme (ed.), *Cornish Wills 1342–1540*, DCRS new ser. 50 (2007), 202, 207.

3 R. Carew, *The Survey of Cornwall* (1602, repr. 2004), f. 140r.

4 i.e. John Fulford, archdeacon of Totnes, in 1500 (*Cal. Papal Regs*, XVII(1), 182), and William Fawell, suffragan bishop of Hippo, from 1537 (ECA, D&C 3688, f. 30r).

5 *Valor Eccl.* (Rec. Com. 1810–34), II, 397.

6 TNA, E 301/15, ff. 56v–57r, printed in L. S. Snell, *Documents towards a History of the Reformation in Cornwall: vol. I, The Chantry Certificates for Cornwall* (c.1953, 44).

7 E 301/9, m. 5; Snell, *Chantry Certificates*, 43, 44–5, with additional material in Bodleian, Rawl. D 363, ff. 248v–9v.

8 *Cal. Pat.* 1549–51, 104; Henderson, 'The Ecclesiastical History of the 109 Parishes of West Cornwall', 414.

9 CRO, TA/194; J. Polsue, *A Complete Parochial History of the County of Cornwall* (1867–72), III, 93.

10 For site information, see CCC, HER 22543.

11 *Rot. Litt. Pat.*, 111; *Cur. Reg.* XI, 407. He had also been archdeacon of Totnes and dean of St Buryan before being elected bishop of Worcester on 20 Jan 1214.

12 *Rot. Litt. Pat.*, 111; *Cur. Reg.* XI, 407. He succeeded to his predecessor's three benefices, and was replaced in another of them, the deanery of St Buryan, in December 1220 (*Rot. Litt. Claus.*, 444). For his career, see above, St Buryan, p. 00.

13 *Cur. Reg.* XI, 407; Hull (ed.), *Cartulary of St. Michael's Mount*, 57.

14 *Cal. Pat.* 1216–25, 415.

15 Barlow (ed.), *English Episcopal Acta*, XII, 306; he is not known to have been dean.

16 Ibid.; he too is not recorded as dean.

17 *Reg. Bronescombe*, ed. Hingeston-Randolph, 177, 187; ed. Robinson, II, 29, 94.

18 For the names of treasurers from 1300, see J. Le Neve, *Fasti Ecclesiae Anglicanae 1300–1541*, vol. IX: *Exeter Diocese*, ed. J. M. Horn (1964), 10–12.

SCILLY

BENEDICTINE PRIORY

The priory of St Nicholas Scilly, located on the island of Tresco, was a cell of the Benedictine abbey of Tavistock (Devon), an abbey founded in the 970s.[1] The linkage of Tavistock with the Isles of Scilly (which were often regarded as one island in the Middle Ages) is first securely attested on 13 September 1114, when King Henry I granted 'all the churches of Scilly with their appurtenances' to the abbey, to be held 'just as well as ever monks or hermits held them in the time of King Edward and Burgald, bishop of Cornwall'.[2] The grant was made to Osbert, abbot of Tavistock, and Turold his monk, and included an order that Turold 'and all the monks of Scilly' should enjoy the king's peace. This points to the existence of a small monastic community by this date, with Turold as its head. The royal grant professed to be granting traditional rights and properties rather than new ones, but the two historical figures whom it mentions did not live at the same time. Buruhwold was not bishop after 1027, while Edward the Confessor was king from 1042 to 1066. There may have been clergy on the Scillies before Turold's time but they are unlikely to have been monks during the 10th or 11th centuries, since communities of such men are not recorded in Cornwall in that period. Henry's charter is in fact the earliest clear reference to a monastery in the county after the Norman Conquest, and Turold's priory was probably a new enterprise founded in or shortly before 1114.

EARLY HISTORY

Further information about Tavistock and its presence on the Scillies comes from two charters of Henry I's son Reginald earl of Cornwall, dated between 1140 and 1175. The first confirmed his father's grant,[3] and the second gave the monks of Scilly all rights of wreck on the islands that they held 'totally', except for whales or whole ships. The islands are specified as *Rentemen* (perhaps Tresco and Bryher), *Nurcho* (perhaps St Martin), St Elide (now St Helen), Sampson, and Tean.[4] This indicates that Tavistock held both temporal and spiritual authority over the northern islands of the Scillonian archipelago. The two southern islands, St Mary (or Ennor) and St Agnes, were in the hands of a lay lord from the 12th century onwards, who held his land as a tenant of the earldom (later the duchy) of Cornwall. Here Tavistock claimed only spiritual rights but these at first caused friction with the lords of St Mary, who seem also to have had claims to lordship over parts of the northern islands. The friction is first mentioned between 1161 and 1184 when Bishop Bartholomew of Exeter received a complaint that Richard of Week, the lay lord of St Mary, had built a chapel there without the abbey's consent in which a priest celebrated divine service although the church and parish of St Mary belonged to Tavistock. The bishop ordered the suspension of the service and the appearance of Richard and the priest before him.[5] Richard also resisted Tavistock's claim to tithes in his fee. Between 1161 and 1177 Bartholomew commanded him to pay tithes from all his possessions in Scilly to the prior and brethren of what was now referred to as St Nicholas of Scilly, especially tithes of rabbits.[6] Eventually Richard made concessions. First he granted his tithes on Scilly, including rabbits, to Tavistock abbey, a grant confirmed by Bartholomew in 1176–7.[7] Later, between 1199 and 1207, he issued two charters, one of which renounced any rights over the possessions of Tavistock abbey in Scilly except for the island of *Nurcho* with its appurtenances, two bescates of land on St Agnes, and three on St Mary,[8] while the other formally granted *Nurcho* and the other excepted properties to the abbey.[9] This seems to have left Tavistock in possession of the temporal lordship of the northern isles of Scilly and the spiritual lordship of the whole island group.

The island of Tresco, where the monastic church was sited, was also known as the island of St Nicholas in medieval times, after the dedication of the church. The church must have existed there by the early 12th century, and it appears to have been substantially

---

1 On the history of the abbey, see H. P. R. Finberg, *Tavistock Abbey*, 2nd edn (1969), and on the medieval history and archaeology of the Isles of Scilly, [A.] C. Thomas, *Exploration of a Drowned Landscape* (1985) and J. Ratcliffe, *The Archaeology of Scilly* (1989).

2 G. Oliver, *Monasticon Dioecesis Exoniensis* (1846), 73, quoting the now lost 'Maynard cartulary'; *Regesta Regum Anglo-Normannorum*, ed. H. W. C. Davis et al. (1913–59), III, 119. Thomas (*Exploration*, 200) proposed a date of *c*.1120, since Archbishop Thurstan of York, consecrated in 1119, was among the witnesses; but the other witnesses would all fit 1114 and Thurstan was elected archbishop in August of that year.

3 H. P. R. Finberg, 'Some Early Tavistock Charters', *EHR* 62 (1947), 359–60.

4 Oliver, *Monasticon*, 74.

5 F. Barlow (ed.), *English Episcopal Acta*, vol. XI: *Exeter 1046–1184* (1996), 120–1.

6 Ibid., 121–2.

7 Ibid., 122.

8 Finberg, 'Some Early Tavistock Charters', 374–5 (no. 52). A bescate was an area of land that could be dug with a spade on one day.

9 Ibid., 374 (no. 51).

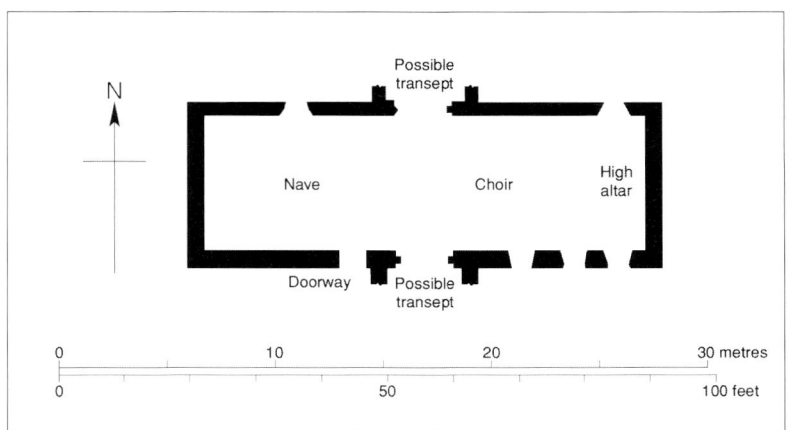

FIG 61. *(right) Scilly Priory, plan.*

FIG 62. *(below) The ruins of the priory of Scilly, as drawn by William Borlase for his* Observations on the Ancient and Present State of the Islands of Scilly *(1756).*

rebuilt at a later date, perhaps in the early 14th century. The antiquary William Borlase, who visited the site in 1756, found ruins consisting of an aisleless choir and nave whose external length was 86 feet (26 metres) with a width of 32 feet (9.6 metres) (Figs. 61–62). A large arch in the centre of the south wall and a corresponding gap in the north wall pointed, he thought, to the presence of transepts, making a cruciform church.[1] Two arches and some walling survive on the site (SV 8945 1424), as do the remains of a font.[2] The church possessed a graveyard, and domestic buildings would have been required to house the monastic community, which consisted of a prior, at least one fellow monk, and presumably some lay staff. The church was a parish church, apparently for the whole of the island group, but there were chapels on all the other major islands, most of which were probably subject to St Nicholas and served by its clergy on an occasional basis.[3] The two most important chapels were those of St Elide on the island now called St Helen, and St Mary on the island of that name. The first contained the shrine of a local saint and was a centre of pilgrimage,[4] while the second,

which lay near the centre of power of the lay lords of Scilly, may have had more status and a chaplain of its own.[5] Benedictine monks did not normally undertake parish duties, and it is possible that in some periods the monks of Scilly employed a chaplain to act for them, but the remoteness of the islands may have drawn the monks into parish work to a greater extent than was common elsewhere. The bishops of Exeter made a number of different arrangements for the hearing of the islanders' confessions, for awarding them penances, and for citing sinners before the Church courts of the diocese. In 1328 Bishop Grandisson commissioned a Dominican friar to do so, in 1330 a chaplain, Richard de Lancastre, and in 1331 the prior of Scilly, Robert Deneys.[6] In 1375 Bishop Brantingham gave similar powers to another prior, Richard Auncell, in both the island of St Mary and that of St Nicholas.[7]

Tavistock's possessions on Scilly must have generated some income from wreck, fishing, and trade. The 13th-century *Orkneyinga Saga* tells how an early 12th-century Viking from Orkney, Svein Asleifarson, went to Ireland with three ships and robbed a merchant

---

1 Penzance, Morrab Library, BOR/11 p. 76, printed in W. Borlase, *Observations on the Ancient and Present State of the Islands of Scilly* (1756), 43–4 and plate IV; C. G. Henderson, 'The Ecclesiastical History of the 109 Parishes of West Cornwall', *JRIC* new ser. 3 (1957–60), 493–4. The internal dimensions were about 6 feet (1.8 metres) less in each case.

2 For site information, see CCC, HER 7324.1.

3 On the chapels of Scilly, see Thomas, *Exploration of a Drowned Landscape*, 173–93.

4 N. Orme, *The Saints of Cornwall* (2000), 111–12; Thomas, *Exploration*, 181–2, 204–7.

5 The terms church and parish are used of it in 1161×1184 (Barlow (ed.), *English Episcopal Acta*, XI, 120–1). Compare also the mention of a cleric in 1363 who held 'the church of Scilly… of small value' (*Cal. Papal Pets.*, I, 434).

6 *Reg. Grandisson*, I, 357, 568, 594.   7 *Reg. Brantyngham*, I, 363.

ship belonging to the monks of Scilly.¹ Equally, the islands lay open to attack and plunder by mariners because of their location near shipping routes between Britain, Ireland, and France, especially the outer islands which were further away from the castle of the lay lord on St Mary. The history of the islands from the 12th century onwards is punctuated by reports and complaints of such depredations. The *Orkneyinga Saga* relates how another Orcadian of that period, Thorbjorn Clerk, 'won a great victory and a massive share of plunder' by attacking the island of St Mary,² and some annals of Tavistock abbey record the decapitation of 112 'pirates' on the island of St Nicholas in 1209.³ It must have taken courage and skill to run the affairs of the priory, which may explain why two 13th-century priors of Scilly, Alan in 1233 and John in 1262, were elected as abbots of Tavistock.⁴

By the end of the 13th century the monks of Tavistock were interested in withdrawing from Scilly if they could do so with advantage. They petitioned Edward I, saying that they had little power to cope with felonious mariners in times of war, and suggested exchanging their lands in Scilly with him for an endowment of similar value, which they estimated at £60 per annum. They pointed out that the islands had anchorage for a thousand ships and were frequented by vessels from France, Normandy, Spain, and Gascony, an indication of how hard it must have been to keep law and order. The king ordered an inquiry into the proposal, but nothing resulted and Tavistock was obliged to retain its responsibilities for a further two and a half centuries.⁵ On one occasion we glimpse the monks of Scilly taking action against an interloper who threatened their rights: in this case the Cornish coroner who visited the islands in 1305 to enquire into homicides, felonies, and a wreck on the island of Tresco. Subsequently, he claimed, a large number of named local people attacked him, imprisoned him, and forced him to pay £5 for his freedom. The documents relating to the affair name the culprits as including John, prior of St Nicholas, Brother John of Yalmeton (perhaps an alias of the prior), Brother John of Exeter, and Oliver of Sullye, chaplain.⁶

THE LATER MIDDLE AGES

The wars between the English and French in the 14th century brought further problems to the monks of Scilly. In 1342 six hundred Welshmen, voyaging to campaign in Brittany, were driven by storms to the islands where they stayed for twenty days, carrying away crops, animals, and goods said to be worth more than £500.⁷ Three years later Tavistock abbey told Edward III that although it was bound to maintain two monks in the islands to pray for the king and his predecessors, monks did not dare to dwell there on account of the war with the French. The king therefore conceded that while the war lasted the abbey might staff the church with two chaplains, provided that these did the duties of the monks.⁸ In 1351 Bishop Grandisson permitted Tavistock to appropriate the tithes of Whitchurch (Devon) on account of misfortunes that the house had suffered, including the fact that pirates had greatly destroyed the Scillies from which part of the monastery's support was derived.⁹ Grandisson's sympathy for the abbey later turned to annoyance when nothing was done to send back monks to the islands after the kings of England and France made peace in 1360. On 20 October 1363 the official in charge of the archbishop of Canterbury's Court of Arches in London summoned the abbot of Tavistock and a chaplain named Stephen Haldu to appear in the court in the following November. It appears from the summons that the abbey had reduced its staffing to a single chaplain and that Grandisson had objected to this, but that he had been unable to bring the abbey to obedience without recourse to the archbishop's court.¹⁰

Grandisson's intervention appears to have succeeded. By October 1367 there was again a prior on the island, who is mentioned in a letter of Edward III stating that the priory was founded by the king's ancestors, belonged to his patronage, and existed to pray for his own and his ancestors' souls. The king observed that the institution had been so destroyed and impoverished by the presence of mariners from various regions that the prior could not sustain his priory and had asked the king to defend him against the evildoers. Edward accordingly extended his protection to the prior, monks, chaplains, servants, and possessions, and ordered his subjects (particularly the constable of the castle of St Mary) to support and defend them.¹¹ Something of a return to normality may be suggested by the grant of two leases of tenements on Tresco, made by the abbot of Tavistock at Michaelmas 1383. The rent in each case was the tiny sum of 12*d*. per annum, payable to the prior, together with the duty of attending his court twice a year.¹² Wreck continued to be a valuable commodity for the priory, and the actions of the monks against the coroner in 1305 are readily explicable in terms of the latter's attempt to seize a wreck on Tresco. In 1410 an inquisition held at

---

1 H. Pálsson and P. Edwards (ed.), *Orkneyinga Saga* (1978), 132.
2 Ibid., 184.
3 Bodleian, Digby 81, f. 88r; H. P. R. Finberg, 'Pirate Gore in Scilly', *DCNQ* 22 (1942–6), 250–1.
4 *Close Rolls* 1231–4, 241; *Close Rolls* 1261–4, 132.
5 TNA, SC 8/75/3720; Finberg, *Tavistock Abbey*, 15.
6 *Cal. Pat.* 1301–7, 350–1, 538; *Cal. Pat.* 1307–13, 40, 85, 258.
7 *Cal. Pat.* 1343–5, 494; TNA, SC 8/34/1680 (a subsequent petition for redress for the damage).
8 Oliver, *Monasticon*, 74; *Cal. Pat.* 1343–5, 480.
9 *Reg. Grandisson*, II, 1107.
10 DRO, Bedford Estates, W1258 M/E31.
11 Oliver, *Monasticon*, 74.
12 W1258 M/E32–3.

Penzance by the king's deputy havener of Cornwall found that the prior of Scilly had held, time out of mind, the right of wreck, jetsam, and flotsam, whether found on sand or stone, on the islands of Sampson, St Nicholas, *Nothowe* (St Martin?), St Elide (St Helen), and Tean.[1]

The restored priory continued to suffer from difficulties. In 1373 Bishop Brantingham of Exeter ordered the recall to Tavistock of the prior, John Duraunte, on account of age and feebleness that left the priory destitute of government in both spiritual and temporal matters. Brantingham took the unusual step of choosing a Tavistock monk as Duraunte's successor, Richard Auncell, and ordered him to be given possession of the cell. A colleague monk was to be sent to live there with him, and the other ministers and parishioners of the priory and the churches belonging to it were to be told to obey him.[2] Auncell must himself have encountered problems, since in 1380 Richard II renewed the protection that his grandfather had granted in 1367, and by 1385 the prior had left Scilly to head the monastery of St Michael's Mount.[3] Successors continued to be appointed in the first half of the 15th century. In 1443 John Denyngton, then prior, was commissioned by Bishop Lacy to correct sins on the islands, with power to excommunicate and absolve,[4] and in 1452 the abbot of Tavistock wrote to the parishioners of the islands informing them that he had appointed Richard Salter from the abbey as prior.[5] It appears as if Salter replaced a monk who had been forcibly removed, since the letter forbade the people of the Scillies to deal with any other monk of the abbey previously appointed.

The wars of the English and French subsided after 1453, but the Scillies remained a lawless place. In 1461 Tavistock abbey and Sir John Colshill, the lay lord of the islands, appealed to the pope for support. On 10 July in that year Pius II issued a papal bull, setting out the grounds of their appeal. Pirates had assaulted, killed, captured, and held to ransom the people of the islands: clergy, laity, fishermen, pilgrims, and shipwrecked mariners. They had plundered and destroyed churches, houses, and other buildings, and taken ecclesiastical goods and produce belonging to the abbey and the lay lord. Ecclesiastical services were being disrupted, including worship, the sacraments, and hospitality to the poor and sick. Other persons, living in cities and castles elsewhere, received the perpetrators of these crimes and the people and goods that they had carried off. The pope forbade such deeds under pain of excommunication, and ordered the publication of his bull by the bishops of Exeter and St Malo – a provision suggesting that the evildoers were identified with men from south-west England and Brittany. As a favour he granted a large indulgence of seven years and seven lents to pilgrims visiting the chapel of St Elide. This chapel, the pope observed, belonged to Tavistock and was governed by its monks, but its buildings, books, and ornaments had much deteriorated. The indulgence was granted to all who gave alms to the chapel, or who visited it at Christmas, Midsummer, or the feast-day of St Elide (8 August).[6]

The papal bull was endorsed by the archbishop of Canterbury on 30 July, with an order to enforce it, and a copy of the bull and endorsement survives among the former archives of Tavistock.[7] When William Worcester the antiquary visited Tavistock in 1478 he learnt that the Scillies lay 'under the *appotasmento* [power or supervision?] of Pope Pius' and referred to the bull, which he seems to have seen since he noted its date and the names of the petitioners.[8] At about the same time he wrote down the names of two of the Scilly islands, St Mary and Tresco, stating that both belonged to Tavistock and recording that the latter was 'uncultivated'.[9] In 1492, when a representative of the archbishop of Canterbury held a visitation of Tavistock abbey, he recorded that 'Nicholas Rewe, monk, residing in the Isles of Scilly, did not appear [at Tavistock], nor could he because of the peril of the sea and the distance and because of other business essential to the house'.[10] Rewe may have been temporarily on his own while awaiting the arrival of a colleague, but we shall presently encounter evidence from the 1530s that also mentions a single monk, and it may well be that the abbey reduced the monastic presence from two monks to one during the second half of the 15th century, technically putting an end to the priory. On 17 September 1501 Tavistock leased 'the isles, churches, and chapels of Scilly, with all their tithings, oblations, fruits, and emoluments, concerning and pertaining there to us by the priory of Scilly'. The lease was granted to William Trewynnard and his son James for a period of seven years at an annual rent of £3 13s. 4d., five dozen puffins, and a seal, the latter two commodities probably being meant to enrich the diet of the abbey. The Trewynnards were to find 'a sufficient curate or curates duly and truly to minister divine service, sacraments, and sacramentals to the inhabitants of the said isles of Scilly' and 'to pay and to bear all manner of charges ordinary and extraordinary concerning the foresaid priory of Scilly'.[11] Monks were no longer primarily responsible for administering the abbey's revenues on the islands.

---

1 W1258 M/E34.
2 *Reg. Brantyngham*, I, 30.
3 *Cal. Pat.* 1377–81, 470; *Cal. Pat.* 1385–9, 62; *Reg. Brantyngham*, I, 94.
4 *Reg. Lacy*, ed. Dunstan, II, 281–2.
5 W1258 M/E35.
6 *Cal. Pap. Regs.*, XI, 603–4.
7 W1258 M/E36.
8 W. Worcester, *Itineraries*, ed. J. H. Harvey (1969), 114–15.
9 Ibid., 24–5.
10 *Reg. Morton, Canterbury*, II, 81.
11 W1258 M/E37.

LAST YEARS

The next evidence about the monastic presence comes from the antiquary John Leland, who travelled through Cornwall in about 1533 and in 1542. Like Worcester he did not visit the islands but heard or read about them. On his first visit he noted that 'In the biggest isle (called St Nicholas Isle) of the Scillies is a little pile or fortress and a parish church that a monk of Tavistock in peace[time] doth serve as a member to Tavistock abbey. There be in that parish about 60 households.' He went on to talk of another island called 'Inisschawe', i.e. Tresco.[1] In 1542 he mentioned St Mary as being five miles in circuit and having a 'meately strong pile' (a moderately strong castle), while Tresco was six miles in circuit and the biggest of the islands. It 'belonged to Tavistock, and there was a poor cell of monks of Tavistock'.[2] Both these accounts regarded Tresco as the largest island although it is smaller than St Mary, which also had the major fortification. It is difficult to be sure whether Leland distinguished the islands accurately, and whether the monk mentioned in the first account was operating at the church on Tresco or had moved to St Mary. His reports confirm the impression, however, that the cell had been reduced to a single monk, who may well have been acting as parish priest of the islands. The second account was written after the dissolution of Tavistock abbey, and what it says about the cell relates to the past as a whole; it does not prove that the cell had existed in recent times.

The income of Tavistock abbey was assessed by the Crown in 1535, but no mention was made of the Scillies, perhaps because their value was so small.[3] The abbey surrendered to the Crown on 3 March 1539, and the last monk must have left the islands by or before that date.[4] Unlike the abbey's Devon lands, most of which passed to John Lord Russell, the Crown retained the properties in Scilly; it was, by this time, already lord of the southern islands by right of the duchy of Cornwall. From the 1540s the Crown made a series of grants of leases of the islands to important lay people, one of which, in favour of Sir Thomas Arundell in 1545, required him to maintain a minister on the islands.[5] In this way the single monk of the last years of the Tavistock era was replaced by a single parish clergyman.

PRIORS OF SCILLY

Turold	occurs 13 Sept 1114[6]
Hugh	occurs 1161 × 1184[7]
Alan	vac. by 8 June 1233[8]
John Chubbe	vac. 1262[9]
John [of Yalmeton?]	occurs 1305[10]
Robert Deneys	occurs 4 Jan 1331[11]
John Duraunte	replaced 28 Sept 1373[12]
Richard Auncell	appointed 28 Sept 1373; occurs 11 Oct 1375; vac. by 7 Dec 1385[13]
John Denyngton	occurs 23 March 1443[14]
Richard Salter	appointed 28 Oct 1452[15]

ST TEATH

PREBENDAL CHURCH

The parish church of St Teath (SX 0643 8059) takes its name from a saint originally known as 'Tedda' or 'Tetha', and is first recorded in about 1190.[16] By the 1260s it supported three clergy: two prebendaries, appointed by the bishop of Exeter from at least 1266, and a vicar. The earliest known vicar was instituted by the bishop in 1259 at the presentation of Bodmin priory, but from 1279 onwards this appointment belonged to the bishop alone.[17] The vicar was responsible for the care of the parish, and occupied a house that stood, until the 19th century, over a mile north of the church and outside the village of St Teath, near the present Vicarage Farm. In 1259 Bishop Bronescombe of Exeter granted him the glebe and all the altarage (small tithes and offerings in church), and freed him from payment of dues to the archdeacon and bishop.[18] Ten years later this allowance was cut down to the profits of the glebe with 2s. worth of altarage, and he became liable to bear all the burdens

---

1 J. Leland, *Itinerary*, ed. L. Toulmin Smith (1907–10), I, 318.
2 Ibid., 190.
3 *Valor Eccl.* (Rec. Com. 1810–34), II, 381–4.
4 *8th Deputy Keeper's Report* (1847), App. II, 44; *L &P Hen. VIII*, XIV(1), p. 172.
5 *L &P Hen. VIII*, XX(1), p. 439.
6 Oliver, *Monasticon*, 73.
7 Barlow (ed.), *English Episcopal Acta*, XI, 120–1.
8 *Close R.* 1231–4, 241.
9 *Close R.* 1261–4, 132.
10 *Cal. Pat.* 1301–7, 350–1, 538.
11 *Reg. Grandisson*, I, 594.
12 *Reg. Brantyngham*, I, 30.
13 Ibid., I, 30, 363; I, 94.
14 *Reg. Lacy*, ed. Dunstan, II, 281–2.
15 W1258 M/35.
16 N. Orme, *The Saints of Cornwall* (2000), 244–5; Bodleian, James 23, p. 165, printed with translation in J. Blair, *The Church in Anglo-Saxon Society* (2005), 522.
17 *Reg. Bronescombe*, ed. Hingeston-Randolph, 178–9; ed. Robinson, I, 30–1; II, 126.
18 *Reg. Bronescombe*, ed. Hingeston-Randolph, 256; ed. Robinson, I, 50–1.

of the church.[1] In 1291 the papal taxation of the English Church estimated the vicar's annual income at 20s. – probably, as usual, a large underestimate.[2] The two prebendaries each held a prebend or endowment, which did not have a geographical name but, as at Crantock and Probus, was called after the man who currently held it: for example 'Luson's' and 'Harman's' in 1548. Each prebendary had an identical stipend, presumably because they shared their assets in common; in 1291 their incomes were valued at £4 each.[3]

The only contemporary explanations of why the church was staffed in this way come from the Reformation period. In 1546 the chantry commissioners of Henry VIII stated that the prebends were founded 'to find two priests in perpetuity to be assistant in the ministry of divine service within the parish church', and two years later similar commissioners acting for Edward VI reported that the prebends had been founded by the predecessors of the bishop of Exeter.[4] When and how the prebends originated is unknown, except that it was before 1266. Bishop William Warelwast had interests in this area in the early 12th century, when he gave the neighbouring church of St Kew to Plympton priory, and the church of St Kew claimed rights of burial and tithe over certain estates in St Teath parish in about the 1190s.[5] The involvement of Bodmin priory in St Teath recalls the fact that its canons were patrons of one of the prebends in the next-door parish of St Endellion and of the parish church of St Minver, further south.[6] Why its patronage passed to the bishop is also unclear. Despite the statement of 1546 that the prebendaries helped to say services in the church, there is no sign that they and the vicar formed a religious community at St Teath, at least after about the mid 13th century. No directions survive requiring the prebendaries to reside there, and the earliest recorded appointments to the prebends, by Bishop Bronescombe, relate to men who spent their careers elsewhere. They included his chaplain, Peter of Gyllefort; his chamberlain, Richard of the Grange; Henry of Cristinstowe, a clerk of the previous bishop, Richard Blund; and two men, Roger Barat and William of Bisimano, whose benefices included prebends at Crediton and Exeter Cathedral.[7] The prebends of St Teath were primarily sources of income with which the bishops of Exeter rewarded their servants or other men in their favour.

The records of the Reformation period are not consistent about the revenues of the church of St Teath. According to the *Valor Ecclesiasticus* of 1535, the rectory was appropriated to Exeter Cathedral – a term normally meaning that the 'great tithes' of grain were appropriated, more accurately in this case by the two prebendaries. However the *Valor* also states that the vicar received the greater tithes and the lesser (those of all other kinds of agricultural produce). It estimated the income of the prebends at £6 10s. each and that of the vicar at £12.[8] When the chantry commissioners of Edward VI investigated the church in 1548 they reported that the prebends consisted of lands and tenements, which the prebendaries had leased for an annual rent of £13 6s. 8d. This time the incomes were estimated at £8 17s. each. The prebendaries were said to be 'never resident' and they were not involved with schooling, preaching, or poor relief.[9] It is possible that the endowments of the prebends included some glebe land, as was so at St Endellion, but they probably consisted chiefly of the corn and grain tithes of the parish, notwithstanding the evidence of the *Valor*. In 1839 the tithe survey of St Teath parish records that the corn and grain tithes were in the hands of a lay impropriator (evidently as a consequence of the Reformation), while the vicar received the other tithes.[10] The crown seized the endowments of the prebends in the spring of 1548, as it did at St Endellion, although prebends that were not associated with a religious community sometimes survived the Reformation as they did at such places as Chulmleigh and Exeter Castle (Devon). The last two prebendaries of St Teath were granted pensions of £6 each.[11] During the reign of Elizabeth I the crown continued to lease the prebends, but in 1583 it granted the properties to Theophilus and Robert Adams. Further grants were made in 1588, 1590, and 1607, without apparent effect, since the prebends were still being leased by the crown between 1618 and 1630.[12] The Chantry Act, on the other hand, did not affect the parish church, the vicarage, or their assets, and the parish church survives.[13] There are no visible remains connected with the prebends or prebendaries.

---

1 *Reg. Bronescombe*, ed. Hingeston-Randolph, 256; ed. Robinson, II, 34.

2 *Reg. Bronescombe*, ed. Hingeston-Randolph, 471.

3 Ibid.

4 TNA, E 301/15, ff. 55v–56r; E 301/9, m. 4; printed in L. S. Snell, *Documents towards a History of the Reformation in Cornwall: vol. I, The Chantry Certificates for Cornwall* (c.1953), 48–9.

5 F. Barlow (ed.), *English Episcopal Acta,* vol. XI: *Exeter 1046–1184* (1996), 24; Bodleian, James 23, p. 165; Blair, *Church in Anglo-Saxon Society*, 522.

6 *Reg. Bronescombe*, ed. Hingeston-Randolph, 171, 175; ed. Robinson, II, 60. In addition, Bodmin had once owned the manor of Trevilley in St Teath (W. M. M. Picken, 'Tremail and Turgoil in Domesday Book', *DCNQ*, 38.8 (1990), 271–2).

7 *Reg. Bronescombe*, ed. Hingeston-Randolph, 178–9; ed. Robinson, II, 19, 44–5, 55, 96, 98.

8 *Valor Eccl.* (Rec. Com. 1810–34), II, 401.

9 E 301/9, m. 4; Snell, *Chantry Certificates*, 49; Bodleian, Rawl. D 363, f. 240v.

10 CRO, TA/219, p. 1. The impropriator held no land in the parish that might be identifiable with the prebends.

11 E 301/10; Snell, *Chantry Certificates*, 49, 49–50.

12 J. Maclean, *The Parochial and Family History of the Deanery of Trigg Minor*, 3 vols. (1873–9), III, 97–8.

13 For site information, see CCC, HER17867.02.

TEMPLE

KNIGHTS TEMPLARS' PROPERTY

Temple in Cornwall takes its name from the members of the Order of the Temple, or Knights Templars, who established themselves in England in 1128, making their headquarters at the Temple outside the western edge of the city of London.[1] By 1185 the order held possessions in Cornwall, which are listed in the inquest into the Templars' properties throughout England made in that year at the time of the appointment of Geoffrey FitzStephen as master of the order's bailiwick of England. The inquest identified them as follows: a piece of land at Fowey Moor 'that returns half a mark [6s. 8d.]'; a virgate at Connerton, in Gwithian, the gift of Richard the Butler, held by Robert Black [*Niger*] for 5s; a messuage at Launceston, the gift of Richard FitzWilliam, held by Walter for 12d.; and 3s. from the mill at Launceston, also the gift of Richard FitzWilliam, paid by the canons of the same town.[2] Richard the Butler occurs in documents between about 1157 and 1164, while Richard FitzWilliam held five knights' fees in Cornwall in 1166.[3] This suggests that the Templars gained their Cornish possessions in or after the middle of the 12th century, and the inquest shows that these were neither extensive nor wealthy; nor is there any evidence to suggest that they grew after 1185. The knights also received an annual grant of one mark [13s. 4d.] from the king's revenues in the county of Cornwall, a charge that was laid by the Crown upon each of the counties of England in or before 1156.[4]

The principal piece of property was the holding on Fowey Moor, or Bodmin Moor as it is nowadays called. This property, eventually known as Temple, lay astride the main road between Bodmin and Launceston, and was probably of a similar size to the parish that later developed from it, containing 843 acres. Privileges granted to the Templars by the popes in the 12th century gave their lands immunity from the power of bishops and local clergy, and their possessions were often exempted from clerical and lay taxation.[5] In due course a chapel was built on the Templars' property (SX 1461 7323), probably during the 12th century, and the property gained the status of a separate parish served by the chapel. The medieval dedication of the chapel is unknown, but it has been named in honour of St Catherine since the late 19th century.[6] The chapel and parish did not necessarily share the immunities of the Templars' lay property, and in the papal taxation of 1291 the chapel was valued at 10s. and taxed at one tenth of that sum.[7] No record mentions any religious house or institution at Temple other than the chapel. The inquest of 1185 lists the Templar possessions in Cornwall after a section dealing with those of the order's house in Bristol, and it is likely that they were administered from that city. The Cornish properties were too poor to have supported an establishment of Templar knights or servants, and although Temple lay in a remote place on a main road, the order did not play a significant role in caring for travellers. Even the location of the chapel, a little way off the highway, does not suggest that the building was sited, like some hospital chapels, to minister to passers by or to solicit their offerings. Despite the many historical works that have inferred the presence of a Templar house at Temple, it is safer to envisage the place merely as a piece of property belonging to the order and named after it.

In 1308 the property of the Templars in England was seized by the Crown, as a result of which the income of the Cornish properties was reckoned (perhaps incompletely) at £2 12s. 7d.[8] The formal dissolution of the order by Pope Clement V followed in 1312, with the proviso that its possessions should be transferred to the Order of St John of Jerusalem, or Hospitallers, whose base in Cornwall was the preceptory of Trebeigh in the parish of St Ive.[9] It took the Hospitallers years to gain control of some of the Templar properties, and others they never recovered, but in 1332 they held the chapel of Temple, probably with the adjoining land, and they acquired the mill rent from Launceston.[10] The Hospitallers normally ran their Cornish properties themselves until 1524, through a preceptor based first at Trebeigh and later at Ansty (Wilts.), and the payment of 'Temple rents' each Michaelmas is

---

1 On the order and its houses, see E. Lord, *The Knights Templars in Britain* (2002).
2 B. A. Lees (ed.), *Records of the Templars in England in the Twelfth Century: The Inquest of 1185*, British Academy, Records of Social and Economic History 9 (1935), 60, 62–3.
3 Ibid., 60.
4 *Pipe R* 1156–8 (Rec. Com. 1844), 3, 6, 8, etc. The payment from Cornwall is first recorded in *Pipe R* 1176 (PRS 26), 9.
5 Lord, *Knights Templars*, 9–10.
6 CRO, TA/220; N. Orme, *English Church Dedications* (1996), 119.
7 *Reg. Bronescombe*, ed. Hingeston-Randolph, 472.
8 C. Perkins, 'The Wealth of the Knights Templars in England and the Disposition of it after the Dissolution', *American Hist. Review* 15 (1910), 253.
9 See the article on Trebeigh that follows.
10 *Reg. Grandisson*, II, 640, 793–4; *Valor Eccl.* (Rec. Com. 1810–34), II, 403.

mentioned in 1505.[1] The chapel and parish continued to exist after 1308, with a somewhat indeterminate status. No clergy were presented to the bishop for institution to the benefice during the Middle Ages, but that was also true of some Cornish churches belonging to monasteries. It is likely that the Templars and Hospitallers both hired chaplains without tenure to serve the chapel. On the other hand we have seen that the chapel was taxed in the papal taxation of 1291, where it was listed in the rural deanery of Trigg Minor, and Bishop Grandisson of Exeter regarded Temple as lying in that deanery under his jurisdiction. He even imposed an interdict upon it for some reason, which he relaxed in 1332 at the request of the Order of St John.[2] In the taxation of 1341, known as the *Inquisitio Nonarum*, Temple was described as a chapel and linked with the neighbouring parish of Blisland, perhaps because it was served by a cleric from that place.[3] Some such arrangement seems to have existed in 1371 when the Hospitallers' representative at Trebeigh petitioned Bishop Brantingham of Exeter to allow a priest named William Libbe, who was serving another church in the vicinity, to celebrate a second mass on Sundays and on one weekday so that he could also minister at Temple, a request that was granted.[4]

Temple remained in the possession of the Hospitallers until the dissolution of their order in England in 1540, but in 1524 they leased all their Cornish property to Sir John Chamond for forty years, receiving a rent instead.[5] After the Dissolution Temple belonged to the Crown (with a brief interval in 1558–9 when it was restored to the Hospitallers), but in practice the property continued to be leased until the late 16th century when it passed with Trebeigh to John Wraye of Trebeigh (d. 1597).[6] After the Reformation the parish of Temple developed a reputation as having an anomalous status, and in 1602 the Cornish historian Richard Carew regarded it as 'a place exempted from the bishop's jurisdiction', where marriages could take place without the formalities required in other parishes.[7] The chapel was served, after 1540, by a succession of curates who appeared at bishops' visitations from about the 1630s but who were not admitted or licensed by the bishops of Exeter until 1744. The chapel building, by the end of the Middle Ages, consisted of a chancel, nave, transept, and western tower, and possessed a font and burial ground. It was rebuilt in 1883.[8]

TREBEIGH

KNIGHTS HOSPITALLERS' PRECEPTORY

The brothers of the Hospital of St John of Jerusalem, or Hospitallers, established their first house in England at Clerkenwell outside London in about 1144. During the second half of the 12th century they acquired possessions throughout England, enabling them to open other houses, known as preceptories or commanderies, including Trebeigh in the parish of St Ive.[9] Their earliest known property in Cornwall was granted to them by Henry (II) de Pomeroy, of the prominent landholding family of that name based at Berry Pomeroy (Devon). This consisted of the advowson of the church of Madron and can be dated between about 1165, when Henry succeeded to the headship of the family, and 1184, the year of the death of Bishop Bartholomew of Exeter who is mentioned in the grant.[10] John Stillingfleet, a brother of the order who compiled a list of the founders of the order in England in 1434, recorded Pomeroy's gift along with the information that 'Reginald de Marisco, knight, gave [the Hospitallers] the advowson of the church of St Cleer in the same county'.[11] Reginald was the son of William, brother of Reginald earl of Cornwall, and

---

1 BL, Cotton Claud. E.vi, ff. 15v–16r.
2 *Reg. Grandisson*, II, 640.
3 *Inquisitio Nonarum* (Rec. Com. 1807), 345.
4 *Reg. Brantyngham*, I, 253.
5 Cotton Claud. E.vi, f. 260r–v.
6 J. Maclean, *The Parochial and Family History of the Deanery of Trigg Minor* (1873–9), III, 178–9.
7 R. Carew, *The Survey of Cornwall* (1602, repr. 2004), f. 227v.
8 For site information, see CCC, HER 1707. The post-Reformation history of Temple is covered by Maclean, *Trigg Minor*, III, 178–82.
9 D. Knowles and R. N. Hadcock, *Medieval Religious Houses: England and Wales* (1971), 298–309. For the history of the order in England, especially in the century before the Reformation, see G. O'Malley, *The Knights Hospitallers of the English Langue,*

1460–1565 (2005). I am grateful to Dr H. Nicholson, Dr O'Malley, and Dr S. Phillips for their generous help and advice in compiling this article and for communicating most of the references to the archives of the National Library of Malta.
10 F. W. Weaver (ed.), *A Cartulary of Buckland Priory*, Somerset Record Soc. 25 (1909), 121, 169–70. For Henry de Pomeroy's dates, see I. J. Sanders, *English Baronies* (1960), 106–7, and for his acquisition of the property, the imperilment of his grant after his rebellion, and the ultimate confirmation of the grant by King John in 1206, J. Carne and L. E. Courtney, 'On the Identification of the *Ridwri* of the Tregothnan Charter', *JRIC* 1.2 (1864–5), 1–5 at 4–5, and *Rot. Litt. Pat.*, 60.
11 London, College of Arms, L 17, f. 154r (a 16th-century transcript), printed in W. Dugdale, *Monasticon Anglicanum* (1817–30), VI(2), 838.

occurs as a witness to charters in the late 12th century.[1] No evidence survives about the donor of the order's other chief possessions in the county, the manor of Trebeigh and its adjoining church of St Ive, but Reginald de Marisco is a possible candidate since both places lay close to St Cleer. A further small piece of property at Tresarrett in St Mabyn parish belonged to the Hospitallers by 1195, and is still commemorated by the name Spittal.[2]

EARLY HISTORY

It is likely that the preceptory was founded in the last decade or two of the 12th century, after these acquisitions. The first mention of its existence occurs in June 1201 in connection with an atrocious crime that came before the king's justices of assize at Launceston. A local jury reported that Brother Simon the Hospitaller and Nicholas, his serving boy, had been discovered slain in their house of Trebeigh, and that Walter the miller, William of Sideham, and William of Rutha were suspected of their death. The first two had fled and were vagabonds; William of Rutha appeared at the assize and claimed benefit of clergy as a clerk and acolyte. He was ordered to be kept in custody. The jurors went on to say that the body of another Hospitaller named Hugh had been found in the stream at Trebeigh on the day after the former murders, and that Geoffrey Sireve and Roger of Rue were suspected of drowning him. Roger, who came from Trebeigh, had fled, while Geoffrey also claimed benefit of clergy as a clerk and acolyte. Two others, Gilbert the chaplain of St Ive and Alice his servant, were suspected of receiving the criminals, and both were arrested. The evidence suggests not merely an affray by passing villains but the involvement of local people including clergy, the motives for which are not clear. More certainly the episode points to the establishment of a fully working preceptory at Trebeigh by about 1200, staffed by two Hospitaller brothers and at least one servant.[3]

The preceptory was sited on the manor of Trebeigh, a little way west of St Ive church and north of the road from Liskeard to Callington (SX 3037 6718). The manor is recorded in the Domesday survey of 1086,[4] and the road had some importance since it provided a route in and out of Cornwall complementing that which led through Bodmin and Launceston. It took travellers to the River Tamar at Gunnislake, which they crossed by water until the early 16th century when Gunnislake bridge was built, before going on to Tavistock in Devon and thence to Exeter. In the early 19th century Trebeigh was approached from the west by a track that left the main road near the River Tiddy, and the tithe map of 1840 shows another track leading eastwards from Trebeigh to St Ive church.[5] It appears therefore to have been possible for passers-by to turn aside to the preceptory without retracing their steps. The purpose of the establishment, like that of other small religious houses, was to maintain worship, the religious life, and hospitality, while supervising the property and affairs of the order in Cornwall. Privileges granted to the Hospitallers by 12th-century popes exempted their lay property from the authority of local bishops and from the payment of tithes and taxes, but this did not extend to the parish churches in their ownership.[6] The early 18th-century Cornish historian William Hals believed that the manor of Trebeigh had been 'a kind of franchise royal, exempted and privileged in some respects against the common law, and within its precincts held pleas of debt and damages... and had its prison and bailiff for the public service, as the hundred courts have'.[7] In 1840 the land around Trebeigh, north of the main road, formed a tithe-free area of 308 acres, which probably represents the barton or home-farm of the preceptory.[8]

In the 12th and 13th centuries grants of property to religious bodies were sometimes disputed by lay people who claimed to have rights to inherit them. In 1239 the advowson of St Cleer was the subject of a suit by Ingelram of Bray and his wife Beatrice, descendants of Reginald de Marisco, but they failed to make good their case and withdrew it in return for being received into the benefits and prayers of the Order of St John.[9] A further attempt to claim the advowson by Michael of Bray in 1311 was defeated when the order produced evidence of the agreement of 1239.[10] In due course the Hospitallers followed other ecclesiastical bodies in seeking to extract revenues from the churches they held. St Cleer was the first to have its great tithes (of grain) appropriated to the order in an arrangement sanctioned by Bishop Quinil of Exeter (1280–1291).[11] At the papal taxation of 1291 the value of this church to the order was stated to be £6 13s. 4d., over and above £2

---

1 P. L. Hull (ed.), *The Cartulary of Launceston Priory*, DCRS new ser. 30 (1987), 158–9, 161.

2 RIC, Henderson 23, p. 42; J. Maclean, *The Parochial and Family History of the Deanery of Trigg Minor* (1873–9), II, 489, 491; below, p. 302. It may have become part of the Hospitallers' property at Temple (Henderson 23, p. 39), but was not tithe-free by the nineteenth century (CRO, TA/132).

3 D. M. Stenton (ed.), *Pleas before the King or his Justices 1198–1202*, vol. II, Selden Soc. 68 (1952), 70–1.

4 C. and F. Thorn (ed.), *Domesday Book*, vol. X: *Cornwall* (1979), sections 3/7, 5/1/20.

5 J. B. Harley and Y. O'Donoghue (ed.), *The Old Series Ordnance Survey Maps of England and Wales*, vol. II (Lympne, 1977), plate 43; CRO, TA/90.

6 J. Delaville Le Roulx (ed.), *Cartulaire général de l'Ordre des hospitaliers de saint-Jean de Jerusalem* (1894–1906), I, 29–30, 101–2, 166–8, 173–5.

7 J. Polsue, *A Complete Parochial History of the County of Cornwall* (1867–72), II, 244.

8 TA/90; TNA, IR 30/6/77.

9 J. H. Rowe (ed.), *Cornwall Feet of Fines* (1914), I, 36.

10 G. J. Turner (ed.), *Year Books of Edward II*, vol. VI, Selden Soc. 26 (1911), 182.

11 Ibid. The bishop's licence for appropriation does not survive.

received by the vicar of the parish.¹ At Madron the Hospitallers drew an annual pension from the rectory by 1291, estimated at £6 13s. 4d., compared with £5 6s. 8d. received by the rector.² In 1309 Bishop Stapledon of Exeter agreed to the appropriation of Madron, by which the order took all the major revenues including the tithes of fish, and the local clergyman became a vicar entitled only to the glebe and altarage (offerings and probably some small tithes). He and his successors were obliged to pay the annual fees called procurations due to the archdeacon, to maintain the church furnishings, windows, and chancel roof, and to accommodate the brethren of the order or their proctor when they visited.³

In 1336 the head of the order in England, the prior of England at Clerkenwell, applied to Bishop Grandisson to vary the terms of the appropriation of Madron. An agreement was concluded on 30 October by which the bishop allowed the Hospitallers to take a portion of the glebe of Madron in order to construct a barn and other necessary buildings, with free ingress and egress, and the vicars of Madron were exonerated from their duty of accommodating the brethren and their proctor.⁴ The third advowson, St Ive, had probably passed to the order along with Trebeigh, which was the principal manor of its parish. It had a long-serving rector during the first half of the 14th century, Bartholomew de Castro (1314–c.1349), who had links with Grandisson and may have been responsible for the refurbishment of the church's chancel that took place at this time in the manner of work at Exeter cathedral (Fig. 19). Early in 1350, a year after the probable date of Castro's death, the Hospitallers approached Grandisson about appropriating St Ive to their use, and he asked the canons of the cathedral to meet him in the chapter house on 5 April to discuss the matter.⁵ It seems that this meeting refused the application, since St Ive remained a rectory for the rest of the Middle Ages.⁶ The order acquired some further pieces of property in Cornwall, however, in about the 1310s or 20s, following the suppression of the Order of Knights Templars by Pope Clement V in 1312. Many of the Templars' possessions were subsequently transferred to the Hospitallers, and these included their estate and church at Temple together with their mill in Launceston.⁷

In 1338 the prior of England, Philip of Thame, drew up a detailed statement of the Hospitallers' income and expenditure in England for the benefit of the grand master of the order, which gives us the fullest account of the Hospitallers' affairs in Cornwall and at Trebeigh in particular.⁸ At this time the order's property in the county constituted 'the bailiwick of Trebeigh' and was administered from that house. The preceptory itself was valued at 16s. 8d. per annum, and a nearby water-mill at 10s. 8d. The house included a garden and dovecote, and we also know of a chapel, probably with a burial ground, although these are not mentioned in the statement. The surrounding estate consisted of 200 acres of arable land and pasture, and 3½ of meadow. Rented land produced 30s. per annum, and small sums of 3d., 9d., and 13s. 4d. resulted from letting the glebes of St Ive, Madron, and St Cleer respectively. The church of Madron returned £32 per annum and St Cleer £18 13s. 4d. Each English preceptory raised money through a *confraria*, which was a voluntary association of contributors. The members probably gave a regular sum each year and received the benefit of the order's prayers and the papal indulgences granted to it.⁹ This collection had formerly generated £21 6s. 8d. per annum in the bailiwick of Trebeigh, but was now worth £18 13s. 4d. – a decline that was reported all over England in varying degrees and explained as the result of heavier taxation caused by the wars with France.¹⁰ The staffing of Trebeigh in 1338 consisted of two sergeants, one of whom was preceptor, together with a chaplain and an unspecified number of servants, two of whom were assigned to the preceptor. Sergeants ranked below knights in the hierarchy of the order, and small houses like Trebeigh were often wholly staffed by such men at this time. Hospitality was offered to visitors. The expenses of the preceptory amounted to £20 10s. 8d. per annum, which was spent on corn, rye, meat, and fish for food; robes and mantles for the brothers; the stipends of the chaplain and servants; and fodder for the horses of the preceptor and the visitors. Altogether the Hospitallers valued their Cornish income at £75 11s. 4d. per annum which, after deducting the expenses of the preceptory, left available a surplus of about £55.

THE LATER MIDDLE AGES

The Hospitallers resembled the orders of friars in being a centralised and international body ruled, in their case, by the grand master based at Rhodes during the 14th and 15th centuries, and by the prior of England at Clerkenwell, assisted from time to time by a chapter of the brethren. Like friars, the brothers of the order were not permanently linked to any house but were sent to serve wherever they were needed, sometimes in England and sometimes abroad, including Rhodes itself. Since Trebeigh was one of the order's lesser

---

1 *Reg. Bronescombe*, ed. Hingeston-Randolph, 468.
2 Ibid., 470.
3 *Reg. Stapeldon*, 336.
4 *Reg. Grandisson*, II, 830–1.   5 Ibid., II, 1088.
6 Grandisson had previously clashed with the Hospitallers over the parish of Temple (ibid., II, 640).
7 Ibid., II, 640, 793–4; *Valor Eccl.* (Rec. Com. 1810–34), II, 403.

8 L. B. Larking (ed.), *The Knights Hospitallers in England*, Camden Soc. 65 (1857), 15–16.
9 Their names are not recorded, but in 1477 the corporation of Launceston paid 2s. 3d. to the 'clerk' of Trebeigh for prayers for the souls of two named men who, perhaps, had left money to the order in return for prayers (CRO, B/LAUS/162).
10 Larking (ed.), *Knights Hospitallers*, 4.

establishments, its preceptors were generally in charge of a house for the first time and would hope to move up the scale to a more valuable property after a few years. By the 15th century they were usually knights, due to the dying out of the lesser grades of sergeants and chaplain-brothers. Nearly all the preceptors and other brothers assigned to Trebeigh must have come from outside Cornwall. Robert of Langeton, the preceptor's colleague in 1338, had previously been stationed in Yorkshire,[1] while Simon of Myneworth, who occurs as a chaplain-brother at Trebeigh in 1351,[2] had been *custos* (keeper) of a small Hospitaller establishment at Harefield (Middx.) in 1338.[3] In 1371 the preceptor, Tilman Nydek, gained the bishop's permission for a priest whom he was employing at Temple to celebrate mass twice on two days every week, presumably because the priest was functioning in another church or chapel.[4] Nydek appears to have been a German, but spent most of his career in England.[5] In 1386 he was confirmed in office (or in a second term of office) by the grand master of the order, and was still in the kingdom in 1410 when he was confirmed as preceptor of the Hospitaller houses at Baddesley (Hants.) and Mayne (Dorset).[6]

In 1371 Pope Gregory XI permitted the order's brothers to hold up to three preceptories together in order to meet the higher costs of running them, and this practice became common in England during the 15th century. The next recorded preceptor after Nydek, John Seyvill (1408–15), held Trebeigh along with Temple Bruer (Lincs.),[7] which may explain why Michael Joce, a chaplain-brother, is mentioned as *custos* of Trebeigh in 1411.[8] He remained as such for at least the next seven years while acting as a penitentiary or confessor in the rural deanery of East, probably deputising for Seyvill and for his successor Roger Inglose. In 1433 Edmund Asshton occurs as preceptor of Trebeigh and of Ansty (Wilts.),[9] and he was succeeded in both places by Robert Botyll in 1439.[10] This pairing then became a permanent union in which Ansty probably served as the preceptor's principal residence.[11] In 1452 Bishop Lacy of Exeter, being asked to report on the Hospitallers' possessions in his diocese, referred to Trebeigh as 'formerly a cell', which suggests that the order had reduced its activities there.[12] The preceptor at Ansty continued to run the estate at Trebeigh and to collect the Cornish revenues as if he lived in the county, but only chaplains are recorded on the site after this time, chaplains who were probably chiefly priests from outside the order serving the chapel there. Two such men are named in the 1450s.[13]

Towards the end of the 15th century registers of the business of the order in England begin to survive, which throw more light on the management of Trebeigh and the Cornish property. In 1495 the Hospitallers granted Walter Trethew, chaplain, custody of the chapel of Trebeigh and a chamber at the end of the chapel, in return for his good service to the order and on condition of celebrating divine service in the chapel in person or by a deputy. He was to receive sufficient fuel for his chamber, an acre of land called *Freren Acre*, and a stipend of £4 13s. 4d.[14] Trethew was rector of St Ive from 1475 until his death in 1520, and evidently held the chaplaincy of Trebeigh in plurality with that post. In 1496 the order granted the next presentation of the church of Madron to Thomas Hobson, gentleman, Nicholas Nynys, citizen and tailor of London, and Peter Bevill of Cornwall, probably in return for money.[15] In 1505 it made a lease of a kind called an *anticipacio* in order to raise money for the preceptor, a device often used for the purpose of financing a journey to Rhodes. These leases were short-term and involved the lessee paying a sum of money at the outset. That of 1505 granted Trebeigh to Bevill for two years, including all its lands, rents, tithes, offerings, and *fraryes* (i.e. the *confraria* collections), excluding woodlands, advowsons of churches, and control of wards, marriages, and bondmen. Bevill paid £90 for the lease and undertook to reimburse the rector of St Ive or his deputy for providing divine service in the chapel, to maintain all houses, walls, and buildings with thatching and daubing, and to take care of hedges and ditches.[16]

Further leases of this kind were made in subsequent years. In 1508 Richard Weston and George Dalison, esquires and relatives of Hospitallers, paid £26 6s. 10¾d. for a grant of both Ansty and Trebeigh to last for one

---

1 TNA, SC 8/194/9686.
2 Also Meneworth (*Cal. Papal. Regs.* III, 448, when granted papal permission to choose a confessor and receive a plenary indulgence at the hour of his death).
3 Larking (ed.), *Knights Hospitallers*, 125.
4 *Reg. Brantyngham*, I, 253.
5 *Cal. Pat.* 1370–4, 4, 8, 188; 1388–92, 205–6. There are places called Niedeck in Alsace and Hannover.
6 Valetta, National Library of Malta, Archives of the Knights (hereafter NLM, Arch.), 323, f. 144v; 336, ff. 137v–138r.
7 NLM, Arch. 334, f. 108r.
8 DRO, Chanter VIII, ff. 115v, 238r.
9 NLM, Arch. 349, f. 62r. A reference of 1434 calls him preceptor of Trebeigh alone (BL, Cotton Nero E.vi, ff. 5v–6v) but this may simply have omitted Ansty.
10 NLM, Arch. 353, f. 141v. Botill was also preceptor of Melchbourne (Beds.), and was elected prior of the order in England in 1440.
11 For a brief history of the Ansty preceptory, see *VCH Wiltshire*, III, 328–9.
12 *Reg. Lacy*, ed. Dunstan, III, 134–5.
13 William Symon, 1452 (*Cal. Pat.* 1452–61, 59); Robert Knollys, 1456 (*Reg. Bourgchier*, 175).
14 BL, Lansdowne 200, f. 24v (pencil foliation).
15 Ibid., f. 33r–v.
16 BL, Cotton Claud. E.vi, ff. 15v–16r (pencil foliation).

year. They were required to maintain chaplains at both houses and hospitality at Ansty.¹ The two preceptories were granted for identical sums to John Babington, preceptor of Dalby and Rothley, and Francis Bell, gentleman, for one year in 1524, and to Antonio Vivaldo, merchant, and Bartholomew Hussey, gentleman, for three years in 1529.² However, on 7 July 1524 (the same day as the grant to Babington and Bell) the order, for the first recorded time in its history, granted a long lease of Trebeigh alone for forty years to John Chamond, knight, of Efford, Cornwall, and John Walshe of Truro, clerk, at an annual rent of £60. This represented a leasehold arrangement similar to that employed by monasteries, and meant that the order took little further part in running the Cornish property. Chamond's and Walshe's grant, like Bevill's, carried the obligation to maintain a chaplain, undertake repairs, and bear costs, and further specified that they should make copies of court rolls at their own expense and send them to the prior of Clerkenwell.³ Further grants of the next presentation to the Hospitallers' churches in Cornwall were made in the case of Madron (1515) to Michael Bray of Cornwall, gentleman; St Ive (1515) to James Cokkar, Thomas Hartyshede, and Thomas Grove; Madron (1526) to John, Richard, and Edward Arundell of Trerice; and St Cleer (1529) to William Mablesteyn and others.⁴ The Hospitallers' own records appear to have been more accurate about the value of their property in Cornwall than assessments made for royal taxation. In 1522 the royal valuation of property known as the 'Military Survey' reported that the Hospitallers' possessions in Cornwall consisted of the rectory of St Cleer, worth £23, the rectory of Madron, worth £18, land in St Ive parish, i.e. Trebeigh, worth £7, and land in Menheniot worth 13s. 4d.⁵ The total of these sums fell well below the leasehold rent, and must therefore have overlooked some assets such as Temple. In the valuation of 1535 the income of the combined preceptory of Ansty and Trebeigh was put at £90 1s. 9½d.⁶ A small payment to Trebeigh by Launceston priory, as rent of the mill in Launceston, occurs separately under the entry for that priory.⁷

SUPPRESSION

The order of St John was dissolved in England by an act of Parliament concluded in May 1540. This transferred its possessions to the Crown, but the preceptors were allowed to occupy their properties until 29 September.⁸ The prior of England and a number of his brethren were granted pensions, of whom Cuthbert Layton, the last preceptor of Ansty and Trebeigh, received one of £60.⁹ At that date Trebeigh and the Hospitallers' other Cornish possessions were still leased to Chamond and Walshe for £60 per annum. A royal audit of their lease, from Michaelmas 1540 to Michaelmas 1541, notes that they had continued to collect the *frary* of Trebeigh, valued at £12 per annum, 'from the devotion of the subjects of the lord king' under indulgences issued by the pope, until Parliament abolished all papal jurisdiction in 1536.¹⁰ In 1551 the king's court of Augmentations granted the reversion of the Chamond-Walshe lease to a royal servant, Robert Gardyner, at a yearly rent of £48 for a period of 21 years from the expiry of the previous lease.¹¹ On 2 April 1558 the order was re-established in England by Mary I and received back some of its former property, including the lordship and manor of the late preceptory of Trebeigh.¹² Some preceptors were appointed (Layton to Newland in Yorkshire),¹³ but the order did not regain Ansty and no one is recorded being put in charge of Trebeigh. In any case the order's revival was brief, since the new prior of England, Sir Thomas Tresham, died on 1 March 1559, and in the following May the first parliament of Elizabeth I passed a statute annexing to the Crown all religious foundations and their property established during Mary's reign, including the order of St John.¹⁴

In December 1573 the Crown granted the reversion of Gardyner's lease to Henry Welbye of Lincolnshire and George Blythe of London, and then in January 1574 to Peter Coryton, esquire.¹⁵ Eventually the possession of the manor of Trebeigh came to Henry Killigrew of Woolstone in Poundstock, and passed by marriage through his daughter Elizabeth to John Wraye, esquire, of Bridestowe (Devon), who made Trebeigh his residence and died there in 1597.¹⁶ The site was later developed as a private house and farm, and there are no substantial visible remains of the preceptory.¹⁷

PRECEPTORS OF TREBEIGH

William of Cosynton	occurs 1281¹⁸
Vincent of Herdwyck	occurs 1338¹⁹

---

1 Ibid., f. 57r.–v.
2 Ibid., f. 238r–v; TNA, LR 2/62, f. 5r–v.
3 Cotton Claud. E.vi, f. 260r–v.
4 Ibid., ff. 152v–3r, 286v–7r; LR 2/62, f. 53r.
5 T. L. Stoate (ed.), *The Cornwall Military Survey 1522* (Almondsbury, 1987), 15, 57, 108, 110. No land in Menheniot was tithe free in the nineteenth century (CRO, TA/144).
6 *Valor Eccl.*, II, 108.
7 Ibid., II, 403.
8 O'Malley, *Knights Hospitallers*, 224.
9 32 Hen. VIII, c. 24; *Statutes of the Realm*, III, 778–80.
10 TNA, SC6/Hen.VIII/7262.
11 *Cal. Pat.* 1572–5, 220.
12 *Cal. Pat.* 1557–8, 317, 321.
13 Ibid., 313, 317.
14 1 Eliz. I, c. 24; *Statutes of the Realm*, IV(1), 397–400; *Cal. S. P. Venetian* 1558–80, 46–7, 79.
15 *Cal. Pat.* 1572–5, 212, 220–1.
16 J. Maclean, *The Parochial and Family History of the Deanery of Trigg Minor* (1873–9), III, 178–9.
17 For site information, see CCC, HER 6849.
18 Weaver (ed.), *Cartulary of Buckland*, 150–1. He was still a brother of the order in 1289 (ibid., 138).
19 Larking (ed.), *Knights Hospitallers*, 16.

Tilman Nydek	occurs 30 Dec 1371; conf. 22 Feb 1386[1]	William Weston, senior	granted 5 April 1470; occurs 17 Feb 1482[9]
John Seyvill	occurs 10 Nov 1408; res. by 3 June 1415[2]	Richard Dalison	prob. granted 25 March 1483 × 24 March 1487; occurs 28 Oct 1493[10]
Michael Joce	occurs 31 Jan 1411, 27 Jan 1418[3]	William Weston, junior	prob. occurs 17 Sept 1498; occurs Nov 1500; vac. 28 Sept 1507[11]
Roger Inglose	granted 3 June 1415; vac. by 16 July 1417[4]		
Robert Dangeas	conf. 16 July 1417[5]	Robert Newport	occurs 17 June 1514; died by 1 Sept 1517[12]

PRECEPTORS OF ANSTY AND TREBEIGH

		John Bothe	granted 1 Sept 1517; vac. 1520 × 1521[13]
Edmund Asshton	occurs 5 July 1433 (Ansty and Trebeigh), 6 July 1434 (Trebeigh); res. by 31 Jan 1439[6]	Edward Hill(s)	prob. granted 1520 × 1521; vac. 26 Aug 1524[14]
		Nicholas Hussey	granted 26 Aug 1524; died 20 Feb 1531[15]
Robert Botyll	granted 31 Jan 1439 (Trebeigh), 5 Feb 1439 (Ansty); died Sept 1468[7]	Cuthbert Layton	granted 25 Feb 1531; till dissolution 1540[16]
Robert Eaglesfield	granted 21 Jan 1469; vac. by 5 April 1470[8]		

TREGONY

AUGUSTINIAN PRIORY

The priory of St James, Tregony, originated as a dependency of the abbey of Sainte-Marie-du-Val, Le Val for short, a house of Augustinian canons situated in the parish of Saint-Omer near Caen, in the department of Calvados (Normandy).[17] The abbey was given property in the early 12th century by Goscelin or Joscelin de Pomeroy (or Pomeray), an important landowner both in Normandy and in the south-west of England, where Berry Pomeroy (Devon) was his principal seat.[18] Grants to the abbey by him, or members of his family, included the churches of Cuby (Cornwall) and Berry Pomeroy, Clyst St George, and other places

---

1 Also Nydegge (*Reg. Brantyngham*, I, 253; NLM, Arch. 323, f. 144v).

2 NLM, Arch. 334, f. 108r; 338, f. 127v. He was also preceptor of Temple Bruer (Lincs.)

3 Designated *custos* or 'keeper', perhaps in the absence of a resident preceptor (DRO, Chanter VIII, ff. 115v, 238r).

4 NLM, Arch. 338, f. 127v; 340, f. 116r–v.

5 NLM, Arch. 340, f. 116r–v. He had been promised Trebeigh on 11 March 1416 at the next round of promotions (NLM, Arch. 340, ff. 116v–117r), which may indicate that he was in dispute with Inglose about the preceptory until his confirmation. In 1425–6 he occurs as preceptor of Ossington (Notts.) (TNA, E 210/11259).

6 NLM, Arch. 349, f. 62r; Cotton Nero E.vi, ff. 5v–6v (cf. NLM, Arch. 351, f. 135r); NLM, Arch. 353, f. 141v.

7 NLM, Arch. 353, f. 141v; 377, f. 143r; J. Stevenson (ed.), *Letters and Papers Illustrative of the Wars of the English in France* (RS, 1861–4), II(2), 791. He was also preceptor of Melchbourne (Beds.), and was elected prior of the order in England in 1440. Consequently Trebeigh was annexed to the office of prior until his death, in effect as a prioral resource or *camera*.

8 NLM, Arch. 377, f. 143r; Arch. 379, ff. 143v–144r. He moved to the Beverley (Yorks.) preceptory in 1470.

9 NLM, Arch. 379, ff. 143v–144r; O'Malley, *Knights Hospitallers*, 358; *Reg. Bourgchier*, 351.

10 The probable date of grant is deduced from a gap in the series of the order's *Libri Bullarum*; BL, Lansdowne 200, f. 28r.

11 NLM, Arch. 384, f. 2v; BL, Lansdowne 200, f. 76v; NML, Arch. 398, f. 117r. He was promoted to Baddesley and Mayne in 1507.

12 NLM, Arch. 403, ff. 163r–v; 404, f. 147r–v; 406, f. 164r–v.

13 NLM, Arch. 406, f. 164r–v; O'Malley, *Knights Hospitallers*, 346. He was also preceptor of Quenington (Gloucs.) throughout his tenure of Ansty and Trebeigh, and continued to hold it after exchanging the latter two houses for Dinmore (Herefs.) after the death of its preceptor, Lancelot Docwra, on 4 May 1520. He died in battle at Rhodes.

14 He followed Bothe at Ansty and Trebeigh; for his replacement, see NLM, Arch. 411, f. 154r; cf. Cotton Claud. E.vi, f. 238r–v. He moved to Shingay (Cambs.) in 1524.

15 NLM, Arch. 411, f. 154v; 54, f. 184v; cf. LR 2/62, f. 5r–v (15 Jan 1529). He died at Malta.

16 NLM, Arch. 414, f. 194v; O'Malley, *Knights Hospitallers*, 351; *L&P Hen. VIII*, VII, p. 620; *Valor Eccl.*, II, 108; *Statutes of the Realm*, III, 778–80.

17 On the history of the abbey, see A. L. Léchaudé d'Anisy, *Les Anciennes abbayes de Normandie* ([1904]), II, 263–72, and C. Beaunier, *Abbayes et prieurés de l'ancienne France*, vol. VII, ed. J. M. Besse (1914), 133.

18 On the family, see I. J. Sanders, *English Baronies* (1960), 106–7.

in Devon.¹ The Pomeroys built a castle at Tregony and established a borough alongside it in the late 11th or 12th centuries.² The borough probably lay at first in the parish of Cuby, but in due course it acquired its own parish church with a diminutive parish covering the borough and a small area on its north side. This church, St James, stood at the western approach to Tregony and outside it, north of the road that traversed the borough; the suggested site is SW 9221 4487.³ In 1841 the field on the north side of the road was called St James Park, and the two fields further north were still glebe land.⁴ The site of the church was a prominent one at the lower end of the town, close to the River Fal which was once navigable to this point, and to the bridge which by 1382 carried the road from Tregony to Truro over the river.⁵

A priory of Augustinian canons was founded in Tregony, staffed by canons from Le Val, at some point during the 12th or early 13th centuries. The date of the foundation is unknown, and the priory does not appear in the list of Cornish monasteries ascribed to Gervase of Canterbury, compiled in about 1200.⁶ It certainly existed by 1231, when the prior of St James of Tregony and two other Cornish clergy were sued by a layman for having given a judgment in a Church court concerning the possession of an advowson.⁷ There seems to be no evidence in documents about the priory's site or buildings. These are often assumed to have lain away from the parish church, and to have stood close to the castle: the conjectured location is SW 9231 4482.⁸ Two records of 1267 indeed talk of the priory and the parish church in separate terms, but this may have been to encompass all their buildings, rights, and properties rather than to indicate that they occupied different locations.⁹ Another document of 1282 refers to a single church of St James in Tregony, at a time when both the priory and parish church still existed,¹⁰ and it is noteworthy that when the priory was closed shortly afterwards, St James was united with Cuby under a single incumbent, as if it had not previously had one of its own. The registers of the bishops of Exeter are also silent about the existence of a rector of St James before the end of the priory. It may be that St James was both priory church and parish church, with the canons organising worship in the chancel and the prior acting as rector of the parish. The site would have suited a priory, being prominent, not far from the castle, and sufficiently spacious for monastic buildings as well as for a parochial churchyard. Similar small houses of Augustinian canons and even Benedictine monks acted as parish churches in other places.¹¹

The Pomeroy family regarded itself as patron of the priory,¹² and the institution was subject to the authority of the bishop of Exeter. On 30 March 1260 two canons of Le Val appeared before Bishop Bronescombe, one being Nicholas de St Remy and the other Geoffrey, requesting authority to administer the abbey's property. The bishop instituted Nicholas to rule the priory, on condition that he kept residence there, and gave Geoffrey charge of the goods of the abbey in Devon.¹³ Four years later, on 27 January 1264, Bronescombe granted Geoffrey d'Eu (*de Algia*), probably the same man, custody of the priory until the following Easter, on condition that he acquired no rights in the place.¹⁴ One might assume that this arrangement was intended to cover a vacancy until Le Val could send a successor, were it not that within a short time the abbey decided to rid itself of its possessions in Cornwall and Devon. On 29 May 1266 Bronescombe gave permission for Le Val to exchange property with the priory of Merton (Surrey), another Augustinian house.¹⁵ A year later, on 14 and 15 July 1267, Merton conveyed to Le Val its dependency in Normandy, the priory of Cahanges (Calvados), and received in return the churches of Cuby, Tregony, and others in Devon and Somerset. It agreed to pay a further annual sum of £8 13*s.* 4*d.* to equalise the value of the exchange.¹⁶ On the following 4 August the proctor of Le Val in the diocese of Exeter, Richard de Ponte,

---

1 A. Heales, *The Records of Merton Priory in the County of Surrey* (1898), 147–8; *Reg. Bronescombe*, ed. Hingeston-Randolph, 253; ed. Robinson, I, 38–9, 56–7; ECA, D&C 2100.

2 On the town, see P. Sheppard, *The Historic Towns of Cornwall* (1980), 27–9.

3 For site information, see CCC, HER 24307.

4 Evidence for the location of St James church in this vicinity is provided by John Leland in 1533 (*Itinerary*, ed. L. Toulmin Smith (1907–10), I, 323); a 1539 map of the south coast of Cornwall (BL, Cotton Aug. I.i.35, 36, 38, 39); CRO, ARD/TER/409 (mentioning glebe land adjacent to St James's churchyard); TNA, E 134/2 William and Mary Mich./21 (deposition of Melchisedech Libbye in 1686: 'St James church was a little above the said Tregony Bridge'); and CRO, TA/ and TM/227/1.

5 C. G. Henderson and H. Coates, *Old Cornish Bridges and Streams* (1928), 86–9.

6 Gervase of Canterbury, *Historical Works*, ed. W. Stubbs, vol. II (RS 1880), 424.

7 *Cur. Reg.* XIV, 358.

8 C. G. Henderson, 'The Ecclesiastical History of the 109 Parishes of West Cornwall', *JRIC* new ser. 2 (1953–6), 136–7; 3 (1957–60), 451–2; P. Sheppard, 'Parochial Check-List of Antiquities: Hundred of Powder, 7, Parish of Cuby', *Cornish Archaeology* 7 (1968), 97; CCR, HER 24309.

9 Heales, *Records of Merton Priory*, 149; ECA, D&C 2099.

10 *Reg. Bronescombe*, ed. Hingeston-Randolph, 379.

11 Compare St Anthony-in-Roseland, Minster, and Scilly, in the present volume.

12 Henderson, 'Ecclesiastical History', 451.

13 *Reg. Bronescombe*, ed. Hingeston-Randolph, 187–8; ed. Robinson, I, 72–5.

14 *Reg. Bronescombe*, ed. Hingeston-Randolph, 274–5; ed. Robinson, II, 6–7.

15 Heales, *Records of Merton Priory*, 149.

16 Ibid., 147–9. On Cahanges, see Beaunier, *Abbayes et Prieurés*, VII, 142.

resigned the priory of Tregony, the parish church, and other properties into Bronescombe's hands for the benefit of Merton priory, reserving for Le Val certain moveable goods of the churches concerned.[1]

At first it was envisaged that Tregony priory would continue in being as a house of canons. In 1278 Bishop Bronescombe wrote to Merton, acknowledging its request that Tregony be placed under the Augustinian rule 'as formerly', and granting Merton the right to send one of its canons at a time to the bishop of Exeter to be instituted as prior of Tregony. The prior was to swear obedience to the bishop, be content with the possessions of Tregony, use them to maintain the priory, and live there with a fellow canon.[2] A prior named William de la Lee is mentioned during the period of Merton's ownership, and a canon called Nicholas of Tregony became prior of Merton in 1292, possibly taking his surname from a period of service in Cornwall.[3] But this arrangement was of short duration; presumably Merton found it too expensive to maintain a dependent house. On 26 April 1282 Bronescombe's successor as bishop, Peter Quinil, issued a document recalling that Merton had acquired the churches of Cuby and St James Tregony (only one church in Tregony being specified) and that Bronescombe had committed their rule to two canons of Merton. Quinil now permitted Merton either to recall the canons to the mother house and to substitute others, or to serve the churches by a vicar presented to the bishop and assigned by him with a suitable stipend.[4] In the event Merton ceased to provide canons and the bishop agreed to new arrangements. The two churches were combined into one benefice, Merton was allowed to appropriate some of the revenues for its own use, and the rest were assigned to a vicar responsible for serving both parishes, which continued to be regarded as distinct entities. On 19 November 1286 Quinil instituted William of St Melan to the churches of Cuby and St James Tregony, the latter being now described as dependent on Cuby and both churches as belonging to the patronage of Merton priory. The document of institution also allocated the revenues of the parishes. Merton received the great tithes (tithes of corn) of Cuby parish, the barns situated there, a piece of land called New Park, the rents of all the priory's tenants in Cuby, and pensions from the churches of St Austell and Lesnewth. The vicar was granted the glebe and the lesser tithes of Cuby, and the glebe and the whole tithes of Tregony. Merton was to repair the chancels, church ornaments, and books in the first instance, and the vicar to do so thereafter.[5]

The priory of Tregony, then, came to an end between 1282 and 1286. No complete record of its properties or revenues has survived, and they are only partially recoverable from the papal taxation records of 1291. These assessed the spiritual revenues of Cuby and St James at £6 6s. 8d. (an assessment undervalued by half or more, as usual), and the pension from Lesnewth at 5s.[6] The taxation does not mention any temporal property of Merton in Cornwall in 1291, so the value of the rents of tenants remains elusive, as does the amount of the pension from St Austell. These unrecorded revenues were probably fairly small. The parish church of St James remained in use until the Reformation.[7] When the antiquary John Leland made his first visit to Cornwall in about 1533, he noted 'an old castle and a parish church of St James standing in a moor by the castle', but by 1602 the church was described as 'long time in decay and unfrequented'.[8] A witness of 1686 stated that it had largely disappeared, but another source refers to parts of the walls as standing in the early 18th century.[9] There are no visible remains today.

PRIORS OF TREGONY

Nicholas de Saint Remy	inst. 30 March 1260[10]
Geoffrey d'Eu (de Algia)	granted custody 27 Jan 1264[11]
Walter de Bello	occurs before 1267 × 1287[12]
William de la Lee	occurs 1267 × 1287[13]

---

1 D&C 2099; G. Oliver, *Additional Supplement to the Monasticon* (1854), 7.

2 *Reg. Bronescombe*, ed. Hingeston-Randolph, 275; ed. Robinson, II, 119–20.

3 Private archive; D. M. Smith and V. C. M. London (ed.), *The Heads of Religious Houses: England and Wales. II. 1216–1377* (2001), 422.

4 *Reg. Bronescombe*, ed. Hingeston-Randolph, 379.

5 Ibid., 379–80.   6 Ibid., 468, 472.

7 E.g. in 1502 Thomas Poyle of Tregony asked to be buried in it and gave money to the store of the church, while Stephen Lelley and Marion made bequests in 1525 (N. Orme (ed.), *Cornish Wills 1348–1540*, DCRS new ser. 50 (2007), 113, 174–5).

8 Leland, *Itinerary*, ed. Toulmin Smith, I, 323; CRO, ARD/TER/409.

9 E 134/2 William and Mary Mich./21 (deposition of Melchisedech Libbye); D. Gilbert, *The Parochial History of Cornwall* (1838), I, 299.

10 *Reg. Bronescombe*, ed. Hingeston-Randolph, 188; ed. Robinson, I, 72–5.

11 *Reg. Bronescombe*, ed. Hingeston-Randolph, 274–5; ed. Robinson, II, 6–7.

12 He preceded William de la Lee (private archive).

13 Private archive.

TRURO

DOMINICAN FRIARY

The Dominican Friars (alternatively Friars Preachers or Black Friars) established their house in Truro by 29 September 1259, when its church was dedicated by Bishop Bronescombe of Exeter.[1] There was a Dominican friary in Exeter by 1232, the only other such site in the diocese, and since church dedication depended on the coming of a bishop, it is possible that the Truro foundation was made a little earlier than 1259. In 1375 Edward III claimed that the house was founded by his ancestors, but a rival claim of the same kind was made in 1462 by Ralph Reskymer, a Cornish esquire of Roskymmer in Mawgan-in-Meneage and Merthen in Constantine.[2] Friars gravitated to towns, because they lived from alms and donations which were more readily available there, and because there was more scope for them to minister to people through preaching and hearing confessions. The reasons for the Dominicans' choice of Truro are unknown. Negatively the Franciscans may already have taken Bodmin and a settlement of friars in Launceston may have been discouraged by Launceston priory. Positively Truro was a seaport and had possessed the status of a borough since the end of the 12th century.[3] It also had good access to central and western Cornwall, enabling the friars to extend their ministry into these parts if they wished, and lay in the area of Cornish speech if they desired to work among its speakers. The friary was located in Kenwyn Street, the name of the suburb of Truro beyond the River Kenwyn, near the main road leading into western Cornwall.[4] The suggested site is SW 8236 4484.

The original friary buildings were restored or extended during the 14th century. In 1354 the Black Prince, duke of Cornwall, ordered the keeper of his park at Restormel to deliver ten oaks to the friars towards the making of their houses, and in the following year he granted them a stretch of his quarry at Pentuan in St Austell, fifty feet long and twelve broad, for the construction of their church and houses.[5] The buildings were large enough for William Courtenay, archbishop of Canterbury, and his retinue to dine and sleep there on 12 and 16 August 1384, during his visitation of Cornwall.[6] By the Reformation the church consisted of a choir with a high altar and a nave with two further altars, one of which was perhaps the Trinity altar mentioned in the 15th century.[7] Dominican churches were often dedicated to St Dominic, the founder of the order, but there is no specific evidence about Truro in this respect. Adjoining the church was a cemetery, which accommodated not only the friars but some lay people, since all the orders of friars were allowed to grant burial to outsiders. In 1328 Bishop Grandisson of Exeter ordered the church and cemetery to be reconciled after their status had been violated, presumably by the spilling of blood.[8]

The friary came to possess a few small pieces of property to supplement its reliance on voluntary gifts. In about 1297 the prior of Truro (the head of the friary) and eight laymen were reported to have acquired a house and toft at Carvedras in Kenwyn parish from Thomas Tresour.[9] In 1375 the friars were given a royal pardon for obtaining two plots of land from Richard Cristofre 100 feet in length and 50 in breadth, which they had enclosed and added to their precinct without permission.[10] In 1462 Ralph Reskymer promised them a close or meadow, a dovecote, and two gardens adjoining the friary, but although Ralph's son William repeated the promise in 1465, he made the proviso that an annuity of 13s. 4d. might be substituted, and the Reskymers appear to have been paying this sum by 1470.[11] By 1480 the prior held a close of land at Truro Vean in St Clement parish from the Arundell family, at a rent of 10s.,[12] and in 1517 Tristram Colen, a wealthy layman of Truro and Kea, bequeathed the friars half of a tin work at Forest near Carn Brea.[13] In 1539 the friary's

---

1 *Reg. Bronescombe*, ed. Hingeston-Randolph, 65; ed. Robinson, I, 44–5.

2 *Cal. Pat.* 1374–7, 163; *Cal. Close* 1461–8, 148–9; Oliver, *Monasticon* (1846), 68. On the Reskymer family, see C. G. Henderson, *A History of the Parish of Constantine in Cornwall*, ed. G. H. Doble (1937), 95–110.

3 C. G. Henderson, 'Records of the Borough of Truro before A.D.1300', *JRIC* 23 (1929–32), 103–36, especially 112–13; M. W. Beresford and H. P. R. Finberg, *English Medieval Boroughs: a handlist* (1973), 82; P. Sheppard, *The Historic Towns of Cornwall* (1980), 23–6.

4 J. Leland, *Itinerary*, ed. L. Toulmin Smith (1907–10), I, 198, 322; the former reference mistakenly attributed the house to the White Friars.

5 *Black Prince's Reg.*, II, 65, 81.

6 Lambeth Palace Library, Reg. Courtenay, f. 115r.

7 *L&P Hen. VIII*, XIII(2), 157.

8 *Reg. Grandisson*, I, 395.

9 Henderson, 'Records of the Borough of Truro', 113.

10 *Cal. Pat.* 1374–7, 163; Oliver, *Monasticon*, 68.

11 *Cal. Close* 1461–8, 148–9, 312; Oliver, *Monasticon*, 68; *Cat. Ancient Deeds*, IV, no 9898 (pp. 474–5).

12 H. S. A. Fox and O. J. Padel (ed.), *The Cornish Lands of the Arundells of Lanherne*, DCRS new ser. 41 (2000), 77.

13 E. H. W. Dunkin, *The Monumental Brasses of Cornwall* (1882), 38.

possessions were said to comprise its site and five tenements, worth £4 1s. 4d. per annum.[1]

As these donations indicate, the friars received support from people of rank, although we must remember that the surviving records favour their contacts with the wealthy and tell us nothing about their links with the poor. The executors of Bishop Bitton of Exeter gave them £7 in 1307–10, and the Black Prince a tun of wine in 1363.[2] Gifts of money to them often occur in Cornish wills during the 15th and early 16th centuries, generally coupled with ones to the Franciscans of Bodmin.[3] William Worcester, who visited the Truro friary in 1478, learnt of seven members of the county gentry who were buried or commemorated in the church. They included Sir John and Lady Matilda Arundell, Sir John and Sir Ralph Beaupré, Sir Ralph [Ranulph?] Blanchminster, Sir Otho Bodrugan, and Ralph Reskymer.[4] Reskymer planned his burial in the friary in 1462 but he died at Bicester (Oxon.) three years later, after which his son undertook to bring his body for reburial to the friary within three years so that it might be interred before the altar of the Holy Trinity.[5] A further request for burial in the friary was made by John Hariwell in 1515, who asked for a marble stone to be placed on his grave.[6] Friars requited the gifts they received with prayers, especially trentals (sets of thirty masses said for souls after death), and requests for such masses at the Truro friary are found in some of the wills already mentioned. Two permanent endowments for prayers are also recorded. The Reskymer benefaction was intended to finance a daily mass at the Trinity altar at about 10.00am, with intercessions for the soul of Ralph and his family. This was the latest time in the morning that mass was usually celebrated, and may have been chosen to attract leisured local people as were similar masses in other towns.[7] In 1526 John Cavell of Penryn arranged for a sum of 10s. to be paid to the friars annually to support a solemn mass for his soul and those of his wives every 10 October.[8]

The Dominicans of Truro, like their counterparts at Bodmin, recruited some of their members locally. Friars of the house ordained in Exeter diocese during the 1310s bore topographical surnames such as Boskennyis, Landege, Landwynnec, Trevenith, Treweleck, and Withiel.[9] At the same time the Dominicans resembled all the major orders of friars in being part of a centralised international organisation. Their English houses were organised into four districts called 'visitations', under which Truro probably belonged to that of London or Oxford.[10] Friars did not necessarily remain in the friary that they joined, so that the Cornish were liable to be sent elsewhere while friars from outside Cornwall came to Truro. Each Dominican friary would have provided education in Latin for young recruits and regular lectures in basic theology lectures for their adult members. More academic studies – logic, philosophy, and advanced theology – were offered to appropriate students at selected houses in England. In 1397 the leadership of the order appointed Master Thomas Truro as lecturer at Truro, a place described as being 'his native convent'.[11] The appointment was probably to lecture in theology. Thomas had been associated with the friary since 1381,[12] and the title 'master' suggests that he had graduated at a university. Another academically distinguished figure of the same period was Benedict Lugans, who occurs as prior of Truro from 1374 to 1389. A probable native of Cornwall, he had been ordained from the Winchester convent of the order in 1350 and was a doctor of theology, probably of Oxford.[13] A similar doctor, David Carnu, resident at Oxford between 1430 and 1448, may also have been a Cornishman and if so, like Lugans, a possible recruit to the order via the Truro friary.[14]

The friary must have possessed books for teaching and study, but only one of these survives: a 14th-century copy of Witelo's treatise on perspective.[15] Friars like the above were often better educated than the parish clergy, and the Truro Dominicans were sometimes employed by the bishops of Exeter to do

---

1 TNA, SC 6/HenVIII/7300.

2 W. H. Hale and H. T. Ellacombe (ed.), *Accounts of the Executors of Richard Bishop of London 1303, and… Thomas Bishop of Exeter 1310*, Camden Soc. new ser. 10 (1874), 28, 30; *Black Prince's Reg.*, II, 201.

3 N. Orme (ed.), *Cornish Wills 1342–1540*, DCRS new ser. 50 (2007), indexed on 285. They include bequests by gentry such as John Dabernon of Calstock, 1368, Nicholas Tremayn of Sydenham Damerel (Devon), 1438, Sir John Treffry of Fowey, 1500, and Peter Bevill of St Allen, 1512.

4 W. Worcester, *Itineraries*, ed. J. H. Harvey (1969), 98–9.

5 *Cal. Close* 1461–8, 148–9, 312.

6 Orme (ed.), *Cornish Wills*, 157.

7 Compare William Langland, *Piers Plowman*, ed. W. W. Skeat, 2 vols (1969), B.V.418–19.

8 *Cat. Ancient Deeds*, V, 422.

9 All known Dominican ordinations are listed in A. B. Emden, *A Survey of Dominicans in England* (Rome, Istituto Storico Domenicano Santa Sabina, Dissertationes Historicae 18, 1967), especially 93–103.

10 D. Knowles and R. N. Hadcock, *Medieval Religious Houses: England and Wales* (1971), 213.

11 T. Kaeppeli (ed.), *Registrum Litterarum fr. Raymundi de Vineis Capuani, Magistri Ordinis 1380–1399*, Monumenta Ordinis Fratrum Praedicatorum Historia 19 (1937), 196. In 1398 a Thomas Trurii (perhaps better read as Truru) is described as a 'master of theology' living in the papal court at Rome (*Cal. Papal Regs.* V, 153).

12 *Reg. Brantyngham*, I, 455–6.

13 His surname is identical with the place-name Loggans in Phillack. For his career, see *BRUO*, III, 2192; *Reg. Brantyngham*, I, 322, 357, 364, 414–15, 440, 447; II, 637, 688.

14 *BRUO*, I, 359 s.n. Carnu (Carne). The surnames Carne, Carnow, and Cornew are found in Cornwall, and Carnu received a bequest from the will of the Cornishman Reginald Mertherderwa (Orme (ed.), *Cornish Wills*, 76).

15 M. R. James, *The Western Manuscripts in the Library of Emmanuel College* (1904), 16.

pastoral tasks in western Cornwall. In 1309 Bishop Stapledon commissioned two of them, Martin of Carogan (modern Crohans?) and Ralph of Tredaeck (modern Tredeague) to hear confessions inside the friary, presumably of outsiders.[1] Bishop Grandisson licensed Richard de Ponte as a confessor in the Isles of Scilly in 1328 and John the prior of Truro as a penitentiary in Cornwall in 1330, while Roger Tyrel of the Truro friary was commissioned in 1355 to act as a penitentiary 'for the merely Cornish [speakers] who do not know English'.[2] Penitentiaries heard the confessions of the clergy and dealt with major sins of the laity. The next bishop, Thomas Brantingham, commissioned Thomas Truro as a confessor once and Benedict Lugans on at least eight occasions,[3] while his successor but two, Edmund Lacy, authorised Thomas Berwyk to hear confessions in 1425 and William Berwyk to do the same and to preach in 1435.[4] In 1474 a Dominican friar, Philip Arundell, was serving as the parish chaplain of Penzance, apparently with a stipend.[5] Some of these men, like Tyrel, must have been fluent in Cornish, a fact that may have assisted in bringing contemporary learning to the Cornish-speaking community.

The orders of friars in England were all dissolved in 1538, and the Truro Dominicans surrendered their house to the king's visitor on 22 September.[6] Eleven friars witnessed the surrender, the only evidence for the size of the community which may have been larger in earlier centuries. The list was headed by John Reskarnon, perhaps the prior but not identified as such, followed by John de Coloribus, the senior friar in academic standing and a man of distinction in the history of the Truro house. John came from the Lille area of north-western France, where he first occurs in 1502 at the Dominican friary in the town, later studying and teaching philosophy and theology there and at Paris. In 1511 he left France without permission, allegedly having committed a serious theft, and went to Oxford where he took the degrees of BD in 1511 and DD in 1522.[7] He became a naturalised Englishman in 1527 and was favourably regarded by the authorities in the late 1520s as someone who might write against Luther and advise on the king's divorce. By the early 1530s he had been seconded to the friary in Truro and became acquainted with the Arundells of Lanherne. A letter survives from him to Sir Thomas Arundell reporting that he had been drafted to the household of the bishop of Lincoln, and asking for help to return to Cornwall.[8] He duly did so since he is recorded as a preacher at Bodmin priory, which granted him an annuity of £4 for his services in 1537.[9] At least three more of the last eleven friars had passed part of their careers outside Cornwall: Thomas Pascaw and Peter Tomkyn, who had been ordained priests at Exeter, and Martin Jeffrey likewise at London.[10]

A survey of English friary buildings made at the time of the Dissolution mentions Truro among those 'with no substance of lead [i.e. as roofing], save only some of them have small gutters'. It was evidently roofed with more humble materials: slate or thatch.[11] An indenture of the friary's moveable property in 1538 tells us that the choir of the church contained a high altar embellished with a 'table' (probably a reredos, carved or painted with religious imagery), a pair of organs, service books of the Dominican 'use' or format, and stalls for the friars – the latter described as 'poor and old'. In the nave there were two old altars and some seating. The 'steeple' (meaning a tower or turret) contained three bells.[12] All the stuff in the vestry (vestments and altar cloths) was 'very poor'. The house had debts to the tune of £16 13s. 4d., and the visitor sold the contents of the vestry to help discharge them. He confiscated silver plate weighing 360 ounces, and found a chest containing documents belonging to various men that had presumably been deposited in the friary for safety.[13] Like friars elsewhere the Truro Dominicans did not receive pensions because they were regarded as having had no property, but all save two (Uryin Blybyn and Thomas Pascaw) received permission to become secular priests and to hold benefices.[14] John de Coloribus, as a former monastic employee, was entitled to have his £4 annuity confirmed by the Crown, but when he arranged for this to be done in 1542, the confirmation document fell into the hands of George Rolles, keeper of the king's records, who drew the pension himself. About five years later John, describing himself as poor and sickly, was obliged to petition the lord chancellor for redress; he was apparently successful, since he is named as receiving the pension in 1555.[15]

The Crown leased the friary in 1541 to Nicholas

---

1 *Reg. Stapeldon*, 395.
2 *Reg. Grandisson*, I, 357, 558; II, 1146.
3 *Reg. Brantyngham*, 322, 357, 364, 414–15, 440, 447, 455–6; II, 637, 688.
4 *Reg. Lacy*, ed. Dunstan, I, 114, 290.
5 TNA, C 85/81/25; Emden, *Survey of Dominicans*, 100.
6 *L&P Hen. VIII*, XIII(2), 157.
7 Biography in *ODNB*; *BRUO*, I, 470; and W. A. Hinnebusch, 'Foreign Dominican Students' in *Oxford Studies Presented to Daniel Callus*, Oxford Hist. Soc. n.s. 16 (1964), 113–14; for his Bodmin employment, above p. 152.
8 *L&P Hen. VIII*, V, 100.

9 TNA, E 315/102, f. 158r.
10 Emden, *Survey of Dominicans*, 103, 167.
11 *L&P Hen. VIII*, XIII(2), 190.
12 The church is conventionally drawn with a four-sided tower on a map of the south coast of Cornwall in 1539 (BL, Cotton Aug. I.i.35, 36, 38, 39).
13 *L&P Hen. VIII*, XIII(2), 157; H. Michell Whitley, 'Inventories of the Cornish Friaries at the Time of their Dissolution', *JRIC* 8 (1883–5), 23–4. Peter Bevill's will of 1512 mentions an indenture of his kept in the friary (Orme (ed.), *Cornish Wills*, 140).
14 D. S. Chambers, *Faculty Office Registers 1534–1549* (1966), 167.
15 C 1/1207/33; BL, Add. 8102, f. 35v.

Randall of Truro for twenty-one years.[1] In 1553 it sold the house and site as part of a large parcel of religious property to two Warwickshire gentlemen, Edward Auglionby of Balsall and Henry Higforde of Solihull.[2] Parts of the church were said to be standing in about 1750, but the site was built over in the 19th century and there are now no visible remains.[3] Excavations in about 1840 found the capital of a column, later presented to Truro Museum, together with stone fragments and human bones.[4] The matrix of the friary seal was discovered in 1842 in the garden of the vicarage of the church of St Nicholas, Sturry (Kent). It showed a seated Christ and bore the legend S[IGILLVM] CONVENT[VS] FRATRV[M] PREDICATOR[VM] DE TRIVERV ('the seal of the convent of the Friars Preachers of Truro').[5]

PRIORS OF TRURO

John	occurs 15 Apr 1330[6]
Benedict Lugans	occurs 15 Feb 1374–22 Nov 1389[7]
Nicholas Mewen	occurs 20 Sept 1419[8]
John Reskarnon	occurs 22 Sept 1538[9]

TYWARDREATH

BENEDICTINE PRIORY

The priory of St Andrew at Tywardreath was founded by Richard fitz Turold or his family in the late 11th or early 12th century.[10] Richard was one of the largest landholders in Cornwall after the Norman Conquest.[11] In the Domesday survey of 1086 he is credited with holding twenty-eight manors in the county as a tenant of the count of Mortain, one as a tenant of the bishop of Exeter, and five in Devon. He also owned a house in Exeter.[12] His Cornish property stretched from Landulph to Kelynack near St Just-in-Penwith, but lay especially in central and north Cornwall (the hundreds of Lesnewth, Powder, Stratton, Trigg, and West). In due course the family built a castle at Cardinham, a middle point among these properties. Richard died between 1103 and 1123, leaving a son, William fitz Richard, who died before 1149 and was succeeded by his son, Robert fitz William, who died *c.*1175. Robert's son Robert, also known as Robert of Cardinan (the original spelling of Cardinham), occurs in records of about 1176–80. He is referred to as Robert II in the following pages, and was the father of a second Robert of Cardinan (Robert III), who is recorded in documents by about 1200 and died in about 1227. Robert III's successor was his (probably second) son Andrew, who lived until about 1253 and had a daughter Isold, who married Thomas de Tracy and later William de Ferrers. During the 1260s and 70s the Cardinan family properties were dispersed, their original centre, Cardinham, being granted to Oliver Dinham, lord of Hartland (Devon), in 1268.[13]

In the 1150s or 60s Robert fitz William issued a charter confirming the donations made by his grandfather Richard and his father William to the monastery of St Sergius and St Bacchus at Angers (France) and to the monastery of Tywardreath, naming various churches and pieces of lay property.[14] Another charter of confirmation, issued for the benefit of Angers by Thomas Becket, archbishop of Canterbury (1162–70), lists the properties that it held or claimed in Cornwall, including the church of Tywardreath which is stated to have been granted by Richard fitz Turold, William his son, and William's son Robert.[15] These two charters open the possibility that Richard fitz Turold

---

1 *L&P Hen. VIII*, XVI, 720.
2 *Cal. Pat.* 1553, 239.
3 For site information, see CCC, HER 18921.
4 E. J. Spry, 'Notes relating to the Dominican Friary, in Kenwyn Street, and to St Mary's Church', *22nd Annual Report of the Royal Institution of Cornwall* (1840), 40–55.
5 A. Way, 'Seal of the Friars Preachers of Truro', *Archaeologia* 31 (1846), 459–60; W. Haslam, 'Description of the Ancient Seal of the Dominican Friars of Truro', *29th Annual Report of the Royal Institution of Cornwall* (1847), 61–2.
6 *Reg. Grandisson*, I, 558.
7 *Reg. Brantyngham*, I, 322; II, 688.
8 *Reg. Chichele*, ed. Jacob, II, 173.
9 Perhaps prior but not described as such (*L&P Hen. VIII*, XIII(2), 157).
10 Previous works on the history of the priory include G. Oliver, *Monasticon Dioecesis Exoniensis* (1846), 33–47; L. Guilloreau, *Prieurés anglais de la dépendance de Saint-Serge d'Angers* (Ligugé, 1909); and O. J. Padel and L. McCann, 'Catalogue of Arundell Deeds: Tywardreath Priory', 2 vols (CRO, typescript), with valuable introductions. The CRO now holds the Arundell deeds (hereafter AR), which include the major surviving collection of Tywardreath deeds and documents (hereafter ART). Some further documents, apparently once part of the collection but not now in it, were printed by Oliver, and ten Tywardreath deeds (some additional, some duplicates) are preserved in the Dinham Cartulary (BL, Add. 34792 (A), ff. 17r–19v).
11 On the family, see I. J. Sanders, *English Baronies* (1963), 110; I. N. Soulsby, 'Richard Fitz Turold, Lord of Penhallam, Cornwall', *Medieval Archaeology* 20 (1976), 146–8; and *ODNB*.
12 C. and F. Thorn (ed.), *Domesday Book*, vol. IX: *Devon* (1985), I, 15/42, 16/115, 30/1–4; C. and F. Thorn (ed.), *Domesday Book*, vol. X: *Cornwall* (1979), 2/5, 5/3.
13 Add. 34792 (A), ff. 3r–v.
14 Oliver, *Monasticon*, 39 (No. VII).
15 Ibid., 41 (No. XIV).

gave Tywardreath church to the abbey of St Sergius, perhaps with other Cornish property, and that St Sergius founded the priory of Tywardreath in Richard's lifetime.[1] The grant would have to be dated after 1086, since the abbey is not mentioned as holding any Cornish land in Domesday Book. On the other hand no charter issued by Richard himself survives in relation to St Sergius or Tywardreath, and no later charter establishes that the priory existed before his death.

The evidence is a little stronger in relation to Richard's son William. He too has left no extant charter granting property to either St Sergius or Tywardreath, but a charter made by his great-grandson Robert III in or after about 1200 confirms a grant allegedly made by William to the monks of Tywardreath of a tithe (tenth share) of the provisions of William's household, excluding luxury items.[2] Such a grant suggests the presence of a community able to use such provisions. A charter witnessed by Robert fitz William, in which Jordan of Otham granted property to the priory in return for burial there with his ancestors, also points to its existence well before the middle of the 12th century.[3] All the earliest surviving charters of Tywardreath, however, were issued by Robert fitz William or during his lifetime. He 'was the first founder' according to the Tudor antiquary John Leland, who visited the monastery in about 1533 and 1542,[4] and the first record of the monastic personnel relates to a prior named Osbert, who was in office by 1149.[5] In short although the foundation of the priory could have taken place at any point between 1086 and 1149, its existence can only be traced for certain from the latter end of this period.

St Mary Vale Other Norman lords who founded or patronised religious houses in Cornwall at Launceston, Minster, and Tregony did so near their castles. Tywardreath does not fit this pattern. Instead a religious link was made between the monastery and the castle through the chapel of St Mary Vale (*de Valle*), which stood in a valley about a mile west of the castle (SX 1054 6754).[6] The reason why the chapel was sited there is unknown, but although the place appears remote, it is only about three miles by paths from Bodmin. St Mary Vale is first mentioned in Becket's charter as a church (*ecclesia*) belonging to St Sergius.[7]

In about 1180 Robert II of Cardinan confirmed its possession of a small tenement at 'Lebiri' and granted another at 'Leslof', both in Cardinham parish.[8] By a further charter, dating from about 1200, he gave the mill of Cardinham and the milling rights of the manor to the church of St Mary and to the monks of Tywardreath.[9] By the early 13th century St Mary was served by a monk from the priory, and between about 1200 and 1225 Robert III added 9s. per annum from his mills at Luxulyan to fund a second monk there, praying for the souls of Robert, his wife, and their family.[10] Shortly afterwards the prior of Tywardreath undertook to maintain both monks and to increase their income by 15s.[11] St Mary Vale seems to have been at its most flourishing while Andrew of Cardinan was lord of Cardinham in the 1230s and 40s. A charter by which Andrew confirmed its property and privileges speaks of a 'prior of the Vale', presumably the senior of the two monks there, and refers to the prior's duty of celebrating one mass each week for the soul of Andrew's father Robert.[12] The monks who served the chapel must have lived in the vicinity, but whether they did so in the Vale or at Cardinham Castle is not known.

After Oliver Dinham acquired the Cardinham property in 1268, the church of the Vale probably declined in importance. His family had wider interests, and the castle was not their principal residence. Between 1268 and 1270 he disposed of his rights of patronage over Tywardreath Priory to Richard, earl of Cornwall and king of the Romans, although he reserved them in respect of the 'chantry of Blessed Mary of the Vale, due by a certain monk of the priory of Tywardreath'.[13] In the papal taxation of 1291 St Mary Vale was described not as a priory but as the 'chapel of the monks of the Vale', and its income was valued at only 10s.[14] The falling size of the community at Tywardreath during the 14th century makes it unlikely that monks (let alone a prior) were stationed there after about the 1370s, at the very latest. By the 15th century St Mary was described merely as an 'oratory' or 'chapel'.[15] It still existed in the latter sense in 1494 when Thomas Cornish, bishop of Tenos, granted it an indulgence of forty days at the request of Thomas Roger, clerk and notary public, who had a devotion to the place.[16]

---

1 The view of D. Knowles and R. N. Hadcock, *Medieval Religious Houses, England and Wales*, 2nd edn (1971), 79.

2 Oliver, *Monasticon*, 39 (No. V). Robert calls William his *atavus*.

3 CRO, Arundell Deeds: Tywardreath Priory (hereafter ART) /1/3, printed in Oliver, *Monasticon*, 41–2 (No. XVII).

4 J. Leland, *Collectanea*, ed. T. Hearne (1774), I, 76; cf. J. Leland, *Itinerary*, ed. L. Toulmin Smith (1907–10), I, 202, 322. Leland miscalled the monks 'Cluniacs' on his first visit.

5 P. L. Hull (ed.), *The Cartulary of Launceston Priory*, DCRS new ser. 30 (1987), 111.

6 For site information, see CCC, HER 2960. St Mary Vale had no connection (as is sometimes suggested) with the Augustinian abbey of Le Val in Normandy, the mother house of Tregony priory (on which see above, p. 278–80).

7 Oliver, *Monasticon*, 41 (No. XIV).

8 ART/1/6; W. M. M. Picken, 'Trezance, Lahays and the Manor of Cardinham', *DCNQ* 26 (1954–5), 203–8 at 205.

9 ART/1/7, printed in Oliver, *Monasticon*, 38–9 (No. IV).

10 ART/1/59.

11 ART/1/60.

12 Add. 34792 (A), ff. 18v–19r.

13 G. Oliver, *Additional Supplement to the Monasticon Dioecesis Exoniensis* (1854), 5 (No. III).

14 *Reg. Bronescombe*, ed. Hingeston-Randolph, 468.

15 ART/5/8, 6/7.

16 ART/5/8. Cornish was a suffragan bishop in Exeter diocese.

EARLY HISTORY AND ENDOWMENTS

The choice of Tywardreath as the site of the Cardinan family's monastery reflected the fact that the manor had been in the family's possession since at least 1086.[1] Since the priory was also given the churches and tithes of Fowey, Lanlivery, and Tywardreath, the location was an appropriate one, which offered the monks resources close at hand. Tywardreath was not an ancient Cornish church site dedicated to a Brittonic saint, unless such a site and saint were obliterated by the monastic foundation. The monastery and the parish church did not share a single building as was the case at Minster and probably Tregony, but were separate structures a short distance apart.[2] Both were dedicated to St Andrew, and the monastery also to St Benedict. Its site lay off main highways, although it was connected by lanes to the roads from Lostwithiel to Fowey and to St Austell. On the other hand it was near the sea, reflected in the name Tywardreath, which means 'the house on the strand'. The priory and its village stood only a short distance from the estuary of the Luxulyan River, which was a small landing place, and they were not far from the port of Fowey. This maritime situation left the priory open to attacks from ships, and in 1338 (during the Hundred Years War) the bishop of Exeter permitted the monks to withdraw to a safer place because of assaults by pirates.[3] In the 1510s the prior complained to the pope of the vulnerability of his house to pirates and men of war.[4]

The priory was endowed with temporal and religious property (Fig. 63). In the first of these categories Robert fitz William's confirmation charter included the manors of Trenant in Fowey, Trevennen in Goran, and numerous lesser pieces of land.[5] During the 12th and 13th centuries the priory received further small grants of property from the Cardinan family and others.[6] Manorial court rolls, rentals, and leases reveal that the priory organised its lands as eight manors for administrative purposes.[7] Two of these, St Austell and Fowey, consisted of properties that were concentrated in the two parishes concerned. Fentrigan in Warbstow included scattered lands in the north-east Cornish parishes of Altarnun, Davidstow, Lesnewth, Otterham, Treneglos, Warbstow, Week St Mary, and Whitstone. Gready in Lanlivery gathered possessions of the priory in St Austell, Cardinham, Lanivet, Lanlivery, and Luxulyan, while Porthia (the modern St Ives) encompassed those in St Anthony-in-Meneage, Gulval, St Ives, Lelant, Madron, Manaccan, Towednack, Zennor, and possibly Ludgvan. Trenant in Fowey incorporated some tenements in Tywardreath, and Trevennen in Goran took in properties in St Erme, Goran, St Michael Caerhays, and Probus. Finally Tywardreath Prior comprised the holdings in the priory's home parish along with ones in St Austell, St Endellion, St Enoder, Golant, Lanlivery, St Martin-by-Looe, and Menheniot. The monastery owned only part of the land in Tywardreath, the rest of which lay in other hands. In 1839 the tithe survey reported upwards of 267 acres in the parish of Tywardreath as being free of tithe. They included the land of the farm later known as Newhouse, between the roads leading south and west of the village, as well as holdings on Bishop's Down and at Caruggat in the far north of the parish. These areas probably represent the 'home farm' worked directly by the priory's servants up to the Reformation.[8]

The priory's churches are listed in Robert fitz William's confirmation charter as St Austell, Fowey, Lanlivery (with the chapel of 'Boswithgy', i.e. Luxulyan), Lelant, Treneglos, Tywardreath, and Zennor. Lanlivery is stated to have been given by Baldwin fitz Turstan and Zennor by Ralph de Sechville.[9] Other charters of Robert granted the churches of St Austell and Treneglos, apparently as his own gifts.[10] Thomas Becket's confirmation (dated between 1162 and 1170) mentions a somewhat different list of churches: St Anthony (-in-Meneage), Fowey, Lanlivery (with *Boswithgy*), Lelant, St Mary Vale, 'St Stephen' (-in-Brannel?), and Week St Mary.[11] In the late 12th or early 13th century William Peverel granted the church of St Breward.[12] The monastery did not manage to gain or keep hold of all these churches, and lost St Breward, St Stephen, Week St Mary, and Zennor at an early date. Lelant was conveyed to Bishop Bronescombe of Exeter between 1261 and 1272.[13] In 1281 Archbishop Pecham of Canterbury confirmed the monastery's possession of St Anthony-in-Meneage, St Austell with the chapel of St Blazey (also known as Landreath), Fowey, Lanlivery with the chapels of Lostwithiel and Luxulyan, Treneglos with the chapel of Warbstow, and Tywardreath with the chapel of St Samson at Golant.[14] These six parishes remained in the

---

1 Thorn (ed.), *Domesday Book: Cornwall*, 5/8.

2 Either because the parish church preceded the founding of the priory, or from a wish to keep the priory secluded. Population can hardly have been an issue, as it was at Bodmin and Launceston.

3 *Reg. Grandisson*, II, 870–1.

4 ART/4/10.

5 Oliver, *Monasticon*, 39 (No. VII).

6 For the charters relating to the priory's possessions, see above, p. 284 note 10.

7 Padel and McCann, 'Catalogue of Arundell Deeds: Tywardreath Priory', vol. I.

8 CRO, TA/242, pp. 18–19.

9 Oliver, *Monasticon*, 39 (No. VII). Oddly, St Austell is not mentioned in two later twelfth-century charters of Tywardreath's possessions (ibid., 37–8 (No. 1) and 41 (No. XIV), so its acquisition by the priory may have been delayed or interrupted.

10 ART/1/57; Oliver, *Monasticon*, 40 (No. XI), 40–1 (No. XIII).

11 Oliver, *Monasticon*, 41 (No. XIV). On Week St Mary, see also Oliver, *Additional Supplement*, 4 (No. I).

12 Oliver, *Monasticon*, 42 (No. XVIII).

13 *Reg. Bronescombe*, ed. Hingeston-Randolph, 60–2, 150; ed. Robinson, II, 58, 99.

14 Oliver, *Monasticon*, 43 (No. XXI).

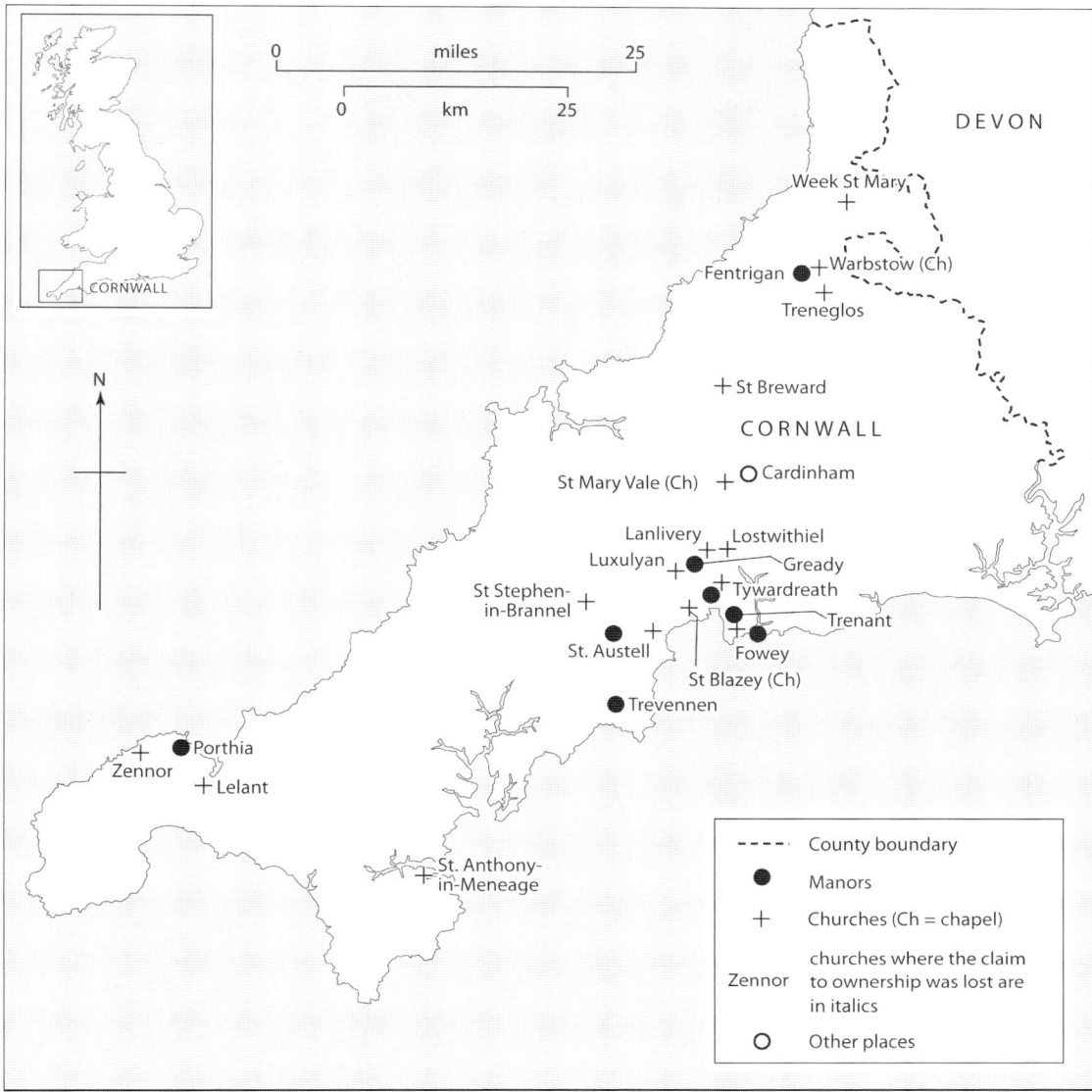

FIG 63. *The property of Tywardreath Priory.*

priory's patronage down to the Reformation, all being 'appropriated' so that the monastery received the 'great tithes' of grain while the lesser tithes went to the vicars who served the parishes. In about 1200 Gervase of Canterbury compiled a gazetteer of religious houses in England in which he listed a house of St Anthony in Cornwall, staffed by Benedictine monks subject to Angers.[1] Taken literally this would indicate that Angers or Tywardreath maintained a cell of monks at St Anthony-in-Meneage, but although Tywardreath owned the church and some lay property in the latter parish, there is no evidence for such a cell. The reference may reflect confusion with the cell of Augustinian canons at St Anthony-in-Roseland.[2]

Tywardreath's property gave it a commanding position in the region between St Austell, Fowey, and Lostwithiel, based not only on rural manors and churches but on the town and port of Fowey, where the prior held the rights over public affairs known as the assize of bread and ale and the view of frankpledge.[3] In the early 13th century Prior Theobald granted a charter recognising Fowey as a borough and granting privileges to its burgesses, including the rights to bequeath their tenements to their heirs, to have their children married freely, and to be exempt from tolls. If the priory decided to institute an office of provost, the burgesses could elect him. Judicial power, however, remained in the hands of the priory and its bailiff.[4] In 1316 Tywardreath secured from the king a grant of a weekly market in the town and two yearly fairs of three days,[5] but the

1 Gervase of Canterbury, *Historical Works*, ed. W. Stubbs, vol. II (RS 1880), 424.
2 Above, p. 137.
3 *Placita de Quo Warranto* (Rec. Com. 1818), 109.
4 Oliver, *Monasticon*, 40 (No. XII).
5 *Cal. Chart.* 1300–26, 306.

townspeople had no significant rights of self-government, and did not send representatives to Parliament, until after the Reformation. The monastery also benefited from the diffusion of its property beyond its neighbourhood, especially in Goran, St Ives, and north-east Cornwall. This balanced its relatively peripheral location away from major roads, and helped it to make links with important people over much of the county. These links are reflected in the wide range of families that appear in the priory's obituary list as benefactors or as members of its confraternity.[1]

The earliest evidence about Tywardreath's income is that of the papal taxation of 1291 which, as has been noted elsewhere, fell short of true values by a half or more. This assessed the total annual revenue as £73 9s. 4d., of which the majority (£42 2s.) was attributed to the priory's churches. The latter, in descending order of value (chiefly from tithes), consisted of St Austell at £10 13s. 4d., Lanlivery £9 11s. 8d., Treneglos £7, Tywardreath £5 6s. 8d., St Anthony-in-Meneage £4 13s. 4d., Fowey £4, and St Mary Vale 10s. There was a pension from the church of Lesnewth worth 5s. and tithes from property in Tresmeer worth 2s. The temporal lands, totalling £31 7s. 4d., were led by Porthia (£9 13s. 6d.), followed by Trenant (£7 12s. 8½d.), Treneglos (£5 19s. 6d.), Tywardreath (£4 15s. 4d.), and Trevennen (£3 6s. 4½d.). Tywardreath's values, both temporal and ecclesiastical, may omit certain revenues that supported the monastic community.[2] These figures suggest that the priory ranked about fourth among the Cornish religious houses in terms of wealth: lower than Launceston, Bodmin, and St Germans, and roughly equal with Glasney.

INSTITUTIONAL LIFE AND BUILDINGS

The priory was subject to the authority of its mother house until the outbreak of the Hundred Years War in the early 14th century. Up to that time the priors were chosen by the abbot and monks of St Sergius, and all are likely to have been French, as are the monks. Monks from the priory with French surnames were ordained in Exeter diocese between 1311 and 1317, and others are mentioned in 1331 as having been sent from France.[3] Men with English names are not recorded until the 1370s.[4] The prior and monks, however, had power to administer their property and affairs, and by 1328 they possessed their own seal for authenticating documents.[5] Tywardreath also lay in the diocese of Exeter, whose bishops instituted each new prior to office and received from him an oath of obedience. In 1263 Bishop Bronescombe stipulated that priors should not be removed without his consent, and subsequent bishops insisted that they should ask for permission to be absent from the priory, even to visit Angers.[6] A third important overlord was the patron who represented the founder. Until the second half of the 13th century this was the head of the Cardinan family, but soon after Oliver Dinham acquired the Cardinham property from Isold in 1268, he disposed of his rights of patronage over Tywardreath priory to Richard, earl of Cornwall.[7] In 1270 Prior Roger de Fontibus was instituted as prior of Tywardreath on the presentation both of St Sergius and of Earl Richard.[8] Thereafter the patron of the priory was the earl, later the duke, of Cornwall, and the king when the duchy was vacant or when control of the priory was assumed by the Crown in times of war with France.[9]

The priory and its associated buildings lay to the south of the present parish churchyard on what was later the site of Newhouse Farm (SX 0840 5410).[10] Amateur excavations of about 1822 suggested that the church had a semi-circular east end, and measured 80 feet (24.1 metres) long by 50 feet (15.1 metres) wide. It is not clear whether this represents all or part of the church. The building stone was said to include porphyry from Pentewan and hornblende from Duporth (both nearby places), and the floor to have been paved with beach pebbles; there was also some tiling.[11] Carved stones and a pillar base from the site are preserved at the parish church. The core of the monastic church, as elsewhere in Cornwall, consisted of a choir and a nave, divided by a screen surmounted by a crucifix. A document of 1444 refers to an altar below the crucifix in the nave of the church, very likely against and in the middle of the screen.[12] Leland states that Robert fitz William was buried 'before the crucifix' in 'the west part of the church', signifying the east end of the nave – a place of honour in medieval churches,

---

1 Below, p. 292.

2 *Reg. Bronescombe*, ed. Hingeston-Randolph, 468–9, 472, 479.

3 *Reg. Stapeldon*, 478, 481, 492, 502, 513; *Reg. Grandisson*, II, 695–6.

4 Below, p. 290.

5 Below, p. 289.

6 *Reg. Bronescombe*, ed. Hingeston-Randolph, 277–8; ed. Robinson, II, 1. Permissions for the prior to be absent survive in *Reg. Stapeldon*, 395, and *Reg. Stafford*, 359.

7 G. Oliver, *Additional Supplement to the Monasticon Dioecesis Exoniensis* (1854), 5 (No. III).

8 *Reg. Bronescombe*, ed. Hingeston-Randolph, 188; ed. Robinson, II, 41.

9 P. L. Hull (ed.), *The Caption of Seisin of the Duchy of Cornwall (1337)*, DCRS new ser. 17 (1971), 140.

10 For site information, see CCC, HER 20625, and P. A. Sheppard, 'Checklist of Antiquities: 17, Parish of Tywardreath', *Cornish Archaeology* 17 (1978), 126–8.

11 J. R., 'Priory of Tywardreath', *The Gentleman's Magazine* 92/2 (1822), 602; J. Polsue, *A Complete Parochial History of the County of Cornwall* (1867–72), IV, 276–7. More exact measurements are needed. For tiles, see E. S. Eames, *catalogue of Medieval Lead-Glazed Earthenware in the... British Museum* (1980), I, nos. 1351, 1361.

12 Oliver, *Monasticon*, 44 (No. XXIII). Launceston priory had a similar nave altar.

although less honourable than the choir.¹ There was a Lady Chapel by 1522, when the monks appointed a clerk to look after it.² This chapel may have been housed in a transept off the nave, as has been conjectured at St Germans.³ The church contained at least one other important grave besides Robert fitz William's: that of Sir Henry Champernown in 1329.⁴

In 1333 it was said that the number of monks ought to be seven, a figure that is likely to go back to the 12th or 13th centuries.⁵ Later, as we shall see, it was not always sustained. The community's domestic and ancillary buildings included a cloister, chapter-house, refectory, dormitory, prior's chamber, guest hall, kitchen, and stable.⁶ By 1507 there was a 'great chamber', presumably that of the prior, and a former prior was allowed to build a new chamber and parlour for his use next to it.⁷ In 1339 the guest hall (*aula hospitium*) was said to have suffered destruction, causing the bishop to license the prior, monks, and their guests to eat meat in any room of the priory other than the church.⁸ This hall was later restored and embellished in 1504 with a seven-light window of Pentewan stone.⁹ Other people lived on the premises outside the cloister area. In 1261 the vicar of Tywardreath was assigned a chamber with the food and drink of a monk, and his successor still resided there in 1390.¹⁰ The monastery employed servants of various ranks. One man retained in 1487 was granted the privileges of other gentlemen in the household, and allowed a servant on a par with the grooms.¹¹ The chapel clerk appointed in 1522 was allocated his own dwelling, 'the shelled corner house', adjoining the monastery garden.¹² There were also some pensioners. In 1520 the monks contracted with William Higman, merchant, that he should receive a chamber, food, drink, a gown, fuel, and pasture for his horse in return for bequeathing all his goods to the priory.¹³ From time to time the king sent former members of his household to be supported, as he did to other Cornish monasteries. The earliest known of them, Walter Bray, died in 1376, and a series of others came, one at a time, until the monastery was dissolved in 1536.¹⁴

THE HUNDRED YEARS WAR

The history of the priory in the 12th and 13th centuries is confined to its acquisitions of property and to the names of its priors. At the end of the 13th, with the outbreak of the Hundred Years War between the English and French, it became caught up in politics like other 'alien' daughter-houses of French abbeys. From time to time, when there was war with France, the kings from Edward I to Henry IV took the priory into their hands, sequestrating its goods and revenues except for those required to support the monks. During these periods, 1295–1303, 1324–7, 1337–61, 1369–99, and from 1402 onwards, the Crown also appointed the priors (except in 1333) and presented clergy to the priory's parish churches.¹⁵ The sequestrated revenues were leased to Englishmen, and the Crown granted pensions out of them on at least two occasions.¹⁶ In 1324 royal officials compiled inventories of Tywardreath's grain and animals,¹⁷ and in 1337 a fuller list was made of its income and possessions. The latter estimated their total value at £266 6s. 10½d., including the tithes of the priory's churches (£119 6s. 8d.), rents from temporal property (£68 0s. 3¼d.), moveable goods in the priory (£30 6s.), pensions from churches (£24 13s. 4d.), goods at Trenant (£16 18s. 2d.), and goods at Trevennen (£7 2s. 4d.). Particular items included two chalices, vestments, ornaments, and books in the church; a few silver cups and spoons and some maple-wood bowls; three beds in the prior's chamber and six in the monks' dormitory; and kitchen equipment. There were three horses in the stable, and oxen and pigs on the monastery farm.¹⁸

The royal interventions weakened the priory's economy and its links with France. John Grandisson made interventions with a view to improving matters. In 1328 he ordered the priory's goods and seal to be sequestrated for a time, until the house's finances were in better order.¹⁹ Two years later he ordered an enquiry into the consumption of goods by certain monks through dissolute living, and by 1331 he had appointed William de Bouges, the prior of Minster, as coadjutor to the aged Prior Philip of Tywardreath.²⁰ Philip died in

---

1 Leland, *Collectanea*, ed. Hearne, I, 76; idem, *Itinerary*, ed. Toulmin Smith, I, 202.

2 TNA, E 315/100, f. 233r; N. Orme, 'Music and Teaching at Tywardreath Priory, 1522–1536', *DCNQ* 36.8 (1990), 277–80.

3 Above, p. 188. A semicircular east end, if correct, would rule out a chapel east of the choir.

4 *Reg. Grandisson*, I, 524.

5 Ibid., II, 695.

6 For references to these rooms, see TNA, E 106/9/30; *Cal. Pat.* 1399–1401, 281; ART/4/4, /8; and Oliver, *Monasticon*, 45 (No. XXIV).

7 ART/4/8.

8 *Reg. Grandisson*, II, 899.

9 Oliver, *Monasticon*, 35, without mentioning the source.

10 *Reg. Bronescombe*, ed. Hingeston-Randolph, 188; ed. Robinson, 125; *Reg. Brantyngham*, II, 702.

11 ART/3/138; cf. 139.

12 E 315/100, f. 233r; Orme, 'Music and Teaching', 277–80.

13 ART/3/148.

14 *Cal. Close* 1374–7, 470; 1381–5, 630; 1389–92, 549; 1399–1402, 556; 1402–5, 493, 499–500; 1441–7, 370; *Cal. Pat.* 1399–1401, 281; *L & P Hen. VIII*, I(1), 508; IV(1), 772; IV(2), 1947; ART 3/137, 150; ART 5/13.

15 C. W. New, *History of the Alien Priories in England to the Confiscation of Henry V* (1916), 55–82; D. J. A. Matthew, *The Norman Monasteries and their English Possessions* (1962); *Cal. Pat.* 1338–40, 413; 1343–5, 34, 135, 211; 1348–50, 356, 512.

16 *Cal. Pat.* 1348–50, 93; 1405–8, 98, 381.

17 TNA, E 106/6/11, mm. 3, 6, 23.

18 TNA, E 106/9/30, printed in Oliver, *Monasticon*, 34–5.

19 *Reg. Grandisson*, I, 364–5, 411, 454–5.

20 Ibid., I, 588; II, 631.

1333, freeing the bishop to take further action. He ordered Bouges, now the administrator, to economise by paying 18*d*. per monk per week from the priory's revenues, and to ensure that they all ate and slept together.¹ He asked the abbot of Angers to recall two monks who had been recently sent to Cornwall, in order to lessen the charges on the monastery, along with Brother John Miral who had committed many faults. Five shillings each was allocated for their journey money.² Miral was still at Tywardreath in 1334, when the bishop ordered him to return to France, asserting that Miral had engaged in a gross lapse of modesty and honesty.³ Meanwhile Grandisson personally appointed Bouges as prior, claiming that the right to do so had lapsed to him; presumably Angers had been unable to fill the post because of the war.⁴

When Edward III made peace with France in 1361, he restored the priory into the hands of the prior, only to seize it again when the war resumed in 1369.⁵ Meanwhile the monks of St Sergius attempted to appoint a prior between 1365 and 1370 in the person of Astère de Cremande and, when this appointment was obstructed, they appealed to the papal court against the king and the bishop of Exeter.⁶ This did not prevent Edward from nominating another Frenchman, William de la Haye, a monk of Tywardreath, as prior in 1370, although the patronage was attributed to the prince of Wales as duke of Cornwall.⁷ Two years later the pope recognised Haye as prior, implying that the challenge by Angers failed.⁸ During the early 1370s three monks of Tywardreath were ordained in Exeter diocese: Richard Brounscombe in 1370, Robert le Feutrer in 1371, and Nicholas Notman in 1373, the first and third of whom were presumably English.⁹ The community remained small, however, and apparently mainly French. In 1374 the bishop of Exeter reported that Haye resided at the priory together with four monks,¹⁰ and when in 1378 foreign monks were ordered to leave England, four French monks of Tywardreath were given safe-conducts for the purpose.¹¹ This seems to have extinguished the community. In 1381, when the clergy of Cornwall paid a poll-tax, only the prior, the vicar, and three priests were listed as paying it in Tywardreath. It looks as if the prior was the sole remaining monk, and that he had replaced his colleagues by hiring priests.¹²

For the next sixty years the only recorded monks of the house are its priors. Haye died in 1399 and the new Lancastrian king, Henry IV, nominated John Maslyn to succeed him, in the name of the king and the prince of Wales (later Henry V).¹³ Maslyn was a monk of the abbey of St Pierre-sur-Dives (Calvados, Normandy), with which the king had links because he was patron of the abbey's daughter priory of Tutbury (Staffs.). On 19 March 1400, following a truce between the English and the French in 1396, the king gave back the priory to Maslyn, an act that released the patronage into the hands of the prince of Wales alone, who appointed the next prior, John Roger, in 1406.¹⁴ Roger was a former monk of Tutbury, originally from St Pierre-sur-Dives, who had become prior of Modbury (Devon), another dependency of St Pierre, in 1399. After moving to Tywardreath he retained his links with Modbury until 1422 as the person responsible for farming its revenues.¹⁵ A late attempt was made to revive the link with Angers in 1410, when Roger received a royal licence to bring six monks from St Sergius to Tywardreath to stay there for life.¹⁶ This project looks like an attempt to restore the priory to its status prior to the Hundred Years War, but it is not known if the plan was effective. Meanwhile the truce with France did not hold, and in 1405 the king granted £80 per annum from the monastery to his brother-in-law, Sir John Cornewall, who received other alien priory property at this time. The grant was to hold good for as long as the war should last.¹⁷

The priory could easily have suffered the fate of other small alien houses during this period. Elsewhere in Cornwall Minster became a parish church and St Michael's Mount was granted to Syon abbey. Roger was not faultless in his personal life (as prior of Modbury he committed fornication with a woman named Joan Bayle),¹⁸ but he played an important part in ensuring Tywardreath's survival, perhaps because of the services

---

1 Ibid., II, 695–6.
2 Ibid.
3 Ibid., II, 750.
4 Ibid., III, 1296
5 *Cal. Pat.* 1358–61, 558–9; 1367–70, 301.
6 Paris, Bibl. nat., lat. 11 818 (a history of the abbey, by Dom Fournerau) gives the date as 1365, while P. Rangeard, *L'Histoire de l'Université d'Angers* (1877), 267–8, implies *c*.1370.
7 *Cal. Pat.* 1370–4, 5; *Reg. Brantyngham*, I, 12, 194.
8 *Cal. Papal Regs* IV, 174.
9 Ibid., II, 753, 756, 774. Notman died, probably at Tywardreath, on a 17 June (CRO, RS/60 (Tywardreath Collation Book), p. 32).
10 *Reg. Brantyngham*, I, 195.
11 TNA, C 76/61, m. 8. They were John Powelart, John Mirebeau, Thomas Coupe, and John Renard.
12 TNA, E 179/25/5. At least one of the priests, John Waty, was a secular chaplain, ordained priest in 1370 (*Reg. Brantyngham*, II, 761).
13 *Reg. Stafford*, 216.
14 *Cal. Pat.* 1399–1401, 72; *Reg. Stafford*, 216. Maslyn was allowed to be non-resident for eight months in 1402 (ibid., 359).
15 *Cal. Pat.* 1396–9, 480; *Reg. Stafford*, 188; J. M. Jones, 'The Norman Benedictine Alien Priory of St George, Modbury, AD *c*.1135–1480', *TDA* 131 (1999), 94–5. Roger's appointment to Modbury was made not by Henry IV, as stated in *Reg. Stafford*, 188, but by Richard II, who had seized the Lancastrian possessions, including the patronage of Tutbury. A third Tutbury monk, William Lambert, was appointed prior of St Michael's Mount in 1410 (above, p. 233).
16 *Cal. Papal Regs* VI, 348; *Cal. Pat.* 1408–13, 159–60.
17 *Cal. Pat.* 1405–8, 98, 381. On Cornewall, see also Matthew, *The Norman Monasteries*, 123–4, 127, 141, 164–5.
18 TNA, C 85/78/10, 18.

that he seems to have rendered to the English Crown in France when Henry IV and Henry V resumed the Hundred Years War. In 1410 he was given the right to remain in England for life, in 1414 he is mentioned going abroad, in 1418 Henry V gave him custody of the lands of the abbey of Troarn in Normandy, and in 1421 he was granted protection while on royal service.[1] Meanwhile, during the 1410s, he entered a plea in the court of chancery for the annulment of the grant to Cornewall, and obtained a certificate from the bishop of Exeter that the priory was conventual (i.e. a community). In 1416 the chancery judged in his favour, and the grant to Cornewall was revoked.[2] In effect Tywardreath became a 'denizen' or naturalised and independent monastery, although it is still not clear if it contained any monks apart from the prior. No ordinations of clergy from the house are recorded in the early 15th century, and it may be significant that Roger entrusted the monastery's seal and certain of its deeds and goods to John Tullok, a local man – an odd transaction unless the prior had no colleagues.[3] Roger made at least two further visits abroad, in 1423 and 1428,[4] and continued as prior until he resigned the post in 1433.[5] His successor, John Brentyngham, was an Englishman but a Benedictine monk of the abbey of St Vigor at Cerisy-la-Forêt (Calvados, Normandy), not far from St Pierre-sur-Dives which it resembled in having a cell in England, in its case at Monk Sherborne (Hants.). The documents survive by which Brentyngham gained his abbot's permission to leave and a papal dispensation to circumvent his illegitimate birth.[6] He was presented to the priorship by Henry VI on 31 July 1433 and instituted by proxy, in the person of Tullok, by the bishop of Exeter on 24 October.[7]

THE 15TH-CENTURY REVIVAL

Under Brentyngham the priory not merely survived but began to revive. He extracted the seal from Tullok, and was probably responsible in 1440 for securing an indulgence from the bishop of Exeter for visitors to a chapel of St Andrew in his parish and for those praying for the souls of his predecessor Roger and of Joan Cheynedrit.[8] According to his successor, Walter Barnecote, he had at one time no fellow-monks,[9] and he too may have employed secular priests to maintain religious services. In 1444 he entered into an agreement with the family of the late Sir John Cornewall to erect a chantry in the monastery. The agreement states that Cornewall had promised to relieve the priory's poverty and that his executors had given it a sum of £100 together with vestments and ornaments. In return the priory undertook to celebrate mass, either by a monk or a secular chaplain, for the souls of Cornewall, his wife, and son at the altar before the crucifix, and to keep an anniversary for the family every 11 December, consisting of three masses celebrated in the choir of the monastery.[10] Within three years of this, however, the monastery contained monks capable of celebrating mass. Barnecote was made a priest in 1447, the first recorded monk to be ordained from the monastery in the 15th century, and he was followed by three others – John Hoper, Richard Ollerton, and John Tomme – in 1452.[11] Meanwhile Brentyngham had died in the previous year, and Barnecote had been presented by the king to succeed him.[12]

Barnecote reigned for forty-four years, building on Brentyngham's foundations and doing much to restore the priory to its ancient staffing and activities.[13] Both priors deserve credit for creating a community of Benedictine monks from local recruits in a county that, by this time, had no other house of such monks other than the tiny cells of St Carroc and Scilly. Barnecote was evidently an active and intelligent man. In 1454 he was licensed to study for two years at an English university, and did so at Oxford where he was allowed to prolong his residence until Easter 1457.[14] In 1468 he was appointed a penitentiary, with extraordinary power to hear confessions, in the rural deanery of Powder.[15] He worked hard to recover assets that he regarded the priory as having lost unlawfully. In 1453 he retrieved from John Tullok and Robert Treveryon a quantity of silver plate, including ten cups, twelve spoons, two salt cellars, a gilded knife, and a gold ring.[16] In 1461 he cited Tullok's widow Joan and her second husband into the court of chancery, alleging that the Tulloks had used the priory seal while it was in their custody to grant themselves a messuage, three orchards, and five acres of land in Tywardreath. The defendants refuted the charge

---

1 *Cal. Pat.* 1408–13, 213; TNA, C 76/97, m. 18; C 64/10, m. 25; C 64/15, m. 25.
2 *Cal. Pat.* 1416–22, 12–13.
3 Oliver, *Monasticon*, 43–4 (No. XXII).
4 TNA, C 76/106, m. 14; C 76/110, m. 7.
5 Oliver (*Monasticon*, 35) states that he resigned to become abbot of Cerisy-la-Forêt, but the basis for this is unknown. Roger is not clearly identifiable in the list of abbots in D. Sammarthanus, *Gallia Christiana*, XI (Paris, 1874), 411.
6 ART/5/3–4.
7 *Cal. Pat.* 1429–36, 285; *Reg. Lacy*, ed. Hingeston-Randolph, I, 158.
8 *Reg. Lacy*, ed. Dunstan, II, 198.
9 Oliver, *Monasticon*, 43–4 (No. XXII).
10 Ibid., 44 (No. XXIII).

11 *Reg. Lacy*, ed. Dunstan, IV, 209–12, 238–42. A certain John Pryny, described as a 'regular canon' was also attributed to Tywardreath when ordained deacon in 1429 (ibid., 129).
12 *Cal. Pat.* 1446–52, 495; *Reg. Lacy*, ed. Hingeston-Randolph, I, 364.
13 There is a Barnacott in Kilkhampton and other such places in Devon, but Kilkhampton is not very far from Tywardreath's properties in north Cornwall.
14 *Reg. Lacy*, ed. Dunstan, III, 196; DRO, Chanter XII(i), f. 34r. Both grants required him to appoint a deputy to run the monastery.
15 DRO, Chanter XII(ii) (Reg. Bothe), f. 75r.
16 ART/3/68. For other documents involving Barnecote and the Tulloks, see TNA, C 1/27/502, C 1/31/26, and C 1/43/91.

but waived any right in the disputed property, and Barnecote had their waiver registered by the court.[1] By 1468 he was attempting to regain the former monastery of Minster and its property from Lady Hungerford, on the grounds that the monastery had belonged to his priory up to the time of John Maslyn.[2] There is no evidence that Minster had ever been legally subject to Tywardreath, however, and the attempt failed. When the priory was visited by the archbishop of Canterbury's commissary in 1492 Barnecote typically used the occasion to complain that a local man was unjustly detaining one of his tenements. By that time there were again six monks besides the prior – the number stated as proper in 1333.[3]

Records about late-medieval monasteries are largely economic, legal, and disciplinary. In contrast their spiritual and cultural life is usually obscure. Nothing is recorded about the internal education of the monks of Tywardreath until 1513, when Bishop Oldham ordered that the novices and other members of the house should be instructed in grammar.[4] Barnecote is the only one known to have attended university. The sole surviving book from the priory is the so-called 'collation book', a 15th- and early 16th-century Latin miscellany in five parts.[5] The first is a calendar of obits (death-dates) of monks and outsiders – clergy and laity – who were benefactors or friends of the monastery. This is followed by directions for creating monks and by a collection of thirty-three homilies for reading at collations (certain meals during Lent). The fourth part is Usuard's *Martyrology* (a list of saints and their days throughout the year), and the fifth is the Rule of St Benedict. The priory's music would have consisted largely of the chanted daily services in the choir, but by 1522 Tywardreath was trying to broaden this by providing 'pricksong' (harmonised music) in its Lady Chapel, thereby imitating the practice of cathedrals and larger monasteries. In that year it appointed Thomas Rayne, yeoman, as clerk of the chapel in return for board, a robe, and a salary of £2 13s. 4d. He undertook to sing and play the organs in the chapel and elsewhere in the church, and to provide two boy scholars with unbroken voices, able to sing pricksong, to help perform the Lady mass each day. These musical arrangements were modest ones, since larger monasteries had more boys and sometimes adult clerks to sing as well. Moreover Rayne was charged rent for his accommodation and had to act as a barber, shaving the prior each week.[6] Two of his former scholars gave evidence in a Church court case in 1584.[7]

Tywardreath had close relationships with many of the wealthier laity of Cornwall. Like most other religious houses the priory organised a confraternity or league of friends to which outsiders were admitted in return for gifts or out of respect for their status. Such people were prayed for, sometimes with obit masses on the anniversary of their death. In 1500 John Treffry, knight, of Fowey bequeathed goods and money to the priory on condition that his name was set 'in the martyrology with the founders',[8] and Elizabeth Horde (died c.1516) is mentioned as a 'sister' of Tywardreath, 'registered and admitted upon the martyrology'.[9] The martyrology was a calendar of saints, similar to or identical with the collation book, the latter of which contains some hundreds of names of monks and 'friends' (*familiares*), ranging from the 12th to the 16th centuries, with the dates on which their deaths were remembered. Most were local people, apart from a few public figures such as Richard, earl of Cornwall and king of the Romans, Queen Isabella, wife of Edward II, and Cardinal Beaufort. Many of the early names exist only as forenames, but the later ones can often be identified. They included, in the years around 1500, Sir Reginald Bray, privy councillor of Henry VII, and his wife; Sir John Percival, sometime lord mayor of London, and his wife Thomasine, foundress of Week St Mary grammar school; and several Cornish gentry: Peter and Thomasine Bevill of St Allen, Sir Thomas and Lady Grenville of Stowe, Treffry of Fowey, and John Tregian, sheriff of Cornwall, and his wife Joan. The Brays were described as 'special benefactors', and one or two gifts by others are specified. Robert and Tybot Pedder gave four liturgical books, and John Nyvet, priest, a silver chalice and a pair of priest's vestments.[10] In 1524 John Porth, a servant of Henry VIII who had been born at St Blazey, left money for masses to be said in the priory, 'wherein I was brought up in my youth'.[11] This may have been as a page-boy or boarder in the prior's household.

On the death of Barnecote in 1496 the duke of Cornwall, Prince Arthur, presented the subprior, Richard Martyn.[12] Martyn's reign, which lasted for only ten years, was notable for the new window that he added to the guest hall and for a visitation of the priory in 1504 by Thomas Woodington, vicar general of the archbishop of Canterbury, during a vacancy in the bishopric of Exeter. Woodington followed his visit with injunctions ordering the celebration of the daily services by day and by night, the observance of

1 Oliver, *Monasticon*, 43–4 (No. XXII).
2 ART/6/3–5; above, p. 243.
3 *Reg. Morton, Canterbury*, II, 81.
4 Oliver, *Monasticon*, 35.
5 CRO, RS/60, pp. 2–67. A psalter (BL, Add. 44949), has been stated as belonging to the priory (e.g. Oliver, *Monasticon*, 36), but it was written in the north of England and contains no references to its medieval ownership.
6 E 315/100, f. 233r; Orme, 'Music and Teaching', 277–80.

7 TNA, E 134/26 Eliz./Easter 14.
8 Treffry gave a gown, silver plate, and money with a total value of 20 marks in return for this (N. Orme (ed.), *Cornish Wills 1342–1540*, DCRS new ser. 50 (2007), 108).
9 ART/3/36.
10 RS/60, pp. 11–66. William Martyn of Lostwithiel gave a share of a tin-works in 1493 (Orme (ed.), *Cornish Wills*, 103), and Peter Bevill vestments worth £5 in 1512 (ibid., 140).
11 Ibid., 171.
12 Oliver, *Monasticon*, 35.

monastic discipline, the reading of the Rule of St Benedict three times a week, and the repair of the monastic buildings – decayed through negligence. An inventory was to be made of all goods and jewels, while the priory seal should be kept in a locked chest and used only with the consent of the whole community. The brothers, apart from the prior, were all to sleep in the same dormitory – one to a bed, to eat in the refectory, and not to leave the premises without the prior's leave.[1] Prohibitions against private bedrooms, individual meals, and unauthorised wandering are commonly found after monastic visitations. Martyn sought to retire in April 1506, and the bishop gave him permission to discuss the matter with the subprior, Thomas Colyns.[2] Colyns agreed to pay Martyn a substantial pension of £40 per annum, and in return Martyn asked Oldham to recommend Colyns to Henry VII as his successor, calling him 'an able man, virtuous, and of good disposition'.[3] The appointment duly went ahead. Colyns was instituted on 25 November, and a month later Oldham ratified Martyn's pension but reduced it to £20.[4]

LAST YEARS

Colyns ruled the priory for almost the whole of its remaining history. He was probably the Thomas Colyns, monk of Glastonbury abbey, ordained acolyte and subdeacon in Somerset in March 1486, and certainly the Thomas Colyn granted a 'title' (or guarantee of support) for ordination by Tavistock abbey in May of that year.[5] The title described him as a 'clerk' of Exeter diocese, of free and legitimate birth, and implies that he came to Tywardreath from outside Cornwall and in adulthood rather than adolescence. His rule as prior was marked by a liking for grandeur. In 1523 he obtained a coat of arms from the king's heralds in London, thereby rivalling his contemporary, Thomas Vivian, prior of Bodmin, who also possessed such a coat, without having Vivian's justification of being a suffragan bishop.[6] He acquired a private seal displaying Laocoon and his sons being strangled by serpents – a gesture at the new fashion for classical art and literature.[7] The appointment of the Lady chapel clerk and prior's barber belongs to his time.

Such a life-style cost money, and Colyns sought to improve his income by gaining a papal licence in 1510 allowing him to hold a parish benefice and to remain outside the cloister to serve it.[8] On the strength of this he became incumbent of a series of churches belonging directly or indirectly to the priory: St Anthony-in-Meneage until 1514, St Clether from 1514 to 1518, and Fowey from 1518 to 1528. Between 1513 and 1521 he drafted petitions to Pope Leo X requesting further aid for the priory. He claimed that it had declined in value to £160 per annum because of the negligence of its foreign priors and through attacks from the sea, so that it could not maintain its staffing, give hospitality, or defend itself. The pope was asked to endow the house with some special privilege or indulgence, and to allow Colyns to hold benefices to the value of £100 per annum.[9] A similar request was sent to Cardinal Wolsey.[10] The priory also raised money, or gained favour, by granting to other people the right of presenting the next clergyman to one or other of its parish churches. Nine such grants are recorded between 1514 and 1533.[11] In 1528 Colyns resigned Fowey in favour of a relative, Henry Collins, reserving for himself a pension of £8, and when Henry died in 1530 he organised the succession of another member of his family, Edward Collins alias Harris.

Bishop Oldham of Exeter visited Tywardreath in 1513, and found several matters in need of correction.[12] He ordered that the prior should render a financial account to the community once a year. Meat should be eaten only according to the Rule of St Benedict, decent meals should be provided, and the servants should be of good character. The direction about teaching grammar to the novices was followed by a stipulation that the monks should leave the monastery only with the prior's permission, and then only in pairs. They were not to visit taverns, converse with women, or admit women into the house. The next bishop, John Veysey, visited in 1521 and issued further injunctions based on what he found and on reports that the community was falling away from its rule. Veysey commanded that the daily services should be devoutly celebrated, beginning with matins soon after midnight. Silence should be kept at times and in places where it was customary, especially after the final service of compline. Monks should not leave the monastery without reasonable cause, and must always be accompanied by colleagues. Doors, windows, and other ways by which women might enter

---

1 ART/4/4.
2 ART/4/5.
3 ART/4/6. Henry VII was in effect the patron, since the duke of Cornwall (later Henry VIII) was a minor.
4 ART/4/7–8. The latter is a further agreement by Colyns that Martyn should receive the pension and that a new chamber and parlour should be erected for his use.
5 Taunton, Somerset Record Office, D/D/B. Reg. 7, f. 193(ii); ART/5/6. ART/5/7 is a letter dimissory of March 1487 allowing him, as a subdeacon, to receive further ordination in another diocese. Monks could move from one house to another.
6 Bodleian, Ashmole 763, f. 47 left hand; London, College of Arms, M 3, f. 79v. The arms were: azure, on a chevron argent between three bezants or, three choughs proper (sable and gules); in chief or a griffin passant parted per pale gules and sable (gules alone in the Ashmole MS).
7 C. W. King, 'Seal Set with an Intaglio of Laocoon', *Archaeological Journal* 24 (1867), 45–54.
8 *Cal. Papal Regs* XIX, 213–14.
9 ART/4/10–11.
10 ART/4/12.
11 ART/3/124/1, 3/125, 3/127, 3/130–5.
12 ART/4/9; Oliver, *Monasticon*, 35.

or monks might leave should be closed. Monks should not be paid money for clothing and other necessities but supplied with what they needed, and none of them should be allocated more than £5 worth of food and clothing per annum. Finally the prior was to correct and reform those brothers guilty of incontinence with women.[1] Clearly the house was not in a perfect state and there appears to have been poor discipline. On the other hand problems of these kinds were common in late-medieval and early-Tudor monasteries, and Tywardreath need not have been significantly worse than other houses. Colyns later claimed that he had kept Veysey's injunctions faithfully.

By the end of the 1520s, however, his position was in danger. Reform of monasteries was becoming a political issue, and Colyns's personal state appears to have caused concern. Contemporaries drew attention to his age and infirmity (he was about sixty), and elderly witnesses at an inquisition in 1589 recalled his addiction to alcohol. One of them, Richard Gynnis 'did well know Prior Collyns, and saith that he would be overcome with drink', while another, John Wattes, 'did divers tymes know Prior Collyns' butler to fetch divers bottels of wine' from a merchant of Lostwithiel, and said that 'it was much reported by divers credible persons that... the said prior would be oftentymes overcome with drinck'.[2] Rumour appears to have spread in the summer of 1529 that Colyns would be deposed, and Robert Hamlyn, a monk of Tavistock abbey, claimed that he was urged by neighbours of Colyns to propose himself for the post.[3] Hamlyn consulted Edward Willoughby, son and heir of Lord Broke, and the marquess of Exeter, Henry Courtenay, whom Colyns had made honorary steward of the monastery.[4] Henry VIII granted the next presentation of a prior to Bishop Veysey and the marquess, and Veysey immediately resigned his rights to the latter.[5] Wolsey showed an interest in the proceedings, interviewing Hamlyn and asking about the priory's value and Colyns's character. Hamlyn replied that the value was £200 per annum and praised the prior's previous government, or so he said. On 26 September Wolsey wrote to Colyns, complimenting him on his rule, referring to his poor health and age, and urging him to resign for a suitable pension. Six days later the marquess wrote on identical lines, and Willoughby carried a similar message in person.

Monks were not as vulnerable in 1529 as they would be a few years later. Colyns refused to commit himself, and expressed displeasure with Hamlyn for trying to depose him. Hamlyn excused himself in two letters to Colyns, and tried to coax the prior to give way. Ball, another monk of Tywardreath, alleged that Colyns had promised to resign in his favour. Eventually two gentlemen of the marquess's household came to the priory on the night of 29 November, along with William Kendall, bailiff of Fowey and friend of the prior. The prior claimed that they told him that the marquess desired him to resign his place to Hamlyn immediately, in return for a pension. If he did so the marquess would be his good lord; otherwise charges would be brought to make him leave whether he wished or not. They demanded a plain answer. Colyns said that he hoped the marquess would continue to be his good lord, that he had no intention of resigning, and that if his intention was such he would have resigned as the marquess commanded. The gentlemen left, warning him that he 'should hear other things before long'. Colyns then wrote to the subdean of Exeter, Robert Weston, beseeching his favour and asking him to enrol the support of Colyns's 'good master' Sir Thomas Denys, a prominent figure in Devon, and the bishop's chancellor, John Gybbons. Gybbons had allegedly promised that Colyns would not be in danger if he kept the bishop's injunctions. Either the prior's friends intervened in his favour or his opponents lacked the ground or will to proceed, since Colyns survived the crisis. Hamlyn got a better post as abbot of Athelney (Somerset).

On 13 August 1534 Colyns and five other monks acknowledged the supremacy of Henry VIII as head of the Church of England.[6] This coincided with the arrival of a more dynamic figure on the scene in the person of Thomas Cromwell, the king's vicar general of the Church, who did not waste time on inadequate or obstinate clergy. In about 1534–5 Cromwell wrote to Colyns complaining that the prior's jurisdiction over the town of Fowey had led to its decay. 'No manner good order, equity, nor justice is executed and used within the same town'. He ordered Colyns to allow the inhabitants liberty, in other words self-government, in return for retaining his lawful revenues from them, and told him to certify his decision by the hands of Thomas Treffry of Fowey, who carried the letter. Cromwell left Colyns in no doubt that he meant business. He accused the prior of having had 'little or no regard neither to the good order, rule, and defence [of the town], nor yet to the good rule and governance of yourself, your monastery, and religion, as you be bound. Wherefore his highness [Henry VIII] thinketh that you be very unworthy to have rule of any town that cannot well rule

---

1 DRO, Chanter XV, ff. 7v–8r.

2 TNA, E 134/31Eliz/Hil24, m. 2; A. L. Rowse, *Tudor Cornwall* (1941), 162.

3 What follows is based on six contemporary letters, ART/4/14–19, printed in Oliver, *Monasticon*, 45–7 (Nos. XXV–XXX).

4 The stewardship was granted in 1527 (ART/16/14/1–2).

5 ART/4/14. There is no record of this grant in the patent rolls, but another was made to Veysey and Robert Hill in 1532; perhaps the first grant was never officially registered (ART/5/14; *L&P Hen. VIII*, V, 430).

6 TNA, E 25/110/4, printed in *7th Deputy Keeper's Report* (1846), App. II, 302.

yourself.' He warned that he would report the prior's reply to the king.[1] Colyns was still prior on 18 July 1535,[2] but he had been deprived of office by the following March, probably by the commissioners of Henry VIII who visited the monasteries of the South West in the winter of 1535–6.[3] No pension appears to have been assigned to him, but he still had his pension from Fowey and may have received support from his family. The ledger stone of his tomb, dated 1539 and decorated with a foliated cross, survives in the parish church of Tywardreath where it formerly lay in the chancel, implying that he died in the neighbourhood and was given a relatively honourable burial.[4]

In 1535 the priory's revenues were assessed by the royal commissioners who drew up the *Valor Ecclesiasticus*, its gross income being reckoned at £151 16s. 1d. The largest element of this, £83 4s. 2d., came from tithes, those of St Austell being valued at £23 7s. 6d., Luxulyan at £9 6s. 8d., Fowey at £9 3s. 4d., and St Anthony-in-Meneage at £5 6s. 8d. The remaining tithes (St Blazey, Lanlivery, St Samson (Golant), Tywardreath, Treneglos, and Warbstow) were reckoned together at £36. A further £16 13s. 8d. came from other ecclesiastical pensions and revenues. The temporal lands of the priory, still organised in eight major groupings, produced £51 18s. 3d., of which Trenant accounted for £11 13s. 8d., Gready £10 5s. 4d., Tywardreath £8 7s. 11d., Trevennen £6 5s. 4d., Porthia £5 11s. 9d., Fentrigan £3 11s. 1d., St Austell £3 7s., and Fowey £1 11s. 10d., while a further £1 4s. 4d. was attributed to St Anthony-in-Meneage. Fees were paid to two auditors, two bailiffs, and to Sir John Chamond, now the chief steward. The vicar of Tywardreath received a salary of £14 6s. 8d. and the last royal pensioner, William Huchyn, £3 6s. 8d. The total net income was £123 9s. 3d.[5] As usual this assessment, although detailed, was an underestimate. Even Colyns had reported the income as £160 and Hamlyn as £200. When the king's administrators produced accounts for the priory's property in 1539–40, they returned an income of £110 17s. 11d. from ecclesiastical sources and £91 12s. 11½d. from temporal ones: a total of just over £200.[6]

The priory did not long survive Colyns's removal. In March and April 1536 Parliament enacted a statute dissolving monasteries worth less than £200 net per annum, and Tywardreath fell victim to this since its nominal income lay below that level. Meanwhile on 18 March 1536 a new prior took office: Nicholas Guest, the former cellarer and subprior of St Germans.[7] Guest, in his late fifties, was an Augustinian canon not a monk, but suitable Benedictines may have been scarce and a prior was needed either because the house was not yet marked for closure or else to wind up its affairs.[8] On 12 May he was granted permission to change his monastic habit and to hold a parish benefice,[9] and on 2 July he was awarded a pension of £16 per annum for life or until he gained a benefice of an equivalent value.[10] He was allowed to maintain his household until 10 August which, in the absence of a document of surrender, may be taken as the date of the priory's dissolution.[11] Two years later he became vicar of St Winnow and died in 1545. The other monks were allowed the choice of working in the world as secular clergy or moving to another monastery, but it is not known what choices they made.[12] One had previously been serving the chapel of St Samson at Golant.[13] On 6 October 1536 the king leased the priory site and the adjoining lands for twenty-one years to John Grenville of Stowe, royal serjeant-at-arms, at a rent of £9 9s. 4d.[14] Grenville transferred the lease to Sir John Arundell, and Arundell conveyed it to Laurence Courtenay in 1542, reserving for himself the stone and timber of the church, cloister, dormitory, and chapter house.[15] During the same year the Crown granted the site and nearby property, when the lease should expire, to Edward Seymour, earl of Hertford.[16] Later in the 16th century they were variously held by the families of Kendall, Young, Copleston, St. Aubyn, and Rashleigh.[17] Six of the priory's manors were awarded by act of parliament in 1540 to Prince Edward (Edward VI) as duke of Cornwall.[18]

Nothing of the priory buildings now remains above ground, apart from the carved stones at the parish church. Four different versions of the priory seal are

---

1 Polsue, *Parochial History*, II, 23.   2 ART/1/42–3.

3 TNA, SC 6/HenVIII/451: references to the visitors making arrangements for Colyns's expenses as prior. A later local witness stated that Colyns was deprived (TNA, E 134/31Eliz/Hil24).

4 BL, Add. 29762, printed in D. Gilbert, *The Parochial History of Cornwall* (1838), IV, 103; Polsue, *Parochial History*, IV, 273.

5 *Valor. Eccl.* II (Rec. Com. 1810–34), 396.

6 W. Dugdale, *Monasticon Anglicanum* (1817–30), IV, 658.

7 SC 6/HenVIII/451.

8 Perhaps Bishop Veysey made the appointment, by virtue of the king's grant of presentation in 1532. For Guest's age and signature (he used this spelling, although Gyst occurs in other documents), see TNA, E 315/118, f. 232r.

9 D. S. Chambers, *Faculty Office Registers 1534–1549* (1966), 55.

10 TNA, E 315/232, f. 35v; *L & P Hen. VIII*, XIII(1), 576.

11 SC 6/HenVIII/451.

12 They were Robert Mortymer, subprior, Henry Bobyt, Madern Wylliam, William John, and John Stevyn (above, p. 294 note 6); the names and pensions in Rowse, *Tudor Cornwall*, 210, are incorrect. William John may be identical with a chantry priest of St Cleer recorded in 1548 (L. S. Snell, *Documents towards a History of the Reformation in Cornwall:* vol. I, *The Chantry Certificates for Cornwall* (c.1953), 18–19).

13 TNA, E 318/340; cf. RS/60, p. 31.

14 TNA, E 318/773; *L & P Hen. VIII*, XIII(1), 578.

15 Oliver, *Monasticon*, 45 (No. XXIV).

16 *L & P Hen. VIII*, XVII, 322.

17 Rowse, *Tudor Cornwall*, 209–11.

18 St Austell, Fentrigan, Fowey, Gready, Porthia Prior, and Trevennen (*L & P Hen. VIII*, XV, 213).

known, all featuring St Andrew, together with Prior Colyns's personal seal.[1] A coat of arms is also recorded, based on St Andrew's cross: gules, a saltire or between four fleurs-de-lys of the last.[2]

PRIORS OF TYWARDREATH[3]

Osbert	occurs before 1149[4]
Osbern	occurs 1158 × c.1160[5]
Baldwin	occurs 1171[6]
Hamelin	occurs late 12th century[7]
Andrew	occurs late 12th or early 13th century[8]
Theobald	occurs c.1225[9]
Simon	occurs c.1230 × 1251[10]
Michael	occurs 11 June 1251, died 4 or 6 March 1263[11]
Geoffrey	adm. 22 May 1263; occurs 26 Aug 1263[12]
Roger de Fontibus	adm. 13 June 1270[13]
John [Loenter?]	occurs 14 May 1284[14]
James	occurs Easter 1288[15]
Philip de Trembleyon	occurs 8 Sept 1293, Nov 1296 × Nov 1297; died 25 May 1333[16]
William de Bouges	coll. 17 Nov 1333; died 18 Oct 1355 or a later year[17]
John Brid	provided *in commendam* 28 Apr 1334[18]
Astère de Cremande	pres. c.1365 × 1370[19]
William de la Haye	occurs as *custos* 2 May 1370; pres. 25 Oct 1370; inst. 1 Nov 1370; papal confirmation 25 Apr 1372; died 18 June 1399[20]
John Maslyn	pres. 3 Nov 1399; inst. 9 Dec 1399; died 7 Aug 1406[21]
John Roger	inst. 14 Dec 1406; res. by 24 Oct 1433[22]
John Brentyngham	pres. 31 July 1433; inst. 24 Oct 1433; died 11 Oct 1451[23]
Walter Barnecote	pres. 23 Oct 1451; inst. 31 Oct 1451; died 20 Nov 1496[24]
Richard Martyn	elected 13 Dec 1496; res. by 25 Nov 1506[25]
Thomas Colyns	inst. 25 Nov 1506; occurs 18 July 1535; depr. by 18 March 1536[26]
Nicholas Guest	app. 18 March 1536, vac. 10 August 1536[27]

---

1 Oliver, *Monasticon*, 36.

2 Bodleian, Ashmole 763, f. 47 left hand (dated 1531). The coat appears in a window of Tywardreath parish church.

3 The assistance of D. Knowles, C. N. L. Brooke, and V. C. M. London (ed.), *The Heads of Religious Houses: England and Wales*, vol. I, 2nd edn (2001), and D. M. Smith and V. C. M. London (ed.), *The Heads of Religious Houses: England and Wales* vol. II (2001), is gratefully acknowledged.

4 Hull (ed.), *Cartulary of Launceston*, 111; cf. Oliver, *Monasticon*, 41 (No. XVI). Possibly the same as the next.

5 ART/1/4; F. Barlow (ed), *English Episcopal Acta, XI: Exeter 1046–1184* (1996), 59–60.

6 ART/1/45; Barlow (ed), *English Episcopal Acta*, XI, 127–8.

7 ART/1/58; Add. 34792 (A), f. 17r; Oliver, *Monasticon*, 38 (No. I). His obit was kept on 1 Apr (RS/60, p. 18).

8 Oliver, *Monasticon*, 42 (No. XVIII).

9 AR/1/60–1; Add. 34792 (A), f. 17r–v; Hull (ed.), *Cartulary of Launceston*, 194.

10 AR/1/815; Add. 34792 (A), ff. 3v, 17v, 19r.

11 AR/1/841; *Reg. Bronescombe*, ed. Hingeston-Randolph, 277; ed. Robinson, I, 160–1 (4 March); RS/60, p. 12 (obit kept on 6 March).

12 *Reg. Bronescombe*, ed. Hingeston-Randolph, 156, 277–8; ed. Robinson, II, 1, 3.

13 *Reg. Bronescombe*, ed. Hingeston-Randolph, 188; ed. Robinson, II, 41. Obits of a prior or priors named Roger were kept on 12 and 31 Oct (RS/60, pp. 56, 60).

14 J. H. Rowe (ed.), *Cornwall Feet of Fines*, DCRS (1914–50), I, 175. The obit of a prior named John Loenter was kept on 6 Apr (RS/60, p. 18).

15 TNA, CP 40/72, m. 35d. His obit was kept on 24 March (RS/60, p. 16).

16 BL, Egerton 2657, f. 136r (a transcript of a deed communicated to William Borlase; cf. RIC, Henderson 19, p. 363); TNA, E 106/4/2, m. 6; RS/60, p. 28.

17 *Reg. Grandisson*, III, 1296; RS/60, p. 58. The latter gives the date of Bouges's death as 1355; on the other hand the next prior, de la Haye, was appointed after the death of Bouges, who may therefore have died nearer to 1370 (*Reg. Brantyngham*, I, 12). Bouges had previously been prior of Minster.

18 *Cal. Papal Regs* II, 400. The provision, by the pope, was probably ineffective. Brid was a Cistercian monk, bishop of Cloyne (Ireland).

19 Above, p. 290 note 6.

20 *Cal. Fine 1368–77*, 76; *Cal. Pat. 1370–4*, 5, 7; *Reg. Brantyngham*, I, 12; *Cal. Papal Regs* IV, 174; RS/60, p. 26.

21 *Cal. Pat. 1399–1401*, 138; *Reg. Stafford*, 216; RS/60, p. 42.

22 *Reg. Stafford*, 216; *Reg. Lacy*, ed. Hingeston-Randolph, I, 158. He died by 29 June 1440 (*Reg. Lacy*, ed. Dunstan, II, 198).

23 *Cal. Pat. 1429–36*, 285; *Reg. Lacy*, ed. Hingeston-Randolph, I, 158; RS/60, p. 56.

24 *Cal. Pat. 1446–52*, 495; *Reg. Lacy*, ed. Hingeston-Randolph, I, 364; RS/60, p. 63.

25 Oliver, *Monasticon*, 35; DRO, Chanter XIII, f. 10r–v. He died on 11 Nov 1510 (RS/60, p. 62).

26 Chanter XIII, f. 10r–v; ART 1/42–3.

27 SC 6/Hen VIII/451; E 134/31Eliz/Hil24.

ST VEEP

CLUNIAC PRIORY OF ST CARROC

The priory of St Carroc in the parish of St Veep was a cell of the Cluniac priory of Montacute in Somerset, and its early history shares the obscurity of that of its mother house. Montacute priory may have been founded in about 1078 by Robert count of Mortain (d. 1090), but Montacute tradition regarded his son William, count from 1190 to 1106, as the founder. William fell out of favour with Henry I in 1104 and forfeited his power, leaving Montacute in a weak position. Few records of the priory's possessions seem to have survived from the early and mid 12th century, and its cartulary, which was compiled in the early 14th century, contains a number of 12th-century charters that look like reconstructions.[1] By the time that the cartulary was compiled the monks believed that Count William had given them the churches of Altarnun, Crantock, and St Neot in Cornwall, and that he or Alured the Butler had granted them Veryan.[2] The cartulary, however, contains no charter conveying either the site of the priory of St Carroc or its chief possession, the adjacent parish church of St Veep.

The earliest mention of St Carroc in the cartulary occurs in a charter of Henry II, allegedly issued between 1154 and 1161, confirming various possessions of Montacute including 'in Cornwall St Carroc with all its [appurtenances]'.[3] This may refer to property at St Carroc rather than to a priory there, and the document may not be authentic in all respects. A more reliable reference is to be found in a charter of about 1192 granted by John count of Mortain (later King John), in which he confirmed the gifts of his ancestors to Montacute including 'the priory of St Carroc'.[4] The priory is likely to have been established in the second half of the 12th century, either to administer Montacute's four Cornish churches for which it was centrally situated, or in response to gifts of land in its vicinity. One such gift was made by a knight named Warin Haccombe, lord of Penpoll, who granted Montacute and the monks of St Carroc all his land at 'Trauaylward' and 'Bothele' in the fee of Manely, which lay immediately north of St Carroc.[5] This was in the late 12th or the 13th century, but apparently followed the establishment of the priory. Montacute also came to possess or claim some other small pieces of temporal property in east Cornwall, including land at 'Polgrum' and 'Trewen', disputed and lost in 1201;[6] four acres in Morval, surrendered in 1238;[7] and a tenement called 'La Hilonde' in the manor of Treglasta in Davidstow, held by 1300.[8] In 1291 the prior of St Carroc was assessed as holding 40s. of rent in the rural deaneries of West and Trigg Major,[9] and in 1535 the priory's lands were said to lie in 'Gonam' and St Ive.[10] Two years later they were reported as consisting of a capital messuage (the priory itself) with appurtenances in the parishes of Duloe and Lanteglos-by-Fowey, and the manors of 'Govan' and St Carroc.[11]

St Carroc enjoyed two further revenues from ecclesiastical sources. Until 1236 it received a pension of £4 4s. 3d. from the church of Altarnun, and when in that year Montacute gave up the church to Bishop Brewer of Exeter, the bishop agreed to pay St Carroc an annual sum of £3 6s. 8d. from the income of his see until some equivalent provision could be made.[12] The other revenue came from St Carroc's parish church of St Veep. This church was apparently still in lay hands in the early years of the priory's history, since Robert, lord of the manor of Manely, is stated to have presented a certain John son of the Reeve to be its rector in the reign of King John (1199–1216). The monks of Montacute had acquired it by 1236 when Bishop Brewer repaid them for the gift of Altarnun by allowing them to appropriate the tithes of various churches in Exeter diocese including St Veep.[13] In 1284 Robert fitz Walter, a nephew of the earlier Robert, claimed the advowson of St Veep against the prior of Montacute, citing his uncle's presentation of a rector and arguing that since Robert had died without issue, his property should have passed to his brother Walter and thence to himself, Walter's son. Fitz

---

1 Bodleian, Trinity College Oxford D 85; T. S. Holmes (ed.), *Two Cartularies of the Augustinian Priory of Bruton and the Cluniac Priory of Montacute*, Somerset Record Soc. 8 (1894).

2 Trinity College Oxford D 85, ff. 1r, 9r; Holmes (ed.), *Two Cartularies*, 119, 125–6.

3 Trinity College Oxford D 85, f.23r; Holmes (ed.), *Two Cartularies*, 124.

4 Trinity College Oxford D 85, f.26v; Holmes (ed.), *Two Cartularies*, 128.

5 Trinity College Oxford D 85, f.92v; Holmes (ed.), *Two Cartularies*, 191.

6 D. M. Stenton (ed.), *Pleas before the King or his Justices 1198–1202*, vol. II, Selden Soc. 68 (1952), 126, 144, 180.

7 J. H. Rowe (ed.), *Cornwall Feet of Fines*, DCRS (1914–50), I, 36.

8 Trinity College Oxford D 85, f.92r; Holmes (ed.), *Two Cartularies*, 190.

9 *Reg. Bronescombe*, ed. Hingeston-Randolph, 479.

10 *Valor Eccl.* (Rec. Com. 1810–34), I, 196. Dr O. J. Padel suggests that *Gonam* or *Govan* may be Tregunnon in Altarnun parish (private information).

11 G. Oliver, *Monasticon Dioecesis Exoniensis* (1846), 69, quoting TNA, Augmentation Office, roll of 31 Henry VIII.

12 F. Barlow (ed.), *English Episcopal Acta*, XII: *Exeter 1186–1257* (1996), 252–3.

13 Ibid., 251–2.

Walter's claim was sufficiently strong to cause the prior of Montacute to settle the case out of court and to buy off the claimant with the large sum of 120 marks (£80), after which Montacute retained possession of St Veep until the Reformation.[1] The papal taxation of 1291 reckoned the priory's share of the income of St Veep at £5, which with the 40s. of rent made a total of £7; no mention was made of a pension from the bishop.[2]

The priory was situated on the edge of Penpoll creek (SX 1346 5459) in the vicinity of the modern house of St Cadix – a name adopted in the 18th century, probably through confusion with the Welsh saint Cadoc. Two factors are likely to have influenced the choice of site. One was the presence of a chapel there, dedicated to a Cornish saint Carroc, whose name (in this form) was unique within Cornwall.[3] The chapel was evidently older than the priory but lay by the 12th century within the parish of St Veep and was subordinate to its church.[4] It was an obvious site for the priory at a time when the parish church had not come into Montacute's hands. A second advantage of the chapel was its riverside location on a branch of the River Fowey, from which it was possible to travel by boat to Lostwithiel, Fowey, and the English Channel. The chapel was apparently retained in a modest form to serve as the priory church. It appears as a small chapel-like building on a map of the south coast of Cornwall made in 1539,[5] and is referred to as a chapel in a grant of the St Carroc property in 1545.[6] It also bears the symbol of a chapel, not a church, on John Norden's maps of Cornwall in the 1590s.[7] A field east of St Cadix was known as 'Chapel Meadow' in 1839, and another near the parish church as 'Prior Park'.[8] The area on either side of Penpoll creek, leading up to the road near St Veep church and covering just over 67 acres, constituted a tithe-free area in the 18th and 19th centuries, and doubtless represented the home farm that supplied the needs of the priory.[9]

St Carroc belonged to Montacute and had no legal existence of its own. In 1340, however, there was considered to be an advowson carrying the right to appoint its prior, which was granted by Edward III in that year to William de Montague, earl of Salisbury.[10] Later, in 1535, the prior was stated to be removable by the prior of Montacute.[11] Since Montacute was a Cluniac house, dependent on the French abbey of Cluny, its rights and revenues (including those of St Carroc) were taken into the king's hands during the wars with France in the late 13th and 14th centuries. Inventories of St Carroc's property and revenues were duly made in 1324 and 1337, the former giving the value as £28 and the latter as £40 14s. 5d.[12] The king also appropriated the patronage of the vicarage of St Veep at such times,[13] but royal interference ceased when Montacute was recognised as an English or 'denizen' house in 1407. Cells like St Carroc were normally staffed by a prior and one other monk, in this case sent from Montacute, but in 1381 only the prior is mentioned there,[14] and towards the end of the 15th century Prior John Bristowe may have been the sole monastic resident. Being on his deathbed he entrusted muniments, jewels, and money to a local man, John Seggemore of Manely, who later (Montacute complained) refused to hand them back.[15] When the tithes of St Veep were appropriated to Montacute in 1236, the bishop of Exeter ordered that the vicar of St Veep should have meals at the prior's table, although he was awarded a dwelling house near the church.[16] The duties of the prior and his colleague, apart from daily prayer, were probably to administer the affairs of Montacute in Cornwall. No pastoral work would have been necessary, but one prior, Thomas Cherell in 1500, received papal permission to hold an additional benefice with or without cure.[17]

By about 1200 the chapel saint, Carroc, was becoming reinterpreted as 'Cyriac' or 'Cyricus', in other words as the well-known Roman child-saint, and in later times the priory and chapel were sometimes given his name.[18] In 1336 Bishop Grandisson dedicated the parish church, whose saint Veep was equally obscure, in honour of SS Cyricus and his mother Julitta.[19] There seems to have been some local cult of the chapel saint. In 1385 the prior of St Carroc complained to the bishop that the vicar of St Veep had unlawfully appropriated tithes in the parish and impeded the offerings that the parishioners were accustomed to

---

1 TNA, JUST 1/111, m. 2d; Rowe (ed.), *Cornwall Feet of Fines*, I, 181.

2 *Reg. Bronescombe*, ed. Hingeston-Randolph, 468, 479.

3 On the saint, see N. Orme, *The Saints of Cornwall* (2000), 85–6; the name may be a variant of Carantoc, patron saint of Crantock.

4 The question has been raised as to whether St Carroc was a pre-Conquest monastery (L. Olson, *Early Monasteries in Cornwall* (1989), 97–8), but there is no evidence for this. Such a monastery might be expected to have retained its status as a parish church, and have established a larger parish.

5 BL, Cotton Aug. I.i.35, 36, 38, 39.

6 *L&P Hen. VIII*, XX(2), p. 215.

7 *John Norden's Manuscript Maps of Cornwall and its Nine Hundreds*, ed. W. L. D. Ravenhill (1972), facsimiles 2, 5, 10.

8 CRO, TA/243, p. 36.

9 Ibid.; R. Potts (ed.), *A Calendar of Cornish Glebe Terriers 1673–1735*, DCRS new ser. 19 (1974), 167.

10 *Cal. Pat.* 1338–40, 475; *Cal. Pat.* 1340–3, 196.

11 *Valor Eccl.*, I, 196.

12 TNA, E 106/6/11, mm. 4, 26; E 106/9/30.

13 E.g. *Cal. Close* 1370–4, 254–5.

14 TNA, E 179/24/5.

15 TNA, C 1/213/104.

16 F. Barlow (ed.), *English Episcopal Acta*, XII, 251–2.

17 *Cal. Papal Regs*, XVII(1), 173. No such person is recorded with a benefice in Exeter diocese in this period; if Cherell is a mistake for Cherd, the person concerned may have been Thomas Chard, later prior of Montacute (*BRUO*, I, 389–90).

18 Gervase of Canterbury, *The Historical Works*, ed. W. Stubbs, 2 vols (RS 1879–80), ii. 424; Orme, *Saints of Cornwall*, 101.

19 *Reg. Grandisson*, II, 819.

make in the priory of St Carroc on the feast-day of Cyricus and Julitta.[1] When the antiquary William Worcester visited Cornwall in 1478 he was told that 'St Sirus, priest, lies in the church of the priory of the religious men of St Carroc', a statement which, if true, may indicate that there was a shrine in the chapel and that the saint was regarded as both a local and a universal figure.[2] There are parallels for such a belief elsewhere in Cornwall and Wales.[3] In 1301 a friar named Walter of Exeter made a copy of the *Life of Guy of Warwick*, still extant in the 16th century, which stated that it was written at St Carroc at the request of Baldwin of Windsor, citizen of Exeter.[4] The *Life* was probably in French or English, but the reason for its execution at the priory is unknown.

The priory still existed when John Leland made his first visit to Cornwall in about 1533 and described it as 'a cell of two black monks of Montacute'.[5] Two years later the royal valuation of Church property, the *Valor Ecclesiasticus*, assessed its income as £11 1s. 0d., made up of tithes (£7 13s. 4d), rent of land in 'Gonam' and St Ive (£2 18s. 0d.), and rent of demesne land (9s. 8d.).[6] In 1537 Montacute leased the property to John Tubbe, John Kaylleway, and Roger Tubbe in return for a similar annual rent of £11 1s. 0d., the lease including the temporal properties with the tithes and profits of the rectory of St Veep.[7] The priory came to an end at or before 20 March 1539, when Montacute surrendered to the Crown.[8] On 3 September 1545 the Crown granted the priory and all its properties, together with the rectory of St Veep and its tithes, to Laurence Courtney and his wife Dorothy on payment of £199 7s. 6d.[9] The priory site subsequently became a domestic house but the chapel, as stated above, was still standing in the 1590s. In about 1700 William Hals wrote that the original house and chapel were dilapidated, that the burial ground had been made into a garden, and that a new dwelling house had been erected nearby, using materials from its predecessor.[10] Numerous worked stones have since been found on the site, dating from the 12th to the 16th centuries. They include sections of window tracery, probable jambs from doorways, and part of a cresset stone that once held cups for lights in the chapel. A small copper-gilt crucifix was found on the site in the 19th century,[11] and the upper half of a stone crucifix was recovered from Penpoll Creek in the late 20th.[12]

PRIORS OF ST CARROC

Henry	no date; perhaps 14th century[13]
Robert	occurs 1339[14]
John	occurs 1381[15]
William Smethe	occurs 29 July 1385[16]
William	occurs 5 May 1396[17]
John Hoper	no date; perhaps 15th century[18]
John Bristowe	died before 1493 × 1500[19]
Thomas Cherell	occurs 20 Jan 1500[20]
Laurence Casteltown	occurs 1535[21]

VERYAN

'SHEEPSTALL' LEPER HOUSE

'Sheepstall' (now Shipstors) was a medieval settlement half a mile south-west of Tregony on the south bank of the River Fal and just inside the parish of Veryan (SW915 440). In the early 14th century it included messuages and at least two mills (one corn, one fulling), and may have had access by water to the Fal estuary; in 1335 its lord, Sir John Lercedekne, secured it a royal grant of a weekly market and a three-day fair at the festival of St Margaret.[22] A leper house is first recorded there in 1301 when it stood close to the two mills – an

---

1 *Reg. Brantyngham*, II, 582.
2 W. Worcester, *Itineraries* (1969), 106–7.
3 Orme, *Saints of Cornwall*, 60, 243–4.
4 R. L. Poole and M. Bateson (ed.), *Index Britanniae Scriptorum: John Bale's Index of British and other Writers*, 2nd edn (1990), pp. xxv, 104.
5 J. Leland, *Itinerary*, ed. L. Toulmin Smith (1907–10), I, 324.
6 *Valor Eccl.*, I, 196; the same total is given after the dissolution (TNA, SC 6/HenVIII/3137), where *Gonam* is rendered *Govam*.
7 W. Dugdale, *Monasticon Anglicanum* (1817–30), V, 172–3.
8 *8th Deputy Keeper's Report* (1847), Appendix II, 32. No prior of St Carroc is mentioned at the surrender of Montacute although the priors of two other cells are identified.
9 *L&P Hen. VIII*, XX(2), p. 215.
10 BL, Add. 29762, f. 232v, printed in D. Gilbert, *The Parochial History of Cornwall* (1838), IV, 111; cf. BL, Egerton 2657, f. 176r.
11 J. Polsue, *A Complete Parochial History of the County of Cornwall* (1867–72), IV, 288–9; it is now in private ownership.
12 The stone crucifix is currently in St Veep church. For site information on St Carroc, see CCC, HER 26760.
13 CRO, RS/60, p. 40 (Tywardreath obituary, where his death is noted on 22 July).
14 *Reg. Grandisson*, II, 908.
15 E 179/24/5.
16 *Reg. Brantyngham*, II, 582; possibly the same as the next.
17 CRO, ART/1/55; possibly the same as the preceding.
18 RS/60, p. 38 (where his death is noted on 4 July).
19 C 1/213/104.
20 *Cal. Papal Regs*, XVII(1), 173.
21 *Valor Eccl.*, I, 196. He was a senior monk of Montacute, having been ordained priest in 1490: DRO, ChanterXII (ii), f. 155.
22 *Cal. Chart. R 1327–1341*, 322; C. G. Henderson, 'The Ecclesiastical History of the 109 Parishes of West Cornwall', *JRIC* new ser. 3 (1957–60), 429–30; M. I. Somerscales, 'Lazar Houses in Cornwall', *JRIC* new ser. 5 (1965), 84–5.

unusual location for an institution that was usually set apart from other people.¹ A chapel of St Margaret is mentioned in the same year, but it is not known whether this was a place of worship for the lepers, the public, or both.² Shortly afterwards, in 1307–10, the executors of Bishop Bitton of Exeter granted 12s. 6d. to the lepers of 'Sheepstall',³ and the leper community still existed in 1419 when John Megre, a London pewterer who was the father-in-law of the lord of the manor (another Sir John Lercedekne), bequeathed 6d. to each lazar at 'Sheepstall'.⁴ This is the last such reference, leaving it unclear how far the community acquired the organisation and status of a hospital, or when it disappeared. The chapel still existed at the end of the 16th century.⁵ There are now no visible features.⁶

UNCERTAIN HOSPITALS AND LEPER COMMUNITIES

Lepers are recorded in several places in medieval Cornwall, in addition to the small number of institutional leper hospitals. These records are chiefly due to a unique source: the accounts of the executors of Bishop Bitton of Exeter who died in 1307.⁷ Between that date and 1310 the executors arranged for the payment of money to lepers in Cornwall and Devon, as far as Sancreed near Land's End. Contacts were made with lepers in 23 places in Cornwall, and the payments made to them were subsequently recorded, in topographical order, in the executors' accounts. It is not clear that that the agents actively sought out every possible leper. One group that probably existed, at 'Nan(s)clergy' in St Keverne parish, is not mentioned,⁸ and there is no example from the north-east of the county. Moreover the accounts talk only of payments 'to the lepers' of the places concerned, and although in some places, such as Bodmin, Launceston, and Liskeard, this related to the inmates of organised leper hospitals, in most cases there is no evidence that the lepers who received money belonged to such institutions. They may have been living in informal communities, or privately and individually, and the references to them cannot be safely regarded as indicating the existence of leper hospitals.

A few other references to lepers or 'lazars' in Cornwall occur in the 16th century, particularly in parish records as a result of small sums of money being given to them out of charity. Lazars may have been lepers, or people of apparently similar afflictions. These groups may sometimes have had a common building, like the example at Marazanvose, or may have been living dispersedly. The evidence currently available about early leper groups in Cornwall is listed below, in alphabetical order of places. It is restricted to documentary evidence. There has been a temptation to deduce the presence of lepers in Cornwall from the place-name 'Clodgy', but although this word may sometimes be derived from a presumed Cornish word *clav-jy, meaning 'sick house', it may also represent the dialect word 'clidgy', meaning 'sticky'.⁹ Places have not been included in this list on that ground, unless supported by other evidence. Other uncertain and conjectural information about hospitals and leper communities is collected and discussed at the end of this section.

Bodmin: Dunmere   In 1307–10 the Bitton executors paid 22s. 6d. to the lepers of 'Dynmur', a place that occurs between Liskeard and Bodmin in their list and evidently refers to what is nowadays called Dunmere in the parish of Bodmin, one and a half miles north-west of Bodmin on the road to Camelford, Padstow, and Wadebridge (SX 054 676).¹⁰ The place was on a main highway and by a bridge over the River Camel that existed as early as 1220.¹¹ The executors made a donation to another group of lepers in Bodmin, probably those in the hospital of St Laurence, but although the lepers of Dunmere received more than those of Bodmin, no later evidence has been found about them. A tenement at Dunmere called 'St Ann's Chapel Hays' hints at a chapel of St Anne in the vicinity,¹³ but the cult of St

---

1 Henderson, 'The Ecclesiastical History', 429–30.
2 Ibid.
3 W. H. Hale and H. T. Ellacombe (ed.), *Accounts of the Executors... of Thomas Bishop of Exeter 1310*, Camden Soc. new ser. 10 (1874), 28.
4 N. Orme (ed.), *Cornish Wills 1342–1540*, DCRS new ser. 50 (2007), 52.
5 H. M. Jeffrey, 'A Map of the River Fal and its Tributaries from a Survey Made in 1597 by Baptista Boazio', *JRIC* 9 (1886–9), 165–70; map opposite p 165.
6 For site information, see CCC, HER 24283.2.
7 W. H. Hale and H. T. Ellacombe (ed.), *Accounts of the Executors of Richard Bishop of London 1303, and...Thomas Bishop of Exeter 1310*, Camden Soc. new ser. 10 (1874), 28–9, discussed in N. Orme and M. Webster, *The English Hospital* (1995), 170–7.   8 Above, p. 195.
9 For discussion of the word see O. J. Padel, *Cornish Place-Name Elements*, English Place-Name Society 56/57 (1985), 59–60.
10 Hale and Ellacombe (ed.), *Accounts of Executors*, 28.
11 C. G. Henderson and H. Coates, *Old Cornish Bridges and Streams* (1972), 112.
13 J. Maclean, *The Parochial and Family History of the Deanery of Trigg Minor* (1873–9), I, 199. The connection between the lepers and the chapel is urged by Somerscales, 'Lazar Houses', 82.

Anne did not reach Cornwall until the late 14th century, and there is no evidence that the chapel (if it existed) had any connection with a leper community.

St Breock   The lepers of St Breock received 12*s*. 6*d*. from the executors of Bishop Bitton in 1307–10.[1]

Budock: Argal   The lepers of 'Argol' received 8*s*. from the Bitton executors in 1307–10, the place being listed between Truro and Helston.[2] It was evidently identical with Argal or Argol in Budock parish, nowadays represented by houses called Higher Argal and Argol Manor (SW 76 32). A place called Clodgy Moor between Higher Argal and Kergilliack may preserve the memory of the lepers.[3] The location was a roadside one, on or near the highway from Truro to Helston, and since the lepers were only two miles from Penryn, they may have had a relationship with that settlement and with the surrounding manors which belonged to the bishop of Exeter. No other reference to them is recorded.

St Clement: Kiggon   A payment of 3*s*. to the lepers of 'Coygon' was made by Bishop Bitton's executors in 1307–10, the payment being recorded in the list of places between Freewater and Truro.[4] The place-name is preserved in the modern Kiggon Bridge (SW 855 455), which carries the main highway from Truro eastwards across the Trevella Stream. As so often, the lepers were associated with a bridge and road.[5]

Crantock   In 1597 the wardens of Blanchminster's charity at Stratton (Cornwall) paid 4*d*. 'to one licensed to gather for the lazar people of Crantock being ix [i.e. nine]'.[6] This may be an example of a post-Reformation community of lepers or leper-like people, resembling those that occur at St Ives and Marazanvose; the site, if they all occupied one, is not known.

Creed: Grampound   Grampound emerged as a borough towards the end of the 13th century, taking its name from the 'great bridge' that carried the main road from Truro eastwards across the River Fal.[7] The Bitton executors donated 15*s*. 'to the lepers of 'Ponsmur' in 1307–10, using the Cornish form of the name Grampound.[8]

Fowey   Fowey had the status of a borough after the early 13th century,[9] and Bishop Bitton's executors gave 12*s*. 6*d*. to the lepers of Fowey in 1307–10.[10]

St Germans   The sum of 9*s*. 6*d*. was paid to the lepers of St Germans by the Bitton executors in 1307–10; the place was the site of an important manor and residence of the bishops of Exeter, as well as that of the Augustinian priory.[11]

Goran   In 1596 the wardens of Blanchminster's charity at Stratton (Cornwall) paid 4*d*. 'to a poor man of St Goran that gathered for three lazar children'.[12] This suggests a family of lepers or leper-like people in the parish, but not necessarily a community.

Gulval: Glas   The lepers of 'Glas' received 9*s*. from the executors in 1307–10, the place being listed between Helston and Mousehole.[13] This lost place-name was in Gulval parish and is mentioned in 1392 as lying in Tolver (SW 490 323). Tolver is on a lane off the main roads from Hayle and Marazion to Penzance, rather than on a roadside location as has been suggested.[14]

Illogan: Nancecuke   A catalogue of deeds compiled in 1930 mentions a grant of property at Tehidy in Illogan parish, with an approximate date of 1280. The deed, originally in Latin but summarised in the catalogue in English, was witnessed by 'Richard de Methrol, Master of the Friars of Nanscoyt'.[15] 'Nanscoyt' is best interpreted as modern Nancecuke, and 'Methrol' as Methrose, both in that parish,[16] while 'Friars' presumably translates *fratrum* in Latin, a word that could

---

1 Hale and Ellacombe (ed.), *Accounts of Executors*, 29.
2 Ibid.
3 C. G. Henderson, 'The Ecclesiastical History of the 109 Parishes of West Cornwall', *JRIC* new ser. 2–3 (1953–60), 51; Somerscales, 'Lazar Houses', 88. For site information, see CCC, HER 18542.
4 Hale and Ellacombe (ed.), *Accounts of Executors*, 28.
5 For further discussion, see Henderson, 'Ecclesiastical History', 77–8; Somerscales, 'Lazar Houses', 87. A site has been suggested at SW 8560 4550, but the suggestion is based on the supposed identification of a leper chapel, for which there is no documentary evidence (CCC, HER 22505).
6 R.W. Goulding, *Records of Blanchminster's Charity* (1898) 78; Somerscales, 'Lazar Houses', 95–6.
7 M. W. Beresford and H. P. R. Finberg, *English Medieval Boroughs* (1973), 78; Henderson and Coates, *Old Cornish Bridges*, 85.
8 Hale and Ellacombe (ed.), *Accounts of Executors*, 28. There is no evidence for a chapel of the community, as suggested by Somerscales, 'Lazar Houses', 84, and her proposed dedication to St Anne is too early for 1307–10.
9 Beresford and Finberg, *English Medieval Boroughs*, 78.
10 Hale and Ellacombe (ed.), *Accounts of Executors*, 28; Somerscales, 'Lazar Houses', 83.
11 Hale and Ellacombe (ed.), *Accounts of Executors*, 28. Somerscales, 'Lazar Houses', 74–5, conjectured a site at Bonyalar (SX 30 59), and suggests that the lepers had a chapel but none is known.
12 Goulding, *Records of Blanchminster's Charity*, 77; Somerscales, 'Lazar Houses', 98.
13 Hale and Ellacombe (ed.), *Accounts of Executors*, 29.
14 Henderson, 'Ecclesiastical History', 192. This distinguishes *Glas* from the location suggested by Somerscales, 'Lazar Houses', 90. She also drew attention to fields described as 'part of Clodgy Downs' in the Gulval Tithe Apportionment of 1843 (CRO, AD/59/33, p. 33).
15 H. R. Moulton, *Palaeography, Genealogy and Topography: selections from the collection of H. R. Moulton* (1930), 179.
16 I am grateful for the advice of Dr O. J. Padel on this matter.

equally well be rendered as 'brothers'. A settlement of friars at Nancecuke, in the sense of one of the mendicant orders, seems unlikely. A community of hospital inmates with a master is possible, in which case it would have been a relatively secluded body off main roads (compare 'Nan(s)clergy' in St Keverne), but hospital communities in Cornwall were usually made up of lepers and one might expect them to have been to be described as such rather than as brothers. An equally good solution might be a religious guild of local men, such as existed in Truro by 1278.[1] There was a chapel at Nancecuke by 1352.[2]

St Ives   The borough accounts of St Ives mention the names of lazars and describe the support given to them between 1577 and 1597.[3] The borough built and repaired dwellings for them, and provided occasional alms and clothes, maintenance during sickness, and shrouds after death. The lazars' names were John, Mary, Philip, John Nyclis and his mother Joan, John Saundrie, and Joan (or John) Wats. Two of them, John Saundrie and Joan (or John) Nyclis, died during the period. The houses may have been on or near Clodgy Point (SW 50 41), if that name was taken from the presumed Cornish word for a sick house.[4]

St Mabyn: Spittal   Spittal is a hamlet on the lane from St Mabyn to Blisland (SX 077 731), first mentioned by that name in a conveyance of lands in 1331. The place is close to Tresarrett where the Order of St John, or Hospitallers, held property by 1195, and more probably takes its name from them than from a local hospital, an institution that was normally sited near a town or on a main road. There is a parallel in Devon, where Spittle in Chulmleigh refers to property formerly held by the Hospitallers.[5]

Madron   In 1307–10 the Bitton executors distributed the sum of 6s. to the lepers of 'Madern', placed in their list between Mousehole and Sancreed.[6]

Newlyn East: Mitchell   Bishop Bitton's executors gave 14s. 'to the lepers of 'Medeschole' in 1307–10.[7] M. I. Somerscales wished to identify this place with Michaelstow,[8] but the name is undeniably that of Mitchell, a small borough created on the main Bodmin to Redruth road during the 13th century, on the border of the parishes of Newlyn East and St Enoder (SW 86 54).[9]

Padstow   Padstow appears to have had the status of a borough in the early 14th century,[10] and this coincides with the payment of 6s. to the lepers of 'Oldestowe' by Bishop Bitton's executors in 1307–10.[11] 'Oldestowe' is a well-attested name for Padstow. No other reference to the lepers is known, and it is consequently not yet possible to link them with any of the several chapels known to have existed in and near the town.[12]

Paul: Mousehole   The lepers of Mousehole received 13s. 6d. from Bishop Bitton's executors in 1307–10.[13] Mousehole was another small Cornish borough in the late 13th and early 14th centuries.[14] Somerscales conjectured that they occupied a site at the fields called Higher and Lower Park Clodgy and Clodgy Moor, west of Sheffield (SW455 266).[15] These are near, but not on, the road from Mousehole and Penzance to St Buryan.

Perranzabuloe: Marazanvose   A description of the parish boundaries of St Allen in 1613 refers to 'the lazar house at the end of Gone Satha Downes' and 'the lazar house at the entry into the lane that leadeth to Marazanvose from Gowen-Satha Downes, where the three parishes meet, viz. Allen, Kenwyn, and St Piran in the sands'.[16] The meeting point is about a mile southwest of Marazanvose proper, by the side of the main road through Cornwall from Bodmin to Redruth (SW789 445), where Martin's map of Cornwall (1748) and that of the Ordnance Survey (1809) show a building called 'Perran [or Piran] Almshouses'. The building was just inside Perranzabuloe parish. Its origin and constitution are not known, but like the post-Reformation references to Crantock and St Ives it indicates the existence of a humble house or houses for lazars at a late date, which seems to have been adapted in due course as an almshouse for other infirm people.

Probus: Freewater   The same executors paid 20s. in 1307–10 to the lepers of 'Resureghy', a place that occurs in

---

1   Above, p. 43.
2   Henderson, 'Ecclesiastical History', 226–7; *Black Prince's Reg.*, II, 37.
3   J. H. Matthews, *A History of the Parishes of Saint Ives, Lelant, Towednack and Zennor* (1892), 150, 158–9, 163–6; Somerscales, 'Lazar Houses', 93–4.
4   Somerscales, 'Lazar Houses', 93–4.
5   RIC, Henderson 23, p. 42; Maclean, *Trigg Minor*, II, 489, 491; Orme and Webster, *English Hospital*, 209; above, p. 274.
6   Hale and Ellacombe (ed.), *Accounts of Executors*, 29. Somerscales, 'Lazar Houses', 92, conjectured that the lepers occupied land at Higher and Lower Clodgy (SW 438 305), which she incorrectly described as being tithe free in 1841; in fact this land paid tithe to the (by then lay) rector (CRO, TA/133, pp. 19, 22). Clodgy, here as elsewhere, may come from the Cornish word for 'sticky'.

7   Hale and Ellacombe (ed.), *Accounts of Executors*, 29.
8   Somerscales, 'Lazar Houses', 97. She overemphasised the argument that Bitton's executors listed their donations in an absolutely topographical sequence; this argument cannot outweigh the normal meaning of the place-name.
9   Beresford and Finberg, *English Medieval Boroughs*, 80.
10   Ibid.
11   Hale and Ellacombe (ed.), *Accounts of Executors*, 29.
12   For conjectures, see Somerscales, 'Lazar Houses', 96.
13   Hale and Ellacombe (ed.), *Accounts of Executors*, 29.
14   Beresford and Finberg, *English Medieval Boroughs*, 80.
15   Somerscales, 'Lazar Houses', 91–2.
16   RIC, HC 62, p. 95.

their list between Tregony and Kiggon near Truro.[1] 'Resureghy' is nowadays Freewater, a name adapted from 'Suffree-water', about one and a half miles north-west of Tregony on the road to Truro (SW 906 459). This payment was one of five to lepers within a fairly small area east of Truro.

Redruth   The Bitton executors gave 9s. to the lepers of Redruth in 1307–10, a place that was not a borough but lay on the main road from Bodmin to west Cornwall.[2] No further evidence about lepers there has been found in the Middle Ages, but references to lazars occur in the parish registers during the late 16th century. Jane, daughter of the poor lazar woman, was buried on 16 September 1592; Harry, son of Sydwel the lazar woman, on 2 October 1592; and Siblye the lazar woman on 10 October 1592.[3] The information could be interpreted economically as indicating the presence of one lazar woman named Sybil or Sidwell living with her children.

Saltash: Trematon   The lepers of Trematon received 7s. 6d. from Bishop Bitton's executors in 1307–10, the place being listed between Launceston and St Germans.[4] Trematon had an important castle, belonging in the 14th century to the earls (later dukes) of Cornwall, and was a borough in its own right in 1298, separate from that of Saltash nearby.[5] It is not known where the lepers lived, and the suggestion that they did so at Trevollard (SX 39 59) assumes that they possessed a chapel, which is not certain.[6]

Sancreed   The Bitton executors gave a mere 6d. to the lepers of 'St Sancreed' in 1307–10, a donation that may relate to a single person rather than a community.[7]

Truro   The Bitton executors distributed 12s. to the lepers of Truro in 1307–10.[8] Much later than this, in 1657, a lease of a close of land called Park Vedras in Kenwyn parish, on the north side of the road from Truro to Penryn, mentioned 'an old pair of walls heretofore called 'The Leaper's House'; in 1697 the place was written 'Leopards House'.[9] This site, which M. I. Somerscales identified with Richmond Hill, is a possible candidate for a leper community in the 14th century or later, standing as it does outside the settlement and on a main road.[10]

OTHER POSSIBLE SITES

Several other hospitals and leper communities have been conjectured in Cornwall as well as those for which there is substantive evidence. 'Clodgy' place-names of uncertain meaning are found in Breage,[11] Constantine,[12] Devoran,[13] Mawnan,[14] Paul,[15] and Perranuthnoe.[16] A folk tradition about a hospital is recorded at Carwithenack in Constantine.[17] A field near Trewolvas in St Columb Major in 1617 was called Lazar Park and may relate to a leper community, since it lay near a road junction.[18]

Several references to otherwise unknown hospitals seem to be the result of mistakes in documents or by historians. The will of John Megre in 1419 refers to the lazars of St Margaret (Helston) and St Margaret (Launceston), which are probably errors for the hospitals of St Mary Magdalene and St Leonard respectively. Megre had Cornish connections but had lived for a long time in London.[19] A hospital of St Margaret (Bodmin) referred to by R. M. Clay is a misunderstanding of a passage in the work of the 19th-century historian George Oliver.[20] He mentions a chapel of St Margaret in the town immediately after references to the hospitals of St Anthony and St George there, but he does not refer to a hospital and none is recorded.[21] An allusion by Richard Carew to a hospital of St Thomas (Launceston) seems to have been another mistake for St Leonard, but has been reproduced in some modern histories.[22] Finally it has been supposed that the chapels of St Margaret at Trelower in St Mewan and St Benedict at Lanivet belonged to leper houses.[23] In neither case is there either documentary or archaeological evidence. St Benedict is mentioned on several occasions between 1411 and 1535, as well as after the Reformation, but always simply as a chapel.[24]

---

1   Hale and Ellacombe (ed.), *Accounts of Executors*, 28. The suggested site is SW 9073 4593, based on archaeological finds (Henderson, 'Ecclesiastical History', 423; Somerscales, 'Lazar Houses in Cornwall', 86; CCC, HER 22995).
2   Hale and Ellacombe (ed.), *Accounts of the Executors*, 29; Somerscales, 'Lazar Houses', 94–5.
3   CRO, P/194/1/1.
4   Hale and Ellacombe (ed.), *Accounts of Executors*, 28.
5   Beresford and Finberg, *English Medieval Boroughs*, 82.
6   Somerscales, 'Lazar Houses', 74.
7   Hale and Ellacombe (ed.), *Accounts of Executors*, 29. For conjectures about a site, see Somerscales, 'Lazar Houses', 92–3.
8   Hale and Ellacombe (ed.), *Accounts of Executors*, 28–9.
9   Henderson, 'Ecclesiastical History', 257.
10 Somerscales, 'Lazar Houses', 87–8. For site information, see CCC, HER 18888–9.
11 At Trewavas Head (SW 5955 2678) (CCC, HER 29276).
12 C. G. Henderson, *A History of the Parish of Constantine in Cornwall* (1937), 17. For possible site information, see CCC, HER 24575.
13 Somerscales, 'Lazar Houses', 98. For possible site information, see CCC, HER 18492.
14 Somerscales, 'Lazar Houses', 98.
15 V. Russell, *West Penwith Survey* (1971), 78.
16 Somerscales, 'Lazar Houses', 99. For possible site information, see CCC, HER 29015.
17 J. Polsue, *A Complete Parochial History of Cornwall* (1867–72), I, 246.
18 C. G. Henderson, *St Columb Major Church and Parish, Cornwall* (1930), 56; Somerscales, 'Lazar Houses', 98.
19 N. Orme (ed.), *Cornish Wills 1342–1540*, DCRS new ser. 50 (2007), 52.
20 R. M. Clay, *The Mediaeval Hospitals of England* (1909), 283.
21 G. Oliver, *Monasticon Dioecesis Exoniensis* (1846), 15.
22 Above, p. 223–4.
23 Somerscales, 'Lazar Houses', 98.
24 Henderson, 'Ecclesiastical History', 287–8; N. Orme, *The Saints of Cornwall* (2000), 70.

ANCHORITES AND HERMITS

The evidence listed here is confined to documentary references. It does not include possible remains of anchorites' or hermits' cells preserved in parish churches or other places.[1]

Bodmin In 1361 the register of Edward the Black Prince, duke of Cornwall, records an order for the delivery of two oaks from Restormel park to Serlo of Cornwall who wished to lead a hermit's life, for the purpose of building him a hermitage at the end of the town of Bodmin.[2] In 1406 Richard Tyttesbury, canon of Exeter, bequeathed 40d. 'to the anchorite of Bodmin'.[3] This person or a successor, named Margaret, living as a recluse 'near Bodmin', was granted permission by Bishop Stafford of Exeter in 1416 to migrate to Henry V's new abbey of Bridgettine nuns at Sheen, later Syon, west of London and to be professed as a member of their order.[4]

St Germans In 1590 the crown granted the property of an alleged hermitage of St Mary in Tideford and St Germans, worth 2s. per annum, to Edward Dyer in a large body of properties said to have been concealed from confiscation during the Reformation.[5]

St Just-in-Penwith In 1302 a jury in the hundred of Penwith, west Cornwall, resolved that Thomas of Penmargh should be tried before the king's justices because 'he entered by night the house of Andrew Paugan, hermit, within the chapel of St Just and killed the same Andrew, and immediately fled.' We are also told that Andrew had a son, John.[6] The incident evidently relates to the parish of St Just-in-Penwith, but since that parish had a church which should have been described as such, the hermit may have lived at a subsidiary chapel in the parish, dedicated to the saint.[7] There were such chapels in some other Cornish parishes, including Gwinear and Madron.

Liskeard The chapel of Our Lady in the Park stood a little way west of Liskeard (SX 2382 6476), and was noted by John Leland in 1542 as a place where, up to 1538, 'was wont to be great pilgrimage'.[8] In 1339 Roger Godman, hermit of the chapel, was granted royal protection to collect alms for his support throughout the kingdom.[9] A successor of his, John Stokysley, also described as hermit of the chapel, occurs in 1440 when he and two other men were granted a licence by Bishop Lacy for services to be held in the chapel in their presence on three days of the week.[10]

Lostwithiel A charter of the late 12th century, in which Robert (II) of Cardinan confirmed grants by his ancestors to Tywardreath Priory, refers to 'the hermitage of Baldwin's Bridge (*de Ponte Baldewyni*) with the gardens and lands belonging to the same hermitage and necessaries from the wood to be held by the brother dwelling in the same place'.[11] This bridge, apparently in the vicinity of Lanlivery, has been conjectured as the bridge across the River Fowey at Lostwithiel.[12] If so, the hermitage there may be identical with one that was functioning in the late 13th century, when Edmund earl of Cornwall (1272–1300) granted to Brother Robert of Penlyn, hermit, an island surrounded by the waters of the Fowey, the houses on the island, and an annuity of £2 16s. 2d. from his property at Penknight near Lostwithiel.[13] An inquisition into the earl's property taken in November 1300 reported that the annuity was still being paid and described Robert as hermit 'of the island of Penlyn', evidently an island in the river and possibly at the bridge.[14] King Edward I, who inherited the earl's property, confirmed the grant in May 1301.[15]

There was another hermitage in Lostwithiel parish in the park adjoining the castle of Restormel. Here Earl Edmund was supporting a hermit by 1296–7, named Brother Philip of Restormel, with an annuity of £2 13s. 4d. that was still being paid in 1300.[16] In 1337 a description

---

1 The following accounts include information collected by the late Rotha Mary Clay and the late Basil Cottle, kindly conveyed to me by Dr E. Jones.
2 *Black Prince's Reg.*, II, 180–1.
3 N. Orme (ed.), *Cornish Wills 1342–1540*, DCRS new ser. 50 (2007), 200.
4 Chanter VIII, f. 218r; *Reg. Stafford*, 25, 328. In 1428 seven nuns of Syon were called Margaret or Margery, of whom Margaret Browne (or Brome) or Margery Philips might be relevant here (G. J. Aungier, *The History and Antiquities of Syon Monastery* (1840), 51–2). See also the mid 15th-century necrology of Syon (Cambridge, Magdalene College, F.4.23, ff. 7–12v).
5 *Cal. Pat. 33 Elizabeth I (1590–1591)*, List & Index Soc. 308 (2005), 103.
6 TNA, JUST 1/118, m. 52.
7 For possibilities, see C. G. Henderson, 'The Ecclesiastical History of the 109 Parishes of West Cornwall', *JRIC* new ser. 3 (1957–60), 239–41.
8 J. Leland, *Itinerary*, ed. L. Toulmin Smith (1907–10), I, 208.
9 *Cal. Pat.* 1338–40, 254.
10 *Reg. Lacy*, ed. Dunstan, II, 248–9.
11 G. Oliver, *Monasticon Dioecesis Exoniensis* (1846), 38.
12 C. Henderson and H. Coates, *Old Cornish Bridges and Streams* (1928), 13.
13 *Cal. Close 1296–1302*, 448.
14 *Cal. Inq. p. m.* III, 458.
15 *Cal. Close 1296–1302*, 448.
16 L. M. Midgley (ed.), *Ministers' Accounts of the Earldom of Cornwall, 1296–7*, vol. II, Royal Historical Society, Camden 3rd ser. 67 (1945), 241; *Cal. Inq. p. m.* III, 458.

of the castle mentions a bell there 'which belonged to the hermitage, formerly that of Brother Robert',[1] and in 1346 the Black Prince, now lord of the castle and park, ordered the payment of an annuity of £2 10s. for life to Brother Eustace 'hermit of the Trinity' in the park of Restormel.[2] The description suggests that he served or lived at the chapel of the Trinity known to have stood in the park. A fourth hermit in this sequence occurs in 1354 when the Black Prince agreed to increase the sum of £2 10s. per annum that he was paying to a chaplain named William Pruet, hermit of Restormel, by a further 16s. 8d. in return for a promise by Pruet that he would spend the rest of his life at the hermitage singing masses for the prince's ancestors.[3]

Marhamchurch   In May 1403 Bishop Stafford commissioned two clergy to place a woman named Cecily Moys of his diocese in a newly constructed house in the churchyard of the parish church of Marhamchurch where she wished to live a 'contemplative or anchoritic life'. She was allowed to remain there on probation until the following Christmas.[4] The remains of a window on the former north wall of the chancel of the church have been conjectured to be part of this cell. In 1405 the bishop granted *Lucy* Moys, anchorite of Marhamchurch, permission to choose a confessor,[5] and in 1406 Richard Tyttesbury, canon of Exeter, bequeathed 40d. 'to the anchorite of Marhamchurch', probably the same woman.[6]

St Michael's Mount   A hermit named Stephen Gildeford was granted an annuity of £4 by Syon Abbey in 1435, evidently to live at the Mount which belonged to the abbey. The same man or a successor, Stephen Treher' alias Symond, hermit of the Mount, is recorded receiving the annuity between 1456 and 1479.[7]

1   P. L. Hull (ed.), *The Caption of Seisin of the Duchy of Cornwall*, DCRS new ser. 17 (1971), 41.
2   *Black Prince's Reg.*, I, 22, 138
3   Ibid., II, 63.
4   Chanter VIII, f. 64r; *Reg. Stafford*, 251.
5   Chanter VIII, f. 76v; *Reg. Stafford*, 251.
6   Orme (ed.), *Cornish Wills*, 251.
7   Above, p. 235.

GLOSSARY

advowson – the right to choose and present the clergyman of a parish church and present him to the bishop for **institution**, or to be involved in choosing the head of a religious house; the owner of the right was known as the **patron**.

aisle – a subdivision of a church, usually alongside and parallel with the **nave**, **chancel**, or **choir**.

alien priory – a priory owned and ruled by an abbey in France.

altarage – a name for the lesser revenues of a **benefice**, including offerings made in church and small **tithes**.

altar – a stone table at which **mass** was celebrated. The high altar was the principal altar of a church, placed at the east end of the **chancel** or **choir**.

anchorite – a man or woman who took vows to live celibately and permanently in an enclosed room or house, as opposed to having some freedom of movement like a **hermit**.

anniversary – *see* **obit**.

annuellar – an alternative name for a **chantry priest**.

appropriation – the practice by which a religious house was allowed to make itself rector of a parish and to take **tithes** from the parish.

archdeacon – a cleric in charge of an archdeaconry, a subdivision of a diocese.

archpriest – a title sometimes given to the cleric in charge of a small **college** of priests.

assize of bread and ale – the right to fix the prices and quality of bread and ale.

bailiwick – an administrative area, a term used by the Knights Templars and the Order of St John of Jerusalem.

benefice – a remunerated post held by a cleric such as a **rector**, **vicar**, or secular **canon**.

breviary – a book containing the daily offices or services said by the clergy.

canon, regular – a cleric, similar to a monk, who belonged to an abbey or priory that followed the Rule of St Augustine or other similar rules.

canon, secular – a senior cleric serving a cathedral or **college**.

canon law – the law of the Church.

cell – a small religious house owned and ruled by an abbey or priory elsewhere.

chancel – the eastern part of a parish church where services were said, usually occupied only by clergy or important laity. In the case of cathedrals, monasteries, and colleges the term **choir** is generally used instead.

chantry – the saying of a daily mass by a priest for the good estate of a living person, or the soul of a dead one, either for a limited period or perpetually. The term is also used for the endowment that paid the priest, and for the place where the masses were said, such as a chapel inside a church

chantry priest – the priest of a **chantry**, also known in Devon and Cornwall as an annuellar.

chapel – an area within a church containing an altar, or a separate building with an altar that did not have the status of a parish church.

chaplain – a term used in the middle ages for priests who worked in parishes (but who were not **rectors** or **vicars**) and in private households.

chapter – a meeting of clergy.

choir – the eastern part of a cathedral, monastery, or college, where services were said, equivalent to the **chancel** of a parish church; also the collective term for the clergy who perform the service in that part of the church.

chorister – a boy singer in a cathedral or **college**.

chrism – a mixture of oil and balm used in baptism and in other rites.

churching – a ceremony by which a mother gave thanks after a birth, and was led back into the parish church by the priest.

clerestory – the upper part of a church, above the aisles, which carries a row of windows to light the church.

civil law – Roman law (as distinct from **canon law** and **common law**).

clerk – originally and usually a cleric who was not a priest, but of lower status; later also applied to priests.

collation – an act similar to an **institution**, in the case of a benefice of which the bishop was patron, so that he both nominated and instituted the person he appointed.

college, collegiate church – a church staffed by a resident group of secular clergy who governed it together. The word originally applied to a collection of clergy, not to any academic function.

commendation, '*in commendam*' – the grant of a benefice to somebody as a temporary measure, pending the appointment of a permanent occupant.

common law – the law of the courts of the king of England.

communion – *see* **mass**.

confession – the process of confessing one's sins to the rector or vicar of the parish at least once a year during Lent.

consistory – the court of the bishop of the diocese.

corrody – a pension charged on a monastery, which had to provide the pensioner with board and lodging for life.

crossing – the part of a church at the east end of the nave, between the transepts.

curate – originally the **rector** or **vicar** of a parish who exercised the **cure of souls**. After the Reformation the term came to mean a priest who assisted or deputised for a rector or vicar, but until the middle of the sixteenth century such men were usually known as **chaplains**.

cure of souls – the right and duty to care for the souls of the inhabitants of a parish.

dean – the title given to the chief cleric of a cathedral and of some colleges, as well as the presiding cleric of a **rural deanery**.

diocese – the territory ruled by a bishop. The diocese of Exeter covered Cornwall and Devon.

Dirige – the service of mattins for the dead.

donative – a term used after the Reformation of benefices to which the **patron** could appoint a clergyman without reference to the bishop.

escheat – the reversion of a piece of property to its overlord, after the death of a holder who did not have a recognised heir.

escheator – a royal officer in each county who dealt with **escheats** that reverted to the king.

excommunication – a punishment imposed by a cleric, usually a bishop, which forbade a sinner to attend church, receive the sacraments, or mix with other people.

frankpledge, view of – the right to enforce the medieval system of frankpledge, by which people in a community were obliged to take responsibility for one another's behaviour.

friar – a cleric who lived from voluntary donations, unlike monks and parish clergy who received their support from lands and other endowments.

gloss – a translation or note in a manuscript, placed between the lines or in the margins.

glebe – land belonging to the rector or vicar of a parish.

havener – an official in charge of harbours and shipping.

hermit – a person, usually male, who took a vow of celibacy and lived alone but was able to travel about, unlike an **anchorite**.

high altar – *see* **altar**

holywater clerk – *see* **parish clerk**

hospital – in medieval times a religious or semi-religious institution offering long-term care for lepers or the infirm, or short-term accommodation, rather than medical treatment.

incumbent – the occupant of a benefice such as a **rector** or **vicar**.

indulgence – a remission of **penance** granted by a pope or a bishop, in return for doing a good deed such as a crusade, pilgrimage, prayer, or contribution to a church or a hospital.

infangthief – the right of a landowner to try a thief caught within the boundaries of the landowner's property.

institution (also **admission**) – the act by which a bishop gave possession of a benefice to a clergyman presented to him by a **patron**.

ledger-stone – a flat stone laid over a grave in a church.

manual – a book containing the pastoral services done by clergy, such as baptisms, marriages, and funerals, so called because they took it around in their hands for these purposes.

mass – the service of the eucharist or holy communion.

mendicant – a friar; the term means a beggar.

minster – in modern use, a church (especially in the tenth, eleventh, and twelfth centuries) staffed by a group of canons, priests, or clerks, rather than monks; in later centuries such churches are known as **colleges** or collegiate churches.

missal – a book containing the service of the mass.

monk – a cleric who lived in a monastery that observed the Rule of St Benedict, or another similar rule.

mortuary – a due paid to a **rector** or **vicar** after someone's death.

nave – the western part of a church, also called the 'body', open to lay people.

nun – the female equivalent of a monk, living in a nunnery.

obit – a mass celebrated on the anniversary of someone's death, also known as an anniversary.

official – the deputy of a bishop or archdeacon who managed their legal affairs.

pardon, pardoner – an **indulgence** and the person who advertised it.

parish – the area belonging to a parish church, whose inhabitants had the duty to support that church and its clergyman and the right to receive care in return.

parish clerk – the assistant of a rector or vicar at the services in a parish church, usually a young man until the fifteenth century; the original term was 'holywater clerk'.

patron – the person with the right to appoint or be involved with the appointment of the rector or vicar of a parish church, or the head of a religious house. This right was known as an **advowson** or as 'patronage', and could be held by clergy or lay people.

peculiar, peculiar jurisdiction – a territory consisting of one or more parishes which had its own system of administration, separate from the normal administration of the diocese.

penance – the penalty due to a sin, which had to be discharged before the sin would be obliterated.

piscina – a drain in a church wall for disposing of holy water.

Placebo – the service of vespers for the dead.

prebend – a share of the income of a church, equivalent to a stipend or salary.

prebendal church – a church staffed by two or more prebendaries, differing from a **college** in that they did not generally live together as a community.

prebendary – the holder of a **prebend**, a member of the **secular clergy**.

presbytery – the eastern part of a choir of a church, near the high altar, where the clergy celebrated mass.

priest – a cleric with the power to say mass, baptise, and administer the other **sacraments**.

prior – the head of a **priory**, sometimes of a **hospital**.

priory – a monastery, generally less large and wealthy than an abbey. There were no abbeys in medieval Cornwall.

proctor – a legal representative or agent.

provision, papal provision – an appointment of a bishop, abbot, prior, cathedral canon, rector, or vicar by the pope instead of by the person(s) normally responsible for making the appointment. Such appointments were common in fourteenth-century England, but only replaced the rights of other clergy, never challenging those of lay people.

provost – the title given to some heads of **colleges**, including Glasney in Cornwall.

rector – the clergyman of a parish who received all its revenues, as opposed to a **vicar**. His benefice and house were known as a rectory.

regular clergy – monks, regular canons, friars, and nuns.

requiem – a mass including prayers for the soul of a dead person.

retrochoir – the area behind the high altar of a large church, similar to choir aisles.

rural deanery – a group of parishes administered by a rural **dean**.

sacraments – one of the seven solemn rites of the medieval Church: baptism, confirmation, marriage, confession, communion, ordination, and the anointing of the sick.

sanctuary – the part of the church around the high altar at the east end of the chancel or choir; also the name of a privilege by which people accused of a crime could take refuge in a church or on certain pieces of Church property; also an alternative name for glebe.

Sarum, Use of – **breviaries**, **manuals**, **missals**, and other service books following the usages of Salisbury Cathedral, commonly used in southern England in the fourteenth, fifteenth, and early sixteenth centuries.

secular clergy – clergy who did not follow the monastic life, such as parish clergy and the clergy of cathedrals and colleges.

sequestrate – to remove on a temporary basis the control and income of a property from the person who normally enjoys it.

sexton – a sacristan who helped look after a church, eventually coming to mean someone who did physical tasks such as ringing bells and digging graves.

sheriff – the chief officer of the king in each county, usually chosen from among the local gentry to serve for one year.

Sir – a title given to all priests, as well as to knights; it did not necessarily signify possession of a university degree.

stipend – the income of a **benefice** received by the cleric who held it.

suffragan – an assistant bishop.

tithe – the obligation of all householders to pay the rector of their parish one tenth of the produce of their land, including all crops and young animals. Fish, dairy products, and the milling of grain were also tithed. Tithes of grain were known as 'great tithes' or 'garb tithes'; other tithes as 'small tithes'.

tympanum – a panel within an archway above a church door or between the chancel and the nave.

vicar – the clergyman of an appropriated parish, who received part but not all of its revenues, unlike a **rector**. His benefice and house were known as a vicarage.

vicar choral – a clergyman in a collegiate church who deputised for a canon in saying the daily services.

vicar general – the deputy of a bishop, with general responsibility for administering his affairs, other than confirmations and ordinations which were done by his **suffragan**.

BIBLIOGRAPHY

UNPUBLISHED SOURCES

ABERYSTWYTH, NATIONAL LIBRARY OF WALES
    MS NLW 22253A (Lanteglos-by-Fowey, prayer book)
    MS NLW 23849D (*Bewnans Ke*)
    MS Peniarth 105 (*Bewnans Meriasek*)

ANTONY HOUSE, CORNWALL (archives administered by Cornwall Record Office)
    HD/11/92–101 (Henderson Deeds, Hospital of St John, Helston)

AVRANCHES (MANCHE), PUBLIC LIBRARY
    MS 159 (Mont St Michel, manuscript)

BARNSTAPLE, NORTH DEVON RECORD OFFICE
    B1/3960 (John Arundell, account book)

CAMBRIDGE, CORPUS CHRISTI COLLEGE
    MS 97, ff. 156r–183r (Bishop Alley, Return of clergy)

CAMBRIDGE, KING'S COLLEGE
    KCAR/3/3/1 (Ledger books)
    SBU/1–9 (St Buryan, documents)
    SMM/1–10 (St Michael's Mount, documents)

CAMBRIDGE, UNIVERSITY LIBRARY
    MS Ee.5.34 (St Buryan, register)

CANTERBURY CATHEDRAL ARCHIVES
    DCc MSSB/A/7 (Cornish crusaders)

EXETER, CATHEDRAL ARCHIVES
    D&C 606 (Altarnun church, contract)
    D&C 1006 (Glasney College, office of provost)
    D&C 1145 (William Bauceyn, chantry ordinance)
    D&C 1403 (St Merryn, account)
    D&C 1469 (William Holcombe, petition)
    D&C 2073 (King Stephen, charter)
    D&C 2080 (King John, charter)
    D&C 2099 (Tregony Priory, grant)
    D&C 2100 (Henry de Pomeroy, grant)
    D&C 2125 (Bodmin Priory, churches)
    D&C 2331 (Launceston Priory, injunctions)
    D&C 2672A (Visitations of churches, 1281)
    D&C 2851 (Visitations of churches, 1331)
    D&C 3498 (Letters)
    D&C 3688 (List of diocesan clergy, 1537)

EXETER, DEVON RECORD OFFICE
    158M/T3 (John Dabernon, will)
    158M/T6 (Nicholas Tremayn, will)
    Bedford Estates, W1258 M/E 31–7 (Scilly Priory, documents)
    Chanter II (Walter Stapledon, episcopal register)
    Chanter VIII (Edmund Stafford, episcopal register, vol. I)
    Chanter IX (Edmund Stafford, episcopal register, vol. II)
    Chanter XII(ii) (Episcopal registers, 1465–1504)
    Chanter XIII (Hugh Oldham, episcopal register)
    Chanter XIV (John Veysey, episcopal register, vol. I)
    Chanter XV (John Veysey, episcopal register, vol. II)
    Chanter XVI (John Veysey, episcopal register, vol. III)
    Chanter XVIII (James Turberville and William Alley, episcopal registers, vol. I)
    Chanter XIX (James Turberville and William Alley, episcopal registers, vol. II)
    CR 163 (Menheniot, court rolls)
    CR 655 (Bodmin Priory, rental)
    ED/M/1036 (Cowley Bridge, indulgence)
    Exeter City Archives, Book 51 (John Hooker, annals)
    Z 19/10/1a–b (Photostat of Cambridge, Corpus Christi College, MS 97, ff. 156r–183r)

EXETER, WEST COUNTRY STUDIES LIBRARY
    Hennessy's Register of Parish Clergy, Devon and Cornwall

HATFIELD HOUSE, HERTS.
    Court rolls, deeds, and general, 10/2, 14/20–24, 20/7, 35/5, 104/2–4, 104/6–9, 108/4 (St Michael's Mount, account rolls)

IPSWICH, SUFFOLK RECORD OFFICE
    IC/AA1/2/1/83 (Will of Robert Hoberd)

LAUNCESTON, BOROUGH ARCHIVES
    Rental, 1474–5

LONDON, BRITISH LIBRARY
    Additional Charter 29000 (Tavistock Abbey, deed)
    Additional MS 2657 (Miscellany, philosophy and medicine)
    Additional MS 7138 ('Plegmund letter' or 'Crediton claim')
    Additional MS 8102 (Exchequer, pensions and grants)
    Additional MS 9381 (Bodmin, gospels)
    Additional MS 10628 (John Somer, 'Kalendar')

Additional MS 29436 (Winchester Cathedral, cartulary)
Additional MS 29762 (William Hals, 'History of Cornwall')
Additional MSS 32243–4 (Stratton, churchwardens' accounts)
Additional MS 33420 (Thomas Tonkins, collections)
Additional MS 34792 (A) (Dinham family, cartulary)
Cotton MS Augustus I.i.35, 36, 38, 39 (Portfolio of maps)
Cotton MS Claudius E.vi (Priory of St John of Jerusalem, register 1503–26)
Cotton MS Julius A.vii (Miscellany, including 'Revelation of St Michael')
Cotton MS Nero E.vi (Priory of St John of Jerusalem, cartulary)
Cotton MS Vespasian A.xiv (Lives of Welsh saints)
Egerton 2104 (A) (Wherwell Abbey, cartulary)
Egerton 2657 (William Borlase, 'Parochial Memorandums, 1740')
Harley Charter 44 B 45 (King's College, Cambridge, petition)
Harley MS 597 (Miscellany, including the will of Thomas Tretherffe)
Harley MS 2252 (Miscellany, including legend of Holy Cross)
Harley MS 2399 (John Bowyer, miscellany)
Harley MS 6600 (St Buryan and Probus, tithes)
Harley MS 7048 (Miscellany, including St Buryan)
Lansdowne MS 160 (Privy Council and other records)
Lansdowne MS 200 (Priory of St John of Jerusalem, register 1492–1500)
Lansdowne MS 418 (Transcripts of Irish ecclesiastical records)
Lansdowne MS 966 (White Kennett, collections)
Royal MS 12.C.XII (Miscellany, including prophecies)
Royal MS 18 D.III (Christopher Saxton, maps)
Stowe MS 1023 (John Anstis, 'Imagines seu Figura')

LONDON, COLLEGE OF ARMS
MS L 10 (Heraldic miscellany)
MS L 17 (Priory of St John of Jerusalem, John Stillingfleet's register)
MS M 3 (Heraldic miscellany)

LONDON, DUCHY OF CORNWALL
E/6/1 (Ministers' Accounts, 1559–60)

LONDON, GUILDHALL LIBRARY
MS 9531/4 (Episcopal registers)

LONDON, LAMBETH PALACE LIBRARY
Simon Sudbury, archi-episcopal register
William Courtenay, archi-episcopal register
John Morton, archi-episcopal register
William Warham, archi-episcopal register

LONDON, THE NATIONAL ARCHIVES (formerly Public Record Office), KEW
C 1 (Chancery, Early chancery proceedings)
C 76 (Chancery, Treaty rolls and Norman rolls)
C 81 (Chancery, Warrants for the great seal)
C 84 (Chancery, Ecclesiastical petitions)
C 85 (Chancery, Significations of excommunication)
C 143 (Chancery, Inquisitions ad quod damnum)
C 258 (Chancery, Files, Certiorari corpus cum causa)
C 270 (Chancery, Ecclesiastical miscellanea)
CP 40 (Court of Common Pleas, Plea rolls)
DL 43 (Duchy of Lancaster, Rentals and surveys)
E 25 (Exchequer, T.R., Acknowledgements of supremacy)
E 36 (Exchequer, T.R., Miscellaneous books)
E 40 (Exchequer, T.R., Ancient deeds)
E 106 (Exchequer, K.R., Extents of alien priories)
E 117 (Exchequer, K.R. Church goods)
E 134 (Exchequer, K.R., Depositions taken by commission)
E 154 (Exchequer, K.R., Inventories of goods and chattels)
E 159 (Exchequer, K.R., Memoranda rolls)
E 163 (Exchequer, K.R., Miscellanea)
E 178 (Exchequer, K.R., Special commissions)
E 179 (Exchequer, K.R., Clerical subsidy rolls)
E 210 (Exchequer, K.R., Ancient deeds, series D)
E 301 (Exchequer, Augmentation Office, Chantry certificates)
E 315 (Exchequer, Augmentation Office, Miscellaneous books)
E 322 (Exchequer, Augmentation Office, Surrenders of monasteries)
E 326 (Exchequer, Augmentation Office, Ancient deeds, series B)
E 329 (Exchequer, Augmentation Office, Ancient deeds, series BS)
E 334 (Exchequer, First Fruits and Tenths, Composition books)
IR 29 (Board of Inland Revenue, Tithe apportionments)
IR 30 (Board of Inland Revenue, Tithe maps)
JUST 1 (Justices Itinerant, Assize rolls)
KB 9 (Court of King's Bench, Crown Side, Indictments files)
KB 27 (Court of King's Bench, Plea and Crown Sides, *Coram Rege* rolls)
LR 2 (Office of the Auditors of Land Revenue, Miscellaneous books)
MPF 1 (Maps and Plans)
PROB 11 (Prerogative Court of Canterbury, Registered copy wills)
REQ 2 (Court of Requests, Pleadings)
SC 2 (Special Collections, Court rolls)
SC 6 (Special Collections, Ministers' accounts)
SC 8 (Special Collections, Ancient petitions)
SC 11 (Special Collections, Rentals and surveys, rolls)
SP 1 (State Papers, Henry VIII, General series)

SP 11 (State Papers, Domestic, Mary)
SP 12 (State Papers, Domestic, Elizabeth I)
STAC 2 (Court of Star Chamber, Proceedings, Henry VIII)

OXFORD, BODLEIAN LIBRARY
MS Ashmole 763 (Heraldic miscellany)
MS Bodley 315 (Miscellany, including Launceston Priory verses)
MS Bodley 572 (*Codex Oxoniensis Posterior*)
MS Bodley 791 (Cornish Ordinalia)
MS Digby 81 (Tavistock Abbey, annals)
MS Digby 196 (Miscellany, including prophecies)
MS Douce 22 (Bodmin Priory, manual)
MS Dugdale 47 (Book of hours)
MS James 23 (Plympton Priory, cartulary)
MS Rawlinson A 315 (Peter Mundy, 'Itinerarium Mundi')
MS Rawlinson D 363 (Church property in Cornwall, 1548)
MS Rawlinson D 997 (Edward Lhuyd, Notes on Cornish parishes)
MS Tanner 196 (Launceston Priory, miscellany)
MS Tanner 221 (Records of the Guild of Jesus, St Paul's Cathedral)
MS Trinity College Oxford D 85 (Montacute Priory, cartulary)
MS Wood C 11 (Ralph Sheldon, church notes)
(printed book) Gough Cornwall 22 (R. Carew, *The Survey of Cornwall*, annotated)

PARIS, BIBLIOTHÈQUE NATIONALE
MS lat. 11,818 (Monasticon Gallicanum)

PENZANCE, MORRAB LIBRARY
Borlase manuscripts

ROUEN (SEINE MARITIME), BIBLIOTHÈQUE MUNICIPALE
MS A.27 (368) (Lanalet Pontifical)

TAUNTON, SOMERSET RECORD OFFICE
D/D/B Reg. 7 (The register of Robert Stillington)
DD/WO/23/1 (Charter of Hasculf de Soligny)
DD/WO/24/1/14 (Will of Thomas Whalesborough)

TOURS (INDRE ET LOIRE), BIBLIOTHÈQUE MUNICIPALE
MS 520 (Miscellany, including prophecies)

TRURO, CORNWALL RECORD OFFICE
AD/59/33 (Tithe apportionment, Gulval)
AD/103/2 (Maintenance and legacies of Joyce Flamank)
AR/1/793–5 (Arundell documents, Bodmin Priory)
AR/1/800–2 (Arundell documents, Bodmin)
AR/14/21 (Arundell documents, tin and mining records)
AR/21/7 (Arundell documents, Katherine Arundell, will)
AR/50/1 (Arundell documents, hospital of *Lamford*)
ARD/TER/84, 189–91, 409 (Archdeaconry of Cornwall, terriers)
ART/1–6 (Arundell documents, Tywardreath Priory)
AU/1 (St Michael's Mount, account roll)
B/BOD/244, /314/3–6, 22, 42 (Bodmin, borough records)
B/LAUS/105–7, 148–72 (Launceston, borough records)
B/LIS 171 (Liskeard, borough records)
CF/3582 (Coode and French, documents)
CL/52 (Clifden of Lanhydrock, documents)
ME/335 (Mount Edgcumbe, documents)
ME/595, /596 (Bodrugan family, cartulary and transcript)
P/7/5/1 (Antony, churchwardens' accounts)
P/13/1/1 (Bodmin, parish registers)
P/19/5/1 (St Breock, churchwardens' accounts)
P/102/5/1 (Kilkhampton, churchwardens' accounts)
P/126/1/1 (Liskeard, parish registers)
P/144/5/2 (Menheniot, churchwardens' accounts)
P/162/5/1 (St Neot, churchwardens' accounts)
P/167/5/1 (North Petherwin, churchwardens' accounts)
P/192/5/1 (Poughill, churchwardens' accounts)
P/194/1/1 (Probus, churchwardens' accounts)
PD/322/1 (Camborne, churchwardens' accounts)
R/3143–58 (Rashleigh of Menabilly, documents)
RS/59/1 (Glasney College, cartulary)
RS/60 (Tywardreath Priory, collation book)
TA/ and TM/ (Tithe apportionments and tithe maps) 6, 13, 22, 55, 68, 90, 99, 109, 111, 132–3, 144, 153, 194, 209, 213, 218–21, 227/1–2, 242–3
TF/677, /678/2 (Treffry accounts)
Padel, O. J., and McCann, L. 'Catalogue of Arundell Deeds' (CRO, typescript)

TRURO, TRURO COUNTY COUNCIL, HISTORIC ENVIRONMENT SERVICE
Historic Environment Register
Report No. 2005R061: *see below*, Cole, D.

TRURO, ROYAL INSTITUTION OF CORNWALL, COURTNEY LIBRARY
HC 19, 23, 62, 66 (Henderson collection)
MMP/22,1 (Map of Bodmin, 1822–3)

VALETTA, ARCHIVES OF MALTA, ARCHIVES OF THE KNIGHTS OF ST JOHN
MSS 54, 323, 334, 336, 338, 340, 349, 351, 353, 377, 379, 395, 398, 403–4, 406, 411, 414

YORK, BORTHWICK INSTITUTE OF HISTORICAL RESEARCH
Reg. 18 (Register of Henry Bowet)

PRINCIPAL PUBLISHED SOURCES

Adams, J. H. 'The Mediaeval Chapels of Cornwall,' *JRIC* new ser. 3 (1957–60), 48–65.

Aldhelm: the Prose Works, trans. M. Lapidge and M. Herren (Ipswich, 1979).

Allan, J. *Archaeological Recording at Minster Church Boscastle*, Exeter Archaeology, Report No. 05.19 (Exeter, 2005).

Allan, J. *Notes towards an Architectural History of Launceston Priory*, Exeter Archaeology, Report No. 09.58 (Exeter, 2009).

Andrews, C. T. *The Dark Awakening: a history of St Laurence's Hospital, Bodmin* (Bodmin, 1978).

The Anglo-Saxon Chronicle, trans. D. Whitelock (London, 1965).

Asser. *Asser's Life of King Alfred*, ed. W. H. Stevenson, new edn (Oxford, 1959).

Audin, P. *Guide des fontaines guérisseuses du Finistère* (Paris, 1983).

Audin, P. *Guide des fontaines guérisseuses du Morbihan* (Paris, 1983).

Bakere, J. *The Cornish Ordinalia: a critical study* (Cardiff, 1980).

Ballard, A., and Tait, J. *British Borough Charters, 1216–1307* (London, 1923).

Barlow, F. (ed.) *English Episcopal Acta*, vol. XI: *Exeter 1046–1184* (London and Oxford, 1996).

Barlow, F. (ed.) *English Episcopal Acta*, vol. XII: *Exeter 1186–1257* (London and Oxford, 1996).

Beresford, M. W., and Finberg, H. P. R. *English Medieval Boroughs: a handlist* (Newton Abbot, 1973).

Bewnans Ke, ed. C. G. Thomas and N. J. A. Williams (Exeter, 2007).

Bewnans Meriasek – see Stokes, W.

Birch, W. de G. *Cartularium Saxonicum*, 3 vols and index (1885–99), II, 527–8.

Black Prince, Register of Edward the, 4 parts (London, Public Record Office, 1930–3).

Blair, J. *The Church in Anglo-Saxon Society* (Oxford, 2005).

Blair, J. and Sharpe, R. (eds.) *Pastoral Care before the Parish* (Leicester, 1992).

Boardman, S. et al. (eds.) *Saints' Cults in the Celtic World* (Woodbridge, 2009).

Boase, C. W. *Registrum Collegii Exoniensis*, Oxford Hist. Soc. 27 (1894).

The Book of Fees, 3 vols (London, Public Record Office, 1920–31).

Bøgholm et al. N. (eds.) *Grammatical Miscellany offered to Otto Jespersen* (Copenhagen 1930).

Bowen, E. G. *The Settlements of the Celtic Saints in Wales* (Cardiff, 1954).

Bowen, E. G. *Saints, Seaways and Settlements in the Celtic Lands* (Cardiff, 1969).

Calendar of Chancery Rolls, Various: 1277–1326 (London, Public Record Office, 1912).

Calendar of Charter Rolls, 6 vols (London, Public Record Office, 1903–27).

Calendar of Close Rolls, 47 vols (London, Public Record Office, 1892–1963).

Calendar of Fine Rolls, 22 vols (London, Public Record Office, 1911–63).

Calendar of Documents Preserved in France, vol. I, ed. J. H. Round (RS, 1899).

Calendar of Inquisitions Miscellaneous, 8 vols (London, Public Record Office, 1916–2003).

Calendar of Inquisitions Post Mortem (London, Public Record Office, 1904–, in progress

Calendar of Papal Petitions, vol. I (London, Public Record Office, 1897).

Calendar of Papal Registers (London, Public Record Office, and Dublin, Irish Historical Manuscripts Commission, 1894–, in progress).

Calendar of Patent Rolls (London, Public Record Office, 1891–, in progress).

Calendar of State Papers, Venetian, 38 vols in 40 (London, Public Record Office, 1864–1947).

Carew, R. *The Survey of Cornwall* (London, 1602; 1603 modern style); repr. with introduction and index, ed. J. Chynoweth, N. Orme, and A. Walsham, DCRS new ser. 47 (2004).

Carey, J. et al. (eds.) *Studies in Irish Hagiography: Saints and Scholars* (Dublin, 2001).

Catalogue of Ancient Deeds, 6 vols (London, Public Record Office, 1890–1915).

Chambers, D. S. *Faculty Office Registers 1534–1549* (Oxford, 1966).

Charles-Edwards, T. 'The seven bishop-houses of Dyfed', *Bulletin of the Board of Celtic Studies* 24 (1970–2), 247–62.

Chédeville, A. and Guillotel, H. *La Bretagne des saints et des rois* (Rennes, 1984).

Clay, R. M. *The Mediaeval Hospitals of England* (London, 1909).

Clay, R. M. *The Hermits and Anchorites of England* (London, 1914).

Close Rolls: Henry III, 14 vols (London, Public Record Office, 1902–38).

Cockerham, P. D. *Continuity and Change: Memorialisation and the Cornish Funeral Monument Industry, 1497–1660* (Oxford, 2006).

Cokayne, G. E. *The Complete Peerage*, ed. V. Gibbs and H. A. Doubleday, 13 vols in 14 (1910–59).

Cole, D., et al. *Glasney College, Penryn, Cornwall* (Truro, Cornwall County Council, Historic Environment Service, Report No. 2005R061, 2005).

Colker, M. L. 'The Life of Guy of Merton by Rainald of Merton', *Mediaeval Studies* 31 (1969), 250–61.

Combellack, M. (ed.) *The Camborne Play: a translation of Beunans Meriasek* (Truro, 1988).

Conner, P. W. *Anglo-Saxon Exeter: a Tenth-Century Cultural History* (Woodbridge, 1993).

Coomber, J. E. 'Medieval Painting in Cornwall' (University of Exeter, unpublished MA thesis 1980).

Cooper, J. P. D. *Propaganda and the Tudor State* (Oxford, 2003).

Cornwall, John of – see Curley.

Councils and Synods I: A.D. 871–1204, ed. Dorothy Whitelock, M. Brett, and C. N. L. Brooke, 2 vols (Oxford, 1981).

Councils and Synods II: 1205–1313, ed. F. M. Powicke and C.R. Cheney, 2 vols (Oxford, 1964).

Cox, J. C. *Churchwardens' Accounts* (London, 1913).

Cox, J. C. *The Sanctuaries and Sanctuary Seekers of Mediaeval England* (London, 1911).

Cramp, R. et al. *Corpus of Anglo-Saxon Stone Sculpture*, VII, *South-West England* (Oxford, 2006).

Crossing, W. *Guide to Dartmoor*, 2nd edn. (Plymouth, 1912).

Curia Regis Rolls: Richard I to Henry III (London, Public Record Office, 1923–, in progress).

Curley, M. J. 'A New Edition of John of Cornwall's *Prophetia Merlini*', *Speculum* 57 (1982), 217–49.

Davis, J. L. and Kirby, D. P. (eds.) *Cardiganshire County History*, I, *From the Earliest Times to the Coming of the Normans* (Cardiff, 1994).

Davies, W. 'The Celtic Church' (review article), *Journal of Religious History* 8 (1974–5), 406–11.

De Labriolle, P. *Les Sources de l'histoire du montanisme* (Fribourg, 1913).

Deputy Keeper's Report – see Report of the Deputy Keeper

Dickinson, J. C. *The Origins of the Austin Canons and their Introduction into England* (London, 1950).

Doble, G. H. *Saint Melor, Patron of Mylor and Linkinhorne, and of Amesbury (Wilts.)*, Cornish Saints 13 (Long Compton, 1927).

Doble, G. H. *Saint Mewan and Saint Austol*, Cornish Saints 8, 2nd edn. (Long Compton, 1929).

Doble, G. H. *Saint Neot, Abbot and Confessor*, Cornish Saints 21 (Exeter,1929).

Doble, G. H. *Four Saints of the Fal*, Cornish Saints 20 (Exeter, 1929).

Doble, G. H. *Saint Perran, Saint Keverne, and Saint Kerrian*, Cornish Saints 29 (1931), 36–68.

Doble, G. H. *Saint Meriadoc, Bishop and Confessor*, Cornish Saints 34 (Truro, 1935).

Doble, G. H. (ed.) *Pontificale Lanaletense (Blbliothèque de la Ville de Rouen, A.27 cat. 368)* Henry Bradshaw Society 74 (1937).

Doble, G. H. *Saint Mawes, Abbot and Confessor*, Cornish Saints 1, 2nd edn (Long Compton, 1938).

Doble, G. H. *Saint Petrock, Abbot and Confessor*, Cornish Saints 11, 3rd edn (1938), 51–9.

Doble, G. H. 'The Relics of St Petroc', *Antiquity* 13 (1939), 403–15.

Domesday Book – see Farley, A.; Ellis, H.; Thorn, C. and F.

Dugdale, W. *Monasticon Anglicanum*, ed. J. Caley, H. Ellis, and B. Bandinel, 6 vols. in 8 (London, Rec. Com., 1817–30).

Dumville, D. N. *English Caroline Script and Monastic History* (Woodbridge, 1993).

Dumville, D. N. *Liturgy and the Ecclesiastical History of Late Anglo-Saxon England* (Woodbridge, 1992).

Dunkin, E. H. W. *The Church Bells of Cornwall* (London and Derby, 1878).

Dunkin, E. H. W. *The Monumental Brasses of Cornwall* (London, 1882).

Eames, E. S. *Catalogue of Medieval Lead-Glazed Earthenware Tiles in the Department of Medieval and Later Antiquities, British Museum*, 2 vols (London, 1980).

Edwards, N. and Lane, A. (eds.) *The Early Church in Wales and the West* (Oxford, 1992).

Ehwald, R. (ed.) *Aldhelmi Opera*, Monumenta Germaniae Historica, Auctores Antiquissimi, 15 (Berlin, 1919).

Ellis, H. (ed.) *Domesday Book: Additamenta* (London, Rec. Com., 1816).

Emden, A. B. *A Biographical Register of the University of Oxford to AD 1500*, 3 vols (Oxford, 1957–9).

Emden, A. B. *A Biographical Register of the University of Cambridge to 1500* (Cambridge, 1963).

Emden, A. B. *A Survey of Dominicans in England*, Institutum Historicum FF. Praedicatorum, Dissertationes Historicae 18 (Rome, 1967).

Emden, A. B. *A Biographical Register of the University of Oxford AD 1501 to 1540* (Oxford, 1974).

Enys, J. D., et al., 'Mural Painting in Cornish Churches', *JRIC* 15 (1901–2), 136–60.

Ernault, É. (ed.) *L'ancien mystère de saint-Gwénolé* (Rennes, 1932–4).

Etchingham, C. 'The implications of *paruchia*', *Ériu* 44 (1993), 139–62.

Etchingham, C. *Church Organisation in Ireland A.D. 650 to 1000* (Maynooth, 1999).

Evans, D. E. et al. (eds.) *Proceedings of the Seventh International Congress of Celtic Studies* (Oxford, 1986).

Farley, A. (ed.) *Domesday Book*, 2 vols (London, 1783); index, ed. H. Ellis (London, Rec. Com., 1816).

Farmer, D. H. (ed.) *The Oxford Dictionary of Saints* (Oxford, 1978), 398.

Feudal Aids. Inquisitions and Assessments relating to Feudal Aids, 6 vols (London, Public Record Office, 1899–1021).

Finberg, H. P. R. *The Early Charters of Devon and Cornwall*, University of Leicester, Department of English Local History, occasional papers 2, 2nd edn (1963).

Fizzard, A. D. *Plympton Priory* (London and Boston, Ma, 2008).

Fletcher, J. R., and Stéphan, J. *Short History of St. Michael's Mount Cornwall* (St Michael's Mount, 1951).

Flobert, P. (ed.) *La Vie ancienne de Saint Samson de Dol* (Paris, 1997).

Förster, M. 'Die Freilassungsurkunden des Bodmin-Evangeliars', in N. Bøgholm, A. Brusendorff, and C. Bodelsen (ed.), *A Grammatical Miscellany offered to Otto Jespersen* (Copenhagen and London, 1930), 77–99.

Fowler, D. C. *John Trevisa* (Aldershot, 1993).

Fowler, D. C. *The Life and Times of John Trevisa, Medieval Scholar* (Seattle and London, 1995).

Fox, H. S. A., and Padel, O. J. (ed.) *The Cornish Lands of the Arundells of Lanherne*, DCRS new ser. 41 (2000).

Foxe, J. *Acts and Monuments*, ed. J. Pratt, 8 vols (4th edn, London, 1877).

Frere, W. H., and Kennedy, W. M. (ed.) *Visitation Articles and Injunctions of the Period of the Reformation*, 3 vols, Alcuin Club 14–16 (1908–10).

Frost, D. H. '*Sacrament an Alter*: a Tudor Cornish Patristic Catena', *Cornish Studies*, new ser. 11 (2003), 291–307.

Frost, D. H. 'Glasney's parish clergy and the Tregear manuscript', *Cornish Studies*, 2nd series, 15 (2007) 27–89.

Fryde, E. B., Greenway, D. E., Porter, S., and Roy, I. (ed.) *Handbook of British Chronology* (3rd edn, London, Royal Historical Society, 1986).

Gascoyne, J. *A Map of the County of Cornwall*, ed. W. L. D. Ravenhill and O. J. Padel, DCRS new ser. 34 (1991).

Gilbert, C. S. *Historical and Topographical Survey of the County of Cornwall*, 2 vols (Plymouth and London, 1817–20).

Gilbert, D. *The Parochial History of Cornwall*, 4 vols (London, 1838).

Gildas. *The Ruin of Britain and Other Works*, ed. M. Winterbottom (London, 1978).

Giot. P. R. et al., *The British Settlement of Brittany* (Stroud, 2003).

Golding, B. 'Robert of Mortain', *Anglo-Norman Studies* 13 (1990), 19–44.

Goulding, R. W. *Records of the Charity known as Blanchminster's Charity* (Louth, Stratton, and Bude, 1898).

Graham, R. *English Ecclesiastical Studies* (London, 1929).

Graves, E. van T. (ed.) 'The Old Cornish Vocabulary' (Columbia University, New York, PhD thesis, 1962).

Grosjean, P. 'Vie et Miracles de. S. Petroc', *Analecta Bollandiana* 74 (1956), 131–88, 470–96.

Gwara, S. *Education in Wales and Cornwall in the Ninth and Tenth Centuries: Understanding* De raris fabulis (Cambridge, Kathleen Hughes Memorial Lectures, 4, 2004).

Haines, R. M. 'A Confraternity Document of St Mary Magdalene's Hospital, Liskeard', *Bulletin of the Institute of Historical Research* 45 (1972), 128–35, repr. with an illustration and additions in idem, *Ecclesia Anglicana: Studies in the English Church of the Later Middle Ages* (Toronto, 1989), 192–200.

Hale, W. H., and Ellacombe, H. T. (ed.) *Accounts of the Executors of Richard Bishop of London 1303, and of the Executors of Thomas Bishop of Exeter 1310*, Camden Society new ser. 10 (1874).

Harding, P. A., and others. 'The Evaluation of a Medieval Leper Hospital at St Leonard's, Cornwall', *Cornish Archaeology* 36 (1997), 138–50.

Harley, J. B., and O'Donoghue, Y. (ed.) *The Old Series Ordnance Survey Maps of England and Wales*, vol. II (Lympne, 1977).

Harvey, J. H. (ed.) *William Worcestre: Itineraries* (Oxford, 1969).

Heales, A. *The Records of Merton Priory in the County of Surrey* (London, 1898).

Henderson, C. G. *The Cornish Church Guide* (Truro, 1927).

Henderson, C. G. 'Records of St John's Hospital near Helston', *JRIC* 22 (1928), 382–407.

Henderson, C. G. *Records of the Church and Priory of St Germans* (Long Compton, 1929).

Henderson, C. G. *St. Columb Major Church and Parish, Cornwall* (Shipston-on-Stour, 1929; Long Compton, [1930]).

Henderson, C. G. 'Records of the Borough of Truro before A.D.1300', *JRIC* 23 (1929–32), 103–36.

Henderson, C. G. 'Rialton', *Old Cornwall* 2/12 (1931–6), 1–10.

Henderson, C. G. *Essays in Cornish History* (Oxford, 1935).

Henderson, C. G. 'Concerning Bodmin Priory', *Journal of the Royal Polytechnic Society of Cornwall* new ser. 8/3 (1936), 27–39.

Henderson, C. G. *A History of the Parish of Constantine in Cornwall*, ed. G. H. Doble (Long Compton, 1937).

Henderson, C. G. 'The Ecclesiastical History of the 109 Parishes of West Cornwall', *JRIC* new ser. 2 (1953–6), 1–210; 3 (1957–60), 211–382, 383–497. Pagination is independent of the rest of these volumes.

Henderson, C. G. 'The ecclesiastical antiquities of the four western hundreds of Cornwall', *Journal of the Royal Institution of Cornwall*, n.s. 2 (1953–6) and 3 (1957–60).

Henderson, C. G., and Coates, H. *Old Cornish Bridges and Streams* (Exeter, 1928, repr. Truro, 1972).

Herring, P. *An Archaeological Evaluation of St Michael's Mount* (Truro, Cornwall Archaeology Unit, 1993).

Hingeston-Randolph, F.C. *Register of Bishop Grandisson*, 3 vols.

Hobbs, S. (ed.) *The Cartulary of Forde Abbey*, Somerset Record Soc. 85 (1998).

Hooke, D. *Pre-Conquest Charter-Bounds of Devon and Cornwall* (Woodbridge, 1994).

Hooker, J. *A Catalog of the Bishops of Excester* (London, 1584).

Hughes, K. 'The Celtic Church: is this a valid concept?' *Cambridge Medieval Celtic Studies* 1 (1981), 1–20.

Hughes, P. L., and Larkin, J. F. *Tudor Royal Proclamations*, 3 vols (1964–9).

Hull, P. L. (ed.) *The Cartulary of St Michael's Mount*, DCRS new ser. 5 (1962).

Hull, P. L. 'The Foundation of St.-Michael's Mount in Cornwall: a Priory of the Abbey of Mont St.-Michel', in *Millénaire monastique du Mont Saint-Michel: mélanges commemoratifs: I. Histoire et vie monastique* (Paris, 1967), 703–24.

Hull, P. L. (ed.) *The Caption of Seisin of the Duchy of Cornwall (1337)*, DCRS new ser. 17 (1971).

Hull, P. L. 'Thomas Chiverton's Book of Obits', *DCNQ* 33 (1974–7), 97–102, 143–7, 188–93, 236–9, 277–82, 337–41; 34 (1978–81), 5–11, 52–5.

Hull, P. L. (ed.) *The Cartulary of Launceston Priory*, DCRS new ser. 30 (1987).

Hull, P. L., and Sharpe, Richard. 'Peter of Cornwall and Launceston', *Cornish Studies* 13 (1985), 5–53.

Iago, W. 'The Ecclesiastical Seals of Cornwall', *JRIC* 8 (1883–5), 28–79.

James, J. 'The Medieval Chapels of Devon' (University of Exeter, unpublished MPhil thesis, 1997).

Jankulak, K. *The Medieval Cult of St Petroc* (Woodbridge, 2000).

Jeffrey, H. M. 'A Map of the River Fal and its Tributaries from a Survey Made in 1597 by Baptista Boazio', *JRIC* 9 (1886–9), 165–70.

Jenner, H. 'The Bodmin Gospels', *JRIC* 21 (1922–5), 113–45.

Jenner, H. 'The Manumissions in the Bodmin Gospels', *JRIC* 21 (1922–5), 235–60.

Jenner, H. 'The Lannaled mass of St Germanus in Bodl. MS. 572', *Journal of the Royal Institution of Cornwall* 23 (1929–32), 477–92.

Jenner, H., and Taylor, T. 'The Legend of the Church of the Holy Cross in Cornwall', *JRIC* 20 (1915–21), 295–309.

Jones, F. *The Holy Wells of Wales* (Cardiff, 1954).

Jülicher, A. 'Ein gallisches Bischofsschreiben des 6. Jahrhunderts als Zeuge für die Verfassung der Montanistenkirche', *Zeitschrift für Kirchengeschichte*, 16 (1986), 664–71.

Kain, R. J. P., and Oliver, R. R. *The Tithe Maps of England and Wales: a cartographic analysis and county-by-county catalogue* (Cambridge, 1995).

Kain, R. J. P., and Prince, H. C. *The Tithe Surveys of England and Wales* (Cambridge, 1985).

Kain, R. J. P., and Prince, H. C. *Tithe Surveys for Historians* (Chichester, 2000).

Kain, R. J. P., and Ravenhill, W. L. D. (ed.) *Historical Atlas of South-West England* (Exeter, 1999).

Kemble, J. M. (ed.) *Codex Diplomaticus Aevi Saxonici*, 6 vols (London, 1839–48).

Ker, N. R. *Medieval Libraries of Great Britain* (2nd edn, London, 1964); *Supplement to the Second Edition*, ed. A. G. Watson (London, 1987).

Keynes S. and Lapidge, M. *Alfred the Great: Asser's Life of King Alfred and other Contemporary Sources* (Harmondsworth, 1983).

Knight, J. K. 'Seasoned with Salt: insular-Gallic contacts in the early memorial stones and cross slabs', in K. R. Dark (ed.), *External Contacts and the Economy of Late Roman and Post-Roman Britain* (Woodbridge, 1996), pp. 109–20.

Knowles, D., Brooke, C. N. L., and London, V. C. M. (ed.), *The Heads of Religious Houses: England and Wales. I, 940–1216* (2nd edn, Cambridge, 2001).

Knowles, D., and Hadcock, R. N. *Medieval Religious Houses: England and Wales*, (2nd edn, London, 1971).

Lack, W., Stuckfield, H. M., and Whittemore, P. *The Monumental Brasses of Cornwall* (London, 1997).

Lane-Davies, A. *Holy Wells of Cornwall* (No place, 1970).

Langdon, A. *Stone Crosses in North Cornwall* (2nd edn, [St Austell,] 1996).

Langdon, A. *Stone Crosses in West Penwith* ([St Austell,] 1997).

Langdon, A. *Stone Crosses in West Cornwall* ([St Austell,] 1999).

Langdon, A. *Stone Crosses in Mid Cornwall*, 2nd edn ([St Austell,] 2002).

Langdon, A. *Stone Crosses in East Cornwall*, 2nd edn ([St Austell,] 2002).

Langdon, A. G. *Old Cornish Crosses* (Truro, 1896).

Largillière, R. *Les Saints et l'organisation chrétienne primitive dans l'Armorique bretonne* (Rennes, 1923).

Latham et al. R. E. (eds.) *Dictionary of Medieval Latin from British Sources* (Oxford, 1975–).

Leach, A. F. *English Schools at the Reformation, 1546–8* (Westminster, 1896).

Le Berre, Y. et al. (eds.) *Buez santez Nonn, mystère breton: vie de sainte* Nonne (Treflevenez, 1999).

Leland, J. *Collectanea*, ed. T. Hearne, 6 vols (2nd edn, London, 1774).

Leland, J. *The Itinerary of John Leland*, ed. L. Toulmin Smith, 5 vols (London, 1907–10).

Le Neve, J. *Fasti Ecclesiae Anglicanae 1066–1300*, vol. X: *Exeter*, ed. D. E. Greenway (London, 2005).

Le Neve, J. *Fasti Ecclesiae Anglicanae 1300–1541*, vol. IX: *Exeter Diocese*, ed. J. M. Horn (London, 1964).

Lepine, D. *A Brotherhood of Canons Serving God: English Secular Cathedrals in the Later Middle Ages* (Woodbridge, 1995).

Lepine, D., and Orme, N. (ed.) *Death and Memory in Medieval Exeter*, DCRS new ser. 46 (2003).

Letters and Papers, Foreign and Domestic, Henry VIII, ed. S. J. Brewer, J. Gairdner, and R. H. Brodie, 21 vols in 33 parts (London, 1864–1932).

Letters Relating to the Hospitals in the Diocese of Exeter, communicated at the instance of Bishop Seth Ward (No place, 1665).

Lettres Communes des Papes du XIVe Siècle: Urbain V, Lettres Communes, ed. M. H. Laurent et al., 12 vols (Paris, 1954–85).

Lysons, D. and S. *Magna Britannia*, vol. III: *Cornwall* (London, 1814).

Lloyd, J. E. *A History of Wales, from the Earliest Times to the Norman Conquest*, 3rd edn, 2 vols (London, 1939).

Maclean, Sir J. *The Parochial and Family History of the Deanery of Trigg Minor*, 3 vols. (London and Bodmin, 1873–9).

Matthew, D. J. A. *The Norman Monasteries and their English Possessions* (London, 1962).

Matthews, J .H. *A History of the Parishes of Saint Ives, Lelant, Towednack and Zennor* (London, 1892).

Mattingly, J. 'The Medieval Parish Guilds of Cornwall', *JRIC* new ser. 10/3 (1989), 290–329.

Mattingly, J. 'The Dating of Bench-ends in Cornish Churches', *JRIC* new ser. II, 1/1 (1991), 58–72.

Mattingly, J. 'Stories in the Glass: reconstructing the St Neot pre-Reformation glazing scheme', *JRIC* new ser. II, 3/3–4 (2000), 9–55.

Mattingly, J., et al., 'A Tin Miner and a Bal Maiden: further research on the St Neot windows', *JRIC* (2001), 96–100.

Mattingly, J. 'Pre-Reformation Saints' Cults in Cornwall, with particular reference to the St Neot windows', in J. Cartwright (ed.), *Celtic Hagiography and Saints' Cults* (Cardiff, 2003), 249–70.

Mattingly, J. 'Going A-Riding: Cornwall's late-medieval guilds revisited', *JRIC* (2005), 78–103.

Meyrick, J. *A Pilgrim's Guide to the Holy Wells of Cornwall* (Falmouth, 1982).

Napier, A. S., and Stevenson, W. H. (ed.) *The Crawford Collection of Early Charters and Documents now in the Bodleian Library* (Oxford, 1895).

New, C. W. *History of the Alien Priories in England to the Confiscation of Henry V* (Chicago, 1916).

Nonarum Inquisitiones in Curia Scaccarii, ed. G. Vanderzee (London, Record Commission, 1807).

Norden, J. *Speculi Britanniae Pars: Cornwall* (London, 1728).

Norden, J. *John Norden's Manuscript Maps of Cornwall and its Nine Hundreds*, ed. W. L. D. Ravenhill (Exeter, 1972).

Norris, E. (ed.) *The Ancient Cornish Drama*, 2 vols (Oxford, 1859).

Okasha, E. *Corpus of Early Christian Inscribed Stones of South-West Britain* (London, 1993).

Okasha, E. 'A Supplement to Corpus of Early Christian Inscribed Stones of South-West Britain', *Cornish Archaeology* 37–8 (1998–9), 137–52.

Oliver, G. *Monasticon Dioecesis Exoniensis*, with supplement (Exeter and London, 1846).

Oliver, G. *Additional Supplement to the Monasticon Dioecesis Exoniensis* (Exeter, 1854).

Olson, L. *Early Monasteries in Cornwall* (Woodbridge, 1989).

Olson, L. 'Cornish rural religious processions', *Australian Celtic Journal* 1 (1988), 22–9.

Olson, L., and Padel, O. J. 'A Tenth-Century List of Cornish Parochial Saints', *Cambridge Medieval Celtic Studies* 12 (1986), 33–71.

Ó Riain, P. 'Towards a methodology in early Irish hagiography', *Peritia* 1 (1982).

Orme, N. *Education in the West of England, 1066–1548* (Exeter, 1976).

Orme, N. 'The Early Musicians of Exeter Cathedral', *Music and Letters* 59 (1978), pp. 395–410.

Orme, N. *The Minor Clergy of Exeter Cathedral* (Exeter, 1979).

Orme, N. 'The Dissolution of the Chantries in Devon, 1546–8', *TDA* 111 (1979), 78–80.

Orme, N. 'The Church in Crediton from Saint Boniface to the Reformation', in T. A. Reuter (ed.), *The Greatest Englishman: essays on St Boniface and the Church at Crediton* (Exeter, 1980), 97–131.

Orme, N. 'The Medieval Clergy of Exeter Cathedral: I, the Vicars Choral and Annuellars', *TDA* 113 (1981), 79–102.

Orme N. 'The Medieval Clergy of Exeter Cathedral: II, the Secondaries and Choristers', *TDA* 115 (1983), 79–100.

Orme, N. 'St Michael and his Mount', *JRIC* new ser. 10/1 (1986–7), 32–43.

Orme, N. 'Indulgences in the Diocese of Exeter', *TDA*, 120 (1988), 15–32.

Orme, N. 'Music and Teaching at Tywardreath Priory, 1522–1536', *DCNQ* 36/8 (1990), 277–80.

Orme, N. 'Sufferings of the Clergy': illness and old age in Exeter diocese, 1300–1540, in M. Pelling and R. M. Smith (ed.), *Life, Death, and the Elderly: historical perspectives* (London, 1991), 62–73.

Orme, N. 'Indulgences in Medieval Cornwall', *JRIC* new ser. II, 1/2 (1992), 149–70.

Orme, N. 'Bishop Grandisson and Popular Religion', *TDA* 124 (1992), 107–18.

Orme, N. 'Saint Breage; a medieval virgin saint of Cornwall', *Analecta Bollandiana* 110 (1992), 341–52.

Orme, N. 'Education in the Cornish Play *Beunans Meriasek*', *Cambridge Medieval Celtic Studies* 25 (1993), 1–13.

Orme, N. 'The Clergy of Clyst Gabriel, 1312–1508', *TDA* 126 (1994), 107–121.

Orme, N. *English Church Dedications* (Exeter, 1996).

Orme, N. 'Church and Chapel in Medieval England', *Transactions of the Royal Historical Society* 6th ser. 6 (1996), 75–102.

Orme, N. 'A Fifteenth-Century Prayer-Book from Cornwall: MS NLW 22253A', *JRIC* n.s. II, 3/2 (1999), 69–73.

Orme, N. *The Saints of Cornwall* (Oxford, 2000).

Orme, N. 'The Lanteglos Prayer-Book: a further note', *JRIC* new ser. II, 3/3–4 (2000).

Orme, N. *Medieval Children* (New Haven and London, 2001).

Orme, N. 'Confession in a Fifteenth-Century Devon Parish', *TDA* 134 (2002), 57–68.

Orme, N. 'Popular Religion and the Reformation in England: a View from Cornwall', in J. A. Tracy and M. Ragnow (ed.), *Official Religion and Lived Religion* (Cambridge, 2004), 351–75.

Orme, N. *Medieval Schools* (New Haven and London, 2006).

Orme, N. 'The Other Parish Churches: Chapels in Late Medieval England', in C. Burgess and E. Duffy (ed.), *Parish Churches in Late Medieval England* (Donington, 2006), 78–94.

Orme, N. 'The Church and Clergy of St Buryan, c.1200–c.1574', *JRIC* (2006), 32–44.

Orme, N. 'Prayer and Education in Fifteenth-Century Camborne', *JRIC* (2006), 95–104.

Orme, N. (ed.) *Cornish Wills 1342–1540*, DCRS new ser. 50 (2007).

Orme, N. *Cornwall and the Cross: 500–1560* (London, 2007).

Orme, N. *Exeter Cathedral : the first thousand years* (Exeter, 2009).

Orme, N. 'The Cornish at Oxford University, 1180–1540', *JRIC* (2010).

Orme, N., and Padel, O. J. 'The Medieval Lepers of Lamford, Cornwall', *Historical Research* 69 (1995), 102–7.

Orme, N., and Padel, O. J. 'Cornwall and the Third Crusade', *JRIC* (2005), 71–7.

Orme, N., and Webster, M. *The English Hospital, 1070–1570* (New Haven and London, 1995).

The Oxford Dictionary of National Biography, ed. C. Matthew and B. Harrison, 60 vols (Oxford, 2004); updated electronic edition http://www.oxforddnb.com

Padel, O. J. 'Cornish Language Notes: 5. Cornish Names of Parish Churches', *Cornish Studies* 4–5 (1976–7), 15–27.

Padel, O. J. 'Two New Pre-Conquest Charters for Cornwall', *Cornish Studies* 6 (1978), 20–7.

Padel, O. J. *Cornish Place-Name Elements*, English Place-Name Society 56/57 (1985).

Padel, O. J. *A Popular Dictionary of Cornish Place-Names* (Penzance, 1988).

Padel, O. J. 'Glastonbury's Cornish Connections', in L. Abrams and J. P. Carley (ed.), The *Archaeology and History of Glastonbury Abbey* (Woodbridge, 1991), 245–56.

Padel, O. J. 'The nature of Arthur', *Cambrian Medieval Celtic Studies* 27 (1994), 1–31.

Padel, O. J. 'Notes on the New Edition of the Middle Cornish "Charter Endorsement"', *Cambrian Medieval Celtic Studies* 30 (1995), 123–7.

Padel, O. J. 'Local Saints and Place-Names in Cornwall' in A. Thacker and R. Sharpe (ed.), *Local Saints and Local Churches in the Early Medieval Period* (Oxford, 2002), 303–60.

Padel, O. J. 'Oral and Literary Culture in Medieval Cornwall', in H. Fulton (ed.), *Medieval Celtic Literature and Society* (Dublin, 2005), 95–116.

Padel, O. J. 'The Charter of Lanlawren (Cornwall)', in K. O'Brien O'Keeffe and A. Orchard (ed.), *Latin Learning and English Lore*, 2 vols (Toronto and London, 2005), II, 74–85.

Padel, O. J. *Slavery in Saxon Cornwall: the Bodmin Manumissions* (Cambridge, 2009).

Page, M. 'The Ownership of Advowsons in Thirteenth-Century Cornwall', *DCNQ*, 37/10 (1996), 336–41.

The Parliament Rolls of Medieval England 1275–1504, ed. Chris Given-Wilson et al., 16 vols (Woodbridge and London, 2005).

Parliamentary Papers, *Commissions of Inquiry into Charities in England and Wales, Thirty-second Report*, Part I (London, 1837), 401–516 [covers Cornwall].

Pearce, S. M. (ed.) *The Early Church in Western Britain and Ireland*, British Archaeological Reports, British Series 102 (Oxford, 1982).

Peter, O. B. *Launceston Priory: The Substance of a Lecture* (Launceston, 1889).

Peter, R. and O. B. *The Histories of Launceston and Dunheved* (Plymouth, 1885).

Peter, T. C. *The History of Glasney Collegiate Church, Cornwall* (Camborne, 1903).

Petts, D. 'Cemeteries and Boundaries in Western Britain', in S. Lucy and A. Reynolds (ed.), *Burial in Early Medieval England and Wales* (London, 2002), 24–46.

Picken, W. M. M. 'The "Landochou" Charter', in W.G. Hoskins, *The Westward Expansion of Wessex*, University of Leicester, Department of Local History, Occasional Papers 13 (1960), 36–44.

Picken, W. M. M. 'The Manor of Tremaruustel and the Honour of St Keus', *JRIC* new ser. 7 (1973–7), 220–30.

Picken, W. M. M. 'Light on Lammana', *DCNQ* 35/8 (1985), 281–6.

Picken, W. M. M. 'Bishop Wulfsige Comoere: an unrecognised tenth-century gloss in the Bodmin Gospels', *Cornish Studies* 14 (1986), 34–8.

Picken, W. M. M. *A Medieval Cornish Miscellany*, ed. O. J. Padel (Chichester, 2000).

Pipe Rolls:

Magnum Rotulum Scaccarii vel Magnum Rotulum Pipae… 33 Hen. I, ed. J. Hunter (London, Rec. Com.., 1844; reissued, London, HMSO, 1929)

The Great Rolls of the Pipe… 2, 3, and 4 Henry II, ed. J. Hunter, (London, Rec. Com., 1844).

The Great Roll of the Pipe… 23 Henry II, PRS 26 (1905).

Placita de Quo Warranto temporibus Edw. I, II & III, ed. W. Illingworth (London, Rec. Com., 1818).

Plummer, C. (ed.) *Vitae Sanctorum Hiberniae*, 2 vols (Oxford, 1910), I, 232.

[Polsue, J.] *A Complete Parochial History of the County of Cornwall*, 4 vols (Truro and London, 1867–72).

Pool, P. A. S. 'The Ancient and Present State of St. Michael's Mount, 1762', *Cornish Studies* 3 (1976), 29–47.

Potts, R. (ed.) *A Calendar of Cornish Glebe terriers 1673–1735*, DCRS new ser. 19 (1974).

Pounds, N. J. G. (ed.) *The Parliamentary Survey of the Duchy of Cornwall*, 2 parts, DCRS new ser. 25, 27 (1982–4).

Powicke, F. M., and Cheney, C. R. (ed.) *Councils and Synods II: A.D. 1205–1313*, 2 vols (Oxford, 1964).

Preston-Jones, A. 'Decoding Cornish Churchyards', in N. Edwards and A. Lane (ed.), *The Early Church in Wales and the West* (Oxford, 1992), 104–24, repr. in *Cornish Archaeology* 33 (1994), 71–95.

Preston-Jones, A. and Langdon, A. 'St Buryan crosses', *Cornish Archaeology* 36 (1997), 107–28.

Preston-Jones, A., and Rose, P. 'Medieval Cornwall', *Cornish Archaeology* 25 (1986), 155–85.

Probert, D. W. 'Church and Landscape: a study in social transition in south-western Britain A.D. *c*.400–*c*.1200' (Birmingham University, unpublished PhD thesis, 2002).

Pryce, H. *Native Law and the Church in Medieval Wales* (Oxford, 1993).

Pryce, H. 'Ecclesiastical sanctuary in thirteenth-century Welsh law', *Journal of Legal History* 5 (1984), 1–13.

Quiller-Couch, M. and L. *Ancient and Holy Wells of Cornwall* (London, 1894, repr. Liskeard, 1994).

Rashleigh, J., and Vincent, J. A. C. (ed.) *Abstract of the Glasney Cartulary* (Truro, 1879).

Ratcliffe, J. *The Archaeology of Scilly* (Truro, Cornwall Archaeology Unit, 1989).

Rattue, J. *The Living Stream: Holy Wells in Historical Context* (Woodbridge, 1995).

Regesta Regum Anglo-Normannorum, ed. H. W. C. Davis et al., 4 vols. (Oxford, 1913–59); vol. I, ed. D. Bates (2nd edn, Oxford, 1998).

The Register of Thomas de Brantyngham, Bishop of Exeter, ed. F. C. Hingeston-Randolph, 2 vols (London and Exeter, 1901–6).

The Registers of Walter Bronescombe and Peter Quivil, Bishops of Exeter, ed. F. C. Hingeston-Randolph (London and Exeter, 1889).

The Register of Walter Bronescombe Bishop of Exeter 1258–1280, ed. O. F. Robinson, 3 vols, Cant. & York Soc. 82, 87, 94 (1995–2003).

The Register of Henry Chichele, Archbishop of Canterbury, 1414–1443, ed. E. F. Jacob, 4 vols, Cant. & York Soc. 42, 45–7 (1937–47).

The Register of John de Grandisson, Bishop of Exeter, ed. F. C. Hingeston-Randolph, 3 vols (London and Exeter, 1894–9).

The Register of Edmund Lacy, Bishop of Exeter, ed. F. C. Hingeston-Randolph, 2 vols (London and Exeter, 1901–15). Vol. II is now superseded by the edition of G. R. Dunstan, next following.

The Register of Edmund Lacy, Bishop of Exeter: Registrum Commune, ed. G. R. Dunstan, 5 vols, DCRS new ser. 7, 10, 13, 16, 18 (1963–72).

The Register of John Morton, Archbishop of Canterbury 1486–1500, ed. C. Harper-Bill, 3 vols, Cant. & York Soc. 75, 77, 89 (1987–2000).

The Register of Edmund Stafford, ed. F. C. Hingeston-Randolph (London and Exeter, 1886).

The Register of Walter de Stapeldon, Bishop of Exeter, ed. F. C. Hingeston-Randolph (London and Exeter, 1892).

Registrum Thome Bourgchier Cantuariensis Archiepiscopi A.D.1454–1486, ed. F. R. H. Du Boulay, Cant. and York Soc. 54 (1957).

Reiss, A. *The Sunday Christ: Sabbatarianism in English medieval wall painting*, British Archaeological Reports, British Series 292 (Oxford, 2000).

Report of the Deputy Keeper of the Public Records (London, 1865–, in progress).

Rivet, A. L. F., and Smith, C. *The Place-Names of Roman Britain* (London, 1979).

Robbins, A. F. 'The Closing Days of Launceston Priory', *Notes and Gleanings... Devon and Cornwall* 4 (1891), 3–7, 20–4, 42–5, 53–6, 71–5, 84–7.

Robinson, D. M. *The Geography of Augustinian Settlement*, 2 parts, British Archaeological Reports, British Series 80 (Oxford, 1980).

Robinson, J. A. *The Saxon Bishops of Wells* (London, 1918).

Roscarrock, N. *Lives of the Saints: Cornwall and Devon*, ed. N. Orme, DCRS new ser. 35 (1992).

Rose-Troup, F. *The Western Rebellion of 1549* (London, 1913).

Rotuli Chartarum, ed. T. D. Hardy (London, Rec. Com., 1837).

Rotuli Litterarum Clausarum in Turri Londinensi asservati, ed. T. D. Hardy, 2 vols (London, Rec. Com., 1833–44).

Rotuli Litterarum Patentium, 1201–1216, ed. T. D. Hardy (London, Rec. Com., 1835).

Rotuli Parliamentorum, ed. J. Strachey, 6 vols (London, 1767–77).

Rouse, R. H. and M. A. (ed.) *Registrum Anglie de Libris Doctorum et Auctorum Veterum*, Corpus of British Medieval Library Catalogues 2 (London, 1991).

Rowe, J. H. (ed.) *Cornwall Feet of Fines*, 2 vols, DCRS (1914–50).

Rowse, A. L. *Tudor Cornwall* (London, 1941).

Russell, V. *West Penwith Survey* (Truro, 1971).

Salter, H. E. (ed.) *Chapters of the Augustinian Canons*, Cant. & York Soc. 29 (1922).

Sanders, I. J. *English Baronies* (Oxford, 1960).

Sawyer, P. H. *Anglo-Saxon Charters: an annotated list and bibliography* (London, Royal Historical Society, 1968); online updated version http://www.trin.cam.ac.uk/kemble

Sedding, E. H. *Norman Architecture in Cornwall* (London, 1909).

Sharpe, R. *A Handlist of the Latin Writers of Great Britain and Ireland before 1540* (Brussels, 1997).

Sheppard, P. *The Historic Towns of Cornwall: an archaeological survey* (Truro, 1980).

Sims-Williams, P. *The Celtic Inscriptions of Britain: phonology and chronology, c.400–1200* (Oxford, 2003).

Smith, B. (ed.) *Britain and Ireland 900–1300* (Cambridge, 1999).

Smith, D. M., and London, V. C. M. (ed.), *The Heads of Religious Houses: England and Wales. II. 1216–1377* (Cambridge, 2001); *III. 1377–1540* (Cambridge, 2008).

Smith, J. 'Oral and written: saints, miracles, and relics in Brittany, *c.* 850–1250', *Speculum* 65 (1990), 309–43.

Smith, L. T. (ed.) *The Itinerary of John Leland in or about the Years 1535–1543*, 5 vols (London, 1906–10).

Snell, L. S. *Documents towards a History of the Reformation in Cornwall:* vol. I, *The Chantry Certificates for Cornwall* (Exeter, *c.*1953).

Snell, L. S. *Documents towards a History of the Reformation in Cornwall:* vol. II, *The Edwardian Inventories of Church Goods for Cornwall* (Exeter, *c.*1955).

Somerscales, M. I. 'Lazar Houses in Cornwall', *JRIC* new ser. 5/1 (1965), 61–99.

Sowell, C. R. 'The Collegiate Church of St. Thomas of Glasney', *JRIC* 1/3 (1864–5), 21–34 with 4 plates.

Spriggs, M. 'Where Cornish Was Spoken and When: a provisional synthesis', *Cornish Studies* new ser. 11 (2003), 228–69.

The Statutes of the Realm, from Magna Carta to the end of the Reign of Queen Anne, ed. A. Luders, T. E. Tomlins, J. Raithby, et al., 11 vols (London, Record Commission, 1810–28).

Stenton, D. M. (ed.) *Pleas before the King or his Justices, 1198–1202*, vol. II, *Rolls or Fragments of Rolls from the Years 1198, 1201 and 1202*, Selden Society 68 (1952), 48–9.

Stevenson, J. 'Introduction' to a reprint of F. E. Warren, *The Liturgy and Ritual of the Celtic Church* (Woodbridge, [1881]1987).

Stevenson, W. H. (ed.) *Asser's Life of King Alfred* (Oxford, 1904).

Stoate, T. L. (ed.) *Cornwall Subsidies in the Reign of Henry VIII* (Almondsbury, 1985).

Stoate, T. L. (ed.) *The Cornwall Military Survey 1522* (Almondsbury, 1987).

Stoate, T. L. (ed.) *Cornwall Manorial Rentals and Surveys* (Almondsbury, 1988).

Stokes, W. (ed.) *The Passion* (London, 1861).

Stokes, W. (ed.) *Beunans Meriasek: The Life of St Meriasek* (London, 1872).

Storrs, C. M. *Jacobean Pilgrims from England to St. James of Compostella* (Compostella, 1994; repr. London, 1998).

Street, G. E. 'The Restoration of the Church of St. Michael Penkevel, Cornwall', *Journal of the Royal Institute of British Architects*, 1st ser. 13 (1862–3), 32–53.

Tanguy, B. 'Les cultes de saint Gildas, sainte Trifine et saint Trémeur et les abbayes de Saint-Gildas-de-Rhuys et de Saint-Gildas-des-Bois', *Mémoires de la Société d'histoire et d'archéologie de Bretagne* 83 (2006), 5–27.

Taylor, T. *St. Michael's Mount* (Cambridge, 1932).

Thacker, A. and Sharpe, R. (eds.) *Local Saints and Local Churches* (Oxford, 2002).

Thomas, C. *Christian Antiquities of Camborne* (St Austell, 1967).

Thomas, C. *Christianity in Britain to AD 500* (London, 1981).

Thomas, C. *Exploration of a Drowned Landscape* (London, 1985).

Thomas, C. *And Shall These Mute Stones Speak? Post-Roman inscriptions in western Britain* (Cardiff, 1994).

Thomas, G. and Williams, N. (eds.) *Bewnans Ke: the Life of St Kea* (Exeter, 2007).

Thompson, A. Hamilton. 'Diocesan Organization in the Middle Ages: archdeacons and rural deans', *Proceedings of the British Academy* 29 (1943), 153–94.

Thompson, A. Hamilton. *The English Clergy and their Organization in the Later Middle Ages* (Oxford, 1947).

Thorn, C. and F. (ed.) *Domesday Book*, vol. X: *Cornwall* (Chichester, 1979) (modern translation).

Todd, M. *The South West to AD 1000* (London, 1987).

Toorians, L. (ed.) *The Middle Cornish Charter Endorsement: the making of a marriage in medieval Cornwall*, Innsbrucker Beiträge zur Sprachwissenschaft, 67 (Innsbruck, 1991).

Turner, S. *Making a Christian Landscape: the countryside in early medieval Cornwall, Devon and Wessex* (Exeter, 2006).

Turner, S. (ed.) *Medieval Devon and Cornwall: shaping an ancient countryside* (Macclesfield, 2006).

Valor Ecclesiasticus tempore Henrici VIII auctoritate regia institutus, ed. J. Caley, 6 vols (London, Rec. Com., 1810–24).

Wade-Evans, A. W. (ed.) *Vitae Sanctorum Britanniae et Genealogiae* (Cardiff, 1944).

Wallis, J. *The Bodmin Register* (Bodmin, 1827–38).

Way, A. 'Charter of Queen Elizabeth to the Hospital of St Laurence de Ponteboy, Bodmin, AD 1582', *JRIC* 3 (1868–70), 1–33.

Whetter, J. *The History of Glasney College* (Padstow, 1988).

Whetter, J. 'The Thomas Killigrews', *Old Cornwall* 10/7 (1988), 338–49.

Whitaker, J. *The Ancient Cathedral of Cornwall Historically Surveyed*, 2 vols (London, 1804).

Whitley, H. Michell. 'Inventories of the Cornish Friaries at the Time of their Dissolution', *JRIC* 8 (1883–5), 22–7.

Wilkinson, J. J. 'The Receipts and Expenses in the Building of Bodmin Church', *The Camden Miscellany: Vol. VII*, Camden Society new ser. 14 (1875).

Willis, B. *Notitia Parliamentaria*, 3 vols (London, 1715–50).

Worcester, W. *Itineraries*, ed. J. H. Harvey (Oxford, 1969).

Wormald, F. 'The Calendar of the Augustinian Priory of Launceston in Cornwall', *The Journal of Theological Studies* 39 (1938), 1–21.

Wright, A. R. *British Calendar Customs: England*, ed. T. E. Lones, 3 vols, Folk-Lore Society 97, 102, 106 (1936–40).

Yorke, B. *Wessex in the Early Middle Ages* (London, 1995).

INDEX

Places are in Cornwall unless otherwise stated. The word 'St' is ignored when indexing places in Cornwall, but not elsewhere. Place-names in Cornwall other than those of parishes are listed separately, with the name of the parish in which they are located in brackets and cross-references to them under the parish names. People of whom only a forename or surname is known are not generally indexed unless they are well-known figures. In describing clergy, 'canon' denotes Augustinian canons, 'cleric' all non-monastic clergy, and 'prior' heads of monastic houses.

Abbott, William, courtier 159
Aclond, Reginald de, prior 140
Acy, William de 209
Adam, John, cleric 159
Adams, Theophilus and Robert 271
Advent 26, 74, 97
advowsons 25, 37, 99 – *see also* patronage
Ælfeah Gerent 6
Ælfsige, possible bishop 12
Æthelgar, bishop 10
Æthelheard, king 4
Æthelred the Unready, king 10–11, 122–3, 126, 129
Æthelstan, king 6, 10–11, 14, 16, 113, 121, 124, 128–30, 132, 150, 164, 166, 168, 190
St Agnes 17, 26–7, 42, 80
Aldhelm, saint 3–5, 9, 121, 123
Alfred, king 5, 10, 120–1, 133
Algar, prior and bishop 35, 139–40
alien priories 46–7, 50, 166, 232, 242–3, 289–91, 298
St Allen 23, 48, 67, 105, 142, 247–8, 259 – *see also* Gwarnick; Lanner
Alley, William, bishop of Exeter 106–7
almshouses 56, 159–60, 262
altarage 38
altars 39, 41–2, 71, 103, 105, 107 and passim
Altarnun 20, 27, 41–2, 44, 68, 79, 88, 94, 115, 173, 286, 297 – *see also* Drywork; Tredaule; Trevage
Alured the Butler 297
Alverton (Madron) 231
Alyn, John, cleric 173
Amesbury, Michael of, abbot 198
Amon, monk 8, 135
anchorites 31, 56–7, 304–5
Andreas, Miletus, prior 242–3
Angers (France), abbey of St Serge 30, 46, 51, 240, 242–3, 284–5, 288, 290
Annales Cambriae 4–5
Anstewylle, Simon, canon 211
Ansty (Wilts.), preceptory 51, 93, 272, 276–7
St Anthony-in-Meneage 45, 93, 137, 286–8, 293, 295
St Anthony-in-Roseland, priory and parish 126, 136–9; mentioned 26–7, 30, 32, 34–5, 39, 44, 46, 50–1, 92–3, 98, 108, 287

Antony, East 48, 73, 80, 105, 191
Antrenon, Joce of 247
appropriation of benefices 38, 48, 99, 110 and passim
archdeacons 24 – *see also* Cornwall
Arches family 187
archpriests 55, 226–8, 234–5, 238–40
Argal (Budock), lepers of 301
Argenton, William d', prior 239
Arles, council of 7
Arscott, John, cleric 101, 235, 239–40, 260
Assanus alias Suffianus, Sir Emmanuel 173
Arthur, king 37, 90, 114, 140, 238
Arthur, prince of Wales 292
Arundell families
 of Helland 152
 of Lanherne 171–2; mentioned 37, 53–6, 71, 83–4, 88, 94, 106, 151, 156–7, 270, 281–3, 295
 of Tolverne 83, 171–2
 of Trerice 277
Arundell, Benedict, cleric 261
Arundell, Humphrey, rebel 102
Arundell, Joan, prioress 31
Arundell, John, senior, bishop of Chichester 58, 60–1
Arundell, John, junior, bishop of Exeter 60–1, 91
Arundell, Philip, friar 54, 283
Arwenack (Budock) 159
Ashburton (Devon) 212
Ashbury (Devon) 210, 218
Asshton, Edmund, Hospitaller 276, 278
Asser, bishop 5, 9–10, 121–2, 133
Athelstan – *see* Æthelstan
Aude, Peter, rioter 146
Aufred son of Ruald 241
Auglionby, Edward, gentleman 284
Augustinian Order of canons 30, 34–5, 140, 145, 148–9, 151, 184, 189–90, 203, 211, 213, 217, 280
Aumarle, Thomas, cleric 65
Auncell, Richard, prior 51, 233, 240, 267, 269–70
St Austell 14–15, 63, 107, 112, 280, 286, 288, 295 – *see also* Pentuan
St Austell, Philip of, cleric 37
Austell, Thomas, cleric 265

Austyn, John, prior 138–9
Averay, John, prior 189, 191
Aysshton, Nicholas, judge 88

Babington, John, Hospitaller 277
Bake (St Germans) 185
Baker, John, prior 217–18, 221
Baldwin, archbishop 184
Balsam, John, cleric 65
Bante, Oger, prior 148, 154, 211, 215
Bantham (Devon) 7
baptism 18, 43, 70, 77, 82, 96, 101–2, 107, 110
Barat, Roger, cleric 271
Barclay, Alexander, poet and friar 158, 190, 219
Barnecote, Walter, prior 51, 53, 243–4, 291–2, 296
Barnstaple (Devon) 70
Bartholomew, bishop of Exeter 30, 141, 184, 221, 266
Basset family 183, 239
Bassett, Gregory, friar 158
Bate, Leonard 179
Bauceyn, William, cleric 206
Baugh, David 168–9
Baugh alias Williams, Thomas, cleric 168–9, 171
Bawdyn, John, canon 152
Bayle, Joan 290
bead–rolls 71, 86
Beaufort, Henry, cardinal 216, 292
Beaulieu (Hants.), abbey 32, 44, 46, 93, 124, 131
Beaupré family 157, 250, 256, 259, 282
Beaupré, Richard of, cleric 165, 253
Beaworthy (Devon) 209–10
Bede, historian 7, 123
Bell, Francis, gentleman 277
Bell, Sir Thomas 199
Bello, Walter de, prior 280
bells and bell-towers
 of parish churches and chapels 41–2, 77, 103, 153, 172
 of religious houses 143, 153, 159, 206, 219, 235–6, 239, 255–6, 258, 260
 of saints 18
Benedictine Order 30
Bent, Walter, canon 217

Beroul, author 89, 238
Berwyk, Thomas and William, friars 283
Bevill family 53, 67, 94, 235, 265, 276, 282–3, 292
Bewnans Ke, drama 90, 113–14, 119, 258 – *see also* Kea
Bewnans Meriasek, drama 90, 114, 119, 258 – *see also* Camborne; Meriasek
Bible 36, 41, 96, 100, 104
Bikelegh, Osbert de 209
Binnerton (Crowan) 77
bishops – *see* Cornwall, Crediton, Exeter, Sherborne
 suffragans 49, 91, 103–4, 149–50
Bisimano, Geoffrey of, cleric 37, 174
Bisimano, William of, 271
Biskyr, John, hospital inmate 226
Bitton, Thomas, bishop of Exeter 48, 164, 252
 executors of 33, 156, 160, 164–5, 194, 200, 222, 224, 250, 282, 299, 300–3
Black Death 46–7; mentioned 51, 55, 62, 142, 145, 148, 157, 176, 215, 227, 256
Black Prince – *see* Edward
Black, Robert 272
Blanchminster family 83, 89, 282
St Blazey 26, 286, 292, 295
Bleuet family 157
Blisland 65, 69, 273
Bloyou family 141, 199
Blohiou (i.e. Bloyou), John, cleric 180
Bloyou, William, cleric 261
Blund, Richard, bishop of Exeter 24, 221, 271
Blybyn, Uryin, friar 283
Blythe, George 277
Bobyt, Henry, monk 295
Boconnoc 27, 42, 48
Bodardle (Lanlivery) 200
Bodbrane (Duloe) 171
Bodigga (St Martin-by-Looe) 132, 202
Bodiniel (Bodmin) 99, 128, 152–3
Bodmin 32–4, 46, 57, 67–8, 78, 101, 104, 108, 146, 155 – *see also* Bodiniel; Boscarne; Callywith; Dunmere; Kingswood; Ruthern
 St Anthony, almshouse 159–60; mentioned 56, 73
 borough community 54, 56, 80, 98, 146, 150, 152–3, 157, 159
 chapels 76, 150
 Franciscan friary 155–9; mentioned 31, 33, 39, 50, 53–4, 84, 92, 108, 149, 161
 St George, almshouse 160; mentioned 56, 73
 Gospels 17–19, 127, 149
 guilds 73, 159–60
 hermits and anchorites 304
 St Laurence, leper hospital 160–2; mentioned 33, 56
 St Margaret, house and chapel 52, 144, 148
 manumissions in Bodmin Gospels 12, 20, 122, 127,
 minster 126–8, 139–40; mentioned 9, 11–14, 16–18, 20–1, 23, 39, 119, 121–4, 134
 parish church and vicar 65–9, 85, 88, 94, 144–5, 151, 161
 priory 140–54; mentioned 30, 35, 38–9, 44–6, 48, 50–3, 64, 66, 83–5, 91–3, 98–9, 158, 161, 181–2, 270–1, 283
 school 88, 94, 101, 155
Bodmin Moor, formerly Fowey Moor 272
Bodrugan family 37, 87, 183, 247, 250, 255, 259, 282
Bodrugan, William of, cleric 49, 248, 261
Bodulgate, Henry, cleric 182
Body, William, archdeacon's deputy 91, 101
Boia, dean 127, 139
Boia, pupil 12
Bolevill, William of, monk and *custos* 198–9
Bolleit or Bollegh family 84, 88, 168, 192
Bollegh, Henry of, archdeacon 37, 192, 245, 248, 254, 261, 263, 265
Bologna (Italy), university 60
Bolter, Roger, cleric 177, 265
Bolton, Roger, cleric 166
Bonallack (Constantine) 84
Boniface, saint 3
Bonner, Edmund, bishop 105
Bonyalva (St Germans) 132, 202, 209, 219
Book of Common Prayer 101, 103–4, 106–7
books and writings
 education and scholarship 12, 18, 35–6, 53–4, 88, 90, 130, 158, 213, 258, 282
 financial accounts 80
 hagiography 53, 213 – *see also* saints, Lives of
 law (unspecified) 217
 literature, Cornish language 90–1, 105, 114
 literature, Latin 18, 35–7
 literature, French and English 47, 53, 88–90, 150, 299
 liturgy 17–18, 41–2, 61–2, 71, 83, 85, 89, 101, 103–5, 129–30, 149, 158, 237, 256, 264, 280, 283, 292
 medicine 53, 150
 music 52, 80
 printed 95
Boor, John, cleric 171
Booth, John, bishop of Exeter 243
Borlase, William, historian 150, 160, 267
Boscarn, Richard, friar 157, 159
Boscarne (Bodmin) 146
Boscastle (Forrabury, Minster) 74, 100, 241
Boscawen family 57, 83, 167
Bossiney (Tintagel) 127
Boteler family 183
Boteler, Giles, cleric 183
Bothe, John, Hospitaller 278
Botreaux family 43, 48, 207, 209–10, 212, 240–1, 243–4
Botyll, Robert, Hospitaller 276, 278
Bouges, William de, prior 242, 289–90, 296
Bovyle, Richard, cleric 84
Bowyer, John, canon 53, 90, 150
boys in churches and religious houses 55, 57, 145, 166, 177, 212, 246, 252, 254, 257, 259–60, 292
Boyton 38, 99, 106, 132, 202, 209–10, 219 – *see also* Bradridge; Northcott
Bradford (Devon) 209, 219
Bradoc 26–7, 42, 48, 159

Bradridge (Boyton) 209–10, 218–19
Brandon, Charles, duke of Suffolk 169
Brandwellan, saint 111
Brantingham, Thomas, bishop of Exeter 49
 and collegiate churches 177, 254–7
 and friars 54, 158, 283
 and hospitals and military orders 161, 225, 273
 and monasteries 148, 186, 189, 233, 243, 267, 269
brasses, monumental 64–5
Bray family 274, 277, 289, 292
Braybrook family 86, 237
Braylegh, Richard of, cleric 261
Breage, saint 8
Breage, church and parish 26, 32, 69–70, 80, 93, 112, 128, 303 – *see also* Methleigh; Pengersick; Pengwedna
Brentingham, John, prior 51, 291, 296
St Breock 23, 27, 80, 88, 103, 134, 162, 223, 225 – *see also* Burlawn Eglos; Pawton; Wadebridge
 lepers of 301
St Breward 40–2, 44, 286 – *see also* Hamatethy; Rough Tor
Brewe, William, cleric 161
Brewer, William, bishop of Exeter 24, 164, 166, 173–4, 179, 245, 248, 263, 297
 statutes of 36, 38, 41, 43
Brian, Breton lord 20, 221
Brid, John, monk 296
Bridgerule (Devon) 209–11, 219
bridges 83–4, 160, 194, 200, 206, 222, 248, 254, 274, 304
Bridgwater (Som.)
 friary 158
 hospital 32, 93
Brigge, Thomas atte, cleric 180
Brimmore, Nicholas of, cleric 175
Bristol (Gloucs.) 157
 St James, priory 32
 Templars 272
Bristowe, John, prior 298–9
Brittany 7–9, 14–18, 20, 88, 98, 113–15, 118, 120–1, 124–5, 134–5, 141, 163, 269
Broccan, legendary king 116
Bronescombe, Walter, bishop of Exeter 23–4
 founder of Glasney college 25, 33, 244–8, 250, 252–5, 259
 and friaries 155, 157, 281
 and monasteries 24, 138, 146, 187, 185–6, 213, 279–80, 286, 288
 and parish churches 195–6, 270–1
 register of 37–8, 164, 180
Brounscombe, Richard, monk 290
Bruton (Som.), priory 217
Bruton, Richard, cleric 182
Bryan alias Cornwall, John, schoolmaster 89–90
Brykevile, Richard of, prior 220
Bryvyth, saint 111
Bucklawren (St Martin-by-Looe) 132, 202, 209–10, 219
Budoc, saint 15
Budock 15, 26–7, 45, 245, 247–8, 253, 259 – *see also* Argal; Arwenack; Falmouth; Penryn

Burdon, Thomas of, prior 214–15, 220
burials – *see* funerals and burial rites, tombs
Burlawn Eglos (St Breock) 18, 77
Burniere (Egloshayle) 11, 23, 93
Buruhwold, bishop 11–12, 266
St Buryan, minster, church, parish 128, 163–71; mentioned 6, 11–15, 20–1, 27, 32–3, 39, 44, 47–8, 50, 54–5, 82, 84, 87, 92–3, 99–100, 108, 119, 120, 124, 234 – *see also* Rospannel
Bury St Edmunds (Suffolk) 237

St Cadix – *see* St Carroc
Cadoc, saint 8, 15, 232, 238
St Cadoc (Padstow) – *see* Padstow
Cællincg or *Caellwic*, estate 9, 123
Caerhays (St Michael Caerhays) 160
Caerhays family 160–1
calendars, church 17, 54, 149, 157, 212, 292
Calle, Reynold, cleric 257, 261
Callestick (Perranzabuloe) 127
Callington 26, 78, 88, 189–90 – *see also* Dupath; Hingston Down
Callywith (Bodmin) 146
Calstock 87, 103 – *see also* Cotehele
Camborne 14, 18, 71, 73, 80, 90–1, 105, 114, 119, 193, 258 – *see also* Reskajeage
chapels in 14, 76–7
Cambridge, university of 53, 145, 149, 213
King's College 166–7, 234–6
Camelford 74, 87, 100
Cancale, Ralph de, prior 240
Canonsleigh (Devon), priory 31, 211
Canterbury 176, 244
pilgrimage to 86
Canterbury, archbishops of 9–10, 107, 126, 129
confirmation of charters by 184, 284, 286
appeals to 52, 216, 243, 268
visitations by 149, 177–8, 189–90, 217, 259, 269, 281, 291–2
Capell, Robert, canon 191
Caradon Prior (Linkinhorne) 209–10, 219
Carantoc, saint 111, 178
Carbura, John, cleric 180
Cardinan family 30, 43, 197, 200, 207, 284–5, 304
Cardinham 16, 30, 65, 74, 109, 284–6 – *see also* St Mary Vale
Carew family 98, 185, 220, 223
Carewe, John, cleric 193–4
Carew, Richard, historian 81, 110, 162, 185, 226, 238, 265, 273, 303
Cargoll (Newlyn East) 23, 93, 127
Carleton, Adam, archdeacon 61, 253
Carlyon, John, prior 180, 217
Carlyon, Richard, cleric 180, 218–19, 221, 223
Carmelite Order 32, 53
Carminow family 144, 156–7, 159–61
Carn Brea (Illogan) 76
Carnegie (Minster) 241
Carnehille, Ralph, cleric 60
Carnellow, William, prior 145, 148, 154
Carnu, David, friar 60, 282
Carogan, Martin of, friar 283
Carracawn (St Germans) 185
St Carroc (St Veep), priory and chapel 297–9; mentioned 18, 30, 32, 34, 38–9, 43–4, 50–2, 84, 92–3, 98, 108
Carslake, William, cleric 250
Carslegh, James, archdeacon 216
Carter alias Smyth, Benedict, canon 152
Carter, Richard, merchant 162
Carteret, Ralph de, prior 240
Carthusian Order 31, 83, 153
cartularies 140, 211, 233, 244, 252, 266, 284, 297
Caruggat (Tywardreath) 286
Carvanion, William 259
Carvedras (Kenwyn) 281
Carville, Peter de, prior 232, 240
Casteltown, Laurence, prior 299
Castro, Bartholomew de, cleric 62, 275
Catisby, Benedict, cleric 264
Cavell family 183, 282
Cavell, William, cleric 183
Cecil, Robert, earl of Salisbury 239
'Celtic Church' 110
cemeteries – *see* funerals and burial rites
Centwine, king 3
Cergeaux family 157, 183
Cerisy-la-Forêt (France), abbey 51, 291
Chamond family 99, 152–3, 218–19, 273, 277, 295
Champernown family 191, 289
chantries and chantry priests
certificates and dissolution (1546–8) 99–100, 162, 169, 172–3, 179, 183, 193–4, 199, 223, 252, 259–60, 265, 271
in collegiate and parish churches 36, 47, 55, 62–3, 67, 92–4, 99–101, 144, 168–9, 171–3, 199, 228, 244, 246, 254–6, 259–60
in monasteries, hospitals, friaries 144, 193–4, 206, 285, 291
Chapel Amble (St Kew) 77
Chapel Euny (Sancreed) 114
Chapelyn, William, leper 223
chapels
in churches 63, 70–1 and passim
freestanding 26–7, 74–7, 112, 119; mentioned 19, 21, 26–7, 43, 82, 88, 94, 97 and passim
licences for 76–7
Chard, Thomas, prior 298
'Charter Endorsement' 90
charters, Anglo-Saxon 9–10, 120, 127–31, 133, 228
Cherell, Thomas, prior 298–9
Cheynedrit family 291
Chichele, Henry, archbishop 216
children 43, 77, 81, 83–4, 274 – *see also* baptism; boys; schools
chi-rho – *see* stones, inscribed
Christ and Jesus, cults of 60, 71, 73, 75, 79–81, 86–7, 90, 106, 168, 207, 235 – *see also* images; relics; rood screens
Christmas 81, 107, 222
Chubbe, John, prior 270
church ales 80, 110
church houses 80–1
churches, parish – *see* parish churches
churching of women 70, 107
churchwardens 80, 94
accounts of 80, 94
Chyverston family 83–4
Chyverton, Henry, of Bodmin 260

Cistercian Order 30–2
St Cleer 5–6, 27, 72, 78, 84, 87, 120, 273–5, 277, 295 – *see also* Fursnewth; Trengale
Cleeve (Som.), abbey 32, 46, 93, 210
Clegher, Richard, cleric 172
St Clement 45, 230–2, 234–5 – *see also* Kiggon; Truro Vean
clergy, parish – *see* parish clergy
Clerk, William, friar 53–4
clerks, parish – *see* parish clerks
St Clether 48, 78–9, 120, 293 – *see also* Trefoward
Cleverton family 157
Climsland Prior (Stoke Climsland) 209–10, 219
Cluniac Order 30 – *see also* St Carroc; Montacute
Clynk, John, havener 211
Clyst Gabriel (Devon), hospital 64
Cnut, king 130, 186
Coan, saint 111–12
Cobbethorn, John, cleric 60
Coche, Ralph, chapel clerk 258
Cokkar, James 277
Colan 37, 45, 79, 247–8, 255, 259 – *see also* Coswarth
Cole, John, hospital prior 161–2
Colen, Tristram 281
colleges and collegiate churches 33, 54–5, 92, 100, 163–71, 172, 173–80, 226–8
clerks of 168–9, 177, 179, 235, 246, 254–6, 258, 260
incomes of 163, 169, 174, 179, 226, 239, 248, 259–60, 264–5
liturgy in 250, 254–6, 258–9
numbers of staff 168–9, 174, 177, 179, 226, 234–5, 239, 246, 260
stipends and wages in 163, 168–9, 174, 179, 181, 183, 226, 235, 238–9, 246, 253, 255, 259–60, 265
Collins alias Harris, Edward 293
Collins, Henry, cleric 293
Collins – *see also* Colyns
Coloribus, John de, friar 152, 219, 283
Colshill, Sir John 269
Columb, saint 8, 90
St Columb Major 37, 44–5, 54, 66, 69, 78, 88, 92–3, 162, 303 – *see also* Reterth; Tregoose
Arundell chantry 171–3; mentioned 55–6
St Columb Minor 26, 129, 174–5, 179 – *see also* Treloy
St Columb, Richard of, friar 158
Colyns, Thomas, prior 293–6
Combe, John, cleric 167
Combrygge, Roger, prior 211, 221
communion – *see also* mass
pre-Reformation 71, 81–2
post-Reformation 101–3, 107, 239
Comoere, bishop – *see* Wulfsige
Compostella (Spain) 86–7, 229
compulsions 63
Conan, bishop 6, 10, 12, 129–30
Concorès, Ithier de, cleric 176
confession 18, 35, 43, 77, 82, 96, 99, 157–8, 211, 216, 222, 253–4, 267, 269, 276, 283, 291
confirmation 43, 82

confraternities of religious houses 53, 275–7, 292
Connerton (Gwithian) 272
Constantine, church and parish 12, 19, 21, 32, 42, 84, 119, 128, 192, 303 – see also Bonallack
Constantine, emperor 7
Constantine, ruler of the Dumnonii 1–2, 7
St Constantine, Roger of, cleric 248
Conwenian, Thomas 195
Cook, Thomas, cleric 63
Copleston family 295
Copplestone (Devon) 120
Corke, John, cleric 258, 262
Cornedon, Elizabeth, hospital inmate 223
Cornelly 26, 262–3
Cornewall family 290–1
Cornish language
  personal names in 6, 111
  place-names in 116–19
  spoken 6, 11–12, 14, 16, 33, 54, 61, 90, 96, 102, 122, 158, 165–6, 242, 246, 258, 281, 283
  written 18, 36, 87, 90–1, 105, 114–15, 237–8, 258
Cornish, Thomas, bishop 285
'Cornish Vocabulary' 36
Cornu, David, friar 60
Cornwall, origins of 1, 3, 5
  archdeacons of 24–5, 33, 49, 61, 91, 147, 175, 192–3, 221, 233, 248, 253, 260, 263–4, 275
  diocese and bishops of 9–12, 20, 121–3, 127, 129–30, 188, 201
  diocese proposed (1539) 99, 153
  duchy and dukes in general 47, 98, 143, 163, 211, 220, 231, 243, 270, 288, 292 – see also Arthur; Edward VI; Edward the Black Prince; Henry V
  earldom and earls in general 31–2, 37, 164, 206, 209, 231, 288 – see also Edmund; John; Reginald; Richard
Cornwall, John of, cleric and author 36
Cornwall, John, schoolmaster – see Bryan
Cornwall, Michael of, cleric and poet 37
Cornwall, Peter of, canon and author 34–5, 43, 204
  family of 34, 43, 204
Cornwall, Peter of, friar 35
Cornwall, Richard of, two such clerics 37
Cornwall, Serlo of, hermit 304
Cornwall, Stephen of, cleric 60
Cornworthy (Devon), priory 31
corrodies – see monasteries
Coryton family 277
Cosawes (St Gluvias) 75, 86, 105
Coswarth (Colan) 127–8
Cosyn, Joan, of Launceston 214
Cosynton, William of, Hospitaller 277
Cotehele (Calstock) 74, 76
Courtenay family 190, 217–18, 295
Courtenay, Henry, marquess of Exeter 218, 294
Courtenay, Peter, bishop of Exeter 188
Courtenay, William, archbishop 189, 281
Courtney family 299
Courteys, Thomas, prior 149, 154
courts, Church 24–5
Coutances (France) 35
Coverdale, Miles, bishop of Exeter 104

Coynt, John, hospital prior 194
Crabbe, Ralph, cleric 234–5, 240
Crackington (St Gennys), chapel 210
Crane, Henry, cleric 105
Cranewell, William, sheriff 157
Cranmer, Thomas, archbishop 101, 169
Crantock, minster, collegiate church, parish 128–9, 173–80; mentioned 12–13, 21, 27, 30, 32–3, 39, 41, 44, 50, 54–5, 57, 61, 63, 67, 82, 92–3, 99–100, 105, 158, 192, 194, 206, 297–8 – see also Halwyn; Langurrow; Treago; Vosporth
  lazars of 301
Crediton (Devon), church of 4, 24, 32, 57, 74, 245–6, 249
  bishops of 10, 12, 122–3
Creed 14, 41, 60, 71, 83 – see also Grampound
Cremande, Astère de, monk 290, 296
crime 60–1, 73, 189, 193, 218, 274 – see also rebellion
Cristinstowe, Henry of, cleric 271
Cristofre, Richard 281
Cromwell, Thomas, king's minister 96–7, 151–2, 190, 218–19, 238, 294–5
Crosse, Thomas of, cleric 170
crosses, standing 14–15, 20, 79–80, 108, 119–20
Crowan 32, 114 – see also Binnerton
Crown, English, in relation to the Church in Cornwall
  pre-Conquest period 9–12, 121–4
  and alien priories – see alien priories
  grants of Cornish churches by 51, 152, 163, 166, 191, 233–4
  legal proceedings of 148, 156, 193, 195–6, 199, 215–16, 217–18, 237, 222, 257, 262–3, 268,
  patronage claims 27, 37, 48–9, 55, 142–3, 164–70, 186, 211, 231, 242–3, 257, 262, 290
  pensioners of – see pensioners
  at Reformation 95–110, 151–3, 182, 190–1, 218–19, 260, 265, 270–1, 277, 294–5
  and Templars – see Templars
crusades 43–4, 46, 83
Cubert 21, 78, 82, 105, 141, 145, 152 – see also Ellenglaze
Cuby 32, 48, 278–80
Cuddenbeak (St Germans) 186
Cullyng, William, cleric 180, 257, 261
Curtys, William, hospital prior 162
Cury 26
Cuthred, king 5
Cybi or Cuby, saint 16
Cynewulf, king 5

Dabernon, John, of Calstock 87, 157, 161, 185, 200, 222, 225, 282
Dalison, George, esquire 276
Dalison, Richard, Hospitaller 278
Dangeas, Robert, Hospitaller 278
Daniel, bishop 10, 12, 129
Dartmoor (Devon), crosses on 120
Daune family 157
David, saint 16
David of Cornwall, cleric 37
Davidstow 32, 63, 73, 82, 107–8, 286 – see also Treglasta

St Day (Gwennap), Trinity chapel 75, 84, 86, 105, 112, 115, 236, 239
deaneries, rural 25, 27, 43, 243, 273, 276, 291, 297
Decimarius, William, prior 242–4
dedications, church 15–16, 111–14 – see also saints
Degeman or Degaman, saint 112–13, 119
St Degaman (Wendron) 84
Degendon, John, canon 216
Denbawde, John, canon 217
Deneys, Robert, prior 267, 270
Denisel, Odo, canon 147
St Dennis 26
Denyngton, John, prior 269–70
Derwa, saint 18
Devon
  contrasted with Cornwall 111, 116
  earls of 199
Devoran (Feock) 303
Dinham family 187, 190, 212
Dinuurrin, place 9, 121, 126
Diptford (Devon) 209
Docco, saint 15–16, 115
Docco, church of – see St Kew
Dolbear, Ralph 212
Dollson, John 162, 223, 225
Domesday Book 13, 21, 127–33, 139, 163, 173, 184, 202–3, 229, 262, 284
Dominican Order 31, 281–4
Doniert, 'king' 5, 20
Doune, William, cleric 182, 215, 250
drama, Cornish 90–1, 114, 258
Drefe, Alfred of, friar 54, 158
Drift (Sancreed) 158
Drywork (Altarnun), chapel 210–11
Dudley, Sir Andrew 103
Duke, Richard, of London 199
Duloe 45, 71–2, 297 – see also Bodbrane
Dumnonia, Dumnonii 1–4, 14, 121
Dungarth, king 5, 120
Dunmere (Bodmin) 146, 150, 153
  lepers of 300–1
Dunmow, John, cleric 167
Dunstan, archbishop and saint 10–11, 123, 129
Dupath (Callington), well 78, 120
Duraunte, John, prior 269–70
Dyer, Edward 304
Dyfed (Wales) 9, 121

Eadred, king 10
Eadwulf, bishop 10
Eaglesfield, Robert, Hospitaller 278
Ealdred, bishop 12, 122–3
Easter 9, 81–2, 101, 107, 123, 199, 222
Eastway (Morwenstow) 209–10
Ecgberht, king 5, 9–11, 121, 126
Edgar, king 11, 131, 195
Edgcumbe family 218
Edmund (I), king 128
Edmund, earl of Cornwall 32, 155, 164, 209, 304
Edmund, John, cleric 178, 180
Edneves alias Souffere, John, cleric 257, 261
education – see schools, universities
Edward the Confessor, king 20–1, 133, 228, 266
Edward the Elder, king 16
Edward I, king 33, 48, 156, 164, 186, 196,

226, 264, 268, 304
Edward II, king 147, 165
Edward III, king 142–3, 145, 164–6, 212, 238, 257, 268, 281, 290
Edward IV 61, 145, 167, 234, 238
Edward VI, duke of Cornwall later king 100–4, 220, 295
Edward the Black Prince 53, 142, 146, 156–7, 166, 186, 236, 281–2, 304–5
Edwards, Thomas, hospital inmate 223
Efford (Stratton), chapel 209
eglos-, place-name element 14, 113–14
Egloshayle 14–15, 27, 45, 142, 150 – see also Burniere; Pendavey; Wadebridge
Egloskerry 14, 38, 41, 132, 202, 209–10, 213, 219 – see also Penheale
Eir, Richard, rioter 146
Elide, saint and chapel (Scilly) 267, 269
Eliot family 191
Elizabeth I, queen 106, 162, 169, 239, 271, 277
Ellenglaze (Cubert) 127, 139, 142, 152
Elys, John, pensioner 212
St Elvan (Sithney) 18
Endelient, saint 180, 182
St Endellion, church and parish 180–4; mentioned 14, 18, 33, 65, 80, 92, 99–100, 104, 129, 142, 150, 271, 286 – see also St Illick; Roscarrock; Scarrabine
English language 47, 87–9, 96, 100–2, 104, 165–6
St Enoder 21, 41, 67, 90, 127, 192, 194, 247–8, 253, 259, 286 – see also Mitchell
St Enodoc (St Minver) 26, 41, 76, 97, 149
Entenin, saint 14, 137
Enys, Richard, cleric 250–1
St Erme 61, 286 – see also Treworgan
St Erney 26–7
St Erth 42, 44, 87 – see also Trelissick
St Ervan 27, 72, 105, 134
Esse, John of, cleric 37, 174
estates of early churches 4–6, 9–13, 19, 113–14
Estone, Nicholas of, canon 147
Eu, Geoffrey d', canon 279
Eu, William d', archdeacon 25
Euny, saint 17, 112, 114
St Eval 27, 134
Evelyng, John, cleric 258, 261
St Ewe 61, 162
Exeter (Devon) 1, 6–7, 25, 30, 34, 102, 106, 207, 210, 299
churches at 2, 7
friaries 157, 283
marquess of – see Courtenay
Exeter, bishops of, 23–5, 27, 33, 44–5, 48–9, 86, 91, 93, 114–21, 135, 142, 170, 174, 184–91, 201, 211, 248, 260, 262–4 – see also individual names
Exeter, minster later cathedral
churches and income in Cornwall 27, 42, 44, 46, 67–8, 93, 114, 121–2, 135, 262–3
consulted by bishop 175, 216, 275
influence on Cornish churches 33, 65, 246, 249–55, 275
personnel with Cornish links 25, 63, 167, 178, 257, 294
Exeter, John of, monk 268

Exeter, Walter of, friar 299
Eynesbury (Hunts.) 112, 115

Falmouth (Budock) 87, 248, 252, 258
Fawell, William, cleric 265
Fawton (St Neot) 197, 202, 210
Fayne, friar of Bodmin 157
Fentongollan (St Michael Penkevil) 226
Fentrigan (Warbstow) 286, 295
Feock 45, 109, 245, 247–8, 253, 259 – see also Devoran
Fermesham, Walter of, cleric 254, 261
Fertrer, Joel le, prior 242
Feutrer, Robert le, monk 290
Fili, saint 14
Fissacre, Robert, prior 34, 213, 220
FitzPeter, Walter, cleric 263, 265
FitzRalph, John, of Caerhays 155
FitzRoges, William, cleric 261
FitzStephen, Geoffrey, Templar 272
FitzWalter family 157
FitzWilliam, Richard 272
Flamank family 146, 159–60, 162
Fontevrault (France), abbey 32, 46
Fontibus, Roger de, prior 288, 296
fonts 41–2, 69–70, 112
Ford, William, craftsman 156
Forde (Devon), abbey 221
Formosus, pope 10
Forest (Illogan) 281
Forrabury 44–5, 93, 241 – see also Boscastle
Fort, Thomas, canon 53, 61, 149
Forte, John, canon 217
Forthe, William, cleric 170
Fortescue family 139
Fowey 30, 33, 80, 87, 98, 153, 286–7, 294, 298 – see also Trenant
church and parish 41, 45, 83, 135, 286, 293, 295
lepers of 301
Fowey Moor – see Bodmin Moor
France 22, 30, 32, 34–5, 38, 46, 50, 61, 156, 176, 232–3, 240–3, 268–9, 283, 288, 290–1 – see also French language; Hundred Years War
Franciscan Order 31, 35, 219
Observants 94
Freewater (Probus), lepers of 302–3
French language 47, 83, 87–9
friars 31–2, 35, 53–4, 86, 98, 237, 267, 299, 302
education of 54, 282
numbers of 32, 53, 92, 157–8, 283
recruitment of 157, 282
Froste, Walter, of Launceston 212
Fulford, John, cleric 265
funerals and burial rites – see also tombs
in parish churches 18, 82, 80, 84, 101, 110, 118–19, 210, 226
in religious houses 18, 107, 207–8, 210, 230, 234–5, 241, 281–2, 285
Fursnewth (St Cleer) 99, 127, 142, 153

Galford (Devon), battle 5
Gardyner, Robert, royal servant 277
Gascoyne, Joel, cartographer 27, 200
Gayer family 169
Geffrey, Alexander, cleric 260
Genesius of Arles, saint 212

Gennys or Guinas, saint 212
St Gennys 21, 41, 131, 209–10, 212–13, 219 – see also Crackington; Hill; Treworgie
Gennys, William, canon 217–19
Gentill, James, cleric 169, 178–80, 259, 262
Gentill, John, cleric 60–1
Genver (Tintagel) 113
Geoffrey fitz Robert, founder 140
Geoffrey of Monmouth, author 36, 88, 114, 238
Gerent or Geruntius, king 3–5, 9, 11, 121, 123
Gerent, saint 14
St Germans 22–3, 27, 83, 93, 132, 208–9, 304 – see also Bake; Bonyalva; Carracawn; Cuddenbeak; Lethiock; Long Colling; Tideford
bishops of – see Cornwall, diocese and bishops
lepers of 301
early cathedral and minster 129–30; mentioned 6, 9–12, 20–1, 118, 121–2
priory and parish church 184–91; mentioned 30, 33, 38–9, 44–5, 48–51, 65, 84, 92–3, 98–9, 108
German of Auxerre, saint 111, 115, 122–3, 129–30, 188, 190
Germanus, abbot 12
Germany 158, 276
Germoe, church and saint 26, 74, 80, 84, 97, 112, 120
Gerrans 27, 66, 105, 136–8 – see also Tregaire
Gervase of Canterbury, topographer 137, 279, 287
Gervays, John 210
Gildas, historian 1–2, 7–8
Gildeford, Stephen, hermit 235, 305
Gill, Gervase, hospital prior 223–4
Gilmartin (Launceston) 222–3
Glas (Gulval), lepers of 301
Glasney – see Penryn
Glastonbury (Som.) 86, 230, 232
abbey 2, 4, 30, 33, 112, 132, 196–9, 293
glazing, church 41–2, 53, 67, 70, 88–9, 100, 108–9, 111–12, 144, 150
glebes 19–21, 181, 241, 255, 265, 270, 275, 279
Gloucester, earls of 32
St Gluvias 26–7, 45, 70–1, 75, 245, 247–8, 253, 259–60 – see also Cosawes; Penryn
Godfrey of Cornwall, friar 53, 60
Godman, Roger, hermit 304
Godman, William, cleric 146
Godolphin family 97
Godwyn, Thomas 139
Gody, John, cleric 161
Golant or St Samson 26, 135, 286, 295
Goldsithney (Perranuthnoe) 230
Goldsmyth, Thomas le, of Bodmin 156
Goldson, Robert 189
Gomersale, Richard of, cleric 256, 261
Good Friday 81, 101
Goran 12, 14, 19, 61, 119, 130, 247–8, 253, 259, 286, 288 – see also Trevennen
lazars of 301
St Goran, John of, cleric 37
Gorges, Sir Ferdinando 251

Gosse, Nicholas, cleric 167
Gourge, Stephen, canon 98, 213
Grade 84, 87, 168
Grampound (Creed) 74
  lepers of 301
Grandisson, John, bishop of Exeter 49
  and collegiate churches 48, 55, 164–8, 175–6, 245, 248–50, 252–3, 255–6
  and friars 54, 156, 158, 267, 281, 283
  and monasteries 51–2, 138, 145, 147–8, 150, 186, 207–8, 212, 214–15, 232, 268, 275, 289–90
  and parishes and parish clergy 46, 54, 57, 60, 84–5, 115, 273, 298
  and saints' lives 111, 114
graveyards 14–15
Gray family 183
Gray, Walter de, cleric 163, 170, 262–3, 265
Gready (Lanlivery) 286, 295
Gregory the Great, pope 129, 190
Gregory, John, cleric 63
Greke, Thomas, cleric 62
Grenville family 53, 292, 295
Greston, Eleanor, laundress 223
Grove, Thomas 276
Gueriir, saint 5, 115
Guest, Nicholas, prior 98, 190, 295–6
guilds 43, 67, 72–3, 77, 94, 100, 105, 111, 159–60, 168, 213, 250, 302 – see also confraternities
Gulval 11, 21, 79, 86, 185, 190, 193, 232, 286 – see also Glas
Gunwalloe 26
Gurde, John, leper 223
Guy of Merton, prior 34, 140
Guyer, John, cleric 169–70
Gwarnick (St Allen) 73
Gwennap 42, 44, 75 – see also St Day
Gwinear, saint 8, 88
Gwinear, church and parish 42, 48, 78, 80
Gwithian, saint 15
Gwithian, church and parish 14–15, 26, 77 – see also Connerton
Gybbons, John, cleric 217–18
Gyllefort, Peter of, cleric 271
Gynnis, Richard 294

Haccombe family 30, 297
Hailes (Gloucs.), abbey 32, 93
Haldu, Stephen, cleric 268
Hale, John of, cleric 170
Hals, William, historian 150, 156, 226, 228, 274, 299
Halwyn (Crantock) 127
Hamatethy (St Breward) 161
Hambleton, William of, cleric 164, 166, 170
Hamley family 187
Hamlyn, Robert, monk 294
Hancock, William, prior 191
Hardy, John, prior 233, 240
Harepath, Richard, prior 51, 189, 191, 233, 240
Hariwell, John 282
Harold II, earl and king 11, 20, 128, 131–2
Harpedene, William of, cleric 264
Harry alias Henry, Nicholas, cleric 258, 261
Harry, Nicholas, of Bodmin 162

Harrys, John, cleric 193–4
Harrys, Robert, hospital prior 223–4
Harrys, Thomas, archdeacon 193
Hartland (Devon), minster and abbey 13, 32, 45–6, 93, 112, 180, 202, 217
Hartopp, Ralph, cleric 183
Hartyshede, Thomas 277
Hastings family 244
Hawke, Richard 172
Hawkyn, John, prior 191
Haye, William de la, prior 290, 296
Haym, Stephen, cleric 37, 170, 247, 252
healing 15, 79, 115, 119–20 – see also miracles; wells
Heghes, William, cleric 261
Heldris de Cornuälle, author 89
Helland, parish 21, 152
Helland (Mabe) 118
Helston 26, 97, 110, 194, 237
  St John hospital 192–4; mentioned 27, 33, 56, 92, 99–100
  St Mary Magdalene leper hospital 194; mentioned 33, 56, 83, 192
Helstone (Lanteglos-by-Camelford) 202–3
Helygan family 77
Hendeman, Thomas, cleric 180
Henoc, cleric 7
Henry I, king 22, 30, 129, 135, 163, 173, 195, 203, 262, 266, 297
Henry II, king 36, 141, 195–6, 297
Henry III, king 164, 174, 244, 262
Henry IV, king 51, 215, 233
Henry V, duke of Cornwall, later king 51, 211, 233, 235, 243, 290–1
Henry VI, king 61, 73, 86, 166–7, 212, 234, 236, 238, 291
Henry VII, king 48, 61, 150, 152, 293
Henry VIII, king 92, 95–9, 150–1, 219, 239, 292, 294–5
Henry of Avranches, poet 37
Henry fitz William, three such men 192
Henry, Thomas, clerk 171
Henton, Thomas of, cleric 264
heraldry 150–1, 183, 187–8, 191, 206, 220, 239, 293, 296
Herdwyck, Vincent of, Hospitaller 277
Hereford (Herefs.) 86, 232
heresy 48, 60, 101–2, 104, 106
Heriz, Henry de 209
Herle, Sir John, 171
hermits 56, 235, 266, 304–5
Hertford, Thomas of, cleric 262–3, 265
Hesyll, John, cleric 255
Hewet, John 159
Heynson, Richard, cleric 178–9
Hicks, Thomas, mayor 218
Higforde, Henry, gentleman 284
Higman, William, merchant 289
St Hilary 61, 66, 82, 231–2, 234–6 – see also Marazion; Trevabyn; Truthwall
Hill (St Gennys), chapel 210
Hill(s), Edward, Hospitaller 278
Hingston Down (Callington), battle 5
Hobson, Thomas, gentleman 276
Hogge, Thomas, of Bodmin 161
Hoggs, John, scholar 87
Holcomb, William, cleric 265
Holcote, Robert, friar 53, 213
Hole, William, canon 147

Hollacombe (Devon) 127, 139, 142, 152
Holland, Arnold of, cleric 37, 163, 170
Holland, John, earl of Huntingdon 215
Holwood (Quethiock?) 241
Honiton, Roger, canon 148
Honyland, John, prior 206, 211, 215–16, 221
Hoo, Robert, cleric 256–7, 261
Hooker, John, historian 105
Hoper, John, monk 291
Hoper, John, prior 299
Hopkyn, John, hospital prior 161–2
Hopkyn, William, prior 217, 221
Horde, Elizabeth 292
Horton, Roger of, prior 64, 206, 214, 220
Hospitallers – see St John, Order of
hospitals 33, 44, 56, 64, 160–2, 192–5, 299–300
Howard of Bindon family 183
Hull, Robert 255
Humphrey, duke of Gloucester 216
hundreds 25
Hundred Years War 46, 50, 138, 167, 232–3, 242–3, 275, 286, 289–91
Hune, William de la, prior 242
Hungerford family 243–4, 292
Huntingdon (Hunts.), priory 150
Hussey, Bartholomew, gentleman 277
Hussey, Nicholas, Hospitaller 278
Hyckeling, Hugh, cleric 251
Hygo, Richard, cleric 238
Hynkley, David, cleric 199
Hywel, king 6
Hywys family 157

Ia, saint 16
Ildiern, saint 111
Ildrayth, saint 112
St Illick (St Endellion) 18, 63, 76, 112, 119
Illogan 43, 72 – see also Carn Brea; Forest; Nancecuke; Tehidy
Illtud, saint 8
images 85
  divine (Trinity, Christ) 68–70, 86, 288 – see also rood screens
  saints and angels 69, 72, 144, 168, 188, 206, 237, 250, 283
  at the Reformation 96–7, 100–1, 105, 108
Indract, saint 112
indulgences
  in general 83–4, 234
  abolition of 96–7
  hospitals 161, 194, 224–5, 277
  parish churches and chapels 164, 206, 227, 269, 285
  personal 83–4, 94, 168, 291
  religious houses 86–8, 177, 188, 229, 236, 293
Ine, king 3–4
Inglose, Roger, Hospitaller 276, 278
Inistioge (Co. Kilkenny, Ireland), priory 140
Inkpen family 160
inscriptions in churches and elsewhere 88, 109, 172, 250 – see also stones, inscribed
Instantius, bishop 7
Ireland 2, 8–9, 16, 35, 37, 49, 53, 61, 113, 116, 123, 140, 149, 224–5, 227, 296

Isabel, Nicholas, prior 240
Isabella, queen of Edward II 292
St Issey 27, 42, 44, 65, 78, 83–4, 134
St Ive 62, 65, 82, 274–7, 297 – *see also* Trebeigh
St Ives or Porthia 16, 26, 76, 112, 258, 286, 288, 295
   lazars of 302

Jacobstow 255
James I, king 162, 179, 239, 265
James II, king 224
Jamys, John, canon 190
Jaune alias Trebursy, William 180
Jeffrey, Martin, friar 283
Jerusalem 83, 86–7
Jesus – *see* Christ
Jewel, John, bishop 106
Joan, princess of Wales 231
Joce, Michael, Hospitaller 276, 278
St John, church 39, 41
John of Bridlington, saint 206, 213
John, count of Mortain later king 142, 146, 163–4, 209, 229, 262–3, 273, 297
John the Chanter, bishop of Exeter 136
John of Eltham, earl of Cornwall 157
John alias William, William, prior 53, 149–50, 154
John, William, monk 295
St Juliot 21, 48, 210, 219
Just, saint 14
St Just-in-Penwith 48, 61, 165, 247–8, 256, 259–60, 284
   hermitage 304
St Just-in-Roseland 136–8, 260 – *see also* St Mawes

Kaer, John, cleric 165
Kaylleway, John 299
Kea or Ke, saint 90, 111, 113–14, 119, 258
Kea, church and parish 12, 21, 90–1, 113, 116, 118, 130–1, 194, 247–8, 253, 259 – *see also* Tregavethan
Kells (Co. Kilkenny, Ireland) 140
Kelly, John, cleric 180
Kellygreen (St Tudy) 192
Kellygore, John, cleric 243
Kembell, John, cleric 194
Kendall family 99, 153, 218–19, 294–5
Kenegy, Alan, prior 53, 148–9, 154
Kenstec, bishop 9, 121, 123, 126
Kent family 157
Kentysbery, John, friar 157
Kenwyn, saint 15
Kenwyn. church and parish 15, 26, 131, 259 – *see also* Carvedras
St Keran, John of, cleric 175
St Keverne 12–15, 21, 27, 32–3, 45, 70, 97–8, 101, 119, 124, 131, 195, 230 – *see also* Nan(s)clegy; Traboe
St Kew, earlier *Docco*, minster, church, parish 8, 11–12, 20, 23, 27, 32, 70, 88–9, 103, 105, 109, 115, 119, 131, 137, 181, 271 – *see also* Chapel Amble; Treroosel
   alleged Augustinian house 195–6
Keyne, saint 238
St Keyne 28, 105
Kiggon (St Clement), lepers of 301

Kilkhampton 41, 80, 291 – *see also* Stowe
Kilkhampton, John of, prior 145, 147, 154
Killigrew family 70, 84, 159–61, 251, 255, 262, 277
King Harry Ferry (Philleigh) 238
Kingswood (Bodmin) 99, 146, 153
Kirkeby, John of, cleric 170
Knyfton, Matthew, cleric 235, 240
Knolle, Adam of, prior 52, 214, 220
Knolles, Robert, cleric (St Buryan) 167, 171
Knollys, Robert, cleric (Trebeigh) 276
Kylkeham, John, prior 191

Lacy, Edmund, bishop of Exeter 49
   and parishes and parish clergy 54, 60, 77, 145, 148, 181, 269, 283, 304
   and religious houses 52, 54, 187,, 206, 215–17, 238, 251, 254, 257–8, 269, 276, 283
   indulgences of 83, 161, 194, 225, 234
Ladock 135, 165
Lady chapels 52, 66, 85, 143–4, 149, 188, 206–7, 212, 235, 245, 249–50, 255, 289, 292
Lamb, William, cleric 105
Lambert, William, prior 233, 240
Lambest (Menheniot) 185
Lammana or Looe Island (Talland), priory and chapels 196–9; mentioned 26, 28, 30, 33–4, 76, 99–100, 132, 237
Lamorran 11, 44, 118
Lamprey, Stephen, cleric 218–19
Lancastre, Richard de, cleric 267
Landewarnek, John, friar 53
Landewednack 69 – *see also* Lizard Point
Landkey (Devon) 113
Landrake 21, 27, 184–6, 189–91
Landreyne, John, cleric 60
landscape 14–15, 17, 34, 76, 78–80, 108, 116–20, 160, 197, 204, 241, 260, 285
Landulph 21, 72, 87, 185, 190–1, 284 – *see also* Tinnel
Laneast 21, 26, 38, 132, 202, 209–10, 213, 219
Langa, John, of Launceston 214
Langeton, Robert of, Hospitaller 276
Langunnet (St Veep) 21
Langurrow (Crantock) 174
Lanherne (St Mawgan-in-Pydar) 11, 171–2
Lanhydrock 26, 142, 149, 152–3, 200
Lanivet 153, 160–1, 286, 303 – *see also* Reperry
Lanlawren (Lanteglos-by-Fowey) 132
Lanlivery 26, 41, 48, 69, 98, 111, 153, 200, 286, 288, 295 – *see also* Bodardle; Gready; Penknight; Restormel
   Maudlin hospital 200–1; mentioned 33, 56
lann, place-name element 14, 116–19
Lannaled – *see* St Germans
Lannargh family 84, 168
Lanner (St Allen) 23
Lanrake, John, friar 53
Lanreath 14, 21, 72, 193
Lansallos 6, 12, 19, 21, 111, 132, 206
Lanteglos-by-Camelford 26, 152 – *see also* Helstone
Lanteglos-by-Fowey 32, 48, 61–2, 75, 77, 81, 87, 297 – *see also* Lanlawren; Polruan

Lantokai (Som.) 113
Laon (France), canons of 139
Lapford (Devon) 210
Latimer, Hugh, bishop 238
Latin language 12, 18, 34, 36, 43, 53, 62, 65, 71, 83, 87–8, 95–6, 100, 104, 140, 207, 213
Launcells 21, 32
Launceston 60, 74, 91, 274 – *see also* Gilmartin
   almshouse 56, 224
   chapels, including castle 76, 185, 202, 206, 208–9, 211, 219, 222
   guilds 73, 83, 223
   Newport 208
   new town, Dunheved 12, 33–4, 36, 73, 108, 201, 204, 206–8, 225, 275
   old town, St Stephens 12–14, 16, 21–3, 34, 201, 207
   property of Templars and Order of St John 272–3, 275, 277
   St Leonard, leper hospital 221–4; mentioned 33, 56, 219
   St Mary Magdalene church 26, 28, 38, 65–6, 73, 80, 94, 208, 210, 218
   St Stephen, priory 203–21; mentioned 30, 34, 38–9, 44–6, 48, 50–2, 66, 84, 87, 92–3, 98–9, 151–2, 198–9, 221–2
   St Stephen–by–Launceston, minster later parish church 132, 201–4, 208–10, 214, 219; mentioned 12–14, 16, 21–3, 27, 34, 38, 43, 64
   St Thomas–by–Launceston church 26, 28, 38, 204, 206, 208–10, 212, 218–20
   schools 87–8, 94, 98, 100–1, 213
Launcestonland, manor 209–10, 219
Laurence, John, canon 218
Lawhitton 9, 11, 21, 23, 27, 41, 48, 53, 68, 93, 107, 122, 201
lay people, religion of 43, 47, 65–91, 94–5, 99, 101–2, 105–6, 109
Layton, Cuthbert, Hospitaller 277–8
lazars – *see* lepers
Lechlade, Walter of, cleric 264
Ledes, John of, cleric 242
Lee, William de la, prior 280
Leigh, Silvester 179
Leland, John, antiquary
   on collegiate and parish churches and chapels 85, 97, 167–8, 178, 206, 252, 280, 304
   on friaries 155, 158, 285
   on hospitals and almshouses 159, 161–2, 193
   on islands 198, 270
   on monasteries 10, 64, 129, 138, 141, 144, 146, 150, 161, 184, 186, 188–90, 204, 207, 229, 288, 299
Lelant 32, 77, 112, 146, 175, 259, 286
Lelley family 280
Lent 81, 96, 110, 219, 222
Leofric, bishop of Exeter 12, 21, 86, 123, 130, 184, 189, 229
lepers and lazars 33, 47, 56, 160–2, 194–5, 200–1, 221–4, 299–300, 300–3
Lercedekne family 201, 299–300
Lercedekne, Martin, cleric 258
Lercevesque family 37
Lesnewth 45, 241, 280, 286, 288

Lethiock (St Germans) 185
Leucum, monk 12
Le Val – see Ste-Marie-du-Val
St Levan 14, 26, 48, 79–80, 128, 163, 167–9 – see also Treen
Lewannick 209–10, 219–20 – see also Polyphant; Trewanta
Lewannick, Richard of 209
Leye, Roger, prior 215, 220
Lezant 27, 76
Lhuyd, Edward, antiquarian 160
Libbe, William, cleric 273
Lifton (Devon) 48, 209
Linkinhorne 61, 83, 106, 206, 209–11, 213, 215, 219 – see also Caradon Prior; Rillaton; Trefrize
Liskeard 21–2, 68, 73, 83–4, 189, 202, 209–11, 215, 218–19
  St Mary Magdalene leper hospital 224–6; mentioned 33, 56
  park, St Mary chapel, hermitage 56, 75–6, 85, 97, 100, 304
Little Petherick 27, 88, 134
liturgy – see parish churches: services
Lizard Point (Landewednack) 1
Llandough (Glam.) 8, 131
Llandygai (Caerns.) 113
Llantwit Major (Glam.) 8
Lloyd, Owen, cleric 167
Lochard, William, cleric 167, 171
Loenter [?], John, prior 296
Lollards 48
London 24, 37, 48–9, 86, 151, 153, 161, 169, 216, 236, 257, 260, 268, 272, 276–7
  Dominican friary 282–3
  Holy Trinity, Aldgate, priory 34–5, 203
  Order of St John, Clerkenwell 273, 275
  St Mary Rounceval hospital 83
  St Paul's cathedral 83
London, John of 155
London, Siger of, cleric 179
Long Colling (St German) 185
Looe, East and West 43, 74, 197–8
Looe Island – see Lammana
Lostwithiel 80, 84, 142, 161, 294, 298
  church and parish 26, 28, 48, 66–7, 93
  hermits of 304
Lovell, John, of Launceston 215–16
Lovocat and Catihern, letter to 121
Lucow or Lycow, John, cleric 173
Lucy family 32
Ludewan, saint 15
Ludgvan 15, 228, 286
Luer, Richard, canon 153
Luffincott (Devon) 209–10
Lugans, Benedict, friar 54, 282–4
Luke, William, cleric 161
Lunday, William of, cleric 176, 179
Luxulyan 26, 48, 67, 286, 295
Lybbe, John, cleric 260, 262
Lydford (Devon) 5
Lyfing, bishop 12, 123
Lyhert, Walter, bishop 60–1
Lytelton family 99, 153

Mabe 26–7, 77, 105 – see also Helland; Treliever
Mabelsteyn, William 277
St Mabyn 148 – see also Spittal; Tresarrett

Macclesfield, John, cleric 243
Madron 45, 48, 78–9, 93, 120, 273, 275–7, 286 – see also Alverton; Penzance
  lepers of 302
Maenchi, nobleman 6, 20, 132
Maidstone (Kent), college 169
Maker 9, 11, 32
Manaccan alias Minster 45, 48, 93, 132–3, 247–8, 254, 259, 286
Manely (St Veep) 297–8
Manton, Ralph of, cleric 164, 170
manumissions 127
Marazanvose (Perranzabuloe), lazars 302
Marazion, including Market Jew (St Hilary) 84, 97, 169, 228, 230–2, 234
Margaret of Anjou, queen 61
Margaret of France, queen 167
Marhamchurch 21, 56, 93, 105, 156, 305
Marisco, Reginald de, knight 31, 273
Marke, John, collector 226
Market Jew – see Marazion
Marny family 183
marriage 18, 41, 70, 82, 96, 101, 103, 105, 107–8, 110
Marsely, Henry, cleric 61, 165–6
Marsh, Robert of, cleric 175
Marshal, Henry, bishop of Exeter 24, 136, 142, 225, 230, 234, 241, 263
St Martin-by-Looe 22, 132, 209, 286 – see also Bodigga; Bucklawren
St Martin-in-Meneage 26, 228
Martyn, Richard, prior 292–3, 296
Martin, Thomas, cartographer 200, 302
Martyn, William 292
Mary I, queen 104–6, 183, 219, 223, 239, 277
St Mary Vale (Cardinham), priory and chapel 285; mentioned 30, 33–4, 74, 76, 288
Maslyn, John, prior 243, 290, 292, 296
mass 18, 70–1, 102, 105, 172, 250 – see also communion
Matilda, empress 204
Maunte, John de, cleric 165–7, 170
Maunte, Matthew de, cleric 167, 170
St Mawes (St Just-in-Roseland) 80
Mawgan, saint 111, 133
Mawgan-in-Meneage 14, 21, 32, 133, 192, 230
St Mawgan-in-Pydar 21, 169 – see also Lanherne
Mawnan 303
Maynard, David, cleric 171
Mayrinhac, Bernard de, cleric 176, 179
Megre, John, pewterer 161, 194, 201, 222, 225, 300, 303
men as a specific group 43, 67, 70, 72–3, 80–1, 87, 110, 217 – see also boys; friars; monasteries, parish clergy
St Melan, William of, cleric 280
Menaclidgey (Sithney) 192, 194
Meneage, district 133
Menheniot 32, 48, 64–5, 71, 80, 105, 225, 286 – see also Lambest; Treviddo
  St Mary Magdalene hospital – see Liskeard
Meriasek, saint 87, 114–15, 258
Merryfield, John 172
St Merryn 26–7, 67, 78

Merston, Henry, cleric 166
merther, place-name element 14
Merther 26, 78, 111–12, 262–3
Mertherderwa, Reginald, cleric 60, 79, 88
Merthérian, saint 43
Merthereuny (Wendron) 14, 114
Merton (Surrey), priory 32–4, 45, 93, 140, 151, 217, 279–80
Methleigh (Breage) 11
Meubred, saint 16
Mevagissey 14, 48, 247–8, 255, 259–60
St Mewan 14, 61, 112 – see also Trelower
Mewen, Nicholas, friar 284
Michael, archangel, cult of 86, 97, 111, 198, 232, 237, 250
Michael, Richard, prior 191
St Michael Caerhays 26, 28, 41, 286 – see also Caerhays
St Michael Penkevil 226–8; mentioned 55, 65, 103 – see also Fentongollan
St Michael's Mount, church and priory 228–40; mentioned 16–17, 21–2, 26, 30, 33, 35, 38–9, 43–4, 46, 48, 50, 55–6, 74, 76, 80, 82, 84–8, 92, 100, 105, 115, 119–20, 133, 165, 195, 198, 263, 305
Michaelstow 76
Michell, James, cleric 55, 250, 258
Michell, John, cleric 180
Michell, William, cleric 235, 240
Michell – see also Mychel
Militon family 238–9
Milton Abbot (Devon) 211
mining 67, 281
Minster or Talcarn – see also Boscastle; Carnegie; Trela
  priory and church 240–4; mentioned 20, 30, 33–5, 38–9, 43–4, 46, 48, 50–1, 61, 84, 98, 133, 190–1, 207, 289, 292
Minster – see also Manaccan
minsters, Anglo-Saxon and Norman 12–14, 18, 32, 112, 119, 126–35, 139–40, 163, 173, 201–3, 210
Minstre, William de la, monk 242
St Minver 66, 79, 97, 142, 149, 152, 180–1, 271 – see also St Enodoc
miracles 8, 34, 43, 84–6, 141, 232, 241
Miral, John, monk 290
Mirk, John, canon 237
Mitchell (St Enoder) 74
  lepers of 302
Modbury (Devon), priory 290
Modred family 183
Mohun family 87
Moleyns, Adam, cleric 167, 171
Molines, William des, cleric 263, 265
monasteries of monks and regular canons 22, 26, 30–5, 47, 50–3, 98
  corrodies in 147, 149, 153, 189, 193, 207, 231–2, 289 – see also monasteries: pensioners
  dissolution of 98–9, 102
  early medieval 7–9
  incomes of 137–8, 142, 151–2, 184–5, 190, 199, 210–11, 219, 231, 242, 244, 280, 288–9, 294–5, 298–9
  liturgy in 52, 144, 147, 212, 291, 293
  numbers of clergy 30, 51, 92, 145, 151, 153, 189–90, 211, 217, 289, 292, 295
  pensioners 49, 145, 189–90, 212, 231–2,

289, 295 – *see also* monasteries: corrodies
   recruitment of clergy 52, 211, 229
   servants of 147–8, 150, 189, 207, 212, 214, 217, 242, 289
Monk Sherborne (Hants.), priory 291
monks – *see* monasteries
Montacute (Som.), priory 22, 30, 32, 51, 93, 129, 133, 173–4, 297–9
Montague, William de, earl of Salisbury 298
Mont St Michel (France), abbey 22, 30, 46, 86, 133, 228–33, 237
Moren, saint 11
Moretonhampstead (Devon) 69
Morice, Francis 179
Morlegh, John, canon 217–18
Mortain, counts of 210 – *see also* John; Robert; William
Mortymer, Robert, monk 295
Morton, William, cleric 234–6, 240
Morvah 26
Morval 45, 185, 190, 297
Morwenstow 41, 48, 53, 61, 67 – *see also* Eastway
Mottisfont (Hants.), priory 32
Mousehole (Paul)
   lepers of 302
   St Clement's Island 76
Moyle family 188
Moys, Cecilia or Lucy, anchoress 56, 305
Mullion 32, 37, 42, 48
Mullyng, William, canon 149
Mundy family 153
Mundy, Peter, voyager 260
Mundy, Thomas – *see* Wandsworth
music 52, 55, 80, 178, 258, 292
Mychel, John, canon 189
Mylor 27, 39, 239, 247–8, 255, 259
Myn, Walter, cleric 257, 261
Myneworth or Menewrth, Simon of, Hospitaller 276

names
   hypocoristic 113, 298
   personal 6, 111
   place-names 14–15, 112–13, 115–19
Nancecuke (Illogan) 43, 127, 141, 301–2
Nans, John, cleric 60, 114, 193–4, 251, 258–9, 261
Nan(s)clegy (St Keverne) lepers of 195; mentioned 33, 300
Nanskevell, Richard, cleric 173
Nansmuer, Henry, cleric 243
Naylor, John, of Bodmin 144
Nectan, saint 8, 112, 119, 180, 213
Neot, saint 11, 16–17, 88, 213, 297
St Neot 5, 12, 21, 26, 30, 32, 62, 67, 70, 88–9, 108–9, 111–12, 115, 119, 133, 162, 209 – *see also* Fawton
St Neot's (Hunts.) 11
Netherbury (Dorset) 86, 237
Neville, George, bishop of Exeter 236–7, 253, 258
Newenham (Devon), abbey 32, 46
Newlyn East 23, 75, 82, 105, 112, 142, 192 – *see also* Cargoll
Newport, Robert, Hospitaller 278
Newquay (St Columb Minor) 84

Newton St Petrock (Devon) 127, 139, 142, 152
Nicolls, Nicholas, cleric 105
Noe, William, cleric 254
Noel, Pascow, cleric 60
Nonn or Nonnita, saint 88, 213
non-residence of clergy 32, 55, 92, 107, 167, 175–6, 182–3, 253, 255, 258
Norden, John, topographer 86, 298
Northamtone, Michael of, cleric 174
Northcott (Boyton) 106
Northecote, John, leper 223
North Hill 103, 191
North Lew (Devon) 68
North Petherwin 25–6, 32, 41, 79–80, 133–4
North Tamerton 21, 38, 73, 99, 202, 206, 209–10, 219, 223
Nortone, John of, cleric 179
Nottingham 86, 237
nunneries and nuns 31, 150, 304 – *see also* Syon; Wilton
Nydek, Tilman, Hospitaller 276, 278
Nynys, Nicholas, Londoner 276
Nyvet, John, priest 292

Oby, John, cleric 259, 261
Offe, Ellen, of Launceston 218
'official', archdeacon's deputy 25, 49
Oldham, Hugh, bishop of Exeter 91, 150, 188, 217, 258, 292–3
Oldstowe, John, cleric 148
Ollerton, Richard, monk 291
Olyver, Richard, cleric (Glasney) 254
Oliver, Richard, cleric (Minster) 243–4
Olyver, Richard, canon 153
Olyver, Robert, of Bodmin 53, 144
Ordinalia – see drama
ordination 37, 57, 104–5, 109, 157, 166
organs 80
Orkneyinga Saga 267–8
Osbern, bishop of Exeter 21–2
Otham, Jordan of 285
Otterham 286
Otterton (Devon) 229
Ottery St Mary (Devon), collegiate church 245, 249, 253
Oxford (Oxon.)
   Exeter College 48, 59, 93
   friaries 149, 158, 213, 282–3
   Rewley, abbey 32, 93
   schools at 90, 107
   university 36–7, 53, 57–60, 149, 158, 193, 213, 235, 258, 291

Padstow 41, 80, 99, 126–7, 130, 139, 148, 152–3
   early minster 11–12, 17–18, 122–4, 134
   later church and parish 14, 20–1, 27, 45, 83, 142
   St Cadoc and other chapels 15, 61, 75–6, 78–9, 91, 119, 149
   lepers 302
paganism 8, 16
papacy and popes
   early missions to England 129, 190
   indulgences 83, 86, 188, 224–5, 229, 236, 269, 293
   legal acts 12, 166, 168, 196–7, 209, 213, 215, 241, 290

and military orders 272, 274–6
   protection by 51, 269
   provisions to benefices 46–7, 256–7
   Reformation period 95–6, 102, 104, 106
   taxation of Pope Nicholas IV (1291) 44–6 and passim
pardoners 83
Paris, university of 35–7
parish churches 14, 18, 21
   bells – *see* bells
   buildings 38–41, 47, 62–3, 65–70, 94, 108
   dedications – *see* dedications
   estates of – *see* estates
   fonts – *see* fonts
   furnishings 41, 94, 103, 105, 108–9
   images in – *see* images
   inscriptions in – *see* inscriptions
   ornaments and plate 41–2, 97, 103, 105
   porches 70, 109
   processions from – *see* processions
   screens – *see* rood screens
   seating in 42, 69, 71, 80, 94–5, 109–10
   served by members of religious orders 145, 152, 211–12, 267, 283
   services 42, 70–1, 77, 101, 107, 109, 123
   sites of 14, 116–19
   values and income 26, 28, 77, 91–2, 244, 253, 271
   windows – *see* glazing
parish clergy – *see also* rectors; vicars
   beneficed clergy 17–21, 36–8, 42, 46–7, 57–65, 109
   chantry priests – *see* chantries
   chaplains 37, 61–3, 92–3, 100, 108, 138, 150, 168–9, 188, 193, 212, 214, 222, 242–3, 264, 267–70, 272
   education of 36, 57
   houses 20, 25, 38, 62, 241, 244, 252, 264
   marriage of 103, 105, 107
   non-residence by – *see* non-residence
   numbers 26, 63, 92
   pre-Conquest 17–18, 121, 127
   retirement and pensions 64
   stipends of beneficed clergy – *see* parish churches: values and income
   wages of chaplains 63, 93–4, 171, 173
parish clerks 36, 42, 57, 63, 70, 80, 107, 109, 168, 171, 212
parishes, origins and characteristics 18, 25–9, 48, 116–19, 170
Parker, Matthew, archbishop 107
Parkyn, Henry, hospital prior 162
Parlaben, Ralph, friar 157
Parys, Robert, canon 211, 216–17
parochia, meaning of 9, 121–2
Pascon agan Arluth, poem 90
Pascaw, Thomas, friar 283
Pascow, John, cleric 258–9, 261
patronage of churches
   collegiate churches 48–9, 163–4, 173–4, 226, 247–8, 256–7, 263–4
   monasteries, friaries, hospitals 20, 142–3, 160–1, 186, 192, 200, 201–3, 211, 231, 234, 279, 281, 294, 298
   parish churches and chantries 20, 25, 37, 99, 141–2, 171, 182–3, 185, 209–10, 230, 243–4, 256–7, 270–1, 273–4, 277, 286
Paugan, Andrew, hermit 304
Paul, church 48

Paul of Léon, saint 8, 16
Paul, parish 303 – *see also* Mousehole
Pawton (St Breock) 9, 11, 23, 27, 93, 103, 123, 126
Payne, Richard, cleric 173
Peasants' Revolt 48, 146
Pecche, John, merchant 236
peculiar jurisdictions 23, 27, 48, 164–6, 175, 186, 229, 231, 248, 253
Pedder family 292
Pelynt 21, 32, 103, 105 – *see also* Trelawne
Pempel, Stephen, cleric 60–1
Pendavey (Egloshayle) 139, 142, 145, 152
Penels, Richard, cleric 49
Pengersick (Breage) 238
Pengwedna (Breage) 171
Penhal, Henry of, cleric 193
Penheale (Egloskerry), chapel 219
Penhyll, Alexander, cleric 258, 261
penitentiaries – *see* confession
Penknight (Lanlivery) 304
Penlyn, Robert of, hermit 304
Penpons family 58, 173
Penros, Richard of 165
Penryn (Budock, St Gluvias) 11, 23, 27, 61, 84, 93, 108, 114–15, 245–6, 258, 282
   almshouse 262; mentioned 56
   Glasney college 244–62; mentioned 25, 27, 33, 38–9, 41, 44–6, 48–50, 55, 57, 60–1, 66, 84, 88, 91–3, 99–100, 114–15, 193, 263–4
   St Thomas church 246
   schools 55, 87, 258–60
pensioners in monasteries – *see* monasteries
Pentecost 81, 101, 107
Pentuan (St Austell) 281
Penventon (Sithney) 192
Penzance (Madron) 54, 74, 87, 97, 269, 283
Percival, Thomasine, foundress 88, 101, 144, 292
Perer, Richard, prior 240
Perranarworthal 26, 134
Perranuthnoe 28, 82, 134, 236, 303 – *see also* Goldsithney
Perranzabuloe 12–13, 15–16, 18, 21–3, 27, 42, 44, 82, 84, 105, 110, 113, 115, 119, 134–5, 168, 236, 239 – *see also* Callestick; Marazanvose; Tywarnhayle
Peryent, Sir John 260
Petit, le, Robert, bishop 49
Petroc, saint 8, 11, 15–18, 20, 34–5, 39, 52, 88, 113–15, 119, 122, 126, 134, 140, 144, 149, 213
Peverel family 156–7, 161
Peyntone, Nicholas of, cleric 263
Phelips, Francis 179
Philippa, queen 61
Phillack 14, 116, 193
Philleigh 21, 136 – *see also* King Harry Ferry; Tolverne
pilgrimage 84–7; mentioned 17, 43, 83, 94, 96–8, 105, 115, 198, 229, 232, 236–9, 267
Piper, John, prior 189, 191
Piran, saint 8, 17–18, 82, 84, 88, 113, 115, 213
place-names – *see* names
Plymouth (Devon) 257
   Carmelite friary 32, 53, 84
Plympton (Devon) 84

St Mary, church 69
   priory 10, 23, 30, 32, 46, 93, 119, 126, 129, 136–8, 140, 195–6, 217, 257
Plympton, William of, canon 34, 147
Pole, Reginald, cardinal 102
Pole, Richard, friar 157–8
Polgover, Richard of, prior 191
Pollard, John, archdeacon 91, 104
Polmarke, John, cleric 61
Polmorva, William, cleric 60–1
Polroad (St Tudy) 127
Polruan (Lanteglos-by-Fowey) 75–7
Polsloe (Devon), priory 31
Polyphant (Lewannick) 241, 244
polyphony – *see* music
Pomeroy family 30–1, 43, 169, 194, 229, 265, 273, 278–9
Ponte, Richard de, friar 283
Ponte, Richard de, proctor 279
Portel, Richard, prior 242
Porth, John, royal servant 292
Porthia – *see* St Ives
Portlemouth (Devon) 113
Portlooe (Talland) 197–9
Portlooe, Sir Odo of 198
Poughill 32, 45, 70, 73, 80, 210, 213, 219–20
Pounde, John, teacher 258
Poundstock 16, 48, 54, 61, 80–1, 131
Powlerde, Richard 219
Powtrayn, Martin, canon 190
Poyle, Thomas, of Tregony 159, 280
'Prayer Book Rebellion' 101–2
Prechour, John, prior 186, 191
Prest, Agnes, nonconformist 106
preaching 54, 71, 82, 100, 107, 157–8, 166, 254
Prideaux family 99, 151, 153
Prideaux, Edmund, illustrator 156
Probus, minster, church, parish 135, 262–5; mentioned 4, 12–14, 21–2, 32, 44, 92, 94–5, 99–100, 112, 124, 248, 286 – *see also* Freewater; Ventontinny
processions, parish 81–2, 100, 105, 107, 112, 115, 168
prophecy 238
Prospidnick (Sithney) 171
provisions, papal – *see* papacy
Prowse, Thomas 239
Pruet, William, hermit 305
Pryny, John, canon 291
psalm singing 107
Ptolemy, geographer 1
Pullo, Ralph, cleric 203, 220
pulpits 69, 71, 107
Pultone, John of, cleric 179
Pycot, John, cleric 248, 264
Pydar or Pyder, hundred 128, 146

Quethiock 48 – *see also* Holwood
Quinil, Peter, bishop of Exeter 38, 174, 195–6, 247–8, 255, 263–4, 274, 280
   statutes of 36, 41–3, 68, 80

Raddon, Richard of 209, 212
Randall, Nicholas, of Truro 284
Rashleigh family 153, 295
Rauf, John, cleric 257, 261
Rauff, Stephen, friar 157

Raulyn, John, of Bodmin 161
Rawlyns, Thomas, of Bodmin 153
Rayne, Thomas, chapel clerk 292
rebellions 48, 101–2, 146, 150, 215, 219, 237, 259
rectors and rectories 37–8, 44–5, 46–7, 93, 199, 226
Reddew, Richard, cleric 60, 258, 261
Redman, Richard, bishop of Exeter 77
Redruth 114
   lepers and lazars of 303
Redruth, Richard, cleric 60
Reformation, English, 95–110
Reginald de Dunstanville, earl of Cornwall 22–3, 30, 163, 204, 207, 209–10, 221–2, 229, 273–4
   Beatrice or Mabilia, wife of 207
relics, undefined 34–5, 96, 168, 177, 250
   of Christ 84, 106, 168
   of saints 16–17, 35, 82, 105–6, 112, 115, 126, 140, 153, 188, 212, 238
Reperry (Lanivet) 171
Reskajeage (Camborne) 80, 231
Reskarnon, John, friar 283–4
Reskymer family 31–2, 83, 192–3, 281–2
Restormel (Lanlivery), park of 56, 76, 281, 304–5
Restormel, Philip of, hermit 304
Reterth (St Columb Major) 99, 142, 152–3
Reve, Thomas 260
Rewe, Nicholas, monk 269
Rewley – *see* Oxford
Rhodes (Greece) 275–6
Rialton (St Columb Minor) 52, 99, 108, 127, 139, 142, 144, 150, 152–3
Richard II, king 167, 186, 212, 215, 222, 233, 243, 257, 269, 290
Richard III, king 238
Richard, earl of Cornwall, king of the Romans 131, 141, 146, 155, 163–4, 174, 198, 206, 208–9, 222, 285, 288, 292
Richard the Butler 272
Richard fitz Turold – *see* Cardinan family
Richard, John, canon 149
Richardson family 183
Rillaton (Linkinhorne) 202
Robartes family 183
Robert, count of Mortain 20–2, 128–9, 131–5, 163, 173, 201–3, 228–9, 297
Robert fitz Walter, of Manely 297–8
Roche 67, 76, 97, 237 – *see also* Tremoddrett
Rochester (Kent), cathedral 32, 164, 166
Rodde, John, hospital prior 223–4
Rodde, Walter, friar 158–9
Rodney family 157
Rof, John, archdeacon
Rogationtide 81–2, 98, 100, 107, 112, 168
Roger, John, prior 51, 84, 290–1, 296
Roger, Thomas, notary 285
Rolles, George, royal servant 283
Roman Britain 1, 7, 196
Rome 17, 83, 86–7, 282
rood and choir screens 39–41, 68–71, 94, 105, 107, 143, 168, 206, 250, 288, 291
Roscarrock (St Endellion) 181
Roscarrock family 106, 182
Roscarrock, Nicholas, hagiographer 80, 82, 90, 105, 182

Rosemelian, Roger, friar 159
Rosmeber, William of, hospital prior 194
Rospannel (St Buryan) 163, 166, 169
Rough Tor (St Breward) 76
rounds 14
Rous, le, Hugh, bishop 35, 140
Ruan Major 107
Ruan Minor 93
Rue, Roger of 274
Rufus, Richard, friar 35
Rumon, saint 11, 14, 115, 213
Russell, John, lord 270
Rutha, William of, cleric 274
Ruthern (Bodmin) 146
Ryse, John, cleric 167–8, 171

St Aubin, William of, cleric 163, 170
St Aubyn family 239, 295
St Giles-in-the-Heath (Devon) 25–6, 38, 210, 219
St John of Jerusalem or Hospitallers, Order of 26, 31, 35, 44–6, 50–1, 83, 98, 104, 272–3, 273–8
St Leger, Sir John 182–3
St Mathieu-de-Fineterre (France), abbey 163
St Méen (France), abbey 141
St Pierre-sur-Dives (France), abbey 51, 290
St Quay (France) 113
St Remy, Nicholas of, prior 279
St Vigor (France), abbey – *see* Cerisy-la-Forêt
Ste-Marie-du-Val (France), abbey 30, 33, 278–80, 285
saints 96, 104
  chairs of 80, 120
  Cornish, Breton, and Welsh 7–8, 14–17, 43, 72, 78–9, 111–13, 213
  feast days 81, 84, 96, 98–9, 110
  images – *see* images
  international 43, 62, 68–70, 72–3, 85–6, 111, 168, 235, 238 and passim
  Irish 8–9, 16, 113, 116
  Lives of 7–8, 15–17, 34, 62, 88, 111, 113–14, 140–1, 238
  miracles by – *see* miracles
  relics of – *see* relics
Salisbury (Wilts.) 239 – *see also* Sarum
Saltash (St Stephen-by-Saltash) 87–8, 94, 101, 188
Salter, Richard, prior 269–70
Sampford Courtenay (Devon), 101
Samson, saint 7–8, 15–16, 118–19, 131
  monastery of 8, 135
St Samson – *see* Golant
Sancey, John, cleric 171
Sancreed 42, 48, 78–9 – *see also* Chapel Euny; Drift
  leper of 303
sanctuary (legal) 14, 124–5, 128, 131, 134–5, 164, 168, 177, 223, 262
sanctuary (church land) – *see* glebes
Sarum, Use of 70, 172
Sativola, saint 111
Saunders, Christopher, cleric 179–80
Scarrabine, Higher and Lower (St Endellion) 181
schools
  pre-Conquest 18, 130
  in monasteries and friaries 54, 149, 157, 213, 282, 292–3
  non-monastic, private and public 36, 42, 55, 57, 87–8, 94, 98, 100–1, 172, 258–60
Scilly, Isles of 1, 7, 26, 33, 54, 76, 92–3, 97–8, 266–70, 283
  priory of 266–70; mentioned 30, 34–5, 39, 44–6, 50–1, 233
screens – *see* rood screens
script, Carolingian 123–4
seals
  of collegiate churches 169, 179, 256, 260
  of hospitals 161, 200, 223
  of monasteries and friaries 144, 148, 153, 191, 220, 231, 239, 284, 288–9, 291, 293, 295–6
Seggemore, John 298
Seneschal, Richard, cleric 261
Senhouse, Richard 170
Sennen 26, 32, 48, 128, 163, 167–9
Serle, John, prior 190–1
Servon, Geoffrey de, prior 240
Seymour, Edward, earl of Hertford 295
Seyntmaur family 83
Seyvill, John, Hospitaller 276, 278
Sheepstall (Veryan) hospital 299–300; mentioned 33, 56
Shene, Henry of, pensioner 212
Sherborne (Dorset), church and abbey 4–5, 9, 135
  bishops of 6, 10, 20, 121–3
Shere, John, prior 98, 217–19, 221
Shessel, Lewis, almshouse master 162
Shyre, William, prior 52–3, 211, 213, 216–17, 221
Sideham, William of 274
Silvester, saint, Life of 114
Simon of Apulia, bishop of Exeter 142, 234, 263
Simon the Clerk, cleric 263, 265
Sireve, Geoffrey, cleric 274
Sithney, saint 15–16
Sithney 15–18, 45, 48, 84, 88, 192, 194, 247–8, 253, 259 – *see also* St Elvan; Menacliday; Penventon; Trelissick
Skewys, John of 212
Skyburiow, Roger of 247
Skyn(n)ard, William, cleric 175–6, 179
Slake, Nicholas, cleric 167, 171
Smethe, William, prior 299
Smith, John, friar 157
Soligny family 30, 196–8
Somer, John, friar 54, 158–9
Somerset, links or similarities with 112, 116, 118
Soor family 136
Sore, John, cleric 63, 180
Southcote, John 260
South Hill 19, 135
South Petherwin 27, 73, 132–4, 185, 190, 202, 204, 208
Sparke, Adam, cleric 257, 261
Spitel, Wulfric of 221
Spittal (St Mabyn) 274, 302
Stafford, Edmund, bishop of Exeter 49, 188
  and anchorites 304–5
  and collegiate churches 177, 250, 254, 256
  and hospitals 161, 194, 225
  indulgences 83, 161, 177, 194
  and monasteries 148, 189, 215
Stanbury, John, friar and bishop 53, 60–1
Stanley, William, Lord Mounteagle 169
Stapledon, Walter, bishop of Exeter 49, 57
  founder and benefactor 59, 64
  and collegiate and parish churches 48, 55, 164–5, 175, 230, 253, 255, 264, 275
  and other religious houses 147, 189, 206, 212, 214, 224, 230, 275, 283
Stephen, saint 16, 111, 220
St Stephen-by-Launceston – *see* Launceston
St Stephen-by-Saltash 48, 63 – *see also* Saltash; Trematon
St Stephen-in-Brannel 286
Stephen, king 23, 203–4, 262
Stephen, Laurence, cleric 48
Stephens, John, friar 159
Sternhold, Thomas, courtier 98, 153
Stevyn, John, monk 295
Stevyns, John, canon 53, 150
Stillingfleet, John, Hospitaller 273
Stithians 32, 48
Stoke Climsland 106 – *see also* Climsland Prior
Stoke, William, leper 223
Stokes, Alan, cleric 171
Stokysley, John, hermit 304
stones, inscribed 2, 5–7, 14, 20, 79, 116, 120
  ogham inscriptions 2, 116
stores, church 72, 77, 94
stow, place-name element 119
Stowe (Kilkhampton), chapel 94
Stradbroke (Suffolk) 237
Stratford, John, bishop 224
Stratton 68, 73, 80, 162, 208–10, 218–19, 223, 225, 301 – *see also* Efford
Stratton, John, prior 51, 243–4
Stubbes, John, cleric 217–18
Stukeley, Peter, cleric 166–7, 171
Sullye, Oliver of, cleric 268
Sunday Christ, St Sunday 70
Suttone, Martin of, cleric 264
Swavesey, Geoffrey of, prior 242
Swymmer, Robert, prior 98, 190–1
Sylke, William, cleric 167
Symon, John, prior 151, 154
Symon, William, canon 217
Symon, William, cleric 276
Symons, William, leper 223
Symphorian, saint 18
Syon (Middx.), abbey 31, 51, 55–7, 86, 93, 233–9, 304–5

Talcarn – *see* Minster
Talkarn, William, cleric 180
Talland 190, 196, 198–9, 210, 213, 215, 219 – *see also* Lammana; Portlooe; Trenant
Talland, Gilbert de 210
Tamworth, Sir Nicholas 188
Taunton (Som.), 259
  priory 140, 217
Tauton, Robert of, canon 34, 141
Tavistock (Devon) 39, 187
  abbey of 11–12, 22, 26, 30, 32–3, 46, 51, 92–3, 98, 115, 202, 210, 233, 266–70, 293–4

taxation
   immunity from 14, 119, 127–8, 130, 132–5, 163, 272, 274
   papal – *see* papacy
Taylour, John, cleric 237
Taylour alias Cardmaker, John, friar 219
St Teath, church and parish 270–1; mentioned 33, 92, 99–100, 142, 180–1 – *see also* Trevilley
Tehidy (Illogan) 231
Teignterer, William, prior 34, 214, 220
Templars, Knights 26, 31, 44, 46, 50, 272, 275
Temple 272–3; mentioned 26, 28, 31, 50, 275
'Tenth–Century List' of saints 14
Teoric, prior 34, 203, 220
Terri fitz Simon, cleric 174, 179
Teudar, legendary ruler 8
Tewkesbury (Gloucs.), abbey 32, 93
Thame, Philip of, Hospitaller 275
Thomas fitz Anthony, founder 140
Thomas alias Kyllavoes, Henry 138
Thomas, John, canon 145, 149
Thomas, Robert, cleric 235
Thorbjorn Clerk 268
Tiberianus, bishop 7
Tideford (St Germans), alleged hermitage 304
tiles, floor 70, 144, 187, 206, 249, 288
Tinnel (Landulph) 184, 190
Tintagel 7, 14–15, 20–1, 32, 36, 40–1, 45–6, 63, 113, 241 – *see also* Bossiney; Genver; Treknow; Trethevy
Tintagel, Robert of 209
tithes 20–1, 38, 77, 99, 110
   tithe-free areas 20, 99, 138, 162, 185, 198, 209, 222, 274, 286, 298, 302
tithe maps 27
Todeworth, Richard of, cleric 261
Toker, John, canon 216
Toker, John, hospital inmate 223
Tolverne (Philleigh) 136, 171
tombs – *see also* funerals and burial rites
   in parish churches 42, 64–5, 84, 110, 168, 172, 182, 197, 227
   in religious houses 64, 138, 144, 151, 156–7, 177, 188, 193, 197, 206–8, 250, 282, 288–9, 295
Tomkyn, Peter, friar 283
Tomme, John, monk 291
Tomyowe, Richard, merchant 173
Tomyowe, Thomas, cleric 60
Ton, Richard, cleric 114
Towednack 26, 286
Traboe (St Keverne) 195, 228, 230–4
Tracy, Sir Thomas 200
Tragev, William of, cleric 180
Treago (Crantock) 174
Trebeigh (St Ive), preceptory of 273–8; mentioned 31, 50–1, 83, 98, 104, 108, 272–3
Tredaeck, Ralph of, friar 283
Tredaule (Altarnun) 241, 244
Tredenek family 159–61
Trediddan, Stephen, prior 64, 206, 211, 215, 221
Tredowel, Ribert of, cleric 255
Treen or *Trethyn* (St Levan) 163

trees, holy 80, 245
Trefeuwa, Henry of, cleric 175, 179
Treffry family 53, 157, 185, 282, 292
Trefolyn, John, friar 157
Trefoward (St Clether) 241
Trefrize (Linkinhorne) 209
Tregaire (Gerrans) 11, 23, 93, 136
Tregavethan (Kea) 130
Tregawythan, William, canon 148
Tregear, John, cleric 105
Tregian family 53, 292
Treglasta (Davidstow) 202, 297
Tregonwell, John, royal servant 97–8, 153, 190, 219
Tregony 28, 32–3, 159, 279
   priory and church of 278–80; mentioned 30, 33–5, 43, 48
Tregony, Nicholas of, canon 280
Tregoose (St Columb Major) 173
Tregoz family 87
Tregrisiow, Ralph, cleric 60
Tregury, Michael, archbishop 60–1, 86, 237
Trehaverock family 183
Treher' alias Symond, Stephen, hermit 235, 305
Treiagu family 55, 226–7, 247
Trekelad, Adam of, friar 158–9
Treknow (Tintagel) 127, 139, 141–2
Trela (Minster) 241
Trelawne (Pelynt) 197
Trelawny family 188
Treliever (Mabe) 11
Trelissick (St Erth or Sithney) 146
Trelobys, Ralph, cleric 114
Trelothryk family 157
Trelower (St Mewan) 303
Treloy (St Columb Minor) 127
Tremaine 16, 26, 38–40, 210, 213
Tremayn family 282
Trematon (St Stephen-by-Saltash) 185, 230
   lepers of 303
Trembleyon, Philip de, prior 289–90, 296
Trembras, John, cleric 65
Tremoddrett (Roche) 77
Tremur, Ralph, cleric 48, 60–1
Trenakys, Richard, canon 145
Trenant (Fowey) 286, 288–9, 295
Trenant (Talland) 198
Treneglos 26, 41, 286, 288, 295
Trengale (St Cleer) 127
Trengoff, Walter, cleric 49, 60, 258, 261
Trenowth family 228
Treroosel (St Kew) 130–1
Tresarrett (St Mabyn) 274
Tresco – *see* Scilly, priory of
Tresham, Sir Thomas, Hospitaller 277
Tresham, William, cleric 99
Tresithney, John 171
Treskelly, William, prior 186, 189, 191
Tresmeer 38, 132, 202, 209–11, 219, 288
Tresour, Thomas 281
Tresuswal, Benedict of, cleric 227–8
Tretherff family 67
Trethevy (Tintagel) 134
Trethevyn, William, friar 53
Trethew, Walter, cleric 276
Treueygon, Laurence of, bailiff 160
Trevabyn (St Hilary) 230

Trevage (Altarnun) 241, 244
Trevalga 63
Trevanion family 161
Trevarak, Isabel, prioress 31
Trevelles, William, cleric 60
Trevennen (Goran) 286, 288–9, 295
Trevenwythe, William of, cleric 180
Treverbyn, Walter of 199
Trevers, Richard, friar 158
Treveryon, Robert 291
Treviddo (Menheniot) 94
Trevilian, Henry, cleric 49
Trevilian, John, friar 158
Trevilley (St Teath) 127, 271
Trevisa, John, cleric and translator 60, 90
Trewanta (Lewannick) 209
Trewen 26–7
Trewethenek family 83
Treworgan (St Erme) 231, 263
Treworgie (St Gennys) 209, 219
Trewynnard family 269
Trewynnard, Michael, cleric 60, 258–9, 261
Trewinnek, Henry of, canon 211
Trewynt family 157
Trigg, district 6, 8, 25
Troarn (France), abbey 291
Truro 33, 94, 98, 101, 108, 130, 161, 192, 194, 277
   Dominican friary 281–4; mentioned 31, 33, 50, 53–4, 67, 84, 92, 155
   lepers of 303
   parish church and parish 28, 43, 63, 65, 83
   St Mary of the Portal 86
Truro Vean (St Clement) 281
Truro, Thomas, friar 54, 282–3
Truthwall (St Hilary) 229–9
Tubbe family 99, 153, 298
St Tudy 11, 126 – *see also* Kellygreen; Polroad
Tullok, John 291
Turberville, James, bishop of Exeter 105–6, 183
Tutbury (Staffs.), priory 233, 290
Tyrel, Roger, friar 54, 283
Tyttesbury, Richard, cleric 304–5
Tywardreath – *see also* Caruggat
   parish church 103, 286, 295–6
   priory 284–96; mentioned 30, 33–5, 38, 43–6, 48, 50–3, 67, 87, 92–3, 98, 108, 137, 240, 242–3, 247, 304
Tywarnhayle (Perranzabuloe) 15, 127–8, 202–3

universities 36–7, 45, 53–4, 57–60, 100, 107, 145, 149, 158 – *see also* Bologna; Cambridge; Oxford; Paris
Uppeton, Richard of, prior 214, 220
Urban, John, of Kent 71, 144, 193
Uryn, William, cleric 261

Valcan, William de, prior 239
Valor Ecclesiasticus 92–3, 96 and passim
St Veep 18, 32, 45, 297–9 – *see also* St Carroc; Langunnet; Manely
Ventontinny (Probus) 137
Vere, John de, earl of Oxford 237
Veryan 18, 33, 42, 44, 56, 62, 297, 299–300 – *see also* Sheepstall

Veysey, John, bishop of Exeter 74, 91, 96, 103–5, 150–1, 218, 251, 293
vicars and vicarages 37–8, 44–5, 46–8, 93, 145, 215, 263–5, 270, 289, 295, 298
vicars choral 175–9, 246, 250–6, 259–60
Vikings 5, 11, 16, 112, 123, 126, 134, 267–8
visitations, ecclesiastical
   of the Cornwall archdeaconry 25, 91, 165, 281
   of Exeter Cathedral's churches 42, 44
   of religious houses 147, 165, 167, 177, 189–90, 214, 217, 256–7, 259, 292–3
Vivaldo, Antonio, merchant 277
Vivian or Vyvyan, families 31, 150, 159, 165, 169
Vyvyan, Honora, prioress 31
Vyvyan, Richard, cleric 172–3
Vivian, Thomas, prior and bishop 64, 91, 144–5, 150–1, 154, 183
Vivian, Thomas, vicar of Bodmin 150
Vivian, William, prior 53, 148–9, 154
Volant, John le, prior 233, 240
Vosporth (Crantock) 174
Vyel, Ralph, prior 240

Wadebridge (St Breock, Egloshayle) 74
Wagett, William, cleric 167
Walforde, Nicholas, priory *custos* 138–0
Walker, Christopher, cleric 108
Walkington, Thomas, cleric 257, 261
Wales 2, 6, 8–9, 12, 15–16, 112–13, 115, 118, 120–1, 123–5, 129, 134, 178, 232
wall paintings 41, 69–70
Walshe, John, cleric 276
Walter of Coutances, bishop 35–7, 141
Walter of Cowick, saint 111
Walter of St Omer, cleric 163, 170, 262–3, 265
Wandsworth alias Mundy, Thomas, prior 98–9, 151–4, 217
Warbeck, Perkin 48, 238, 259
Warbstow 26, 286, 295 – *see also* Fentrigan
Ward, Seth, bishop of Exeter 226
Ware (Herts.) 86, 237
Warelwast, Robert, bishop of Exeter 23–4, 136–7, 229
Warelwast, William, bishop of Exeter 22, 24, 30, 126, 136, 140–1, 150, 179, 195–6, 201, 203, 271
Warleggan 44, 47, 60
Wars of the Roses 48
Waryn, John, cleric (Menheniot) 53, 62, 64–5, 88, 213
Waryn, John, cleric (Crantock) 180
Waryn, Robert, prior 221
Watchet (Som.) 112
Wattes, John 294
Webb, William, hospital inmate 226
Week St Mary 25, 68, 83, 286
   grammar school 88, 93–4, 101
Week, Richard of 266
Welbye, Henry 277
Wellesleigh, Reginald, cleric 243
wells, holy 15–16, 78–9, 108, 110, 119–20, 137
Wells (Som.) 5, 11, 61
Wells, Hugh of, cleric 174, 179
Wendron 14, 27, 32 – *see also* St Degaman; Merthereuny
Wenilla, Richard de, prior 231, 239
St Wenn 32, 45, 61
Wente, John, cleric 239
Weras, saint 18
Werdour, Geoffrey 158
Werrington 21, 25–6, 32, 38, 76, 202, 206, 209–10, 219
Wessex, kings and territory of 1–6, 9–11
Westminster (Middx.), abbey 243
Weston, Richard, esquire 276
Weston, Robert, cleric 294
Weston, William, two such men, Hospitallers 278
Whalesborough family 87, 156
Wherwell (Hants.), abbey 32
Whitstone 61, 84, 286
Whit Sunday – *see* Pentecost
Whytby, Richard, cleric 238
William the Conqueror, king 11, 20–1, 128, 131, 201
William, count of Mortain 22, 129, 133, 135, 163, 173, 203, 297
William of Malmesbury, historian 6
William son of Nicholas, founder 240
William, James, friar 157
William, Richard, cleric 193
William – *see also* Wylliam
Williams, Hugh, collector 223
Willis, Browne, antiquary 188
Willoughby, Edward, nobleman 294
wills 24, 48, 62, 77, 86, 248, 250
Wilton (Wilts.), abbey 32, 93
Winchester (Hants.) 11
Winchester, John of, cleric 180
Windsor (Berks.), St George's chapel 86, 93, 191, 238
Windsor, Baldwin of 299
Winifred, saint 115
St Winnow 11, 15, 21, 26–7, 42, 44, 70, 97–8, 109, 135, 188, 190, 295
Winslade family 102
Winter, Thomas, archdeacon 91
Winwaloe, saint 16, 113–14
Witham (Som.), priory 83
Withiel 99, 105, 127, 139, 142, 150–3
Withiel, Simon, cleric 253
Witney, Thomas of, master mason 249
Wolsey, Thomas, cardinal 293–4
Wolveston, Richard of, cleric 170
women – *see also* churching; marriage; nunneries
   anchoresses 304–5
   charitable needs of 150, 159–60, 162, 220, 223–4
   church companies of 67, 72
   foundresses and patrons 88, 101, 144, 228, 231
   heterodoxy of 106
   reading by 83
   religious involvement of 20, 43, 77, 80, 86, 212, 223–4, 226, 232, 292
   tombs 83–4, 88, 207
   undesirable relations with clergy 43, 148, 165, 214, 217–18, 256, 290, 293–4
Woodington, Thomas, vicar general 292–3
Woolstone (Poundstock) 241, 244, 277
Worcester, William, antiquary
   on books and documents 53–4, 88, 149–50, 250, 282
   on buildings and places 86, 143–4, 155, 157, 199, 212, 235, 237–8, 244, 249, 259, 269, 282, 299
Wray, John, of Trebeigh 273, 277
Wulfnoth Rumuncant 6
Wulfsige Comoere, bishop 6, 11–12, 122–3
Wycliffe, John, reformer 48, 60
Wydeslade, Richard, cleric 232
Wylliam, Madern, monk 295
Wynard, William 185
Wythiel family 157

Yalmeton, John of, monk 268, 270
Yerle, John, canon 52, 216
Ymbe, Michael, hospital inmate 223
Yokeflete, Thomas, cleric 257, 261
Young family 295

Zennor 247–8, 253, 259, 286